KT-177-211

BARBARA JEAN

THE ROUGH GUIDE TO
ENGLAND

This eleventh edition updated by
**Rob Andrews, Samantha Cook, Matthew Hancock,
Phil Lee, David Leffman, Rachel Mills, Alice Park,
Claire Saun**

with additional
Greg Dickins

ROUGH
GUIDES

C016560077

Contents

Introduction to
England

No one enjoys knocking England more than the English, but – modesty and self-deprecation aside – this nation retains a boundless capacity to surprise, charm and thrill. For a small country, England has a regional diversity with few parallels – from rugged coasts to ancient woodlands, cricket-green villages to post-industrial towns – but what draws most visitors to England is its long and colourful history, grisly and glorious in equal measure, as brought to life through the country's trail of wonderful heritage sights and museums. While the 2016 Brexit vote hints at a nation hung up on those glory days, much of England remains progressive and forward-looking – the national character is defined as much by multiethnic urban communities, international arts festivals and sky-piercing architecture as by afternoon tea, BBC dramas and fish 'n' chips.

Whether you're in the market for city breaks and shopping sprees, or hanker after a muddy weekend in the country, there's an abundance of options for a fabulous break. You'll eat well, too. England has an ever-expanding choice of excellent food and drink – locally sourced and seasonally produced, championed in cafés, restaurants and pubs, at food festivals and farmers' markets in every corner of the nation – challenging every outmoded stereotype about dreary British cuisine.

The English do **heritage** amazingly well. There are first-class museums all over the country (many of them free), and what's left of the nation's green and pleasant land is protected with passion and skill. Indeed, ask an English person to define their nation in terms of what's worth seeing and you're most likely to have your attention drawn to the golden rural past – the village green, the duck pond, the hedgerow-fringed winding lane. And it really is impossible to overstate the bucolic attractions of the various regions, from Cornwall to the Lake District, or the delights they provide – from hiking trails and prehistoric stone circles to rickety pubs and arcane festivals. Don't be entirely misled by

ABOVE ROBIN HOOD'S BAY, NORTH YORKSHIRE **RIGHT** ANGEL OF THE NORTH, GATESHEAD the chocolate boxes and the postcards, however – farming today forms just a tiny proportion of the national income and there's a marked dislocation between the urban population and the small rural communities, many of which are struggling.

England's **towns and cities** also have more than their fair share of heritage and historic attractions, which, when matched with the buzzy energy of regeneration and innovation, can make a very heady mix – for every person who wants to stand outside the gates of Buckingham Palace or visit the Houses of Parliament, there's another who makes a beeline for the latest show at Tate Modern, the bars of Manchester's Northern Quarter or Brighton's winding Lanes. Urban civic pride is not a new phenomenon for the English, however. In fact, it's been steady since the Industrial Revolution, and **industry** – and the Empire it inspired – has provided a framework for much of what you'll see as you travel around. Virtually every town bears a mark of former wealth and power, be it a magnificent Gothic cathedral financed from a monarch's treasury, a parish church funded by the tycoons of the medieval wool trade, or a triumphalist civic building raised on the back of the slave and sugar trades. In the south of England you'll find old dockyards from which the Royal Navy patrolled the oceans, while in the north there are vast, hulking mills that employed entire towns. England's **museums and galleries** – several of them ranking among the world's finest – are full of treasures trawled from its imperial conquests. And in their grandiose stuccoed terraces and wide esplanades, the old seaside **resorts** bear testimony to the heyday of English holiday towns, at one time as fashionable as any European spa.

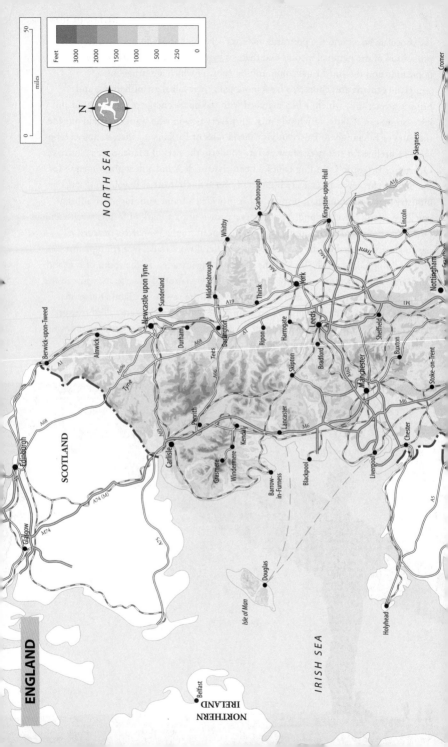

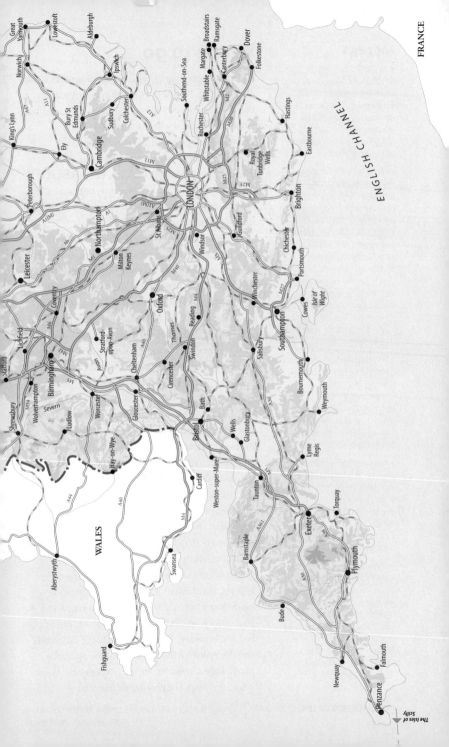

FACT FILE

• As part of the United Kingdom of Great Britain and Northern Ireland ("the UK"), **England** is a parliamentary democracy, with Queen Elizabeth II – Britain's longest-reigning monarch – as its head of state.

• Bordered by Scotland to the north and Wales to the west, England is the largest country in Great Britain, occupying an area of 50,085 square miles (129,720 sq km). The **terrain** is diverse, from plains to peaks, cliffs to beaches, though the superlatives, much like the natives, are all modest on a world scale – the largest lake, Windermere, is 10 miles (16km) long, the highest mountain, Scafell, just 3205ft (978m) above sea level.

• The **population** of around 54 million is dense for a country of this size. Settlement is concentrated in the southeast around London, and in the large industrial cities of the Midlands and the North.

• You can always plan a day out at the **seaside** – nowhere in England is more than 70 or so miles from the sea. The farthest point is near the tiny village of Coton in the Elms, in southern Derbyshire.

• England is one of the world's most **multiethnic** countries, made up largely of people of Anglo-Saxon, Scots, Welsh and Irish descent, plus sizeable communities from the Caribbean, Africa, the Indian subcontinent, China, Southeast Asia and Eastern Europe.

Where to go

To begin to get to grips with England, **London** is the place to start. Nowhere else in the country can match the scope and innovation of the capital city, a colossal, vibrant metropolis whose increasingly cluttered skyline features some of the most recognizable buildings in the world. It's here that you'll find England's best spread of nightlife, cultural events, museums, galleries, pubs, shops and restaurants, its most mixed population, and its most fully developed tourist infrastructure.

The capital is an irresistible destination and should not, on any account, be missed. However, each of the other large cities – **Birmingham**, **Bristol**, **Newcastle**, **Leeds**, **Sheffield**, **Manchester** and **Liverpool** among them – makes its own claim for historic and cultural diversity, and you certainly won't have a representative view of England's urban life if you venture no further than London. And to some extent it's in these regional centres that the most exciting architectural and social developments are taking place, though for many visitors, as tourist attractions, they rank well behind ancient cities like **Canterbury**, **York**, **Salisbury**, **Durham**, **Lincoln** and **Winchester** – to name a few of those with the most celebrated of England's cathedrals – the gorgeous Georgian ensemble in **Bath**, or the venerable university cities of **Cambridge** and **Oxford**, arguably the two most beautiful seats of learning in the world. These all, in their different ways, provide a glimpse of England's history and heritage in a less frenetic environment than the capital.

Cities can be tiring, and nobody should visit England without spending some time in its old **villages**, hundreds of which amount to nothing more than a pub, a shop, a gaggle of cottages and, if you're lucky, an old farmhouse or wayside inn offering bed and breakfast. **Devon**, **Cornwall**, the **Cotswolds** and the **Yorkshire Dales** harbour some especially picturesque specimens, but every county can boast a decent showing of photogenic hamlets.

CLOCKWISE FROM TOP LEFT BOROUGH MARKET, LONDON; AFTERNOON TEA AT *CLARIDGE'S*, LONDON; MOUNTAIN BIKING IN THE YORKSHIRE DALES, LOWER WINSKILL

ENGLAND'S BEACHES

Although rarely mentioned in the same breath as the sun-baked sands of the Mediterranean or Caribbean, England's **beaches** can compare with the best of them, both in terms of natural beauty and for cleanliness. For a combination of decent climate and good sand, coastal **Cornwall** and **Devon**, in the southwest, are hard to beat. England's largely pebbly southeastern coast is perhaps less suitable for lounging, though it does boast the surreal shingle stretch of **Dungeness** and some glorious sandy strands around **Thanet** in Kent, while the low cliffs and gravel of East Anglia's shore give way to a string of wide sandy beaches between **Cromer** and **Hunstanton**. There are spectacular stretches of sand in the northeast, notably around Scarborough in Yorkshire and in **Northumberland**, though the stiff North Sea breezes may require a degree of stoicism. Offshore islands, too, have some stunning coves and beaches, notably the Isles of Scilly and the Isle of Man.

Almost every stretch of English coast is **walkable**, and mostly waymarked – check out in particular the Norfolk Coast Path, the Cleveland Way along the Yorkshire coast, or the 630-mile South West Coast Path, which takes in some of the country's wildest and most picturesque scenery. The England Coast Path, set for completion in 2020, will soon bring all the above together in the country's longest National Trail (2795 miles). And then there are the quintessentially English **resorts**: a good beach, a pier or two, the piercing screech of gulls, fish and chips, saucy postcards and lobster-red flesh at every turn. Blackpool in the northwest is the pinnacle – full-on and tawdry, and with seven miles of clean beach to boot. Other resorts blend the same basic family-friendly ingredients with, in varying degrees, old-fashioned gentility (including Scarborough, in Yorkshire – said to be the country's oldest resort – and Broadstairs in Kent); elegance (classy Southwold, in Suffolk); and vintage hipster appeal (Kent's Margate and Morecambe in Lancashire). On the south coast, meanwhile, Brighton has a fiercely independent identity that combines the Georgian charm of its architecture with a bohemian appeal and a strong LGBT+ scene.

Evidence of England's pedigree is scattered between its settlements, as well. Wherever you're based, you're never more than a few miles from a majestic **country house** or **ruined castle** or **monastery**, and in many parts of the country you'll come across the sites of civilizations that thrived here long before England existed as a nation. In the southwest there are remnants of a **Celtic** culture that elsewhere was all but eradicated by the **Romans**, and from the south coast to the northern border you can find traces of **prehistoric** settlers, the most famous being the megalithic circles of Stonehenge and Avebury.

Then of course there's the English **countryside**, a diverse terrain from which Constable, Turner, Wordsworth, the Brontë sisters and a host of other native luminaries took inspiration. Most dramatic and best known are the moors and uplands – **Exmoor**, **Dartmoor**, **Bodmin Moor**, the **North York Moors** and the **Lake District** – each of which has its over-visited spots, though a brisk walk will usually take you out of the throng. Quieter areas are tucked away in every corner, from the flat wetlands of the eastern Fens to the chalk downland of Sussex. It's a similar story on the coast, where a number of resorts take advantage

OPPOSITE FROM TOP *GOLDEN LION*, PORT ISAAC, CORNWALL; PORT ERIN, ISLE OF MAN

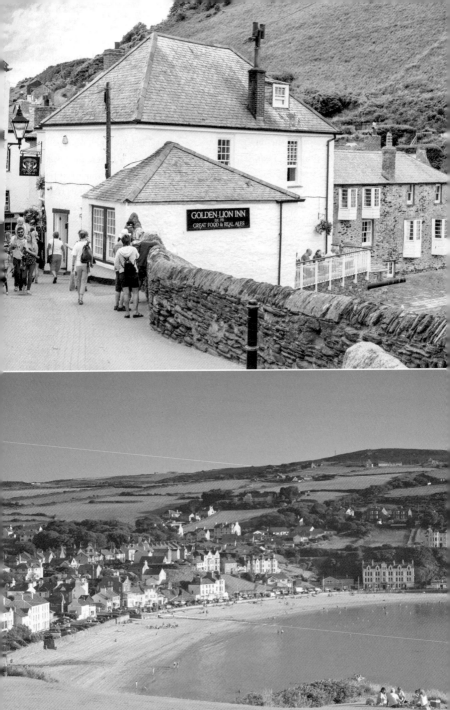

of the finest spots, but it also offers blissful pockets of peace and quiet – along the exposed strands of **Northumberland**, for example, the flat horizons of **East Anglia** or the crumbling headlands of **Dorset**.

When to go

Considering how temperate the English **climate** is it's amazing how much mileage the locals get out of the subject – a two-day cold snap is discussed as if it were the onset of a new Ice Age, and a week above 25°C (over 77°F) starts rumours of drought. In recent years, however, the Brits' weather obsession has had some grounding in serious reality: summer temperatures have been known to soar into the 30s (over 90°F) before dropping drastically the next day, while catastrophic winter and spring flooding, and violent coastal storms, are now common occurrences in parts of the country.

However, as a rule, English summers rarely get very hot and the winters don't get very cold. There's not a great deal of regional variation (see box below), though there are small microclimates; in general it's wetter in the west than the east, and the south gets more hours of sunshine than the north. Regional differences are more marked in winter, when the south tends to be milder and wetter than the north.

The bottom line is that it's impossible to say with any certainty that the weather will be pleasant in any given month. Obviously, if you're planning to camp or go to the beach, you'll want to visit between June and September. That said, even August has been known to present weeks of rain on the trot. Elsewhere, if you're balancing the likely fairness of the weather against the density of the crowds, the best time would be between **April and early June** or in **September** or **October**. England in the springtime, and in the autumn, can be a very beautiful place.

AVERAGE DAILY MAXIMUM TEMPERATURES

	Jan	Feb	Mar	Apr	May	Jun	Jul	Aug	Sep	Oct	Nov	Dec
BIRMINGHAM												
°F	42	43	48	54	61	66	68	68	63	55	48	44
°C	5	6	9	12	16	19	20	20	17	13	9	7
LONDON												
°F	43	44	50	56	62	69	71	71	65	58	50	45
°C	6	7	10	13	17	21	22	22	19	14	10	7
PLYMOUTH												
°F	47	47	50	54	59	64	66	67	64	58	52	49
°C	8	8	10	12	15	18	19	19	18	14	11	9
YORK												
°F	43	44	49	55	61	67	70	69	64	57	49	45
°C	6	7	9	13	16	19	21	21	18	14	9	7

Author picks

Our indefatigable authors are always on the lookout for the best travel experiences in the country – here are some places to start.

Fish and chips You can get a lip-smacking seaside supper at *Yorkshire Fisheries*, Blackpool (p.542), *Maggie's* (p.163), on the beach in Hastings' Fishing Quarter – which has the biggest beach-launched fleet in Europe – or at Whitby's *Magpie Café* (p.635), one of Rick Stein's favourites.

Marvellous markets Manchester's German Christmas Market is a magical wonderland, with Glühwein too (p.525). Norwich's huge open-air market is always bustling (p.396), but for the best foodie shopping in England it has to be Borough Market in London (p.130).

Boutique boltholes In a pretty Somerset village, *Lord Poulett Arms* combines history with contemporary chic (p.308), while London's *Hazlitts* offers ravishing Georgian elegance in the heart of Soho (p.112). You can luxuriate in Lincoln at the *Old Palace* (p.500) or enjoy a posh retreat at *Randy Pike*, a cosy Lake District hideaway (p.564).

Glorious gardens Vita Sackville-West's Sissinghurst, in Kent, is the artistic cottage garden to end them all (p.154), while Stourhead in Wiltshire (p.231) offers a slice of traditional England at its best. Find French and Italian influences at Mount Edgcumbe garden near Plymouth (p.340) and offbeat charm at Alnwick Garden in Northumberland, with its topiary snakes and a poison garden (p.660).

Seaside stars You're spoilt for choice for glorious strands in the southwest, but top spots include Studland Bay (p.216) and Par Beach in the Isles of Scilly (p.364). For vast sandy expanses, head to Holkham Bay, where three miles of pancake-flat sands (p.406) lie beyond the pines and dunes, or Northumberland's Bamburgh, which offers acres of sky, sea and dunes with a dramatic castle backdrop (p.662).

> Our author recommendations don't end here. We've flagged up our favourite places – a perfectly sited hotel, an atmospheric café, a special restaurant – throughout the Guide, highlighted with the ★ symbol.

FROM TOP *RANDY PIKE*; SISSINGHURST; PAR BEACH, ISLES OF SCILLY

30

things not to miss

It's not possible to see everything England has to offer in one trip – and we don't suggest you try. What follows is a selective taste of the country's highlights: stunning architecture, dramatic landscapes, fun activities and world-class museums. All highlights are colour-coded by chapter and have a page reference to take you straight into the Guide, where you can find out more.

1

1 STONEHENGE
Page 229

Redolent of mystery and myth, this is the most important stone circle in England, attracting crowds of thousands, including white-robed druids, for the summer solstice.

2 EDEN PROJECT
Page 351

The vast, eco-friendly "biomes" that form the centre of the Eden Project are filled with weird and wonderful plants from around the world.

3 SURFING IN NORTH DEVON
Page 344

The beaches strung along the northern coast of Devon offer some great breaks, with Woolacombe, Croyde and Saunton the places to see and be seen.

4 MALHAM
Page 603

A jewel of the Yorkshire Dales National Park, this pretty village is the perfect base for walks into the spectacular scenery of Malham Cove, Malham Tarn and Gordale Scar.

11 NORTHERN QUARTER AND ANCOATS, MANCHESTER

Manchester's old garment district is a buzzing area packed with indie shops, vintage emporiums and cool bars; for food and drink, the hippest places are in Ancoats' red-brick factory buildings.

12 OXFORD COLLEGES

Admire the dreaming spires of this glorious historic university town.

13 BLACKPOOL PLEASURE BEACH

Donkey rides, illuminations and roller coaster thrills at the mother of all English seaside resorts.

14 DARTMOOR

Southern England's great expanse of wilderness is perfect for hikers and riders.

15 BRADFORD CURRY HOUSES

Bradford's excellent curry restaurants run the gamut from cheap and cheerful balti houses to upmarket contemporary dining rooms.

16 SHOPPING IN BRIGHTON

Brighton's Lanes and quirky North Laine, packed with shops, cafés and bars, are at the heart of this warm-hearted, alternative seaside resort.

17 HAWORTH

This atmospheric Yorkshire village was home to the Brontë sisters; their Georgian home is now a museum.

18 WINDERMERE, LAKE DISTRICT
The bucolic Lake District National Park boasts sixteen major lakes and scores of mountains.

19 HAMPTON COURT
The finest of Tudor palaces, this splendid red-brick pile makes a spectacular day-trip from London.

20 VIA FERRATA, LAKE DISTRICT
High-level thrills on this exhilarating mountain climb, following the old miners' path up Fleetwith Pike.

21 TATE MODERN
The world's largest modern art gallery is housed in a spectacular former power station.

22 CHIPPING CAMPDEN
Impossibly pretty honey-stone village with rolling hills and great walking all around.

23 ALDEBURGH
Lovely, low-key Suffolk coastal town with a world-class classical music festival and a vibrant cultural scene.

24 DURDLE DOOR
This distinctive limestone arch is the highlight of Dorset's Jurassic Coast and is close to some lovely beaches.

25 SOUTHWOLD
Page 393

George Orwell didn't like the place, but everyone else does: Southwold is a charming seaside town with a wide sandy beach and brightly painted beach huts.

26 NEW FOREST
Page 206

Famed for its wild ponies, this ancient hunting ground is a fabulous destination for cyclists and walkers.

27 ST IVES, CORNWALL
Page 361

Sunny seaside resort with great beaches and the best arts collection in southwest England.

28 HADRIAN'S WALL
Page 652

Walk or cycle the length of this atmospheric Roman monument, which snakes its way for 84 miles over rough, sheep-strewn countryside.

29 LONDON'S MARKETS
Page 130

From the vintage stores and food stalls of Brick Lane to the floral abundance of Columbia Road and the grand old Victorian hall at Spitalfields, London's markets could fill a weekend.

30 LIVERPOOL VISUAL ARTS
Page 529

Liverpool is home to some mind-blowing galleries and exhibitions, not least the Walker and the Tate, plus the cutting-edge Liverpool Biennial contemporary arts festival.

Itineraries

England may be a small country, but between the bracing Cornish coast and the misty northern peaks, it has an astonishing amount to offer. The following itineraries give you a taster of its top destinations, its offbeat corners, and its literary highlights.

THE GRAND TOUR

You'll need at least a couple of weeks to really enjoy the big-hit destinations, but if time is at a premium you could pick and mix from this round-up of England's must-sees.

❶ **London** Give yourself at least three nights in London, quite simply one of the world's greatest cities. **See p.48**

❷ **Cambridge** Head to The Backs, a green swathe of land along the River Cam, for views of the spectacular old colleges (and, hopefully, someone falling in the river while punting). See p.413

❸ **Brighton** Submerge yourself, both in the sea and in Brighton's maze of bohemian boutiques, bars and brunch spots. **See p.167**

❹ **St Ives** Cornwall's dramatic coastline is breathtaking; base yourself in this artistic little town to enjoy the best of it. **See p.361**

❺ **Bath** Few people can resist this elegant Georgian city, with its Roman baths, luxury spa and excellent foodie scene. **See p.282**

❻ **Liverpool** You don't have to be a Beatles fan to love "the Pool", which not only has some fantastic Fab Four sights, but also an excellent food and nightlife scene. **See p.529**

❼ **The Peak District** The Peaks offer wonderfully rugged outdoors country just a short hop away from the nearby cities. See p.460

❽ **York** This picturesque medieval city, with its glorious minster, is one of the most beautiful in the country. **See p.586**

❾ **Lake District** The pretty village of Grasmere makes a perfect base for forays into the dramatic hills and lakes of the Lake District National Park. **See p.552**

QUIRKY ENGLAND

This offbeat itinerary, which focuses on some loopy sights in some lovely places, will help uncover another side to England beyond Big Ben and Beefeaters. Allow a good two weeks to explore.

❶ **Sir John Soane's Museum, London** Quite simply the most intriguing, unusual and eccentric small museum in London. This eclectic collection of art and antiquities is enhanced by mirrors, domes and other works of spatial trickery. **See p.75**

❷ **Dungeness, Kent** This wild shingle stretch, splashed with wildflowers, is home to a mix of artists, traditionalists and free spirits, all living in the shadow of a colossal nuclear power station. It's unlike anywhere else in England. See p.153

❸ **Postcard Museum, Isle of Wight** The Isle of Wight has an atmosphere all of its own – for a taster, check out the cheeky, and often surreal, British seaside humour at Ryde's retro postcard museum. **See p.194**

ABOVE ROYAL CRESCENT, BATH

4 Cerne Abbas Giant, Dorset No visit to England, with its love of *Carry On* films and double-entendres, would be complete without a gawp at this large naked man carved into a green hillside. **See p.219**

5 Pitt Rivers Museum, Oxford Eyes glazing over at the fancy china and Old Masters at stately home no. 32? Come here to peruse exhibits arranged like an exotic junk shop. Past "objects of the month" include a disease demon mask from Sri Lanka and Siberian reindeer knickers. **See p.247**

6 Southwold, Suffolk Suffolk's poshest seaside town may seem frightfully refined, but head to the Under the Pier Show for offbeat arcade games and handmade slot machines – an inventive take on the traditional seaside pier. **See p.393**

7 Kinema in the Woods, Lincolnshire A charmingly nostalgic picture house in a woodland setting, and home of the Mighty Compton Organ, which chimes through the interval. **See p.502**

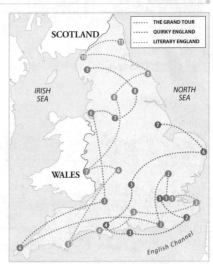

LITERARY ENGLAND

This itinerary, which touches upon the most famous of England's extraordinary literary highlights, could take at least two weeks – or longer, if you use the sites as jumping-off points for some of England's loveliest countryside.

1 Shakespeare's Globe, London Shakespeare as it was meant to be experienced, outdoors, with a raucous crowd, full of verve. **See p.88**

2 Dickens Museum, Broadstairs Dickens spent a lot of time in this Kentish seaside resort; this little clifftop house, inspiration for Miss Trotwood's house in *David Copperfield*, is full of memorabilia. **See p.142**

3 Chawton, Hampshire The pretty village where Jane Austen lived in her later years is packed with sights relating to the perennially popular author. **See p.204**

4 Dorchester, Dorset Thomas Hardy's town is a good base for the surrounding "Hardy country" that features so evocatively in his novels. **See p.217**

5 Greenway, Devon Agatha Christie fans won't want to miss her former holiday mansion on the banks of the Dart, with its lovely river views. **See p.329**

6 Stratford-upon-Avon, West Midlands Not only can you see the Bard's works performed in the RSC theatres of his hometown, but you can also visit his birthplace and Anne Hathaway's picturesque cottage. **See p.436**

7 Hay-on-Wye, Herefordshire Well worth a trip even if you can't make it to the world-famous literary festival, this riverside border town boasts a huge array of secondhand book stores. **See p.449**

8 Haworth, Yorkshire A pilgrimage site for every Brontë fan: wander around the Parsonage where the sisters grew up – and stroll across the wild Yorkshire moorland that features so powerfully in their works. **See p.609**

9 Whitby, Yorkshire Bram Stoker found spooky inspiration in this dramatically set fishing town – lure out your inner Goth and follow the Dracula trail around all the key sites. **See p.632**

10 Cockermouth, Cumbria The Lake District, where Wordsworth wandered lonely as a cloud, is full of places related to the poet; a visit to his childhood home is a great starting point. **See p.578**

11 Seven Stories, Newcastle upon Tyne Seven storeys crammed full of stories, focusing on the fine art of children's literature. **See p.645**

RURAL POSTBOX, LAKE DISTRICT NATIONAL PARK

Basics

Getting there

London is one of the world's busiest transport hubs, and there are good deals from around the world on flights into the UK's capital. However, if you're planning to tour the southwest or north of England consider flying directly to more convenient international airports such as Manchester, Birmingham or Bristol.

London's biggest and best-known airports – **Heathrow** and **Gatwick** – take the bulk of transatlantic and long-haul flights into the UK, though there are also three smaller London airports (**Stansted**, **Luton** and **City**) and a host of useful regional British airports, many of which are served by numerous low-cost airlines from mainland Europe and Ireland. Principally, in England these are **Manchester** and **Liverpool** in the northwest; **Birmingham** in the West Midlands; **Bristol**, Newquay and Exeter in the West Country; **Leeds-Bradford** and Doncaster-Sheffield in Yorkshire; **Newcastle** and Durham Tees Valley in the northeast; **East Midlands**; and **Bourne-mouth** and **Southampton** in the south. There are also airports at Blackpool, Humberside, Nottingham and Norwich. The cheapest deals need to be booked well in advance and tend to have little or no flexibility.

Overland routes from mainland Europe include high-speed trains into London (with onward connections) through the Channel Tunnel – either passenger-only Eurostar services or the drive-on drive-off **Eurotunnel** shuttle train. There's also a range of useful **ferry** routes.

Flights from the US and Canada

Many airlines fly nonstop to London, Manchester and other British airports – flight time is around seven hours from the east coast, ten hours from the west. Flights on European airlines might be cheaper but tend to route through their respective European hubs, adding to the journey time.

From the US, low-season round-trip fares from New York are most competitive, starting at US$500–

700; from Chicago they start at around US$1000 direct (cheaper non-direct). There are some good deals from New York with Iceland's WOW air (ⓦwowair.us), changing at Reykjavik, and direct with Norwegian Air Shuttle (ⓦnorwegian.com). Fares from the west coast can start from between US$700 (with Norwegian offering cheap deals from LA) and US$1000.

From Canada, the best deals involve flying to London out of Toronto or Montreal: from Toronto flights are around Can$750, while from Vancouver they start around Can$1000.

Flights from Australia and New Zealand

Flight time from **Australia** and **New Zealand** to England is at least 22 hours. Flights via Southeast Asia or the Middle East to London are generally the cheapest. Return **fares** start at Aus$1200 from Sydney. From Auckland to London return fares start at around NZ$1800.

Flights from Ireland

You can get a one-way flight between **Ireland** and England for around €40–70. There are routes out of Dublin, Cork, Knock, Kerry and Shannon to many English airports; airlines include Aer Lingus, British Airways, Flybe and Ryanair. The cheapest options **from Belfast** and Derry are usually easyJet, Flybe and Ryanair.

Ferries

There are several ferry routes from mainland Europe and Ireland to England. The quickest, cheapest services are on the traditional cross-Channel routes **from the French ports** of Calais, and Dunkerque to **Dover** in Kent, plus routes to Portsmouth from Le Havre, Cherbourg and St Malo and from Spain (Santander and Bilbao). From Zeebrugge (Belgium) and Rotterdam (the Netherlands) ferries go to Hull; from the Hook of Holland they go to Harwich, while from Amsterdam they arrive in Newcastle.

A BETTER KIND OF TRAVEL

At Rough Guides we are passionately committed to travel. We believe it helps us understand the world we live in and the people we share it with – and of course tourism is vital to many developing economies. But the scale of modern tourism has also damaged some places irreparably, and climate change is accelerated by most forms of transport, especially flying. All Rough Guides' flights are carbon-offset, and every year we donate money to a variety of environmental charities.

Ferry services **from Ireland** (Dublin, Rosslare and Belfast) run to England's northwest (Liverpool and the Isle of Man) and **Wales** (Holyhead, Fishguard and Pembroke).

Fares vary considerably, according to time of year, and time and type of crossing – some high-speed ferry services can cut journey times on the same route by up to half – while accommodation is often obligatory (and welcome) on night crossings from the continent.

For **information** on routes and operators, see ⓦ aferry.co.uk.

Trains

Direct **Eurostar trains** (ⓦ eurostar.com) run roughly hourly to London St Pancras International from Calais (1hr 10min), Lille (1hr 20min), Brussels (2hr) and Paris (2hr 20min), with connections into those cities from across Europe and direct seasonal services from southern France (Lyon, Avignon and Marseille in summer and over Christmas; Bourg St Maurice, Aime La Plagne and Moutiers in winter), as well as Disneyland Paris, and a direct Amsterdam–London service as of 2018. Fares start from around €50 one-way, though you'll have to book well in advance. There are discounts on standard fares for travellers under 26 and over 60.

For drivers, the fastest and most convenient cross-Channel option is the **Eurotunnel** (ⓦ euro tunnel.com) drive-on-drive-off shuttle train from Calais to Folkestone (around 75 miles southeast of London), which runs 24 hours and takes 35–45 minutes. Booking is advised, especially at weekends or if you want the best prices. The standard fare for a car and all its passengers is from €85 one-way (with cheap deals available for short trips); more if booked at short notice. **Irish Ferries** (ⓦ irishferries .com) offer SailRail return fares of around €100 to London (via Holyhead) from anywhere in the Republic; journey time is around eight hours from Dublin. For the best train information online, check the **Man in Seat 61** at ⓦ seat61.com and ⓦ loco2 .com for journey planning.

Buses

Eurolines (ⓦ eurolines.co.uk) coordinates inter-national bus services to London (with connections onwards) from dozens of **European cities**. This is the cheapest way of travelling, but you really do have to ask yourself how long you want to spend cooped up in a bus. Only routes from northern European cities are anything like bearable: the

journey from Paris, for example, which takes around six hours to London Victoria Coach Station and costs from €18 one-way.

Tours and organized holidays

Package tours of England, where all flights, accom-modation and ground transport are arranged for you, can sometimes be cheaper than organizing things yourself. Many companies, for example, offer **coach tours** of the country's historic highlights, or help you explore some aspect of its heritage, such as art and architecture, or gardens and stately homes. Other operators specialize in **activity holidays** (see box, p.40).

AGENTS AND OPERATORS

STA Travel UK ☎ 0333 321 0099, US ☎ 1800 781 4040, Australia ☎ 134 782, New Zealand ☎ 0800 474 400, South Africa ☎ 0861 781 781, ⓦ statravel.co.uk. Worldwide specialists in independent travel; also student IDs, travel insurance, car rental, rail passes, and more. Good discounts for students and under-26s.

Trailfinders UK ☎ 020 7368 1200, Ireland ☎ 01 677 7888, ⓦ trailfinders.com. One of the best-informed and most efficient agents for independent travellers.

Travel CUTS Canada ☎ 1800 667 2887, ⓦ travelcuts.com. Canadian youth and student travel firm.

PACKAGE TOURS

Abercrombie & Kent US ☎ 1800 554 7016, ⓦ abercrombiekent .com. Classy travel specialist, with no-expense-spared escorted and independent trips, from London-highlights trips to nine-day tours of English gardens.

Contiki Holidays UK ☎ 0808 281 1120, ⓦ contiki.com. Lively, reasonably priced, budget-accommodation adventure tours for 18–35s, including London trips and a nine-day England and Scotland tour.

Martin Randall Travel UK ☎ 020 8742 3355, ⓦ martinrandall.com. Wide-ranging all-inclusive historical and cultural tours led by experts – for example, seven days walking Hadrian's Wall, nine days exploring England's cathedrals or four days soaking up the Arts and Crafts heritage of the Cotswolds, plus one-day lecture/tours in London.

Getting around

Almost every town and larger village in England can be reached by train or – if you have time and flexibility – bus, but public transport costs are among the highest in Europe and travel can eat up a large part of your budget. Rural destin-ations are often poorly served, too. It pays to investigate all the special deals and passes, some of which are only

available outside the UK and must be bought before you arrive. It may be cheaper and easier to drive, especially if you're in a group, though traffic can be bad in the cities and on the motorways. If you want to find if a particular route is feasible by public transport, ⓦtraveline .info is a good first port of call.

By plane

Given the time it takes getting to and from many airports (particularly London if not flying from City Airport), there are few domestic journeys where **flying** is worthwhile, with some exceptions, say, if you are travelling from the southwest to the north of England (Newquay to Newcastle takes 1hr 30min by plane, 9hr 30min by train, for example, though there aren't flights every day). However, sometimes flight prices are competitive compared with expensive on-the-spot train tickets for journeys such as London–Newcastle or Manchester–Newquay. Domestic airlines include British Airways (ⓦba.com), easyJet (ⓦeasyjet.com), Ryanair (ⓦryanair.com), flybe (ⓦflybe.com) and Cityjet (ⓦcityjet.com). Fares on popular routes such as London to Newcastle, with journey times of around an hour, can cost as little as £75 return.

By train

Despite grumbles about the rail network, and the high cost of travel compared to other European rail systems, getting around England by train is still the best, most scenic and – usually – most painless way to travel. Most major towns in England have rail links (though coverage of small towns is woeful compared with other European countries), and mainline routes out of London in particular are **fast and frequent** – the 200-mile trips to York and Exeter, for instance, are covered in two hours. The fastest journeys head north from London on east- and west-coast mainline routes (to Birmingham, Manchester, Leeds and Newcastle, among others), and there are high-speed services to Kent from King's Cross St Pancras; other journeys, however, can be more complicated, particularly if you're travelling east–west, which might involve a train change or two.

England's trains are run by myriad **operators**, but all are required to work as a single network with integrated ticketing. The **National Rail Enquiries** website (ⓦnationalrail.co.uk) is a useful first call for timetable, route and fare information; it lists all the regional operators and offers ticket-buying links from

TOP 5 TRAIN JOURNEYS
Dartmouth Steam Railway See p.328
Swanage Steam Railway See p.215
North Yorkshire Moors Railway See box, p.629
Ravenglass and Eskdale Railway See p.575
Settle to Carlisle Railway See box, p.604

its journey planner. For an exhaustive rundown of train travel in the UK, check the excellent **Man in Seat 61** website (ⓦseat61.com).

Buying tickets

As a rule, the earlier you book, the less you will pay. Always look out for **online offers** with **booking sites** like ⓦloco2.com, ⓦticketclever.com and ⓦmegatrain.com (the last of which is frustrating to use, but can help you find low fares on a few routes). It's also worth checking the websites of the individual operators, as usually their fares will match those offered by the booking sites. A **seat reservation** is usually included with the ticket. Just turning up and buying a ticket at the station is always the most expensive way to go (sometimes phenomenally so); it's always worth asking at the ticket desk about the options, as you may get discounts on groups or couples travelling together. If the ticket office is closed, or the automatic machines aren't working, you may buy your ticket on board from the inspector. In some cases, though, buying a ticket on the train when you had the opportunity to buy one beforehand could lead to a penalty of £20 – the stations from which penalty fares apply will have large posters advertising that fact.

Cheapest are **advance tickets**, which are only available several weeks ahead of time and sell out quickly. They can only be used on the specified train booked – miss it, and you pay a surcharge or have to buy another ticket. Off-peak fares can be bought in advance or on the day of travel, but are only valid for travel at quieter times (generally outside Mon–Fri 5–10am & 3–8pm). Most expensive are the fully flexible anytime tickets.

Rail passes

For overseas visitors planning to travel widely by train, a **BritRail England pass** could be a wise investment (ⓦbritrail.net). It gives unlimited travel throughout England and is valid for varied periods of from two to fifteen days in two months (not necessarily consecutive). There are first- and second-class versions, discounted Youth Passes and

Senior Passes, and for every adult buying a full-priced ticket one child (aged 5 to 15) receives the same pass for free. Note that BritRail passes have to be bought before you enter the UK.

If you've been resident in a European country other than the UK for at least six months, an **InterRail pass** (🌐interrail.eu), allowing unlimited train travel in England, Wales and Scotland (for 3, 4, 6 or 8 days within one month), might be worth it – but note that you can't use the pass for travel in your country of residence. **Eurail** passes are not valid in the UK, though they do provide discounts on Eurostar trains to England and on some ferry routes.

National Rail Enquiries (🌐nationalrail.co.uk) details the many regional rail passes that can be bought by both locals and visitors in England itself. **Rover and Ranger passes** offer unlimited travel in single, multi-day or flexi-day formats – the Ride Cornwall Ranger, for example, which costs £13 for one day of off-peak train travel in that county. There are numerous options when it comes to **annual railcards**, including the 16–25 Railcard for full-time students and people aged between 16 and 25; the Senior Railcard for travellers over 60; the Two Together card for a couple travelling together; and the Family & Friends Railcard for groups of up to four adults and four children travelling together. Each costs £30 for the year and gives up to a third off most adult fares in England (more for children's fares).

By bus

Travel by bus – long-distance services are known as "coaches" – is usually much cheaper than by train, though less comfortable, and traffic congestion can make the same journey much longer. The biggest **inter-city** bus operators in England are **National Express** (🌐nationalexpress.com) and **Megabus** (🌐megabus.com). On busy routes, and on any route at weekends and holidays, it's advisable to book ahead to get the best deal. Fares are very reasonable, with discounts for under-26s, over-60s and families, plus various advance-purchase fares and special deals. **Regional and urban** bus services are run by a huge array of companies. Check **Traveline** (🌐traveline.info) for information and routes. In many cases, timetables and routes are well integrated, but more remote, rural spots are neglected.

By car

Your English driving experience will depend very much on where you drive. Slogging through the traffic from major city to major city is rarely an illuminating way to see the nation – motorways ("M" roads) and main "A" roads may have up to four lanes in each direction, but even these can get very congested, with long traffic jams, especially at peak travel times and on public holidays. Driving in the countryside is far more agreeable, though on "B" roads and minor roads there might only be one lane (single track) in both directions. Keep your speed down, and be prepared for abrupt encounters with tractors, sheep and other hazards in remote spots. Don't underestimate the English **weather**, either. Snow, ice, fog and wind can cause havoc – and there has been major flooding in the past few years – and driving conditions, on motorways as much as in rural areas, can deteriorate quickly. Local radio stations feature regularly updated traffic bulletins, as does the **Highways Agency** (🌐highways.gov.uk or 🌐trafficengland.com).

England just has one **Toll Road**, the M6 in the Midlands, as well as tolls on the Dartford crossing and various bridges, but **congestion charges** apply in London (see box, p.110). **Fuel** is pricey – unleaded petrol (gasoline) and diesel in particular. Out-of-town supermarkets usually have the lowest prices, while the highest prices are charged by motorway service stations.

Parking in towns, cities and popular tourist spots can be a nightmare and often costs a small fortune. A yellow line along the edge of the road indicates **parking restrictions**; check the nearest sign to see exactly what they are. A double-yellow line means no parking at any time, though you can stop briefly to unload or pick up people or goods, while red lines signify no stopping at all. Fines for parking illegally are high – as much as £130 (though reduced if you pay within fourteen days) – and if you're wheel-clamped it will cost you £200 or so to have your vehicle released.

Rules and regulations

Drive on the left. **Seatbelts** must be worn by everyone in a vehicle, front and back, while motorcyclists and their passengers must wear a helmet. You are not permitted to make a kerbside turn against a red light and must always give way to traffic (circulating clockwise) on a **roundabout** – this applies even for mini-roundabouts, which may be no more than a white circle painted on the road. **Speed limits** are 20 miles per hour in many residential streets, 30 miles per hour in built-up areas, 70 miles per hour on dual carriageways and motorways and 60 miles per hour on most other roads – as a rule, assume that in any area with street lighting the speed limit is 30 miles per hour unless otherwise stated. Be alert to the signs, as **speed cameras** are everywhere.

Most foreign nationals can get by with their **driving licence** from home, but if you're in any doubt, obtain an **international driving permit** from a national motoring organization. Anyone bringing their own vehicle into the country should also carry vehicle registration, ownership and insurance documents.

The AA (W theaa.com), RAC (W rac.co.uk) and Green Flag (W greenflag.com) all operate **24-hour emergency breakdown** services, and offer useful online route planners. You may be entitled to free assistance through a reciprocal arrangement with a motoring organization in your home country – check before setting out. You can make use of these emergency services if you are not a member, but you will need to join at the roadside and will incur a hefty surcharge.

Vehicle rental

Car rental is best booked online through one of the large multinational chains (Avis, Budget, easycar, Hertz or National, for example) or through a site such as W auto-europe.co.uk. **North Americans** might want to contact the independently owned Europe by Car (T 1800 223 1516, W europeby carblog.com), which has good deals on short and longer-term rentals.

If you rent a car from a company in the UK, expect to pay around £30 per day, £50 for a weekend, or £100–160 per week. Few companies will rent to drivers with less than one year's experience and most will only rent to people between 21 or 23 and 70 years of age. Rental cars will be manual (stick shift) unless you specify otherwise – if you want an **automatic transmission**, book well ahead and expect to pay at least £170 a week. **Motorbike rental** is more expensive – around £80 a day or £400 a week. Try London-based Raceways (W raceways.net) or RoadTrip in Woking, near Heathrow (W roadtrip.uk).

By bike

Cycling around England can be a pleasant option, as long as you stick to the quieter "B" roads and country lanes – or, best of all, follow one of the **traffic-free trails** of the extensive National Cycle Network (see p.40).

Cycle helmets are not compulsory – but you're well advised to wear one, especially if you're hell-bent on tackling the congestion, pollution and aggression of city traffic. You do have to have a **rear reflector** and front and back **lights** when

riding at night, and you are not allowed to carry children without a special **child seat**. It is also illegal to cycle on pavements and in most public parks, while **off-road** cyclists must stick to bridleways and by-ways designated for their use.

Bike rental is available at cycle shops in most large towns, and at villages within National Parks and other scenic areas. Expect to pay around £20–25 per day, or more for specialist mountain bikes and less for multi-day rents; you may need to provide credit card details or leave a passport as a deposit.

Accompanied bikes are allowed free on mainline trains, but you usually need to book the space in advance; check W nationalrail.co.uk for individual company regulations. Bus and coach companies rarely accept cycles, and even then only if they are dismantled and boxed.

Accommodation

Accommodation in England ranges from corporate chain hotels to crumbling castles, from budget backpacker hostels to chic boutique hotels. Often they're in interesting old buildings – former coaching inns, converted mansions and manor houses – which offer heaps of historic atmosphere. Accommodation does tend to be quite expensive, but there are bargains to be had.

A nationwide **grading system**, annually upgraded, awards **stars** to hotels, guesthouses and B&Bs. There's no hard and fast correlation between rank and price, but the system does lay down minimum levels of standards and service. However, not every establishment participates, and you shouldn't assume that a particular place is no good simply because it doesn't. In the rural backwaters in particular some of the best accommodation is to be found in **farmhouses** and other simple properties whose facilities may technically fall short of official standards.

Hotels

English hotels vary wildly in size, style, comfort and price. The starting price for a basic hotel is around £80 per night for a double or twin room, breakfast usually included; anything more upmarket, or with a bit of boutique styling, will be around £100 a night, while at the top-end properties the sky's the limit, especially in London or in resort or country-house hotels. Many city hotels in particular charge a room rate only.

ACCOMMODATION PRICES

Throughout this Guide we give a headline price for every accommodation reviewed, which indicates the lowest price you could expect to pay per night for a **double or twin room in high season** (basically, from Easter to the end of September, though local variations apply). We also give the high-season price for a dorm bed in a **hostel** – note that for YHA hostels, prices quoted are for non-members (members get a £3/night discount). Prices given for **self-catering** options indicate the minimum per-night price in high season. For **campsites** we give the cost of a pitch for two people bringing their own tent, unless otherwise indicated. **Single occupancy** rates vary widely: though they're typically around three-quarters of the price of a double, some places charge almost the full double rate and others charge only a little over half that. Rates in hotels and B&Bs may well drop between Sunday and Thursday, or if you stay more than one night, and some places will require a minimum stay of two or more nights at the weekend and/or in high season; we indicate when an establishment has a general rule on this.

Breakfast is generally included in rates, and free **wi-fi** is usually available throughout the property (except when camping, of course). Reviews in the Guide note when that isn't the case.

Budget hotel chains – including Premier Inn (Ⓦpremierinn.com), Holiday Inn Express (Ⓦhi express.com), Jurys Inn (Ⓦjurysinns.com), Travelodge (Ⓦtravelodge.co.uk), Ibis (Ⓦibishotel.com) and Comfort/Quality/Sleep Inns (Ⓦchoicehotelsuk.co.uk) – have properties across the country. With no frills (and with breakfast charged extra), they are not always automatically the cheapest option, but they can be a good deal for families and small groups, and rates can get down to a bargain £40–50 per night if booked well in advance. Point A Hotels (London; Ⓦpointahotels.com) and easyHotel (London, Liverpool, Manchester and Birmingham; Ⓦeasyhotel.com) can be even cheaper, offering a simple "add-on" system whereby you book a minimal room online with the option of adding niceties including cleaning, windows, TVs, wi-fi and baggage storage.

B&Bs, guesthouses and pubs

At its most basic, the typical English **bed and breakfast** (**B&B**) is an ordinary private house with a couple of bedrooms set aside for paying guests. Larger establishments with more rooms, particularly in resorts, style themselves as **guesthouses**, but they are pretty much the same thing.

TOP 5 QUIRKY HOTELS

Belle Tout Beachy Head. See p.165
Cley Windmill Norfolk. See p.404
Millers at the Anchor Porlock Weir, Somerset. See p.314
Old Dungeon Ghyll Langdale. See p.565
Pelirocco Brighton. See p.172

At the extreme budget end of the scale – basic B&Bs under £70 a night – you'll normally experience small rooms, fairly spartan facilities and shared bathrooms (though there are some fantastic exceptions). You'll pay a few pounds more for en-suite shower and toilet, while at the top end of the range you can expect real style, fresh flowers, gourmet breakfasts, king-sized beds and luxurious bathrooms. Many top-notch B&Bs – say around £100–120 or more per night – offer more luxury and far better value pound for pound than more impersonal hotels. In this category you can also count **pubs** (or inns), and the increasingly popular "**restaurants with rooms**". Both will often have only a handful of rooms, but their atmosphere – and the lazy option of laying your head in the same place that you eat and drink – may make them a good choice.

Hostels

The **Youth Hostels Association** (Ⓦyha.org.uk) has hundreds of hostels across England, ranging from lakeside mansions to thatched country cottages. There are still shared bathrooms and traditional single-sex bunk-bed dormitories in most, though the majority now also offer smaller rooms (sometimes en suite) of two to six beds for couples, families and groups. Some hostels have been purpose-built, or have had expensive refurbishments, and in cities, resorts and National Park areas the facilities are often every bit as good as budget hotels. Most offer self-catering kitchens, laundry facilities and lounges, while wi-fi access, cafés, bars, tour bookings and bike rental and storage are common. The hostel will usually provide bed linen,

TOP 5 HOSTELS

Grasmere Independent Hostel. See p.566
Kipps Canterbury. See p.146
Safestay Holland Park London. See p.115
YHA Boggle Hole See p.632
YHA Boscastle. See p.372

pillows and duvet; towels and other necessities can often be rented.

You don't have to be a member to stay at a YHA hostel but non-members are charged an extra £3 a night. One year's membership, which is open only to residents of the EU, costs £15 per year for England and Wales and can be bought online or at any YHA hostel. Members gain automatic membership of the hostelling associations of the ninety countries affiliated to **Hostelling International** (HI; Ⓦ hihostels.com).

Prices are calculated according to season, location and demand, with adult dorm beds usually £15–30 per night – prices can get higher than that in London and at peak holiday periods. A private twin room in a hostel goes for around £40–80, and family rooms sleeping four start from around £75 (much more in London). **Meals** are good value – breakfast or a packed lunch for around £5–7, or £9–13 for dinner. Advance **booking** is recommended, and essential at Easter, Christmas and from May to August.

A large number of **independent hostels** offer similar prices. With no membership fees, more relaxed rules, mixed dorms and no curfew, many of them, in the cities at least, tend to attract a predominantly young, keen-to-party crowd, but there are family-friendly options, too. For news and reviews, check Ⓦ independenthostelguide.co.uk, which also lists primitive bunkhouses, bunk barns and camping barns in the most rural locations.

Camping

England has hundreds of **campsites**, ranging from small, family-run places to large sites with laundries, shops and sports facilities. Prices start at around £5 per adult in the simplest sites, though at larger, more popular locations you can pay far more, and sometimes there are separate charges per car and tent. Many campsites also have accommodation in permanently fixed, fully equipped caravans, or in wooden cabins or similar. Perhaps in part due to the unreliable weather, Brits have taken

glamping to their hearts, with more tipis, yurts, bell tents and camping pods than you can shake a billycan at. Some are downright lavish (with beds, plump duvets, private loos and wood burners) and are priced accordingly: Ⓦ coolcamping.co.uk, Ⓦ campingandcaravanningclub.co.uk and Ⓦ uk campsite.co.uk are useful online resources for finding sites.

In England's wilder places you will find **camping barns** and **bunkhouses**, many administered by the YHA, though with plenty of others operated by individual farmers and families. They are pretty basic – often in converted agricultural buildings, old crofters' cottages and the like – but they are weatherproof and cheap (from around £8 a night). **Farmers** may offer field-and-tap pitches for around £3 per night, but setting up a tent without asking first is counted as trespassing and not recommended. Camping wild is illegal in most National Parks and nature reserves, though Dartmoor is one exception; check Ⓦ nationalparks.gov.uk/visiting /camping for more information.

Self-catering

Holiday self-catering properties range from city penthouses to secluded cottages. **Studios and apartments**, available by the night in an increasing number of cities, offer an attractive alternative to hotels, with prices from around £90 a night (more in London). Rural **cottages and houses** work out cheaper, though the minimum rental period may be a week. Depending on the season and location, expect to pay from around £350 for a week in a small cottage, perhaps three or four times that for a larger property in a popular tourist spot.

ACCOMMODATION CONTACTS

B&BS, HOTELS, FARMS AND STUDENT ROOMS

Cool Places Ⓦ coolplaces.co.uk. Good selection of unusual places to stay, from hostels and glamping to farmouse B&Bs.

Distinctly Different Ⓦ distinctlydifferent.co.uk. B&B or self-catering in converted buildings across England, from cowsheds to lighthouses.

Farm Stay Ⓦ farmstay.co.uk. The UK's largest network of farm-based accommodation – B&B, self-catering and camping.

University rooms Ⓦ universityrooms.co.uk. Student halls of residence in university towns from Cornwall to Northumberland, offering good-value rooms (mostly single) or self-catering apartments over the summer (July–Sept), Easter and Christmas holidays.

Wolsey Lodges Ⓦ wolseylodges.com. Superior B&B in grand properties throughout England, from Elizabethan manor houses to Victorian rectories.

SELF-CATERING

Airbnb ⓦ airbnb.com. Cool self-catering, with a huge variety of properties – seaside cottages to farmhouses, canal barges to warehouse apartments, and rooms in private houses.

Landmark Trust ⓦ landmarktrust.org.uk. A preservation charity that lists pricey, rather special accommodation in distinctive historic properties – castles, ruins, follies, towers and cottages.

National Trust Holiday Cottages ⓦ nationaltrustcottages.co.uk. Self-catering holiday cottages, houses and farmhouses, most of which are set in the gardens or grounds of National Trust properties.

Rural Retreats ⓦ ruralretreats.co.uk. Upmarket accommodation in restored historic buildings.

Under the Thatch ⓣ 0844 500 5101, ⓦ underthethatch.co.uk. A select choice of self-catering cottages and cabins, many beautifully restored, from traditional thatched cottages to Romany caravans and yurts.

Food and drink

England no longer has to feel ashamed of its culinary offerings. Over the last twenty years, changing tastes have transformed supermarket shelves, restaurant menus and pub blackboards, with an increasing importance placed on good-quality and sustainable eating – not only sourcing products locally, but also using free-range, organic, humanely produced ingredients. London continues to be the main centre for all things foodie and fashionable, though great restaurants, gastropubs, farmers' markets and interesting local food suppliers can be found across England, often in surprisingly out-of-the-way places.

English cuisine

For some visitors the quintessential English meal is **fish and chips**, a dish that can vary from the succulently fresh to the indigestibly greasy: local knowledge is the key, as most towns, cities and resorts have at least one first-rate fish-and-chip shop ("chippie") or restaurant. Other **traditional English dishes** (steak and kidney pie, bacon sandwiches, roast beef, sausage and mash, pork pies) have largely discarded their stodgy image and been poshed up to become restaurant, and particularly gastropub, staples – comfort food still, but often cooked with the best ingredients and genuinely tasty. Many hitherto neglected or previously unfashionable English foods – from brawn to brains – are finding their way into top-end restaurants, too, as inventive restaurateurs, keen on using good, seasonal produce, reinvent the classics. The principles of this "nose to tail" eating cross over with the increasingly modish **Modern British** cuisine, which marries local produce with ingredients and techniques from around the world. **Vegetarians** need not worry, either, despite all this emphasis on meat – veggie restaurants are fairly easy to find in towns and cities, and practically every restaurant and pub will have at least one vegetarian option. You'll find that Italian, Indian and Chinese restaurants usually provide a decent range of meat-free dishes, too.

The wealth of **fresh produce** varies regionally, from hedgerow herbs to fish landed from local boats, and, of course, seasonally. Restaurants are increasingly making use of seasonal ingredients – and in rural areas many farms offer "Pick Your Own" sessions, when you can come away with armfuls of delicious berries, orchard fruits, beetroot and the like. Year-round you'll find superlative seafood – from crabs to cockles, oysters to lobster – fine cheeses and delicious free-range meat. Check out the growing profusion of farmers' markets and farm shops, usually signposted by the side of the road in rural areas, to enjoy the best local goodies and artisan products.

Cafés, tearooms and coffee shops

Though still a nation of tea-heads, Brits have become bona fide **coffee** addicts, and international chain outlets such as *Starbucks*, *Costa* and *Caffè Nero* line every high street. However, there will usually be at least one independent coffee shop,

---

A FOODIE LEXICON

Whether you're curious about Cornish pasties or Lancashire hotpots, puzzled by Yorkshire puddings or interested in Eccles cakes, you may have to learn a whole **lexicon** to figure out what you're eating. Foodie bafflers range from faggots (offal meatballs) to bubble-and-squeak (fried leftover potato-and-cabbage patties), toad in the hole (sausages in a batter pudding) and spotted dick (suet-pudding dessert with currants). Even the basics aren't straightforward – a simple bread roll, for example, may be referred to as a roll, cob, bap, barmcake, teacake or bread-bun, depending on which part of England you're in.

ENGLISH BREAKFAST

The traditional **Full English** will keep you going all day. It consists of eggs, bacon, sausage, tomatoes, mushrooms, baked beans and toast – all fried, though you some places also offer the eggs scrambled or poached. Especially in northern England, it may also include black pudding (ie, blood sausage). Veggie alternatives are commonly available. Though less common, you may also be served kippers (smoked herring) for a traditional breakfast. B&Bs and hotels will also serve cereals, toast, and many other breakfast standards. A "**continental**" **breakfast** usually means cereal, toast and preserves, though often croissants, fruit and yoghurt too. Though the staple early-morning drink is tea, drunk strong, hot and with cold milk, coffee is just as popular.

even in the smallest places, and artisan coffee, brewed with obsessive care by super-cool baristas, can be found in London, especially, along with some of the bigger cities. Despite the encroaching grip of the coffee chains, every town, city and resort in England should also have a few cheap **cafés** offering non-alcoholic drinks, all-day breakfasts, snacks and meals. Most are only open during the daytime, and have few airs and graces; the quality is not guaranteed, however. A few more genteel **teashops** or **tearooms** serve sandwiches, cakes and light meals throughout the day, as well, of course, as tea – the best of them will offer a full afternoon tea, including sandwiches, cakes and scones with cream and jam.

Pubs and gastropubs

The old-fashioned English **pub** remains an enduring social institution, and is often the best introduction to town or village life. In some places, it might be your only choice for food. While occasionally the offerings can be terrible, England's foodie renaissance, and a commercial need to diversify, means that many have had to up their game. The umbrella term **gastropub** can refer to anything from a traditional country inn with rooms and a restaurant to a slick city-centre pub with upmarket dining room, but generally indicates a pub that puts as much emphasis on the food as the drink. Some are really excellent – and just as expensive as a regular restaurant, though usually with a more informal feel – while others simply provide a relaxed place in which to enjoy a gourmet pork pie or cheese platter with your pint.

Restaurants

Partly by dint of its size, London has the broadest selection of **top-class restaurants**, and the widest choice of cuisines, but there are some seriously fine dining options in most major cities. Indeed,

wherever you are in England you're rarely more than half an hour's drive from a really good meal. Heston Blumenthal's Michelin-star-studded *Fat Duck*, for example, touted as one of the world's best restaurants, is in the small Berkshire village of Bray, where you will also find the equally lauded *Waterside Inn* – while the best Indian food outside the Asian subcontinent is found in unsung cities like Bradford and Leicester.

While a great curry in Birmingham's Balti Triangle or a Cantonese feast in Manchester's Chinatown might **cost** you just £15–20 a head, the going rate for a meal with drinks in most modest restaurants is more like £25–30 per person. If a restaurant has any sort of reputation, you can expect to be spending £40–60 each, and much, much more for the services of a top chef – tasting menus (excluding drinks) at the best-known Michelin-starred restaurants cost upwards of £80 per person. However, **set meals** can be a steal, even at the poshest of restaurants, where a limited-choice two- or three-course lunch or "pre-theatre" menu might cost less than half the usual price.

Drinking

Originating as wayfarers' hostelries and coaching inns, **pubs** – "public houses" – have outlived the church and marketplace as the focal points of many a British town and village. They are as varied as the townscapes: in larger market towns you'll find huge

TOP 5 DESTINATION RESTAURANTS

Le Champignon Sauvage Cheltenham. See p.272

Clove Club London. See p.118

L'Enclume Cartmel. See p.559

The Pilgrims Lovington, Somerset. See p.308

Waterside Inn Bray. See p.277

oak-beamed inns with open fires and polished brass fittings; in remoter upland villages there are stone-built pubs no larger than a two-bedroomed cottage. In towns and cities corner pubs still cater to local neighbourhoods, the best of them stocking an increasingly varied list of local beers and craft brews, while chain pubs, cocktail bars, independent music venues and wine bars all add to the mix. Most pubs and bars serve food, in some shape or form.

Most pubs are officially open from 11am to 11pm, though cities and resorts have a growing number of places with extended licences, especially at weekends. The legal **drinking age** is 18 and though many places will have a special family room (particularly outside cities) or a beer garden, young children may not always be welcome in the evenings (often after 8pm or 9pm).

Beer and cider

Beer, sold by the pint (generally £3.20–5) and half pint (often just a touch over half the price), is England's staple drink, and has been a mainstay of the local diet for centuries, dating back to times when water was too dangerous to drink. Ask simply for a "beer", though, and you'll cause no end of confusion. While lager is sold everywhere, in recent years there's been a huge resurgence in regional beer brewing, and England's unique glory is its **real ale** or **cask ale**, a refreshing beer brewed with traditional ingredients, without additional carbonation, pumped by hand from a cask and served at cellar temperature (not "warm", as foreign jibes have it). If it comes out of an electric pump it isn't the real thing (though it might be a craft beer). The most common ale is known as **bitter**, with a colour ranging from straw-yellow to dark brown, depending on the brew. Other real ales include golden or **pale ales**, plus darker and maltier **milds**, **stouts** and **porters**. Controversy exists over the head of foam on top: in southern England, people prefer their pint without a head, and brimming to the top of the glass; in the north, flat beer is frowned on and drinkers prefer a short head of foam. For more on cask ales, check the website of the influential **Campaign for Real Ale** (Ⓦcamra .org.uk), who remain the bastions of this traditional brewing scene.

Complementary to real ale – and with the distinction between them contentious – are the **craft beers** produced by hundreds of small, independent breweries that have flourished in recent years, influenced by the American craft-brewing scene. Though hoppy pale ales predominate – generally carbonated and so served chilled from kegs not casks – the range of English craft beers is overwhelming. They cover everything from German-style lagers to IPAs (Indian Pale Ales) and Belgian-influenced sour saisons – name a beer style and an independent English brewer will have tried making it, in small batches, probably in a shed in the suburbs or under the railway arches in a former industrial zone. Scotland's BrewDog (Ⓦbrewdog .com) were at the forefront and are now going global, while London's Kernel (Ⓦthekernelbrewery .com) and Manchester's Cloudwater Brew Co. (Ⓦcloudwaterbrew.co) are two names to look out for. The resurgence of independent breweries – both real-ale traditionalists and craft brewers – means that, unlike a decade ago, in many pubs across the country you'll see a row of quirky hand pumps and keg clips lined up along the bar, boasting local provenance and unusual names. It's always worth asking if there's a good local brewery whose beers you should try (and a good pub will let you taste first).

BREWERIES TO VISIT

England has a fantastic selection of beers, and there's no more quintessentially English experience than to sample a pint or two in the nation's one great surviving social institution: the pub. However, in many places you can also visit the breweries themselves – tiny microbreweries sometimes open up a basic taproom once a week for tastings, while others you can tour.

Cumbria alone has more than thirty small breweries, with Jennings in Cockermouth (see p.578), offering guided tours – with the inevitable free tipple at the end. It's also home to the pioneering one-pub outlet the *Bitter End* (see p.579).

The Hook Norton Brewery in **Oxfordshire** (Ⓦhooky.co.uk) still uses a working steam engine in its beer production, while there can't be many more remote ale-making locations than that of the Dent Brewery (Ⓦdentbrewery.co.uk), hidden in a secluded corner of the **Yorkshire Dales National Park**; you can drop in on its own pub, the *George & Dragon*, for a tipple (see p.605), and visit nearby Masham's Theakston's and Black Sheep breweries (see box, p.606).

Though many pubs are owned by large breweries who favour their own beers, this beer revolution has increased the choice in most places. Still best, however, is a **free house** – an independently run pub that can sell whichever beer it pleases.

England's other traditional pint is **cider**, made from fermented apple juice and usually sparkling, with most brewers based in the west of England. There's also a variant made from pears, called **perry**, and, particularly in the West Country, **scrumpy**, a potent and cloudy beverage, usually flat, dry and very apple-y. In most pubs you'll only find a few of the big-name brands. However, in recent years "real" cider – which CAMRA defines as containing a minimum of ninety percent fresh apple juice, along with a few other requirements – has been gaining popularity, ranging from sweet, sparkling golden ciders to cloudy, unfiltered ones from small local producers.

Wine

Now is the time for English **wine**. It has firmly shucked off its image as inferior to its longer-established European counterparts, with nearly five hundred small-scale vineyards producing delicious tipples, mainly in southern England, where the conditions – and rising temperatures – are favourable. The Southwest has a couple of notable wineries, including Sharpham, outside Totnes in Devon (see p.330), but most are in the Southeast; there are several excellent vineyards for visiting in Kent, Sussex and Surrey (see box, p.157). The speciality is sparkling wine, and the best of these have beaten French champagnes in international blind-tasting competitions. For more, see Ⓦ englishwineproducers.co.uk.

Festivals and events

England's showpiece events – from the military pageant of Trooping the Colour to the jolly bombast of the Last Night of the Proms – portray one side of England: formal, patriotic, royal... and stuck in the past. However, that typifies just a fraction of the festivities you'll find. There are quirky village fêtes that date back centuries with customs that defy explanation; major music festivals that cover the countryside in tent cities each summer; popular book festivals and other cultural soirées; and large, loud and fabulous street parties like Notting Hill's carnival and the LGBT+ Pride festivals of London, Manchester and Brighton. All are different, but all show that the English like to let their hair down, and if there's music, drink and a touch of the absurd – cheese rolling, pancake racing? – so much the better.

A festival calendar

This list just scratches the surface – most regions will have major arts and cultural festivals, a music festival or two, plus country shows, food and drink festivals and sporting events. Check with the local tourist office, or see Ⓦ visitengland.com/things-to-do/upcoming-events for more information.

JAN–MARCH

London New Year's Day Parade (Jan 1) Ⓦ lnydp.com; admission charge for grandstand seats in Piccadilly, otherwise free. A procession of floats, marching bands, cheerleaders and clowns wends its way from Parliament Square to Green Park.

Chinese New Year (Late Jan/Early Feb). Processions, fireworks and festivities in England's three main Chinatowns – London, Liverpool and Manchester.

Shrove Tuesday (47 days before Easter Sunday). The last day before Lent is also known as "Pancake Day" – it's traditional to eat thin pancakes, usually with sugar and lemon; public events include pancake races.

Shrovetide Football (Shrove Tuesday & Ash Wednesday) Ⓦ ashbourne-town.com. The world's oldest, largest, longest, craziest football game takes place in and around Ashbourne, Derbyshire.

Rye Bay Scallop Week (10 days end Feb/early March) Ⓦ scallop.org.uk. Ten days of foodie events in the pretty Sussex town of Rye: scallop tastings, cookery demos, barrow races and special menus.

Six Nations Rugby tournament (Feb & March) Ⓦ rbs6nations.com. Tournament between England, Scotland, Wales, Ireland, France and Italy.

APRIL & MAY

St George's Day (April 23). The day that commemorates England's patron saint is also, by chance, the birthday of William Shakespeare, so in addition to Morris dancing and other traditional festivities in towns and villages – with celebrations in London's Trafalgar Square and at other major destinations – there are also Bard-related events at Stratford-upon-Avon (Ⓦ shakespeare.org.uk).

Padstow 'Obby 'Oss (May 1) Ⓦ padstowlive.com. Processions, music and May Day dancing in Padstow, Cornwall, centring on the 'oss itself, a curious costumed and masked figure with obscure origins. See p.368

Exeter Festival of South West Food and Drink (early May) Ⓦ exeterfoodanddrinkfestival.co.uk. See box, p.323

Glyndebourne Opera Festival (mid-May to late Aug) Ⓦ glyndebourne.com. One of the classiest arts festivals in the country, in East Sussex. See box, p.166

Bath Festival (late May) ⓦ bathfestivals.org.uk. Top-class, ten-day music and literature jamboree, ranging from orchestral, jazz and world music to author talks, workshops and debates.

Hay Festival (last week in May) ⓦ www.hayfestival.com. Bibliophiles descend on this Welsh border town for a big literary shindig and its offshoot HowTheLightGetsIn, a festival of philosophy and music. See p.449

JUNE & JULY

Trooping the Colour (Second Sat in June) ⓦ householddivision .org.uk. Massed bands, equestrian pageantry, gun salutes and fly-pasts for the Queen's Official Birthday on Horse Guards Parade, London.

Aldeburgh Festival (mid- to end June) ⓦ snapemaltings.co.uk. Suffolk festival of classical music, established by Benjamin Britten. See box, p.391

Glastonbury (late June) ⓦ glastonburyfestivals.co.uk. This five-day music and performing arts festival, taking place over the last weekend in June on a beautiful site in Somerset, has grown from its hippy roots to become the greatest music festival on the planet. No festival in 2018, returning 2019. See box, p.306

Pride London (end June/early July) ⓦ prideinlondon.org. England's biggest LGBT+ event, with parade, music and parties, plus two weeks of events preceding the parade. Brighton (ⓦ brighton-pride.org), Manchester (ⓦ manchesterpride.com) and other cities have big Pride events of their own in Aug.

Latitude (mid-July) ⓦ latitudefestival.com. Set near the lovely Suffolk seaside town of Southwold, Latitude festival is laidback and family-friendly with a good mix of music stages, comedy, talks and other performances, and attracts some pretty big names. See p.393

Liverpool International Music Festival (mid-July) ⓦ limfestival.com. Four days of free events in Sefton Park, with an eclectic line-up of music, plus other gigs around the city.

The Proms (mid-July to mid-Sept) ⓦ bbc.co.uk/proms. Top-flight international classical music festival at the Royal Albert Hall, London, ending in the famously patriotic Last Night of the Proms. See box, p.128

WOMAD (late July) ⓦ womad.org. Renowned four-day world music festival outside Malmesbury, Wiltshire.

Whitstable Oyster Festival (last week July) ⓦ whitstable oysterfestival.com. Seafront procession and a beachside "blessing of the oysters" – and heaps of fresh bivalves to snack on, of course. See p.139

Cambridge Folk Festival (end July/early Aug) ⓦ cambridgefolkfestival.co.uk. Superb festival encompassing folk music in its broadest sense, with a good mix of big names and interesting newcomers. See p.421

AUG & SEPT

Cowes Week (1st week Aug) ⓦ cowesweek.co.uk. Sailing extravaganza in the Isle of Wight, with partying and star-studded entertainment. See p.199

Boardmasters, Newquay (five days in early Aug) ⓦ boardmasters .co.uk. Cornish seaside music and surfing festival. See box, p.323

Sidmouth FolkWeek (1st week Aug) ⓦ sidmouthfolkweek.co.uk. The country's longest-running folk festival, with events throughout the town. See p.327

Great British Beer Festival (mid-Aug) ⓦ gbbf.org.uk. Colossal booze-fest in London, featuring more than nine hundred real ales and ciders from around the world.

Notting Hill Carnival (last Sun & bank hol Mon Aug) ⓦ thelondonnottinghillcarnival.com. Vivacious two-day carnival led by London's Caribbean community with parades and floats, thumping sound systems, food stalls and huge crowds taking over the whole neighbourhood. See box, p.124

Blackpool Illuminations (late Aug or early Sept to early Nov) ⓦ visitblackpool.com. Initiated to extend the traditional Blackpool holiday season, the Blackpool lights have been a tourist attraction for over a century. Switch-on weekend is celebrated with free events and music (register for wristband).

Abbots Bromley Horn Dance (early Sept) ⓦ abbotsbromley.com. Vaguely pagan mass dance in mock-medieval costume – one of the most famous of England's ancient customs, in Staffordshire.

Heritage Open Days (2nd week Sept) ⓦ heritageopendays.org. uk. Annual opportunity to peek inside hundreds of buildings in England that don't normally open their doors to the public, from factories to Buddhist temples.

Ludlow Food Festival (mid-Sept) ⓦ foodfestival.co.uk. High-profile fest in this foodie Shropshire town, with local producers, Michelin chefs and scores of events and masterclasses.

St Ives September Festival (2 weeks mid-Sept) ⓦ stivesseptemberfestival.co.uk. Eclectic Cornish festival of art, poetry, literature, jazz, folk, rock and world music.

WEIRD AND WONDERFUL FESTIVALS

National nuttiness is displayed at dozens of local festivals around England every year. **Easter** is particularly big on eccentricity, from the **Hare Pie Scramble and Bottle-Kicking** (Easter Mon), a chaotic village bottle-kicking contest at Hallaton, Leicestershire, to Gawthorpe in Yorkshire's **World Coal-Carrying Championship** (Easter Mon; ⓦ gawthorpemaypole.org.uk), an annual race to carry 50kg of coal a mile through the village. May brings a host of ancient spring rites, including the **Helston Furry Dance** (May 8), a courtly procession and "Floral Dance" through the Cornish town (see p.356). There's more odd racing at the **Brockworth Cheese Rolling** (late May, bank hol Mon; ⓦ cheese-rolling.co.uk) when crowds of daredevils chase a large cheese wheel down a murderous Gloucestershire incline. Later in the year, thousands flock to Ashton, Northamptonshire, to watch modern-day gladiators fight for glory armed only with a nut and twelve inches of string, in the **World Conker Championship** (mid-Oct).

OCT–DEC

Battle of Hastings reenactment (weekend in mid-Oct) Ⓦ www.english-heritage.org.uk. Annual reenactment of the famous 1066 battle in Battle, featuring over 1000 soldiers and living history encampments.

Halloween (Oct 31). Last day of the Celtic calendar and All Hallows Eve: pumpkins, plus a lot of ghoulish dressing-up, trick-or-treating and parties.

Guy Fawkes Night/Bonfire Night (Nov 5). Nationwide fireworks and bonfires commemorating the foiling of the Gunpowder Plot in 1605 – atop every bonfire is hoisted an effigy known as the "guy" after Guy Fawkes, one of the conspirators. Many events stick to fireworks nowadays, but notable traditional events include those in York (Fawkes's birthplace), Ottery St Mary in Devon, and Lewes, East Sussex.

Lord Mayor's Show (2nd Sat in Nov) Ⓦ lordmayorsshow.org. Held annually in the City of London since 1215, and featuring a daytime cavalcade and night-time fireworks to mark the inauguration of the new Lord Mayor.

New Year's Eve (Dec 31). Big parties all over England; in London, there's a massive fireworks display over the Thames, centred on the London Eye (tickets required for riverside locations).

Sports and outdoor activities

As the birthplace of football, cricket, rugby and tennis, England boasts a series of sporting events that attract a world audience. For those who wish to participate, the UK caters for just about every outdoor activity, in particular walking, cycling and watersports, but there are also opportunities for anything from rock climbing to pony trekking.

Spectator sports

Football (soccer) is the national game in England, with a wide programme of professional league matches taking place every Saturday afternoon from early August to mid-May, with plenty of Sunday and midweek fixtures too. It's very difficult to get tickets to Premier League matches involving the most famous teams (Chelsea, Arsenal, Manchester United, Liverpool), but tours of their grounds are feasible. You could also try one of the lower-league games.

Rugby comes in two codes – 15-a-side **Rugby Union** and 13-a-side **Rugby League**, both fearsomely brutal contact sports that can make entertaining viewing even if you don't understand the rules. In England, rugby is much less popular than football, but Rugby League has a loyal and dedicated fan base in the north – especially Yorkshire and Lancashire – while Union has traditionally been popular with the English middle class. Key Rugby Union and League games are sold out months in advance, but ordinary fixtures present few ticketing problems. The Rugby Union season runs from September to just after Easter, Rugby League February to September.

Cricket is English idiosyncrasy at its finest. People from non-cricketing nations – and most Brits for that matter – marvel at a game that can last several days and still end in a draw, while many people are unfamiliar with its rules. International, five-day "Test" matches, pitting the English national side against visiting countries, are played most summers at grounds around the country, and tickets are usually fairly easy to come by. The domestic game traditionally centres on four-day County Championship matches between English county teams, though there's far bigger interest – certainly for casual watchers – in the "Twenty20" (T20) format, designed to encourage flamboyant, decisive play in three-hour matches.

Finally, if you're in England at the end of June and early July, you won't be able to miss the country's annual fixation with **tennis** in the shape of the Wimbledon championships. It's often said that no one gives a hoot about the sport for the other fifty weeks of the year, though the success of Scottish champion Andy Murray (who has won the men's singles twice), has changed that somewhat, and has meant the crowds at Wimbledon and watching on screens across the country are no longer rooting for an underdog. Advance tickets for main courts are hard to come by, but you can join the queue for ground passes (Ⓦ wimbledon.com).

Walking

Walking routes track across many of England's wilder areas, amid landscapes varied enough to suit any taste. Turn up in any National Park area and local information offices will be able to advise on anything from a family stroll to a full day out on the mountains. For shorter walks, you could check out the **National Trust** website (Ⓦ nationaltrust.org.uk), which details picturesque routes of varying lengths that weave through or near their properties. If you're travelling on public transport, consult the user-generated site **Car Free Walks** (Ⓦ carfreewalks .org), which details hundreds of routes that set off and finish at train stations and bus stops, providing OS map links and elevation profiles for each.

ACTIVITY TOUR OPERATORS

There are numerous activity tours available taking in the best of the English outdoors. We've listed some of the top choices below for getting out on the water, on two wheels or just on foot.

BOATING AND SAILING

Blakes Holiday Boating UK ☎ 0345 498 6184, ⓦ blakes.co.uk. Cruisers, yachts and narrowboats on the Norfolk Broads, the River Thames and various English canals.

Classic Sailing UK ☎ 01872 580022, ⓦ classic-sailing.co.uk. Hands-on sailing holidays on traditional wooden boats and tall ships, including Cornwall and the Isles of Scilly.

CYCLING

The Carter Company UK ☎ 01296 631671, ⓦ the-carter -company.com. Gentle self-guided cycling and walking tours, including in London, Kent, Oxford and the Cotswolds, Devon, Cornwall and Dorset, in simple or luxury accommodation.

Saddle Skedaddle UK ☎ 01912 651110, ⓦ skedaddle.co.uk. Biking adventures and classic road rides – including guided, self-guided and tailor-made tours in Cornwall, the Cotswolds, Northumberland and the New Forest, lasting from a weekend to a week, or a 22-day Land's End to John O'Groats tour.

SWIMMING

Swim Trek ☎ 01273 739 713, ⓦ swimtrek.com. Guided wild-swimming holidays and trips, including one day on the Thames or along the Dorset coast, and Lake District trips.

SURFING

Surfers World UK ☎ 07540 221089, ⓦ surfersworld.co.uk. Short breaks with surfing courses in Woolacombe, Croyde, and on the north Cornwall coast, as well as coasteering and paddleboarding and group holidays.

WALKING

Contours Walking Holidays UK ☎ 01629 821900, ⓦ contours .co.uk. Excellent short breaks or longer walking holidays and self-guided hikes in every region of England, from famous trails to lesser-known local routes.

English Lakeland Ramblers US ☎ 1800 724 8801, ⓦ ramblers.com. Escorted and self-guided walking tours in the Lake District and the Cotswolds, either inn-to-inn or based in a country hotel.

Ramblers Worldwide Holidays UK ☎ 01707 331133, ⓦ ramblersholidays.co.uk. Sociable guided walking tours all over the UK, on a variety of themes, and for various fitness levels.

For walks within day-trip distance of London by public transport, check out the *Rough Guide to Walks in London & the Southeast*. Various **membership associations**, including the Ramblers Association (ⓦ ramblers.org.uk) and Walkers are Welcome (ⓦ walkersarewelcome.org.uk), also provide information and route ideas online.

Even for short hikes you need to be **properly equipped**, follow local advice and listen out for local weather reports – British weather is notoriously changeable and increasingly extreme. You will also need a good **map** – in most cases one of the excellent and reliable Ordnance Survey (OS) series (see p.45), usually available from local tourist offices or outdoor shops.

Hiking trails

England's finest **walking areas** are the granite moorlands and spectacular coastlines of Devon and Cornwall in the southwest, and the highlands of the north – notably the Yorkshire Dales, the North York Moors and the Lake District. Keen hikers might want to tackle one of England's twelve **National Trails** (ⓦ nationaltrail.co.uk). The most famous – certainly the toughest – is the **Pennine Way** (268 miles; usual walking time 16–19 days), stretching from the Derbyshire Peak District to the Scottish Borders (see box, p.467), while the challenging **South West Coast Path** (630 miles; from 30 days) through Cornwall, Devon, Somerset and Dorset tends to be tackled in shorter sections (see box, p.313). This is currently the most comprehensive stretch of coastal walkway, though plans are underway to create a complete **England Coast Path** (ⓦ nationaltrail.co.uk /england-coast-path), expanding access and joining together existing coastal footpaths into a 2800-mile waymarked path by 2020. Other English trails are less gung-ho in character, like the **South Downs Way** (100 miles; 8 days) following the chalk escarpment and ridges of the South Downs (see box opposite) or the fascinating **Hadrian's Wall footpath** (84 miles; 7 days).

Cycling

The **National Cycle Network** is made up of 14,500 miles of signed cycle route, mainly on traffic-free paths (including disused railways and canal towpaths) and country roads. You're never far from one of the numbered routes, all of which are detailed on the **Sustrans** website (ⓦ sustrans.org.uk), a charitable trust devoted to the development of environmentally sustainable transport. Sustrans also publishes an excellent

ENGLAND'S NATIONAL PARKS

England has ten National Parks (ⓦ www.nationalparks.gov.uk), from Dartmoor in the southwest to Northumberland in the north.

- **The Broads** See box, p.400. The best place for a boating holiday – the rivers, marshes, fens and canals of Norfolk (and stretching into Suffolk) make up one of the most important wetlands in Europe, and are also ideal for birdwatching. A car isn't much use – cyclists and walkers have the best of it. Don't miss: the long-distance footpath, Weavers' Way (see box, p.400).

- **Dartmoor** See p.333. Southern England's largest wilderness attracts back-to-nature hikers – the open moorland walking can be pretty hardcore, and Dartmoor is famous for its standing stones, Stone Age hut circles and hill forts. Don't miss: Grimspound Bronze Age village (see p.335).

- **Exmoor** See p.311. Exmoor straddles the Somerset/Devon border and on its northern edge overlooks the sea from high, hogback hills. Crisscrossed by trails and also accessible from the South West Coast Path, it's ideal for walking and pony trekking. Don't miss: the four-mile hike to Dunkery Beacon, Exmoor's highest point (see p.312).

- **Lake District** See p.552. The Lake District (in Cumbria, in northwest England) is an almost alpine landscape of glacial lakes and rugged mountains. It's great for hiking, rock climbing and watersports, but also has strong literary connections and thriving cultural traditions. Don't miss: Honister's hard-hat mine tour and Via Ferrata mountain traverse (see p.574).

- **New Forest** See p.206. In the predominantly domesticated landscape of Hampshire, the country's best surviving example of a medieval hunting forest can be surprisingly wild. The majestic woodland is interspersed by tracts of heath, and a good network of paths and bridleways offers plenty of scope for biking and pony rides. Don't miss: camping in one of the stunning New Forest sites (see p.206).

- **Northumberland** See p.655. Where England meets Scotland, remote Northumberland in England's northeast is adventure country. The long-distance Pennine Way runs the length of the park, and the Romans left their mark in the shape of Hadrian's Wall, along which you can hike or bike. Don't miss: the Chillingham cattle wildlife safari (see p.658).

- **North York Moors** See p.625. A stunning mix of heather moorland, gentle valleys, ruined abbeys and wild coastline. Walking and mountain biking are the big outdoor activities here, but you can also tour the picturesque stone villages or hang out with goths in Whitby. Don't miss: a day out at Ryedale Folk Museum (see p.628).

- **Peak District** See p.460. England's first National Park (1951) is also the most visited, because it sits between the major population centres of the Midlands and the northwest. It's rugged outdoors country, with some dramatic underground caverns, tempered by stately homes and spa and market towns. Don't miss: a trip down Treak Cliff Cavern (see p.466).

- **South Downs** See box, p.172. England's newest National Park (established 2010) might not be as wild as the others – about 85 percent is farmland – but it offers a rural escape into West and East Sussex from one of the most densely populated parts of the country. Don't miss: a walk along the South Downs Way, which covers over 100 miles of the chalk uplands between Winchester and Beachy Head (see box, p.163).

- **Yorkshire Dales** See p.599. The best choice for walking, cycling and pony trekking, Yorkshire's second National Park spreads across twenty dales, or valleys, at the heart of the Pennines. England's most scenic railway – the Settle to Carlisle line – is another great draw, while caves, waterfalls and castles provide the backdrop. Don't miss: the walk to dramatic Malham Cove (see p.603).

series of waterproof cycle maps (1:100,000) and regional guides.

Major routes include the **C2C** (Sea-to-Sea), which runs for 140 miles between Whitehaven/Workington on the English northwest coast and Tynemouth/Sunderland on the northeast; the **Cornish Way** (123 miles), from Bude to Land's End; and the classic cross-Britain route from **Land's End to John O'Groats**, the far southwest of England to the northeast tip of Scotland – roughly 1000 miles, which can be covered in two to three weeks, depending on which route you choose.

England's biggest cycling organization, **Cycling UK** (ⓦ cyclinguk.org), provides lists of tour operators and rental outlets, and supplies members with touring and technical advice, as well as insurance.

Watersports

Sailing and **windsurfing** in England are especially popular along the south coast (particularly the Isle of Wight and Solent) and in the southwest (around Falmouth in Cornwall, and around Salcombe and Dartmouth in Devon). Here, and in the Lake District, you'll be able to rent dinghies, boats and kayaks, either by the hour or for longer periods of instruction – from around £30 for a couple of hours of kayaking to about £150 for a two-day nonresidential sailing course.

Newquay in Cornwall is England's undisputed **surfing** centre, whose main break, Fistral, regularly hosts international contests. But there are quieter spots all along the north coast of Cornwall and Devon, as well as a growing scene on the more isolated northeast coast from Yorkshire up to Northumberland, with lots of action at the pretty seaside town of Saltburn. For more **information** on surfing in England, including a directory of surf schools and an events calendar, check ⓦ surfinggb.com.

Another option is **coasteering**, a thrilling extreme sport that involves climbing, swimming, scrambling and cliff jumping – with a guide – along the more spectacular stretches of rocky coast; Cornwall is a particularly good coasteering hotspot. Finally, if you can brave the often chilly temperatures, consider **wild swimming**, which has really taken off and is a wonderful way to experience England's many beautiful rivers, lakes, waterfall pools and sea caves. Check ⓦ wildswimming.co.uk for a run-down of good places plus safety tips – you should always heed local advice.

Travel essentials

Climate

Though it has seen some extreme storms, flooding and snowfall in recent years, England has a generally temperate, maritime climate, which means largely moderate temperatures (see box, p.12) and a decent chance of at least some rain whenever you visit. If you're attempting to balance the clemency of the weather against the density of the crowds, even given regional variations and microclimates the best months to come to England are April, May, September and October.

Costs

Faced with another £4 pint, a £40 theatre ticket and a £20 taxi ride back to your £100-a-night hotel, England might seem like the most expensive place in Europe – in the cities, at least. Even if you're camping or hostelling, using public transport, buying picnic lunches and eating in pubs and cafés, your minimum expenditure will be around £40 per person per day. Couples staying in B&Bs, eating at local pubs and restaurants and sightseeing should expect to splash out £70 per person, while if you're renting a car, staying in hotels and eating at fancier places, budget for at least £120 each. Double that last figure if you choose to stay in a stylish city or grand country-house hotel, while on any visit to London work on the basis that you'll need an extra £30 per day.

Discounts and admission charges

Many of England's **historic attractions** – from castles to stately homes – are owned and/or operated by either the **National Trust** (☏ 0344 800 1895, ⓦ nationaltrust.org.uk; denoted as NT in the Guide) or **English Heritage** (☏ 0370 333 1181, ⓦ www.english -heritage.org.uk; EH). Both these organizations usually charge entry fees, though some sites are free. If you plan to visit more than half a dozen places owned by one of them, it's worth considering an annual membership (£65 for the National Trust; £54 for English Heritage) – you can join on your first visit to any attraction. For non-UK visitors, English Heritage's nine- or sixteen-day **overseas visitors passes** (£31/£37; family passes available) are good value if you are planning on visiting more than two of their properties. The National Trust touring pass is similar (7 days £29; 14 days £34; buy online in advance), though some NT properties are not included. US members of the **Royal Oak Foundation** (ⓦ royal-oak.org) get free admission to all National Trust properties.

Municipal art galleries and museums across the UK often have free admission, as do the world-class **state museums** in London, Birmingham, Manchester and elsewhere, from the British Museum (London) to York's National Railway Museum. Private and municipal museums and other collections rarely charge more than £10 admission. Some **cathedrals** and churches either charge admission or ask for voluntary donations.

The admission charges given in the Guide are the full adult rate, unless otherwise stated. Concessionary rates – generally a few pounds less – for **senior citizens** (over 60), under-26s and **children** (generally from 5 to 17) apply almost everywhere, from tourist attractions to public transport. Family

TIPPING

Although there are no fixed rules for **tipping**, a 10 to 15 percent tip is anticipated by restaurant waiters. Tipping taxi drivers ten percent or so is optional, but most people at the very least round the fare up to the nearest pound. Some restaurants levy a "discretionary" or "optional" **service charge** of 10 or 12.5 percent, which must be clearly stated on the menu and on the bill. However, you are not obliged to pay it, and certainly not if the food or service wasn't what you expected. It is not normal to leave tips if you order at the bar in pubs, though more likely if there's table service in bars, when some people choose to leave a few coins. The only other occasions when you'll be expected to tip are at the hairdressers, and in upmarket hotels where porters and bell boys expect and usually get a pound or two per bag or for calling a taxi.

tickets are often available, and children under 5 are usually free.

Full-time students can benefit from an International Student ID Card (ISIC; 🌐 isic.org), and those under 30 from an International Youth Travel Card (IYTC), while **teachers** qualify for the International Teacher Identity Card (ITIC). Available from STA Travel (see p.28), all cost £12 and are valid for special air, rail and bus fares, and discounts at museums and other attractions.

Crime and personal safety

Terrorist attacks in England may have changed the general perception of how safe the country feels, but it's still extremely unlikely that you'll be at any risk as you travel around, though you will be aware of heightened **security** in place at airports, major train stations and high-profile sights. You can walk more or less anywhere without fear of harassment, though the big cities can have their edgy districts and it's always better to err on the side of caution, especially late at night. Leave your passport and valuables in a hotel or hostel safe (carrying **ID** is not compulsory, though if you look particularly youthful and intend to drink in a pub or buy alcohol in a shop it can be a good idea to carry it, and some clubs require ID for entry), and exercise the usual caution on public transport. If you're taking a taxi, always make sure that it's officially licensed and never pick one up in the street – unless it's an official black taxi in London (see p.110). Bar or restaurant staff can usually provide a reliable recommendation or direct you to the nearest taxi rank.

Other than asking for directions, most visitors rarely come into contact with the **police**, who as a rule are approachable and helpful. Most wear chest guards and carry batons, though regular street officers do not carry guns. If you are robbed, report it straight away to the police; your insurance company will require a **crime report number**. For **police**, **fire** and **ambulance** services phone ❶999.

Electricity

The **current** is 240V AC. North American appliances will need a transformer and adaptor; those from Europe, South Africa, Australia and New Zealand only need an adaptor.

Entry requirements

At the time of writing citizens of all European countries – except Albania, Bosnia and Herzegovina, Macedonia, Montenegro, Serbia and all the former Soviet republics (other than the Baltic states) – can enter England with just a **passport**, for up to three months (and indefinitely if you're from the EU, European Economic Area or Switzerland). Americans, Canadians, Australians and New Zealanders can stay for up to six months, providing they have a return ticket and funds to cover their stay. Citizens of most other countries require a **visa**, obtainable from their British consulate or mission office. Check with the **UK Border Agency** (🌐 ukvisas.gov.uk) for up-to-date information about visa applications, extensions and all aspects of residency.

The 2016 referendum, when the UK voted **to leave the European Union**, has, in theory, put many visa and entry requirements to the UK in flux, particularly for work or longer stays for citizens of the EU, EEA and Switzerland. The UK is set to leave the EU by March 2019, at which point new arrangements will need to be in place. In reality, the status quo will most likely continue for short-term visits, when visas are unlikely to be required, but check in advance; work, study and longer-term visa requirements may change. Until 2019, EU, EEA and Swiss citizens can work in the UK without a permit (other nationals need a work permit in order to work legally in the UK).

Note that visa regulations are subject to frequent changes, so it's always wise to contact the nearest British embassy or High Commission before you travel.

Health

No vaccinations are required for entry into England. Citizens of all EU and EEA countries and Switzerland are entitled to free medical treatment within the National Health Service (**NHS**), which includes the vast majority of hospitals and doctors, on production of their **European Health Insurance Card** (EHIC) or, in extremis, their passport or national identity card. However, this could change when the UK leaves the EU, estimated for 2019, so check in advance. Some Commonwealth countries also have reciprocal healthcare arrangements with the UK – for example Australia and New Zealand. If you don't fall into either of these categories, you will be charged for all medical services – except those administered by accident and emergency units at NHS hospitals – so health insurance is strongly advised.

Pharmacists (known as **chemists** in England) can advise you on minor conditions but can dispense only a limited range of drugs without a doctor's prescription. Most are open standard shop hours, though there are also late-night branches in large cities and at 24-hour supermarkets. For generic pain relief, cold remedies and the like, the local supermarket is usually the cheapest option.

Minor complaints and injuries can be dealt with at a **doctor's (GP's) surgery** – your hotel should be able to point you in the right direction, though you may not be seen immediately. For serious injuries, go to the 24-hour **Accident and Emergency (A&E)** department of the nearest **hospital**, and in an **emergency**, call an ambulance on ☎999. If you need medical help fast but it's not a 999 emergency you can also get free advice from the NHS's 24-hour **helpline** on ☎111.

Insurance

It's a good idea to take out an **insurance policy** before travelling to cover against theft and loss, as well as illness or injury if not covered by reciprocal arrangements with your home country. Most exclude so-called dangerous sports unless an extra premium is paid: in England this can mean most watersports, rock climbing and mountaineering, though hiking, kayaking and jeep safaris would probably be covered.

Internet

Most hotels and hostels in England have free **wi-fi** (we indicate in the Guide if they do not). In addition, many museums, public buildings, tourist offices and some train stations provide free wi-fi, as do numerous cafés, restaurants and bars. Less common are dedicated internet cafés, but some public libraries also offer free access.

LGBT+ travellers

England offers one of the most diverse and accessible **LGBT+** scenes anywhere in Europe. Nearly every sizeable town has some kind of organized LGBT+ life – from bars and clubs to community groups – with the major scenes found in London, Manchester and Brighton. Listings, news and reviews can be found at *Gay Times* (𝕎 gaytimes.co.uk) and *Pink News* (𝕎 pinknews.co.uk). The website of the campaigning organization Stonewall (𝕎 stonewall.org.uk) is also useful, with directories of local groups and advice on reporting hate crimes, which, unfortunately, continue to be a concern. The age of consent is 16.

Mail

The postal service (**Royal Mail**) is pretty efficient. First-class **stamps** to anywhere in the UK currently cost 65p and post should arrive the next day; if the item is anything approaching A4 size, it will be classed as a "Large Letter" and will cost 98p; if you want to guarantee next-day delivery, ask for Special Delivery (from £6.45). Second-class stamps cost 56p, taking up to three days; airmail to the rest of

ROUGH GUIDES TRAVEL INSURANCE

Rough Guides has teamed up with WorldNomads.com to offer great **travel insurance** deals. Policies are available to residents of over 150 countries, with cover for a wide range of adventure sports, 24-hour emergency assistance, high levels of medical and evacuation cover and a stream of travel safety information. Roughguides.com users can take advantage of their policies online 24/7, from anywhere in the world – even if you're already travelling. And since plans often change when you're on the road, you can extend your policy and even claim online. Roughguides.com users who buy travel insurance with WorldNomads.com can also leave a positive footprint and donate to a community development project. For more information go to 𝕎 roughguides.com/travel-insurance.

DISTANCES, WEIGHTS AND MEASURES

Distances (and speeds) on English signposts are in miles, and beer is still served in pints. For everything else – money, weights and measures – a confusing mixture of the **metric and imperial** systems is used: fuel is dispensed by the litre, while meat, milk and vegetables may be sold in either or both systems. Throughout this Guide distances are given in feet, yards and miles.

Europe and the world costs £1.17 and should take three days within Europe, five days further afield. Stamps can be bought at post offices, but also from newsagents, many gift shops and supermarkets, although they usually only sell books of four or ten first-class UK stamps.

To find out your nearest **post office**, see ⓦpost office.co.uk.

Maps

Petrol stations in England stock large-format **road atlases** produced by the AA, RAC, Collins, Ordnance Survey and others, which cover all of Britain, at a scale of around 1:250,000, and include larger-scale plans of major towns. The best of these is the Ordnance Survey road atlas, which handily uses the same grid reference system as their folding maps. Overall, the **Ordnance Survey** (OS; ⓦordnancesurvey.co.uk) produces the most comprehensive maps, renowned for their accuracy and clarity. Their 1:50,000 (pink) *Landranger* series shows enough detail to be useful for most walkers and cyclists, and there's more detail still in the full-colour 1:25,000 (orange) *Explorer* series – both cover the whole of Britain. The full OS range is only available at a few big-city stores or online, but you can get the OS app.

The Media

For television, radio and online news, the UK's **British Broadcasting Corporation** (**BBC**; ⓦbbc.co.uk), paid for by a licence fee levied on viewers, remains the biggest media provider, with both national and regional coverage. The BBC's website is useful for news headlines and weather forecasts. Two terrestrial channels, **BBC1** and **BBC2**, plus digital **BBC4**, covers the full swathe of television broadcasting from international, national and local news to world-famous drama and entertainment, such as *Doctor Who*.

The BBC's **radio network** (ⓦbbc.co.uk/radio) has five nationwide stations: **Radio 1** (chart and dance music); **Radio 2** (light pop and rock for an older audience); **Radio 3** (classical and jazz); **Radio 4** (current affairs, arts and drama); and **5 Live** (sports, news, discussions and phone-ins). Digital-only BBC stations include the alternative-music 6 Music, and the BBC Asian Network, and there are stations for all regions. You can find many of the BBC's best radio shows as **podcasts**.

Beyond the BBC, there are three terrestrial channels: ITV (ⓦitv.com), Channel 4 (ⓦchannel4 .com) and Channel 5 (ⓦchannel5.com), plus dozens of digital and satellite options. Live sport is often shown on satellite provider Sky, whose 24-hour rolling Sky News programme rivals that of CNN. Most English homes and hotels get around forty "freeview" channels spread across the networks, including dedicated news, film, sports, arts and entertainment channels.

The major **newspapers**, providing print and online news, include the higher-end traditional papers, *The Times* (ⓦthetimes.co.uk; paywall), the staunchly Conservative *Daily Telegraph* (ⓦtelegraph .co.uk; paywall), the left-of-centre *Guardian*, with its Sunday sister paper the *Observer* (ⓦtheguardian .com), and the *Independent* (ⓦindependent.co.uk; online only). Of the **tabloid titles**, the most popular is the *Sun* (ⓦthesun.co.uk), a muck-raking right-wing paper whose chief rival is the traditionally left-leaning *Mirror* (ⓦmirror.co.uk). The middlebrow daily tabloids – the *Daily Mail* (ⓦdailymail.co.uk) and the *Daily Express* (ⓦexpress.co.uk) – are particularly partisan and noticeably xenophobic.

Money

England's currency is the **pound sterling** (£), divided into 100 pence (p). Coins come in denominations of 1p, 2p, 5p, 10p, 20p, 50p, £1 and £2. Bank of England notes are in denominations of £5, £10, £20 and £50. At the time of writing, £1 was worth US$1.29, €1.15, Can$1.74, Aus$1.95 and NZ$2.10. For current **exchange rates**, visit ⓦxe.com.

The easiest way to get hold of cash is to use your **debit card** at an **ATM**; there's usually a daily withdrawal limit, which varies depending on the money issuer, but starts at around £250. You'll find ATMs outside banks, at all major points of arrival and motorway service areas, at large supermarkets, petrol stations and even inside some pubs, rural post offices and village shops (though a charge of a few pounds may be levied on cash withdrawals at small, stand-alone ATMs – the screen will tell you).

Credit cards are widely accepted in hotels, shops and restaurants – MasterCard and Visa are almost universal, charge cards like American Express and Diners Club less so.

Paying by plastic involves inserting your credit or debit card into a "chip-and-pin" terminal, beside the till in shops, or brought to your table in restaurants, and then keying in your PIN to authorize the transaction. **Contactless payments**, where you simply hold your credit or debit card on or near a card reader without having to key in a PIN, are prevalent for transactions for up to £30, including on London transport (see box, p.109). Note that the same overseas transaction fees will apply to contactless payments as to those made with a PIN. Contactless has increased the number of establishments that take card – even market stalls may do – though some smaller places, such as B&Bs and shops, may accept cash only, and occasionally there's a minimum amount for card payments (£5 or £10 ususally).

You can change currency or cheques at **post offices** and **bureaux de change** – the former charge no commission, while the latter tend to be open longer hours and are found in most city centres and at major airports and train stations.

Opening hours and public holidays

Though traditional office hours are Monday to Saturday from around 9am to 5.30pm or 6pm, many businesses, shops and restaurants throughout England will open earlier – or later – and close later. The majority of shops are open daily, and in the towns at least might stay open late on a Thursday evening, but some places – even the so-called "24hr supermarkets" – are closed or have restricted hours on Sunday, and businesses in remote areas and villages might even have an "early closing day" – often

---

PUBLIC HOLIDAYS

Jan 1 (New Year's Day)
Good Friday
Easter Monday
First Mon in May ("May Day")
Last Mon in May
Last Mon in Aug
Dec 25 (Christmas Day)
Dec 26 (Boxing Day)

Note that if January 1, December 25 or December 26 falls on a Saturday or Sunday, the next weekday becomes a public holiday.

Wednesday – when they shut at 1pm. Banks are not open at the weekend. We have given full **opening hours** for everything we review – museums, galleries and tourist attractions, cafés, restaurants, pubs and shops – throughout the Guide, noting where they're especially complex or prone to change and you should check before visiting.

While many local shops and businesses close on **public holidays**, few tourist-related businesses observe them, particularly in summer. However, nearly all museums, galleries and other attractions are closed on Christmas Day and New Year's Day, with many also closed on Boxing Day (Dec 26). England's public holidays are usually referred to as **bank holidays** (though it's not just the banks who have a day off).

Phones

Every English landline number has a prefix, which, if beginning ☎01 or 02, represents an **area code**. The prefix ☎07 is for mobile phones/cellphones. A variety of ☎08 prefixes relate to the cost of calls – some, like ☎0800, are free to call from a landline, others (like ☎0845 and ☎0870) are more expensive than landlines, the actual price depending on your phone or phone operator; ☎03 numbers are charged at local rates. Beware, particularly, **premium-rate ☎09 numbers**, common for pre-recorded information services (including some tourist authorities), which can be charged at anything up to £3.60 a minute.

For directory enquiries, there are numerous companies offering the service, all with six-figure numbers beginning with ☎118, but charges are extortionate (with minimum charges of £5-plus and costs quickly escalating) and so best avoided.

Most hotel rooms have telephones, but there is almost always an exorbitant surcharge for their use. Public **payphones** – telephone boxes – are still found, though with the ubiquity of mobile phones, they're seldom used.

Mobile phone access is universal in towns and cities, and rural areas are well served too, though coverage can be patchy. To use your own phone, check with your provider that international roaming is activated – and that your phone will work in the UK. Any EU-registered phones will be charged the same rates for calls, text messages and data as your home tariff (at least until March 2019 when the UK leaves the EU). Calls using non-EU phones are still unregulated and can have prohibitively expensive roaming charges. If you're staying in England for any length of time, it's often easiest to **buy a mobile** and local SIM card in the UK – basic prepay ("pay as you go") models start at around £30, usually including some calling credit.

CALLING ABROAD FROM ENGLAND

Australia ☎ 0061 + area code minus the initial zero + number.
New Zealand ☎ 0064 + area code minus the initial zero + number.
US and Canada ☎ 001 + area code + number.
Republic of Ireland ☎ 00353 + area code minus the initial zero + number.
South Africa ☎ 0027 + area code + number.

Smoking

Smoking is banned in all public buildings and offices, restaurants and pubs, and on all public transport. In addition, the vast majority of hotels and B&Bs no longer allow it. **E-cigarettes** are not allowed on public transport and are generally prohibited in museums and many other public buildings; for restaurants and bars it depends on the individual proprietor.

Time

Greenwich Mean Time (GMT) – equivalent to Coordinated Universal Time (UTC) – is used from the end of October to the end of March; for the rest of the year Britain switches to **British Summer Time** (BST), one hour ahead of GMT.

Tourist information

England's tourism authority, VisitEngland (Ⓦ visit england.com), is a reasonable first stop for general information, while regional tourism boards concentrate on particular areas.

Tourist offices (also called Tourist Information Centres, or "TICs") exist in major tourist destinations, though local cuts have led to closures over recent years, and services can depend on volunteers. They tend to follow standard shop hours (roughly Mon–Sat 9am–5.30pm), though are sometimes also open on Sundays, with hours curtailed during the winter season (Nov–Easter). We've listed opening hours in the Guide.

The **National Parks** usually have their own dedicated information centres, which offer similar services to tourist offices but can also provide expert guidance on local walks and outdoor pursuits.

Travellers with disabilities

On the whole, England has good facilities for travellers with disabilities. All new public buildings – including museums, galleries and cinemas – are obliged to provide **wheelchair access**; airports and (generally) train stations are accessible; many buses have easy-access boarding ramps; and dropped kerbs and signalled crossings are the rule in every city and town. However, old buildings and Victorian infrastructure still creates problems for accessibility in some places (not all of London's tube system is wheelchair accessible, for example). The number of accessible hotels and restaurants is growing, and reserved parking bays are available almost everywhere, from shopping centres to museums. If you have specific requirements, it's always best to talk first to your travel agent, chosen hotel or tour operator.

Wheelchair users and blind or partially sighted people are automatically given thirty to forty percent reductions on train fares, and people with other disabilities are eligible for the Disabled Persons Railcard (£20/year; Ⓦ disabledpersons-railcard.co.uk), which gives a third off the price of most tickets for you and someone accompanying you. There are no bus discounts for disabled tourists. In addition to the resources listed below, for detailed reviews of some of England's leading attractions – museums, markets, theatres – written by and for disabled people, download the free **Rough Guide to Accessible Britain** (Ⓦ accessibleguide.co.uk).

USEFUL CONTACTS

Open Britain Ⓦ openbritain.net. Accessible travel-related information, from accommodation to attractions.
Tourism For All Ⓦ www.tourismforall.org.uk. Listings, guides and advice for access throughout England.

Travelling with children

Facilities in England for travellers with children are similar to those in the rest of Europe. Breast-feeding is permitted in all public places, including restaurants and cafés, and **baby-changing** rooms are widely available, including in shopping centres and train stations. Children aren't allowed in certain **licensed (alcohol-serving) premises**, though this doesn't apply to restaurants, and many pubs and inns have family rooms or beer gardens where children are welcome. Some **B&Bs and hotels** won't accept children under a certain age (usually 12). Under-5s generally travel free on public transport and get in free to attractions; 5- to 16-year-olds are usually entitled to concessionary rates. Many public museums and attractions have kids' activity packs, family events, play areas and so on, and you can generally find a playground in any neighbourhood.

London

THE LONDON EYE AND HOUSES OF PARLIAMENT

1

London

For the visitor, London is a thrilling place. Monuments from the capital's glorious past are everywhere, from medieval banqueting halls and the great churches of Christopher Wren to eclectic Victorian architecture. You can relax in the city's quiet Georgian squares, explore the narrow alleyways of the City of London, wander along the riverside walkways, and uncover the quirks of what is still identifiably a collection of villages. The largest capital in Europe, stretching for more than thirty miles from east to west, and with a population just short of nine million, London is also incredibly diverse, ethnically and linguistically, offering cultural and culinary delights from right across the globe.

The capital's great historical **landmarks** – Big Ben, Westminster Abbey, Buckingham Palace, St Paul's Cathedral, the Tower of London and so on – draw in millions of tourists every year. Things change fast, though, and the regular emergence of new attractions ensures there's plenty to do even for those who've visited before. With Tate Modern and the Shard, the city boasts the world's most popular modern art museum and Western Europe's tallest building. And the city continues to grow, its cultural, nightlife and culinary scenes pushing ever onwards into neighbourhoods once well beyond the tourist radar – into East London in particular.

You could spend days just **shopping** in London, mixing with the upper classes in the "tiara triangle" around Harrods, or sampling the offbeat weekend markets of Portobello Road, Brick Lane and Camden. The city's **pubs** have always had heaps of atmosphere, and **food** is now a major attraction too, with more than fifty Michelin-starred restaurants and the widest choice of cuisines on the planet. The **music**, **clubbing** and **LGBT+** scenes are second to none, and mainstream **arts** are no less exciting, with regular opportunities to catch outstanding theatre companies, dance troupes, exhibitions and opera.

London's special atmosphere comes mostly, however, from the life on its streets. A cosmopolitan city since at least the seventeenth century, when it was a haven for Huguenot immigrants escaping persecution in Louis XIV's France, today it is truly **multicultural**, with over half its permanent population originating from overseas. The last hundred years has seen the arrival of thousands from the Caribbean, the Indian subcontinent, the Mediterranean, the Far East and Eastern Europe, all of whom play an integral part in defining a metropolis that is unmatched in its sheer diversity.

COLUMNBIA ROAD FLOWER MARKET

Highlights

❶ **British Museum** Quite simply one of the world's greatest museums. **See p.72**

❷ **The Shard** Feel the breeze in your hair as you take in the breathtaking views from the 72nd floor. **See p.81 & p.90**

❸ **Tate Modern** London's huge modern art gallery is housed in a spectacularly converted power station. **See p.87**

❹ **Borough Market** London's upmarket larder, this historic market has an irresistible selection of gourmet goods to sample. **See p.89 & p.130**

❺ **South Kensington's museums** A trio of superb museums, with everything from whales to rockets and Wedgwood to Raphael to pique your interest. **See p.95**

❻ **Hampstead Heath** With ponds to swim in, sublime views and mile upon mile of lush heathland, Hampstead is possibly London's loveliest green space. **See p.99**

❼ **Greenwich** Picturesque riverside spot, with a weekend market, the National Maritime Museum and old Royal Observatory. **See p.100**

❽ **Hampton Court Palace** Tudor interiors, architecture by Wren and vast gardens make this a great day out. **See p.107**

❾ **East End markets** Best visited on a Sunday – start at Spitalfields, head towards Brick Lane and end up at Columbia Road. **See p.130**

HIGHLIGHTS ARE MARKED ON THE MAPS ON P.52 & P.56

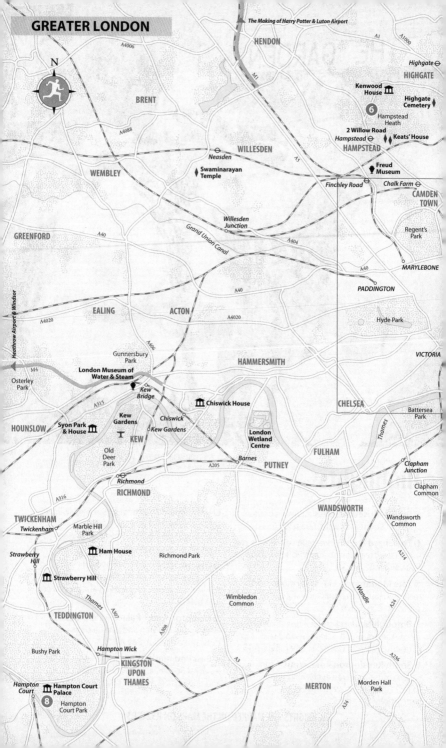

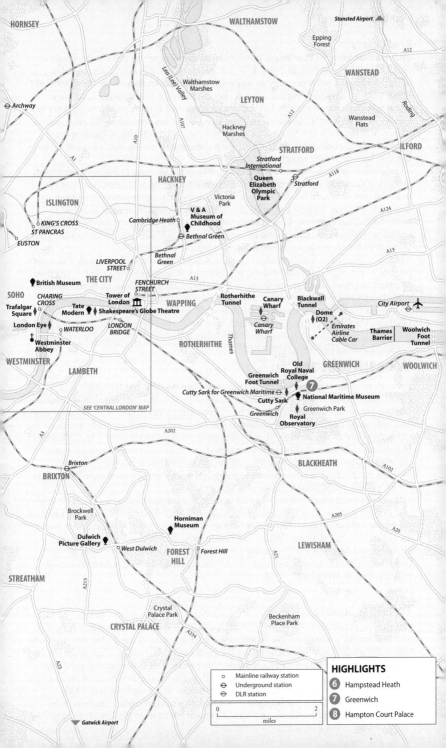

HORNSEY

WALTHAMSTOW

Stansted Airport

Epping
Forest

A12

Archway

Lea (Lee) Valley

Walthamstow
Marshes

LEYTON

WANSTEAD

Roding

A12

Hackney
Marshes

Wanstead
Flats

A107

A10

A1

ILFORD

STRATFORD

Stratford
International

A118

A124

Stratford

ISLINGTON

HACKNEY

KING'S CROSS
ST PANCRAS

EUSTON

Victoria
Park

Queen
Elizabeth
Olympic
Park

Cambridge Heath

V & A
Museum of
Childhood

Bethnal Green

A13

Bethnal
Green

LIVERPOOL
STREET

British Museum

THE CITY

SOHO

CHARING
CROSS

Trafalgar
Square

Tate
Modern

London Eye

WATERLOO

Westminster
Abbey

WESTMINSTER

FENCHURCH
STREET

Tower of
London

Shakespeare's Globe Theatre

LONDON
BRIDGE

WAPPING

Rotherhithe
Tunnel

Canary
Wharf

Canary
Wharf

Thames

Blackwall
Tunnel

Dome
(O2)

City Airport

Emirates
Airline
Cable Car

Thames
Barrier

Woolwich
Foot
Tunnel

ROTHERHITHE

GREENWICH

WOOLWICH

LAMBETH

Old
Royal Naval
College

Greenwich
Foot Tunnel

7

Cutty Sark for Greenwich Maritime

Cutty Sark

Greenwich

National Maritime Museum

Greenwich Park

Royal
Observatory

SEE 'CENTRAL LONDON' MAP

A202

Brixton

BRIXTON

Brockwell
Park

Dulwich
Picture Gallery

West Dulwich

BLACKHEATH

A102

LEWISHAM

A205

A20

Horniman
Museum

FOREST
HILL

Forest Hill

A21

STREATHAM

A215

Crystal
Palace Park

Beckenham
Place Park

CRYSTAL PALACE

A234

A23

Gatwick Airport

HIGHLIGHTS

○ Mainline railway station
⊖ Underground station
⊖ DLR station

0   2
miles

6 Hampstead Heath

7 Greenwich

8 Hampton Court Palace

1

Brief history

The Romans founded **Londinium** in 47 AD as a stores depot on the marshy banks of the Thames. Despite frequent attacks – not least by Queen Boudica, who razed it in 61 AD – the port became secure in its position as capital of Roman Britain by the end of the century. London's expansion really began, however, in the eleventh century, when it became the seat of the last successful invader of Britain, the Norman duke who became **King William I of England** (aka "the Conqueror"). Crowned in Westminster Abbey, William built the White Tower – centrepiece of the Tower of London – to establish his dominance over the merchant population, the class that was soon to make London one of Europe's mightiest cities.

Little is left of medieval or Tudor London. Many of the finest buildings were wiped out in the course of a few days in 1666 when the **Great Fire of London** annihilated more than thirteen thousand houses and nearly ninety churches, completing a cycle of destruction begun the year before by the Great Plague, which killed as many as a hundred thousand people. Chief beneficiary of the blaze was Christopher Wren, who was commissioned to redesign the city and rose to the challenge with such masterpieces as St Paul's Cathedral and the Royal Naval Hospital in Greenwich.

Much of the public architecture of London was built in the Georgian and Victorian periods of the eighteenth and nineteenth centuries, when grand structures were raised to reflect the city's status as the financial and administrative hub of the **British Empire**. And though postwar development peppered the city with some undistinguished Modernist buildings, more recent experiments in high-tech architecture, such as the Gherkin, the Cheesegrater and the Shard, have given the city a new gloss.

Westminster

Political, religious and regal power has emanated from **Westminster** for almost a millennium. It was Edward the Confessor (1042–66) who first established Westminster as London's royal and ecclesiastical power base, some three miles west of the City of London. The embryonic English parliament used to meet in the abbey and eventually took over the old royal palace of Westminster. In the nineteenth century, Westminster – and Whitehall in particular – became the "heart of the Empire", its ministries ruling over a quarter of the world's population. Even now, though the UK's world status has diminished, the institutions that run the country inhabit roughly the same geographical area: Westminster for the politicians, Whitehall for the civil servants.

The monuments and buildings in and around Westminster also span the millennium, and include some of London's most famous landmarks – **Nelson's Column**, **Big Ben** and the **Houses of Parliament**, **Westminster Abbey**, plus two of the city's finest permanent art collections, the **National Gallery** and **Tate Britain**. This is a well-trodden tourist circuit since it's also one of the easiest parts of London to walk round, with all the major sights within a mere half-mile of each other, linked by one of London's most majestic streets, **Whitehall**.

Trafalgar Square

Despite the persistent noise of traffic, **Trafalgar Square** is still one of London's grandest architectural set pieces. John Nash designed the basic layout in the 1820s, but died long before the square took its present form. The Neoclassical National Gallery filled up the northern side of the square in 1838, followed five years later by the central focal point, **Nelson's Column**, topped by the famous admiral; the very large bronze lions didn't arrive until 1868, and the fountains didn't take their present shape until the late 1930s.

As one of the few large public squares in London, Trafalgar Square has been both a tourist attraction and a focus for **political demonstrations** since the Chartists assembled

LONDON ORIENTATION: WHERE TO GO

Although the majority of the city's sights are situated north of the **River Thames**, which loops through the centre of the city from west to east, there is no single focus of interest. That's because London hasn't grown through centralized planning but by a process of agglomeration. Villages and urban developments that once surrounded the core are now lost within the amorphous mass of Greater London.

Westminster, the country's royal, political and ecclesiastical power base for centuries, was once a separate city. The grand streets and squares to the north of Westminster, from **St James's** to **Covent Garden**, were built as residential suburbs after the Restoration in 1660, and are now the city's shopping and entertainment zones known collectively as the **West End**, with **Soho** long the seedy heart of London after dark, now packed with restaurants, pubs and bars. To the east is the original City of London – known simply as **The City** – founded by the Romans, with more history than any other patch of the city, and now one of the world's great financial centres.

East of the City, the neighbourhoods of **East London** draw in visitors for the markets and nightlife of Brick Lane, Spitalfields and Shoreditch, with the creative scene spreading ever outwards to places like Bethnal Green, Hackney and Dalston. In its far reaches, East London is home to the **Olympic Park**, and the second financial centre of Canary Wharf.

The **south bank** of the Thames is perfect for exploring on foot, from the London Eye, in the west, to Tate Modern and the pubs and markets of Borough beyond, with the Shard looming overhead. To the west, the **museums** of South Kensington are a must, as is Portobello Road market in trendy Notting Hill. Literary Hampstead and Highgate in north London are refined neighbourhoods to wander, standing either side of half-wild **Hampstead Heath**. To the southeast, **Greenwich**, downstream of central London, with its nautical associations, royal park and observatory, makes a great day out – especially if visited by boat. Finally, there are plenty of rewarding day-trips in west London along the Thames, most notably to **Hampton Court Palace** and Windsor Castle.

here in 1848 before marching to Kennington Common. Since then, countless demos and rallies have taken place, and nowadays various free events, commemorations and celebrations are staged here.

Stranded on a traffic island to the south of the column, and predating the entire square, is an **equestrian statue of Charles I**, erected shortly after the Restoration on the very spot where eight of those who had signed the king's death warrant were disembowelled. Charles's statue also marks the original site of the thirteenth-century **Charing Cross**, from where all distances from the capital are measured – a Victorian imitation now stands outside Charing Cross train station.

St Martin-in-the-Fields

Trafalgar Square, WC2N 4JH • Mon, Tues, Thurs & Fri 8.30am–1pm & 2–6pm, Wed 8.30am–1.15pm & 2–5pm, Sat 9.30am–6pm, Sun 3.30–5pm; concerts Mon, Tues & Fri 1pm • Free • ☎ 020 7766 1100, ⓦ stmartin-in-the-fields.org • ⊖ Charing Cross

The northeastern corner of Trafalgar Square is occupied by James Gibbs's church of **St Martin-in-the-Fields**, fronted by a magnificent Corinthian portico. Designed in 1721, the interior is purposefully simple, though the Italian plasterwork on the barrel vaulting is exceptionally rich; it's best appreciated while listening to one of the church's free lunchtime **concerts**. There's a licensed café (see p.115) in the roomy **crypt**, along with a shop, gallery and brass-rubbing centre.

National Gallery

Trafalgar Square, WC2N 5DN • Daily 10am–6pm, Fri till 9pm • Guided tours daily 11.30am & 2.30pm, plus Fri 7pm • Free • ☎ 020 7747 2885, ⓦ nationalgallery.org.uk • ⊖ Charing Cross

The **National Gallery** was begun in 1824 by the British government. The gallery's canny acquisition policy has resulted in more than 2300 paintings, but the collection's virtue is not so much its size as its range, depth and sheer quality. To view the collection chronologically, begin with the **Sainsbury Wing**, to the west. With more than one

1

HIGHLIGHTS

1. British Museum
2. The Shard
3. Tate Modern
4. Borough Market
5. South Kensington's museums
9. East End markets

Hampstead, **1**, **0**, **2**, **1** & **3** ▲

Chalk Farm ⊖
Swiss Cottage ⊖
Roundhouse **4** CHALK FARM ROAD
Camden Town ⊖ Camden Road
ADELAIDE ROAD
KING HENRY'S ROAD
PRIMROSE HILL ROAD
GLOUCESTER AVENUE
BELSIZE ROAD
BOUNDARY ROAD
AVENUE ROAD
FINCHLEY ROAD
ELSWORTHY ROAD
REGENT'S PARK ROAD
Primrose Hill
CAMDEN HIGH STREET
ST PANCRAS WAY
ROYAL COLLEGE STREET
PRATT STREET
CAMDEN STREET
Camden Town ⊖
4
8 CAMDEN TOWN ⊖
Jewish Museum
DELANCEY STREET
10
Mornington Crescent ⊖
EVERSHOLT STREET
HAMPSTEAD ROAD
SEE "BLOOMSBURY AND KING'S CROSS" MAP FOR DETAIL

PRINCE ALBERT ROAD
St John's Wood ⊖
ACACIA ROAD
WELLINGTON ROAD
MARLBOROUGH PLACE
ABBEY ROAD
HAMILTON TERRACE
CARLTON VALE
London Zoo
Regent's Park
ALBANY STREET
Euston Station

Maida Vale ⊖
MAIDA VALE
ELGIN AVENUE
SUTHERLAND AVENUE
Warwick Avenue ⊖
Little Venice
Regent's Canal
London Central Mosque
ST JOHN'S WOOD ROAD
Lord's Cricket Ground
PARK ROAD
Open Air Theatre
Warren Street ⊖ EUSTON ROAD
Euston Square ⊖
Great Portland Street ⊖ **2**
Regent's Park ⊖
MARYLEBONE ROAD
Goodge Street ⊖
MORTIMER STREET
Baker Street ⊖
Marylebone ⊖
Madame Tussauds
BAKER STREET
GLOUCESTER PLACE
MARYLEBONE HIGH STREET
PORTLAND PLACE
NEW CAVENDISH ST
Edgware Road ⊖
WESTWAY
Royal Oak ⊖
GLOUCESTER TERRACE
Paddington Station
Paddington ⊖
SUSSEX GARDENS
EDGWARE ROAD
SEYMOUR STREET
Wallace Collection
Wigmore Hall
WIGMORE STREET
John Lewis
OXFORD CIRCUS
Oxford Circus ⊖
OXFORD STREET
Marble Arch ⊖
Marble Arch
Bond Street ⊖
BROOK STREET
NEW BOND STREET
REGENT STREET
PICCADILLY CIRCUS
Bayswater ⊖
Queensway ⊖
Lancaster Gate ⊖
BAYSWATER ROAD
Hyde Park
PARK LANE
SOUTH AUDLEY STREET
Royal Academy
Piccadilly Circus ⊖
CURZON STREET
St James's Palace
Kensington Gardens
Serpentine Sackler Gallery
Serpentine Gallery
The Serpentine
PICCADILLY
Green Park
Green Park ⊖
THE MALL
Kensington Palace
Wellington Arch
CONSTITUTION HILL
Buckingham Palace
BIRDCAGE WALK
KENSINGTON ROAD
Hyde Park Corner ⊖
St James's Park
High Street Kensington ⊖
Royal Albert Hall
Knightsbridge ⊖
BELGRAVE SQUARE
BUCKINGHAM PALACE ROAD
Westminster Cathedral
Victoria ⊖
Science Museum
Victoria & Albert Museum
Harrods
BROMPTON ROAD
PONT STREET
ECCLESTON ST
EATON SQUARE
4
Victoria Station
Natural History Museum
5
SLOANE STREET
EBURY STREET
Victoria Coach Station
BELGRAVE ROAD
CROMWELL ROAD
Gloucester Road ⊖
South Kensington ⊖
SLOANE SQUARE
Sloane Square ⊖
PIMLICO ROAD
5
Earl's Court ⊖
OLD BROMPTON ROAD
FULHAM ROAD
KING'S ROAD
Royal Hospital
ROYAL HOSPITAL ROAD
GROSVENOR ROAD
CHELSEA EMBANKMENT
ALBERT BRIDGE
CHELSEA BRIDGE
River Thames
BELGRAVE ROAD
SEE "CHELSEA TO NOTTING HILL" MAP FOR DETAIL
Battersea Park

Kew Gardens ◄
Hammersmith & Fulham ◄

1

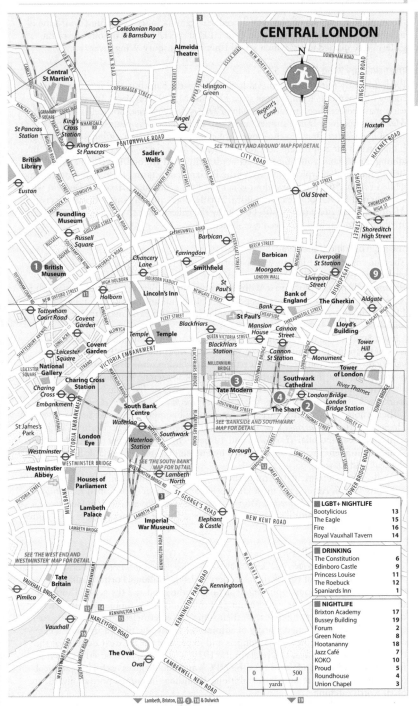

CENTRAL LONDON

N

Caledonian Road & Barnsbury

Almeida Theatre

Central St Martin's

Islington Green

Regent's Canal

Hoxton

St Pancras Station

King's Cross Station

Angel

King's Cross-St Pancras

Sadler's Wells

SEE 'THE CITY AND AROUND' MAP FOR DETAIL

British Library

Euston

Old Street

Shoreditch High St

Foundling Museum

Barbican

Shoreditch High Street

Russell Square

Chancery Lane

Farringdon

Barbican

Liverpool St Station

Liverpool Street

1 British Museum

Smithfield

Moorgate

London Wall

Lincoln's Inn

St Paul's

Bank of England

The Gherkin

Aldgate

Tottenham Court Road

Holborn

Bank

Mansion House

Lloyd's Building

Aldgate High St

Covent Garden

Temple

Temple

Blackfriars

Cannon Street

Tower Hill

Leicester Square

National Gallery

Charing Cross Station

Blackfriars Station

Cannon St Station

Monument

London Bridge

Tower of London

Charing Cross

Embankment

South Bank Centre

MILLENNIUM BRIDGE

3 Tate Modern

Southwark Cathedral

4 London Bridge

2 The Shard

London Bridge Station

River Thames

St James's Park

London Eye

Waterloo

Southwark

SEE 'BANKSIDE AND SOUTHWARK' MAP FOR DETAIL

Westminster

Waterloo Station

Borough

Westminster Abbey

Houses of Parliament

SEE 'THE SOUTH BANK' MAP FOR DETAIL

Lambeth North

12

Lambeth Palace

Imperial War Museum

Elephant & Castle

NEW KENT ROAD

SEE 'THE WEST END AND WESTMINSTER' MAP FOR DETAIL

Tate Britain

Kennington

Pimlico

Vauxhall

The Oval

Oval

CAMBERWELL NEW ROAD

■ LGBT+ NIGHTLIFE	
Bootylicious	13
The Eagle	15
Fire	16
Royal Vauxhall Tavern	14

■ DRINKING	
The Constitution	6
Edinboro Castle	9
Princess Louise	11
The Roebuck	12
Spaniards Inn	1

■ NIGHTLIFE	
Brixton Academy	17
Bussey Building	19
Forum	2
Green Note	8
Hootananny	18
Jazz Café	7
KOKO	10
Proud	5
Roundhouse	4
Union Chapel	3

0   500
yards

▼ Lambeth, Brixton, **17**, **5**, **18** & Dulwich   ▼ **19**

1

thousand paintings on display, you'll need real stamina to see everything, so if time is tight your best bet is to home in on your areas of special interest or join one of the gallery's free **guided tours**, which set off from the Sainsbury Wing foyer.

The Sainsbury Wing (1200–1500)

Predominantly filled with medieval Italian works, the Sainsbury Wing's sixteen rooms start with fragments from Sienese artist Duccio's Maestà altarpiece. The collection's early masterpieces here include Uccello's *Battle of San Romano*, Botticelli's *Venus and Mars* (inspired by a Dante sonnet) and Piero della Francesca's beautifully composed *Baptism of Christ*. Drawing the crowds is Leonardo's melancholic *Virgin of the Rocks*, hung next to the exquisitely delicate *Burlington House Cartoon* preparatory sketch. In among the Italians, you'll find the extraordinarily vivid **Wilton Diptych**, one of the few British medieval altarpieces to survive the Puritan iconoclasm of the Commonwealth, while in room 56 another standout is Jan van Eyck's intriguing *Arnolfini Portrait*, which is celebrated for its complex symbolism. Finally, don't miss the small, pristinely crisp *Madonna of the Pinks* (room 60), bought by the gallery for £22 million, once its attribution to Raphael had been established.

The main building (1500–1930)

The fine collection of Italian works continues into the much grander main building with large-scale paintings including Veronese's lustrous *Family of Darius before Alexander* displayed in the vast Wohl Room (room 9). Beyond, Holbein's masterful *Ambassadors* is hung alongside his portrait of Erasmus and works by Cranach the Elder. Numerous works by Titian on display include his early masterpiece *Bacchus and Ariadne*.

From **Spain** there are dazzling pieces by El Greco, Goya, Murillo and Velázquez, among them the provocative *Rokeby Venus*, while from the Dutch Golden Age, the gallery owns numerous Rembrandt paintings, including some of his most searching portraits – two of them self-portraits – and a typically serene Vermeer, as well as abundant examples of Rubens' expansive, fleshy canvases. The gallery owns several works by Caravaggio, including *Salome receives the head of John the Baptist*.

There's home-grown **British** art, too, represented by important works such as Hogarth's satirical *Marriage à la Mode*, Gainsborough's translucent *Morning Walk*, Constable's ever-popular *Hay Wain*, and Turner's *Fighting Temeraire*. Highlights of the **French** contingent include superb works by Poussin, Claude, Fragonard, Boucher, Watteau and David.

Finally, there's a particularly strong showing of **Impressionists** and **Post-Impressionists** in rooms 43–46. Among the most famous works are Manet's unfinished *Execution of Maximilian*, Renoir's *Umbrellas*, Monet's *Thames below Westminster*, Van Gogh's *Sunflowers*, Seurat's pointillist *Bathers at Asnières*, a Rousseau junglescape and Cézanne's proto-Cubist *Bathers*.

National Portrait Gallery

St Martin's Place, WC2H 0HE • Daily 10am–6pm, Thurs & Fri till 9pm • Free • ☎ 020 7306 0055, ⓦ npg.org.uk • ⊖ Charing Cross

Around the east side of the National Gallery lurks the **National Portrait Gallery**, founded in 1856 to house uplifting depictions of the good and the great. Though it undoubtedly has some fine works among its collection of ten thousand portraits, many of the studies are of less interest than their subjects. Nevertheless, it's fascinating to trace who has been deemed worthy of admiration at any one time: aristocrats and artists in previous centuries, warmongers and imperialists in the early decades of the twentieth century, writers and poets in the 1930s and 1940s, and, latterly, retired footballers, and film and pop stars. The NPG's **audioguide** gives useful biographical information, and the temporary exhibitions, including the annual portrait award, are often worth catching.

Whitehall

Whitehall, the unusually broad avenue connecting Trafalgar Square to Parliament Square, is synonymous with the faceless, pinstriped bureaucracy charged with the day-to-day running of the country, who inhabit the governmental ministries which line the street. During the sixteenth and seventeenth centuries, however, Whitehall was the permanent residence of the kings and queens of England.

The statues dotted about recall the days when Whitehall stood at the centre of an empire on which the sun never set. Halfway down, in the middle of the road, stands Edwin Lutyens' **Cenotaph**, a memorial to the war dead, erected after World War I and the centrepiece of the Remembrance Sunday ceremony in November. Close by are the gates of Downing Street, home to London's most famous address, **Number 10 Downing Street**, the seventeenth-century terraced house that has been the official residence of the prime minister since it was presented to Sir Robert Walpole, Britain's first PM, by George II in 1732.

Banqueting House

Whitehall, SW1A 2ER • Daily 10am–5pm but frequent early closures so ring or check website before visiting; last entry 4.30pm • £6.50 • ⓣ 020 3166 6154, ⓦ hrp.org.uk • ⊖ Charing Cross

Whitehall Palace was originally the London seat of the Archbishop of York, confiscated and greatly extended by Henry VIII after a fire at Westminster forced him to find alternative accommodation. The chief section of the old palace to survive the 1698 fire was the **Banqueting House** begun by Inigo Jones in 1619 and the first Palladian building to be built in England. The one room open to the public has no original furnishings, but features superlative Rubens ceiling paintings glorifying the Stuart dynasty, commissioned by Charles I in the 1630s. Charles himself walked through the room for the last time in 1649 when he stepped onto the executioner's scaffold from one of its windows.

Horse Guards and the Household Cavalry Museum

Whitehall, SW1A 2AX • Daily: April–Oct 10am–6pm (part-day closures through May & June); Nov–March 10am–5pm • £7 • ⓣ 020 7930 3070, ⓦ householdcavalrymuseum.co.uk • ⊖ Charing Cross or Westminster

Two mounted sentries of the Queen's Household Cavalry and two horseless colleagues are posted to protect **Horse Guards**, originally the main gateway to St James's Park and Buckingham Palace. Round the back of the building, you'll find the **Household Cavalry Museum** where you can learn about the regiments' history. With the stables immediately adjacent, it's a sweet-smelling place, and – horse-lovers will be pleased to know – you can see the beasts in their stalls through a glass screen. Don't miss the pocket riot act on display, which ends with the wise warning: "must read correctly: variance fatal".

Churchill War Rooms

King Charles St, SW1A 2AQ • Daily 9.30am–6pm; June–Aug till 7pm • £19 • ⓣ 020 7416 5000, ⓦ iwm.org.uk • ⊖ Westminster

In 1938, in anticipation of Nazi air raids, the basements of the civil service buildings on the south side of King Charles Street, south of Downing Street, were converted into

CHANGING THE GUARD

The Queen is Colonel-in-Chief of the seven **Household Regiments**: the Life Guards and the Blues and Royals are the two Household Cavalry regiments; while the Grenadier, Coldstream, Scots, Irish and Welsh Guards make up the Foot Guards.

Changing the Guard takes place at two London locations: the Foot Guards march with a band to Buckingham Palace (May–July daily 11.30am; Aug–April alternate days; no ceremony if it rains; ⓦ royal.gov.uk) – they're best sighted coming down the Mall around 11.15am. The Household Cavalry have a ceremony at Horse Guards on Whitehall (Mon–Sat 11am, Sun 10am, with an elaborate inspection at 4pm), and they don't care if it rains or shines. A ceremony also takes place regularly at Windsor Castle (see p.276).

1

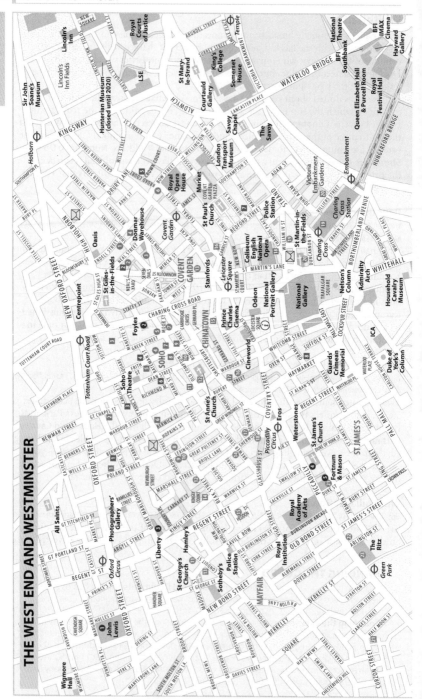

THE WEST END AND WESTMINSTER

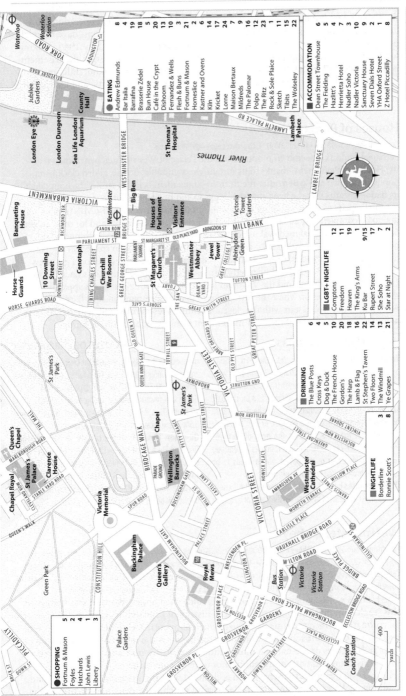

● **EATING**

Andrew Edmunds	8
Bar Italia	4
Barrafina	19
Brasserie Zedel	18
Bun House	5
Café in the Crypt	20
Dishoom	13
Fernandez & Wells	10
Flesh & Buns	3
Fortnum & Mason	21
Homeslice	6
Kastner and Ovens	14
Kiln	17
Kricket	24
Lorne	9
Maison Bertaux	7
Mildreds	16
The Palomar	12
Polpo	23
The Ritz	1
Rock & Sole Plaice	11
Sketch	15
Tibits	2
The Wolseley	22

■ **ACCOMMODATION**

Dean Street Townhouse	6
The Fielding	5
Hazlitt's	4
Henrietta Hotel	7
Nadler Soho	3
Nadler Victoria	10
Sanctuary House	9
Seven Dials Hotel	2
YHA Oxford Street	1
Z Hotel Piccadilly	8

■ **LGBT+ NIGHTLIFE**

Comptons	12
Freedom	11
Heaven	19
The Harp	16
The King's Arms	9/15
Ku Bar	17
Rupert Street	7
She Soho	13
Star at Night	21

■ **DRINKING**

The Blue Posts	6
Cross Keys	4
Dog & Duck	5
The French House	10
Gordon's	20
The Harp	18
Lamb & Flag	16
St Stephen's Tavern	22
Two Floors	14
The Windmill	13
Ye Grapes	21

■ **NIGHTLIFE**

Borderline	3
Ronnie Scott's	8

● **SHOPPING**

Fortnum & Mason	5
Foyles	2
Hatchards	4
John Lewis	1
Liberty	3

River Thames

0 yards 400

the **Cabinet War Rooms**. It was here that Winston Churchill directed operations and held Cabinet meetings for the duration of World War II, and the rooms have been left pretty much as they were when they were finally abandoned on VJ Day 1945, making for an atmospheric underground trot through wartime London. Also in the basement is the excellent **Churchill Museum**, where you can hear snippets of Churchill's most famous speeches and check out his trademark bowler, spotted bow tie and half-chewed Havana, not to mention his wonderful burgundy zip-up "romper suit".

Houses of Parliament

Parliament Square, SW1A 0AA • ☎ 020 7219 4114, ⓦ parliament.uk • ⊖ Westminster

Perhaps London's best-known monument is the Palace of Westminster, better known as the **Houses of Parliament**, thanks to its instantly recognizable, ornate, gilded clocktower popularly known as **Big Ben**, after the thirteen-tonne main bell that strikes the hour. Such is its national status that the news that the bongs would be silenced for four years during essential repairs to the tower brought howls of protest from traditionalist MPs (repairs are due to be completed in 2021, though it will still ring out at New Year and for other major occasions). The original medieval palace burned down in 1834, and everything you see now – save for Westminster Hall – is the work of **Charles Barry**, who created an orgy of honey-coloured pinnacles, turrets and tracery that attempts to express national greatness through the use of Gothic and Elizabethan styles. It's undoubtedly the city's finest Victorian Gothic Revival building, and the Victorian love of mock-Gothic detail is as apparent throughout the interior, where the fittings were largely the responsibility of Barry's assistant, **Augustus Pugin**. Tours start with the eleventh-century **Westminster Hall**, with its huge oak hammer-beam roof: one of the most magnificent secular medieval halls in Europe.

INFORMATION AND TOURS   HOUSES OF PARLIAMENT

Tours Saturday year-round, plus Mon–Fri during parliamentary recess (usually 9.20am–4.30pm; 1hr 15min self-guided audio tours £18.50 advance/£20.50 on the day; 1hr 30min guided tours £25.50 advance/£28 on the day; ☎ 020 7219 4114; ⓦ parliament.uk/visiting). Advance booking is recommended and cheaper, or buy tickets on the day from the ticket office at the front of Portcullis House, on Victoria Embankment. UK residents are entitled to a free guided tour of the palace, which needs to be organized through your local MP's office.

Public galleries To watch proceedings in either the House of Commons – the livelier of the two – or the House of Lords, join the queue for the public galleries at the Cromwell Green visitor entrance during sitting times. For a full schedule of debates phone ☎ 020 7219 4272, or visit ⓦ parliament.uk. For the House of Commons, regular sitting times are Mon 2.30–10.30pm, Tues & Wed 11.30am–7.30pm, Thurs 9.30am–5.30pm and occasionally Fri 9.30am–3pm.

Question Time UK citizens can attend Prime Minister's Question Time (Wed noon–12.30pm) – when the House of Commons is at its liveliest – and ministerial Question Times (Mon 2.30pm, Tues 11.30am, Thurs 9.30am); book in advance with your MP's office, though members of the public will be let in if there's space.

Westminster Abbey

Parliament Square, SW1P 3PA • **Abbey** Mon–Sat 9.30am–4.30pm, Wed until 7pm, last admission on any day 1hr before closing • £20 in advance or £22 on the day, including audioguide • **Verger tours** Mon–Sat times vary • £5 • **Great Cloisters** Daily 9.30am–4.30pm **College Garden** Tues–Thurs: April–Sept 10am–6pm; Oct–March 10am–4pm • Entry to cloisters and garden included in cost of ticket to abbey but free on Sundays when entry is via Dean's Yard • ☎ 020 7222 5152, ⓦ westminster-abbey.org • ⊖ Westminster

The Houses of Parliament dwarf their much older neighbour, **Westminster Abbey**, yet this single building embodies much of the history of England: it has been the venue for all coronations since the time of William the Conqueror, and the site of more or less every royal burial for some five hundred years between the reigns of Henry III and George II. Scores of the nation's most famous citizens are honoured here, too, and the interior is crammed with hundreds of monuments and statues.

Entry is via the north transept, which is cluttered with monuments to politicians and traditionally known as **Statesmen's Aisle**, beyond which is the main **nave**: narrow, light and, at over 100ft in height, one of the tallest in the country. The most famous monument in this section is the **Tomb of the Unknown Soldier**, near the west door. Passing through the choir, you reach the central sanctuary, site of the coronations, and the wonderful **Cosmati floor mosaic**, constructed in the thirteenth century by Italian craftsmen.

Henry VII's Chapel and Shrine of Edward the Confessor

The abbey's most dazzling architectural set piece, the **Lady Chapel**, is better known as **Henry VII's Chapel**, after the Tudor monarch who added it in 1503 as his future resting place. With its intricately carved vaulting and fan-shaped gilded pendants, the chapel represents the last spectacular gasp of English Perpendicular Gothic.

As you leave Henry VII's Chapel, look out for Edward I's **Coronation Chair**, a decrepit oak throne dating from around 1300 and used in every coronation since 1308. Behind the high altar, the **Shrine of Edward the Confessor** is the sacred heart of the building, now only accessible on a guided tour.

Poets' Corner

Nowadays, the abbey's royal tombs are upstaged by **Poets' Corner**, in the south transept, though the first occupant, Geoffrey Chaucer, was in fact buried here not because he was a poet, but because he lived nearby. By the eighteenth century this zone had become an artistic pantheon; those buried here include Charles Dickens and Thomas Hardy, while there are memorials to Shakespeare, Oscar Wilde and William Blake.

Great Cloisters

Doors in the south choir aisle (plus a separate entrance from Dean's Yard) lead to the **Great Cloisters**. On the east side lies the octagonal Chapter House, where the House of Commons met from 1257, boasting thirteenth-century apocalyptic wall paintings. Also worth a look is the museum, filled with generations of royal funereal effigies.

Tate Britain

Millbank, SW1P 4RG · Daily 10am–6pm; usually first Fri of month until 10pm · Free; charge for some temporary exhibitions (around £16–18) · ☎ 020 7887 8888, ⓦ tate.org.uk · ⊖ Pimlico

A purpose-built gallery half a mile south of Parliament, founded in 1897 with money from sugar baron Henry Tate, **Tate Britain** is devoted to British art. The collection covers 1500 to the present, and the gallery also puts on large-scale temporary exhibitions that showcase British artists.

The pictures are largely hung chronologically, so you begin with the richly bejewelled portraits of the Elizabethan nobility, before moving on to Britain's most famous artists – Hogarth, Constable, Gainsborough, Reynolds – plus foreign-born artists like Van Dyck who spent much of their career in Britain. The ever-popular **Pre-Raphaelites** are always well represented, as are established twentieth-century greats such as Stanley Spencer and Francis Bacon alongside living artists such as David Hockney and Bridget Riley. Lastly, don't miss the Tate's outstanding **Turner collection**, displayed in the Turner Wing, and the room dedicated to William Blake on its upper floor.

Westminster Cathedral

Victoria St, SW1P 1LT · **Cathedral** Mon–Fri 7am–7pm, Sat 8am–7pm, Sun 8am–8pm · Free · **Tower** Mon–Fri 9.30am–5pm, Sat & Sun 9.30am–6pm · £6 · ☎ 020 7798 9055, ⓦ westminstercathedral.org.uk · ⊖ Victoria

Begun in 1895, the stripy neo-Byzantine concoction of the Roman Catholic **Westminster Cathedral** was one of the last and wildest monuments to the Victorian era. It's constructed from more than twelve million terracotta-coloured bricks, decorated with hoops of Portland stone – "blood and bandages" style, as it's known – and culminates in a magnificent tapered tower which rises to 274ft, served by a lift. The **interior** is only half

1

finished, so to get an idea of what the place will look like when it's finally completed, explore the series of **side chapels** whose rich, multicoloured decor makes use of more than one hundred different marbles from around the world.

St James's

St James's, the exclusive little enclave sandwiched between St James's Park and Piccadilly, was laid out in the 1670s close to St James's Palace. Regal and aristocratic residences overlook Green Park, gentlemen's clubs cluster along Pall Mall and St James's Street, while jacket-and-tie restaurants and expense-account gentlemen's outfitters line Jermyn Street, giving the area an air of exclusivity that's rare in London. Open to all, though, is **St James's Park**, with large numbers heading for the Queen's chief residence, **Buckingham Palace**, and the adjacent Queen's Gallery and Royal Mews.

The Mall

Laid out as a memorial to Queen Victoria, the tree-lined sweep of **The Mall** is at its best on Sundays, when it's closed to traffic. The bombastic **Admiralty Arch** was erected to mark the entrance at the Trafalgar Square end of The Mall, while at the Buckingham Palace end stands the ludicrous **Victoria Memorial**, Edward VII's overblown 2300-ton marble tribute to his mother, which is topped by a gilded statue of Victory. Four outlying allegorical groups in bronze confidently proclaim the great achievements of her reign.

St James's Park

SW1A 2BJ • Daily 5am–midnight • Free • ☎ 0300 061 2350, ⓦ royalparks.org.uk

Flanking nearly the whole length of the Mall, **St James's Park** is the oldest of the royal parks, having been drained and enclosed for hunting purposes by Henry VIII. It was landscaped by Nash in the 1820s, and today its lake is a favourite picnic spot. Pelicans – originally a gift from the Russians to Charles II – can still be seen at the eastern end of the lake, and there are exotic ducks, swans and geese aplenty.

Buckingham Palace

The Mall, SW1A 1AA • Late July to late Aug 9.30am–7.30pm, last admission 5.15pm; Sept 9.30am–6.30pm, last admission 4.15pm • State Rooms: £23, including garden highlights: £32.50 • ☎ 030 3123 7300, ⓦ royalcollection.org.uk • ⊖ Green Park or Victoria

The graceless colossus of **Buckingham Palace** has served as the monarch's permanent London residence only since the accession of Victoria. Bought by George III in 1762, the building was overhauled in the late 1820s by Nash and again in 1913, producing a palace that's as bland as it's possible to be.

For a few months a year, the hallowed portals are grudgingly nudged open. The interior, however, is a bit of an anti-climax: of the palace's 750 rooms you're permitted to see twenty or so, and there's little sign of life, as the Queen decamps to Scotland every summer. For the rest of the year the only draw is to watch **Changing the Guard** (see box, p.59), in which a detachment of the Queen's Foot Guards marches to appropriate martial music from St James's Palace and Wellington Barracks to the palace forecourt (unless it rains, that is).

Queen's Gallery

Buckingham Palace Rd, SW1A 1AA • Daily: Aug & Sept 9.30am–5.30pm; Oct–July 10am–5.30pm • £11 • ☎ 030 3123 7301, ⓦ royalcollection.org.uk • ⊖ Victoria

A Doric portico on the south side of Buckingham Palace forms the entrance to the **Queen's Gallery**, which puts on temporary exhibitions drawn from the **Royal Collection**,

1

TOP 5 QUIRKY MUSEUMS

Dennis Severs' House Spitalfields. See p.84
Horniman Museum Forest Hill. See p.104
Old Operating Theatre and Herb Garret
Borough. See p.90

Sir John Soane's Museum Holborn.
See p.75
Wellcome Collection Euston. See p.73

a superlative array of art that includes works by Michelangelo, Raphael, Holbein, Reynolds, Gainsborough, Vermeer, Van Dyck, Rubens, Rembrandt and Canaletto, as well as the world's largest collection of Leonardo drawings, the odd Fabergé egg and heaps of Sèvres china.

Royal Mews

Buckingham Palace Rd, SW1W 1QH • April–Oct daily 10am–5pm; Feb, March & Nov Mon–Sat 10am–4pm • £10; combined ticket with Queen's Gallery £19 • ☎ 030 3123 7302, ⓦ royalcollection.org.uk • ⊖ Victoria

Royal carriages are the main attraction at the Nash-built **Royal Mews**, in particular the Gold State Coach, made for George III in 1762 and used in every coronation since. It's smothered in 22-carat gilding and weighs four tonnes, its axles supporting four life-size figures.

St James's Palace

Marlborough Rd, SW1A 1BS • **Chapel Royal** Oct–Good Friday services Sun 8.30am & 11.15am **Queen's Chapel** Easter Sun–July services Sun 8.30am & 11.15am • ⊖ Green Park

St James's Palace's main red-brick gate-tower is pretty much all that remains of the Tudor palace erected here by Henry VIII. When Whitehall Palace burned down in 1698, St James's became the principal royal residence and, in keeping with tradition, every ambassador to the UK is still accredited to the "Court of St James's", even though the court has since moved down the road to Buckingham Palace. The modest, rambling, crenellated complex is off limits to the public, with the exception of the **Chapel Royal**, situated within the palace, and the **Queen's Chapel**, on the other side of Marlborough Road; both are open for services only.

Clarence House

The Mall, SW1 1BA • Aug Mon–Fri 10am–4.30pm, Sat & Sun 10am–5.30pm, last admission 1hr before closing; visits (by guided tour) must be booked in advance • £10 • ☎ 020 7766 7303, ⓦ royalcollection.org.uk • ⊖ Green Park

Clarence House, connected to the palace's southwest wing, was home to the Queen Mother, and now serves as the official London home of Charles and his second wife, Camilla, but a handful of rooms can be visited over the summer when the royals are in Scotland. The interior is pretty unremarkable, so apart from a peek behind the scenes in a working royal palace, or a few mementos of the Queen Mum, the main draw is the twentieth-century British paintings on display by the likes of Walter Sickert and Augustus John.

Mayfair

Piccadilly, which forms the southern border of swanky **Mayfair**, may not be the fashionable promenade it started out as in the eighteenth century, but a whiff of exclusivity still pervades **Bond Street** and its tributaries, where designer clothes emporia jostle for space with jewellers, bespoke tailors and fine art dealers. **Regent Street** and **Oxford Street**, meanwhile, are home to the flagship branches of the country's most popular chain stores.

1

OXFORD STREET: THE BUSIEST STREET IN EUROPE

As wealthy Londoners began to move out of the City in the eighteenth century in favour of the newly developed West End, so **Oxford Street** – the old Roman road to Oxford – gradually became London's main shopping thoroughfare. Today, despite successive recessions and sky-high rents, Oxford Street remains Europe's busiest street, simply because this two-mile hotchpotch of shops is home to (often several) flagship branches of Britain's major retailers. The street's only real architectural landmark is **Selfridges** (see p.130), which opened in 1909 and has a facade featuring the Queen of Time riding the ship of commerce and supporting an Art Deco clock.

Regent Street

Regent Street, drawn up by John Nash in 1812 as both a luxury shopping street and a triumphal way between George IV's Carlton House and Regent's Park, was the city's earliest attempt at dealing with traffic congestion, slum clearance and planned social segregation, something that would later be perfected by the Victorians. The increase in the purchasing power of the city's middle classes in the last century brought the tone of the street "down" and heavyweight stores now predominate. Among the best known are **Hamley's**, reputedly the world's largest toyshop, and **Liberty**, the upmarket department store that popularized Arts and Crafts designs.

Piccadilly

Piccadilly apparently got its name from the ruffs or "pickadills" worn by the dandies who used to promenade here in the late seventeenth century. It's not much of a place for promenading today, however, with traffic nose to tail most of the day and night. Infinitely more pleasant places to window-shop are the various **nineteenth-century arcades** that shoot off to the north and south, grandest of which is the Burlington Arcade, built to protect shoppers from the mud and horse dung on the streets, but now equally useful for escaping exhaust fumes.

Royal Academy of Arts

Piccadilly, W1J 0BD • Daily 10am–6pm, Fri till 10pm • Special exhibitions from £12 • Regular guided tours of building (check online) • ☎ 020 7300 8000, ⓦ royalacademy.org.uk • ⊖ Green Park

The **Royal Academy of Arts** occupies one of the few surviving aristocratic mansions that once lined the north side of Piccadilly. Rebuilding in the nineteenth century destroyed the original curved colonnades beyond the main gateway, but the complex has kept the feel of a Palladian *palazzo*. The country's first-ever formal art school, founded in 1768, the RA hosts a wide range of art exhibitions, and an annual **Summer Exhibition** whereby anyone can enter paintings in any style, and the lucky winners get hung, in rather close proximity, and are for sale. RA "Academicians" are allowed to display six of their own works – no matter how awful. The result is a bewildering display, which gets panned annually by highbrow critics, but enjoyed happily by everyone else. Other temporary exhibitions range from Rubens to Ai Weiwei, while the **Collections Gallery** in the rear building – connected by a David Chipperfield-designed concrete bridge and opening in 2018 – displays highlights from the Royal Academy's eclectic permanent collection, including Michelangelo's marble relief, the *Taddei Tondo*.

Bond Street

Bond Street, which runs parallel with Regent Street and is lined with designer shops, art galleries and auction houses, carefully maintains its exclusivity. It is, in fact, two streets rolled into one: the southern half, laid out in the 1680s, is known as Old Bond Street; its northern extension, which followed less than fifty years later, is known as New Bond Street. They are both pretty unassuming streets architecturally, yet the shops that line them are among the flashiest in London, dominated by perfumeries, jewellers and designer clothing stores. In addition to fashion, Bond Street is also renowned for its fine art galleries and its **auction houses**, the oldest of which is Sotheby's, 34–35 New Bond St, whose viewing galleries are open free of charge.

Marylebone

Marylebone, which lies to the north of Oxford Street, is, like Mayfair, another grid-plan Georgian development. Marylebone High Street retains a leisurely, village-like ambience, and has some good independent shops. The area boasts a very fine art gallery, the **Wallace Collection**, and, in its northern fringes, one of London's biggest tourist attractions, **Madame Tussauds**, plus the ever-popular **Sherlock Holmes Museum**.

Wallace Collection

Manchester Square, W1U 3BN · Daily 10am–5pm · Free · Free guided tours daily 2.30pm, Sat & Sun also 11.30am · ☎ 020 7563 9500, ⓦ wallacecollection.org · ⊖ Bond Street

Housed in a well-preserved, eighteenth-century manor, incongruously situated not far from the hubbub of Oxford Street, the splendid **Wallace Collection** is best known for its eighteenth-century French paintings, Franz Hals' *Laughing Cavalier*, Titian's *Perseus and Andromeda*, Velázquez's *Lady with a Fan* and Rembrandt's affectionate portrait of his teenage son, Titus. It was bequeathed to the nation in 1897 by the widow of Richard Wallace, an art collector and the illegitimate son of the fourth Marquess of Hertford, and the museum has preserved the feel of a grand stately home, its exhibits piled high in glass cabinets, and paintings covering almost every inch of wall space. The fact that these exhibits are set amid priceless Boulle furniture – and a bloody great armoury – makes the place even more remarkable.

Madame Tussauds

Marylebone Rd, NW1 5LR · Times vary, but generally: Sept–June Mon–Fri 9am–4pm, Sat & Sun 9am–5pm; July, Aug & peak times daily 8.30am–6pm · Advance booking online £29/on the day £35 · ⓦ madametussauds.com · ⊖ Baker Street

Madame Tussauds has been pulling in the crowds ever since the good lady arrived in London from Paris in 1802 bearing the sculpted heads of guillotined aristocrats. The entrance fee might be extortionate and the waxwork likenesses of the famous occasionally dubious, but you can still rely on finding London's biggest queues here (book online to avoid waiting). Inside, they change exhibits regularly, but one of the more original experiences is the **Spirit of London**, an irreverent five-minute romp through the history of London in a miniaturized taxicab.

Sherlock Holmes Museum

239 Baker St, NW1 6XE · Daily 9.30am–6pm · £15 · ☎ 020 7224 3688, ⓦ sherlock-holmes.co.uk · ⊖ Baker Street

Baker Street is synonymous with Sherlock Holmes, the fictional detective who lived at no. 221b (the number on the door of the museum, though it's actually at no. 239). Unashamedly touristy, the **Sherlock Holmes Museum** is stuffed full of Victoriana and life-size models of characters from the books. It's an atmospheric and competent exercise in period reconstruction, though it won't take you long to see everything.

Soho

Bounded by Regent Street to the west, Oxford Street to the north and Charing Cross Road to the east, **Soho** is very much the heart of the West End. It was the city's premier red-light

1

district for centuries and, even as major developments encroach, it retains an unorthodox and slightly raffish air that's unique in central London. It has an immigrant history as rich as that of the East End and a louche nightlife that has attracted writers, musicians and revellers of every sexual persuasion since the eighteenth century. Conventional sights are few, yet, away from the big tourist junctions of Piccadilly Circus and Leicester Square, there's probably more interesting street life here than anywhere in the city centre, whatever the hour. Today it's London's most high-profile LGBT+ quarter, especially around **Old Compton Street**, with Greek, Frith and Dean streets, which cut across it, home to a mix of old-style Soho venues, such as *Ronnie Scott's* on Frith Street – London's longest running jazz club – cellar bars and some good restaurants. At the north end is Soho Square, the area's main green space. Dividing Soho in two is busy **Wardour Street**, with nearby **Berwick Street** known for its street market, record and fabric stores. At the western end, near Regent Street, you'll find **Carnaby Street**, made famous as the place to buy your miniskirts in the swinging 1960s, when Mary Quant had a shop here. Nowadays, it has a decent mix of chain stores, while you can find some more interesting one-off boutiques and places to eat just off it along **Foubert's Place** and **Newburgh Street** and in **Kingly Court**.

Piccadilly Circus

Anonymous and congested, **Piccadilly Circus** is a much-altered product of Nash's grand 1812 Regent Street plan and now a major traffic interchange. It may not be a picturesque place, but thanks to its celebrated aluminium statue, popularly known as **Eros**, it's prime tourist territory. The fountain's archer is one of the city's top attractions, a status that baffles all who live here. Despite the bow and arrow, the figure is not the god of love at all but his lesser-known brother, Anteros, god of requited love, commemorating the selfless philanthropic love of the Earl of Shaftesbury, a Bible-thumping social reformer who campaigned against child labour.

Leicester Square

When the big cinemas and nightclubs are doing good business, and the buskers are entertaining the crowds, **Leicester Square** is one of the most crowded places in London, particularly on a Friday or Saturday when huge numbers of tourists and half the youth of the suburbs seem to congregate here. It wasn't until the mid-nineteenth century that the square actually began to emerge as an entertainment zone; cinema moved in during the 1930s, a golden age evoked by the sleek black lines of the Odeon on the east side.

Chinatown

Chinatown, hemmed in between Leicester Square and Shaftesbury Avenue, is a self-contained jumble of shops, cafés and restaurants. Only a minority of London's Chinese live in these three small blocks, but it remains a focus for the community, a place to do business or the weekly shop, celebrate a wedding, or just meet up for meals, particularly on Sundays, when the restaurants overflow with Chinese families tucking into *dim sum*. **Gerrard Street** is the main drag, where you'll see telephone kiosks rigged out as pagodas and fake Chinese gates or *paifang*.

Old Compton Street

If Soho has a main road, it would be **Old Compton Street**, which runs parallel with Shaftesbury Avenue. The shops, boutiques and cafés here are typical of the area and a good barometer of the latest fads. Soho has been a permanent fixture on the **LGBT+ scene** for the better part of a century, and you'll find a profusion of gay bars, clubs and cafés jostling for position here and at the junction with Wardour Street.

Photographers' Gallery

16–18 Ramillies St, W1F 7LW • Mon–Sat 10am–6pm, Thurs till 8pm, Sun 11–6pm • £4, free before noon • ☎ 020 7087 9300, ⓦ thephotographersgallery.org.uk • ⊖ Oxford Circus

Established in 1971, the **Photographers' Gallery** was the first independent gallery devoted to photography in London, and is now the city's largest public photographic gallery. This former warehouse hosts three floors of exhibitions that change regularly and are invariably worth a visit, as are the bookshop and café. There's also a **camera obscura** in the third-floor studio (open when the studio isn't in use).

Covent Garden and Strand

More sanitized and commercial than neighbouring Soho, the shops and restaurants of **Covent Garden** today are a far cry from the district's heyday when the piazza was the great playground (and red-light district) of eighteenth-century London. The buskers in front of St Paul's Church, the theatres round about, and the **Royal Opera House** on Bow Street are survivors of this tradition, and on a balmy summer evening, **Covent Garden Piazza** is still an undeniably lively place to be, while the streets to the north, around Neal Street, and the Seven Dials junction, including Monmouth Street and the tucked-away **Neal's Yard**, are better for browsing and people-watching. On the area's southern edge, the **Strand**, a busy thoroughfare connecting Westminster to the City, was once famous for its riverside mansions, though only **Somerset House**, on the north side of Waterloo Bridge, remains.

Covent Garden Piazza

London's oldest planned square, laid out in the 1630s by Inigo Jones, **Covent Garden Piazza** was initially a great success, its novelty value alone attracting a rich and aristocratic clientele, but over the next century the tone of the place fell as the fruit and vegetable market expanded, and theatres, coffee houses and brothels began to take over the peripheral buildings. When the market closed in 1974, the piazza narrowly survived being turned into an office development. Instead, the elegant Victorian market hall and its environs were restored to house shops, restaurants and arts-and-crafts stalls. Of Jones's original piazza, the only remaining parts are the two rebuilt sections of north-side arcading, and **St Paul's Church**, to the west.

London Transport Museum

Covent Garden Piazza, WC2E 7BB • Daily 10am–6pm, Fri opens 11am • Adults £17.50, under-16s free; tickets are valid for unlimited entries for a year • ☎ 020 7379 6344, ⓦ ltmuseum.co.uk • ⊖ Covent Garden

A former flower-market shed on Covent Garden Piazza's east side is home to the **London Transport Museum**, a sure-fire hit for families. To follow the displays chronologically, head for Level 2, where you'll find a reconstructed 1829 Shillibeer's Horse Omnibus, which provided the city's first regular horse-bus service. Level 1 tells the story of the world's first underground system and contains a lovely 1920s Metropolitan Line carriage in burgundy and green with pretty, drooping lamps. On the ground floor, one double-decker **tram** is all that's left to pay tribute to the world's largest tram system, dismantled in 1952. Look out, too, for the first **tube** train, from the 1890s, whose lack of windows earned it the nickname "the padded cell".

Royal Opera House

Bow St, WC2E 9DD • Backstage tours (booked in advance): usually Mon–Sat 10.30am, 12.30pm & 2.30pm • ☎ 020 7304 4000, ⓦ roh.org.uk • ⊖ Covent Garden

The arcading on the northeast side of the piazza was rebuilt as part of the redevelopment of the **Royal Opera House**, whose main Neoclassical facade dates from 1811 and opens

1

onto Bow Street. The adjoining Victorian wrought-iron-and-glass structure is the Floral Hall, once home to Covent Garden's flower market and now the **Paul Hamlyn Hall**, a spectacular setting for the theatre's champagne bar (open 1hr 30min before performances). Some areas of the Opera House are closed for limited periods for refurbishment, which, once complete, will create more public spaces looking out onto the piazza and Bow Street.

Somerset House

The Strand, WC2R 1LA • **Fountain Court** Daily 7.30am–11pm • Free **Riverside terrace** Daily 8am–11pm • Free • **Guided tours** Thurs 1.15pm & 2.45pm, Sat 12.15pm, 1.15pm, 2.15pm & 3.15pm • Free • **Embankment Galleries** Mon, Tues, Sat & Sun 10am–6pm, Wed–Fri 11am–8pm • £6 **East and West Wing Galleries** Daily 10am–6pm during exhibitions • Usually free • ☎ 020 7845 4600, ⓦ somersethouse.org.uk • ⊖ Temple or Covent Garden

Somerset House is the sole survivor of the grandiose river palaces that once lined the Strand. Although it looks like an old aristocratic mansion, the present building was purpose-built in 1776 to house government offices. Nowadays, Somerset House's granite-paved courtyard, which has a 55-jet **fountain** that spouts little syncopated dances straight from the cobbles, is used for open-air performances, concerts, installations and, in winter, an ice rink.

The interior is a network of corridors and exhibition spaces, also housing half a dozen cafés and restaurants. The south wing has a lovely riverside terrace with a café/restaurant and the **Embankment Galleries**, which host special exhibitions on contemporary art and design. You can also admire the Royal Naval Commissioners' superb gilded eighteenth-century barge in the **King's Barge House**, below ground level in the south wing.

Courtauld Gallery

Somerset House, The Strand, WC2R 1LA • Daily 10am–6pm, last entry 5.30pm, Thurs occasionally open until 9pm • £8, more during temporary exhibitions • ☎ 020 7848 2526, ⓦ courtauld.ac.uk • ⊖ Temple or Covent Garden

In the north wing of Somerset House is the **Courtauld Gallery**, chiefly known for its dazzling collection of Impressionist and Post-Impressionist paintings. Among the most celebrated is a small-scale version of Manet's *Déjeuner sur l'herbe*, Renoir's *La Loge*, and Degas' *Two Dancers*, plus a whole heap of Cézanne's canvases, including one of his series of *Card Players*. The Courtauld also boasts a fine selection of works by the likes of Rubens, Van Dyck, Tiepolo and Cranach the Elder, as well as top-notch twentieth-century paintings and sculptures by, among others, Kandinksy and Matisse.

Bloomsbury and King's Cross

Bloomsbury was built over in grid-plan style from the 1660s onwards, and the formal bourgeois Georgian squares laid out then remain the area's main distinguishing feature. In the twentieth century, Bloomsbury acquired a reputation as the city's most learned quarter, dominated by the dual institutions of the **British Museum** and **London University**, but perhaps best known for its literary inhabitants, among them T.S. Eliot and Virginia Woolf. Today, the British Museum is clearly the star attraction, but there are other minor sights, such as the **Charles Dickens Museum**. Only in its northern fringes does the character of the area change dramatically, as you near the hustle and bustle of **Euston**, **St Pancras** and **King's Cross** train stations, beyond which one section of the Regent's Canal is the focus for an imaginatively designed new quarter that has adapted former industrial structures – gasholders and warehouses – into galleries, parks and luxury apartments.

FROM TOP GREENWICH PARK (P.101); LITTLE VENICE (P.98) >

1

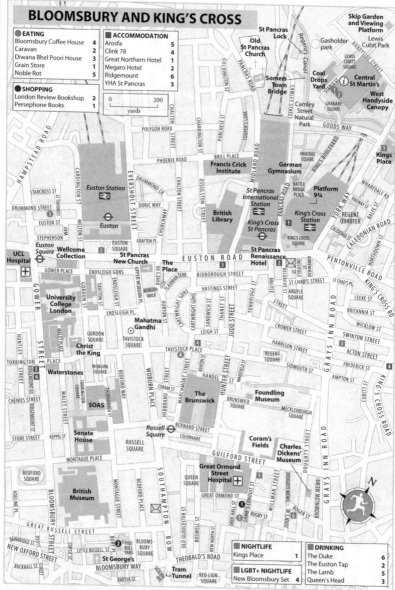

BLOOMSBURY AND KING'S CROSS

● EATING
Bloomsbury Coffee House	4
Caravan	2
Diwana Bhel Poori House	3
Grain Store	
Noble Rot	5

■ ACCOMMODATION
Arosfa	5
Clink 78	4
Great Northern Hotel	1
Megaro Hotel	2
Ridgemount	6
YHA St Pancras	3

● SHOPPING
London Review Bookshop	2
Persephone Books	1

■ NIGHTLIFE
Kings Place	1

■ LGBT+ NIGHTLIFE
New Bloomsbury Set	4

■ DRINKING
The Duke	6
The Euston Tap	2
The Lamb	5
Queen's Head	3

0   200
yards

British Museum

Great Russell St, WC1B 3DG • Daily 10am–5.30pm, Fri till 8.30pm • Free; special exhibitions £12–17; audioguides £6 • **Eye-opener tours** Numerous each day, ask at information desks; 30–40min • Free • **Highlights tour** Fri–Sun 11.30am & 2pm; 1hr 30min • £12 • ☏ 020 7323 8181, �ⓦ britishmuseum.org • ⊖ Tottenham Court Road, Russell Square or Holborn

The **British Museum** is one of the great museums of the world. With more than seventy thousand exhibits ranged over several miles of galleries, it boasts a huge collection of antiquities, prints and drawings. Its assortment of Roman and Greek art is unparalleled, its Egyptian collection is the most significant outside Egypt, and there are fabulous treasures from Anglo-Saxon and Roman Britain, and from China, Japan, India and Mesopotamia.

The building itself, begun in 1823, is the grandest of London's Greek Revival edifices, dominated by the giant Ionian colonnade and portico that forms the main entrance. At the heart of the museum is the **Great Court**, with its remarkable, curving glass-and-steel roof, designed by Norman Foster. At the centre stands the copper-domed former **Round Reading Room**, built in the 1850s to house the British Library, where Karl Marx penned *Das Kapital* (unfortunately currently closed to the public).

The museum is vast, immensely popular and, on first visit, overwhelming, so it's worth focusing on one or two sections. There are **information desks** in the Great Court, where you can get audioguides and find out about **tours**: the Eye-opener tours, which concentrate on just one or two rooms, are particularly recommended.

The collections

To get a sense of the origins of the collection, start at the ground-floor **Enlightenment gallery** (room 1). Originally the King's Library, this imposing 300ft Neoclassical room was built to house George III's library (now at the British Library), and looks like a very large cabinet of curiosities, full of unusual items that formed the nucleus of the collection.

The most famous of the **Roman and Greek antiquities** are the Parthenon sculptures, better known as the **Elgin Marbles**, after the British aristocrat who acquired the reliefs in 1801. There's a splendid series of **Assyrian reliefs**, depicting events such as the royal lion hunts of Ashurbanipal, in which the king slaughters one of the cats with his bare hands. The **Egyptian collection** of monumental sculptures is impressive, with the ground-floor centrepiece the **Rosetta Stone**, which finally unlocked the secret of Egyptian hieroglyphs. On the first floor, it's the remarkable collection of **mummies** that draws the biggest crowds.

The leathery half-corpse of the 2000-year-old **Lindow Man**, discovered in a Cheshire bog, and the Anglo-Saxon treasure from the **Sutton Hoo** ship burial, are among the highlights of the prehistoric and Romano-British section. The medieval and modern collections, meanwhile, include the exquisite twelfth-century **Lewis chessmen**, carved from walrus ivory.

Further rooms cover European Renaissance treasures, Mexico and North America, plus Africa, Islamic art, Japan, Korea and China – including a remarkable collection of Chinese porcelain. There are also changing exhibits from the museum's large collection of prints and drawings, and rooms devoted to money and clocks.

Charles Dickens Museum

48 Doughty St, WC1N 2LX • Tues–Sun 10am–5pm, last admission 4pm • £9 • ☎ 020 7405 2127, ⓦ dickensmuseum.com • ⊖ Russell Square

Charles Dickens moved to Doughty Street in 1837, shortly after his marriage to Catherine Hogarth, and they lived here for two years, during which time he wrote *Nicholas Nickleby* and *Oliver Twist*. Much of the house's furniture belonged, at one time or another, to Dickens. Also on display are numerous portraits, including the earliest known portrait of the writer (a miniature painted by his aunt in 1830), and original, heavily annotated manuscripts. The museum puts on special exhibitions, and you'll also find a café here.

Wellcome Collection

183 Euston Rd, NW1 2BE • Tues–Sat 10am–6pm, Thurs till 10pm, Sun 11am–6pm • Free • ☎ 020 7611 2222, ⓦ wellcomecollection.org • ⊖ Euston or Euston Square

The **Wellcome Collection** is the foundation established by American-born pharmaceutical magnate Henry Wellcome (1853–1936). It puts on thought-provoking scientifically themed exhibitions, and has various permanent displays, the one unmissable one being

1

Medicine Man, which showcases the weird and wonderful collection of historical and scientific artefacts amassed by Henry Wellcome. These range from Florence Nightingale's moccasins to a mummified human body from the Chima people of Peru (1200–1400). Don't leave without taking a look at the top-floor **reading room** – a fantastically quirky library and gallery, where you could happily spend a few hours perusing the exhibits. A café, bookshop and restaurant are all on site.

British Library

96 Euston Rd, NW1 2DB • Building Mon–Thurs 9.30am–8pm, Fri 9.30am–6pm, Sat 9.30am–5pm, Sun 11am–5pm; Treasures Gallery closes 6pm on Mon • Free; charge for some special exhibitions • ☎ 0330 333 1144 or ☎ 020 7412 7332, ⓦ bl.uk • ⊖ King's Cross

As one of the country's most expensive public buildings, the **British Library** took flak from all sides during its protracted construction, and finally opened in 1998. Yet while it's true that the building's uncompromising red-brick edifice is resolutely unfashionable, the library's interior has met with general approval, and the exhibition galleries are superb. At its centre, a huge multistorey glass-walled tower houses the vast **King's Library**, collected by George III.

With the exception of the reading rooms, the library is open to the public and puts on a wide variety of exhibitions and events, and has several cafés, a restaurant and free wi-fi. In the **Treasures Gallery** is a selection of the BL's ancient manuscripts, maps, documents and precious books, including the richly illustrated Lindisfarne Gospels and the Magna Carta, along with changing displays of early literary editions and manuscripts.

King's Cross and St Pancras stations

Euston Rd, N1C 4QP • ⊖ King's Cross St Pancras

The area around King's Cross and St Pancras stations is always buzzing with buses, cars, commuters, tourists and, with the massive development behind, construction workers. Architecturally, the area is dominated by **St Pancras Station**, the most glorious of London's red-brick Victorian edifices, with the neo-Gothic former *Midland Grand Hotel* designed by George Gilbert Scott, now the *St Pancras Renaissance*, forming its facade. It overshadows neighbouring **King's Cross Station**, opened in 1852, a mere shed in comparison, albeit one that has been beautifully restored. It is, of course, the station from which Harry Potter and his wizarding chums leave for school aboard the *Hogwarts Express* from platform 9¾. The film scenes were shot between platforms 4 and 5, and a station trolley is now embedded in the new concourse wall, providing a perfect photo opportunity for Potter fans (expect to queue), next to a Harry Potter-themed shop.

Granary Square and the canal

Granary Square, N1C 4AA • **King's Cross Visitor Centre** Stable St • Mon–Fri 10am–5pm, Sat 10am–4pm • ☎ 020 3479 1795, ⓦ kingscross .co.uk • **Camley Street Natural Park** 12 Camley St, N1C 4PW • Daily: April–Sept 10am–5pm; Oct–March 10am–4pm • Free • ☎ 020 7833 2311, ⓦ wildlondon.org.uk • ⊖ King's Cross St Pancras

From King's Cross station, walk north up King's Boulevard and you reach the Regent's Canal and the district that once serviced the industries dependent on the canal and railways. The relocation of Eurostar to St Pancras kick-started redevelopment here, which is now well underway, transforming 67 acres into a new city quarter. It will ultimately include twenty new streets and ten new public squares, with around twenty venerable former industrial structures, mostly designed by Lewis Cubitt, surviving. Beyond the canal is the centrepiece **Granary Square**, a large open space almost entirely taken over by a grid of playful dancing fountains that are irresistible to children on hot days. The former Granary building itself is home to **Central Saint Martins**, part of the University of the Arts.

To find out more about the development, visit **King's Cross Visitor Centre** to the side of the Granary building, which has a model of the development and from where you can take a guided tour (1hr 30min; free; book online). Largely car-free, with plenty of green spaces and frequent pop-up markets and events, the whole area is fun to explore. Walk along the canal, past the picturesque **St Pancras Lock**, and you reach a cluster of brooding Victorian gasholders, one framing a landscaped park with mirrored pergola, **Gasholder Park**. On the other side of the canal, connected by a pedestrian bridge, is **Camley Street Natural Park**, which was transformed into a wildlife haven of woodland sand ponds in the 1980s.

Holborn

Holborn, on the periphery of the financial district of the City, has long been associated with the law, and its **Inns of Court** make for an interesting stroll, their archaic, cobbled precincts exuding the rarefied atmosphere of an Oxbridge college, and sheltering one of the city's oldest churches, the twelfth-century **Temple Church**. Holborn's gem, though, is the **Sir John Soane's Museum**, one of the most memorable and enjoyable of London's small museums, packed with architectural illusions and an eclectic array of curios.

Temple

Temple is the largest and most complex of the Inns of Court, where every barrister in England must study (and eat) before being called to the Bar. A few very old buildings survive here and the maze of courtyards and passageways are still redolent of Dickens's London, as described in *Bleak House*.

Middle Temple Hall

Middle Temple Lane, EC4Y 9AT • **Hall** Mon–Fri 10am–noon & 3–4pm, though sometimes closed for events • Free • **Gardens** May–July & Sept Mon–Fri noon–3pm • ☎ 020 7427 4800, ⓦ middletemplehall.org.uk • ⊖ Temple or Blackfriars

Medieval students ate, attended lectures and slept in the **Middle Temple Hall**, still the Inn's main dining room. The present building, constructed in the 1560s, provided the setting for many great Elizabethan masques and plays – probably including Shakespeare's *Twelfth Night*, which is believed to have been premiered here in 1602. The hall is worth a visit for its fine hammer-beam roof, wooden panelling and decorative Elizabethan screen.

Temple Church

Temple, EC4Y 7HL • Mon, Tues, Thurs & Fri 10am–4pm, Wed usually term time 2–4pm & summer 10am–4pm, but times and days vary; check online • £5 • ☎ 020 7353 3470, ⓦ templechurch.com • ⊖ Temple or Blackfriars

The complex's oldest building is **Temple Church**, built in 1185 by the Knights Templar, and modelled on the Church of the Holy Sepulchre in Jerusalem. The interior features striking Purbeck marble piers, recumbent marble effigies of medieval knights and tortured grotesques grimacing in the spandrels of the blind arcading. The church makes an appearance in both the book and the film of Dan Brown's *The Da Vinci Code*.

Sir John Soane's Museum

12–14 Lincoln's Inn Fields, WC2A 3BP • Tues–Sat 10am–5pm, candlelit eve first Tues of month 6–9pm (very popular, so you may have to queue) • Free • **Guided tours** (including the private apartment) Tues & Sat 11am & noon, Thurs & Fri noon; book ahead • £10 • **Private apartment tours** Tues–Sat 1.15pm & 2pm; no advance booking, sign up ahead of time on the day • Free • ☎ 020 7405 2107, ⓦ soane.org • ⊖ Holborn

A trio of buildings on the north side of Lincoln's Inn Fields houses the fascinating **Sir John Soane's Museum**. Soane (1753–1837), a bricklayer's son who rose to be architect of the Bank of England, was an avid collector who designed this house not only as a home and

1

office, but also as a place to show his large collection of art and antiquities. Arranged much as it was in his lifetime, the ingeniously planned house – with mirrors, domes and skylights creating space and light as if out of nowhere – reveals surprises in every alcove. Standouts among the thousands of objects and artworks are the Egyptian sarcophagus of Seti and Hogarth's mercilessly satirical series *Election* and *The Rake's Progress* (in the picture room, the latter hung hidden behind the former; the room guides will show you). To get a real sense of the man and architect who created this curious place, take one of the private apartment tours of the upper floor.

The City

Stretching from Temple Bar in the west to the Tower of London in the east, **The City** is where London began. It was here, nearly two thousand years ago, that the Romans first established a settlement on the Thames; later the medieval City emerged as the country's most important trading centre and it remains one of the world's leading financial hubs. However, in this Square Mile (as the City is sometimes referred to), you'll find few leftovers of London's early days, since four-fifths burnt down in the Great Fire of 1666. Rebuilt in brick and stone, the City gradually lost its centrality as London swelled westwards. What you see now is mostly the product of three fairly recent building phases: the Victorian construction boom; the postwar reconstruction following World War II; and the building frenzy that began in the 1980s and has continued ever since, most recently adding a cluster of dizzingly high skyscrapers.

When you consider what has happened here, it's amazing that anything has survived to pay witness to the City's 2000-year history. Wren's spires still punctuate the skyline and his masterpiece, **St Paul's Cathedral**, remains one of London's geographical pivots. At the City's eastern edge, the **Tower of London** still boasts some of the best-preserved medieval fortifications in Europe. Other relics, such as Wren's **Monument** to the Great Fire and London's oldest synagogue and church, are less conspicuous, and even locals have problems finding modern attractions like the **Museum of London** and the **Barbican** arts complex.

St Paul's Cathedral

St Paul's Churchyard, EC4M 8AD • Cathedral Mon–Sat 8.30am–4.30pm, last admission 4pm; galleries Mon–Sat 9.30am–4.15pm • £18; £16 online • ☎ 020 7236 4128, ⓦ stpauls.co.uk • ⊖ St Paul's

Designed by Christopher Wren and completed in 1710, **St Paul's Cathedral** remains a dominating presence in the City, despite the encroaching tower blocks. Topped by an enormous lead-covered dome, its showpiece west facade is particularly magnificent.

The best place from which to appreciate St Paul's is beneath the **dome**, decorated (against Wren's wishes) with Thornhill's trompe-l'oeil frescoes. The most richly decorated section of the cathedral, however, is the **chancel**, where the gilded mosaics of birds, fish, animals and greenery, dating from the 1890s, are spectacular. The intricately carved oak and limewood **choir stalls**, and the imposing organ case, are the work of Wren's master carver, Grinling Gibbons.

The galleries

A series of stairs, beginning in the south aisle, lead to the dome's three **galleries**, the first of which is the internal **Whispering Gallery**, so called because of its acoustic properties – words whispered to the wall on one side are distinctly audible over 100ft away on the other, though the place is often so busy you can't hear much above the hubbub. The other two galleries are exterior, with suitably breathtaking views: the wide **Stone Gallery**, around the balustrade at the base of the dome, and, ultimately, the tiny **Golden Gallery**, below the golden ball and cross which top the cathedral.

1

TOP 5 CITY CHURCHES

The City of London is crowded with **churches** (w london-city-churches.org.uk), the majority of them built or rebuilt by Wren after the Great Fire. Weekday lunchtimes are a good time to visit, when many put on free concerts of classical and chamber music; others have branched out and host cafés during the week.

St Bartholomew-the-Great Cloth Fair; w greatstbarts.com; ⊖ Barbican. The oldest surviving pre-Fire church, established in 1123, in the City and by far the most atmospheric, with a Norman chancel. Mon–Fri 8.30am–5pm, Sat 10.30am–4pm, Sun 8.30am–8pm; mid-Nov to mid-Feb Mon–Fri closes 4pm; £5.

St Mary Abchurch Abchurch Lane; ⊖ Cannon Street or Bank. Unique among Wren's City churches for its huge, painted, domed ceiling, plus the only authenticated reredos by Grinling Gibbons. Mon–Fri 11am–3pm.

St Mary Aldermary Bow Lane/Watling Street; ⊖ Mansion House. Wren's most successful stab at

Gothic, with fan vaulting in the aisles and a panelled ceiling in the nave. Mon–Fri 9am–4.30pm.

St Mary Woolnoth Lombard St; ⊖ Bank. Hawksmoor's only City church, sporting an unusually broad, bulky tower and a Baroque clerestory that floods the church with light from its semicircular windows. Mon–Fri 7.30am–5.15pm.

St Stephen Walbrook Walbrook; ⊖ Bank. Wren's dress rehearsal for St Paul's, with a wonderful central dome and plenty of original woodcarving. Mon, Tues & Thurs 10am–4pm, Wed 11am–3pm, Fri 10am–3.30pm.

The crypt

Although the nave is crammed full of overblown monuments to military types, burials in St Paul's are confined to the whitewashed **crypt**, reputedly the largest in Europe. Immediately to your right is Artists' Corner, which boasts as many painters and architects as Westminster Abbey has poets, including Christopher Wren himself, who was commissioned to build the cathedral after its Gothic predecessor, Old St Paul's, was destroyed in the Great Fire. The crypt's two other star tombs are those of **Nelson** and **Wellington**, both occupying centre stage and both with even more fanciful monuments upstairs.

Museum of London

150 London Wall, EC2Y 5HN • Daily 10am–6pm • Free • ☎ 020 7001 9844, w museumoflondon.org.uk • ⊖ Barbican or St Paul's

Over the centuries, numerous Roman, Saxon and medieval remains have been salvaged or dug up and are now displayed in the **Museum of London**, whose permanent galleries provide an educational and imaginative trot through London's past, from prehistory to the present day. Specific exhibits to look out for include the Bucklersbury Roman mosaic, marble busts from the Temple of Mithras (uncovered in the City) and the model of Old St Paul's, but the prize possession is the **Lord Mayor's Coach**, built in 1757 and rivalling the Queen's in sheer weight of gold decoration. Look out, too, for the museum's excellent temporary exhibitions, gallery tours, lectures and walks.

Guildhall

Gresham St, EC2V 5AE • Great Hall May–Sept daily 10am–4.30pm; Oct–April Mon–Sat 10am–4.30pm; gallery Mon–Sat 10am–5pm, Sun noon–4pm • Free • ☎ 020 7332 1313, w cityoflondon.gov.uk • ⊖ Bank

Despite being the seat of the City governance for over 800 years, **Guildhall** doesn't exactly exude municipal wealth. Nevertheless, it's worth popping inside the **Great Hall**, which miraculously survived both the Great Fire and Blitz. The hall is still used for functions, though only the walls survive from the original fifteenth-century building, which was the venue for several high-treason trials, including that of Lady Jane Grey. The purpose-built **Guildhall Art Gallery** contains one or two exceptional works, most notably Rossetti's *La Ghirlandata*. In the basement, you can view the remains of a

1

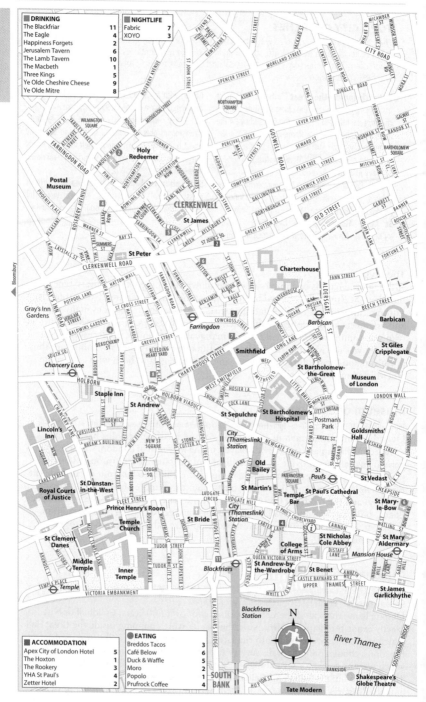

DRINKING	
The Blackfriar	11
The Eagle	4
Happiness Forgets	2
Jerusalem Tavern	6
The Lamb Tavern	10
The Macbeth	1
Three Kings	5
Ye Olde Cheshire Cheese	9
Ye Olde Mitre	8

NIGHTLIFE	
Fabric	7
XOYO	3

ACCOMMODATION	
Apex City of London Hotel	5
The Hoxton	1
The Rookery	3
YHA St Paul's	4
Zetter Hotel	2

EATING	
Breddos Tacos	3
Café Below	6
Duck & Waffle	5
Moro	2
Popolo	1
Prufrock Coffee	4

1

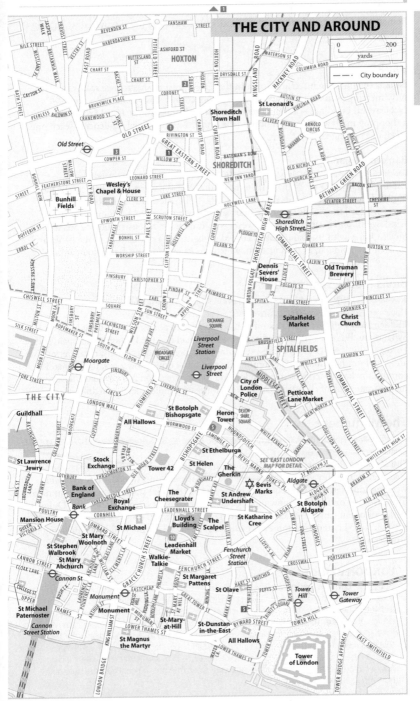

THE CITY AND AROUND

0 | yards | 200

– – – City boundary

HOXTON

St Leonard's

Shoreditch Town Hall

SHOREDITCH

Old Street

Wesley's Chapel & House

Bunhill Fields

Shoreditch High Street

Dennis Severs' House

Old Truman Brewery

Spitalfields Market

Christ Church

SPITALFIELDS

Moorgate

Exchange Square

Liverpool Street Station

Liverpool Street

City of London Police

Petticoat Lane Market

THE CITY

Guildhall

St Botolph Bishopsgate

Heron Tower

All Hallows

St Lawrence Jewry

Stock Exchange

Tower 42

St Ethelburga

St Helen

The Gherkin

Bevis Marks

Aldgate

Bank of England

Royal Exchange

Bank

The Cheesegrater

St Andrew Undershaft

St Botolph Aldgate

Mansion House

St Michael

Lloyd's Building

The Scalpel

St Katharine Cree

St Mary Woolnoth

St Stephen Walbrook

St Mary Abchurch

Leadenhall Market

Walkie-Talkie

Fenchurch Street Station

Cannon St

Monument

St Margaret Pattens

St Olave

Tower Hill

Tower Gateway

Monument

St Michael Paternoster

St-Mary-at-Hill

St-Dunstan-in-the-East

All Hallows

Tower Hill

Cannon Street Station

St Magnus the Martyr

Tower of London

SEE 'EAST LONDON' MAP FOR DETAIL

1

Roman amphitheatre, dating from around 120 AD, which was discovered when the gallery was built in 1988.

Bank

Bank is the finest architectural arena in the City. Heart of the finance sector and the busy meeting point of eight streets, it's overlooked by a handsome collection of Neoclassical buildings – among them, the **Bank of England**, the **Royal Exchange** (now a shopping mall) and **Mansion House** (the Lord Mayor's official residence) – each one faced in Portland stone.

Bank of England

Threadneedle St, EC2R 8AH • Mon–Fri 10am–5pm • Free • ☎ 020 7601 5545, ⓦ bankofengland.co.uk • ⊖ Bank

Established in 1694 by William III to raise funds for the war against France, the **Bank of England** wasn't erected on its present site until 1734. All that remains of the building on which Sir John Soane spent the best part of his career from 1788 onwards is the windowless, outer curtain wall. However, you can view a reconstruction of Soane's Bank Stock Office, with its characteristic domed skylight, see a virtual tour of the bank, and touch a real gold bar, in the **museum**, which has its entrance on Bartholomew Lane.

Bevis Marks Synagogue

Bevis Marks, EC3A 7LH • Mon, Wed & Thurs 10.30am–2pm, Tues & Fri 10.30am–1pm, Sun 10.30am–12.30pm; guided tours Wed & Fri 11.30am, Sun 11am • £5; tours free • ☎ 020 7626 1274, ⓦ sephardi.org.uk/bevis-marks • ⊖ Aldgate

Hidden away behind a red-brick office block in a little courtyard is the **Bevis Marks Synagogue**. Built in 1701 by Sephardic Jews who had fled the Inquisition in Spain and Portugal, this is the country's oldest surviving synagogue, and its roomy, rich interior gives an idea of just how wealthy the community was at the time. Nowadays, the Sephardic community has dispersed across London and the congregation has dwindled, though the magnificent array of chandeliers makes it popular for candlelit Jewish weddings.

The Monument

Fish St Hill, EC3R 8AH • April–Sept daily 9.30am–6pm; Oct–March 9.30am–5.30pm • £5; joint ticket with Tower Bridge £12 • ☎ 020 7403 3761, ⓦ themonument.org.uk • ⊖ Monument

The Monument was designed by Wren to commemorate the Great Fire of 1666. Crowned with spiky gilded flames, this plain Doric column stands 202ft high; if it were laid out flat it would touch the bakery where the Fire started, east of Monument. The bas-relief on the base, now in very bad shape, depicts Charles II and the Duke of York in Roman garb conducting the emergency relief operation. Views from the gallery, accessed by 311 steps, are somewhat dwarfed nowadays by the buildings springing up around it.

LONDON BRIDGE

Until 1750, **London Bridge** was the only bridge across the Thames. The medieval bridge achieved world fame: built of stone and crowded with timber-framed houses, a palace and a chapel, it became one of the great attractions of London – there's a model in the nearby church of **St Magnus the Martyr** (Tues–Fri 10am–4pm). The houses were finally removed in the mid-eighteenth century, and a new stone bridge, erected in 1831, lasted until the 1960s; that one was bought by an American industrialist and now stands reconstructed in the Arizona desert. It was transported there to be the focus of a new settlement, where it remains, now a curious centrepiece in a sprawling desert town. The present concrete structure dates from 1972.

1

AIMING HIGH: CITY SKYSCRAPERS

Throughout the 1990s, most people's favourite modern building in the City was Richard Rogers' **Lloyd's Building**, on Leadenhall Street – a vertical version of his Pompidou Centre in Paris – an inside-out array of glass and steel piping. Lloyd's was upstaged in 2003 by Norman Foster's 590ft-high glass diamond-clad **Gherkin**, which endeared itself to Londoners with its cheeky shape. In recent years, the City skyline has sprouted yet more skyscrapers, with the **Cheesegrater** (officially the Leadenhall Building), Richard Rogers' 737ft wedge-shaped office block, opposite the Lloyd's Building, and the **Scalpel**, a 620ft angular shard of glass, clustering near the Gherkin. Set away from this tight grouping and so more controversial is Rafael Viñoly's ugly, unsympathetic 525ft **Walkie Talkie**, on Fenchurch Street, which features a public **Sky Garden** on the top floor (20 Fenchurch St, EC3M 8AF; Mon–Fri 10am–6pm, Sat & Sun 11am–9pm; book free tickets in advance; ☎020 7337 2344, ⊛skygarden.london), and several restaurants and bars.

More are planned, with the vast block of the 219ft **22 Bishopsgate** currently under construction and, tallest of all, **1 Undershaft**, planned for completion in the 2020s, which will be the tallest construction in the Square Mile, at 951ft. It'll remain second tallest in London (and Europe) to Renzo Piano's 1016ft **Shard**, by London Bridge (see p.90).

Tower of London

EC3N 4AB • Mon & Sun 10am–5.30pm, Tues–Sat 9am–5.30pm; Nov–Feb closes 4.30pm; last admission 30min before closing; 1hr guided tours every 30min • £28; £24.80 online in advance; tours free • ☎ 0844 482 7799, ⊛ hrp.org.uk • ⊖ Tower Hill

One of Britain's main tourist attractions, the **Tower of London** overlooks the river at the eastern boundary of the old city walls. Despite all the hype, it remains one of London's most remarkable buildings, site of some of the goriest events in the nation's history, and somewhere all visitors and Londoners should explore at least once. Chiefly famous as a place of imprisonment and death, it has variously been used as a royal residence, armoury, mint, menagerie, observatory and – a function it still serves – a safe-deposit box for the Crown Jewels.

The lively free **guided tours** given by the Tower's **Beefeaters** (officially known as Yeoman Warders) are useful for getting your bearings. Visitors enter the Tower by the Middle Tower and the Byward Tower, in the southwest corner, but in times gone by most prisoners were delivered through **Traitors' Gate**, on the waterfront. Immediately, they would have come to the **Bloody Tower**, which forms the main entrance to the Inner Ward, and which is where the 12-year-old Edward V and his 10-year-old brother were accommodated "for their own safety" in 1483 by their uncle, the future Richard III, and later murdered. It's also where **Walter Raleigh** was imprisoned on three separate occasions, including a thirteen-year stretch.

Tower Green and the White Tower

At the centre of the Inner Ward is village-like **Tower Green**, where, over the years, seven highly placed but unlucky individuals have been beheaded, among them Anne Boleyn and her cousin Catherine Howard (Henry VIII's second and fifth wives). The **White Tower**, which overlooks the Green, is the original "Tower", begun in 1078, and now home to displays from the **Royal Armouries**. Even if you've no interest in military paraphernalia, you should at least pay a visit to the **Chapel of St John**, a beautiful Norman structure on the second floor that was completed in 1080 – making it the oldest intact church building in London.

Crown Jewels

The **Waterloo Barracks**, to the north of the White Tower, hold the **Crown Jewels**; queues can be painfully long, however, and you only get to view the rocks from moving walkways. The vast majority of exhibits post-date the Commonwealth (1649–60), when many of the royal riches were melted down for coinage or sold off. Among the jewels are some of the largest cut diamonds in the world, plus the legendary **Koh-i-Noor**, which was set into the Queen Mother's Crown in 1937.

1

Tower Bridge

SE1 2UP • Daily: April–Sept 10am–5.30pm; Oct–March 9.30am–5pm • £9.80; joint ticket with Monument £12 • ☎ 020 7403 3761,
Ⓦ towerbridge.org.uk • ⊖ Tower Hill

Tower Bridge ranks with Big Ben as the most famous of all London landmarks. Completed in 1894, its neo-Gothic towers are clad in Cornish granite and Portland stone, but conceal a steel frame, which, at the time, represented a considerable engineering achievement, allowing a road crossing that could be raised to give tall ships access to the upper reaches of the Thames. The raising of the bascules remains an impressive sight (check the website for times). If you buy a ticket, you get to walk across the elevated walkways that link the summits of the towers, and which have glass-floor sections, and visit the Tower's Victorian Engine Rooms, on the south side of the bridge, where you can see the now defunct giant coal-fired boilers which drove the hydraulic system until 1976, and play some interactive engineering games.

East London

Few places in London have engendered so many myths as the **East End**, an area long synonymous with slums, sweatshops and crime, its dark mythology surrounding the likes of Jack the Ripper and the Kray twins. It was also the first port of call for wave after wave of **immigrants**, including the French Huguenots, Jewish eastern Europeans and those from the Indian subcontinent. Now, however, visitors arriving here are most likely to be those in search of the next London scene. Art previews, experimental cocktail bars and edgy nightlife all find a space in the sprawl of neighbourhoods – Spitalfields, Whitechapel, Bethnal Green, Shoreditch, Hoxton, Dalston, Hackney – that make up the wider East London.

For day-time visitors, Sunday morning is the best time to visit for the network of famous **Sunday markets** – clothes and crafts in Spitalfields, hip vintage gear around Brick Lane and flowers on Columbia Road – while further afield the **Olympic Park** has some fun spots for families.

Spitalfields

Spitalfields, within sight of the sleek tower blocks of the financial sector, lies at the old heart of the East End, where the French Huguenots settled in the seventeenth century, where the Jewish community was at its strongest in the late nineteenth century, and where today's Bengali community eats, sleeps, works and prays. If you visit just one

---

THE EVOLUTION OF EAST LONDON

Since the 1990s, the northern fringe of the City has been colonized by artists, designers and architects. This has evolved into a distinctive look, scene and attitude found across East London – think vintage markets, revamped old pubs, speakeasy-style bars, hipster coffee shops and street art. You'll find a swathe of neighbourhoods where cheap Turkish, Bangladeshi or Vietnamese restaurants, plus the occasional traditional East End café (such as *E. Pellicci* in Bethnal Green), sit alongside high-end boutique hotels, art galleries and street fashion stores. **Hoxton** (to the north of Old Street) and **Shoreditch** (to the south) kicked off the East End transformation, but they have since been upstaged by **Dalston** (up Kingsland Road) and **Hackney** beyond. To get a taste of the area try these East London favourites:

AN EAST LONDON TOP 5

Bethnal Green Working Men's Club See
p.125
Columbia Road Flower Market See p.130
Culpeper See p.113

E. Pellicci See p.118
First Thursdays at Whitechapel Gallery
See p.85

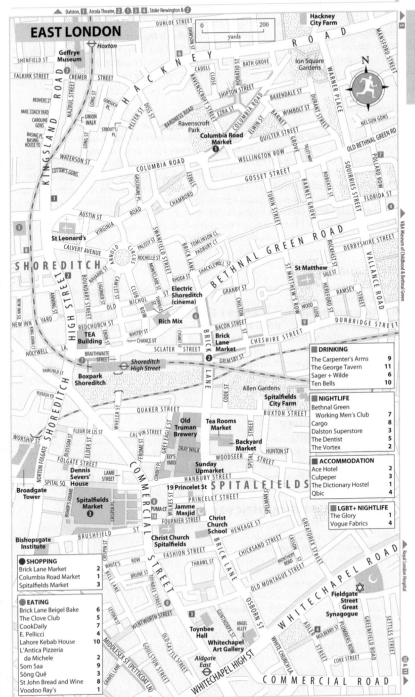

EAST LONDON

Dalston, Arcola Theatre, Stoke Newington &

Hackney City Farm

Geffrye Museum

Hoxton

SHENFIELD ST

FALKIRK STREET

CREMER STREET

REDVERS ST

MAIL COACH YARD

CAROLINE GDNS

BASING PL BASING HOUSE YD

WATERSON ST

COTTON'S GDNS

KINGSLAND ROAD

HACKNEY ROAD

NAZRUL STREET

LONG ST

GORSUCH PL

UNION WALK

LONG ST

STROUT'S

GASCOIGNE PL

COLUMBIA ROAD

CHAMBORD STREET

DUNLOE STREET

DAWSON ST

CADELL CLOSE

BARONESS ROAD

RAVENSCROFT STREET

PELTER ST

DISS ST

Ravenscroft Park

EZRA ST

BATH GROVE

HORATIO ST

SHIPTON STREET

COLUMBIA ROAD

ELWIN ST

BARNET GROVE

Columbia Road Market **1**

QUILTER STREET

WELLINGTON ROW

GOSSET STREET

TURIN STREET

Ion Square Gardens

WARNER PLACE

BAXENDALE ST

WIMBOLT ST

DURANT STREET

TILLEY WAY

OLD BETHNAL GREEN RD

POLLARD ROW

SQUIRRIES STREET

ROBERTA ST

BARNET GROVE

FLORIDA ST

MANSFORD STREET

NELSON GDNS

N

AUSTIN ST

VIRGINIA ROAD

St Leonard's

CALVERT AVENUE

SWANFIELD STREET

ARNOLD CIRCUS

NAVARRE ST

ROCHELLE ST

PALISSY ST

MONTCLARE ST

CLUB ROW

NICHOL ROW

BRICK LANE

TOMLINSON CL.

PADBURY CT

RHODA ST

BETHNAL GREEN ROAD

SHACKLEWELL LA

GRANBY ST

St Matthew

ST MATTHEW'S ROW

CHILTON ST

HEREFORD STREET

SALE ST

WOOD CLOSE

BUCKFAST ST

DERBYSHIRE STREET

RAMSEY STREET

DUNBRIDGE STREET

VALLANCE ROAD

V&A Museum of Childhood & Bethnal Green

SHOREDITCH

HIGH STREET

NEW INN YARD

NEW INN SQ

GT EASTERN ST

KINGS JN JOHN

BOUNDARY STREET

OLD NICHOL ST

REDCHURCH STREET

EBOR ST

WHITBY ST

CHANCE ST

SCLATER STREET

TEA Building

HOLYWELL LA.

BRAITHWAITE STREET

FAIRCHILD ST

PLOUGH YD

WORSHIP ST

NORTON FOLGATE

SHOREDITCH

Electric Shoreditch (cinema)

Rich Mix **6**

Brick Lane Market **2**

GRIMSBY ST

CHESHIRE STREET

BACON STREET

BRICK LANE

CYGNET ST

CODE ST

Shoreditch High Street **7**

Boxpark Shoreditch

Broadgate Tower

FLEUR DE LIS ST

BLOSSOM ST

ELDER ST

FOLGATE STREET

SPITAL SQ

Dennis Severs' House

LAMB STREET

Bishopsgate Institute

Spitalfields Market **3**

QUAKER STREET

CALVIN STREET

ELY'S YARD

CORBET PL

HANBURY STREET

19 Princelet St

PRINCELET STREET

JS NISBED

CRISPIN ST

WHITE'S ROW

BRUSHFIELD ST

Old Truman Brewery

DRAY WALK

WOODSEER STREET

Sunday Upmarket

WILKES ST

PUMA CT **10**

FOURNIER STREET

Jamme Masjid

Christ Church School

Tea Rooms Market

Backyard Market

HUNTON ST

Spitalfields City Farm

BUXTON STREET

SPELMAN STREET

Allen Gardens

WHEELER ST

SPITAL STREET

COMMERCIAL STREET

SPITALFIELDS

HEBS ST

HEBS ST

HENEAGE ST

Christ Church Spitalfields

FASHION STREET

THRAWL ST

FLOWER & DEAN ST

CHICKSAND STREET

WENTWORTH STREET

TOYNBEE ST

TONBEE STREET

BRUNE ST

LEYDEN ST

BELL LANE

OLD MONTAGUE STREET

CASSON STREET

MONTHOPE ROAD

GREATOREX STREET

CHICKSAND STREET

OSBORN ST

GREATOREX STREET

MIDDLESEX ST (PETTICOAT LN)

WHITE CHURCH LANE

OLD CASTLE STREET

GUNTHORPE ST

ANGEL ALLEY

Toynbee Hall

Whitechapel Art Gallery

Aldgate East

WHITECHAPEL HIGH STREET

GRAVEL LANE

GOULSTON STREET

COMMERCIAL

WHITECHAPEL ROAD

ADLER STREET

PLUMBERS ROW

MULBERRY ST

COKE STREET

GREENFIELD ROAD

SETTLES STREET

ROAD

Fieldgate Street Great Synagogue

Royal London Hospital

DRINKING
The Carpenter's Arms	9
The George Tavern	11
Sager + Wilde	6
Ten Bells	10

NIGHTLIFE
Bethnal Green Working Men's Club	7
Cargo	8
Dalston Superstore	3
The Dentist	5
The Vortex	2

ACCOMMODATION
Ace Hotel	2
Culpeper	3
The Dictionary Hostel	1
Qbic	4

LGBT+ NIGHTLIFE
The Glory	1
Vogue Fabrics	4

SHOPPING
Brick Lane Market	2
Columbia Road Market	1
Spitalfields Market	3

EATING
Brick Lane Beigel Bake	6
The Clove Club	5
CookDaily	7
E. Pellicci	4
Lahore Kebab House	10
L'Antica Pizzeria da Michele	2
Som Saa	9
Sông Quê	3
St John Bread and Wine	8
Voodoo Ray's	1

0 200 yards

1

area in the East End, it should be this, which preserves mementos from each wave of immigration. The focal point of the area is **Spitalfields Market**, the red-brick and green-gabled market hall built in 1893; the west end has been extensively remodelled and holds glass-fronted chain stores and restaurants, but the original facades survive on the northern and eastern sides. Within, you can find a daily changing mix of crafts, arts and food stalls (see p.131).

Dennis Severs' House

18 Folgate St, E1 6BX • Mon noon–2pm (last admission 1.15pm), Sun noon–4pm (last admission 3.15pm); Mon, Wed & Fri "Silent Night" visits 5–9pm • £10; "Silent Night" visits £15 • ☎ 020 7247 4013, ⓦ dennissevershouse.co.uk • ⊖ Shoreditch High Street or Liverpool Street

You can visit one of Spitalfields' characteristic eighteenth-century terraced houses at 18 Folgate St, where the American artist **Dennis Severs** lived until 1999. Eschewing all modern conveniences, Severs lived under candlelight, decorating his house as it would have been two hundred years ago. The public were invited to share in the experience that he described as like "passing through a frame into a painting". Today visitors are free to explore the cluttered, candlelit rooms, which resonate with the distinct impression that the resident Huguenot family has just popped out, not least due to the smell of cooked food and the sound of horses' hooves on the cobbles outside.

Brick Lane

Truman Brewery, Brick Lane, E1 6QL • Various markets Sat 11am–6pm, Sun 10am–5pm • ⓦ trumanbrewery.com • ⊖ Aldgate East, Shoreditch High Street, Liverpool Street

Brick Lane gets its name from the brick kilns situated here after the Great Fire to help rebuild the City. By 1900, this was the high street of London's unofficial Jewish ghetto, but from the 1960s, Brick Lane became the heart of the Bangladeshi community; latterly it has gentrified into a mix of hip vintage shops and music venues, intermingled with the Bangladeshi curry houses. The Sunday flea market (8am–3pm) occupies the northern stretch of the road, while craft, vintage and food markets fill every corner of the **Old Truman Brewery** complex, halfway up Brick Lane, at weekends.

Whitechapel Gallery

77–82 Whitechapel High St, E1 7QX • Tues–Sun 11am–6pm, Thurs until 9pm • Free • ☎ 020 7522 7888, ⓦ whitechapel.org • ⊖ Aldgate East

Near the south end of Brick Lane, the **Whitechapel Art Gallery** is housed in its original beautiful, crenellated 1899 Arts and Crafts building by Charles Harrison Townsend, its facade embellished with a smattering of gilded leaves by the sculptor Rachel Whiteread,

---

QUEEN ELIZABETH OLYMPIC PARK

The focus of the 2012 Olympics was the **Olympic Park**, laid out over a series of islands formed by the River Lee and various tributaries and canals. Since the Olympics, it has been renamed the **Queen Elizabeth Olympic Park** and the whole area has been replanted with patches of grass, trees and flowers, with waterways meandering through it, and it's peppered with cafés, making it a great new park in which to hang out on a sunny day (ⓦ queenelizabeth olympicpark.co.uk; ⊖ Stratford). The centrepiece is the **Olympic Stadium**, now home to West Ham United football club and UK Athletics; it also serves as a major events venue. Standing close to the stadium is the **ArcelorMittal Orbit** tower (daily: April–Sept 10am–6pm; Oct–March 10am–5pm, sometimes later during peak periods; tower £11.50, tower and slide £16.50; book online in advance; ⓦ arcelormittalorbit.com), a 377ft-high continuous loop of red recycled steel designed by Anish Kapoor, with the world's longest tunnel slide spiralling down it. But the most eye-catching venue is Zaha Hadid's wave-like **Aquatics Centre**, where a swim costs under £5. To the north of the site, you can try out track, BMX and mountain biking at the **Velodrome** (ⓦ visitleevalley.org.uk).

and an extension into a former library next door. Founded by one of the East End's many Victorian philanthropists, Samuel Barnett, the gallery has an illustrious history of showing innovative exhibitions of contemporary art. There's also a great bookshop, reading room and café-bar. Its **First Thursdays** initiative is a perfect way to soak up the East London buzz: on the first Thursday of every month, some 150 East London galleries, small and large, stay open till 9pm.

V&A Museum of Childhood

Cambridge Heath Rd, E2 9PA • Daily 10am–5.45pm • Free • ☎ 020 8983 5200, ⓦ vam.ac. uk/moc • ⊖ Bethnal Green

The wrought-iron hall that houses the **V&A Museum of Childhood** was originally part of the V&A in South Kensington (see p.95) and was transported here in the 1860s to bring art to the East End. On the ground floor you'll see clockwork **toys** – everything from classic robots to a fully functioning model railway – marionettes and puppets, teddies and Smurfs, and even Inuit dolls. The most famous exhibits are the remarkable antique **dolls' houses** dating back to 1673, displayed upstairs, where you'll also find a play area for very small kids, and the museum's special exhibitions.

Docklands

Built in the nineteenth century to cope with the huge volume of goods shipped along the Thames from all over the Empire, **Docklands** was once the largest enclosed cargo-dock system in the world. When the docks closed in the 1960s the area was generally regarded as having died forever, but regeneration in the 1980s brought luxury flats and, on the Isle of Dogs, a huge high-rise office development. Here, at **Canary Wharf**, César Pelli's landmark stainless steel tower **One Canada Square** remains an icon on the city's eastern skyline. The excellent **Museum of London Docklands** (daily 10am–6pm; free; ⓦ museumoflondon.org.uk/docklands), in an old warehouse in Canary Wharf, charts the history of the area from Roman times to the present day.

The South Bank

Drawing in huge numbers of visitors for its high-profile tourist attractions, including the enormously popular **London Eye**, the **South Bank** forms a waterside cluster of London's finest cultural institutions, while further south is the impressive **Imperial War Museum**. With most of London's major sights sitting on the north bank, the views from here are the best on the river, and, thanks to the wide, traffic-free riverside boulevard, the area can be happily explored on foot, while for much of the year outdoor festivals take place along the riverbank.

Southbank Centre

Belvedere Rd, SE1 8X • Foyers daily 10am–11pm; occasional closures for events • ☎ 020 3879 9555, ⓦ southbankcentre.co.uk • ⊖ Waterloo

In 1951, the South Bank Exhibition, on derelict land south of the Thames, formed the centrepiece of the national **Festival of Britain**, an attempt to revive postwar morale by celebrating the centenary of the Great Exhibition. The site's most striking features were the saucer-shaped Dome of Discovery (inspiration for the Millennium Dome), the Royal Festival Hall (which still stands) and the cigar-shaped steel-and-aluminium Skylon tower (yet to be revived).

The Festival of Britain's success provided the impetus for the creation of the **Southbank Centre**, home to a string of venerable artistic institutions: the Royal Festival Hall and Queen Elizabeth Hall concert venues; the Hayward Gallery, known for its

1

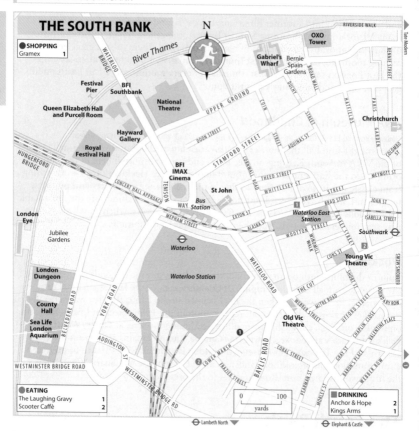

THE SOUTH BANK N

Tate Modern

● SHOPPING
Gramex   1

RIVERSIDE WALK

OXO
Tower

River Thames

Gabriel's   Bernie
Wharf   Spain
        Gardens

Festival   BFI
Pier   Southbank

Christchurch

Queen Elizabeth Hall   National
and Purcell Room   Theatre

UPPER GROUND

Hayward
Gallery

Royal
Festival Hall

BFI
IMAX
Cinema

St John

MEYMOTT ST

London
Eye

Jubilee
Gardens

Bus
Station

Waterloo East
Station

Southwark ⊖

ISABELLA STREET

London
Dungeon

Waterloo

Young Vic
Theatre

Waterloo Station

County
Hall

Sea Life
London
Aquarium

Old Vic
Theatre

❶

WESTMINSTER BRIDGE ROAD

❷ LOWER MARSH

0   100
      yards

● EATING
The Laughing Gravy   1
Scooter Caffè   2

■ DRINKING
Anchor & Hope   2
Kings Arms   1

⊖ Lambeth North ▼   ⊖ Elephant & Castle ▼

large temporary exhibitions of modern art; the BFI Southbank arts cinema, and the National Theatre (see p.127). Its uncompromising concrete brutalism is softened by its riverside location, its avenue of trees, its buskers and skateboarders, the weekend food stalls behind the RFH, and the busy secondhand bookstalls outside the BFI. In summer, the roof garden tucked away above the Queen Elizabeth Hall is a delightful spot, while there are often free events and live music in the Festival Hall's main public spaces, plus seasonal outdoor bars and pop-up venues that host summer-long festivals of cabaret and theatre.

London Eye

County Hall, SE1 7PB • Daily: Jan–May & Sept–Dec 11am–6pm; Easter holidays & June–Aug 10am–8.30pm; closed two weeks in Jan for maintenance • £26; £23.45 online • ☎ 0871 781 3000, ⓦ londoneye.com • ⊖ Waterloo or Westminster

Having graced the skyline since the start of the twenty-first century, the **London Eye** is one of the city's most famous landmarks. Standing an impressive 443ft high, it's the largest Ferris wheel in Europe, weighing over two thousand tonnes, yet as simple and delicate as a bicycle wheel. It's constantly in slow motion, which means a full circuit in one of its 32 pods (one for each of the city's boroughs) should take around thirty minutes. Booking online is cheaper, but note that unless you've paid extra you'll still have to queue to get on. Tickets are sold from the box office at the eastern end of County Hall.

Sea Life London Aquarium

County Hall, SE1 7PB • Mon–Fri 10am–6pm, last entry 5pm; Sat, Sun & school holidays 9.30am–7pm, last entry 6pm • £26; £20.40 online • Ⓦ visitsealife.com • ⊖ Waterloo or Westminster

The most popular attraction in County Hall – the giant building beside the London Eye – is the **Sea Life London Aquarium**, spread across three subterranean levels. With some super-large tanks, and everything from sharks in the biggest tank and eerie large rays that glide over the walk-through glass tunnel, to turtles and Gentoo penguins, this is an attraction that is almost guaranteed to please kids, albeit at a price (book online; multi-attraction tickets, including the London Eye and Madame Tussauds, are also available).

London Dungeon

County Hall, SE1 7PB • Mon–Wed & Fri 10am–5pm, Thurs 11am–5pm, Sat & Sun 10am–6pm; school holidays closes 7pm or 8pm • £30; £21–28.50 online • ❶ 020 7654 0809, Ⓦ thedungeons.com • ⊖ Waterloo or Westminster

Gothic horror-fest the **London Dungeon** remains one of the city's major crowd-pleasers – to shorten the amount of time spent queuing (and save money), buy your ticket online. Young teenagers and the credulous probably get the most out of the various ludicrous live-action scenarios, each one hyped up by the team of costumed ham-actors; a couple of horror rides and a drink at a mock-Victorian pub complete the experience.

Imperial War Museum

Lambeth Rd, SE1 6HZ • Daily 10am–6pm • Free • ❶ 020 7416 5000, Ⓦ london.iwm.org.uk • ⊖ Lambeth North

Housed in a domed building that was once the infamous lunatic asylum "Bedlam", the superb **Imperial War Museum** holds by far the best military museum in the capital. The treatment of the subject is impressively wide-ranging and fairly sober, with the main atrium's large exhibits described not as weapons but as **Witnesses to War**, contrasting Harrier jets and a Spitfire with, for example, a bomb-blasted car from Baghdad. Galleries cover the full scope of World War I, in a fully immersive, gruelling display, while the most interesting section on World War II is a look at a local Lambeth family and their wartime lives. The museum also has a harrowing **Holocaust Exhibition** (not recommended for children under 14). Pulling few punches, it chronicles the history of anti-Semitism in Europe and the Holocaust, as well as focusing on individual victims, interspersing archive footage with eyewitness accounts from contemporary survivors.

Bankside

In Tudor and Stuart London, the chief reason for crossing the Thames to Bankside was to visit the disreputable Bankside entertainment district around the south end of London Bridge. Four hundred years on, Londoners are heading to the area once more, thanks to a wealth of top attractions – led by the mighty **Tate Modern** – that pepper the traffic-free riverside path between Blackfriars Bridge and Tower Bridge. The area is conveniently linked to St Paul's and the City by the fabulous Norman Foster-designed **Millennium Bridge**, London's first pedestrian-only bridge.

Tate Modern

Bankside, SE1 9TG • Daily 10am–6pm, Fri & Sat till 10pm • Free; special exhibitions around £17–18 • ❶ 020 7887 8888, Ⓦ tate.org.uk • ⊖ Southwark or Blackfriars

Bankside is dominated by the awesome **Tate Modern**. Designed as an oil-fired power station by Giles Gilbert Scott, this austere, brick-built "cathedral of power" was

1

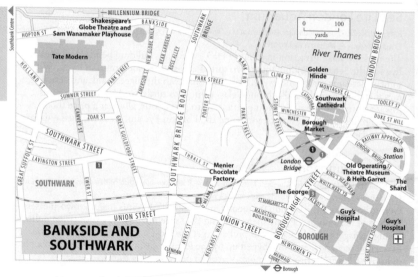

BANKSIDE AND SOUTHWARK

converted into a splendid modern art gallery in 2000. Such was its phenomenal success that in 2016 Tate opened a vast new extension, the **Blavatnik Building**, a distorted prism of latticed bricks that rises to 215ft, above the power station's three original circular tanks; this extension is topped by a superb, open-air, tenth-floor **viewing level**. At the centre of this huge art complex is the original, stupendously large **Turbine Hall**, used for large installations. The original building, the riverside **Boiler House**, and the extension are connected at the Turbine Hall at Level 0 and via bridges on levels 1 and 4.

Initially, Tate Modern can overwhelm in its size and scope. To ease yourself in, go to the **Start Display** at the centre of Boiler House's Level 2. Here, three modest rooms hold some of the Tate's most illustrious works, including Matisse's late work *The Snail* (1953), in order to introduce you to key ideas in modern art. Beyond here you'll find permanent displays on levels 2 and 4 of the Boiler House and levels 2, 3 and 4 of the Blavatnik Building, where the focus is specifically post-1960s.

The Tate's **permanent collection** dates back to 1900, but the curators have largely eschewed a chronological approach and have instead displayed work thematically. They also re-hang spaces regularly, so even big names may not be on show. The Tate has growing collections by artists from Africa, Latin America, the Middle East and across the globe; women artists also tend to be well represented. The consequence is that many names will be unfamiliar, but one of the joys of Tate Modern is coming across surprising juxtapositions of instantly recognizable artworks – a Monet water lily, Warhol's Marilyn or one of the gallery's numerous Picassos – next to artists about whom you know very little. Several artists get rooms to themselves, among them **Mark Rothko**, whose abstract "Seagram Murals", originally destined for a posh restaurant in New York, have their own shrine-like room in the heart of the collection.

Shakespeare's Globe

21 New Globe Walk, SE1 9DT • Exhibition and tours daily 9am–5pm; tours every 30min (no Globe tours summer Tues–Sat after 12.30pm) • £15; £11.50 with Bankside tour • ☎ 020 7902 1500, ⓦ shakespearesglobe.com • ⊖ Southwark or London Bridge

Dwarfed by Tate Modern, but equally remarkable in its own way, **Shakespeare's Globe** is a reconstruction of the open-air polygonal playhouse where most of the Bard's later

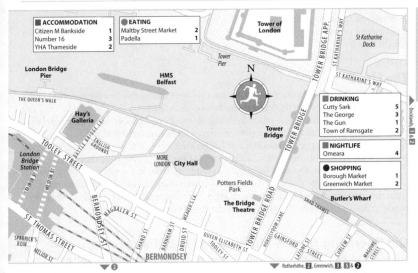

works were first performed. The theatre, which boasts the first new thatched roof in central London since the Great Fire of 1666 – and the first candlelit indoor theatre since the advent of electricity – puts on plays by Shakespeare and his contemporaries, both outside and in the indoor Sam Wanamaker Playhouse. To find out more about Shakespeare and the history of Bankside, the Globe's stylish **exhibition** is well worth a visit. You can have a virtual play on medieval instruments such as the crumhorn or sackbut, prepare your own edition of Shakespeare, and see some exquisitely authentic costumes up close. Included in the ticket is an informative half-hour **guided tour** of the theatre; during the summer season, if you visit in the afternoon, you'll be taken on a tour of the Bankside area instead.

Southwark Cathedral

London Bridge, SE1 9DA • Mon–Fri 8am–6pm, Sat & Sun 8.30am–6pm • Free • ☎ 020 7367 6700, ⓦ cathedral.southwark.anglican.org • ⊖ London Bridge

Built as the medieval Augustinian priory church of St Mary Overie, **Southwark Cathedral** was given cathedral status only in 1905. Of the original thirteenth-century church, only the choir and retrochoir now remain, separated by a tall and beautiful stone Tudor screen, making them probably the oldest Gothic structures left in London. The nave was entirely rebuilt in the nineteenth century, but the cathedral contains numerous interesting monuments, from a thirteenth-century oak effigy of a knight to an early twentieth-century memorial to Shakespeare.

Borough Market

Borough High St & Stoney St, SE1 1TL • Mon & Tues some stalls 10am–5pm, Wed & Thurs 10am–5pm, Fri 10am–6pm, Sat 8am–5pm • ☎ 020 7407 1002, ⓦ boroughmarket.org.uk • ⊖ London Bridge

There has been a produce market near the southern end of London Bridge since medieval times. **Borough Market**, beneath the railway arches between Borough High Street and Southwark Cathedral, and now sprawling out over a fairly large area, is now best known for its busy specialist food market (see p.131), with stalls selling top-quality produce from around the world – pungent cheeses, unusual wild

1

mushrooms, oysters, game, charcuterie and far more besides – along with hot food stalls (some of which operate Mon–Sat). It's very popular on Friday and Saturday so get there early.

The Shard

Railway Approach, SE1 9QU • April–Oct daily 10am–10pm; Nov–March Mon–Wed & Sun 10am–7pm, Thurs–Sat 10am–10pm • £30.95; £25.95 online in advance • ☎ 0844 499 7111, ⓦ theviewfromtheshard.com • ⊖ London Bridge

London's – and the country's – tallest building, Renzo Piano's 1016ft, tapered, glass-clad tower **the Shard** rises directly above the remodelled and expanded London Bridge station. In the years since it topped out in 2012, it has become a favourite city landmark, not least because it's considerably more elegant than some of the towers that have shot up since. Though pricey to visit, the view from the two public galleries at the top is sublime, the highest one open to the elements. From up here everything else in London looks small, from the unicycle of the London Eye to the tiny box that is St Paul's Cathedral, while the model railway of London Bridge is played out below you.

Old Operating Theatre Museum and Herb Garret

9a St Thomas St, SE1 9RY • Daily 10.30am–5pm; closed mid-Dec to early Jan • £6.50; NT members half-price • ☎ 020 7188 2679, ⓦ oldoperatingtheatre.com • ⊖ London Bridge

By far the most educational and the strangest of Southwark's museums is the **Old Operating Theatre Museum and Herb Garret**. Built in 1821 in a church attic, where the hospital apothecary's herbs were stored, this women's operating theatre, reached via a narrow spiral staircase, was once adjacent to the women's ward of St Thomas' Hospital (now in Lambeth). Despite being gore-free, the museum is a stomach-churning place: the surgeons would have concentrated on speed and accuracy (most amputations took less than a minute), but there was still a thirty percent mortality rate. The instruments on display are gruesome, while the apothecary's supplies include snail water and other intriguing concoctions.

HMS Belfast

The Queen's Walk, SE1 2JH • Daily: March–Oct 10am–6pm; Nov–Feb 10am–5pm • £16, including audioguide • ☎ 020 7940 6300, ⓦ iwm.org.uk/visits/hms-belfast • ⊖ London Bridge

HMS Belfast, a World War II cruiser, is permanently moored between London Bridge and Tower Bridge. Armed with six torpedoes, and six-inch guns with a range of more than fourteen miles, the *Belfast* spent over two years of the war in the Royal Naval shipyards after being hit by a mine in the Firth of Forth at the beginning of hostilities. Later in the war it saw action in the Barents Sea before supporting the D-Day landings. The ship was also operational during the Korean War, before being decommissioned. It's fun to explore the maze of cabins, through galleys and workrooms and up to the very top Flag Deck for the views, and right down to the claustrophobic lowest reaches of the ship containing the Boiler and Engine rooms, a spaghetti of pipes and valves that descend for three levels below water level.

City Hall

The Queen's Walk, SE1 2AA • Mon–Thurs 8.30am–6pm, Fri 8.30am–5.30pm • Free • ☎ 020 7983 4000, ⓦ london.gov.uk • ⊖ London Bridge

East of the *Belfast*, overlooking the river, Norman Foster's startling glass-encased **City Hall** looks like a giant car headlight or fencing mask, and serves as the headquarters for the Greater London Authority and the Mayor of London. Visitors are welcome to stroll up the helical walkway, visit the café and watch proceedings from the second floor.

Kensington and Chelsea

Hyde Park and **Kensington Gardens** cover a distance of a mile and a half from Oxford Street in the northeast to Kensington Palace, set in the Royal Borough of **Kensington** and **Chelsea**. Other districts go in and out of fashion, but this area has been in vogue ever since royalty moved into **Kensington Palace** in the late seventeenth century.

The most popular tourist attractions lie in **South Kensington**, where three of London's top **museums** – the Victoria and Albert, Natural History and Science museums – stand on land bought with the proceeds of the 1851 Great Exhibition. Chelsea, to the south, once had a slightly more bohemian pedigree. In the 1960s, the **King's Road** carved out its reputation as London's catwalk, while in the late 1970s it was the focus for the city's punk explosion, though nothing so rebellious could be imagined in Chelsea now.

Hyde Park and Kensington Gardens

Hyde Park Daily 5am–midnight • **Kensington Gardens** Daily 6am–dusk • **Lido** May Sat & Sun 10am–6pm; June–Aug daily 10am–6pm • £4.80 • **Memorial fountain** Daily: March & Oct 10am–6pm; April–Aug 10am–8pm; Sept 10am–7pm; Nov–Feb 10am–4pm • **Playground** Daily: Feb & late Oct 10am–4.45pm; March & early Oct 10am–5.45pm; April & Sept 10am–6.45pm; May–Aug 10am–7.45pm; Nov–Jan 10am–3.45pm • ☎ 0300 061 2114, ⓦ royalparks.org.uk • ⊖ Hyde Park Corner, Marble Arch, Knightsbridge or Lancaster Gate

Hangings, muggings, duels and the 1851 Great Exhibition are just some of the public events that have taken place in **Hyde Park**, which remains a popular spot for political demonstrations and pop concerts. For most of the time, however, the park is simply a lazy leisure ground – a wonderful open space that allows you to lose all sight of the city beyond a few persistent tower blocks.

The park is divided in two by the **Serpentine**, which has a pretty upper section known as the **Long Water**, which narrows until it reaches a group of four fountains. In the southern section, you'll find the popular **Lido** on its south bank and the **Diana Memorial Fountain**, less of a fountain and more of a giant oval-shaped mini-moat. The western half of the park is officially **Kensington Gardens**. In the northwest is the **Diana Memorial Playground**, featuring a ship stuck in sand and other imaginative playthings; at busy times you may have to queue to get in. The other two most popular attractions are the **Serpentine Galleries** and the overblown **Albert Memorial**.

Marble Arch

At Hyde Park's treeless northeastern corner is **Marble Arch**, erected in 1828 as a triumphal entry to Buckingham Palace, but now stranded on a busy traffic island at the west end of Oxford Street. This is a historically charged piece of land, as it marks the site of **Tyburn gallows**, the city's main public execution spot until 1783. It's also the location of **Speakers' Corner**, a peculiarly English Sunday-morning tradition, featuring an assembly of ranters and hecklers.

Wellington Arch

Hyde Park Corner, W1J 7JZ • Daily: April–Sept 10am–6pm; Oct 10am–5pm; Nov–March 10am–4pm • £5; EH • ⊖ Hyde Park Corner

At the southeast corner of Hyde Park, the **Wellington Arch** stands in the midst of **Hyde Park Corner**, one of London's busiest traffic interchanges. Erected in 1828, the arch was originally topped by an equestrian statue of the Duke himself, later replaced by Peace driving a four-horse chariot. Inside, you can view an exhibition on the history of the arch, and the Battle of Waterloo, and take a lift to the top of the monument where the exterior balconies offer a bird's-eye view of the swirling traffic.

Apsley House

149 Piccadilly, W1J 7NT • April–Oct Wed–Sun 11am–5pm; Nov–March Sat & Sun 10am–4pm • £9.30; EH • ⊖ Hyde Park Corner

Overlooking the traffic whizzing round Hyde Park Corner is **Apsley House**, Wellington's London residence and now a museum to the "Iron Duke". The highlight is

1

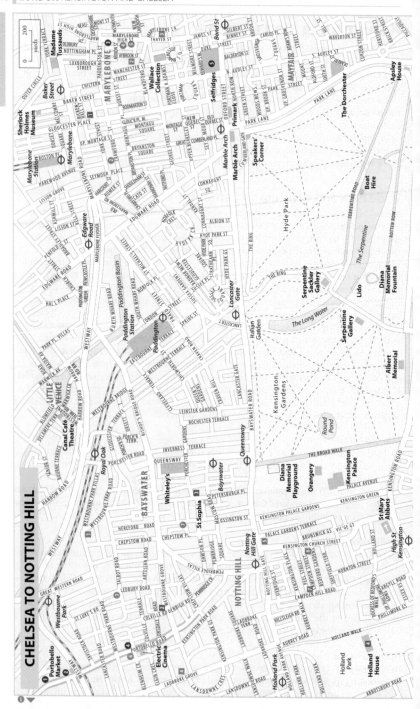

CHELSEA TO NOTTING HILL

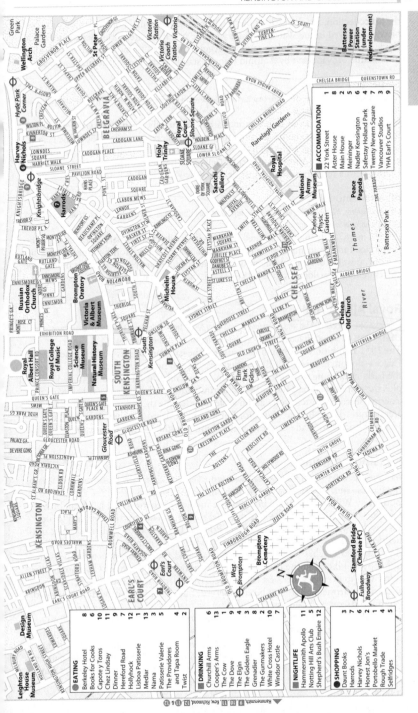

▲ Hammersmith, ◆ ⊕ Kew, Richmond, ◆ ⊕ &

■ ACCOMMODATION

22 York Street	1
Aster House	8
Main House	2
Meininger	5
Nadler Kensington	6
Safestay Holland Park	4
Twenty Nevern Square	7
Vancouver Studios	3
YHA Earl's Court	9

● EATING

Berkeley Hotel	8
Books for Cooks	6
Capote y Toros	10
Chez Lindsay	9
Dinner	7
Hereford Road	12
Hollyhock	11
Lisboa Patisserie	1
Medlar	13
Nama	3
Patisserie Valerie	5
The Providores and Tapa Room	4
Twist	2

■ DRINKING

Churchill Arms	6
Cooper's Arms	13
The Cow	1
The Dove	9
The Elgin	4
The Golden Eagle	3
Grenadier	2
The Gunmakers	8
White Cross Hotel	10
Windsor Castle	7

■ NIGHTLIFE

Hammersmith Apollo	11
Notting Hill Arts Club	5
Shepherd's Bush Empire	12

● SHOPPING

Daunt Books	3
Harrods	7
Harvey Nichols	6
Honest Jon's	2
Portobello Market	1
Rough Trade	4
Selfridges	5

1

the **art collection**, much of which used to belong to the King of Spain. Among the best pieces, displayed in the Waterloo Gallery on the first floor, are works by de Hooch, Van Dyck, Velázquez, Goya, Rubens and Correggio. The famous, more than twice life-size, nude statue of Napoleon by Antonio Canova stands at the foot of the main staircase.

Serpentine Galleries

Kensington Gardens, W2 3XA • Tues–Sun 10am–6pm; Pavilion mid-June to mid-Oct • Free • ☎ 020 7402 6075, ⓦ serpentinegalleries.org • ⊖ Knightsbridge or South Kensington

In the southeast corner of Kensington Gardens stands the **Serpentine Gallery**, built as a tearoom in 1908, but used as a contemporary art gallery since the 1960s. The gallery commissions a leading architect to design a summer pavilion each year. A second exhibition space, the **Serpentine Sackler Gallery**, is housed in a former munitions depot nearby, with a restaurant on the side designed by Zaha Hadid.

Albert Memorial

Kensington Gardens, W2 2UH • Guided tours March–Dec first Sun of month 2pm & 3pm; 45min • Tours £9 • ☎ 020 8969 0104 • ⊖ Knightsbridge or South Kensington

Erected in 1876, the richly decorated, High Gothic **Albert Memorial** is as much a hymn to the glorious achievements of Britain as to its subject, Queen Victoria's husband, who died in 1861, possibly of typhoid. Albert occupies the central canopy, gilded from head to toe and clutching a catalogue for the 1851 Great Exhibition that he helped to organize.

Royal Albert Hall

Kensington Gore, SW7 2AP • Guided tours depart from Door 12 every 30min: April–Oct 9.30am–4.30pm; Nov–March 10am–4pm • £12.25 • ☎ 0845 401 5045, ⓦ royalalberthall.com • ⊖ South Kensington or High Street Kensington

The 1851 Exhibition's most famous feature – the gargantuan glasshouse of the Crystal Palace – no longer exists, but the profits were used to buy a large tract of land south of the park, now home to South Kensington's remarkable cluster of museums and colleges, plus the vast **Royal Albert Hall**, a splendid iron-and-glass-domed concert hall with an exterior of red brick, terracotta and marble that became the hallmark of South Ken architecture. The hall is the venue for Europe's most democratic music festival, the Henry Wood Promenade Concerts, better known as the **Proms** (see box, p.128).

Kensington Palace

Kensington Gardens, W8 4PX • Daily: March–Oct 10am–6pm; Nov–Feb 10am–5pm; last admission 1hr before closing • £17 March–Oct; £16.50 Nov–Feb • ☎ 020 3166 6000, ⓦ hrp.org.uk • ⊖ Queensway or High Street Kensington

Bought by William and Mary in 1689, the modestly proportioned Jacobean brick mansion of **Kensington Palace** was the chief royal residence for the next fifty years. It's best known today as the place where Princess Diana lived from her marriage until her death in 1997, and is now the official residence of a number of royals including the Duke and Duchess of Cambridge (William and Kate). **Queen Victoria** spent an unhappy childhood in the palace, under the steely gaze of her strict German mother. According to her diary, her best friends were the palace's numerous "black beetles". Victoria's apartments have not been preserved, but the permanent **Victoria Revealed** exhibition traces and examines her life.

The palace is home to the **Royal Ceremonial Dress Collection**, which means you usually get to see a few of the frocks worn by Diana, as well as several of the Queen's dresses. The highlights of the **King's State Apartments** are the trompe-l'oeil ceiling paintings by William Kent, particularly those in the Cupola Room, and the paintings in the King's Gallery by, among others, Tintoretto. The more modest **Queen's State Apartments** are lined with royal portraits, all part of the Royal Collection and rotated periodically.

Victoria and Albert Museum (V&A)

Entrances on Cromwell Rd and Exhibition Rd, SW7 2RL • Daily 10am–5.45pm, Fri till 10pm • Free; charge for some exhibitions • **Guided tours** (meet at main entrance) Daily 10.30am, 12.30pm, 1.30pm & 3.30pm • Free • ☎ 020 7942 2000, ⓦ vam.ac.uk • ⊖ South Kensington

For sheer variety and scale, the **Victoria and Albert Museum** is the greatest museum of applied arts in the world. Beautifully displayed across a seven-mile, four-storey maze of rooms, the V&A's treasures are impossible to survey in a single visit; get hold of a floor plan to help you decide which areas to concentrate on, or join a free tour. And if you're flagging, head for the edifying café in the museum's period-piece **Morris, Gamble & Poynter Rooms**.

Perhaps the most precious of the V&A's many exhibits are the **Raphael Cartoons** (room 48a, level 1), from the Italian *cartone* meaning a large piece of paper. They comprise seven vast, full-colour paintings in distemper, which are, in fact, designs for tapestries ordered in 1515 by Pope Leo X for the Sistine Chapel. Also on the ground floor, you'll find one of the more disorientating sights in the museum, the two enormous **Cast Courts**, filled with plaster casts of famous sculptural works, created to allow Victorian Londoners to experience the glories of ancient art and including the colossal Trajan's Column, sliced in half to fit in the room, and a life-sized replica of Michelangelo's *David*.

Beyond these, you'll find the finest collection of Italian sculpture outside Italy, the world's largest collection of Indian art outside India, plus extensive Chinese, Islamic and Japanese galleries. Among the other highlights are the justifiably popular jewellery section, the beautifully designed Medieval and Renaissance galleries, the British Galleries and the costume and fashion collections. In addition, the V&A's temporary shows on art, photography and fashion are among the best in Britain, and are now housed in new subterranean gallery spaces built below the gleaming porcelain-tiled Sackler Courtyard, separated from Exhibition Road by the museum's original Portland stone screen.

Science Museum

Exhibition Rd, SW7 2DD • Daily 10am–6pm; school holidays 10am–7pm • Free; charge for some activities; Wonderlab £8, £6 under-17s • ☎ 0870 870 4868, ⓦ sciencemuseum.org.uk • ⊖ South Kensington

With galleries large enough to display jet planes and a phenomenal range of interactive exhibits that appeal to all ages, the **Science Museum** is impressive in its scope, covering every conceivable area of science. Major refurbishments have created some fantastic new displays, including the Zaha Hadid-designed Maths Gallery, though with redesigns ongoing, some areas are closed for the foreseeable future.

On the ground floor, **Exploring Space** follows the history of rockets and space, with a full-size replica of the Apollo 11 landing craft which deposited US astronauts on the moon in 1969. **Making the Modern World** displays iconic inventions of modern science and technology, including Robert Stephenson's *Rocket* of 1829. Other galleries cover flight – including flight simulators and a vast gallery of flying machines – energy and materials. One of the most popular galleries is the **Wonderlab** on floor 3, also known as **The Statoil Gallery**; aimed at 5- to 15-year-olds, it's packed with dozens of hands-on activities and experiments with magnetism, electric circuits, light and sound.

Natural History Museum

Cromwell Rd, SW7 5BD • Daily 10am–5.50pm • Free • ☎ 020 7942 5000, ⓦ nhm.ac.uk • ⊖ South Kensington

Alfred Waterhouse's purpose-built mock-Romanesque colossus ensures the status of the **Natural History Museum** as London's most handsome museum, both an important resource for serious zoologists and a major tourist attraction.

The central **Hintze Hall** is dominated by a full-size, 25m blue-whale skeleton, dramatically suspended from the ceiling. The rest of the museum is divided into four colour-coded zones. The **Blue Zone** includes the ever-popular Dinosaur gallery, with its fossils and grisly life-sized **animatronic dinosaurs**. Popular sections over in the

1

Green Zone include the Creepy-Crawlies, and the excellent **Investigate** centre, where children aged 7 to 14 get to play at being scientists (you need to obtain a timed ticket; reserved for school groups in term-time mornings).

Less visited, the **Darwin Centre** – also known as the **Orange Zone** – is dominated by the giant concrete **Cocoon**, home to more than twenty million specimens, where visitors can learn more about the scientific research and specimen collections. In the nearby **Zoology spirit building**, you can view a small selection of bits and bobs pickled in glass jars.

If you enter the museum via the side entrance on Exhibition Road, you start at the **Red Zone**, a visually exciting romp through the earth's evolution, with the solar system and constellations writ large on the walls and the most intact Stegosaurus skeleton ever found. Boarding the central escalator will take you through a partially formed globe to the top floor and an exhibition on volcanoes and earthquakes, including the slightly tasteless Kobe earthquake simulator.

Design Museum

224–238 Kensington High St, W8 6AG • Daily 10am–6pm • Free; charge for some temporary exhibitions (up to £16) • ☎ 020 3862 5900, Ⓦ designmuseum.org • ⊖ High Street Kensington

One of the most striking 1960s buildings in London, a concrete-framed structure with a sweeping hyperbolic paraboloid roof clad in copper, the former home of the Commonwealth Institute next to Holland Park has been, appropriately enough, taken over by the **Design Museum**, which moved in at the end of 2016. It hosts numerous temporary exhibitions and events, along with a slightly cramped permanent exhibition, **Designer Maker User**, which features highlights from the museum's collection of design classics and everyday objects.

Leighton House Museum

12 Holland Park Rd, W14 8LZ • Mon & Wed–Sun 10am–5.30pm • £9 • ☎ 020 7602 3316, Ⓦ rbkc.gov.uk • ⊖ High Street Kensington

Several wealthy Victorian artists rather self-consciously founded an artists' colony in the streets that lay to the west of Kensington Gardens. "It will be opulence, it will be sincerity", Lord Leighton opined before starting work on the remarkable **Leighton House** in the 1860s – he later became President of the Royal Academy and was ennobled on his deathbed. The big attraction here is the domed **Arab Hall**, decorated with Saracen tiles, gilded mosaics and latticework drawn from all over the Islamic world. The other rooms are hung with paintings by Lord Leighton and his Pre-Raphaelite chums, and there's even a Tintoretto.

Chelsea

From the Swinging Sixties up until the era of Punk, **Chelsea** had a slightly bohemian pedigree; these days, it's just another wealthy west London suburb. Among the most nattily attired of all those parading down the King's Road nowadays are the scarlet- or navy-blue-clad Chelsea Pensioners, army veterans from the nearby **Royal Hospital**.

Saatchi Gallery

Duke of York's HQ, King's Rd, SW3 4RY • Daily 10am–6pm • Free • Ⓦ saatchigallery.com • ⊖ Sloane Square

On the south side of the King's Road, a short stroll from Sloane Square, the former **Duke of York's HQ**, built in 1801, is now the unlikely home of the **Saatchi Gallery**, which puts on changing exhibitions of contemporary art in its whitewashed rooms. Charles Saatchi, the collector behind the gallery, was the man who promoted the Young British Artists (YBAs) beyond the art world, though these days you'll find a global roster of contemporary artists represented, along with commercial photography exhibitions.

Royal Hospital

Royal Hospital Rd, SW3 4SR • **Grounds** Daily: May–Sept 10am–8pm; Oct–April 10am–4.30pm • Free **Great Hall & Chapel** Mon–Sat 10am–noon & 2–4.40pm, Sun 2–4pm • Free **Museum** Mon–Fri 10am–4pm • Free • ☎ 020 7881 5516, Ⓦ chelsea-pensioners.co.uk • ⊖ Sloane Square

Founded as a retirement home for army veterans by Charles II in 1682, and designed by Christopher Wren, the **Royal Hospital**'s majestic red-brick wings and grassy courtyards became a blueprint for institutional and collegiate architecture all over the English-speaking world. The public are welcome to view the austere hospital chapel, and the equally grand, wood-panelled dining hall opposite, where three hundred or so uniformed Pensioners still eat under the royal portraits and the vast allegorical mural of Charles II. On the east side of the hospital, a small **museum** displays Pensioners' uniforms, medals and two German bombs.

National Army Museum

Royal Hospital Rd, SW3 4HT • Daily 10am–5.30pm; open until 8pm on first Wed of the month • Free • ☎ 020 7730 0717, Ⓦ nam.ac.uk • ⊖ Sloane Square

The concrete bunker next door to the Royal Hospital, on Royal Hospital Road, houses the **National Army Museum**. After a complete redesign, the coverage and range of army exhibits is wide-ranging and thoughtful, considering army life and subjects like the ethics of warfare alongside a plethora of historical artefacts, including a huge scale model of the Battle of Waterloo and interactive exhibits such as strategy games.

North London

Stretching north from the Regent's Canal and **Regent's Park**, home to **London Zoo**, North London's neighbourhoods are a historically rich, attractive and eclectic series of villages, now subsumed into the general mass of the city, and with a reputation for a certain sort of wealthy liberal bohemianism. Drawing the tourist hordes, **Camden Town** has its markets, pubs and live music. The highlights, however, are the village-like suburbs of **Hampstead** and **Highgate**, on the edge of London's wildest patch of greenery, **Hampstead Heath**.

Regent's Park

Daily 5am–dusk • Free • ☎ 0300 061 2300, Ⓦ royalparks.org.uk • ⊖ Regent's Park, Baker Street, Great Portland Street, St John's Wood or Camden Town

Regent's Park is one of London's smartest parks, with a boating lake, ornamental ponds, waterfalls and some lovely gardens. Under the reign of the Prince Regent (later George IV), the park was to be girded by a continuous belt of terraces, and sprinkled with a total of 56 villas, including a magnificent royal palace. Inevitably, the plan was never fully realized, but enough was built to create something of the idealized garden city that Nash and the Prince Regent had envisaged. Within the Inner Circle, the **Queen Mary's Gardens** are by far the prettiest section of the park. Prominent on the skyline is the shiny copper dome of **London Central Mosque** at 146 Park Road, an entirely appropriate addition given the Prince Regent's taste for the Orient.

London Zoo

Outer Circle, Regent's Park, NW1 4RY • **Zoo** Daily: April–Aug 10am–6pm (5pm during Sunset Safaris); March, Sept & Oct 10am–5.30pm; Nov–Feb 10am–4pm • March–Oct £27.04; £24.30 online; Nov–Feb £22.73; £20.45 online • **Sunset Safaris** June to mid-July Fri 6–10pm • £20.80 online; buy in advance • ☎ 020 7722 3333, Ⓦ zsl.org/zsl-london-zoo • ⊖ Camden Town

The northeastern corner of Regent's Park is occupied by **London Zoo**. Founded in 1826 with the remnants of the royal menagerie, the enclosures here are as humane as any inner-city zoo could make them. In recent years, many of the animals have been moved

1

REGENT'S CANAL

The **Regent's Canal**, completed in 1820, was constructed as part of a direct link from Birmingham to the newly built London Docks in the East End, covering nine miles, with 42 bridges, twelve locks and two tunnels. The lock-less stretch **between Little Venice and Camden Town** is the busiest, most attractive section, tunnelling through to Lisson Grove, skirting Regent's Park, offering back-door views of the aviary at London Zoo and passing straight through the heart of Camden Market. You can walk, jog or cycle along the towpath, but this section of the canal is also served by scheduled narrowboats.

Three companies run daily **boat services** between Camden and Little Venice, passing through the Maida Hill tunnel. The narrowboat *Jenny Wren* (March Sat & Sun; April–Oct daily; 2–3 daily; £14 return; ☎020 7485 4433, ⓦ walkersquay.com) starts off at Camden, goes through a canal lock (the only company to do so) and heads for Little Venice (with live commentary) before returning; while you can embark on *Jason's* narrowboats (April–early Nov 3–4 daily; £9.50 one-way, £14.50 return; ⓦ jasons.co.uk) at either end (live commentary to Camden); the London Waterbus Company (April–Sept daily; Oct Thurs–Sun; Nov to mid-Dec & Jan–March Sat & Sun, weather permitting; up to 8 daily; £9 one-way, £14 return; with zoo visit £25 from Camden, £27 from Little Venice; ☎020 7482 2550, ⓦ londonwaterbus.com) sets off from both places and calls at London Zoo. Journey times are around 45 minutes one-way.

from their classic, architecturally listed homes, such as the famous penguin pool, into more spacious, modern enclosures. Among the biggest hits is the impressive 2500-square-metre **Land of the Lions**, a scaled-down recreation of an Indian village, that allows for surprisingly close encounters with the big cats. Likewise, **Gorilla Kingdom** has large viewing areas, while for smaller animals there are some imaginative walk-through enclosures, such as **Rainforest Life**, with its sleepy sloths, **Meet the Monkeys** and **In with the Lemurs**.

Camden Market

Off Chalk Farm Road, NW1 8A · Camden Lock Market and Stables Market daily 10am–7pm · ⓦ camdenmarket.com · ⊖ Camden Town or Chalk Farm

For all its tourist popularity, **Camden Market** remains a genuinely offbeat place. It began life in the 1970s, as a small craft market in the cobbled courtyard by Camden Lock, and now encompasses several sections; the sheer variety of what's on offer – from jewellery to furniture, along with a mass of street fashion and clubwear, and plenty of food stalls – is what makes Camden Town so special. More than 100,000 shoppers turn up here each weekend, and most parts of the market now stay open week-long, alongside a crop of shops, cafés and bistros.

Jewish Museum

129–131 Albert St, NW1 7NB · Daily 10am–5pm, Fri until 2pm · £8.50 · ☎020 7284 7384, ⓦ jewishmuseum.org.uk · ⊖ Camden Town

Camden is home to London's purpose-built **Jewish Museum**. On the first floor, there's an engaging exhibition explaining Jewish practices, illustrated by cabinets of Judaica. On the second floor, there's a special Holocaust gallery which tells the story of Leon Greenman (1920–2008), one of only two British Jews who suffered and survived Auschwitz. The museum also puts on a lively programme of special exhibitions, discussions and concerts, and has a café on the ground floor.

Hampstead

Perched on a hill to the west of Hampstead Heath, **Hampstead** village developed into a fashionable spa in the eighteenth century, and was not much altered thereafter. Later, it became one of the city's most celebrated literary *quartiers* and even now it retains its reputation as a bolthole of the high-profile intelligentsia and discerning pop stars. Proximity to **Hampstead Heath** is, of course, the real joy of Hampstead; this mixture of woodland, smooth pasture and landscaped garden is quite simply the most exhilarating patch of greenery in London.

Keats' House

10 Keats Grove, NW3 2RR • March–Oct Wed–Sun 11am–5pm; Nov–Feb Fri–Sun 1–5pm; tours 3pm (30min) • £6.50 (including tour); garden free • ☎ 020 7332 3868, ⓦ cityoflondon.gov.uk/keats • Hampstead Heath Overground or ⊖ Hampstead

The English Romantic poet John Keats is celebrated at **Keats' House**, an elegant, whitewashed Regency double villa off Downshire Hill at the bottom of the High Street. Inspired by the tranquillity of Hampstead and by his passion for girl-next-door Fanny Brawne (whose house is also part of the museum), Keats wrote some of his most famous works here before leaving for Rome, where he died of consumption in 1821, aged just 25. The neat, simple interior contains books, letters and Fanny's engagement ring, as well as listening posts and a film of Keats' life.

2 Willow Road

2 Willow Rd, NW3 1TH • March–Oct Wed–Sun 11am–5pm; note that before 3pm, visits are by hourly guided tour • £6.50; NT • ☎ 020 7435 6166, ⓦ nationaltrust.org.uk/2-willow-road • Hampstead Heath Overground or ⊖ Hampstead

An unassuming red-brick terraced house built in the 1930s by the Hungarian-born architect **Ernö Goldfinger** (1902–87), **2 Willow Road** gives a fascinating insight into the Modernist mindset. This was a state-of-the-art pad when Goldfinger moved in, and as he changed little during the following fifty years, what you see today is a 1930s avant-garde dwelling preserved in aspic, a house both modern and old-fashioned. An added bonus is that the rooms are packed with works of art by the likes of Bridget Riley, Duchamp, Henry Moore and Man Ray.

Freud Museum

20 Maresfield Gardens, NW3 5SX • Wed–Sun noon–5pm • £8; 50 percent discount for NT • ☎ 020 7435 2002, ⓦ freud.org.uk • ⊖ Finchley Road

The **Freud Museum** is one of the most poignant of London's house museums. Having lived in Vienna for his entire adult life, the psychotherapist, by now semi-disabled and with only a year to live, was forced to flee the Nazis, arriving in London in the summer of 1938. The ground-floor study and library look exactly as they did when Freud lived here; the collection of erotic antiquities and the famous couch, sumptuously draped in Persian rugs, were all brought here from Vienna. Upstairs, home movies of family life are shown continually, and a small room is dedicated to Freud's daughter, Anna, herself an influential child analyst, who lived in the house until her death in 1982.

Hampstead Heath

Daily 24hr • Free • **Hill Garden** Daily 8.30am–dusk • ☎ 020 7332 3322, ⓦ cityoflondon.gov.uk • **Men's and women's bathing ponds** Daily year-round from 7am, closing time varies • **Mixed pond** Mid-May to mid-Sept daily 7am–6.30pm • £2 • Hampstead tube and Hampstead Heath or Gospel Oak Overground; bus #210 from ⊖ Hampstead or Golders Green or #24 from central London, including Tottenham Court Rd and Camden

Hampstead Heath may not have much of its original heathland left, but it packs a wonderful variety of bucolic scenery into its eight hundred acres. At its southern end are the rolling green pastures of **Parliament Hill**, north London's premier spot for kite flying, and with unrivalled views over the London skyline. On either side are numerous **ponds**, three of which – one for men, one for women and one mixed – you can swim in. The thickest woodland is to be found in the **West Heath**, beyond Whitestone Pond, also the site of the most formal section, **Hill Garden**: a secluded and romantic little gem with eccentric balustraded terraces and 800ft pergola, which create an alluring sense of faded grandeur. Beyond lies **Golders Hill Park**, where you can gaze at pygmy goats and fallow deer, and inspect the impeccably maintained aviaries, home to flamingos, cranes and other exotic birds.

1

Kenwood House

Hampstead Lane, NW3 7JR • Daily: April–Oct 10am–5pm; Nov–March 10am–4pm • Free • ☎ 020 8348 1286, ⓦ english-heritage.org.uk • Bus #210 from ◉ Archway or Golders Green

Hampstead Heath's most celebrated sight is the whitewashed Neoclassical mansion of **Kenwood House**, set within landscaped grounds dotted with sculptures. The house is home to a collection of seventeenth- and eighteenth-century art, including a handful of real masterpieces by Vermeer, Rembrandt, Boucher, Gainsborough and Reynolds. Of the period interiors, the most spectacular is Robert Adam's sky-blue and pink library.

Highgate Cemetery

Swain's Lane, N6 6PJ • **East Cemetery** March–Oct Mon–Fri 10am–5pm, Sat & Sun 11am–5pm; Nov–Feb closes 4pm; guided tours Sat 2pm • £4, guided tours £8 **West Cemetery** Guided tours only: March–Oct Mon–Fri 1.45pm, Sat & Sun every 30min 11am–3pm; Nov–Feb Sat & Sun hourly 11am–3pm • £12; no under-8s • ☎ 020 8340 1834, ⓦ highgatecemetery.org • ◉ Archway

Highgate Cemetery, ranged on both sides of Swain's Lane, is London's best-known graveyard. The most illustrious incumbent of the **East Cemetery** is Karl **Marx**. Marx himself asked for a simple grave topped by a headstone, but by 1954 the Communist movement decided to move his grave to a more prominent position and erect the hulking bronze bust that now surmounts a granite plinth. To visit the more atmospheric and overgrown **West Cemetery**, with its spooky Egyptian Avenue and sunken catacombs, you must take a guided tour. Among the prominent graves usually visited are those of artist Dante Gabriel Rossetti, and lesbian novelist Radclyffe Hall.

The Swaminarayan temple

105–119 Brentfield Rd, NW10 8LD • **Temple** Daily 9am–6pm • Free • **Exhibition** Mon–Fri 9am–5pm, Sat & Sun 9am–6pm • £2 • ☎ 020 8965 2651, ⓦ londonmandir.baps.org • ◉ Neasden

Perhaps the most remarkable building in the whole of London lies just off the North Circular, in the glum suburb of Neasden. Here, rising majestically above the surrounding semi-detached houses, is the **Shri Swaminarayan Mandir**, a traditional Hindu temple topped with domes and *shikharas*, erected in 1995 in a style and scale unseen outside of India for over a millennium. You enter through the Haveli (cultural complex) and, after taking off your shoes, proceed to the Mandir (temple) itself, carved entirely out of Carrara marble, with every possible surface transformed into a honeycomb of arabesques, flowers and seated gods. Beneath the Mandir, an **exhibition** explains the basic tenets of Hinduism, details the life of Lord Swaminarayan, and includes a video about the history of the building.

South London

Spreading out from the river that marks the city's great divide – both real and imagined – South London is formed by a series of distinctive, often underrated neighbourhoods, villages subsumed into the city with the railways and industrialization. It includes one outstanding area for sightseeing, **Greenwich**, with its fantastic ensemble of the Royal Naval College, the *Cutty Sark*, the National Maritime Museum, the Royal Observatory and the beautifully landscaped royal park. Other standouts are the **Dulwich Picture Gallery**, a superb public art gallery older than the National Gallery, and the eclectic **Horniman Museum** in neighbouring Forest Hill, plus a few diverse, busy neighbourhoods worth exploring, **Brixton** chief among them.

Greenwich

Greenwich draws tourists out from the centre in considerable numbers. At its heart is the outstanding architectural set piece of the **Old Royal Naval College** and the

1

Queen's House, courtesy of Christopher Wren and Inigo Jones respectively. Most visitors, however, come to see the **Cutty Sark**, the **National Maritime Museum** and Greenwich Park's **Royal Observatory**. With the added attractions of its parkland, covered market of crafts, antiques and food stalls (see p.130), riverside pubs and walks – plus startling views across to Canary Wharf and Docklands – it makes for one of the best days out in the capital. To reach Greenwich, you can take a **train** from London Bridge (every 30min) or the **DLR** to Cutty Sark station (every 4–10min), but by far the most scenic option is by **boat** from one of the piers in central London (every 20–30min), with Thames Clippers (see p.110).

Cutty Sark

King William Walk, SE10 9HT • Daily 10am–5pm • £13.50; combined ticket with Observatory £18.50 • ☎ 020 8312 6608, ⓦ rmg.co.uk • Cutty Sark DLR

Wedged in a dry dock by the river is the majestic **Cutty Sark**, the world's last surviving tea clipper. Launched in 1869, the *Cutty Sark* was actually more famous in its day as a wool clipper, returning from Australia in just 72 days. The vessel's name comes from Robert Burns' *Tam O'Shanter*, in which Tam, a drunken farmer, is chased by Nannie, an angry witch in a short Paisley linen dress, or "cutty sark"; the clipper's figurehead shows her clutching the hair from the tail of Tam's horse. After a devastating fire in 2007, the ship has been beautifully restored, and you can explore the bunks, officers' quarters and below-deck storage, where there are interactive displays.

Old Royal Naval College

SE10 9NN • Daily: grounds 8am–11pm; buildings 10am–5pm • Free • ☎ 020 8269 4747, ⓦ ornc.org • Cutty Sark DLR

Making the most of its riverbank location, the **Old Royal Naval College** is a majestic Baroque ensemble designed, for the most part, by Wren. Initially built as a royal palace, but eventually converted into the Royal Hospital for Seamen, the complex was later home to the Royal Naval College, but now houses the University of Greenwich and the Trinity Laban. The two grandest rooms, situated underneath Wren's twin domes, are open to the public and well worth visiting. The **Chapel**, in the east wing, has exquisite pastel-shaded plasterwork and spectacular, decorative detailing on the ceiling, all designed by James "Athenian" Stuart after a fire in 1799 destroyed the original interior. Opposite the chapel is the magnificent **Painted Hall** in the west wing, which is dominated by James Thornhill's gargantuan allegorical ceiling painting, and his trompe-l'oeil fluted pilasters (reopening after renovation in 2019). Over in the Pepys Building, you can get a good overview of Greenwich's history in **Discover Greenwich**, where there's an information desk and historical displays.

National Maritime Museum

Romney Rd, SE10 9NF • Daily 10am–5pm; Ahoy! and All Hands: Tues, Sat, Sun & hols 10am–5pm, Mon & Wed–Fri 2–5pm, open other times if no school groups • Free; charge for special exhibitions • ☎ 020 8312 6608, ⓦ rmg.co.uk • Cutty Sark DLR

The main building of the **National Maritime Museum** is centred on a glass-roofed courtyard, which houses the museum's largest artefacts, among them the splendid 63ft-long gilded **Royal Barge**, designed in Rococo style by William Kent for Prince Frederick, the much unloved eldest son of George II. The various themed galleries are superb, and stuffed full of model ships and curious artefacts, including Nelson's coat. Several well-designed sections are just for kids: **Ahoy!** is a nautically themed play area for under-7s on the ground floor; while the second-floor **All Hands** gallery gives older kids a taste of life on the seas.

Inigo Jones's **Queen's House**, originally built amid a rambling Tudor royal palace, is now the focal point of the Greenwich ensemble, and is part of the Maritime Museum. As royal residences go, it's an unassuming country house, but as the first Neoclassical building in the country, it has enormous architectural significance. You enter via the beautiful **Tulip Staircase**, Britain's earliest cantilevered spiral staircase – its name derives from the floral

1

patterning in the wrought-iron balustrade – which takes you to the Great Hall, a perfect cube. The rooms here show the museum's **art collection**, ranging from royal portraits and scenes of Greenwich to nautical scenes, plus a few navigational instruments.

Royal Observatory

Greenwich Park, SE10 9NF • **Flamsteed House** Daily 10am–5pm • £9.50, including audioguide; combined ticket with Cutty Sark £18.50 • **Astronomy Centre** Daily 10am–5pm • Free • **Planetarium** Shows every 45min • £7.50; combined ticket with Flamsteed House £12.50 • ☎ 020 8312 6565, ⓦ rmg.co.uk • Greenwich DLR/train station

Perched on the crest of Greenwich Park's highest hill – and so with sublime views over to Canary Wharf – the **Royal Observatory** was established by Charles II in 1675. It's housed in a rather dinky Wren-built red-brick building, whose northeastern turret sports a bright-red time-ball that climbs the mast at 12.58pm and drops at 1pm GMT precisely; it was added in 1833 to allow ships on the Thames to set their clocks.

Greenwich's greatest claim to fame, of course, is as the home of **Greenwich Mean Time** (GMT) and the **Prime Meridian**. Since 1884, Greenwich has occupied zero longitude, the **Meridian Line** marked by the strip in the observatory's main courtyard. The observatory housed the first Astronomer Royal, John Flamsteed, whose chief task was to study the night sky in order to discover an astronomical method of finding the longitude of a ship at sea. Beyond the Octagon Room, where the king used to show off to his guests, are the Time galleries, which display four of the clocks designed by **John Harrison**, including "H4", which helped win the Longitude Prize in 1763.

The free **Astronomy Centre** galleries give a brief rundown of some of the big questions of the universe, and you can also watch one of the thirty-minute presentations in the **Planetarium**.

Brixton

Market stalls Mon–Sat 8am–6pm, Wed till 3pm • **Brixton Village and Market Row** Mon 8am–6pm, Tues–Sun 8am–11.30pm (shops shut earlier; check individual café and restaurant times) • **Farmers' market** Sun 9.30am–2.30pm • ⓦ brixtonmarket.net • **Pop Brixton** Mon–Wed & Sun 9am–11pm, Thurs–Sat 9am–midnight • ⓦ popbrixton.org • ⊖ Brixton

Brixton is a classic Victorian suburb, transformed from open fields into bricks and mortar in a couple of decades following the arrival of the railways in the 1860s. The viaducts dominate central Brixton, with shops and arcades hidden under their arches, but it's the West Indian community, who arrived here in the 1950s and 1960s, who define the character of the place. These days the area's revived indoor markets attract increasing numbers of visitors to a plethora of small restaurants and bars, making this always busy, noisy neighbourhood even more frenetic. As you leave the tube, directly opposite, you'll see the bright mural of **David Bowie**, who was born in Brixton in 1947; it became a shrine to Bowie on his death in January 2016.

The main axis for the market is **Electric Avenue**, which runs behind the tube station, so called as it was one of the first London shopping streets to be lit by electricity in the 1880s. From here you can find the arcades of **Market Row** and **Brixton Village**, which create a maze of activity. Nearby, **Pop Brixton**, on the corner of Pope's Road and Brixton Station Road, is a shipping-container-built mini village of shops and street-food traders, plus a couple of tiny but excellent restaurants, outdoor bars and an events space.

Dulwich Picture Gallery

Gallery Rd, SE21 7AD • Tues–Fri 10am–5pm, Sat & Sun 11am–5pm • Permanent collection £7; exhibitions (including entry to permanent collection) around £15.50 • ☎ 020 8693 5254, ⓦ dulwichpicturegallery.org.uk • West Dulwich (from Victoria) or North Dulwich (from London Bridge) train stations

Dulwich Picture Gallery, the nation's oldest public art gallery, was designed by John Soane in 1814, who created a beautifully spacious building, awash with

CLOCKWISE FROM TOP LEFT HIGHGATE CEMETERY (P.100); DESIGN MUSEUM (P.96); KEW GARDENS (P.105); BUCKINGHAM PALACE (P.64) >

1

natural light. The collection was acquired on behalf of the King of Poland, who lost his kingdom before he could take possession of it; it was then bequeathed to the foundation of Dulwich, and is crammed with superb paintings: elegiac landscapes by Cuyp, one of the world's finest Poussin series, and splendid works by Gainsborough, Van Dyck, Canaletto and Rubens, plus **Rembrandt**'s beautiful *Girl at a Window*. At the centre of the museum, look out for the tiny mausoleum designed by Soane for the sarcophagi of the gallery's founders. The temporary exhibitions are often excellent and there's a good café, overlooking the museum's well-tended gardens.

Horniman Museum

100 London Rd, SE23 3PQ • Daily 10.30am–5.30pm • Free; aquarium £4; butterfly house £5.40; charge for temporary exhibitions (around £7) • ☎ 020 8699 1872, ⓦ horniman.ac.uk • Forest Hill train station from Victoria or London Bridge

The wonderful **Horniman Museum** was purpose-built in 1901 by Frederick Horniman, a tea trader with a passion for collecting. In addition to the museum's natural history collection of stuffed birds and animals – with a majestic, overstuffed walrus its centrepiece – there's an eclectic ethnographic collection, and a music gallery with more than 1500 instruments from Chinese gongs to electric guitars. The gardens, with animal trail, butterfly house, bandstand and glasshouse, and with views over South London, are charming, and there's an aquarium in the basement.

West London

Running through the swathes of green, suburban West London is the **River Thames**, once the "Great Highway of London" and still the most pleasant way to travel in these parts during summer. Boats plough up the Thames all the way from central London via the **Royal Botanic Gardens** at **Kew** and the picturesque riverside at **Richmond**, as far as **Hampton Court**. In among the commuter-belt suburbs are several picturesque former country retreats. The Palladian villa of **Chiswick House** is perhaps the best known, as well as popular **Syon House**, a showcase for the talents of Robert Adam.

Chiswick House

Burlington Lane, W4 2RP • **House** April–Oct Mon–Wed & Sun 10am–6pm; Oct closes 5pm; March Sat & Sun 10am–4pm • £7.20; EH • **Gardens** Daily 7am–dusk • Free • ☎ 020 8995 0508, ⓦ chgt.org.uk • Chiswick train station from Waterloo or ⊖ Turnham Green

Chiswick House is a perfect little Neoclassical villa, designed in the 1720s by the Earl of Burlington, and set in one of the most beautifully landscaped gardens in London. Like its prototype, Palladio's Villa Rotonda near Vicenza, the house was created as a "temple to the arts" where, amid his fine art collection, Burlington could entertain artistic friends such as Swift, Handel and Pope. Entertaining took place on the **upper floor**, a series of cleverly interconnecting rooms, each enjoying a wonderful view out onto the gardens – all, that is, except the Tribunal, the domed octagonal hall at the centre of the villa, where the earl's finest paintings and sculptures are displayed.

London Museum of Water and Steam

Green Dragon Lane, TW8 0EN • Daily 11am–4pm • £12.50 • ☎ 020 8568 4757, ⓦ waterandsteam.org.uk • Bus #237 or #267 from ⊖ Gunnersbury or Kew Bridge train station (from Waterloo)

Difficult to miss, thanks to its stylish Italianate standpipe tower, the **Museum of Water and Steam** occupies a former Victorian pumping station, 100 yards west of Kew

1

Bridge. At the heart of the museum is the Steam Hall, which contains a triple expansion steam engine and four gigantic nineteenth-century Cornish beam engines. The museum also has a hands-on **Waterworks** gallery in the basement, devoted to the history of the capital's water supply, and **Splash Zone**, ideal for younger kids. The best time to visit is at weekends, when each of the museum's industrial dinosaurs is put through its paces, and the small narrow-gauge steam **Waterworks Railway** runs back and forth round the yard.

Syon House

London Rd, TW8 8JF • **House** Mid-March to Oct Wed, Thurs & Sun 11am–5pm • £12.50 (includes gardens) • **Gardens** Mid-March to Oct daily 10.30am–5pm • £7.50 • ☎ 020 8560 0882, Ⓦ syonpark.co.uk • Bus #237 or #267 from ➏ Gunnersbury or Kew Bridge train station (from Waterloo)

From its rather plain castellated exterior, you'd never guess that **Syon House** contains the most opulent eighteenth-century interiors in London. The splendour of Robert Adam's refurbishment is immediately revealed, however, in the pristine **Great Hall**, an apsed double cube with a screen of Doric columns at one end and classical statuary dotted around the edges. There are several more Adam-designed rooms to admire in the house, in particular the **Long Gallery** – 136ft by just 14ft – plus a smattering of works by Lely, Van Dyck and others.

While Adam beautified Syon House, Capability Brown laid out its **gardens** around an artificial lake, surrounding it with oaks, beeches, limes and cedars. The gardens' chief focus now, however, is the crescent-shaped **Great Conservatory**, an early nineteenth-century addition which is said to have inspired Joseph Paxton, architect of the Crystal Palace.

Kew Gardens

Kew Green or Kew Road, TW9 3AE • April–Sept Mon–Thurs 10am–6.30pm, Fri–Sun 10am–7.30pm (till 9pm June; till 8.30pm mid-July to Aug); Oct daily 10am–6pm; Nov & Jan daily 10am–4.15pm; Dec daily 10am–3.30pm; March daily 10am–5.45pm • £16.50; £15.50 online • ☎ 020 8332 5655, Ⓦ kew.org • ➏ Kew Gardens, then a short walk down Lichfield Rd to Victoria Gate

Established in 1759, Kew's **Royal Botanic Gardens** manage the extremely difficult task of being both a world leader in botanic research and an extraordinarily beautiful and popular public park. There's always something to see, whatever the season, but to get the most out of the place come some time between spring and autumn, bring a picnic and stay for the day.

Of all the glasshouses, by far the most celebrated is the **Palm House**, a curvaceous mound of glass and wrought iron, designed by Decimus Burton in the 1840s. Its drippingly humid atmosphere nurtures most of the known palm species. Elsewhere in the gardens, you'll find the **Treetop Walkway**, which lifts you 60ft off the ground, and gives you a novel view of the tree canopy, a 163ft-high **Pagoda**, an art gallery, and

---

RIVER TRANSPORT: HEADING WEST

From April to October **Westminster Passenger Services** runs a scheduled service from Westminster Pier to Kew, Richmond and Hampton Court (departure times vary, but the first boat from Westminster usually leaves around 10.30am and the last around 2pm; your last chance to get back from Kew to Westminster is usually 5.30pm; 1hr 30min to Kew, around 3hr to Hampton Court; £13 single to Kew, £20 return; £17 to Hampton Court, £25 return; ☎ 020 7930 2062, Ⓦ wpsa.co.uk). In addition, **Turks** runs a regular service from Richmond to Hampton Court (around 3 daily; to mid-Sept Tues–Sun; Aug daily; £9 single, £10.80 return; 1hr 45min; ☎ 020 8546 2434, Ⓦ turks.co.uk). For the latest on boat services on the Thames, see Ⓦ tfl.gov.uk.

1

various follies and semi-wild areas. The newest addition is the **Hive**, a 17m-high honeycomb structure that takes you inside the world of honeybees using 900 LED lights and the sound of 40,000 bees.

The three-storey red-brick mansion of **Kew Palace** (April–Oct only), to the northwest of the Palm House, was bought by George II as a nursery and schoolhouse for his umpteen children. Later, George III was confined to the palace and subjected to the dubious attentions of doctors who attempted to find a cure for his "madness".

Richmond

Richmond, upriver from Kew, basked for centuries in the glow of royal patronage, with Plantagenet kings and Tudor monarchs frequenting the riverside palace. Although most of the courtiers and aristocrats have gone, it is still a wealthy district, with two theatres, riverside walks and spacious, leafy upmarket residential streets.

Richmond Park

Daily: March–Sept 7am–dusk; Oct–Feb 7.30am–dusk • Free • ☎ 0300 061 2200, ⓦ royalparks.org.uk • Bus #371 from ⊖ Richmond to Richmond Gate or #65 from ⊖ Richmond to Petersham Gate

Richmond's greatest attraction is the enormous **Richmond Park**, at the top of Richmond Hill – 2500 acres of undulating grassland and bracken, dotted with coppiced woodland and as wild as anything in London. Eight miles across at its widest point, this is Europe's largest city park, famed for its red and fallow deer, which roam freely, and for its ancient oaks. For the most part untamed, the park does have a couple of deliberately landscaped plantations that feature splendid springtime azaleas and rhododendrons.

Ham House

Ham St , TW10 7RS • House April–Oct daily noon–4pm; Jan–March visits by guided tour only (Mon–Fri hourly noon–3pm, Sat & Sun noon–4pm); gardens daily 10am–5pm • £10.80; NT • ☎ 020 8940 1950, ⓦ nationaltrust.org.uk/ham-house-and-garden • Bus #371 or #65 from ⊖ Richmond

Leave the rest of London far behind at **Ham House**, home to the earls of Dysart for nearly three hundred years. Expensively furnished in the seventeenth century, but little altered since then, the house is blessed with one of the finest Stuart interiors in the country, from the stupendously ornate Great Staircase to the Long Gallery, featuring six "Court Beauties" by Peter Lely. Elsewhere, there are several fine Verrio ceiling paintings, some exquisite parquet flooring and works by Van Dyck and Reynolds. Also glorious are the formal seventeenth-century **gardens**, especially the Cherry Garden, laid out with an aromatic lavender parterre. The Orangery, overlooking the original kitchen garden, serves as a tearoom.

Strawberry Hill

268 Waldegrave Rd, TW1 4ST • **House** March–Oct Mon–Wed & Sun hours vary but generally 11am–5pm • £12.50 • **Garden** Daily 10am–6pm • Free • ☎ 020 8744 1241, ⓦ strawberryhillhouse.org.uk • Strawberry Hill train station from Waterloo

In 1747 writer, wit and fashion queen Horace Walpole, youngest son of former prime minister Robert Walpole, bought this "little play-thing house … the prettiest bauble you ever saw … set in enamelled meadows, with filigree hedges", renamed it **Strawberry Hill** and set about inventing the most influential building in the Gothic Revival. Walpole appointed a "Committee of Taste" to embellish his project with details from other Gothic buildings: screens from Old St Paul's and Rouen cathedrals, and fan vaulting from Henry VII's Chapel in Westminster Abbey. Walpole wanted visits of Strawberry Hill to be a theatrical experience, and, with its eccentric Gothic decor, it remains so to this day.

Hampton Court

Hampton Court Rd, KT8 9AU · **Palace** Daily: April–Oct 10am–6pm; Nov–March closes 4.30pm; last entry 1hr before closing · £20.90
(tickets £1–3 cheaper online) · **Magic Garden** April–Oct daily 10am–6pm, last admission 5.15pm · £7.70, kids aged 3–15 £5.50
(includes Maze) · ☎ 020 3166 6000, ⓦ hrp.org.uk · Hampton Court train station from Waterloo

Hampton Court Palace, a sprawling red-brick ensemble on the banks of the Thames thirteen miles southwest of London, is the finest of England's royal abodes. Built in 1516 by the upwardly mobile **Cardinal Wolsey**, Henry VIII's Lord Chancellor, it was purloined by Henry himself after Wolsey fell from favour. In the second half of the seventeenth century, Charles II laid out the gardens, inspired by what he had seen at Versailles, while William and Mary had large sections of the palace remodelled by Wren a few years later.

Audioguides are available and free guided tours are led by period-costumed historians who bring the place to life. It's worth taking a day to explore fully – Hampton Court is huge – but the most rewarding sections are: **Henry VIII's Apartments**, which feature the glorious double-hammer-beamed Great Hall and Chapel Royal, with vaulted ceiling adorned with gilded cherubs; **William III's Apartments**, covered in militaristic trompe-l'oeil paintings; **Henry VIII's Kitchens**; and the **Cumberland Art Gallery**, which display a superb selection of works from the Royal Collection.

Overlooked by Wren's magnificent South Front is the formal **Privy Garden**, laid out as it would have been under William III. Here is the palace's celebrated **Great Vine**, whose grapes are sold at the palace each year in September. Close by is the gallery housing *The Triumphs of Caesar*, a series of heroic canvases by **Andrea Mantegna** from around 1486. To the west, the magnificent **Broad Walk** runs north for half a mile from the Thames. Halfway along lies the indoor **Royal Tennis Court**, used for real tennis, an arcane precursor of the modern game.

To the north of the palace the informal **Wilderness** area contains the famous trapezoidal **Maze**, laid out in 1714. Also on this side of the palace grounds is the gorgeous **Rose Garden** and an elaborate adventure playground for kids called the **Magic Garden**.

ARRIVAL AND DEPARTURE   LONDON

BY PLANE
The capital's five international airports – Heathrow, Gatwick, Stansted, Luton and City Airport – are all less than an hour from the city centre.

HEATHROW
Some 15 miles west of central London, Heathrow (ⓦ heathrowairport.com) has five terminals and three train/tube stations: one for terminals 1, 2 and 3, and separate ones for terminals 4 and 5; Oyster and contactless can be used on the Underground and Elizabeth Line, and Heathrow Express (as of mid-2018).
Heathrow Express High-speed trains travel nonstop to Paddington Station (Mon–Sat 5.15am–11.20pm, Sun 6.20am–11.20pm; every 15min; journey 15min; £22–25 one-way off-peak, £37 return, more if you purchase your ticket on board; ⓦ heathrowexpress.com).
Elizabeth Line Formerly Heathrow Connect, the new Elizabeth Line (Crossrail) service will run four trains an hour from terminals 2, 3 and 4 to Paddington from May 2018 (with a service from terminal 5 from December 2019 onwards), with several stops on the way.
Underground The Piccadilly tube line runs directly into central London (daily 5am–11pm; Fri & Sat 24hr from

terminals 1, 2, 3 & 5 only; every 5min; journey 50min–1hr); £3.10 off-peak, £5.10 peak (Mon–Fri 6.30–9.30am) with Oyster card (see box, p.109).
National Express Bus services run direct to Victoria Coach Station (daily 4.20am–10.10pm; every 20min–1hr; journey 40min–1hr; £6–£13.50 one-way; ⓦ nationalexpress.com).

GATWICK
Around 30 miles south of London, Gatwick Airport (ⓦ gatwickairport.com) has good transport connections; you can pay by Oyster and contactless on train services (though it's cheaper to buy returns in advance).
Gatwick Express Nonstop service between the airport's South Terminal and Victoria Station (daily 5.50am–11.20am; every 15min; journey 30min; £17.80 one-way, £31.60 return, if bought online; group savings and other discounts available; ⓦ gatwickexpress.com).
Southern and Thameslink trains Other train options include Southern services to Victoria (daily 5.40am–11pm, roughly every 15min; Fri & Sat hourly night service; 35min) and Thameslink services to various stations (24hr; every 15–30min; journey 30–45min), including Blackfriars and St Pancras; one-way tickets with Oyster: peak £16.50, off-peak £10.30; return £19.80.

1

National Express Buses run from Gatwick direct to central London (daily 24hr; 1–2 hourly; 1hr 30min; £6–£10 one-way).

STANSTED

Roughly 35 miles northeast of the capital, Stansted (ⓦ stanstedairport.com) is mainly used by the budget airlines.

Stansted Express The most convenient way to get into town is by train on the Stansted Express to Liverpool Street (daily 5.30am–12.30am; every 15–30min; journey 45min; £16.60 one-way, £28 return; ⓦ stanstedexpress.com).

National Express Buses to Liverpool Street, Stratford, Waterloo, Victoria Coach Station and Paddington (daily 24hr; every 20–30min; journey 1hr–1hr 45min), with tickets around £8–13 one-way.

CITY AIRPORT

London's smallest airport, City Airport, which handles almost entirely domestic and European flights (ⓦ london cityairport.com), is in Docklands, 10 miles east of central London. Docklands Light Railway (DLR) will take you straight to Bank in the City (Mon–Sat 5.30am–12.15am, Sun 7am–11.15pm; every 8–15min; journey 20min); pay by Oyster or contactless (see opposite).

LUTON

Around 30 miles north of London, Luton (ⓦ london-luton .co.uk) handles mostly charter flights.

Luton Airport Parkway A free shuttle bus (every 10min; 5min) transports passengers to Luton Airport Parkway train station, connected to St Pancras (daily 24hr; every 15–30min; journey 25–45min; one-way £14) and other stations in central London.

Buses Green Line runs the #757 coach from Luton Airport to Victoria Coach Station (daily 24hr; every 20min–1hr; journey 1hr–1hr 30min; one-way £10, return £17; ⓦ www .greenline.co.uk), stopping at several locations en route. National Express runs buses to Victoria Coach Station (daily 24hr; every 20min–1hr; journey 1hr 5min–1hr 20min; £6–12 one-way).

BY TRAIN

From Europe Eurostar (ⓦ eurostar.com) trains arrive at St Pancras International, next door to King's Cross.

From Britain Arriving by train from elsewhere in Britain, you'll come into one of London's mainline stations, all of which have adjacent Underground stations. As a rough guide, Charing Cross handles services to Kent; Euston to the Midlands, northwest England and Glasgow; Fenchurch Street to south Essex; King's Cross to northeast England and Scotland; Liverpool Street to eastern England; Marylebone to the Midlands; Paddington to west and southwest England, including Oxford, Bath and Bristol; St Pancras for Eurostar and the southeast, plus trains to the East Midlands

and South Yorkshire; Victoria to destinations south, including Brighton; and Waterloo directly southwest of London, including Southampton and Salisbury.

Information National Rail Enquiries (☎ 0345 748 4950, ⓦ nationalrail.co.uk).

DESTINATIONS

Charing Cross to: Canterbury West (hourly; 1hr 40min); Dover Priory (every 30min; 1hr 40min–2hr); Hastings (every 30min; 1hr 35min–1hr 50min); Rochester (every 30min; 1hr 15min).

Euston to: Birmingham New Street (every 20min; 1hr 25min); Carlisle (hourly; 3hr 25min); Lancaster (hourly; 2hr 30min); Liverpool Lime Street (hourly; 2hr 10min); Manchester Piccadilly (every 20min; 2hr 5min).

King's Cross to: Cambridge (every 30min; 45min); Durham (hourly; 2hr 55min); Leeds (every 30min; 2hr 15min); Newcastle (every 30min; 2hr 50min–3hr 15min); York (every 20–30min; 1hr 50min–2hr 30min).

Liverpool Street to: Cambridge (every 30min; 1hr 15min); Norwich (every 30min; 1hr 45min–1hr 55min).

London Bridge to: Brighton (every 30min; 1hr).

Paddington to: Bath (every 30min; 1hr 30min); Bristol (every 15–30min; 1hr 20min–1hr 40min); Cheltenham (every 2hr; 2hr 15min); Exeter (every 30min–1hr; 2hr 15min–2hr 50min); Gloucester (every 2hr; 2hr); Oxford (every 30min; 55min); Penzance (every 1–2hr; 5hr 30min); Plymouth (hourly; 3hr 15min–3hr 40min); Worcester (hourly; 2hr 20min–2hr 50min).

St Pancras to: Brighton (every 30min; 1hr 15min); Canterbury (every 30min–1hr; 55min); Dover Priory (every 30min–hourly; 1hr 5min); Leicester (every 15–30min; 1hr–1hr 35min); Nottingham (2 hourly; 1hr 40min–2hr); Rochester (every 30min; 35min); Sheffield (every 30min; 2hr–2hr 20min).

Victoria to: Arundel (Mon–Sat every 30min, Sun hourly; 1hr 30min); Brighton (every 30min; 50min); Canterbury East (every 30min–1hr; 1hr 40min); Chichester (1–2 hourly; 1hr 30min); Dover Priory (Mon–Sat every 30min; 2hr–2hr 15min); Lewes (Mon–Sat every 30min, Sun hourly; 1hr–1hr 10min); Rochester (every 30min; 40min–1hr).

Waterloo to: Portsmouth Harbour (every 15–30min; 1hr 40min–2hr 15min); Southampton Central (every 30min; 1hr 15min); Winchester (every 30min; 1hr).

BY BUS

Victoria Coach Station Coming into London by coach, you're most likely to arrive at Victoria Coach Station, a couple of hundred yards south down Buckingham Palace Rd from the train and Underground stations of the same name. Journey times leaving London can vary considerably: maximum times are given, but avoid travelling by coach during the afternoon rush hour if you can.

Information Traveline (☎ 0871 200 2233, ⓦ traveline

.info) or National Express (☎ 0871 781 8181, ⓦ national express.com).

Destinations Bath (hourly–every 1hr 30min; 3hr 15min); Birmingham (every 30min; 3hr 20min); Brighton (every 30min–1hr 30min; 3hr); Bristol (every 2hr; 3hr); Cambridge (every 30min–1hr 30min; 2hr); Canterbury (hourly–every 1hr 30min; 2hr 40min); Dover (8 daily; 3hr–3hr 30min); Exeter (every 2–3hr; 4hr 30min); Gloucester (every 1–2hr; 3hr 25min); Liverpool (every 1–2hr; 6hr 15min); Manchester (every 1hr 30min; 6hr 25min); Newcastle (4 daily; 7hr 55min); Oxford (every 20min; 2hr); Plymouth (5 daily; 6hr 20min); Stratford (3 daily; 3hr 45min).

GETTING AROUND

London's **transport network** is complex and expensive, but will get you wherever you want at most hours of the day or night. Avoid travelling during the **rush hour** (Mon–Fri 8–9.30am & 5–7pm), when tubes become unbearably crowded, and some buses get so full that they won't let you on. You're best using Oyster or a contactless payment card (see box below).

INFORMATION

Transport for London (TfL) For maps, route planning and information see ⓦ tfl.gov.uk, or call ☎ 0343 222 1234.

Visitor Centres TfL has Visitor Centres, where you can buy Oyster cards and get information, at: Piccadilly Circus (daily 9.30am–4pm); Liverpool Street (daily 9am–5pm); Victoria (daily 8am–6pm); Euston, King's Cross Underground and Paddington (all Mon–Sat 8am–6pm, Sun 8.30am–6pm); Heathrow terminals 2 & 3 Underground station (daily 7.30am–8.30pm); and Gatwick North and South Arrivals (daily 9.15am–4pm).

Apps The best mobile phone app for route planning, including finding live bus times, is Citymapper (ⓦ city mapper.com).

BY TUBE

Except for very short journeys, the Underground – or tube – is by far the quickest way to get about.

Tube lines Eleven different lines cross much of the metropolis, although south of the river is not very well covered. Each line has its own colour and name – all you need to know is which direction you're travelling in (northbound, eastbound, southbound or westbound), and the final destination (plus sometimes which branch).

Services Frequent Mon–Sat 5.30am–12.30am, Sun 7.30am–11.30pm; you rarely have to wait more than 5min for a train between central stations.

Night Tube The 24hr Night Tube service runs every 10–20min on Friday and Saturday on five main lines: Central, Jubilee, Piccadilly, Victoria and Northern (Charing Cross branch), plus an East London section of the Overground (see p.110).

Fares An Oyster card or contactless payment (touched in and out at the barrier at each station) is by far your best option (see box below); one-way fares with paper tickets are never the best choice – a journey in zone 1 costs £4.90 with a paper ticket, £2.40 with an Oyster or contactless card.

GETTING ABOUT: OYSTER CARDS AND CONTACTLESS PAYMENT

For all London transport, the cheapest, easiest ticketing option is an **Oyster card**, London's transport smartcard, available from all tube stations and TfL Visitor Centres. Use it either to store a weekly/monthly **travelcard**, or as a **pay-as-you-go** card. As you enter the tube or bus, simply touch in your card at the card reader. On a tube or train, you need to touch out again, or a maximum cash fare of up to £7.80 will be deducted; on a bus, you only touch in. A pay-as-you-go Oyster operates daily and weekly price-capping; you will stop being charged when you have this (£6.60 for zones 1–2 for a day; £33 for a week, running Mon–Sun), but you still need to touch in (and out). Unless you're buying a monthly or yearly Oyster card, it costs £5 for the card (refundable on return), or visitors can buy a Visitor Oyster card for £3, plus the amount of credit you want.

If you have a debit or credit card or smart phone with a **contactless payment** function, you can use this in the same way as a pay-as-you-go Oyster card, with the same fares and price-capping (make sure that you use the same card all day). British Visa, MasterCard and American Express cards work; for cards issued outside the UK, American Express and most but not all MasterCard and Visa with contactless payment should work. However, any **overseas bank charges** will apply to each use.

Children under 11 travel for free; children aged 11–15 travel free on all buses and at child rate on the tube; children aged 16 or 17 can travel at half the adult rate on all forms of transport. Children 11 years old and over must have a Zip Oyster photocard; apply in advance online (£15 for 11–15 year olds; £20 for 16–17 year olds). Visitors from outside the UK will need to pick this up from a TfL Visitor Centre (see above).

Other travelcards and passes are available, too; check ⓦ tfl.gov.uk for details.

1

THE CONGESTION CHARGE

All vehicles entering central London on weekdays between 7am and 6pm are liable to a **congestion charge** of £11.50 per vehicle (£10.50 if you sign up online to pay automatically each time you travel in the zone; vehicles that don't meet certain emission standards have to pay an additional £10/day emissions surcharge). Pay the charge online or over the phone (lines open Mon–Fri 8am–10pm, Sat 9am–3pm; ☎0343 222 2222, ⓦtfl.gov.uk), before midnight; paying the following day costs £14; 24 hours later, you'll be liable for a £130 Penalty Charge Notice (reduced to £65 if you pay within fourteen days). Disabled travellers, motorcycles, minibuses and some alternative-fuel vehicles are exempt from the charge, but you must register in order to qualify. For more details, visit ⓦtfl.gov.uk.

BY BUS

London's red buses – most, but not all, of them, double-deckers – are fun to ride on and a cheap way of sightseeing. For example, the #11 bus from Victoria station will take you past Westminster Abbey and the Houses of Parliament, up Whitehall, round Trafalgar Square, along the Strand and on to St Paul's Cathedral. You can also take an old-fashioned double-decker Routemaster, on "heritage" route #15 (daily 9.30am–6.30pm; every 20min) from Trafalgar Square to Tower Hill. At many stops you need to stick your hand out to get the bus to stop, and press the bell in order to get off.

Services Some buses run a 24hr service, but most run between about 5am and midnight, with a network of night buses (prefixed with the letter "N") operating outside this period (every 20–30min).

Fares A one-way fare is £1.50, any time and for any distance travelled, including if you transfer to another bus within an hour (the Hopper fare). You must touch in every time you alight (though you don't touch out); cash is not accepted – you need an Oyster card, contactless debit card or travelcard.

BY OVERGROUND AND DLR

Overground The orange Overground line is a large network that connects with the tube system and stretches out to Richmond in the west, Stratford in the east, forming an orbital railway, a sort of outer Circle Line. It's particularly useful for reaching parts of East London (every 5–15min roughly). From New Cross Gate to Dalston Junction there's a night service (Fri & Sat), with plans to extend it to Highbury & Islington.

DLR The Docklands Light Railway is a network of driverless trains from Bank in the City, and from Tower Gateway (close to Tower Hill tube and the Tower of London) above ground to the financial centre of Docklands, plus other areas in the East End, and also below ground to Greenwich. It's integrated with the tube; pay by Oyster.

BY TRAIN

Large areas of London's outskirts are best reached by the suburban train network, departing from one of the main central termini (see p.108); they all accept Oyster, and main routes generally run every 15–30min.

BY BOAT

Boat trips on the Thames are a fun way of sightseeing, and there are several tours and speedboats as well as Thames Clippers.

Thames Clipper Runs a regular commuter service between the London Eye and Greenwich (every 15–30min Mon–Fri 7am–10.30pm, Sat & Sun 8.30am or 9.30am–10.30pm, then one final eastbound service around 11.30pm; ⓦthamesclippers.com). There are piers on both sides of the river, including Embankment, Bankside, Blackfriars, London Bridge and Tower. You can buy tickets at a pier, but there is a discount if you buy online in advance or use an Oyster card. Typical fares are £6.30 for a central zone single with a pay-as-you-go Oyster card or online (£8.10 otherwise), with an unlimited hop-on hop-off day River Roamer costing £16.30 online, £18.50 from the pier.

BY TAXI

Black cabs Compared to most cities, London's metered black cabs are expensive unless there are three or more of you, though black-cab drivers have unparalleled knowledge of the city's streets. The minimum fare is £2.60, and a ride from Euston to Victoria, for example, costs around £15–20 (Mon–Fri 5am–8pm). After 8pm on weekdays and all day during the weekend, a higher tariff applies, and after 10pm it's higher still. A yellow light over the windscreen tells you if the cab is available – just stick your arm out to hail it. To order a black cab in advance (£2 extra), phone ☎0871 871 8710.

Minicabs and apps Private minicabs are much cheaper than black cabs, but cannot be hailed from the street. They must be licensed and able to produce a TfL ID on demand. Apps like Hailo and Uber can come in handy, too, though at the time of going to print TfL had decided not to renew Uber's licence to operate in London; check for updates before you travel.

BY BIKE

Boris bikes The city's cycle rental scheme – or Boris bikes, as they're universally known, after former Mayor of London Boris Johnson – has over 700 docking stations across central London. With a credit or debit card, you can buy 24hr access for just £2. You then get the first 30min on a bike free, so if you hop from docking station to docking station you don't pay another penny. Otherwise, it's £2 for each additional 30min. For more details see ⓦtfl.gov.uk.

Bike rental London Bicycle Tour Company, 1a Gabriel Wharf on the South Bank (ⓣ020 7923 6838, ⓦlondon bicycle.com), has bikes for rent (£3.50–4/hr; £20–24/day).

INFORMATION AND TOURS

Visit London The official tourist information body, though they don't run any tourist offices. Check ⓦvisit london.com for information.

City of London Information Centre The City's central information office, situated on the south side of St Paul's Cathedral (Mon–Sat 9.30am–5.30pm, Sun 10am–4pm; ⓦcityoflondon.gov.uk; ⊖St Paul's); several walking tours of the City run daily from here (most £7).

London Pass and discounts The London Pass (ⓦlondonpass.com) covers a hop-on hop-off bus tour, Thames river cruise and entry to around 70 of London's top charging attractions, including Hampton Court Palace, London Zoo, St Paul's Cathedral, the Tower of London, Westminster Abbey and Windsor Castle. The pass costs £62 for one day (£42 for kids), rising to £139 for six days (£96 for kids), with all-zone Oyster card options available too. Buy online or from a TfL Visitor Centre and other outlets. If you've travelled to London by National Rail train (not Eurostar) you can get two-for-one tickets on numerous attractions (see ⓦdaysoutguide.co.uk).

Bus tours Standard sightseeing tours are run by several rival bus companies, with open-top double-deckers every 30min from Victoria station, Trafalgar Square, Piccadilly and other tourist spots. You can hop on and off several different routes with the Original Tour for £29 (daily 8.20am–6pm; every 15–30min; ⓣ020 8877 1722, ⓦtheoriginaltour.com). Golden Tours' (ⓦgoldentours.com) bus tour is included in the London Pass.

Boat tours City Cruises run from Westminster to Greenwich (every 40min; tickets £10–16, one-day ticket included in London Pass, if bought online; ⓣ020 7928 3132, ⓦcitycruises.com).

Walking tours Numerous walking tours are offered, including those departing from the City of London information centre (see above). They normally cost around £10 and take around 2hr; often you can simply show up at the starting point. Original London Walks (ⓣ020 7624 3978, ⓦwww.walks.com) are a well-established company.

ACCOMMODATION

London **accommodation** is expensive. The **hostels** are among the costliest in the world, while venerable institutions such as the *Ritz*, the *Dorchester* and the *Savoy* charge the very top international prices – from £300 per luxurious night. For a decent **hotel** room, don't expect much change out of £110 a night, and even **B&Bs** struggle to bring their tariffs down to £90 for a double with shared facilities. The **chain hotels** are a safe bet – but they'll offer less character than the places that we've reviewed below and, depending on the season or location, may not always be that much cheaper. Premier Inn (ⓦpremierinn .com), Travelodge (ⓦtravelodge.co.uk), easyHotel (ⓦeasyhotel.com) and Point A (ⓦpointahotels.com) all have properties in central locations. Whatever the time of year, you should book as early as possible if you want to stay within a couple of tube stops of the West End. Among the many price comparison sites and booking portals, ⓦlondontown.com often offers good discounts.

HOTELS, GUESTHOUSES AND B&BS

When choosing your area, bear in mind that the West End – Soho, Covent Garden, St James's, Mayfair and Marylebone – and the western districts of Knightsbridge and Kensington are dominated by expensive, upmarket hotels; for central hotels at a good price, Bloomsbury remains a safe bet, while a number of less expensive options are popping up on the fringes. Free wi-fi is almost universally standard, and is free in all the establishments we review. While anywhere categorized as a B&B automatically includes breakfast, our reviews specify where breakfast is included in hotel rates (which is unusual) and guesthouses (which is less so).

WESTMINSTER AND ST JAMES'S

★**Artist Residence** 52 Cambridge St, SW1V 4QQ ⓣ020 7828 6684, ⓦartistresidence.co.uk; ⊖Pimlico; map p.56. Boutique guesthouse offering relaxed luxury and cool style. The ten rooms – exposed brick, bare wood, stylish prints and upcycled furnishings – feature lots of extras, but the cheapest are small. There's a Modern British restaurant and a cocktail bar on site. **£265**

LONDON POSTCODES

A brief word on **London postcodes**: the name of each street is followed by a letter giving the geographical location (E for "east", WC for "west central" and so on) and a number that specifies the postal area. However, this is not a reliable indication of the remoteness of the locale – W5, for example, lies beyond the more remote-sounding NW10 – so it's always best to check a map before taking a room in what may sound like a fairly central area.

1

B&B Belgravia 64–66 Ebury St, SW1W 9QD ☎020 7259 8570, ⓦbb-belgravia.com; ⊖Victoria; map p.56. Welcoming B&B near Victoria train and coach stations. The small, simple, en-suite rooms are comfortable, with some original features; those on the ground floor can get street noise. There's a lounge with hot drinks and a guest laptop, plus a garden and bike loan. **£160**

Nadler Victoria 10 Palace Place, SW1E 5BW ☎020 3540 8800, ⓦnadlerhotels.com; ⊖Victoria; map p.60. One of a sophisticated mini-chain – well-designed, comfortable rooms with kitchenettes, plus friendly service – very near Buckingham Palace. The cheapest rooms are small, but still prove excellent value in this part of town. Branches in Soho (see below) and Earl's Court (see p.113). **£195**

Sanctuary House 33 Tothill St, SW1H 9LA ☎020 7799 4044, ⓦsanctuaryhousehotel.co.uk; ⊖St James's Park; map p.60. Fuller's Brewery runs a number of hotels in London; this one has a terrific location by St James's Park. The 34 smart rooms, despite being above the drinking action, are quiet enough, and kitted out in an uncontroversially contemporary style. **£166**

Z Hotel Piccadilly 2 Orange St, WC2H 7DF ☎020 3551 3700, ⓦthezhotels.com; ⊖Piccadilly Circus; map p.60. While this modern hotel is convenient for Piccadilly, it's also a hop away from Trafalgar Square. With properties all over London, the Z chain specializes in well-designed, teeny rooms – they're en suite, with storage space, but the cheapest don't have windows (rooms with windows cost £15 more). Free nightly wine and cheese buffets. **£164**

MARYLEBONE

22 York Street 22 York St, W1U 6PX ☎020 7224 2990, ⓦ22yorkstreet.co.uk; ⊖Baker Street; map p.92. This ten-room B&B, in a family house, delivers a home from home with heart. The Georgian building is antique-bedecked, with comfortable public spaces for reading and board games. Breakfasts are communal. **£150**

SOHO

Dean Street Townhouse 69–71 Dean St, W1D 3SE ☎020 7434 1775, ⓦdeanstreettownhouse.com; ⊖Tottenham Court Road; map p.60. One of a set of hotels owned by the Soho House members' club, this 1730s beauty is in a great location. The split-level "broom cupboard" is OK for one night – after that rooms increase in size up to the relatively capacious "bigger" (£470). All are luxurious, with nice touches including home-made biscuits; many have standalone tubs. **£220**

★**Hazlitt's** 6 Frith St, W1D 3JA ☎020 7434 1771, ⓦhazlittshotel.com; ⊖Tottenham Court Road; map p.60. This early eighteenth-century building, off Soho Square, is a hotel of character and charm. Creaky, crooked old stairs lead up to romantic en-suite rooms, decorated with period furniture and antique books. Continental breakfast (not included) is served in your room; there's also a small library with real fire and honesty bar. **£299**

Nadler Soho 10 Carlisle St, W1D 3BR ☎020 3697 3697, ⓦthenadler.com; ⊖Tottenham Court Road; map p.60. Attention to detail, lovely service and good prices for this location. The smart, modern rooms are businesslike (the cheapest are small), with a microwave, fridge, coffee machine and kettle, so you could effectively self-cater. There are (cheaper) branches in St James's (see above) and near Earl's Court (see p.113). **£209**

COVENT GARDEN

The Fielding 4 Broad Court, Bow St, WC2B 5QZ ☎020 7836 8305, ⓦthefieldinghotel.co.uk; ⊖Covent Garden; map p.60. In an old building (there's no lift) on a pedestrianized court behind the Royal Opera House, this little hotel offers simple, en-suite rooms – a little tired in places, but clean, comfortable and great value for this location, with tea- and coffee-making facilities. Rates increase by £20 at the weekend. **£140**

Henrietta Hotel 14–15 Henrietta St, WC2E 8QH ☎020 3794 5313, ⓦhenriettahotel.com; ⊖Covent Garden; map p.60. Opulent boutique hotel spread across two historic townhouses, with an on-site restaurant helmed by star chef Ollie Dabbous. With a hipster-boudoir feel, the rooms include a minibar stocked with cocktails created by the mixologists at *Experimental Cocktail Club*. **£238**

Seven Dials Hotel 7 Monmouth St, WC2H 9DA ☎020 7240 0823, ⓦsevendialshotel.com; ⊖Covent Garden; map p.60. Welcoming, eighteen-room guesthouse on one of Covent Garden's nicest streets. It's in no way fancy: the staircase is narrow and steep (no lift) and the basic en-suite rooms are very small, but all are clean and comfy, and rates include breakfast. **£110**

BLOOMSBURY AND KING'S CROSS

Arosfa 83 Gower St, WC1E 6HJ ☎020 7636 2115, ⓦarosfalondon.com; ⊖Goodge Street; map p.72. The fifteen en-suite rooms in this popular, friendly guesthouse aren't big, but they're clean and comfortable. There's a homely guest lounge/bar and a walled garden – and breakfasts (Full English and buffet) are included. **£160**

Great Northern Hotel King's Cross St Pancras Station, Pancras Rd, N1C 4TB ☎020 3388 0800, ⓦgnhlondon.com; ⊖King's Cross St Pancras; map p.72. Gussied-up station hotel with a vaguely Deco feel and lots of extras – Nespresso coffee, pastries and fresh fruit offered on each floor. The boutique rooms are bijou; the smallest, called "couchettes", evoke the romance of a train sleeper, while others are tucked beneath the eaves. **£230**

Megaro Hotel Belgrove St, WC1H 8AB ☎020 7843 2222, ⓦhotelmegaro.co.uk; ⊖King's Cross St Pancras; map p.72. Unfussy contemporary choice opposite the train station. The rooms – fifty or so, including family options

– are relatively spacious, with good bathrooms and espresso machines. **£200**

★ **Ridgemount** 65–67 Gower St, WC1E 6HJ ☎ 020 7636 1141, ⓦ ridgemounthotel.co.uk; ⊖ Goodge Street; map p.72. Old-fashioned, friendly and popular family-owned guesthouse, faded but clean. Around half of the 32 rooms have washbasins but share facilities, which are spotless, and are sizeable; en-suites cost about £20 more. Full breakfast included. **£95**

THE CITY

Apex City of London Hotel 1 Seething Lane, EC3N 4AX ☎ 020 7702 2020, ⓦ apexhotels.co.uk; ⊖ Tower Hill; map p.78. Sleek and nicely appointed modern hotel on a secluded street near the Tower of London. It's geared towards a corporate clientele, but welcoming to all – and every guest gets a free rubber duck. Book early for the best rates. **£152**

The Rookery 12 Peter's Lane, Cowcross St, EC1M 6DS ☎ 020 7336 0931, ⓦ rookeryhotel.com; ⊖ Farringdon; map p.78. Rambling Georgian townhouse, all panelled walls, flagstoned floors and creaky timeworn floorboards. The rooms, some of which are a little dark, offer faded Baroque glam. There's a comfy conservatory and an honesty bar, but breakfast, not included in the price, is served in your room. **£240**

★ **Zetter Hotel** 86–88 Clerkenwell Rd, EC1M 5RJ ☎ 020 7324 4567, ⓦ thezetter.com; ⊖ Farringdon; map p.78. In a stylishly converted warehouse, the *Zetter* epitomizes good-value boutique style. Rooms are colourful and bold, with extras such as hot-water bottles and vintage paper-backs. Free bike rental. Their more expensive sister hotels *Zetter Townhouse* (opposite, on St John's Square) and *Zetter Townhouse Marylebone* are even more whimsical. **£145**

EAST LONDON

Ace Hotel 100 Shoreditch High St, E1 6JQ ☎ 020 7613 9800, ⓦ acehotel.com/london; ⊖ Liverpool Street; map p.83. This branch of the US hipster hotel chain is a party-animal choice. Hosting exhibitions, talks, gigs and DJ nights, it also has various artisan coffee and snack bars and a Modern British restaurant, with a club in the basement and a rooftop bar. Rooms are as cool as you'd expect, all subdued dark colours, retro styling and quirky touches – deluxe options include turntables and vinyl. **£219**

Culpeper 40 Commercial St, E1 6LP ☎ 020 7247 5371, ⓦ theculpeper.com; ⊖ Aldgate East; map p.83. Simple, artfully distressed en-suite rooms above a gastropub near Brick Lane (don't expect peace and quiet during pub hours). There's a plant-filled terrace on the roof, where you can sit with a drink overlooking the City, and a good hot breakfast is included. **£120**

The Hoxton 81 Great Eastern St, EC2A 3HU ☎ 020 7550 1000, ⓦ hoxtonhotels.com; ⊖ Old Street; map p.78.

"The Hox" was one of the first hotels in this nightlife neighbourhood, and despite a change in ownership it remains a stalwart, with buzzy communal areas and two hundred or so attractive rooms. Downstairs, the *Hoxton Grill* and the DJ bar are popular hangouts – ask for a quiet room if you value your sleep. A light breakfast is delivered to your room. **£199**

★ **Qbic** 42 Adler St, E1 1EE ☎ 020 3021 2644, ⓦ london .qbichotels.com; ⊖ Aldgate East; map p.83. Bright, youthful hotel – the eye-popping colour blocks and kitschy photos are not for everyone. Rooms feature fab bathrooms and comfortable beds; the cheapest are very small, though, with no windows, for which you'll pay around £15 more. Bikes for loan, free hot drinks, and a Modern British restaurant/bar hosting monthly gigs and DJ sets. **£130**

SOUTH BANK

★ **Captain Bligh Guest House** 100 Lambeth Rd, SE1 7PT (no phone), ⓦ captainblighhouse.co.uk; ⊖ Lambeth North; map p.56. Captain Bligh's former residence can be your home from home – a cosy Georgian building, opposite the Imperial War Museum, run by a friendly, unobtrusive couple. The five en-suite rooms each have kitchenettes stocked with simple breakfast provisions. The three-night minimum may be the only snag. No cards. **£100**

BANKSIDE

Citizen M Bankside 20 Lavington St, SE1 0NZ ☎ 020 3519 1680, ⓦ citizenm.com; ⊖ Southwark; map p.88. One of a slick European chain that also has branches near Tower Hill and Shoreditch. The modern rooms are pod-like, but well designed, with big windows, big beds and touch-tablet controls, and the buzzy canteen/bar is handy. **£160**

KENSINGTON AND CHELSEA

Aster House 3 Sumner Place, SW7 3EE ☎ 020 7581 5888, ⓦ asterhouse.com; ⊖ South Kensington; map p.92. Set on a white-stuccoed South Ken street, this upmarket B&B has thirteen rooms, all en suite but of varying sizes, decorated in a chintzy, traditional style. One opens out onto the pretty back garden. A copious buffet breakfast is served in a sunny conservatory. **£240**

★ **Main House** 6 Colville Rd, W11 2BP ☎ 020 7221 9691, ⓦ themainhouse.co.uk; ⊖ Notting Hill Gate; map p.92. Homely, and a tad bohemian, this guesthouse offers huge suites (one with two bedrooms), covering a floor each. No breakfast, but there's a fridge for guests' use (along with all manner of extras) and you can have tea/ coffee brought to your room. Three-night minimum. **£130**

Nadler Kensington 25 Courtfield Gardens, SW5 0PG ☎ 020 7244 2255, ⓦ thenadler.com/kensington.shtml; ⊖ Earl's Court; map p.92. Good-value contemporary accommodation, with attention to detail but no fussy extras. The 65 rooms range from bijou singles via "luxury bunks" to

1

deluxe; all have mini-kitchens and a choice of pillows. A good choice for families. There are two more Nadlers, in St James's (see p.112) and Soho (see p.112). **£165**

Twenty Nevern Square 20 Nevern Square, SW5 9PD ☎ 020 7565 9555, ⓦ 20nevernsquare.mayflower collection.com; ⊖ Earl's Court; map p.92. In an area of bog-standard B&Bs, this small hotel is a more interesting alternative, strewn with Oriental and European antiques. Rooms are en suite; some, however, are teeny, and others can be noisy. Buffet breakfast included. **£150**

Vancouver Studios 30 Prince's Square, W2 4NJ ☎ 020 7243 1270, ⓦ vancouverstudios.co.uk; ⊖ Bayswater; map p.92. Good-value self-catering suites (some with balconies) in a grand old Victorian townhouse with maid service, a walled garden and a resident cat. Those at the back are quietest. **£149**

NORTH LONDON

Hampstead Village Guesthouse 2 Kemplay Rd, NW3 1SY ☎ 020 7435 8679, ⓦ hampsteadguesthouse.com; ⊖ Hampstead; map p.56. Prettily located on a quiet residential street between Hampstead Village and the Heath, this is an unconventional guesthouse in a family home. Rooms (most en suite) are full of character, crammed with books, pictures and personal mementos. Breakfast costs £10. One-night bookings cost £5 (Mon–Fri) or £10 (Sat) more. **£105**

SOUTH LONDON

Number 16 16 St Alfege Passage, SE10 9JS ☎ 020 8853 4337, ⓦ st-alfeges.co.uk; ⊖ Cutty Sark DLR; map p.88. Behind Hawksmoor's St Alfege church, this Greenwich B&B – owned by a flamboyant ex-antique dealer/actor – offers a warm welcome, offbeat flair and the feel of being in a slightly eccentric home from home. **£140**

HOSTELS

Youth Hostel Association (YHA) hostels (ⓦ yha.org.uk) are generally the cleanest, most efficiently run in the capital. However, they often charge more than private hostels, and tend to get booked up months in advance. Independent hostels are cheaper and more relaxed, but can be less reliable in terms of facilities – some are noisy, not that clean, and essentially little more than places to flop after partying all night. A good website for booking independent places online is ⓦ hostelworld.com/hostels/London.

YHA HOSTELS

★ **Central** 104 Bolsover St, W1W 5NU ☎ 0345 371 9154, ⓦ yha.org.uk/hostel/london-central; ⊖ Great Portland Street; map p.56. Secure, clean 300-bed hostel, in a surprisingly quiet West End location, with a kitchen, 24hr café and bar. Most dorms, and some doubles, are en-suite; others have showers next door. Dorms **£35**, doubles **£89**

Earl's Court 38 Bolton Gardens, SW5 0AQ ☎ 0345 371 9114, ⓦ yha.org.uk/hostel/london-earls-court; ⊖ Earl's Court; map.p.92. Buzzy, busy 186-bed hostel with kitchen, café, lounge and patio garden. Some doubles are en suite. Dorms **£32**, doubles **£79**

Oxford Street 14 Noel St, W1F 8GJ ☎ 0345 371 9133, ⓦ yha.org.uk/hostel/london-oxford-street; ⊖ Oxford Circus; map p.60. The Soho location and modest size (around 105 beds) mean this hostel tends to be full year-round. The atmosphere can be party central, but it's pretty family-friendly. There's a café, kitchen, dining room and bar. No en suites. Dorms **£35**, doubles **£85**

St Pancras 79–81 Euston Rd, NW1 2QE ☎ 0345 371 9344, ⓦ yha.org.uk/hostel/london-st-pancras; ⊖ King's Cross St Pancras; map p.72. This hostel, near the train station on the busy Euston Rd, has nearly two hundred beds. Dorms and private rooms are clean, bright and double-glazed, and some are en suite. No kitchen, but there's a café. Dorms **£34**, doubles **£85**

St Paul's 36 Carter Lane, EC4V 5AB ☎ 0345 371 9012, ⓦ yha.org.uk/hostel/london-st-pauls; ⊖ St Paul's; map p.78. A 213-bed hostel in a grand old school building opposite St Paul's Cathedral. Dorms sleep up to eleven; all facilities are shared, including for the private rooms. Café, but no kitchen. Dorms **£30**, doubles **£79**

Thameside 20 Salter Rd, SE16 5PR ☎ 0345 371 9756, ⓦ yha.org.uk/hostel/london-thameside; ⊖ Rotherhithe; map p.88. Huge purpose-built hostel in a quiet spot near the river. A 15min walk from the tube, it often has space when more central places are full. All dorms (sleeping up to eleven) and private rooms are en suite. Self-catering is available, and there's a simple café-bar. Dorms **£25**, doubles **£69**

INDEPENDENT HOSTELS

Clink 78 78 King's Cross Rd, WC1X 9QG ☎ 020 7183 9400, ⓦ clinkhostels.com; ⊖ King's Cross St Pancras; map p.72. Occupying a Victorian magistrates' court, this huge party hostel has plenty of jazzed-up period features (you can even stay in one of the tiny old prison cells). It can get noisy – and there's a lively DJ bar – but it's fun if you're feeling sociable. Dorms (four to fourteen beds; some pods; some en suite) include women-only options, and there are private singles/twins (some en suite). Kitchen facilities (not for breakfast), internet lounge and travel shop, plus continental breakfast for £1. They have a smaller, quieter sister property, *Clink 261*, down the road. Dorms **£25**, twins **£90**

The Dictionary Hostel 10–20 Kingsland Rd, E2 8DA ☎ 020 7613 2784, ⓦ thedictionaryhostel.com; ⊖ Old Street; map p.83. This is a friendly, party hostel, as you'd expect from its Shoreditch location. There's a café, bar, kitchen and roof terrace, plus a good free breakfast. The dorms (four to sixteen beds, some women-only) and doubles (with TVs and tea- and coffee-making facilities) look good, with whitewashed walls and timber floors – most options are en suite. Dorms £22, doubles £70

Meininger 65–67 Queen's Gate, SW7 5JS ☎020 3318 1407, ⓦmeininger-hotels.com; ⊖Gloucester Road; map p.92. Secure, family-friendly hostel, one of a German chain, near the South Ken museums. The 48 rooms include dorms (four to twelve beds), some en suite and some women-only, plus singles and doubles (some en suite, with TV). No kitchen, but there's a bar/bistro, laundry and table tennis. Minimum two-night stay in summer. Dorms £27,

doubles £200

★**Safestay Holland Park** Holland Walk, W8 7QU ☎020 7870 9629, ⓦsafestay.com; ⊖Holland Park; map p.92. This bright hostel, within Holland Park, is a smart choice. The unisex dorms, which sleep four to 33, are clean, with good beds (with curtains and reading lights) and showers; the private twins (some en suite) have TVs. There's a garden, lounge and pool room, a café-bar and laundry, but no self-catering. Families welcome. Dorms £23, twins £80

EATING

London is a great city for eating out. You can sample any kind of **cuisine** here, from Pakistani to Japanese, Modern British to fusion. And it needn't be expensive – even in the fanciest restaurants, set menus (most often served at lunch) can be a great deal, and sharing plates can be a godsend if you want to cut costs. The city's dynamic **street food** scene, meanwhile, with food trucks, carts and pop-up stalls dishing up artisan food at low prices, offers an amazing diversity. Keep track of the ever-shifting scene on ⓦkerbfood.com, ⓦstreetfeastlondon.com and ⓦrealfoodfestival.co.uk. Bear in mind also that many pubs serve food, from simple pub grub to haute cuisine – check out the **gastropubs** in our Drinking section (see p.120).

WESTMINSTER

CAFÉ

Café in the Crypt St Martin-in-the-Fields, Trafalgar Square, WC2N 5DN ☎020 7766 1158, ⓦstmartin-in-the-fields.org; ⊖Charing Cross; map p.60. This handy café – below the church, in the eighteenth-century crypt – is a nice spot at which to fill up. The daily-changing selection focuses on home-made British comfort food, plus soups, salads and puds. Live jazz Wed 8pm. Mon & Tues 8am–8pm, Wed 8am–10.30pm (jazz ticket holders only after 6.30pm), Thurs–Sat 8am–9pm, Sun 11am–6pm.

RESTAURANT

★**Lorne** 76 Wilton Rd, SW1V 1DE ☎020 3327 0210, ⓦlornerestaurant.co.uk; ⊖Victoria; map p.60. Modern British food made with farm-fresh seasonal ingredients; the intriguing menu lists dishes such as cod with curried peas, sea herbs, mussels and onion rings. Mains from £19; one-/two-course lunch menus £15/£22. Mon 6.30–9.30pm, Tues–Sat noon–2.30pm & 6.30–9.30pm.

MAYFAIR AND MARYLEBONE

CAFÉS

Patisserie Valerie 105 Marylebone High St, W1U 4RS ☎020 7935 6240, ⓦpatisserie-valerie.co.uk; ⊖Bond Street; map p.92. Founded as Swiss-run *Maison Sagne* in the 1920s, and preserving its glorious decor, the café is now run by Soho's fab patissiers (see p.116). They do light lunches and brunch dishes (£6–14), but the plump, creamy cakes are the stars. Mon–Fri 7am–8pm, Sat 8am–8pm, Sun 8.30am–7pm.

Tibits 12–14 Heddon St, W1B 4DA ☎020 7758 4112, ⓦtibits.co.uk; ⊖Piccadilly Circus; map p.60. Rather glam veggie/vegan café (Tues is totally vegan) in a restaurant-packed lane, offering self-service salads, soups,

hot dishes and desserts from around the world. Pay by weight (£2.40/100g before 6pm, £2.70 after). There's another branch in Southwark. Mon–Wed 9am–10.30pm, Thurs & Fri 9am–midnight, Sat 11.30am–midnight, Sun 11.30am–10.30pm.

The Wolseley 160 Piccadilly, W1J 9EB ☎020 7499 6996, ⓦthewolseley.com; ⊖Green Park; map p.60. The 1920s interior is a major draw at this opulent brasserie, which started its days as the showroom for Wolseley cars. The European comfort food is good, if pricey – come for a big breakfast, a bowl of chicken soup with dumplings (£8.75), a half-dozen oysters (from £17), or afternoon tea. Mon–Fri 7am–midnight, Sat 8am–midnight, Sun 8am–11pm.

RESTAURANTS

The Providores and Tapa Room 109 Marylebone High St, W1U 4RX ☎020 7935 6175, ⓦtheprovidores .co.uk; ⊖Baker Street; map p.92. New Zealand chef Peter Gordon serves elegant fusion cuisine at *Providores* (mains from £16 at lunch; £23 at dinner) and, downstairs, anything from cheese platters to beef pesto (£5–22) at the casual *Tapa Room* (no reservations). Providores: Mon–Fri noon–2.45pm & 6–10pm, Sat 10am–2.30pm & 6–10pm, Sun 10am–2.30pm & 6–9.45pm; Tapa Room: Mon–Fri 8am–10.30pm, Sat 9am–3pm & 4–10.30pm, Sun 9am–3pm & 4–10pm.

★**Twist** 42 Crawford St, W1H 1JW ☎020 7723 3377, ⓦtwistkitchen.co.uk; ⊖Edgware Road; map p.92. Superb, rustic-chic restaurant where the Mediterranean/ Eastern/Latin American fusion tapas menu (£10–13), lists such dishes as black-ink gnocchi with langoustine cream or ricotta-stuffed courgette flowers. Charcuterie, cheeses and Josper-grilled meats are also on offer. Mon–Thurs noon–3pm & 6–11pm, Fri noon–3pm & 6–11.30pm, Sat noon–3pm & 6pm–midnight.

1

MORE THAN JUST A CUPPA: AFTERNOON TEA

The capital's most popular venues for a classic **afternoon tea** – sandwiches, scones and cream, cakes and tarts, and, of course, pots of leaf tea – are the top hotels and swanky department stores, though many restaurants offer their own version. Wherever you go, you should book well in advance. Most hotels will expect at least "smart casual attire"; only *The Ritz* insists on jacket and tie. Prices quoted here are for the standard teas; champagne teas, or more substantial high teas, are more expensive.

Berkeley Hotel Wilton Place, SW1X 7RL ☎020 7235 6000, ⊚the-berkeley.co.uk; ⊖Knightsbridge; map p.92. Daily 1.30–5.30pm. £52.

Fortnum & Mason 181 Piccadilly, W1A 1ER ☎020 7734 8040, ⊚fortnumandmason.com; ⊖Green Park; map p.60. Mon–Sat 11am–7pm, Sun 11.30am–6pm. £44.

The Ritz 150 Piccadilly, W1J 9BR ☎020 7300 2345, ⊚theritzlondon.com; ⊖Green Park; map p.60. Daily 11.30am, 1.30pm, 3.30pm, 5.30pm & 7.30pm. £54.

Sketch 9 Conduit St, W1S 2XG ☎020 7659 4500, ⊚sketch.london; ⊖Oxford Circus; map p.60. Daily noon–4.30pm. £58.

SOHO

CAFÉS

★**Bar Italia** 22 Frith St, W1D 4RF ☎020 7437 4520, ⊚baritaliasoho.co.uk; ⊖Leicester Square; map p.60. Tiny espresso bar that's been a Soho institution since the 1950s, keeping many of its original features. Check out the Gaggia coffee machine and the iconic neon sign. Daily 7am–5am.

★**Bun House** 24 Greek St, W1D 4DZ ☎020 8017 9888, ⊚bun.house; ⊖Leicester Square; map p.60. Pretty corner spot for fresh steamed Cantonese buns (all £2.50). Most are filled with umami-packed meats, but there's one veggie option and a couple of decadent dessert buns. Mon–Wed 11am–11pm, Thurs 11am–midnight, Fri & Sat 11am–late, Sun noon–10pm.

Fernandez & Wells 43 Lexington St, W1F 9AL ☎020 734 1546, ⊚fernandezandwells.com; ⊖Piccadilly Circus; map p.60. With its hanging hams and urban-rustic ambience, this café is popular for coffee, breakfasts and cakes to take away or eat in, plus small plates/sandwiches piled high with the best Iberian ingredients. There are four more branches around Central London. Mon–Fri 7.30am–11pm, Sat 9am–11pm, Sun noon–6pm.

★**Maison Bertaux** 28 Greek St, W1D 5DQ ☎020 7437 6007, ⊚maisonbertaux.com; ⊖Leicester Square; map p.60. Open since 1871, this charming, ramshackle and *très* French patisserie is an unmissable Soho experience. The decor is simple, bohemian and a little dog-eared; the cakes, tarts and croissants are to die for. No cards. Mon–Sat 9am–10pm, Sun 9am–8pm.

RESTAURANTS

★**Andrew Edmunds** 46 Lexington St, W1F 0LP ☎020 7437 5708, ⊚andrewedmunds.com; ⊖Piccadilly Circus; map p.60. Romantic, though usually packed, dining room in a Regency townhouse, candlelit at night, with a neighbourhood feel and simple food – roast pigeon

with Swiss chard, say, or fennel, butterbeans and roast tomato. Mains £14–25. No mobile phones. Mon–Fri noon–3.30pm & 5.30–10.45pm, Sat 12.30–3.30pm & 5.30–10.45pm, Sun 1–4pm & 6–10.30pm.

Brasserie Zédel 20 Sherwood St, W1F 7ED ☎020 7734 4888, ⊚brasseriezedel.com; ⊖Piccadilly Circus; map p.60. Huge, opulent Art Deco brasserie offering French classics – onion soup, cassoulet, choucroute – in an irresistibly Gallic atmosphere. There's a street-level café, too, which opens at 8am (Sat and Sun 9am) for coffee and patisserie. Mains from £13; all-day menus £9.75/£12.75/£19.95. Mon–Sat 11.30am–midnight, Sun 11.30am–11pm.

★**Kiln** 58 Brewer St, W1F 9TL (no phone) ⊚kilnsoho .com; ⊖Piccadilly Circus; map p.60. Sophisticated Thai food with twists – a dash of Myanmar here, a little Yunnan there – and amazingly fresh ingredients. Typical dishes (£6–22) on the small-plates menu include jungle curry of turbot and snake beans or five-spice duck and offal with aged soy. Reservations taken for parties of four or more only. Mon–Sat noon–2.30pm & 5–10.30pm, Sun 1–8pm.

Kricket 12 Denman St, W1D 7HH (no phone) ⊚kricket .co.uk; ⊖Piccadilly Circus; map p.60. Born from a pop-up, this terrific Indian place now has a permanent Soho home, all exposed pipes, bare brick and open kitchen. Mix and match creative dishes (£5.50–12) like Keralan fried chicken with curry leaf mayonnaise or smoked aubergine with sesame raita. Reservations are only accepted for groups of four or more. Mon–Sat noon–2.30pm & 5.30–10.30pm.

Mildreds 45 Lexington St, W1F 9AN ☎020 7494 1634, ⊚mildreds.co.uk; ⊖Piccadilly Circus; map p.60. This veggie restaurant, serving tasty, home-made world cuisine – Sri Lankan curries, burritos, stir-fried Asian veg, burgers – is a Soho standby. It's petite, and can get busy, but takes no bookings. Mains £7–12. Branches in Camden and King's Cross. Mon–Sat noon–11pm.

The Palomar 34 Rupert St, W1D 6DN ☎ 020 7439 8777, ⓦ thepalomar.co.uk; ⊖ Piccadilly Circus; map p.60. Contemporary Jerusalem food in a noisy, slick space, with counter seating around the busy kitchen and a dining room at the back. It's a sociable sharing-plate experience, full of hefty flavours – octopus with burnt courgette, labneh and chimichurri, for example. Dishes £4–15. Mon–Sat noon–2.30pm & 5.30–11pm, Sun 12.30–3.30pm & 6–9pm.

★**Polpo** 41 Beak St, W1F 9SB ☎ 020 7734 4479, ⓦ polpo.co.uk; ⊖ Piccadilly Circus; map p.60. The first in what has become a mini-chain, this branch of Polpo serves delicious *cicheti* (bar snacks) and small plates from £3 to £10 – try the crab and chilli linguine or any of the meatballs. Reservations are taken for lunch; dinner bookings are limited. The other London Polpos – in Covent Garden (two branches), Chelsea, Notting Hill and Smithfield – along with, from the same team, *Polpetto* on Berwick St, and *Spuntino*, a hip take on American diner food on Rupert St, are also recommended. Mon–Thurs 8am–11pm, Fri 8am–midnight, Sat 11.30am–midnight, Sun 11.30am–10pm.

COVENT GARDEN
CAFÉS
Homeslice 13 Neal's Yard, WC2H 9DP ☎ 020 3151 7488, ⓦ homeslicepizza.co.uk; ⊖ Covent Garden; map p.60. Rustic-cool pizza joint offering thin-crust, wood-fired gourmet pizzas – pig cheek, collard greens and crackling, say – plus sparkling wine on tap; £4/slice (some varieties only) or £20 for a 20-inch pizza. Branches in Shoreditch and Fitzrovia. Daily noon–11pm.

★**Kastner and Ovens** 52 Floral St, WC2E 9DA ☎ 020 7836 2700, ⓦ facebook.com/kastnerandovens; ⊖ Covent Garden; map p.60. Tiny takeaway turning out home-made fresh salads and heart-warming pies, quiches, soups and hot specials, and an irresistible selection of cakes. Around £7 for three salads. Mon–Fri 8am–4pm.

Rock & Sole Plaice 47 Endell St, WC2H 9AJ ☎ 020 7836 3785, ⓦ rockandsoleplaice.com; ⊖ Covent Garden; map p.60. This venerable fish-and-chip shop is an appealing, no-nonsense place, but it's not cheap – cod and chips costs around £15. Eat in or at a pavement table, or take away. Mon–Sat 11.30am–10.30pm, Sun noon–10pm.

RESTAURANTS
★**Barrafina** 10 Adelaide St, WC2N 4HZ (no phone) ⓦ barrafina.co.uk; ⊖ Charing Cross; map p.60. This terrific tapas bar has won bucketloads of accolades for doing simple food impeccably well. It's fairly meaty – suckling pig, braised ox tongue and herb-crusted rabbit shoulder are typical. Branches in Drury Lane and Soho. No reservations; no groups larger than four. Mon–Sat noon–3pm & 5–11pm, Sun 1–3.30pm & 5.30–10pm.

Dishoom 12 Upper St Martin's Lane, WC2H 9FB ☎ 020 7420 9320, ⓦ dishoom.com; ⊖ Leicester Square; map p.60. Re-creating the atmosphere of the Persian cafés of Old Bombay, *Dishoom* is buzzy and stylish but, most importantly, serves great food – don't miss the black dhal. Mains from £6.50. Very limited reservations. Branches in Shoreditch, King's Cross and near Carnaby Street. Mon–Thurs 8am–11pm, Fri 8am–midnight, Sat 9am–midnight, Sun 9am–11pm.

Flesh & Buns 41 Earlham St, WC2H 9LX ☎ 020 7632 9500, ⓦ bonedaddies.com; ⊖ Covent Garden; map p.60. The boozy, rock'n'roll vibe at this noisy Japanese *izakaya*-style basement restaurant belies the quality of the food: the rice buns are the stars, served with succulent toppings (crispy duck leg £14.20; miso-grilled aubergine £9.70). Mon & Tues noon–3pm & 5–10pm, Wed–Fri noon–3pm & 5–11pm, Sat noon–11pm, Sun noon–9.30pm.

BLOOMSBURY AND KING'S CROSS
CAFÉS
Bloomsbury Coffee House 20 Tavistock Place, WC1H 9RE ☎ 020 7837 2877, ⓦ bloomsburycoffeehouse.co.uk; ⊖ Russell Square; map p.72. Cosy basement café, a popular student haunt, serving breakfasts, home-made savoury dishes, Allpress coffee and cakes. Mon–Fri 8am–4.30pm, Sat & Sun 8am–1.30pm.

Caravan 1 Granary Square, N1C 4AA ☎ 020 7101 7661, ⓦ caravanrestaurants.co.uk; ⊖ King's Cross; map p.72. A trailblazer on the King's Cross dining scene, this buzzy spot, occupying a huge old grain store, serves tempting Modern European/fusion breakfasts, brunches, small plates (from £6.50), gourmet pizza (from £9) and larger mains (from £17.50) to a lively crowd. Expect to see anything from molasses-roasted beets to chaat-masala-braised oxtail. There are branches in Exmouth Market and near Bankside. Mon–Fri 8am–10.30pm, Sat 10am–10.30pm, Sun 10am–4pm.

Diwana Bhel Poori House 121–123 Drummond St, NW1 2HL ☎ 020 7387 5556, ⓦ diwanabph.com; ⊖ Euston; map p.72. On a street lined with cheap Indian restaurants, this South Indian veggie diner wins for its enormous all-you-can-eat lunchtime buffet (£7) – dinners are not nearly as good value. Mon–Sat noon–11.30pm, Sun noon–10.30pm.

RESTAURANTS
Grain Store Granary Square, N1C 4AB ☎ 020 7324 4466, ⓦ grainstore.com; ⊖ King's Cross; map p.72. Warehouse-style restaurant with a strong focus on fresh veg; try oyster mushrooms in vegan XO sauce with wasabi pea coulis and herb tofu. Mains from £13.50; small plates (£3.50–16) served all day. Mon–Fri noon–10.30pm, Sat 10am–10.30pm, Sun 10.30am–3.30pm.

1

★**Noble Rot** 51 Lamb's Conduit St, WC1N 3NB ☎020 7242 8963, ⓦnoblerot.co.uk/wine-bar; ⊖ Russell Square; map p.72. Superlative seasonal food served in a cosy wine bar in a lovely old townhouse. Many dishes have a European accent (Auvergne guinea fowl with sweetcorn and girolles, say). Small plates from £9; mains from £18. Mon–Sat noon–2.30pm & 6–9.30pm.

THE CITY
CAFÉS

★**Breddos Tacos** 82 Goswell Rd, EC1V 7DB ☎020 3535 8301, · ⓦbreddostacos.com; ⊖Barbican; map p.78. High-spirited fusion taqueria, born from an East London food shack, that uses the best British produce in everything from crunchy sweetbread tacos to chanterelle mushroom tostadas. Tacos £2.50–4.50; tostadas around £7; grills £7–20. No reservations. Mon–Sat noon–3pm & 5–10.30pm.

Café Below St Mary-le-Bow Church, Cheapside, EC2V 6AU ☎020 7329 0789, ⓦcafebelow.co.uk; ⊖ St Paul's; map p.78. A rare City gem: a cosy, family-owned café in a Norman church crypt, serving home-cooked bistro-style dishes with creative veggie choices and good hot breakfasts. Lunch mains from £11. Mon–Fri 7.30–10am & 11.30am–2.30pm.

Prufrock Coffee 23–25 Leather Lane, EC1N 7TE ☎020 7242 0467, ⓦprufrockcoffee.com; ⊖Chancery Lane; map p.78. This pared-down shrine to the coffee bean pioneered London's artisan coffee craze. The coffee is great, of course – and there's a short menu of breakfast, lunch and pastries. Mon–Fri 8am–6pm, Sat & Sun 10am–5pm.

RESTAURANTS

Duck & Waffle Heron Tower, 110 Bishopsgate, EC2N 4AY ☎020 3640 7310, ⓦduckandwaffle.com; ⊖Aldgate; map p.78. Forty floors up, this smart place offers amazing City views and hipster comfort food (the signature dish features waffles, duck confit, fried duck egg and mustard maple syrup; £17). Small plates £8–13. Daily 6am–5am.

★**Moro** 34–36 Exmouth Market, EC1R 4QE ☎020 7833 8336, ⓦmoro.co.uk; ⊖ Angel; map p.78. This lovely, lively and warmly decorated restaurant is a place of pilgrimage for disciples of Sam and Sam Clark's Moorish/Mediterranean/ Middle Eastern cuisine. The changing menus are outstanding, especially the lamb dishes and the yoghurt cake. Mains £17.50–24; tapas (from £3.50) are served at the bar all day Mon–Sat. Mon–Sat noon–2.30pm & 5.15–10.45pm (tapas all day), Sun 12.30–3pm.

EAST LONDON
CAFÉS

Brick Lane Beigel Bake 159 Brick Lane, E1 6SB ☎020 7729 0616, ⓦfacebook.com/beigelbake; ⊖Shoreditch High Street; map p.83. Fresh bagels baked on the spot in a basic, much-loved takeaway. They're delicious, and cheap; by far the priciest is the hot salt beef (£4.10), and even smoked salmon and cream cheese is a mere £1.90. Daily 24hr.

★**CookDaily** Shoreditch, 2–10 Bethnal Green Rd, E1 6GY ☎07498 563168, ⓦcookdaily.co.uk; ⊖Shoreditch High Street; map p.83. Among many good eating options in the Boxpark shipping container complex, this cool vegan place is a massive hit for its big, flavour-packed bowls of global food (all £9), served over a half rice/half quinoa mix. Mon–Wed & Sat noon–9pm, Thurs & Fri noon–9.30pm, Sun noon–7pm.

★**E. Pellicci** 332 Bethnal Green Rd, E2 0AG ☎020 7739 4873, ⓦepellicci.com; ⊖Bethnal Green; map p.83. *Pellicci's* caff (open since 1900) is an iconic, family-owned and jubilantly friendly East End institution with its stunning 1940s decor intact, serving hefty fry-ups and good home-made Anglo-Italian grub. Mon–Sat 7am–4pm.

Voodoo Ray's 95 Kingsland High St, E8 2PB ☎020 7249 7865, ⓦvoodoorays.com; ⊖Dalston Junction; map p.83. Grungy late-night drinking dens come and go in Dalston, but *Voodoo Ray's* seems set to stay – a post-party pizza/Margarita joint where the pizzas (from £3.50/slice) are huge and the Margaritas are strong. Branches in Shoreditch, Camden and Peckham. Mon–Wed 5pm–midnight, Thurs 5pm–1am, Fri & Sat noon–3am, Sun noon–midnight.

RESTAURANTS

The Clove Club 380 Old St, EC1V 9LT ☎020 7729 6496, ⓦthecloveclub.com; ⊖Old Street; map p.83. This relatively relaxed, Michelin-starred restaurant offers flawless set menus (lunch five courses, £75; dinner five/nine courses, £75/£110; veggie menus same price), listing innovative British dishes with Scottish accents – the buttermilk-fried chicken with pine salt is a hit. Small plates are served at the bar from 6pm (£5–50), and you can go a la carte at lunch (mains £18–35). Beware, though: the "ticketing" system requires you to pay in advance. Mon 6–10.30pm, Tues–Sat noon–2.15pm & 6–10.30pm.

Lahore Kebab House 2–10 Umberston St, E1 1PY ☎020 7481 9737, ⓦlahore-kebabhouse.com; ⊖Aldgate East; map p.83. Legendary Pakistani kebab house. Go for the lamb cutlets and roti, and turn up hungry. BYOB. Mains £8–16. Daily noon–1am.

★**L'Antica Pizzeria da Michele** 125 Stoke Newington Church St, N16 0UH ☎020 7687 0009, ⓦfacebook.com /damichelelondon; ⊖Stoke Newington; map p.83. In 2016 the best pizza restaurant in Naples (for which read the best pizza restaurant in the world) made its second home in a simple little Stoke Newington space. Just two pizzas are served: the Margherita and the Marinara (without cheese, but with lashings of garlic). In both, the smoky, blistered base perfectly balances that terrific, nuanced tomato sauce. From £8. No reservations; arrive early. Tues–Sat noon–11pm, Sun noon–10.30pm.

Popolo 6 Rivington St, EC2A 3DU ☎020 7729 4299, ⓦpopoloshoreditch.com; ⊖Old Street; map p.78. Convivial spot dishing up gutsy Italian tapas with Spanish and Moorish influences – fresh pasta or risotto, Dorset crab and bottarga salad, labneh with deep-fried olives – around a busy open kitchen or in an upstairs dining room. Plates £4–14. No reservations. Tues & Wed noon–3pm & 5.30–10.30pm, Thurs–Sat noon–3pm & 5.30–11pm.

★**Som Saa** 43a Commercial St, E1 6BD ☎020 7324 7790, ⓦsomsaa.com; ⊖Aldgate East; map p.83. The short menu of regional Thai food served in this revamped warehouse is outstanding (and spicy): try the jungle curry of guinea fowl with garlic and kajron flowers. Sharing plates £7.50–14.50 at lunch, more at dinner. Reservations only for groups larger than four. Mon 6–10.30pm, Tues–Fri noon–2.30pm & 6–10.30pm, Sat noon–3pm & 6–10.30pm.

Sông Quê 134 Kingsland Rd, E2 8DY ☎020 7613 3222, ⓦsongque.co.uk; ⊖Hoxton; map p.83. In a street heaving with budget Vietnamese restaurants, this basic place is a favourite for steaming *phô* (from £9) and spicy seafood. Mon–Fri noon–3pm & 5.30–11pm, Sat noon–11pm, Sun noon–10.30pm.

St John Bread and Wine 94–96 Commercial St, E1 6LZ ☎020 7251 0848, ⓦstjohngroup.uk.com/spitalfields; ⊖Liverpool Street; map p.83. A simpler offshoot of the famed *St John*, serving the same superlative British food on a regularly changing menu – featuring offal, pig's cheek and the like, but also wonderful veg and fish dishes, and simple breakfasts. Sharing plates £5–21. Mon 8–11.30am, noon–4pm & 6–10pm, Tues–Fri 8–11.30am, noon–4pm & 6–11pm, Sat 8.30am–noon, 1–4pm & 6–11pm, Sun 8.30am–noon, 1–4pm & 6–10pm.

THE SOUTH BANK AND BANKSIDE
CAFÉS
Maltby Street Market Maltby St, SE1 3PA ⓦmaltby .st; ⊖London Bridge; map p.88. Within walking distance of Borough Market (see p.130), this smaller foodie hotspot huddles under the railway arches south of Tower Bridge. The stalls – plus some good bars and restaurants – spread along Maltby and Druid streets (ⓦdruid.st) down to the Spa Terminus (ⓦwww.spa -terminus.co.uk); most action is on the Ropewalk. Sat 9am–4pm, Sun 11am–4pm.

Scooter Caffè 132 Lower Marsh, SE1 7AE ☎020 7620 1421, ⓦfacebook.com/scootercaffe; ⊖Waterloo; map p.86. This quirky little coffee house, filled with bric-a-brac, vintage furniture and scooter memorabilia, is a relaxed spot to drink good coffee and linger. At night it morphs into a boho bar. Mon–Thurs 8.30am–11pm, Fri 8.30am–midnight, Sat 10am–midnight, Sun 10am–11pm.

RESTAURANTS
Laughing Gravy 154 Blackfriars Rd, SE1 8EN ☎020 7998 1707, ⓦthelaughinggravy.co.uk; ⊖Southwark; map p.86. There's a cosy neighbourhood vibe at this upmarket brasserie, which serves bistro food – braised duck pappardelle; pan-fried cod; roast dinners – in a brick-walled dining room. Mains £12.50–25. Mon–Thurs noon–3pm & 5–10pm, Fri noon–3pm & 5–10.30pm, Sat noon–4pm & 5–10.30pm, Sun noon–4.30pm.

★**Padella** 6 Southwark St, SE10 1TQ (no phone) ⓦpadella.co; ⊖London Bridge; map p.88. The open kitchen at this bright, contemporary pasta place by Borough Market turns out wonderful, authentic fresh pasta. A small plate of gnocchi with sage and butter costs just £4, while tagliarini with crab, chilli and lemon is one of the most expensive dishes at £11.50. BYOB; no reservations. Mon–Sat noon–4pm & 5–10pm, Sun noon–5pm.

KENSINGTON AND CHELSEA
CAFÉS
★**Books for Cooks** 4 Blenheim Crescent, W11 1NN ☎020 7221 1992, ⓦbooksforcooks.com; ⊖Ladbroke Grove; map p.92. There's a cute dining area inside this excellent cookery bookshop. Get there early to grab a seat for the three-course set lunch (£7). Tues–Sat 10am–6pm; food noon–1.30pm.

Capote y Toros 157 Old Brompton Rd, SW5 0LJ ☎020 7373 0567, ⓦcambiodetercio.co.uk; ⊖Gloucester Road; map p.92. The emphasis at this tapas bar is on Spain's sherries, with 125 on offer, along with modern tapas (£6–29). Nightly flamenco guitar. Tues–Sat 6–11.30pm.

Lisboa Patisserie 57 Golborne Rd, W10 5NR ☎020 8968 5242; ⊖Ladbroke Grove; map p.92. Authentic Portuguese *pastelaria*, a perfect post-Portobello Rd pit stop, with coffee, croissants and the best *pasteis de nata* (custard tarts) this side of Lisbon. Daily 7.30am–7.30pm.

RESTAURANTS
Dinner Mandarin Oriental Hotel, 66 Knightsbridge, SW1X 7LA ☎020 7201 3833, ⓦdinnerbyheston.com; ⊖Knightsbridge; map p.92. Though this is a Heston Blumenthal restaurant, he doesn't actually cook here – the head chef worked with him at the *Fat Duck* – and there is less emphasis on flashy molecular cuisine. However, the creative food, using old English recipes, is as intriguing as you'd expect; try the salamagundy or the "meat fruit". Mains £28–90; three-course weekday lunch menu £45. Mon–Fri noon–2pm & 6–10.15pm, Sat & Sun noon–2.30pm & 6.30–10.30pm.

Hereford Road 3 Hereford Rd, W2 4AB ☎020 7727 1144, ⓦherefordroad.org; ⊖Baywsater; map p.92. The contemporary dining room, with bustling open kitchen, is a smart setting for accomplished English cooking – beetroot, sorrel and boiled egg; braised duck leg with turnips, and

1

such like. Mains £12–16.50; two-/three-course weekday lunch menus £13.50/£15.50. Mon–Sat noon–3pm & 6–10.30pm, Sun noon–4pm & 6–10pm.

★**Medlar** 438 Kings Rd, SW10 0LJ ☎020 7349 1900, ⓦmedlarrestaurant.co.uk; ⊖Fulham Broadway; map p.92. Superlative Modern European food – roast stone bass with palourde clams and pancetta, for example – served in a relaxed, elegant dining room. It's prix fixe, and excellent value: one-/two-/three-course lunch menus £25/£30/£35, two-/three-course dinner £41/£49 (£35 on Sun). Mon–Fri noon–3pm & 6.30–10.30pm, Sat noon–3pm & 6–10.30pm, Sun noon–3pm & 6–9.30pm.

Nama 110 Talbot Rd, W11 1JR ☎020 7313 4638, ⓦnamafoods.com; ⊖Westbourne Park; map p.92. Creative raw vegan food with global accents – raspberry gazpacho; truffle pasta; kohlrabi ravioli – with lots of juices, smoothies and infusions. Mains £9–16.50. Tues & Wed noon–10pm, Thurs noon–11pm, Fri & Sat 9am–11pm, Sun 9am–6pm.

NORTH LONDON
CAFÉS
Brew House Kenwood House, Hampstead Lane, NW3 7JR ☎020 8348 4073, ⓦsearcyskenwoodhouse.co.uk; ⊖Highgate; map p.56. The food isn't amazing – though they do a good line in cakes – but the location, in the huge, sunny garden courtyard of Kenwood House, more than compensates. Daily: spring & summer 9am–6pm; rest of year 9am–4pm.

Louis Patisserie 32 Heath St, NW3 6TE ☎020 7435 9908; ⊖Hampstead; map p.56. For more than fifty years this tiny tearoom/patisserie has been serving sticky cakes, tea and coffee to a local crowd. They may now play background music, and some Hungarian specialities have dropped off the menu, but it's still a refreshingly uncorporate choice. Daily 8am–6pm.

RESTAURANTS
Jin Kichi 73 Heath St, NW3 6UG ☎020 7794 6158, ⓦjinkichi.com; ⊖Hampstead; map p.56. Book ahead for this tiny, homely and busy neighbourhood Japanese diner,

which specializes in charcoal-grilled *yakitori* (skewers). The sushi, noodles and other Japanese staples are good, too. Skewers from £2; other dishes from £4. Tues–Sat 12.30–2.10pm & 6–11pm, Sun 12.30–2.10pm & 6–10pm.

Namaaste Kitchen 64 Parkway, NW1 7AH ☎020 7485 5977, ⓦnamaastekitchen.co.uk; ⊖Camden Town; map p.56. You'll find unusual dishes, including wild rabbit *achari* with aubergine compote, at this superb contemporary Indian and Pakistani restaurant. Mains £12–23; one-/two-/three-course lunch menus £8.50/£10/£12.50. Mon–Thurs noon–3pm & 5.30–11.30pm, Fri & Sat noon–11.30pm, Sun noon–11pm.

SOUTH LONDON
RESTAURANT
Naughty Piglets 28 Brixton Water Lane, SW2 1PE ☎020 7274 7796, ⓦnaughtypiglets.co.uk; map p.56. Small, convivial restaurant with a cosy local vibe, dishing up flavour-packed small plates (£7–16) – pork belly with Korean spices, say, or sardine lasagne with black olives – and "low intervention" wines. Tues & Wed 6–10pm, Thurs noon–2.30pm & 6–10pm, Fri & Sat noon–3pm & 6–10pm, Sun noon–3pm.

WEST LONDON
CAFÉ
Hollyhock Terrace Gardens, Petersham Rd, TW10 6UX ☎020 8948 6555; ⊖Richmond; map p.92. This laidback fairtrade vegetarian café, hidden away in Richmond's flower-filled Terrace Gardens, is perfect for light lunches or coffee and cakes on the shady terrace overlooking the river. Daily 9am–dusk.

RESTAURANT
Chez Lindsay 11 Hill Rise, Richmond, TW10 6UQ ☎020 8948 7473, ⓦchezlindsay.co.uk; ⊖Richmond; map p.92. Small, bright, riverside Breton restaurant, serving *galettes*, crêpes and French mains including steak frites and oysters. *Galettes* from £5.25, mains £12.50–25; two-/three-course menus (Mon–Fri noon–7pm) £12.75/£15.75. Mon–Sat noon–11pm, Sun noon–10pm.

DRINKING

WESTMINSTER
St Stephen's Tavern 10 Bridge St, SW1A 2JR ☎020 7925 2286, ⓦststephenstavern.co.uk; ⊖Westminster; map p.60. Opulent Victorian pub opposite the Houses of Parliament and wall to wall with civil servants and MPs. Good real ales, plus fish and chips and pies. Mon–Sat 10am–11pm, Sun 10am–10pm.

MAYFAIR AND MARYLEBONE
The Golden Eagle 59 Marylebone Lane, W1U 2NY ☎020 7935 3228; ⊖Bond Street; map p.92. Proper

old one-room neighbourhood pub – a delight in this swanky area – with a good range of real ales, and regular singalongs around the piano (Tues, Thurs & Fri). Mon–Sat 11am–11pm, Sun noon–10pm.

The Gunmakers 33 Aybrook St, W1U 4AP ☎020 7487 4937, ⓦthegunmakersmarylebone.co.uk; ⊖Bond Street; map p.92. This place is all wood panelling, Churchill memorabilia and an awful lot of framed bullets. Decent range of ales (including a few crafts), plus a brief menu of dirty burgers. Mon–Sat 10am–11pm, Sun noon–10pm; kitchen Mon–Sat noon–9pm, Sun noon–5pm.

1

The Windmill 6–8 Mill St, W1S 2AZ ☎ 020 7491 8050, ⓦ windmillmayfair.co.uk; ⊖ Oxford Circus; map p.60. Convivial pub just off Regent St, a perfect retreat for exhausted shoppers. The Young's beers are good, as are the award-winning pies. Mon–Fri 11am–11pm, Sat noon–11pm, Sun noon–6pm.

Ye Grapes 16 Shepherd Market, W1J 7QQ ☎ 020 7493 4216; ⊖ Green Park; map p.60. Located in Shepherd Market, a charming corner of Mayfair, it's the location that really makes this pub. If it's too busy, try the *King's Arms*, also in Shepherd Market. Mon–Sat 11am–11pm, Sun noon–10pm.

SOHO

The Blue Posts 22 Berwick St, W1F 0QA ☎ 020 7437 5008; ⊖ Tottenham Court Road; map p.60. Real old-school Soho – the "governor" wears a tie, pulls pints from a relatively small selection of ales and lagers, and offers only the finest selection of peanuts and crisps. Popular with the local media crowd. Mon–Fri 11am–11pm.

Dog & Duck 18 Bateman St, W1D 3AJ ☎ 020 7494 0697, ⓦ bit.ly/DogDuck; ⊖ Tottenham Court Road; map p.60. Tiny Nicholson's pub that retains much of its old character, beautiful Victorian tiling and mosaics, a range of real ales and a loyal clientele. If it gets too busy downstairs, head upstairs to the George Orwell Bar (he used to drink here). Daily 10am–11pm.

★**The French House** 49 Dean St, W1D 5BG ☎ 020 7437 2799, ⓦ frenchhousesoho.com; ⊖ Leicester Square; map p.60. This cosy pub has been a boho-Soho institution since Belgian Victor Berlemont bought the place shortly before World War I. Strictly no music or TV, but plenty of classic Soho barflies and no end of Free French and literary associations. Beer – lager only – famously comes by the half pint; wine and champagne a speciality. Mon–Sat noon–11pm, Sun noon–10pm.

Two Floors 3 Kingly St, W1B 5PD ☎ 020 7439 1007, ⓦ twofloors.com; ⊖ Oxford Circus; map p.60. An unlikely combo: craft ales and cocktails in the pubby street-level bar and a dimly lit tiki bar in the basement – yet this place pulls it off with aplomb. Mon–Thurs noon–11pm, Fri & Sat noon–midnight, Sun noon–10pm.

COVENT GARDEN AND THE STRAND

Cross Keys 31 Endell St, WC2H 9BA ☎ 020 7836 5185, ⓦ crosskeyscoventgarden.com; ⊖ Covent Garden; map p.60. You'll do well to find a seat in this cosy, foliage-drenched Covent Garden favourite, which is stuffed with copper pots, brass instruments, paintings and memorabilia. Most beer is from Brodie's in Leyton. Mon–Sat 11am–11pm, Sun noon–10pm.

Gordon's 47 Villiers St, WC2N 6NE ☎ 020 7930 1408, ⓦ gordonswinebar.com; ⊖ Charing Cross; map p.60.

Cavernous, shabby, atmospheric old wine bar, open since 1890 and specializing in ports, sherries and Madeiras; the cheese platters are legend. It's a favourite with local office workers, who spill outdoors in the summer. Mon–Sat 11am–11pm, Sun noon–10pm.

★**The Harp** 47 Chandos Place, WC2N 4HS ☎ 020 7836 0291, ⓦ harpcoventgarden.com; ⊖ Leicester Square; map p.60. For such a sliver of a pub, they pack in an excellent array of ales and ciders. The tiny bar is invariably packed; there's more room in the comfortably battered upstairs. Mon–Thurs 10am–11pm, Fri & Sat 10am–midnight, Sun noon–10pm.

Lamb & Flag 33 Rose St, WC2E 9EB ☎ 020 7497 9504, ⓦ lambandflagcoventgarden.co.uk; ⊖ Leicester Square; map p.60. More than three hundred years old, this agreeably tatty Fuller's pub, tucked down an alley between Garrick and Floral streets, is perennially popular. Mon–Sat 11am–11pm, Sun noon–10pm.

BLOOMSBURY AND KING'S CROSS

The Duke 7 Roger St, WC1N 2PB ☎ 020 7242 7230, ⓦ dukepub.co.uk; ⊖ Russell Square; map p.72. Lovely little neighbourhood pub with an unusual, unforced Art Deco flavour and lots of interwar design details. Its discreet location keeps the crowd in the small bar manageable. Mon–Sat noon–11pm.

★**The Euston Tap** 190 Euston Rd, NW1 2EF ☎ 020 3137 8837, ⓦ eustontap.com; ⊖ Euston; map p.72. A pleasingly peculiar set-up, the *Euston Tap* comprises two of the station's original entrance lodges, separated by a bus lane. A pair of taprooms are tucked within these somewhat tomb-like little spaces, serving cask and keg ales plus ciders and perries. Daily noon–11pm.

The Lamb 94 Lamb's Conduit St, WC1N 3LZ ☎ 020 7405 0713, ⓦ thelamblondon.com; ⊖ Russell Square; map p.72. Well-preserved Victorian pub with mirrors, polished wood, leather banquettes and etched-glass "snob" screens. Rather peaceful, as there's no music or TV. Mon–Wed 11am–11pm, Thurs–Sat 11am–midnight, Sun noon–10pm.

Queen's Head 66 Acton St, WC1X 9NB ☎ 020 7713 5772, ⓦ queensheadlondon.com; ⊖ King's Cross; map p.72. Attractive and laidback local offering cheese, chunky pies and charcuterie alongside craft beers and ciders. Occasional live jazz and piano. Mon & Sun noon–11pm, Tues–Sat noon–midnight.

HOLBORN

Princess Louise 208 High Holborn, WC1V 7EP ☎ 020 7405 8816, ⓦ princesslouisepub.co.uk; ⊖ Holborn; map p.56. This Sam Smith's pub features six rooms of gold-trimmed mirrors, gorgeous mosaics and fine moulded ceilings – even the toilets are listed. Mon–Fri 11am–11pm, Sat noon–11pm, Sun noon–6pm.

Ye Olde Mitre 1 Ely Court, EC1N 6SJ ☎ 020 7405 4751, ⓦ yeoldemitreholburn.co.uk; ⊖ Chancery Lane; map p.78. Hidden down a tiny alleyway off Hatton Garden, this Fuller's pub dates back to 1546, although it was rebuilt in the eighteenth century. The low-ceilinged, wood-panelled rooms are packed with history and the ales are good. Mon–Fri 11am–11pm.

THE CITY

The Blackfriar 174 Queen Victoria St, EC4V 4EG ☎ 020 7236 5474; ⊖ Blackfriars; map p.78. Quirky, relaxing Nicholson's pub, with Art Nouveau marble friezes of boozy monks and a highly decorated alcove – all original, dating from 1905. Mon–Fri 10am–11pm, Sat 9am–11pm, Sun noon–10pm.

★ **The Eagle** 159 Farringdon Rd, EC1R 3AL ☎ 020 7837 1353, ⓦ theeaglefarringdon.co.uk; ⊖ Farringdon; map p.78. The original and still arguably the best of London's gastropubs. They offer a fairly limited selection of beers – but, wow, the food. Prepared in the tiny kitchen behind the bar, the Mediterranean-tinged dishes come out perfect time after time. Mon–Sat noon–11pm, Sun noon–5pm.

★ **Jerusalem Tavern** 55 Britton St, EC1M 5UQ ☎ 020 7490 4281, ⓦ stpetersbrewery.co.uk; ⊖ Farringdon; map p.78. Tiny converted Georgian coffee house – the frontage dates from 1810 – with a raffish, sociable character. The excellent draught beers are from St Peter's Brewery in Suffolk. Mon–Fri 11am–11pm.

The Lamb Tavern 10–12 Leadenhall Market, EC3V 1LR ☎ 020 7626 2454, ⓦ lambtavernleadenhall.com; ⊖ Monument; map p.78. In Leadenhall Market, this historic Young's pub is almost exclusively standing room only (both inside and out) for a suited local crowd. The basement bar, *Old Tom's*, is a little more on trend, serving London beers and artisan cheese and meat platters. Mon–Fri 11am–11pm.

Three Kings 7 Clerkenwell Close, EC1R 0DY ☎ 020 7253 0483, ⓦ bit.ly/ThreeKingsClerk; ⊖ Farringdon; map p.78. Perennial favourite north of Clerkenwell Green, with an eclectic interior, big windows and two small rooms upstairs perfect for lingering. Interesting craft beers and food, too. It's next to *The Crown*, which is also worth a trip. Mon–Fri noon–11pm, Sat 5–11pm.

Ye Olde Cheshire Cheese 145 Fleet St, EC4A 2BU ☎ 020 7353 6170, ⓦ bit.ly/YeOldeCheshire; ⊖ Temple; map p.78. This seventeenth-century watering hole – famous for its historic literary associations, with patrons including Dickens and Dr Johnson – is now a Sam Smith's pub. Its dark-panelled bars and real fires make it a cosy maze, popular – some would say too popular – with tourists and locals alike. Mon–Fri 11am–11pm, Sat noon–11pm.

EAST LONDON AND DOCKLANDS

The Carpenter's Arms 73 Cheshire St, E2 6EG ☎ 020 7739 6342, ⓦ carpentersarmsfreehouse.com; ⊖ Shoreditch High Street; map p.83. Iconic East End pub – the Kray twins bought it for their dear old mum – with an excellent range of craft lagers and ales and home-made food. A friendly, relaxed, low-lit place that feels wonderfully set apart. Mon–Wed 4–11pm, Thurs & Sun noon–11pm, Fri & Sat noon–midnight.

★ **The George Tavern** 373 Commercial Rd, E1 0LA ☎ 020 7790 7335, ⓦ bit.ly/GeorgeTav; ⊖ Whitechapel; map p.83. Arty, shabby, dilapidated pub, packed with history and lovely period detail. There's a bohemian theatre space, and regular, very cool, live music. Mon–Thurs & Sun 4pm–midnight, Fri & Sat 4pm–3am.

The Gun 27 Coldharbour, E14 9NS ☎ 020 7515 5222, ⓦ thegundocklands.com; ⊖ Canary Wharf DLR; map p.88. Legendary dockers' pub, once the haunt of Lord Nelson, *The Gun* is now a classy Fuller's gastropub, with a cosy back bar and a deck offering unrivalled views. Mon–Sat 11am–midnight, Sun 11am–11pm.

Happiness Forgets 8–9 Hoxton Square, N1 6NU ☎ 020 7613 0325, ⓦ happinessforgets.com; ⊖ Old Street; map p.78. Candlelit, bare-brick bar with a Hoxton-via-New York vibe, serving fashionably obscure, serious cocktails to a cool crowd. Has an excellent sister bar in Stoke Newington (ⓦ originalsin.bar). Daily 5–11pm.

Sager + Wilde 193 Hackney Rd, E2 8JL ☎ 020 8127 7330, ⓦ sagerandwilde.com; ⊖ Hoxton; map p.83. Gentrification doesn't get much starker. What was formerly an England flag-draped, locals-only boozer is now this sleek wine bar that makes a lovely stop post-Columbia Road flower market. Across the road, *The Marksman* has won plaudits for its food. Mon–Wed 5pm–midnight, Thurs & Fri 5pm–1am, Sat noon–1am, Sun noon–midnight.

Ten Bells 84 Commercial St, E1 6LY ☎ 020 7247 7532, ⓦ tenbells.com; ⊖ Shoreditch High Street; map p.83. Stripped-down pub with Jack the Ripper associations, great Victorian tiling and a hip, young crowd. Meat and cheese plates are on offer, and there's a cocktail bar upstairs. Pub Mon–Wed noon–midnight, Thurs–Sat noon–1am, Sun 1–9pm; bar Tues & Wed 5pm–midnight, Thurs & Fri 5pm–1am, Sat noon–1am, Sun 1–9pm.

Town of Ramsgate 62 Wapping High St, E1W 2PN ☎ 020 7481 8000; ⊖ Wapping; map p.88. Narrow, medieval pub by Wapping Old Stairs, which once led down to Execution Dock. Captain Blood was discovered here with the Crown Jewels under his cloak. Mon–Sat noon–midnight, Sun noon–10pm.

SOUTH BANK AND BANKSIDE

★ **Anchor & Hope** 36 The Cut, SE1 8LP ☎ 020 7928 9898, ⓦ anchorandhopepub.co.uk; ⊖ Southwark; map p.86. Superb gastropub dishing up excellent, comforting grub – slow-roasted meats, terrines, soufflés, heritage veggies and mouth-watering puds. You can't book (except on Sun), so the bar is basically the waiting room. Mon 5–11pm, Tues–Sat 11am–11pm, Sun 12.30–3.15pm; kitchen Mon 6–10.30pm, Tues–Sat noon–2.30pm & 6–10.30pm, Sun 12.30–3.15pm.

The George 77 Borough High St, SE1 1NH ☎ 020 7407 2056, ⓦ george-southwark.co.uk; ⊖ Borough; map p.88. London's only surviving galleried coaching inn, dating from the seventeenth century and owned by the National Trust. Managed by Greene King, it serves a decent range of real ales (stick to drinks), and is usually mobbed by tourists. Mon–Sat 11am–11pm, Sun noon–10pm.

★**Kings Arms** 25 Roupell St, SE1 8TB ☎ 020 7207 0784, ⓦ thekingsarmslondon.co.uk; ⊖ Waterloo; map p.86. Set on one of Waterloo's impossibly cute terraced Georgian backstreets, this terrific local has a traditional drinking area with an excellent range of beers at the front, and a conservatory-style space with a large open fire and long wooden tables at the rear, where they also serve Thai food. Mon–Sat 11am–11pm, Sun noon–10pm.

The Roebuck 50 Great Dover St, SE1 4YG ☎ 020 7357 7324, ⓦ theroebuck.net; ⊖ Borough; map p.56. Big, airy pub with distressed walls covered with colourful prints. There's an excellent range of beers and a real mix of drinkers; the upstairs room – where Charlie Chaplin performed as a boy – hosts lively events. Above-average pub grub (£10–15) and lots of pavement seating. Mon–Thurs noon–midnight, Fri & Sat noon–1am, Sun noon–11pm; kitchen Mon–Fri noon–2pm & 5–10pm, Sat noon–4pm & 5–10pm, Sun noon–9pm.

KENSINGTON AND CHELSEA

Churchill Arms 119 Kensington Church St, W8 7LN ☎ 020 7727 4242, ⓦ churchillarmskensington.co.uk; ⊖ Notting Hill Gate; map p.92. Justifiably popular, flower-festooned local serving Fuller's beers and passable Thai food in a quirky, eclectic space. Mon–Wed 11am–11pm, Thurs–Sat 11am–midnight, Sun noon–10pm.

Cooper's Arms 87 Flood St, SW3 5TB ☎ 020 7376 3120, ⓦ coopersarms.co.uk; ⊖ Sloane Square; map p.92. This revamped pub is bright and airy, with Mediterranean tiles behind the bar, ornithological paintings everywhere and gramophone horns for light shades. There's a decent range of ales and ambitious pub grub. Mon–Sat noon–11pm, Sun noon–10pm.

★**The Cow** 89 Westbourne Park Rd, W2 5QH ☎ 020 7221 0021, ⓦ thecowlondon.co.uk; ⊖ Royal Oak; map p.92. This handsome gastropub pulls in a cool, slightly raffish crowd. Tasty British food, including shellfish platters, is served both in the bar and in a more formal dining room. Mon–Thurs noon–11pm, Fri & Sat noon–midnight, Sun noon–10pm (kitchen closes 3pm Sun).

The Elgin 96 Ladbroke Grove, W11 1PY ☎ 020 7229 5663, ⓦ theelginnottinghill.co.uk; ⊖ Ladbroke Grove; map p.92. Enormous pub with a riot of original features and modish decorative touches. Buzzy, with regular events, from comedy and live music to life drawing. Mon–Thurs 11am–11pm, Fri & Sat 11am–midnight, Sun noon–10pm.

Grenadier 18 Wilton Row, SW1X 7NR ☎ 020 7235 3074, ⓦ bit.ly/GrenadierSW1X; ⊖ Hyde Park Corner; map p.92. Hidden in a private mews, this charming little Greene King pub was Wellington's local and his officers' mess; the original pewter bar survives, and there's plenty of military paraphernalia on display. Daily noon–11pm.

Windsor Castle 114 Campden Hill Rd, W8 7AR ☎ 020 7243 8797, ⓦ thewindsorcastlekensington.co .uk; ⊖ Notting Hill Gate; map p.92. A country pub in the backstreets of one of London's poshest neighbourhoods, this is a pretty, popular, early Victorian wood-panelled place with a great beer garden. They serve craft beers and grub with ideas above its station. Mon–Sat noon–11pm, Sun noon–10pm.

NORTH LONDON

The Constitution 42 St Pancras Way, NW1 0QT ☎ 020 7380 0767, ⓦ conincamden.com; ⊖ Camden Town; map p.56. Light seems to pour into this canal-side pub, while the beer garden overlooking the water is ideal for fine weather. Its lovely location makes it ripe for gentrification but, for now, it's very much a locals' haunt. Mon–Sat 11am–midnight, Sun noon–10pm.

Edinboro Castle 57 Mornington Terrace, NW1 7RU ☎ 020 7255 9651, ⓦ edinborocastlepub.co.uk; ⊖ Camden Town; map p.56. The main draw at this big, high-ceilinged pub is the leafy beer garden, which hosts summer-weekend barbecues and hog roasts. Mon–Fri noon–11pm, Sat 11am–11pm, Sun noon–10pm.

Spaniards Inn Spaniards Rd, NW3 7JJ ☎ 020 8731 8406, ⓦ thespaniardshampstead.co.uk; ⊖ Hampstead; map p.56. Rambling sixteenth-century coaching inn near the Heath, once frequented by everyone from Dick Turpin to John Keats. With a garden of heath-rivalling proportions and good food, it really draws the crowds at weekends, especially Sun afternoons. Mon–Sat noon–11pm, Sun 11am–10pm.

SOUTH LONDON

Cutty Sark Ballast Quay, off Lassell St, SE10 9PD ☎ 020 8858 3146, ⓦ cuttysarkse10.co.uk; ⊖ Cutty Sark DLR; map p.88. This three-storey Georgian pub, not too touristy, is a good place for a riverside pint – food, however, is overpriced. Mon–Sat 11am–11pm, Sun noon–10pm.

WEST LONDON

★**The Dove** 19 Upper Mall, W6 9TA ☎ 020 8748 9474, ⓦ dovehammersmith.co.uk; ⊖ Ravenscourt Park; map p.92. Very old, low-beamed Fuller's pub with literary

1

NOTTING HILL CARNIVAL

Notting Hill's three-day free **festival** (ⓦthelondonnottinghillcarnival.com), held over the August bank holiday weekend, is the longest-running street party in Europe. Dating back to 1959, the Caribbean carnival is a tumult of elaborate parade floats, eye-catching costumes, chest-thumping sound systems, live bands, irresistible food and huge crowds. Bringing revellers from all over London – it can become unbelievably crowded – it is still at heart a major celebration of Notting Hill's West Indian community, with steel bands, calypso and soca to the fore.

associations, the smallest bar in the UK (4ft by 7ft), popular Sunday roasts and a riverside terrace. Mon–Sat 11am–11pm, Sun noon–10pm.

White Cross Hotel Water Lane, Richmond, TW9 1TH ⓣ020 8940 6844, ⓦthewhitecrossrichmond.com; ⊖Richmond; map p.92. With a longer pedigree and more character than its rivals, the *White Cross* has a large, popular garden overlooking the river, and an open fire in winter. It's a hub for rugby fans. Mon–Sat 10am–11pm, Sun 10am–10pm.

NIGHTLIFE

LIVE MUSIC
LARGE VENUES

Brixton Academy 211 Stockwell Rd, SW9 9SL ⓣ020 7771 3000, ⓦo2academybrixton.co.uk; ⊖Brixton; map p.56. The Academy has seen them all, from mods and rockers to Chase and Status. The 4900-capacity Victorian hall's sound quality isn't immaculate, but it remains a cracking place to see bands.

Hammersmith Apollo 45 Queen Caroline St, W6 9QH ⓣ020 8563 3800, ⓦeventimapollo.com; ⊖Hammersmith; map p.92. The former Hammersmith Odeon is a cavernous space (downstairs can be seating or standing), hosting everyone from Sigur Ros to Regina Spektor and nostalgia acts.

Shepherd's Bush Empire Shepherd's Bush Green, W12 8TT ⓣ020 8354 3300, ⓦo2shepherdsbushempire .co.uk; ⊖Shepherd's Bush; map p.92. Great mid-league bands play here. Views from the vertigo-inducing balconies are great, but downstairs lacks atmosphere if you're not at the front.

SMALL AND MID-SIZED VENUES

Borderline Orange Yard, Manette St, W1D 4JB ⓣ020 3871 7777, ⓦborderline.london; ⊖Tottenham Court Road; map p.60. One of the last central venues still standing, with a guitar-infused music rota, some indie club nights and good sound.

Cargo 83 Rivington St, EC2A 3AY ⓣ020 7739 3440, ⓦcargo-london.com; ⊖Old Street; map p.83. Small, popular venue in what was once a railway arch. Hosts a variety of live acts, including jazz, hip-hop, indie and folk, and excellent club nights.

★**The Dentist** 33 Chatsworth Rd, E5 0LH (no phone) ⓦtheolddentist.com; ⊖Homerton; map p.83. Tasteful guitars, experimental music, cool crowds and a laidback atmosphere in a barely renovated old surgery that puts you and the musicians face to face.

Forum 9–17 Highgate Rd, NW5 1JY ⓣ020 7428 4080, ⓦo2forumkentishtown.co.uk; ⊖Kentish Town; map p.56. The programming at this mid-sized venue has moved towards a reliance on nostalgia acts, but it still occasionally surprises with special events.

Green Note 106 Parkway, NW1 ⓣ020 7485 9899, ⓦgreennote.co.uk; ⊖Camden Town; map p.56. Bijou music venue that punches way above its weight with its excellent line-up of roots, folk, acoustic and world music.

Hootananny 95 Effra Rd, SW2 1DF ⓣ020 7737 7273, ⓦhootananybrixton.co.uk; ⊖Brixton; map p.56. Charismatic world music, ska, reggae, folk and dancehall merge in this once-grand, raucous venue. Over-21s only.

Jazz Café 5 Parkway, NW1 7PG ⓣ020 7485 6834, ⓦthejazzcafelondon.com; ⊖Camden Town; map p.56. There's the odd cheesy pop night, but a combination of big names (at big prices) and clubbier acts from jazz, soul and beyond keep the dancefloor and balcony buzzing.

Kings Place 90 York Way, N1 9AG ⓣ020 7520 1490, ⓦkingsplace.co.uk; ⊖King's Cross St Pancras; map p.72. Two halls host sophisticated classical, jazz and world music gigs at this rather swish development – the acoustics are excellent.

KOKO 1a Camden High St, NW1 7JE ⓣ020 7388 3222, ⓦkoko.uk.com; ⊖Mornington Crescent; map p.56. An atmospheric Camden institution, hosting gigs and weekend club nights, with a cracking assortment of Radio 1-friendly hit-makers dominating proceedings for young crowds.

★**The Macbeth** 70 Hoxton St, N1 6LP ⓣ020 7749 0600, ⓦthemacbeth.co.uk; ⊖Old Street; map p.78. Beautiful venue, good sound system and a great schedule, from buzzing rock and indie gigs to imaginative club nights. Try the roof terrace if you need a break from the dancefloor.

Omeara 6 O'Meara St, SE1 1TE ☎020 3179 2900, ⓦ omearalondon.com; ⊖ London Bridge; map p.88. Fantastic under-arch venue with a lively atmosphere, high-profile DJs and cutting-edge indie acts.

Ronnie Scott's 47 Frith St, W1D 4HT ☎020 7439 0747, ⓦ ronniescotts.co.uk; ⊖ Leicester Square; map p.60. London's most famous jazz club, this small, smart Soho stalwart hosts the really big names as part of its ambitious programme. The Sun jazz lunches are a hit.

★**Roundhouse** Chalk Farm Rd, NW1 8EH ☎0300 678 9222, ⓦ roundhouse.org.uk; ⊖ Chalk Farm; map p.56. This magnificent listed Victorian steam engine shed is one of London's premier performing arts centres, pulling in huge names like Bob Dylan and John Cale alongside more eclectic acts.

★**Union Chapel** Compton Terrace, N1 2UN ☎020 7226 1686, ⓦ unionchapel.org.uk; ⊖ Highbury & Islington; map p.56. Handsome, intimate venue in a beautiful old church (seating is on pews); acts range from contemporary folk via comedy to world music, r'n'b and indie legends. Free Sat lunchtime sessions.

The Vortex 11 Gillett Square, N16 8AZ ☎020 7254 4097, ⓦ vortexjazz.co.uk; ⊖ Dalston Kingsland; map p.83. This small venue is a serious player on the contemporary jazz scene, combining a touch of urban style with a cosy, friendly atmosphere.

CLUBS

Disco tunnels, sticky-floored rock clubs and epic house nights: London has it all. While the capital has lost most of its superclubs, the spread of mid-sized venues gives more choice than ever. Places tend to open between 10pm and midnight – check online. All-nighters and anywhere with a dress code will be pricey, but elsewhere £5–10 is standard, and finding a place to dance for free midweek isn't hard (though prices at the bar may be outrageous).

★**Bethnal Green Working Men's Club** 42–44 Pollard Row, E2 6NB ☎020 7739 7170, ⓦ workersplaytime .net; ⊖ Bethnal Green; map p.83. Postwar kitsch sets the backdrop for some serious playtime: choose from Fifties dress-up, burlesque, disco, rock'n'roll and high-camp gay nights. Thurs–Sat 9pm–2am, check listings for other days.

★**Bussey Building** 133 Rye Lane, SE15 4ST ☎020 7732 5275, ⓦ clfartcafe.org; ⊖ Peckham Rye; map p.56. The very heart of Peckham's cool scene, with three floors of mixed bills – lots of afrobeat and disco – with a friendly crowd and loads of space to dance. The fortnightly Soul Train is big fun. Usually Thurs 5pm–2.30am, Fri & Sat 5pm–6am.

★**Dalston Superstore** 177 Kingsland High St, E8 2PB ☎020 7254 2273, ⓦ dalstonsuperstore.com; ⊖ Dalston Kingsland; map p.83. Dalston's nightlife hub, with picky door staff, fashionable straight/gay clientele and a hedonistic mix of disco, house and party tunes. Bar daily, club usually Wed–Sun 9pm–2.30am.

Fabric 77a Charterhouse St, EC1M 6HJ ☎020 7336 8898, ⓦ fabriclondon.com; ⊖ Farringdon; map p.78. Despite long queues (buy tickets online) and a maze-like layout, this 1600-capacity club gets in the big names. Music booming from the devastating sound system includes drum'n'bass, techno and house. Fri 11pm–7am, Sat 11pm–8am, Sun 11pm–5.30am.

Notting Hill Arts Club 21 Notting Hill Gate, W11 3JQ ☎020 7460 4459, ⓦ nottinghillartsclub.com; ⊖ Notting Hill Gate; map p.92. Groovy dressed-down basement club-bar playing everything from funk through to soul and guitar music. Usually Wed–Sun 7pm–2am.

Proud Camden Stables Market, Chalk Farm Rd, NW1 8AH ☎020 7482 3867, ⓦ proudcamden.com; ⊖ Camden Town; map p.56. Crossing the dance/rock spectrum, the club nights at this former horse hospital have an enduringly student vibe. Club usually 10pm–2.30am.

XOYO 32–37 Cowper St, EC2A 4AP ☎020 7608 2878, ⓦ xoyo.co.uk; ⊖ Old Street; map p.56. This nine-hundred-capacity venue and club has an annoying layout, with convoluted corridors, but the programming is big-time fun, often delivered by Radio 1's roster of dance DJs. Club nights 9pm–4am.

LGBT+ NIGHTLIFE

London's **queer scene** is so huge, diverse and well established that it's easy to forget just how much – and how fast – it has grown over the last couple of decades. **Soho** remains its spiritual heart, with a mix of traditional gay pubs, designer café-bars and a range of gay-run services, while Vauxhall and Shoreditch/Dalston are also good stomping grounds. The major **outdoor event** of the year is **Pride** (ⓦ prideinlondon.org) in late June, a colourful, whistle-blowing parade that takes over central London and features a massive rally in Trafalgar Square; the newer July event **UK Black Pride** (ⓦ ukblackpride.org.uk) also has a large following, with a star-studded rally in Vauxhall Pleasure Gardens.

BARS AND CLUBS

Many gay venues act as pubs by day and transform into raucous parties by night. Lots have cabaret or disco nights and are open until the early hours, making them an affordable alternative to clubs. Admission can be free or fairly cheap, though a few levy a charge after 10pm or 11pm (usually £5–10) for music, cabaret or a disco. We use "mixed" below to mean places for both gays and lesbians, though most are primarily frequented by men.

1

MIXED BARS

Freedom 66 Wardour St, W1F 0TA ☎ 020 7734 0071, ⓦ freedombarsoho.com; ⊖ Piccadilly Circus; map p.60. Hip, metrosexual place, popular for cheap afterwork drinks and a fun dance spot at the weekend. Mon–Thurs 4pm–3am, Fri & Sat 2pm–3am, Sun 2–10.30pm.

Ku Bar 30 Lisle St, WC2H 7BA ☎ 020 7437 4303; 25 Frith St, W1D 5LB ☎ 020 7437 4303, ⓦ ku-bar .co.uk; ⊖ Leicester Square; map p.60. The Lisle St original is one of Soho's largest and best-loved gay bars, serving a scene-conscious yet attitude-free clientele. Ruby Tuesdays are for lesbians only. The Frith St sister bar is a calmer cocktail spot. Lisle St: Mon–Sat noon–3am, Sun noon–midnight; Frith St: Mon–Thurs noon–11.30pm, Fri & Sat noon–midnight, Sun noon–10.30pm.

New Bloomsbury Set 76 Marchmont St, WC1N 1AG ☎ 020 7383 3084, ⓦ newbloomsburyset.net; ⊖ Russell Square; map p.72. Hit happy hour at the right time and get cheap and cheerful cocktails in this tasteful basement bar; secure a cute and cosy snug to enjoy its speakeasy vibe. Mon–Sat 4–11.30pm, Sun 4–10.30pm.

★ **Royal Vauxhall Tavern** 372 Kennington Lane, SE11 5HY ☎ 020 7820 1222, ⓦ vauxhalltavern.com; ⊖ Vauxhall; map p.56. This iconic, disreputable, divey drag and cabaret pub is home to legendary alternative club night Duckie on Sat. The rest of the week brings a changing calendar of performance that attracts a varied, often older crowd. Mon–Thurs 7pm–midnight, Fri 7pm–3am, Sat 9pm–2am, Sun 2pm–2am.

Rupert Street 50 Rupert St, W1D 6DR ⓦ rupert-street. com; ⊖ Piccadilly Circus; map p.60. See and be seen at this smart, mainstream bar with a mixed after-work crowd and more of a pre-club vibe at weekends. The ideal place to start a Soho night out; happy hour lasts until 8pm. Mon–Thurs noon–11pm, Fri & Sat noon–11.45pm, Sun noon–10.30pm.

LESBIAN BARS

★ **She Soho** 23a Old Compton St, W1D 5JL ☎ 020 7437 4303, ⓦ she-soho.com; ⊖ Tottenham Court Road; map p.60. Remarkably, this is Old Compton Street's only lesbian bar, relatively smart and with DJs at the weekend. Mon–Thurs 4–11.30pm, Fri & Sat noon–midnight, Sun noon–10.30pm.

Star at Night 22 Great Chapel St, W1F 8FR ☎ 020 7494 2488, ⓦ thestaratnight.com; ⊖ Tottenham Court Road; map p.60. Mixed, female-led venue, popular with a slightly older crowd who want somewhere to sit, a decent glass of wine and good conversation. Tues–Fri 4–11.30pm, Sat noon–11.30pm.

GAY MEN'S BARS

Comptons 51–53 Old Compton St, W1D 6HN ☎ 020 7096 5470; ⊖ Leicester Square; map p.60. This large, traditional-style pub attracts a butch, cruising yet relaxed 25-plus crowd. Upstairs is more chilled and draws younger drinkers. Mon–Sat noon–11.30pm, Sun noon–10.30pm.

The King's Arms 23 Poland St, W1F 8QL ☎ 020 7734 5907, ⓦ kingsarms-soho.co.uk; ⊖ Oxford Circus; map p.60. London's best-known and perennially popular bear bar, with a traditional pub atmosphere. Sun is (raucous) karaoke night. Mon & Tues noon–11pm, Wed & Thurs noon–11.30pm, Fri & Sat noon–midnight, Sun 1–10.30pm.

CLUBS

Bootylicious Club Union, 66 Albert Embankment, SE1 7TP ☎ 07973 628585, ⓦ bootylicious-club.co.uk; ⊖ Vauxhall; map p.56. Despite having a large black community, London offers just one dedicated gay and lesbian urban music/BME night, held monthly and featuring r'n'b, hip-hop, dancehall, house and classic vibes. Last Sat of the month 11pm–4am.

★ **The Eagle** 349 Kennington Lane, SE11 5QY ☎ 020 7793 0903, ⓦ eaglelondon.com; ⊖ Vauxhall; map p.56. Home to the excellent Sunday-night Horse Meat Disco, this club's vibe is a loose, friendly re-creation of late 1970s New York, complete with facial hair, checked shirts and a pool table. Mon–Wed 4pm–midnight, Thurs 4pm–2am, Fri 4pm–4am, Sat 9pm–4am, Sun 8pm–3am.

Fire South Lambeth Rd, SW8 1RT ☎ 020 3242 0040, ⓦ firelondon.net; ⊖ Vauxhall; map p.56. London's superclub of choice for disco bunnies and hardboyz, with all-nighters – and often all-dayers if you're making a proper weekend of it. Fri, Sat & occasionally Sun from 10pm or 11pm.

★ **The Glory** 281 Kingsland Rd, E2 8AS ⓦ theglory.co; ⊖ Haggerston; map p.83. Drag legend Jonny Woo's meld of lip-syncingly excellent performance, booze and a basement club for disco queens. Days and hours vary.

Heaven Villiers St, WC2N 6NG ☎ 020 7930 2020, ⓦ heavennightclub-london.com; ⊖ Charing Cross; map p.60. Said to be the UK's most popular gay club, this two thousand-capacity venue is home to G-A-Y (Thurs–Sat), with big-name DJs and PAs – expect lots of Drag Race rejects – and Popcorn Monday, which prolongs the weekday fun till 5.30am. Thurs–Sat & Mon hours vary.

★ **Vogue Fabrics** 66 Stoke Newington Rd, N16 7XB (no phone) ⓦ vfdalston.com; map p.83. Dalston's favourite disco basement offers an array of arts events and disco fun for a fashion crowd. Highlights include genderqueer performance night Icy Gays and the mega all-nighter Anal House Meltdown. Days and hours vary.

THEATRE AND COMEDY

1

London has enjoyed a reputation for quality **theatre** since the time of Shakespeare and, along with huge popular hits, still provides platforms for innovation and new writing. The **West End** is the heart of "Theatreland", with Shaftesbury Avenue its main drag, but the term is more conceptual than geographical. Less mainstream work is performed in **Off-West End** theatres and **fringe** venues, where ticket prices are lower and quality more variable. The capital's **comedy** scene is lively, too, whether you want to keep things low-key in an intimate pub or pay top dollar for big-name shows.

INFORMATION AND COSTS

Websites Good starting points for comedy gigs include ⓦ rabbitrabbitcomedy.com, ⓦ alwaysbecomedy.com, ⓦ amusedmoose.com and ⓦ laughoutlondoncomedyclub.co.uk. Consult *Time Out* for weekly, citywide listings (ⓦ timeout.com/london/comedy). For details and news about West End shows, along with tickets and promotions, see ⓦ officiallondontheatre.co.uk and ⓦ londontheatre.co.uk. And for weekly listings for theatre of all stripes, check *Time Out* (ⓦ timeout.com/london/theatre).

Prices Most comedy shows cost around £5–15, but there's plenty of free comedy to be found – often upstairs at pubs. Tickets for O2 and Wembley Arena tours cost anything from £35 up to £125 and beyond. For West End shows the box-office average is around £25–40, with £50–110 the usual top price, but bargains can be found. If you want to buy from the theatre direct it's best to go to the box office; you'll probably be charged a fee for booking over the phone or online. Ticket agencies such as Ticketmaster (ⓦ ticketmaster.co.uk) get seats for West End shows well in advance, but can add hefty booking fees.

Discounts Whatever you do, avoid the touts and the ticket agencies that abound in the West End – there's no guarantee that they are genuine. The Society of London Theatre (ⓦ officiallondontheatre.co.uk) offers online discounts on West End shows; their booth in Leicester Square, "tkts" (Mon–Sat 10am–7pm, Sun 11am–4.30pm; ⓦ tkts.co.uk), sells on-the-day tickets for the big shows at discounts of up to fifty percent. These tend to be in the top end of the price range and are limited to four/person; there's a service charge of £3/ticket. Cheap standby, "first look" and standing tickets can be very good value, and some major theatres sell a few on the door on the day; check the venue's website, and be prepared to put up with a restricted view.

THEATRES

Almeida Almeida St, N1 1TA ☎020 7359 4404, ⓦ almeida.co.uk; ⊖ Highbury & Islington; map p.56. Popular little Islington venue that premieres excellent new plays and excitingly reworked classics from around the world. It often attracts big names, including Benedict Cumberbatch and Ben Whishaw.

★ **Arcola** 24 Ashwin St, E8 3DL ☎020 7503 1646, ⓦ arcolatheatre.com; ⊖ Dalston Junction; map p.83. Exciting fringe theatre in an old Dalston factory and a tent space. Politically charged plays – classics and contemporary

– with shows from young, international companies and cabaret in the tent.

Barbican Silk St, EC2Y 8DS ☎020 7638 8891, ⓦ barbican.org.uk; ⊖ Barbican; map p.78. Theatre, dance and performance by leading international companies and emerging artists, with excellent post-show talks.

The Bridge Theatre 1 Tower Bridge, SE1 2SD ☎0333 320 0052, ⓦ bridgetheatre.co.uk; ⊖ London Bridge; map p.88. Major new venue masterminded by Nicholas Hytner, formerly director at the National. The innovative performance space can be moulded to suit the performance.

Donmar Warehouse 41 Earlham St, WC2Y 9LX ☎0844 871 7624, ⓦ donmarwarehouse.com; ⊖ Covent Garden; map p.60. Long home to excellent writing, the Donmar has also garnered attention with big-name performers.

Menier Chocolate Factory 53 Southwark St, SE1 1RU ☎020 7378 1713, ⓦ menierchocolatefactory.com; ⊖ London Bridge; map p.88. Great name, great venue, with a decent bar; the restaurant's food is inconsistent. Plays tend towards showy casting but interesting works do appear here.

★ **National Theatre** South Bank, SE1 9PX ☎020 7452 3000, ⓦ nationaltheatre.org.uk; ⊖ Waterloo; map p.86. The country's top actors and directors produce an ambitious programme in the three NT theatres: the raked, 1150-seat Olivier, the classic "proscenium" Lyttelton and the experimental Dorfman. Cheap deals are available; on "Travelex" performances seats can cost just £15. Some shows sell out months in advance, but £15/£18 day tickets go on sale on the morning of each performance – get there early (two tickets/person).

Open Air Theatre Inner Circle, Regent's Park, NW1 4NU ☎0844 826 4242, ⓦ openairtheatre.com; ⊖ Baker Street; map p.56. Lovely alfresco space in Regent's Park hosting a tourist-friendly summer programme of Shakespeare, musicals, plays and concerts, many of which are geared towards children.

Roundhouse Chalk Farm Rd, NW1 8EH ☎0300 678 9222, ⓦ roundhouse.org.uk; ⊖ Chalk Farm; map p.56. Camden's most exciting cultural venue, in an old – round – engine repairs shed, the Roundhouse puts on cutting-edge theatre, circus, cabaret and spoken word.

Royal Court Sloane Square, SW1W 8AS ☎020 7565 5000, ⓦ royalcourttheatre.com; ⊖ Sloane Square; map p.92. The Royal Court's programme includes arguably the most ambitious and radical new writing in town; £12 tickets on Mon.

1

★**Shakespeare's Globe** 21 New Globe Walk, SE1 9DT ☎ 020 7401 9919, ⓦ shakespearesglobe.com; ⊖ London Bridge; map p.88. This open-roofed replica Elizabethan theatre stages superb Shakespearean shows as they were originally conceived, as well as works from the Bard's contemporaries and new writing. Seats £20–45, with seven hundred standing tickets for around a fiver. The Globe Theatre season runs April–Oct, but the site's indoor Jacobean theatre, the Sam Wanamaker Playhouse, hosts a candlelit winter theatre season Oct–April, plus concerts and events in summer.

★**Soho Theatre** 21 Dean St, W1D 3NE ☎ 020 7478 0100, ⓦ sohotheatre.com; ⊖ Tottenham Court Road; map p.60. Great central theatre featuring new writing from around the globe at affordable prices. It's renowned for its comedy and cabaret, too, and has a popular, starry bar.

CINEMA

There are a lot of cinemas in London, especially the **West End**, with the biggest on and around Leicester Square. A few classy independent chains show more offbeat screenings, in various locations – check the **Picturehouse** (ⓦ picturehouses .co.uk), **Curzon** (ⓦ curzoncinemas.com) and **Everyman** (ⓦ everymancinema.com). **Tickets** at the major screens cost at least £13, although concessions are offered for some shows at virtually all cinemas, usually off-peak.

★**BFI Southbank** Belvedere Rd, South Bank, SE1 8XT ☎ 020 7928 3232, ⓦ bfi.org.uk; ⊖ Waterloo; map p.86. Eclectic themed seasons, showing between seven and fourteen films daily on four screens. The BFI, in association with Odeon, also runs the nearby IMAX (☎ 0330 333 7878, ⓦ bfi.org.uk/imax), a huge glazed drum where the colossal screen is not recommended for anyone with vertigo.

Electric 191 Portobello Rd, W11 2ED ☎ 020 7908 9696, ⓦ electriccinema.co.uk; ⊖ Notting Hill Gate; map p.92. The Notting Hill Electric – quirky mainstream hits and offbeat offerings – is one of the oldest cinemas in the country (opened 1911). Its current, luxurious incarnation even includes a few double beds. There's a second branch in Shoreditch.

ICA Cinema Nash House, The Mall, SW1Y 5AH ☎ 020 7930 3647, ⓦ ica.org.uk; ⊖ Charing Cross; map p.60. Shows avant-garde, world, underground movies and docs on two screens in the seriously hip HQ of the Institute of Contemporary Arts, some with talks. There's a bar, too.

★**Prince Charles** 7 Leicester Place, WC2H 7BY ☎ 020 7494 3654, ⓦ princecharlescinema.com; ⊖ Leicester Square; map p.60. Two screens in the heart of the West End, with great prices (from £8.50) and a daily changing, lively programme of newish movies, classics and cult favourites, plus all-nighters and sing-a-long romps.

CLASSICAL MUSIC

On most days you should be able to attend a **classical concert** in London for around £15 (the usual range is about £12–50). During the week there are also numerous **free concerts**, often at lunchtimes, in London's churches or given by the city's two leading conservatoires, the Royal College of Music (ⓦ rcm.ac.uk) and Royal Academy of Music (ⓦ ram.ac.uk).

Barbican Silk St, EC2Y 8DS ☎ 020 7638 8891, ⓦ barbican .org.uk; ⊖ Barbican; map p.78. With the outstanding resident London Symphony Orchestra (ⓦ lso.co.uk) and the BBC Symphony Orchestra (ⓦ bbc.co.uk/symphonyorchestra) as associate orchestra, plus top foreign orchestras and big-name soloists in regular attendance, the Barbican is an excellent venue for classical music.

Kings Place 90 York Way, N1 9AG ☎ 020 7520 1490, ⓦ kingsplace.co.uk; ⊖ King's Cross St Pancras; map p.72. Modern, purpose-built venue, by the canal behind King's Cross, featuring new and interesting work in its two performance spaces.

THE PROMS

The **Proms** (Royal Albert Hall; ☎ 0845 401 5040, ⓦ bbc.co.uk/proms; ⊖ South Kensington) provide a summer-season feast of classical music, much of it at bargain prices; uniquely, there are up to 1350 **standing places** available each evening, which cost just £6, even on the famed last night. They're sold from 9am each day; a few are available online but most are at the door. Promming **passes**, which guarantee you entrance up to thirty minutes before a show, cost from £11 (for two proms) up to £240 (for the entire season). **Seated tickets** are £7.50–100; those for the **last night**, which start at £62, are largely allocated by ballot. While the magnificence of the Royal Albert Hall is undeniable, the acoustics aren't the best – OK for orchestral blockbusters, less so for small-scale pieces – but the performers are outstanding, the atmosphere is uplifting and the hall is so vast that everyone has a good chance of getting in.

Southbank Centre Belvedere Rd, South Bank, SE1 8XX ☎ 020 7960 4200, ⓦ southbankcentre.co.uk; ⊖ Embankment; map p.86. Three spaces: the 2500-seat Royal Festival Hall (RFH), home to the Philharmonia (ⓦ philharmonia.co.uk) and the London Philharmonic (ⓦ lpo.co.uk), is tailor-made for large-scale choral and orchestral works, while the Queen Elizabeth Hall (QEH) and intimate Purcell Room are used for chamber concerts, solo recitals, opera and choirs.

Wigmore Hall 36 Wigmore St, W1U 2BP ☎ 020 7935 2141,. ⓦ wigmore-hall.org.uk; ⊖ Bond Street; map p.60. With its near-perfect acoustics, the Wigmore Hall – built in 1901 as a hall for the adjacent Bechstein piano showroom – is a favourite, so book well in advance. It's brilliant for piano recitals, early music and chamber music, but best known for its song recitals by some of the world's greatest vocalists.

OPERA

In addition to the major venues below, a number of **fringe companies**, including Size Zero (ⓦ sizezeroopera.com), Erratica (ⓦ erratica.org), Diva Opera (ⓦ divaopera.com) and Opera Up Close (ⓦ operaupclose.com), produce consistently interesting work.

English National Opera London Coliseum, St Martin's Lane, WC2N 4ES ☎ 020 7845 9300, ⓦ eno.org; ⊖ Leicester Square; map p.60. The ENO is committed to keeping opera accessible, with operas sung in English, an adventurous repertoire, dazzling new productions, non-prohibitive pricing (£12–150) and various discount options.
Royal Opera House Bow St, WC2E 9DD ☎ 020 7304

4000, ⓦ roh.org.uk; ⊖ Covent Garden; map p.60. The ROH, one of the world's leading opera houses, puts on lavish productions, performed in the original language with surtitles. Most tickets are more than £40 (reaching as high as £270), though there is some restricted-view seating (or standing room), which isn't at all bad, from around £10, and various special offers.

DANCE

London's biggest dance festival is **Dance Umbrella** (Oct; ⓦ danceumbrella.co.uk), a season of new work. For a **roundup** of all the major dance events, check ⓦ londondance.com.

The Place 17 Duke's Rd, WC1H 9PY ☎ 020 7121 1100, ⓦ theplace.org.uk; ⊖ Euston; map p.72. The Place, home to a conservatoire and a touring company, presents the work of contemporary choreographers and student performers.
Royal Opera House Bow St, WC2E 9DD ☎ 020 7304 4000, ⓦ roh.org.uk; ⊖ Covent Garden; map p.60. Based at the Opera House, the world-renowned Royal Ballet puts on the very best in classical dance; tickets (£10–150) may be slightly cheaper than for opera. Book early.

Sadler's Wells Rosebery Ave, EC1R 4TN ☎ 020 7863 8000, ⓦ sadlerswells.com; ⊖ Angel; map p.56. With resident dance companies including Matthew Bourne's New Adventures and the ZooNation hip-hop outfit, Sadler's Wells also hosts many international troupes and celebrates everything from flamenco to Bollywood. The Lilian Baylis Theatre, around the back, stages smaller productions, while the Peacock Theatre in Holborn adds populist shows to the mix.

SHOPPING

DEPARTMENT STORES

Fortnum & Mason 181 Piccadilly, W1A 1ER ☎ 020 7734 8040, ⓦ fortnumandmason.com; ⊖ Piccadilly Circus; map p.60. Beautiful 300-year-old store that started out as a humble grocer. It's famous for its pricey food, luxury hampers and fancy afternoon teas (see p.116), but is also good for designer clothes, furniture, luggage and stationery. Mon–Sat 10am–9pm, Sun noon–6pm.
Harrods 87–135 Brompton Rd, SW1X 7XL ☎ 020 7730 1234, ⓦ harrods.com; ⊖ Knightsbridge; map p.92. Vast, expensive and a little stuffy, Harrods is most notable for its Art Nouveau tiled food hall – and of course, its memorial statue of Princess Diana and Dodi, erected by Mohamed Al-Fayed, the store's previous owner and Dodi's father. Mon–Sat 10am–9pm, Sun noon–6pm.

Harvey Nichols 109–125 Knightsbridge, SW1X 7RJ ☎ 020 7235 5000, ⓦ harveynichols.com; ⊖ Knightsbridge; map p.92. Absolutely fabulous, sweetie, "Harvey Nicks" has eight floors of designer collections and casual wear, with a renowned cosmetics department and luxury food hall. Mon–Sat 10am–8pm (July & Aug closes 9pm), Sun noon–6pm.
John Lewis 300 Oxford St, W1C 1DX ☎ 020 7629 7711, ⓦ johnlewis.co.uk; ⊖ Oxford Circus; map p.60. "Never knowingly undersold", this much-loved institution can't be beaten for basics. Mon–Wed, Fri & Sat 9.30am–8pm, Thurs 9.30am–9pm, Sun noon–6pm.
★ **Liberty** 210–220 Regent St, W1B 5AH ☎ 020 7734 1234, ⓦ liberty.co.uk; ⊖ Oxford Circus; map p.60. A glorious emporium of luxury infused with a dash of Art Nouveau bohemia, this exquisite store, with its mock-Tudor

1

exterior, is most famous for its fabrics, designer goods and accessories, but also has an excellent reputation for mainstream and high fashion. Mon–Sat 10am–8pm, Sun noon–6pm.

★ **Selfridges** 400 Oxford St, W1A 1AB ☎ 0800 123 400, ⓦ selfridges.com; ⊖ Bond Street; map p.92. This huge, airy palace of clothes, food and furnishings was London's first great department store and remains its best. The food hall is the finest in town. Mon–Sat 9.30am–10pm, Sun noon–6pm.

BOOKS

★ **Daunt Books** 83 Marylebone High St, W1U 4QW ☎ 020 7224 2295, ⓦ dauntbooks.co.uk; ⊖ Baker Street; map p.92. Inspirational range of travel writing, guidebooks, maps, literary fiction and more, in the galleried interior of this famous Edwardian store. Other branches. Mon–Sat 9am–7.30pm, Sun 11am–6pm.

Foyles 107 Charing Cross Rd, WC2H 0DT ☎ 020 7437 5660, ⓦ foyles.co.uk; ⊖ Tottenham Court Road; map p.60. It may have moved down the road, but this huge and famous store continues to offer a splendid selection of titles – including antiquarian books – on all subjects across its four miles of shelves. Smaller branches under the RFH on the South Bank and in Waterloo Station. Mon–Sat 9.30am–9pm, Sun noon–6pm.

Hatchards 187 Piccadilly, W1J 9LE ☎ 020 7439 9921, ⓦ hatchards.co.uk; ⊖ Piccadilly Circus; map p.60. A little overshadowed by the colossal Waterstones down the road, and actually part of the Waterstones group, the venerable Hatchards holds its own when it comes to quality fiction, biography, history and travel. Mon–Sat 9.30am–8pm, Sun noon–6.30pm.

London Review Bookshop 14 Bury Place, WC1A 2JL ☎ 020 7269 9030, ⓦ lrbshop.co.uk; ⊖ Tottenham Court Road; map p.72. All the books reviewed in the august literary journal and many more are available in this excellent Bloomsbury store. Nice little coffee (and cake) shop, too. Mon–Sat 10am–6.30pm, Sun noon–6pm.

Persephone Books 59 Lamb's Conduit St, WC1N 3NB ☎ 020 7242 9292, ⓦ persephonebooks.co.uk; ⊖ Russell Square; map p.72. Lovely bookshop offspring of a publishing house that specializes in neglected early and mid-twentieth-century writing, mainly by women. Mon–Fri 10am–6pm, Sat noon–5pm.

MUSIC

Gramex 104 Lower Marsh, SE1 7AB ☎ 020 7401 3830, ⓦ gramex.co.uk; ⊖ Waterloo; map p.86. A splendid find for classical music and jazz fans, this friendly, eccentric store – "it might not be good, but it's rare!" – is a treasure-trove of new and secondhand CDs, LPs and 78s. Mon–Sat 11am–6.30pm.

★ **Honest Jon's** 278 Portobello Rd, W10 5TE ☎ 020 8969 9822, ⓦ honestjons.com; ⊖ Ladbroke Grove; map p.92. West London stalwart offering a choice selection of reggae, blues, soul, jazz, funk, R&B, rare groove, world music and more, with current releases, secondhand finds and reissues. Mon–Sat 10am–6pm, Sun 11am–5pm.

Rough Trade 130 Talbot Rd, W11 1JA ☎ 020 7229 8541, ⊖ Ladbroke Grove; ⓦ roughtrade.com; map p.92. This historic indie specialist has a dizzying array – not all of it obscure – from electronica to hardcore and beyond. A second branch, in East London's Truman Brewery, hosts big-ticket live bands. Mon–Sat 10am–6.30pm, Sun 11am–5pm.

MARKETS

★ **Borough** 8 Southwark St, SE1 1TL ☎ 020 7407 1002, ⓦ boroughmarket.org.uk; ⊖ London Bridge; map p.88. Gourmet suppliers from all over the UK converge to sell organic and artisan goodies from around the world at this bustling, historic and utterly enjoyable food market, while street trucks and restaurants do a roaring trade. Mon & Tues 10am–5pm (some stalls only), Wed & Thurs 10am–5pm, Fri 10am–6pm, Sat 8am–5pm, sometimes Sun 10am–4pm.

Brick Lane Brick Lane, E1 6QL ⓦ visitbricklane.org, ⓦ trumanbrewery.com/cgi-bin/markets.pl; ⊖ Shoreditch High Street; map p.83. Sprawling and frenzied, the famous East End market, spreading through Dray Walk, Cygnet and Sclater streets, has become a must-do for hipsters and tourists both – it's hard to say what you can't find here. The coolest gear is sold in and around the Old Truman Brewery (with various markets open Thurs–Sun). Sun 10am–5pm.

Camden Camden High St to Chalk Farm Rd, NW1 ⓦ camdenmarket.com; ⊖ Camden Town; map p.56. Once beloved of hippies, punks and goths, and still a firm favourite with young European tourists, this huge, sprawling mass of stalls, including excellent vintage/antique stuff, segues into one enormous shopping district. Daily, roughly 10am–7pm, with more stalls at the weekend.

Columbia Road Columbia Rd, E2 ⓦ columbiaroad.info; ⊖ Hoxton; map p.83. This pretty East End street spills over in a profusion of blooms and resounds with the bellows of Cockney barrow boys during its glorious market. Come late for the best bargains, or early to enjoy a coffee and brunch in one of the groovy local cafés. It's an excellent shopping area, abounding in indie, arty and vintage stores. Sun 8am–3pm.

Greenwich Greenwich Church St, SE10 9HZ ⓦ greenwichmarketlondon.com; ⊖ Cutty Sark DLR; map p.88. Sprawling set of covered flea markets selling everything from bric-a-brac to board games, with antiques

1

THE MAKING OF HARRY POTTER

Kids and Harry Potter fans will love **The Making of Harry Potter** tour in the Warner Bros studios in Leavesden (20 miles northwest of London); but impressively, they've managed to keep it interesting for everyone else, too. The self-guided **tour** (typically Mon–Fri 8.30/10.30am–6/10pm, Sat & Sun 8.30am–10pm; closed late Jan to early Feb, mid-Nov & around Christmas; last tour 3–4hr before closing; check website for latest hours and tour times; £39, under-16s £31; book far in advance; ☎0345 084 0900, ⓦwbstudiotour.co.uk) takes you around the studios where much of the footage for the eight Harry Potter movies was shot, and every space is crammed with paraphernalia from filming. You can geek out over individual characters' wands and original costumes, or marvel at the films' creature technology – like the animatronic spiders – and the hand-drawn, hyper-detailed architectural plans.

Allow a few hours to get the most out of the tour and avoid rushing at the end – they save the best for last. If you can, time your visit to coincide with one of the **seasonal events**; these include Dark Arts at the end of October, and Hogwarts in the Snow, when the sets are decked out with fake snow and Christmas trees.

To get to the studios, take the train to Watford Junction from Euston (around 8/hr; 15–45min), then shuttle bus (around every 30min; 15min; £2.50, cash only).

and crafts, food and vintage clothes. The surrounding streets, and the shops inside the market, offer more treasures. Daily 10am–5.30pm.

Portobello Portobello and Golborne rds, W10 and W11 ⓦshopportobello.co.uk; ⊖Ladbroke Grove/ Notting Hill Gate; map p.92. Probably the best way to approach this enormous market, or rather markets – beloved of tourist crowds – is from the Notting Hill end, winding your way through the antiques (Fri & Sat) and bric-a-brac down to the fruit and veg, and then via the fashion stalls under the Westway to the vintage (Fri & Sun) and fashion scene (Sat) at Portobello Green (ⓦportobello

fashionmarket.com). The Golborne Rd market is cheaper and less crowded, with antique and retro furniture on Fri and Sat (food Mon–Thurs). Roughly 8am–6pm, till 1pm on Thurs; Golborne Rd closed Sun.

Spitalfields Commercial St, between Brushfield and Lamb sts, E1 6AA ⓦspitalfields.co.uk; ⊖Liverpool Street; map p.83. The East End's Victorian fruit and veg hall feels more like an upmarket mall nowadays, but there are interesting things to be found among its crafts, gifts and clothes stalls. Plenty of bars and restaurants, too, plus independent shops and street food. Mon–Fri 10am– 5pm, Sat 11am–5pm, Sun 9am–5pm.

DIRECTORY

Hospitals Central A&Es include: St Thomas' Hospital, Westminster Bridge Rd, SE1 7EH (⊖Westminster); and University College London Hospital, 235 Euston Rd, NW1 2BU (⊖Euston Square or Warren Street).

Left luggage Left luggage is available at all airports and major train terminals; the Excess Baggage Company (ⓦexcess-baggage.com) runs many of them. All facilities cost around £10–12/24hr.

Police Central 24hr Metropolitan Police stations include

Charing Cross, Agar St, WC2N 4JP (⊖Charing Cross) and West End Central, 27 Savile Row, W1S 2EX (⊖Oxford Circus). The City of London has its own police force, and a 24hr station at 182 Bishopsgate, EC2M 4NP (ⓦcityoflondon .police.uk; ⊖Liverpool Street).

Post offices Conveniently near Trafalgar Square is the post office at 24–28 William IV St, WC2N 4DL (Mon & Wed–Fri 8.30am–6.30pm, Tues 9.15am–6.30pm, Sat 9am–5.30pm).

The Southeast

SEVEN SISTERS

2

The Southeast

The southeast corner of England was traditionally where London went on holiday. In the past, trainloads of East Enders were shuttled to the hop fields and orchards of Kent for a working break from the city; boats ferried people down the Thames to the beaches of north Kent; while everyone from royalty to cuckolding couples enjoyed the seaside at Brighton, a blot of decadence in the otherwise sedate county of Sussex. Although many of the old seaside resorts have struggled to keep their tourist custom in the face of ever more accessible foreign destinations, the region still has considerable charm, its narrow country lanes and verdant meadows appearing, in places, almost untouched by modern life.

The proximity of **Kent** and **Sussex** to the continent has dictated the history of this region, which has served as a gateway for an array of invaders. **Roman remains** dot the coastal area – most spectacularly at Fishbourne in Sussex and Lullingstone in Kent – and many roads, including the main A2 London to Dover, follow the arrow-straight tracks laid by the legionaries. When Christianity spread through Europe, it arrived in Britain on the Isle of Thanet – the northeast tip of Kent, then an island but since rejoined to the mainland by silting. In 597 AD Augustine moved inland and established a monastery at **Canterbury**, still the home of the Church of England and the county's prime historic attraction.

The last successful invasion of England took place in 1066, when the Normans overran King Harold's army near **Hastings**, on a site now marked by Battle Abbey. The Normans left their mark all over this corner of the kingdom, and Kent remains unmatched in its profusion of medieval castles, among them **Dover**'s sprawling clifftop fortress guarding against continental invasion and **Rochester**'s huge, box-like citadel, close to the old dockyards of **Chatham**, power base of the formerly invincible British navy. Gentler reminders of history can be found in pretty **Sandwich** and **Rye**, two of the best-preserved medieval towns in the country.

You can spend unhurried days in elegant old towns such as **Royal Tunbridge Wells**, **Arundel**, **Midhurt** and **Lewes**, or enjoy the less elevated charms of the traditional resorts. **Whitstable** is an arty getaway famed for its oysters, **Deal** has a laidback vibe, and cheeky **Margate** goes from strength to hipster strength, but chief among them all is **Brighton**, combining the buzz of a university town with a good-time atmosphere. The rolling chalk uplands of the **South Downs National Park** get you away from it all, as much as anywhere can in the crowded southeast, with the soaring white cliffs of the **Sussex Heritage Coast** the unmissable scenic highlight. Kent and Sussex also harbour some of the country's finest **gardens** – ranging from the lush flowerbeds of Sissinghurst in the **High Weald** to the great landscaped estate of Petworth House – and a string of excellent **galleries**, among them the Pallant Gallery in **Chichester**, the Turner Contemporary in Margate, the Towner in **Eastbourne** and the tiny Ditchling Museum of Art + Craft just outside Brighton. **Folkestone**, meanwhile, with its high-profile triennial art show, is building a strong cultural reputation.

TURNER CONTEMPORARY, MARGATE

Highlights

❶ The Sportsman, Seasalter Savour impeccable, locally sourced, Michelin-starred food in this simple gastropub by the sea. **See p.140**

❷ Margate With its quirky Old Town, its broad sandy beach and the fabulous Turner Contemporary gallery, this brash old resort is an increasingly hip destination. **See p.140**

❸ Canterbury Cathedral The destination of the pilgrims in Chaucer's *Canterbury Tales*, with a magnificent sixteenth-century interior that includes a shrine to the murdered Thomas Becket. **See p.145**

❹ The White Cliffs of Dover Immortalized in song, art and literature, the famed chalky

cliffs offer walks and vistas over the Channel. **See p.151**

❺ Rye Ancient hilltop town of picturesque cobbled streets, with some great places to eat, shop and sleep. **See p.159**

❻ Walking the South Downs Way Experience the best walking in the southeast – and some fantastic views – on this national trail, which spans England's newest National Park. **See p.163**

❼ The Lanes and North Laine, Brighton Explore the café- and shop-crammed streets of the maze-like Lanes and the buzzy, hip North Laine: Brighton at its best. **See p.172**

HIGHLIGHTS ARE MARKED ON THE MAP ON P.136

The portion of **Surrey** within and around the M25 orbital motorway has little for tourists, but beyond the ring road it takes on a more rural aspect, with miles of beautiful countryside and woodlands to explore; the market towns of **Guildford** and **Dorking** make handy hubs.

GETTING AROUND THE SOUTHEAST

By train Southeastern (Ⓦ southeasternrailway.co.uk) covers Kent and the easternmost part of Sussex, and runs the high-speed services from London St Pancras to the North Kent coast and Chichester. The rest of Sussex, and parts of Surrey, are served by Southern Railway (Ⓦ southern railway.com). Surrey is mainly served by South West Trains (Ⓦ southwesttrains.co.uk).

By bus National Express services from London and other main towns are pretty good, though local bus services are less impressive, and tend to dry up completely on Sundays outside of the major towns. Traveline (Ⓦ travelinesoutheast. org.uk) has route details and timetables. The Discovery Ticket (£8.50, family ticket £16) allows a day's unlimited bus travel across most bus services in the southeast; see

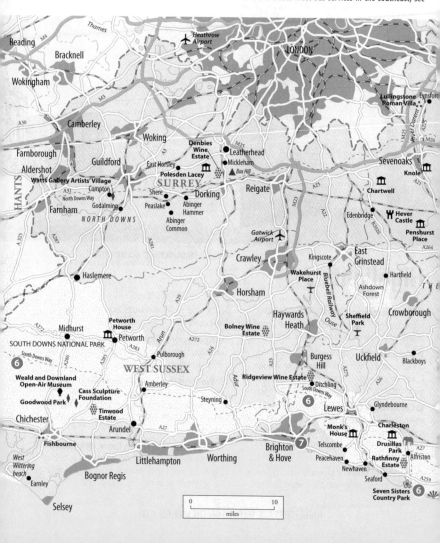

ⓦ southdowns.gov.uk /discovery-ticket for details.
By car Outside of the main towns, driving is the easiest way to get around, although commuter traffic in this corner of England is very heavy. The A2, M2 and M20 link the capital with Dover and Ramsgate, while the M23/A23 provides a quick run to Brighton. The A27 runs west–east across the Sussex coast, giving access to Chichester, Arundel, Brighton, Lewes, Eastbourne and Hastings, but can be slow-going.

North Kent

North Kent has a good share of appealing destinations, all easily accessible from London. The attractive little town of **Rochester** has historic and literary interest, but it's the seaside resorts that really pull in the visitors: arty **Whitstable**; appealingly old-fashioned **Broadstairs**; and **Margate**, which combines a dash of offbeat bucket-and-spade charm with the big-name Turner Contemporary gallery and a thriving vintage scene.

THE SOUTHEAST

HIGHLIGHTS

1. The Sportsman, Seasalter
2. Margate
3. Canterbury Cathedral
4. The White Cliffs of Dover
5. Rye
6. Walking the South Downs Way
7. The Lanes and North Laine, Brighton

2

Rochester and around

The handsome Medway town of **ROCHESTER** was first settled by the Romans, who built a fortress on the site of the existing castle. The town's most famous son is **Charles Dickens**, who spent his youth and final years near here – mischievously, it appears as "Mudfog" in *The Mudfog Papers*, and "Dullborough" in *The Uncommercial Traveller* as well as featuring in *The Pickwick Papers* and much of his last, unfinished novel, *The Mystery of Edwin Drood*. Many of the buildings Dickens described can still be seen today.

In neighbouring Chatham, the colossal **Chatham Historic Dockyard** records more than four hundred years of British maritime history – even if ships don't float your boat, it is well worth a trip.

Huguenot Museum

95 High St, ME1 1LX • Wed–Sat 10am–5pm, bank hol Mon 10am–4pm; last admission 30min before closing • £4 • ☎ 01634 789347, ⓦ huguenotmuseum.org

Above the tourist office on Rochester's historic High Street, the **Huguenot Museum** makes interesting connections between the fifty thousand French Protestants who fled France for Britain between 1685 and 1700 and modern-day refugees. The small display focuses on the dire religious persecution that drove them to flee their homes, the hostility they faced on arrival, and the huge contribution they made to British culture. Though many Huguenots settled in east London, there were significant populations in Kent – including an important silk-weaving community in Canterbury.

Guildhall Museum

17 High St, ME1 1PY • Tues–Sun 10am–5pm • Free • ☎ 01634 332900, ⓦ medway.gov.uk

The best section in the **Guildhall Museum**, in two buildings at the riverside end of the High Street, is its chilling exhibition on the decommissioned prison ships – or hulks – used to house convicts and prisoners of war in the late eighteenth century. The **Dickens Discovery Rooms**, in the adjoining building, include a wordy display about his life, and a short film about the locations that feature in his work.

Rochester Castle

Northwest end of the High St, ME1 1SW • Daily: April–Sept 10am–6pm; Oct–March 10am–4pm; last entry 45min before closing • £6.40; EH • ☎ 01634 335882, ⓦ www.english-heritage.org.uk/visit/places/rochester-castle

Built around 1127 by William of Corbeil, Archbishop of Canterbury, **Rochester Castle**, though now ruined, remains one of the best-preserved examples of a Norman fortress in the country. The stark 113ft-high ragstone keep glowers over the town, while the interior is all the better for having lost its floors, allowing clear views up and down the dank shell. The outer walls and two of the towers retain their corridors and spiral stairwells, allowing you to scramble up rough and uneven damp stone steps to the uppermost battlements.

Rochester Cathedral

Boley Hill, ME1 1SX • Mon–Fri 7.30am–6pm, Sat & Sun 7.30am–5pm • Free • ☎ 01634 843366, ⓦ rochestercathedral.org

Rochester Cathedral, built on Anglo-Saxon foundations, dates back to the eleventh century – though the structure has been much modified since. Plenty of Norman features have endured, however, particularly in the nave and on the cathedral's west front, with its pencil-shaped towers and richly carved portal and tympanum. Some fine paintings survived the Dissolution; look out for the thirteenth-century depiction of the Wheel of Fortune (only half survives) on the walls of the quire.

Restoration House

17–19 Crow Lane, ME1 1RF • June–Sept Thurs & Fri 10am–5pm • £8.50; gardens only £4 • ☎ 01634 848520, ⓦ restorationhouse.co.uk

An elegant Elizabethan mansion, the inspiration for Miss Havisham's Satis House in *Great Expectations*, **Restoration House** was given its current name after Charles II stayed here just before his restoration. Delightfully, the owners have avoided the manicured renovations of so many old houses; its ragged, crumbling beauty reveals far more about the house's long life and many alterations than would something more formal.

Chatham Historic Dockyard

About 1 mile north of Chatham along Dock Rd, ME4 4TE • Daily: mid-Feb to end March & Nov 10am–4pm; end March to Oct 10am–6pm; Victorian Ropery and *Ocelot* tours by timed ticket only • £24; under-15s £14; tickets valid for a year • ☎ 01634 823800, ⊛ thedockyard.co.uk • Bus #190 runs to the docks from Rochester (every 7–20min; 5min); there are also trains to Chatham station from Rochester (see below) and St Pancras International (every 30min; 40min) – from the station you can walk (30min), catch a bus (#101; 15min) or take a taxi (£7)

Two miles east of Rochester, the **Chatham Historic Dockyard**, founded by Henry VIII, was by the time of Charles II the major base of the Royal Navy. The dockyards were closed in 1984, with the end of the shipbuilding era, but reopened soon afterwards as a tourist attraction. The eighty-acre site, with its array of historically and architecturally fascinating ships and buildings, is too big to explore in one trip. Highlights include the interactive **Command of the Oceans** displays, the Victorian sloop **HMS Gannet**, the **Victorian Ropery** and the **Ocelot submarine**, the last warship to be built at the yard.

ARRIVAL AND INFORMATION ROCHESTER

By train Trains arrive in the heart of town just east of the High St, opposite the back entrance of the tourist office. Destinations Canterbury (every 20–45min; 40–50min); Chatham (every 5–25min; 3min); London Charing Cross (Mon–Fri every 30min; 1hr 20min); London St Pancras (every 30min; 35–40min); London Victoria (every 10–20min; 45min–1hr 20min); Ramsgate (every 5–40min; 1hr 10min).

Tourist office 95 High St (April–Sept Mon–Sat 10am–5pm, Sun 10.30am–5pm; Oct–March Mon–Sat 10am–5pm; ☎ 01634 338141, ⊛ visitmedway.org).

ACCOMMODATION

Golden Lion 147–151 High St, ME1 1EL ☎ 01634 405402, ⊛ jdwetherspoon.com. Rochester's most central option, with nine well-equipped en-suite rooms above a busy Wetherspoons pub. Breakfast is available in the pub (for an extra fee). **£80**

Ship & Trades Maritime Way, Chatham, ME4 3ER ☎ 01634 895200, ⊛ shipandtradeschatham.co.uk. Fifteen contemporary B&B rooms in a great location above a waterside brasserie-bar near the dockyard. Many rooms have marina views and some have terraces. **£100**

EATING

The Deaf Cat 83 High St, ME1 1LX ⊛ thedeafcat.com. A hop away from the cathedral, this coffee shop, dedicated to the memory of Dickens's deaf cat, is a laidback place serving espresso drinks, cookies, cakes and sandwiches to tourists and locals. Mon–Sat 9am–5pm, Sun 10am–5pm.
Topes 60 High St, ME1 1JY ☎ 01634 845270, ⊛ topes restaurant.com. Rochester's best restaurant, near the cathedral, in a wood-panelled dining room with sloping ceilings. Lunch sees gourmet burgers (£8) and inventive dishes (from £12) – basil gnocchi with Jerusalem artichoke and salsify, perhaps – with a two-/three-course set menu on Sun (£19.50/25); dinner is also prix fixe (£28/£35). Afternoon tea Wed–Sat 3–4pm (from £12.50). Wed–Fri & Sun noon–4pm, Sat noon–4pm & 6.30–9pm.

Whitstable

Fishermen, artists, yachties and foodies rub along in lively, laidback **WHITSTABLE**. The **oysters** for which the town is famed have been farmed here since Roman times, and today the annual **Oyster Festival** (end July; ⊛ whitstableoysterfestival.co.uk) is a high-spirited party of parades, live music, the "Landing of the Oysters" ceremony and raucous oyster-eating competitions.

Formal sights are few, which is part of the appeal. Follow the signs from the lively **High Street** and trendy **Harbour Street**, with its delis, restaurants and boutiques, to reach the **seafront**, a quiet shingle beach punctuated by weathered groynes and backed for most of its length by seaside houses and colourful beach huts in varying states of repair.

The Victorian **harbour**, a mix of pretty and gritty that defines Whitstable to a tee, bustles with a fish market, whelk stalls and a couple of seafood restaurants, and offers plenty of places to sit outside and watch the activity. The handsome 1892 Thames sailing barge, **Greta** (☎ 07711 657919, ⊛ greta1892.co.uk), offers boat trips around the estuary.

ARRIVAL AND INFORMATION

WHITSTABLE

By train From the train station it's a 15min walk to the centre, along Cromwell Road to Harbour St, the northern continuation of High St.

Destinations Broadstairs (every 10–45min; 25min); London St Pancras (hourly; 1hr 15min); London Victoria (hourly; 1hr 30min); Margate (every 10–45min; 20min); Ramsgate (every 10–45min; 35min).

By bus Buses to Canterbury (every 15min; 30min) stop on the High St.

Tourist information The Whitstable Shop, 34 Harbour St (Jan–March Mon–Sat 10am–4pm, Sun 11am–4pm; April–Dec Mon–Fri 10am–4pm, Sat 10am–5pm, Sun 11am–5pm; ☎ 01227 770060).

ACCOMMODATION

★ **Duke of Cumberland** High St, CT5 1AP ☎ 01227 280617, ⊛ thedukeinwhitstable.co.uk. Eight comfortable, good-value en-suite B&B rooms above a friendly, boho music pub. It can be noisy on weekend nights, when they have live bands, but the music (which is invariably excellent) usually winds up around midnight. On sunny mornings breakfast in the garden is a treat. **£80**

Fishermen's Huts Near the harbour ☎ 01227 280280, ⊛ whitstablefishermanshuts.com. Thirteen two-storey weatherboard cockle-farmers' stores (sleeping 2–6 people), offering cute, characterful accommodation near the harbour. Most have sea views, and some have basic self-catering facilities. Rates include breakfast, served at the nearby *Continental Hotel*, and drop considerably out of season. Mon–Thurs & Sun **£125**, Fri & Sat (two-night minimum) **£195**

EATING

★ **The Sportsman** Faversham Rd, Seasalter, CT5 4BP ☎ 01227 273370, ⊛ thesportsmanseasalter.co.uk. The drab exterior belies the Michelin-starred experience inside this fabulous gastropub, in a lonesome seaside spot four miles west of town. The deceptively simple food takes local sourcing to the extreme: fresh seafood, marsh lamb, seaweed from the beach, bread and butter made right here – even the salt comes from the sea outside. Mains from £21 – roast gurnard with bouillabaisse and green olive tapenade, say. Reservations essential. Tues–Sat noon–2pm & 7–9pm, Sun noon–2.30pm.

★ **Wheeler's Oyster Bar** 8 High St, CT5 1BQ ☎ 01227 273311, ⊛ wheelersoysterbar.com. A Whitstable institution dating back to 1856, this is one of the best restaurants in Kent. It's an informal, friendly little place, with just four tables in a back parlour and a few stools at the fish counter, but the inventive, super-fresh seafood is stunning, whether you choose raw oysters or more substantial mains (from £16) like roasted bass with coriander mash in a prawn and mussel broth with samphire. Delicious quiches available from the counter, too. BYO; cash only; reservations essential. Mon & Tues 10.30am–9pm, Thurs 10.15am–9pm, Fri 10.15am–9.30pm, Sat 10am–10pm, Sun 11.30am–9pm.

Windy Corner Stores 110 Nelson Rd, CT5 1DZ ☎ 01227 771707, ⊛ facebook.com/windycornerstoresandcafe. Homely neighbourhood café with a couple of outdoor tables on the quiet residential street. The home-made food includes breakfasts (£3–7) from a full veggie to a bacon sarnie, creative salads, sandwiches and daily specials (lasagne, perhaps, or vegetable gratin; from £7), and good coffee and cakes. Daily 8am–4.30pm.

DRINKING

Black Dog 66 High St, CT5 1BB ⊛ facebook.com/The BlackDog13. Don't be deceived by the vaguely Goth exterior – this quirky micropub is a cheery place, with (mainly) Kentish ales, ciders and wines, inexpensive local snacks, and a friendly regular crowd. No cards, no vaping, no children. Mon–Wed noon–11pm, Thurs–Sun noon–midnight.

Old Neptune Marine Terrace, CT5 1EJ ☎ 01227 272262, ⊛ thepubonthebeach.co.uk. A white weatherboard landmark standing alone on the beach, the "Neppy" is the perfect spot to enjoy a sundowner at a picnic table on the shingle, or to hunker down with a pint after a bracing beach walk. Some real ales, plus live music on Sat & Sun. Mon–Wed 11.30am–10.30pm, Thurs–Sat 11.30am–11.30pm, Sun noon–10.30pm.

Margate

After a few decades in decline, the tide in **MARGATE** is undoubtedly turning. It may not be the prettiest town on the Kent coast, but its energetic combination of eccentricity, nostalgia and cheery seaside fun give it a definite appeal. With the splendid **Turner Contemporary** gallery, the retro-cool **Dreamland** amusement park, a cluster of **vintage shops** and indie galleries in the Old Town and some superb places to eat and stay – not to mention the big, sandy **beach** – Margate is a must-see.

Dreamland

Marine Terrace/Belgrave Rd, CT9 1XG • Days and hours vary widely, depending on school holidays and special events: check website •
Free entry; attractions £1.50–3.50 – buy an unlimited wristband (£13.50/children £9.50) or load cash onto a rechargeable "Dream Pass"
and pay as you go • ☎ 01843 295887, ⓦ dreamlandmargate.com

Dreamland, which grew from Victorian pleasure gardens to become a wildly popular
theme park in the 1920s, stood derelict on the seafront for nearly ten miserable years
following its closure in 2003. Restored in 2015 under the guiding eye of designers
Wayne and Geraldine Hemingway, it's become the flagbearer for the new, improved
Margate – a hit with hipsters and hen dos alike. There's more here than knowing
vintage cool, however. Certainly the look of the place – old-school **roller disco** and
retro **pinball machines**, jaunty **helter skelter** and 1920s wooden **rollercoaster** – plays
on beloved memories of the traditional British seaside, but there's lots for today's
kids, too, from the Octopus's Garden playground to the gravity-defeating Barrel of
Laughs ride. It also hosts a lot of cool music events, featuring acts from Slaves to
the Dub Pistols.

2

Turner Contemporary

Rendezvous, CT9 1HG • Tues–Sun 10am–6pm • Free • ☎ 01843 233000, ⓦ turnercontemporary.org

Rearing up on the east side of the harbour, the opalescent **Turner Contemporary** is a
seafront landmark. Named for J.M.W. Turner, who went to school in the Old Town in
the 1780s, and who returned frequently as an adult to take advantage of the dazzling
light, the gallery is built on the site of the lodging house where he created some of his
famous sea paintings. Offering fantastic views of the ever-changing seascape through its
enormous windows, the gallery hosts temporary exhibitions of contemporary art –
previous shows have featured Yinka Shonibare and Grayson Perry.

Shell Grotto

Grotto Hill, CT9 2BU • Easter–Oct daily 10am–5pm; Nov–Easter Sat & Sun 11am–4pm • £4 • ☎ 01843 220008, ⓦ shellgrotto.co.uk

Discovered, or so the story goes, in 1835, Margate's bizarre **Shell Grotto** has been
captivating visitors ever since. Accessed via a damp subterranean passageway, the
grotto's hallways and chambers are completely covered with mosaics made from
shells – more than 4.5 million of them, tinted silvery grey and black by the fumes
of Victorian gas lamps. The origins of the grotto remain a mystery – some believe
it to be an ancient pagan temple, others a Regency folly – which only adds to its
offbeat charm.

ARRIVAL AND INFORMATION

MARGATE

By train The station is near the seafront on Station Rd.
Destinations Broadstairs (every 5–30min; 5min); Canterbury
(hourly; 30min); London St Pancras (every 25min–1hr; 1hr
30min); London Victoria (Mon–Sat hourly; 1hr 50min);
Ramsgate (every 5–30min; 15min); Whitstable (every
10–45min; 20min).
By bus Buses pull in at the clocktower on Marine Terrace.

Destinations Broadstairs (every 10–30min; 30min);
Canterbury (every 30min; 1hr); Herne Bay (hourly; 50min);
London (7 daily; 2hr–2hr 30min); Ramsgate (every 10–
15min; 45min).
Tourist office Droit House, Harbour Arm (April–Oct daily
10am–5pm; Nov–March Tues–Sat 10am–5pm; ☎ 01843
577577, ⓦ visitthanet.co.uk).

ACCOMMODATION

Sands Hotel 16 Marine Drive, CT9 1DH ☎ 01843
228228, ⓦ sandshotelmargate.co.uk. This airy boutique
refurb of an old seafront hotel has twenty luxe, tasteful
rooms, some with little balconies and sea views. The
swanky restaurant has glorious sunset views, and there's
a roof terrace for relaxing. **£200**

★**Walpole Bay Hotel** Fifth Ave, Cliftonville, CT9
2JJ ☎ 01843 221703, ⓦ walpolebayhotel.co.uk. This

family-run hotel has changed little since Edwardian times,
and exudes an air of shabby gentility from its pot-plant-
cluttered dining room to its clanky vintage elevator.
Don't miss the museum of, well, everything – including a
collection of napery (household linen) art. Rooms vary, but
most have sea views, many have small balconies and all are
comfy, clean and well equipped. **£85**

EATING

Cheesy Tiger 7–8 Harbour Arm, CT9 1AP ☎01843 448550, ⓦfacebook.com/cheesytigermargate. Rickety, boho little deli/café/wine bar offering small plates (pea and wild garlic risotto, for example) and cheese dishes made with the finest ingredients. Choose a sinfully unctuous toastie – or just sit with a simple cheese platter and glass of red gazing across at the sands. Dishes from £6. Hours vary; usually Mon & Wed 6–9pm, Thurs 6–10pm, Fri & Sat noon–10pm, Sun noon–9pm.

GB Pizza Co 14 Marine Drive, CT9 1DH ☎01843 297700, ⓦgreatbritishpizza.com. A buzzing contemporary pizza joint on the seafront, with smiley staff and a lively vibe, dishing up gourmet crispy pizza (£5–9.50) made with ingredients from small producers. Mon–Fri 11.30am–9.30pm, Sat & Sun 10am–9.30pm; shorter hours in autumn/winter.

★**Hantverk & Found** 18 King St, CT9 1DA ☎01843 280454, ⓦhantverk-found.co.uk. Tiny Old Town gallery café serving fabulous, inventive fish. It's hard to choose – prawn and squid ink croquettes? Plaice with seaweed and caper butter? Clams in dashi miso? – but you simply can't go wrong. Starters/small plates from £7, large plates £13–20. Thurs & Fri noon–4pm & 6.30–11pm, Sat noon–4pm & 6–11pm, Sun noon–4pm.

DRINKING

Fez 40 High St, CT9 1DS. Relaxed and eccentric pub, stuffed with recycled vintage memorabilia – young mods and old soulboys alike perch on Waltzer ride carriages, barber chairs or cinema seats to enjoy a good chat and a pint of real ale or speciality cider. Mon–Sat noon–10.30pm, Sun noon–10pm.

Harbour Arms Harbour Arm, CT9 1JD ☎07776 183273, ⓦthe-harbour-arms.co.uk. This cosy, cluttered micropub, with a nautical, sea-salty atmosphere, serves cask ales and ciders to a loyal local crowd. In warm weather the outside benches are at a premium, especially at sunset. Daily from noon; closing hours vary.

Broadstairs

Overlooking its golden sandy beach – Viking Bay – from its clifftop setting, **BROADSTAIRS** is the smallest and most immediately charming of the resort towns in northeast Kent. A fishing village turned Victorian resort, it's within walking distance of several sandy **bays** and has an excellent **folk festival**. It also has strong **Charles Dickens** connections: the author stayed here frequently, and rented an "airy nest" overlooking the sea, where he finished writing *David Copperfield*. A small **museum** and, in June, the **Dickens Festival** (ⓦbroadstairsdickensfestival.co.uk), play up the associations.

Dickens House Museum

2 Victoria Parade, CT10 1QS • Easter to mid-June & mid-Sept to mid-Oct daily 1–4.30pm; mid-June to mid-Sept daily 10am–4.30pm; Nov Sat & Sun 1–4.30pm • £3.75 • ☎01843 861232, ⓦdickensmuseumbroadstairs.co.uk

The broad, balconied cottage that houses the **Dickens House Museum** was once the home of Miss Mary Pearson Strong, on whom Dickens based the character of Betsey Trotwood in *David Copperfield*. Its small rooms are crammed with memorabilia, including Dickens' correspondence, illustrations from the original novels and a reconstruction of Betsey Trotwood's parlour.

ARRIVAL AND DEPARTURE

BROADSTAIRS

By train Broadstairs station is at the west end of the High St, a 10min walk to the seafront.
Destinations Canterbury (hourly; 25min); London St Pancras (every 25min–hourly; 1hr 20min–1hr 45min); London Victoria (Mon–Sat hourly; 1hr 50min); Margate (every 5–30min; 5min); Ramsgate (every 5–30min; 6min); Whitstable (every 10–45min; 25min).

By bus Buses stop along the High St.
Destinations Canterbury (hourly; 1hr–1hr 30min); London (7 daily; 2hr 45min–3hr 20min); Margate (every 10–30min; 30min); Ramsgate (every 5–20min; 15min).

Tourist information There's a small information kiosk on the Promenade by the *Royal Albion* hotel terrace (ⓦvisitthanet.co.uk).

ACCOMMODATION

★**Belvidere Place** 43 Belvedere Rd, CT10 1PF ☎01843 579850, ⓦbelvidereplace.co.uk. This stylish, quirky boutique B&B earns extra points for its warm, friendly management and gourmet breakfasts. The five lovely rooms feature sleek bathrooms, contemporary art and one-off vintage furniture finds. **£160**

EATING AND DRINKING

Tartar Frigate Harbour St, CT10 1EU ☎01843 862013, ⓦtartarfrigate.co.uk. In an unbeatable location right on the harbour, this eighteenth-century flint pub is a relaxed, friendly hangout, with regular folk bands. Book ahead for the restaurant, which offers classic seafood dishes from £17. Sun lunch sees things go off-piste, with a traditional four-course roast (£19). Pub Mon–Sat 11am–11pm, Sun 11am–10.30pm; restaurant Mon–Sat noon–1.45pm & 7–9.45pm, Sun seatings 12.30pm & 3.30pm.

★**Wyatt & Jones** 23–27 Harbour St, CT10 1EU ☎01843 865126, ⓦwyattandjones.co.uk. Stylish, airy restaurant a pebble's throw from the beach, dishing up superb Modern British food – try roasted hake with cauliflower, crab, shredded ham hock and beans – using mainly Kentish ingredients. Mains from £14 at lunch (small plates also available from £6), a little more in the evening. Wed & Thurs 9–11am, noon–3pm & 6.30–9pm, Fri & Sat 9–11am, noon–3pm & 6–10pm, Sun 9–11am & noon–4pm.

Ramsgate

RAMSGATE is the largest of the resorts in northeast Kent, its robust Victorian red-brick architecture and elegant Georgian squares set high on a cliff linked to the seafront by broad, sweeping ramps. Down by the **harbour** (ⓦportoframsgate.co.uk) cafés and bars overlook the bobbing yachts, while the town's small, busy **Ramsgate Sands** lies just a short stroll away. Sights include the **Maritime Museum**, on the quayside, which chronicles local maritime history (Easter–Sept Tues–Sun 10.30am–5.30pm; £2.50; ⓦramsgatemaritime museum.org) and the **Ramsgate Tunnels**, on Marina Esplanade (tours Wed–Sun 10am, noon, 2pm & 4pm; 1hr; £6.50; ☎01843 588123, ⓦramsgatetunnels.org), a subterranean warren of air-raid shelters – equipped with bunk beds, electric lights and lavatories – that saved thousands of lives during World War II.

ARRIVAL AND DEPARTURE   RAMSGATE

By train Ramsgate's station lies about 1.5 miles northwest of the centre, at the end of Wilfred Rd, at the top of the High St. Destinations Broadstairs (every 5–30min; 6min); Canterbury (every 20–40min; 20min); London St Pancras (every 10min–1hr; 1hr 15min–1hr 45min); London Charing Cross (hourly; 2hr 10min); London Victoria (Mon–Sat hourly; 2hr); Margate

(every 5–30min; 15min); Whitstable (every 10–45min; 35min).
By bus Buses pull in at the harbour.
Destinations Broadstairs (every 5–20min; 15min); Canterbury (hourly; 45min); London (7 daily; 2hr 30min–3hr); Margate (every 10–15min; 45min).

ACCOMMODATION

Albion House Albion Place, CT11 8HQ ☎01843 606630, ⓦalbionhouseramsgate.co.uk. Boutique hotel in an elegant clifftop Regency house. Most of the fourteen rooms, decorated in soothing contemporary style, offer

sea views and some have balconies. *Townleys*, their brasserie/bar, is good, too, serving anything from afternoon tea to cheeseboards or Modern British mains. Two-night minimum stay at weekends. **£155**

EATING AND DRINKING

Belgian Café 98 Harbour Parade, CT11 8LP ☎01843 587925, ⓦwww.belgiancafe.co.uk. Big, brash, casual place near the seafront, its outside tables spilling over with an eclectic crowd enjoying breakfasts, brunches, Belgian beers, real ales and marina views. Mon–Thurs & Sun 7am–2am, Fri & Sat 7am–3am.

Vinyl Head Café 2 The Broadway, Addington St, CT11 9JN ☎07901 334653, ⓦfacebook.com/vinylheadramsgate. Cool, chilled-out neighbourhood café offering home-made cakes, crêpes and veggie food, plus interesting events, from haircuts to live music – and vinyl for sale, of course. Mon–Thurs & Sun 9am–5pm, Fri & Sat 9am–10pm.

Canterbury

The fine old city of **CANTERBURY** offers a rich slice through two thousand years of English history, with Roman and early Christian remains, a ruined Norman **castle** and a famous **cathedral** that looms over a medieval warren of time-skewed Tudor buildings. Its compact centre, partly ringed by ancient **walls**, is virtually car-free, but this doesn't stop the High Street seizing up in high summer with the milling crowds.

2

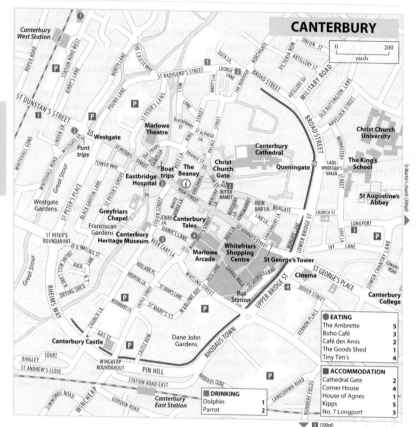

Brief history

The city that began as a Belgic settlement was known as **Durovernum Cantiacorum** to the Romans, who established a garrison and supply base here, and was renamed **Cantwaraburg** by the Saxons. In 597 the Saxon King Ethelbert welcomed the monk Augustine, despatched by the pope to convert England to Christianity; one of the two Benedictine monasteries that Augustine founded – Christ Church, raised on the site of the Roman basilica – was to become England's first cathedral.

After the Norman invasion, a power struggle ensued between the archbishops, the abbots from the nearby monastery – now **St Augustine's Abbey** – and King Henry II. This culminated in the assassination of Archbishop **Thomas Becket** in the cathedral in 1170, a martyrdom that created one of Christendom's greatest shrines and made Canterbury one of the country's richest cities. Believers from all over Europe flocked to the cathedral on pilgrimages to Becket's tomb – ribald events portrayed to great effect in Geoffrey Chaucer's fourteenth-century **Canterbury Tales**.

Becket's tomb was later destroyed on the command of Henry VIII, who also ordered the dissolution of St Augustine's Abbey, and the next couple of centuries saw a downturn in Canterbury's fortunes. The city suffered extensive damage from German bombing in 1942 during a "Baedeker Raid" – a Nazi campaign to destroy Britain's most treasured historic sites as identified in the eponymous German travel guides. The cathedral survived, however, and today, along with St Augustine's Abbey and St Martin's Church (at the corner of B. Holmes Rd and St Martin's Lane), has been designated a **UNESCO World Heritage Site**.

Canterbury Cathedral

Buttermarket, CT1 2EH • April–Oct Mon–Sat 9am–5.30pm (crypt from 10am), Sun 12.30–2.30pm; Nov–March Mon–Sat 9am–5pm (crypt from 10am), Sun 12.30–2.30pm; last entry 30min before closing • £12 • ☎ 01227 762862, ⓦ canterbury-cathedral.org

Mother Church of the Church of England, **Canterbury Cathedral** dominates the northeast quadrant of the city. A cathedral has stood here since 602, established by Augustine, but the structure you see today owes most to the **Normans**, who rebuilt it in 1070 after a huge fire. Modified over successive centuries, today it is characterized by the puritanical lines of the late medieval Perpendicular style.

The spot where Thomas Becket was murdered, known as the **Martyrdom**, is just off the nave in the northwest transept, marked by a modern-day flagstone etched with the name "Thomas". Next to it, the **Altar of the Sword's Point** – where, in medieval times, the shattered tip of the sword that hacked Becket's scalp was displayed as a relic – is marked by a modern sculpture of the assassins' weapons. From the Martyrdom you descend to the low, Romanesque **crypt**, one of the few surviving parts of the Norman cathedral and the finest of its type in the country. Amazingly well-preserved **carvings** adorn the capitals of the sturdy columns, showing flowers, animals, scallops, sea monsters and winged beasts. Becket's original shrine stood down here until 1220, when it was moved to a more resplendent position in the **Trinity Chapel**, beyond the Quire. The new shrine, far more ornate than the earlier tomb, studded, according to the writer Erasmus in 1513, with jewels as big as goose eggs, was demolished during the Dissolution of the Monasteries in 1538; a candle marks where it once stood. You can get a sense of what the shrine looked like in the thirteenth-century stained-glass **Miracle Windows**, on the north side of the chapel.

2

The Beaney

18 High St, CT1 2RA • Tues–Sat 10am–5pm, Sun noon–5pm • Free • ☎ 01227 862162, ⓦ canterburymuseums.co.uk/beaney

A sturdy terracotta, brick and mock-Tudor ensemble built in 1898, the **Beaney** – officially the **Beaney House of Art and Knowledge** – has the not unlikeable feel of a Victorian collection. The stuffed animals, pinned beetles and cases of **antiquities and archeological finds** are intriguing, but make sure to spend time with the **paintings**. Highlights include the Van Dyck portrait of Kent MP Sir Basil Dixwell (1638), a Walter Sickert landscape (1936) painted during his four-year stay on the Kent coast, and the vigorous images of 1930s Kentish hop-pickers by English Impressionist Dame Laura Knight.

Roman Museum

Butchery Lane, CT1 2JR • Daily 10am–5pm • £8; joint ticket with Canterbury Heritage Museum (see p.146) £12 • ☎ 01227 785575, ⓦ canterburymuseums.co.uk/romanmuseum

Following the devastating German bombings of 1942, excavations of the destroyed Longmarket area, off the High Street, exposed the foundations of a Roman townhouse complete with mosaic floors. These are now preserved *in situ* in the subterranean **Roman Museum**, but it's the rich haul of **artefacts**, domestic and military, that proves to be the big attraction.

Canterbury Tales

St Margaret's St, CT1 2TG • April–Aug daily 10am–5pm; Sept & Oct daily 10am–4pm; Nov–March Wed–Sun 10am–4pm • £9.95 • ☎ 01227 696002, ⓦ canterburytales.org.uk

Based on Geoffrey Chaucer's medieval stories, the **Canterbury Tales** is a quasi-educational, and fun, attraction. Costumed guides set you on your way through odour-enhanced galleries depicting a series of fourteenth-century tableaux as you follow the progress of a group of pilgrims (or rather, suitably scrofulous mannequins) from London to Becket's fabulously ornate shrine. Each space provides a setting for one of the famous tales.

Canterbury Heritage Museum

Stour St, CT1 2NR • 11am–5pm: April–Sept Wed–Sun; Oct & some hol weeks daily • £8; joint ticket with Roman Museum (see p.145) £12 •
☎ 01227 475202, ⊚ canterburymuseums.co.uk/heritagemuseum

The **Canterbury Heritage Museum** provides a lively jaunt through local history, with particularly strong sections on the Roman city, the medieval pilgrimage era and the Tudors and Stuarts – and interesting sections on local literary figures Christopher Marlowe, Joseph Conrad and Oliver Postgate (originator, in the 1970s, of children's television programmes *Bagpuss* and *The Clangers*).

St Augustine's Abbey

Longport, CT1 1PF • April–Sept daily 10am–6pm; Oct daily 10am–5pm; Nov–March Sat & Sun 10am–4pm • £6.20; EH • ☎ 01227 767345,
⊚ www.english-heritage.org.uk/visit/places/st-augustines-abbey

St Augustine's Abbey, founded as a monastery by Augustine in 598, was vastly altered and enlarged by the Normans before being destroyed in the Dissolution. Today, it is an atmospheric site, with more to see than its ruinous state might suggest. Ground plans, delineated in stone on soft carpets of grass, along with scattered semi-intact chapels, altar slabs and tombstones, powerfully evoke the original buildings, while illustrated information panels recount the abbey's changing fortunes.

ARRIVAL AND INFORMATION
CANTERBURY

By train Canterbury has two train stations: Canterbury East (in the south) and Canterbury West (in the north), each a 15min walk from the cathedral. Canterbury West is used by the high-speed train from London St Pancras.
Destinations from Canterbury East Chatham (every 20–40min; 45min); Dover (every 30min–1hr; 15–30min); London Victoria (every 30–40min; 1hr 35min); Rochester (every 20–40min; 40min–1hr).
Destinations from Canterbury West Ashford (every 10–30min; 15–25min); Broadstairs (hourly; 25min); London Charing Cross (Mon–Sat hourly; 1hr 45min); London St Pancras (hourly; 55min); Margate (hourly; 30min); Ramsgate (every 20–40min; 20min).

By bus National Express services and local Stagecoach East Kent buses use the station just inside the city walls on St George's Lane beside the Whitefriars shopping complex.
Destinations Broadstairs (hourly; 1hr–1hr 30min); Deal (Mon–Sat every 30min–1hr; 45min–1hr 20min); Dover (every 15min–1hr; 45min); Folkestone (every 15min–1hr; 45min); London Victoria (hourly; 2hr); Margate (every 30min; 1hr); Ramsgate (hourly; 45min); Sandwich (every 20min; 40min); Whitstable (every 15min; 30min).
Tourist office In the Beaney, 18 High St (Mon–Wed & Fri 9am–6pm, Thurs 9am–8pm, Sat 9am–5pm, Sun 10am–5pm; ☎ 01227 862162, ⊚ canterbury.co.uk).

ACCOMMODATION

Cathedral Gate 36 Burgate, CT1 2HA ☎ 01227 464381, ⊚ cathgate.co.uk; map p.144. Built in 1438 and with a fantastic location next to the cathedral, this ancient pilgrims' hostelry – all crooked, creaking floors and narrow, steep staircases – is in no way fancy, but it's comfortable, with cathedral views from many of the rooms and a simple continental breakfast. The cheapest rooms share toilets and showers, but have basins and tea- and coffee-making facilities. **£81.50**

Corner House 1 Dover St, CT1 3HD ☎ 01227 780793, ⊚ cornerhouserestaurants.co.uk; map p.144. Set on a busy corner just outside the city wall, these three gorgeous B&B rooms combine rustic charm and contemporary cool. The same people run the superb Modern British restaurant downstairs. **£99**

★ **House of Agnes** 71 St Dunstan's St ☎ 01227 472185, ⊚ houseofagnes.co.uk; map p.144. You can't fail to be charmed by the crooked exterior of this quirky B&B, which has eight individually designed rooms in the main fifteenth-century house (mentioned in *David Copperfield*), and another eight options in the old stable block in the walled garden (£95). **£115**

★ **Kipps** 40 Nunnery Fields, CT1 3JT ☎ 01227 786121, ⊚ kipps-hostel.com; map p.144. A 10min walk from Canterbury East station, this excellent self-catering hostel – with mixed en-suite dorms plus single and double rooms – is clean and very friendly, with homely touches and a large cottage garden. Regular events mean you can be sociable, but it's more a home from home than a party place. No curfew. Breakfast £3.50. Dorms **£24**, doubles **£75**

No. 7 Longport 7 Longport, CT1 1PE ☎ 01227 455367, ⊚ 7longport.co.uk; map p.144. This fabulous little hideaway – a tiny, luxuriously decorated fifteenth-century

2

cottage with a double bedroom, wet room and lounge – is tucked away in the courtyard garden of the friendly owners' home, opposite St Augustine's Abbey. Breakfasts are wonderful, with lots of locally sourced ingredients, and can be eaten in the main house, in the cottage or in the courtyard. **£100**

EATING

The Ambrette 14–15 Beer Cart Lane, CT1 2NY ☎01227 200777, ⓦtheambrette.co.uk; map p.144. Smart nouvelle Indian cuisine with a strong focus on local produce, with delicious flavours infusing everything from quinoa and mushroom biryani to goat stew with jasmine rice. Mains £17–30; two-/three-course lunch menus (Mon–Sat) £21.95/£24.95. Mon–Thurs 11am–2.30pm & 6–9.30pm, Fri & Sat 11am–2.30pm & 5.30–10pm, Sun noon–2.30pm & 5.30–10pm.

Boho Café 27 High St, CT1 2AZ ☎01227 458931, ⓦbohocafecanterbury.co.uk; map p.144. This funky café-bar, with its paintbox-bright, mismatched decor, has an informal feel. The Mediterranean-accented menu (mains from £8) ranges from big breakfasts via tapas to home-made burgers, with coffee and cake all day. There's a little suntrap garden at the back. Mon–Thurs 9am–6pm, Fri & Sat 9am–9pm, Sun 10am–5pm.

Café des Amis 95 St Dunstan's St, CT2 8AD ☎01227 464390, ⓦcafedez.com; map p.144. Lively Mexican/Tex-Mex/South American place with eclectic, carnivalesque decor and delicious food. Try the paella (£26.95 for two) followed by a bubbling chocolate *fundido*. Mon–Thurs noon–10pm, Fri noon–10.30pm, Sat 11am–10.30pm, Sun 11am–9.30pm.

★**The Goods Shed** Station Rd West, CT2 8AN ☎01227 459153, ⓦthegoodsshed.co.uk; map p.144. It doesn't get any more locally sourced than this – a buzzing, shabby-chic Modern British restaurant in the fabulous Goods Shed farmers' market, where most of the ingredients are provided by the stalls themselves. The regularly changing menu might feature dishes such as pressed leek and goat curd with herb salad (£7) or steamed hake with wilted chard (£17.50). Great breakfasts, too. Tues–Fri 8–10.30am, noon–2.30pm & 6–9.30pm, Sat 8–10.30am, noon–3pm & 6–9.30pm, Sun 9–10.30am & noon–3pm.

★**Tiny Tim's** 34 St Margaret's St, CT1 2TG ☎01227 450793, ⓦtinytimstearoom.com; map p.144. This incongruously named, elegant, 1930s-inspired tearoom offers some thirty blends of tea as well as all-day breakfasts, light lunches (from £7), cakes and filling afternoon teas (all day, from £18.50). In good weather sit in the cute back garden. Tues–Sat 9.30am–5pm, Sun 10.30am–4pm.

DRINKING

Canterbury is a nice place for a drink, with a number of pubs serving **real ales** in cosy, historic buildings. The Kentish Shepherd Neame-owned places are in the majority, but look out, too, for beers from Canterbury's own Wantsum, Canterbury Brewers and Canterbury Ales breweries.

Dolphin 17 St Radigund's St, CT1 2AA ☎01227 455963, ⓦthedolphincanterbury.co.uk; map p.144. Likeable, unpretentious 1930s-built pub with a good selection of local real ales, a roaring fire in winter and a big, grassy beer garden. Tasty modern pub grub, too (mains from £9). Mon–Wed noon–11pm, Thurs–Sat noon–midnight, Sun noon–10pm; kitchen Mon–Wed noon–2pm & 6–9pm, Thurs & Fri noon–2pm & 6–10pm, Sat noon–

10pm, Sun noon–3pm & 6–9pm.

Parrot 1–9 Church Lane, CT1 2AG ☎01227 454170, ⓦtheparrotonline.com; map p.144. Ancient hostelry – among the oldest in Canterbury – in a quiet location, with loads of character, a decent selection of ales and a gastropub menu (mains from £9). There's a beer terrace at the back. Daily noon–11pm; kitchen Mon–Sat noon–10pm, Sun noon–9.30pm.

Sandwich

SANDWICH, one of the best-preserved medieval towns in England, is a sleepy, picturesque place, with some fine half-timbered buildings lining its narrow streets and a lovely location on the willow-lined banks of the River Stour. It's also a major destination for **golfers** – the **Royal St George's**, perhaps the finest link course in England, fringes the coast to the east (ⓦroyalstgeorges.com).

Sandwich's riverfront **quayside**, peaceful today, was once the heart of a great medieval port. While the river estuary began silting up in the sixteenth century, and the sea is now miles away, the waterfront gives the place a breezily nautical atmosphere, with small boats moored by the toll bridge, open countryside stretching out across the river

THE CINQUE PORTS

In 1278 Dover, Hythe, Sandwich, Romney and Hastings – already part of a long-established but unofficial confederation of defensive coastal settlements – were formalized under a charter by Edward I as the **Cinque Ports** (pronounced "sink", despite the name's French origin). In return for providing England with maritime support, the five ports were granted trading privileges and other liberties – including self-government, exemption from taxes and tolls and "possession of goods thrown overboard" – that enabled them to prosper while neighbouring ports struggled.

Rye, Winchelsea and seven other **"limb" ports** on the southeast coast were later added to the confederation. The ports' privileges were eventually revoked in 1685; their maritime services had become increasingly unnecessary after Henry VIII had founded a professional navy and, due to a shifting coastline, several of their harbours had silted up anyway, stranding some of them miles inland. Today, of all the Cinque Ports, only Dover is still a major working port.

2

and the cry of seagulls raking the air. Seal- and bird-spotting **boat trips** (£7–35; ☏07958 376183, ⓦsandwichriverbus.co.uk) run from the toll bridge over the Stour.

ARRIVAL AND INFORMATION

SANDWICH

By train Sandwich station is off St George's Rd, from where it's a 10min walk north to the town centre and the quay.

Destinations Deal (every 30min–1hr; 6min); Dover (every 30min–1hr; 25min); Ramsgate (hourly; 15min).

By bus Buses pull in and depart from outside the tourist office.

Destinations Canterbury (every 20min–1hr; 45min); Deal (every 20min–1hr; 25–35min); Dover (every 45min–1hr; 45min–1hr); Ramsgate (hourly; 45min–1hr).

Tourist office Guildhall, Cattle Market, in the town centre (April–Oct Mon–Sat 10am–4pm; ☏01304 613565, ⓦsandwichtowncouncil.gov.uk or ⓦwhitecliffscountry.org.uk).

ACCOMMODATION

Bell Hotel The Quay, CT13 9EF ☏01304 613388, ⓦbellhotelsandwich.co.uk. Rambling hostelry that has stood on this site since Tudor times; today's buildiing is largely Edwardian. Rooms are comfy, in an uncontroversial, contemporary style; the priciest have balconies overlooking the Stour. There's a good restaurant serving Modern European food (mains from £13). Minimum two-night stay on summer weekends. **£130**

EATING AND DRINKING

★George and Dragon 24 Fisher St, CT13 9EJ ☏01304 613106, ⓦgeorgeanddragon-sandwich.co.uk. A fifteenth-century inn and popular, unpretentious gastro-pub, with delicious Modern British food (mains £11–18), cask ales, roaring fires in winter and a courtyard for alfresco dining. Booking advised for dinner. Mon–Sat 11am–11pm, Sun 11am–4pm; kitchen Mon–Sat noon–2pm & 6–9.15pm, Sun noon–2pm.

No Name 1 No Name St, CT13 9AJ ☏01304 612626, ⓦnonameshop.co.uk. For picnic supplies, including baguettes, look no further than this excellent French deli near the Guildhall. You can also eat in, from a daily-changing menu (£7–14) of light dishes – salads, soups, quiches – and heartier mains such as confit de canard or *tartiflette*. Mon–Sat 8am–5pm, Sun 9am–4pm.

Deal

The low-key seaside town of **DEAL**, six miles southeast of Sandwich, was the site of Julius Caesar's first successful landfall in Britain in 55 BC. Today it's an appealing place, with a broad, steeply shelving shingle **beach** backed by a jumble of faded Georgian townhouses, a picturesque **Old Town** redolent with maritime history and a striking concrete **pier** lined with hopeful anglers casting their lines. Henry VIII's two seafront **castles**, linked by a seaside path, are the main attractions, and there are enough good places to eat, drink and stay to make the town an appealing weekend destination.

2

Deal Castle

Marine Rd, CT14 7BA • April–Sept daily 10am–6pm; Oct daily 10am–5pm; Nov–March Sat & Sun 10am–4pm • £6.60; EH • ☎ 01304 372762, ⓦ www.english-heritage.org.uk/visit/places/deal-castle

Diminutive **Deal Castle**, at the south end of town, is one of the most striking of Henry VIII's forts. Its distinctive shape – viewed from the air it looks like a Tudor rose – owes less to aesthetics than to sophisticated military engineering: the squat rounded walls were good at deflecting missiles. Self-guided **audio tours** outline every detail of the design, with the bare rooms revealing how the castle changed over the years and giving a good sense of how the soldiers lived.

Walmer Castle

Kingsdown Rd, 1 mile south of Deal, CT14 7LJ • Jan to mid-Feb Sat & Sun 10am–4pm; mid-Feb to March Wed–Sun 10am–4pm; April–Sept daily 10am–6pm; Oct daily 10am–5pm; Nov & Dec Sat & Sun 10am–6pm • £10.70; EH • ☎ 01304 364288, ⓦ www.english-heritage.org.uk/visit/places/walmer-castle-and-gardens • Hourly buses (#82/#82A) from Deal; also accessible on foot or by bike along the seafront (30min) or from Walmer train station, a mile away

Walmer Castle is another of Henry VIII's Tudor-rose-shaped defences, built to protect the coast from its enemies across the Channel. Like Deal Castle it saw little fighting, and changed use when it became the official residence of the Lords Warden of the Cinque Ports in 1708 (which it remains, though the title itself is now strictly ceremonial). Adapted over the years, today the castle resembles a heavily fortified stately home; the best-known resident was the Duke of Wellington, who was given the post of Lord Warden in 1828 and who died here in 1852. You can see the armchair in which he expired and a pair of original Wellington boots.

ARRIVAL AND INFORMATION   DEAL

By train The station is on Queen St, a 10min walk from the sea.
Destinations Dover (every 15min–1hr; 15min); Ramsgate (every 30min–1hr; 20min); Sandwich (every 30min–1hr; 6min); Walmer (every 30min–1hr; 3min).
By bus Buses run from South St, Queen St and Victoria Rd, all near each other in the centre.
Destinations Canterbury (hourly; 1hr 15min); Dover (every

30min–1hr; 45min); London Victoria (2 daily; 2hr 50min–3hr 45min); Sandwich (every 20min–1hr; 25–35min); Walmer (every 15min–1hr; 15–30min).
Tourist office Town Hall, High St (April–Sept Mon–Fri 10am–2pm, Sat 10am–2pm; Oct–March Mon–Fri 10am–2pm; ☎ 01304 369576, ⓦ deal.gov.uk or ⓦ whitecliffs country.org.uk).

ACCOMMODATION AND EATING

Bear's Well 10 St George's Rd, CT14 6BA ☎ 01304 694144, ⓦ bearswell.co.uk. In a central but peaceful Old Town house, this airy boutique B&B has three lovely en-suite rooms with views of the church or the pretty back garden. Breakfasts, made using local produce, are great. **£120**

★**Frog and Scot** 86 High St, CT14 6EG ☎ 01304 379444, ⓦ frogandscot.co.uk. Delightful neighbourhood haven serving superlative French-inspired dishes, from sea bass with bouillabaisse to chestnut soup with goose

confit, and a fabulous wine list. Mains from £15; two-/three-course lunch menus £13.95/£16.95. Wed–Sat noon–2.30pm & 6.15–9.15pm, Sun noon–3.30pm.
Poppy's Kitchen 119 High St, CT14 6BB ☎ 01304 371719, ⓦ poppyskitchen.co.uk. Simple, fresh and delicious food, with a focus on organic ingredients. Dishes (from £5.50) might include chard and Cheddar tart or kale, apple, spelt and hazelnut salad, while breakfasts range from home-made granola to a Full English. Gorgeous cakes, too. Mon–Sat 9am–5.30pm, Sun 10am–3pm.

Dover and around

Given its importance as a travel hub – it's the busiest ferry port in Europe – **DOVER** is surprisingly small and, badly bombed during World War II, the town centre is unprepossessing. The nearby attractions, however, are big ones: **Dover Castle**, looming proudly above town, and the iconic **White Cliffs**.

Dover Castle

Castle Hill, CT16 1HU • Mid-Feb to March Wed–Sun 10am–4pm; April–July & Sept daily 10am–6pm; Aug daily 9.30am–6pm; Oct daily 10am–5pm; Nov to mid-Feb Sat & Sun 10am–4pm • £19.40, under-16s £11.60; EH • ☎ 0370 333 1181, ⓦ www.english-heritage.org.uk /visit/places/dover-castle • Buses #15, #15X, #80, #80A & #93 from Dover town centre (hourly; 20min)

No historical stone goes unturned at **Dover Castle**, an astonishingly imposing defensive complex that has protected the English coast for more than two thousand years. In 1068 **William the Conqueror**, following the Battle of Hastings, built over the earthworks of an Iron Age hillfort here; a century later, the Normans constructed the handsome **keep**, or Great Tower, that now presides over the heart of the complex. The grounds also include a **Roman lighthouse**, a **Saxon church** – with motifs graffitied by irreverent Crusaders still visible near the pulpit – and all manner of later additions, including a network of **tunnels** dug during the Napoleonic Wars and extended during World War II.

You should allow a **full day** for a visit. If time is short, head first for the **Operation Dynamo tunnel tours** (at regular intervals; 40min), which are affecting immersive experiences that, accompanied by the muffled sound of anti-aircraft guns and screaming Spitfires, shed light on the build-up to the war and the Dunkirk evacuation. From there, make your way to Henry II's **Great Tower**. Here the opulent medieval royal court has been painstakingly re-created, with everything from the pots and pans in the kitchen to the richly coloured furniture in the King's Chamber.

White Cliffs of Dover

Stretching sixteen miles along the coast, a towering 350ft high in places, the vast **White Cliffs of Dover** are composed of chalk plus traces of quartz, shells and flint. A large area of the cliffs lies within the Kent Downs Area of Outstanding Natural Beauty, and with their grasslands home to rare plants, butterflies and migrant birds, have been designated a Site of Special Scientific Interest. A **walk** along the cliffs affords you amazing views of the Straits of Dover – and on a clear day you may well even see France.

A significant stretch is owned by the **National Trust**, which has a visitor centre on Upper Road, Langdon Cliffs (daily: March–June, Sept & Oct 10am–5pm; July & Aug 10am–5.30pm; Nov–Feb 11am–4pm; parking £3.50; ⓦ nationaltrust.org.uk/white-cliffs -dover). The NT manages two clifftop attractions: **Fan Bay Deep Shelter**, an underground labyrinth that housed troops during World War II (tours every 30min April–Oct Mon & Fri–Sun 11am–3pm; 45min; £10); and the **South Foreland lighthouse**, above St Margaret's Bay, built in 1843 to guide ships past the perilous Goodwin Sands (tours leave regularly 11am–5pm: mid-March to mid-July, Sept & Oct Mon & Fri–Sun; mid-July to Aug daily; 30min; £6; ⓦ nationaltrust.org.uk/south-foreland-lighthouse) – there's a good tearoom in the lighthouse, too.

ARRIVAL AND INFORMATION

DOVER AND AROUND

By train Dover Priory station is off Folkestone Rd, a 10min walk west of the centre.
Destinations Canterbury (every 30min–1hr; 15–30min); Deal (every 15min–1hr; 15min); London Victoria (every 30min–1hr; 2hr); Sandwich (every 30min–1hr; 25min).
By bus The town-centre bus station is on Pencester Rd.
Destinations Canterbury (every 15min–1hr; 45min);

Deal (every 30min–1hr; 45min); London Victoria (11 daily; 1hr 55min–3hr 20min); Sandwich (every 45min–1hr; 45min–1hr).

Tourist office Dover Museum, Market Square (April–Sept Mon–Sat 9.30am–5pm, Sun 10am–3pm; Oct–March Mon–Sat 9.30am–5pm; ☎ 01304 201066, ⓦ whitecliffs country.org.uk).

ACCOMMODATION

Maison Dieu 89 Maison Dieu Rd, CT16 1RU ☎ 01304 204033, ⓦ maisondieu.co.uk. Welcoming, central guest-house with six spotless single, double, twin and family rooms, most of which are en suite. A few have views over the garden to Dover Castle. Optional breakfast £6.50 extra. **£85**

White Cliffs Hotel High St, St-Margaret's-at-Cliffe, 4 miles northeast of Dover, CT15 6AT ☎ 01304 852229, ⓦ thewhitecliffs.com. Friendly place – a hit with walkers and cyclists – with a sociable restaurant/bar. The seven rooms tucked away in the main building – a sixteenth-century

2

weatherboard house – come in all shapes, sizes and styles, from rustic and cosy to glamorous and huge; there are nine

less expensive options (£90) in outbuildings around the spacious beer garden. Tasty full breakfast included. **£120**

EATING AND DRINKING

★**Allotment** 9 High St, CT16 1DP ☎ 01304 214467, ⓦ facebook.com/allotmentdover. The best option on Dover's high street, this bistro serves tasty, unpretentious food in a light space. Try a simple breakfast or lunch (wild boar sausages in Kentish cider; baguettes), or fancier dinner mains including Whitstable fish stew or partridge in perry sauce. Mains £10–16. Tues–Thurs 10.30am–9.30pm, Fri 9am–9.30pm, Sat 9am–10pm, Sun noon–4pm.

The Coastguard St Margaret's Bay, 4 miles northeast

of Dover, CT15 6DY ☎ 01304 853051, ⓦ thecoastguard .co.uk. This nautically themed beachside pub/restaurant, at the bottom of the White Cliffs, is a good spot for a Kentish cask ale, either on the large terrace or in the small beer garden. They serve traditional English dishes (fish and chips, burgers, pies) and interesting daily specials (razor clams with garlic and toasted nuts, say); mains £10–20. Mon–Sat 10am–11pm, Sun 10am–10pm; kitchen Mon–Sat noon–2.45pm & 6–8.45pm, Sun noon–2.30pm & 6–8pm.

Folkestone

In the early 2000s, depressed after the demise of its tourist industry and the loss of its ferry link to France, **FOLKESTONE** was a doleful place. Thus began a concerted effort to start again, with hopes pinned on the arts and the creative industries. Cue Folkestone's **Triennial** (ⓦ folkestonetriennial.org.uk), a contemporary art show that since its premier in 2008 has been gradually bringing Folkestone out of its extended limbo. With the regenerating **Creative Quarter** and the salty little fishing **harbour**, the gloriously landscaped **Lower Leas Coastal Park**, a sandy town **beach**, and the wild **Warren** cliffs and beach nearby, Folkestone has plenty to offer.

ARRIVAL AND INFORMATION

By train Folkestone Central station is off Cheriton Rd, just under a mile northwest of the Creative Quarter.
Destinations Dover (every 10–50min; 20min); London Charing Cross (every 30min–1hr; 1hr 40min); London St Pancras (every 30min–1hr; 55min).

By bus The bus station is in the centre of town.
Destinations Dover (every 20–30min; 30min); London Victoria (4 daily; 2hr 10min–3hr).
Tourist office 1–2 Guildhall St (Mon–Fri 9am–5pm; ☎ 01303 257946, ⓦ discoverfolkestone.co.uk).

ACCOMMODATION AND EATING

★**Rocksalt Rooms** 1–3 Back St, CT19 6NN ☎ 01303 212070, ⓦ rocksaltfolkestone.co.uk. Four "boutique bolt holes" (they're small) in an unbeatable harbourside location. It's run by the people who own the excellent *Smokehouse* chippy downstairs, and the sophisticated *Rocksalt* restaurant, footsteps away. Rooms at the front are the best, with French windows and water views, but they're all chic and super-comfy. Continental breakfast is

delivered to your room in a hamper. **£85**
Steep Street 18–24 Old High St, CT10 1RL ☎ 01303 247819, ⓦ steepstreet.co.uk. This gorgeous coffee house, lined ceiling to floor with books, buzzes with a Creative Quarter crowd. They serve simple, good food, from sandwiches to salads, quiches to cakes (cakes from £2; savoury tarts £4). Mon–Fri 8.30am–6pm, Sat 9am–6pm, Sun 9am–5pm.

Romney Marsh

In Roman times, what is now the southernmost chunk of Kent was submerged beneath the English Channel. The lowering of the sea levels in the Middle Ages and later reclamation created a hundred-square-mile area of shingle and marshland, now known as **Romney Marsh**. Once home to important Cinque and limb ports (see box, p.149), and villages made wealthy from the wool trade, this rather forlorn expanse now presents a melancholy aspect, given over to agriculture and with few sights – unless you count the sheep, the birdlife and several curious medieval **churches**. While this flat, depopulated area makes good walking and cycling country, its salt-speckled, big-skied strangeness can also be appreciated on the dinky **Romney, Hythe & Dymchurch Railway** (RH&DR; mid-March to Oct daily; Nov to mid-March Sat & Sun, plus special events and tours; £18 Hythe–Dungeness return, less for shorter journeys; ☎01797 362353, ⊚rhdr.org.uk), a fifteen-inch-gauge line whose miniature steam trains run the 13.5 miles between the lonesome shingle spit of **Dungeness** and the seaside town of **Hythe**. Around five miles west of the latter, **Port Lympne Reserve**, working on a conservation and breeding programme for wild and endangered species, is home to more than seven hundred animals, including spectacled bears, Western Lowland gorillas and black rhino (daily: April–Oct 9.30am–6.30pm, last admission 3.30pm; Nov–March 9.30am–5pm, last admission 2.30pm; £25, under-16s £21; ☎01303 264647, ⊚aspinallfoundation.org/port-lympne).

Dungeness

An end-of-the-earth eeriness pervades **DUNGENESS**, the windlashed shingle headland at the marsh's southernmost tip. Dominated by two hulking nuclear power stations (one of them disused), "the Ness" is not conventionally pretty, but there's a strange beauty to this lost-in-time spot, where a scattering of weatherboard shacks and disused railway carriages houses fishermen, artists and recluses drawn to the area's bleak, otherworldly allure. The late Derek Jarman, artist and filmmaker, made his home here, at **Prospect Cottage** – on Dungeness Road, a twenty-minute walk from the RH&DR station – and the shingle garden he created from beachcombed treasures and tough little plants remains a poignant memorial. Panoramic views over the headland can be had from the decommissioned **Old Lighthouse** (10.30am–4.30pm: March–May & late Sept to Oct Sat & Sun; June Tues–Thurs, Sat & Sun; July to late Sept daily; £4; ⊚dungenesslighthouse.com), built in 1904.

The unique ecology around here attracts huge colonies of gulls, terns, smews and gadwalls; you can see them, and all manner of waterbirds, waders and wildfowl, from the **RSPB visitor centre** (daily: March–Oct 10am–5pm; Nov–Feb 10am–4pm; free; ⊚rspb.org.uk) on the Lydd road three miles from Dungeness.

The High Weald

The **Weald** stretches across a large area between the North and South Downs and includes parts of both Kent and Sussex. The central part, the **High Weald**, is epitomized by gentle hills, sunken country lanes and somnolent villages as well as some of England's most beautiful gardens, including **Sissinghurst**, **Great Dixter**, **Wakehurst Place** and **Sheffield Park** – the last of these the southern terminus of the vintage **Bluebell Railway**. The bracken and gorse-speckled heathland that makes up nearby **Ashdown Forest** – setting for the Winnie-the-Pooh stories – is a lovely spot for longer walks. The Weald also offers a wealth of picturesque historical sites, including a couple of picture-book castles – **Hever Castle** and **Bodiam Castle** – as well as stately homes at **Penshurst** and **Knole**, a well-preserved Roman villa at **Lullingstone**, the fascinating home of wartime leader Winston Churchill at **Chartwell** and Rudyard Kipling's countryside retreat at **Bateman's**. **Tunbridge Wells**, set in the heart of the beautiful High Weald countryside, makes a good base.

Royal Tunbridge Wells

The handsome spa town of **ROYAL TUNBRIDGE WELLS** was established after a bubbling ferrous **spring** discovered here in 1606 was claimed to have curative properties, and reached its height of popularity during the Regency period when restorative cures were in vogue. It remains an elegant place, with some smart places to stay and eat and three lovely urban parks: the **Grove** and **Calverley Grounds** offer formal gardens, while the wilder **Common**, spreading out to the west, is laced with historic pathways.

2

The Pantiles

Tucked off the southern end of the High Street, the colonnaded **Pantiles** – named for the clay tiles, shaped in wooden pans, that paved the street in the seventeenth century – is a pedestrianized parade of independent shops, delis and cafés that exudes a faded elegance. Here, at the original **Chalybeate Spring**, outside the 1804 Bath House, a costumed "dipper" will serve you a cup of the iron-rich waters (Easter–Sept Wed–Sun 10.30am–3.30pm; £1), a tradition dating back to the eighteenth century.

Tunbridge Wells Museum

Mount Pleasant Rd, TN1 1JN • Tues–Sat 9.30am–5pm • Free • ☎ 01892 554171, ⊛ tunbridgewellsmuseum.org

Sitting above the town library, **Tunbridge Wells Museum** offers an intriguing mishmash of local history, its old glass cabinets filled with everything from fossils to dandy Georgian glad rags, fading maps and scruffy stuffed animals. Take a look at its exquisite Tunbridge ware, the finely crafted wooden marquetry, dating from the late eighteenth century and popular until the 1920s, that was applied to everything from boxes to book covers to furniture.

ARRIVAL AND INFORMATION   ROYAL TUNBRIDGE WELLS

By train The train station stands where the High St becomes Mount Pleasant Rd.
Destinations Hastings (every 30min–1hr; 40–50min); London Charing Cross (every 15–30min; 55min); Sevenoaks (every 20min; 20–25min).
By bus Buses set down and pick up along the High St and Mount Pleasant Rd.

Destinations Brighton (every 30min–1hr; 1hr 50min); Hever (Mon–Sat 2 daily; 40–50min); Lewes (every 30min–1hr; 1hr 20min); London Victoria (1 daily; 1hr 40min); Sevenoaks (every 30min–2hr; 45min).
Tourist office Corn Exchange, The Pantiles (10am–3pm: April–Sept Mon–Sat; Oct–March Tues–Sat 3pm; ☎ 01892 515675, ⊛ visittunbridgewells.com).

ACCOMMODATION

Hotel du Vin Crescent Rd, TN1 2LY ☎ 01892 320749, ⊛ hotelduvin.com. Elegantly set in a Georgian mansion overlooking Calverley Grounds, this member of the luxe

Hotel du Vin chain is quietly classy, with a cosy bar, romantic French restaurant and a beautifully sloping old staircase leading up to the rooms. **£175**

EATING AND DRINKING

The Black Pig 18 Grove Hill Rd, TN1 1RZ ☎ 01892 523030, ⊛ theblackpig.net. Smart gastropub, where locally sourced dishes might include slow-roast pork belly, crispy squid or honey-roasted butternut squash risotto. On a sunny day, settle down with a steak sandwich and a glass of wine in the beer garden. Mains from £11. Daily noon–11pm; kitchen Mon–Thurs noon–2.30pm & 6.30–9.30pm, Fri noon–2.30pm & 6.30–10pm, Sat noon–3pm & 6–10pm, Sun noon–3pm.
Mount Edgcumbe The Common, TN4 8BX ☎ 01892 618854, ⊛ themountedgcumbe.com. Hidden away in an old Georgian house, this food pub has a deliciously rural feel, with a nice garden. It makes a cosy, offbeat place for a Modern British meal – from veggie sharing plates to fish

and chips – or a pint of local ale. Check out the real cave in the bar area, strewn with fairy lights. Mains from £12. Mon–Wed 11am–11pm, Thurs–Sat 11am–11.30pm, Sun noon–10.30pm; kitchen Mon–Thurs noon–3pm & 6–9.30pm, Fri & Sat noon–9.30pm, Sun noon–8pm.
Sankey's 39 Mount Ephraim, TN4 8AA ☎ 01892 511422, ⊛ sankeys.co.uk. Lively pub, decked out with enamel signs, brewery mirrors, squishy sofas and a wood-burning stove. It has a host of specialist beers and a good pub-grub menu (burgers, bangers, salads) but is best known for its seafood. Mains from £7. Mon–Wed & Sun noon–11pm, Thurs–Sat noon–1am; kitchen Mon noon–3pm, Tues–Fri noon–3pm & 6–9pm, Sat noon–9pm, Sun noon–8pm.

Sissinghurst

Biddenden Rd, 15 miles east of Tunbridge Wells, TN17 2AB • Gardens mid-March to Oct daily 11am–5.30pm, last admission 45min before closing; estate daily dawn–dusk • Mid-March to Oct £12.50; Nov & Dec £9; NT • ☎ 01580 710700, ⊛ nationaltrust.org.uk/sissinghurst

When she and her husband took it over in 1930, the writer Vita Sackville-West described the neglected Tudor estate of **Sissinghurst** as "a garden crying out for rescue".

Over the following thirty years they transformed the five-acre plot into one of England's greatest country gardens, the romantic abundance of flowers, spilling over onto narrow brick pathways, defying the formality of the great gardens that came before. Don't miss the magical **White Garden**, with its pale blooms and silvery-grey foliage, and, in summer, the lush, overblown **Rose Garden**. In the Tudor **tower** that Vita used as her quarters you can climb 78 steep stairs to get a bird's-eye view of the gardens and the ancient surrounding woodlands; halfway up, peep into Vita's study, which feels intensely personal still, with rugs on the floor and a photo of her lover, Virginia Woolf, on her desk.

2

Great Dixter

Near Northiam, TN31 6PH, 22 miles southeast of Tunbridge Wells • April–Oct Tues–Sun & bank hols: gardens 11am–5pm; house 2–5pm • £11, gardens only £9 • ☎ 01797 252878, ⓦ greatdixter.co.uk • Stagecoach bus #2 passes through Northiam on its way from Hastings to Tenterden (Mon–Sat hourly; 45min from Hastings)

One of the best-loved gardens in the country, **Great Dixter** was the creation of gardener and writer **Christopher Lloyd**, who lived here until his death in 2005. Exuberant and informal, the gardens – now maintained by Lloyd's friend and head gardener **Fergus Garrett** – spread around a splendid medieval half-timbered house in a series of intimate garden "rooms" and sweeps of wildflower-speckled meadow.

Bodiam Castle

Bodiam, TN32 5UA, 18 miles southeast of Tunbridge Wells • Daily 10.30am–5pm, or dusk if earlier • £9.30; NT • ☎ 01580 830196, ⓦ nationaltrust.org.uk/bodiam-castle • Bus #349 from Hastings (Mon–Fri every 2hr; 40min); steam train from Tenterden (April–Sept up to 5 services a day; ☎ 01580 765155, ⓦ kesr.org.uk)

One of the country's most picturesque castles, **Bodiam** is a classically stout square block with rounded corner turrets, battlements and a wide moat. When it was built in 1385 to guard what were the lower reaches of the River Rother, Bodiam was state-of-the-art military architecture, but during the Civil War, a company of Roundheads breached the fortress and removed its roof, and over the following centuries Bodiam fell into neglect. Inside the castle walls there are plenty of nooks and crannies to explore, and steep spiral staircases leading up to the crenellated battlements; look out for the castle's portcullis, claimed to be the oldest in the country.

Bateman's

Bateman's Lane, Burwash, TN19 7DS, 13 miles southeast of Tunbridge Wells off the A265 • Daily: garden 10am–5pm or dusk; house April–Oct 11am–5pm, Nov–March 11am–3pm • £10.40; NT • ☎ 01435 882302, ⓦ nationaltrust.org.uk/batemans

Half a mile south of the picturesque village of Burwash, **Bateman's** was the idyllic home of the writer and journalist Rudyard Kipling from 1902 until his death in 1936. The house is set amid attractive gardens, which feature a still-working watermill converted by Kipling to generate electricity. Inside, the house displays Kipling's letters, early editions of his work and mementos from his travels.

Penshurst Place

Penshurst, TN11 8DG, 5 miles northwest of Tunbridge Wells • April–Oct daily: house noon–4pm; gardens noon–6pm • £11, gardens only £9 • ☎ 01892 870307, ⓦ penshurstplace.com • Bus #231 or #233 from Tunbridge Wells (Mon–Sat); Penshurst train station is 2.5 miles north (no taxis)

Tudor timber-framed houses and shops line the pretty main street of **Penshurst**. Presiding over it all is fourteenth-century **Penshurst Place**, home to the Sidney family since 1552 and birthplace of the Elizabethan soldier and poet, Sir Philip Sidney. The jaw-dropping Baron's Hall is the glory of the interior, with its 60ft-high chestnut-beamed roof still in place. The 48 acres of grounds offer good parkland walks, while the eleven-acre walled **garden** is a beautiful example of Elizabethan garden design.

Hever Castle

Hever, TN8 7NG, 10 miles northwest of Tunbridge Wells • Daily: castle April–Oct noon–6pm, Nov noon–4.30pm; gardens April–Oct 10.30am–6pm, Nov 10.30am–4.30pm; last entry 1hr 30min before closing • £16.90, gardens only £14.20 • ☎ 01732 865224, ⓦ hevercastle.co.uk • Hever train station is a mile west (no taxis)

The moated **Hever Castle** was the childhood home of Anne Boleyn, second wife of Henry VIII, and where Anne of Cleves, Henry's fourth wife, lived after their divorce. In 1903, having fallen into disrepair, the castle was bought by William Waldorf Astor, American millionaire-owner of *The Observer*, who had it assiduously restored in mock-Tudor style. Today, Hever has an intimate feel, and though it does display some intriguing Elizabethan and Jacobite artefacts it tells you more about the aspirations of American plutocrats than the lifestyle of Tudor nobles. **Anne Boleyn's room** is the most affecting; small and bare, dominated by a wooden chest carved with the words "Anne Bullen". You can also see the book of prayers she carried to the executioner's block, inscribed in her own writing and with references to the pope crossed out. Outside is Waldorf Astor's beautiful **Italian Garden**, decorated with statues, some more than two thousand years old, as well as a traditional yew-hedge maze, adventure playground, splashy water maze and boating lakes.

Chartwell

Mapleton Rd, Westerham, TN16 1PS, 17.5 miles northwest of Tunbridge Wells • **House** March–Oct Mon–Fri 11.30am–5pm, Sat & Sun 11am–5pm; Dec (some rooms only) Sat & Sun 11am–3pm • **Studio** Daily: March–Oct noon–4pm; Nov & Dec noon–3.30pm • **Gardens** Daily: March–Oct 10am–5pm; Nov–Feb 10am–4pm • £13.50; studio & gardens only £6.75; NT • ☎ 01732 868381, ⓦ nationaltrust.org.uk/chartwell

Packed with the wartime prime minister's possessions – including his rather contemplative paintings – there is something touchingly intimate about **Chartwell**, the country residence of **Winston Churchill** from 1924 until his death in 1965. The house is set up to look largely as it would have in the 1920s and 1930s, revealing the personal side of this gruff statesman; don't miss the sweet series of notes between him and his wife, and a letter from his father written when he was a young man, expressing his fears that he was to become "a social wastrel". In the rolling **gardens**, dotted with lakes and ponds and shaded by mature fruit trees, you can see Churchill's **studio**, which is lined with more than one hundred canvases.

Knole

Sevenoaks, entered from the south end of Sevenoaks High St, TN15 0RP • **House** March–Oct Tues–Sun noon–4pm • £8.15; NT • **Gatehouse tower** Daily: mid-March to Oct 10am–5pm; Nov–Feb 10am–4pm • £3.15; NT • **Parkland** Daily dawn–dusk • Free; NT • ☎ 01732 462100, ⓦ nationaltrust.org.uk/knole • The High St entrance is a mile south of Sevenoaks train station and half a mile south of the bus station; it's a 15min uphill walk from the entrance through the estate to the house

Covering a whopping four acres, **Knole** palace, in the commuter town of **Sevenoaks**, is an astonishingly handsome ensemble. Built in 1456 as a residence for the archbishops of Canterbury, it was appropriated in 1538 by Henry VIII, who loved to hunt in its thousand acres of **parkland** (still today home to several hundred wild deer). Elizabeth I gave the estate to her Lord Treasurer, Thomas Sackville, who remodelled the house in Renaissance style in 1605; it has remained in the family's hands ever since. Bloomsbury Group writer and gardener Vita Sackville-West was raised here, and her lover Virginia Woolf derived inspiration for her novel *Orlando* from frequent visits. Highlights of this endlessly fascinating treasure-trove range from the lustrous **Venetian Ambassador's Room** with its staggering carved and gilded eighteenth-century bed, to the **Gatehouse**

WINE IN THE SOUTHEAST: A SPARKLING SUCCESS STORY

With almost identical soil and geology to the Champagne region, and increased temperatures due to global warming, the Southeast is home to many of the country's best **vineyards**, several of which offer **tours** and **tastings**. For more details of vineyards throughout Kent, Sussex and Surrey – including a downloadable wine routes **map** – check the website of the Southeastern Vineyard Association. ⓦ seva.uk.com.

KENT

Biddenden Gribble Bridge Lane, Biddenden, TN27 8DF ☎ 01580 291726, ⓦ biddendenvineyards.com. Kent's oldest commercial vineyard, producing wines from eleven varieties of grape, plus traditional ciders and juices – there's a shop/café on site. Short, self-guided tours and occasional themed tours are all free. Jan & Feb Mon–Sat 10am–5pm; March–Dec Mon–Sat 10am–5pm, Sun 11am–5pm.

Chapel Down Small Hythe, Tenterden, TN30 7NG ☎ 01580 763033, ⓦ chapeldown.com. Multi-award-winning winemaker – they do a great lager, too – with a wine and produce store on site, and a smart terrace restaurant overlooking the vines. Pop in for a wander, or take a guided tour. Daily 10am–5pm; guided tours & tastings (1hr 45min; £10) April–Nov daily.

Hush Heath Five Oak Lane, Staplehurst, TN12 0HT ☎ 01622 832794, ⓦ hushheath.com. Family-owned estate devoting around twenty of its four hundred acres to Chardonnay, Pinot Noir and Pinot Meunier vineyards. It's famed for its sparkling wines, made using traditional methods, and in particular the Balfour Brut Rosé. The free self-guided trail through the glorious estate is stunning, as are the free tastings. Daily 11am–5pm.

SUSSEX

Bolney Wine Estate Foxhole Lane, Bolney, RH17 5NB ☎ 01444 881894, ⓦ bolneywineestate.co.uk. This small, family-run vineyard has a lovely setting and offers a variety of tours, plus an on-site café. The vineyard has won awards for its sparkling wines, but is also known – unusually for the UK – for its red wines. Shop Mon–Sat 9am–5pm, Sun 10am–3pm; café Tues–Fri 9am–5pm, Sun 10am–3pm; tours £10–42.50 (see website for dates).

Ridgeview Wine Estate Fragbarrow Lane, Ditchling Common, off the B2112, BN6 8TP ☎ 01444 241441, ⓦ ridgeview.co.uk. Multi-award-winning vineyard, known for its sparkling wines. Try one of the tours (pre-booking essential), or just turn up at the cellar door and taste before you buy. 11am–4pm: Jan & Feb Mon–Fri & Sun, March–Dec daily; tours (1hr 30min–2hr; £15) regularly in summer.

Tinwood Estate Tinwood Lane, Halnaker, PO18 0NE ☎ 01243 537372, ⓦ tinwoodestate.com. Smart vineyard near Chichester producing sparkling wines from classic Champagne-variety grapes. There are tours (pre-booking essential) in summer, plus there's a stylish, modern tasting room. Daily 9am–6pm; tours (1hr 30min; £15) regularly in summer.

SURREY

Denbies Wine Estate London Rd, Dorking, RH5 6AA ☎ 01306 876616, ⓦ denbies.co.uk. Vast commercial vineyard specializing in sparkling wines and whites. Indoor tours lead you through the winery; outdoor options include a truck ride through the estate, which also has public footpaths. Tastings and meals can be added to some tours. Tours (50min–1hr; £6.50–16.95) March–Oct daily 11am, noon, 2pm, 3pm & 4pm (occasionally more on Sat); Nov–Feb limited options.

2

---

tower, filled with the private possessions of Eddy Sackville-West, a Bloomsbury Group stalwart, who lived here from 1926 to 1940. Knole is undergoing a **major restoration**, slated for completion in 2018; until then some rooms will be closed for conservation. Admission prices will increase once the work is complete.

Lullingstone Roman Villa

Eynsford, DA4 0JA, 8 miles north of Sevenoaks • April–Sept daily 10am–6pm; Oct daily 10am–5pm; Nov–March Sat & Sun 10am–4pm • £7.60; EH • ☎ 01322 863467, ⓦ www.english-heritage.org.uk/visit/places/lullingstone-roman-villa • The villa is a 2-mile walk from Eynsford train station

Located in a rural spot alongside the trickle of the River Darent, **Lullingstone Roman Villa**, believed to have started as a farm around 100 AD, grew to become an important estate and remained occupied until the fifth century. The site is known for its brilliantly preserved mosaics, including a fine **mosaic floor** depicting Bellerophon riding Pegasus and slaying the Chimera, a fire-breathing she-beast, but displays throughout – including a couple of human skeletons – offer lively and often poignant glimpses into Roman domestic life.

Ashdown Forest

Information Barn Wych Cross, RH18 5JP, 14 miles southwest of Tunbridge Wells • April–Sept Mon–Fri 2–5pm, Sat & Sun 11am–5pm; Oct–March Sat & Sun 11am–dusk • ☎ 01342 823583, ⓦ ashdownforest.org • There are dozens of free parking sites on the main roads through the Forest; Metrobus # 291 runs between Tunbridge Wells and East Grinstead, stopping at Hartfield and Coleman's Hatch (Mon–Sat hourly, Sun every 2hr) and #270 runs from Brighton to East Grinstead via Wych Cross (Mon–Sat hourly)

The ten-square-mile expanse of **Ashdown Forest** – which is in fact almost two-thirds heathland – is best known as the home of the much-loved fictional bear **Winnie-the-Pooh**. A.A. Milne wrote his famous children's books from his weekend home at the northeastern edge of the forest, modelling the stories closely on the local area. Today you can visit Pooh Bridge and many other spots described in the stories; download a leaflet from the website, or, for Pooh Bridge, park at the dedicated car park just off the B2026.

Sheffield Park and Garden

On the A275 East Grinstead–Lewes main road, TN22 3QX, 18 miles southwest of Tunbridge Wells • **Garden** Daily 10am–5pm, or dusk if earlier • £11.20; NT • **Parkland** Daily dawn–dusk • Free; NT • ☎ 01825 790231, ⓦ nationaltrust.org.uk/sheffield-park-and-garden • Bus #121 from Lewes (Sat every 2hr; 30min); Bluebell Railway (see below) Sheffield Park station is a 10min walk away

First laid out by Capability Brown in the eighteenth century, the beautifully landscaped gardens at **Sheffield Park and Garden** are set around five deep lakes, linked by cascades and waterfalls, and are particularly famed for their autumn colours. On the other side of the access road lies the estate's 265-acre parkland, dotted by grazing sheep, and home to a natural play trail.

Bluebell Railway

Sheffield Park Station, on the A275 East Grinstead–Lewes main road, TN22 3QL, 18 miles southwest of Tunbridge Wells • April–Oct daily; Nov–March Sat, Sun & school hols • Day ticket with unlimited travel £19, station admission £1.50 Kingscote, £2.50 Horsted Keynes, £3 Sheffield Park • ☎ 01825 720800, ⓦ bluebell-railway.com • The railway is connected to the mainline station at East Grinstead; bus #121 from Lewes (Sat every 2hr; 30min) runs to Sheffield Park station

A mile southwest of Sheffield Park lies the southern terminus of the **Bluebell Railway**, whose vintage steam locomotives chuff eleven miles north via Horsted Keynes and Kingscote stations to the mainline station at East Grinstead. The stations have all been beautifully restored in period style, and Sheffield Park station is also home to the railway sheds and a small museum.

Wakehurst Place

On the B2028 between Ardingly and Turners Hill, RH17 6TN, 20 miles west of Tunbridge Wells • Daily: March–Oct 10am–6pm; Nov–Feb 10am–4.30pm; Millennium Seed Bank closes 1hr earlier • £12.50 (includes parking); NT members and others groups with reciprocal arrangements get free entry but are required to pay for parking (£2/1hr 30min, £10/day) • ☎ 01444 894066, ⓦ kew.org/visit-wakehurst • Metrobus #272 from Haywards Heath (Mon–Sat every 2hr; 15min)

The country home of Kew Royal Botanic Gardens, **Wakehurst Place** sprawls over 465 acres and encompasses formal gardens, lakes and ancient woodland; you'll need a whole day to explore it properly. Wakehurst Place is also home to the **Millennium Seed Bank**, the world's largest seed conservation project, which aims to safeguard 25 percent of the Earth's plant species by 2020.

Rye and around

Perched on a hill overlooking Romney Marsh, the pretty, ancient town of **RYE** was added as a "limb" to the original Cinque Ports (see box, p.149), but was subsequently marooned two miles inland by the retreat of the sea and the silting-up of the River Rother. It is now one of the most visited places in East Sussex – half-timbered, skew-roofed and quintessentially English, with plenty of interesting independent shops to poke around in and some excellent places to eat.

Rye's most picturesque street – and the most photographed – is the sloping cobbled **2** **Mermaid Street**, the town's main thoroughfare in the sixteenth century. At the top of Mermaid Street, just around the corner in West Street, lies **Lamb House** (mid-March to Oct Tues, Fri & Sat 11am–5pm; £5.85; NT; ☎01580 762334, ⓦnationaltrust.org.uk /lamb-house), home of the authors Henry James and (subsequently) E.F. Benson. Just a few cobbled yards away is the peaceful oasis of Church Square, where **St Mary's Church** boasts the oldest functioning pendulum clock in the country; the ascent of the church tower (£3.50) offers fine views over the rooftops. In the far corner of the square stands the stout **Ypres Tower** (daily: April–Oct 10.30am–5pm; Nov–March 10.30am–3.30pm; £4; ☎01797 227798, ⓦryemuseum.co.uk), built to keep watch for cross-Channel invaders; it now houses a number of relics from Rye's past, including paraphernalia from the town's smuggling heyday.

Rye's acclaimed **literary festival** (ⓦryeartsfestival.co.uk) takes place over two weeks in September and also features a wide range of musical and visual arts events. The other big annual event is **Rye Bay Scallop Week** (ⓦscallop.org.uk), held at the end of February.

Rye Harbour Nature Reserve

Rye Harbour Rd, TN31 7TU • Nature Reserve open access; Information centre most days 10am–4/5pm • Free • ☎ 01797 227784, ⓦ sussexwildlifetrust.org.uk • Bus #313 runs from Rye station to Rye Harbour (roughly hourly)

A few miles south of town is **Rye Harbour Nature Reserve**, by turns bleak and beautiful. Miles of footpaths meander around the shingle ridges, salt marsh and reed beds; you can download walks from the website, or pick up a map from the **information centre** situated down the path opposite the car park.

Winchelsea

Perched on a hill two miles southwest of Rye, **Winchelsea** was rebuilt by Edward I after the original settlement, Old Winchelsea – one of the Cinque Ports (see box, p.149) – was washed away in the great storm of 1287. Today the tiny town (no more than a few streets arranged around a central square) feels positively deserted, but it's well worth the trip from Rye to visit the ruined Gothic **Church of St Thomas à Becket**, with its beautiful 1930s stained-glass windows.

Camber Sands

Around three miles east of Rye, on the other side of the River Rother estuary, **Camber Sands** is a two-mile stretch of gorgeous dune-backed sandy beach that has become a renowned centre of wind- and watersports. The nicest way to reach it from Rye is by bike, on the three-mile dedicated **cycle path**.

ARRIVAL AND GETTING AROUND

RYE AND AROUND

By train Rye's train station is at the bottom of Station Approach, off Cinque Ports St; it's a 5min walk up to High St.

Destinations Ashford (hourly; 20min); Hastings (hourly;

20min); London St Pancras (hourly; 1hr 25min).

By bus Bus #100 runs into the centre of Rye from Hastings (Mon–Sat every 30min, Sun hourly; 40min), passing through Winchelsea en route. Bus #101 (Mon–Sat hourly,

2

Sun every 2hr; 15min) runs from Rye station to Camber Sands (Mon–Sat hourly, Sun every 2hr; 15min).
By bike You can rent bicycles from Rye Hire, 1 Cyprus Place

(Mon–Fri 8am–5pm, Sat 8am–noon, Sat afternoon & Sun by appointment only; £13/half-day, £18/day; ☎01797 223033, ⓦ ryehire.co.uk).

INFORMATION

Rye Heritage and Information Centre Strand Quay, TN31 7AY (daily 10am–5pm; check website for winter hours; ☎01797 226696, ⓦ ryeheritage.co.uk). This privately run information centre sells town maps (30p) and rents out

walking tour audioguides (£4). Its excellent sound-and-light show (every 30min; 20min; £3.50) gives you a potted history of Rye using a model of the town as it would have looked in the early nineteenth century.

ACCOMMODATION

The George 98 High St, TN31 7JT ☎01797 222114, ⓦ thegeorgeinrye.com. This luxurious small hotel manages to get everything just right, from the cosy, wood-beamed bar and excellent restaurant to the tasteful, individually furnished rooms: there are 34 to choose from, ranging from an Arts and Crafts-styled room decked out in William Morris textiles to a Miami-themed hangout with circular bed. **£145**

★**Hayden's** 108 High St, TN31 7JE ☎01797 224501, ⓦ haydensinrye.co.uk. Friendly, popular B&B with seven

elegant, contemporary rooms set above a restaurant in the heart of town. Rooms at the back have lovely views out over Romney Marsh. **£125**

Rye Windmill Off Ferry Rd, TN31 7DW ☎01797 224027, ⓦ ryewindmill.co.uk. Great value for Rye, this 300-year-old Grade II listed smock windmill contains eight smart en-suite rooms, plus two suites in the windmill itself; splash out on the Windmill Suite (£170) for panoramic views over Rye. Minimum two-night stay at weekends. **£90**

EATING AND DRINKING

★**Knoops** Tower Forge, Hilders Cliff, Landgate ☎01797 225838, ⓦ facebook.com/KnoopsChocolateBar. This little place only offers one thing – hot chocolate – but it does it with style. Choose your chocolate (from 27 to 80 percent solids; £3), add your extras (various spices, peppers, fruits, even flowers – all 50p, or a shot of something stronger for £1) and wait to be presented with your own bowl of made-to-order chocolately loveliness. Mon & Fri–Sun 10am–6pm, plus Tues & Wed same hours in school hols.

Landgate Bistro 5–6 Landgate, TN31 7LH ☎01797 222829, ⓦ landgatebistro.co.uk. Perhaps the best restaurant in Rye, this small, intimate place – housed in

two interconnected Georgian cottages – is known for its traditionally British food: there's plenty of fish from the local fishing fleet, Romney Marsh lamb and game in season (mains £11–20). Wed–Fri 7–11pm, Sat noon–3.30pm & 6.30–11pm, Sun noon–3.30pm.

Standard Inn The Strand, TN31 7EN ☎01797 225231, ⓦ thestandardinnrye.co.uk. Beautifully restored inn, with bare brick walls and beams. There's a good selection of craft beer and local ale, including the pub's own Standard Inn Farmer's Ale, plus excellent food (mains £10–16). Mon–Thurs noon–11pm, Fri & Sat noon–midnight, Sun noon–10pm; kitchen daily noon–3/4pm & 6–9/9.30pm.

Hastings and around

The seaside town of **HASTINGS** has all the ingredients for a perfect break: a picturesque Old Town crammed with independent shops and cafés; a seafront that combines plenty of tacky seaside amusements with a sleek modern art gallery and a splendid new pier; a still-working fishing quarter supplying a multitude of excellent fish and seafood restaurants; and miles of lovely countryside right on its doorstep.

Just inland is the town of **Battle**, where William, Duke of Normandy, marched to meet King Harold's army in the famous battle of 1066. Bexhill's striking **De La Warr Pavilion** lies a few miles west of Hastings along the coast.

Old Town

The pretty **Old Town** is the nicest part of Hastings. **High Street** and pedestrianized **George Street** are the focus, both lined with antiques shops, galleries, restaurants and pubs. Running parallel to the High Street is **All Saints Street**, punctuated with the odd, rickety, timber-framed dwelling from the fifteenth century. Midway along George Street, the **West Hill Cliff Railway** (March–Sept daily 10am–5.30pm; Oct–Feb Sat &

Sun 11am–4pm; return ticket £2.60) ascends West Hill, depositing you a short walk from **Hastings Castle** (hours vary but generally April–Oct daily 10am–4pm; £4.75; ☎01424 422964, ⓦsmugglersadventure.co.uk/hastings-castle-experience), of which very little remains bar a few crumbling walls.

The Stade

Down by the seafront, the area known as **The Stade** is characterized by its tall, black weatherboard **net shops**, most dating from the mid-nineteenth century, and still in use today. The Stade is home to the town's fishing fleet – the largest beach-launched fleet in Europe – and many of the net shops sell fresh-off-the-boat fish. Just west of the net huts, the wide expanse of the **Stade Open Space** is used for various events throughout the year.

2

Jerwood Gallery

Rock-a-Nore Rd, TN34 3DW • Feb–Dec Tues–Sun & bank hols 11am–5pm; first Tues of month open until 8pm • £9, free first Tues of month 4–8pm • ☎01424 425809, ⓦjerwoodgallery.org

Adjacent to the fishing quarter, the sleek **Jerwood Gallery**, covered in shimmering dark-glazed tiles, provides a home for the Jerwood Foundation's modern art collection, which includes works by Stanley Spencer, Walter Sickert and Augustus John. A **café** up on the first floor overlooks the fishing boats on the beach.

East Hill and Hastings Country Park

Just behind the net shops, the venerable **East Hill Cliff Railway** (March–Sept daily 10am–5.30pm; Oct–Feb Sat & Sun 11am–4pm; return ticket £2.60) climbs up to **East Hill**, for wonderful views over the town and access to **Hastings Country Park** (ⓦhastingscountrypark.org.uk), a beautiful expanse of heathland, sandstone cliffs and ancient woodland ravines which spreads east for three miles.

Hastings Pier

Open daily; hours vary depending on season, weather and events – check website • Free • ⓦhastingspier.org.uk

West of The Stade, the beautifully restored **Hastings Pier** has risen phoenix-like from the ashes of an arson attack in 2010. Wide expanses of bare deck allow it to be used for everything from markets to concerts to open-air film screenings – check the website to see what's on. The centrepiece is The Deck, a beautifully designed visitor centre and café.

St Leonards-on-Sea

Shabby, arty, quirky and a bit rough around the edges, **St Leonards** – once a separate town but now more or less absorbed into Hastings – lies at the western end of the seafront. It's worth spending a morning or afternoon checking out some of the cool art galleries, shops, cafés and restaurants along **Norman Road** and **Kings Road**.

HASTINGS FESTIVALS

The biggest weekend of the year is the **Jack-in-the-Green Festival** (May Day weekend; ⓦhastingsjack.co.uk), three days of festivities culminating in a riotous parade of dancers, drummers and leaf-bedecked revellers through the streets of the Old Town up to Hastings' hilltop castle, where "the Jack" – a garlanded, leaf-covered figure whose origins date back to the eighteenth century – is ritually slain and the spirit of summer released.

Other events include three separate **food festivals** celebrating Hastings' fishing industry; **Hastings Week** in October; and **Fat Tuesday** (ⓦhastingsfattuesday.co.uk) held over four days in February, which sees hundreds of gigs taking place around town, many of them free.

Battle Abbey and Battlefield

At the south end of High St, Battle, TN33 0AD · Feb half term daily 10am–4pm; mid-Feb to March Wed–Sun 10am–4pm; April–Sept daily 10am–6pm; Oct daily 10am–5pm; Nov to mid-Feb Sat & Sun 10am–4pm · £11.20; EH · ☎ 01424 775705, ⓦ www.english-heritage.org.uk /visit/places/1066-battle-of-hastings-abbey-and-battlefield · Buses #304 and #305 from Hastings (Mon–Sat hourly; 15min), or regular trains from Hastings and London Charing Cross to Battle station, a 10min walk away

Six miles inland from Hastings in the small town of Battle, the remains of **Battle Abbey** occupy the site of the most famous land battle in British history. Here, or hereabouts, on October 14, 1066, the invading Normans swarmed up the hillside from Senlac Moor and overcame the army of King Harold, spelling an end to Anglo-Saxon England. Before the battle took place, William vowed that, should he win, he would build a religious foundation on the very spot of Harold's slaying to atone for the bloodshed, and, true to his word, Battle Abbey was built four years later and subsequently occupied by a fraternity of Benedictines.

The abbey, once one of the richest in the country, was partially destroyed in the Dissolution and much rebuilt and revised over the centuries. The magnificent 1330s gatehouse (topped by a rooftop viewing platform) still survives, along with the thirteenth-century rib-vaulted dormitory range, but all that remains of William's original abbey church is an outline on the grass, with the site of the high altar – the spot where Harold was supposedly killed – marked by a memorial stone. An excellent **visitor centre** shows a film about the battle and the events leading up to it. Audioguides (40min) take you round the site of the **battlefield**, vividly re-creating the battle and its aftermath.

De La Warr Pavilion

Marina, Bexhill-on-Sea, TN40 1DP · Daily: April–Oct 10am–6pm; Nov–March 10am–5pm · Free · ☎ 01424 229111, ⓦ dlwp.com · Bus #98 from Hastings (Mon–Sat every 30min, Sun hourly; 40min); train from Hastings (every 20min; 10min); or seafront cycle path from Hastings to Bexhill

The seaside town of Bexhill-on-Sea, five miles west of Hastings, is home to the iconic **De La Warr Pavilion**, a sleek Modernist masterpiece overlooking the sea. Built in 1935 by architects Erich Mendelsohn and Serge Chermayeff, the Pavilion slid gradually into disrepair after World War II, but today it has been restored to its original glory, hosting contemporary art **exhibitions** and **live performances**.

ARRIVAL AND INFORMATION

HASTINGS AND AROUND

By train Hastings station is a 10min walk from the seafront along Havelock Road. There's another station, St Leonards Warrior Square, at the north end of Kings Rd. Destinations Ashford (hourly; 40min); Battle (every 30min; 15min); Brighton (every 30min; 1hr 5min); Eastbourne (every 20min; 25min); Lewes (every 20min; 55min); London Victoria (hourly; 2hr–2hr 15min); Rye (hourly; 20min); Tunbridge Wells (every 30min; 35–50min).
By bus Bus services operate from outside the train station. Destinations Battle (Mon–Sat hourly; 15min); Dover

(Mon–Sat every 30min, Sun hourly; 2hr 50min); Eastbourne (Mon–Sat every 20–30min, Sun hourly; 1hr 15min); London Victoria (1 daily; 2hr 35min); Rye (Mon–Sat every 30min, Sun hourly; 40min).
Tourist office On the seafront at Aquila House, Breeds Place, TN34 3UY (April–Oct Mon–Fri 9am–5pm, Sat 9.30am–5.30pm, Sun 10.30am–4pm; Nov–March Mon–Fri 9am–5pm, Sat 9.30am–4.30pm, Sun 11am–3pm; ☎ 01424 451111, ⓦ visit1066country.com).

ACCOMMODATION

★**The Laindons** 23 High St, TN34 3EY ☎ 01424 437710, ⓦ thelaindons.com. Set in a Georgian townhouse, this friendly boutique B&B has five gorgeous rooms, all with a crisp Scandi vibe. Breakfast includes coffee from *The Laindons'* own coffee bar and roastery, *No. 23*, below the B&B. **£120**
Senlac Guesthouse 46–47 Cambridge Gardens, TN34 1EN ☎ 01424 435767, ⓦ senlacguesthouse.co.uk. Stylish yet affordable, this friendly guesthouse with smart,

contemporary rooms and located near the station, is fantastic value. The cheapest rooms share bathrooms. Breakfast costs £8.50 extra. **£60**
Swan House 1 Hill St, TN34 3HU ☎ 01892 430014, ⓦ swanhousehastings.co.uk. Beautiful B&B in a half-timbered fifteenth-century building on one of the Old Town's most picturesque streets. Rooms are luxurious and tasteful, and there's a pretty decked patio garden for sunny breakfasts. Minimum two-night stay at weekends. **£120**

EATING AND DRINKING

The Crown 64–66 All Saints St, TN34 3BN ☎01424 465100, ☻thecrownhastings.co.uk. Great pub with a lovely ambience and a trendy crowd. There's plenty of local produce on the menu (Hastings fish, Bodiam ice cream, Rye Bay coffee, and so on) and behind the bar (Sussex ales, gins and ciders). Mon–Sat 11am–11pm, Sun 11am–10.30pm; kitchen Mon–Fri noon–5pm & 6–9.30pm, Sat & Sun 11am–5pm & 6–9.30pm.

Maggies Above the fish market, Rock-a-Nore Rd ☎01424 430205. The best fish and chips in town can be found at this first-floor café, right on the beach. It's open for lunch only, and is very popular, so book ahead. Mon–Sat noon–2pm.

Webbe's 1 Rock-a-Nore Rd, TN34 3DW ☎01424 721650, ☻webbesrestaurants.co.uk. Good seafood restaurant opposite the Jerwood Gallery. Mains such as steamed panache of Hastings fish cost around £15, or you can pick and choose from tasting dishes at £3.75 each. There's plenty of outside seating in summer. Mon–Fri noon–2pm & 6–9pm, Sat & Sun noon–9.30pm.

Eastbourne

Like so many of the southeast's seaside resorts, **EASTBOURNE** was kick-started into life in the 1840s, when the Brighton, Lewes and Hastings Rail Company built a branch line from Lewes to the coast. Nowadays Eastbourne has a solid reputation as a retirement town by the sea, and though the contemporary **Towner Gallery** has introduced a splash of modernity, the town's charms remain for the most part sedate and old-fashioned. The Towner Gallery lies in the **Cultural Quarter**, centred on Devonshire Park; three theatres sit on the park's fringes, while the park itself is home to **lawn tennis courts**, which play host to big-name players during the Aegon International Eastbourne in June. The focus of the elegant seafront is the Victorian **pier**; just to the west is the splendid **bandstand** (☻eastbournebandstand.co.uk), which hosts various musical events throughout the year. Continue west to the end of the seafront and you'll come to the start of the steep two-mile-long path climbing up to Beachy Head (see p.164), one of the scenic splendours of the South Downs National Park.

Towner Art Gallery and Museum

Devonshire Park, BN21 4JJ • Tues–Sun & bank hols 10am–5pm • Free • ☎ 01323 434670, ☻townereastbourne.org.uk

Housed in a sleek modern edifice by Devonshire Park, the excellent **Towner Art Gallery and Museum** puts on four or five exhibitions a year, which are shown alongside rotating displays of modern and contemporary art from its own permanent collection; it's especially well known for its modern British art.

ARRIVAL AND INFORMATION
EASTBOURNE

By train Eastbourne's splendid Italianate station is a 10min walk from the seafront up Terminus Rd.
Destinations Brighton (every 20min; 35min); Hastings (every 20min; 30min); Lewes (every 20min; 30min); London Victoria (Mon–Sat 4 hourly, Sun 2 hourly; 1hr 20min–1hr 50min).

By bus The National Express coach station is on Junction Rd, right by the train station. Most local bus services are run by Stagecoach.
Destinations Brighton (every 10–15min; 1hr 15min); Hastings (Mon–Sat every 20min, Sun hourly; 1hr 10min); London Victoria (2 daily; 3hr 15min); Tunbridge Wells

THE SOUTH DOWNS WAY

The long-distance **South Downs Way** rises and dips over one hundred miles along the chalk uplands between the city of Winchester and the spectacular cliffs at Beachy Head, and offers the southeast's finest walks. The OS *Explorer* **maps** OL11 and OL25 cover the eastern end of the route; you'll need OL10, OL8, OL3 and OL32 as well to cover the lot. Several **guidebooks** are available (some covering the route in just one direction); you can also check out the **website** ☻nationaltrail.co.uk/south-downs-way.

2

(Mon–Sat hourly; 50min).

Tourist office 3 Cornfield Rd, just off Terminus Rd (March, April & Oct Mon–Fri 9am–5.30pm, Sat 9am–4pm; May–Sept Mon–Fri 9am–5.30pm, Sat 9am–5pm, Sun 10am–1pm; Nov–Feb Mon–Fri 9am–4.30pm, Sat 9am–1pm; ☎01323 415415, ⌨ visiteastbourne.com).

ACCOMMODATION AND EATING

Beach Deck Royal Parade, BN22 7AE ☎01323 720320, ⌨ thebeachdeck.co.uk. The perfect spot for an alfresco lunch, with a big suntrap deck overlooking the beach. Food (including gluten-free options) ranges from burgers to fresh fish. Summer Mon–Wed & Sun 8.30am–6pm, Thurs–Sat 8.30am–late; winter hours vary – check website.

Fusciardi's 30 Marine Parade, BN22 7AY ☎01323 722128, ⌨ fusciardiicecreams.co.uk. This ice-cream parlour is an Eastbourne institution, with piled-high sundaes that are a work of art. Daily 9am–7pm; June &

Aug generally open until 10/10.30pm.

Pebble Beach 53 Royal Parade ☎01323 431240, ⌨ pebblebeacheastbourne.com. Boutique B&B at the eastern end of town, with six stylish, good-value rooms set across three floors of a Victorian seafront townhouse. **£80**

Urban Ground 2a Bolton Rd, BN21 3JX ☎01323 410751, ⌨ urbanground.co.uk. Fab little independent coffee shop with great coffee and a range of tasty sandwiches, soups and cakes. There's a second branch in the Towner Gallery. Mon–Sat 7.30am–6pm, Sun 9am–5pm.

Sussex Heritage Coast and around

Just west of Eastbourne lies the most dramatic stretch of coastline in the South Downs National Park, the **Sussex Heritage Coast**, where the chalk uplands are cut by the sea into a sequence of splendid cliffs that stretch for nine pristine miles. The most spectacular of these is **Beachy Head** (575ft high), the tallest chalk sea-cliff in the country. A couple of miles to the west of here the cliffs dip down to **Birling Gap**, where's there's access to the beach, and a National Trust-run café and information centre. Birling Gap marks the eastern end of a series of magnificent undulating chalk cliffs known as the **Seven Sisters**, which end three miles further west at the meandering River Cuckmere – an area encompassed by the **Seven Sisters Country Park**. This stretch of coast provides some of the most impressive walks in the region; head to one of the visitor centres (see below) for advice and route maps.

Alfriston and around

Three miles inland from the Seven Sisters Country Park along the River Cuckmere is the picture-perfect village of **ALFRISTON**, with plenty of creaky old smuggling inns, a picturesque village green ("The Tye") and some lovely riverside walks. On The Tye sits the fourteenth-century timber-framed and thatched **Clergy House** (mid-March to Oct Mon–Wed, Sat & Sun 10.30am–5pm; Nov & Dec Sat & Sun 11am–4pm; £5.35; NT; ☎01323 871961, ⌨ nationaltrust.org.uk/alfriston-clergy-house), the first property to be acquired by the National Trust, in 1896. At the other end of the green is the Gun Room (daily 10am–4pm; ☎01323 870 022, ⌨ rathfinnyestate.com), the shop-cum-cellar door of the **Rathfinny Wine Estate**, which sprawls over the hillsides on the southern outskirts of Alfriston; tours of the vineyard are available.

A mile or so up the valley, the excellent **Drusillas Park** (daily: March–Oct 10am–6pm; Nov–Feb 10am–5pm; £18.50–19.50 depending on season, under-2s free; cheaper tickets available if booked online; ☎01323 874100, ⌨ drusillas.co.uk) has penguins, meerkats, lemurs and more, plus a miniature railway, paddling pool and an adventure playground.

ARRIVAL AND INFORMATION   SUSSEX HERITAGE COAST AND AROUND

By bus Bus #13X runs from Eastbourne and Brighton via Beachy Head, Birling Gap and the Seven Sisters Country Park Visitor Centre (late April to mid-June Sat & Sun hourly; mid-June to mid-Sept Mon–Fri 3 daily, Sat & Sun hourly; 35min). The Cuckmere Valley Ramblerbus operates an hourly circular service (50min) from Berwick train station – with hourly connections to Eastbourne, Lewes and Brighton – to the Seven Sisters Country Park via Alfriston (April–Oct Sat, Sun & bank hols; ⌨ cuckmerebuses.org.uk).

Tourist information Beachy Head Countryside Centre, Beachy Head (Easter–Oct Mon 1–4pm, Tues–Sun 10am–4pm; Nov Sat & Sun 11am–3pm; volunteer-run, so opening times can vary, especially in winter; ☎01323 737273, ⓦ beachyhead.org). Birling Gap Information Centre, Birling Gap (daily 10am–5pm, or 4pm in winter; ☎01323 423197, ⓦ nationaltrust.org.uk/birling-gap-and-the-seven-sisters). Seven Sisters Country Park Visitor Centre, Exceat, on the A259 between Seaford and Eastbourne (March & Nov Sat & Sun 11am–4pm; April–Sept daily 10.30am–4.30pm; Oct daily 11am–4pm; volunteer-run, so opening times can vary, especially in winter; ☎0345 608 0194, ⓦ sevensisters .org.uk).

ACCOMMODATION

Belle Tout Beachy Head ☎01323 423185, ⓦ belletout .co.uk. For a real treat book into this fabulous lighthouse, perched high up on the dramatic cliffs just west of Beachy Head. The cosy rooms boast stupendous views, there's a snug residents' lounge and – best of all – there's unrestricted access to the lamproom at the top of the lighthouse, where you can sit and watch the sun go down. **£190**

2

Lewes and around

LEWES, the county town of East Sussex, straddles the River Ouse as it carves a gap through the South Downs on its final stretch to the sea. Though there's been some rebuilding, the core of Lewes remains remarkably good-looking: replete with crooked older dwellings, narrow lanes – or "twittens" – and Georgian houses. With numerous traces of its long history still visible (not least a medieval castle), plus a lively cultural scene, plenty of independent and antiques shops, and some of England's most appealing chalkland on its doorstep, Lewes makes a great Sussex base. Nearby are the Bloomsbury Group's country home at **Charleston**, Virginia Woolf's former home **Monk's House**, and the **Ditchling Museum of Art + Craft** – all a short hop by car.

Lewes Castle

169 High St • Mon & Sun 11am–5.30pm (dusk in winter), Tues–Sat 10am–5.30pm (dusk in winter); closed Mon in Jan • £7.70, joint ticket with Anne of Cleves House £12.30 • ☎01273 486290, ⓦ sussexpast.co.uk

Both **Lewes Castle** and St Pancras Priory (see p.166) were the work of William de Warenne, who was given the land by William I following the Norman Conquest. Inside the castle complex – unusual for being built on two mottes, or mounds – the shell of the eleventh-century keep remains, and can be climbed for excellent views over the town to the surrounding Downs. Tickets include admission to the **museum** (same hours as castle) by the entrance, where exhibits include archeological artefacts and a town model.

LEWES BONFIRE NIGHT

Each November 5, while the rest of Britain lights small domestic bonfires or attends municipal firework displays to commemorate the 1605 foiling of a Catholic plot to blow up the Houses of Parliament, Lewes puts on a more dramatic show, whose origins lie in the deaths of the Lewes Martyrs, the seventeen Protestants burned here in 1556 at the height of Mary Tudor's militant revival of Catholicism. The town's six tightly knit **bonfire societies** spend much of the year organizing the spectacular Bonfire Night extravaganza, when their members dress up in traditional costumes and parade through the narrow streets carrying flaming torches and flares, before marching off to the outskirts of town for their society's individual bonfire and fireworks display.

Boisterous and anarchic, the **Lewes Bonfire Night** experience is brilliant, but it does get packed, especially on years when November 5 falls on a weekend. Roads close early, parking is restricted and there can be horrendously long queues for trains at the end of the night; it's best to stay over if you can (book early). With loud bangs, flying sparks and lots of open flames, the event is definitely not suitable for small children. If the 5th falls on a Sunday the celebrations take place on the 4th. For more, see ⓦ lewesbonfirecouncil.org.uk.

GLYNDEBOURNE

Founded in 1934, **Glyndebourne**, three miles east of Lewes, off the A27 (☎01273 812321, ⓦglyndebourne.com), is Britain's only unsubsidized opera house, and the Glyndebourne season (mid-May to Aug) is an indispensable part of the high-society calendar. Tickets for the season's six productions are pricey, but there are some standing-room-only ones available at reduced prices, and discounts for under-30s (register in advance).

Southover

From the High Street, the steep, cobbled and much photographed **Keere Street** leads to **Southover**, the southern part of town. At the foot of Keere Street, tranquil **Grange Gardens** (daily dawn–dusk; free) sprawl around Southover Grange, childhood home of the diarist John Evelyn. Nearby on Southover High Street is the timber-framed **Anne of Cleves House** (Feb–Nov Mon & Sun 11am–5pm, Tues–Sat 10am–5pm; closes 4pm in Feb & Nov; sometimes closed for private functions – call to check; £5.60, joint ticket with Lewes Castle £12.30; ☎01273 474610, ⓦsussexpast.co.uk), a fifteenth-century hall house laid out as it would have looked in Tudor times. Cross the road and head down Cockshut Lane to reach the evocative ruins of **St Pancras Priory** (open access; free); in its heyday it was one of Europe's principal Cluniac institutions, with a church the size of Westminster Abbey.

Monk's House

Rodmell, BN7 3HF, 3 miles south of Lewes • Easter–Oct Wed–Sun & bank hols: house 1–5pm; garden 12.30–5.30pm • £5.75; NT • ☎01273 474760, ⓦ nationaltrust.org.uk/monks-house

The pretty, weatherboard **Monk's House** was the home of novelist **Virginia Woolf** and her husband, Leonard. Like nearby Charleston (see below), where Virginia's much-loved sister Vanessa Bell lived, Monk's House hosted gatherings of the Bloomsbury Group, and the house is unmistakably "Bloomsbury" in style, with painted furniture and artworks by Vanessa and her partner Duncan Grant in every room. The real highlight, though, is the tranquil **garden**, with its beautiful views over the Ouse Valley.

Charleston

Signposted off the A27, BN8 9LL • March–June, Sept & Oct Wed–Sun & bank hols noon–5pm; July & Aug Wed–Sat 11.30am–5.30pm, Sun & bank hols noon–5.30pm; note that Wed–Sat entry is by 1hr guided tour only, while on Sun & bank hols rooms are stewarded and you can move about freely; garden open same hours as house (not part of tour); last entry 1hr before closing • House and garden £12.50, garden only £4.50 • ☎01323 811626, ⓦ charleston.org.uk

Six miles east of Lewes lies **Charleston**, the country home and gathering place of the writers, intellectuals and artists known as the Bloomsbury Group. Virginia Woolf's sister Vanessa Bell, Vanessa's husband, Clive Bell, and her lover, Duncan Grant, moved here during World War I so that the men, both conscientious objectors, could work on local farms. Almost every surface of the farmhouse interior is painted and the walls are hung with paintings by Picasso, Renoir and Augustus John, alongside the work of the residents. The guided tours give a fascinating insight into the lives of the unconventional group of friends and lovers; try to visit on a day when a tour is running if you can. Elsewhere on the site, the purpose-built **Wolfson Gallery** hosts changing exhibitions exploring the Bloomsbury Group's artistic and literary heritage.

Ditchling Museum of Art + Craft

Lodge Hill Lane, BN6 8SP • Tues–Sat 10.30am–5pm, Sun & bank hols 11am–5pm • £6.50 • ☎01273 844744, ⓦ ditchlingmuseumartcraft.org.uk

The pretty village of **Ditchling** lies eight miles west of Lewes at the foot of the Downs, overlooked by beauty spot Ditchling Beacon – one of the highest spots on the escarpment. On the village green, the beautifully designed two-room **Ditchling Museum**

of Art + Craft houses a fascinating assortment of prints, paintings, weavings, sculptures and other artefacts from the artists and craftspeople who lived in Ditchling in the last century, among them typographer and sculptor Eric Gill, printer and writer Hilary Pepler, weaver Ethel Mairet and calligrapher Edward Johnson, who designed the iconic London Underground typeface.

ARRIVAL AND INFORMATION

By train The train station is south of High Street down Station Rd.

Destinations Brighton (every 10–20min; 15min); Eastbourne (every 20min; 30min); London Victoria (Mon–Sat every 30min, Sun hourly; 1hr 10min).

By bus The bus station is on Eastgate St, near the foot of School Hill.

Destinations Brighton (Mon–Sat every 15min, Sun every

LEWES AND AROUND

30min; 30min); Tunbridge Wells (Mon–Sat every 30min, Sun hourly; 1hr 10min).

Tourist office At the junction of High St and Fisher St (April–Sept Mon–Fri 9.30am–4.30pm, Sat 9.30am–4pm, Sun 10am–2pm; Oct–March Mon–Fri 9.30am–4.30pm, Sat 10am–2pm; ☎01273 483448, ⓦ staylewes.org). They hold copies of the excellent free monthly magazine *Viva Lewes* (ⓦ vivalewes.com).

ACCOMMODATION

The Corner House 14 Cleve Terrace, BN7 1JJ ☎01273 567138, ⓦ lewescornerhouse.co.uk. Super-friendly B&B on a quiet Edwardian terrace, close to Grange Gardens. The two en-suite rooms have lovely homely touches such as patchwork quilts and plenty of books, and the owner is a great source of information on the town and area. __£85__

YHA South Downs Itford Farm, Beddingham, 5 miles

from Lewes ☎0870 371 9574. The nearest hostel to Lewes is a gem, newly renovated from an old farm, and in a fabulous location right on the South Downs Way footpath, with great transport connections (Southease station – with regular connections to Lewes – is under 200m away). Camping pods (sleeping 3) and bell tents (sleeping 5) are available, and there's a café and licensed bar too. Dorms __£25__, doubles __£55__, camping pods __£49__, bell tents __£89__

EATING AND DRINKING

Flint Owl 209 High St, BN7 2DL ☎01273 472769, ⓦ flintowlbakery.com. The café of the Glynde-based Flint Owl Bakery – which supplies its pastries and artisan bread around Sussex – is a stylish space with a small courtyard garden out the back, and counters piled high with freshly baked goodies. Mon–Sat 9am–5pm.

The Hearth Pizzeria Eastgate, BN7 2LP ☎01273 470755, ⓦ thehearth.co. The wood-fired sourdough pizzas at this down-to-earth pizzeria were voted among the best in the UK by the BBC's *Good Food* magazine. If you

can't decide which to go for try the Dalai Lama ("one with everything"). Mon & Tues 5–10pm, Wed–Fri noon–2pm & 5–10pm, Sat noon–10pm.

Lewes Arms Mount Place, BN7 1YH ☎01273 473252, ⓦ lewesarms.co.uk. This characterful local is a good spot to sample a pint of Sussex Best, produced down the road at Harvey's brewery. The home-cooked pub food is great value, too. Mon–Thurs 11am–11pm, Fri & Sat 11am–midnight, Sun noon–11pm; kitchen Mon–Fri & Sun noon–8.30pm, Sat noon–9pm.

Brighton

Vibrant, quirky and cool, **BRIGHTON** (or **Brighton & Hove**, to give it its official name) is one of the country's most popular seaside destinations. The essence of the city's appeal is its faintly bohemian vitality, a buzz that comes from a mix of holiday-makers, foreign-language students, a thriving LGBT+ community, and an energetic local student population from the art college and two universities.

Any trip to Brighton inevitably begins with a visit to its two most famous landmarks – the exuberant **Royal Pavilion** and the wonderfully tacky **Brighton Pier** – followed by a stroll along the seafront promenade or the pebbly beach. Just as fun, though, is an exploration of Brighton's car-free **Lanes** – the maze of narrow alleys marking the old town – or a meander through the more bohemian streets of **North Laine**. Brighton's other great draw is its **cultural life**: you're spoilt for choice when it comes to live music, theatre, comedy and concerts, especially if you coincide your visit with the **Brighton Festival** (see box, p.171), the largest arts festival in England.

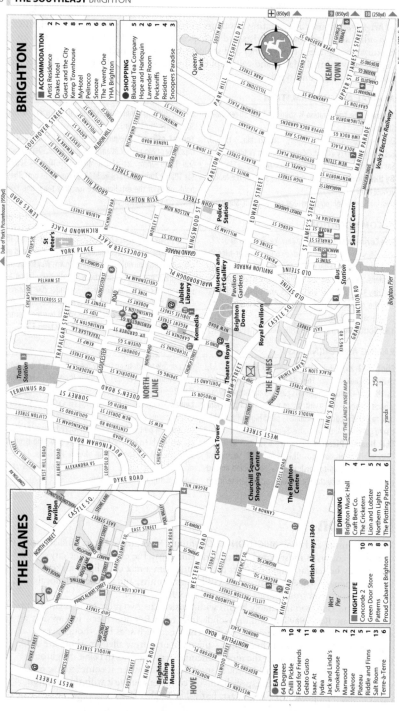

BRIGHTON

ACCOMMODATION
Artist Residence	2
Drakes Hotel	7
Guest and the City	4
Kemp Townhouse	8
MyHotel	1
Pelirocco	3
Snooze	6
The Twenty One	9
YHA Brighton	5

SHOPPING
Bluebird Tea Company	5
Hope and Harlequin	2
Lavender Room	6
Pecksniffs	1
Resident	4
Snoopers Paradise	3

THE LANES

EATING
64 Degrees	3
Chilli Pickle	10
Food for Friends	11
Gelato Gusto	8
Isaac At	9
Iydea	7
Jack and Linda's	2
Smokehouse	
Marwood	12
Melrose	5
Plateau	1
Riddle and Finns	13
Salt Room	4
Terre-à-Terre	6

DRINKING
Brighton Music Hall	7
Craft Beer Co.	4
The Cricketers	1
Lion and Lobster	5
Northern Lights	2
The Plotting Parlour	6

NIGHTLIFE
Concorde 2	10
Green Door Store	3
Patterns	8
Proud Cabaret Brighton	9

The Royal Pavilion

4/5 Pavilion Buildings, BN1 1EE • Daily: April–Sept 9.30am–5.45pm; Oct–March 10am–5.15pm; last entry 45min before closing • £13, audioguides £2 • ☎ 0300 029 0900, ⓦ brightonmuseums.org.uk/royalpavilion

In any survey to find England's most loved building, there's always a bucketful of votes for Brighton's exotic extravaganza, the **Royal Pavilion**. The building was the south-coast pied-à-terre of the fun-loving Prince Regent (the future George IV), who first visited the seaside resort in 1783 and spent much of the next forty years partying, gambling and frolicking with his mistress here. The building you see today is the work of John Nash, architect of London's Regent Street, who in 1815 redesigned the Prince's original modest dwelling into an extraordinary confection of slender minarets, twirling domes, pagodas, balconies and miscellaneous motifs imported from India and China. The result defined a genre of its own – Oriental Gothic.

2

Inside, the **Banqueting Room** erupts with ornate splendour and is dominated by a one-tonne chandelier hung from the jaws of a massive dragon cowering in a plantain tree. The stunning **Music Room**, the first sight of which reduced George to tears of joy, has a huge dome lined with more than 26,000 individually gilded scales and hung with exquisite umbrella-like glass lamps. After climbing the famous cast-iron staircase with its bamboo-look banisters, you can go into Victoria's sober and seldom-used bedroom and the **North-West Gallery**, where the king's portrait hangs, along with a selection of satirical cartoons. More notable, though, is the **South Gallery**, decorated in sky-blue with trompe l'oeil bamboo trellises and a carpet that appears to be strewn with flowers.

Brighton Museum

Royal Pavilion Gardens, BN1 1EE • Tues–Sun & bank hols 10am–5pm • £5.20 • ☎ 0300 029 0900, ⓦ brightonmuseums.org.uk/brighton

Across the gardens from the Pavilion stands the **Brighton Museum** – once part of the royal stable block – which houses a wonderful and eclectic mix of modern fashion and design, archeology, painting and local history. Among the highlights are Dalí's famous sofa (1938) based on Mae West's lips, the 13,000-object ethnographic collection, and the mummified animals and painted coffins of the Ancient Egypt galleries.

The Lanes

Tucked between the Pavilion and the seafront is a warren of narrow, pedestrianized alleyways known as **The Lanes** – the core of the old fishing village from which Brighton evolved. Long-established jewellers' shops, boutiques and several cafés, pubs and restaurants make this a great place to wander.

North Laine

Vibrant, buzzy **North Laine** (ⓦ northlaine.co.uk), which sprawls west and north of the Royal Pavilion as far as Trafalgar Street, bordered by Queens Road to the west and the A23 to the east, is more offbeat than the Lanes. Here the eclectic shops, selling secondhand records, vintage gear, homeware, upmarket fashion and New Age objects, mingle with cool coffee shops and pavement cafés and bars.

The seafront

To soak up the tackier side of Brighton, head down to the **seafront** and take a stroll along **Brighton Pier** (daily: April–Oct 10am–10pm; Nov–March 11am–5pm; opening hours can vary depending on weather; free; ☎ 01273 609361, ⓦ brightonpier.co.uk), completed in 1899, its every inch devoted to cacophonous fun. Opposite Brighton Pier, on Marine Parade, is the **Sea Life Centre** (daily: May–Aug 10am–6pm; Sept–April

2

10am–5pm; last entry 1hr before closing; times can change so check website; £10.50–17.50 depending on ticket type; ☎01273 604234, ⒲visitsealife.com/Brighton), which is the world's oldest operating aquarium, opened in 1872; its wonderfully atmospheric Victorian aquarium hall is the main attraction.

West of Brighton Pier

The busiest section of the seafront lies between Brighton Pier and the derelict **West Pier**, half a mile west along the seafront; here, down at beach level underneath the old fishermen's arches, the **Lower Esplanade** is lined with cafés, gift shops, galleries, bars and clubs. The Lower Esplanade is also home to the **Brighton Fishing Museum** (normally daily 9am–5pm; free; ⒲brightonfishingmuseum.org.uk), which displays old photos and video footage of the golden days of the local fishing industry. By the West Pier, there's no missing the **British Airways i360** (open daily – check website for hours; £15; ☎0333 772 0360, ⒲britishairwaysi360.com), which at 162m high is the world's tallest moving observation tower. Step aboard the saucer-shaped pod to be whisked aloft for 360-degree views over the city and beyond.

East of Brighton Pier

Just east of Brighton Pier, the 300m-long twin zipwires of **Brighton Zip** (daily 10am–9pm, weather dependent; £16; ⒲brightonzip) whisk thrill-seekers along the seafront. If you prefer a more sedate form of transport, try the antiquated locomotives of **Volk's Electric Railway** (Easter–Sept open daily; trains run every 15min; £3.60 return; ⒲volkselectricrailway.co.uk) – the world's oldest electric railway – which trundle eastward towards **Brighton Marina** (⒲brightonmarina.co.uk), stopping off en route at the fabulous **Yellowave** beach sports venue (summer Mon–Fri 10am–10pm, Sat & Sun 10am–8pm; winter Tues–Thurs 10am–9pm, Fri–Sun 10am–5pm; court rental £22/hr; ☎01273 672222, ⒲yellowave.co.uk), the perfect spot for a taster of beach volleyball, with six sand courts, plus an excellent café.

Kemp Town

East of the city centre, **Kemp Town** is the heart of the city's LGBT+ community and one of Brighton's liveliest, most colourful neighbourhoods. From the Old Steine, head along busy, bustling **St James's Street** (Brighton's "Gay Village"), and its quieter continuation, **St George's Road**, where you'll find a clutch of antique and vintage shops, cosy pubs and laidback coffee shops.

Hove

West of the city centre, **Hove** – which started life as a separate resort in the 1820s and only merged with Brighton in 1997 – is a stylish neighbourhood, with some beautiful Regency architecture and an elegant, lawn-backed seafront. The main sight is **Hove Museum** (19 New Church Rd; Mon, Tues & Thurs–Sat 10am–5pm, Sun & bank hols 2–5pm; free; ☎0300 029 0900, ⒲brightonmuseums.org.uk/hove; bus #1, #1A, #6, #49 or #49A), which houses a fascinating and eclectic collection that covers everything from contemporary crafts to a 3500-year-old Bronze Age cup.

ARRIVAL AND DEPARTURE	BRIGHTON

By train Brighton train station is at the top of Queen's Rd, which descends to the clocktower and then becomes West St, eventually leading to the seafront, a 10min walk away. Destinations Arundel (hourly; 1hr 10min); Chichester (every 30min; 45–55min); Eastbourne (every 20min; 35min); Hastings (every 30min; 1hr 5min); Lewes (every

10–20min; 15min); London Bridge (Mon–Sat 2 hourly; 1hr); London St Pancras (every 30min; 1hr 15min); London Victoria (1–2 hourly; 55min); Portsmouth Harbour (Mon–Sat every 30min, Sun hourly; 1hr 30min).

By bus The long-distance bus station is just in from the seafront on the south side of the Old Steine.

Destinations Arundel (Mon–Sat every 30min, Sun hourly; 2hr); Chichester (every 20–30min; 1hr 45min); Eastbourne (every 10–15min; 1hr 15min); Lewes (Mon–Sat every 15min, Sun every 30min; 30min); London Victoria (hourly; 2hr 20min); Tunbridge Wells (Mon–Sat every 30min, Sun hourly; 1hr 50min).

GETTING AROUND

By bus A one-day CitySaver ticket (£5) allows you unlimited travel on the city bus network (ⓦ buses.co.uk). Short-hop journeys cost £2.20.

By taxi For a city taxi, call ⓣ 01273 202020 or ⓣ 01273 204060. There are central ranks at Brighton station, East St, Queens Square near the clocktower and outside St Peter's Church.

By tour For details of city tours, which range from ghost walks to food tours to a "Piers and Queers" tour, see ⓦ visitbrighton.com/things-to-do/tours-and-sightseeing.

The Brighton Greeters scheme pairs up visitors with a volunteer Brighton resident tour guide for a free two-hour tour; see ⓦ visitbrighton.com/greeters for more information.

By bike There's a downloadable cycling map of the city at ⓦ brighton-hove.gov.uk/content/cycle-facilities-map. Bike rental is available from Brighton Cycle Hire, Unit 8, under the station, off Trafalgar Street (£7/3hr, £10/24hr; ⓣ 01273 571555, ⓦ brightoncyclehire.com); and Brighton Beach Bike Hire, Madeira Drive, by Yellowave (£12 for 3hr, £16 for 4+ hours; ⓣ 07917 753794, ⓦ brightonbeachbikes.co.uk).

INFORMATION

Visitor information There are fifteen staffed Visitor Information points (ⓣ 01273 290337, ⓦ visitbrighton.com) throughout the city, including at Brighton Pier, the Royal Pavilion shop and Jubilee Library in the North Laine.

Useful apps, magazines and websites VisitBrighton produces a free app for smartphones (ⓦ visitbrighton.com /apps). The best listing magazine is *Source* (ⓦ brighton source.co.uk), but *XYZ* (ⓦ xyzmagazine.co.uk) and *BN1* (ⓦ bn1magazine.co.uk) are also worth a look. *Viva Brighton* (ⓦ vivabrighton.com) is a monthly magazine of articles and reviews, distributed free around the city.

ACCOMMODATION

Brighton's **accommodation** is pricey, with rates often rising substantially at weekends. The listings below quote weekend, high-season rates; at many places these prices will fall dramatically out of season and midweek, so it pays to check around. Note that at weekends there's generally a two-night-minimum stay. Much of the city's nicest B&B accommodation is found in **Kemp Town**, east of the city centre.

Artist Residence 33 Regency Square, BN1 2GG ⓣ 01273 324302, ⓦ artistresidencebrighton.co.uk; map p.168. Cool and quirky, this uber-stylish hotel has 23 rooms – some of them decorated by local and international artists – plus a cocktail bar and two very good restaurants. **£170**

Drakes Hotel 33–34 Marine Parade, BN2 1PE ⓣ 01273 696934, ⓦ drakesofbrighton.com; map p.168. The unbeatable seafront location is the big draw at this chic, minimalist boutique hotel. The most expensive rooms come with freestanding baths by floor-to-ceiling windows. There's an excellent in-house restaurant too. Breakfast £7.50–15 extra. **£160**

★**Guest and the City** 2 Broad St, BN2 1TJ ⓣ 01273 698289, ⓦ guestandthecity.co.uk; map p.168. Lovely B&B in a great central location a minute from the pier, with stylish rooms (the two feature rooms – £140 – come with stained-glass windows of classic Brighton scenes), and super-friendly owners. **£90**

Kemp Townhouse 21 Atlingworth St, BN2 1PL ⓣ 01273 681400, ⓦ kemptownhouse.com; map p.168. Stylish five-star B&B with excellent service and nine chic rooms decked out with black-and-white photos of the city. A complimentary carafe of port in the room is a nice touch. **£155**

MyHotel 17 Jubilee St ⓣ 01273 900300, ⓦ myhotels .com/my-hotel-brighton; map p.168. Hip boutique hotel in the heart of North Laine, with rooms designed along feng shui lines, and a great bar, *Merkaba*, downstairs. Rates fluctuate with demand, so check online for last-minute bargains. **£120**

BRIGHTON FESTIVAL

Every May the three-week-long **Brighton Festival** (ⓦ brightonfestival.org) takes over various venues around town. This arty celebration includes over two hundred events, ranging from exhibitions and street theatre to concerts and talks. Running at the same time is the **Brighton and Hove Fringe Festival** (ⓣ 01273 709709, ⓦ www.brightonfestivalfringe.org.uk), which puts on over 700 events, and the biannual **Artists' Open Houses Festival** (ⓦ aoh.org.uk; also runs in Dec), when hundreds of private homes fling open their doors to show the work of local artists. For details of Brighton's many other festivals and events, check out ⓦ visitbrighton.com.

2

Pelirocco 10 Regency Square ☎ 01273 327055, ⓦ hotel pelirocco.co.uk; map p.168. "England's most rock'n'roll hotel" is a real one-off, featuring extravagantly themed rooms inspired by pop culture and pin-ups. There's a Fifties-style boudoir, a Pop Art "Modrophenia" room featuring bedside tables made from scooters, and even a twin room styled as Lord Vader's Quarters, complete with light sabre, Darth Vader costume and Star Wars DVDs. **£145**

★**Snooze** 25 St George's Terrace, BN2 1JJ ☎ 01273 605797, ⓦ snoozebrighton.com; map p.168. Quirky, characterful guesthouse in Kemp Town, with eight funky rooms that range in style from "Brighton Bollywood" or French flea market to full-on 1970s glamour. **£140**

The Twenty One 21 Charlotte St, BN2 1AG ☎ 01273 686450, ⓦ thetwentyone.co.uk; map p.168. Popular Regency townhouse B&B, with stylish rooms and super-friendly owners. Rooms come with iPads, bathrobes and a well-stocked hospitality tray. **£135**

YHA Brighton Old Steine, BN1 1NH ☎ 01273 738674, ⓦ yha.org.uk/hostel/brighton; map p.168. Less than a minute's walk from the pier, this hostel has 51 en-suite rooms (including 20 doubles, some with roll-top baths), plus a self-catering kitchen and a good café-bar. Prices drop midweek and out of season; book well ahead for weekend stays. Breakfast £5.75 extra. Dorms **£33**, doubles **£80**

EATING

Brighton has the greatest concentration of **restaurants** in the southeast after London and a thriving **café** culture, especially in the buzzy North Laine area. There are plenty of good **coffee shops** in the city, including those belonging to Brighton-based chains Ground and the Small Batch Coffee Company; the latter has its own roastery in Hove.

THE SEAFRONT

Jack and Linda's Smokehouse 197 Kings Arches; map p.168. This tiny beachfront smokehouse is run by a lovely couple who've been traditionally smoking fish here for over a decade. Grab a fresh crab sandwich or hot mackerel roll (£4.40) to eat on the beach for a perfect summer lunch. April–Sept daily 10am–5pm; Oct Sat & Sun 10am–5pm; March & Nov weather dependent.

Melrose 132 King's Rd, BN1 2HH ☎ 01273 326520, ⓦ melroserestaurant.co.uk; map p.168. Traditional seafront establishment that's been serving up tasty, excellent-value fish and chips (£7.25), local seafood, roasts and custard-covered puddings for over forty years. The next-door *Regency Restaurant* is smaller and similar. Daily 11.30am–10.30pm.

Salt Room 106 King's Rd, BN1 2FU ☎ 01273 929488, ⓦ saltroom-restaurant.co.uk; map p.168. One of the city's best fish and seafood restaurants, with a stylish exposed-brick interior, sea views and fantastic charcoal-grilled fish and seafood (mains £20 and up). Daily noon–4pm & 6–10pm.

THE LANES

★**64 Degrees** 53 Meeting House Lane, BN1 1HB ☎ 01273 770115, ⓦ 64degrees.co.uk; map p.168. The best seats in the house at this tiny restaurant in the Lanes are up at the counter of the open kitchen: the idea is that you choose several small plates of food (£6–12) and share them, to create your own tasting menu. The food's inventive, delicious and prepared in front of you, and the whole experience is brilliant fun. Daily noon–3pm & 6–9.45pm.

Food for Friends 18 Prince Albert St, BN1 1HF ☎ 01273 202310, ⓦ foodforfriends.com; map p.168. Brighton's original vegetarian restaurant – on this spot for over 35 years – serves up sophisticated veggie dishes (mains £12–14) that are imaginative enough to please die-hard

meat-eaters too. Mon–Thurs & Sun noon–10pm, Fri & Sat noon–10.30pm.

Marwood 52 Ship St, BN1 1AF ☎ 01273 382063, ⓦ themarwood.com; map p.168. Quirky, laidback café with great coffee and food (mains around £7) and splendidly bonkers decor that runs from stuffed animals and skateboards on the walls to Star Wars spaceships dangling from the ceiling. Mon 8am–7pm, Tues–Fri 8am–11pm, Sat 9am–11pm, Sun 10am–7pm.

Plateau 1 Bartholomews, BN1 1HG ☎ 01273 733085, ⓦ plateaubrighton.co.uk; map p.168. Laidback little restaurant-cum-wine bar serving cocktails, organic beers and biodynamic wine, and food that ranges from small "bites" (£5–9) to bigger "plats" (from £11), so you can stop by for a nibble and a drink, or a full-blown meal. Daily noon–late; kitchen noon–3.30pm & 6–10pm.

Riddle and Finns 12b Meeting House Lane, BN1 1HB ☎ 01273 721667, ⓦ riddleandfinns.co.uk; map p.168. Bustling champagne and oyster bar where you can tuck into a huge range of shellfish and fish (mains £13–19) at communal marble-topped tables in a white-tiled, candle-lit dining room with an open kitchen. No bookings. Sat 11.30am–11pm, Mon–Fri & Sun noon–10pm.

★**Terre-à-Terre** 71 East St, BN1 1HQ ☎ 01273 729051, ⓦ terreaterre.co.uk; map p.168. One of the country's best vegetarian restaurants, serving up inventive global veggie cuisine (mains around £15/16). The taster plate for two (£30) is a good place to start if you're befuddled by the weird and wonderful creations on offer. Mon–Fri noon–10.30pm, Sat 11am–11pm, Sun 11am–10pm.

NORTH LAINE

Chilli Pickle 17 Jubilee St, BN1 1GE ☎ 01273 900383, ⓦ thechillipickle.com; map p.168. Stylish, buzzing

restaurant in North Laine serving sophisticated, authentic Indian food – everything from masala dosas to Chennai seafood stew (mains £10–17). At lunchtimes they offer a range of thalis and street food. Daily noon–3pm & 6–10.30pm.

★**Gelato Gusto** 2 Gardner St, BN1 1UP ☎01273 673402, ⓦgelatogusto.com; map p.168. Splendid *gelateria*, with regularly changing flavours that run from Turkish Delight to blood-orange *sorbetto*. Mon–Fri 11.30am–6pm, Sat & Sun 11am–6pm.

★**Isaac At** 2 Gloucester St, BN1 4EW ☎07765 934740, ⓦisaac-at.com; map p.168. A fun fine-dining experience, with food – inspired by Sussex and all sourced locally – prepared in front of you in the open kitchen: for the full experience, opt for the six-course tasting menu (£50) paired with Sussex wines or juices (£29/22 respectively). Tues–Fri 6.30–10.30pm, Sat 12.30–2.30pm & 6.30–10.30pm.

Iydea 17 Kensington Gardens, BN1 4AL ☎01273 667992, ⓦiydea.co.uk; map p.168. Good-value, tasty veggie food served up cafeteria-style. What's on offer changes every day, but there tends to be a quiche, a lasagne, a curry and enchiladas, alongside half a dozen other dishes (£4.70–7.70). Daily 9.30am–5.30pm; lunch served Mon–Thurs & Sun 11.30am–4.30pm, Fri & Sat 11.30am–5pm.

DRINKING

Brighton Music Hall 127 King's Rd Arches, BN1 2FN ☎01273 747287, ⓦbrightonmusichall.co.uk; map p.168. Beachfront bar with a huge open-air heated terrace, and free live music when the sun shines. Hours vary but generally summer daily 9/10am–late; winter most days from noon.

Craft Beer Co. 22–23 Upper North St, BN1 3FG ☎01273 723736, ⓦthecraftbeerco.com; map p.168. One for beer lovers, this friendly pub has nine daily-changing cask ales and over 200 bottled varieties. The house Craft Pale Ale is brewed for them by Kent Brewery. Mon–Thurs noon–11pm, Fri & Sat noon–1.30am, Sun noon–11pm.

The Cricketers 15 Black Lion St BN1 1ND ☎01273 329472, ⓦcricketersbrighton.co.uk; map p.168. Brighton's oldest pub, immortalized by Graham Greene in *Brighton Rock*, has a traditional feel, with good daytime pub grub, real ales and a cosy courtyard bar. Mon–Thurs 11am–midnight, Fri & Sat 11am–1am, Sun 11am–11pm.

Lion and Lobster 24 Sillwood St, BN1 2PS ☎01273 327299, ⓦthelionandlobster.co.uk; map p.168. One of the city's best pubs, with a traditional feel but a young, fun atmosphere. Pub quiz on Mon nights, and live jazz on Sun. Good food is served until late. Mon–Thurs 11am–1am, Fri & Sat 11am–2am, Sun noon–midnight.

Northern Lights 6 Little East St, BN1 1HT ☎01273 747096, ⓦnorthernlightsbrighton.co.uk; map p.168. Laidback, ever-popular bar with a Scandinavian theme: choose from two dozen different flavoured vodkas, aquavit, and beers from Denmark, Sweden and Finland. The Nordic menu features reindeer, Smörgåsbord and pickled herring. Mon–Thurs 5pm–midnight, Fri 3pm–2am, Sat noon–2am, Sun noon–midnight.

★**The Plotting Parlour** 6 Steine St BN2, 1TE ☎01273 621238, ⓦtheplottingparlour-brighton.co.uk; map p.168. This dimly lit, snug cocktail bar is a real treat, with exquisite cocktails (£8 and up), table service and stylish decor. Mon–Thurs & Sun 3pm–midnight, Fri & Sat 3pm–1am.

NIGHTLIFE

Concorde 2 Madeira Shelter, Madeira Drive, BN2 1EN ☎01273 673311, ⓦconcorde2.co.uk; map p.168. A Victorian tearoom in a former life, this intimate live music venue features up-and-coming acts, big names and varied club nights.

Green Door Store Trafalgar Arches, Lower Goods Yard ⓦthegreendoorstore.co.uk; map p.168. Uber-cool club and live music venue in the arches under the train station, playing anything from psych to blues, punk or powerdisco. The bar is free entry; live gig entry varies.

Patterns 10 Marine Parade, BN2 1TL ☎01273 894777, ⓦpatternsbrighton.com; map p.168. Trendy seafront hangout that boasts a terrace with sea views and a basement club. The range of club nights is broad but specializes in electronic music and attracts internationally renowned DJs.

Proud Cabaret Brighton 83 St Georges Rd, BN2 1EF ☎01273 605789, ⓦproudcabaretbrighton.com; map p.168. Opulent venue in a former ballroom hosting dinner and cabaret/burlesque shows, plus diverse club nights.

LGBT+ BRIGHTON

Brighton has one of the longest established and most thriving **gay scenes** in Britain, centred around St James's Street in Kemp Town, and with a variety of lively clubs and bars drawing people from all over the southeast; for **listings** and events check out *Gscene Magazine* (ⓦgscene.com). The annual **Brighton Pride** (date varies each summer; ⓦbrighton-pride.org) is an LGBT+ parade and ticketed party in Preston Park. Information, advice and support about the scene is available from **Brighton and Hove LGBT Switchboard** (☎01273 204050, ⓦswitchboard.org.uk).

ENTERTAINMENT

Brighton Dome 29 New Rd, BN1 1UG ☎01273 709709, ⓦ brightondome.org; map p.168. Home to three venues – Pavilion Theatre, Concert Hall and Corn Exchange – offering theatre, concerts, dance and performance.

Duke of Yorks Picturehouse Preston Circus, BN1 4NA ☎0871 704 2056, ⓦ picturehouses.co.uk; map p.168. Grade II listed cinema with a licensed bar showing art-house, independent and classic films. Dukes at Komedia is its sister cinema, based at the Komedia arts centre (see below).

★**Komedia** 44–47 Gardner St, BN1 1UN ☎0845 293 8480, ⓦ komedia.co.uk/brighton; map p.168. A Brighton institution, this highly regarded arts venue hosts stand-up comedy, live music and cabaret, as well as fun club nights.

Theatre Royal New Rd, BN1 1SD ☎01273 764400, ⓦ atgtickets.com/venues/theatre-royal-brighton; map p.168. Venerable old theatre – going since 1807 – offering predominantly mainstream plays, opera and musicals.

SHOPPING

Most of Brighton's high street chains are found in and around **Churchill Square** (ⓦ churchillsquare.co.uk) and **East Street**. The best areas for independent shops are the **Lanes** and **North Laine** (ⓦ northlaine.co.uk); it's also worth wandering over to **Kemp Town** for a browse around its antiques shops.

Bluebird Tea Company 41 Gardner St, BN1 1UN ☎01273 325523, ⓦ bluebirdteaco.com; map p.168. The UK's only tea mixologist, selling a huge variety of fine leaf teas from Gingerbread Chai to Enchanted Narnia (with Turkish Delight). Mon–Fri 10.30am–6pm, Sat 10am–6.30pm, Sun 10.30am–5.30pm.

Hope and Harlequin 31 Sydney St, BN1 4EP ☎01273 675222, ⓦ hopeandharlequin.com; map p.168. Upmarket vintage shop, stocking clothes and collectables up to the 1970s, with a special emphasis on the 1930s and 1940s. Mon & Wed–Sat 10.30am–6pm, Sun 11am–5pm; call ahead to check Tues opening.

Lavender Room 16 Bond St, BN1 1RD ☎01273 220380, ⓦ lavender-room.co.uk; map p.168. Stylish boutique selling fragrances, lingerie, jewellery and vintage-inspired home accessories. Mon–Sat 10am–6pm, Sun 11am–5pm.

Pecksniffs 45–46 Meeting House Lane, BN1 1HB ☎01273 723292, ⓦ pecksniffs.com; map p.168. Independent British fragrance house in the Lanes, selling a range of perfumes, bespoke blends and body products. Mon–Sat 10am–5pm, Sun 10.30am–4pm.

Resident 28 Kensington Gardens, BN1 4AL ☎01273 606312, ⓦ resident-music.com; map p.168. Award-winning independent record shop in North Laine; it also sells tickets for local venues. Mon–Sat 9am–6.30pm, Sun 10am–6pm.

Snoopers Paradise 7–8 Kensington Gardens ☎01273 602558; map p.168. Huge North Laine flea market containing over ninety different stalls over two floors; don't miss Snoopers Attic (ⓦ snoopersattic.co.uk), a "vintage makers' boutique" up on the first floor. Mon–Sat 10am–6pm, Sun 11am–4pm.

Arundel

The hilltop town of **ARUNDEL**, eighteen miles west of Brighton, has for seven centuries been the seat of the dukes of Norfolk, whose fine **castle** looks over the valley of the River Arun. The medieval town's well-preserved appearance and picturesque setting draws in the crowds on summer weekends, but at any other time a visit reveals one of West Sussex's least spoilt old towns. The main attraction is the castle, but the rest of Arundel is pleasant to wander round, with some good independent shops, cafés and restaurants on the High Street and Tarrant Street.

Arundel Castle

Mill Rd, BN18 9AB • April–Oct Tues–Sun & bank hols: keep 10am–4.30pm; Fitzalan Chapel & grounds 10am–5pm; castle rooms noon–5pm • Castle rooms, keep, grounds & chapel £18; keep, grounds & chapel £13; grounds & chapel £11 • ☎01903 882173, ⓦ arundelcastle.org

Despite its medieval appearance, much of what you see of **Arundel Castle** is comparatively new, the result of a series of lavish reconstructions from 1718 onwards, after the original Norman structure was badly damaged during the Civil War. One of the oldest parts is the twelfth-century **keep**, from which you can peer down onto the current duke's spacious residence. Inside the main castle, highlights include the impressive **Barons Hall** and the **library**, which has paintings by Gainsborough, Holbein and Van Dyck. On the edge of the castle grounds, the fourteenth-century **Fitzalan Chapel** houses tombs of past dukes of Norfolk, including twin effigies of the seventh duke – one as he looked when he died and, underneath, one of his emaciated corpse. Nearby, the **Collector Earl's Garden** is a playfully theatrical take on a Jacobean garden, with exotic planting, and pavilions, obelisks and urns made from green oak rather than stone.

Arundel Cathedral

Corner of Parson's Hill & London Rd, BN18 9AY • Daily 9am–6pm or dusk • Free • ☎ 01903 882297, ⓦ arundelcathedral.net

The flamboyant **Arundel Cathedral** was constructed in the 1870s by the fifteenth duke of Norfolk over the town's former Catholic church; its spire was designed by John Hansom, inventor of the hansom cab. Inside are the enshrined remains of St Philip Howard, the canonized thirteenth earl, who was sentenced to death in 1585, accused of Catholic conspiracy against Elizabeth I's Protestant court. He died of dysentery in the Tower of London ten years later.

WWT Arundel Wetland Centre

Mill Rd, BN18 9PB • Daily: April to mid-Oct 9.30am–5.30pm; mid-Oct to March 9.30am–4.30pm • £11, under-17s £5.50 • ☎ 01903 883355, ⓦ wwt.org.uk/visit/arundel

The **WWT Arundel Wetland Centre**, a mile out of town, is home to endangered waterfowl from around the world, but a wander around the scenic 65-acre site can also turn up sightings of native wildlife, including water voles, kingfishers, sand martins, dragonflies and peregrines. Don't miss the tranquil, rustling **reedbed boardwalks** or the boat trips, probably your best chance of spotting water voles.

ARRIVAL AND INFORMATION   ARUNDEL

By train Arundel's station is half a mile south of the town centre over the river on the A27.
Destinations Brighton (hourly; 1hr 10min); Chichester (Mon–Sat 2 hourly, Sun hourly; 30–50min); London Victoria (every 30min; 1hr 20min).

By bus Buses from Brighton (Mon–Sat every 30min, Sun hourly; 2hr) arrive on either the High St or River Rd.
Tourist information There's a Visitor Information Point at Arundel Museum, opposite the castle entrance on Mill Road (daily 10am–4pm; ⓦ sussexbythesea.com).

ACCOMMODATION AND EATING

Bay Tree 21 Tarrant St, BN18 9DG ☎ 01903 883679, ⓦ thebaytreearundel.co.uk. Cosy and relaxed little restaurant squeezed into three low-beamed rooms, with a small terrace out the back. Mains such as pheasant breast wrapped in bacon cost £16–18 at dinner; lunch features simpler dishes. Mon–Fri 11.30am–2.45pm & 6.30–9.30pm, Sat & Sun 10.30am–4.30pm & 6.30–9.30pm.

George and Dragon Inn Burpham ☎ 01903 883131, ⓦ georgeatburpham.co.uk. Three miles from Arundel (a lovely walk up the east bank of the river), this seventeenth-century pub has bags of character, plenty of

Sussex ales on tap and a seasonal, local menu that runs from ciabattas (£6.50) to burgers (£12.50), fish, salads and steaks. Mon–Fri 10.30am–3pm & 6–11pm, Sat 10.30am–11pm, Sun 10.30am–10pm; kitchen Mon–Fri noon–2.30pm & 6–9pm, Sat noon–3pm & 6–9.30pm, Sun noon–4pm & 6–8.30pm.

Swan Hotel 27–29 High St, BN18 9AG ☎ 01903 882314, ⓦ swanarundel.co.uk. Fifteen smart rooms above a pub, decked out in shabby-chic style, with shutters and bare boards or coir carpets, and seaside prints on the wall. Prices fluctuate according to demand. **£99**

Midhurst and around

Lying right in the centre of the South Downs National Park, and home to the park's headquarters, the small market town of **MIDHURST** has plenty of charm and a lovely location, surrounded by swathes of gorgeous countryside. Midhurst grew up around the medieval market in **Market Square**, still the most attractive corner of town. If you're visiting on a summer weekend, don't miss the atmospheric **Cowdray Ruins** at the

THE SOUTH DOWNS NATIONAL PARK

The **South Downs National Park** came into being in 2010. Covering over six hundred square miles, it stretches for 70 miles from eastern Hampshire through to the chalk cliffs of East Sussex, encompassing rolling hills, heathland, woodland and coastline. More than 112,000 people live and work in the national park – more than in any other – and it is crisscrossed by a dense network of over 1800 miles of footpaths and bridleways.

The park's headquarters and visitor centre, the South Downs Centre (see below), is in Midhurst. ⓦ **southdowns.gov.uk** has comprehensive information on public transport, walks, cycling, horseriding and other activities, plus an events calendar.

2

northern end of town (June–Aug Sat, Sun & bank hols 11am–4pm; £6.50; ☎01730 810781, ⓦcowdray.org.uk); before it was gutted by fire in 1793, the house was one of the grandest homes in the country.

Petworth House

Petworth, GU28 9LR • **House** Mid-March to early Nov daily 11am–5pm; rest of year opening hours vary – check website • **Pleasure Ground** Daily: Feb 10am–4pm; early March 10am–4.30pm; mid-March to Oct daily 10am–5pm; Nov–Jan 10am–3.30pm • House and Pleasure Ground mid-March to early Nov £13.50, rest of year £7.20; NT • ☎ 01798 342207, ⓦ nationaltrust.org.uk/petworth • Train to Pulborough, then Stagecoach Coastline #1 bus (Mon–Sat hourly, Sun every 2hr)

Seven miles east of Arundel, the pretty little town of Petworth is dominated by **Petworth House**, one of the southeast's most impressive stately homes. Built in the late seventeenth century, the house is stuffed with treasures – including the 1592 Molyneux globe, believed to be the earliest terrestrial globe in existence – and contains an outstanding art collection, with paintings by Van Dyck, Titian, Gainsborough, Bosch, Reynolds, Blake and Turner (the last a frequent guest here). The 700-acre **grounds**, home to a large herd of fallow deer, were landscaped by Capability Brown and are considered one of his finest achievements.

ARRIVAL AND INFORMATION

By train and bus The closest stations are at Haslemere (connected by bus #70 to Midhurst: Mon–Sat hourly; 25min), Petersfield (bus #92: Mon–Sat hourly; 25min) and Chichester (bus #60: Mon–Sat every 30min, Sun hourly; 40min).

South Downs Centre Capron House, North St, GU29 9DH (Mon–Thurs 9am–5pm, Fri 9am–4.30pm; May–Sept also

MIDHURST AND AROUND

Sat 9am–1pm; ☎01730 814810, ⓦsouthdowns.gov.uk). The visitor centre of the South Downs National Park contains a small exhibition about the National Park, and has plenty of leaflets and information on walks and public transport. There's also information on Midhurst (ⓦ visit midhurst.com), including town maps and trails.

ACCOMMODATION AND EATING

The Church House Church Hill, GU29 9NX ☎01730 812990, ⓦchurchhousemidhurst.com. A great location by Market Square, five gorgeous rooms, and home-made cake on arrival are just some of the things to love about this B&B. **£140**

★ **Horse Guards Inn** Upperton Rd, Tillington, GU28 9AF ☎01798 342332, ⓦthehorseguardsinn.co.uk. Lovely little gastropub between Midhurst and Petworth; in summer you can grab a deckchair (or hay-bale) in the idyllic garden. Harveys and guest ales on tap, plus excellent seasonal food

(mains around £15). Daily noon–midnight; kitchen Mon–Thurs noon–2.30pm & 6.30–9pm, Fri noon–2.30pm & 6–9.30pm, Sat noon–3pm & 6–9.30pm, Sun noon–3.30pm & 6.30–9pm. **£100**

The Olive & Vine North Street, GU29 9DJ ☎01730 859532, ⓦtheoliveandvine.co.uk. Popular, contemporary restaurant-bar that covers all bases, from morning coffee through to evening meals (burgers, salads, *moules frites*) and late-night cocktails. Daily 9am–late; kitchen daily noon–9pm.

Chichester and around

The handsome city of **CHICHESTER** has plenty to recommend it: a splendid twelfth-century **cathedral**, a thriving cultural scene and an outstanding collection of modern British art on show at **Pallant House Gallery**. The city began life as a Roman settlement, and its Roman cruciform street plan is still evident in the four-quadrant symmetry of the town centre. The main streets lead off from the Gothic **Market Cross**, a bulky octagonal rotunda topped by ornate finials and a crown lantern spire, built in 1501 to provide shelter for the market traders. The big attraction outside Chichester is **Fishbourne Roman Palace**, the largest excavated Roman site in Britain, though for families a day at dune-backed **West Wittering beach** will be hard to beat.

Chichester Festivities (☎01243 528356, ⓦchifest.org.uk) is Chichester's annual arts festival, taking place at a range of venues over two weeks in late June, and featuring music, talks, theatre, comedy and other events.

Chichester Cathedral

West St, PO19 1RP • Mon–Sat 7.15am–6.30pm, Sun 7.15am–5pm; tours (45min) Mon–Sat 11.15am & 2.30pm • Free • ☎01243 782595, ⓦ chichestercathedral.org.uk

The city's chief attraction is the fine Gothic **Chichester Cathedral**. Building began in 1076, but the church was extensively rebuilt following a fire a century later and has been only minimally modified since about 1300, except for the slender spire and the unique, freestanding fifteenth-century bell tower. The **interior** is renowned for its modern devotional art, which includes a stained-glass window by Marc Chagall and an altar-screen tapestry by John Piper. Older treasures include a sixteenth-century painting in the north transept of the past bishops of Chichester, and the fourteenth-century Fitzalan tomb that inspired Philip Larkin to write *An Arundel Tomb*. However, the highlight is a pair of carvings created around 1140, the **Chichester Reliefs**, which show the raising of Lazarus and Christ at the gate of Bethany; originally brightly coloured, with semiprecious stones set in the figures' eyes, the reliefs are among the finest Romanesque stone carvings in England.

Pallant House Gallery

9 North Pallant, PO19 1TJ • Tues, Wed, Fri & Sat 10am–5pm, Thurs 10am–8pm, Sun & bank hols 11am–5pm • £10, Tues £5, Thurs 5–8pm permanent collection free (£5 for temporary exhibitions) • ☎01243 774557, ⓦ pallant.org.uk

Off South Street, in the well-preserved Georgian quadrant of the city known as the Pallants, you'll find **Pallant House Gallery**, a superlative collection of twentieth-century British art housed in a Queen Anne townhouse and award-winning contemporary extension. Artists whose works are on display in the permanent collection include Henry Moore, Lucian Freud, Walter Sickert, Barbara Hepworth and Peter Blake, and there are also excellent temporary exhibitions.

Fishbourne Roman Palace

Salthill Rd, Fishbourne, PO19 3QR, 2 miles west of Chichester • Daily: Feb & Nov to mid-Dec 10am–4pm; March–Oct 10am–5pm • £9.20 • ☎01243 789829, ⓦ sussexpast.co.uk • Train from Chichester to Fishbourne (hourly; 3min); turn right from the station and the palace is a few minutes' walk away

Fishbourne is the largest and best-preserved Roman dwelling in the country. Roman relics have long been turning up hereabouts, and in 1960 a workman unearthed their source – the site of a depot constructed by the invading Romans in 43 AD, which is thought later to have become the vast, hundred-room palace of a Romanized Celtic aristocrat. The one surviving wing, the north wing, displays floor mosaics depicting Fishbourne's famous dolphin-riding cupid as well as the more usual geometric patterns. An audiovisual programme portrays the palace as it would have been in Roman times, and the extensive gardens attempt to re-create the palace grounds.

GLORIOUS GOODWOOD

Four miles north of Chichester, the **Goodwood Estate** (☎01243 775055, ⓦgoodwood
.co.uk) is most famous for its racecourse and its motor-racing circuit, and for its three big
sporting events: the **Festival of Speed** (late June/early July), a long weekend of vintage
and special cars; **Glorious Goodwood** (late July/Aug), one of *the* social events of the
horse-racing year; and the **Goodwood Revival** (mid-Sept), a motor-racing meeting
staged in the 1940s, 1950s and 1960s. All three events are very popular; buy tickets and book
accommodation well in advance.

2

Cass Sculpture Foundation

Goodwood, PO18 0QP, 5 miles north of Chichester • Easter–Oct daily 10.30am–4.30pm • £12.50 • ☎01243 538449, ⓦsculpture.org.uk •
No public transport

Cass Sculpture Foundation is an absolute must for anyone interested in contemporary
art, with more than fifty large-scale works – some of which have been specially
commissioned – sited in a 26-acre woodland environment. The selection of pieces
on display changes from year to year as they are sold; past artists have included
Antony Gormley, Thomas Heatherwick, Eduardo Paolozzi, Andy Goldsworthy and
Rachel Whiteread.

Weald and Downland Open-Air Museum

Singleton, PO18 0EU, 6 miles north of Chichester • March, Nov & Dec daily 10.30am–4pm; April–Oct daily 10.30am–6pm; Downland
Gridshell tour (30min–1hr 30min) daily 1.30pm • £13 • ☎01243 811363, ⓦwealddown.co.uk • Stagecoach Coastline bus #60 from
Chichester or Midhurst (Mon–Sat 2 hourly, Sun hourly)

More than fifty old buildings from sites around the Southeast – from a Tudor market
hall to a medieval farmstead – have been dismantled and reconstructed at the fifty-acre
Weald and Downland Open-Air Museum, where there are stewards on hand to bring
the buildings to life. There's a daily guided **tour** of the Downland Gridshell building,
the museum's workshop and store, and there are also numerous special events and
activities throughout the year.

West Wittering beach

8 miles south of Chichester • Daily: mid-March to mid-Oct 6.30am–8.30pm; mid-Oct to mid-March 7am–6pm • Parking £1–8 depending
on season, day & time • ☎01243 514143 (Estate Office), ⓦwestwitteringbeach.co.uk • Buses #52 & #53 run from Chichester bus station
to West Wittering village (15–25min), a 10min walk from the beach

Unspoilt **West Wittering beach** is one of the loveliest beaches in Sussex, with acres of
dune-backed soft sand, and warm, shallow lagoons at low tide. A brilliant watersports
outfit, X-Train (☎01243 513077, ⓦx-train.co.uk), offers windsurfing, kitesurfing,
stand-up paddleboarding and more. The beach gets very busy on summer weekends;
come early, or be prepared for traffic jams.

ARRIVAL AND INFORMATION   CHICHESTER AND AROUND

By train Chichester's train station lies on Stockbridge Rd;
it's a 10min walk north to the Market Cross.
Destinations Arundel (Mon–Sat 2 hourly, Sun hourly;
30–50min); Brighton (2 hourly; 45–55min); London
Victoria (Mon–Sat 2 hourly, Sun hourly; 1hr 35min);
Portsmouth Harbour (Mon–Sat every 15min, Sun every
30min; 25–40min).
By bus The bus station is across the road from the train
station, on Southgate.

Destinations Brighton (every 20–30min; 1hr 45min);
Midhurst (Mon–Sat every 30min, Sun hourly; 40min);
Portsmouth (hourly; 55min).
Tourist information There's a Visitor Information Point
at the Novium Museum, Tower Street (April–Oct Mon–Sat
10am–5pm, Sun 10am–4pm; Nov–March Mon–Sat
10am–5pm, Sun 10am–4pm; ☎01243 775888, ⓦvisit
chichester.org).

ACCOMMODATION AND EATING

4 Canon Lane 4 Canon Lane, PO19 1PX ☎01243 813586, ⓦchichestercathedral.org.uk. Eight-bedroom Victorian house owned by the cathedral and located in its grounds. Rooms are big and comfortable, with art on the walls lent by the Pallant House Gallery. Breakfast costs extra (£8.95). **£99**

Field & Fork 4 Guildhall St, PO19 1NJ ☎01243 789915, ⓦfieldandfork.co.uk. One of the best places to eat in the city, serving up imaginative, locally sourced food, such as wild sea trout with local broad beans or maple-glazed short rib of beef (£12–19). Tues–Sat 11.30am–3pm & 5pm–late.

★**Musgrove House B&B** 63 Oving Rd, PO19 7EN ☎01243 790179, ⓦmusgrovehouse.co.uk. Great-value boutique B&B, just a short walk from the centre, with three lovely rooms and super-friendly owners. **£90**

Park Tavern 11 Priory Rd ☎01243 785057, ⓦpark tavernchichester.co.uk. Overlooking Priory Park, this is one of the city's nicest pubs. Good-value home-made food (around the £10 mark), plus sandwiches and ploughman's. Fuller's on tap, plus a guest ale. Live music on Sun afternoons. Mon–Sat 11am–11pm, Sun noon–10.30pm; kitchen Mon noon–3pm, Tues–Fri noon–3pm & 6–9pm, Sat 11am–9pm, Sun noon–4pm.

ENTERTAINMENT

Chichester Festival Theatre Oaklands Park, PO19 6AP ☎01243 781312, ⓦcft.org.uk. Highly regarded

theatre, with a season running roughly between Easter and Oct; in the shorter winter season it hosts touring shows.

Guildford and around

Set on the River Wey, in rolling Surrey countryside, **GUILDFORD** is an attractive county town, its cobbled high street lined with half-timbered buildings. For good views, walk up to the medieval **Guildford Castle** (March & Oct Sat & Sun 11am–4pm; April–Sept daily 10am–5pm; £3.20; ⓦguildford.gov.uk/castle), which has a viewing platform in the tower.

Watts Gallery Artists' Village

Down Lane, Compton, 3 miles southwest of Guildford, GU3 1DQ • **Gallery** Tues–Sun 11am–5pm • £9.50; half-price on Tues • **Limnerslease tours** Check website and book in advance; 1hr • £5 • **Chapel** Mon–Fri 9am–5pm, Sat & Sun 10am–5pm • Free • ☎01483 810235, ⓦwattsgallery.org.uk • #46 bus (hourly Mon–Sat; 15min) from Guildford town centre

Surrey played a key role in the Arts and Crafts movement of the late nineteenth and early twentieth centuries, with many artists finding inspiration in its quintessentially English countryside. Established in 1903 by influential artists Mary and George Frederic Watts, the **Watts Gallery** displays a variety of George's work – from light-infused metaphysical landscapes to socially conscious portraits and vigorous sculpture.

A ten-minute woodland walk away, **Limnerslease**, the couple's home, is visitable only on **guided tours** that are rich in personal snippets. The real star, though, is the **Watts Chapel**, Mary's masterpiece. Within this little red-brick and terracotta building, reminiscent of a Byzantine church, every patch of wall and vaulted ceiling is covered in a riot of imagery – lustrous jewel colours, natural motifs, Celtic knots, Art Nouveau styling and spiritual symbols combining to create an affecting, profoundly spiritual whole.

ARRIVAL AND INFORMATION	GUILDFORD AND AROUND

By train Trains from London Waterloo (every 30min; 35min) run to Guildford station, a mile west of the centre, across the River Wey.

Tourist office 155 High St (May–Sept Mon–Sat 9.30am–5pm, Sun 11am–4pm; Oct–April Mon–Sat 9.30am–5pm; ☎01483 444333, ⓦwww.guildford.gov.uk/visitguildford).

ACCOMMODATION AND EATING

★**Hurtwood Hotel** Walking Bottom, Peaslake, GU5 9RR ☎01306 730514, ⓦhurtwoodhotel.co.uk. This 1920s inn in the pretty hamlet of Peaslake, 8 miles southeast of Guildford, makes a great base for cycling and

walking breaks. There are stylish, comfy boutique B&B rooms and a pub/Italian restaurant (ⓦhurtwoodinn.com) – run by different people – downstairs. The front terrace is a sociable suntrap. **£100**

Dorking and around

Set at the mouth of a gap carved by the River Mole through the North Downs, the historic market town of **DORKING** is surrounded by glorious Surrey Hills countryside. **Box Hill**, north of Dorking on a chalk escarpment above the River Mole, draws streams of walkers and cyclists; there are more good walks to be had through the Edwardian **Polesden Lacey** estate.

2

Box Hill

Box Hill Rd, 3 miles northeast of Dorking, KT20 7LB • Daily dawn to dusk • Free, but parking £1.50/hr for first 2hr, £4 for up to 4hr; NT • ☏ 01306 885502, ⓦ nationaltrust.org.uk/box-hill • Box Hill & Westhumble train station is 1.5 miles west; #465 bus from Dorking (daily)

Box Hill, a mile from the North Downs Way, offers walking trails and cycle paths through woodlands of rare wild box trees, yew, oak and beech, and across chalk grasslands scattered with wildflowers and fluttering with butterflies. Trails include a "natural play trail" for kids, a two-mile Stepping Stones walk along the River Mole, and some longer, more strenuous options. Brilliant views abound, most famously from the **Salomons' Memorial** viewpoint near the café, where on a clear day you can see across the Weald to the South Downs.

Polesden Lacey

Near Great Bookham, 4 miles northwest of Dorking, RH5 6BD • Daily: March–Oct 11am–5pm; Nov–Feb 11am–4pm; entry by guided tour only 11am–12.30pm, with self-guided visits after that; gardens open 10am • £13.60; NT • ☏ 01372 452048, ⓦ nationaltrust.org.uk /polesden-lacey • Box Hill & Westhumble station is 3 miles east

Minutes from the North Downs Way, the grand Edwardian estate of **Polesden Lacey** practically begs you to while away the day with a picnic. Take a wander around the **gardens** – which include a lavender garden, apple orchard and walled rose garden – and the 1400-acre surrounding estate, with its woodlands and waymarked trails.

The **house** – remodelled in 1906 by the architects of the *Ritz* – is worth a look. It's largely set up to appear as it would have in the 1930s, when owned by wealthy socialite Margaret Greville.

ARRIVAL AND INFORMATION

By train Dorking's main station is a mile north of the centre.

Destinations Box Hill & Westhumble (hourly; 2min);

DORKING AND AROUND

London Victoria (every 30min; 1hr); London Waterloo (every 30min; 50min).

Website ⓦ visitdorking.com.

ACCOMMODATION AND EATING

Duke of Wellington Guildford Rd, East Horsley, KT24 6AA ☏ 01483 282312, ⓦ dukeofw.com. This smart gastropub conversion of a sixteenth-century inn, handy for Polesden Lacey, has plump armchairs and an open fire. The seasonal menu ranges from superfood salad via pan-fried sea bream with Bombay potatoes to sirloin steak; mains £14–28, two/three-course daytime menu £13.75/£16.75. Mon–Thurs & Sun noon–11pm, Sat noon–midnight; kitchen daily 11am till late.

Running Horses Old London Rd, Mickleham, RH5 6DU

☏ 01372 372279, ⓦ therunninghorses.co.uk. Old coaching inn near Box Hill, with six luxurious B&B rooms, Brakspear ales in the bar and British food, both traditional and contemporary in the restaurant (mains from £13). Mon–Fri 7.30–9.30am & 11am–11pm, Sat 8–10am & 11am–11pm, Sun 11am–10.30pm; kitchen Mon–Thurs 7.30–9.30am, noon–3pm & 6–9pm, Fri 7.30–9.30am, noon–3pm & 6–10pm, Sat 8–10am, noon–3pm & 6–10pm, Sun noon–8pm. **£110**

Hampshire, Dorset and Wiltshire

NEW FOREST PONY AT LATCHMORE BOTTOM

Hampshire, Dorset and Wiltshire

The distant past is perhaps more tangible in Hampshire (often abbreviated to "Hants"), Dorset and Wiltshire than in any other part of England. Predominantly rural, these three counties overlap substantially with the ancient kingdom of Wessex, whose most famous ruler, Alfred, repulsed the Danes in the ninth century and came close to establishing the first unified state in England. And even before Wessex came into being, many earlier civilizations had left their stamp on the region. The chalky uplands of Wiltshire boast several of Europe's greatest Neolithic sites, including Stonehenge and Avebury, while in Dorset you'll find Maiden Castle, the most striking Iron Age hillfort in the country, and the Cerne Abbas Giant, source of many a legend.

The Romans tramped all over these southern counties, leaving the most conspicuous signs of their occupation at the amphitheatre of **Dorchester** – though that town is more closely associated with the novels of Thomas Hardy and his vision of Wessex. None of the landscapes of this region could be described as grand or wild, but the countryside is consistently seductive, not least the crumbling fossil-bearing cliffs around **Lyme Regis**, the managed woodlands of the **New Forest** and the gentle, open curves of Salisbury Plain. The area's historic country towns such as **Sherborne**, **Shaftesbury** and **Bridport** are generally modest and slow-paced, with the notable exceptions of the two major maritime bases of **Portsmouth** and **Southampton**, a fair proportion of whose visitors are simply passing through on their way to the more genteel pleasures of the **Isle of Wight**. The two great cathedral cities in these parts, **Salisbury** and **Winchester**, and the seaside resorts of **Bournemouth** and **Weymouth** see most tourist traffic, while the great houses of Wilton, Stourhead, Longleat and Kingston Lacy also attract the crowds. You don't have to wander far off the beaten track, however, to find attractive villages such as **Lacock** and the appealing town of **Bradford-upon-Avon** – and, of course, some of the region's most dramatic coastal cliff scenery around the **Isle of Purbeck**.

Portsmouth and around

Britain's foremost naval station, **PORTSMOUTH** occupies the bulbous peninsula of Portsea Island, on the eastern flank of a huge, easily defended harbour. Billing itself as Britain's only island city, it is also its most densely populated city, with more than 15,000 people per square mile. The ancient Romans raised a fortress on the northernmost edge of this inlet, but this strategic location wasn't fully exploited until Tudor times, when Henry VII established the world's first dry dock here and made Portsmouth a royal dockyard. It has flourished ever since and nowadays Portsmouth is

KAYAKING AROUND OLD HARRY ROCKS, STUDLAND BAY

Highlights

❶ Osborne House Wander around the stunning gardens and get an insight into royal family life at Queen Victoria's former seaside home. **See p.199**

❷ The New Forest William the Conqueror's old hunting ground, home to wild ponies and deer, is ideal for walking, biking and riding. **See p.206**

❸ Sea kayaking in Studland View the rugged Old Harry Rocks up close on a guided kayak tour through sea arches and below towering chalk cliffs. **See p.216**

❹ Durdle Door Famous natural arch at the end of a splendid beach, accessed by a steep cliff path – a great place for walkers and swimmers alike. **See p.217**

❺ Seaside Boarding House, Burton Bradstock Down a Daiquiri on the terrace while watching the sun set over this stunning stretch of coast. **See p.224**

❻ Lyme Regis Enjoy one of the most historic and picturesque villages on the south coast. **See p.225**

❼ Stonehenge Marvel at one of Britain's most iconic sites, which is now much enhanced by an informative, environmentally friendly visitor centre. **See p.229**

HIGHLIGHTS ARE MARKED ON THE MAP ON P.186

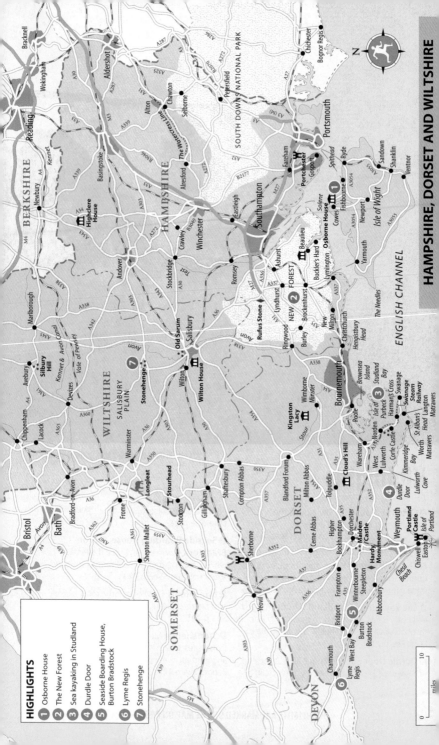

HAMPSHIRE, DORSET AND WILTSHIRE

HIGHLIGHTS

1. Osborne House
2. The New Forest
3. Sea kayaking in Studland
4. Durdle Door
5. Seaside Boarding House, Burton Bradstock
6. Lyme Regis
7. Stonehenge

TOP 5 OUTINGS FOR KIDS

Visit **Beaulieu Motor Museum**, paradise for petrolheads. See p.207

Take a boat to **Brownsea Island**. See p.213

Explore a 1940s schoolroom at **Tyneham** deserted village. See p.217

Go on a **fossil-hunting tour** at Charmouth. See box, p.225

Check out the lions, giraffes and rhino in deepest rural Wiltshire, at **Longleat Safari Park**. See p.231

---

a large industrialized city, its harbour clogged with naval frigates, ferries bound for the continent or the Isle of Wight, and swarms of tugs.

Due to its military importance, Portsmouth was heavily bombed during World War II, and bland tower blocks now give the city an ugly profile. Only **Old Portsmouth**, based around the original harbour, preserves some Georgian and a little Tudor character. East of here is **Southsea**, an attractive residential suburb of terraces facing a large common and a shingle beach.

3

Portsmouth Historic Dockyard

Victory Gate, HM Naval Base, PO1 3LJ • Daily: April–Oct 10am–5.30pm; Nov–March 10am–5pm; last entry 1hr before closing • All-inclusive ticket £35, under-16s £15 (online £28/£12); individual attraction tickets £18; all tickets valid for one year • ☎ 023 9283 9766, ⊕ historicdockyard.co.uk

For most visitors, a trip to Portsmouth begins and ends at the **Historic Dockyard**, in the **Royal Naval Base** at the end of Queen Street. The complex comprises three ships and several museums, with the main attractions being HMS *Victory*, HMS *Warrior*, the National Museum of the Royal Navy, the Mary Rose Museum, and a boat tour around the harbour. In addition, the Dockyard Apprentice exhibition gives insights into the working of the docks in the early twentieth century, while Action Stations provides interactive activities and simulators, plus the UK's tallest indoor climbing tower.

HMS Warrior

Portsmouth Historic Dockyard's youngest ship, **HMS Warrior**, dates from 1860. It was Britain's first armoured (iron-clad) battleship, complete with sails and steam engines, and was the pride of the fleet in its day. The ship displays a wealth of weaponry, including rifles, pistols and sabres, though the *Warrior* was never challenged nor even fired a cannon in her 22 years at sea.

Mary Rose Museum

The impressive, boat-shaped **Mary Rose Museum** was built around Henry VIII's flagship, the **Mary Rose**, and houses not only the ship itself, but also thousands of objects retrieved from or near the wreck, including guns, gold and the crew's personal effects. The ship capsized before the king's eyes off Spithead in 1545 while engaging French intruders, sinking swiftly with almost all her seven-hundred-strong crew. In 1982 a massive conservation project successfully raised the remains of the hull, which silt had preserved beneath the seabed, and you can now view the world's only remaining sixteenth-century warship through protective glass windows.

HMS Victory

Currently undergoing restoration (though still open to the public), **HMS Victory** was already forty years old when she set sail from Portsmouth for Trafalgar on September 14, 1805, returning in triumph three months later, but bearing the corpse of Admiral Nelson. Shot by a sniper from a French ship at the height of the battle, Nelson expired below deck three hours later, having been assured that victory was in sight. A plaque on

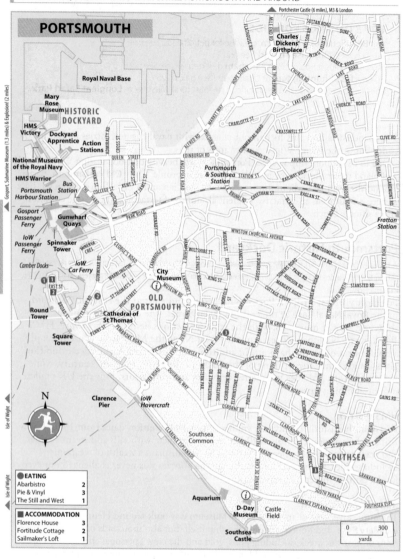

PORTSMOUTH

the deck marks the spot where Nelson was fatally wounded and you can also see the wooden cask in which his body was preserved in brandy for the return trip to Britain. Although badly damaged during the battle, the *Victory* continued in service for a further twenty years, before being retired to the dry dock where she rests today.

National Museum of the Royal Navy

Opposite the *Victory*, various buildings house the exhaustive **National Museum of the Royal Navy**. Tracing naval history from Alfred the Great's fleet to the present day, the collection includes some jolly figureheads, Nelson memorabilia, including the only surviving sail from HMS *Victory*, and nautical models, though there's scant coverage of

BOATS TO GOSPORT

Gosport can be reached by taking the **passenger ferry** from Harbour train station jetty between the historic dockyard and Gunwharf Quays (daily 5.30am–midnight every 10–15min; 5min; £3.40 return; ☎023 9252 4551, ⓦgosportferry.co.uk). If you have an all-inclusive ticket for Portsmouth Historic Dockyard, you can take the **Waterbus** which shuttles hourly (10.15am–4.15pm, Sat & Sun only from Nov–March) between the Historic Dockyard, Gunwharf Quays, the Submarine Museum and Explosion!

more recent conflicts. The Trafalgar Experience is a noisy, vivid re-creation of the battle itself, with gory bits to thrill the kids.

Royal Navy Submarine Museum

Haslar Jetty, Gosport, PO12 2AS · Daily: April–Oct 10am–5.30pm; Nov–March Wed–Sun 10am–4.30pm (daily in school hols); last HMS *Alliance* tour 1hr before closing · £13.50 · ☎023 9251 0354, ⓦsubmarine-museum.co.uk

Portsmouth's naval theme persists throughout otherwise humdrum Gosport, where the **Royal Navy Submarine Museum** displays, unsurprisingly, submarines – four in total, some of which you can enter. Allow a couple of hours to explore these slightly creepy vessels – a guided **tour** inside HMS *Alliance* gives you a gloomy insight into how cramped life was on board, and the museum elaborates evocatively on the history of submersible craft.

Explosion! The Museum of Naval Firepower

Priddy's Hard, Gosport, PO12 4LE · April–Oct daily 10am–5pm; Nov–March Sat & Sun 10am–4pm; last entry 1hr before closing · £10.80 · ☎023 9250 5600, ⓦexplosion.org.uk

Near the Royal Submarine Museum, housed in an old armaments depot, **Explosion!** tells the story of naval warfare from the days of gunpowder to the present, with weapons of all descriptions, including mines, big guns and torpedoes, all backed up by vivid computer animations.

Spinnaker Tower

Gunwharf Quays, PO1 3TT · Daily 10am–5.30pm; open from 9.30am in the school summer hols · £10.50, or £8.90 online · ☎023 9285 7520, ⓦwww.spinnakertower.co.uk

From Portsmouth Harbour train station, it's a short walk along the historic waterfront to the sleek modern **Gunwharf Quays** development, where you'll find a multitude of cafés, restaurants, nightspots and shops. Here you'll find **Spinnaker Tower**, an elegant, 557ft-high sail-like structure, offering **views** of up to twenty miles over land and sea. Its three viewing decks can be reached by a high-speed lift, the highest one being open to the elements, though most people stick to View Deck 1, which has one of Europe's largest glass floors.

Old Portsmouth

It's a well-signposted fifteen-minute walk south of Gunwharf Quays to what remains of **Old Portsmouth**. Along the way, you pass the simple **Cathedral of St Thomas** (ⓦportsmouthcathedral.org.uk) on the High Street, whose original twelfth-century features have been obscured by rebuilding after the Civil War and again in the twentieth century. The High Street ends at a maze of cobbled Georgian streets huddling behind a fifteenth-century wall protecting the **Camber**, or old port, where Walter Raleigh landed the first potatoes and tobacco from the New World. Nearby, the Round and Square towers, which punctuate the Tudor fortifications, are popular vantage points for observing the comings and goings of the boats.

D-Day Museum

Clarence Esplanade, Southsea, PO5 3NT • Daily: April–Sept 10am–5.30pm; Oct–March 10am–5pm; last entry 30min before closing •
£6.80 • ☎ 023 9282 6722, ⊛ ddaymuseum.co.uk

Located in the suburb of **Southsea**, southeast of Old Portsmouth, the **D-Day Museum**
focuses on Portsmouth's role as the principal assembly point for the Normandy beach
landings in World War II, code-named "Operation Overlord". The museum's most
striking exhibit is the 295ft-long Overlord Embroidery, a sort of twentieth-century
equivalent of the Bayeux Tapestry, which took five years to complete. The museum
was °sundergoing substantial refurbishment at the time of going to press, so check the
website for the latest details.

Southsea Castle

Clarence Esplanade, Southsea, PO5 3PA • March–Oct Tues–Sun & bank hols 10am–5pm • Free • ☎ 023 9282 6722, ⊛ southseacastle.co.uk

Next door to the D-Day Museum, Southsea's most historic building, marked by a little
lighthouse, is the squat **Southsea Castle**, built from the remains of Beaulieu Abbey (see
p.207). You can go inside the keep and learn about Portsmouth's military history, and can
climb up to the spot from where Henry VIII is said to have watched the *Mary Rose* sink
in 1545 (see p.187). There's also an appealing café inside the castle walls and courtyard.

Charles Dickens' Birthplace

393 Old Commercial Rd, PO1 4QL • April–Sept Fri–Sun 10am–5.30pm, last entry 5pm • £4.20, free for Portsmouth residents • ☎ 023 9282 7261,
⊛ charlesdickensbirthplace.co.uk

Just over a mile northeast of Old Portsmouth, **Charles Dickens' Birthplace** is set up to look
much as it would have when the famous novelist was born here in 1812. Charles's father,
John, moved to Portsmouth in 1809 to work for the Navy Pay Office before he was
recalled to London in 1815, so Charles only lived here for three years, but nevertheless he
is said to have returned often and set parts of *Nicholas Nickleby* in the city. The modest
house not only contains period furniture (including the couch on which he died) but also
a wealth of information about the time when Dickens lived here.

Portchester Castle

Church Rd, Portchester, PO16 9QW • April–Sept daily 10am–6pm; Oct daily 10am–5pm; Nov–March Sat & Sun (daily in Feb half term)
10am–4pm • £6.20; EH • ☎ 02392 378291, ⊛ www.english-heritage.org.uk/visit/places/portchester-castle • Bus #3 stops a quarter of a
mile from the castle and Portchester train station is a mile away

Six miles northwest of the city centre, just past the marina development at Port Solent,
Portchester Castle was built by the Romans in the third century, and boasts the finest
surviving example of Roman walls in northern Europe – still over 20ft high and
incorporating some twenty bastions. The Normans felt no need to make any substantial
alterations when they moved in, but a keep was later built within Portchester's precincts
by Henry II, which Richard II extended and Henry V used as his garrison when
assembling the army that was to fight the Battle of Agincourt.

ARRIVAL AND INFORMATION

By train Portsmouth's main station is in the city centre,
but the line continues to Harbour Station, the most
convenient stop for the dockyard sights and old town.
Destinations Brighton (every 30min; 1hr 20min–1hr
30min); London Waterloo (every 15–20min; 1hr 35min–
2hr 15min); Salisbury (hourly; 1hr 15min); Southampton
(every 20min; 45min–1hr); Winchester (hourly; 1hr).
By bus National Express buses stop at The Hard

Interchange, right by Harbour Station.
Destinations London Victoria (hourly; 1hr 50min–2hr
30min); Southampton (hourly; 40min–1hr).
By ferry Wightlink passenger catamarans leave from
the jetty at Harbour Station for Ryde (see p.194), while car
ferries depart from the ferry port off Gunwharf Rd, just
south of Gunwharf Quays, for Fishbourne (see p.178).
Hovercraft link Southsea with Ryde (see p.194), while

ferries run regularly from the Harbour Station to Gosport, on the other side of Portsmouth Harbour (see box, p.189).
Tourist offices There are two tourist offices in Portsmouth

(☎ 023 9282 6722, ⓦ visitportsmouth.co.uk), one in the City Museum, 2 Museum Rd (daily 10am–5.30pm), the other in the D-Day Museum (see opposite).

ACCOMMODATION

Florence House 2 Malvern Rd, Southsea, PO5 2NA ☎ 023 9200 9111, ⓦ florencehousehotel.co.uk; map p.188. Tasteful boutique B&B in an Edwardian townhouse with a range of rooms over three floors, all spick and span and with flatscreen TVs. There's a tiny downstairs bar and communal lounge, and parking permits can be provided. If it's full, check out the other boutique-style hotels in the area run by the same group (the Mercer Collection). **£95**

Fortitude Cottage 51 Broad Street, PO1 2JD ☎ 023 9282 3748, ⓦ fortitudecottage.co.uk; map p.188. Stylish B&B in Portsmouth Old Town overlooking the ferry

terminal and Gunwharf Quays. The top-floor room has its own roof terrace with fantastic views of the water, and three others have harbour views (though not all do). Free parking. **£170**

Sailmaker's Loft 5 Bath Square, PO1 2JL ☎ 023 9282 3045, ⓦ sailmakersloft.org.uk; map p.188. Recently renovated, this modern B&B is set just back from the waterfront, right opposite *The Still* pub, with top-floor rooms overlooking the water. Most rooms have their own bathroom. **£70**

EATING

Abarbistro 58 White Hart Rd, PO1 2JA ☎ 023 9281 1585, ⓦ abarbistro.co.uk; map p.188. Lively bar/restaurant with an outside terrace on the edge of Old Portsmouth. The menu features popular classics such as pork belly (£16.50) and steaks (£22.50), plus daily-changing fish specials. Mon–Sat 11am–11pm, Sun noon–10pm.

Pie and Vinyl 61 Castle Road, Southsea, PO5 3AY ☎ 023 9275 3914 ⓦ pieandvinyl.co.uk; map p.188. Part café, part hip shop selling – as the name suggests – records and pies. It's a great space for browsing and chilling, with a wide range of tasty pies on offer (from £6; extra for

mash, peas and gravy) – there are also vegan options. Mon–Sat 11am–9pm, Sun 11am–5pm.

The Still and West 2 Bath Square, Old Portsmouth, PO1 2JL ☎ 023 9282 1567, ⓦ stillandwest.co.uk; map p.188. A waterfront terrace and cosy interior with views over the harbour make this pub worth stopping by: the food ranges from the traditional fish and chips (£13.50) to sea trout (£19) and thyme-roasted chicken (£14). Mon–Sat 9.30am–11pm, Sun 9.30am–10.30pm; kitchen Mon–Fri noon–9pm, Sat noon–10pm, Sun noon–8pm.

Southampton

A glance at the map gives some idea of the strategic maritime importance of **SOUTHAMPTON**, which stands on a triangular peninsula formed at the place where the rivers Itchen and Test flow into Southampton Water, an eight-mile inlet from the Solent. Sure enough, Southampton has figured in numerous stirring events: it witnessed the exodus of Henry V's Agincourt-bound army, the Pilgrim Fathers' departure in the *Mayflower* in 1620 and the maiden voyages of such ships as the *Queen Mary* and the *Titanic*. Despite its pummelling by the Luftwaffe and some disastrous postwar urban sprawl, the thousand-year-old city has retained some of its medieval charm in parts and has reinvented itself as a twenty-first-century shopping centre in others, with the giant glass-and-steel **West Quay** as its focus. A short stroll north of here, Southampton's new **Cultural Quarter** is worth a visit, with its open squares, excellent art gallery and superb Sea City Museum.

City Art Gallery

Civic Centre, Commercial Rd • Mon–Fri 10am–3pm, Sat 10am–5pm • Free • ☎ 02380 833007, ⓦ southamptoncityartgallery.com

Core of the modern town is the Civic Centre, a short walk east of the train station and home to the excellent **City Art Gallery**. Though not always on show at the same time, its collection is particularly strong on contemporary British artists, with works by Gilbert and George, Chris Ofili and Lucian Freud. You can also see works by older masters: Gainsborough, Joshua Reynolds and the Impressionists – Monet and Pissaro included.

Sea City Museum

Civic Centre, Havelock Rd, SO14 7FY • Daily 10am–5pm • £8.50, joint ticket with Tudor House £12 • ☎ 02380 833007, ⓦ seacitymuseum.co.uk

The purpose-built **Sea City Museum** is a triumph of design that succeeds in being both moving and fun. Opened on April 10, 2012, the hundredth anniversary of the day that the *Titanic* sailed from Southampton's Town Quay on its maiden voyage, the museum provides a fascinating insight into the history of the ship, its crew, its significance to Edwardian Southampton and, of course, an account of the fateful journey, which started in high excitement and ended only four days later in tragedy. Impressive **interactive displays** give you the chance to steer the *Titanic* around the icebergs, while re-creations of a second-class cabin and the boiler room allow you to imagine life as both crew and passenger. **Interviews with survivors** of the disaster are particularly moving, with tales of children being put into hessian sacks and hauled up from the lifeboats onto the rescue ship, the *Carpathia*.

Upstairs, the Gateway to the World gallery details the history of Southampton and its **maritime heritage**, from its beginnings as a small Roman port to the modern day. Exhibits as diverse as an early log boat, found in nearby Hamble, a collection of prehistoric flints, and a giant model of the *Queen Mary* are on display.

Medieval Merchants House

58 French St, SO1 0AT • April–Sept Sat & Sun 11am–4pm • £4.80; EH • ☎ 02380 221503, ⓦ www.english-heritage.org.uk/visit/places/medieval-merchants-house

Standing in one of Southampton's busiest streets in medieval times, the **Medieval Merchants House** was built in 1290 by John Fortin, a merchant who made his money trading with Bordeaux. The house has been restored to its fourteenth-century condition, with replica furniture such as a canopied four-poster bed, the kind that a wealthy merchant would have enjoyed languishing in.

Tudor House Museum and Garden

St Michael's Square, SO14 2AD • Mon–Thurs 10am–3pm, Sat & Sun 10am–5pm • £5, joint ticket with Sea City Museum £12 • ☎ 02380 834242, ⓦ www.tudorhouseandgarden.com

The excellent **Tudor House Museum and Garden** was built in 1492 by the wealthy John Dawtrey, who worked on Henry VIII's shipping fleet and who could afford to embellish his home with the best glass and oak available. The house then passed on to other city bigwigs, including artist George Rogers, who added a new Georgian wing at the back. By the early 1800s, it sat in the middle of a district of slums and was earmarked for demolition until saved by philanthropist and collector William Spranger, whose collection of Victorian curios were left here when the house became a museum in 1912. Today, the museum houses an intriguing mishmash of high-tech interactive displays, historic paintings, and artefacts including a Greek amphora and a re-created **Victorian kitchen**. You can also visit the beautifully landscaped **Tudor garden**, which contains a good café and the ruins of the Norman St John's Palace, built in the 1300s by a wealthy merchant when this part of town sat right on the quayside.

ARRIVAL AND INFORMATION   SOUTHAMPTON

By train Southampton's central station is in Blechynden Terrace, west of the Civic Centre.

Destinations Bournemouth (every 15–20min; 30min–1hr 10 min); London Waterloo (every 15–20min; 1hr 20min–1hr 35min); Portsmouth (every 20min; 45min–1hr); Salisbury (every 30min; 30–40min); Weymouth (every 30min; 1hr 20min–1hr 40min); Winchester (every 15min; 15–30min).

By bus National Express buses run from the coach station on Harbour Parade.

Destinations Bournemouth (roughly hourly; 45min–1hr); London Victoria (15 daily; 2hr–2hr 20min–2hr 45min); Portsmouth (13 daily; 50min–1hr); Salisbury (1 daily; 45min); Weymouth (3 daily; 2hr 40min–3hr) and Winchester (10 daily; 25–45min).

Tourist information The main tourist information point

TOP 5 FOOD WITH A VIEW

Kuti's Royal Thai Southampton. See below
The Salt Cellar Shaftesbury. See p.222
The Scott Arms Kingston. See p.215

The Seaside Boarding House Burton
Bradstock. See p.224
Urban Reef Boscombe. See p.211

is in the Central Library of the Civic Centre, 8 Civic Centre Rd (Mon–Thurs 10am–6pm, Fri 10am–5pm, Sat 10am–4pm; ☎02380 833333, ⓦdiscoversouthampton.co.uk), where you can pick up leaflets, maps and guides to the city.

ACCOMMODATION

Ennios Town Quay Rd, SO14 2AR ☎02380 221159, ⓦennios.co.uk. In a former warehouse right on the waterfront, this boutique-style hotel has plush rooms with comfortable beds and smart bathrooms. The stylishly decorated rooms come with L'Occitane toiletries, and there's an excellent Italian restaurant downstairs. **£120**

★**Pig in the Wall** 8 Western Esplanade, SO14 2AZ ☎02380 636900, ⓦthepighotel.com. Built into the city walls, Southampton's most stylish boutique hotel has been cleverly renovated and beautifully decorated in a shabby-chic style. All the rooms have powerful showers and top-of-the range coffee machines – the large (pricier) rooms boast glamorous roll-top baths in the rooms themselves. There's a great bar/lounge/deli downstairs, or you can jump in one of the hotel Land Rovers, which will take you to their sister hotel/ restaurant in the New Forest for dinner (see p.209). **£145**

EATING AND DRINKING

The Arthouse Gallery Café 178 Above Bar St, SO14 7DW ☎02380 238582, ⓦthearthousesouthampton .org. Friendly, community-run café which serves delicious home-made vegan and vegetarian dishes, such as sharing platters and Greek meze with hummus, pitta and stuffed vine leaves (both £9), as well as organic rum and craft beers. The café also hosts workshops, art exhibitions, knitting circles and live music; upstairs, there's a piano, comfy sofas and plenty of board games. Tues–Sat 10.30am–10pm, Sun noon–5pm.

Kuti's Royal Thai Pier Gate House, Royal Pier, SO14 2AQ ☎02380 339211, ⓦroyalthaipier.co.uk. Choose from the Thai tapas menu (mains from £9), the set menus or, best of all, the excellent five-course Sun lunch buffet (£12) at this superbly ornate waterside restaurant. The building was once a pier opened by the then Princess

Victoria in 1833, and has fine views over the water from the outside deck on summer evenings. Mon–Thurs noon–2.30pm & 5–10pm, Fri & Sat noon–2.30pm & 5pm–11pm, Sun noon–3pm & 5–10pm.

The Dancing Man Brewery Wool House, Town Quay, SO14 2AR ☎02380 836666, ⓦdancingmanbrewery .co.uk. The atmospheric fourteenth-century Wool House, a medieval warehouse, now houses a lively pub and micro-brewery, with the beers brewed on site in vast stills. The food is good – pies, burgers, steaks (£11–18) plus tasty sandwiches at lunch (£5–8) – with waiter service upstairs and bar service downstairs. There are tables outside and dogs are welcome too. Mon–Wed & Sun noon–11pm, Thurs–Sat noon–midnight; kitchen Mon–Sat noon–3pm & 6–9pm, Sun noon–5pm.

The Isle of Wight

The lozenge-shaped **ISLE OF WIGHT** has begun to shake off its old-fashioned image and attract a younger, livelier crowd, with a couple of major annual **rock festivals** and a scattering of fashionable hotels. Despite measuring less than 23 miles at its widest point, the island packs in a surprising variety of landscapes and coastal scenery. Its **beaches** have long attracted holiday-makers, and the island was a favourite of such eminent Victorians as Tennyson, Dickens, Swinburne, Julia Margaret Cameron and Queen Victoria herself, who made **Osborne House**, near Cowes, her permanent home after Albert died.

ARRIVAL AND DEPARTURE   THE ISLE OF WIGHT

There are three **ferry** departure points from the mainland – Portsmouth, Southampton and Lymington. **Fare** structures and **schedules** on all routes are labyrinthine, from £16 for a day-return foot-passenger ticket on the Southampton–West Cowes route in low season to over £100 for a high-season return for a car and four passengers on the Lymington–Yarmouth route: check the companies' websites for full details of current fares and schedules.

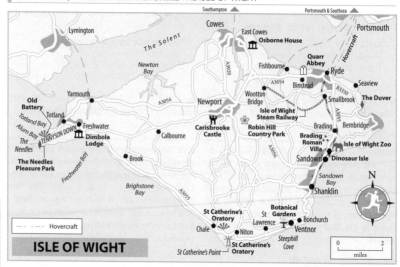

3

ISLE OF WIGHT

From Portsmouth Wightlink (ⓦwightlink.co.uk) runs car ferries from the Gunwharf Terminal to Fishbourne (45min), and a high-speed catamaran from the Harbour to Ryde (passengers only; 20min). Hovertravel (ⓦhovertravel.co.uk) runs hovercraft from Clarence Esplanade in Southsea to Ryde (passengers only; 10min).

From Southampton Red Funnel (ⓦredfunnel.co.uk) operates a high-speed catamaran to West Cowes (passengers only; 25min) and a car ferry to East Cowes (1hr).
From Lymington Wightlink (ⓦwightlink.co.uk) runs car ferries to Yarmouth (40min).

INFORMATION

Tourist information The helpful Visit Isle of Wight (ⓣ01983 521555, ⓦvisitisleofwight.co.uk) is a good source of information and runs the island's only tourist office; it's in The Guildhall, High St, Newport (Mon–Fri 10am–3pm).

GETTING AROUND

By train There are two train lines on the island: the seasonal Isle of Wight Steam Railway (ⓣ01983 882204, ⓦiwsteamrailway.co.uk) runs from Wootton Bridge to Smallbrook Junction, where it connects with the east-coast Island line from Ryde to Shanklin (every 20–40min; 25min; ⓦislandlinetrains.co.uk).
By bus Local buses are run by Southern Vectis (ⓣ01983 827000, ⓦislandbuses.info), who sell good-value tickets offering unlimited travel on their network (£10/day, £24/week).

By bike Cycling is a popular way of getting around the island, though in summer the narrow lanes can get very busy. For bike rental, contact Wight Cycle Hire (ⓣ01983 761800, ⓦwightcyclehire.co.uk, from £12/half-day, £16/day): its office is in Yarmouth, but it can deliver bikes anywhere on the island (minimum hire fee £50).

Ryde

As a major ferry terminal, **RYDE** is the first landfall many visitors make on the island, but one where few choose to linger, despite some grand nineteenth-century architecture and a fine sandy town **beach**.

Donald McGill Postcard Museum

The Royal Victoria Arcade, Union St, PO33 2LQ · Mon–Sat 11am–4pm · £3 · ⓣ01983 717435, ⓦsaucyseasidepostcards.com

Ryde's quirky little **Postcard Museum** crams in a good proportion of the twelve thousand saucy postcards created by artist Donald McGill. The cards, produced throughout the first half of the twentieth century, reached their peak of popularity in the 1930s. Packed with daft double entendres, the collection here also shows how far things have moved since the Obscene Publications Act regularly tried to have McGill's cards banned.

ARRIVAL AND DEPARTURE   RYDE

The **bus station**, **hovercraft** terminal and Esplanade **train station** are all near the base of the pier, while **catamarans** from Portsmouth dock at the Pier Head.

ACCOMMODATION AND EATING

The Boathouse Springvale Rd, Seaview, PO34 5AW, 2 miles east of Ryde ☎ 01983 810616, ⓦ theboathouse iow.co.uk. It's a pleasant 2-mile walk along the coast to this classy gastropub, whose garden boasts fantastic views across the Solent. A great spot for a drink, it also serves scampi and chips (£12), seafood platters (£10.50) and fresh fish of the day. It also has spacious en-suite rooms decorated in a contemporary style with iPod docks; superior rooms have sea views. Mon–Sat 9am–11pm, Sun 9am–10.30pm; kitchen Mon–Sat 9–11am & noon–9.30pm, Sun 9–11am & noon–9pm. **£130**

Olivo 32–33 Union St, PO33 2LE ☎ 01983 611118, ⓦ olivorestaurant.co.uk/ryde. Tasty Italian dishes in a buzzy, stylish restaurant with bare-brick walls and an open kitchen. There are decent pizzas (£10–13) and pasta dishes (£10–15), plus some less usual main courses, such as seared duck breast (£17). Daily 9am–9pm.

Sorrento Lodge 11 The Strand PO33 2LG ☎ 01983 812813 ⓦ sorrentolodge.co.uk. Very well kept B&B in a large townhouse with a seafront garden, run by a helpful couple. Some of the rooms have sea views, all are en suite, and the breakfasts are good. **£80**

Three Bouys Appley Lane, PO33 2DU ☎ 01983 811212, ⓦ threebuoys.co.uk. Excellent food in a lovely setting in this upstairs restaurant with a large balcony overlooking Ryde beach. The decor is contemporary, with wooden floors and tables and big picture windows giving fantastic views over the Solent, and the food is well-cooked and -presented. Dishes include seared scallops (£9) and St Austell mussels (£15), and there are good vegetarian options. Mon–Fri noon–2.30pm & 6–9pm, Sat noon–3pm & 6–9.30pm, Sun noon–9pm.

Quarr Abbey

Just outside the village of Binstead, PO33 4ES • Tearoom and farm shop Mon–Sat 10am–5pm, Sun 11.15am–5pm; closes 4pm in winter • Free • ☎ 01983 882420, ⓦ quarrabbey.org • Buses #4 and #9 from Ryde stop outside the abbey

Two miles west of Ryde's centre, **Quarr Abbey** was founded in 1132 by Richard de Redvers as one of the first Cistercian monasteries in Britain. Its name derives from the nearby quarries, where stone was extracted for use in the construction of Winchester and Chichester cathedrals. Only stunted ruins survived the Dissolution and ensuing plunder of ready-cut stone. In 1907 a new Benedictine abbey was founded just west of the ruins – a striking rose-brick building with Byzantine overtones, which can only be visited on guided **tours** (check the website for times). You can wander freely around the grounds, where you'll find a very fine tea garden, farm shop and visitor centre.

Brading Roman Villa

Morton Old Rd, PO36 0PH • Daily 10am–5pm; last entry 4pm • £9.50 • ☎ 01983 406223, ⓦ bradingromanvilla.org.uk • Bus #3 from Ryde or Sandown

Just south of the ancient village of **Brading**, on the busy Ryde to Sandown A3055, are the remains of **Brading Roman Villa**, which are renowned for their **mosaics**. This is the more impressive of two such villas on the island, both of which were probably sites of

THE ISLE OF WIGHT STEAM RAILWAY

The seasonal **Isle of Wight Steam Railway** (☎ 01983 882204, ⓦ iwsteamrailway.co.uk) makes the delightful ten-mile return trip from Smallbrook Junction (where it connects with the Island line) to Wootton Bridge, between Ryde and Newport. Its impeccably restored carriages in traditional green livery run through lovely unspoilt countryside, stopping at Ashey and Havenstreet, where there's a small museum of railway memorabilia. The adult return fare (£13, or £11.50 online) is valid for any travel on that day.

bacchanalian worship. The Brading site is housed in an attractive modern museum and its superbly preserved mosaics include intact images of Medusa and depictions of Orpheus. There's also a good café here.

Sandown

The traditional seaside resort of **SANDOWN** merges with its neighbour Shanklin across the sandy reach of Sandown Bay, representing the island's holiday-making epicentre. Appropriately enough, this traditional 1960s bucket-and-spade resort possesses the island's only surviving pleasure **pier**, bedecked with various traditional amusements and a large theatre with nightly entertainment in season.

Isle of Wight Zoo

Yaverland Seafront, PO36 8QB • Daily: Jan to mid-Feb & Dec 11am–3pm; mid-Feb to March & Oct 10am–4pm; April–Sept 10am–5.30pm; closed in adverse weather • £11, under-15s £10 • ☎ 01983 403883, ☜ isleofwightzoo.com

At the northern end of the Esplanade, and built into the walls of a Victorian fort, the **Isle of Wight Zoo** houses Britain's largest collection of tigers including some endangered species that are virtually extinct in the wild. It's also home to panthers and other big cats, as well as some frisky lemurs, monkeys and reptiles.

Dinosaur Isle

Culver Parade, PO36 8QA • Daily: April–Aug 10am–6pm; Sept–Oct 10am–5pm; Nov–March 10am–4pm; last entry one hour before closing • £5, under-16s £4 • ☎ 01983 404344, ☜ www.dinosaurisle.com

Situated on Sandown's seafront esplanade, **Dinosaur Isle** is housed in a purpose-built museum shaped like a giant pterosaur. Inside, you'll find robotic dinosaurs and life-size replicas of the various species once found on the island, while the museum's collection also showcases some of the prehistoric finds on the island, one of Europe's richest sites for dinosaur remains.

ARRIVAL AND DEPARTURE

SANDOWN

By train The Island line train station, served by trains from Ryde and Shanklin, is on Station Ave, about a 10min walk inland from the pier.

By Bus Buses #2 from Newport via Shanklin, or #3 & #8 from Ryde.

ACCOMMODATION AND EATING

The Belmore 101 Station Avenue PO36 8HD ☎ 01983 404189, ☜ belmorebandb.com. On a quiet street a short walk from the beach, this large Victorian house has been converted into a smart B&B. The comfortable rooms are decorated with stylish furnishings and have a marine vibe. Two-night minimum stay in summer. **£80**

The Reef The Esplanade, PO36 8AE ☎ 01983 403219, ☜ thereefsandown.co.uk. A bright bar/restaurant right on the seafront, with great views. It serves up a range of mid-priced dishes including pizzas, pasta and burgers (from £10), steaks (£18) and fresh fish (from £11). Daily 11am–11pm; kitchen daily noon–9pm.

Shanklin

SHANKLIN, with its auburn cliffs, Old Village and scenic Chine, has a marginally more sophisticated aura than its northern neighbour. The rose-clad, thatched **Old Village** may be syrupy, but the adjacent **Shanklin Chine** (daily: April to late May 10am–5pm; late May to Sept 10am–10pm; late Oct 10am–8pm; £4.50 single visit, £5.50 return ticket valid for a week; ☎ 01983 866432, ☜ shanklinchine.co.uk), a twisting pathway descending a mossy ravine and decorated on summer nights with fairy lights, is undeniably picturesque; former resident John Keats once drew inspiration from the environs.

ARRIVAL AND DEPARTURE

SHANKLIN

By train The final stop on the Island Line from Ryde, Shanklin train station is about half a mile inland at the top of Regent St.

By bus The bus station (buses #2 & #3 from Ryde and Newport) is a little south of the train station, on Landguard Rd.

ACCOMMODATION, EATING AND DRINKING

Fisherman's Cottage Southern end of the Esplanade, at the bottom of Shanklin Chine, PO37 6BN ☎01983 863882, ⓦfishermanscottageshanklin.co.uk. An atmospheric nineteenth-century thatched pub right on the seafront, with outside tables: it's child-friendly and serves wholesome pub food, such as fish pie and cod and chips (mains around £11). Mid-March to Oct daily: pub 11am–10pm; kitchen noon–9pm.

Pendleton's 85 High Street, PO37 6NR ☎01983 868727, ⓦpendletons.org. Well-regarded restaurant serving local produce where possible, in dishes such as duck leg with champ mash, pork medallions (around £16) and pasta (from £12). Tues–Sat 6pm–11pm.

Rylstone Manor Rylstone Gardens, PO37 6RG ☎01983 862806, ⓦwww.rylstone-manor.co.uk. This superb Victorian pile, with period decor, sits right in the middle of the leafy public gardens at the top of the cliff. It has its own bar and dining room, though children under 16 are not allowed and in high season there is a 3-night minimum stay. **£145**

Ventnor

The seaside resort of **VENTNOR** and its two village suburbs of **Bonchurch** and **St Lawrence** sit at the foot of St Boniface Down, the island's highest point at 787ft. The Down periodically disintegrates into landslides, creating the jumbled terraces known locally as the **Undercliff**, whose sheltered, south-facing aspect, mild winter temperatures and thick carpet of undergrowth have contributed to the former fishing village becoming a fashionable health spa. Thanks to these unique factors, the town possesses rather more character than the island's other resorts, its Gothic Revival buildings clinging dizzily to zigzagging bends.

The floral terraces of the Cascade curve down to the slender Esplanade and narrow beach, where some of the former boat-builders' cottages now house shops, cafés and restaurants. From the Esplanade, it's a pleasant mile-long stroll to Ventnor's rolling **Botanical Gardens**, filled with exotic plants and impressive glasshouses (daily 10am–5pm; £9.50, valid for one week; ☎01983 855397, ⓦbotanic.co.uk).

ACCOMMODATION   VENTNOR

Hambrough Hotel Hambrough Rd, PO38 1SQ ☎01983 856333, ⓦthehambrough.com. Small, stylish, modern hotel with a chic bar. The comfortable rooms come with all the luxuries, including flatscreen TV and espresso machines; most have sea views, and some have balconies. **£150**

★**The Leconfield** 85 Leeson Rd, Upper Bonchurch, PO38 1PU ☎01983 852196, ⓦleconfieldhotel.com. Friendly and comfortable B&B in attractive grounds overlooking the sea. The well-kept rooms are spacious, light and airy, and many have free-standing baths and sea views. The breakfast's delicious, and there's a heated pool in summer in the lovely garden. **£90**

EATING AND DRINKING

El Toro Contento 2 Pier St, PO38 1ST ☎01983 857600, ⓦeltorocontento.co.uk. A cosy restaurant dishing up home-made tapas, such as chorizo in cider and spicy mussels, most for under a fiver. Also serves Spanish hams and cheeses and will cook paella (around £11 a head, minimum 4 people) with 24hr notice. Summer daily 5–10pm; winter Thurs–Sun 4–10pm.

Spyglass Inn Ventnor Esplanade, PO38 1JX ☎01983 855338, ⓦthespyglass.com. Lively pub, with a terrace, in a great location on the seafront. You can eat giant portions of pub grub, such as fisherman's pie (most mains £10–12). Frequent live music, too. Daily 10am–11pm; kitchen daily noon–9.30pm.

★**Wheelers Crab Shed** Steephill Cove, PO38 1AF ☎01983 855819. Delicious home-made crab pasties, sandwiches and mackerel ciabattas served from a pretty shack on the seashore. Also tasty local lobster salads and daily fish specials. Easter to October Mon & Wed–Sun (plus sunny weekends & hols in other months) noon–3pm.

The southwest coast

The western Undercliff begins to recede at the village of Niton, where a footpath continues to the most southerly tip of the island, **St Catherine's Point**, marked by a modern lighthouse. A prominent landmark on the downs behind is **St Catherine's Oratory**, known locally as the "Pepper Pot": originally a lighthouse, it reputedly dates from 1325.

Seven miles northwest along the coast, Military Road ascends the flank of Compton Down before descending into Freshwater Bay. If you're walking this way, you might stop off at the National Trust-owned **Compton Bay**, a splendid spot for a swim or a picnic that's frequented by local surfers and accessed by a steep path leading down from the dark red cliffs.

Dimbola Lodge

Terrace Lane, Freshwater Bay, PO40 9QE • April–Oct daily 10am–5pm; Oct–March Tues–Sun 10am–4pm • £5 • ☎ 01983 756814, ⓦ dimbola.co.uk

On the coastal road at Freshwater Bay, **Dimbola Lodge** was the home of pioneer photographer **Julia Margaret Cameron**, who settled here after visiting local resident Tennyson in 1860. The building now houses a gallery of her work plus changing exhibitions, as well as a room devoted to memorabilia from the Isle of Wight festival. There's also a bookshop and tearoom/restaurant.

Tom's Eco Lodge Tapnell Farm, Newport Rd, PO41 0YJ ☎ 07717 666346, ⓦ tomsecolodge.com. Set next to the Tapnell Farm animal park and activity centre (ⓦ tapnell farm.com) with stunning views over the distant Solent, these ready-erected, upmarket tents are the ultimate in glamping – they come complete with fridges, electricity, private hot-water showers and flushing toilets. Great for families. Minimum three-night stay. From **£192**

The Needles and Alum Bay

The breezy four-mile ridge of **Tennyson Down** running from Freshwater Bay to **The Needles** is one of the island's most satisfying walks, with vistas onto rolling downs and vales. On top of the Down, there's a monument to the eponymous poet, who lived on the island for forty years from 1853 until his death. At its western tip sits the **Needles Old Battery**, a gun emplacement built 250ft above the sea in 1863 (April–Oct daily 10.30am–5pm; fort may be closed in bad weather; £6.50, NT; ☎ 01983 754772, ⓦ nationaltrust.org.uk/the-needles-old-battery-and-new-battery). There are fabulous views from here over the three tall chalk stacks known as **The Needles**, which jut out into the English Channel. Needles Pleasure Cruises runs **boat trips** round the Needles (April–Oct; £6; ☎ 01983 761587, ⓦ www.needlespleasurecruises.co.uk) from **Alum Bay**, a twenty-minute walk away. To catch the boat, you can walk down the cliff path or take the chairlift (daily 10am–4pm; £6 return; ⓦ www.theneedles.co.uk), which descends the polychrome cliffs to ochre-hued sands.

Yarmouth

Four miles east of the Needles and linked to Lymington in the New Forest by car ferry, the pleasant north-coast town of **YARMOUTH** makes a lovely entrance to the island and is the best base for exploring its western tip. Although razed by the French in 1377, the port prospered after **Yarmouth Castle** (Easter–Oct daily 10am–4pm; £5.20, EH; ☎ 01983 760678, ⓦ www.english-heritage.org.uk/visit/places/yarmouth-castle), tucked between the quay and the pier, was commissioned by Henry VIII. Inside, some of the rooms have re-created life in a sixteenth-century castle, and there's also a display on the many wrecks that floundered here in the Solent, while the battlements afford superb views over the estuary. Yarmouth's only other real sight is the Grade II listed **pier**, England's longest wooden pier still in use.

The Blue Crab High St, PO41 0PL ☎ 01983 760014, ⓦ thebluecrab.co.uk. A simply decorated restaurant, with cosy booths, that offers fish and shellfish dishes such as hake with mussel and leek sauce (£15). Also does top-quality fresh fish and chips from £8. Mon–Wed, Fri & Sat 11am–3pm & 6–11pm, Thurs 10am–3pm & 6–11pm, Sun 6–11pm.

The George Hotel Quay St, PO41 0PE ☎01983 760331, ⓦthegeorge.co.uk. In a great position right by the ferry dock, with a lovely garden overlooking the Solent, this seventeenth-century hotel has hosted the likes of Charles II in its time. The rooms are comfortable and elegantly furnished, some with balconies looking out over the water, and there are two excellent restaurants downstairs, specializing in local produce. Minimum two-night stay at weekends. **£200**

Off the Rails Station Rd, PO41 0QT ☎01983 761600, ⓦofftherailsyarmouth.co.uk. In the former station on a disused railway line that is now a popular cycle path, this cosy café has train-style banquettes and a wood-burner inside, while outside there are tables on the platform overlooking the River Yar. The food is good, if slightly pricey, with breakfasts such as smoked salmon and scrambled eggs (£10.50), tasty burgers (£12), and more unusual options for dinner such as duck cassoulet (£16). Wed, Thurs & Sun 9am–4pm, Fri & Sat 9am–10pm.

Cowes

COWES, at the island's northern tip, is associated with sailing craft and boat building: Henry VIII installed a castle to defend the Solent's expanding naval dockyards from the French and Spanish, and in the 1950s the world's first hovercraft made its test runs here. In 1820 the Prince Regent's patronage of the yacht club gave the port its cachet, and the Royal Yacht Squadron is now one of the world's most exclusive sailing clubs. The first week of August sees the international yachting festival **Cowes Week** (ⓦlendycowesweek.co.uk), where serious sailors mingle with visiting royalty; most summer weekends see some form of nautical event taking place in or around town.

The town is bisected by the River Medina, with **West Cowes** being the older, more interesting half. At the bottom of the meandering High Street, **boat trips** around the harbour and the Solent leave from Thetis Wharf, near the Parade (☎01983 564602, ⓦsolentcruises.co.uk). The more industrial **East Cowes**, where you'll find Osborne House, is connected to West Cowes by a "floating bridge", or chain ferry (approx every 10–15min, Mon–Sat 5–12.30am, Sun 6.30–12.30am; pedestrians £1.50 return, cars £2.60 single; ⓦiwfloatingbridge.co.uk, ☎01983 293041).

Osborne House

East Cowes, PO32 6JX • April–Sept daily 10am–6pm; Oct daily 10am–5pm; Nov–March Sat & Sun 10am–4pm • £16.20; EH • ☎01983 200022, ⓦwww.english-heritage.org.uk/visit/places/osborne • Bus #4 from Ryde or #5 from Newport, or either from East Cowes

The only place of interest in East Cowes is Queen Victoria's family home, **Osborne House**, signposted one mile southeast of town. The house was built in the late 1840s by Prince Albert and Thomas Cubitt in the style of an Italianate villa, with balconies and large terraces overlooking the landscaped gardens towards the Solent. The **state rooms**, used for entertaining visiting dignitaries, exude formality as one would expect – the Durbar Room, clad almost entirely in ivory, is particularly impressive – while the **private apartments** feel homely in a manner appropriate to the affluent family holiday residence that Osborne was. Following Albert's death, the desolate Victoria spent much of her time here, and it's where she eventually died in 1901. Since then, according to her wishes, the house has remained virtually unaltered, allowing an intimate glimpse into Victoria's family life. In the **grounds**, you can see the remains of a barracks with its own drawbridge, built by Prince Albert as a place where the boys could play soldiers, and Queen Victoria's original bathing machine, next to her private beach.

ACCOMMODATION COWES

Albert Cottage York Ave, East Cowes, PO32 6BD ☎01983 299309, ⓦalbertcottagehotel.com. Adjacent to and once part of the Osborne estate, this lovely mansion, set in its own grounds, has a country house feel to it. Rooms are very comfortable, and have flatscreen TVs; it has its own highly rated restaurant, too. **£140**

★ Into the Woods Lower Westwood, Brocks Copse Rd, Wootton, PO33 4NP ☎07769 696464, ⓦisleofwight treehouse.com. Lovely, luxury treehouse (sleeps 4) and shepherds' huts (sleep 6) to rent on a farm in a secluded wood, three miles south of East Cowes. Both are beautifully finished and eco-friendly, and come complete with wood-burning stoves, en-suite showers, and even wi-fi. The location is peaceful, with chickens and geese, rope swings to play on and woods to run around in – the perfect combination of nature and home comforts. There's a

two-night minimum stay off-season, up to seven nights minimum in Aug. Treehouse **£175**, shepherds' huts **£150**
Villa Rothsay Baring Rd, West Cowes, PO31 8DF ☎01983 295178, ⓦvilla-rothsay.co.uk. Upmarket boutique hotel that's maintained its Victorian roots with period decor throughout – think curtains, ornate stairways and stained-glass windows. Some of the rooms have sea views and balconies (£10 extra) and there are great views from the grounds and raised patio area. **£145**

EATING AND DRINKING

The Coast Bar & Dining Room 14–15 Shooters Hill, West Cowes, PO31 7BG ☎01983 298574, ⓦthecoastbar .co.uk. Light and airy bar/restaurant with wooden floors and a lively, informal vibe. The menu features wood-fired pizzas (£9–12), plus the likes of loin of venison (£16.50), seafood linguine (£14) and a good selection of steaks (from £19). Daily 9am–1am.

Folly Inn Folly Lane, Whippingham, PO32 6NB ☎01983 297171. A mile from Osborne House, this attractive waterside pub has the river lapping at its decks and is said to have replaced a French smuggler's barge that sold produce here in the 1700s. It serves decent pub food such as beef and ale pie (£11), plus tasty fajitas (£12). The Folly Waterbus (☎07974 864627) runs a taxi service from Cowes to the jetty next to the pub. Daily 9am–10pm.

The Mess Canteen & Bar 63 High St, West Cowes, PO31 7RL ☎01983 280083. Completely decorated with recycled materials, this lively place serves up great burgers – try tempura soft-shell crab or halloumi – and unusual salads such as calamari or goats' cheese, all around £9–12. There's a good range of cocktails – the Isle of Wight jam-jar tea is tasty – the service is friendly and the vibe is fun. Mon–Thurs 11am–2.30pm & 6–9pm, Sat 11am–9.30pm, Sun 11am–3.30pm.

Newport

The capital of the Isle of Wight, **NEWPORT**, sits in the centre of the island at a point where the River Medina's commercial navigability ends. Though worth a visit to see the hilltop fortress of **Carisbrooke Castle**, the town itself isn't particularly engaging.

Carisbrooke Castle

Castle Hill, southwest of Newport, PO30 1XY • Feb half term daily 10am–4pm; late Feb & March Wed–Sun 10am–4pm; April–Sept daily 10am–6pm; Oct daily 10am–5pm; Nov to early Feb Sat & Sun 10am–4pm • £9.40; EH • ☎01983 523112, ⓦwww.english-heritage.org.uk /visit/places/carisbrook-castle • Bus #7 from Newport

The most famous resident of **Carisbrooke Castle**, a rather austere Norman pile, was Charles I, detained here (and caught one night ignominiously jammed between his room's bars while attempting escape) before his execution in London. The **museum** features relics from his incarceration, as well as those of the last royal resident, Princess Beatrice, Queen Victoria's youngest daughter. There's also a sixteenth-century well-house, where you can watch donkeys trudge around a huge treadmill to raise a barrel 160ft up the well shaft.

Winchester and around

Nowadays a tranquil, handsome market town, **WINCHESTER** was once one of the mightiest settlements in England. Under the Romans it was Venta Belgarum, the fifth-largest town in Britain, but it was **Alfred the Great** who really put Winchester on the map when he made it the capital of his Wessex kingdom in the ninth century. For the next two hundred years or so Winchester ranked alongside London, its status affirmed by William the Conqueror's coronation in both cities and by his commissioning of the local monks to prepare the **Domesday Book**. It wasn't until after the Battle of Naseby in 1645, when Cromwell took the city, that Winchester began its decline into provinciality.

Hampshire's county town now has a scholarly and slightly anachronistic air, embodied by the ancient almshouses that still provide shelter for senior citizens of "noble poverty" – the pensioners can be seen walking round the town in medieval black or mulberry-coloured gowns with silver badges. It also makes a good base from

Map labels:

A272 & Stockbridge ▲ ▲ Train Station (200yd) & 🚉 (3.5 miles) ▲ A3090 & A33 Basingstoke

NORTH WALLS

WINCHESTER

@ Library

■ **DRINKING**
The Black Boy 2
Wykeham Arms 1

SUSSEX STREET
TOWER STREET
STAPLE GARDENS
JEWRY STREET
ST PETER'S STREET
PARCHMENT STREET
UPPER BROOK STREET
MIDDLE BROOK STREET

■ **ACCOMMODATION**
29 Christchurch Road 3
Lainston Country
House Hotel 1
The Old Vine 2

● **EATING**
Forte Kitchen 1
River Cottage Canteen 2

CLIFTON HILL
CLIFTON TERRACE
UPPER HIGH ST

ROMSEY ROAD
Westgate
☒ Museum
@
HIGH STREET
ST GEORGE'S STREET
FRIARSGATE
LOWER BROOK ST

A3090, A31 Romsey

ST JAMES TERRACE
Gurkha
Museum
Great
Hall
CASTLE AVE
ST CLEMENT STREET
N
THE SQUARE
City
Museum
GREAT MINSTER ST
MARKET LANE
THE BROADWAY
Bus
Station
EASTGATE STREET
WATER LANE
City
Mill

ST JAMES LANE
SOUTHGATE STREET
ST THOMAS STREET
SYMONDS STREET
Cathedral
Guildhall
King
Alfred's
Statue
ⓘ

CHRISTCHURCH ROAD
ST JAMES VILLAS
COMPTON ROAD
EDGAR ROAD
ST CROSS ROAD
CANON STREET
ST SWITHUN STREET
COLEBROOK STREET
THE CLOSE

B3404 Alton
CHESIL STREET

3

BEAUFORT ROAD
St Michael's Road
Kings
☒ Gate
Jane
Austen's
House
COLLEGE STREET
Wolvesey
Castle
Chesil
Theatre
River Itchen

CULVER ROAD
KINGSGATE STREET
Winchester
College
WHARF HILL

0   50
yards

3
M3 & A33 Southampton ▼   Hospital of St Cross (0.7 miles) ▼   M3 Southampton & London ▼ 2

which to explore the nearby towns of **Chawton** and **Selborne**, homes, respectively, to Jane Austen and the eminent naturalist, Gilbert White.

Winchester Cathedral

9 The Close, SO23 9LS • Mon–Sat 9.30am–5pm, Sun 12.30–3pm • £8, including a guided tour of cathedral, treasury and crypt (ticket valid for one year) • **Tower tours** Jan–May, Oct & Nov Wed 2.15pm, Sat 11.30am & 2.15pm; June–Sept Mon, Wed & Fri 2.15pm, Sat 11.30am & 2.15pm; 1hr 30min • £6.50 • ☏ 01962 857275, ⓦ winchester-cathedral.org.uk

The first minster to be built in Winchester was raised by Cenwalh, the Saxon king of Wessex in the mid-seventh century, and traces of this building have been unearthed near the present **cathedral**, which was begun in 1079 and completed some three hundred years later. The exterior is not its best feature – squat and massive, it crouches stumpily over the tidy lawns of the Cathedral Close. The interior is rich and complex, however, and its 556ft **nave** makes this Europe's longest medieval church. Outstanding features include the carved Norman font of black Tournai marble, the fourteenth-century misericords (the choir stalls are the oldest complete set in the country) and some amazing monuments – **William of Wykeham's Chantry**, halfway down the nave on the right, is one of the most ornate.

Jane Austen, who died in Winchester, is commemorated close to the font by a memorial brass and slab beneath which she's interred, though she's recorded simply as the daughter of a local clergyman. Above the high altar lie the mortuary chests of pre-Conquest kings, including **Cnut** (though the bones were mixed up after Cromwell's Roundheads broke up the chests in 1645); **William Rufus**, killed while hunting in the New Forest in 1100, lies in the presbytery.

Behind the impressive Victorian screen at the end of the presbytery, look out for the memorial shrine to **St Swithun**. Originally buried outside in the churchyard, his remains were later interred inside, where the "rain of heaven" could no longer fall on him, whereupon he took revenge and the heavens opened for forty days – hence the legend that if it rains on St Swithun's Day (July 15) it will do so for another forty. His exact burial place is unknown.

Accessible from the north transept, the Norman **crypt** – often flooded – is home to Antony Gormley's contemplative figure *Sound II*, which is frequently ankle-deep in the waters. The cathedral's original foundations were dug in marshy ground, and at the beginning of the last century a steadfast diver, William Walker, spent five years replacing the rotten timber foundations with concrete.

City Museum

The Square, SO23 9ES • April–Oct Mon–Sat 10am–5pm, Sun noon–5pm; Nov–March Tues–Sat 10am–4pm, Sun noon–4pm • Free • ☎ 01962 863064, Ⓦ www.winchester.gov.uk/museums

Just off the High Street on the Square, the **City Museum** recounts Winchester's history with archeological and historical displays. Set on three floors, it is an imaginative medley of local artefacts including re-created traditional shopfronts, some impressive Roman mosaics, medieval coins and skeletons.

Great Hall

At the top of the High St on Castle Ave, SO23 8UJ • Daily 10am–5pm • Free, donation requested • ☎ 01962 846476, Ⓦ hants.gov.uk/greathall

The **Great Hall** is all that remains of a thirteenth-century castle destroyed by Cromwell. Sir Walter Raleigh heard his death sentence here in 1603, though he wasn't finally dispatched until 1618, and Judge Jeffreys held one of his Bloody Assizes (see p.218) in the castle after Monmouth's rebellion in 1685. The main interest now is a large, brightly painted disc slung on one wall like some curious antique dartboard. This is alleged to be King Arthur's Round Table, but the woodwork is probably fourteenth-century, later repainted as a PR exercise for the Tudor dynasty – the portrait of Arthur at the top of the table bears an uncanny resemblance to Henry VIII.

College Street

College Street is home to the buildings of **Winchester College**, the oldest public school in England – established in 1382 by William of Wykeham for "poor scholars", it now educates few but the wealthy and privileged. You can look round the medieval college buildings, its cloisters and Gothic chapel on a **guided tour** (2–4 daily; 1hr; £8; ☎01962 621209, Ⓦwinchestercollege.org).

At no.8 College Street stands the house where **Jane Austen** died. She moved here from Chawton in 1817 (see p.204), when she was already ill with Addison's Disease, and died later the same year, aged 42. The house is privately owned, though, so you can't look round. At the top of the street, the thirteenth-century **Kings Gate** is one of the city's original medieval gateways, housing the tiny St Swithun's Church.

Wolvesey Castle

Entrance off College St, SO23 9NB • April–Sept daily 10am–5pm • Free; EH • Ⓦ www.english-heritage.org.uk/visit/places /wolvesey-castle-old-bishops-palace

East of the cathedral, the remains of Winchester's Saxon walls bracket the ruins of the twelfth-century **Wolvesey Castle** – actually the palace for the Bishops of Winchester, who once wielded great clout over England's religious and political affairs. As a result, this was once one of the most important buildings in Winchester, encompassing its own stables, prison, chapel and gardens. Today, the castle ruins remain impressive, dwarfing the current dwelling place of the Bishop of Winchester, a relatively modest house built in 1680, which sits alongside it.

Hospital of St Cross

St Cross Rd, SO23 9SD • April–Oct Mon–Sat 9.30am–5pm, Sun 1–5pm; Nov–March Mon–Sat 10.30am–3.30pm • £4.50 • ☎01962 878218,
ⓦ hospitalofstcross.co.uk

About a mile south of College Walk, reached by a pleasant stroll across the water
meadows of the Itchen, lies the **Hospital of St Cross**, which featured in the BBC's
historical drama *Wolf Hall*. Founded in 1136 as a hostel for poor brethren, it boasts a
fine church, begun in that year and completed a century or so later, where you can see
a triptych by the Flemish painter Mabuse. Needy wayfarers may still apply for the
"dole" at the porter's lodge – a tiny portion of bread and beer.

ARRIVAL AND INFORMATION   WINCHESTER

By train The station is about a mile northwest of the
cathedral, on Stockbridge Rd.
Destinations Bournemouth (every 15–20min; 45min–
1hr); London Waterloo (every 15–20min; 1hr–1hr 10min);
Portsmouth (hourly; 1hr); Southampton (every 15min;
15–30min).
By bus National Express buses pull in at and depart from
the conveniently located bus station on the Broadway,

opposite the tourist office.
Destinations Bournemouth (8 daily; 1hr 20min–1hr
55min); London (8 daily; 1hr 55min–2hr 30min);
Southampton (10 daily; 25–45min).
Tourist office In the imposing Guildhall, High St (May–
Sept Mon–Sat 10am–5pm, Sun & bank hols 11am–4pm;
Oct–April Mon–Sat 10am–5pm; ☎01962 840500, ⓦvisit
winchester.co.uk).

3

ACCOMMODATION

29 Christchurch Road 29 Christchurch Rd, SO23 9SU
☎01962 868 661, ⓦbedbreakfastwinchester.co.uk;
map p.201. Well-furnished, comfortable B&B in a charming
Regency house located in a quiet, residential part of town.
No smoking. **£100**
Lainston Country House Hotel Woodman Lange,
Sparshot, SO21 2LT ☎01962 776088, ⓦexclusive.co.uk
/lainston-house; map p.201. Around a 10min drive from
Winchester towards Stockbridge, this seventeenth-century

mansion sits in 63 acres of grounds – it's luxurious and
comfortable, with huge bedrooms and friendly staff. It has its
own quality restaurant, specializing in local produce. **£175**
The Old Vine 8 Great Minster St, SO23 9HA ☎01962
854616, ⓦoldvinewinchester.com; map p.201. Lovely,
big rooms that combine period decor with modern touches
such as widescreen TVs, above a fine bar/restaurant, and
right opposite the cathedral. The street can be noisy at
night. **£120**

EATING

Forte Kitchen 78 Parchment St SO23 8AT ☎01962
856840, ⓦfortekitchen.co.uk; map p.201. The best
place in town for lunch. There's a good selection of
sandwiches plus more hearty mains such as smoked
mackerel with spinach, poached eggs and sourdough,

or Hampshire beef burger (both £11.50). The large upstairs
dining room attracts a lively, arty clientele. Mon–Fri
8am–4pm, Sat 9am–5pm, Sun 9am–4pm.
★ **River Cottage Canteen** Abbey Mill, Abbey Mill
Gardens, The Broadway, SO23 9GH ☎01962 457747,

THE REAL DOWNTON ABBEY

Tucked away in the northern reaches of Hampshire, twenty miles north of Winchester,
Highclere Castle (9.30am–5pm: Easter, early April & May bank hol weekends daily, mid-July
to mid-Sept Mon–Thurs & Sun; castle, exhibition and gardens £22, castle and gardens £15,
gardens £7; ☎01635 253210, ⓦhighclerecastle.co.uk) will be very familiar to fans of ITV's hit
period drama, **Downton Abbey**, which was filmed here. Home to Lord Carnarvon and his
family, the house is approached via a long drive that winds through a stunning 5000-acre
estate, and is surrounded by beautiful **gardens** designed by Capability Brown. Inside the
house, *Downton Abbey* aficionados will enjoy loitering in the **Drawing Room** and the **Library**,
scene of many a drama and quivering stiff-upper-lip of Lord Grantham and his family, while
upstairs you can peer into the bedrooms of the Crawley girls. In the castle cellars, an **Egyptian
Exhibition** celebrates the real-life fifth Earl of Carnarvon, who, in 1922, discovered the tomb of
Tutankhamun with Howard Carter, and who funded many of Carter's expeditions. Since the
house is still a family home and is also sometimes closed for filming, its opening hours vary
from month to month and year to year; call or check the website for details.

THE WATERCRESS LINE

Alresford, six miles east of Winchester, is the departure point for the **Watercress Line** (Feb–July, Sept & Oct days vary; Aug & school hols daily; call or check website for details; £16; ☎01962 733810, ⓦwatercressline.co.uk), a steam-powered railway so named because it passes through the former watercress beds that once flourished here. The train chuffs ten miles to **Alton**, with gourmet dinners served on board on Saturday evenings, plus traditional Sunday lunches, and Real Ales Trains serving ales from local breweries on some Saturday evenings.

ⓦrivercottage.net/canteens; map p.201. Located in a converted mill building, this is a great venue spread over several floors, with outside seating by the millstream. The menu features local ingredients, such as pan-fried gurnard (£16), and plenty of veggie options like roasted squash and spinach curry (£14). The cocktails are good, too. Mon–Fri 11am–10.30pm, Sat 10am–10pm, Sun 10am–4pm.

DRINKING

The Black Boy Wharf Hill, SO23 9NP ☎01962 861754, ⓦtheblackboypub.com; map p.201. Fantastic old pub with log fires in winter, walls lined with books and low ceilings hung with old coins and miniature bottles. Good cask ales from local breweries are on draught and there's reasonable pub grub from around £10, as well as a small outdoor terrace. Mon–Thurs noon–11pm, Fri & Sat noon–midnight, Sun noon–11.30pm.

Wykeham Arms 75 Kingsgate St, SO23 9PE ☎01962 853834, ⓦwykehamarmswinchester.co.uk; map p.201. This highly atmospheric eighteenth-century pub has a warren of cosy rooms, with open fireplaces, good bar snacks and decent beers. Daily 11am–11pm.

Chawton

A mile southwest of Alton and sixteen miles northeast of Winchester, the village of **CHAWTON** was home to Jane Austen from 1809 to 1817, during the last and most prolific years of her life – it was here that she wrote or revised almost all of her six books, including *Sense and Sensibility* and *Pride and Prejudice*.

Jane Austen's House Museum

Winchester Road, GU34 1SD • Daily: March–May & Sept–Dec 10.30am–4.30pm; June–Aug 10am–5pm • £8 ☎01420 83262, ⓦwww .jane-austens-house-museum.org.uk

A plain red-brick building in the centre of the village, **Jane Austen's House** contains first editions of some of her greatest works and provides a fascinating insight into the daily life of the author. You can see a lock of her hair, pieces of her jewellery and the desk where she wrote her books. The gardens include a learning centre that shows a short film about her life.

Chawton House

GU34 1SJ • Late March to Oct Mon–Fri noon–4.30pm, Sun 11am–5pm; last entry 30mins before closing • £8 • ☎01420 541010, ⓦwww.chawtonhouse.org

A short walk from Jane Austen's house is **Chawton House**, which belonged to Jane's brother, Edward Austen Knight. It remained in the Austen family until 1987, when it was bought by American IT millionaire Sandy Lerner. She opened the **Chawton House Library**, which contains an impressive collection of women's writing in English from 1600 to 1830; it also hosts frequent events.

ARRIVAL AND DEPARTURE

CHAWTON

By train The village is accessible on the Watercress Line steam train (see box above).

By bus From Winchester or Alton train station, take the #64 to Chawton roundabout (1–2 hourly; 15min from Alton; 40min from Winchester), then it's a 12min walk.

FROM TOP SEA VIEW, BURTON BRADSTOCK, NEAR BRIDPORT (P.224); DEER, ISLE OF PURBECK (P.214); STONEHENGE (P.229) >

The New Forest

Covering about 220 square miles, the **NEW FOREST** is one of southern England's favourite rural playgrounds, attracting some 13.5 million day-visits annually. The land was requisitioned by William the Conqueror in 1079 as a hunting ground, and the rights of its inhabitants soon became subservient to those of his precious deer. Fences to impede their progress were forbidden and terrible punishments were meted out to those who were caught poaching – hands were lopped off, eyes put out. Later monarchs less passionate about hunting than the Normans gradually restored the commoners' rights, and today the New Forest enjoys a unique patchwork of ancient laws and privileges alongside the regulations applying to its National Park status.

The **trees** here are now much more varied than they were in pre-Norman times, with birch, holly, yew, Scots pine and other conifers interspersed with the ancient oaks and beeches. One of the most venerable trees is the much-visited **Knightwood Oak**, just a few hundred yards north of the A35, three miles southwest of Lyndhurst, which measures about 22ft in circumference at shoulder height. The most conspicuous species of **fauna** is the New Forest **pony** – you'll see them grazing nonchalantly by the roadsides and ambling through some villages. The local deer are less visible now that some of the faster roads are fenced, although several species still roam the woods, including the tiny **sika deer**, descendants of a pair that escaped from nearby Beaulieu in 1904.

ARRIVAL AND DEPARTURE
THE NEW FOREST

By train The main London to Weymouth line passes through the New Forest, with fast trains stopping at Brockenhurst (see p.209); slower trains also stop at Ashurst, Sway and New Milton. From Brockenhurst a branch line runs to Lymington (every 30min; 10min) to link with the Isle of Wight ferry.

GETTING AROUND

Though the southern forest stretches have a reasonably efficient bus network, to get the best from the New Forest, you need to walk or ride through it, avoiding the places cars can reach.

By bus Useful routes through the forest include the #6 from Southampton to Lymington via Lyndhurst and Brockenhurst; the coastal routes #X1 and #X2 from Bournemouth and Christchurch to Lymington; and in summer the hop-on hop-off open-top New Forest Tour bus which runs on three different circular routes around the forest, taking in all the main settlements, and can carry up to four bikes for free (July to mid-Sept; £14.40 for a one-day ticket, valid on all three routes; ⓦthenewforesttour.info). Other services are run by More Buses (☎01202 338420, ⓦmorebus.co.uk) and Blue Star (☎01202 338421, ⓦbluestarbus.co.uk).

By bike There are 150 miles of car-free gravel roads in the forest, making cycling an appealing prospect – pick up a book of route maps from tourist offices or bike rental shops. Bikes can be rented in several places: for details of cycle routes and bike-hire outfits, check ⓦww.new-forest-national-park.com/bike-hire-in-the-new-forest.html.

INFORMATION

Information offices There are two information centres in the forest, one in Lyndhurst (see opposite), and the other in Lymington (see p.208), in the St Barbe Museum, New St, off the High St (Mon–Sat 10am–5pm, Sun 11am–4pm; ☎01590 689000, ⓦlymington.org).

Maps The Ordnance Survey Leisure Map 22 of the New Forest is best for exploring. Shops in Lyndhurst sell specialist walking books and natural history guides.

ACCOMMODATION

Camping There are ten campsites throughout the forest run by Camping in the Forest (☎024 7642 3008, ⓦcampingintheforest.co.uk); most are open from Easter to late Sept, though some are open year-round. Some are very simple, with few or no facilities, others have electricity and hot shower blocks, but they all have open access to the forest. Many even have streams and fords running through them, with ponies and donkeys wandering freely.

Lyndhurst

LYNDHURST, its town centre skewered by an agonizing one-way system, isn't a particularly interesting place, though the brick **parish church** is worth a glance for its William Morris glass and the grave of Mrs Reginald Hargreaves, better known as Alice Liddell, Lewis Carroll's model for Alice. The town is of most interest to visitors for the **New Forest Museum and Visitor Centre** in the central car park off the High Street (daily: April–Oct 10am–5pm; Nov–March 10am–4pm; ☎023 8028 3444, ⓦnewforestcentre.org.uk), and the adjoining **museum** (free, donations welcome), which focuses on the history, wildlife and industries of the New Forest. The forest's most visited site, the **Rufus Stone**, stands three miles northwest of Lyndhurst. Erected in 1745, it marks the putative spot where the Conqueror's son and heir, **William II** – aka William Rufus, after his ruddy complexion – was killed by a crossbow bolt in 1100.

ACCOMMODATION	LYNDHURST
Forest Lodge Hotel Pikes Hill, Romsey Rd, SO43 7AS ☎023 8028 3677, ⓦnewforesthotels.co.uk/forest-lodge -hotel. Attractive Georgian building in a good location – a short walk from Lyndhurst High St but away from the main road, so there's less traffic noise. The rooms are comfortable and there's an indoor pool and sauna. **£150**	**Rufus House** Southampton Rd, SO43 7BR ☎023 8028 2930, ⓦrufushouse.co.uk. A couple of minutes out of town on the Ashurst road, opposite some fine New Forest country-side, this good-value place has plenty of character. Its tower room has a four-poster bed (£15 extra), though front rooms face a busy road. Minimum two-night let in high season. **£95**

3

EATING AND DRINKING	
★**The Oak Inn** Pinkney Lane, Bank, SO43 7FD ☎023 8028 2350, ⓦoakinnlyndhurst.co.uk. Fantastic little country pub a mile out of Lyndhurst, with low wooden ceilings, a roaring fire for winter and a garden for the summer. It's popular with walkers and cyclists and there's decent food (mains from £14.50), featuring local ingredients – it's best to book in advance. Mon–Sat 11.30am–11pm, Sun noon–10.30pm; kitchen Mon–Fri noon–5pm & 6–9pm, Sat	noon–5pm & 6–9.30pm, Sun noon–5pm & 6–8pm. **La Pergola** Southampton Rd, SO43 7BQ ☎023 8028 4184, ⓦla-pergola.co.uk. Lively Italian restaurant in an attractive building with its own garden. Sizzling meat and fish dishes cost around £15–20, and there's tasty pasta and pizza from £10 and superb home-made desserts, as well as daily specials. Tues–Sun & bank hols 11am–2.30pm & 6–10.30pm.

Beaulieu

The village of **BEAULIEU** (pronounced "Bewley"), in the southeast corner of the New Forest, was the site of one of England's most influential monasteries, a Cistercian house founded in 1204 by King John – in remorse, it is said, for ordering a group of supplicating monks to be trampled to death. Built using stone ferried from Caen in northern France and Quarr on the Isle of Wight, the **abbey** managed a self-sufficient estate of ten thousand acres, but was dismantled soon after the Dissolution. Its refectory now forms the parish church, which, like everything else in Beaulieu, has been subsumed into the Montagu family estate – they have owned a large chunk of the New Forest since one of Charles II's illegitimate progeny was named duke of the estate.

Beaulieu House and the National Motor Museum

Beaulieu, SO42 7ZN • Daily: June–Sept 10am–6pm; Oct–May 10am–5pm • £24.75, or £19.50 online • ☎01590 612435, ⓦbeaulieu.co.uk

Beaulieu estate comprises **Palace House**, the attractive if unexceptional family home of the Montagus, a ruined Cistercian **abbey** and the main attraction, the **National Motor Museum**, all set in fine grounds. The Motor Museum's collections of over 250 vehicles includes spindly antiques, recent classics and Formula I cars rubbing shoulders with land-speed racers, vintage Rolls-Royces, Ferraris and a Sinclair C5, as well as some of *Top Gear*'s more outlandish vehicles. A monorail runs through the museum and round the grounds, towards the Palace House, formerly the abbey's gatehouse, which contains masses of Montagu-related memorabilia, while the undercroft of the abbey houses an exhibition depicting medieval monastic life.

ACCOMMODATION AND EATING   BEAULIEU

The Montagu Arms Lyndhurst Rd, SO42 7ZL ☎ 01590 612324, ⓦ montaguarmshotel.co.uk. You can stay in smart and comfortable rooms, some with four-poster beds, in this seventeenth-century building with open fires and a lovely garden. There's good-quality pub food at the on-site *Monty's Inn*, or you can push the boat out for a meal at *The Terrace*, one of the New Forest's top restaurants. The attractive dining room overlooks a pretty garden, where you can eat in the summer. The three-course *Terrace* lunch menu is good value at £23, while the full tasting menu costs £90 a head. Monty's: Mon–Fri 11am–3pm & 6–11pm, Sat 11am–11pm, Sun 11am–10.30pm; The Terrace: Tues 7–9.30pm, Wed–Sun noon–2.30pm & 7–9.30pm. **£190**

Buckler's Hard

Daily: April–Sept 10am–5pm; Oct–March 10am–4.30pm • Free (if you walk or cycle), £6.90 (covers parking and Maritime Museum entrance) • ☎ 01590 616203, ⓦ bucklershard.co.uk

The hamlet of **BUCKLER'S HARD**, a couple of miles downstream from Beaulieu, has a wonderful setting. A row of picturesque thatched shipwrights' cottages, some of which are inhabited, leads down to the Beaulieu River; it doesn't look much like a **shipyard** now, but from Elizabethan times onwards dozens of men o' war were assembled here from giant New Forest oaks. Several of Nelson's ships were launched here, to be towed carefully by rowing boats past the sandbanks and across the Solent to Portsmouth. The largest house in the hamlet, which forms part of the Montagu estate, belonged to Henry Adams, the master builder responsible for most of the Trafalgar fleet; it's now a hotel, pub and restaurant (see below). At the top of the village is the **Maritime Museum**, which traces the history of the great ships and incorporates buildings preserved in their eighteenth-century form. The hamlet is also the starting point for a bucolic **river cruise** down the Beaulieu River (Easter to Oct daily, roughly hourly 11am–4.30pm; 30min; £5, or £4.50 online).

ACCOMMODATION AND EATING

The Master Builder's Hotel SO42 7XB ☎ 0844 815 3399, ⓦ hillbrookehotels.co.uk/the-master-builders. Picturesque and peaceful, this wonderful quirky hotel is in a sixteenth-century building with open fires and a superb location overlooking the river. The rooms are a mixed bunch; some have east Asian flourishes and individually designed furniture, and some have views of the river. There's also a decent restaurant and pub – the *Yachtsman's Bar* menu features standard pub grub, with sandwiches (£6.50), pizzas (£12–14) and fish and chips (£13), while the *Riverview Restaurant* is a more upmarket affair, serving starters such as salt-fired Solent mackerel (£7), followed by roast sea bass with Lymington crab risotto (£19.50). You can take drinks and food from the bar menu outside onto the lawns in nice weather. Bar daily noon–9pm; restaurant Mon–Sat noon–2.30pm & 7–9pm, Sun 12.30–3pm & 7–9pm. **£120**

Lymington

The most pleasant point of access for ferries to the Isle of Wight (see p.193) is **LYMINGTON**, a sheltered haven that's become one of the busiest leisure harbours on the south coast. Rising from the quay area, the cobbled street of the old town is lined with Georgian houses. At the top of the High Street (opposite Church Lane) is the partly thirteenth-century **Church of St Thomas the Apostle**, which has a cupola-topped tower built in 1670.

ARRIVAL AND DEPARTURE   LYMINGTON

By train A branch line runs from Brockenhurst to Lymington (every 30min; 10min). Trains call first at Lymington Town station, a short walk from the High St, then run onto Lymington Pier to link with the Isle of Wight ferry.

By bus Bus #6 runs roughly hourly from Southampton to Lymington (1hr 15min) via Lyndhurst (40min) and Brockenhurst (55min); the coastal routes #X1 and #X2 (1–2 hourly) run here from Christchurch (1hr 10min) and Bournemouth (1hr 45min).

ACCOMMODATION AND EATING

Britannia House Mill Lane, SO41 3BA ☎ 01590 672091, ⓦ britannia-house.com. A well-kept, friendly and central B&B, right by the train station. The comfortable rooms are on the small side but there's a fine sitting room commanding views over the waterfront. **£99**

Lanes Ashley Lane, SO41 3RH ☎01590 672777, ⓦlanesoflymington.com. Set in an old chapel and former school, with some tables on an internal balcony, this bright buzzy restaurant and bar serves locally sourced fish and meats (£16–24) including halibut steak, rack of lamb and less pricey burgers (£13). Tues–Sat 11.30am–2.30pm & 6.30–9.30pm.

The Haven King Saltern Rd, SO41 3QD ☎01590 679971, ⓦhavenrestaurant.co.uk. Wedged among the luxury yachts in Lymington harbour, this is, not surprisingly, a favoured haunt for the local sailing fraternity. The smart but laidback café-restaurant has a nautical-themed bar area, tables inside and a great raised terrace with views across the Solent. Fresh fish is the speciality, with dishes such as seafood bouillabaisse (£18.50), or swordfish steaks (£19.50), though it also does burgers and steaks. Daily 8am–midnight (food served until 9.30pm).

Stanwell House 14–15 High St, SO41 9AA ☎01590 677123, ⓦstanwellhousehotel.co.uk. The most upmarket choice in town, this handsome boutique-style hotel has an array of individually designed rooms boasting roll-top baths, flatscreen TVs and the like. Its main restaurant, Burcher & Co, is also the top spot to eat, in a dining room with a distinctly colonial feel (mains from around £16); there is also a less formal bistro serving modern European cuisine, and light snacks and afternoon teas are also available. Daily 7am–9pm. **£135**

Brockenhurst

You'll frequently find New Forest ponies strolling down the High Street of **BROCKENHURST**, undoubtedly the most attractive and liveliest town in the forest. Surrounded by idyllic heath- and woodland and with a ford at one end of the High Street, it's a picturesque spot and a useful travel hub.

ARRIVAL AND DEPARTURE   BROCKENHURST

By train The station is on the eastern edge of town – from here, turn left and left again onto Brookley Rd, and you'll find the bulk of shops, banks and places to eat and drink. Mainline services run every 15–20min from/to Southampton (15–20min), Winchester (30min) and London Waterloo (1hr 30min). In addition, a branch line runs to Lymington (every 30min; 10min) to link with the Isle of Wight ferry.

ACCOMMODATION AND EATING

★**The Pig** Beaulieu Rd, SO42 7QL ☎01590 622354, ⓦthepighotel.co.uk. Brockenhurst's best restaurant by a mile is in a fabulous New Forest country house with chic rooms, set in stunning grounds. The innovative menu uses ingredients from its gardens or from the surrounding area – fish is smoked on site, eggs come from its own chickens, and the herbs and vegetables are home-grown. All the ingredients are sourced from within 25 miles and the results, such as New Forest wood pigeon with locally foraged mushrooms (around £16), are delicious. Daily 12.30–2.30pm & 6.30–9.30pm. **£185**

Rosie Lee 6 Brookley Rd, SO42 7RBA ☎01590 622797. Lovely tearoom serving delicious and inexpensive home-made cakes and tasty sandwiches on vintage china. You can sit outside – they provide blankets and hot water bottles when it's cold – or at one of the cosy tables inside; dogs welcome. Daily 9am–4.30pm.

Bournemouth and around

Renowned for its pristine sandy beach (one of southern England's cleanest) and its gardens, the resort of **BOURNEMOUTH** dates from 1811, when a local squire, Louis Tregonwell, built a summerhouse on the wild, unpopulated heathland that once occupied this stretch of coast, and planted the first of the pine trees that now characterize the area. The mild climate, sheltered site and glorious beach encouraged the rapid growth of a full-scale family-holiday resort, complete with piers, cliff railways and boat trips. Today Bournemouth has a rather genteel image, counterbalanced by a thriving university scene and burgeoning numbers of language students and clubbers.

Bournemouth's beach spreads either side of the Victorian **pier**, which was built in 1880, then extended in 1894 and 1909 to more than 300m long, and used as a landing stage for steamers. Today, it's home to the usual arcades and amusements plus the world's first pier-to-shore **zipwire**, a quick but exhilarating ride with dual wires so you can race down with a friend (April–Sept £18; Oct–March £15; ⓦrockreef.co.uk/pier).

Russell-Cotes Art Gallery and Museum

Russell-Cotes Rd, East Cliff, BH1 3AA • Tues–Sun & bank hols 10am–5pm • April–Sept £6; Oct–March free • ☏ 01202 451858, ⓦ russellcotes.com

Surrounded by lovely gardens on a clifftop, the **Russell-Cotes Art Gallery and Museum** has one of the UK's best collections of Victoriana, collected from around the world by the wealthy Russell-Cotes family. The quirky assortment of artworks, Asian souvenirs and curios, such as the ornate loo used by royal mistress Lily Langtry, are displayed in an ornately decorated mansion, once the family home. Highlights of the collection are Rossetti's *Venus Verticordia* (1864) and England's most important collection of Victorian nudes, which scandalized much of society at the time.

St Peter's Church

Hinton Rd, BH1 2EE • ☏ 01202 290986, ⓦ stpetersbournemouth.org.uk

In the centre of town, the graveyard of **St Peter's Church** is where **Mary Shelley**, author of the Gothic horror tale *Frankenstein*, is buried, together with the heart of her husband, the Romantic poet Percy Bysshe Shelley. The tombs of Mary's parents – radical thinker William Godwin and early feminist **Mary Wollstonecraft** – are also in the graveyard.

ARRIVAL AND INFORMATION
BOURNEMOUTH

By train The station is about a mile inland, connected to the town centre and seafront by frequent buses, or you can walk there in around 15–20min.
Destinations Brockenhurst (every 15–20min; 15–25min); Dorchester (every 30min–1hr; 45min); London Waterloo (every 30min; 2hr); Poole (every 20min; 10min); Southampton (every 15–20min; 30min–1hr 10min); Weymouth (hourly; 55min); Winchester (every 15min; 45min–1hr).

By bus Opposite the train station (see above).
Destinations Direct National Express buses run to London (hourly; 2hr 30min); Southampton (hourly; 45min–1hr); Weymouth (5 daily; 1hr 15min–1hr 20min); and Winchester (8 daily; 1hr 20min–1hr 55min).
Tourist office Pier Approach (Jan–March & Nov–Dec daily 10am–4pm; April–June & Sept–Oct daily 10am–5pm; July–Aug Mon–Sat 9am–6pm, Sun 9am–5pm; ☏ 01202 451734, ⓦ bournemouth.co.uk).

ACCOMMODATION

★**Beach Lodges** Seafront Promenade, Boscombe, BH5 1BN ☏ 01202 451781, ⓦ bournemouthbeach lodges.co.uk. If you want to sleep right on the beach, opt for these deluxe beach huts which sleep up to six and come complete with hot showers, loos, fridges and kitchens. Set back slightly from the promenade, they boast terrific views. There are good low-season discounts, and with their own heating, they're magical even in winter. Minimum three-night stay. £210

★**The Greenhouse Hotel** 4 Grove Rd, BH1 3AX ☏ 01202 498900, ⓦ thegreenhousehotel.co.uk. Boutique-style, eco-friendly hotel in a Grade II listed Victorian villa a short walk from the town centre. The stylish rooms come with all the latest mod cons, ultra-comfy beds, and free home-made biscuits. The environmental standards are very high – water is solar-heated, and much of the electricity is generated on site. There's also an excellent bar and restaurant. £160

Urban Beach Hotel 23 Argyll Rd, Boscombe, BH5 1EB ☏ 01202 301509, ⓦ urbanbeachhotel.co.uk. A short (but steep) walk from Boscombe's beach, and close to the shops, this old Victorian townhouse has been given a boutique makeover. There's a variety of rooms, all of them stylish with designer furniture, comfy beds and DVDs. The downstairs bar/restaurant serves great cocktails. £145

EATING AND DRINKING

Koh Thai Tapas Daimler House, 38–40 Poole Hill, BH2 5PS ☏ 01202 294723, ⓦ koh-thai.co.uk. Lively restaurant done out with stylish Thai decor – all dark-wood furniture, comfy sofas and fresh orchids. The Thai food is beautifully presented and can be eaten in tapas size (£6–8.50) or full portions. Mains (£8–18) include Thai curries, stir fries and noodles. The cocktails are great too. Mon 5.30–10pm, Tues–Sun 12.30–3pm & 5.30–10pm.

★**Sixty Million Postcards** 19–21 Exeter Rd, BH2 5AF ☏ 01202 292697, ⓦ sixtymillionpostcards.com. One of Bournemouth's best bars, attracting an unpretentious but trendy student crowd. There are board games, various alcoves for cosy chats and comfy sofas. Offers a good range of beers, drinks and good-value burgers, with occasional DJs and live music. Mon–Thurs noon–midnight, Fri & Sat noon–2am, Sun 11am–midnight.

★**Urban Reef** Undercliff Drive, Boscombe, BH5 1BN 📞01202 443960, ⓦurbanreef.com. Art Deco-style restaurant/bar/café in a fabulous position on Boscombe seafront. Designed to give great sea views from both floors, its quirky decor features a mock-up beach hut hanging on the wall, and there's a large deck for drinks on the front and an adjacent takeaway serving wood-fired pizzas (£10). Food varies from cooked breakfast (£8.50) to New Forest mushroom risotto (£12) and pan-seared salmon (£17).

Daily 8am–10pm.

West Beach Pier Approach, BH2 5AA 📞01202 587785, ⓦwest-beach.co.uk. Close to the pier, this seafood restaurant has a prime position on the beach, with decking out on the promenade. It's smart and stylish, and you can watch the chefs at work in the open kitchen. Fish and seafood dishes start at around £18, and there are also some meat and veg dishes. Daily 9am–10pm; closed Mon eves in winter.

Wimborne Minster

An ancient town on the banks of the River Stour, just a few minutes' drive north from the suburbs of Bournemouth, **WIMBORNE MINSTER** is an attractive little town, worth an hour or two's wander around its narrow alleys, or along the riverbank. It's home to southern England's largest covered **market** (Fri–Sun; ⓦwimbornemarket.co.uk), though its main point of interest is the great **church**, the Minster of St Cuthberga.

3

Minster of St Cuthberga

High St, BH21 1HT • Mon–Sat 9.30am–5.30pm, Sun 2.30–5.30pm; Chained Library Easter–Oct Mon 2–4pm, Tues–Fri 10.30am–12.30pm & 2–4pm; phone for winter opening times • Free • 📞01202 884753, ⓦwimborneminster.org.uk

Built on the site of an eighth-century monastery, the **Minster of St Cuthberga**'s massive twin towers of mottled grey and tawny stone dwarf the rest of town. At one time the church was even more imposing – its spire crashed down during morning service in 1602. What remains today is basically Norman with later additions, such as the Perpendicular west tower; this bears a figure dressed as a grenadier of the Napoleonic era, who strikes every quarter-hour with a hammer. The **Chained Library** above the choir vestry, dating from 1686, is Wimborne's most prized possession and one of the oldest public libraries in the country. Its collection of ancient books includes a manuscript written on lambskin dating from 1343.

Kingston Lacy

2 miles northwest of Wimborne Minster; BH21 4EA • **House** Mid-March to Oct Wed–Sun 11am–5pm; Nov to mid-March 11am–4pm • £12.70 (includes grounds); NT • **Grounds** Daily: mid-March to Oct 10am–6pm; Nov to mid-March 10am–4pm • £7 • 📞01202 883402, ⓦnationaltrust.org.uk/kingston-lacy

The glorious seventeenth-century mansion of **Kingston Lacy** stands in 250 acres of parkland grazed by a herd of Red Devon cattle. Designed for the Bankes family, who were exiled from Corfe Castle (see p.215) after the Roundheads reduced it to rubble, the brick building was clad in grey stone during the nineteenth century by Sir Charles Barry, co-architect of the Houses of Parliament. William Bankes, then owner of the house, was a great traveller and collector, and the **Spanish Room** is a superb scrapbook of his Grand Tour souvenirs. Kingston Lacy's **picture collection** is also outstanding, featuring Titian, Rubens, Velázquez and many other old masters.

Christchurch

CHRISTCHURCH, five miles east of Bournemouth, is best known for **Christchurch Priory** (Mon–Sat 9.30am–5pm, Sun 2.15–5.30pm; donation requested; 📞01202 485804, ⓦchristchurchpriory.org), England's longest parish church at 311ft. The oldest parts of the current church date back to 1094, and its fan-vaulted North Porch is impressively large. Fine views can be gained from the top of the 120ft-high **tower** (£3; call ahead to book).

The area round the old town quay has a carefully preserved charm, with the **Red House Museum and Gardens** on Quay Road (Tues–Fri 10am–5pm, Sat 10am–4pm; free; ☎01202 482860, ⊛www.hampshireculturaltrust.org.uk) containing an affectionate collection of local memorabilia. **Boat trips** (Easter–Oct daily; ☎01202 429119, ⊛bournemouthboating.co.uk) leave from the grassy banks of the riverside quay, heading east to the sandspit at Mudeford (30min; £8 return) or upriver to Tuckton (15min; £3 return).

ARRIVAL AND INFORMATION
CHRISTCHURCH

By train Christchurch is on the main London Waterloo to Weymouth line; the train station is on Stour Rd, a mile north of the town centre.

By bus Local buses from Bournemouth in the east, Lymington in the west and Ringwood in the north pull up at the bus stop close to the tourist office.

Tourist office Regent Centre, 51 High St (Mon 9am–4.30pm, Tues–Sat 10am–4.30pm; ☎01202 499199, ⊛visitdorset.com).

ACCOMMODATION

Captains Club Hotel Wick Lane, BH23 1HU ☎01202 475111, ⊛captainsclubhotel.com. Although the modern glass exterior resembles a car showroom, this upmarket hotel is very comfortable inside and there's a fine riverside terrace, bar, restaurant and spa. The contemporary rooms come with great river views. Website offers and last-minute deals can reduce the price dramatically. **£280**

Kings Hotel 18 Castle St, BH23 1DT ☎01202 588933, ⊛thekings-christchurch.co.uk. An attractive place in the centre of town right opposite the castle ruins. The twenty rooms are well furnished in boutique style, complete with flat-screen TVs, and some have views over the castle at the front. There's a good restaurant and lively bar downstairs, too, and guests have free use of the spa facilities at a sister hotel. **£135**

EATING AND DRINKING

The Boathouse 9 Quay Rd, BH23 1BU ☎01202 480033, ⊛boathouse.co.uk. This modern café-bar/restaurant is in a lovely location overlooking the river with a large outdoor terrace, and a modern wood-burner inside. Main courses include salmon and monkfish skewers with couscous (£16.50) or Cornish mussels and chips (£15.50), as well as a selection of tasty stone-baked pizzas (£11–13). Mon–Thurs & Sun 9am–9pm, Fri & Sat 9am–10pm.

The Jetty Christchurch Harbour Hotel, 95 Mudeford, BH23 3NT ☎01202 400950, ⊛thejetty.co.uk. Renowned chef Alex Aitken uses local seasonal produce in this contemporary wooden restaurant with stunning views of Christchurch harbour. Interesting main courses include a mixed fish grill served with garlic and seaweed mayonnaise (£24.50), and the local-produce lunch/early-evening menu is good value at £25 for three courses. Mon–Sat noon–2.30pm & 6–10pm, Sun noon–8pm.

Ye Olde George Inn 2a Castle St, BH23 1DT ☎01202 479383, ⊛yeoldegeorgeinnchristchurch.co.uk. Christchurch's oldest pub, the *George* is an attractive former coaching inn with a great courtyard garden, and a warren of small rooms inside. Serves reasonably priced pub grub (from £11), tasty pizzas (£7–10) and a selection of real ales. Mon–Thurs & Sun 11am–11pm, Fri & Sat 11am–midnight; kitchen daily noon–10pm.

Poole

West of Bournemouth, **POOLE** is an ancient seaport on a huge, almost landlocked harbour. The town developed in the thirteenth century and was successively colonized by pirates, fishermen and timber traders. The old quarter by the quayside contains more than one hundred historic buildings, as well as the contemporary Poole Museum.

Poole Museum

4 Old High St, BH15 1BW • Easter–Oct daily 10am–5pm; Nov–Easter Mon–Sat 10am–4pm, Sun noon–4pm • Free • ☎01202 262600, ⊛poolemuseum.co.uk

Poole Museum traces the town's development through the centuries, with displays of local ceramics and a rare Iron Age log boat that was dug out of the harbour in 1964: carved out of a single tree trunk, the 33ft-long boat dates from around 300 BC. Look out, too, for the fascinating footage of the flying boats that took off from Poole harbour during the 1940s for east Asia and Australia.

Brownsea Island

BH13 7EE • Feb & March Sat & Sun 10am–4pm; April–Oct daily 10am–5pm • £6.75; NT • ☎ 01202 707744, ⓦ nationaltrust.org.uk /brownsea-island • Access by boat: Feb & March from Sandbanks only (Sat & Sun 10am–4pm, every 30min); April–Oct from Sandbanks and Poole Quay (daily 10am–5pm, every 30min); from Sandbanks £6.50 return, from Poole Quay £10.75 return

Brownsea Island is famed for its red squirrels, wading birds and other **wildlife**, which you can spot along themed trails. The landscape is surprisingly diverse for such a small island – much of it is heavily wooded, though there are also areas of heath and marsh, and narrow, shingly beaches – and it's pretty easy to escape from the boat-trippers and find a peaceful corner to picnic.

Compton Acres

164 Canford Cliffs Rd, BH13 7ES • Daily: Easter–Oct 10am–6pm; Nov–Easter 10am–4pm; last entry 1hr before closing • £8.45 • ☎ 01202 700778, ⓦ comptonacres.co.uk • Bus #50 from Bournemouth and #52 from Poole

One of the area's best-known gardens, **Compton Acres**, lies on the outskirts of Poole, signposted off the A35 Poole Road towards Bournemouth. Spectacularly sited over ten acres on steep slopes above Poole Harbour, each of the five gardens here has a different international theme, including a formal Italian garden and the elegantly understated Japanese Garden, its meandering streams crossed by stone steps and wooden bridges.

3

ARRIVAL AND INFORMATION   POOLE

By train Poole's train station is on Serpentine Rd, about a 15min walk from the waterfront along the High St.
Destinations Bournemouth (every 20min; 10min); London Waterloo (every 30min; 2hr–2hr 10min); Weymouth (every 30min; 35–45min).
By bus The bus station is in front of the Dolphin Centre on

Kingland Rd, with regular National Express services to London Victoria (11 daily; 3–4hr).
Tourist office At Poole Museum, 4 High St (April–Oct daily 10am–5pm; Nov–March Mon–Sat 10am–4pm, Sun noon–4pm; ☎ 01202 262600 ⓦ pooletourism.com).

ACCOMMODATION

★**Hotel du Vin** Thames St, BH15 1JN ☎ 01202 685666, ⓦ hotelduvin.com. Inside a fine old mansion with a double staircase, this stylish hotel has plush, comfortable rooms, an atmospheric restaurant and wine cellar, and a very cosy bar with its own log fire – great in winter. The location is ideal, in the pretty old town, a minute's walk from the Quay. **£160**
The Old Townhouse 7 High St, BH15 1AB ☎ 01202

670950, ⓦ theoldtownhouse.co.uk. Attractive little Victorian-style B&B in a great location opposite the museum, with a wood-panelled tearoom/breakfast room on the ground floor. The decor in the four rooms may be rather traditional, but they are spotless and comfortable – one has its own terrace – and the owners go out of their way to be helpful. **£95**

EATING AND DRINKING

Deli on the Quay Unit D17 Dolphin Quays, The Quay, BH15 1HH ☎ 01202 660022, ⓦ delionthequay.com. Bright, light harbourfront café-deli stacked with delicious preserves, wines and the like. The café serves fresh croissants, sandwiches and decent coffee. Mon & Wed–Fri 8.30am–5pm, Tues 8.30am–8pm, Sat & Sun 9am–5pm; Nov–March closes 4pm Mon–Fri.
★**The Guildhall Tavern** 15 Market Street, BH15 1NB, ☎ 01202 671717, ⓦ guildhalltavern.co.uk. Fantastic French seafood restaurant with marine-themed decor and a small patio at the back, serving local fish and shellfish – scallops, crab, lobster and oysters among them – as well as traditional French dishes such as snails in garlic butter (six for £7) and boeuf bourguignon (£18). There's a very reasonable lunchtime set menu (two courses for £17, three for £20.50). Tues–Thurs 11.30am–3.30pm & 6–9.30pm,

Fri & Sat 11.30am–3.30pm & 5.30–10pm.
Karma 22 High St, BH15 1BP ☎ 01202 6701818, ⓦ karma-mediterranean.co.uk. Atmospheric dining room with quirky decor, bare brick arches and wooden tables. The food is Mediterranean/Middle Eastern; the tasty meze include aubergine dip and falafel (starter platter to share £16), and there are mains such as hearty grills (chicken or lamb kebab and rice), moussaka and kleftiko (£14–16). Tues–Thurs 5.30–9pm, Fri & Sat 5.30–10pm.
Poole Arms 19 The Quay, BH15 1HJ ☎ 01202 673450 ⓦ poolearms.co.uk. Completely covered with green tiles, this wonderfully atmospheric sixteenth-century pub is reassuringly old-fashioned, with decent beers and great fish dishes (£11–15). There's outdoor seating facing the waterfront, too. Mon–Sat 11am–11pm, Sun noon–11pm; kitchen daily noon–9pm.

The Isle of Purbeck

Though not actually an island, the **ISLE OF PURBECK** – a promontory of low hills and heathland jutting out beyond Poole Harbour – does have an insular and distinctive feel. Reached from the east by the ferry from Sandbanks at the narrow mouth of Poole Harbour, or by a long and congested landward journey via the bottleneck of **Wareham**, Purbeck can be a difficult destination to reach, but its villages are immensely pretty, none more so than **Corfe Castle**, with its majestic ruins. From **Swanage**, a low-key seaside resort, the Dorset Coast Path provides access to the oily shales of **Kimmeridge Bay**, the spectacular cove at **Lulworth** and the much-photographed natural arch of **Durdle Door**.

The whole coast from Purbeck to Exmouth in Devon – dubbed the **Jurassic Coast** (ⓦjurassiccoast.org) – is a World Heritage Site on account of its geological significance and fossil remains; walkers can access it along the South West Coast Path.

ARRIVAL AND GETTING AROUND   THE ISLE OF PURBECK

By ferry There are regular ferries from Sandbanks (7am–11pm every 20min; pedestrians & bikes £1, cars £4.30; ☎01929 450203, ⓦsandbanksferry.co.uk).

By train Wareham is the only place served by mainline trains, though a steam train also runs between Swanage and Norden (see opposite). The train track has now been fully restored between Swanage and Wareham, with a trial diesel service running the full route from 2018 (4 trains daily on 90 selected days; see ⓦswanagerailway.co.uk for details of schedule).

By bus The Purbeck Breezer (ⓦmorebus.co.uk) runs two services around the Purbecks – route #40 from Poole to Swanage via Wareham and Corfe Castle, and route #50 from Bournemouth to Swanage via the Sandbanks ferry and Studland. In summer, some services are open-top.

By bike Cycling is a great way to get around, though be prepared for steep hills; bikes can be rented from Cycle Experience at Norden Car Park, Corfe Castle (☎01929 481606, ⓦpurbeckcyclehire.co.uk) and Charlie the Bikemonger, 5 Queen's Rd, Swanage (☎01929 475833, ⓦcharliethebikemonger.com).

Wareham

The grid pattern of its streets indicates the Saxon origins of **WAREHAM**, and the town is surrounded by even older earth ramparts known as the Walls. A riverside setting adds greatly to its charms, though the place gets fairly overrun in summer. Nearby lies an enclave of quaint houses around **Lady St Mary's Church**, which contains the marble coffin of Edward the Martyr, murdered at Corfe Castle in 978 (possibly by his stepmother, to make way for her son Ethelred).

St Martin's Church, at the north end of town, dates from Saxon times and contains a faded twelfth-century mural of St Martin offering his cloak to a beggar. The church's most striking feature, however, is a romantic effigy of T.E. Lawrence in Arab dress, which was originally destined for Salisbury Cathedral, but was rejected by the dean there who disapproved of Lawrence's sexual proclivities. Lawrence was killed in 1935 in a motorbike accident on the road from Bovington (six miles west); his simply furnished cottage is at **Clouds Hill**, seven miles northwest of Wareham (late May to Oct daily 11am–5pm; £6.30, NT; ☎01929 405616, ⓦnationaltrust.org.uk/clouds-hill). The small **Wareham Town Museum**, next to Wareham's town hall on East Street (Easter–Oct Mon–Sat 10am–4pm; free; ☎01929 553448, ⓦgreenacre.info/WTM) focuses on local history and Lawrence memorabilia.

ARRIVAL AND INFORMATION   WAREHAM

By train Wareham station, a 15min walk north of the town, sees regular trains from London (every 30min; 2hr 20min) and Weymouth (every 20–40min; 25–35min), with a limited train service to Swanage (see opposite).

Tourist office Wareham Library, South St (Easter–Oct Mon 10am–5pm, Tues–Sat 9.30am–5pm; Nov–Easter Mon 10am–4pm, Tues–Sat 9.30am–4pm; ☎01929 552740, ⓦvisit-dorset.com).

Corfe Castle

The Square, Corfe Castle, BH20 5EZ • Daily: March & Oct 10am–5pm; April–Sept 10am–6pm; Nov–Feb 10am–4pm • £9; NT • ☎ 01929 481294, ⓦ nationaltrust.org.uk/corfe-castle • A few minutes' walk from Corfe Castle station (on the Swanage Steam Railway)

The romantic ruins of **Corfe Castle**, crowning the hill behind the village of the same name, are perhaps the most evocative in England. The family seat of Sir John Bankes, Attorney General to Charles I, this Royalist stronghold withstood a Cromwellian siege for six weeks, gallantly defended by Lady Bankes. One of her own men, Colonel Pitman, eventually betrayed the castle to the Roundheads, after which it was reduced to its present gap-toothed state by gunpowder. Apparently the victorious Roundheads were so impressed by Lady Bankes' courage that they allowed her to take the keys to the castle with her – they can still be seen in the library at the Bankes' subsequent home, Kingston Lacy (see p.211).

ACCOMMODATION   CORFE CASTLE

Mortons House 45 East St, BH20 5EE ☎ 01929 480988, ⓦ mortonshouse.co.uk. In a sixteenth-century manor house with a beautiful walled garden and log fires in winter, this award-winning small hotel has snug rooms, some with four-poster beds and stone fireplaces. The restaurant offers top local cuisine. **£160**

Norden Farm Norden, BH20 5DS, 1 mile from Corfe Castle ☎ 01929 480098, ⓦ nordenfarm.com. Tucked into a tranquil valley, this working farm has extensive fields for tents and caravans, good facilities, its own shop and a menagerie of animals. Closed Nov–Feb. **£14.50**

EATING AND DRINKING

The Greyhound The Square, BH20 5EZ ☎ 01929 480205, ⓦ greyhoundcorfe.co.uk. One of England's oldest coaching inns, with frequent live music and a pleasant garden at the back with views of the castle. The food is good, with simple dishes such as pulled pork sandwiches or fish and chips (£9–14), and more elaborate meals like langoustine risotto (£16). Daily 11am–11pm; kitchen Mon–Sat noon–9pm, Sun noon–8pm.

★ **The Scott Arms** West St, Kingston, BH20 5LH, 2 miles from Corfe Castle ☎ 01929 480270, ⓦ thescottarms.

com. In the neighbouring village, a steep climb above Corfe Castle, this is a wonderful old inn with a warren of cosy rooms at the front and a large, modern-looking back room that doubles as its restaurant. The biggest draw is its garden, which commands a stupendous view over Corfe Castle in the valley below. The food is substantial, varied and good value at around £13 for mains; in summer the *Jerk Shak* sells fantastic Caribbean food in the garden. Daily 11am–11pm; kitchen Mon–Fri noon–2.30pm & 6–8.30pm, Sat & Sun noon–2.45pm & 6–8.45pm.

Swanage and around

Purbeck's largest town, **SWANAGE**, is a traditional seaside resort with a pleasant sandy beach and an ornate town hall. The town's station is the southern terminus of the **Swanage Steam Railway** (April–Oct daily; Nov– March Sat, Sun & school hols; £12.50 return; ☎ 01929 425800, ⓦ swanagerailway.co.uk), which runs for six miles to Norden, just north of Corfe Castle. There are plans to extend the service to Wareham. West of Swanage, you can pick up the coastal path to **Durlston Country Park**, (daily sunrise–sunset; free) around a mile out of town. Set in 280 acres of coastal woodland and crisscrossed with clifftop paths, it's a great place for a picnic or for wind-blown walks.

ACCOMMODATION   SWANAGE AND AROUND

The Swanage Haven 3 Victoria Rd, BH19 1LY ☎ 01929 423088, ⓦ swanagehaven.com. Good-value boutique-style guesthouse: the smart rooms have flatscreen TVs and the decked garden has a great outdoor hot tub. Breakfasts are made from locally sourced ingredients. No children. **£90**

★ **Tom's Field Campsite** Langton Matravers, BH19 3HN, a couple of miles west of Swanage ☎ 01929 427110,

ⓦ tomsfieldcamping.co.uk. Wonderfully sited and well run, this is the best campsite in the region, with sea views from some of the pitches and direct access to the coast path. It also lets out bunks in a converted Nissen hut – The Walker's Barn – and a converted pigsty called The Stone Room. The campsite has a well-stocked shop, but only takes reservations for longer stays – turn up early to bag a pitch. Walker's Barn **£13**, camping **£16**, Stone Room **£30**

3

3

EATING AND DRINKING

Gee Whites The Old Stone Quay, 1 High St, BH19 2LN ☎01929 425720, ⓦgeewhites.co.uk. Fashionable seafood bar right on the quay serving local lobster, crabs, mussels and oysters. The menu changes daily according to what's been caught (most dishes £7–10), but usually features the likes of *moules marinières*, tempura prawns and dressed crab. Summer daily 9am–9.30pm; rest of year hours are weather dependent.

★**Seventh Wave** Durlston Castle & Country Park, Lighthouse Rd, BH19 2JL ☎01929 421111, ⓦ7eventh wave.com. Inside Durlston Castle with stunning views over the coast, this is an unmissable stop – either for a coffee, snack or full meal. There are paninis and sandwiches for around £7.50, fresh fish or mains for £11–15, and cream teas for £10. Easter–Sept Mon–Thurs & Sun 9.30am–4pm,

Fri & Sat 9.30am–4pm & 6–9pm; Oct–Easter daily 9.30am–4pm.

★**Square and Compass** Worth Matravers, BH19 3LF, 4 miles west of Swanage ☎01929 439229, ⓦsquareand compasspub.co.uk. In a quintessential Purbeck village, with stunning views over the surrounding Downs and sea, this is one of England's finest pubs: the bar is a tiny hatch, the interior is a winter fug of log fires, walkers and dogs (and the occasional live band), while outside there's a motley collection of stone seats and wooden benches. Regularly winning CAMRA awards for its local ales and ciders, and with its own little fossil museum, it also serves delicious home-made pies. April–Sept daily noon–11pm; Oct–March Mon–Thurs noon–3pm & 6–11pm, Fri–Sun noon–11pm.

Studland

East of Swanage, you can follow the South West Coast path over Ballard Down to descend into the pretty village of **STUDLAND** at the southern end of **Studland Bay**. The most northerly stretch of the beach, **Shell Bay**, is a magnificent strand of icing-sugar sand backed by a remarkable heathland ecosystem which is home to all six British species of reptile – adders are quite common, so be careful. On Middle Beach, you can **hire kayaks** from the **Studland Sea School** (☎01929 450430, ⓦstudlandseaschool. co.uk), or take one of their excellent guided kayak or snorkelling tours round Old Harry Rocks, through rock arches.

ACCOMMODATION AND EATING   STUDLAND

★**Bankes Arms** Manor Rd, BH19 3AU ☎01929 450225, ⓦbankesarms.com. Lovely location, good food, and a great range of real ales, some from local independent breweries and others from its own on-site Purbeck Brewery. The pub food costs slightly more than average, but the portions are big, and frankly it's worth it for the joy of sitting in the grassy front garden with fantastic bay views, or by the roaring log fire in the cosy Purbeck stone interior. Daily 11am–11pm; kitchen May–Sept Mon–Sat noon–9.30pm & Sun noon–9pm, Oct–April daily noon–9pm.

The Pig on the Beach Studland Bay, BH19 3AU

☎01929 450288, ⓦthepighotel.com. An eighteenth-century manor house in a fantastic location with lovely gardens leading down to the sea: renovated in *The Pig's* signature shabby-chic style, it has very comfortable rooms – some have sea views, all have luxurious showers – or you can stay in a converted shepherd's hut in the grounds (£240). The restaurant is great too, specializing in locally caught or foraged ingredients, plus herbs and veg grown in the cottage garden – expect dishes such as south coast hake with marsh samphire (£18); it's very popular so booking is recommended. Daily noon–2.30pm & 6.30–9.30pm. **£180**

Kimmeridge Bay and around

Towards the western half of the Isle of Purbeck the coastal geology changes as the grey-white chalk and limestone cliffs give way to darker beds of shale. **Kimmeridge Bay** may not have a sandy beach but it does have a remarkable marine wildlife reserve much appreciated by divers. The pretty village of **KIMMERIDGE** lies about a mile inland from the bay, and is home to the **Etches Collection** (daily 10am–5pm; £8; ☎01929 270000, ⓦtheetchescollection.org) a fascinating purpose-built museum housing 2000 Jurassic-era fossils. West of Kimmeridge are the Lulworth artillery ranges, which are inaccessible during weekdays but generally open at weekends and in school holidays – watch out for the red warning flags and notices, and always stick to the path.

Tyneham

Beyond Kimmeridge, the coastal path passes close to the deserted village of **Tyneham** (within the Lulworth artillery ranges, so the same restrictions apply; ⓦtynehamopc.org. uk), whose residents were summarily evicted by the army in 1943. You can wander around the abandoned stone cottages, which have an eerie fascination, while an exhibition in the church explains the history of the village. Some of the buildings, such as the **schoolhouse**, have been restored to their 1940s condition.

Lulworth Cove and around

The quaint thatch-and-stone villages of **EAST LULWORTH** and **WEST LULWORTH** form a prelude to **Lulworth Cove**, a perfect shell-shaped bite formed when the sea broke through a weakness in the cliffs and then gnawed away at them from behind, forming a circular cave that eventually collapsed to leave a bay enclosed by sandstone cliffs. West of the cove is **Stair Hole**, a roofless sea cave riddled with arches that will eventually collapse to form another Lulworth Cove. The mysteries of local geology are explained at the **Lulworth Heritage Centre** (daily 10am–5pm; free) by the car park at the top of the lane leading down to the cove.

Durdle Door

A mile west of Lulworth Cove, the iconic limestone arch of **Durdle Door** can be reached via the steep uphill path that starts from Lulworth Cove's car park. The arch itself sits at the end of a long shingle beach (which can be accessed via steep steps), a lovely place for catching the sun and swimming in fresh, clear water. There are further steps to a bay just east of Durdle Door, **St Oswald's Bay**, with another shingle beach and offshore rocks that you can swim out to.

ACCOMMODATION AND EATING   **LULWORTH COVE AND AROUND**

Castle Inn 8 Main Rd, West Lulworth, BH20 5RN ☎01929 400311, ⓦthecastleinn-lulworthcove.co.uk. Up in the village, this sixteenth-century thatched pub has a lovely terraced garden, a good range of local real ales and a selection of traditional pub games. High-quality pub grub features home-made steak and ale pie (£14) and salmon steaks (£13). It's also very dog-friendly. Daily noon–10pm; kitchen daily noon–9pm.

Durdle Door Holiday Park West Lulworth, BH20 5PU ☎01929 400200, ⓦlulworth.com. Superbly positioned up on the cliffs above Durdle Door, this campsite has fabulous views from its touring field, while tents can be pitched in the

more sheltered wooded field. It's a 20min walk across fields to Lulworth Cove and there's also a shop and café-bar on site. **£42**

Lulworth Cove Inn Main Rd, Lulworth Cove, BH20 5RQ ☎01929 400333, ⓦlulworth-coveinn.co.uk. With a great location right on the main street leading down to the cove and overlooking the duck pond, this is the first choice in Lulworth itself, especially if you can bag one of the front rooms that come with their own cove-view terraces (£10 extra). The pub downstairs offers local Blandford ales, real fires, a pleasant garden and decent food, including steak and ale pie (£13.50) and smoked mackerel (£11.50). Daily 11am–11pm; kitchen noon–9pm. **£110**

Dorchester and around

For many, **DORCHESTER**, county town of Dorset, is essentially **Thomas Hardy**'s town; he was born at Higher Bockhampton, three miles east, his heart is buried in Stinsford, a couple of miles northeast (the rest of him is in Westminster Abbey), and he spent much of his life in Dorchester itself (see box, p.218). The town appears in his novels as Casterbridge, and the local countryside is evocatively depicted, notably the wild heathland of the east (Egdon Heath) and the eerie yew forest of Cranborne Chase. The real Dorchester – liveliest on Wednesday, market day – has a pleasant central core of mostly seventeenth-century and Georgian buildings, though the town's origins go back to the Romans, who founded "Durnovaria" in about 70 AD. The Roman walls were replaced in the eighteenth century by tree-lined avenues called "Walks", but some traces of the Roman period have survived. On the southeast edge of town, **Maumbury Rings** is where the Romans held vast gladiatorial combats in an amphitheatre adapted from a Stone Age site.

In addition to its Hardy connections, Dorchester is also associated with the notorious **Judge Jeffreys**, who, after the ill-fated rebellion of the Duke of Monmouth (one of Charles II's illegitimate offspring) against James II, held his "**Bloody Assizes**" in the Oak Room of the former Antelope Hotel (now offices) on Cornhill in 1685. A total of 292 men were sentenced to death, though most got away with a flogging and transportation to the West Indies, while 74 were hung, drawn and quartered, their heads stuck on pikes throughout Dorset and Somerset.

Shire Hall

58–60 High St, DT1 1UZ • Daily 10am–5pm • £8, ticket valid for one year • ☏ 01305 267992

Shire Hall, also known as the **Old Crown Courts**, are where the **Tolpuddle Martyrs** (see opposite), were sentenced to transportation for forming what was in effect Britain's first trade union. The room in which the Martyrs were tried (and where Thomas Hardy later served as a magistrate) has been preserved almost unchanged from when it first opened in 1796; it is now the centrepiece of a fascinating courthouse museum, with changing exhibitions and events linked to the history of justice. You can also visit the original cells.

Dorset County Museum

High West St, DT1 1XA • April–Oct Mon–Sat 10am–5pm (daily in school summer hols); Nov–March Mon–Sat 10am–4pm • £6.35 • ☏ 01305 262735, ⊛ dorsetcountymuseum.org

The best place to find out about Dorchester's history is the engrossing Victorian **Dorset County Museum**, where archeological and geological displays trace Celtic and Roman history, including a section on nearby Maiden Castle (see opposite), and a Jurassic Coast gallery, complete with fossils and animated flying dinosaurs. Pride of place goes to the re-creation of Thomas Hardy's study, where his pens are inscribed with the names of the books he wrote with them. In early 2018, the museum was the first venue to host London's Natural History Museum's diplodocus skeleton (aka Dippy) on its nationwide tour, in advance of a substantial renovation project. Parts of the museum will be closed during the construction of a £13 million extension, including new galleries, a library and a café, which is due to open in 2020.

HARDY'S WESSEX

Thomas Hardy (1840–1928) resurrected the old name of **Wessex** to describe the region in which he set most of his fiction. In his books, the area stretched from Devon and Somerset ("Lower Wessex" and "Outer Wessex") to Berkshire and Oxfordshire ("North Wessex"), though its central core was Dorset ("South Wessex"), the county where Hardy spent most of his life. His books richly depict the life and appearance of the surroundings, often disguised under fictional names. Thus Salisbury makes an appearance as "Melchester", Weymouth (where he briefly lived) as "Budmouth Regis", and Bournemouth as "Sandbourne" in *Tess of the d'Urbervilles*. But it is **Dorchester**, the "Casterbridge" of his novels, that is portrayed in most detail, to the extent that many of the town's landmarks that still remain can be identified in the books (especially *The Mayor of Casterbridge* and *Far From the Madding Crowd*). Hardy was born and lived in Higher Bockhampton (1840–62 and 1867–70), three miles northeast of the town, in what is now **Hardy's Cottage** (11am–5pm: mid-March to Oct daily; Nov to mid March Thurs–Sun; £6.30, NT; ☏ 01305 262366, ⊛ nationaltrust .org.uk/hardys-cottage), where a few bits of period furniture and some original manuscripts are displayed. Having worked as an architect, Hardy returned to Dorchester in 1885, and spent the rest of his life in **Max Gate**, in Alington Avenue, which he designed himself (11am–5pm: mid-March to Oct daily; Nov to mid March Thurs–Sun; £6.30, NT; ☏ 01305 262538, ⊛ nationaltrust.org.uk /max-gate). Here, he completed *Tess of the D'Urbervilles*, *Jude the Obscure* and much of his poetry.

Maiden Castle

Around 2 miles southwest of Dorchester, DT2 9EY • Daily 24hr • Free; EH • ⓦ www.english-heritage.org.uk/visit/places/maiden-castle

One of southern England's finest prehistoric sites, **MAIDEN CASTLE** stands on a hill southwest of Dorchester. Covering about 115 acres, it was first developed around 3000 BC by a Stone Age farming community and then used during the Bronze Age as a funeral mound. Iron Age dwellers expanded it into a populous settlement and fortified it with a daunting series of ramparts and ditches, just in time for the arrival of Vespasian's Second Legion. The ancient Britons' slingstones were no match for the more sophisticated weapons of the Roman invaders, however, and Maiden Castle was stormed in a massacre in 43 AD. What you see today is a massive series of grassy concentric ridges about 60ft high, creasing the surface of the hill. The main finds from the site are displayed in the Dorset County Museum (see opposite).

Cerne Abbas giant

Cerne Abbas, 7 miles north of Dorchester, DT2 7AL • Daily 24hr • Free; NT • ☎ 01297 489481, ⓦ nationaltrust.org.uk/cerne-giant

The village of **CERNE ABBAS** has bags of charm, with gorgeous Tudor cottages and abbey ruins, but its main attraction is the enormously priapic **Cerne Abbas giant** carved in the chalk hillside just north of the village, standing 180ft high and brandishing a club over his disproportionately small head. The age of the monument is disputed, though it is likely that the giant originated as some primeval fertility symbol. Folklore has it that lying on the outsize member will induce conception, but the National Trust, who now own the site, do their best to stop people wandering over it and damaging the 2ft-deep trenches that form the outlines. Although you can walk round the giant, the carving itself is fenced off to avoid erosion and you don't get the full impact when you are so close – for the best view, follow signs to the car park and **viewpoint** on the hillside opposite.

Milton Abbas

12 miles northeast of Dorchester • Bus #311 from Dorchester (3 daily; 45min)

The village of **MILTON ABBAS** is an unusual English rural idyll. It owes its model-like neatness to the First Earl of Dorchester who, in the eighteenth century, found the medieval squalor of former "Middleton" a blot on the landscape of his estate. He had the village razed and rebuilt in its present location as thirty semi-detached, whitewashed and thatched cottages on wide grassy verges. No trace remains of the old village that once surrounded the fourteenth-century **abbey church** (now part of Milton Abbey school), which is a mile's walk away near the lake at the bottom of the village.

Tolpuddle Martyrs Museum

Tolpuddle, DT2 7EH, 8 miles east of Dorchester • April–Oct Tues–Sat 10am–5pm, Sun 11am–5pm; Nov–March Thurs–Sat 10am–4pm, Sun 11am–4pm • Free • ☎ 01305 848237, ⓦ tolpuddlemartyrs.org.uk

The delightful Dorset village of **TOLPUDDLE** is of interest principally because of the **Tolpuddle Martyrs**. In 1834, six villagers, George and James Loveless, Thomas and John Standfield, John Brine and James Hammett, were sentenced to transportation for banding together to form the Friendly Society of Agricultural Labourers, in order to petition for a small wage increase on the grounds that their families were starving. The men spent three years in Australia's penal colonies before being pardoned following a public outcry – and the Martyrs passed into history as founders of the **trade union** movement. Six memorial cottages were built in 1934 to commemorate the centenary of the Martyrs' conviction. The middle one has been turned into the little **Tolpuddle Martyrs Museum**, which charts the story of the men, from their harsh rural lives before their conviction to the horrors of transportation in a convict ship and the brutal conditions of the penal colonies.

ARRIVAL AND INFORMATION

DORCHESTER AND AROUND

By train Dorchester has two train stations, Dorchester South and Dorchester West, both south of the centre.
Destinations (Dorchester South) Bournemouth (every 30min; 40–45min); London Waterloo (every 30min; 2hr 35min–2hr 50min); Weymouth (every 15–30min; 10–15min).
Destinations (Dorchester West) Bath (5 daily; 2hr); Bristol (5 daily; 2hr 10min–2hr 25 min).
By bus Most local buses stop around the car park on Acland Rd, to the east of South St, though long-distance

buses pull in next to Dorchester South train station.
Destinations Bournemouth (4 daily; 1hr–1hr 45min); London Victoria (1 daily; 4hr); Weymouth (at least hourly; 25min–1hr).
Tourist Information Centre Dorchester Library, South Walks House, Charles St (April–Oct Mon 10am–5.30pm, Tues & Fri 9.30am–7pm, Wed 9.30am–1pm, Thurs 9.30am–5.30pm, Sat 9am–4pm; Nov–March Mon 10am–4pm, Tues, Thurs & Fri 9.30am–4pm, Wed 9.30am–1pm, Sat 9am–4pm; ☏ 01305 267992, ⓦ visit-dorset.com).

ACCOMMODATION

The Old Rectory Winterbourne Steepleton, DT2 9LG, 4 miles west of Dorchester ☏ 01305 889468, ⓦ theold rectorybandb.co.uk. A lovely former rectory in a tiny, pretty village. Dating from 1850, the B&B has four comfortable en-suite rooms, one with a four-poster, and attractive well-kept gardens. **£80**

Westwood House 29 High West St, DT1 1UP ☏ 01305 268018, ⓦ westwoodhouse.co.uk. Comfortable Georgian townhouse on the busy high street, with well-furnished rooms complete with flatscreen TVs. The breakfasts are great, and there's an inexpensive car park nearby. **£100**

EATING AND DRINKING

Potters Café 19 Durngate St, DT1 1JP ☏ 01305 260312. Very appealing café/restaurant with a log fire in winter and a small garden. It serves a range of inexpensive dishes such as fish soup, quiche and salads, as well as the likes of tempura red mullet (£10). Mon–Sat 9.30am–4pm, Sun 10am–2.30pm.
Sienna 36 High West St, DT1 1UP ☏ 01305 250022, ⓦ siennadorchester.co.uk. Former Masterchef contestant Marcus Wilcox is the chef at this small upmarket restaurant which specializes in locally sourced British cuisine, with innovative dishes such as sea trout with artichoke and lamb

with aubergine and yoghurt (£17–20). Wed–Fri noon–2pm & 7–9pm, Sat 10am–2pm & 7–9pm, Sun noon–3pm.
Yalbury and Yvons Café & Wine Bar Dukes Auction House, Brewery Square, DT1 1GA ☏ 01305 260185, ⓦ ycscafe.com. In the modern cultural quarter of Brewery Square, this friendly café-restaurant serves a good range of sandwiches and pastries by day, and evening meals at weekends such as wild boar and faggots and Portland crab (mains £10–14). Mon–Thurs 8.30am–5pm, Fri & Sat 8.30am–11pm, Sun 9am–3pm.

Sherborne

Tucked away in the northwest corner of Dorset, ten miles north of Cerne Abbas, the pretty town of **SHERBORNE** was once the capital of Wessex, its church having cathedral status until Old Sarum (see p.229) usurped the bishopric in 1075.

Abbey Church

3 Abbey Close, ST9 3LQ • Daily: April–Oct 8am–6pm; Nov–March 8am–4pm • Free, but donation welcome • ☏ 01935 812452, ⓦ sherborneabbey.com

Sherborne's former historical glory is embodied by the magnificent **Abbey Church**, founded in 705 and later becoming a Benedictine abbey. Most of its extant parts date from a rebuilding in the fifteenth century. Among the abbey church's many tombs are those of Alfred the Great's two brothers, Ethelred and Ethelbert, and the Elizabethan poet Thomas Wyatt, all in the northeast corner.

The castles

Sherborne boasts two "castles", both associated with Sir Walter Raleigh. Queen Elizabeth I first leased, then gave, Raleigh the twelfth-century **Old Castle**, on Castletom (April–June, Sept & Oct daily 10am–5pm; July & Aug daily 10am–6pm; £4.30, EH;

☎03703 331181, ⓦwww.english-heritage.org.uk/visit/places/sherborne-old-castle), but it seems that he despaired of feudal accommodation and built himself a more comfortably domesticated house, **Sherborne Castle**, in adjacent parkland accessed from New Road (April–Oct Tues–Thurs, Sat & Sun 11am–5pm, gardens 10am–6pm; castle and gardens £12, gardens only £6.50; ☎01935 812072, ⓦsherbornecastle.com). When Sir Walter fell from the queen's favour by seducing her maid of honour, the Digby family acquired the house and have lived here ever since. The Old Castle fared less happily, and was pulverized by Cromwellian cannon fire for the obstinately Royalist leanings of its occupants.

ARRIVAL AND INFORMATION   SHERBORNE

By train The station is 5min south of the town centre, and is served by hourly trains between London and Exeter, with some services continuing on to Plymouth.

By bus Buses from Dorchester, Yeovil and Blandford Forum

pull in outside the train station.

Tourist office 3 Tilton Court, Digby Rd (Mon–Sat: Easter–Aug 9am–5pm; Sept–Nov 9.30am–4pm; Dec–Easter 10am–3pm; ☎01935 815341, ⓦsherbornetown.com).

ACCOMMODATION AND EATING

The Eastbury Long St, DT9 3BY ☎01935 813131, ⓦtheeastburyhotel.co.uk. In a fine Georgian house, with its own highly regarded restaurant, bar and lovely walled gardens. The front rooms are on the small side; it's worth paying extra for one of the executive rooms, which are spacious and boutique in feel, overlooking the gardens. The restaurant specializes in dishes made from seasonal and locally sourced ingredients. Daily

noon–2pm & 6.30–9pm. **£150**

★**Oliver's** 19 Cheap St, DT9 3PU ☎01935 815005, ⓦoliverscoffeehouse.co.uk. With long wooden benches laid out in a former Victorian butcher's, adorned with the original tiles, this friendly café-deli serves great cakes and coffee, accompanied by oodles of atmosphere. Mon–Fri 9am–5pm, Sat 9.30am–5pm, Sun 10am–4pm.

Shaftesbury

Fifteen miles east of Sherborne on the A30, **SHAFTESBURY** perches on a spur of lumpy hills, with severe gradients on three sides of the town. On a clear day, views from the town are terrific – one of the best vantage points is **Gold Hill**, quaint, cobbled and very steep. At its crest, the **Gold Hill Museum and Garden** (April–Oct daily 10.30am–4pm; free; ☎01747 852157, ⓦgoldhillmuseum.org.uk) displays items ranging from locally made buttons, for which the area was once renowned, to a mummified cat.

Pilgrims used to flock to Shaftesbury to pay homage to the bones of Edward the Martyr, which were brought to the **abbey** in 978, though now only the footings of the abbey church survive, just off the main street on Park Walk (April–Oct daily 10am–5pm; £3; ☎01747 852910, ⓦshaftesburyabbey.org.uk). **St Peter's Church** on the marketplace is one of the few reminders of Shaftesbury's medieval grandeur, when it boasted a castle, twelve churches and four market crosses.

ARRIVAL AND INFORMATION   SHAFTESBURY

By bus Shaftesbury has services from Salisbury (Mon–Sat 2–3 daily; 1hr 15min) and Blandford Forum (Mon–Sat 4 daily; 45min).

Tourist office 8 Bell St (Mon–Sat 10am–4pm; ☎01747 853514, ⓦshaftesburydorset.com).

ACCOMMODATION AND EATING

The Grosvenor Arms The Commons, SP7 8JA ☎01747 850580, ⓦgrosvenorarms.co.uk. This former coaching inn in the centre of town has had a successful makeover into a buzzy, boutique-style hotel. The rooms are stylish, with comfy beds, coffee machines and flatscreen TVs, and the downstairs restaurant is good too, with a wood-fired

pizza oven, plus local fish and meat dishes (£10–15). Daily noon–3pm & 6–10pm. **£90**

Number 5 Bimport 5 Bimport, SP7 8AT ☎01747 228490, ⓦfivebimport.co.uk. Small, friendly B&B in an attractive, classily renovated Georgian townhouse in the centre of Shaftesbury. There are just two rooms – the larger

3

one opens onto the garden. £135
★**The Salt Cellar** Gold Hill, SP7 8JW ☎01747 851838. Right at the top of the hill itself and with great views, this

place serves inexpensive snacks and daily specials from around £8, including home-made pies, in the pillar-lined interior or at outdoor tables on the cobbles. Mon–Sat 9am–5pm.

Weymouth and around

Whether George III's passion for sea bathing was a symptom of his eventual madness is uncertain, but it was at **WEYMOUTH** in 1789 that he became the first reigning monarch to follow the craze. Sycophantic gentry rushed into the waves behind him, and soon the town, formerly a busy port, took on the elegant Georgian stamp that it bears today. Weymouth's highlight, of course, is its long sandy beach, and it makes a lively family holiday destination in summer, reverting to a more sedate rhythm out of season.

The Esplanade

Weymouth's most imposing architectural heritage stands along the **Esplanade**, a dignified range of bow-fronted and porticoed buildings gazing out across the graceful bay. At the far southern end of the Esplanade, the Quay juts out into the sea, housing the town's ferry terminals and its newest attraction, the 173ft-high **Jurassic Skyline** (daily: April, May & late Oct 11am–3pm; June to late July & mid-Sept to mid-Oct 11am–5pm; late July to early Sept 11am–6pm; check website for half-term and bank hol hours; £7.50, £6.50 online; ⓦjurassicskyline.com), which provides stunning views over the town and coastline. At the northern end of the promenade, in Lodmoor Country Park, the excellent **Sea Life Park** (daily March–Oct 10am–5pm, Nov–Feb 10am–4pm; last admission 1hr before closing; £23.50, £16.50 online, includes entry to Jurassic Skyline; ⓦvisitsealife.com/weymouth) is home to turtles, penguins, otters and seals, as well as a seahorse breeding centre, and water play areas.

The Old Harbour

The pedestrianized **St Mary's Street** heads south from the Esplanade to the Town Bridge, beyond which is the more intimate quayside of the **Old Harbour**. Here, a few buildings survive from pre-Georgian times, including the restored **Tudor House** at 3 Trinity Street (Feb–April, Nov & Dec first Sun of month 2–4pm; May–Oct Tues–Fri 1–4pm, Sun 2–4pm; £4; ☎01305 779711).

ARRIVAL AND INFORMATION

WEYMOUTH AND AROUND

By train Weymouth is served at least hourly by trains from London (2hr 45min–3hr), Southampton (1hr 20min–1hr 40min), Bournemouth (50min) and Poole (35–45min), with less regular services from Bristol (2hr 30min) and

Bath (2hr 10min). Trains arrive at the station on King St, a short walk back from the seafront.
By bus Buses from Dorchester (at least hourly; 25min– 1hr) pull in at the stops by King George III's statue.

ACCOMMODATION

★**Bay View House** 35 The Esplanade, DT4 8DH ☎01305 782083, ⓦbayview-weymouth.co.uk. Clean, friendly and well-kept guesthouse right on the seafront. All the rooms are comfortable, but the front ones overlooking the sea are great value at £65. Also has family rooms and free private garage parking. £60

Old Harbour View 12 Trinity Rd, DT4 8TJ ☎01305 774633, ⓦoldharbourview.co.uk. Cosy guesthouse in a great harbourfront location. It consists of just two rooms in a Georgian townhouse, but it's worth paying a few pounds extra for the one at the front with a harbour view. The breakfasts are great, using locally sourced and free-range ingredients. £98

EATING AND DRINKING

Enzo 110 The Esplanade, DT2 7EA ☎01305 778666, ⓦenzo-ristorante.co.uk. Traditional Italian restaurant

with clean, contemporary decor, tiled floors and modern furnishings; it's right on the seafront, but slightly away from the hubbub of the main drag. It serves a range of pasta dishes (£9–12) and pizzas (£8–13), plus other main courses such as veal escalope (£15.50). Excellent value and friendly service. Daily 12.30–2.30pm & 5.30–10.30pm.

Manbo's Bistro 46 St Mary St, DT4 8PU ☎01305 839839, ⓦ manbosbistro.com. They serve good-value fish, pasta and meat dishes, such as prawn and pesto linguine (£10) and fish chowder (£13), plus tasty daily fish and game specials, at this friendly family-run bistro. The dining area is narrow with an open kitchen at the back, and there are a few tables on the pedestrianized street in front. Mon 6–9pm, Tues–Thurs noon–2.30pm & 6–9pm, Fri noon–2.30pm & 6–9.30pm, Sat noon–3pm & 6–9.30pm.

★ **The Hive Café** 20 Park St, DT4 7DQ ☎07867 898498. Great veggie and vegan café with friendly service, a little courtyard at the back and a cosy upstairs room with a wood-burner. The food is fantastic – home-made quiche and filo pastries, falafel and a great-value meze plate with a pasty and a selection of salads for £6. Tasty cakes are made with honey from their own hives, and the hot lemon, ginger and honey drink (£2) is delicious. Wed–Sat 10.30am–4pm, Sun 11am–3.30pm.

Isle of Portland

Just south of Weymouth stretch the giant arms of Portland Harbour, where a long causeway links the mainland to the stark, wind-battered and treeless **Isle of Portland**. It's famed above all for its hard white limestone, which has been quarried here for centuries – Wren used it for St Paul's Cathedral, and it clads the UN headquarters in New York. It was also used for the 6000ft breakwater that protects Portland Harbour – the largest artificial harbour in Britain, built by convicts in the nineteenth century and the main centre for the 2012 Olympic Games sailing events. It is still surveyed by **Portland Castle** (daily: April–Sept 10am–6pm; Oct 10am–5pm; £5.70, EH; ☎01305 820539, ⓦ www.english-heritage.org.uk/visit/places/portland-castle), which was commissioned by Henry VIII. Southeast of here, the craggy limestone of the Isle rises to 496ft at Verne Hill. At **Portland Bill**, the southern tip of the island, you can climb the 153 steps of **Portland Lighthouse** (10am–5pm: Easter–Oct daily; Nov–Easter Sat & Sun; £7, includes entry to visitor centre; ☎01305 821050, ⓦ trinityhouse.co.uk), which dates from 1906, for superb views in all directions.

ARRIVAL AND DEPARTURE ISLE OF PORTLAND

By bus First Bus service #1 runs every 20–30min from Weymouth King's Statue to Portland (30–40min).

EATING AND DRINKING

Cove House Inn 91 Chiswell, DT5 1AW ☎01305 820895, ⓦ thecovehouseinn.co.uk. A good spot for food or a quick drink, with pub staples such as burgers (£9.25) as well as a daily local fish menu, featuring such treats as scallops with chorizo and garlic (£13). It's cosy inside, with its wood-burner and big windows with sea views, while the outside tables look over Chesil Beach. Mon–Sat 11am–11pm, Sun noon–10.30pm; kitchen daily noon–2.30pm & 6–9pm.

Crab House Café Ferrymans Way, Portland Rd at the entrance to the Portland causeway, DT4 9YU ☎01305 788867, ⓦ crabhousecafe.co.uk. In a great location overlooking Chesil Beach, this upmarket beach shack is renowned for its superb, locally caught fresh fish and seafood (from around £14), including oysters from its own beds. The menu changes daily according to the catch, but expect dishes like turbot steak with samphire. There are tables outside; reservations advised. Wed & Thurs noon–2.30pm & 6–9pm, Fri & Sat noon–2.30pm & 6–9.30pm, Sun noon–3.30pm.

Chesil Beach

Chesil Beach is the strangest feature of the Dorset coast, a 200yd-wide, 50ft-high bank of pebbles that extends for eighteen miles, its component stones gradually decreasing in size from fist-like pebbles at Portland to "pea gravel" at Burton Bradstock in the west. This sorting is an effect of the powerful coastal currents, which make this one of the most dangerous beaches in Europe – churchyards in the local villages display plenty of evidence of wrecks and drownings. Though not a swimming beach, Chesil is popular with sea anglers, and its wild, uncommercialized atmosphere makes an appealing antidote to the south-coast resorts. Behind the beach, **The Fleet**, a brackish lagoon, was the setting for J. Meade Faulkner's classic smuggling tale, *Moonfleet*.

ACCOMMODATION

★**East Shilvinghampton Farm** Portesham, DT3 4HN ☎01420 80804, ⓦfeatherdown.co.uk. A lovely farm in a beautiful valley, a couple of miles inland from the Fleet Lagoon. It has various spacious, luxurious tents to rent – ready-erected, with running water, a toilet, a wood-burning stove and comfortable beds – in an idyllic field that looks down the valley, with horses, goats and chickens in the paddock next door. Three-night minimum stay. From **£145**

Abbotsbury

At the point where Chesil Beach attaches itself to the shore is the pretty village of **ABBOTSBURY**, all tawny ironstone and thatch. The village has three main attractions, which can be visited individually or on a combined "Passport" ticket for £18, with discounts on the website (☎01305 871130, ⓦabbotsbury-tourism.co.uk). The most absorbing is the **Swannery** (daily mid-March to Oct 10am–5pm; £12.50), a wetland reserve for mute swans dating back to medieval times, when presumably it formed part of the abbot's larder. If you visit in late May or June, you'll see baby cygnets waddling around and squabbling at your feet. The eel-grass reeds through which the swans paddle were once harvested to thatch roofs throughout the region. One example can be seen on the fifteenth-century Tithe Barn, the last remnant of the abbey and today housing the **Children's Farm** (10am–5pm: mid-March to early Sept daily; late Sept & Oct Sat & Sun; £11, under-16s £9.50), whose highlights include goat-racing and pony rides. Lastly, in the **Subtropical Gardens** (daily: Nov–March 10am–4pm; April–Oct 10am–5pm; closed over Christmas period; £12.50) delicate species thrive in the microclimate created by Chesil's stones, which act as a giant radiator to deter all but the worst frosts.

Bridport and around

Ten miles west of Abbotsbury is pretty **BRIDPORT**, mentioned in the Domesday Book of 1086 and an important port before the rivers silted up in the early 1700s, leaving it stranded inland. It's a pleasant old town of solid brick buildings with very wide streets, a hangover from its days as a major rope-making centre when cords were stretched between the houses to be twisted and dyed. Today, it's a lively **market** town (Wed & Sat) with an arty, alternative vibe. The harbour lies a mile or so south at **West Bay**, which has a fine sandy beach sheltered below majestic red cliffs – the sheer East Cliffs are a tempting challenge for intrepid walkers – and it made a suitably brooding location for the ITV murder series, *Broadchurch*.

ACCOMMODATION AND EATING · BRIDPORT AND AROUND

The Bull 34 East St, DT6 3LF ☎01308 422878, ⓦthebullhotel.co.uk. Friendly, boutique-style hotel in a former seventeenth-century coaching inn in the centre of town. The rooms are comfortable and modern, some with roll-top baths: there are also some family rooms. The restaurant and bar are good, too: try *moules marinières* (£9) to start, followed by an 8oz rib-eye steak (£22). Daily noon–3pm & 6.30–9.30pm. **£135**

★**Seaside Boarding House** Cliff Rd, Burton Bradstock, DT6 4RB ☎01308 897205, ⓦtheseaside boardinghouse.com. Smart and stylish, this beachside bolthole has a relaxed vibe, great cocktails, and comfortable contemporary rooms, with lovely sea or countryside views. Set up by the founders of London's Groucho Club, it's a wonderful place to chill out and the location is hard to beat – a short walk from the beach, with a large terrace giving fantastic views along the coast. The restaurant, with French windows opening onto the terrace, is highly recommended for its tasty Modern British dishes, such as halibut with shellfish bisque (mains £14–20), with fresh fish and local, seasonal produce featuring strongly. Daily 10am–10pm. **£195**

The Riverside West Bay, DT6 4EZ ☎01308 422011, ⓦthefishrestaurant-westbay.co.uk. Reservations are recommended for this renowned restaurant which offers fresh, sumptuous fish and seafood and fine river views.

There is a daily changing menu, but expect the likes of lemon sole fillets with sea salt and lemon (£22.25). There are also meat and vegetarian options. Tues–Thurs noon–2.30pm & 6.30–8.30pm, Fri & Sat noon–2.30pm & 6.30–9pm, Sun noon–2.30pm.

★**Watch House Café** West Bay, DT6 4EL ☎01308 459330, ⓦ hivebeachcafe.co.uk/watch-house-caf. Nestled into a bank of shingle right on the beach, and with an appealing outdoor terrace, this rightly popular café-restaurant is a must-visit. You can just have a coffee and cake or ice cream, but the real draw is the fresh fish and seafood, including a superb fish soup (£12) and Lyme Bay hake fillets with samphire (£17). There is also a wood-fired oven which churns out good-sized pizzas (£10–15). July & Aug Mon–Wed & Sun 10am–5pm, Thurs–Sat 10am–5pm & 6–8pm; Sept–June daily 10am–5pm.

Lyme Regis

LYME REGIS, Dorset's most westerly town, shelters snugly between steep, fossil-filled cliffs. Its intimate size and photogenic qualities make this a popular and congested spot in high summer, with some upmarket literary associations – Jane Austen summered in a seafront cottage and set part of *Persuasion* in Lyme (the town appears in the 1995 film version), while novelist John Fowles lived here until his death in 2005 (the film adaptation of his book, *The French Lieutenant's Woman*, was also shot here).

Colourwashed cottages and elegant Regency and Victorian villas line its seafront and flanking streets, but Lyme's best-known feature is a practical reminder of its commercial origins: **the Cobb**, a curving harbour wall originally built in the thirteenth century. It has suffered many alterations since, most notably in the nineteenth century, when its massive boulders were clad in neater blocks of Portland stone.

On Bridge Street, the excellent **Lyme Regis Museum** (daily 10am–5pm; £4.95; ☎01297 443370, ⓦ lymeregismuseum.co.uk) displays artefacts related to the town's literary connections, including John Fowles' office chair, with the new Mary Anning Wing telling the story of Anning's life and her incredible fossil finds (see below). Meanwhile **Dinosaurland** on Coombe Street (late Feb to late Oct daily 10am–5pm; sporadic openings at other times; £5; ☎01297 443541, ⓦ dinosaurland.co.uk), fills out the story of ammonites and other local fossils. The town is also something of a foodie destination, with lots of superb fish restaurants and good pubs, plus the **Town Mill Complex** (ⓦ townmill.org.uk) in Mill Lane, just off Coombe Street, where there's a fantastic cheese shop, local brewery and café, as well as a working mill, pottery and art gallery.

ARRIVAL AND INFORMATION
LYME REGIS

By train Lyme's nearest station is in Axminster, 5 miles north, served by regular trains from London Waterloo and Exeter: bus #X54 runs from the station to Lyme.

By bus First Buses (ⓦ firstgroup.com) runs a daily

LYME'S JURASSIC COAST

The cliffs around Lyme are made up of a complex layer of limestone, greensand and unstable clay, a perfect medium for preserving **fossils**, which are exposed by landslips of the waterlogged clays. In 1811, after a fierce storm caused parts of the cliffs to collapse, 12-year-old **Mary Anning**, a keen fossil-hunter, discovered an almost complete dinosaur skeleton, a 30ft ichthyosaurus now displayed in London's Natural History Museum.

Hands-off inspection of the area's complex **geology** can be enjoyed all around the town: as you walk along the seafront and out towards The Cobb, look for the outlines of ammonites in the walls and paving stones. To the west of Lyme, the **Undercliff** is a fascinating jumble of overgrown landslips, now a nature reserve, where a great path wends its way through the undergrowth for around seven miles to neighbouring Seaton in Devon. East of Lyme, a huge landslip in 2008 closed the Dorset Coast Path to **Charmouth** (Jane Austen's favourite resort), as well as blocking the two-mile beach route to the resort, which was previously walkable at low tide. At Charmouth, you can take the coastal path leading to the headland of **Golden Cap**, whose brilliant outcrop of auburn sandstone is crowned with gorse.

#X52 bus service from Exeter (1hr 45min) and Bridport (25min).

Tourist office Church St (April–July & Sept–Oct Mon–Sat 10am–5am; Aug Mon–Sat 10am–5am, Sun 10am–4pm; Nov–March Mon–Sat 10am–3pm; ☎01297 442138, ⓦlymeregis.org).

ACCOMMODATION

★**Alexandra Hotel** Pound St, DT7 3HZ ☎01297 442010, ⓦhotelalexandra.co.uk. Popular with honeymooners and good for families, this is the town's top hotel, located inside an eighteenth-century manor house with bleached wood floors and lovely gardens overlooking the sea. Many of the comfortable rooms have sea views, and there is also a highly rated restaurant. **£180**

Old Lyme 29 Coombe St, DT7 3PP ☎01297 442929, ⓦoldlymeguesthouse.co.uk. Central guesthouse right in the town centre in a lovely 300-year-old stone former post office. There are six smallish but spruce bedrooms – one is a triple room and all are en suite, or with a private bathroom. **£90**

EATING AND DRINKING

Hix Oyster and Fish House Cobb Rd, DT7 3JP ☎01297 446910, ⓦhixoysterandfishhouse.co.uk. In a lovely location overlooking the town and sea, this airy restaurant, owned by acclaimed chef Mark Hix, specializes in local fish and seafood: sublime main courses include Torbay cod with shrimps (£21.50), though there are cheaper options, like huss curry (£13.50). April–Oct daily noon–10pm; Nov–March Tues–Sat noon–10pm, Sun noon–4pm.

Royal Standard 25 Marine Parade, DT7 3JF ☎01297 442637, ⓦtheroyalstandardlymeregis.co.uk. Beachside inn dating back four hundred years, with a log fire inside, and a great sea-facing beer garden that leads onto the beach. There are real ales on tap, brewed by Palmers in nearby Bridport, and decently priced pub grub (from £11). Daily 10am–11pm; kitchen April–Sept daily noon–9pm, Oct–March daily noon–3pm & 5.50–9pm.

★**Tierra Kitchen** 1a Coombe St, DT7 3PY ☎01297 445189, ⓦtierrakitchen.co.uk. Overlooking the mill-stream, *Tierra Kitchen* is a bright vegetarian restaurant serving a range of tasty seasonal lunches such as courgette-flower fritters or vegetable tagine (around £10), plus evening meals such goat's cheese and beetroot tarte tatin, with delicious desserts (two courses for £20). Tues 6–9pm, Wed–Sat noon–2.15pm & 6–9pm.

Town Mill Bakery 2 Coombe St, DT7 3PY ☎01297 444754, ⓦtownmillbakery.wordpress.com. A wonderful bakery/café serving a superb array of breads and cakes freshly baked on the premises. The ingredients are mostly local and largely organic, with sublime breakfasts of home-made jam, boiled eggs and local honey – choose your bread and toast it yourself, then sit at the communal long wooden tables. Lunch includes home-made soup and pizzas (from £7.50). Daily: Aug 8.30am–8pm; Sept–July 8.30am–5pm.

Salisbury and around

SALISBURY, huddled below Wiltshire's chalky plain in the converging valleys of the Avon and Nadder, sprang into existence in the early thirteenth century, when the bishopric was moved from nearby **Old Sarum** (see p.229). Today, it looks from a distance very much as it did when Constable painted his celebrated view of it, and though traffic may clog its centre, this prosperous and well-kept city is designed on a pleasantly human scale, with no sprawling suburbs or high-rise buildings to challenge the supremacy of the cathedral's immense spire. The city's inspiring silhouette is best admired by taking a twenty-minute walk through the water meadows southwest of the centre to the suburb of **Harnham**.

North of Salisbury stretches a hundred thousand acres of chalky upland, known as **Salisbury Plain**; it's managed by the Ministry of Defence, whose presence has protected it from development and intensive farming, thereby preserving species that are all but extinct elsewhere in England. Though largely deserted today, in previous times Salisbury Plain was positively overrun with communities. Stone Age, Bronze Age and Iron Age settlements left hundreds of burial mounds scattered over the chalklands, as well as major complexes at Danebury, Badbury, Figsbury, **Old Sarum**, and, of course, the great circle of **Stonehenge**, England's most famous historical monument. To the west, Salisbury's hinterland also includes one of Wiltshire's great country mansions, **Wilton House**, as well as **Stourhead** and **Longleat Safari Park**.

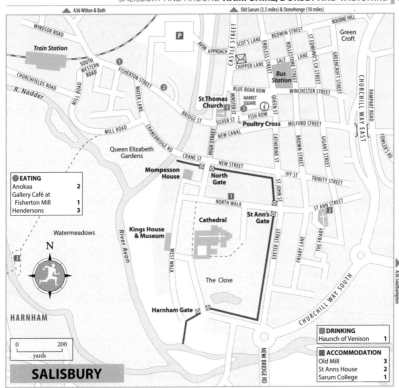

EATING

Anokaa	2
Gallery Café at Fisherton Mill	1
Hendersons	3

DRINKING

Haunch of Venison	1

ACCOMMODATION

Old Mill	3
St Anns House	2
Sarum College	1

SALISBURY

Salisbury Cathedral

The Close, SP1 2EJ • Cathedral daily Mon–Sat 9am–5pm, Sun noon–4pm; chapter house April–Oct Mon–Sat 9.30am–5pm & Sun 11am–4pm, Nov–March Mon–Sat 10am–4.30pm & Sun 11am–4pm • £7.50 suggested donation • **Tower tours** April–Sept Mon–Sat at least 2 daily, usually at 11.15am & 1.15pm, up to 5 a day at busy times; 1hr 45min; book ahead • £12.50 • ☎ 01722 555120, ⓦ salisburycathedral.org.uk

Begun in 1220, **Salisbury Cathedral** was mostly completed within forty years and is thus unusually consistent in its style, with one prominent exception – the **spire**, which was added a century later and, at 404ft, is the highest in England. Its survival is something of a miracle, for the foundations penetrate only about six feet into marshy ground, and when Christopher Wren surveyed it he found the spire to be leaning almost two and a half feet out of true. He added further tie rods, which finally arrested the movement.

The interior is over-austere, but there's an amazing sense of space and light in its high nave, despite the sombre pillars of grey Purbeck marble, which are visibly bowing beneath the weight they bear. Monuments and carved tombs line the walls. Don't miss the octagonal **chapter house**, which displays a rare original copy of the Magna Carta, and whose walls are decorated with a frieze of scenes from the Old Testament.

The Close

Surrounding the cathedral is the **Close**, a peaceful precinct of lawns and mellow old buildings. Most of the houses have seemly Georgian facades, though some, like the Bishop's Palace and the deanery, date from the thirteenth century. **Mompesson House** (mid-March to Oct daily 11am–5pm; £6.50, garden only £1, NT; ☎ 01722 420980, ⓦ nationaltrust.org .uk/mompesson-house), built by a wealthy merchant in 1701, contains some beautifully furnished eighteenth-century rooms and a superbly carved staircase. Also in the Close is the **King's House**, home to the **Salisbury and South Wiltshire Museum** (Oct–May Mon–Sat 10am–5pm; April–Oct Mon–Sat 10am–5pm & Sun noon–5pm; £7.50; ☎01722 332151, ⓦsalisburymuseum.org.uk) – an absorbing account of local history.

Around the Market Square

The Close's **North Gate** opens onto the centre's older streets, where narrow pedestrianized alleyways bear names like Fish Row and Salt Lane, indicative of their trading origin. Many half-timbered houses and inns have survived, and the last of four market crosses, **Poultry Cross**, stands on stilts in Silver Street, near the Market Square. The market, held on Tuesdays and Saturdays, still serves a large agricultural area, as it did in earlier times when the city grew wealthy on wool. Nearby, the **Church of St Thomas** – named after Thomas Becket – is worth a look inside for its carved timber roof and "Doom painting" over the chancel arch, depicting Christ presiding over the Last Judgement. Dating from 1475, it's the largest of its kind in England.

ARRIVAL AND DEPARTURE

SALISBURY AND AROUND

By train Trains from London arrive half a mile west of Salisbury's centre, on South Western Rd.
Destinations Bath (2–4 daily; 1hr); Bradford-Upon-Avon (2–4 daily; 45min); Bristol (2–4 daily; 1hr 10min); London Waterloo (every 30min; 1hr 30min); Portsmouth (hourly; 1hr 15min); Southampton (every 30min; 30min–40min).
By bus Buses stop at various sites around the city centre.
Destinations Bournemouth (Mon–Sat every 30min, Sun hourly; 1hr 15min); London (5 daily; 3hr 15min–4hr); Southampton (Mon–Sat every 1–2hr; 1hr 10min).

INFORMATION AND TOURS

Tourist office Fish Row, just off Market Square (Mon–Fri 9am–5pm, Sat 10am–4pm, Sun & bank hols 10am–2pm; ☎01722 3428606, ⓦvisitwiltshire.co.uk). It's also the starting point for informative and inexpensive guided walks of the city.

Bus tours Tours to Stonehenge and Old Sarum depart from the train station (bus only £14, with entry to Old Sarum and Stonehenge £29; ☎01722 336855, ⓦthestonehengetour .info) every 30min in summer, and hourly at other times.

ACCOMMODATION

★**Old Mill** Town Path, Harnham, SP2 8EU ☎01722 512139, ⓦoldmillhotelsalisbury.co.uk; map p.227. The fully equipped rooms of this riverside pub in a former sixteenth-century papermill have great views across the meadows to the cathedral. The location feels really rural but is just a short walk from the city centre. Real ales are on tap in the bar, and there's an adjoining restaurant serving good local food. <u>£125</u>
St Anns House 32–34 St Ann St, SP1 2DP ☎07715 213146, ⓦstannshouse.co.uk; map p.227. A well-restored

Georgian townhouse with stylish, comfortable rooms in a quiet street a short walk from the cathedral. <u>£110</u>
★**Sarum College** 19 The Close, SP1 2EE ☎01722 424800, ⓦsarum.ac.uk; map p.227. By no means luxurious but in the best location in Salisbury, this friendly ecumenical college (parts of which were designed by Sir Christopher Wren) rents out simple en-suite doubles with views over The Close, plus others without private facilities (£45). There's also a decent common room, and breakfast is included. <u>£105</u>

EATING

Anokaa 60 Fisherton Street, SP2 7RB ☎01722 341717, ⓦanokaa.com; map p.227. Attractive Indian restaurant with smart decor – fresh orchids and contemporary painting on the walls – and waiters in traditional, brightly coloured Indian dress. The food is a cut above the average too, with unusual dishes such as rum-soaked wild venison starter (£8) and main courses including Chardonnay-soaked duck breast (£16) and marinated Portobello mushrooms with masala mash (£11.25). Daily noon–2pm & 5.30–11pm.

★**Gallery Café at Fisherton Mill** 108 Fisherton St, SP2 7QY ☎01722 500200, ⓦfishertonmill.co.uk; map p.227. Great café within a renovated mill/art gallery serving delicious soups (£4.50), sandwiches on sourdough (£6) and main courses such as lemon roast chicken (£13.50), as well as tasty home-made cakes. Upstairs, you can watch artists at work in their studios, weaving and making jewellery. Mon–Fri 10am–5pm, Sat 9.30am–5pm.
Hendersons Artisan Bakery and Café 19 Oatmeal Row, SP1 1TH ☎01722 341717; map p.227. Lovely

bakery/café, which makes its own breads (including organic), quiches and pastries on site. They use local and seasonal ingredients, so you may find specials such as beetroot bread, rosemary and sea-salt focaccia and wild

garlic tart on the menu (tart with salad £5). There's plenty of space upstairs, or you can sit at the tables outside in the square with a made-to-order sandwich and coffee for lunch. Mon–Sat 8am–5pm.

DRINKING

★ **Haunch of Venison** 1 Minster St, SP1 1TB ☎ 01722 411313 ⓦ haunchpub.co.uk; map p.227. One of the city's most atmospheric and historic pubs, with a wonderful warren of rooms, a fireplace dating from 1588, and a

former bread oven containing a mummified hand. The quirky, sloping-floored restaurant serves interesting dishes such as pulled haunch of venison burgers (£16) and Wiltshire pork belly (£15). Daily 11am–11pm.

Old Sarum

Castle Rd, SP1 3SD, 2 miles north of Salisbury • Daily: April–Sept 10am–6pm; Oct 10am–5pm; Nov–March 10am–4pm • £4.80; EH • ☎ 01722 335398, ⓦ www.english-heritage.org.uk/visit/places/old-sarum

The ruins of **Old Sarum** occupy a bleak hilltop site. Possibly occupied up to five thousand years ago, then developed as an Iron Age fort whose double protective ditches remain, it was settled by Romans and Saxons before the Norman bishopric of Sherborne was moved here in the 1070s. Within a couple of decades a new **cathedral** had been consecrated at Old Sarum, and a large religious community was living alongside the soldiers in the central castle. Old Sarum was an uncomfortable place, parched and windswept, and in 1220 the dissatisfied clergy – additionally at loggerheads with the castle's occupants – appealed to the pope for permission to decamp to Salisbury (still known officially as New Sarum). When permission was granted, the stone from the cathedral was commandeered for Salisbury's gateways, and once the church had gone the population waned. By the nineteenth century Old Sarum was deserted, and today the dominant features of the site are huge earthworks, banks and ditches, with a broad trench encircling the rudimentary remains of the Norman palace, castle and cathedral.

Stonehenge

Near Amesbury, SP4 7DE, 9 miles north of Salisbury • Daily: mid-March to May & Sept to mid-Oct 9.30am–7pm; June–Aug 9am–8pm; mid-Oct to mid-March 9.30am–5pm; last entry 2hr before closing; advance booking of timed tickets essential • £16.50; EH • ☎ 0870 333 1181, ⓦ www.english-heritage.org.uk/visit/places/stonehenge • Shuttle buses to the site (every 10min; 10min) leave from the visitor centre

No ancient structure in England arouses more controversy than **Stonehenge**, a mysterious ring of monoliths. While archeologists argue over whether it was a place of ritual sacrifice and sun-worship, an astronomical calculator or a royal palace, the guardians of the site have struggled for years to accommodate its enormous visitor numbers, particularly during the summer **solstice**, when crowds of 35,000 or more gather to watch the sunrise.

Access to the stones themselves is via a **shuttle-bus service** from a sleek **visitor centre** that opened in 2013, after years of debate and planning. This low-rise, environmentally

---

THE GREAT BUSTARDS OF SALISBURY PLAIN

The empty expanses of Salisbury Plain are home to the country's only colony of **Great Bustards**, the world's heaviest flying bird, which became extinct in the UK in the 1840s. Chicks were reintroduced here from Russia in 2004 to a secret location, and the first Great Bustard to be born in the UK in nearly two hundred years appeared in 2009. Visits can be arranged to see the 3ft-high birds: you will be taken in a Landrover to a hide, from where you can view the birds in their natural habitat (£15/person; call ☎ 07817 971327 or see ⓦ greatbustard.org for details).

STONEHENGE – A BRIEF HISTORY

Some people may find **Stonehenge** underwhelming, but understanding a little of its history and ancient significance gives an insight into its mystical appeal. What exists today is only a small part of the original prehistoric complex, as many of the outlying stones were probably plundered by medieval and later farmers for building materials. The **construction** of Stonehenge is thought to have taken place in several stages. In about 3000 BC the outer circular bank and ditch were built, just inside which was dug a ring of 56 pits, which at a later date were filled with a mixture of earth and human ash. Around 2500 BC the first stones were raised within the earthworks, comprising approximately forty great blocks of dolerite (bluestone), whose ultimate source was Preseli in Wales. Some archeologists have suggested that these monoliths were found lying on Salisbury Plain, having been borne down from the Welsh mountains by a glacier in the last Ice Age, but the lack of any other glacial debris on the plain would seem to disprove this theory. The most likely explanation is that the stones were cut from quarries in Preseli and dragged or floated here on rafts, a prodigious task that has defeated recent attempts to emulate it.

The crucial phase in the creation of the site came during the next six hundred years, when the incomplete bluestone circle was transformed by the construction of a circle of 25 **trilithons** (two uprights crossed by a lintel) and an inner horseshoe formation of five trilithons. Hewn from Marlborough Downs sandstone, these colossal stones (called sarsens), ranging from 13ft to 21ft in height and weighing up to thirty tons, were carefully dressed and worked – for example, to compensate for perspectival distortion the uprights have a slight swelling in the middle, the same trick as the builders of the Parthenon were to employ hundreds of years later. More bluestones were arranged in various patterns within the outer circle over this period. The purpose of all this work remains baffling, however. The symmetry and location of the site (a slight rise in a flat valley with even views of the horizon in all directions) as well as its alignment towards the points of sunrise and sunset on the summer and winter solstices tend to support the supposition that it was some sort of observatory or time-measuring device. The site ceased to be used at around 1600 BC, and by the Middle Ages it had become a "landmark". Recent excavations have revealed the existence of a much larger settlement here than had previously been thought (the most substantial Neolithic village of this period to be found on the British mainland, in fact), covering a wide area.

sensitive pair of buildings includes a shop, café and **exhibition** space combining archeological remains from the area with high-tech interactive displays explaining the significance and history of it all. Outside, you can look round a cluster of re-created Neolithic houses, and try your hand at pulling a life-size Preseli bluestone. Perhaps a more fitting way to approach the site, however, is on foot – it's a pleasant, way-marked thirty-minute walk from the visitor centre across fields (once part of a World War I airfield) to the stones.

Wilton House

Wilton, SP2 0BJ, 5 miles west of Salisbury • **House** Easter & May–Aug Mon–Thurs, Sun & bank hols Sat 11.30am–5pm • £15 (includes grounds) • **Grounds** Easter to mid-Sept daily 11am–5.30pm • £6.25 • ☎ 01722 746714, ⓦ wiltonhouse.co.uk

The splendid **Wilton House** dominates the village of **WILTON**, renowned for its carpet industry. The original Tudor house, built for the first earl of Pembroke on the site of a dissolved Benedictine abbey, was ruined by fire in 1647 and rebuilt by Inigo Jones, whose classic hallmarks can be seen in the sumptuous Single Cube and Double Cube rooms, so called because of their precise dimensions.

The easel **paintings** are what makes Wilton really special, however – the collection includes works by Van Dyck, Rembrandt, two of the Brueghel family, Poussin, Andrea del Sarto and Tintoretto. In the grounds, the famous **Palladian Bridge** has been joined by various ancillary attractions including an adventure playground and restaurant. Note, too, that the grounds host frequent events which can restrict access; check the website for details.

Stourhead

Near Mere, BA12 6QF, 25 miles west of Salisbury • **House** Mid-Feb to mid-March Sat & Sun 11am–3pm; mid-March to Oct daily 11am–4.30pm; first two weeks of Nov & Dec daily 11am–3.30pm • **Gardens** Daily: mid-April to Oct 9am–6pm; Nov to mid-April 9am–5pm • House and gardens £16; NT • **King Alfred's Tower** Aug daily noon–4pm • £4.20; NT • ☎ 01747 841152, ⓦ nationaltrust.org.uk/stourhead

Landscape gardening was a favoured mode of display among the grandest eighteenth-century landowners, and **Stourhead** is one of the most accomplished examples of the genre. The Stourton estate was bought in 1717 by Henry Hoare, who commissioned Colen Campbell to build a new villa in the Palladian style. Hoare's heir, another Henry, returned from his Grand Tour in 1741 with his head full of the paintings of Claude and Poussin, and determined to translate their images of well-ordered, wistful classicism into real life. He dammed the Stour to create a lake, then planted the terrain with blocks of trees, domed temples, stone bridges, grottoes and statues, all mirrored vividly in the water. The **house** itself is of minor interest, though it has some good Chippendale furniture, but it is the stunning **gardens** that are the highlight. At the entrance, you can pick up a map detailing a lovely two-mile walk around the lake. The estate itself is vast and includes a pub, a church and a farm shop (a good place to pick up a picnic), plus **King Alfred's Tower**, three miles or so from the main entrance (you can drive round the estate and park by the tower, if you find it too far to walk). Built in 1772, it is one of England's oldest follies, and you can climb the two hundred or so steps up to the top for fine views across the estate and into neighbouring counties.

Longleat

Warminster, BA12 7NW, 27 miles west of Salisbury • Opening hours and closing days vary throughout the season, but are generally 10am–5pm, 6pm or 7pm; check website for exact times and days • House and grounds only £18.95, all attractions £33.95; discounts available online • ☎ 01985 844400, ⓦ longleat.co.uk

The African savanna intrudes into the bucolic Wiltshire countryside at **Longleat** safari and adventure park. In 1946 the sixth marquess of Bath became the first stately-home owner to open his house to the paying public on a regular basis, and in 1966 he caused even more amazement when Longleat's Capability Brown landscapes were turned into England's first drive-through **safari park**, with lions, tigers, giraffes and rhinos on show, plus monkeys clambering all over your car. Other attractions followed, including boat trips on a lake full of sea lions, a large hedge maze, various exhibitions, and high-tech simulators. Beyond the razzmatazz, there's an exquisitely furnished Elizabethan **house**, with an enormous library and a fine collection of pictures, including Titian's *Holy Family*.

Avebury

The village of **AVEBURY** stands in the midst of a **stone circle** (daily 24hr; free) that rivals Stonehenge – the individual stones are generally smaller, but the circle itself is much wider and more complex. A massive earthwork 20ft high and 1400ft across encloses the main circle, which is approached by four causeways across the inner ditch, two of them leading into wide avenues stretching over a mile beyond the circle. It was probably built soon after 2500 BC, and presumably had a similar ritual or religious function to Stonehenge. The structure of Avebury's diffuse circle is quite difficult to grasp, but there are plans on the site, and the **Alexander Keiller Museum** provides further details and background. Further prehistoric sites can be seen at nearby **Silbury Hill** and **West Kennet Long Barrow**, making the sixteenth-century **Avebury Manor** seem youthful in comparison.

Alexander Keiller Museum

SN8 1RF • Daily 10am–6pm • £4.40; NT • ☎ 01672 539250, ⓦ nationaltrust.org.uk/avebury

The nearby **Alexander Keiller Museum** provides an excellent overview of the Avebury stones and their significance, plus information about the role of Keiller himself. A Scottish archeologist and heir to a marmalade fortune, Keiller was responsible for restoring the stones and excavating the surrounding site. The museum is housed in two separate buildings: the **Stables Gallery** houses some of Keiller's original finds, while the seventeenth-century **Barn Gallery** has exhibits on local archeology, interactive displays plus activities for children.

Avebury Manor

SN8 1RF • Daily 11am–5pm • Manor and gardens £10, Manor only £7.20; NT • ☎ 01672 539250, ⊕ nationaltrust.org.uk/avebury

Built on the site of a former priory, the pretty sixteenth-century **Avebury Manor** was refurbished in 2011. Little of the house's original decoration remained, and almost all the furnishings here have been re-created in Tudor, Queen Anne, Georgian or Victorian style. As you wander round the **house**, you can lie on the beds, sit on the sofas and even play billiards in the Billiards Room. The **gardens** have been replanted too, with topiary and walled gardens, and there's a vintage-style tearoom in the former West Library.

Silbury Hill and West Kennet Long Barrow

Just outside Avebury, the neat green mound of **Silbury Hill** is disregarded by the majority of drivers whizzing by on the A4. At 130ft it's no great height, but when you realize that it's the largest prehistoric artificial mound in Europe, and was made using nothing more than primitive spades, it commands more respect. It was probably constructed around 2600 BC, and though no one knows quite what it was for, the likelihood is that it was a burial mound. You can't actually walk on the hill – having admired it briefly from the car park, cross the road to the footpath that leads half a mile to the **West Kennet Long Barrow** (daily 24hr; free; NT & EH). Dating from about 3250 BC, this was definitely a chamber tomb – nearly fifty burials have been discovered here.

ACCOMMODATION AND EATING   AVEBURY

Cirdes Café Next to the Barn Gallery, SN8 1RF ☎ 01672 539250. This National Trust café is your best bet for an inexpensive lunch, offering good meals and snacks, with plenty of veggie options and, of course, tasty cakes and cream teas. There's indoor seating in a converted farm building, plus outdoor tables in the courtyard. Daily 10am–5.30pm.

The Lodge High St, SN8 1RF ☎ 01672 539023, ⊕ aveburylodge.co.uk. An attractive Georgian and vegetarian B&B with just two rooms, one en suite, but both comfortable and overlooking the Stone Circles. Breakfast is served in a grand dining room filled with antiques. Free parking for guests. **£195**

Lacock

LACOCK, twelve miles west of Avebury, is the perfect English feudal village, albeit one gentrified by the National Trust and besieged by tourists all summer, partly due to its fame as a location for several films and TV series – the later *Harry Potter* films and the BBC's *Wolf Hall*, among others. The village's most famous son is photography pioneer **Henry Fox Talbot**, a member of the dynasty that has lived in the local abbey since it passed to Sir William Sharington on the Dissolution of the Monasteries in 1539. The opulent tomb of Sir William Sharington, buried beneath a splendid barrel-vaulted roof, can be seen in the village church of **St Cyriac** (daily 24hr; free).

Lacock Abbey and the Fox Talbot Museum

SN15 2LG • Abbey Jan Sat & Sun 11am–5pm, Feb–Dec daily 11am–5pm; museum, cloisters and grounds Feb–Dec daily 10.30am–5.30pm • £12.70; NT • ☎ 01249 73045, ⊕ nationaltrust.org.uk/lacock

William Henry Fox Talbot was the first person to produce a photographic negative, and the **Fox Talbot Museum**, in a sixteenth-century barn by the gates of Lacock Abbey, captures something of the excitement he must have experienced as the dim outline of an oriel window in the abbey imprinted itself on a piece of silver nitrate paper. The museum also houses the Fenton Collection, featuring photographs and cameras from the birth of photography to the 1980s, which was donated by the British Film Institute. The **abbey** itself boasts a medieval cloister and a few monastic fragments amid the eighteenth-century Gothic.

ARRIVAL AND DEPARTURE   LACOCK

The #X34 **bus** runs hourly from Chippenham and Frome, stopping outside the *George Inn* (🌐 faresaver.co.uk).

ACCOMMODATION AND EATING

Beechfield House Hotel Beanacre, SN12 7PU, 2 miles south of Lacock ☎ 01225 703700, 🌐 beechfieldhouse .co.uk. This lovely country-house hotel has comfortable rooms, an excellent restaurant and a heated outdoor pool, all set in attractive grounds. It has family rooms and the service is friendly but professional. £125

George Inn 4 West St, SN15 2LH ☎ 01249 730263 🌐 georgeinnlacock.co.uk. A rambling, partly fourteenth-century pub with roaring fires and a dog-wheel (the dog powered the wheel to turn a spit over the fire). Good for

a drink, with a variety of guest ales, plus decent pub food, such as fish of the day with chips (£13). Mon–Fri 11am–3pm & 6–11pm, Sat 11am–11pm, Sun 11am–10.30pm; kitchen Mon–Sat noon–2.30pm & 6–9pm, Sun noon–2.30pm & 6–8pm.

Lacock Pottery The Tanyard, Church St, SN15 2LB ☎ 01249 730266, 🌐 lacockbedandbreakfast.com. Three comfortable B&B rooms in a lovely old building overlooking the church and the village. Breakfasts are good, featuring home-made bread and jams. Weekdays £90, weekends £100

Bradford-on-Avon

With its buildings of auburn stone and lovely river- and canalside walks, **BRADFORD-ON-AVON** is the most appealing town in Wiltshire's northwest corner. Sheltering against a steep wooded slope, it takes its name from its "broad ford" across the Avon, though the original fording place was replaced by a **bridge** dating mainly from the seventeenth century. The domed structure at one end is a quaint old jail converted from a chapel.

The local industry, based on textiles, was revolutionized with the arrival of Flemish weavers in 1659, and many of the town's handsome buildings reflect the prosperity of this period. Yet Bradford's most significant building is the tiny **Church of St Laurence** (April–Sept 10am–6pm; Oct–March 10am–4pm) on Church Street, an outstanding example of Saxon church architecture dating from 700 AD. Its distinctive feature is the carved angels over the chancel arch.

ARRIVAL AND INFORMATION   BRADFORD-ON-AVON

By train The station is on St Margaret's St, close to the town centre.
Destinations Bath (2 hourly; 15min); Bristol (2 hourly; 35min); Dorchester (every 2hr; 1hr 30min); Salisbury (hourly; 45min).

Tourist office 50 St Margaret's St (April–Oct Mon–Sat 10am–5pm, Sun 10am–4pm; Nov–March Mon–Sat 10am–4pm, Sun 11am–3pm; ☎ 01225 865797, 🌐 bradfordonavon .co.uk).

ACCOMMODATION AND EATING

Bradford Old Windmill 4 Mason's Lane, BA15 1QN ☎ 01225 866842, 🌐 bradfordoldwindmill.co.uk. An unusual B&B based in a converted windmill, with a variety of quirky rooms, including one in the former grinding room. £100

Lock Inn Café Frome Rd, BA15 1LE ☎ 01225 868068, 🌐 thelockinn.co.uk. This rambling café by the canal is the best place for an inexpensive meal at any time of the day, with interesting dishes such as feta fritters and cajun chicken (most mains around £9) which you can eat in one of a series of Wendy houses or inside a moored canal boat.

They also rent bikes and canoes. Mon & Sun 8.30am–5.30pm, Tues–Sat 8.30am–9pm.

Timbrell's Yard 49 St Margaret's Street, BA15 1DE ☎ 01225 869494, 🌐 timbrellsyard.com. The rooms here are very individually designed (and sized), combining rustic and contemporary flair, with lots of stripped beams and original fittings. The rooms are above a hip restaurant and café-bar, run by ex-*River Cottage* chef Tom Blake, serving dishes such as grilled mackerel with romesco sauce (£15.50), or Cornish hake with Dorset clams (£19.50). Daily 8am–9pm. £110

Oxfordshire, the Cotswolds and around

BIBURY

Oxfordshire, the Cotswolds and around

About sixty miles northwest of London, the small university city of Oxford is one of England's great urban set pieces, presenting as impressive a collection of Gothic, classical and Revival architecture as anywhere in Europe. Oxford anchors a diverse swathe of terrain that reaches across central southern England, straddling the Chiltern Hills, a picturesque band of chalk uplands on the fringes of the capital. Close to the orbital M25 motorway, this is commuter country, but further out a rural spirit survives from England's pre-industrial past, felt most tangibly in the Cotswolds, rolling hills between Oxford and Cheltenham that encompass some of the country's most celebrated landscapes and photogenic villages.

Covering much of **Oxfordshire** and **Gloucestershire**, the picture-postcard **Cotswolds** region sports old churches and handsome stone mansions, with scenic drives galore and plenty of walking opportunities, not least on the long-distance Cotswolds Way. Highlights include the engaging market town of **Chipping Campden**, the delightful village of Northleach and bustling **Cirencester**. Within striking distance of Oxford are handsome Woodstock, a little town that lies alongside one of England's most imposing country homes, Blenheim Palace, and further south, Henley-on-Thames, an attractive spot on the river famous for its regatta. To the west lies **Cheltenham**, an appealing Regency spa town famous for its horse-racing, that serves as a base for visits to **Gloucester** and its magnificent cathedral.

Striking west from the Chilterns across the North Wessex Downs is the 85-mile-long Ridgeway, a prehistoric track – and now a national trail possessing a string of prehistoric sites, the most extraordinary being the gigantic chalk horse that gives the Vale of White Horse its name. Bordering south Oxfordshire, **Berkshire** has the royal residence of **Windsor Castle** as its focus, but can also offer a fine gallery in the Thames-side village of Cookham. Arching round to the north of London are the counties of **Buckinghamshire** and **Bedfordshire** ("Bucks and Beds"), which have lower-key attractions, including a museum of World War II code-breakers at Bletchley, on a looping route to the ancient town of **St Albans**.

GETTING AROUND   OXFORDSHIRE, THE COTSWOLDS AND AROUND

By train Mainline services from London Paddington serve Reading, Oxford, Cheltenham and Gloucester, also stopping midway at Cotswolds villages including Kingham (near Stow-on-the-Wold), Moreton-in-Marsh (between Stow and Chipping Campden) and Kemble (near Cirencester). There are also fast trains from London Marylebone, Birmingham, Reading and Southampton to Oxford, and from Birmingham and Bristol to Cheltenham.

By bus Long-distance buses stick mostly to the motorways, providing an efficient service to all the larger towns,

Highlights

❶ **Oxford** One of Britain's most captivating cities, with dozens of historic colleges, memorable museums and an enjoyably lively undergraduate atmosphere. **See p.239**

❷ **Chipping Campden** Perfectly preserved medieval wool town, with honey-coloured houses lining its historic main street. **See p.263**

❸ **Cirencester** Self-styled "Capital of the Cotswolds", with a bustling marketplace overlooked by the superb Gothic church of St John the Baptist. **See p.267**

❹ **Festivals in Cheltenham** Cheltenham's three-day National Hunt Festival is one of the highlights of the British racing calendar, while the town also boasts lively festivals dedicated to folk, jazz, classical music, literature and science. **See p.271**

❺ **Gloucester Cathedral** The earliest – and one of the finest – examples of English Perpendicular architecture, topped by a magnificent tower. **See p.274**

❻ **Windsor Castle** The oldest and largest inhabited castle in the world – still an important ceremonial residence of the Queen – in the Berkshire countryside outside London. **See p.276**

HIGHLIGHTS ARE MARKED ON THE MAP ON P.238

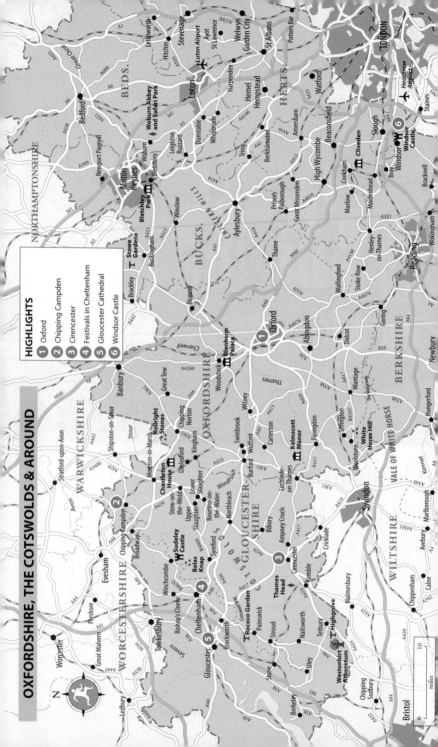

OXFORDSHIRE, THE COTSWOLDS & AROUND

HIGHLIGHTS

1. Oxford
2. Chipping Campden
3. Cirencester
4. Festivals in Cheltenham
5. Gloucester Cathedral
6. Windsor Castle

but local services between the villages are patchy, or sometimes nonexistent.

By car The Cotswolds are enclosed by the M5, M4 and M40, which, along with the M1 and A1(M) to the east, provide easy access.

Oxford

When visitors think of **OXFORD**, they almost always imagine its **university**, revered as one of the world's great academic institutions, inhabiting honey-coloured stone buildings set around ivy-clad quadrangles. The image is accurate enough, but although the university dominates central Oxford both physically and spiritually, the wider city has an entirely different character, its economy built chiefly on the **factories** of Cowley, south of the centre. It was here that Britain's first mass-produced cars were made in the 1920s and, although there have been more downs than ups in recent years, the plants are still vitally important to the area.

Oxford should be high on anyone's itinerary, and can keep you occupied for several days. The **colleges** include some of England's finest architecture, and the city also has some excellent **museums** and a good range of bars and restaurants.

Christ Church College

St Aldates, OX1 1DP • Mon–Sat 10am–5pm, Sun 2–5pm; last entry 4.15pm • July & Aug £9, rest of year £7–8; discounts apply if you visit at times when the hall and/or cathedral are closed • ☎ 01865 276492, ☯ www.chch.ox.ac.uk

Stretching along the east side of St Aldates is the main facade of **Christ Church College**, whose distinctive Tom Tower was added by Christopher Wren in 1681 to house the

4

OXFORD'S COLLEGES

So where, exactly, is **Oxford University**? Everywhere – and nowhere. The university itself is nothing more than an administrative body, setting examinations and awarding degrees. Although it has its own offices (on Wellington Square), they are of no particular interest. What draws all the attention are the university's constituent **colleges** – 38 of them (plus another six religious foundations known as Permanent Private Halls), most occupying historic buildings scattered throughout the city centre. It is these that hold the 800-year-old history of the university, and exemplify its spirit.

The origins of the university are obscure, but it seems that the reputation of **Henry I**, the so-called "Scholar King", helped attract students in the early twelfth century. The first **colleges**, founded mostly by rich bishops, were essentially ecclesiastical institutions and this was reflected in collegiate rules and regulations – until 1877 lecturers were not allowed to marry, and women were not granted degrees until 1920.

There are common **architectural features** among the colleges, with the students' rooms and most of the communal areas – chapels, halls (dining rooms) and libraries – arranged around quadrangles (**quads**). Each, however, has its own character and often a label, whether it's the richest (St John's), most left-wing (Wadham) or most public-school-dominated (Christ Church). Collegiate rivalries are long established, usually revolving around sports, and tension between the city and the university – "Town" and "Gown" – has existed as long as the university itself.

EXPLORING THE COLLEGES

All the more popular colleges have restricted **opening hours** – and may close totally during academic functions. Most now also impose an **admission charge**, while some (such as University and Queens) are out of bounds to outsiders. Regardless of published rules, it's always worth asking at the **porter's lodge**, at the main entrance of each college: porters have ultimate discretion and if you ask they may let you look around. One nice way to gain access is to attend choral evensong, held during term time and offering the chance to enjoy superb music in historic surroundings for free. New College choir is generally reckoned to be the best, but Queen's College and Merton are also good. Some colleges also **rent out student rooms** in the holidays (see p.248).

London (A40/M40) ▲ ▲ 7 (350yd) & 8 (850yd)

100
0   yards

OXFORD

River Cherwell

St Catherine's College

Nelson's Walk

MANOR ROAD

Magdalen Grove

Magdalen College

MAGDALEN BRIDGE

Punts

HIGH STREET

Botanic Gardens

LONGWALL STREET

ROSE LANE

JOWETT WALK

MANSFIELD ROAD

SAVILE ROAD

New College

HOLYWELL STREET

QUEEN'S LANE

Holywell Music Room

Sheldonian Theatre

Clarendon Building

Bridge of Sighs

CATTE STREET

NEW COLLEGE LANE

University College

Queen's College

LOGIC LANE

MERTON STREET

Merton College

Wadham College

History of Science Museum

Radcliffe Camera

All Souls College

HIGH STREET

MAGPIE LANE

Cathedral

PARKS ROAD

SOUTH PARKS ROAD

MUSEUM ROAD

Trinity College

Bodleian Library

RADCLIFFE SQUARE

BRASENOSE LANE

St Mary the Virgin

ORIEL SQUARE

Christ Church Picture Gallery

Christ Church Meadow

St John's College

Exeter College

TURL STREET

Brasenose College

BEAR LANE

ALFRED ST

Christ Church College

War Memorial Garden

Balliol College

BROAD STREET

MARKET STREET

Covered Market

SHIP STREET

CARFAX

BLUE BOAR STREET

ST ALDATES

Broad Walk

ST GILES

MAGDALEN STREET

St Michael-at-the-Northgate

ST MICHAEL'S STREET

Oxford Union

CORNMARKET STREET

Town Hall & Museum of Oxford

Modern Art Oxford

SPEEDWELL STREET

The Ashmolean

Odeon

Oxford Playhouse

New Theatre

NEW INN HALL STREET

Carfax Tower

QUEEN ST

PEMBROKE STREET

BREWER STREET

ROSE PLACE

PUSEY STREET

BEAUMONT STREET

GLOUCESTER STREET

Bikezone

Odeon

GEORGE STREET

Westgate Shopping Centre & Central Library

ST EBBE'S STREET

PUSEY LANE

ST JOHN'S STREET

Gloucester Green Bus Station

NEW ROAD

CASTLE STREET

WELLINGTON SQUARE

WALTON STREET

WORCESTER ST

Oxford Castle

NORFOLK STREET

PARADISE STREET

P

P

Worcester College

Worcester College Lake

Oxford Canal

Castle Mill Stream

NEW ROAD

PARK END STREET

ST THOMAS' STREET

OXPENS ROAD

Ice Rink

RICHMOND ROAD

WALTON CRESCENT

N

HYTHE BRIDGE STREET

7

9

8

Said Business School

FRIDESWIDE SQUARE

BOTLEY ROAD

HOLLYBUSH ROW

BECKET STREET

Train Station

Farmoor & Vale of White Horse

Farringdon & Vale of White Horse

Abingdon, Police Station & River Thames

● EATING
Ben's Cookies	10
Branca	1
Chiang Mai Kitchen	11
Edamame	4
Gee's	3
Missing Bean	9
News Café	6
Pieminister	8
Pierre Victoire	2
Turl Street Kitchen	5
Vaults & Garden	7

● SHOPPING
Albion Beatnik Bookstore	1
Alice's Shop	6
Antiques on High	5
Blackwell	2
Gloucester Green markets	3
Oxford Cheese Company	4

■ DRINKING AND NIGHTLIFE
The Bear	6
The Bullingdon	8
Café Tarifa	7
Eagle & Child	2
Lamb & Flag	3
Raoul's	1
Turf Tavern	4
Wheatsheaf	5

■ ACCOMMODATION
Bath Place	4
Buttery	5
Central Backpackers	9
Malmaison	11
Old Bank	10
Old Parsonage	1
Oxford Backpackers	7
The Randolph	3
Richmond	2
Tower House	6
YHA Oxford	8

weighty "Great Tom" bell. The tower lords it over the main entrance of what is Oxford's largest and arguably most prestigious college, but visitors have to enter from the south, a signed five-minute walk away – just beyond the tiny War Memorial Garden and at the top of Christ Church Meadow. Don't be surprised if you have to queue to get in. This is the most touristy of all the Oxford Colleges, particularly popular thanks to its Harry Potter connections: many scenes from the films were shot here, while a studio recreation of the college's hall provided the set of Hogwarts' Great Hall.

From the entrance it's a few steps to the striking **Tom Quad**, the largest quad in Oxford – so large in fact that the Royalists penned up their mobile larder of cattle here during the Civil War. Guarded by Tom Tower, the quad's soft, honey-coloured stone makes a harmonious whole, but it was actually built in two main phases, with the southern side dating back to Wolsey, and the north finally finished in the 1660s. A wide stone staircase in the southeast corner beneath a stupendous fan-vaulted ceiling leads up to the **Hall**, the grandest refectory in Oxford, with its fanciful hammer-beam roof and a set of stern portraits of past scholars by a roll call of famous artists, including Reynolds, Gainsborough and Millais. As well as Albert Einstein, William Gladstone and no fewer than twelve other British prime ministers were educated here.

Oxford Cathedral

Christ Church's college chapel is otherwise known as **Oxford Cathedral**. The Anglo-Saxons built a church on this site in the seventh century as part of the priory of St Frideswide (Oxford's patron saint), although the present building dates mainly from 1120–80. The priory was suppressed in 1524, but the church survived. It's unusually discordant, with all sorts of bits and bobs from different periods, but fascinating all the same. The dominant features are the sturdy circular columns and rounded arches of the Normans, but there are also early Gothic pointed arches, and the chancel ceiling is a particularly fine example of fifteenth-century stone vaulting.

Christ Church Picture Gallery

June Mon & Wed–Sat 10.30am–5pm, Sun 2–5pm; July–Sept Mon–Sat 10.30am–5pm, Sun 2–5pm; Oct–May Mon & Wed–Sat 10.30am–1pm & 2–4.30pm, Sun 2–4.30pm • £4, or £2 with a Christ Church admission ticket • **Tours** Mon 2.30pm • Free with admission • ☎ 01865 276172, ⓦ www.chch.ox.ac.uk/gallery

Hidden away in Christ Church's pocket-sized Canterbury Quad is the college's **Picture Gallery**. The extensive collection comprises around three hundred paintings and two thousand drawings, with fine works by artists from Italy and the Netherlands including paintings by Tintoretto, Van Dyck and Frans Hals and drawings by da Vinci, Dürer, Raphael and Michelangelo.

Christ Church Meadow

Christ Church Meadow fills in the tapering gap between the rivers Cherwell and Thames. If you decide to delay visiting Christ Church College, you can take a stroll east along Broad Walk for the Cherwell, or keep going straight down tree-lined (and more appealing) New Walk for the Thames.

Merton College

Merton St, OX1 4JD • Mon–Fri 2–5pm, Sat & Sun 10am–5pm • £3 • ☎ 01865 276310, ⓦ www.merton.ox.ac.uk

Merton College is historically the city's most important. Balliol and University colleges may have been founded earlier, but it was Merton – opened in 1264 – which set the model for colleges in both Oxford and Cambridge, being the first to gather its students and tutors together in one place. Furthermore, unlike the other two, Merton retains some of its original medieval buildings, with the best of the thirteenth-century architecture clustered around **Mob Quad**, a charming courtyard with mullioned windows and Gothic doorways to the right of the Front Quad. From the Mob Quad, an archway leads through to the

Chapel, dating from 1290, inside which you'll find the funerary plaque of Thomas Bodley, founder of Oxford's famous Bodleian Library (see opposite).

Magdalen College

High St, OX1 4AU • Daily: July & Aug 10am–7pm; Sept noon–7pm; Oct–June 1–6pm or dusk • £6 • ☎ 01865 276000, ⓦ www.magd.ox.ac.uk

At the east end of the High Street stands **Magdalen College** (pronounced "maudlin"), whose gaggle of stone buildings is overshadowed by its chunky medieval bell tower. Steer right from the entrance and you reach the **chapel**, which has a handsome reredos, though you have to admire it through the windows of an ungainly stone screen. The adjacent **cloisters** are adorned by standing figures, some biblical and others folkloric, most notably a tribe of grotesques. Magdalen also boasts better **grounds** than most other colleges, with a bridge – at the back of the cloisters – spanning the River Cherwell to join **Addison's Walk**. You can hire punts from beneath **Magdalen Bridge**, beside the college.

Botanic Garden

Rose Lane, OX1 4AZ • March, April, Sept & Oct Mon noon–5pm, Tues–Sun 9am–5pm; May Mon noon–6pm, Tues–Sun 9am–6pm; June–Aug daily 9am–6pm; Nov–Feb Mon noon–4pm, Tues–Sun 9am–4pm • £5 • ⓦ www.botanic-garden.ox.ac.uk

Bounded by a curve of the River Cherwell, Oxford's **Botanic Garden** is the oldest of its kind in England, established in 1621. Still enclosed by its original high wall, it comprises several different zones, from a lily pond, a bog garden and a rock garden through to borders of bearded irises and variegated plants. There are also six large **glasshouses** containing tropical and carnivorous species.

New College

New College Lane, OX1 3BN • Daily: Easter–Oct 11am–5pm, rest of year 2–4pm • Easter–Oct £4, rest of year free • ☎ 01865 279555, ⓦ new.ox.ac.uk

Founded in 1379, **New College** is entered via the large but rather plain **Front Quad**. On the left side of the quad rises the magnificent Perpendicular **chapel**, arguably the finest in Oxford. The ante-chapel contains some superb fourteenth-century stained glass and the west window – of 1778 – holds an intriguing Nativity scene based on a design by Sir Joshua Reynolds. Beneath it stands the wonderful 1951 sculpture *Lazarus* by Jacob Epstein. Immediately past the chapel lies the college's peaceful **cloisters**.

TAKING TO THE WATER

Punting is a favourite summer pastime among both students and visitors, but handling a punt – a flat-bottomed boat ideal for the shallow waters of the Thames and Cherwell rivers – requires some practice. The punt is propelled and steered with a long pole, which beginners inevitably get stuck in riverbed mud: if this happens, let go of it and paddle back, or you're likely to be dragged overboard.

There are two central **boat rental** places: Magdalen Bridge Boathouse (☎ 01865 202643, ⓦ oxfordpunting.co.uk), beside the Cherwell at the east end of the High Street; and Salter's Steamers (☎ 01865 243421, ⓦ salterssteamers.co.uk) at Folly Bridge, south of Christ Church. Opening times vary: call for details, or try to arrive early (around 10am) to avoid the queues which build up on sunny summer afternoons. At either, expect to **pay** £20–22 per hour plus a deposit of about £50; ID is required. Punts can take a maximum of five or six people, including the person punting.

Salter's Steamers also runs **passenger boats** downstream along the Thames from Folly Bridge, including to Iffley Lock (April–Oct 7 daily; 40min return; £8). Oxford River Cruises (☎ 01865 987147, ⓦ oxfordrivercruises.com) also run short cruises from Folly Bridge, including upstream as far as Godstow on Port Meadow (April–Oct 2 daily; 2hr 30min; £29).

An archway on the east side of the Front Quad leads through to the modest **Garden Quad**, with the thick flowerbeds of the **College Garden** beckoning beyond. The north side of the garden is flanked by the largest and best-preserved section of Oxford's medieval **city wall**. The conspicuous earthen **mound** in the middle is a later decorative addition, not medieval.

Bridge of Sighs

Spanning **New College Lane** a few paces off Catte Street, you can't miss the iconic **Bridge of Sighs**, an archway completed in 1914 to link two buildings of Hertford College. In truth it bears little resemblance to its Venetian namesake, but nonetheless has a certain Italianate elegance. It was designed, so the story goes, to give residents of Hertford's older buildings to the south a way to reach the newfangled flushing toilets being installed across the road without having to venture outdoors.

New College Lane

Under the Bridge of Sighs, atmospheric, traffic-free **New College Lane**, a favourite cyclists' rat-run, extends east, flanked for the most part by high, medieval stone walls. Squeeze down narrow **St Helen's Passage** – decorously renamed from its original title, Hell's Passage – on the left to reach the famed *Turf Tavern* (see p.250) and the seventeenth-century cottages on Bath Place, insinuated into kinks of the medieval city walls. Just past St Helen's Passage, the modest house on the left, topped by a mini-observatory, was the home of astronomer Edmund Halley (1656–1742), discoverer of the comet that bears his name.

4

Bodleian Library

Broad St, OX1 3BG • Closed to the public; some rooms accessible on tours (see box, p.244) • ☎ 01865 287400, ⓦ www.bodleian.ox.ac.uk

Christopher Wren's pupil Nicholas Hawksmoor designed the **Clarendon Building**, a domineering, solidly symmetrical edifice at the east end of Broad Street, completed in 1713. It now forms part of the **Bodleian Library**. Founded by scholar Sir Thomas Bodley in 1602, the Bodleian is the UK's largest library after the British Library in London, with an estimated 117 miles of shelving. It includes the Modernist 1930s **Weston Library** (formerly known as the **New Bodleian**) directly opposite the Clarendon, designed by Sir Giles Gilbert Scott and linked to the main building by tunnels. As one of the UK and Ireland's six copyright libraries, the Bodleian must find room for a copy of every book, pamphlet, magazine and newspaper published in Britain.

Old Schools Quadrangle

Mon–Fri 9am–5pm, Sat 9am–4.30pm, Sun 11am–5pm • Free

Behind the Clarendon Building you enter the Bodleian's beautifully proportioned **Old Schools Quadrangle**, completed in 1619 in an ornate Jacobean-Gothic style and offering access to all of the university's academic faculties, or schools: the name of each is lettered in gold above the doorways which ring the quad. On the east side rises the handsome **Tower of the Five Orders**, its tiers of columns in ascending order Tuscan, Doric, Ionic, Corinthian and Composite.

The Divinity School

Mon–Sat 9am–5pm, Sun 11am–5pm • £1 • Tours available (see box, p.244)

Entered from the quad, the **Divinity School** is a highlight. Begun in 1424, this exceptional room is a masterpiece of late Gothic architecture, featuring an extravagant vaulted ceiling adorned with a riot of pendants and 455 decorative bosses. Built to house the university's theology faculty, it was, until the nineteenth century, also where degree candidates were questioned about their subject by two interlocutors, with a professor acting as umpire. Few interiors in Oxford are as impressive.

TOURS OF BODLEIAN LIBRARY

An **audioguide** is available for self-guided tours of the Bodleian Library quad and Divinity School (40min; £2.50) – or there's a host of **guided tours** around those few areas of the Bodleian open to the public. It's always advisable to **book in advance** with the tours office (Mon–Sat 9am–4pm, Sun 11am–4pm; ☎01865 287400, ⓦ www.bodleian.ox.ac.uk), located inside the Great Gate on Catte Street.

Mini tour 30min; £6. Divinity School and Duke Humfrey's Library. Mon–Sat 3.30pm, 4pm & 4.40pm, Sun 12.45pm, 2.15pm, 2.45pm, 3.15pm, 4pm & 4.40pm.

Standard tour 1hr; £8. Divinity School, Duke Humfrey's Library and Convocation House. Mon–Sat 10.30am, 11.30am, 1pm & 2pm, Sun 11.30am, 2pm & 3pm.

Extended tour "Upstairs Downstairs" 1hr 30min; £14. Divinity School, Duke Humfrey's Library, Convocation House, Gladstone Link, Radcliffe Camera. Wed & Sat 9.15am.

Extended tour "Reading Rooms" 1hr 30min; £14. Divinity School, Duke Humfrey's Library, Convocation House, Upper Reading Room. Sun 11.15am & 1.15pm.

Duke Humfrey's Library and Convocation House

Only accessible on guided tours (see box above)

Above the Divinity School stands the atmospheric **Duke Humfrey's Library**, in working use as a reading room from its completion in 1487 right through to 2014, when its collections were transferred to the new Weston Library building. The room, extensively added to during the early seventeenth century, is distinguished by its superb beamed ceiling and carved corbels.

Alongside the Divinity School is the **Convocation House**, a sombre wood-panelled chamber where parliament sat during the Civil War, which now sports a fancy fan-vaulted ceiling completed in 1759.

The Sheldonian Theatre

Broad St, OX1 3AZ • Jan & Dec Mon–Sat 10am–3pm; Feb–April & Oct–Nov Mon–Sat 10am–4.30pm; May–Sept daily 10am–4.30pm • £3.50 • ⓦ www.admin.ox.ac.uk/sheldonian

At the east end of Broad Street, the **Sheldonian Theatre** is ringed by railings topped with a line of glum-looking, pop-eyed classical busts. The Sheldonian was Christopher Wren's first major work, a reworking of the Theatre of Marcellus in Rome, semicircular at the back and rectangular at the front. It was conceived in 1663, when the 31-year-old Wren's main job was as professor of astronomy. Designed as a stage for university ceremonies, nowadays it also functions as a concert hall, but the interior lacks much sense of drama, and even the views from the cupola are disappointing.

Museum of the History of Science

Broad St, OX1 3AZ • Tues–Sun noon–5pm • Free • ⓦ www.mhs.ox.ac.uk

The classical heads that shield the Sheldonian Theatre continue along the front of the fascinating **Museum of the History of Science**, whose two floors display an amazing clutter of antique microscopes and astrolabes, sundials, quadrants and sextants. The highlights are Elizabeth I's own astrolabe and a blackboard used by Einstein in 1931, still covered with his scribbled equations.

Trinity College

Broad St, OX1 3BH • Daily 10am–noon & 2–6pm • £3 • ☎01865 279900, ⓦ www.trinity.ox.ac.uk

Trinity College is fronted by three dinky lodge-cottages. Behind them the manicured lawn of the Front Quad stretches back to the richly decorated **chapel**, awash with Baroque stuccowork. Its high altar is flanked by an exquisite example of the work of Grinling Gibbons – a distinctive performance, with cherubs' heads peering out from delicate foliage. Behind the chapel stands **Durham Quad**, an attractive ensemble of old stone buildings begun at the end of the seventeenth century.

Exeter College

Turl St, OX1 3DP • Daily 2–5pm • Free • ☎ 01865 279600, ⓦ www.exeter.ox.ac.uk

In medieval **Exeter College** aim for the elaborate Gothic Revival chapel, conceived by Gilbert Scott in the 1850s. It contains a fine set of **stained-glass windows** illustrating biblical stories – St Paul on the road to Damascus, Samson bringing down the pillars of the Philistine temple – as well as a superb Pre-Raphaelite tapestry, the *Adoration of the Magi*, a collaboration between former students William Morris and Edward Burne-Jones.

The Radcliffe Camera

Radcliffe Sq, OX1 3BG • Closed to the public; accessible only on Bodleian Library's extended tour (see box opposite) • ☎ 01865 287400, ⓦ www.bodleian.ox.ac.uk

The mighty rotunda of the **Radcliffe Camera**, built between 1737 and 1748 by James Gibbs, architect of London's St Martin-in-the-Fields church, displays no false modesty. Dr John Radcliffe, royal physician (to William III), was, according to a contemporary diarist, "very ambitious of glory": when he died in 1714 he bequeathed a mountain of money for the construction of a library. Gibbs was one of the few British architects of the period to have been trained in Rome and his design is thoroughly Italian in style, its limestone columns ascending to a delicate balustrade, which is decorated with pinprick urns and encircles a lead-sheathed dome. Taken over by the Bodleian Library in 1860, it now houses a reading room.

All Souls College

High St, OX1 4AL • Mon–Fri 2–4pm; closed Aug • Free • ☎ 01865 279379, ⓦ www.asc.ox.ac.uk

Running the entire east side of Radcliffe Square, its immense chapel windows the epitome of the Perpendicular Gothic style, **All Souls College** is one of the quietest places in central Oxford – because it has no undergraduates. Uniquely, it admits only "fellows" (that is, distinguished scholars) either by election of existing fellows, or by an exam reputed to be the hardest in the world. The result is that All Souls is generally silent. Sightseers gather at the elaborate gates on Radcliffe Square, wondering how to gain access to the lovely quad beyond: turn right and walk around the corner onto High Street to reach the **college entrance**. This gives onto the modest Front Quad, location of the spectacular fifteenth-century **chapel**, with its gilded hammer-beam roof and neck-cricking reredos (though all its figures are Victorian replacements). Move through to the spacious **North Quad**, the object of all that admiration: Hawksmoor's soaring Gothic twin towers face the Radcliffe Square gates, while ahead, the Codrington Library – also Hawksmoor – sports a conspicuous, brightly decorated sundial designed by Wren.

Church of St Mary the Virgin

High St, OX1 4BJ • Mon–Sat 9am–5pm, Sun noon–5pm (July & Aug until 6pm) • Free; tower £4 • ☎ 01865 279111, ⓦ www.university-church.ox.ac.uk

Mostly dating from the fifteenth century, **St Mary the Virgin** is a hotchpotch of architectural styles. The church's saving graces are its elaborate, thirteenth-century pinnacled spire and its distinctive Baroque **porch**, flanked by chunky corkscrewed pillars. The interior is disappointingly mundane, though the carved poppy heads on the choir stalls are of some historical interest: the tips were brusquely squared off when a platform was installed here in 1555 to stage the heresy trial of Cranmer, Latimer and Ridley, leading Protestants who had run foul of Queen Mary. The church's other diversion is the **tower**, with wonderful views.

FIRST FOR COFFEE

East of St Mary's church, two cafés face each other across the High Street, both claiming to be **England's oldest coffee house**. To the south, the *Grand Café* occupies the site of a coffee house opened by a Lebanese Jew named Jacob in or just after 1650. Opposite, the *Queen's Lane Coffee House* stands where a Syrian Jew named Cirques Jobson launched a competing enterprise at roughly the same time. Whichever was first, Oxford's gentlefolk were drinking coffee – and also hot chocolate – several years ahead of London.

Covered Market

High St, OX1 3DZ • Mon–Sat 8am–5pm, Sun 10am–4pm • ⓦ oxford-coveredmarket.co.uk

For refreshment on the hoof – as well as a fascinating glimpse into the everyday life of Oxford away from the colleges – drop into the **Covered Market**, wedged between the High Street and Market Street. Opened in 1774, it remains full of atmosphere, home to butchers, bakers, fishmongers, greengrocers and cheese sellers as well as cafés, clothes boutiques and shoe shops.

Carfax Tower

Carfax, OX1 1ET • Daily: March 10am–4pm; April–Oct 10am–4.30pm; Nov–Feb 10am–3pm • £3

The busy **Carfax** crossroads is a fulcrum, where chiefly "gown" architecture along the High Street to the east is balanced by the distinctly "town" atmosphere of Cornmarket and Queen Street to the west. This has been a crossroads for more than a thousand years: roads met here in Saxon times, and the name "Carfax" derives from the Latin *quadrifurcus* ("four-forked"). The junction is overlooked by a square thirteenth-century **tower**, adorned by a pair of clocktower jacks. You can **climb** it for wide views over the centre, though other vantage points – principally St Mary's (see p.245) – have the edge.

St Michael-at-the-Northgate

Cornmarket, OX1 3EY • Daily: April–Oct 10.30am–5pm; Nov–March 10.30am–4pm • Free; tower £2.50 • ☎ 01865 240940, ⓦ www.smng.org.uk

North of Carfax is **Cornmarket**, now a busy pedestrianized shopping strip lined with familiar high-street stores. There's precious little here to fire the imagination until you reach **St Michael-at-the-Northgate**, a church recorded in the Domesday Book, with a late fourteenth-century font where Shakespeare's godson was baptized in 1606. The church's Saxon **tower**, built in 1050, is Oxford's oldest surviving building; enter for rooftop views and to see an eleventh-century sheela-na-gig.

Ashmolean Museum

Beaumont St, OX1 2PH • Tues–Sun 10am–5pm • Free • ☎ 01865 278000, ⓦ www.ashmolean.org

Second only to the British Museum in London, the **Ashmolean Museum** occupies a mammoth Neoclassical building on the corner of Beaumont Street and St Giles. It grew from the collections of the magpie-like **John Tradescant**, gardener to Charles I and an energetic traveller, and today it possesses a vast and far-reaching collection covering everything from Minoan vases to Stradivarius violins.

Light and airy modern galleries cover four floors (pick up a **plan** at reception). The "orientation" gallery in the basement provides a thematic overview of the museum, while the ground floor houses the museum's "ancient world" exhibits, including its superb Egyptology collection and an imposing room full of Greek sculptures. Floor 1 is dedicated to Mediterranean, Indian and Islamic artefacts (Hindu bronzes, Iranian pottery and so on) while floor 2 is mainly European, including the museum's wide-ranging collection of Dutch, Flemish and Italian paintings. Floor 3 focuses on European art since 1800, including works by Sickert, Pissarro and the Pre-Raphaelites.

Oxford University Museum of Natural History

Parks Rd, OX1 3PW • Daily 10am–5pm • Free • ☎ 01865 272950, ⓦ www.oum.ox.ac.uk

From the Ashmolean, it's a brief walk north up St Giles to the *Lamb & Flag* pub (see p.250), beside which an alley cuts east through to the **Oxford University Museum of Natural History**. The building, constructed under the guidance of John Ruskin, looks like a cross between a railway station and a church – and the same applies inside, where a High Victorian-Gothic fusion of cast iron and glass features soaring columns and capitals decorated with animal and plant motifs. Exhibits include some impressive dinosaur skeletons, models of exotic beasties, a four-billion-year-old meteorite, and so on.

Pitt Rivers Museum

Parks Rd, OX1 3PP • Mon noon–4.30pm, Tues–Sun 10am–4.30pm; tours (20min) Tues & Wed 2.30pm & 3.15pm; object handling Sat 11am–1pm • Free • ☎ 01865 270927, ⓦ www.prm.ox.ac.uk

Oxford's eye-popping **Pitt Rivers Museum** is housed in the same building as the University Museum of Natural History, accessed via a door at the rear of the ground-floor level. Founded in 1884, this is one of the world's finest ethnographic museums and an extraordinary relic of the Victorian age, arranged like an exotic junk shop with each intricately crammed cabinet labelled meticulously by hand. The exhibits – brought to England by, among others, Captain Cook – range from totem poles and mummified crocodiles to African fetishes and gruesome shrunken heads. Set aside an hour or two to roam the dark corners of this three-storey wonder: look out especially for the brilliant puppets on level 1 and blood-curdling swords and knuckle-dusters on level 2.

Modern Art Oxford

30 Pembroke St, OX1 1BP • Tues–Sat 10am–5pm, Sun noon–5pm • Free • ☎ 01865 722733, ⓦ www.modernartoxford.org.uk

Just south of Carfax, narrow Pembroke Street heads west to the outstanding **Modern Art Oxford** gallery, founded in 1965 and hosting an excellent programme of temporary exhibitions. It's worth stopping by, whatever happens to be showing.

Oxford Castle Unlocked

New Rd, OX1 1AY • Tours daily 10am–5pm, every 20min; last tour starts 4.20pm; 1hr • £10.95; discounted joint tickets with other attractions available, see website • ☎ 01865 260666, ⓦ oxfordcastleunlocked.co.uk

West of Carfax is the site of what was **Oxford Castle**, built in 1071. Only the motte (mound) survives: the buildings atop it were demolished after the Civil War. In later centuries a cluster of stern Victorian edifices beside the mound served chiefly as Oxford's prison, decommissioned in 1996 and now a luxury hotel (see p.249), around which cluster shops, bars and restaurants. To one side, the excellent heritage centre **Oxford Castle Unlocked** offers memorable **guided tours**, during which costumed warders lead you up the Saxon-era **St George's Tower**, show you medieval prison cells and take you down into the Romanesque crypt beneath **St George's Chapel**, telling tales of wars, executions and hauntings along the way.

4

ARRIVAL AND DEPARTURE

OXFORD

By train Oxford station is on the west side of the city centre, a 10min walk along Hythe Bridge St. It's served by direct trains from around the country, including London Paddington and – slightly slower but often cheaper – London Marylebone.

Destinations Bath (2 hourly; 1hr 20min–1hr 40min); Birmingham (2 hourly; 1hr 10min); Bristol (hourly; 1hr 40min); Cheltenham (every 30min; 2hr–2hr 15min); Gloucester (every 30min; 1hr 40min–2hr 20min); London (2–3 hourly; 1hr); Winchester (2 hourly; 1hr 10min–1hr 30min); Worcester (2 hourly; 1hr 15min–1hr 35min).

By bus Most buses are operated by Oxford Bus (☎ 01865 785400, ⓦ oxfordbus.co.uk) and Stagecoach (☎ 01865 772250, ⓦ stagecoachbus.com). Long-distance routes

A WEEKEND IN OXFORD

FRIDAY NIGHT

Toast your weekend with a **champagne cocktail** in the *Randolph's Morse Bar* and a slap-up **dinner** at, say, *Branca* or *Gee's*, sloping off afterwards to *Raoul's* for a nightcap.

SATURDAY

Start the day with a visit to the **Covered Market**, to relax with a coffee while getting a flavour of town life and watch the butchers and fishmongers lay out the new day's wares, then join one of the tourist office's **walking tours**. Grab a bite to eat and devote the afternoon to "gown" life: choose two or three of the **colleges** (such as Christ Church, Merton and New) and pick up the atmosphere of the old city-centre streets (Broad, Merton, Turl) as you go. End the day with a **punt**, before setting off down the **Cowley Road** to sample Oxford's lounge bars and global restaurants, and perhaps find some live music.

SUNDAY

Begin with a lazy brunch in one of **Jericho**'s taverns and cafés – or, if you prefer, a genteel 11.15am "coffee concert" at the Holywell Music Room – before tackling the wonder that is the **Ashmolean Museum**. View ancient weaponry and shamanic artefacts at the **Pitt Rivers Museum** or opt for a country walk in the park behind **Magdalen College** – then hole up at *Pierre Victoire* for fine wines and rich French cooking.

4

terminate at Gloucester Green bus station, in the city centre adjoining George St. Most county buses terminate on Magdalen St, St Giles or St Aldates – the #853 service (Mon–Sat 2–4 daily, Sun daily) covers Burford (45min), Northleach (1hr) and Cheltenham (1hr 30min).
Destinations (from Gloucester Green) London Victoria coach station (Oxford Tube and X90 express coaches daily every 10–30min; 1hr 40min); Heathrow Airport (Airline coach daily every 20–30min; 1hr 30min); Gatwick Airport (Airline coach daily hourly; 2hr).

By car Five big park-and-ride sites (@parkandride.oxfordbus.co.uk) are signposted around the ring road. All offer cheap parking (around £2/day) as well as frequent buses into the centre (usually every 8–15min: Mon–Sat 6am–11pm, Sun 8am–7pm; £2.80 return). Central Oxford is not car-friendly: many streets are pedestrianized and parking is limited. The largest car park is at the Westgate shopping mall, accessed off Thames St (£28 for up to 24hr).

GETTING AROUND

On foot From the rail station to Magdalen Bridge it's roughly a mile and a quarter, and you pass almost everything of interest on the way.
By bike Bainton Bikes at Walton Street Cycles, 78 Walton St (@01865 311610, @baintonbikes.com) rents bikes from £10/day.
By taxi There are taxi ranks at Carfax, Gloucester Green, St Giles and the railway station. Otherwise, call Radio Taxis (@01865 242424, @radiotaxisoxford.co.uk).

INFORMATION AND TOURS

Tourist office 15 Broad Street (July & Aug Mon–Sat 9am–5.30pm, Sun 9.30am–4pm; rest of year Mon–Sat 9.30am–5pm, Sun 10am–3.30pm; @01865 686430, @experienceoxfordshire.org). Staff also sell discounted tickets for a range of nearby attractions, including Blenheim Palace, as well as tickets for coaches to London.
Listings information *Daily Info* (@dailyinfo.co.uk) is the continually updated online version of Oxford's student news sheet. You'll spot the twice-weekly paper version (Tues & Fri) pinned up in colleges and cafés around town.
Guided tours The tourist office offers excellent guided walking tours of the city centre (daily 10.45am & 2pm, plus extra slots if there's sufficient demand; 2hr; £14). Many guides tout for business along Broad St, offering daytime walks and evening ghost tours. A literary walk starts from Carfax Tower (Wed 2pm; 1hr 30min; £15; @oxfordwalkingtours.com).

ACCOMMODATION

As well as the places listed below, another good source of accommodation is the **university**. Outside term time, many colleges let out rooms on a B&B basis at often bargain rates. Expect little or no hotel-style service, but you are free to soak up the college ambience and may score a view over a historic quad. For more information, visit @oxfordrooms.co.uk.

HOTELS

★**Bath Place** 4 Bath Place, OX1 3SU ☎01865 791812, ⓦbathplace.co.uk; map p.240. This unusual hotel is tucked away down an old cobbled courtyard flanked by ancient buildings in an unbeatable central location. The sixteen creaky rooms are each individually decorated in attractive antique style with canopied beds and bare stone walls. **£135**

Malmaison Oxford Castle, 3 New Rd, OX1 1AY ☎01865 268400, ⓦmalmaison.com/locations/oxford; map p.240. Classy designer hotel in what was a Victorian prison, part of the Oxford Castle complex. Rooms – which take up three cells, knocked through – are nothing short of glamorous, featuring contemporary bathrooms and high-tech gadgets. Head through to C wing for bigger, mezzanine suites. **£173**

Old Bank 92 High St, OX1 4BJ ☎01865 799599, ⓦoldbank-hotel.co.uk; map p.240. Great location for a slick hotel in a shiny conversion of an old bank. All 42 bedrooms are decorated in crisp, modern style, some with great views over All Souls College opposite. **£209**

★**Old Parsonage** 1 Banbury Rd, OX2 6NN ☎01865 310210, ⓦoldparsonage-hotel.co.uk; map p.240. This lovely, centrally located hotel occupies a charming, wisteria-clad building from 1660, with 35 tasteful, modern rooms. Free parking, and free walking tours for guests on request. **£195**

The Randolph 1 Beaumont St, OX1 2LN ☎0344 879 9132, ⓦrandolph-hotel.com; map p.240. Oxford's most famous hotel, long the favoured choice of the well-heeled visitor, occupies a neo-Gothic brick building with a distinctive, nineteenth-century interior. It's now part of the Macdonald chain, still with traditional service, well-appointed bedrooms and a distinguished club atmosphere. **£151**

GUESTHOUSES AND B&BS

Buttery 11 Broad St, OX1 3AP ☎01865 811950, ⓦthebutteryhotel.co.uk; map p.240. This friendly sixteen-room guesthouse/hotel has a slap-bang central location, and modest rooms, plain but decent. Choose a back room to avoid the noise of carousing students. **£125**

Richmond 25 Walton Crescent, OX1 2JG ☎01865 311777, ⓦthe-richmond-oxford.co.uk; map p.240. Quiet B&B attached to the excellent *Al-Shami* Lebanese restaurant. Rooms are simple but prices are low – and you can opt for a delicious Lebanese breakfast (hummus, olives, white cheese, pitta bread etc). **£85**

★**Tower House** 15 Ship St, OX1 3DA ☎01865 246828, ⓦtowerhouseoxford.co.uk; map p.240. Lovely guesthouse in a 300-year-old building overlooking Jesus College. The eight double rooms (five en suite) sport fresh, modern decor. Breakfast is at the affiliated *Turl Street Kitchen* (see p.250) next door. Profits support local charities. **£115**

HOSTELS

Central Backpackers 13 Park End St, OX1 1HH ☎01865 242288, ⓦcentralbackpackers.co.uk; map p.240. Independent hostel with fifty beds (including female-only dorms), 24-hour access and a friendly attitude. On a busy street: expect noise from nearby bars. Dorms **£22**

Oxford Backpackers 9a Hythe Bridge St, OX1 2EW ☎01865 721761, ⓦhostels.co.uk; map p.240. Independent hostel with 120 beds in bright, modern dorms (including female-only) and 24-hour access – but just a touch scruffy. Dorms **£15**

YHA Oxford 2a Botley Rd, OX2 0AB ☎0345 371 9131, ⓦyha.org.uk/hostel/oxford; map p.240. Located in a modern block behind the train station, this popular YHA hostel has 187 beds in four- and six-bedded dorms, plus nine doubles, some en suite. There's 24-hour access, with good facilities and a decent café. Dorms **£18**, doubles **£49**

EATING

With so many students and tourists, Oxford has a wide choice of places to eat. Lunchtimes tend to be very busy, though there's no shortage of options. The **restaurant** scene ranges from fine dining to more affordable outlets offering seasonal cooking. The best choice lies on the edge of the centre, along Walton Street and Little Clarendon Street in easygoing Jericho, or southeast on the grungier Cowley Road, buzzing with after-work lounge bars.

CAFÉS

★**Ben's Cookies** 108 Covered Market, OX1 3DZ ☎01865 247407, ⓦbenscookies.com; map p.240. This hole in the wall – the first outlet in a now-global chain – has been churning out the best cookies in Oxford, perhaps England (and some say the world) since 1984, from ginger to peanut butter to triple chocolate chunk. Mon–Sat 9.15am–5.30pm, Sun 10am–4pm.

Missing Bean 14 Turl St, OX1 3DQ ☎01865 794886, ⓦwww.themissingbean.co.uk; map p.240. Plate-glass windows look out onto this pleasant old street, as conversation swirls and Oxford's finest coffee – or so they say – goes down. Mon–Fri 8am–6pm, Sat 9am–

6.30pm, Sun 10am–5.30pm.

News Café 1 Ship St, OX1 3DA ☎01865 242317; map p.240. Breakfasts, bagels and daily specials, plus beer and wine, in this brisk and efficient café. Plenty of local and international newspapers are on hand too. Mon–Thurs & Sun 9am–5pm, Fri & Sat 9am–6pm.

★**Vaults & Garden** Radcliffe Sq, OX1 4AH ☎01865 279112, ⓦthevaultsandgarden.com; map p.240. Occupying atmospheric stone-vaulted chambers attached to St Mary's church, this always-busy café serves up good-quality organic, locally sourced wholefood, as well as coffee and cake. A small outside terrace gazes up at the Radcliffe Camera. Cash only. Daily 8am–6pm.

4

RESTAURANTS

Branca 111 Walton St, OX2 6AJ ☎01865 556111, ⓦ branca.co.uk; map p.240. Large, buzzy bar-brasserie dishing up well-prepared Italian food, from simple pastas, pizzas and risottos through to more elaborate meat and fish mains (£11–18). Mon–Wed & Sun 10am–10pm, Thurs–Sat 10am–10.30pm.

Chiang Mai Kitchen 130a High St, OX1 4DH ☎01865 202233, ⓦ chiangmaikitchen.co.uk; map p.240. An authentically spicy blast of Thai cooking in a homely little timber-framed medieval building tucked down an alleyway off the High St. All the traditional classics are done well, and there's a good vegetarian selection. Mains around £8–10. Mon–Sat noon–10.30pm, Sun noon–10pm.

★**Edamame** 15 Holywell St, OX1 3SA ☎01865 246916, ⓦ edamame.co.uk; map p.240. Voted one of the best Japanese restaurants in Britain, this tiny canteen-style place enjoys a flawless reputation. No bookings are taken, so you may have to queue (and then share a table). Tuck into ramen noodles with pork, chicken or tofu, for instance, or salmon teriyaki. There's plenty for vegetarians. Thurs is sushi night. Mains £6–11; cards not accepted at lunchtime. Wed 11.30am–2.30pm, Thurs–Sat 11.30am–2.30pm & 5–8.30pm, Sun noon–3.30pm.

Gee's 61 Banbury Rd, OX2 6PE ☎01865 553540, ⓦ gees-restaurant.co.uk; map p.240. Formal restaurant occupying chic Victorian conservatory premises. The inventive menu takes in British seasonal dishes such as asparagus and locally reared spring lamb, alongside steaks, fish dishes and more continental cuisine – crab linguine,

bouillabaisse, burrata. Mains £15–26; two-course express menu (Mon–Fri noon–6pm) £13.50. Book ahead. Daily 10am–10.30pm.

Pieminister 56 Covered Market, OX1 3DX ☎01865 241613, ⓦ pieminister.co.uk; map p.240. Your nose will lead you to this pie shop inside the Covered Market. The wide choice includes deerstalker pie (venison and red wine), moo pie (beef and ale), heidi pie (goats' cheese and spinach), and so on, all accompanied by mashed potato, gravy and minty peas, for just £7.50. Gluten-free options, too. Mon–Sat 10am–5pm, Sun 11am–4pm.

Pierre Victoire 9 Little Clarendon St, OX1 2HP ☎01865 316616, ⓦ pierrevictoire.co.uk; map p.240. Much-loved French bistro in a buzzy little Jericho street behind St Giles. The two-course lunch menu (Mon–Sat only) is a steal: £11.50 for great cooking – trout fillet, coq au vin, stuffed peppers – warm service and pleasant ambience. Or go for the dinner menu of steak frites, mussels, duck breast or calves' liver (mains £12–19). Two-course pre-theatre menu £12.50 (6–7pm; not Sat). Mon–Sat noon–2.30pm & 6–11pm, Sun noon–10pm.

★**Turl Street Kitchen** 16 Turl St, OX1 3DH ☎01865 264171, ⓦ turlstreetkitchen.co.uk; map p.240. Much-loved hideaway on a charming backstreet, one of Oxford's top spots for a quiet battery-recharge over coffee and cake. Food is seasonal and hearty – parsnip soup, braised free-range chicken with chickpeas, fennel and wild garlic gratin – served in a cosy setting of sofas and grained wood. Mains £8–15. All profits support local charities. Mon–Thurs & Sun 8am–midnight, Fri & Sat 8am–1am.

DRINKING AND NIGHTLIFE

PUBS AND BARS

The Bear 6 Alfred St, OX1 4EH ☎01865 728164, ⓦ bearoxford.co.uk; map p.240. Tucked away down a narrow side street, this tiny old pub (the oldest in Oxford, founded roughly 800 years ago) offers a wide range of beers and quirkily traditional decor, which includes a collection of ties. Mon–Thurs 11am–11pm, Fri & Sat 11am–midnight, Sun 11.30am–10.30pm.

Café Tarifa 56 Cowley Rd, OX4 1JB ☎01865 256091, ⓦ cafe-tarifa.co.uk; map p.240. Atmospheric lounge bar decked out in Arabian style, with cocktails and cushions, also hosting a variety of generally chilled live music and DJ nights and cult movie screenings. Mon–Thurs 10am–midnight, Fri 10am–12.30am, Sat 10am–1am, Sun 10am–11pm.

Eagle & Child 49 St Giles, OX1 3LU ☎01865 302925, ⓦ nicholsonspubs.co.uk; map p.240. Dubbed the "Bird & Baby", this was once the haunt of J.R.R. Tolkien and C.S. Lewis. The beer is still good and the old wood-panelled rooms at the front are great, but the pub is no longer independently owned – and feels a bit corporate. Mon–Sat 11am–11pm, Sun noon–11pm.

★**Lamb & Flag** 12 St Giles, OX1 3JS ☎01865 515787;

map p.240. Generations of university types have relished this quiet old tavern, owned by St John's College, which comes with low-beamed ceilings and cramped but cosy rooms in which to enjoy hand-drawn ale and genuine pork scratchings. Cash only. Mon–Sat noon–11pm, Sun noon–10.30pm.

Raoul's 32 Walton St, OX2 6AA ☎01865 553732, ⓦ raoulsbar.com; map p.240. Famed Jericho cocktail bar, with a retro Seventies theme, great tunes and a devoted clientele. Navigate the mammoth menu of cocktails to choose a fave or three. Mon, Tues & Sun 4pm–midnight, Wed–Sat 4pm–1am.

★**Turf Tavern** 4 Bath Place, OX1 3SU ☎01865 243235, ⓦ turftavern-oxford.co.uk; map p.240. Small, atmospheric medieval pub, reached via a narrow passageway off Holywell St, with a fine range of beers, and mulled wine in winter. Daily 11am–11pm.

CLUBS AND LIVE MUSIC

The Bullingdon 162 Cowley Rd, OX4 1UE ☎01865 434998, ⓦ thebullingdon.co.uk; map p.240. Popular East Oxford venue for comedy, live music and DJ nights, from punk to grime. The cheap drinks for students pull in a predictable crowd, but the atmosphere rarely disappoints. Mon–Thurs & Sun noon–1am, Fri & Sat noon–3am. **Wheatsheaf** 129 High St, OX1 4DF ☎01865 721156, ⓦfacebook.com/wheatsheaf.oxford; map p.240.

Cramped music pub in a great central location, mainly showcasing local indie and punk bands. Also hosts the Spin Jazz Club (Thurs from 8.30pm; ⓦspinjazz.net). Mon–Wed & Sun noon–11pm, Thurs–Sat noon–midnight.

ENTERTAINMENT

Holywell Music Room 32 Holywell St, OX1 3SD ☎01865 766266, ⓦwww.music.ox.ac.uk; map p.240. This small, plain, Georgian building was opened in 1748 as the first public music hall in England. It offers a varied programme, from straight classical to experimental, with occasional bouts of jazz. Popular Sun morning "coffee

concerts" (ⓦcoffeeconcerts.com) run year-round. **Sheldonian Theatre** Broad St, OX1 3AZ ☎01865 277299, ⓦwww.admin.ox.ac.uk/sheldonian; map p.240. Seventeenth-century edifice that is Oxford's top concert hall, despite rather dodgy acoustics, with the Oxford Philomusica symphony orchestra in residence (ⓦoxfordphil.com).

SHOPPING

Albion Beatnik Bookstore 34 Walton St, OX2 6AA ☎07737 876213, ⓦalbionbeatnik.co.uk; map p.240. Quirky independent bookshop in Jericho that focuses on twentieth-century literature (and jazz). Also has a good secondhand selection, lots of readings and events, and plenty of tea. Mon & Tues 3–8pm, Wed–Fri 1–8pm, Sat 11am–7pm; also Sun 3–6pm in university term time. **Alice's Shop** 83 St Aldates, OX1 1RA ☎01865 723793, ⓦaliceinwonderlandshop.com; map p.240. Tiny Victorian shop that featured in Lewis Carroll's "Through The Looking Glass" – staffed by a sheep – that is now a mini-emporium of all things Alice: books, souvenirs, toys, ornaments, home furnishings and more. July & Aug daily 9.30am–6.30pm; Sept–June Mon–Fri & Sun 10.30am–5pm, Sat 10am–6pm. **Antiques On High** 85 High St, OX1 4BG ☎01865 251075, ⓦantiquesonhigh.co.uk; map p.240. A group of outlets for antiques, prints, books and vintage fashion, as well as an affiliated gallery selling contemporary pieces by the Oxfordshire Craft Guild and Oxford Art Society.

Mon–Sat 10am–5pm, Sun 11am–5pm. **Blackwell** 48 Broad St, OX1 3BQ ☎01865 792792, ⓦblackwell.co.uk; map p.240. Oxford's leading university bookshop, a behemoth of a place that seems to extend for miles, above and below ground, stocking huge general ranges as well as academic titles. Mon–Sat 9am–6.30pm, Sun 11am–5pm. **Gloucester Green markets** Gloucester Green, OX1 2BN ⓦlsdpromotions.com/oxford; map p.240. This city-centre square hosts vibrant open-air food and craft markets: great for browsing and some of the city's best street food on Sat. Food Wed 9am–4pm; food, antiques & crafts Thurs 9am–4pm; food, arts & textiles Sat 10am–5pm; farmers' market 1st & 3rd Thurs of month 9am–3pm. **Oxford Cheese Company** 17 Covered Market, OX1 3DZ ☎01865 721420, ⓦoxfordcheese.co.uk; map p.240. Fantastically aromatic deli in the Covered Market. The perfect place to pick up all sorts of delicious nibbles, including their very own creation: Oxford Blue soft cheese, mellow, creamy and delicious. Mon–Sat 9am–5pm.

4

Around Oxford

From Oxford, a short journey west brings you into the Cotswolds; your first stop could be Burford (see p.257) or Moreton-in-Marsh (see p.260) – but make time, on the way, for the charming little town of **Woodstock** and its imperious country-house neighbour **Blenheim Palace**, birthplace of Winston Churchill. South of Oxford you'll find the pleasantly old-fashioned riverside haunt of **Henley-on-Thames** and open walking country around the **Vale of White Horse**.

Woodstock

WOODSTOCK, eight miles northwest of Oxford, has royal associations going back to Saxon times, with a string of kings attracted by its excellent hunting. The Royalists used Woodstock as a base during the Civil War but, after their defeat, Cromwell never got round to destroying either the town or its manor house: the latter was ultimately given to the Duke of Marlborough in 1704, who razed it to build Blenheim Palace (see p.252). Long dependent on royal and then ducal patronage, Woodstock is now both a well-heeled commuter town for Oxford and a base for visitors to Blenheim. It is also an extremely pretty little place, its handsome stone buildings gathered around the main square, at the junction of Market and High streets.

Oxfordshire Museum

Park St, OX20 1SN • Tues–Sat 10am–5pm, Sun 2–5pm • Free • ☎ 01993 814106, Ⓦ www.tomocc.org.uk

Occupying an eighteenth-century house in the centre of Woodstock, the rather good **Oxfordshire Museum** offers an engaging take on the county's archeology, social history and industry. Its café overlooks the rear garden, which shelters original megalosaurus footprints, recovered from a local quarry and displayed amid a Jurassic garden of ferns, pines and redwoods.

ARRIVAL AND INFORMATION

WOODSTOCK

By bus #S3 for Oxford (every 20min; 30min) and Chipping Norton (hourly; 20min); #500 for Oxford Parkway station (every 30min; 20min); #233 for Burford (Mon–Sat hourly; 55min).

Websites Ⓦ wakeuptowoodstock.com and Ⓦ www.oxfordshirecotswolds.org.

ACCOMMODATION AND EATING

The Bear Park St, OX20 1SZ ☎ 01993 811124, Ⓦ bearhotelwoodstock.co.uk. Behind the ivy-clad walls of this thirteenth-century coaching inn lurks a stylish, modern chain hotel – oak-carved four-poster beds, roaring log fires and all. Grab a table by the bay window for upscale, country-house food: Gressingham duck, Scottish beef and the like. Two-course menu £32. Mon–Thurs noon–2.30pm & 7–9.30pm, Fri & Sat noon–2.30pm & 7–10pm, Sun noon–2.30pm & 7–9pm. **£110**

King's Arms Market St, OX20 1SU ☎ 01993 813636, Ⓦ www.kingshotelwoodstock.co.uk. Chic little hotel, with fifteen contemporary-styled rooms. The fine restaurant (mains £12–17) specializes in Modern British cuisine – leg of lamb or local goats' cheese salad. The bar/restaurant can remain busy until after 11pm: if you want an early night, choose a room at the back. Mon–Fri noon–2.30pm & 6.30–9.30pm, Sat & Sun noon–9pm. **£110**

Blenheim Palace

Woodstock, OX20 1PS • Daily: palace & gardens 10.30am–5.30pm; park 9am–6.30pm or dusk • Palace, park and gardens £24.90; park and gardens £15.30 • ☎ 01993 810530, Ⓦ blenheimpalace.com

In 1704, as a thank-you for his victory over the French at the Battle of Blenheim, Queen Anne gave John Churchill, **Duke of Marlborough** (1650–1722), the royal estate of Woodstock, along with the promise of enough cash to build himself a gargantuan palace.

Work started promptly on **Blenheim Palace** with Sir John Vanbrugh, who was also responsible for Castle Howard in Yorkshire (see p.594), as principal architect. However, the duke's formidable wife, Sarah Jennings, who had wanted Christopher Wren, was soon at loggerheads with Vanbrugh, while Queen Anne had second thoughts, stifling the flow of money. Construction work was halted and the house was only finished after the duke's death at the instigation of his widow, who ended up paying most of the bills and designing much of the interior herself. The end result is England's grandest example of Baroque civic architecture, an Italianate palace of finely worked yellow stone that is more a monument than a house – just as Vanbrugh intended.

The **interior** of the house is stuffed with paintings and tapestries, plus all manner of objets d'art, including furniture from Versailles and carvings by Grinling Gibbons. The **Churchill Exhibition** on the ground floor provides a fascinating introduction to Winston (1874–1965), born at Blenheim as grandson of the seventh Duke of Marlborough, and buried alongside his wife in the graveyard of Bladon church just outside the estate.

Start your exploration of Blenheim's **gardens** by riding the narrow-gauge **miniature train** (March–Oct every 30min; 50p) on a looping journey to the **Pleasure Gardens** a few hundred yards to the east of the palace (also an easy walk). Here, as well as a café, you'll find a butterfly house, lavender garden, maze and other diversions. On the west side of the house, fountains spout beside the terrace of the palace café and paths lead down to the lake past the vivid **Rose Garden**. A path from the front of the house leads you across Blenheim's open **park** down to Vanbrugh's **Grand Bridge** and up to the hilltop **Column of Victory**, topped by a heroic statue of the 1st Duke.

ARRIVAL AND DEPARTURE · BLENHEIM PALACE

Entrances The Blenheim Palace estate has two entrances: the Hensington Gate lies just south of Woodstock on the A44 Oxford Rd, a few minutes on foot from the town centre, while the quieter Woodstock Gate is in the centre of town, at the far end of Park St.

By bus All of Woodstock's main buses (see opposite) stop at the Hensington Gate.

TOURS

Blenheim Palace tours Free guided tours (35min) inside the palace depart about every quarter-hour, though you're free to opt out and stroll at your own pace. On Sun or when the palace is very busy, tours are replaced by guides stationed in every room, who give details as you move through.

Henley-on-Thames

Three counties – Oxfordshire, Berkshire and Buckinghamshire – meet at **HENLEY-ON-THAMES**, long a favourite stopping place for travellers between London and Oxford. Nowadays, Henley is a good-looking, affluent commuter town at its prettiest among the old brick and stone buildings that flank the short main drag, **Hart Street**. At one end of Hart Street is the Market Place and its fetching **Town Hall**, while at the other stand the easy Georgian curves of **Henley Bridge**. Overlooking the bridge is the parish church of **St Mary**, whose square tower sports a set of little turrets worked in chequerboard flint and stone.

River and Rowing Museum

Mill Meadows, RG9 1BF · Daily 10am–5pm · £12.50 · ☎ 01491 415600, ⓦ rrm.co.uk

A five-minute walk south along the riverbank from the foot of Hart Street lies Henley's imaginative **River and Rowing Museum**. Three galleries explore the wildlife and ecology of the Thames along with the history of rowing and the regatta, from ancient triremes to the modern Olympics. A fourth gallery is devoted to models illustrating scenes from the children's classic *Wind in the Willows* by Kenneth Grahame (1859–1932), set near Henley.

ARRIVAL AND DEPARTURE · HENLEY-ON-THAMES

By train Trains arrive from London Paddington (every 30min; 1hr – change at Twyford) and Reading (every 30min; 30min). From the station, it's a 5min walk north to Hart St.

By bus Bus #800/850/X80 from High Wycombe (every 15min; 40min) and Reading (hourly; 40min) stops on Hart St.

INFORMATION AND TOURS

Tourist office In the Town Hall (Mon–Sat 9am–4pm; ☎ 01491 578034, ⓦ visit-henley.com and ⓦ experience oxfordshire.org).

Boat trips Just south of the bridge, Hobbs of Henley offers boat trips along the Thames (Easter–Sept; 1hr; £9.75; ☎ 01491 572035, ⓦ hobbsofhenley.com), and has rowing boats and motor-launches for rent.

ACCOMMODATION AND EATING

★**The Angel** Thameside, RG9 1BH ☎ 01491 410678, ⓦ theangelhenley.com. Of Henley's many pubs, this one stands out for its prime riverside location, with a fine outside deck overlooking the water. Decent food, too: light bites £6–9, mains £11–15. Mon–Sat 11.30am–10pm, Sun 11.30am–7pm; kitchen same hours.

HENLEY ROYAL REGATTA

Henley is best known for its **Royal Regatta**, established in 1839 and now the world's top amateur rowing tournament. The regatta, featuring past and potential Olympic rowers, begins on the Wednesday before the first weekend in July and runs for five days. Contact the Regatta Headquarters on the east side of Henley Bridge for ticket details (☎ 01491 572153, ⓦ hrr.co.uk).

4

Chocolate Café 13 Thameside, RG9 1BH ☎01491 411412, ⓦthechocolatecafe.info. Lovely local café on the water, serving posh all-day breakfasts (eggs benedict £7.50), lunchtime light bites (£6–9), cream teas (from £6.50) and a massive range of hot chocolates, dark and white, with options for nougat, chilli, cinnamon, peppermint and more. Mon–Thurs 8am–5.30pm, Fri–Sun 8am–6pm.

Hotel du Vin New St, RG9 2BP ☎0330 016 0390, ⓦhotelduvin.com. This slick central hotel occupies the creatively revamped old Brakspear Brewery. Rooms are in contemporary boutique style; a few on the top floor have river views. The restaurant serves sumptuous modern European cuisine using local produce. Two-course menu £17.95. Mon–Sat noon–2.30pm & 5.30–10pm, Sun noon–4pm & 6–9.30pm. __£129__

Vale of White Horse

In the southwestern corner of Oxfordshire lies the pretty **Vale of White Horse**, a shallow valley whose fertile farmland is studded with tiny villages and dotted with a striking collection of prehistoric remains. The **Ridgeway National Trail**, running along – or near – the top of the downs, links several of these ancient sites and offers wonderful, breezy views. The Vale is easily visited as a day-trip from Oxford or elsewhere, but you might opt to stay locally in one of the Vale's quaint villages – tiny **Woolstone** is perhaps the most appealing.

White Horse Hill

Uffington, SN7 7UK • Open access • Free • ☎ 01793 762209, ⓦ nationaltrust.org.uk/white-horse-hill • 10min walk from signposted car park. Or, from Oxford, take a bus to Wantage (45min) then change for a Swindon-bound bus to Woolstone (35min), 15min walk away

White Horse Hill, overlooking the B4507 six miles west of the unexciting market town of Wantage, follows close behind Stonehenge (see p.229) and Avebury (see p.231) in the hierarchy of Britain's ancient sites, though it attracts nothing like the same number of visitors. Carved into the north-facing slope of the downs, the 374ft-long **Uffington White Horse** looks like something created with a few swift strokes of an immense brush. The first written record of the horse's existence dates from the time of Henry II, but it was cut much earlier, probably in the first century BC, making it one of the oldest chalk figures in Britain. There's no lack of weird and wonderful theories concerning its origins, but burial sites excavated in the surrounding area point to the horse having some kind of sacred function, though no one knows quite what.

Just below the horse is **Dragon Hill**, a small flat-topped hillock that has its own legend. Locals long asserted that this was where St George killed and buried the dragon, a theory proved, so they argued, by the bare patch at the top and the channel down the side, where blood trickled from the creature's wounds. Here also, at the top of the hill, is the Iron Age earthwork of **Uffington Castle**, which provides wonderful views over the Vale.

THE RIDGEWAY NATIONAL TRAIL

The Iron Age inhabitants of Britain developed the **Ridgeway** (ⓦnationaltrail.co.uk/ridgeway) as a major thoroughfare, a fast route that beetled across the chalky downs of modern-day Berkshire and Oxfordshire, negotiated the Thames and then traversed the Chiltern Hills. It was probably once part of a longer route extending from the Dorset coast to the Wash in Norfolk. Today, the Ridgeway is a National Trail, running from **Overton Hill**, near Avebury in Wiltshire, to **Ivinghoe Beacon**, 87 miles to the northeast near Tring. Crossing five counties, it keeps to the hills and avoids densely populated areas, except where the Thames slices through the trail at **Goring Gap**, marking the transition from the open Berkshire–Oxfordshire downs to the wooded valleys of the Chilterns.

It's fairly easy hiking, and most of the route is accessible to cyclists. The prevailing winds mean that it is best walked in a northeasterly direction. The trail is strewn with prehistoric monuments, though the finest archeological remains are on the downs edging the **Vale of White Horse** (see p.254) and around **Avebury** (see p.231).

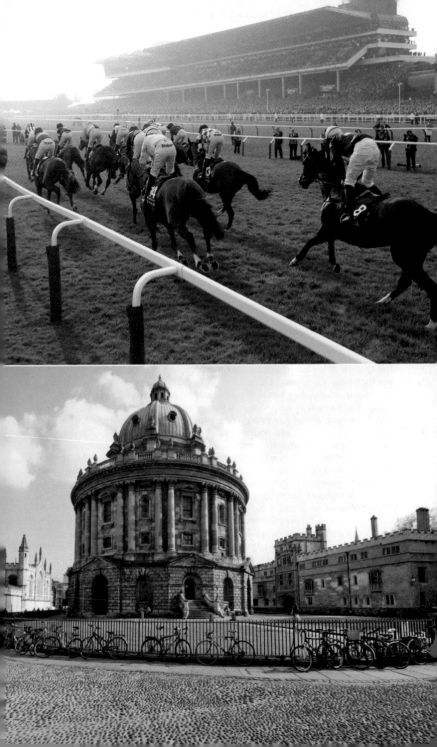

The Ridgeway trail (see box, p.254) runs alongside the white horse and continues west to reach, after one and a half miles, **Wayland's Smithy**, a 5000-year-old burial mound encircled by trees. It is one of the best Neolithic remains in the area, though heavy restoration has rather detracted from its mystery. In ignorance of its original function, the invading Saxons named it after Weland (hence Wayland), an invisible smith who, according to their legends, made impenetrable armour and shod horses without ever being seen.

ACCOMMODATION AND EATING   VALE OF WHITE HORSE

Fox and Hounds Uffington, SN7 7RP ☎ 01367 820680, ⓦ uffingtonpub.co.uk. Friendly local pub in this quiet village a mile and a half north of White Horse Hill. Four well-kept en-suite rooms for B&B, and decent food; mains £10–12. Mon–Sat 11am–11pm, Sun noon–10.30pm; kitchen Mon–Fri noon–2pm & 6–9pm, Sat noon–3pm & 6–9pm, Sun noon–3pm. **£105**

White Horse Inn Woolstone, SN7 7QL ☎ 01367 820726, ⓦ whitehorsewoolstone.co.uk. A mile north of White Horse Hill, this half-timbered, partly thatched old inn offers swanky accommodation, mostly in a modern annexe, and upmarket pub food (mains £11–15). Daily 11am–late; kitchen daily noon–2.30pm & 6–9pm. **£90**

The Cotswolds

The limestone hills that make up the **Cotswolds** are preposterously photogenic, dotted with a string of picture-book villages, many of them built by wealthy cloth merchants between the fourteenth and sixteenth centuries. Largely bypassed by the Industrial Revolution, which heralded the area's commercial decline, the Cotswolds is characterized by handsomely preserved traditional architecture. Numerous churches are decorated with beautiful carving, for which the local limestone was ideal: soft and easy to carve when first quarried, but hardening after long exposure to the sunlight.

For their beauty and ease of access the Cotswolds are a major tourist attraction, with many towns afflicted by plagues of tearooms, antiques shops and coach parties. To see the region at its best, avoid the main towns and instead escape into the countryside. If you have a car, almost any minor road between Oxford and Cheltenham will deliver views, thatched cottages and oodles of rural atmosphere; otherwise, plan day-walks from one of the more attractive centres – **Chipping Campden** is the number-one choice, or opt for **Northleach**, foodie hub **Kingham** or the walkers' haven of **Winchcombe**.

This might be a tamed landscape, but there's good scope for exploring the byways, either in the gentler valleys that are most typical of the Cotswolds or along the dramatic escarpment that marks the western boundary with the Severn Valley. The **Cotswold Way** national trail runs for a hundred miles along the edge of the Cotswold escarpment from Chipping Campden in the northeast to Bath in the southwest, with a number of prehistoric sites providing added interest along the route. The section around Belas Knap is particularly rewarding, offering superb views over Cheltenham and the Severn Valley to the distant Malvern Hills.

GETTING AROUND AND INFORMATION   THE COTSWOLDS

By train Hourly trains from London Paddington via Oxford serve Kingham (1hr 25min) and Moreton-in-Marsh (1hr 35min), access points for the central and northern

Cotswolds between Stow and Chipping Campden. Hourly trains on a different line from London Paddington via Swindon serve Kemble (1hr 15min), useful for Cirencester

TOP 5 COTSWOLDS CHURCHES

St James Chipping Campden. See p.264
St John the Baptist Burford. See p.257
St John the Baptist Cirencester. See p.267

St Mary Tetbury. See p.268
St Peter and St Paul Northleach. See p.262

TOP 5 COTSWOLDS RESTAURANTS

Angel Burford. See below
Eight Bells Chipping Campden. See p.264
Horse and Groom Bourton-on-the-Hill. See p.260

Jesse's Bistro Cirencester. See p.268
Kingham Plough Kingham. See p.259

---

and southerly stretches around Tetbury.

By bus Local buses do a reasonable job connecting the larger towns and villages, but few buses run on Sun; smaller villages are rarely served more than once a week, if at all. Local tourist offices will be able to advise on travel plans – or you can check the public transport info at ⓦescapetothecotswolds.org.uk.

On foot The Cotswolds is prime walking country: wherever you are there's likely to be a marked trail nearby for anything from an hour's rural stroll to a multi-day epic. Loads of routes are downloadable for free from tourism websites (see below), with full descriptions and maps.

Travel pass The one-day "Cotswold Discoverer" (£10) allows unlimited travel on trains (Mon–Fri after 8.50am, Sat & Sun all day) between Oxford, Kingham and Moreton, and between Swindon, Kemble, Cheltenham and Gloucester, and on many of the buses covering main routes in and around Cotswold villages, from Oxford and Stroud in the south to Stratford-upon-Avon in the north. Buy it from local bus drivers or any train station. Details at ⓦescapetothecotswolds.org.uk.

Websites ⓦcotswolds.com, ⓦwww.oxfordshirecotswolds.org and ⓦescapetothecotswolds.org.uk.

Burford

Twenty miles west of Oxford you get your first real taste of the Cotswolds at **BURFORD**, where the long, wide High Street, which slopes down to the bridge over the River Windrush, is simply magnificent, despite the traffic. The street is flanked by a remarkable line of old buildings that exhibit almost every type of classic Cotswolds feature, from wonky mullioned windows and half-timbered facades with bendy beams, through to spiky brick chimneys, fancy bow-fronted stone houses and grand horse-and-carriage gateways.

Church of St John the Baptist

Church Green, near the river, OX18 4RY • Daily 9am–5pm • Free, but donation welcomed • ⓦburfordchurch.org

Of all the Cotswold churches, **St John the Baptist** has the most historical resonance, with architectural bits and pieces surviving from every phase of its construction, beginning with the Normans and ending in the wool boom of the seventeenth century – the soaring Gothic spire built atop the old Norman tower is particularly eye-catching. Thereafter, it was pretty much left alone and, most unusually, its clutter of mausoleums, chapels and chantries survived the Reformation. A plaque outside commemorates three "Levellers" – a loose coalition of political thinkers that blossomed during the English Civil War – who were executed here in 1649 and whose aims are commemorated on **Levellers Day** in May (ⓦlevellersday.wordpress.com).

ARRIVAL AND INFORMATION

BURFORD

By bus #853 (Mon–Sat 3–4 daily, Sun daily) stops by the A40 at the top of Burford, from Northleach (15min), Cheltenham (45min) and Oxford (45min). #233 (Mon–Sat hourly) from Woodstock (55min) and #X10 from Chipping Norton (Mon–Sat hourly; 30min) stop on the High St.

Tourist office 33a High St (Mon–Sat 9.30am–5pm, Sun 10am–4pm; ☏01993 823558, ⓦwww.oxfordshirecotswolds.org).

ACCOMMODATION AND EATING

★**Angel** 14 Witney St, OX18 4SN ☏01993 822714, ⓦtheangelatburford.co.uk. This sixteenth-century inn is highly regarded for its lively, creative menu – black pudding enlivening calves' liver, apricots and salsa adding zip to aubergine tagine, and so on. Mains £15–18. Also three en-suite rooms, tasteful and traditional. Kitchen

daily noon–9.30pm. **£110**

Bay Tree Sheep St, OX18 4LW ☏01993 822791, ⓦcotswold-inns-hotels.co.uk. First-class hotel in a lovely location off the High St, occupying a wisteria-clad stone house dating from the sixteenth century. Its twenty-odd rooms, in the main house and a couple of annexes, are done up in a lavish rendition of period character. Bar meals are excellent (light bites £8–10, mains £13–20), featuring anything from tiger prawns to local pork sausages. Kitchen daily noon–2pm & 7–9.30pm. **£125**

Bull 105 High St, OX18 4RG ☎01993 822220, ⓦbullatburford.co.uk. This venerable old inn has been hosting guests for more than three hundred years

– Charles II dallied here with Nell Gwynne, as did Lord Nelson with Lady Hamilton. Traditionally styled rooms feature panelling and four-poster beds, while the restaurant grafts French and Mediterranean influences onto local ingredients, with emphasis on fish and seafood. Mains £15–23. Kitchen daily noon–2.30pm & 6.30–9pm. **£110**

Kelmscott Manor

Kelmscott, GL7 3HJ • April–Oct Wed & Sat 11am–5pm • £9.50; timed tickets, so call ahead to confirm arrangements • ☎01367 252486, ⓦkelmscottmanor.org.uk • No public transport. The car park is a 10min walk from the house

Kelmscott Manor, amid the Thames-side water meadows about eight miles south of Burford, is a place of pilgrimage for devotees of **William Morris** (see box below), who used this Tudor house as a summer home from 1871 to his death in 1896. The simple beauty of the house is enhanced by the furniture, fabrics and wallpapers created by Morris and his Pre-Raphaelite friends, including Burne-Jones and Rossetti.

Kingham and around

When *Country Life* magazine calls you "England's favourite village", it could easily prompt a downward spiral. But for **KINGHAM**, set in the Evenlode Valley between Chipping Norton (the highest town in Oxfordshire) and Stow-on-the-Wold (the highest town in the Cotswolds), everything's looking up. There's still nothing to do in this cheery, noticeably upmarket village, other than eat well, walk well and sleep well… but that's the point. The stroll in from the railway station is lovely, marked by the Perpendicular tower of **St Andrew's Church**.

WILLIAM MORRIS AND THE PRE-RAPHAELITES

Socialist, artist, writer and craftsman **William Morris** (1834–96) had a profound influence on his contemporaries and on subsequent generations. In some respects he was an ally of Karl Marx, railing against the iniquities of private property and the squalor of industrialized society, but – in contrast to Marx – he believed that machines enslave the individual, and that people would be liberated only through a sort of communistic, crafts-based economy. His prose/poem story *News from Nowhere* vaguely described his Utopian society, but his main legacy turned out to be the **Arts and Crafts movement**.

Morris's career as an artist began at Oxford, where he met **Edward Burne-Jones**, who shared his admiration for the arts of the Middle Ages. After graduating they both ended up in London, painting under the direction of Dante Gabriel Rossetti, the leading light of the **Pre-Raphaelites** – a loose grouping of artists intent on regaining the spiritual purity characteristic of art before Raphael and the Renaissance "tainted" the world with humanism. In 1861 Morris founded **Morris & Co** ("The Firm"), whose designs came to embody the ideas of the Arts and Crafts movement, one of whose basic tenets was formulated by its founder: "Have nothing in your houses that you do not know to be useful or believe to be beautiful." Rossetti and Burne-Jones were among the designers, though Morris's own designs for fabrics, wallpapers and numerous other products were to prove a massive influence in Britain. The Laura Ashley aesthetic is a lineal descendant of Morris's rustic nostalgia.

Not content with his artistic endeavours, in 1890 Morris set up the **Kelmscott Press**, named after (but not located at) his summer home, whose masterpiece was the so-called *Kelmscott Chaucer*, the collected poems of one of the Pre-Raphaelites' greatest heroes, with woodcuts by Burne-Jones. Morris also pioneered interest in the architecture of the Cotswolds and, in response to the Victorian penchant for modernizing churches and cottages, he instigated the **Society for the Protection of Ancient Buildings** (ⓦspab.org.uk), still an active force in preserving the country's architectural heritage.

WALKS AROUND KINGHAM

Kingham has loads of **walking** possibilities – not least within the **Foxholes Nature Reserve** (🕸 bbowt.org.uk), an ancient woodland famed for its spring bluebells. Download maps for longer trails at 🕸 www.oxfordshirecotswolds.org, including Walk 1, a **circular route** to/from Kingham Station (3.5 miles; 2hr 30min), exploring the fields around Bledington.

Daylesford Organic Farm

Daylesford, GL56 0YG • Mon–Sat 8am–8pm, Sun 10am–4pm • ☎ 01608 731700, 🕸 daylesfordorganic.com

A mile north of Kingham, **Daylesford Organic Farm** was founded in the 1980s when a local landowning family converted their farm to organic. Fashions caught up, and now Daylesford not only markets its own-brand produce but has a village **shop** – more like the smartest London food hall, vast, immaculate and expensive. It's a rather absorbing glimpse of Chelsea in the Cotswolds.

ARRIVAL AND DEPARTURE
KINGHAM AND AROUND

By train Kingham has hourly trains from London Paddington (1hr 25min), Oxford (25min), Moreton (10min) and Worcester (50min). The station is a mile west of the village.

ACCOMMODATION AND EATING

Daylesford Organic Daylesford, GL56 0YG ☎ 01608 731700, 🕸 daylesford.com. This super-sleek farm complex includes a spectacularly well-stocked deli and café, where light lunches (£10–16) are filled out by cream teas and informal suppers of wood-fired pizza or chicken teriyaki (£13–19). Absurdly expensive, but very good. Booking essential. Mon–Sat 8am–8pm, Sun 10am–4pm.

★**Kingham Plough** Kingham, OX7 6YD ☎ 01608 658327, 🕸 thekinghamplough.co.uk. The epitome of a Cotswold gastropub. Book ahead for one of Oxfordshire's most atmospheric, upmarket and welcoming restaurants. Local, seasonal produce of all kinds, expertly prepared, is served off a short, daily-changing a la carte menu (mains £18–25) or a less ambitious bar menu: see website for specific menu times. They also have seven country-style rooms. Kitchen Mon–Sat noon–9pm, Sun 11.30am–3pm & 6–8pm. **£145**

Kings Head Bledington, OX7 6XQ ☎ 01608 658365, 🕸 thekingsheadinn.net. Just west of Kingham, this sixteenth-century inn with regulars popping up the bar serves local, ethically sourced Modern British fusion dishes – potted shrimps, steak and ale pie, Cotswold lamb (mains £14–22). The rooms, some floral, some designer-chic, are a snip. Kitchen Mon–Thurs noon–2pm & 6.30–9pm, Fri noon–2pm & 6.30–9.30pm, Sat noon–2.30pm & 6.30–9.30pm, Sun noon–2.30pm & 7–9pm. **£100**

Great Tew

In a region which has beautiful villages and fine old pubs coming out of its ears, **GREAT TEW**, about five miles east of Chipping Norton via the A361 and B4022, takes the biscuit. It has Cotswold character aplenty, its thatched cottages and honey-coloured stone houses weaving around grassy hillocks, flanked on all sides by rolling woodland.

ACCOMMODATION AND EATING
GREAT TEW

★**Falkland Arms** 19–21 The Green, OX7 4DB ☎ 01608 683653, 🕸 falklandarms.co.uk. Idyllic, locally renowned country pub, which rotates guest beers in addition to its Wadworth cask ales, and sells a fine selection of single malts, herbal wines, snuff and clay pipes you can fill with tobacco for a smoke in the flower-filled garden. Little has changed in the flagstone-floored bar since the sixteenth century, although the snug is now a small dining room serving home-made food (mains £10–18). Also with six sympathetically renovated rooms. Mon–Sat 8am–11pm, Sun 9am–10.30pm; kitchen Mon–Sat noon–2.30pm & 6–9.30pm, Sun noon–3pm & 6–8pm. **£85**

The Rollright Stones

Near Little Rollright, OX7 5QB, 5 miles north of Kingham • Open access • Free, but £1 donation in honesty box requested • 🕸 rollrightstones.co.uk

A signed country lane off the A44 leads to the **Rollright Stones**, a scattering of megalithic monuments in the fields either side of the lane. The eerie array consists of large natural stones which were moved here – no one is sure why – plus several burial chambers and barrows. The largest group is the **King's Men**, comprising over seventy irregularly spaced stones forming a circle one hundred feet in diameter, one of the most important such monuments in the country. The circle gets its name from a legend about a witch who turned a king and his army (of unknown identity) into these gnarled rocks to stop them invading England. Across the lane stands the **King's Stone** monolith, offering pensive views, with the **Whispering Knights** in sight on the field margin.

Chastleton House

4 miles east of Moreton-in-Marsh, GL56 0SU • Wed–Sun: April–Sept 1–5pm; March & Oct 1–4pm • £10.50; NT • Timed tickets, pre-bookable on ☏ 01494 755560, ⓦ nationaltrust.org.uk/chastleton-house • No public transport

Built between 1605 and 1612 by Walter Jones, a Welsh wool merchant, **Chastleton House** ranks among England's most splendid Jacobean properties, set amid ornamental gardens that include the country's first-ever croquet lawn. Inside, the house looks stuck in time, with unwashed upholstery, unpolished wood panelling and miscellaneous clutter: the National Trust, who took it on in 1991, wisely decided to stick to the "lived-in" look. Among the highlights are the barrel-vaulted long gallery and, in the beer cellar, the longest ladder (dated 1805) you're ever likely to see. There's also a wonderful topiary garden.

Moreton-in-Marsh

A key transport hub and one of the Cotswolds' more sensible towns, **MORETON-IN-MARSH** is named for a now-vanished wetland nearby. It has always been an important access point for the countryside and remains so with its **railway station**, which is on the line between London, Oxford and Worcester. It also sits astride the A429 Fosse Way, the former Roman road that linked Exeter with Lincoln. On the broad, handsome **High Street**, enhanced with Jacobean and Georgian facades, stands the nineteenth-century **Redesdale Hall**, named for Lord Redesdale, father of the infamous Mitford sisters (among them Diana, wife of British wartime fascist leader Oswald Mosley; and Unity, a close companion of Adolf Hitler), who as children lived at Batsford House near the town.

ARRIVAL AND INFORMATION MORETON-IN-MARSH

By train Moreton has hourly trains from London Paddington (1hr 35min), Oxford (35min), Kingham (10min) and Worcester (40min). The station is a 2min walk from the High St.

By bus #1 (Mon–Sat 4 daily) to/from Broadway (25min), Chipping Campden (45min) and Stratford-upon-Avon (1hr 15min); #2 (Mon–Sat 4 daily) to/from Chipping Campden (30min) and Stratford-upon-Avon (1hr 10min); #801 (Mon–Sat every 1–2hr; June–Sept also 2–3 on Sun) to/ from Stow-on-the-Wold (15min), Bourton-on-the-Water (25min) and Cheltenham (1hr 10min), some also via Northleach (55min).

Tourist office High St (Mon 8.45am–4pm, Tues–Thurs 8.45am–5.15pm, Fri 8.45am–4.45pm, Sat 10am–1pm; Nov–March Sat closes 12.30pm; ☏ 01608 650881, ⓦ cotswolds.com).

ACCOMMODATION AND EATING

Acacia Guest House 2 New Rd, GL56 0AS ☏ 01608 650130, ⓦ acaciainthecotswolds.co.uk. Decent little B&B on the short street connecting the station to the High St – very handy for arrivals and departures by train or bus. **£65**

★ Horse and Groom Bourton-on-the-Hill, GL56 9AQ ☏ 01386 700413, ⓦ horseandgroom.info. Occupying a Georgian building of honey-coloured Cotswold stone two miles west of Moreton, this free house has a reputation for good beer and excellent food. The menu changes frequently, focused on meat sourced from local farmers and seasonal veg. It's popular: book ahead. Mains £13–18. Also

five appealing rooms, one with French doors opening onto the garden. Mon–Sat noon–11pm, Sun noon–10.30pm; kitchen Mon–Sat noon–3pm & 6.30–9.30pm, Sun noon–3pm & 6.30–8.30pm. **£120**

Manor House High St, GL56 0LJ ☏ 01608 650501, ⓦ cotswold-inns-hotels.co.uk. Pleasant four-star hotel occupying a sixteenth-century former coaching inn, with a nice garden and stylish rooms. Its posh restaurant, with muted contemporary styling, serves Modern British cuisine (mains £11–17), with good vegetarian options available. Daily noon–2.30pm & 7–9.30pm. **£120**

WALKS AROUND STOW-ON-THE-WOLD

"Meadows and Mills" is an easy **walk** (4 miles; 2hr 30min; route map at ⓦ escapetothe cotswolds.org.uk) which heads downhill from Stow across fields to Lower Slaughter and Bourton-on-the-Water. The high wolds west of Stow are horse country: aim for the *Plough Inn* at Ford, on the B4077, bedecked in equestrian memorabilia. A pleasant **circular walk** (6 miles; 3hr) starts at the pub, heads to Cutsdean village and follows a back lane to skirt Jackdaw's Castle, ex-jockey Jonjo O'Neill's training yard, returning to Ford alongside the "gallops".

Stow-on-the-Wold

Ambling over a steep hill seven hundred feet above sea level, **STOW-ON-THE-WOLD**, five miles south of Moreton, draws in a quantity of visitors disproportionate to its size and attractions, which essentially comprise an old **marketplace** surrounded by pubs, antique and souvenir shops, and an inordinate number of tearooms. The narrow walled alleyways, or "tchures", running into the square were designed for funnelling sheep into the market, which is itself dominated by an imposing Victorian hall. **St Edward's Church** has a photogenic north porch, where two yew trees flanking the door appear to have grown into the stonework.

ARRIVAL AND INFORMATION

STOW-ON-THE-WOLD

By bus Buses stop just off the main square, including #801 (Mon–Sat every 1–2hr; May–Sept also 2–3 on Sun) to/from Bourton-on-the-Water (10min), Moreton (15min) and Cheltenham (1hr 10min), some also via Northleach (30min); and #802 (Mon–Sat 4–6 daily) to/from Kingham

station (15min).
Tourist office In the library on the main square (April–Oct Mon & Wed 10am–5pm, Tues & Fri 10am–7pm, Thurs 10am–2pm, Sat 10am–4pm; ☎ 01451 870998, ⓦ stowinfo .co.uk and ⓦ cotswolds.com).

ACCOMMODATION AND EATING

★ **Jaffe & Neale** 8 Park St, GL54 1AQ ☎ 01451 832000, ⓦ jaffeandneale.co.uk. Outpost for this much-loved Chipping Norton bookshop/café, which has brought a fresh, contemporary feel to the interior of this old building. Come for the carrot cake, stay for the literary inspiration. Mon–Sat 9.30am–5pm, Sun 10am–4pm.
Number Nine 9 Park St, GL54 1AQ ☎ 01451 870333, ⓦ number-nine.info. Pleasant old house offering quality B&B just down from the town square. The three bedrooms feature low beams but contemporary styling – and the rates are a bargain. **£75**
Porch House Digbeth St, GL54 1BN ☎ 01451 870048, ⓦ porch-house.co.uk. Purportedly the oldest inn in Britain, with parts of the building dated at 947 AD (though

the interiors have been freshly modernized). The thirteen hessian-floored rooms look good, but are on the small side. The restaurant is a comfortably posh affair (mains £13–18), with cheaper nosh in the wonky-beamed pub. Mon–Sat 8am–11pm, Sun 8am–10.30pm; kitchen Mon–Fri noon–3pm & 6–9.30pm, Sat noon–9.30pm, Sun noon–8.30pm. **£115**
★ **Queen's Head** The Square, GL54 1AB ☎ 01451 830563, ⓦ queensheadstowonthewold.com. Traditional old pub that provides good beer, good service and a pleasant chatty atmosphere. Food is a level above standard pub grub (mains £11–15), and they have a few simple, stylish rooms nearby. Mon–Sat 11am–11pm, Sun noon–10.30pm; kitchen daily noon–2.30pm & 6.30–9pm. **£79**

SHOPPING

Borzoi Bookshop Church St, GL54 1BB ☎ 01451 830268, ⓦ borzoibookshop.co.uk. Lovely little independent bookshop in the centre of town, with a great range of stock and knowledgeable staff. Mon–Sat 9.30am–5pm.
Fosse Gallery The Square, GL54 1AF ☎ 01451 831319,

ⓦ fossegallery.com. Long-established, privately owned gallery devoted to contemporary British art. Whatever's showing, it's always worth popping in. Mon–Sat 10.30am–5pm.

Bourton-on-the-Water

BOURTON-ON-THE-WATER is the epicentre of Cotswold tourism. Beside the village green – flanked by photogenic Jacobean and Georgian facades in yellow Cotswold stone – five picturesque little **bridges** span the shallow River Windrush, dappled by

4

shade from overhanging trees. It looks lovely, but its proximity to main roads means that it's invariably packed with people: tourist coaches cram in all summer long and the little **High Street** now concentrates on souvenirs and teashops, interspersed with everything from a Model Village and Motoring Museum to a Dragonfly Maze and Bird Park.

Lower Slaughter

A mile outside Bourton-on-the-Water, **LOWER SLAUGHTER** (as in *slohtre*, Old English for a marshy place, cognate with "slough") is a more enticing prospect, though still on the day-trippers' circuit. Pop by to take in some of the most celebrated village scenery in the Cotswolds, as the River Eye snakes its way between immaculate honey-stone cottages. There is a small **museum** (and souvenir shop) signposted in a former mill, but the main attraction of the stroll through the village is to stop in for a little something at one of the grand hotels occupying gated mansions on both sides of the street.

Northleach

Secluded in a shallow depression, **NORTHLEACH** is one of the most appealing and atmospheric villages in the Cotswolds – a great base to explore the area. Despite the fact that the A40 Oxford–Cheltenham road and A429 Fosse Way cross at a large roundabout nearby, virtually no tourist traffic makes its way into the centre. Rows of immaculate late medieval cottages cluster around the **Market Place** and adjoining **Green**.

The Old Prison

Fosse Way, GL54 3JH • May–Oct daily 10am–5pm; Nov–April Mon, Tues & Thurs–Sun 9.30am–4pm • Free • ☎ 01451 861563, ⓦ escapetothecotswolds.org.uk

Just outside town is the Georgian **Old Prison**, which has interesting displays on the history of crime and punishment, along with the **Cotswolds Discovery Centre**, a visitor centre explaining the work of the Cotswolds Conservation Board in maintaining the Cotswolds Area of Outstanding Natural Beauty.

Church of St Peter and St Paul

Mill End, GL54 3HL • Daily 9am–5pm • Free • ☎ 01451 861132, ⓦ northleach.org

One of the finest of the Cotswolds "wool churches", **St Peter and St Paul** is a classic example of the fifteenth-century Perpendicular style, with a soaring tower and beautifully proportioned nave lit by wide clerestory windows. The floors of the aisles are inlaid with an exceptional collection of memorial **brasses**, marking the tombs of the merchants whose endowments paid for the church. On several, you can make out the woolsacks laid out beneath the owner's feet – a symbol of wealth and power that survives today in London's House of Lords, where a woolsack is placed on the Lord Chancellor's seat.

Mechanical Music Museum

High St, GL54 3ET • Daily 10am–5pm • £8 • ☎ 01451 860181, ⓦ mechanicalmusic.co.uk

Two minutes' walk along the High Street from the Market Place, the **Mechanical Music Museum** holds a bewildering collection of antique musical boxes, automata, barrel organs and mechanical instruments, all stuffed into one room. The entrance fee includes an hour-long **tour**.

ARRIVAL AND DEPARTURE   **NORTHLEACH**

By bus Buses stop by the Green.

Destinations #801 (Mon–Sat 5 daily) to/from Cheltenham (40min), Bourton-on-the-Water (15min), Stow-on-the-Wold (30min) and Moreton-in-Marsh (40min); #853 (Mon–Sat 3–4 daily, 1 on Sun) to Burford (15min), Cheltenham (30min) and Oxford (1hr); #855 (Mon–Sat 5–6 daily) to/from Cirencester (20–40min) and Bibury (20min).

ACCOMMODATION AND EATING

Cotswold Lion Café Old Prison, GL54 3JH ☎01451 861563, ⓦescapetothecotswolds.org.uk. Friendly daytime café on the edge of the town, serving up teas, coffees, cakes and light lunches (under £10). Daily 10am–4.30pm.

Wheatsheaf West End, GL54 3EZ ☎01451 860244, ⓦcotswoldswheatsheaf.com. Excellent former coaching inn, remodelled in a bright modern style softened by period furniture, bookcases and etchings. Its restaurant has upscale Mediterranean-influenced cuisine – polenta with nettles and peas, spiced lamb pie with sultanas, and so forth. Mains £13–19. It also has fourteen comfortable, en-suite guest rooms. Mon–Sat noon–3pm & 6–9pm, Sun noon–3.30pm & 6–9pm. **£120**

Bibury

A detour between Northleach and Cirencester passes through **BIBURY**, dubbed "the most beautiful village in England" by William Morris (see box, p.258). Bibury draws attention for **Arlington Row**, originally built around 1380 as a wool store and converted in the seventeenth century into a line of cottages to house weavers. Their hound's-tooth gables, warm yellow stone and wonky windows stole William Morris's heart – and are now immortalized in the British passport as an image of England.

ARRIVAL AND DEPARTURE
BIBURY

By bus The #855 (Mon–Sat 5–6 daily) runs to Northleach (20min) and Cirencester (20min)

Chipping Campden

4

Situated on the northern edge of the Cotswolds, near Stratford-upon-Avon (see p.436), **CHIPPING CAMPDEN** gives a better idea than anywhere else in the area of how a prosperous wool town might have looked in the Middle Ages. Its name derives from the Saxon term *campadene*, meaning cultivated valley, and the Old English *ceapen*, or market. The elegant **High Street** is hemmed in by mostly Tudor and Jacobean facades – an undulating line of weather-beaten roofs above twisted beams and mullioned windows. The evocative seventeenth-century **Market Hall** has survived too, an open-sided pavilion propped up on sturdy stone piers in the middle of the High Street, where farmers once gathered to sell their produce.

The Old Silk Mill

Sheep St, GL55 6DS • Daily 10am–5pm; Hart Silversmiths Mon–Fri 9am–5pm, Sat 9am–noon • Free • ☎01386 841100, ⓦhartsilversmiths.co.uk

Just off the High Street is the **Old Silk Mill**, where designer Charles Ashbee relocated the London Guild of Handicraft in 1902, introducing the Arts and Crafts movement (see box, p.258) to the Cotswolds. Today, as well as housing galleries of local art, the building rings with the noise of chisels from the resident stone carvers. Upstairs, you're free to wander into the workshop of **Hart**, a silversmith firm – it's like stepping into an old photograph, with metalworking tools strewn everywhere under low ceilings, and staff perched by the windows working by hand on decorative pieces.

Court Barn Museum

Church St, GL55 6JE • Tues–Sun 10am–5pm; Oct–March closes 4pm • £5 • ☎01386 841951, ⓦcourtbarn.org.uk

The history of the Guild of Handicraft, and its leading exponents, is explained at the superb **Court Barn Museum**. Sited opposite a magnificent row of seventeenth-century Cotswold stone **almshouses**, the museum displays the work of Charles Ashbee and eight Arts and Crafts cohorts, placing it all in context with informative displays and short videos. Featured works include the bookbinding of Katharine Adams, the stained-glass design of Paul Woodroffe and furniture by Gordon Russell.

St James' Church

Church St, GL55 6JG · March–Oct Mon–Sat 10am–4.30pm, Sun noon–4pm; Nov–Feb Mon–Sat 11am–3pm, Sun noon–3pm · Free ·
ⓣ 01386 841927, ⓦ stjameschurchcampden.co.uk

At the top of the village rises **St James' Church**. Built in the fifteenth century, the zenith of Campden's wool-trading days, this is the archetypal Cotswold wool church, beneath a magnificent 120ft tower. Inside, the airy nave is bathed in light from the clerestory windows. The South Chapel holds the ostentatious **funerary memorial** of the Hicks family, with fancily carved marble effigies lying on a table-tomb.

Dover's Hill

Panoramic views crown the short but severe hike up the first stage of the Cotswold Way, north from Chipping Campden to **Dover's Hill** (which is also accessible by car). The highest point, 740ft above sea level, affords breathtaking vistas to the Malvern Hills and beyond. This is where, in 1612, local lawyer Robert Dover organized competitions of running, jumping, wrestling and shin-kicking that rapidly became known as the **Cotswold Olimpicks**, still staged here annually (see ⓦ olimpickgames.co.uk).

ARRIVAL AND INFORMATION

CHIPPING CAMPDEN

By train Moreton-in-Marsh station (see p.260) is 8 miles away, connected by bus #1 or #2.

By bus Buses stop on the High St, including the linked routes #1 & #2.

Destinations Broadway (Mon–Sat 4 daily; 20min); Moreton-in-Marsh (Mon–Sat every 1–2hr; 45min);

Stratford-upon-Avon (Mon–Sat every 1–2hr; 40min).

Tourist office High St (March–Oct daily 9.30am–5pm; Nov–Feb Mon–Thurs 9.30am–1pm, Fri–Sun 9.30am–4pm; ⓣ 01386 841206, ⓦ campdenonline.org and ⓦ cotswolds.com).

ACCOMMODATION AND EATING

Badgers Hall High St, GL55 6HB ⓣ 01386 840839, ⓦ badgershall.com. This tearoom in an old stone house has won awards for its traditional English tea and cakes, all freshly made daily. It also does light lunches (under £10). En-suite guest rooms upstairs feature period detail – beamed ceilings and antique pine furniture. Mon–Sat 10am–4.30pm, Sun 11am–4.30pm. **£115**

Bakers Arms Broad Campden, GL55 6UR ⓣ 01386 840515, ⓦ bakersarmscampden.com. From the archway under the *Noel Arms* on the High St, walk a mile or so south to find this gem, named a North Cotswolds Pub of the Year for its ales, its atmosphere and its solid food – fish pie, gammon and good veggie options (mains £10–15). Mon 5–11pm, Tues–Fri noon–3pm & 5–11pm, Sat noon–11pm, Sun noon–10.30pm; kitchen Tues–Thurs noon–2pm & 6–8pm, Fri & Sat noon–2pm & 6–9pm, Sun noon–4pm.

★ **Eight Bells** Church St, GL55 6JG ⓣ 01386 840371, ⓦ eightbellsinn.co.uk. Much-loved old inn with a first-rate restaurant – pheasant with mushrooms, pork with apricots and chestnuts, lamb's liver on bubble and squeak. Mains £13–22. It also has seven individually done-up bedrooms, smartly modern without boutique pretension. Kitchen Mon–Thurs noon–2pm & 6.30–9pm, Fri & Sat noon–2.30pm & 6.30–9.30pm, Sun noon–3pm & 6–9pm. **£120**

Volunteer Inn Lower High St, GL55 6DY ⓣ 01386 840688, ⓦ thevolunteerinn.net. There are nine budget rooms at this lively pub, often used by walkers and cyclists (you can rent bikes here from £12/day; see ⓦ www.cyclecotswolds.co.uk). The on-site *Maharaja* restaurant serves unusual Bangladeshi fish and chicken curries and fruity Kashmiri dishes (mains £8–17). Pub daily 11am–11pm; restaurant Mon–Thurs & Sun 6–10.30pm, Fri & Sat 6–11pm. **£50**

Broadway

BROADWAY, five miles west of Chipping Campden, is a handsome little village at the foot of the steep escarpment that rolls along the western edge of the Cotswolds. It seems likely that the Romans were the first to settle here, but Broadway's high times were as a stagecoach stop on the route from London to Worcester. Its long, broad main street, framed by honey-stone cottages and shaded by chestnut trees, attracts more visitors than is comfortable, but things do quieten down in the evening.

Gordon Russell Design Museum

Russell Square, WR12 7AP • Tues–Sun: Feb, Nov & Dec 11am–4pm; March–Oct 11am–5pm • £5 • ☎ 01386 854695, ⓦ gordonrussellmuseum.org

Just off the village green, the absorbing **Gordon Russell Design Museum** is dedicated to the work of this local furniture-maker (1892–1980), whose factory formerly stood next door. Influenced both by the Arts and Crafts movement but also by modern technology, Russell's stated aim was to "make decent furniture for ordinary people" through "a blend of hand and machine". The museum showcases many of his classic furniture designs, alongside other period artefacts ranging from metalware to mirrors.

Broadway Museum

65 High St, WR12 7DP • Tues–Sun 10am–5pm • £5 • ☎ 01386 859047, ⓦ broadwaymuseum.org.uk

A former coaching inn now holds the **Broadway Museum**, run in partnership with Oxford's mighty Ashmolean Museum. Objects across four floors of displays include embroidered tapestries and furniture in the panelled ground-floor rooms, Worcester porcelain, glass, examples of William Morris tiles, and Cotswold pottery on the upper levels, as well as paintings by Gainsborough and Reynolds.

Broadway Tower

Fish Hill, WR12 7LB • Daily 10am–5pm; shorter hours in bad weather • Tower £5, bunker £4, joint ticket £8 • ☎ 01386 852390, ⓦ broadwaytower.co.uk

A mile southeast of the village, **Broadway Tower**, a turreted folly built in 1798, has become an icon of the Cotswolds, perched at more than 1000ft above sea level with stupendous views that purportedly encompass thirteen counties. Now privately owned, it stands alongside a family activity park with café. The historical displays in the tower are a bit limp: visit to climb the 71 steps to the roof, for those views. Nearby you can venture down into a Cold War-era **nuclear bunker**. A circular **walk** from Broadway heads up to the tower (4 miles; 3hr).

ARRIVAL AND INFORMATION   BROADWAY

By bus #1 (Mon–Sat 4 daily) to/from Chipping Campden (20min), Moreton-in-Marsh (25min) and Stratford-upon-Avon (1hr); #606 (Mon–Sat 4 daily, 2 on Sun) to/from Winchcombe (25min) and Cheltenham (1hr).

Tourist office Russell Square (Feb, March, Nov & Dec Mon–Sat 10am–4pm, Sun 11am–3pm; April–Oct Mon–Sat 10am–5pm, Sun 11am–3pm; ☎01386 852937, ⓦ broadway-cotswolds.co.uk).

ACCOMMODATION AND EATING

Crown and Trumpet 14 Church St, WR12 7AE ☎01386 853202, ⓦ cotswoldholidays.co.uk. This cheery, historic local tavern has decent beers, a lively atmosphere, quality Sun roasts and regular sessions of live blues and jazz. Mains £6–13. Also has five simple en-suite rooms. Kitchen Mon–Fri 11am–3pm & 5–11pm, Sat 11am–11pm, Sun noon–4pm & 6–10.30pm. **£75**

Lygon Arms High St, WR12 7DU ☎01386 852255, ⓦ lygonarmshotel.co.uk. A grand coaching inn that hosted Charles I (in 1645) and Oliver Cromwell (in 1651) in rooms which still retain their original panelling and fittings today. In 2017, they had a top-to-toe refit, which injected much-needed freshness into both the rooms and restaurant, now serving good, upmarket Modern European cuisine (mains £13–21), including in the majestic Great Hall. Food served Mon–Fri

11am–3pm & 5–10pm, Sat & Sun 11am–10pm. **£170**

Olive Branch 78 High St, WR12 7AJ ☎01386 853440, ⓦ theolivebranch-broadway.com. Award-winning guest-house in an old stone house – a touch pastel-and-chintz, but cosy and well run. Some rooms have king-size beds and access to the garden. **£117**

Russell's 20 High St, WR12 7DT ☎01386 853555, ⓦ russellsofbroadway.co.uk. This relaxed, stylish restaurant serves Modern British cooking: Cotswold lamb chops with lemon & caper-crumbed kidney, honey & thyme-glazed duck breast, monkfish with bulgur wheat, and so on. Mains £15–32, or two-course set menu £20. Seven boutique rooms feature mood lighting, designer furniture and huge stand-alone bathtubs and showers-for-two. Food served Mon–Sat noon–2.15pm & 6–9.15pm, Sun noon–2.30pm. **£130**

Winchcombe and around

About eight miles southwest of Broadway – and nine miles northeast of Cheltenham – **WINCHCOMBE** has a long main street flanked by a fetching medley of stone and

> ## WALKS AROUND WINCHCOMBE
>
> Winchcombe sets itself up as the **walking** capital of the Cotswolds. Aside from the **Cotswold Way** there's the **Gloucestershire Way** to Stow or Tewkesbury, and two long-distance routes heading north into Worcestershire, the **Wychavon Way** and **St Kenelm's Way**. The website ⓦ winchcombewelcomeswalkers.com has full information, including details of a scenic loop (5 miles; 3hr) through **Spoonley Wood**, two miles southeast of town. It starts by the war memorial opposite Winchcombe's church.

half-timbered buildings. Placid today, it was an important Saxon town and one-time capital of the kingdom of Mercia, and flourished during the medieval cloth boom, one of the results being **St Peter's** church, a mainly fifteenth-century structure distinguished by forty alarming gargoyles that ring the exterior.

Sudeley Castle

Winchcombe, GL54 5JD · March–Oct daily 10am–5pm · £14.95 · ☎ 01242 604244, ⓦ sudeleycastle.co.uk

Rising amid a magnificent estate on Winchcombe's southern edge, **Sudeley Castle** combines ravishing good looks with a fascinating history. **Richard III** lived at Sudeley for several years, and in 1535 **Henry VIII** spent a week here with Anne Boleyn. **Katherine Parr**, Henry's sixth wife, died at Sudeley in 1548. During the **Civil War** Sudeley acted as a Royalist garrison, coming under repeated attack. The ruins mouldered grandly, attracting the attention of **George III**, who fell down a crumbling flight of stairs on a visit in 1788. Restored in the nineteenth century, battlemented Sudeley now stands amid exquisite **grounds**. Explore the towering ruins of the Elizabethan **Banqueting Hall** – left romantically untouched – and stroll through a grove of mulberry trees to reach the spectacular **Queen's Garden**, which is surrounded by yews and filled with summer roses. Alongside stands the Perpendicular Gothic **St Mary's Church**, housing a beautiful Victorian tomb that marks the final resting place of Katherine Parr.

Belas Knap

2 miles south of Winchcombe, GL54 5AL · Open access · Free; EH · ⓦ www.english-heritage.org.uk/visit/places/belas-knap-long-barrow · On foot from Winchcombe, the path strikes off to the right near the entrance to Sudeley Castle. When you reach the country lane at the top, turn right and then left for the 10min hike to the barrow

The Neolithic long barrow of **Belas Knap** occupies one of the Cotswolds' wildest summits. Dating from around 3000 BC, this is the best-preserved burial chamber in England, stretched out like a strange sleeping beast cloaked in green velvet, more than fifty metres long. The best way to get there is to **walk**.

ARRIVAL AND INFORMATION

By bus #606 from Broadway (Mon–Sat 4 daily; 35min) and Cheltenham (Mon–Sat 4 daily, 5 on Sun; 20min).

Tourist office High St (April–Oct daily 10am–4pm;

WINCHCOMBE AND AROUND

Nov–March Sat 10am–4pm, Sun 10am–3pm; ☎ 01242 602925, ⓦ winchcombe.co.uk and ⓦ cotswolds.com).

ACCOMMODATION AND EATING

Lion Inn 37 North St, GL54 5PS ☎ 01242 603300, ⓦ thelionwinchcombe.co.uk. This fifteenth-century coaching inn is now a family-run bolthole, with eight modern en-suite rooms. The menu relies on seasonal local produce, but also ventures into light European styles for tagines or seafood dishes. Mains £14–18. Kitchen Mon–Thurs noon–3pm & 6–9pm, Fri & Sat noon–3pm & 6–9.30pm, Sun noon–4pm & 6–9pm. **£120**

White Hart High St, GL54 5LJ ☎ 01242 602359, ⓦ whitehartwinchcombe.co.uk. A good-looking old tavern with wooden floors and benches. Eight en-suite rooms are decorated in traditional-meets-folksy manner, and there are also three cheaper "rambler" rooms with shared bath. The restaurant is a great place to eat, focusing on hearty British cooking – especially meaty mains such as duck and pork belly (£11–25). Daily 8am–9pm. **£75**

Cirencester

Self-styled "Capital of the Cotswolds", the affluent town of **CIRENCESTER** lies on the southern fringes of the region, midway between Oxford and Bristol. As Corinium, it became a provincial capital and a centre of trade under the **Romans**, in Britannia second in size and importance only to "Londinium" (London). The Saxons destroyed almost all of the Roman city, and the town only revived with the wool boom of the Middle Ages. Few medieval buildings have survived, however, and the houses along the town's most handsome streets – Park, Thomas and Coxwell – date mostly from the seventeenth and eighteenth centuries. Cirencester's heart is the delightful **Market Place**, packed with traders' stalls every Monday and Friday, and for the fortnightly Saturday farmers' market (⟶cirencester.gov.uk/markets).

Church of St John the Baptist

Market Place, GL7 2NX • Daily 10am–5pm; Oct–March closes 4pm • Free • ☎ 01285 659317, ⟶ cirenparish.co.uk

The magnificent parish church of **St John the Baptist**, built during the fifteenth century, dominates the market place. The church's most notable feature is its huge **porch**, so big that it once served as the local town hall. The flying buttresses that support the tower had to be added when it transpired that the church had been built over the filled-in Roman ditch that ran beside the Gloucester–Silchester road. Inside the church is a colourful wineglass **pulpit**, carved in stone around 1450, and the **Boleyn Cup**, a gilded silver goblet made in 1535 for Anne Boleyn.

Corinium Museum

Park St, GL7 2BX • Mon–Sat 10am–5pm, Sun 2–5pm; Nov–March closes 4pm • £5.40 • ☎ 01285 655611, ⟶ coriniummuseum.org

West of the Market Place, the sleek **Corinium Museum** is devoted to the history of the town from Roman to Victorian times. The collection of Romano-British antiquities is particularly fine, including wonderful **mosaic pavements**. Other highlights include a trove of Bronze Age gold and an excellent video on Cotswold life in the Iron Age.

4

New Brewery Arts Centre

Brewery Court, off Cricklade St, GL7 1JH • Mon–Sat 9am–5pm; April–Dec also Sun 10am–4pm • Free • ☎ 01285 657181, ⟶ newbreweryarts.org.uk

Just south of the Market Place, the **New Brewery Arts Centre** is occupied by more than a dozen resident artists whose studios you can visit and whose work you can buy in the shop. It's worth popping by to see who is working and exhibiting – and, perhaps, to catch some live music.

ARRIVAL AND INFORMATION   CIRENCESTER

By train From Kemble station, about 5 miles southwest – served by hourly trains from London Paddington (1hr 15min) and Cheltenham (1hr) – take bus #882 (Mon–Fri 5 daily, 2 on Sat; 15min) or a taxi (about £10).

By bus National Express coaches from London Victoria and Heathrow Airport stop on London Rd, while local buses stop in or near Market Place.

Destinations Bibury (#855; Mon–Sat 4 daily; 15min); Cheltenham (#51; Mon–Sat hourly; 40min); Gloucester

(#882; Mon–Fri every 1–2hr, 2 on Sat; 45min); Heathrow Airport (National Express; 5 daily; 1hr 30min); London Victoria (National Express; 5–8 daily; 2hr 20min); Northleach (#855; Mon–Sat every 2hr; 20min); Tetbury (#882; Mon–Sat 3 daily; 45min).

Tourist office At Corinium Museum, Park St (Mon–Sat 10am–5pm, Sun 2–5pm; Nov–March closes 4pm; ☎01285 654180, ⟶ cotswolds.com).

ACCOMMODATION

Corinium 12 Gloucester St, GL7 2DG ☎01285 659711, ⟶ coriniumhotel.com. Decent three-star family-run hotel in a historic property a short walk northwest of the centre. Only fifteen rooms, modestly priced and adequately furnished. **£105**

Fleece Market Place, GL7 2NZ ☎01285 658507, ⟶ thefleececirencester.co.uk. This old town-centre inn

has been freshly updated to a smart, contemporary look. The 28 rooms, all beams and low ceilings, feature swanky en-suite bathrooms. **£99**

Ivy House 2 Victoria Rd, GL7 1EN ☎01285 656626, ⟶ ivyhousecotswolds.com. One of the more attractive of a string of B&Bs along this road, a high-gabled Victorian house with four en-suite rooms. **£90**

YHA Cotswolds New Brewery Arts Centre, GL7 1JH ☎01285 657181, ⓦyha.org.uk/hostel/cotswolds. Converted in 2016 from a long-closed brewery warehouse, this new hostel known as the Barrel Store sits alongside a buzzing arts centre, with keenly priced dorms, doubles and family rooms. No food served, but there's a café next door. Dorms £23, doubles £68

EATING AND DRINKING

Indian Rasoi 14 Dollar St, GL7 2AJ ☎01285 644822, ⓦindianrasoi.org. An up-to-date, contemporary styled restaurant serving excellent Indian food. Go for one of the chef's specials – fiery Naga chilli lamb or coconutty Mangalore chicken – or one of the great vegetarian options, such as Bengali aubergine. Mains £9–14. Mon–Sat noon–2pm & 5.30–11.30pm, Sun noon–2pm & 5.30–11pm.

★**Jesse's Bistro** The Stableyard, 14 Black Jack St, GL7 2AA ☎01285 641497, ⓦjessesbistro.co.uk. Wonderful little hideaway, in a courtyard near the museum. The speciality here is fish and seafood, freshly caught and whisked over directly from Cornwall. Expect crab salad or *moules marinière*, oven-roasted mackerel or pepper-crusted bream alongside meaty favourites such as rump steak. Mains £14–23; two-course lunch £19.50. Mon noon–2.30pm, Tues–Sat noon–2.30pm & 7–9.30pm, Sun noon–4pm.

Made By Bob The Corn Hall, 26 Market Place, GL7 2NY ☎01285 641818, ⓦfoodmadebybob.com. Buzzy, hip daytime café/restaurant. Opens for breakfast (Bircher muesli, kippers, eggs Benedict, full English; £6–11), and stays open after lunch for posh tea. Watch the chefs prepare anything from fish soup with gruyère or linguine with cockles to grilled sardines or rib-eye steak (mains £9–21) – or visit the deli section for swanky sandwiches (£6–8). Booking essential for "Bob's Bar" (Wed–Fri 5–11pm), where nibbles (£4–8) accompany drinks. Mon, Tues & Sat 7.30am–6pm, Wed–Fri 7.30am–11pm.

Tetbury and around

With Prince Charles's Highgrove estate and Princess Anne's Gatcombe Park nearby, **TETBURY** is the Cotswolds' most royal town – but this attractive, engaging place has plenty going for it with or without the Windsors. Scenic countryside, good shopping and excellent food make a fine combination. Just down from the central crossroads, marked by the seventeenth-century **Market House**, Tetbury's **church** (daily 10am–4pm; ⓦtetburychurch.co.uk) – curiously dedicated to both St Mary the Virgin and St Mary Magdalene – is one of England's finest examples of **Georgian Gothic**: the view along the eighteenth-century nave, with its dark box pews, candle chandeliers, slender wooden columns and enormous windows, is breathtaking.

Highgrove

Doughton, GL8 8TQ • Garden tours April–Oct selected days & times; 2hr • From £25 • Booking essential: ☎0303 123 7310, ⓦhighgrovegardens.com

Highgrove, home of Prince Charles and Camilla, Duchess of Cornwall, lies about a mile southwest of Tetbury. Tours of the **gardens** – led, needless to say, by a guide rather than HRH himself – operate in the summer, with tales evoking each setting, from the mighty Thyme Walk to the calm of the Cottage Garden, Stumpery and aromatic Kitchen Garden. There's a waiting list of several weeks.

THAMES HEAD

Between Cirencester and Tetbury, **Kemble** is surrounded by water meadows regarded as the **source of the River Thames**. From Kemble station – served by hourly trains from London Paddington (1hr 15min) and Cheltenham (1hr) – walk half a mile north to the *Thames Head Inn* (☎01285 770259, ⓦthamesheadinn.co.uk), by the railway bridge on the A433. At the pub, bar staff and a sketch-map hanging in the porch can point you towards the stroll of about fifteen minutes to **Thames Head**, a point by a copse in open fields, where a stone marker declares a shallow depression to be the river's source. However, the Thames is fed by groundwater, and since the water table rises and falls, the river's source shifts: don't be disappointed if Thames Head is dry when you visit. The **Thames Path** (ⓦnationaltrail.co.uk) starts here: you can follow it all the way to Greenwich in southeast London, 184 miles away.

Westonbirt: the National Arboretum

3 miles southwest of Tetbury, GL8 8QS · Daily 9am–5pm · £10 (Dec–Feb £7) · Guided walks March–Oct Mon, Wed & Fri 11am, Sat & Sun 11am & 2pm; 2hr · Free with admission · ☎ 0300 067 4890, ⓦ forestry.gov.uk/westonbirt · From Tetbury take bus #27 or #69 (Mon–Sat 2/3 daily; 8min)

Everything about **Westonbirt: The National Arboretum** relies on superlatives, from its role as protector of some of the oldest, biggest and rarest trees in the world to the stunning display of natural colours it puts on in autumn. With seventeen miles of paths to roam, across six hundred acres, the best advice is to make a day of it. There are **guided walks**, **self-guided trails** and lots for kids and families.

ARRIVAL AND INFORMATION

By train From Kemble station, about 7 miles northeast – served by hourly trains from London Paddington (1hr 15min) and Cheltenham (1hr) – take bus #882 (Mon–Fri 5 daily, 3 on Sat; 20min).

By bus Buses drop off in the centre, including #882 to/

TETBURY AND AROUND

from Cirencester (Mon–Fri 5 daily, 3 on Sat; 35min).

Tourist office 33 Church St (Mon–Sat: April–Oct 10am–4pm; Nov–March 10am–2pm; ☎ 01666 503552, ⓦ visittetbury.co.uk and ⓦ cotswolds.com).

ACCOMMODATION AND EATING

The Ormond 23 Long St, GL8 8AA ☎ 01666 505690, ⓦ theormondattetbury.co.uk. This inn-restaurant focuses on local suppliers – think honey-roast ham, steak and ale pie or juniper duck with sausage – served in a cheery, informal setting. Mains £11–18. Doubles as a rather nice mid-range hotel, with tasteful, wittily done-up rooms. Kitchen Mon–Sat noon–2.30pm & 6.30–9.30pm, Sun noon–3pm & 7–9pm. £109

★**Priory Inn** London Rd, GL8 8JJ ☎ 01666 502251, ⓦ theprioryinn.co.uk. Although the mains of Gloucester pork or Bibury trout are excellent (£12–19), the speciality at this family-friendly spot is wood-fired pizza (£9–13). Also has fourteen neutral, unfussy rooms. Kitchen Mon–Fri noon–3pm & 5–10pm, Sat & Sun noon–10pm. £99

Snooty Fox Market Place, GL8 8DD ☎ 01666 502436,

ⓦ snooty-fox.co.uk. Traditional coaching inn, renamed by a former owner who was snubbed by the local hunt. Contemporary-styled rooms feature a nod to the traditional here, a touch of playfulness there, and the food is uncomplicated, presented decently and charged moderately. Mains £12–17. Kitchen daily 9–11.30am, noon–2.30pm, 3–5.30pm & 6–9pm. £111

Stargazy Fish Bar At Priory Inn, London Rd, GL8 8JJ ☎ 01666 500690, ⓦ stargazyfishbar.co.uk. National award-winning fish and chips (£9) at this newcomer – part of the *Priory Inn*, with high-quality ingredients, plenty of options (including pies, chicken and batter-free grilled fish) and twice-fried chips. Take away, dine in or scoff at the garden tables. Mon–Thurs, Sat & Sun noon–3pm & 5–9pm, Fri noon–3pm & 5–10pm.

Painswick

PAINSWICK is a beautiful old Cotswolds wool town easily accessible from Cheltenham. The fame of Painswick's **church** stems not so much from the building itself as from the surrounding **graveyard**, where 99 yew trees, trimmed into bulbous lollipops, surround a collection of eighteenth-century table-tombs unrivalled in the Cotswolds.

Rococo Garden

Half a mile north of Painswick, off Gloucester Rd, GL6 6TH · Mid-Jan to Oct daily 10.30am–5pm · £7.20 · ☎ 01452 813204, ⓦ www .rococogarden.org.uk

Created in the early eighteenth century, the **Rococo Garden** has been restored to its original form with the aid of a painting from 1748. This is England's only example of Rococo garden design, a short-lived fashion typified by a mix of formal geometrical shapes and more naturalistic, curving lines. With a vegetable patch as an unusual centrepiece, it spreads across a sheltered gully. For the best views, walk around anti-clockwise.

ARRIVAL AND INFORMATION

By bus #61 runs to/from Cheltenham (hourly; 40min).

Tourist office Painswick's summer-only tourist office (March–Oct Mon & Wed–Fri 10am–4pm, Tues 10am–1pm,

PAINSWICK

Sat 10am–1pm; ☎ 01452 812278, ⓦ painswicktouristinfo .co.uk and ⓦ cotswolds.com) is in the gravedigger's hut in the corner of the churchyard.

ACCOMMODATION AND EATING

Cardynham House Tibbiwell St, GL6 6XX ☎ 01452 814006, ⓦ cardynham.co.uk. Lovely guesthouse with nine modern, themed rooms, most with four-poster beds and all en suite. The bistro has simple, well-cooked nosh – cod loin, lamb cutlets, beef stroganoff and the like (mains £13–17). Tues–Sat noon–3pm & 6.30–9.30pm, Sun noon–3pm. **£110**

★**Olivas** Friday St, GL6 6QJ ☎ 01452 814774, ⓦ olivas .moonfruit.com. Brilliant deli and café that does delicious Mediterranean-style lunches – Spanish soups and stews of chicken, chickpeas and chorizo, stuffed aubergines, loads of tapas including calamari, whitebait, olives, and more, all around £12. Daily 10am–5pm.

Cheltenham

Until the eighteenth century **CHELTENHAM** was a modest Cotswold town like any other, but the discovery of a spring in 1716 transformed it into Britain's most popular **spa**. During Cheltenham's heyday, a century or so later, royalty and nobility descended in droves to take the waters, which were said to cure anything from constipation to worms. These days, the town – still lively, still posh – has lots of good restaurants and some of England's best-preserved Regency architecture.

Cheltenham also has excellent **arts festivals** (ⓦ cheltenhamfestivals.com) – **jazz** (May), **science** (June), **classical music** (July) and **literature** (Oct), plus a separately run **folk** festival (Feb) – as well as world-class **horse racing** (see box opposite).

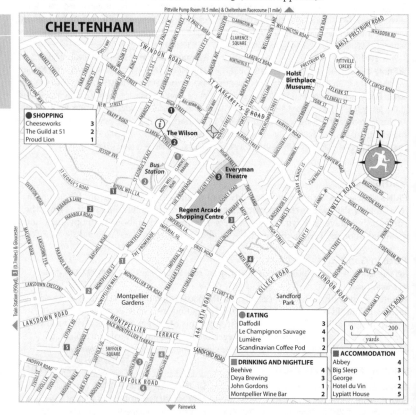

CHELTENHAM

● SHOPPING
Cheeseworks — 3
The Guild at 51 — 2
Proud Lion — 1

● EATING
Daffodil — 3
Le Champignon Sauvage — 4
Lumière — 1
Scandinavian Coffee Pod — 2

■ DRINKING AND NIGHTLIFE
Beehive — 4
Deya Brewing — 3
John Gordons — 1
Montpellier Wine Bar — 2

■ ACCOMMODATION
Abbey — 4
Big Sleep — 3
George — 1
Hotel du Vin — 2
Lypiatt House — 5

CHELTENHAM RACES

Cheltenham racecourse (☎01242 513014, ⓦcheltenham.thejockeyclub.co.uk), on the north side of town, is Britain's main venue for National Hunt racing, also known as "steeplechase" – where the horses jump hurdles or fences. The principal events are the four-day **Festival** in March, which attracts sixty thousand people each day, culminating in the famous **Cheltenham Gold Cup**, and the three-day **November Meeting**, but there are smaller meetings throughout the season, which runs from late October to early May. For what many say is the best view, book ahead for entry to the pen opposite the main stand, known as Best Mate Enclosure (about £10–50, depending on event).

Promenade

Cheltenham's main street, **Promenade**, sweeps majestically south from the High Street, and is lined with some of the town's grandest houses and smartest shops. It leads into Imperial Square, whose greenery is surrounded by proud Regency terraces that herald the handsome squares of the Montpellier district, which stretches south in a narrow block to Suffolk Road, making for a pleasant urban stroll.

The Wilson

Clarence St, GL50 3JT • Mon–Sat 9.30am–5.15pm, Sun 11am–4pm • Free • ☎01242 237431, ⓦthewilson.org.uk

Just off the Promenade stands **The Wilson**, formerly known as the **Cheltenham Art Gallery and Museum**, now housing the tourist office, a shop selling beautiful work by the Gloucestershire Guild of Craftsmen (ⓦguildcrafts.org.uk) and four floors of exhibitions. The rebranding honours Edward Wilson, a Cheltonian who was on Scott's ill-fated Antarctic expedition of 1912. Photographs and some of his Antarctic gear are displayed alongside a collection focused on the Arts and Crafts movement (see box, p.258), ranging from superb furniture to ceramics, jewellery, pottery and exquisitely hand-illustrated books.

Holst Birthplace Museum

4 Clarence Rd, GL52 2AY • Tues–Sat 10am–5pm, Sun 1.30–5pm • £5 • ☎01242 524846, ⓦholstmuseum.org.uk

Housed in a refined Regency terrace house, the **Holst Birthplace Museum** was where the composer of *The Planets* was born, in 1874. Its intimate rooms hold plenty of Holst memorabilia – including his piano in the ground-floor music room – and give a good insight into Victorian family life.

Pittville Pump Room

Pittville Park, GL52 3JE • Wed–Sun 10am–4pm • Free • ☎01242 523852, ⓦcheltenhamtownhall.org.uk/visit-us/pittville-pump-room

About ten minutes' walk north of the centre along handsome Evesham Road brings you into the **Pittville** district, where local chancer Joseph Pitt began work on a grand spa in the 1820s, soon afterwards running out of cash, though he did manage to complete the domed **Pump Room** before he hit the skids. A lovely Classical structure with an imposing colonnaded facade, it is now used mainly as a concert hall, but you can still sample the pungent **spa waters** from the marble fountain in the main auditorium for free.

ARRIVAL AND INFORMATION   CHELTENHAM

By train Cheltenham Spa station is on Queen's Rd, southwest of the centre. Local buses run into town every 10min; otherwise it's a 20min walk.

Destinations Birmingham New Street (2–3 hourly; 40min);

Bristol (every 30min; 40min); London Paddington (hourly, some change at Swindon; 2hr 15min).

By bus National Express coaches for London and Heathrow stop on Royal Well Rd. Local buses stop on Promenade.

Destinations #46 to/from Painswick (hourly; 40min); #51 to/from Cirencester (Mon–Sat hourly; 40min); #94 to/from Gloucester (every 10min; 35min); #606 to/from Winchcombe (Mon–Sat 4 daily, 5 on Sun; 20min) & Broadway (Mon–Sat 4 daily, 2 on Sun; 1hr); #801 to/from Northleach (Mon–Sat 5 daily; 40min), Stow-on-the-Wold (Mon–Sat every 1–2hr; June–Sept also 2–3 on Sun; 55min) & Moreton-in-Marsh (Mon–Sat every 1–2hr; June–Sept also 2–3 on Sun; 1hr 10min); #853 (Mon–Sat 3–4 daily, 1 on Sun) to/from Northleach (30min), Burford (45min) & Oxford (1hr 30min). **Tourist office** In The Wilson, Clarence St (Mon–Wed 9.30am–5.15pm, Thurs 9.30am–7.45pm, Fri & Sat 9.30am–5.30pm, Sun 10.30am–4pm; ☎ 01242 237431, ⓦ visitcheltenham.com and ⓦ cotswolds.com).

ACCOMMODATION

Cheltenham has plenty of **hotels** and **guesthouses**, many of them in fine Regency buildings, but you should book well in advance during the races and festivals.

Abbey 14 Bath Parade, GL53 7HN ☎ 01242 516053, ⓦ abbeyhotel-cheltenham.com; map p.270. There are thirteen individually furnished rooms at this centrally located B&B, with wholesome breakfasts taken overlooking the garden. **£101**

Big Sleep Wellington St, GL50 1XZ ☎ 01242 696999, ⓦ thebigsleephotel.com; map p.270. Contemporary budget hotel with 59 rooms including family rooms and suites, all with a retro designer feel and high-tech gadgetry but no frills – and unusually low prices. **£49**

George St George's Rd, GL50 3DZ ☎ 01242 235751, ⓦ stayatthegeorge.co.uk; map p.270. This Grade II listed building bang in the centre, built in the 1840s, now hosts a stylishly designed 31-room hotel, with contemporary flair to the interiors. Prices are surprisingly competitive. **£89**

Hotel du Vin Parabola Rd, GL50 3AH ☎ 0330 016 0390, ⓦ hotelduvin.com; map p.270. Occupying a splendid old Regency mansion, this glam boutique-style hotel in the sought-after Montpellier district has 49 jazzy rooms and suites and a reputation for excellence. **£109**

Lypiatt House Lypiatt Rd, GL50 2QW ☎ 01242 224994, ⓦ lypiatt.co.uk; map p.270. Splendid, four-square Victorian villa set in its own grounds a short walk from the centre, with spacious rooms, open fires and a conservatory with a small bar. **£111**

EATING

★ **Daffodil** 18–20 Suffolk Parade, GL50 2AE ☎ 01242 700055, ⓦ www.thedaffodil.com; map p.270. Eat in the circle bar or auditorium of this breathtakingly designed 1922 Art Deco ex-cinema, where the screen has been replaced with a hubbub of chefs. Great atmosphere and first-class British cuisine (mains £15–28), as well as cocktails and a swish of style. Two-course set menu (Mon–Sat 5–6.30pm, plus Fri & Sat noon–2.30pm) from £12. Mon–Thurs 5–11pm, Fri & Sat noon–midnight.

Le Champignon Sauvage 24 Suffolk Rd, GL50 2AQ ☎ 01242 573449, ⓦ lechampignonsauvage.co.uk; map p.270. Cheltenham's highest-rated restaurant, whose sensitively updated classic French cuisine has been awarded two Michelin stars, among a welter of other awards. The ambience is chic and intimate, the presentation immaculately artistic. The full menu is £53 (two courses) or £67 (three courses), and there's a smaller set menu at £27 (two courses). Book well ahead. Tues–Sat 12.30–1.15pm & 7.30–8.30pm.

Lumière Clarence Parade, GL50 3PA ☎ 01242 222200, ⓦ lumiere.cc; map p.270. Upscale, contemporary, seasonal British food in a genial ambience of informality, recently named England's Restaurant of the Year. Cornish scallops or sexed-up corned beef prelude mains such as Gloucester Old Spot pork done two ways, partridge or local venison. Three-course menu £65 (or £35 at lunch), with six- and nine-course tasting menus available. Wed & Thurs 7–8.30pm, Fri & Sat noon–1.30pm & 7–8.30pm.

Scandinavian Coffee Pod Royal Well Place, GL50 3DN ⓦ thescandinaviancoffeepod.com; map p.270. Eye-catching little coffee house, in architecturally converted premises, that roasts its own beans and offers exquisitely prepared espressos and lattes, along with cakes and light bites (£4–6). Mon–Fri 8am–5pm, Sat 8.30am–5pm, Sun 9.30am–4pm.

DRINKING AND NIGHTLIFE

Beehive 1–3 Montpellier Villas, GL50 2XE ☎ 01242 702270, ⓦ thebeehivemontpellier.com; map p.270. Popular, easy-going pub with good beer – including locally brewed ales – a friendly ambience and excellent food in the atmospheric restaurant upstairs (mains £10–15). Mon–Thurs & Sun noon–11.30pm, Fri & Sat noon–1am.

Deya Brewing Units 33/34, Lansdown Industrial Estate, Gloucester Rd, GL51 8PL ☎ 01242 269189, ⓦ deya brewing.com; map p.270. Every Fri & Sat this craft brewery, a 2min walk behind the station, opens up its taproom to serve its range of beers on draught – it's a unique way to sample unique beers. Fri 4–9pm, Sat 2–8pm.

★ **John Gordons** 11 Montpellier Arcade, GL50 1SU ☎ 01242 245985, ⓦ johngordons.co.uk; map p.270. Lovely little independent wine bar, hidden off Montpellier's fanciest street. Take a seat in the shop or outside in the old Victorian covered arcade to watch the world go by while sampling a glass or two of wine, alongside a plate of charcuterie, cheeses and/or antipasti (£6–14), or a range of tapas (£2–5). Mon–Wed 11am–10pm, Thurs 10.30am–11pm, Fri & Sat 10.30am–1am.

Montpellier Wine Bar Bayshill Lodge, Montpellier St, GL50 1SY ☎ 01242 527774, ⓦ montpellierwinebar .co.uk; map p.270. Stylish wine bar and restaurant with lovely bow-fronted windows on a busy little corner. Hang out at the bar with a glass of something smooth, or drop in mid-morning for brunch. Mon–Thurs & Sun 9.30am–11pm, Fri & Sat 9.30am–1am.

SHOPPING

Cheeseworks 5 Regent St, GL50 1HE ☎ 01242 255022, ⓦ thecheeseworks.co.uk; map p.270. Posh, aromatic cheesemonger's in the centre of town, selling from local farm cheeses to European varieties, plus ports, chutneys and accessories. Mon–Sat 9.30am–5.30pm.

The Guild at 51 51 Clarence St, GL50 3JT ☎ 01242 245215, ⓦ guildcrafts.org.uk; map p.270. Showroom and shop beside the Wilson gallery for the Gloucestershire Guild of Craftsmen – professional designers working in jewellery, ceramics, textiles, leatherwork, glass, basketry and more. Quality is excellent, which nudges prices up, but these are unusual items. Tues–Sat 10am–5pm, Sun 11am–4pm.

Proud Lion 8 St George's Place, GL50 3JZ ☎ 01242 525636, ⓦ proudlion.co.uk; map p.270. Geeky outlet for comics, graphic novels and gaming, with a wealth of knowledge and enthusiasm to boot. Mon & Sun noon–5.30pm, Tues & Thurs–Sat 10am–5.30pm, Wed 10am–6.30pm.

Gloucester and around

For centuries life was good for **GLOUCESTER**, ten miles west of Cheltenham. The Romans chose this spot for a garrison to guard the River Severn, while in Saxon and Norman times the Severn developed into one of Europe's busiest trade routes. The city became a major religious centre too, but from the fifteenth century onwards a combination of fire, plague, civil war and increasing competition from rival towns sent Gloucester into a decline from which it never recovered – even the opening of a new canal in 1827 between Gloucester and Sharpness failed to revive the town's dwindling

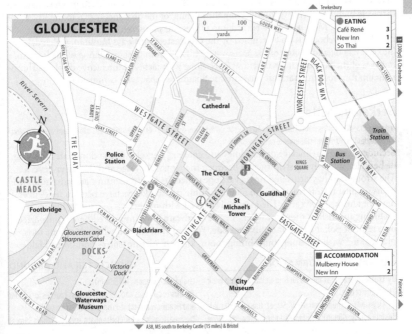

fortunes. Today, the **canal** is busy once again, though this time with pleasure boats, and the Victorian **docks** have undergone a facelift, offering a fascinating glimpse into the region's industrial past. The main reason for a visit, however, remains Gloucester's magnificent **cathedral**, one of the finest in the country.

Gloucester Cathedral

College Green, GL1 2LX • Daily 7.30am–6pm • Free • ☎ 01452 528095, ⓦ gloucestercathedral.org.uk

The superb condition of **Gloucester Cathedral** is striking in a city that has lost so much of its history. The Saxons founded an abbey here, but four centuries later Benedictine monks arrived intent on building their own church; work began in 1089. As a place of worship it shot to importance after the murder of King Edward II in 1327 at nearby Berkeley Castle (see below): Gloucester took his body, and the king's shrine became a place of pilgrimage. The money generated helped finance the conversion of the church into the country's first example of the **Perpendicular style**: the magnificent 225ft tower crowns the achievement.

Beneath the fourteenth- and fifteenth-century construction, some Norman aspects remain, and these are best seen in the **nave**, which is flanked by sturdy pillars and arches adorned with immaculate zigzag carvings. The **choir** provides the best vantage point for admiring the **east window**, completed in around 1350 and – at almost 80ft tall – the largest medieval window in Britain, a stunning cliff face of stained glass. Beneath it to the left is the **tomb of Edward II**, immortalized in alabaster and marble, while below it lies the **Lady Chapel** (closed at the time of writing for restoration), whose delicate carved tracery holds a staggering patchwork of windows. The innovative nature of the cathedral's design can also be appreciated in the beautiful **cloisters**, completed in 1367 and featuring the first fan vaulting in the country – used to represent the corridors of Hogwarts in the *Harry Potter* films.

Gloucester Waterways Museum

Gloucester Docks, GL1 2EH • April–Oct daily 10am–5pm; Nov–March Tues–Sun 11am–3pm • £8.50 • **Boat trips** July, Aug & school hols daily noon, 1.30pm & 2.30pm; rest of year Sat & Sun 1.30pm; 45min • £6.50 • ☎ 01452 318200, ⓦ canalrivertrust.org.uk/gloucester-waterways-museum

Less than half a mile southwest of the city centre, **Gloucester Docks** holds fourteen warehouses that were built for storing grain following the opening of the Sharpness canal to the River Severn in 1827. Most have been turned into offices and shops, but the southernmost Llanthony Warehouse is now occupied by the **Gloucester Waterways Museum**, which delves into every nook and cranny of the area's watery history, from the engineering of the locks to the lives of the horses that trod the towpaths, along with plenty of interactive displays. The museum runs regular **boat trips** out onto the Sharpness canal, with commentary.

Berkeley Castle

Berkeley, GL13 9BQ, 15 miles south of Gloucester • April–Oct Sun–Wed 11am–5pm • £11 • ☎ 01453 810303, ⓦ berkeley-castle.com • If driving, use postcode GL13 9PJ for the main entrance on Canonbury St

Secluded within an enclave of meadows and gardens, **Berkeley Castle** dominates the Vale of Berkeley, a low-lying strip tucked between the Cotswold Edge and the River Severn. The stronghold has a turreted medieval appearance, its twelfth-century austerity softened by its gradual transformation into a family home (the Berkeleys have been in residence here for almost 900 years). The interior is packed with mementos of its long history, including its grisliest moment when, in 1327, **Edward II** was murdered here – purportedly by a red-hot poker thrust into his backside. You can view the cell where the event took place, along with the dungeons, dining room, kitchen, picture gallery and Great Hall.

ARRIVAL AND INFORMATION	GLOUCESTER AND AROUND

By train Gloucester station is on Bruton Way, a 5min walk east of the centre.
Destinations Birmingham New Street (hourly; 50min); Bristol (hourly; 40min); London Paddington (hourly, some

change at Swindon; 1hr 55min).
By bus Local buses and National Express coaches for London and Heathrow Airport stop opposite the train station.
Destinations #94 for Cheltenham (every 10min; 35min);

#882 for Cirencester (Mon–Fri every 1–2hr, 2 on Sat; 45min); #853 (Mon–Sat 2 daily, 1 on Sun) for Northleach (50min), Burford (1hr 5min) & Oxford (2hr).

Tourist office 28 Southgate St (Mon 10am–5pm, Tues–Sat 9.30am–5pm; ☏ 01452 396572, ⊛ thecityofgloucester .co.uk and ⊛ cotswolds.com).

ACCOMMODATION

Mulberry House 2a Heathville Rd, GL1 3DP ☏ 01452 720079, ⊛ the-mulberry-house.co.uk; map p.273. Decent B&B in a modern family home roughly 10min walk northeast of the centre. Two en-suite doubles are enhanced with quality breakfasts. Cash only. **£60**

New Inn 16 Northgate St, GL1 1SF ☏ 01452 522177, ⊛ newinn.relaxinnz.co.uk; map p.273. Though this inn's 33 rooms are pretty basic, with bland decor and corporate furniture, their location above an impressively historic pub (see below) is a big plus. **£55**

EATING

Café René 31 Southgate St, GL1 1TS ☏ 01452 309340, ⊛ caferene.co.uk; map p.273. This lively, fancifully decorated central pub serves decent burgers and steaks, with plenty for vegetarians (mains £9–14), plus lighter lunches and great barbecues in summer (Sun). Live blues, jazz and acoustic music twice a week, and after 11pm on weekend nights the cellar bar turns into a club (£2 admission), with loud local DJs. Mon–Thurs & Sun 11am–midnight, Fri & Sat 11am–4am.

New Inn 16 Northgate St, GL1 1SF ☏ 01452 522177, ⊛ newinn.relaxinnz.co.uk; map p.273. Pop into this fourteenth-century pub in the city centre to sup a pint of one of their several cask ales and have a gander at the preserved interior – this is Britain's most complete surviving medieval courtyard tavern, ringed by galleries (and, reputedly, haunted). You can stay here, too (see above). Mon–Thurs 11am–11pm, Fri & Sat 11am–midnight, Sun noon–10.30pm. **£55**

So Thai Longsmith St, GL1 2HJ ☏ 01452 535185, ⊛ so-thai.co.uk; map p.273. This Thai restaurant is holding onto its reputation for quality and authenticity. The decor features vaulted brickwork, service is attentive and the food – including unusual northern Thai pork curry with pineapple, and lamb massaman curry – is expertly prepared. Mains £10–16, two-course lunch menu £10. Tues–Sun noon–3pm & 6–11pm.

4

Berkshire

One of the "Home Counties" that ring London, **Berkshire** covers a diverse swathe of terrain immediately west of the capital. It is known as a royal county for the presence of **Windsor Castle**, one of the Queen's residences and by far the most important attraction in the area. All around Windsor, the county boundary is formed by the River Thames, on its route into London: a little upstream, at the riverside village of **Cookham**, a gallery displaying works by the local twentieth-century artist Stanley Spencer gives bucolic insight into a now-lost rural idyll. To the north stretch the Chiltern Hills of Buckinghamshire (see p.277), while to the south and west, past Henley-on-Thames (see p.253), the Berkshire Downs rise above humdrum Newbury. The largest town hereabouts is **Reading** – missable, but an important rail crossroads.

Reading

READING, 35 miles west of London, sprawls to a population above 300,000, making it a city in all but name. Prosperous and modern, it is prominent today as a transport hub: the huge train station is the third-busiest in the country outside London, standing at the junction of lines from London, Cornwall, South Wales, the West Midlands and the south coast, and with a direct train to Gatwick Airport and express coach to Heathrow. Reading itself is light on attractions, but boasts a couple of curiosities. First is the **prison** (no public access), a severe-looking structure on Forbury Road, where Oscar Wilde was incarcerated in the 1890s and wrote his poignant *Ballad of Reading Gaol*. The other is a Victorian **replica of the Bayeux Tapestry** recording William the Conqueror's invasion of England in 1066, seventy metres long and now displayed at the **Museum of Reading**, in the town hall on Blagrave Street, two minutes' walk from the station (Tues–Sat 10am–4pm; free; ⊛ readingmuseum.org.uk).

By train The train station is on the north side of town, 5min walk from the centre.

Destinations Birmingham New Street (every 30min; 1hr 35min); Bristol (every 30min; 1hr 15min); Gatwick Airport (hourly; 1hr 15min); London Paddington (every 10min;

25min); Oxford (every 15min; 25min); Southampton (every 30min; 45min); Winchester (every 30min; 30min).

To/from Heathrow The X25 Railair coach shuttles between Reading station and Heathrow Airport (daily every 20min–1hr; 1hr; ⓦ railair.com).

Windsor and Eton

The main reason to visit **WINDSOR**, a royally associated town 21 miles west of London, is to join the human conveyor belt ogling **Windsor Castle**. If you've got the energy or inclination, it's also possible to cross the river to visit **Eton College**, which grew from a fifteenth-century free school for impoverished scholars and choristers to become one of the most elitist schools in the world (for guided tours contact ☎01753 370100, ⓦetoncollege.com). Download details of the **Eton Walkway**, a two-mile circular walk, at ⓦoutdoortrust.com.

Windsor Castle

Windsor, SL4 1NJ • Daily: March–Oct 9.30am–5.30pm; Nov–Feb 9.45am–4.15pm; last entry 1hr 30min before closing • £20.50 • ☎ 0303 123 7304, ⓦ royalcollection.org.uk/visit/windsorcastle

Towering above the town on a steep chalk bluff, **Windsor Castle** is an undeniably imposing sight, its chilly grey walls, punctuated by mighty medieval bastions, continuing as far as the eye can see. Inside, most visitors just gape in awe at the monotonous, gilded grandeur of the **State Apartments**, while the real highlights – the paintings from the Royal Collection that line the walls – are rarely given a second glance. More impressive is **St George's Chapel**, a glorious Perpendicular structure ranking with Henry VII's chapel in Westminster Abbey (see p.62), and the second most important resting place for royal corpses after the Abbey. On a fine day, put aside some time for exploring **Windsor Great Park**, which stretches for several miles south of the castle.

By train London Paddington to Windsor & Eton Central station via Slough (every 30min; 40min) or London Waterloo

to Windsor & Eton Riverside station (every 30min; 55min). From Oxford and Reading, change at Slough.

Cookham and around

Tiny **COOKHAM**, a prosperous Berkshire village five miles northwest of Windsor on the border with Buckinghamshire, was home to **Stanley Spencer** (1891–1959), one of Britain's greatest – and most eccentric – artists. Cliveden (see p.277) is on the doorstep. Much of his work was inspired by the Bible, and many of his paintings depict biblical tales transposed into Cookham – which he once famously described as "a village in Heaven". There's a fine sample of his work at the **Stanley Spencer Gallery** (April–Sept Tues–Sun 10.30am–5.30pm; Oct–March Thurs–Sun 11am–4.30pm; £6; ☎01628 471885, ⓦstanleyspencer.org.uk), which occupies the old Methodist Chapel on the High Street. Three prime exhibits are *View from Cookham Bridge*, the unsettling *Sarah Tubb and the Heavenly Visitors*, and the wonderful (unfinished) *Christ Preaching at Cookham Regatta*. Download details of an hour-long walk round Cookham, visiting places with which Spencer is associated, from the gallery website.

About three miles south of Cookham, on the banks of the Thames, the even smaller village of **BRAY** has the unlikely distinction of hosting two of Britain's four triple-Michelin-starred restaurants – the other two are in London.

By train First get to Maidenhead, served by trains every 15min from London Paddington (40min) and Reading

(15min). Change at Maidenhead for hourly trains to Cookham (7min). Bray is a mile or so from Maidenhead station.

EATING AND DRINKING

Bel & The Dragon High St, Cookham, SL6 9SQ ☎01628 521263, ⊛belandthedragon-cookham.co.uk. This historic half-timbered pub is a nice place for a pint, while the airy modern restaurant offers excellent upmarket international cuisine (mains £9–33), with a more affordable bar menu, backed by an extensive wine list. Also five comfortable rustic-style rooms. Mon–Fri noon–11pm, Sat noon–11.30pm, Sun noon–10.30pm; kitchen Mon–Sat noon–3pm & 6–10pm, Sun noon–9pm. £140

Fat Duck High St, Bray, SL6 2AQ ☎01628 580333, ⊛thefatduck.co.uk. Regularly voted one of the world's top restaurants, showcasing chef Heston Blumenthal's uniquely inventive culinary style. The menu might feature such classic creations as snail porridge and egg-and-bacon ice cream, with whisky wine gums to finish. Reservations (bookable up to four months in advance) are like gold dust. From £265 a head. Tues–Sat noon–1.15pm & 7–8.15pm.

Waterside Inn Ferry Rd, Bray, SL6 2AT ☎01628 620691, ⊛waterside-inn.co.uk. Part of the Roux family's culinary empire, this lovely restaurant has been wowing diners with its idiosyncratic take on French cuisine since 1972. Signature dishes include sumptuous soufflé Suissesse (cheese soufflé with double cream) and tronçonnette de homard (pan-fried lobster with white port sauce). Lunchtime menus £50–80; six-course tasting menu £168. Reserve well in advance. Wed–Sun noon–2pm & 7–10pm.

Bucks and Beds

The muddled landscapes of **Buckinghamshire** (or "Bucks") and **Bedfordshire** ("Beds") mark the transition between London's satellite towns and the Midlands; suburbs now encircle many of the area's once-small country towns. The **Chiltern Hills** extend across the region southwest from the workaday town of Luton, bumping across Bucks as far as the River Thames – this is handsome countryside, characterized by steep forested ridges and deep valleys interrupted by rolling farmland. North Bucks offers a couple of fine attractions: **Stowe Gardens**, dotted with outdoor sculptures and follies, and the World War II code-breaking centre of **Bletchley Park**. Meanwhile, Bedfordshire's most distinctive attraction is whopping **Woburn Abbey** and its safari park.

4

Cliveden

Taplow, SL1 8NS, 1 mile east of Cookham • **Grounds** Daily: mid-Feb to Oct 10am–5.30pm; Nov & Dec 10am–4pm • £11.70; NT • **House tours** April–Oct Thurs & Sun 3–5pm; 30min • £2; NT • ☎01628 605069, ⊛nationaltrust.org.uk/cliveden

Perched on a ridge overlooking the Thames, **Cliveden** (pronounced cliv-dun) is a grand Victorian mansion, designed with sweeping Neoclassical lines by Sir Charles Barry, architect of the Houses of Parliament. Its most famous occupant was **Nancy Astor**, the first female MP, though the house remains best known for the scandalous **Profumo Affair**. Conservative cabinet minister John Profumo met 19-year-old model Christine Keeler at a party at Cliveden in 1961 and had a brief affair with her. Keeler, meanwhile, was also involved with a number of other men, including a Soviet intelligence officer. Profumo was forced to resign in 1963 after having lied to parliament, and Prime Minister Harold Macmillan resigned shortly afterwards.

The National Trust now owns Cliveden. Visits focus on the **grounds**, where a large slice of broadleaf woodland is intercepted by several themed gardens and a maze. The house is now a luxury **hotel** (⊛clivedenhouse.co.uk), with non-guests admitted only on **guided tours**. Its lavish interiors feature acres of wood panelling and portraits of past owners, culminating in the French Dining Room, containing the fittings and furnishings of Madame de Pompadour's own eighteenth-century dining room.

Roald Dahl Museum and Story Centre

81 High St, Great Missenden, HP16 0AL • Tues–Fri 10am–5pm, Sat & Sun 11am–5pm • £6.60 • ☎01494 892192, ⊛roalddahlmuseum.org • Train from London Marylebone to Great Missenden (every 30min; 45min), then 5min walk

A leafy Chiltern commuter town 35 miles northwest of London, **GREAT MISSENDEN** was home for many years to **Roald Dahl** (1916–90), one of the world's greatest children's story writers. His house remains in private hands, but nearby is the **Roald Dahl Museum and Story Centre**, an unmissable treat for Dahl fans. As well as chronicling the author's life, it explores the nature of creative writing, supported by hints from contemporary writers and interactive games.

Stowe Gardens

MK18 5EQ, 3 miles northwest of Buckingham • Daily: March–Oct 10am–5pm; Nov–Feb 10am–4pm • £11.20, joint ticket with Stowe House £17.70; NT • ☎ 01280 817156, ⓦ nationaltrust.org.uk/stowe and ⓦ stowehouse.org

The extensive **Stowe Gardens** contain an extraordinary collection of outdoor sculptures, monuments and decorative buildings by some of the eighteenth century's greatest designers and architects. The thirty-odd structures are spread over a sequence of separate, carefully planned landscapes, from the lake views of the Western and Eastern gardens to the wooded delights of the Elysian Fields and the gentle folds of the Grecian Valley, **Capability Brown**'s first large-scale design. **Stowe House**, with its Neoclassical facade, is used by Stowe School, which offers regular **guided tours**.

Bletchley Park

Sherwood Drive, Bletchley, MK3 6EB, 2 miles south of Milton Keynes • Daily: March–Oct 9.30am–5pm; Nov–Feb 9.30am–4pm • £17.75 (includes audioguide) • ☎ 01908 640404, ⓦ bletchleypark.org.uk • 5min walk from Bletchley station, with trains from London Euston (every 20min; 35min) and Birmingham New St (twice hourly; 1hr; some change at Milton Keynes)

Bletchley Park – now on the edge of Milton Keynes – was the headquarters of Britain's leading code-breakers during World War II, when it was known as "Station X". This was where the British built the first programmable digital computer, Colossus, in 1943, and it was here that they famously broke the German "**Enigma**" code which was encrypting communications within Hitler's armed forces. Much of Station X has survived, its Nissen huts spread over a leafy parcel of land that surrounds the original Victorian mansion. Inside are displays exploring the workings of Station X as well as the stolen Enigma machine that was crucial in deciphering the German code.

Woburn Abbey and Safari Park

Woburn, 5 miles east of Milton Keynes • **Abbey** MK17 9WA • April–Oct daily 11am–5pm • £17 • ☎ 01525 290333, ⓦ woburnabbey.co.uk • **Safari park** MK17 9QN • Feb–Oct daily 10am–6pm • £23 • ☎ 01525 290407, ⓦ woburnsafari.co.uk

The grandiloquent Georgian facade of **Woburn Abbey** overlooks a chunk of landscaped parkland on the eastern edge of Woburn village. Called an abbey because it was built on the site of a Cistercian foundation, the house is the ancestral pile of the dukes of Bedford. The lavish state rooms contain some fine paintings, including an exquisite set of **Tudor portraits**, most notably the famous *Armada Portrait* of Elizabeth I by George Gower. Elsewhere are works by Van Dyck, Velázquez, Gainsborough, Rembrandt, Reynolds and Canaletto. Another part of the duke's enormous estate is home to **Woburn Safari Park**, Britain's largest drive-through wildlife reserve. The animals include African white rhino and bongo antelope. In high season traffic can achieve rush-hour congestion; arrive early for a quieter experience.

St Albans

Just beyond the M25 orbital motorway north of London, **ST ALBANS** in Hertfordshire is one of the most appealing towns on the peripheries of the capital, its blend of medieval and modern features grafted onto the site of **Verulamium**, a town founded by the Romans soon after their successful invasion in 43 AD. After Boudica burned it to the ground eighteen years later, reconstruction was swift and the town grew into a major administrative base. It was here, in 209 AD, that a Roman soldier by the name of Alban became the country's first Christian martyr, when he was beheaded for giving shelter to a priest. Pilgrims later flocked to the town, with the place of execution marked by a hilltop **cathedral** that was once one of the largest churches in the Christian world. St Albans' grand Georgian **town hall** on the central Market Place closed in 2016 for conversion into a new museum and art gallery, which may be open when you visit.

St Albans Cathedral

Off High St, AL1 1BY • Daily 8.30am–5.45pm • Free • ☎ 01727 890210, ⓦ stalbanscathedral.org

An abbey was constructed here in 1077 on the site of a Saxon monastery founded by King Offa of Mercia; despite subsequent alterations, the legacy of the Normans remains the most impressive aspect of the vast brick-and-flint **St Albans Cathedral**. The sheer scale of their design is breathtaking: the **nave**, almost 300 feet long, is the longest medieval nave in Britain. Behind the high altar a stone **reredos** hides the fourteenth-century **shrine of St Alban**. The tomb was smashed up during the Reformation, but the Victorians discovered the pieces and gamely put them all together again.

Verulamium

St Michael's St, AL3 4SW • **Museum** Mon–Sat 10am–5.30pm, Sun 2–5.30pm • £5; joint ticket with theatre £6.50 • ☎ 01727 751810, ⓦ stalbansmuseums.org.uk • **Park** AL3 6AE • Daily 24hr; hypnocaust Mon–Sat 10am–4.30pm, Sun 2–4.30pm • Free • **Theatre** Daily: March–Oct 10am–5pm; Nov–Feb 10am–4pm • £2.50; joint ticket with museum £6.50 • ☎ 01727 835035, ⓦ gorhamburyestate.co.uk /the-roman-theatre

4

Verulamium Museum holds a series of well-conceived displays illustrating life in Roman Britain, but these are eclipsed by the wonderful floor **mosaics** unearthed hereabouts in the 1930s and 1950s. Dating from about 200 AD, the Sea God Mosaic has created its share of academic debate, with some arguing that it depicts a god of nature with stag antler horns rather than a sea god with lobster claws – but there's no disputing the subject of the Lion Mosaic, in which a lion carries the bloodied head of a stag in its jaws. The most beautiful is the Shell Mosaic, whose semicircular design depicts a beautifully crafted scallop shell within a border made up of rolling waves.

The adjacent **Verulamium Park** holds a scattering of Roman remains, including fragments of the old city wall and a building sheltering the **Hypocaust**, comprising the foundations of a townhouse complete with the original underfloor heating system of the bath suite. Just to the west, across busy Bluehouse Hill, is the **Roman Theatre of Verulamium**, which was built around 140 AD, but was reduced to the status of a municipal rubbish dump by the fifth century and is little more than a small hollow now.

ARRIVAL AND INFORMATION

ST ALBANS

By train St Albans City station is off Victoria St, 10min walk east of the centre. Frequent trains from London St Pancras (every 10min; 20min).

Tourist office While the town hall is undergoing remodelling, the tourist office is in the Alban Arena (Mon–Sat 10am–4pm; ☎ 01727 864511, ⓦ enjoystalbans.com).

DRINKING

St Albans hosts the headquarters of **CAMRA**, the Campaign for Real Ale: excellent, hand-pumped beers are available in many a local pub. See ⓦ camra.org.uk for more information.

Ye Olde Fighting Cocks 16 Abbey Mill Lane, AL3 4HE ☎ 01727 869152, ⓦ yeoldefightingcocks.co.uk. This antique hostelry is a good choice – crowded on sunny summer days, but still with lots of enjoyable nooks and crannies in which to nurse a (CAMRA-approved) pint. Mon–Thurs noon–11pm, Fri & Sat noon–midnight, Sun noon–10.30pm.

Bath, Bristol and Somerset

GLASTONBURY FESTIVAL

5

Bath, Bristol and Somerset

Ranging from tidy cricket greens and well-kept country pubs to limestone gorges and windswept moorland, Somerset makes a fitting introduction to England's Southwest. The Georgian, honey-toned terraces of Bath lie at the eastern end of the county, and offers a beautifully preserved set of Roman baths, some first-class museums and a mellow café culture that makes it an unmissable stop on any tour of the region. Just a few miles away, the main city hereabouts is Bristol, one of the most dynamic and cosmopolitan centres outside London, its medieval old quarter and revitalized waterfront supplemented by a superb range of pubs, clubs and restaurants.

Within easy reach to the south lie the exquisite cathedral city of **Wells** and the ancient town of **Glastonbury**, a site steeped in Christian lore, Arthurian legend and New Age mysticism. Nearby, **the Mendips** are fine walking territory and are pocked by cave systems, as at Wookey Hole and Cheddar Gorge. Beyond here, verdant **South Somerset**, with its pretty little Hamstone villages and traditional cider farms, matches the county's bucolic ideal more than any other region. The county town of **Taunton** makes a useful base for exploring the **Quantock Hills**, while further west, straddling the border with Devon, the heathery slopes and wide-open spaces of **Exmoor** offer a range of hikes, with wonderful views from its cliffy seaboard.

Bath

A graceful succession of urban set pieces, **BATH** is a visual feast: harmonious, compact and perfectly complemented by the softly undulating hills that surround it. The city's elegant crescents and Georgian buildings are studded with plaques naming Bath's eminent inhabitants from its heyday as a spa resort; it was here that Jane Austen set *Persuasion* and *Northanger Abbey*, and where Gainsborough established himself as a portraitist and landscape painter.

Bath owes its name and fame to its **hot springs** – the only ones in the country – which made it a place of reverence for the local Celtic population, though it took Roman technology to turn it into a fully fledged bathing establishment. The baths fell into decline with the departure of the Romans, but the town later regained its importance under the Saxons, its abbey seeing the coronation of the **first king of all England**, Edgar, in 973. A new bathing complex was built in the sixteenth century, popularized by the visit of Elizabeth I in 1574, and the city reached its fashionable zenith in the eighteenth century, when **Beau Nash** ruled the town's social scene (see box, p.285). It was at this time, Bath's "Golden Age", that the city acquired its ranks of Palladian mansions and Regency townhouses, all of them built in the local **Bath stone**. The legacy is a city whose

Highlights

① Roman Baths Thermal waters still bubble up in this beautifully restored complex of baths from the Roman era in the UK's original spa town. **See p.285**

② Royal Crescent, Bath In a city famous for its graceful arcs of Georgian terraces, this is the granddaddy of them all, an architectural tour de force with a magnificent view. **See p.288**

③ ss Great Britain, Bristol Moored in the dock in which she was built, the iconic ship is now a museum, an interactive insight into life aboard a nineteenth-century steamer. **See p.296**

④ Wells Cathedral A gem of medieval masonry, this richly ornamented Gothic

masterpiece is the centrepiece of England's smallest city. **See p.300**

⑤ Cheddar Gorge Impressive rockscape with a network of illuminated caves at its base; it's an excellent starting point for wild walks in the Mendip Hills. **See p.303**

⑥ Glastonbury Festival Pack your tent, dust off your wellies and enjoy the ride that is simply Britain's biggest, boldest and best music festival. **See p.306**

⑦ Exmoor Whether you ride it, bike it or hike it, the rolling wilderness of Exmoor offers fine opportunities to experience the great outdoors. **See p.311**

HIGHLIGHTS ARE MARKED ON THE MAP ON P.284

HIGHLIGHTS

1. Roman Baths
2. Royal Crescent, Bath
3. ss Great Britain, Bristol
4. Wells Cathedral
5. Cheddar Gorge
6. Glastonbury Festival
7. Exmoor

BATH, BRISTOL & SOMERSET

WALES

Cardiff
Barry
Bridgend

Bristol Channel

Bridgwater Bay

DEVON
DORSET
SOMERSET

EXMOOR NATIONAL PARK

West Somerset Railway

greatest enjoyment comes simply from wandering its streets, with their pale gold architecture and sweeping vistas.

5

The Roman Baths

Abbey Churchyard, BA1 1LZ • Daily: March to mid-June, Sept & Oct 9am–6pm; mid-June to Aug 9am–10pm; Nov–Feb 9.30am–6pm; last entry 1hr before closing • £15.50, £17 in July & Aug, £21.50 combined ticket with Fashion Museum & Victoria Art Gallery • **Tours** Daily, on the hour; 1hr • Free • ☎ 01225 477785, ⓦ romanbaths.co.uk

There are hours of entertainment in Bath's premier attraction, the **Roman Baths**, which comprises the baths themselves and an informative museum – highlights include the Sacred Spring, part of the temple of the local deity Sulis Minerva, where water still bubbles up at a constant 46.5°C; the open-air (but originally covered) Great Bath, its vaporous waters surrounded by nineteenth-century pillars, terraces and statues of famous Romans; the Circular Bath, where bathers cooled off; and the Norman King's Bath, where people were taking a restorative dip right up until 1978. The free **audioguide** is excellent.

Among a quantity of coins, jewellery and sculpture exhibited are the bronze head of Sulis Minerva and a grand, Celtic-inspired gorgon's head from the temple's pediment. Models of the complex at its greatest extent give some idea of the awe which it must have inspired, while the **graffiti** salvaged from the Roman era – mainly curses and boasts – offer a personal slant on this antique leisure centre.

You can get a free glimpse into the baths from the next-door **Pump Room**, the social hub of the Georgian spa community and still redolent of that era, which houses a formal tearoom and restaurant (see p.290).

Bath Abbey

Abbey Churchyard, BA1 1LT • April–Oct Mon 9.30am–5.30pm, Tues–Fri 9am–5.30pm, Sat 9am–6pm, Sun 1–2.30pm & 4.30–5.30pm (Sun till 6pm in Aug); Nov–March Mon–Sat 9am–4.30pm, Sun 1–2.30pm & 4.30–5.30pm • Free, but £4 donation requested • **Tower tours** From 10/11am: Mon–Fri on the hour, Sat every 30min; 45min • £6 • ⓦ bathabbey.org

Although there has been a church on the site since the seventh century, **Bath Abbey** did not take its present form until the end of the fifteenth century, when Bishop Oliver King began work on the ruins of the previous Norman building, some of which were incorporated into the new church. The bishop was said to have been inspired by a vision of angels ascending and descending a ladder to heaven, which the present facade recalls on the turrets flanking the central window. The west front also features the founder's signature in the form of carvings of olive trees surmounted by crowns, a play on his name.

BEAU NASH

Bath's social renaissance in the eighteenth century was largely due to one man: **Richard "Beau" Nash** (1674–1761), an ex-army officer, ex-lawyer, dandy and gambler, who became Bath's Master of Ceremonies in 1704, conducting public balls of unprecedented splendour. Wielding dictatorial powers over dress and behaviour, Nash orchestrated the social manners of the city and even extended his influence to cover road improvements and the design of buildings. In an early example of health awareness, he banned smoking in Bath's public rooms at a time when pipe-smoking was generally enjoyed among men, women and children. Less philanthropically, he also encouraged gambling and even took a percentage of the bank's takings. According to his rules, balls were always to begin at 6pm and end at 11pm and each one had to open with a minuet "danced by two persons of the highest distinction present". White aprons were banned, gossipers and scandalmongers were shunned, and, most radical of all, the wearing of swords in public places was forbidden. Nash's fortunes changed when gambling restrictions were introduced in 1739, greatly reducing his influence; he died in poverty aged 87, but was treated to a suitably lavish send-off.

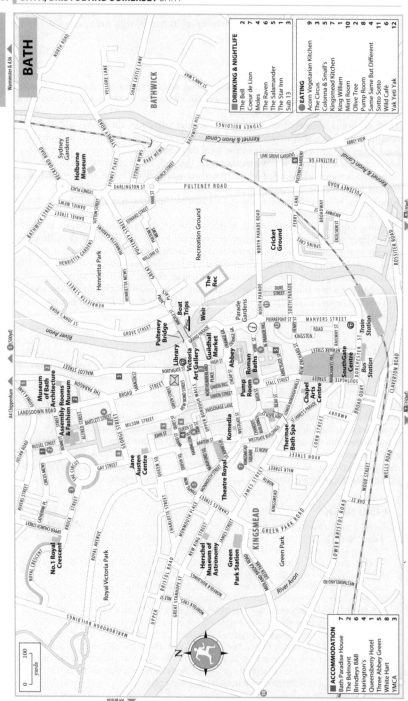

The **interior** is in a restrained Perpendicular style, although it does boast splendid fan vaulting on the ceiling, which was not completed until the nineteenth century. The floor and walls are crammed with elaborate monuments and memorials, and traces of the grander Norman building are visible in the Gethsemane Chapel.

On most days, you can join a **tower tour** to see the massive bells, clock and bell-pulling machinery, and can enjoy a bird's-eye view of Bath – but be prepared for the 212 spiral steps.

Thermae Bath Spa

Hot Bath St, BA1 1SJ • **Baths** Daily: New Royal Bath 9am–9.30pm, last entry 7pm; Cross Bath 10am–8pm, last entry 6pm • £35 for 2hr (Sat & Sun £38), £10 per additional hour • **Visitor centre** April–Sept Mon–Sat 10am–5pm, Sun 11am–4pm • Free • ☎ 01225 331234, ⦿ thermaebathspa.com

At the bottom of the elegantly colonnaded Bath Street, the **Thermae Bath Spa** allows you to take the waters in much the same way that visitors to Bath have done throughout the ages, but with state-of-the-art spa facilities. Heated by the city's thermal waters, the spa includes two open-air pools, one on the roof of its centrepiece, the New Royal Bath, Sir Nicholas Grimshaw's sleekly futuristic "glass cube". Various treatments are offered, from massages to hot-stone therapies, and a small **visitor centre** has displays relating to Bath's thermal waters.

Queen Square and around

North of Hot Bath Street, Sawclose is presided over by the **Theatre Royal** (see p.291), opened in 1805 and one of the country's finest surviving Georgian theatres; Beau Nash had his first house in Bath here from 1743, in what is now the theatre's foyer. Barton Street leads north of Sawclose to **Queen Square**, the first Bath venture of the architect **John Wood the Elder** (1704–54), champion of Neoclassical Palladianism, who lived at no. 15 (not no. 24, as a tablet there asserts). East of the square is the wide shopping strand of **Milsom Street**, which was designed by Wood as the main thoroughfare of Georgian Bath.

Herschel Museum of Astronomy

19 New King St, BA1 2BL • Mid-Jan to mid-Dec Mon–Fri 1–5pm, Sat & Sun 11am–5pm • £6.50 • ☎ 01225 446865, ⦿ herschelmuseum.org.uk

A few minutes west of the centre is the small **Herschel Museum of Astronomy**, former home of the musician and astronomer Sir William Herschel and his sister Caroline, who together discovered the planet Uranus here in 1781. Among the furnishings, musical instruments and knick-knacks from the Herschels' era, you can see a replica of the telescope with which Uranus was identified.

Jane Austen Centre

40 Gay St, BA1 2NT • April–June, Sept & Oct daily 9.45am–5.30pm; July & Aug daily 9.30am–6pm; Nov–March Mon–Fri & Sun 11am–4pm, Sat 9.45am–5.30pm • £11 • ☎ 01225 443000, ⦿ janeausten.co.uk

The **Jane Austen Centre** provides a superficial overview of the author's connections with Bath, illustrated by extracts from her writings, contemporary costumes, furnishings and household items; visits start with a talk every twenty minutes. Austen herself, who wasn't entirely enamoured of the city, lived just down the road at 25 Gay Street – one of a number of places the author inhabited while in Bath.

The Circus

Situated at the top of Gay Street, the elder John Wood's masterpiece, **The Circus**, consists of three crescents arranged in a tight circle of three-storey houses, with a carved frieze running round the entire circle. Wood died soon after laying the foundation stone, and

5

the job was finished by his son, **John Wood the Younger** (1728–82), who was as instrumental as his father in defining Bath's elegant Georgian appearance. The painter Thomas Gainsborough lived at no. 17 from 1760 to 1774.

The Royal Crescent and around

No. 1 Royal Crescent BA1 2LR • Mid-Feb to Dec Mon noon–5.30pm, Tues–Sun 10.30am–5.30pm • £10, or £12.50 with Museum of Bath Architecture • ☎ 01225 428126, ⓦ no1royalcrescent.org.uk

The Circus is connected by Brock Street to the **Royal Crescent**, grandest of Bath's crescents, begun by the younger John Wood in 1767. The stately arc of thirty houses – said to be the country's first – is set off by a spacious sloping lawn from which a magnificent vista extends to green hills and distant ribbons of honey-coloured stone. The interior of **No. 1 Royal Crescent**, on the corner with Brock Street, has been restored to reflect as nearly as possible its original Georgian appearance at the end of the eighteenth century.

At the bottom of the Crescent, Royal Avenue leads onto **Royal Victoria Park**, the city's largest open space, containing an aviary and nine acres of botanical gardens.

The Fashion Museum

Assembly Rooms, Bennett St, BA1 2QH • Daily: March–Oct 10.30am–6pm; Nov–Feb 10.30am–5pm; last admission 1hr before closing • £9, or £21.50 with the Roman Baths & Victoria Art Gallery • ☎ 01225 477789, ⓦ fashionmuseum.co.uk

The younger John Wood's **Assembly Rooms**, east of the Circus, were, with the Pump Room, the centre of Bath's social scene. The building was virtually destroyed by bombing during World War II, but it has since been perfectly restored and houses the **Fashion Museum**, an entertaining collection of clothing from the Stuart era to the latest Milanese designs.

Museum of Bath Architecture

The Vineyards, The Paragon, BA1 5NA • Mid-Feb to Nov Tues–Fri 2–5pm, Sat & Sun 10.30am–5pm • £6, or £12.50 with No. 1 Royal Crescent • ☎ 01225 333895, ⓦ museumofbatharchitecture.org.uk

The Georgian-Gothic Countess of Huntingdon's Chapel houses the **Museum of Bath Architecture**, a fascinating exploration of the construction and architecture of the city and a great place to start your visit. Everything is covered, from the kind of facades associated with the two John Woods to balustrades, door designs and such aspects of interior ornamentation as marbling, stencilling and japanning.

Holburne Museum

Great Pulteney St, BA2 4DB • Mon–Sat 10am–5pm, Sun 11am–5pm • Free • ☎ 01225 388569, ⓦ holburne.org

The River Avon is crossed by the graceful, shop-lined **Pulteney Bridge**, an Italianate structure designed by Robert Adam, from the other side of which a lengthy vista stretches along Great Pulteney Street to the imposing classical facade of the **Holburne Museum**. The building, with a startlingly modern extension at the back, holds an impressive range of decorative and fine art, mostly furniture, silverware, porcelain and paintings, including several works by Gainsborough, notably the famous *Byam Family*, his largest portrait. Look out, too, for works by Constable, Stubbs and Angelika Kauffman.

ARRIVAL AND INFORMATION   **BATH**

By train Bath Spa station is a short walk south of the centre at the bottom of Manvers St.

Destinations Bristol (every 15–30min; 15min); London Paddington (every 30min–1hr; 1hr 30min); Salisbury (every 30min–1hr; 1hr).

By bus The bus station (ⓦ firstgroup.com) lies next to the

train station on Dorchester St.

Destinations Bristol (3–6 hourly; 45min); London (14 daily; 2hr 30min–3hr 15min); Salisbury (Mon–Sat 4 daily; 1hr 35min–2hr 50min); Wells (Mon–Sat every 30min, Sun hourly; 1hr 25min).

By bike/on foot The 13-mile Bristol & Bath Railway Path

(⊕ bristolbathrailwaypath.org.uk) connects the two cities along the route of a disused railway line and the course of the River Avon.

Tourist office Bridgwater House, 2 Terrace Walk (March–Sept Mon–Sat 9am–5.30pm, Sun 10am–4pm; Oct–Feb Mon–Sat 9am–5.30pm; ☎ 01225 322442, ⊕ visitbath.co.uk).

GETTING AROUND AND TOURS

Walking or biking are the best ways to enjoy Bath's Georgian terraces – cars are a hindrance and parking is expensive; drivers should use one of the Park-and-Ride car parks on the periphery of town.

Bike rental Nextbike (☎ 020 8166 9851, ⊕ nextbike .co.uk) operates a rental service for up to 24hr, with bikes available at stands scattered around the city. To use it, you must first register (via the website or on a free app) and pay a £10 deposit; charges are £1/30min or £10 for up to 24hr. Alternatively, there's Bath Bike Hire, Sydney Wharf, Bathwick Hill (£15/day; ☎ 01225 447276, ⊕ bath -narrowboats.co.uk); they also rent narrowboats (from £80/half-day).

Boat tours Hour-long river trips can be made from Pulteney Bridge; operators include Pulteney Cruisers (Easter–Oct 6–12 daily; £9; ☎ 01225 312900, ⊕ pulteney cruisers.com) and Avon Cruising (April–Oct 6 daily; £9; ⊕ pulteneyprincess.co.uk).

Walking tours Mayor's Guides run free 2hr walking tours, starting outside the Pump Room in Abbey Churchyard (⊕ bathguides.org.uk; Mon–Fri & Sun 10.30am & 2pm, Sat 10.30am, May–Aug also Tues & Thurs 7pm).

ACCOMMODATION

Bath is chock-full of **hotels** and **B&Bs**, but most of the latter are small. It's always worth booking early, especially at weekends, when most places demand a two-night minimum and prices rise; rates quoted below are midweek. There are also good-value, central **hostels**, though the nearest **campsites** are some distance outside town. Note that the centre can get noisy at night, so choose a room away from the street for an undisturbed sleep.

Bath Paradise House 86–88 Holloway, BA2 4PX ☎ 01225 317723, ⊕ paradise-house.co.uk; map p.286. Georgian villa an uphill trudge from the centre, but with wonderful views. Open fires in winter, elegant four-posters in some of the rooms, and three rooms opening straight onto the award-winning gardens. **£92**

The Belmont 7 Belmont, Lansdown Rd, BA1 5DZ ☎ 01225 423082, ⊕ belmontbath.co.uk; map p.286. Large doubles, some with tiny, clean, modern en-suite bathrooms, in a centrally located B&B in a house designed by John Wood. No credit cards. **£85**

Brindleys B&B 14 Pulteney Gardens, BA2 4HG ☎ 01225 310444, ⊕ brindleysbath.co.uk; map p.286. Half a dozen light, airy, elegantly decorated bijou rooms that have more than a hint of a French country manor house about them, a feeling that extends to the stylish communal areas. It's set in a quiet residential area just a 5min walk from the centre. **£115**

Harington's Queen St, BA1 1HE ☎ 01225 461728, ⊕ haringtonshotel.co.uk; map p.286. Central hotel in a converted townhouse with friendly service and modern, well-equipped rooms – most are quite small, and some at the top of steep steps. Breakfasts are superlative, and food is available throughout the day. **£130**

Queensberry Hotel Russel St, BA1 2QF ☎ 01225 447928, ⊕ thequeensberry.co.uk; map p.286. Spread across four Georgian townhouses at the top end of town, the *Queensberry* combines a clubhouse feel with a quirky boutique vibe. Rooms are tastefully minimalist – each one different and most with a fabulous bathroom – and there are stylish communal areas, a peaceful walled garden, and a superb basement restaurant (see p.290). **£155**

★**Three Abbey Green** 3 Abbey Green, BA1 1NW ☎ 01225 428558, ⊕ threeabbeygreen.com; map p.286. Top-notch B&B in a superbly renovated Georgian house just steps from the abbey. The airy, spotless rooms are beautifully done; the larger ones overlooking a peaceful square are more expensive. **£120**

★**White Hart** Widcombe Hill, BA2 6AA ☎ 01225 313985, ⊕ whitehartbath.co.uk; map p.286. The comfiest of Bath's hostels has a kitchen, a first-class bar/restaurant and a spacious courtyard. There are clean doubles and twins available, some en suite. Accommodation not available Sun. Dorms **£15**, doubles **£50**

YMCA International House, Broad St, BA1 5LH ☎ 01225 325900, ⊕ bathymca.co.uk; map p.286. Clean, central and spacious, this friendly place has dorms, singles and doubles. No curfew, but no kitchen, either. All rates include breakfast (cooked breakfast £3.50 extra). Dorms **£16**, singles **£32**, doubles **£56**

EATING

CAFÉS

Colonna & Small's 6 Chapel Row, BA1 1HN ☎ 07766 808067, ⊕ colonnaandsmalls.co.uk; map p.286. The highbrowed but helpful brewmasters at this stripped-back coffee specialist serve a serious cup of Joe. Choose from a range of weekly changing single-origin espresso beans

5

and filter coffees. Just don't ask for milk. Or sugar. Mon–Fri 8am–5.30pm, Sat 8.30am–5.30pm, Sun 10am–4pm.

Kingsmead Kitchen 1 Kingsmead Square, BA1 2AA ☎ 01225 329002, ⓦ kingsmeadkitchenbath.co.uk; map p.286. Big breakfasts, snack fodder and dishes such as meze with warm pitta bread (£9) are served at this café tucked away in a corner of one of Bath's most attractive squares. There are beers and wines, and outside seating to boot. Mon–Sat 8.30am–6pm, Sun 9am–5pm.

★ **Wild Café** 10a Queen St, BA1 1HE ☎ 01225 448673, ⓦ wildcafe.co.uk; map p.286. Hidden away down a cobbled side street behind Queen Square, the open kitchen at this popular café does a steady trade in burgers, salads (£8–10) and sandwiches (including an excellent BLT; £6), which can also be bought to take away. Mon–Fri 8am–4.30pm, Sat 9am–6pm, Sun 10am–5pm.

RESTAURANTS

★ **Acorn Vegetarian Kitchen** 2 North Parade Passage, BA1 1NX ☎ 01225 446059, ⓦ acornvegetariankitchen .co.uk; map p.286. Classy veggie and vegan restaurant offering dishes such as butternut squash terrine with pine-nut risotto in an unruffled, arty environment. Set-price lunches are £18 or £23 for two and three courses respectively, while dinners cost £27 or £35 (£20 or £25 before 6.30pm). Mon–Fri & Sun noon–3pm & 5.30–9.30pm, Sat noon–3.30pm & 5.30–10pm.

The Circus 34 Brock St, BA1 2LN ☎ 01225 466020, ⓦ thecircusrestaurant.co.uk; map p.286. There's a refined but relaxed atmosphere at this family-run café/restaurant, just a stroll from the Royal Crescent. It specializes in Modern European dishes such as Sicilian-style braised globe artichokes (£17.50) and tagine of kid goat on saffron couscous (£19.70) – both around £6.50 cheaper at lunch. Mon–Sat 10am–late.

★ **King William** 36 Thomas St, BA1 5NN ☎ 01225 428096, ⓦ kingwilliampub.com; map p.286. North of the centre, the upstairs dining room at the *King William* pub regularly receives accolades for its locally sourced dishes, such as confit pork belly (£19) and gnocchi with Jerusalem artichoke (£14), but the beer and wine list is top-drawer, too. Bar Mon–Fri noon–3pm & 5–11pm, Sat noon–midnight, Sun noon–11pm; restaurant Wed–Fri 6–9pm, Sat 6–10pm, Sun noon–3pm.

Mint Room Longmead Gospel Hall, Lower Bristol Rd, BA2 3EB ☎ 01225 446656, ⓦ themintroom.co.uk; map p.286. Indian food but not as you know it: innovative yet authentic regional cuisine ranging from South Indian king prawn *moilee* (£17) to biryanis served under a pastry crust (£10–12). Mon–Thurs & Sun noon–2pm & 6–11pm, Fri & Sat noon–2pm & 6–11.30pm.

★ **Olive Tree** Queensberry Hotel, Russel St, BA1 2QF ☎ 01225 447928, ⓦ olivetreebath.co.uk; map p.286. One of Bath's top restaurants, this offers exquisite and inventively prepared dishes, a relaxed, contemporary ambience and attentive, friendly service. Whether you order from the tasting menus (£58–80) or opt for individual dishes (mains £19.50–28.50), you can sample such dishes as lobster lasagne, pan-fried turbot and pigeon with asparagus and hazelnut (a vegetarian menu is also available). There are set-price lunch menus Fri & Sat for £26.50 or £32. Mon–Thurs 7–9.30pm, Fri & Sat 12.30–2pm & 6.30–10pm, Sun 12.30–2pm & 7–9.30pm.

Pump Room Abbey Churchyard, BA1 1LZ ☎ 01225 444477, ⓦ romanbaths.co.uk; map p.286. Splash out on a smoked salmon brunch, sample the excellent lunchtime menu (mains around £15) or succumb to a Bath bun or a range of cream teas, all accompanied by a classical trio. It's a bit hammy and overpriced, and you may have to queue, but you get a good view of the Baths. Daily 9.30am–4.30pm; July, Aug & Dec and during major festivals 9.30am–9pm.

Same Same But Different 7a Prince's Buildings, Bartlett St, BA1 2ED ☎ 01225 466856, ⓦ same-same .co.uk; map p.286. Excellent café/restaurant that mixes a laidback ambience with quality food – try some of the unusual tapas dishes (from £4.50), or go for something a bit more substantial, such as smoked haddock kedgeree with duck egg (£10). Mon 8am–6pm, Tues–Fri 8am–11pm, Sat 9am–11pm, Sun 10am–5pm.

Sotto Sotto 10 North Parade, BA2 4AL ☎ 01225 330236, ⓦ sottosotto.co.uk; map p.286. Authentic Italian restaurant in cave-like, brick-vaulted subterranean rooms. The simple but heavenly dishes include orecchiette pasta with spinach and sausage (£9.75), and *pesce spada alla griglia* (grilled swordfish; £16.25). Make sure you sample the excellent antipasti too (around £7.50). Service is superb. It's usually packed, so booking is essential. Daily noon–2pm & 5–10pm.

Yak Yeti Yak 12 Pierrepont St, BA1 1LA ☎ 01225 442299, ⓦ yakyetiyak.co.uk; map p.286. Quality Nepalese restaurant in a series of cellar rooms with a choice of chairs or floor cushions. Meat dishes are stir-fried or spicily marinated, and there's a good vegetarian selection (dishes all £5–9). Mon–Thurs noon–2pm & 6–10.30pm, Fri & Sat noon–2pm & 5–10.30pm, Sun noon–2pm & 6–10pm.

DRINKING AND NIGHTLIFE

★ **The Bell** 103 Walcot St, BA1 5BW ☎ 01225 460426, ⓦ thebellinnbath.co.uk; map p.286. Easy-going, slightly grungy tavern with a great jukebox, live music (Mon & Wed eve, plus Sun lunchtime) and DJs (Fri & Sat). There's bar billiards and a beer garden with table footy. Mon–Sat 11.30am–11pm, Sun noon–10.30pm.

Coeur de Lion 17 Northumberland Place, BA1 5AR ☎ 01225 463568, ⓦ coeur-de-lion.co.uk; map p.286.

BATH'S FESTIVALS

Bath hosts a great range of festivals throughout the year, notably the **Bath Festival** (wbath festivals.org.uk/the-bath-festival), held over ten days in late May and featuring some 130 events taking in jazz, classical and world music, author talks, readings, workshops and debates; the **Bath Fringe Festival** (late May to early June; wbathfringe.co.uk), with the accent on comedy, cabaret and the performance arts; and the **Jane Austen Festival** (wjaneaustenfestivalbath.co.uk), ten days in mid-September. For further information on these and other festivals, contact Bath Box Office, housed in the tourist office at 2 Terrace Walk (☎01225 463362, wbathfestivals.org.uk).

Centrally located tavern on a flagstoned shopping alley, with a few tables outside (and more upstairs). It's Bath's smallest boozer, serves local Abbey Ales, and is a regular tourist stop, with good lunchtime snacks (baguettes £6.50). Mon–Thurs 11am–11pm, Fri & Sat 11am–midnight, Sun noon–10.30pm.

★**Moles** 14 George St, BA1 2EN ☎01225 437537, wmoles.co.uk; map p.286. This much-loved Bath institution features a mix of good live music, DJs and club nights. The cramped basement can get pretty hot and sweaty, though – not for claustrophobes. Mon–Sat 5pm–late.

The Raven 6–7 Queen St, BA1 1HE ☎01225 425045, wtheravenofbath.co.uk; map p.286. A civilized spot with first-rate local ales, served both downstairs and in the less crowded upstairs room (unless one of the story-telling nights is being held there). Food available, including renowned pies (£9.80). Mon–Thurs 8.30am–11pm, Fri & Sat 8.30am–midnight, Sun 8.30am–10.30pm.

The Salamander 3 John St, BA1 2JL ☎01225 428889, wbathales.com; map p.286. Local brewer Bath Ales' pub, with a traditional, dark-wood interior, relaxed atmosphere and tasty dishes available at the bar or in the upstairs restaurant (mains £10–15). Mon–Thurs 11am–midnight, Fri & Sat 11am–1am, Sun 11am–11pm.

★**The Star Inn** 23 The Vineyards, The Paragon, BA1 5NA ☎01225 425071, wabbeyales.co.uk; map p.286. First licensed in 1760, this Abbey Ales pub has a classic Victorian interior, and beers that include the award-winning Bellringer and draught Bass served from a jug. Mon–Thurs noon–2.30pm & 5.30pm–midnight, Fri & Sat noon–1am, Sun noon–midnight.

Sub 13 4 Edgar Buildings, George St, BA1 2EE ☎01225 466667, wsub13.net; map p.286. Settle into a white leather booth in the Champagne Lounge or chill out on the backyard terrace at this trendy basement bar, boasting the best cocktails in town. Mon–Wed 5pm–midnight, Thurs 5pm–2am, Fri & Sat 5pm–3am, Sun noon–11pm.

ENTERTAINMENT

Chapel Arts Centre St James's Memorial Hall, Lower Borough Walls, BA1 1QR ☎01225 461700, wchapelarts.org; map p.286. Nice little venue for all kinds of performing arts, including jazz, folk and comedy. Arrive early to get one of the cabaret-style tables.

Komedia 22–23 Westgate St, BA1 1EP ☎0845 293 8480, wkomedia.co.uk/bath; map p.286. Cabaret and burlesque, comedy, punk and ska bands, tribute acts and more are all staged at this venue. The popular Krater Comedy Club is held on Sat, after which you can stay on for club nights. Meals are available.

Theatre Royal Sawclose, BA1 1ET ☎01225 448844, wtheatreroyal.org.uk; map p.286. Theatre fans should check out what's showing at this historic venue, if only for the atmosphere. More experimental productions are staged in its Ustinov Studio, with family shows at the egg.

Bristol

Just twelve miles from Bath, on the borders of Gloucestershire and Somerset, **BRISTOL** has a very different feel from its sedate neighbour. The city's mercantile roots are overlaid with an innovative, modern culture, fuelled by technology-based industries, a large student population and a lively arts and music scene. As well as its vibrant **nightlife**, the city's sights range from medieval churches to cutting-edge attractions highlighting its maritime and scientific achievements.

Weaving through its centre, the River Avon forms part of a system of waterways that made Bristol a great inland port, in later years booming on the transatlantic trafficking of rum, tobacco and slaves. In the nineteenth century, the illustrious **Isambard Kingdom Brunel** laid the foundations of a tradition of engineering, creating two of Bristol's greatest monuments: the *ss Great Britain* and the lofty Clifton Suspension Bridge.

5

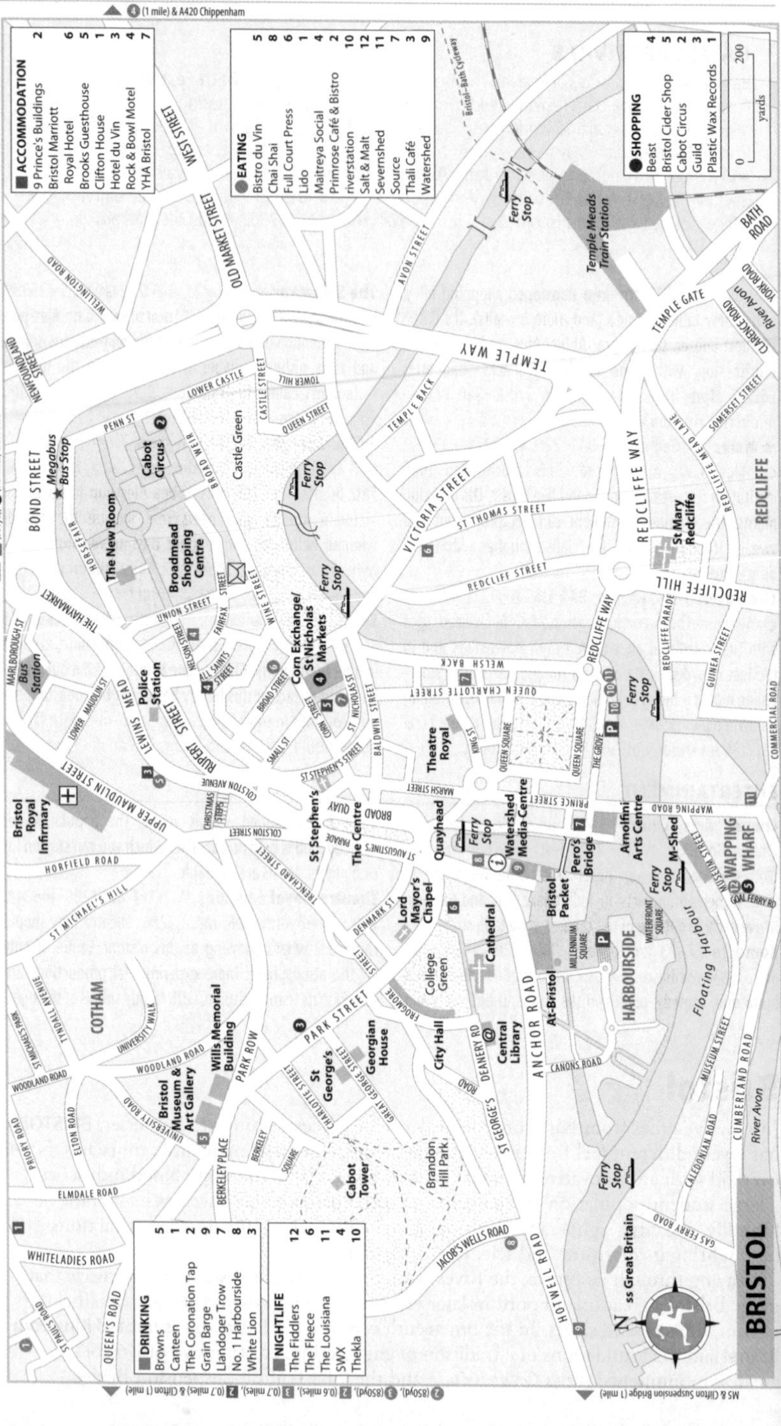

BRISTOL
ACCOMMODATION
9 Prince's Buildings 2
Bristol Marriott Royal Hotel 6
Brooks Guesthouse 5
Clifton House 1
Hotel du Vin 3
Rock & Bowl Motel 4
YHA Bristol 7
EATING
Bistro du Vin 5
Chai Shai 8
Full Court Press 6
Lido 1
Maitreya Social 4
Primrose Café & Bistro 2
riverstation 10
Salt & Malt 12
Severnshed 11
Source 7
Thali Café 3
Watershed 9
SHOPPING
Beast 4
Bristol Cider Shop 5
Cabot Circus 2
Guild 3
Plastic Wax Records 1
DRINKING
Browns 5
Canteen 1
The Coronation Tap 2
Grain Barge 9
Llandoger Trow 7
No. 1 Harbourside 8
White Lion 3
NIGHTLIFE
The Fiddlers 12
The Fleece 6
The Louisiana 11
SWX 4
Thekla 10
0 200 yards
4 (1 mile) & A420 Chippenham
M32, M4 & M5
1 (500yd), 1 (0.8 miles) & St Paul's
2 (850yd), 3 (850yd), 2 (0.6 miles), 3 (0.7 miles), 2 (0.7 miles) & Clifton (1 mile)
M5 & Clifton Suspension Bridge (1 mile)
Bristol–Bath Cycleway
Temple Meads Train Station
Ferry Stop
BATH ROAD
YORK ROAD
CLARENCE ROAD
River Avon
TEMPLE GATE
TEMPLE WAY
SOMERSET STREET
REDCLIFFE MEAD LANE
REDCLIFFE
REDCLIFFE WAY
St Mary Redcliffe
REDCLIFFE HILL
REDCLIFFE PARADE
GUINEA STREET
COMMERCIAL ROAD
WAPPING ROAD
WAPPING WHARF
MUSEUM STREET
GOAL FERRY RD
M-Shed
Arnolfini Arts Centre
Pero's Bridge
Bristol Packet
HARBOURSIDE
WATERFRONT SQUARE
MILLENNIUM SQUARE
Floating Harbour
At-Bristol
ANCHOR ROAD
CANONS ROAD
CUMBERLAND ROAD
CALEDONIAN ROAD
GAS FERRY ROAD
ss Great Britain
HOTWELL ROAD
JACOB'S WELLS ROAD
Brandon Hill Park
Cabot Tower
BERKELEY SQUARE
BERKELEY PLACE
ELMDALE ROAD
WHITELADIES ROAD
QUEEN'S ROAD
ST PAUL'S ROAD
PRIORY ROAD
ELTON ROAD
WOODLAND ROAD
UNIVERSITY ROAD
Bristol Museum & Art Gallery
Wills Memorial Building
PARK ROW
PARK STREET
UNIVERSITY WALK
TYNDALL AVENUE
ST MICHAEL'S PARK
COTHAM
ST MICHAEL'S HILL
HORFIELD ROAD
UPPER MAUDLIN STREET
Bristol Royal Infirmary
LOWER MAUDLIN ST
MARLBOROUGH ST
Bus Station
THE HAYMARKET
LEWINS MEAD
RUPERT STREET
CHRISTMAS STEPS
COLSTON STREET
COLSTON AVENUE
Police Station
NELSON STREET
ALL SAINTS STREET
UNION STREET
FAIRFAX STREET
HORSEFAIR
BOND STREET
Megabus Bus Stop
The New Room
Broadmead Shopping Centre
Cabot Circus
PENN ST
BROAD WEIR
NEWFOUNDLAND STREET
WELLINGTON ROAD
OLD MARKET STREET
WEST STREET
LOWER CASTLE STREET
CASTLE STREET
TOWER HILL
QUEEN STREET
Castle Green
WINE STREET
Corn Exchange/ St Nicholas Markets
BROAD STREET
SMALL ST
CORN STREET
ST NICHOLAS ST
ST STEPHEN'S STREET
St Stephen's
The Centre
BROAD QUAY
ST AUGUSTINE'S PARADE
TRENCHARD STREET
DENMARK ST
Lord Mayor's Chapel
College Green
FROGMORE STREET
ST GEORGE'S ROAD
St George's
Georgian House
GREAT GEORGE STREET
CHARLOTTE STREET
City Hall
DEANERY RD
Central Library
Cathedral
Quayhead
Watershed Media Centre
MARSH STREET
Theatre Royal
KING ST
BALDWIN STREET
QUEEN CHARLOTTE STREET
WELSH BACK
QUEEN SQUARE
THE GROVE
PRINCE STREET
REDCLIFF STREET
ST THOMAS STREET
VICTORIA STREET
TEMPLE BACK
AVON STREET
N

Bristol Cathedral

College Green, BS1 5TJ • Mon–Fri 8am–5pm, Sat & Sun 8am–3.15pm; evensong Mon–Fri 5.15pm, Sat & Sun 3.30pm • Free • **Tours**
Usually Sat 11.30am & 1.30pm; up to 1hr • Free • ⓦ bristol-cathedral.co.uk

Founded as an abbey around 1140 on the supposed spot of St Augustine's convocation with Celtic Christians in 603, venerable **Bristol Cathedral** became a cathedral church with the Dissolution of the Monasteries in the mid-sixteenth century. The two towers on the west front were erected in the nineteenth century in a faithful act of homage to Edmund Knowle, architect and abbot at the start of the fourteenth century. The interior offers a unique example among Britain's cathedrals of a German-style "hall church", in which the aisles, nave and choir rise to the same height. Abbot Knowle's immense **choir** offers one of the country's most exquisite illustrations of the early Decorated style of Gothic, while the adjoining thirteenth-century **Elder Lady Chapel** contains some fine tombs and eccentric carvings of animals, including (between the arches on the right) a monkey playing the bagpipes accompanied by a ram on the violin. The **Eastern Lady Chapel** has some of England's finest examples of heraldic glass. From the south transept, a door leads to the **Chapter House**, a richly carved piece of late Norman architecture.

Georgian House

7 Great George St, BS1 5RR • April–Dec Mon, Tues, Sat & Sun 11am–4pm • Free • ☎ 0117 921 1362, ⓦ bristolmuseums.org.uk/georgian-house-museum

Built in 1791, the deceptively large **Georgian House** is the former home of a local sugar merchant, its spacious and faithfully restored rooms filled with sumptuous examples of period furniture. The basement gives particular insight into domestic times past, while upstairs, illustrated panels tell the story of the family's dealings in the West Indies, including their involvement in slavery.

Bristol Museum and Art Gallery

Queen's Rd, BS8 1RL • Tues–Sun 10am–5pm, daily during school hols • Free • ☎ 0117 922 3571, ⓦ bristolmuseums.org.uk/bristol-museum-and-art-gallery

Housed in a grandiose Edwardian-Baroque building, the **Bristol Museum and Art Gallery** has sections on local archeology, geology and natural history, as well as an important collection of Chinese porcelain and some magnificent Assyrian reliefs carved in the eighth century BC. Artworks by Banksy, the Bristol School and French Impressionists are mixed in with some choice older pieces, including a portrait of Martin Luther by Cranach the Elder and Giovanni Bellini's unusual *Descent into Limbo*.

BANKSY AND THE BRISTOL STREET-ART SCENE

An integral part of Bristol's cultural profile, the street artist known as **Banksy** has (more or less) managed to maintain his anonymity, with exhibitions pulling crowds from London to Los Angeles. It was in Bristol, though, a city known since the 1980s for its **graffiti art**, that he first made his mark, leaving his stencilled daubs and freehand murals on walls throughout the inner city. Websites such as ⓦ bristol-street-art.co.uk will allow you to track down his surviving murals, though it's easy enough to locate his more iconic works such as *The Mild Mild West* (1999) on Stokes Croft and *The Naked Man* (2006) off the bottom of Park Street.

Banksy's global celebrity has led to his works becoming accepted and even protected by the city supremos, and the council has given its blessing to **Upfest** (ⓦ upfest.co.uk), touted as Europe's largest street-art and graffiti festival; it takes place in Bedminster, South Bristol, over a weekend in late July.

5

St Stephen's

21 Stephen's St, off Corn St, BS1 1EQ • Mon–Fri 9.30am–3pm • Free • ☎ 0117 927 7977, ⓦ saint-stephens.com

Hemmed in by characterless modern buildings just east of The Centre (as the elongated traffic intersection northeast of the cathedral is known), **St Stephen's** is one of Bristol's oldest and most graceful churches. It dates from the thirteenth century, was rebuilt in the fifteenth, and was thoroughly restored with plenty of neo-Gothic trimmings in 1875. The church has some flamboyant tombs inside, mainly of various members of the merchant class who were the church's main patrons.

Corn Exchange

Corn St, BS1 1JQ • Mon–Sat 9.30am–5pm • Free

The Georgian **Corn Exchange** was designed by John Wood the Elder of Bath and now contains the covered **St Nicholas Markets**, a lively spot for a wander or a bite to eat. The four engraved brass pillars outside the entrance date from the sixteenth and seventeenth centuries and originally served as trading tables – thought to be the "nails" that gave rise to the expression "pay on the nail".

The New Room

36 The Horsefair, Broadmead, BS1 3JE • Mon–Sat 10am–4pm, Sun 1–4pm • Chapel free, museum £6 • ☎ 0117 926 4740, ⓦ newroombristol.org.uk

Hidden within **Broadmead** shopping centre is the world's first Methodist chapel, **the New Room**. Established by John Wesley in 1739, it looks very much as he left it, with a double-deck pulpit in the chapel, beneath a hidden upstairs window from which the evangelist could observe the progress of his trainee preachers. The rooms where Wesley stayed are now a **museum** illustrating the Bristol connections of John and his brother Charles.

King Street and around

King Street, a short walk southeast from The Centre, was laid out on marshland in 1663 and still holds a cluster of historic buildings, among them the **Theatre Royal**, the oldest working theatre in the country, opened in 1766 and preserving many of its original Georgian features. Further down, and in a very different architectural style, stands the timber-framed **Llandoger Trow** pub (see p.299), once the haunt of seafarers, and reputed to have been the meeting place of Daniel Defoe and Alexander Selkirk, the model for Robinson Crusoe. South of King Street is the elegant, grassy **Queen Square**.

St Mary Redcliffe

Redcliffe Way, Redcliffe, BS1 6RA • Mon–Sat 9am–4.30pm, Sun 8am–8pm • Free • ☎ 0117 231 0060, ⓦ www.stmaryredcliffe.co.uk

Described by Elizabeth I as "the fairest, goodliest and most famous parish church in England", the richly decorated **St Mary Redcliffe**, across Redcliffe Bridge from The Centre, was largely paid for and used by merchants and mariners. The present building was begun at the end of the thirteenth century, though it was added to in subsequent centuries and its tall spire – a distinctive feature on the city's skyline – dates from 1872.

Above the church's north porch is the muniment room, where **Thomas Chatterton** claimed to have found a trove of medieval manuscripts; the poems, distributed as the work of a fifteenth-century monk named Thomas Rowley, were in fact dazzling fakes. The young poet committed suicide after his forgery was exposed, supplying English literature with one of its most glamorous stories of self-destructive genius. The "Marvellous Boy" (according to William Wordsworth) is remembered by a memorial stone in the south transept.

THE SLAVE TRADE IN BRISTOL

Over two hundred years after the abolition of the **British slave trade**, Bristol is still haunted by the instrumental part it played in the trafficking of African men, women and children to the New World – indeed, according to some interpretations, it was Bristol-born Sir John Yeamans, a Barbados planter, who effectively introduced slavery to North America.

The slave trade in Britain was monopolized by the London-based **Royal African Company** until 1698, when the market was opened to all. For the next hundred years, Bristol's merchants were able to participate in the "**triangular trade**" whereby brass pots, glass beads and other manufactured goods were traded for slaves on the coast of West Africa, who were then shipped to plantations in the Americas, the vessels returning to Europe with cargoes of sugar, cotton, tobacco and other slave-labour-produced commodities. By the 1730s, Bristol had become – along with London and Liverpool – one of the main beneficiaries of the trade; in 1750 alone, Bristol ships transported some eight thousand of the twenty thousand slaves sent that year to colonies in the Caribbean and America. The direct profits, together with the numerous spin-offs, helped to finance some of the city's finest Georgian architecture.

Bristol's primacy in the trade had been long supplanted by Liverpool by the time opposition to slavery began to gather force: first the Quakers and Methodists, then more powerful forces voiced their discontent. By the 1780s, the Anglican Dean Josiah Tucker and the Evangelical writer Hannah More had become active abolitionists, and Samuel Taylor Coleridge made a famous anti-slavery speech in Bristol in 1795.

The British slave trade was finally abolished in 1807, but its legacy is still felt strongly in the city, particularly in the divisive figure of **Edward Colston**. The eighteenth-century sugar magnate is revered by many as a great philanthropist – his name given to numerous buildings, streets and schools in Bristol – but also reviled as a leading light in the Royal African Company. His statue in The Centre has more than once been the subject of graffiti attacks and calls for its removal, and famous Bristol band Massive Attack refused to play the Colston Hall because of the connotations of its name, which is scheduled to be changed for the venue's reopening in 2020.

At-Bristol

Anchor Rd, BS1 5DB • Daily 10am–5pm, Sat, Sun & hols 10am–6pm • £13.90, under-15s £8.95 • ☎ 0117 915 1000, Ⓦ at-bristol.org.uk

Occupying a corner of the sleekly modern Millennium Square, marked out by the spherical, stainless-steel planetarium attached to one side, **At-Bristol** deals with all things science. It's chiefly aimed at children, but there's enough interactive wizardry here to entertain and inform everyone, with opportunities to view the blood in your veins, freeze your shadow and create your own short films (with input from Aardman Animations). The **planetarium** has up to eight shows daily, which should be booked when you buy your entry ticket (from £2.50 extra).

M-Shed

Princes Wharf, Wapping Rd, BS1 4RN • Tues–Sun & hols 10am–5pm • Free • Boat, train and crane rides on selected days throughout the year; £2–6 • ☎ 0117 352 6600, Ⓦ bristolmuseums.org.uk/m-shed

Housed in an old harbourside transit shed, the superb **M-Shed** is dedicated to Bristol itself, past and present. It's an enjoyable, unashamedly populist survey, full of memorabilia and anecdotes and casting light on everything from the city's mercantile history to its festivals and street life. On the ground floor, Bristol Places charts the city's changing face, taking in its development as a port and the hardships of World War II. On the floor above, Bristol People and the adjoining Bristol Life look at the (often ordinary) folk who have shaped the city, with the former including a small display on Bristol's links with the transatlantic slave trade (see box above). Afterwards, head out to the long terrace for fantastic harbour views.

5

ss Great Britain

Great Western Dockyard, BS1 6TY • Daily: April–Oct 10am–5.30pm; Nov–March 10am–4.30pm • £14 • ☎ 0117 926 0680,
ⓦ ssgreatbritain.org

Harbourside's major draw, and one of Bristol's iconic sights, the **ss Great Britain** was the first propeller-driven, ocean-going iron ship in the world, built by **Isambard Kingdom Brunel** in 1843. She initially ran between Liverpool and New York, then between Liverpool and Melbourne, circumnavigating the globe 32 times and chalking up over a million miles at sea. Her ocean-going days ended in 1886 when she was caught in a storm off Cape Horn, and she was eventually recovered and returned to Bristol in 1970. On board, you can see restored cabins and peer into the immense engine room, while the adjoining museum gives the background of the vessel and of Bristol's long shipbuilding history.

Clifton

On the western side of the city, **Clifton**, once an aloof spa resort, is now Bristol's stateliest neighbourhood. At the top of Blackboy Hill, the wide green expanses of **Durdham Down** and **Clifton Downs** stretch right up to the edge of the Avon Gorge, a popular spot for picnickers, joggers and kite-flyers. On the southern edge of the Downs is the select enclave of Clifton Village, centred on the Mall, where **Royal York Crescent**, the longest Georgian crescent in the country, offers splendid views over the steep drop to the River Avon below.

Clifton Suspension Bridge

Bridge Rd, BS8 3PA • Free, £1 for motor vehicles • **Visitor Centre** Daily 10am–5pm • Free • **Guided tours** Easter–Oct Sat & Sun 3pm;
45min • Free • ⓦ cliftonbridge.org.uk

A few minutes' walk from Clifton Village is Bristol's most famous symbol, **Clifton Suspension Bridge**, 702ft long and poised 245ft above high water. Money was first put forward for a bridge to span the Avon Gorge by a Bristol wine merchant in 1754, though it wasn't until 1829 that a competition was held for a design – won by **Isambard Kingdom Brunel** in a second round – and not until 1864 that the bridge was completed, five years after Brunel's death. Hampered by financial difficulties, the bridge never quite matched the engineer's original ambitious design, which included Egyptian-style towers topped by sphinxes at each end. You can see copies of his plans in the **Visitor Centre** at the far side of the bridge, alongside designs proposed by Brunel's rivals, some of them frankly bizarre.

ARRIVAL AND DEPARTURE

BRISTOL

By train Temple Meads train station is a 20min walk east of the city centre.
Destinations Bath (every 15–30min; 15min); Birmingham (every 30min; 1hr 25min); Cheltenham (every 30min; 40min); Exeter (1–2 hourly; 1hr); Gloucester (Mon–Sat hourly, Sun every 2hr; 55min); London Paddington (2–3 hourly; 1hr 45min); Taunton (2–4 hourly; 30min–1hr); Yeovil (Mon–Sat 7 daily, Sun 4 daily; 1hr 30min).
By bus Bristol's bus station (ⓦ firstgroup.com) is centrally

located off Marlborough St; at the time of writing, Megabus (ⓦ megabus.com) services to and from London stop outside Black's camping shop on Bond St (near the bus station), though check the website for the current location as this may change.
Destinations Bath (3–6 hourly; 40min); Glastonbury (every 30min; 1hr 40min); London (every 30min–1hr; 2hr 30min–3hr); Wells (every 30min; 1hr).

GETTING AROUND

By ferry A ferry, setting off from the Quayhead, just south of The Centre, connects various parts of the Floating Harbour, including Temple Meads station and the ss Great Britain (every 40min; 10am–6.15pm; from £1.70 single, £2.90 return, £6.50 all-day ticket; ☎ 0117

927 3416, ⓦ bristolferry.com).
By bus Local buses are useful for getting to Clifton's upper reaches; take #8 or #9 from Temple Meads station or The Centre, which also connects the city's train and bus stations.

INFORMATION AND TOURS

Tourist office E-Shed, Canon's Rd (daily 10am–5pm; ☎0906 711 2191, ⓦvisitbristol.co.uk).

Tours Bristol In-Sight (☎0117 971 9279, ⓦbristolinsight .co.uk) runs a hop-on, hop-off, open-top bus tour of the city's key sights (£15, £13 online), while Bristol Packet (☎0117 926 8157, ⓦbristolpacket.co.uk) offers cruises around the harbour, in the Avon Gorge and along the river to Bath (from £6.50).

ACCOMMODATION

With a few notable exceptions, good accommodation in Bristol is surprisingly thin on the ground. Hotels and B&Bs in the centre can suffer from traffic noise and the sound of late-night drinkers; for quieter and more traditional lodgings, choose **Clifton**.

★9 Prince's Buildings 9 Prince's Buildings, Clifton, BS8 4LB ☎0117 973 4615, ⓦ9princesbuildings.co.uk; map p.292. A short walk from the Clifton Suspension Bridge and within staggering distance of several real-ale pubs, this five-storey Georgian B&B, lovingly cared for by its easy-going owners, enjoys a grand view over the Avon Gorge from its antique-filled rooms. Great breakfasts, too. Singles from £72. No credit cards. **£105**

Bristol Marriott Royal Hotel College Green, BS1 5TA ☎0117 925 5100, ⓦbristolmarriottroyal.co.uk; map p.292. Right next to Bristol Cathedral, this Italianate-style Victorian hotel is by far the more attractive of the city's two *Marriotts*, with spacious rooms, two restaurants, a Champagne bar and a lovely swimming pool. **£110**

★Brooks Guesthouse Exchange Ave, off St Nicholas St, BS1 1UB ☎0117 930 0066, ⓦbrooksguesthouse bristol.com; map p.292. Set in the midst of bustling St Nicholas Markets, this boutique B&B has small but comfortable rooms that come with DVD players and iPod docks. The airy, modern breakfast room gives onto a spacious courtyard for relaxing with a book or a drink. You can also stay in an airstream trailer on the roof (£99). **£79**

Clifton House 4 Tyndall's Park Rd, Clifton, BS8 1PG ☎0117 973 5407, ⓦcliftonhousebristol.com; map p.292. This handily sited B&B at the bottom of Clifton and near the centre offers fairly plush rooms with big windows, modern bathrooms and plenty of space – superior rooms, costing £20 extra, are huge – and there's parking too. **£85**

Hotel du Vin The Sugar House, Narrow Lewins Mead, BS1 2NU ☎0330 016 0390, ⓦhotelduvin.co.uk; map p.292. Chic conversion of an old dockside warehouse, centrally located, with dark, contemporary decor. Rooms have big beds and grand bathrooms, and there's an excellent restaurant to boot (see below). **£129**

Rock'n'Bowl Motel 22 Nelson St, BS1 2LA ☎0117 325 1980, ⓦthelanesbristol.co.uk/hostel; map p.292. Clean and efficiently run hostel in an ex-dole office above a busy bowling alley. Single- and mixed-gender dorms (4- to 20-person) and a few en-suite doubles and twins, plus a self-catering kitchen and laundry. Can be noisy. Dorms **£15**, doubles **£65**

YHA Bristol 14 Narrow Quay, BS1 4QA ☎0345 371 9726, ⓦyha.org.uk/hostel/bristol; map p.292. In a refurbished grain house on the quayside, this warm and friendly hostel has mostly four-bed dorms, plus (smallish) private doubles. There's a decent kitchen, and prices include an abundant breakfast. Dorms **£15**, doubles **£39**

EATING

CAFÉS

Full Court Press 59 Broad St, BS1 2EJ ☎07794 808552, ⓦfcpcoffee.com; map p.292. The select menu of superb speciality coffees at this dinky joint near St Nick's Markets have made it an instant hit with local connoisseurs. Mon–Fri 7.30am–5pm, Sat 9am–5pm, Sun 10am–4pm.

Primrose Café 1 Clifton Arcade, Boyces Ave, Clifton, BS8 4AA ☎0117 946 6577, ⓦprimrosecafe.co.uk; map p.292. Homely café in Clifton Village serving a good range of teas, fruit juices and wines, as well as a choice of breakfasts, sandwiches, salads, burgers and pancakes. There's a roof garden open in summer, too. Daily 9/9.30am–5pm.

Watershed 1 Canon's Rd, BS1 5TX ☎0117 927 5101, ⓦwatershed.co.uk; map p.292. Cool café-bar overlooking the boats in one of Bristol's longest-established arts complexes. Good champagne and local beers are supplemented by an appetizing menu, and there's a tiny (non-smoking) terrace. Mon–Fri 9.30am–11pm, Sat 10am–11pm, Sun 10am–10.30pm.

RESTAURANTS

Bistro du Vin Hotel du Vin, The Sugar House, Narrow Lewins Mead, BS1 2NU ☎0117 925 5577, ⓦhotelduvin .com; map p.292. Fine French bistro-style dining, using good seasonal West Country produce in its Modern European menu; most mains around £16. Mon–Sat noon–2.30pm & 5.30–10pm, Fri & Sat noon–2.30pm & 5.30–10.30pm, Sun noon–4pm & 6–9.30pm.

Chai Shai 4 Jacobs Well Rd, BS8 1EA ☎0117 925 0754; map p.292. Small, friendly and laid-back Indian restaurant with an open kitchen and a small menu of light and tasty dishes such as *saag ghosht* (mutton and spinach), *achari* chicken and fish *khata* (all around £8). It's usually busy, so book ahead, or wait in the neighbouring pub for a table to become free. Bring your own beers. Takeaways also available. Mon–Sat 11.30am–3pm & 4–11pm.

★Lido Oakfield Place, Clifton, BS8 2BJ; restaurant entrance on Southleigh Rd ☎0117 332 3970, ⓦlido bristol.com; map p.292. The glass-walled restaurant at this

5

BRISTOL'S FESTIVALS

Try to time your visit to coincide with one of Bristol's numerous festivals, mostly held during the summer. Highlights are **St Paul's Carnival** (wstpaulscarnival.co.uk) on the first Saturday of July, a celebration of the city's Afro-Caribbean culture with floats, stalls and live music; the **Bristol Harbour Festival** (wbristolharbourfestival.co.uk), a weekend of live music, waterside festivities and fireworks over a weekend in late July; and the **Bristol International Balloon Fiesta** (wbristolballoonfiesta.co.uk), at Ashton Court, featuring mass hot-air balloon launches and "night glows" over four days in mid-August.

pool/spa complex overlooks the outdoor pool, which makes dining on dishes like seafood stew (£21) while others exercise a deliciously guilty affair. There are set-price menus (£12–20), while in the poolside bar, breakfast is available until 11.30am and tapas from noon. Daily: restaurant noon–2.45pm & 6–9.45pm; poolside bar 8/9am–10pm.

Maitreya Social 89 St Mark's Rd, BS5 6HY ☎0117 951 0100, wcafemaitreya.co.uk; map p.292. Tucked away in the buzzing heart of the multicultural Easton neighbourhood, this easy-going place serves delicious, inventive vegetarian dishes – falafel with charred aubergine, for example, or smoked shallot tart (both £12). The early-bird menu is great value (£15–17). Tues–Fri 6–11.30pm, Sat 10am–11.30pm, Sun 10am–3pm.

riverstation The Grove, BS1 4RB ☎0117 914 4434, wriverstation.co.uk; map p.292. Two-storey former river-police station, with all-day brunches, tapas and flatbreads at the relaxed ground-floor bar and more refined Modern European dining upstairs, where main courses cost £15–24 and set-price meals £15–19. Try to bag a table by the window for the dockside views. Restaurant Mon–Sat noon–2.30pm & 6–10pm, Sun noon–3pm; bar Mon–Sat 10am–11pm (kitchen until 10pm), Sun 10am–10pm (kitchen until 8pm).

Salt & Malt Cargo 2, Museum St, BS1 6WD ☎01275 333 345, wsaltmalt.com; map p.292. Housed in a shipping container – one of a complex of these in the buzzing Wapping Wharf district behind M-Shed – this smart little fish bar delivers lightly fried cod, haddock and plaice together with crispy chips. Served in a box, it's ideal for mooching along the harbourfront, or you can eat at small tables within view of the boats. Cod and chips is £7.50 to take away, £11.50 at table. Alternatives include battered halloumi, and there's a good choice of beers, ciders and wines. Tues–Sat noon–10pm, Sun noon–8pm.

Severnshed The Grove, BS1 4RB ☎0117 925 1212, wsevernshedrestaurant.co.uk; map p.292. Severnshed, which has a waterside terrace, serves pastas and pizzas (from £8) and grills, including meat and fish firesticks (£17–21), as well as cocktails until late. DJs provide the soundtrack on Sat evenings. Mon–Thurs 10am–11pm, Fri 10am–1am, Sat 9am–1am, Sun 9am–11pm.

★Source 1–3 Exchange Ave, off St Nicholas St, BS1 1JW ☎0117 927 2998, wsource-food.co.uk; map p.292. Almost all the food in this relaxed deli and canteen next to St Nick's Markets is from the West Country, and much of it is organic – for example, fish soup, spiced aubergine and charcuterie-style cold meats (£7–11). Breakfasts, teas and cakes are also available. Mon–Sat 8am–4pm.

Thali Café 1 Regent St, Clifton, BS8 4HW ☎0117 974 3793, wthethalicafe.co.uk; map p.292. Dhaba-style South Asian food in vibrant surroundings. This Clifton branch – there are four others across Bristol – has the trademark deep-pink decor and range of tasty thalis, a balanced selection of dishes served on a stainless-steel platter (from £9.50). Daily 5–10pm, Sat & Sun noon–10pm.

DRINKING

Browns 38 Queen's Rd, BS8 1RE ☎0117 930 4777, wbrowns-restaurants.com; map p.292. Spacious and relaxed place for an evening drink, housed in the Venetian-style former university refectory. The wide choice of tipples includes a range of beers, wines, Champagnes and cocktails. Mon–Thurs 9am–11pm, Fri & Sat 9am–midnight, Sun 9am–10.30pm.

Canteen Hamilton House, 80 Stokes Croft, BS1 3QY ☎0117 923 2017, wcanteenbristol.co.uk; map p.292. Overlooked by one of Banksy's most famous murals, a drab 1960s office block now accommodates this popular collective-style bar. Take a seat at a graffitied table for a coffee or a pint, or try something from the cheap, sustainable menu, accompanied most nights from 9.30pm by live music

(but Sun 4–6pm) and DJs. Mon–Thurs 10am–midnight, Fri & Sat 10am–1am, Sun 10am–11pm.

★The Coronation Tap 8 Sion Place, Clifton, BS8 4AX ☎0117 973 9617, wthecoronationtap.com; map p.292. A proper cider house, the Cori Tap produces its own Exhibition "apple juice", which is sold by the half-pint only, and stocks a wide range of locally produced ciders. Excellent live music, too. Daily 5.30–11.30pm, Sat & Sun 7–11.30pm.

Grain Barge Mardyke Wharf, Hotwell Rd, BS8 4RU ☎0117 929 9347, wgrainbarge.com; map p.292. Floating pub, café and restaurant near the mouth of the harbour, with a tranquil ambience and half a dozen real ales brewed at the Bristol Beer Factory. Interesting calendar of events, including occasional live music on Thurs evenings. Daily noon–11pm, Thurs–Sat noon–11.30pm.

Llandoger Trow 1–3 King St, BS1 4ER ☎0117 926 1650, ⓦbrewersfayre.co.uk; map p.292. Seventeenth-century drinking den full of historical associations (see p.294), with cosy nooks and armchairs, benches outside and a separate restaurant upstairs. Snacks and full meals available. Gets very busy on summer evenings. Mon–Sat 7.30am–11pm, Sun 8am–10.30pm.

No.1 Harbourside 1 Canon's Rd, BS1 5UH ☎0117 929 1100, ⓦno1harbourside.co.uk; map p.292. Laidback lounge bar for drinks, snacks (including plenty of veggie and vegan choices) and live music (Wed–Sun) until late. Sun evenings are for dancing, from flamenco to swing. Mon & Sun 10am–11pm, Tues–Thurs 10am–midnight, Fri & Sat 10am–1am.

The Strawberry Thief 26 Broad St, BS1 2HG ☎0117 925 6925, ⓦstrawberrythiefbar.com; map p.292. Boasting the West Country's largest selection of Belgian beers (around fifty), as well as a good twenty UK craft beers, this relaxed place has a hip, mellow vibe, with small tables and William Morris wallpaper. Food (including brunches and waffles) is gluten-free, mostly vegan and served until 9.30pm. Tues–Thurs 4–11pm, Fri 4pm–midnight, Sat noon–midnight.

White Lion Avon Gorge Hotel, Sion Hill, Clifton, BS8 4LD ☎0117 403 0210, ⓦtheavongorgehotel.com; map p.292. Attached to a hotel perched on the edge of the Gorge in Clifton Village, this modern bar draws in the crowds thanks to its broad terrace, affording magnificent views of the gorge and suspension bridge. Food available. Mon–Sat 11am–11pm, Sun 11am–10.30pm.

NIGHTLIFE

The Fiddlers Willway St, Bedminster, BS3 4BG ☎0117 987 3403, ⓦfiddlers.co.uk; map p.292. Mainly roots bands, good-time retro acts and niche artists perform at this relaxed, family-run venue (formerly a prison) south of the river.

The Fleece 12 St Thomas St, BS1 6JJ ☎0117 945 0996, ⓦthefleece.co.uk; map p.292. Stone-flagged ex-wool warehouse, now a loud, sweaty pub staging everything from acoustic blues and alt-country to punk and deathcore.

The Louisiana Wapping Rd, BS1 6UA ☎0117 926 5978, ⓦwww.thelouisiana.net; map p.292. Established music pub with a well-earned reputation for helping break

bands (The White Stripes, Florence + the Machine) and promoting local artists. It's a mite cramped, but the acoustics and atmosphere are excellent.

SWX 15 Nelson St, BS1 2JY ☎0117 945 0325, ⓦswx bristol.com; map p.292. A real super-club, one of the largest in Bristol, and home to various club nights, as well as live music and comedy.

Thekla The Grove, BS1 4RB ☎0117 929 3301, ⓦthekla bristol.co.uk; map p.292. Ex-cargo boat, now a much-loved venue staging a varied line-up of live bands plus indie, house and club nights.

ENTERTAINMENT

Bristol Old Vic King's St, BS1 4ED ☎0117 987 7877, ⓦbristololdvic.org.uk; map p.292. Britain's oldest working theatre, dating from the 1760s, retains its Georgian interior but has modern facilities. It lays on a full programme of mainstream and more experimental productions in its main auditorium and the Studio.

★**St George's** Great George St, BS1 5RR ☎0845 402 4001, ⓦstgeorgesbristol.co.uk; map p.292. Elegant

Georgian church with superb acoustics, staging a packed programme of lunchtime and evening concerts covering classical, world, folk and jazz music.

Tobacco Factory Raleigh Rd, Southville, BS3 1ET ☎0117 902 0344, ⓦtobaccofactorytheatres.com; map p.292. South of the river, this theatre offers a broad spectrum of drama, dance, comedy and other performing arts on two stages.

SHOPPING

Beast St Nicholas Markets, BS1 1HQ ⓦbeast-clothing .com; map p.292. Amusing T-shirts, hoodies and hats emblazoned with snippets of the local lingo – choose from "Ark At Ee" and "Gert Lush" among others. Mon–Sat 9.30am–5pm.

Bristol Cider Shop Unit 4, Cargo, Gaol Ferry Steps, BS1 6WE ⓦbristolcidershop.co.uk; map p.292. In a converted shipping container, this store stocks over 100 varieties of local cider and perry, including Perry's and the legendary Wilkins, with around eight on tap. Tues–Sat 11am–7pm, Sun 11am–4pm.

Cabot Circus BS1 3BX ⓦcabotcircus.com; map p.292. Ultra-contemporary shopping precinct filled with the usual

big-name brands such as Hollister, Apple, Sony and a three-floor House of Fraser, plus the only Harvey Nichols in the South West. Mon–Sat 10am–8pm, Sun 11am–5pm.

Guild 68–70 Park St, BS1 5JY; map p.292. Quality independent retailer operating here for over a century, containing various departments from designer kitchen goods to a gourmet food hall, plus an outside terrace for a quick coffee break. Mon–Sat 10am–6pm.

Plastic Wax Records 222 Cheltenham Rd, BS6 5QU ⓦplasticwaxrecords.com; map p.292. Bristol's largest record dealer, with wall-to-wall used vinyl and CDs across all genres. Mon 9.30am–4.30pm, Tues–Fri 9.30am–7pm, Sat 9am–6pm, Sun noon–5pm.

Wells

The miniature cathedral city of **WELLS**, 21 miles south of Bristol and the same distance southwest from Bath, has not significantly altered in eight hundred years. Charming and compact, it is eminently walkable, and a stroll around its tightly knit streets reveals a cluster of medieval buildings, archways and almshouses.

Wells Cathedral

Cathedral Green, BA5 2UE • Daily: April–Sept 7am–7pm; Oct–March 7am–6pm • Free, but suggested donation £6 • **Tours** Usually Mon–Sat: April–Oct 11am, noon, 1pm, 2pm & 3pm; Nov–March 11am, noon & 2pm; 1hr • Free • ☎ 01749 674483, ⓦ wellscathedral.org.uk

Hidden from sight until you pass into its spacious close from central Market Place, **Wells Cathedral** presents a majestic spectacle, the broad lawn of the former graveyard providing a perfect foreground. The west front teems with some three hundred thirteenth-century figures of saints and kings, once brightly painted and gilded, though their present honey tint has a subtle splendour of its own. The sensational facade was constructed about fifty years after work on the main building was begun in 1180.

The **interior** is a supreme example of early English Gothic, the long nave punctuated by a dramatic and very modern-looking "scissor arch", one of three that were constructed in 1338 to take the extra weight of the newly built tower. Beyond the arches, there are some gnarled old tombs to be seen in the aisles of the **Quire**, at the end of which is the richly coloured stained glass of the fourteenth-century **Lady Chapel**. The capitals and corbels of the transepts hold some amusing narrative carvings, and in the north transept there's a 24-hour astronomical clock dating from 1390. Opposite the clock, a well-worn flight of steps leads to the **Chapter House**, an octagonal room elaborately ribbed in the Decorated style.

Wells & Mendip Museum

8 Cathedral Green, BA5 2UE • Mon–Sat: Easter–Sept 10am–5pm; Oct–Easter 10am–4pm • £3 • ☎ 01749 673477, ⓦ wellsmuseum.org.uk

The row of clerical houses on the north side of Cathedral Green mainly dates from the seventeenth and eighteenth centuries. The chancellor's house is now the **Wells & Mendip Museum**, displaying some of the cathedral's original statuary as well as a good geological section with fossils from the Mendip area. There are also changing exhibitions, with a focus on World War I until late 2018, then on the history of Wells itself.

Vicars' Close

The cottages that constitute picturesque **Vicars' Close**, linked to the cathedral by the Chain Gate, were built in the mid-fourteenth century to house the men of the choir, and its members still make up most of their inhabitants today. The cobbled close is the oldest continuously inhabited medieval street in Europe but has undergone various alterations over the years – you can get a good idea of its initial appearance at no. 22, which was restored to its original proportions in 1863.

Bishop's Palace

Market Place, BA5 2RA • Daily: Early Jan to March & Nov to late Dec 10am–4pm; April–Oct 10am–6pm • £7.25 • **Tours** Daily 11am & 2pm (palace), noon & 3pm (grounds); palace 30min, grounds 45min • Included in entry fee • ☎ 01749 988111, ⓦ bishopspalace.org.uk

The tranquil grounds of the **Bishop's Palace**, residence of the Bishop of Bath and Wells since 1206, are reachable through the Bishop's Eye archway from Market Place. The palace was walled and moated as a result of a rift with the borough in the fourteenth century, and the imposing gatehouse still features the grooves of the portcullis and a chute for pouring oil and molten lead on would-be assailants. The gardens contain the springs from which

PLEASE
RING
FOR
CIDER

←

5

the city takes its name and the scant but impressive remains of the **Great Hall**, built at the end of the thirteenth century and despoiled during the Reformation. Across the lawn stand the square **Bishop's Chapel** and **Bishop Jocelyn's Hall**, a few state rooms holding displays relating to the history of the site, and the *Undercroft* café.

ARRIVAL AND INFORMATION

WELLS

By bus Buses (☎0345 602 0121, ⓦfirstgroup.com /somerset) pull in at the station off Market St.
Destinations Bath (Mon–Sat 2 hourly, Sun hourly; 1hr 25min); Bristol (every 30min; 1hr); Glastonbury (Mon–Sat every 15min, Sun every 30min; 15min); Taunton (Mon–Sat

every 2hr; 1hr 40min); Wookey Hole (Mon–Sat 1–2 hourly, Sun 4 daily; 5–10min); Yeovil (Mon–Sat hourly; 1hr 20min).
Tourist office Wells & Mendip Museum, 8 Cathedral Green (Mon–Sat: Easter–Sept 10am–5pm; Oct–Easter Mon–Sat 10am–4pm; ☎01749 671770, ⓦwellssomerset.com).

ACCOMMODATION

Beryl Hawkers Lane, BA5 3JP, 1 mile northeast of Wells ☎01749 678738, ⓦwww.beryl-wells.co.uk. Luxury country-house B&B, a former hunting lodge, set in lovely gardens with a children's play area and pool (May–Sept). Decor varies between the fourteen rooms – some are quite twee, others stylishly understated – though all enjoy good views. **£100**
The Crown Market Place, BA5 2RP ☎01749 673457, ⓦcrownatwells.co.uk. Fifteenth-century coaching inn

where William Penn was arrested in 1695 for illegal preaching; it's got a suitably old-fashioned flavour that verges on the fusty and faded. Rooms can be noisy from the bar and bistro below and/or the Wed and Sat markets. **£95**
Swan Hotel Sadler St, BA5 2RX ☎01749 836300, ⓦswanhotelwells.co.uk. This swanky and rambling inn has plenty of antique character, plus friendly service and a rated restaurant (for which booking is essential). Pricier rooms have cathedral views. **£148**

EATING AND DRINKING

Fountain Inn 1 St Thomas St, BA5 2UU ☎01749 672317, ⓦfountaininn.co.uk. Leave the touristy pubs of High Street Wells behind and head under the Chain Gate and beyond Vicar's Close to this rustic-chic gastropub northeast of the cathedral. The interesting menu includes halloumi burger (£11), grilled duck breast with couscous (£16) and spiced lamb cutlets with tabbouleh (£19). Mon 6–10pm, Tues–Fri noon–2pm & 6–10pm, Sat noon–3pm & 6–11pm, Sun noon–2.30pm & 7–9pm.
★**The Good Earth** 4 Priory Rd, BA5 1SY ☎01749 678600, ⓦthegoodearthwells.co.uk. Excellent whole-food restaurant that was making a name for itself with its delicious home-made quiches long before eco food was

in vogue. Soups, salads, veggie pizzas and other organic goodies (mains from £7) available to eat in or take away. Mon–Fri 9am–4.30pm, Sat 9am–5pm.
Square Edge Café 2 Town Hall Buildings, Market Place, BA5 1SE ☎01749 671166, ⓦsquare-edgecafe .co.uk. Close to the sights, this retro-themed café makes a cosy spot to relax over a cup of first-rate coffee and a slice of cake. You can also opt for a full breakfast or a snack lunch, for example a hummus platter (£10.50) or a bun stuffed with beef brisket (£11). The atmospheric interior has two large fireplaces and a range of ancient radios among other curios, and there's an equally quirky courtyard. Mon–Sat 9am–5pm, Sun 10am–4pm.

The Mendips

Northwest of Wells, the ancient woodland, exposed heaths and limestone crags of the **Mendip Hills** are chiefly famous for **Wookey Hole** – the most impressive of many caves in this narrow limestone chain – and for **Cheddar Gorge**, where a walk through the narrow cleft makes a starting point for more adventurous hikes across the Mendips.

Wookey Hole

Two miles northwest of Wells, BA5 1BB • Tours daily every 10–30min: April–Oct 10am–6pm; Nov–March 10am–5pm; last tour 1hr before closing; 1hr • £19, online £17.10 • ☎01749 672042, ⓦwookey.co.uk
It's folklore rather than geology that takes precedence at **Wookey Hole**, a stunning cave complex of deep pools and intricate rock formations hollowed out by the River Axe. Highlight of the **tour** is the alleged petrified remains of the Witch of Wookey, a "blear-eyed hag" who was said to turn her evil eye on crops, young lovers and local farmers. To finish

off, there's a functioning Victorian paper mill and rooms containing speleological exhibits, plus a melange of family "attractions" that range from King Kong to a Clown Museum.

Cheddar Gorge

The nondescript village of **CHEDDAR**, six miles west of Wookey on the A371, has given its name to Britain's best-known cheese – most of it now mass-produced far from here – and is also renowned for **Cheddar Gorge**, lying about a mile to the north.

Cutting a jagged gash across the Mendip Hills, the limestone gorge is an amazing geological phenomenon, though its natural beauty is rather compromised by Lower Gorge's mile of trinket shops and parking areas. Few trippers venture further than the first few curves of the gorge, which holds its most dramatic scenery – at its narrowest, the road squeezes between cliffs towering almost 500ft above – though each turn of the two-mile length presents new, sometimes startling vistas.

Those fit enough can climb the 274 steps of **Jacob's Ladder** to a clifftop tower with views towards Glastonbury Tor, with occasional glimpses of Exmoor and the sea (ladder and tower daily 10am–5pm; £5.50, free to Cheddar Caves ticket-holders). From the tower, there's a circular three-mile clifftop Gorge Walk, and you can branch off along marked paths to such secluded spots as **Black Rock** reserve, just two miles from Cheddar, or **Black Down** and Beacon Batch, at 1068ft the Mendips' highest point.

Cheddar Caves

BS27 3QF • Daily 10am–5pm • £17.95, online £15.25 • ☎ 01934 742343, ⓦ cheddargorge.co.uk

Beneath the towering Cheddar Gorge, the **Cheddar Caves** were scooped out by underground rivers in the wake of the Ice Age, and subsequently occupied by primitive communities. Today, the caves are floodlit to pick out the subtle tones of the rock, and the array of rock formations that resemble organ pipes, waterfalls and giant birds.

ARRIVAL AND INFORMATION   THE MENDIPS

By bus Public transport is essentially limited to #67 from Wells to Wookey Hole (Mon–Fri 7 daily; 10min), and #126 from Wells to Cheddar (Mon–Sat hourly, 4 on Sun; 25min).
By car The Mendip Hills are most easily explored with your own wheels.

Tourist information There's an information desk at the National Trust shop in Cheddar Gorge (Easter to late Oct daily 10am–5pm; late Oct to Christmas & late Feb to Easter Sat & Sun 10am–4pm; ☎ 01934 744689).

ACCOMMODATION AND EATING

Chedwell Cottage 59 Redcliffe St, Cheddar, BS27 3PF ☎ 01934 743268, ⓦ chedwellcottage.co.uk. The charming owners of this homely B&B, in a quiet lane a 10min walk from the gorge, provide three simply furnished en-suite rooms and delicious breakfasts which include home-made bread. No debit/credit cards. £75

The Wookey Hole Inn Wookey Hole, BA5 1BP ☎ 01749 676677, ⓦ wookeyholeinn.com. Very close to the caves, this is a great place to stay the night, with funky, fully

equipped guest rooms and a restaurant (booking essential) that offers a range of expensive but memorable dishes (mains from £13). Mon–Sat noon–2.30pm & 6.30–9pm, Sun noon–3pm. £75

YHA Cheddar Hillfield, Cheddar, BS27 3HN ☎ 0345 371 9730, ⓦ yha.org.uk. Clinically refurbished Victorian house with clean, spacious rooms – four- to six-bed dorms, en-suite doubles and family rooms – and a decent kitchen. Dorms £13, doubles £29

Glastonbury

On the southern edge of the Mendips and six miles south of Wells, **GLASTONBURY**, famed for its annual music festival, is built around the evocative set of ruins belonging to its former abbey. The town lies at the heart of the so-called **Isle of Avalon**, a region rich with mystical associations, and for centuries it has been one of the main Arthurian sites of the West Country – today, it's an enthusiastic centre for all manner of New Age pursuits.

5

GLASTONBURY TALES

At the heart of the complex web of **myths surrounding Glastonbury** is the early Christian legend that the young Jesus once visited this site, a story that is not quite as far-fetched as it sounds. The Romans had a heavy presence in the area, mining lead in the Mendips, and one of these mines was owned by **Joseph of Arimathea**, a well-to-do tin merchant said to have been related to Mary. It's not completely unfeasible that the merchant took his kinsman on one of his many visits to his property, in a period of Christ's life about which nothing is recorded – it was this possibility to which William Blake referred in his *Glastonbury Hymn*, better known as *Jerusalem*: "And did those feet in ancient times/Walk upon England's mountains green?"

Another legend relates how Joseph was imprisoned for twelve years after the Crucifixion, miraculously kept alive by the **Holy Grail**, the chalice of the Last Supper, in which the blood was gathered from the wound in Christ's side. The Grail, along with the spear that had caused the wound, were later taken by Joseph to Glastonbury, where he built the "First Church", around which the abbey later grew, and commenced the conversion of Britain.

Glastonbury is also popularly identified with the mythical **Avalon**. The story goes that King Arthur, having been mortally wounded in battle, sailed to Avalon where he was buried in the abbey's choir, alongside his queen – somehow Glastonbury was taken to be the best candidate for the place.

Glastonbury Abbey

Magdalene St, BA6 9EL • Daily: March–May, Sept & Oct 9am–6pm; June–Aug 9am–8pm; Nov–Feb 9am–4pm • £7.50, online £6.67 • ☎ 01458 832267, ⓦ glastonburyabbey.com

Aside from its mythological origins, **Glastonbury Abbey** can claim to be the country's oldest Christian foundation, dating back to the seventh century and possibly earlier. Enlarged by St Dunstan in the tenth century, it became the richest Benedictine abbey in the country; three Anglo-Saxon kings (Edmund, Edgar and Edmund Ironside) were buried here, and the library had a far-reaching fame. Further expansion took place under the Normans, though most of the additions were destroyed by fire in 1184. Rebuilt, the abbey was the longest in Europe when it was destroyed during the Dissolution of the Monasteries in 1539, and the ruins, now hidden behind walls and nestled among grassy parkland, can only hint at its former extent. The most complete set of remains is the shell of the **Lady Chapel**, with its carved figures of the Annunciation, the Magi and Herod.

The abbey's **choir**, announced by the half-worn but striking transept piers, holds what is alleged to be the tomb of **Arthur and Guinevere**. The discovery of two bodies in an ancient cemetery outside the abbey in 1191 was taken to confirm that here was, indeed, the mystical Avalon; they were transferred here in 1278 but disappeared in the mid-sixteenth century. Elsewhere in the grounds, the fourteenth-century **abbot's kitchen** is the only monastic building to survive intact, with four huge corner fireplaces and a great central lantern above. Behind the main entrance to the grounds, look out for the thorn tree that is supposedly a descendant of the original **Glastonbury Thorn** on Wearyall Hill, said to have sprouted from the staff of Joseph of Arimathea. Big-name **concerts and drama productions** take place in the abbey grounds in summer – check the website for details.

Glastonbury Lake Village Museum

9 High St, BA6 9DP • Mon–Sat 10am–3pm • £3.50; EH • ☎ 01458 832954, ⓦ www.english-heritage.org.uk/visit/places/glastonbury-tribunal

The fifteenth-century **Glastonbury Tribunal** provides an atmospheric setting for the small but interesting **Glastonbury Lake Village Museum**, which has displays from the Iron Age settlements that fringed the former marshland below the Tor. The villages' wattle houses were consistently rebuilt on layers of clay as they slowly submerged into the marshes, and the perfectly preserved finds include jewellery made from animal bones and a 3000-year-old wooden canoe.

Somerset Rural Life Museum

Abbey Farm, Chilkwell St, BA6 8DB • 10am–5pm: Easter–Oct Tues–Sun; Nov–Easter Tues–Sat • £5.45 • ☎ 01458 831197,
Ⓦ somersetrurallifemuseum.org.uk

Centred around the fourteenth-century Abbey Barn, the engaging **Somerset Rural Life Museum** has historically focused on a range of local rural occupations, from cider-making and peat-digging to the unusual practice of mud-horse fishing, named after the sledge shrimpers used to navigate the mud flats of Bridgwater Bay.

Chalice Well

Chilkwell St, BA6 8DD • Daily: April–Oct 10am–6pm; Nov–March 10am–4.30pm • £4.30 • ☎ 01458 831154, Ⓦ chalicewell.org.uk

The **Chalice Well** stands amid a lush garden intended for quiet contemplation at the foot of Glastonbury Tor. The iron-red waters of the well – which is fondly supposed to be the hiding place of the Holy Grail – were considered to have curative properties, making the town a spa for a brief period in the eighteenth century, and they are still prized (there's a tap in Well House Lane).

Glastonbury Tor

Just east of town, BA6 8BG • Free; NT • Ⓦ nationaltrust.org.uk/glastonbury-tor

Towering over the Somerset Levels, the 521ft-high conical hill of **Glastonbury Tor** commands stupendous views as far as the Welsh mountains on very clear days. It is topped by the dilapidated **St Michael's Tower**, sole remnant of a fourteenth-century church, and pilgrims once embarked on the stiff climb up here with hard peas in their shoes as penance – nowadays, people come to picnic, fly kites or feel the vibrations of crossing ley lines.

To get here from Chilkwell St, turn left into Well House Lane and immediately right for the footpath that leads up to the Tor; the shorter, steeper path is accessed from the top of Well House Lane and is served by the Tor Bus (see below)

ARRIVAL AND INFORMATION   GLASTONBURY

By bus Frequent buses (Ⓦ firstgroup.com) #29, #75, #77 and #376 connect Glastonbury with Wells; #376 also goes to Bristol and #29 to Taunton.
Destinations Bristol (every 30min; 1hr 25min); Taunton

(Mon–Sat every 2hr; 1hr 15min); Wells (Mon–Sat 3–4 hourly, Sun every 30min; 15min).
Tourist office Glastonbury Tribunal, 9 High St (Mon–Sat 10am–3.15pm; ☎ 01458 832954, Ⓦ glastonburytic.co.uk).

GETTING AROUND

By bus The Glastonbury Tor Bus (April–Sept daily 10am–5pm; £3, valid all day) runs from the abbey car park to the base of the Tor every 30min, and stops at the Somerset

Rural Life Museum (when open) and Chalice Well.
By bike Lintells Garage, 140 Wells Rd (☎ 01458 832117, Ⓦ lintellsgarage.co.uk), rents bikes for £15/day.

ACCOMMODATION

George & Pilgrim Hotel 1 High St, BA6 9DP ☎ 01458 831146, Ⓦ georgeandpilgrim.relaxinnz.co.uk. This fifteenth-century oak-panelled inn with mullioned windows brims with medieval atmosphere. It's tired and worn in parts and some of the rooms are a bit ordinary – go for one of the older ones, which include frilly four-posters. £86
Isle of Avalon Godney Rd, BA6 9AF ☎ 01458 833618, Ⓦ avaloncaravanpark.co.uk. Convenient campsite a 10min walk from Northload St and within sight of the Tor. The pitches are spacious, and there's a well-stocked shop, plus decent washing facilities and a freezer for

cool-box ice packs. £18
★**Magdalene House** Magdalene St, BA6 9EJ ☎ 01458 830202, Ⓦ magdalenehouseglastonbury.com. In a former convent directly abutting the abbey grounds, this B&B has three stylish and spacious en-suite rooms (one overlooking the abbey, the others with views to Wearyall Hill) with comfy beds. The generous breakfasts use local and organic products. No children under 7. No debit/credit cards. £95
Middlewick Holiday Cottages Wick Lane, BA6 8JW, 1.5 miles north of Glastonbury ☎ 01458 832351, Ⓦ middlewickholidaycottages.co.uk. A dozen self-catering

5

GLASTONBURY FESTIVAL

Glastonbury Festival of Contemporary and Performing Arts (Ⓦglastonburyfestivals.co.uk) takes place most years over four days in late June, with happy campers braving the predictable mudfest at Worthy Farm, outside Pilton, six miles east of Glastonbury itself. Having started as a small hippy affair in the 1970s, "Glasto" has become the biggest and best-organized festival in the country, without shedding too much of its alternative feel. Much more than just a music festival, large parts of the sprawling site are given over to themed "lifestyle" areas, from the meditation marquees of Green Fields to campfire-filled Strummerville and futuristic Arcadia. Bands cover all musical spectrums, from up-and-coming indie groups to international superstars – recent headliners have included Foo Fighters, Radiohead and Ed Sheeran. Despite the steep price (£243), tickets are invariably snapped up within hours of going on sale around October of the previous year.

cottages plus glamping cabins (£81) in rural surroundings, the former with stone walls, oak floors and, in some, cosy wood burners. There's a steam room, indoor pool, BBQ and pizza oven. £90

EATING AND DRINKING

Blue Note Café 4a High St, BA6 8DU ☎01458 832907. A relaxed place to hang out over coffees and cakes with some courtyard seating. It's vegetarian and mostly organic, with nourishing soups, salads and halloumi burgers (mains from £6; three tapas for £10). Mon–Thurs & Sun 9am–5pm, Fri & Sat 9am–11pm.

Hawthorns 8–12 Northload St, BA6 9JJ ☎01458 831255, Ⓦhawthornshotel.co.uk. Homely bar and restaurant whose main draws are its curries (£13) and music sessions (Tues, Thurs, Fri from about 8pm; Sun 5–7pm). Mon–Wed 6–11pm, Thurs noon–3pm & 6–11pm, Fri & Sat noon–11pm, Sun noon–10.30pm; kitchen daily till 9pm.

★**Hundred Monkeys** 52 High St, BA6 9DY ☎01458 833386, Ⓦhundredmonkeyscafe.com. Mellow contemporary café/restaurant whose wholesome offerings include seafood stew (£11.50) and aubergine and tamarind curry (£10), as well as gourmet salads (from £9) and some great cakes. You can sit outdoors at the back. Mon–Thurs & Sun 9am–5pm, Fri 9am–9pm, Sat 8am–9pm.

King Arthur 31–33 Benedict St, BA6 9NB ☎01458 831442. Wood-floored freehouse near St Benedict's Church, serving snacks, burgers (from £7) and a great Sunday roast (£9), plus there's live music most nights and a garden. You'll find Proper Job from Cornwall on tap, as well as local guest beers and ciders. Mon & Tues 3pm–midnight, Wed–Sun noon–midnight; kitchen Mon–Sat till 10pm, Sun till 4.30pm.

South Somerset

Verdant **South Somerset** matches the county's rural image more so than any other region: rolling fields are broken by the occasional isolated farm, while the backcountry lanes that link them are plied by tractors loaded with hay. Majestic **Montacute House** – like many of the villages hereabouts, made in soft honeyed hamstone – is one of the finest stately homes in Somerset, while the region's two destination **museums** provide more adrenalin-fuelled thrills and spills.

Montacute House

Montacute, TA15 6XP • **House** March–Oct daily 11am–4.30pm; Nov–Feb Sat & Sun noon–3pm • £11.40, Nov–Feb £8.20 (includes gardens); NT • **Gardens** Early March to Oct daily 10am–5pm; Nov to early March Wed–Sun 11am–4pm • Nov to early March £5.60, at other times combined ticket only; NT • ☎01935 823289, Ⓦnationaltrust.org.uk/montacute-house • South West Coaches #81 from Yeovil to South Petherton (Mon–Fri hourly, Sat every 2hr) stops a 10min walk from the entrance

Dominating the picture-postcard hamlet of the same name, **Montacute House** still makes the striking statement that Sir Edward Phelips intended when he built it in the late sixteenth century. The beautifully designed mansion, set in formal **gardens** and surrounded by parkland, is today stuffed with fine furniture and tapestries, while its Long Gallery is host to sixty or so of the National Portrait Gallery's vast collection of Tudor and Elizabethan portraits.

Fleet Air Arm Museum

RNAS Yeovilton, BA22 8HW • April–Oct & school hols daily 10am–5.30pm; Nov–March Wed–Sun 10am–4.30pm • £14, online £11.20 •
☎ 01935 840565, ⓦ fleetairarm.com • Nippy Bus N11 from Yeovil (Tues & Fri 3 daily) stops by the entrance

Occupying part of Europe's busiest military air base, the brilliantly interactive **Fleet Air Arm Museum** boasts one of the largest collections of naval aircraft in the world. After working your way through exhibitions that deal with British naval aviation and span World War II and Korea, you're treated to a noisy Phantom fighter launch from the flight deck of an "aircraft carrier" and, in the final hall, the chance to nose around the first Concorde built in Britain.

Haynes International Motor Museum

Sparkford, BA22 7LH • Daily: March–Oct 9.30am–5.30pm; Nov–Feb 9.30am–4.30pm • £14.50 • ☎ 01963 440804, ⓦ haynesmotormuseum
.com • South West Coaches #1/1A/1B from Castle Cary to Yeovil (Mon–Sat 3–8 daily; 15–25min), then 15min walk

Every petrolhead's dream, the **Haynes International Motor Museum** opened in 1985 with the private collection of John Haynes and now houses over four hundred gleaming automobiles. Some of the classiest cars in history are here, but it's worth seeking out the 1905 Daimler Limousine, whose one careful owner was King Edward VII, and the rare 1931 Duesenberg, which takes pride of place on a pedestal in the final hall and is now worth a cool $10 million.

ARRIVAL AND INFORMATION
SOUTH SOMERSET

Most people visit South Somerset by car, but the main gateway on public transport is workaday **Yeovil**. There are also train stations at **Castle Cary** and **Bruton**.

By train The "Heart of Wessex" line runs from Bath (1hr 10min–1hr 25min) and Bristol (1hr 30min–1hr 50min) to Yeovil (Mon–Sat 7 daily, 4 on Sun), via Bruton and Castle Cary. From Taunton, change at Bristol, Castle Cary or Exeter (from Exeter hourly; 1hr).

By bus National Express runs a daily service from Bristol to Yeovil (1hr 30min–1hr 50min).
Tourist information Petters Way, Yeovil (Mon–Fri 9am–4pm; ☎ 01935 462781, ⓦ discoversouthsomerset .com).

SOMERSET CIDER FARMS

Nothing is quite so synonymous with Somerset as **cider**, a drink ingrained in the regional identity. Most pubs across the region stock one or two local ciders, but for the real deal it's hard to beat a visit to a working cider farm itself, where you can sample traditional ciders (around £4.10 for 2 litres) and learn more about the cider-making process.

Burrow Hill Cider Farm Pass Vale Farm, Burrow Hill, TA12 6BU ☎ 01460 240782, ⓦ ciderbrandy.co.uk. Tastings are done in an old, dark cider house dripping with atmosphere – try one of their single-variety, bottle-fermented sparkling ciders (developed in the same way as Champagne) or their highly regarded cider brandy. Tours by arrangement. Mon–Sat 9am–5.30pm.
Perry's Cider Mills Dowlish Wake, TA19 0NY ☎ 01460 55195, ⓦ perryscider.co.uk. Archetypal cider farm and orchards, with a dozen farmhouse and single-variety ciders, plus a small free rural museum. Mon–Fri 9am–5.30pm, Sat 9.30am–4.30pm, Sun 10am–1pm.
Sheppy's Cider Three Bridges, Bradford-on-Tone, TA4 1ER ☎ 01823 461233, ⓦ sheppyscider.com. Complex combining a shop, tearooms, museum (free),

and orchards complete with resident herd of longhorn cattle. Tours (1hr 30min) can be booked (Fri & Sat 2pm; £10). Mon–Sat 9am–5.30pm, Sun 10am–4pm.
Thatchers Myrtle Farm, Sandford, BS25 5RA ☎ 01934 822862, ⓦ thatcherscider.co.uk. Producers of the famous Thatchers Gold, plus eleven other ciders. It's a big operation, but you can still taste their cider straight from the barrel at their shop, or take a walk through the orchards nearby. Book ahead to join a tour of the farm (Wed–Sat 11am; 1hr 30min; £10). Mon–Sat 9am–6pm, Sun 10am–1pm.
Wilkins Lands End Farm, Wedmore, BS28 4TU ☎ 01934 712385, ⓦ wilkinscider.com. Legendary cider-maker Roger Wilkins offers generous tastings in his Banksy-decorated barn up on the Isle of Wedmore. Mon–Sat 10am–8pm, Sun 10am–1pm.

5

GETTING AROUND

By car Public transport in South Somerset is patchy at best; by far the easiest way to tour the region is by car.

By train Trains for Taunton leave from Castle Cary (Mon–Sat 10 daily, 6 on Sun; 20min).

By bus Numerous but sporadic services are run by South West Coaches (ⓦ southwestcoaches.co.uk); Nippy Bus (ⓦ nippybus.co.uk) will probably prove more useful. Slow, infrequent local buses connect the train stations at Yeovil, Castle Cary and Bruton.

ACCOMMODATION AND EATING

South Somerset is blessed with some exceptional places to eat, from converted chapels to award-winning gastropubs. Many of the best places are in the smaller towns and villages, such as **Bruton** and gorgeous little **Hinton St George**, or between them, meaning you'll need your own wheels to get to them.

★**At The Chapel** High St, Bruton, BA10 0AE ☎01749 814070, ⓦ atthechapel.co.uk. Contemporary gem in sleepy Bruton, home to a buzzing restaurant (mains from £12.50; wood-fired pizzas served all day), an artisan bakery, and a cocktail bar where the altar used to be. The eight stripped-back and stylish rooms all have king-sized beds. Mon–Sat 8am–9.30pm, Sun 8am–8pm. £125

★**Lord Poulett Arms** Hinton St George, TA17 8SE ☎01460 73149, ⓦ lordpoulettarms.com. Award-winning pub-restaurant in a beautiful hamstone village, serving game from Exmoor and fish from Dorset (mains £14–20; set menus £16 and £19), plus local ales and cider. Rooms are classy but comfortable. Restaurant Mon–Sat noon–2.30pm & 6.30–9.15pm, Sun noon–3.30pm & 7–9.15pm; bar daily noon–11pm. £85

The Masons Arms 41 Lower Odcombe, Odcombe, BA22 8TX ☎01935 862591, ⓦ masonsarmsodcombe.co.uk. Pretty, thatch-roofed inn four miles west of Yeovil and about a mile south of Montacute, whose friendly owners offer a blend of classic pub grub and a la carte dishes (from £11), served in generous portions. Rooms overlook the garden, and there's also a shepherd's hut and camping (extra charge of £2/person) available. Bar daily 10am–midnight; kitchen daily 8am–2pm & 6.30–9.30pm.

Camping £11, shepherd's hut £75, doubles £95

★**The Pilgrims** Lovington, BA7 7PT ☎01963 240597, ⓦ pilgrimsrestaurant.co.uk. This fantastic place combines the relaxed atmosphere of a country pub with the elegant cooking of a fine-dining restaurant (local-leaning mains £20–24). There are also five modern rooms in the old cider barn (no under-14s). Tues–Thurs 7–11pm, Fri & Sat noon–3pm & 7–11pm, plus last Sun of the month 12.30–3pm. £130

Provender 3 Market Square, South Petherton, TA13 5BT ☎01460 240681, ⓦ provender.co.uk. Chic spot on a pretty square, with a deli stocking farmhouse cheeses, smoked meats and speciality breads, and a light-filled café at the back selling soups and savoury tartlets. Mon 10am–5pm, Tues, Thurs & Fri 9.30am–5pm, Wed 9.30am–3pm, Sat 9am–3pm.

The Queens Arms Corton Denham, DT9 4LR ☎01963 220317, ⓦ thequeensarms.com. Attractive Georgian inn with a range of classy twins and doubles and solid but sophisticated food (seared wild sea trout, smoked duck chop; mains £14–22). Excellent selection of bottled beers and ciders. Mon–Thurs 8am–11pm, Fri & Sat 8am–midnight, Sun 8am–10.30pm; kitchen Mon–Sat noon–3pm & 6–10pm, Sun noon–3pm & 6–8pm. £125

Taunton

West of Glastonbury, the county town of **TAUNTON** makes a handy starting point for excursions into the Quantock Hills, and is home to the excellent **Museum of Somerset**. While in town, take a look at the pinnacled and battlemented towers of its two most important churches – **St James** on Coal Orchard and **St Mary Magdalene** on Church Square – both fifteenth-century structures remodelled by the Victorians.

Museum of Somerset

Taunton Castle, Castle Green, TA1 4AA • Tues–Sat 10am–5pm • Free • ☎ 01823 255088, ⓦ museumofsomerset.org.uk

Started in the twelfth century, **Taunton Castle** staged the trial of royal claimant Perkin Warbeck, who in 1490 declared himself to be the Duke of York, the younger of the "Princes in the Tower" – the sons of Edward IV, who had been murdered seven years earlier. Parts of the structure were pulled down in 1662 and much of the rest has been altered, and it now houses the **Museum of Somerset**, a wide-ranging display that includes

5

finds from Somerset's Lake Villages; the "Frome Hoard", the second-largest collection of Roman coins ever discovered in Britain; and a superb fragment of Roman mosaic found near Langport in the Somerset Levels. The ground-floor Great Hall was where Judge Jeffreys held one of his "Bloody Assizes" following the Monmouth Rebellion of 1685, at which 144 prisoners were sentenced to be hanged, drawn and quartered.

ARRIVAL AND INFORMATION   TAUNTON

By train The station lies a 20min walk north of town. There's also the West Somerset Railway (see box, p.311), which terminates at Bishops Lydeard.

Destinations Bristol (2–3 hourly; 30min–1hr); Exeter (2–3 hourly; 25min).

By bus Taunton's bus station (ⓦfirstgroup.com) is off Castle Green.

Destinations Bishops Lydeard (Mon–Sat every 30min, Sun hourly; 25min); Combe Florey (Mon–Sat every 30min, Sun hourly; 35min); Dulverton (Mon–Sat every 2hr; 1hr

25min); Dunster (Mon–Sat every 30min, Sun hourly; 1hr 15min); Glastonbury (Mon–Sat every 2hr; 1hr 20min); London Paddington (4 daily; 3hr 25min–4hr 20min); Minehead (Mon–Sat every 30min, Sun hourly; 1hr 25min); Wells (Mon–Sat 6 daily; 1hr 40min); Yeovil (Mon–Sat hourly, Sun 2 daily; 1hr–1hr 20min).

Tourist office Market House, Fore St (Mon–Sat 9.30am–4.30pm; ☎01823 340470, ⓦvisitsomerset.co.uk/taunton). Provides information and publications on the whole area, including the Quantocks.

ACCOMMODATION AND EATING

Brookfield House 16 Wellington Rd, TA1 4EQ ☎01823 272786, ⓦbrookfieldguesthouse.uk.com. This B&B close to the centre makes for a clean and comfortable stay, though light sleepers should choose rooms at the back. Evening meals can be arranged, and there's limited off-road parking. No under-8s. **£93**

The Castle Castle Green, TA1 1NF ☎01823 272671, ⓦthe-castle-hotel.com. A wisteria-clad, three-hundred-year-old mansion next to Taunton Castle, this hotel has

atmospheric public rooms, though some of the bedrooms are fairly ordinary, with dated decor. **£130**

The Cosy Club Hunts Court, Corporation St, TA1 4AJ ☎01823 253476, ⓦcosyclub.co.uk. In a converted Victorian arts college, this bar-restaurant has several rooms across two floors, with comfy chairs and delightfully quirky decor. Coffees, teas and meals are available; burgers cost from £9 and tapas are £12 for three. Mon–Wed & Sun 9am–11pm; Thurs–Sat 9am–12.30am; kitchen daily 9am–10pm.

The Quantock Hills

Extending for some twelve miles north of Taunton, the **Quantock Hills** offer some marvellous hiking opportunities off the beaten track. Its snug villages, many of them boasting beautifully preserved churches, are connected by steep, narrow lanes and set in scenic wooded valleys or "combes" that are watered by clear streams and grazed by red deer.

Nether Stowey and around

Eight miles west of Bridgwater on the A39, on the edge of the hills, the pretty village of **NETHER STOWEY** is best known for its association with **Samuel Taylor Coleridge**, who in 1796 walked here from Bristol to join his wife and child at their new home. Coleridge drew inspiration for some of his best-known works while rambling through the surrounding countryside, and you can pick up a leaflet at his former abode for the **Coleridge Way** (ⓦcoleridgeway.co.uk), a walking route that supposedly follows the poet's footsteps between Nether Stowey and Lynmouth (see p.314) on the Exmoor coast; waymarked with quill signs, the 51-mile hike passes through some of the most scenic tracts of the Quantocks and Exmoor.

Coleridge Cottage

35 Lime St, TA5 1NQ • March–Oct Mon & Thurs–Sun 11am–5pm; early to mid-Dec Sat & Sun 11am–3pm • £6.20; NT • ☎01643 821314, ⓦnationaltrust.org.uk/coleridgecottage

At this "miserable cottage", as Sara Coleridge rather harshly called what is now **Coleridge Cottage**, you can see the poet's parlour and reading room, and, upstairs, his

5

COLERIDGE AND WORDSWORTH IN THE QUANTOCKS

Shortly after moving into their new home in **Nether Stowey**, the **Coleridges** were visited by **William Wordsworth** and his sister Dorothy, who soon afterwards moved into the somewhat grander Alfoxden House, near Holford, a couple of miles down the road. The year that Coleridge and Wordsworth spent as neighbours was extraordinarily productive – Coleridge composed some of his best poetry at this time, including **The Rime of the Ancient Mariner** and **Kubla Khan**, and the two poets in collaboration produced the **Lyrical Ballads**, the poetic manifesto of early English Romanticism. Many of the greatest figures of the age made the trek down to visit the pair, among them Charles Lamb, Thomas De Quincey, Robert Southey, Humphry Davy and William Hazlitt, and it was the coming and going of these intellectuals that stirred the suspicions of the local authorities in a period when England was at war with France. Spies were sent to track them and Wordsworth was finally given notice to leave in June 1798, shortly before *Lyrical Ballads* rolled off the press.

---

bedroom and an exhibition room containing various letters and first editions. Rooms, including the kitchen, are laid out as they would have been in the eighteenth century, and there's a re-creation of the poet's "lime-tree bower" in the garden.

The western Quantocks

On the southwestern edge of the Quantocks, the village of **BISHOPS LYDEARD**, terminus of the West Somerset Railway, is worth a wander, not least for **St Mary's** church, which has a splendid tower and carved bench-ends inside. A couple of miles north, pretty **COMBE FLOREY** is almost exclusively built of the pink-red sandstone characteristic of Quantock villages. For over fifteen years (1829–45), the local rector was the unconventional cleric Sydney Smith, called "the greatest master of ridicule since Swift" by the essayist Macaulay; more recently the village was home to Evelyn Waugh.

A little over three miles further north along the A358, **CROWCOMBE** is another typical cob-and-thatch Quantock village, with a well-preserved Church House from 1515 and a lovely old church with a superb collection of pagan-looking carved bench-ends. A minor road from here winds up to **Triscombe Stone**, in the heart of the Quantocks, from where a footpath leads for about a mile to the range's highest point at **Wills Neck** (1260ft).

Stretching between Wills Neck and the village of Aisholt, the moorland plateau of **Aisholt Common** is best explored from **West Bagborough**, where a five-mile path starts at Birches Corner. Lower down the slopes, outside Aisholt, the banks of **Hawkridge Reservoir** make a lovely picnic stop.

GETTING AROUND

THE QUANTOCK HILLS

By public transport The West Somerset Railway (see box opposite) stops near some of the villages along the west flank of the range, though you'll need your own transport or foot-power to reach the best spots, as public transport in the Quantocks is minimal.

ACCOMMODATION AND EATING

★**The Blue Ball Inn** Triscombe, TA4 3HE ☎01984 618242, ⓦ blueball.pub. This secluded inn below Wills Neck has two tastefully decorated B&B rooms, plus meals sourced from neighbouring farms (evening mains £12–16), good local ales and a nice pub garden. Mon–Sat noon–11pm, Sun noon–7pm; kitchen Mon–Sat noon–2.30pm & 6.30–9pm, Sun noon–4pm. £75

Carew Arms Crowcombe, TA4 4AD ☎01984 618631, ⓦ thecarewarms.co.uk. Don't be put off by the stags' heads covering the walls and the riding boots by the fire – this is a delightful rustic pub with a skittles alley and a spacious garden. Local ales complement the top-notch nosh, with mains from £9.50. Half a dozen rooms also available. Easter–Sept daily noon–11pm; Oct–Easter Mon–Sat noon–2.30pm & 5–11pm, Sun noon–6pm. £50

Mill Farm Caravan and Camping Park Fiddington, TA5 1JQ, a couple of miles east of Nether Stowey ☎01278 732286, ⓦ millfarm.biz. This family-friendly campsite has indoor and outdoor pools (open summer only), a boating lake, a gym and pony rides. Advance booking essential at peak times. Closed Dec to mid-March. £13.50

The Old House St Mary St, Nether Stowey, TA5 1LJ

THE WEST SOMERSET RAILWAY

Fringing the western side of the Quantocks, the **West Somerset Railway** (☎01643 704996, ⓦ west-somerset-railway.co.uk) is a restored branch line that runs twenty miles between the station outside the village of Bishops Lydeard, five miles northwest of Taunton, to Minehead on the Somerset coast (see p.313; 1hr 15min; £13.40 one-way, £20 return). Between Easter and October (plus some dates in December), up to six steam and diesel trains depart daily from Bishops Lydeard, stopping at renovated stations on the way. Rover tickets, allowing multiple journeys, cost £20 per day (£18 online), £35 per week (to be purchased at least one day before travel); bikes cost £2 extra. Bus #28 goes to Bishops Lydeard station from Taunton town centre and train station.

☎01278 732392, ⓦtheoldhouse-quantocks.co.uk. This large house in the centre of the village once accommodated Samuel Coleridge. The two rooms – Sarah's Room and the huge Coleridge Suite – are period-furnished, and there's an acre of garden. Self-catering cottages also available (from £350/week). __£85__

★**Parsonage Farm** Over Stowey, TA5 1HA, a mile south of Nether Stowey ☎01278 733237, ⓦparsonage farm.uk. In the shadow of a lovely old Quantock church, this homely B&B with its own orchard and walled kitchen garden has stone floors, brick fireplaces and heaps of character. Run organically and sustainably by a native of Vermont, it offers a Vermont breakfast among other options, and simple candlelit suppers (£12). __£70__

Exmoor

A high, bare plateau sliced by wooded combes and gurgling streams, **EXMOOR** (ⓦwww .exmoor-nationalpark.gov.uk) can present one of the most forbidding landscapes in England, especially when shrouded in a sea mist. On clear days, though, the moorland of this National Park reveals rich bursts of colour and an amazing diversity of wildlife, from buzzards to the unique **Exmoor ponies**, a breed closely related to prehistoric horses and now on the endangered list; in the treeless heartland of the moor in particular, it's not difficult to spot these short and stocky animals. Much more elusive are the **red deer**, England's largest native wild animal, of which Exmoor supports the country's only wild population, currently around three thousand.

Endless **walking routes** are possible along a network of some six hundred miles of footpaths and bridleways, and **horseriding** is another option for getting the most out of Exmoor's desolate beauty. Inland, there are four obvious bases for walks, all on the Somerset side of the county border: **Dulverton** in the southeast, site of the main information facilities; **Simonsbath** in the centre; **Exford**, near Exmoor's highest point at Dunkery Beacon; and the attractive village of **Winsford**, close to the A396 on the east of the moor.

Exmoor's coastline offers an alluring alternative to the open moorland, all of it accessible via the **South West Coast Path**, which embarks on its long coastal journey at **Minehead**, though there is more charm to be found further west at the sister villages of **Lynton** and **Lynmouth**, just over the Devon border.

GETTING AROUND   EXMOOR

In addition to the sketchy scheduled bus service (ⓦwww.filers.co.uk, ⓦfirstgroup.com & ⓦquantockheritage.com), the **Moor Rover** provides on-demand transport to and from anywhere within the National Park (and along the Coleridge Way; see p.309) for walkers and bikers – bikes are hitched on the back; call to book a ride at least one day prior to travel (☎01643 709701, ⓦatwest.org.uk).

Dulverton and the eastern moor

The village of **DULVERTON**, on the southern edge of the National Park, is the Park Authority's headquarters and, with its cafés and shops, makes a good entry point to Exmoor. Five miles north, just west of the A396, **WINSFORD** lays justified claim to being the moor's prettiest hamlet. A scattering of thatched cottages ranged around a sleepy

ACTIVITIES ON EXMOOR

Walking is the obvious activity, and the one that draws most people to Exmoor, but there are plenty of other choices too. Several operators arrange **nature safaris**, usually consisting of small-group 4WD trips taking in wildlife and local history; try Red Stag Safaris (☎01643 841831, ⓦredstagsafari.co.uk; from £35pp). Exmoor Adventures (☎01643 863536, ⓦexmooradventures .co.uk) runs rock climbing, kayaking and other group activities (from £35/person). Consult the National Park website (ⓦwww.exmoor-nationalpark.gov.uk) for other activity operators.

While on the moor, bear in mind that over seventy percent of the National Park is privately owned and that access is theoretically restricted to public rights of way; special permission should certainly be sought before camping, canoeing, fishing or similar.

green, it is watered by a confluence of streams and rivers, giving it no fewer than seven bridges, and it makes a good stopover on the way to nearby **Tarr Steps**, a seventeen-span clapper bridge that is one of the Moor's most famous beauty spots.

Four miles northwest of Winsford, the village of **EXFORD**, an ancient crossing point on the River Exe, is popular with hunting folk as well as with walkers for the four-mile hike to **Dunkery Beacon**, Exmoor's highest point at 1704ft.

INFORMATION

DULVERTON AND THE EASTERN MOOR

National Park Visitor Centre 7–9 Fore St, Dulverton (daily: April–Oct 10am–5pm; Nov–March 10.30am–3pm; ☎01398 323841, ⓦwww.exmoor-nationalpark.gov.uk).

ACCOMMODATION AND EATING

Royal Oak Winsford, TA24 7JE ☎01643 851455, ⓦroyaloakexmoor.co.uk. This thatched and rambling old inn dominates the centre of charming Winsford and offers Exmoor ales, snacks and an extensive restaurant menu (mains from £12). The accommodation is plush (most rooms have four-posters) but does vary, so check first. Mon–Sat noon–2pm & 6.30–8.30pm, Sun (daily in winter) noon–2pm & 6.30–8pm. **£130**

Tongdam 26 High St, Dulverton, TA22 7DJ ☎01398 323397, ⓦtongdam.com. Take a break from English country cooking at this quality Thai outpost (most dishes £12.50–16.50). There's also excellent, modern and tastefully furnished accommodation: two doubles with shared bathroom and a suite with a separate sitting room and a balcony. Mon & Wed–Sun noon–3pm & 6–10.30pm. **£56**

Woods 4 Bank Square, Dulverton, TA22 9BU ☎01398 324007, ⓦwoodsdulverton.co.uk. Decorated with a scattering of antlers, boots and riding whips, this gastro-pub offers Gallic-inspired dishes such as confit duck and foie gras terrine, brill fillet and roast guinea fowl (mains £13.50–18.50). Excellent wine list, too. Mon–Sat noon–2pm & 6–9.30pm, Sun noon–2pm & 7–9.30pm.

YHA Exford Exe Mead, Exford, TA24 7PU ☎01643 831229, ⓦyha.org.uk/hostel/exford. Exmoor's main hostel occupies a gabled Victorian house on the banks of the Exe near the centre of Exford. Camping is also possible, and camping pods (£69) and a bell tent (£95) are available between June and October. The hostel is owned and operated by the *White Horse*, just across the bridge, where you should go to check in. Camping/person **£12**, dorms **£22**, doubles **£54**

Exmoor Forest and Simonsbath

At the heart of the National Park lies **Exmoor Forest**, the barest (and wettest) part of the moor, scarcely populated except by roaming sheep and a few red deer – the word "forest" denotes simply that it was a king's hunting reserve. In the middle of it stands the village of **SIMONSBATH** (pronounced "Simmonsbath"), once home to the Knight family, who bought the forest in 1819 and, by introducing tenant farmers, building roads and importing sheep, brought systematic agriculture to an area that had never before produced any income.

ACCOMMODATION AND EATING

EXMOOR FOREST AND SIMONSBATH

★**Simonsbath House** Simonsbath, TA24 7SH ☎01643 831259, ⓦsimonsbathhouse.co.uk. Cosy bolthole offering spacious and swanky rooms with glorious moorland views and a quality restaurant (three-course meals £25). Self-catering cottages in a converted barn are also available (from £210 for 2 nights). Daily 7–9pm. **£120**

Minehead

5

The Somerset port of **MINEHEAD** quickly became a favourite Victorian getaway with the arrival of the railway, and it has preserved an upbeat holiday-town atmosphere ever since. Steep lanes link the two quarters of **Higher Town**, on the slopes of North Hill, containing some of the oldest houses, and **Quay Town**, the harbour area. Minehead is a terminus for the **West Somerset Railway**, which curves eastwards into the Quantocks as far as Bishops Lydeard (see p.310), and also for the South West Coast Path (see box below), signposted by the harbour.

ARRIVAL AND INFORMATION
MINEHEAD

By bus Bus stops are on or around The Avenue, in the centre of town.

Destinations Bishops Lydeard (Mon–Sat every 30min, Sun hourly; 1hr); Dunster (Mon–Sat every 30min, Sun hourly; 10min); Lynmouth (mid-July to early Sept Mon–Fri & Sun 2 daily; 55min–1hr 5min); Porlock (mid-July to early Sept Mon–Fri & Sun 2 daily; 15–20min); Taunton (Mon–Sat every 30min, Sun hourly; 1hr 20min).

Tourist information The Beach Hotel, The Avenue (Easter–Oct Tues–Sat 10am–4pm, Sun 11am–4pm; Nov–Easter Sat & Sun noon–3pm; ☎01643 702624, ⓦ visit minehead.org).

ACCOMMODATION

Baytree 29 Blenheim Rd, TA24 5PZ ☎01643 703703, ⓦ baytreebandbminehead.co.uk. Victorian B&B facing the public gardens, offering roomy en-suites, including a family unit (£120). Minimum two-night stay at weekends in July & Aug. No debit/credit cards. No children under 10. **£60**

Dunster

Three miles southeast of Minehead, the old village of **DUNSTER** is the area's major attraction. Its impressive castle rears above its well-preserved High Street, where the octagonal **Yarn Market**, dating from 1609, recalls Dunster's wool-making heyday.

Dunster Castle

TA24 6SL • **Castle and watermill** early March to Oct daily 11am–5pm; mid- to late Dec daily 2–7pm; Jan to early March & Nov to mid-Dec daily tours only (call to check times) • £11 (includes grounds); NT • **Grounds** Daily 10am–5pm (or dusk if sooner) • £8 (includes watermill); NT • ☎01643 821314, ⓦ nationaltrust.org.uk/dunster-castle

A landmark for miles around with its towers and turrets, **Dunster Castle** has parts dating back to the thirteenth century, but most of its fortifications were demolished following the Civil War. The structure was subjected to a thorough Victorian restoration in 1868–72, from which it emerged as something of an architectural showpiece, though its interior preserves much from its earlier incarnations. Highlights include a bedroom once occupied by Charles II, a fine seventeenth-century carved staircase, a richly decorated banqueting hall, and various portraits of the Luttrells, owners of the house for six hundred years. The **grounds** feature terraced gardens and riverside walks, all overlooked by a hilltop folly, **Conygar Tower**, dating from 1775.

THE SOUTH WEST COAST PATH

Extending for some **630 miles**, the **South West Coast Path** starts at Minehead and tracks the coastline along the northern seaboard of Somerset and Devon, round Cornwall, back into Devon and on to Dorset, where it finishes close to the entrance to Poole Harbour. Much of the **route** runs on land owned by the National Trust, and all of it is well signposted.

The relevant Ordnance Survey **maps** can be found at most village shops en route, while Aurum Press (ⓦ quartoknows.com) produces four *National Trail Guides* covering the route and the **South West Coast Path Association** (☎01752 896237, ⓦ southwestcoastpath.org.uk) publishes an annual guide to the whole path, including accommodation lists, ferry timetables, tide times and transport details.

5

Tickets also include entry to the eighteenth-century **Dunster Water Mill**, on the River Anvill at the southern end of the village. The mill is still used commercially, grinding the various organic grains that go into making the flour sold in the shop.

INFORMATION **DUNSTER**

National Park Visitor Centre At the top of Dunster Steep, by the main car park (Easter–Oct daily 10am–5pm; Nov–Easter Sat & Sun 10am–2pm; ☎ 01643 821835).

ACCOMMODATION AND EATING

Luttrell Arms 36 High St, TA24 6SG ☎ 01643 821555, ⊛ luttrellarms.co.uk. Traditional, atmospheric fifteenth-century inn with open fires and beamed rooms, some with four-posters (the cheaper rooms are smaller and plainer). The bar and more formal restaurant (mains £15–19) offer decent food, and there's a pleasant garden. Bar daily 11am–11pm; restaurant daily noon–2.30pm & 6–9.30pm. **£140**

Porlock and around

Six miles west of Minehead and cupped on three sides by the hogbacked hills of Exmoor, the thatch-and-cob houses and distinctive charm of **PORLOCK** draw armies of tourists. Many come in search of the village's literary links: according to Coleridge's own less-than-reliable testimony, it was a "man from Porlock" who broke the opium trance in which he was composing *Kubla Khan*, while the High Street's fourteenth-century *Ship Inn* features prominently in the Exmoor romance *Lorna Doone* and, in real life, sheltered the poet Robert Southey when he got caught in a storm while on a ramble. Just two miles west yet feeling refreshingly remote, the tiny harbour of **PORLOCK WEIR** is a tranquil spot for a breath of sea air and a drink.

ARRIVAL AND INFORMATION **PORLOCK AND AROUND**

By bus Porlock's main bus stop is outside St Dubricius church on the High St.
Destinations Lynmouth (mid-July to early Sept Mon–Fri & Sun 2 daily; 50min); Minehead (mid-July to early Sept Mon–Fri & Sun 2 daily; 20min).

Tourist information The Old School Centre, West End, High St (Easter–Oct Mon–Fri 10am–12.30pm & 2–5pm, Sat 10am–5pm; Nov–Easter Tues–Fri 10am–12.30pm, Sat 10am–1pm; ☎ 01643 863150, ⊛ porlock.co.uk).

ACCOMMODATION AND EATING

★**Glen Lodge** Hawkcombe, TA24 8LN ☎ 01643 863371, ⊛ glenlodge.net. At the top of Parson's Lane, running south from St Dubricius on the High St, this beautifully furnished Victorian B&B offers perfect seclusion, comfort and character. There are distant sea views from the rooms and access to the moor right behind. No credit cards. **£100**
Lorna Doone Hotel High St, TA24 8PS ☎ 01643 862404, ⊛ lornadoonehotel.co.uk. This thoroughly Victorian lodging offers rooms of varying sizes (and prices), all clean, comfortable and en suite. The restaurant delivers well-prepared dishes ranging from pasta to steak and ale pie (mains from £9). Mon–Sat 6–9pm, Sun noon–2.30pm. **£65**
★**Millers at the Anchor** Porlock Weir, TA24 8PB ☎ 01643 862753, ⊛ millersattheanchor.co.uk. This eccentric, curio-stuffed hotel, pitched as a "hunting lodge by the sea", enjoys a superb setting on tranquil Porlock Weir's miniature harbourfront. The rooms – it's worth paying more for the lovely harbour views – are great. In the equally atmospheric restaurant, sandwiches, pizzas (in summer) and full meals are served at lunchtime, and dinners are available in the evening (mains around £15). Daily noon–3pm & 6.30–9pm. **£90**

Lynmouth and around

Eleven miles west of Porlock, at the junction and estuary of the East and West Lyn rivers and just inside Devon, **LYNMOUTH** is where the poet Percy Shelley spent his nine-week honeymoon with his 16-year-old bride Harriet Westbrook, writing his polemical *Queen Mab*. The village is linked to Lynton, some 500ft above, by an ingenious water-driven **cliff railway** (mid-Feb to mid-Nov daily, generally 10am–7pm, though closing times vary; £3.80 return; ⊛ cliffrailwaylynton.co.uk), or walkable along an adjacent zigzagging path.

At the top of the village, you can explore the walks and waterfalls and an exhibition on the uses of waterpower in the wooded **Glen Lyn Gorge** (Easter–Oct most days 10am–6pm; call for winter opening; £6; ☎01598 753207, ⓦwww.theglenlyngorge.co.uk), all the more poignant given that the village was almost washed away by flooding in August 1952, when 34 people lost their lives. The owners of the Gorge also run **boat trips** (April–Sept; £10; ☎01598 753207) from the harbour to Lee Bay and back – a great opportunity to view the cliffs and the birdlife that thrives on them.

A beautiful mile-and-a-half walk follows the river east from Lynmouth to where the East Lyn River joins Hoar Oak Water at the aptly named **Watersmeet**, one of Exmoor's most celebrated beauty spots, overlooked by two slender bridges.

ARRIVAL AND INFORMATION

LYNMOUTH AND AROUND

By bus The stop is in Lyndale coach park, next to the Gorge. Destinations Lynton (Mon–Sat 4–5 daily, Sun July & Aug 1 daily; 8min); Minehead (mid-July to early Sept Mon–Fri & Sun 2 daily; 55min–1hr 5min); Porlock (mid-July to early Sept Mon–Fri & Sun 2 daily; 35–50min).

National Park Visitor Centre Lynmouth Pavilion, The Esplanade (daily 10am–5pm; ☎01598 752509).

ACCOMMODATION AND EATING

Rising Sun Harbourside, EX35 6EG ☎01598 753223, ⓦrisingsunlynmouth.co.uk. The stylish rooms in this fourteenth-century harbourfront inn all have the requisite beams and sloping floors. The pub and restaurant are equally atmospheric, and attract crowds with their classic English dishes of steak and lamb, plus plenty of seafood (from £14) – there are few vegetarian options. Bar Mon–Sat 11am–11pm, Sun 11am–10.30pm; kitchen daily noon–2.30pm & 6–9pm in bar, 6.30–8.30pm in restaurant. **£160**

Lynton

The Victorian resort of **LYNTON** perches above a lofty gorge with splendid views over the sea. Almost completely cut off from the rest of the country for most of its history, the village struck lucky during the Napoleonic Wars, when frustrated Grand Tourists – unable to visit their usual continental haunts – discovered in Lynton a domestic piece of alpine landscape, nicknaming the area "Little Switzerland". Samuel Taylor Coleridge and William Hazlitt trudged over to Lynton from the Quantocks, but the greatest spur to the village's popularity came with the publication in 1869 of R.D. Blackmore's Exmoor melodrama *Lorna Doone*, based on the outlaw clans who inhabited these parts in the seventeenth century.

ARRIVAL AND INFORMATION

LYNTON

By bus Buses stop in Castle Hill car park and on Lee Rd. Destinations Barnstaple (Mon–Sat hourly; 50min–1hr 10min); Ilfracombe (early July to Aug Mon–Fri 2 daily, Sun 1 daily; 55min); Lynmouth (Mon–Sat 5–6 daily, Sun July & Aug 1 daily; 6min).

Tourist information Town Hall, Lee Rd (Tues–Thurs & Sat 10am–3pm; ☎01598 752225, ⓦlynton-lynmouth-tourism.co.uk).

ACCOMMODATION AND EATING

★**North Walk House** North Walk, EX35 6HJ ☎01598 753372, ⓦnorthwalkhouse.co.uk. Top-quality B&B in a superb position overlooking the sea, and convenient for the coast path. The spacious, stylish rooms have wooden floors bedecked in rugs, and two have wrought-iron beds. Breakfasts are filling and delicious, and three-course organic dinners are available to guests for £30/person. Self-catering accommodation (from £203 for 3 nights) also available. **£136**

Sunny Lyn Lynbridge, EX35 6NS ☎01598 753384, ⓦsunnylyn.co.uk. You can camp next to the West Lyn River at this tranquil spot within a 20min walk from Lynton, with an on-site shop and café (limited opening in low season), and static caravans and lodges available for rent (minimum two-night stay, or four night in peak season). It's small, so booking is essential. Camping and caravans closed Nov to mid-March. Camping/person **£6.75**, lodges and caravans **£75**

Vanilla Pod 10–12 Queens St, EX35 6AA ☎01598 753706. Good, wholesome meals are served at this friendly place, which is both café-bar and restaurant, with Mediterranean and Middle Eastern leanings. Most mains, such as pork belly and grilled sea bass, cost £12–16. Daily 10am–4pm & 6pm–late; summer school hols daily 10am–late; reduced opening in winter.

Devon and Cornwall

EDEN PROJECT

Devon and Cornwall

6

At England's western extremity, the counties of Devon and Cornwall encompass everything from genteel, cosy villages to vast Atlantic-facing strands of golden sand and wild expanses of granite moorland. The winning combination of rural peace and first-class beaches lends the peninsula a particular appeal to outdoors enthusiasts, and the local galleries, museums and restaurants provide plenty of rainy-day diversions. Together, these attractions have made the region perennially popular, so much so that tourism has replaced the traditional occupations of fishing and farming as the main source of employment and income. The authentic character of Devon and Cornwall may be obscured during the summer season, but avoid the peak periods and you can't fail to be seduced by their considerable charms.

If it's wilderness you're after, nothing can beat the remoter tracts of **Dartmoor**, the greatest of the West Country's granite massifs, much of which retains its solitude despite its proximity to the region's two major cities. Of these, **Exeter** is by far the more interesting, dominated by the twin towers of its medieval cathedral and offering a rich selection of restaurants and nightlife. As for **Plymouth**, much of this great naval port was destroyed by bombing during World War II, though some of the city's Elizabethan core has survived.

The coastline on either side of Exeter and Plymouth enjoys more hours of sunshine than anywhere else on the British mainland, and there is some justification in **South Devon**'s principal resort, Torquay, styling itself the capital of the "English Riviera". St Tropez it ain't, but there's no denying a certain glamour, alloyed with an old-fashioned charm that the seaside towns of **East Devon** and the cliff-backed resorts of **North Devon** share.

Cornwall too has its pockets of concentrated tourist development – chiefly at Falmouth and Newquay, the first of these the chief resort in **Southeast Cornwall**, the second, on **Cornwall's Atlantic coast**, a major draw for surfers due to its fine west-facing beaches. **St Ives** is another crowd-puller, though the town has a separate identity as an arts centre. Further up Cornwall's long north coast, Tintagel's ruined castle and the rock-walled harbour of Boscastle have an almost embattled character in the face of the turbulent sea. However, the full elemental power of the ocean can best be appreciated on the western headlands of Lizard Point and Land's End – on the **Lizard and Penwith peninsulas**, respectively – where the cliffs resound to the constant thunder of the waves, or offshore, on Lundy Island, in the Bristol Channel, and the **Isles of Scilly**, 28 miles west of Land's End.

Highlights

❶ Hiking on Dartmoor Experience this bleakly beautiful landscape along a good network of paths. **See p.333**

❷ Surfing in North Devon The endless ranks of rollers pounding Devon's west-facing northern coast – above all at Woolacombe, Croyde and Saunton – draw surfers of every ability. **See p.344**

❸ The Eden Project Embark on a voyage of discovery around the planet's ecosystems at this disused clay pit, now home to a fantastic array of exotic plants and crops. **See p.351**

❹ Cornish beaches Cornwall has some of the country's best beaches, mostly in fabulous

settings. Beauties include Newquay, Whitesand Bay, the Isles of Scilly, Bude and, overlooked by dramatic black crags, Porthcurno. **See p.359**

❺ St Ives Fine-sand beaches, a brace of renowned galleries and a maze of tiny lanes give this bustling harbour town a feel-good vibe. **See p.361**

❻ Seafood in Padstow The local catch goes straight into the excellent restaurants of the southwestern peninsula. Padstow, where celebrity chef Rick Stein owns a number of places, is a great culinary hotspot. **See p.369**

HIGHLIGHTS ARE MARKED ON THE MAP ON P.320

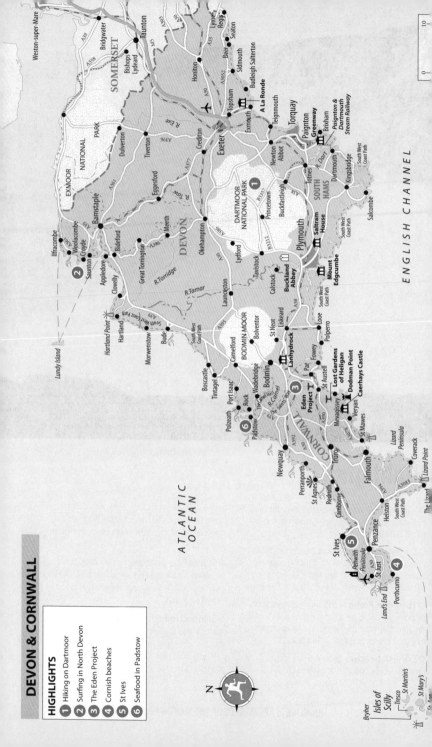

DEVON & CORNWALL

HIGHLIGHTS

1. Hiking on Dartmoor
2. Surfing in North Devon
3. The Eden Project
4. Cornish beaches
5. St Ives
6. Seafood in Padstow

Inland, the mild climate has enabled a slew of gardens to flourish, none quirkier than the **Eden Project**, which imaginatively highlights the diversity of the earth's plant systems with the help of science-fiction-style "biomes". You'll find nature in a rawer guise in **Bodmin Moor**, a great opportunity to escape the crowds.

GETTING AROUND   DEVON AND CORNWALL

Getting around the West Country by **public transport** can be a convoluted and lengthy process, especially in remoter areas.

By train You can reach Exeter, Plymouth, Bodmin, Truro and Penzance by train on the main rail lines from London and the Midlands, with branch lines linking Falmouth (from Truro), Newquay (from Par) and St Ives (from St Erth). The frequent London Waterloo–Exeter service makes several useful stops in Devon, at Axminster, Feniton, Honiton and Pinhoe.

By bus Buses from the chief towns fan out along the coasts and into the interior, though the service can be rudimentary (or completely nonexistent) for the smaller villages.

South West Coast Path The best way of exploring the coast of Devon and Cornwall is on foot along the South West Coast Path (⊕ southwestcoastpath.org.uk), England's longest waymarked trail (at least until the England Coast Path is completed; see p.313) .

6

Exeter

EXETER has more historical sights than any other town in Devon or Cornwall, legacies of an eventful existence dating from its Celtic foundation and the establishment here of the most westerly Roman outpost. After the Roman withdrawal, Exeter was refounded by Alfred the Great and by the time of the Norman Conquest had become one of the largest towns in England, profiting from its position on the banks of the River Exe. The expansion of the wool trade in the Tudor period sustained the city until the eighteenth century. Since then, Exeter has maintained its status as Devon's commercial and cultural hub, despite having much of its ancient centre gutted by World War II bombing.

Exeter Cathedral

The Cloisters, south of Cathedral Close, EX1 1HS • Mon–Sat 9am–5.30pm, Sun 11.30am–5.30pm • £7.50 • **North Tower tours** Usually May–Sept twice weekly, check in advance; 30min • £3.50 • **Roof tours** Usually July–Sept Tues & Sat, check in advance; 1hr 30min–2hr • £5 • ⓣ 01392 255573, ⓦ exeter-cathedral.org.uk

The most distinctive feature of the city's skyline, **Exeter Cathedral** is a stately monument with two great Norman towers flanking the nave. Close up, it's the facade's ornate Gothic screen that commands attention: its three tiers of sculpted (and very weathered) figures – including Alfred, Athelstan, Cnut, William the Conqueror and Richard II – were begun around 1360, part of a rebuilding programme which left only the towers from the original twelfth-century construction.

Entering the cathedral, you're confronted by the longest unbroken **Gothic ceiling** in the world, its **bosses** vividly painted – one, towards the west front, shows the murder of Thomas Becket. The **Lady Chapel** and **Chapter House** – at the far end of the building and off the right transept respectively – are thirteenth-century, but the main part of the nave, including the lavish rib vaulting, dates from a century later. There are many fine examples of sculpture from this period, including, in the minstrels' gallery high up on the left side, angels playing musical instruments, and, below them, figures of Edward III and Queen Philippa. In the **Choir** don't miss the 60ft **bishop's throne** or the **misericords** – decorated with mythological figures and dating from around 1260, they are thought to be the oldest in the country. Outside, a graceful statue of the theologian Richard Hooker surveys **Cathedral Close**, a motley mixture of architectural styles from Tudor to Regency, though most display Exeter's trademark red brickwork. For a glimpse of the cathedral's clock mechanism and spectacular views across the city, consider joining one of the guided **tours** of the roof.

6

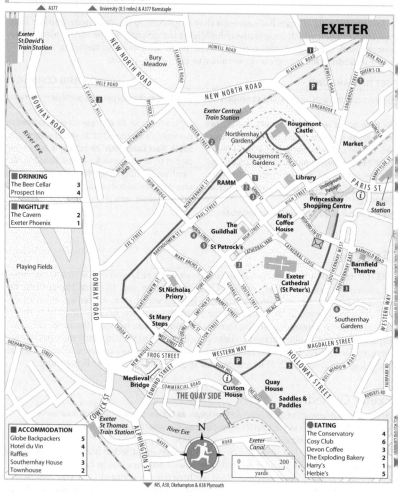

EXETER

Exeter St David's Train Station

A377

University (0.5 miles) & A377 Barnstaple

BONHAY ROAD

River Exe

NEW NORTH ROAD

Bury Meadow

HELE ROAD

ST DAVID'S HILL

ELMGROVE ROAD

HOWELL ROAD

BLACKALL ROAD

HOWELL ROAD

YORK ROAD

QUEEN'S CR.

LONGBROOK STREET

LONGBROOK T.

P

CHURCHIII

NEW NORTH ROAD

MALDON ROAD

RICHMOND ROAD

IRON BRIDGE

Exeter Central Train Station

QUEEN STREET

Northernhay Gardens

Rougemont Castle

Rougemont Gardens

Market

CASTLE ST

BAMPFYLDE ST

NORTHERNHAY ST

PAUL STREET

RAMM

GANDY ST

Library

HIGH STREET

PARIS ST

Underground Passages

i

Princesshay Shopping Centre

Bus Station

DRINKING
The Beer Cellar	3
Prospect Inn	4

NIGHTLIFE
The Cavern	2
Exeter Phoenix	1

EXE STREET

BARTHOLOMEW ST.

BARTHOLOMEW ST

BONHAY ROAD

Playing Fields

NORTH STREET

The Guildhall

St Petrock's

MARY ARCHES ST.

FORE STREET

St Nicholas Priory

SMYTHEN ST

KING ST

MARKET STREET

GEORGE ST

SOUTH STREET

HIGH STREET

Mol's Coffee House

CATHEDRAL YARD

CATHEDRAL CLOSE

Exeter Cathedral (St Peter's)

PALACE

Barnfield Theatre

BARNFIELD ROAD

SOUTHERNHAY WEST

SOUTHERNHAY EAST

WESTERN WAY

St Mary Steps

TUDOR ST

WEST STREET

STEPCOTE HILL

PRESTON STREET

QUAY HILL

Southernhay Gardens

MAGDALEN STREET

OKEHAMPTON STREET

NEW BRIDGE ST

FROG STREET

Medieval Bridge

COWICK ST

EDMUND STREET

COMMERCIAL ROAD

WESTERN WAY

P

i

Custom House

THE QUAY SIDE

Quay House

THE QUAY

Saddles & Paddles

HOLLOWAY STREET

BULL MEADOW ROAD

ROBERTS RD

FAIRPARK RD

ACCOMMODATION
Globe Backpackers	5
Hotel du Vin	4
Raffles	1
Southernhay House	3
Townhouse	2

Exeter St Thomas Train Station

ALPHINGTON ST

HAVEN

River Exe

ROAD

Exeter Canal

N

0   200
yards

EATING
The Conservatory	4
Cosy Club	6
Devon Coffee	3
The Exploding Bakery	2
Harry's	1
Herbie's	5

M5, A30, Okehampton & A38 Plymouth

The Guildhall

High St, EX4 3LN • Generally Mon–Fri 10.30am–1pm & 2–4pm, Sat 10.30am–1pm, but subject to change at short notice; call ahead • Free • ☎ 01392 665500

Some older structures still stand amid the banal concrete of the modern town centre, including, on the pedestrianized High Street, Exeter's finest civic building, the fourteenth-century **Guildhall**, claimed to be England's oldest municipal building in regular use. It's fronted by an elegant Renaissance portico and merits a glance inside for its main chamber, whose arched roof timbers rest on carved bears holding staves, symbols of the Yorkist cause during the Wars of the Roses.

RAMM (Royal Albert Memorial Museum)

Queen St, EX4 3RX • Tues–Sun 10am–5pm • Free • ☎ 01392 265858, ⊚ rammuseum.org.uk

RAMM is the closest thing in Devon to a county museum. Exuding the Victorian spirit of wide-ranging curiosity, it includes everything from a menagerie of stuffed animals to mock-ups of the various building styles used at different periods in the city. The collections of silverware, watches and clocks contrast nicely with the colourful ethnography section, and the picture gallery has some good specimens of West Country art.

Underground passages

Paris St, EX1 1GA • June–Sept & school hols Mon–Sat 9.30am–5.30pm, Sun 10.30am–4pm; Oct–May Tues–Fri 10.30am–4.30pm, Sat 9.30am–5.30pm, Sun 11.30am–4pm; last tour 1hr before closing • £6 • ☎ 01392 665887, ⓦ exeter.gov.uk/passages

Off the top end of the High Street, the Princesshay shopping precinct holds the entrance to a network of **underground passages**. First excavated in the fourteenth century to bring water to the cathedral precincts, they're now visitable on a guided **tour** – not recommended for claustrophobes.

The Quayside

The **River Exe** marks the old city's southwestern boundary; today, the **Quayside** is mostly devoted to leisure activities. Pubs, shops and cafés share space with handsomely restored nineteenth-century warehouses and the smart **Custom House**, built in 1681, its opulence reflecting the former importance of the cloth trade. The area comes into its own at night, but is worth a wander at any time; you can rent bikes and canoes here, too (see p.324).

ARRIVAL AND DEPARTURE **EXETER**

By plane Exeter's airport is 6 miles east of the centre, just off the A30. Stagecoach buses #56A and #56B connect the airport with the bus station on Paris Street (roughly hourly; 20min).
Destinations London City (1–3 daily; 1hr 5min); Manchester (1–3 daily; 1hr 5min); St Mary's, Isles of Scilly (mid-March to early Nov Mon–Sat 1–4 daily; 1hr).

By train Exeter has two main train stations, Exeter Central and St David's, the latter a 15min uphill walk or 10min bus ride from the city centre. South West trains from Salisbury stop at both, as do trains on the branch lines to Barnstaple and Exmouth, but most long-distance trains stop at St David's only.
Destinations Barnstaple (Mon–Sat hourly, Sun 7 daily; 1hr

15min); Bodmin (every 30min–1hr 30min; 1hr 30min–2hr); Liskeard (every 30min–1hr 30min; 1hr 25min–1hr 50min); London (every 30min–1hr; 2hr 10min–3hr 30min); Par (every 30min–1hr 30min; 2hr); Penzance (every 30min–1hr 30min; 3hr–3hr 10min); Plymouth (every 30min–1hr 30min; 1hr); Torquay (1–3 hourly; 40min–1hr); Totnes (1–3 hourly; 35min); Truro (every 30min–1hr 30min; 2hr 30min).

By bus The bus station is on Paris St, one block north of the tourist office.
Destinations Penzance (1 daily; 4hr 50min); Plymouth (every 1–2hr; 1hr 15min–1hr 50min); Sidmouth (1–2 hourly; 55min); Torquay (roughly hourly; 1hr–1hr 15min); Truro (2 daily; 3hr 15min).

TOP 5 DEVON AND CORNWALL FESTIVALS

Boardmasters Festival, Newquay (ⓦ boardmasters.co.uk) Increasingly popular beach festival that takes place annually in early August, combining big-name rock acts with surf and skate competitions – book early.

Exeter Festival of South West Food and Drink (ⓦ exeterfoodanddrinkfestival.co.uk) Held in Northernhay Gardens and the courtyard at Exeter Castle over three days around May 1, this event gives foodies the chance to mingle with local producers and celebrity chefs. In the evening, live music is staged in the castle.

Obby Oss, Padstow (see p.368) Boisterous and deeply traditional May Day caper, permeated with raunchy symbolism.

St Ives September Festival (ⓦ stivesseptemberfestival.co.uk) This knees-up is an essential cultural highlight in Cornwall, with the accent on folk and roots music, plus exhibitions and guided walks.

Sidmouth Folk Week (ⓦ sidmouthfolkweek.co.uk; see box, p.327) Rollicking jamboree of all kinds of folk and roots music held annually in the first week of August in this otherwise genteel resort, with good vibes and smiles all round.

INFORMATION AND ACTIVITIES

Tourist office Dix's Field, off Princesshay (Mon–Sat: April–Sept 9am–5pm, Oct–March 9.30am–4.30pm; ☎01392 665700, ⓦ visitexeter.com).

Saddles & Paddles On the quayside (☎01392 424241, ⓦ sadpad.com). You can rent bikes here (£16/day), as well as kayaks (£10 for the first hour and £5/hr thereafter) to explore the Exeter Canal, which runs 5 miles to Topsham and beyond.

ACCOMMODATION

Globe Backpackers 71 Holloway St, EX2 4JD ☎01392 215521, ⓦ exeterbackpackers.co.uk; map p.322. Clean and central (though a bit of a hike from the stations), this hostel has a kitchen with free tea and coffee. Dorms have six to ten beds and there are a few private rooms too. No check-in 1–3.30pm. Dorms **£17.50**, doubles **£45**

Hotel du Vin Magdalen St, EX2 4HY ☎01392 790120, ⓦ hotelduvin.com/locations/exeter; map p.322. A red-brick former eye hospital has been jazzed up to create a contemporary hotel with quirky details and eye-catching murals. Rooms are full of funky charm – those higher up are bigger and better (and rooms at the back are quieter). There's a French-inspired bistro, a spa and a great indoor/outdoor pool. **£125**

Raffles 11 Blackall Rd, EX4 4HD ☎01392 270200, ⓦ www.raffles-exeter.co.uk; map p.322. The rooms in this elegant Victorian B&B are furnished with Pre-Raphaelite etchings and other items from the owner's antiques business. Breakfasts make use of the B&B's organic home-grown produce. **£85**

★**Southernhay House** 36 Southernhay East, EX1 1NX ☎01392 435324, ⓦ southernhayhouse.com; map p.322. Attractive, individually themed rooms in a renovated nineteenth-century townhouse, with plush carpets and – in the best rooms – freestanding bathtubs. Breakfast is included as standard, but cheaper room-only rates are available. **£125**

Townhouse 54 St David's Hill, EX4 4DT ☎01392 494994, ⓦ townhouseexeter.co.uk; map p.322. This Edwardian guesthouse midway between the train stations backs onto a churchyard and has a garden and generous breakfasts. Rooms are modern but some bathrooms are small. **£77**

EATING

The Conservatory 18 North St, EX4 3QS ☎01392 273858, ⓦ theconservatoryrestaurant.co.uk; map p.322. Centrally located, semiformal restaurant popular for its fresh fish dishes (including grilled sole from Cornwall) and Devon wine. The £10 two-course lunch is great value. Tues–Sat noon–2pm & 5.30–9pm.

Cosy Club 1 Southernhay Gardens, EX1 1SG ☎01392 848744, ⓦ cosyclub.co.uk; map p.322. The institutional setting of this place in a former hospital wing is offset by the zany decor – a retro confection of flouncy lampshades, mismatched furniture, anatomical prints and animal skulls. It's a great spot for brunches, coffees, tapas (£12 for 3) and burgers (£9–14). Daily 9am–11pm; food served until 10pm.

★**Devon Coffee** 88 Queen St, EX4 3RP ☎07796 678559, ⓦ facebook.com/devoncoffeeshop; map p.322. Relaxed, independent coffee shop, where the decor is all stressed wood and chalkboards. The brownies here (£2.80) are exceedingly good, as is the coffee. A second branch at 19 Heavitree Rd serves pizzas Fri & Sat eves. Mon–Sat 8am–6pm, Sun 10am–4pm.

★**The Exploding Bakery** 1b Central Crescent, Queen St, EX4 3SB, next to Exeter Central station ☎01392 427900, ⓦ explodingbakery.com/cafe; map p.322. Slurp top-quality coffee (just £3 a cup) as you watch sweet-smelling cakes being pulled out of the ovens at this busy little wholesale bakery. In case people-watching gets boring, there's plenty of art on the walls. Mon–Fri 8am–4pm, Sat 9am–4pm.

Harry's 86 Longbrook St, EX4 6AP ☎01392 202234, ⓦ harrysrestaurants.co.uk; map p.322. In a converted Victorian stonemason's workshop, this place attracts a cheery crowd with its good-value Mexican and Italian staples (mains £10–15). Daily 9am–2.30pm & 6–11pm.

★**Herbie's** 15 North St, EX4 3QS ☎01392 258473, ⓦ facebook.com/HerbiesVegetarian; map p.322. Friendly, dimly lit place serving up great vegan, vegetarian and wholefood dishes (most mains around £11) plus organic beers and wines and local ice cream. Mon 11am–2.30pm, Tues–Fri 11am–2.30pm & 6–9.30pm, Sat 11am–3.30pm & 6–9.30pm.

DRINKING

The Beer Cellar 2 South St, EX1 1DZ ☎01392 757570, ⓦ facebook.com/thebeercellarexeter; map p.322. This friendly corner bar near the cathedral does great local craft beer on tap and bottled from around the world. Look out for ales from Devon's Branscombe Vale Brewery. Daily 11am–11pm.

Prospect Inn The Quay, EX2 4AN ☎01392 273152, ⓦ heavitreebrewery.co.uk; map p.322. You can eat and drink sitting outside at this seventeenth-century riverside pub, which was the setting for TV drama *The Onedin Line*. Mon–Thurs & Sun 10am–11pm, Fri & Sat 10am–midnight.

NIGHTLIFE

The Cavern 83–84 Queen St, EX4 3RP ☎ 01392 495370, ⓦ exetercavern.com; map p.322. A long-established hub of Exeter's music scene, this subterranean haunt is best known for its live bands (think indie, punk and metal) but it also has more diverse club nights and is open for daytime snacks. Daily 11am–5pm & 8pm–late.

Exeter Phoenix Bradlynch Place, Gandy St, EX4 3LS ☎ 01392 667080, ⓦ exeterphoenix.org.uk; map p.322. Live music and comedy are among the cultural offerings at this arts centre, which also hosts films, exhibitions and readings and has a relaxed café-bar. Mon–Sat 10am–11pm, sometimes Sun for events.

6

East Devon

Quiet, coastal **East Devon** is best known for its elegant nineteenth-century resorts, prime among them **Sidmouth**. But there are plenty of other spots worth visiting along the fossil-rich Jurassic Coast (ⓦ jurassiccoast.org), which stretches from the white sands of **Exmouth** via old-fashioned **Budleigh Salterton** and the smugglers' village of **Beer**, all the way to the Isle of Purbeck in Dorset (see p.214).

Exmouth and around

EXMOUTH, ten miles south of Exeter, started as a Roman port and went on to become the first of the county's resorts to be popularized by holiday-makers in the late eighteenth century. Overlooking lawns, rock pools and a respectable two miles of **beach** – sandy, unlike most others in East Devon – Exmouth's Georgian terraced houses once accommodated the wives of Nelson and Byron, installed at nos. 6 and 19 The Beacon respectively (on a rise overlooking the seafront, above the public gardens). Today it's a relaxed spot that attracts a steady stream of visitors – both from Exeter and, in the summer, from other beach resorts along the south coast.

A La Ronde

Off the A376, EX8 5BD, 2 miles north of Exmouth • Mid-Feb to Oct daily 11am–5pm • £8.90; NT • ☎ 01395 265514, ⓦ nationaltrust.org.uk /a-la-ronde • Take bus #57 from Exmouth or Exeter and get off at the Courtlands Cross stop

The Gothic folly of **A La Ronde** was the creation of two spinster cousins, Jane and Mary Parminter, who in the 1790s were inspired by their European Grand Tour to build a **sixteen-sided house**, possibly based on the Byzantine basilica of San Vitale in Ravenna. The end product is filled with mementos of the Parminters' travels as well as a number of their more offbeat creations, such as a frieze made of feathers culled from game birds and chickens. In the upper rooms are a gallery and staircase completely covered in shells, too fragile to be visited, though part can be glimpsed from the completely enclosed octagonal room on the first floor. Superb views over the Exe estuary extend from the dormer windows on the second floor.

ARRIVAL AND DEPARTURE

EXMOUTH AND AROUND

By train Regular trains to and from Exeter arrive at and leave from the station on Marine Way, a short walk north of the centre.

By bus Buses pull in by the train station; #57 links the town frequently with Exeter.

Destinations Budleigh Salterton (Mon–Sat 2 hourly, Sun hourly; 15–20min); Exeter (Mon–Sat every 15min, Sun every 30min; 40min); Sidmouth (Mon–Sat hourly, Sun 4 daily; 50min–1hr).

Budleigh Salterton

Bounded on each side by red sandstone cliffs, **BUDLEIGH SALTERTON** has a more genteel air than Exmouth – its thatched and whitewashed cottages inspired Noël Coward to write about the place, and John Millais painted his famous *Boyhood of Raleigh* on the shingle beach here (Sir Walter Raleigh was born in pretty **East Budleigh**, a couple of miles inland).

By bus From Exeter take #9A or #57 and change to #157 or #357 (2 hourly; 1hr–1hr 25min).

Sidmouth

Set amid a shelf of crumbling red sandstone, **SIDMOUTH** is the stately queen of East Devon's resorts. The cream-and-white town boasts nearly five hundred buildings listed as having special historic or architectural interest, among them the grand Georgian homes of **York Terrace** behind the Esplanade. Both the mile-long, pebbly main town beach and **Jacob's Ladder**, a cliff-backed shingle and sand strip to the west of town, are easily accessible and well tended. To the east, the coast path climbs steep Salcombe Hill to follow cliffs that give sanctuary to a range of birdlife, including yellowhammers, green woodpeckers and the rarer grasshopper warbler. Further on, the path descends to meet one of the most isolated and attractive beaches in the area, **Weston Mouth**.

By bus Most services depart from Sidmouth Triangle on Station Rd. From Exeter, take bus #9 or #9A (1–2 hourly; 50min).
Tourist office Ham Lane, off the eastern end of the

Esplanade (May–Sept Mon–Sat 10am–5pm, Sun 10am–4pm; Oct–April Mon–Sat 10am–1.30pm; ☎01395 516441, ⓦ visitsidmouth.co.uk). Head here for information on bay cruises and free guided walks around the area.

ACCOMMODATION

Cheriton Guest House 9 Vicarage Rd, EX10 8UQ ☎01395 513810, ⓦ cheriton-guesthouse.co.uk. This B&B has spotless, mostly spacious rooms (one with a balcony), those at the back overlooking a leafy garden leading down to the River Sid. There's a lounge and car park, and the seafront is less than a 10min walk, reached from the High Street or on a riverside path. __£80__
Oakdown Gatedown Lane, Weston, EX10 0PT ☎01297

680387, ⓦ oakdown.co.uk. Spacious, well-maintained campsite some three miles east of Sidmouth off the A3052 (there's some road noise). Camping pods (£50 for 2; max 4 people for £57) and "Shepherd Huts" (£90; max 2 people) are also available for two nights or more, and pubs are nearby. There's a three-night minimum stay on bank hols, or seven nights in Folk Week. Closed early Nov to mid-March. __£21__

EATING AND DRINKING

The Dairy Shop 5 Church St, EX10 8LY ☎01395 513018. Stacked wall to wall with chutneys, gooseberry wine, biscuits and the like, this shop and café is a good spot for soups (£5), savoury crêpes (£6–7) or an ice cream – try the knickerbocker glory. Mon–Sat: April–Sept 9am–5pm; Oct–March 10am–4pm.

Swan Inn 37 York St, EX10 8BY ☎01395 512849, ⓦ rampubcompany.co.uk. Close to the tourist office, this convivial but slightly run-down pub with a garden serves real ales, baguettes, plus meat and fish dishes (sirloin steak £14.95). Mon–Sat 11am–11pm, Sun noon–11pm; kitchen Mon–Sat noon–2pm & 6–9pm, Sun noon–2pm & 7–9pm.

Beer

Eight miles east of Sidmouth, the largely unspoilt fishing village of **BEER** lies huddled within a small sheltered cove between gleaming white headlands. A stream rushes along a deep channel dug into Beer's main street, and if you can ignore the crowds in high summer much of the village looks unchanged since the time when it was a smugglers' haven. While away a sunny afternoon here fishing for mackerel in the bay, for example on the *Lillie May* (☎01297 23455 or ☎07779 040491; £8/person), or pull up a deckchair and tuck into a couple of fresh crab sandwiches on the beach.

Beer Quarry Caves

Quarry Lane, EX12 3AT, a mile west of Beer • Tours daily: April–Sept 10am–4.30pm; Oct 10am–3.30pm; school hols closes 1hr later; last tour 1hr before closing • £8 • ☎01297 680282, ⓦ beerquarrycaves.co.uk

The area around Beer is best known for its quarries, which were worked from Roman times until the nineteenth century: **Beer stone** was used in many of Devon's churches

SIDMOUTH FOLK WEEK

Sidmouth hosts what many consider to be the country's best **folk festival** over eight days in early August. It's an upbeat affair: folk and roots artists from around the country perform in marquees, pubs and hotels around town, and there are numerous ceilidhs and pavement buskers. Accommodation during this period is at a premium but campsites are set up outside town with shuttle buses to the centre. Tickets can be bought for specific days, for the weekend or the entire week. For detailed information, see ⓦsidmouthfolkweek.co.uk. Book early for the main acts.

and houses, and as far afield as London. You can visit the underground **Beer Quarry Caves**, which includes an exhibition of pieces carved by medieval masons.

ARRIVAL AND DEPARTURE

BEER

By bus Beer is connected to Sidmouth by bus #899 (Mon–Sat 3–4 daily; 35min).

ACCOMMODATION AND EATING

Bay View Fore St, EX12 3EE ☎01297 20489, ⓦbayviewguesthousebeer.com. Close to the beach and harbour, most of the rooms in this bright B&B overlook the sea. Abundant breakfasts in the attached café, which does crab sandwiches to take away (£7 with tea or coffee), include smoked haddock and waffles with maple syrup. Closed Nov–Easter. **£80**

Steamers New Cut, EX12 3DU ☎01297 22922, ⓦsteamersrestaurant.co.uk. Family-run restaurant on a quiet alley just up from the harbour. The fresh fish dishes are the main reason to come here, with locally caught monkfish, plaice and brill (£16–18) featuring on the menu; meat and vegetarian dishes are also served. Tues–Sat 10am–1.45pm & 6.45–9pm, Sun call ahead.

South Devon

Southwest of Exeter, the wedge of land that comprises **South Devon** is a mix of traditional seaside resorts, striking coastline and rich agricultural hinterland. With its marina and strings of fairy lights, **Torquay** comes closest to living up to the self-styled "English Riviera" sobriquet of this stretch of coast, while **Brixham**, further south, is still essentially a fishing port, despite the tourist deluge every summer. Inland, things get quieter around **Totnes**, a historic river-port that makes an agreeable base for exploring the whole region. Eight miles downstream, the classic estuary town of **Dartmouth** retains its strong medieval flavour, while the sailing resort of **Salcombe** is a good starting point for exploring the dramatic coast to either side.

Torquay and around

Sporting a mini-corniche and promenades landscaped with palm trees and ornate flowerbeds, **TORQUAY** appealingly blends a quasi-continental flavour with its air of a classic English resort. The town's transformation from a fishing village began with its establishment as a fashionable haven for invalids, among them the consumptive Elizabeth Barrett Browning, who spent three years here.

The resort centres on the small **harbour** and marina, separated by limestone cliffs from its main beach, **Abbey Sands**, which takes its name from Torre Abbey, behind the beachside road.

Torre Abbey

The King's Drive, TQ2 5JE • Tues–Sun 10am–5pm • £8 • ☎01803 293593, ⓦtorre-abbey.org.uk

The Norman abbey that once stood here was razed by Henry VIII, though a gatehouse, tithe barn, chapter house and tower escaped demolition. **Torre Abbey** now contains a good museum, set in pretty ornamental gardens, with collections of silver and glass,

6

window designs by Edward Burne-Jones, illustrations by William Blake, and nineteenth-century and contemporary works of art.

Torquay Museum

529 Babbacombe Rd, TQ1 1HG • 10am–4pm: late June to Aug daily; Sept to mid-June Mon–Sat • £6.45 • ☎ 01803 293975, ⓦ torquaymuseum.org

Torquay Museum, a short walk up from the harbour, includes a section devoted to **Agatha Christie**, who was born and raised in Torquay, though most of the space here is given over to local and natural history displays, including a collection of more than 150,000 plants, birds, insects, shells and reptiles.

Living Coasts

Beacon Quay, TQ1 2BG • Daily: Easter to early July & early Sept to Oct 10am–5pm, last entry 4pm; early July to early Sept 10am–6pm, last entry 4.30pm; Nov–Easter 10am–4pm, last entry 3pm • £11.80 • ☎ 01803 202470, ⓦ livingcoasts.org.uk

At the northern end of Torquay harbour, **Living Coasts** is home to a variety of fauna and flora found on British shores, including puffins, penguins and seals. There are reconstructed beaches, cliff faces and an estuary, as well as underwater viewing areas and a huge meshed aviary. The rooftop café and restaurant have splendid panoramic views.

The beaches

East of Torquay's harbour, you can follow the shore round to some good sand beaches. **Meadfoot Beach**, one of the busiest, is reached by crossing Daddyhole Plain, named after a large chasm in the adjacent cliff caused by a landslide, but locally attributed to the devil ("Daddy"). North of the Hope's Nose promontory, the coast path leads to a string of less crowded beaches, including **Babbacombe Beach** and, beyond, **Watcombe** and **Maidencombe**.

ARRIVAL AND INFORMATION
TORQUAY AND AROUND

By train Torquay's main station is off Rathmore Rd, southwest of Torre Abbey Gardens. There are regular trains to/from Exeter (1–3 hourly; 40min–1hr).

By bus Most buses stop on Lymington Rd (a short walk north of the centre), or on The Strand, close to the marina. Destinations Exeter (12–15 daily; 45min–1hr 10min);

Totnes (Mon–Sat every 30min, Sun hourly; 45min).

Tourist office Vaughan Parade, by the harbour (June–Sept & school hols Mon–Sat 10am–1pm & 1.30–5pm, Sun 10am–1pm & 1.30–3pm; Oct–May Mon–Wed, Fri & Sat 10am–1pm & 1.30–5pm, Sun 10am–1pm & 1.30–3pm; ☎ 0844 474 2233, ⓦ englishriviera.co.uk).

ACCOMMODATION

Exton House 12 Bridge Rd, TQ2 5BA ☎ 01803 293561, ⓦ extonhotel.co.uk. Small, clean and quiet B&B a 10min walk from the train station (free pick-up is usually offered), and just 15min from the centre. The guests' lounge has a balcony, and there's a licensed bar. Book direct for the best rates. **£60**

Torquay Backpackers 119 Abbey Rd, TQ2 5NP ☎ 01803 299924, ⓦ torquaybackpackers.co.uk. Friendly hostel a 15min walk northeast of the train station, with free tea and coffee and convivial common areas (including

space outside for barbecues). Dorms have 4–6 beds. Dorms **£17**, doubles **£38**

★The 25 Boutique B&B 25 Avenue Rd, TQ2 5LB ☎ 01803 297517, ⓦ the25.uk. Rooms in this B&B, a 10min walk from the seafront, feature zebra-striped or purple-hued walls, mood lighting, iPads, smarts TVs with Netflix, rain showers and posh toiletries. The superb breakfasts include home-made yoghurt and smoothies. Book well ahead. No under-18s. **£115**

DARTMOUTH STEAM RAILWAY

Three miles south of Torquay, Paignton's main train station is also the terminus of the **Dartmouth Steam Railway** (April–Oct daily, plus selected dates Nov–March; ☎ 01803 555872, ⓦ dartmouthrailriver.co.uk), which follows the Dart to Kingswear, seven miles south. You could make a day of it by taking the ferry from Kingswear to Dartmouth (see p.331), then taking a riverboat up the Dart to Totnes, from where you can take any bus back to Paignton – a "Round Robin" ticket (£26.50) lets you do this.

EATING AND DRINKING

Hole in the Wall Park Lane, TQ1 2AU ☎01803 200755. This pub is supposed to be one of Torquay's oldest, and was Irish playwright Sean O'Casey's boozer when he lived here. There's a good range of beers, a separate restaurant (mains around £10) and live music on Tues, Thurs and Sun. Daily 11.30am–midnight; kitchen Mon–Sat noon–2.30pm & 6–9pm, Sun 12.30–2.30pm & 6–9pm.

★**Number 7 Fish Bistro** Beacon Terrace, TQ1 2BH ☎01803 295055, ⓦno7-fish.com. Just above the harbour, this place is a must for seafood fans, covering everything from fresh whole crab to grilled turbot – or whatever else the boats have brought in. Most mains cost around £18. Mon, Tues & Sun 6.30–9.45pm, Wed–Sat 12.45–1.45pm & 6.30–9.45pm (closed Mon & Sun eves Nov–May, Sun eve June–Oct).

Brixham and around

BRIXHAM is a major fishing port and the prettiest of the Torbay towns. Among the trawlers on the quayside is moored a full-size reconstruction of the **Golden Hind** (Feb–Oct daily 10.30am–4pm; £7; ☎01803 856223, ⓦgoldenhind.co.uk), the surprisingly small vessel in which Francis Drake circumnavigated the world. The harbour is overlooked by an unflattering statue of William III, who landed in Brixham to claim the crown of England in 1688.

From the harbour, climb King Street and follow Berry Head Road to reach the promontory at the southern limit of Torbay, **Berry Head**, now a conservation area attracting colonies of nesting seabirds. There are fabulous views, and you can see the remains of fortifications built during the Napoleonic Wars.

Greenway

Outside Galmpton, TQ5 0ES, 4 miles west of Brixham • Mid-Feb to Oct daily 10.30am–5pm; Nov & Dec Sat & Sun 11am–4pm • £11; NT • ☎01803 842382, ⓦnationaltrust.org.uk/greenway • Greenway Ferry (☎01803 882811, ⓦgreenwayferry.co.uk) offers services from Dartmouth (6–8/day; £8.50 return); Dartmouth Steam Railway (see box opposite) operates steam trains from Paignton to Greenway Halt (up to 9 daily; 20min; £8.50 return), from where it's a 30min walk through woodland; car parking is free but must be booked a day in advance

The birthplace of Walter Raleigh's three seafaring half-brothers, the Gilberts, and later rebuilt for Agatha Christie, **Greenway** stands high above the Dart amid steep wooded grounds (the ascent from the river landing is challenging). As well as arriving by ferry or steam train, you can reach the house on foot on the waymarked "**Greenway walk**" from Brixham (around 1hr 30min) or via the Dart Valley Trail from Dartmouth or Kingswear (both around 1hr 20min) – Dartmouth's tourist office (see p.332) can supply route maps. Once here, you'll find a low-key collection of memorabilia belonging to the Christie family, including archeological scraps, silverware, ceramics and books, while the grounds afford lovely views over the river.

ARRIVAL AND INFORMATION   BRIXHAM AND AROUND

By bus Most buses arrive at and depart from Town Square and Bank Lane, in the upper town.
Destinations Exeter (2 daily; 1hr 40min); Torquay (every 10–15min; 45min).
Tourist office Hobb Nobs Gift Shop, 19 The Quay (daily 10am–5pm; ☎01803 211211, ⓦenglishriviera.co.uk).

ACCOMMODATION

Quayside Hotel King St, TQ5 9TJ ☎01803 855751, ⓦquaysidehotel.co.uk. Handsome 29-room hotel with superb harbour views, two bars and a good restaurant where meat and seafood dishes are £15–20. It's worth paying extra for a harbour-facing room. **£100**
Sampford House 57–59 King St, TQ5 9TH ☎01803 857761, ⓦsampfordhouse.com. Wake up to stunning views from the front-facing rooms at this B&B, which are smallish but tastefully decorated. Breakfasts include home-made yoghurt and jams. Self-catering accommodation is also available. **£80**

EATING AND DRINKING

Blue Anchor 83 Fore St, TQ5 8AH ☎01803 859373. A great spot for a relaxed pint of local ale, with open fires and low beams. They also offer (rather mediocre) bar food plus live music at weekends. Mon–Sat 11am–midnight,

6

Sun 11am–11.30pm; kitchen daily noon–2.30pm & 6–9.30pm.

★**Rockfish** Fish Market, TQ5 8AJ ☎01803 850872, ⓦtherockfish.co.uk. Set in an airy modern building at one end of the harbour, with lofty views from its curving

deck, this place specializes in the freshest seafood, served with unlimited chips. Apart from the usual cod, haddock and scampi (£12–15), you can order devilled sprats (£7), calamari (£8.50) and roast scallops (£10). There's a takeaway at street level. Daily noon–9.30pm.

Totnes

On the west bank of the River Dart, **TOTNES** has an ancient pedigree, its period of greatest prosperity occurring in the sixteenth century when this inland port exported cloth to France and brought back wine. Some handsome sixteenth-century buildings survive from that era, and there is still a working port down on the river, but these days Totnes has mellowed into a residential market town, popular with the alternative and New Age crowd.

The town centres on the long main street, which changes its name from Fore Street to High Street at the **East Gate**, a much retouched medieval arch. On Fore Street, the town **museum**, occupying a four-storey Elizabethan house, illustrates how wealthy clothiers lived at the peak of Totnes's fortunes (April–Sept Tues–Fri 10am–4pm, also Sat 10am–4pm during summer school hols; last admission 3pm; free; ☎01803 863821, ⓦtotnesmuseum.org). From the East Gate, **Ramparts Walk** trails off along the old city walls, curving round the fifteenth-century church of **St Mary**, a red sandstone building containing an exquisitely carved rood screen. Looming over the High Street, the town's oldest monument, **Totnes Castle**, is a classic Norman structure of the motte and bailey design (April–Sept daily 10am–6pm; Oct daily 10am–5pm; Nov–March Sat & Sun 10am–4pm; £4.30, EH; ☎01803 864406, ⓦwww.english-heritage.org.uk/visit /places/totnes-castle).

ARRIVAL AND INFORMATION

By train Totnes train station lies just off Station Rd, a 10min walk north of the centre; it's served by trains to/from Exeter and Plymouth (both 1–3 hourly; 30min).

By bus Most buses stop on or around two central streets: The Plains and Coronation Rd.

Destinations Exeter (Mon–Sat 12 daily, Sun 5 daily; 1hr 10min–1hr 45min); Plymouth (Mon–Sat every 30min, Sun hourly; 1hr); Torquay (Mon–Sat every 30min, Sun hourly; 40min).

Tourist office See ⓦvisittotnes.co.uk for accommodation, where to eat and local events.

ACCOMMODATION

Great Grubb Fallowfields, Plymouth Rd, TQ9 5LX ☎01803 849071, ⓦthegreatgrubb.co.uk. Leather sofas, restful colours, healthy breakfasts and a patio are the main appeal of this friendly B&B a 10min walk from the centre.

Work by local artists is displayed in the rooms. £85

Royal Seven Stars Hotel The Plains, TQ9 5DD ☎01803 862125, ⓦroyalsevenstars.co.uk. This seventeenth-century coaching inn has had a modern makeover, giving

---

EXCURSIONS FROM TOTNES

The highest navigable point on the **River Dart** for seagoing vessels, Totnes is the starting point for **cruises to Dartmouth**, leaving from Steamer Quay (April–Oct 2–4 daily; 1hr 30min; £14 return; ☎01803 555872, ⓦdartmouthrailriver.co.uk). **Riverside walks** in either direction pass some congenial pubs and, near the railway bridge at Littlehempston, the station of the **South Devon Railway**, where you can board a steam train running along the Dart to Buckfastleigh, on the edge of Dartmoor (late March to Oct 3–9 daily; 30min; £15 return; ☎01364 644370, ⓦsouthdevonrailway.co.uk).

Some of England's finest wines are produced at **Sharpham Wine & Cheese**, near Ashprington, three miles downriver of Totnes (March Mon–Sat 10am–5pm; April–Sept daily 10am–6pm; Oct to late Dec Mon–Sat 10am–3pm; £2.50; ☎01803 732203, ⓦsharpham.com), which you can explore on guided or self-guided tours, with tasting and shopping opportunities aplenty.

it contemporary bedrooms and a stylish bar alongside the traditional *Saloon Bar* and more formal brasserie. The Sunday-night deal, including a carvery meal and breakfast for two, is great value at £100. **£110**

EATING AND DRINKING

★Pie Street 26 High St, TQ9 5RY ☎01803 868674, ⓦpiestreet.co.uk. A purveyor of "British soul food", this place specializes in pies (around £10) made on the premises, to eat in or take away. Choices include curry; chicken, ham and leek; and mushroom *au poivre* – all accompanied by mashed potatoes, chips or salad. Apart from pies, you'll find soup, pork baps and a selection of cheeses on the menu, Timothy Taylor's ale on tap, and a lounge upstairs with board games. Mon–Sat 11.30am–late, Sun noon–6pm; last food orders Mon 6pm, Tues–Thurs 8pm, Fri & Sat 9pm, Sun 3pm.

Totnes Brewing Company 59 High St, TQ9 5PB ☎01803 849290. This pub and microbrewery serves a range of craft ales and ciders from around the world, in addition to its own. It has an authentic, spit-and-sawdust feel, and the small garden occupies the former moat of Totnes Castle. Upstairs, an old ballroom with chandeliers and cinema seats is a venue for live music nights on Fri & Sat (ⓦbarrelhousetotnes .co.uk). Mon–Thurs 5pm–midnight, Fri & Sat noon–midnight, Sun noon–11.30pm.

Willow 87 High St, TQ9 5PB ☎01803 862605. Inexpensive vegetarian snacks, evening meals and organic drinks are served at this mellow café/restaurant. Main dishes are £10–11. There's a courtyard, and live acoustic music on Fri. No credit cards. Mon, Tues & Thurs 10am–5pm, Wed, Fri & Sat 10am–5pm & 6.30–9pm.

Dartmouth and around

South of Torbay, and eight miles downstream from Totnes, **DARTMOUTH** has thrived since the Normans recognized the trading potential of this deep-water port. Today its activities embrace fishing, freight and a booming leisure industry, as well as the education of the Senior Service's officer class at the Royal Naval College, on a hill overlooking the port.

Regular ferries shuttle across the River Dart between Dartmouth and **Kingswear**, terminus of the Dartmouth Steam Railway (see p.328). **Boat cruises** from Dartmouth are the best way to view the deep creeks and grand houses overlooking the river, among them Greenway (see p.329).

The Butterwalk

Duke St, TQ6 9PZ • **Dartmouth Museum** April–Oct Mon & Sun 1–4pm, Tues–Sat 10am–4pm; Nov–March daily 1–3pm • £2 • ☎01803 832923, ⓦdartmouthmuseum.org

Behind the enclosed boat basin at the heart of town, the four-storey **Butterwalk** was built in the seventeenth century for a local merchant. The timber-framed construction, richly decorated with woodcarvings, was restored after bombing in World War II – though it still looks precarious, overhanging the street on eleven granite columns. This arcade now holds shops and the small **Dartmouth Museum**, mainly devoted to maritime curios, including old maps, prints and models of ships.

Dartmouth Castle

Castle Rd, TQ6 0JN • April–Sept daily 10am–6pm; Oct daily 10am–5pm; Nov–March Sat & Sun 10am–4pm • £6.60; EH • ☎01803 833588, ⓦwww.english-heritage.org.uk/visit/places/dartmouth-castle • By boat: Dartmouth Castle Ferry between Dartmouth Quay and castle, Easter–Oct continuous service 10am–4/5pm; £2.50; ⓦdartmouthcastleferry.co.uk

A twenty-minute riverside walk southeast from **Bayard's Cove** – a short cobbled quay lined with eighteenth-century houses, where the Pilgrim Fathers stopped en route to the New World – brings you to **Dartmouth Castle**, one of two fortifications on opposite sides of the estuary dating from the fifteenth century. The castle was the first in England to be constructed specifically to withstand artillery, though was never tested in action, and consequently is excellently preserved.

Blackpool Sands

Two and a half miles southwest of Dartmouth, the coastal path brings you through the pretty hilltop village of Stoke Fleming to **Blackpool Sands**, the best beach in the area.

6

The unspoilt cove, flanked by steep, wooded cliffs, was the site of a battle in 1404 in which Devon archers repulsed a Breton invasion force sent to punish the privateers of Dartmouth for their cross-Channel raiding.

ARRIVAL AND INFORMATION   DARTMOUTH AND AROUND

By ferry Coming from Torbay, visitors to Dartmouth can save time and a long detour through Totnes by using the frequent Higher Ferry (ⓦdartmouthhigherferry.com) or Lower Ferry (ⓦsouthhams.gov.uk) across the Dart from Kingswear (60p–£1.50 foot passengers; £5–5.60 for cars);

the last ones are at around 10.45pm.
Tourist office Mayor's Ave (Easter–Sept Mon, Tues & Thurs–Sat 10am–4pm, Wed 10am–2.30pm; Oct–Easter Mon, Tues & Thurs–Sat 10am–2.30pm; ⓣ01803 834224, ⓦdiscoverdartmouth.com).

ACCOMMODATION AND EATING

Browns 27–29 Victoria Rd, TQ6 9RT ⓣ01803 832572, ⓦbrownshoteldartmouth.co.uk. Boutique-style hotel, with small, stylish rooms decorated with contemporary paintings. Good Mediterranean dishes are served in the bar and restaurant for £10 or less. Mon 10am–6pm, Tues–Sat 10am–11pm (last orders 9pm). **£120**
Café Alf Resco Lower St, TQ6 9AN ⓣ01803 835880, ⓦcafealfresco.co.uk. Funky snack bar that's good for all-day breakfasts, crab sandwiches, steaming coffees and live music at weekends. There's decent accommodation available above the café. Daily 7am–2pm. **£95**
The Captain's House 18 Clarence St, TQ6 9NW ⓣ01803 832133, ⓦcaptainshouse.co.uk. If you don't mind the

lack of both panoramic views and breakfast, this place offers excellent value for money. Bedrooms are simply decorated in white and pale grey, and you'll find plenty of breakfast venues within an easy walk. Parking available. **£72**
The Seahorse 5 South Embankment, TQ6 9BH ⓣ01803 835147, ⓦseahorserestaurant.co.uk. Seafood restaurant facing the river, offering such Italian-inspired dishes as octopus salad and grilled John Dory. It's pricey, with mains costing £20 and up, but the two-course lunch and early-evening menu is more reasonable (£20). The same team also runs *Rockfish*, a couple of doors down (daily noon–9.30pm), which serves first-class fish and chips. Tues–Sat noon–2.30pm & 6–9.30pm.

Salcombe

The area between the Dart and Plym estuaries, the **South Hams**, holds some of Devon's comeliest villages and most striking coastline. The "capital" of the region, **Kingsbridge**, is a useful transport hub but lacks the appeal of **SALCOMBE**, linked to Kingsbridge by a seasonal ferry (late July to Sept most days 2–4 daily; 35min; £7.50 one-way, £12 return; ⓦkingsbridgesalcombeferry.co.uk). Once a nondescript fishing village, Devon's southernmost resort is now a full-blown sailing and holiday centre, its calm waters strewn with small pleasure craft.

You can swot up on boating and local history at **Salcombe Maritime Museum** on Market Street, off the north end of the central Fore Street (April–Oct daily 10.30am–12.30pm & 2.30–4.30pm; £2; ⓣ01548 843080, ⓦsalcombemuseum.org. uk) or take a ferry down to South Sands (April–Oct 2 hourly; £3.70 one-way; ⓣ01548 561035, ⓦsouthsandsferry.co.uk) and climb up to the intriguing **Overbeck's** at Sharpitor (mid-Feb to Oct daily 11am–5pm; £8.80, NT; ⓣ01548 842893, ⓦnationaltrust.org.uk/overbecks), a house and museum that focuses on nineteenth-century curiosities and the area's natural history.

ARRIVAL AND INFORMATION   SALCOMBE

By bus Salcombe is served by regular buses from Kingsbridge (Mon–Sat hourly, Sun 2 daily; 20min), which is where you'll have to change if you're coming from Dartmouth and further afield.

Tourist office Market Street (Easter–Oct Mon–Sat 10am–5pm, Sun 10am–4pm; Nov–Easter Mon–Sat 10am–3pm; ⓣ01548 843927, ⓦsalcombeinformation .co.uk).

ACCOMMODATION AND EATING

Higher Rew Caravan and Camping Park 2 miles west of town, TQ7 3BW ⓣ01548 842681, ⓦhigherrew .co.uk. Large, grassy campsite on a slope surrounded by

attractive farmland. The on-site facilities are good, and there are plenty of places for kids to play. No credit cards. Closed Nov–March. **£22**

Waverley Devon Rd, TQ8 8HL ☎01548 842633, ⓦ waverleybandb.co.uk. With rooms in the main house or in a nautically themed annexe, this B&B offers excellent breakfasts (at a communal table), with lots of choice, and a lounge. It's less than a 10min steep walk from the centre. Self-catering also available. No credit cards. Closed Dec–Feb. **£85**

Winking Prawn North Sands, TQ8 8LD ☎01548

842326, ⓦ winkingprawn.co.uk. Right on the beach, this is an alluring stop for a cappuccino, baguette or ice cream by day, or a chargrilled steak or Cajun chicken salad in the evening, from around 6pm, when booking is advised (mains £17–25). You don't need to book for the summer barbecues (May–Sept 4–8.30pm; £19). Mon–Thurs 9.30am–8.30pm, Fri & Sat 8.45am–8.30pm.

Dartmoor

Occupying the main part of the county between Exeter and Plymouth, **DARTMOOR** is southern England's greatest expanse of wilderness, some 368 square miles of raw granite, barren bogland, sparse grass and heather-grown moor. It was not always so desolate, as testified by the remnants of scattered Stone Age settlements and the ruined relics of the area's nineteenth-century tin-mining industry. Today desultory flocks of sheep and groups of ponies are virtually the only living creatures to be seen wandering over the central fastnesses of the National Park, with solitary birds – buzzards, kestrels, pipits, stonechats and wagtails – wheeling and hovering high above.

The core of Dartmoor, characterized by tumbling streams and high **tors** chiselled by the elements, has belonged to the Duchy of Cornwall since 1307, though there is almost unlimited public access today. However, camping should be out of sight of houses and roads, fires are strictly forbidden, no vehicles are permitted beyond fifteen yards from the road and overnight parking is only allowed in authorized places.

Princetown and around

PRINCETOWN owes its growth to the presence of Dartmoor Prison, a high-security jail originally constructed for POWs captured in the Napoleonic Wars. The grim presence seeps into the village, some of whose functional grey stone houses – as well as the parish church of St Michael – were built by French and American prisoners. The best of the surrounding countryside lies immediately to the north, while two miles northeast, at the intersection of the B3212 and B3357, **Two Bridges** makes a good starting point for an easy, mile-long walk to the dwarfed and misshapen oaks of **Wistman's Wood**, whose cluttered, lichen-covered boulders and dense undergrowth of ferns are an evocative relic of the original Dartmoor Forest. The gnarled old trees are

---

WALKING ON DARTMOOR

Walking is the best way to experience the moor, and a limited network of signposts and painted stones exists to guide **hikers**. Considerable experience is essential for longer distances, however, and map-reading abilities are a prerequisite for any but the shortest strolls (the 1:25,000 Ordnance Survey *Explorer* map OL28 should suffice). Waterproof clothing is also essential.

Broadly speaking, the gentler contours of the southern moor provide less strenuous rambles, while the harsher northern tracts require more skill and stamina. Several walking routes link up with some of Devon's long-distance trails, such as the **Dartmoor Way**, **Tarka Trail**, **Templer Way** and **Two Moors Way**. Information and downloads for these and a range of shorter hikes can be found at ⓦ dartmoor.gov.uk and ⓦ exploredevon.info, while more detailed itineraries are available from local bookshops, National Park visitor centres and tourist offices in Dartmoor's major towns and villages. An extensive programme of **guided walks** (2–6hr; £5–10) is also listed at ⓦ moorlandguides.co.uk.

Beware of **firing schedules** in the northwest quadrant of the moor (see box, p.337).

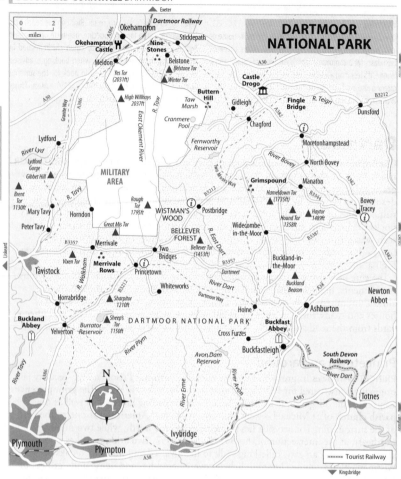

alleged to have been the setting for druidic gatherings, a story unsupported by any evidence but quite plausible in this solitary spot.

ARRIVAL AND INFORMATION

By bus Regular services to Exeter (late May to mid-Sept Sat & Sun 1 daily; 1hr 30min), Moretonhampstead (late May to mid-Sept Sat & Sun 1 daily; 45min) and Tavistock (Mon–Sat 3 daily; 30min).

PRINCETOWN AND AROUND

National Park Visitor Centre Tavistock Rd (April–Oct daily 10am–5pm; Nov–March Tues–Sun 10am–3pm, plus Mon 10am–3pm during school hols; ☎ 01822 890414, ⓦ dartmoor.gov.uk).

ACCOMMODATION AND EATING

Duchy House Tavistock Rd, PL20 6QF ☎ 01822 890552, ⓦ duchyhouse.co.uk. Some 300yd from the centre of Princetown, this Victorian B&B offers staid but reliable accommodation in five traditionally furnished rooms, and there's a spacious guests' lounge. **£75**

Plume of Feathers The Square, PL20 6QQ ☎ 01822 890240 ⓦ theplumeoffeathersdartmoor.co.uk. Pub,

B&B, bunkhouse dorms and a campsite right in the centre of Princetown. Reasonably priced meals are available here, with most mains going for around a tenner. Daily 8am–11pm; kitchen Mon–Thurs & Sun 8am–9pm, Fri & Sat 8am–9.30pm. Camping/person **£7.50**, dorms **£19.50**, doubles **£55**

Postbridge and around

You can see one of Dartmoor's famed **clapper bridges** midway between the crossroads at Two Bridges and the village of **POSTBRIDGE**, while the largest and best preserved of these simple structures is in Postbridge itself, just over five miles northeast of Princetown on the B3212. Used by tin miners and farmers since medieval times, clapper bridges are little more than huge slabs of granite supported by piers of the same material. From Postbridge, you can head south through **Bellever Forest** to the open moor, where **Bellever Tor** (1453ft) affords outstanding views.

6

Grimspound

3 miles northeast of Postbridge, PL20 6TB • Daily 24hr • Free

The Bronze Age village of **Grimspound** lies below Hameldown Tor (1735ft), about a mile off the road. Inhabited some three thousand years ago, this is the most complete example of Dartmoor's prehistoric settlements, consisting of 24 circular huts scattered within a four-acre enclosure. The site is thought to have been the model for the Stone Age settlement where Sherlock Holmes camped in Conan Doyle's *The Hound of the Baskervilles*, while **Hound Tor**, an outcrop three miles to the southeast, provided inspiration for the tale itself. According to local legend, phantom hounds were sighted racing across the moor to hurl themselves on the tomb of a hated squire following his death in 1677.

INFORMATION

POSTBRIDGE AND AROUND

Postbridge National Park Visitor Centre Car park off the B3212 (April–Oct daily 10am–5pm; Nov–March Thurs–Sun 10am–3pm, or daily 10am–3pm during school hols; ☎01822 880272, ⓦdartmoor.gov.uk).

ACCOMMODATION AND EATING

Warren House Inn 2 miles northeast of Postbridge, PL20 6TA ☎01822 880208, ⓦwarrenhouseinn.co.uk. Set in a bleak tract of moorland, this solitary pub offers fire-lit comfort and very basic meals, such as steak and ale pie with chips and veg (£13.50). Easter–Oct daily 11am–10pm, Nov–Easter Mon & Tues 11am–3pm, Wed–Sat 11am–10pm, Sun noon–10pm; kitchen Easter–Oct Mon–Sat noon–9pm, Sun noon–8.30pm, Nov–Easter Mon & Tues noon–2.30pm, Wed–Sat noon–9pm, Sun noon–8.30pm.

YHA Dartmoor Bellever, PL20 6TU ☎0345 371 9622, ⓦyha.org.uk/hostel/dartmoor. One of Dartmoor's two YHA hostels lies a mile or so south of Postbridge on the edge of the forest and on the banks of the East Dart River. Take bus #98 from Tavistock or Princetown (Mon–Sat 1 daily) to Postbridge; it's a mile's walk from the bus stop. Dorms **£19**

The southeastern moor

Four miles east of the crossroads at Two Bridges, crowds home in on the beauty spot of **Dartmeet**, where the valley is memorably lush and you don't need to walk far to leave the car park and ice-cream vans behind. From here the Dart pursues a leisurely course, joined by the River Webburn near the pretty village of **BUCKLAND-IN-THE-MOOR**, one of a cluster of moorstone-and-thatch hamlets on this side of the moor. South of Buckland, the village of **HOLNE** is another rustic idyll, surrounded on three sides by wooded valleys. Two and a half miles north of Buckland, **WIDECOMBE-IN-THE-MOOR** is set in a hollow amid high granite-strewn ridges. Its church of **St Pancras** provides a famous local landmark, its pinnacled tower dwarfing the fourteenth-century main building, whose interior includes a beautiful painted rood screen.

ACCOMMODATION

THE SOUTHEASTERN MOOR

Great Hound Tor Camping Barn Near Manaton, TQ13 9UW ☎01647 221202, ✉greathoundtor@gmail.com. This farmhouse on the eastern edge of Dartmoor offers a cooking area, a woodburner and hot water for showers, but no bedding is provided – you'll basically need all your camping gear except the tent. Per person **£7**

Higher Venton Farm Half a mile south of Widecombe-in-the-Moor, TQ13 7TF ☎01364 621235, ⓦventonfarm .com. A peaceful sixteenth-century thatched longhouse that was once home to the Dartmoor writer Beatrice Chase. The bedrooms are fine (the cheapest double shares a bathroom), and it's close to a couple of good pubs. No wi-fi. **£70**

The northeastern moor

On Dartmoor's northeastern edge, the market town of **MORETONHAMPSTEAD** makes an attractive entry point from Exeter. Moretonhampstead has a historic rivalry with neighbouring **CHAGFORD**, a Stannary town (a chartered centre of the tin trade) that also flourished from the local wool industry. On a hillside overlooking the River Teign, Chagford has a fine fifteenth-century church and some good accommodation and eating options. Numerous **walks** can be made along the Teign and elsewhere in the vicinity.

6

Castle Drogo

2.5 miles northeast of Chagford, near Drewsteignton, EX6 6PB • House Early March to Oct daily 11am–5pm; Nov to mid-Dec Sat & Sun noon–4pm • Garden Daily: early March to Oct 10am–5.30pm; Nov to early March 11am–4pm • House & garden £11; NT • Grounds Daily dawn–dusk • Free, but parking £2/2hr or £4/day; NT • ☎ 01647 433306, ⓦ nationaltrust.org.uk/castle-drogo • Bus #173 from Exeter stops at end of castle drive (Mon–Sat 4 daily; 55min)

The twentieth-century extravaganza of **Castle Drogo** is stupendously sited above the Teign gorge. Having retired at the age of 33, grocery magnate Julius Drewe unearthed a link that suggested his descent from a Norman baron, and set about creating a castle befitting his pedigree. Begun in 1910, to a design by **Edwin Lutyens**, it was not completed until 1930, but the result was an unsurpassed synthesis of medieval and modern elements. Paths lead from Drogo east to **Fingle Bridge**, a lovely spot where shaded green pools shelter trout and the occasional salmon. The castle is undergoing extensive renovation work until around 2019 but remains open to the public, giving visitors a rare chance to see rooms that had long been hidden from view.

ARRIVAL AND INFORMATION

THE NORTHEASTERN MOOR

By bus There are frequent services into Devon.
Destinations from Chagford Exeter (Mon–Sat 5 daily; 1hr); Moretonhampstead (Mon–Sat 3 daily; 15min); Okehampton (Mon–Sat 1 daily; 55min).
Destinations from Moretonhampstead Chagford (Mon–Sat 3 daily; 12min); Exeter (7 daily; 50min–1hr 20min);

Okehampton (Mon–Sat 1 daily; 1hr 10min).
Tourist office New St, Moretonhampstead (April–Oct daily 9.30am–5pm; Nov–March Thurs–Sat 10am–4pm, Sun 11am–3pm; ☎ 01647 440043, ⓦ visitmoretonhampstead .co.uk).

ACCOMMODATION AND EATING

Chagford Inn 7 Mill St, Chagford, TQ13 8AW ☎ 01647 433109, ⓦ thechagfordinn.com. Chic gastropub with slate floors and local art on the walls. Come by at lunchtime for roast-beef baguette (£8.50) or mushroom risotto (£13.50), or in the evening to sample local meat and seafood dishes (£13–17). There's even a separate beef menu, which offers different cuts of a locally reared steer. Three rooms available, too. Kitchen daily noon–2.30pm & 6–9pm. __£80__
Cyprian's Cot 47 New St, Chagford, TQ13 8BB ☎ 01647 432256, ⓦ cyprianscot.co.uk. Comfy, sixteenth-century cottage where you can warm your bones by an inglenook fireplace and, in fine weather, breakfast and take tea in the garden. No debit/credit cards. __£75__

Kestor Inn Manaton, TQ13 9UF ☎ 01647 221626, ⓦ www.kestorinn.com. A popular pub with walkers, serving hot food as well as local ales and ciders, and selling maps, provisions and walking guides. There are en-suite rooms available here too, some with good views. Daily 11am–11pm; kitchen Mon–Sat noon–2pm & 6.30–9pm, Sun noon–4pm & 6.30–9pm. __£95__
Sparrowhawk Backpackers 45 Ford St, Moretonhampstead ☎ 01647 440318, ⓦ sparrowhawk backpackers.co.uk. Excellent, eco-minded hostel with fourteen beds in a light and spacious bunk room, plus a private room sleeping up to four. Good kitchen for self-catering. Dorm __£19__, double __£40__

Okehampton

The main centre on the northern fringes of Dartmoor, **OKEHAMPTON** grew prosperous as a market town for the medieval wool trade, and some fine old buildings survive between the two branches of the River Okement that meet here, among them the prominent fifteenth-century tower of the **Chapel of St James**. Across the road from the seventeenth-century town hall, a granite archway leads into the **Museum of Dartmoor**

FIRING RANGES ON DARTMOOR

A significant portion of northern Dartmoor, containing the moor's highest tors and some of its most famous beauty spots, is run by the **Ministry of Defence**, whose **firing ranges** are marked by red-and-white posts; when firing is in progress, red flags or red lights signify that entry is prohibited. Generally, if no warning flags are flying by 9am between April and September, or by 10am from October to March, there will be no firing on that day; alternatively, check at ☎0800 458 4868 or ⓦmod.uk/access.

6

Life (April to early Dec Mon–Fri 10am–4.15pm, Sat 10am–1pm; £4; ☎01837 52295, ⓦmuseumofdartmoorlife.org.uk), which offers an excellent overview of habitation on the moor since earliest times.

Okehampton Castle

1 mile southwest of Okehampton, EX20 1JA • Daily: April–June, Sept & Oct 10am–5pm; July & Aug 10am–6pm • £4.80; EH • ☎01837 52844, ⓦ www.english-heritage.org.uk/visit/places/okehampton-castle

Perched above the West Okement, **Okehampton Castle** is the shattered hulk of a stronghold laid waste by Henry VIII. The tottering ruins include a gatehouse, Norman keep, and the remains of the Great Hall, buttery and kitchens. Woodland walks and riverside picnic tables invite a gentle exploration of what was once the deer park of the earls of Devon.

ARRIVAL AND DEPARTURE   OKEHAMPTON

By train Okehampton has a useful – if infrequent – rail connection with Exeter (late May to mid-Sept Sun 4 daily; 45min). The station is south of the centre, a 15min walk up Station Rd from Fore St.

By bus There are regular buses to Chagford (Mon–Sat 1 daily; 50min), Exeter (Mon–Sat hourly, Sun 6 daily; 1hr) and Tavistock (Mon–Sat every 1–2hr; 50min).

ACCOMMODATION

Meadowlea 65 Station Rd, EX20 1EA ☎01837 53200, ⓦmeadowleaguesthouse.co.uk. A short walk south of the centre, below the train station and within 550yd of the Granite Way cycling route, this bike-friendly B&B has seven rooms (four en suite) and cycle storage. **£66**
YHA Okehampton Klondyke Rd, EX20 1EW ☎01837

53916, ⓦyha.org.uk/hostel/okehampton. Housed in a converted goods shed at the station, this well-run hostel offers a range of outdoor activities as well as bike rental. Camping also available. Camping/person **£10**, dorms **£27**, doubles **£67**

The western moor

Southwest from Princetown, walkers can trace the grassy path of the defunct rail line to **Burrator Reservoir**, four miles away; flooded in the 1890s to provide water for Plymouth, this is the biggest stretch of water on Dartmoor. The wooded lakeside teems with wildlife, and the boulder-strewn slopes are overlooked by the craggy peaks of **Sharpitor** (1210ft) and **Sheep's Tor** (1150ft). For the best walk from here, strike northwest to meet the valley of the **River Walkham**, which rises in a peat bog five miles north of Princetown at Walkham Head, then scurries through moorland and woods to join the River Tavy at Double Waters, two miles south of Tavistock.

Merrivale

The River Tavy crosses the B3357 Tavistock road four miles west of Princetown at **MERRIVALE**, a tiny settlement amounting to little more than a pub. Merrivale makes another good starting point for moorland walks – it's only half a mile west of one of Dartmoor's most important prehistoric sites, the **Merrivale Rows**. These upright stones form a stately procession, stretching 850ft across the bare landscape. Dating from between 2500 BC and 750 BC, they are probably connected with burial rites.

Lydford

Five miles southwest of Okehampton, the village of **LYDFORD** preserves the sturdy but small-scale **Lydford Castle** (daylight hours; free), a Saxon outpost, then a Norman keep and later used as a prison. The chief attraction here, though – apart from the hotels and restaurants – is the one-and-a-half-mile **Lydford Gorge** (daily: March–Oct 10am–5pm; Nov–Feb restricted access 11am–3.30pm; £8.90, NT; ☎01822 820320, ⌨nationaltrust .org.uk/lydford-gorge), overgrown with thick woods and alive with butterflies, spotted woodpeckers, dippers and herons.

ACCOMMODATION AND EATING   THE WESTERN MOOR

Castle Inn Next to Lydford Castle, EX20 4BH ☎01822 820241, ⌨castleinnlydford.com. Sixteenth-century inn with en-suite cottage rooms, one with a four-poster and one with its own roof terrace looking onto the castle. The oak-beamed, fire-lit bar provides local ales, and there's a beer garden and a restaurant (mains £10–20). Daily noon–11pm; kitchen daily noon–3pm & 6–9pm. **£70**

★**Dartmoor Inn** A386, opposite Lydford turning, EX20 4AY ☎01822 820221, ⌨www.dartmoorinn.com. Three spacious guest rooms furnished with antiques are available above this popular gastropub. The restaurant features tasty options like mushroom risotto and slow-roasted confit of duck leg (£12–19), and there's a set-price Sun lunch (two courses £22). Booking advised. Daily 11am–3pm & 6–11pm; kitchen daily noon–2.30pm & 6–9.15pm. **£115**

Tavistock and around

The main town of the western moor, **TAVISTOCK** owes its distinctive Victorian appearance to the building boom that followed the discovery of copper deposits here in 1844. Originally, however, this market and Stannary town on the River Tavy grew around what was once the West Country's most important Benedictine abbey, established in the eleventh century. Some scant remnants survive in the churchyard of **St Eustachius** (⌨tavistockparishchurch.org.uk), a mainly fifteenth-century building with stained glass from William Morris's studio in the south aisle.

North of Tavistock, a four-mile lane wanders up to **Brent Tor**, 1130ft high and dominating Dartmoor's western fringes. Access to its conical summit is easiest along the path gently ascending through gorse on its southwestern side, leading to the small church of St Michael at the top.

ARRIVAL AND DEPARTURE   TAVISTOCK AND AROUND

By bus Tavistock has good connections with both Okehampton (Mon–Sat every 1–2hr; 50min) and

Princetown (Mon–Sat 3 daily; 30min).

ACCOMMODATION

★**Mount Tavy Cottage** Half a mile east of Tavistock on the B3357, PL19 9JL ☎01822 614253, ⌨mounttavy .co.uk. Set on a beautiful plot with its own lake, this B&B

in a former gardener's cottage has comfortable rooms, organic breakfasts, evening meals by prior arrangement (£20 for two courses) and self-catering options. **£85**

Plymouth and around

PLYMOUTH's predominantly bland and modern face belies its great historic role as a naval base and, in the sixteenth century, the stamping ground of such towering figures as John Hawkins and Francis Drake. It was from here that Drake sailed to defeat the Spanish Armada in 1588, and 32 years later the port was the last embarkation point for the Pilgrim Fathers, whose New Plymouth colony became the nucleus for the English settlement of North America. The importance of the city's Devonport dockyards made the city a target in World War II, when the Luftwaffe reduced most of the old centre to rubble. Subsequent reconstruction has done little to improve the place, though it would be difficult to spoil the glorious vista over **Plymouth Sound**, the basin of calm water at the

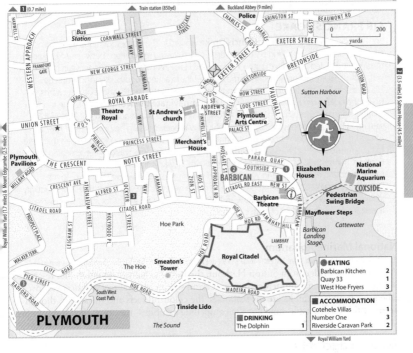

mouth of the combined Plym, Tavy and Tamar estuaries, largely unchanged since Drake played his famous game of bowls on the Hoe before joining battle with the Armada.

One of the best local excursions from Plymouth is to **Mount Edgcumbe**, where woods and meadows provide a welcome antidote to the urban bustle. East of Plymouth, the aristocratic opulence of **Saltram House** includes fine art and furniture, while to the north you can visit Francis Drake's old home at **Buckland Abbey**.

Plymouth Hoe

A good place to start a tour of the city is **Plymouth Hoe**, an immense esplanade with glorious views over the water. Here, alongside various war memorials, stands a rather portly statue of Sir Francis Drake gazing grandly out to the sea. Appropriately, there's a bowling green back from the brow.

Smeaton's Tower

Plymouth Hoe, PL1 2NZ • Daily 10am–5pm; check winter times • £4 • ☎ 01752 304774, ⓦ plymhearts.org/smeatons-tower

One of the city's best-known landmarks, the red-and-white-striped **Smeaton's Tower** was erected in 1759 by John Smeaton on the treacherous Eddystone Rocks, fourteen miles out to sea. When replaced by a larger lighthouse in 1882, it was reassembled here, where it gives lofty views across Plymouth Sound.

Around the Barbican

At the old town's quay at **Sutton Harbour**, the **Mayflower Steps** commemorate the sailing of the Pilgrim Fathers, with a plaque listing the names and professions of the 102 Puritans on board. Edging the harbour, the **Barbican** district is the heart of old Plymouth; most of the buildings are now shops and restaurants.

6

SIR FRANCIS DRAKE

Born around 1540 near Tavistock, **Francis Drake** worked in the domestic coastal trade from the age of 13, but was soon taking part in the first English slaving expeditions between Africa and the West Indies, led by his Plymouth kinsman John Hawkins. Later, Drake was active in the secret war against Spain, raiding and looting merchant ships in actions unofficially sanctioned by Elizabeth I. In 1572 he became the first Englishman to sight the Pacific, and soon afterwards, on board the *Golden Hinde*, became the first to **circumnavigate the world**, for which he received a knighthood on his return in 1580. The following year Drake was made mayor of Plymouth, settling in Buckland Abbey (see opposite), but he was back in action before long – in 1587 he "singed the king of Spain's beard" by entering Cadiz harbour and destroying 33 vessels that were to have formed part of Philip II's **Armada**. When the replacement invasion fleet appeared in the English Channel in 1588, Drake – along with Raleigh, Hawkins and Frobisher – played a leading role in wrecking it. The following year he set off on an unsuccessful expedition to help the Portuguese against Spain, but otherwise most of the next decade was spent in relative inactivity in Plymouth, Exeter and London. Finally, in 1596 Drake left with Hawkins for a raid on Panama, a venture that cost the lives of both captains.

National Marine Aquarium

Rope Walk, PL4 0LF · Daily 10am–5pm; last entry 4pm · £15.95, or £14.35 online · ☎ 0844 893 7938, ⓦ national-aquarium.co.uk

Across the footbridge from Sutton Harbour, the **National Marine Aquarium** has re-created a range of marine environments, from moorland stream to coral reef and deep-sea ocean. The most popular exhibits are the seahorses, the colourful reefs and the sharks, though some of the smaller tanks hold equally compelling exhibits – the anemones, for example.

Mount Edgcumbe

2 miles southwest of the city, PL10 1HZ · **House & Earl's Garden** April–Sept Mon–Thurs & Sun 11am–4.30pm; last entry 4pm · £7.20 · **Lower gardens and country park** Daily 8am–8pm (winter 8am–6pm) · Free · ☎ 01752 822236, ⓦ mountedgcumbe.gov.uk · Plymouth Boat Trips (ⓦ plymouthboattrips.co.uk) operate ferries from Mayflower Steps direct to Mt Edgcumbe (April–Sept Sat & Sun, daily in school hols: 6–7 daily); alternatively, bus #34 from Royal Parade to Admiral's Hard, Stonehouse, from where Plymouth Boat Trips operates a passenger ferry service to Cremyll (every 30min), just outside the country park

Lying on the Cornish side of Plymouth Sound and visible from the Hoe is **Mount Edgcumbe house**, a reconstruction of the bomb-damaged Tudor original; inside, the predominant note is eighteenth-century, the rooms elegantly restored with authentic Regency furniture. Far more enticing are the impeccable **gardens** divided into the formal **Earl's Garden**, next to the house, and the **lower gardens**, including French, Italian and English sections – the first two a blaze of flowerbeds adorned with classical statuary, the last an acre of sweeping lawn shaded by exotic trees. The **park** gives access to the coastal path and the huge **Whitsand Bay**, the best bathing beach for miles around, though subject to dangerous shifting sands and fierce currents.

Saltram House

Near Plympton, 2 miles east of Plymouth, PL7 1UH · **House** Daily: March–Oct 11am–4.30pm; Nov–Feb 11am–3.30pm · **Garden** Daily: March–Oct 10am–5pm; Nov–Feb 10am–4pm · House & garden March–Oct £11, Nov–Feb £8; NT · **Park** Daily dawn–dusk · Free, but parking £3; NT · ☎ 01752 333500, ⓦ nationaltrust.org.uk/saltram · Buses #19, #21, #51 or #200 from Royal Parade to Marsh Mills roundabout, from where it's a walk of a mile (signposted)

The remodelled Tudor **Saltram House** is Devon's largest country house, featuring work by architect Robert Adam and fourteen portraits by **Joshua Reynolds**, who was born in nearby Plympton. The showpiece is the Saloon, a fussy but exquisitely furnished room dripping with gilt and plaster, and set off by a huge Axminster carpet especially woven for it in 1770. Saltram's landscaped **garden** and **park** provide a breather from this riot of interior design.

ARRIVAL AND INFORMATION

By train Plymouth's train station is a mile north of the Hoe off Saltash Rd. Frequent buses run between the station and the city centre.

Destinations Bodmin (every 1–2hr; 40min); Exeter (1–2 hourly; 1hr); Liskeard (1–2 hourly; 25min); Par (1–2 hourly; 50min); Penzance (1–2 hourly; 2hr); Truro (1–2 hourly; 1hr 15min).

By bus Buses pull in at the bus station off Mayflower St, a short walk from Royal Parade.

PLYMOUTH AND AROUND

Destinations Bodmin (4 daily; 1hr 15min); Exeter (10 daily; 1hr 10min); Falmouth (3 daily; 2hr 30min); Newquay (5 daily; 2hr); Penzance (4–5 daily; 3–4hr); St Austell (4 daily; 1hr 15min); St Ives (3 daily; 2hr 50min–3hr 30min); Torquay (2 daily; 55min–2hr 15min); Truro (5 daily; 1hr 40min–2hr 10min).

Tourist office The tourist office is off Sutton Harbour at 3–5 The Barbican (April–Oct Mon–Sat 9am–5pm, Sun 10am–4pm; Nov–March Mon–Fri 9am–5pm, Sat 10am–4pm; ☎ 01752 306330, ⓦ visitplymouth.co.uk).

6

ACCOMMODATION

Cotehele Villas 217 Stuart Rd, PL1 5LQ ☎ 07877 474643, ⓦ cotehelevillas.com; map p.339. This smart and stylish place 10min from the train station is slightly out of the way – a 25min walk to the Barbican – but is worth seeking out for its fresh, uncluttered feel. It has three bright, en-suite rooms with wooden flooring, period features and modern bathrooms; the light breakfasts are served in your room. Two-night minimum stay. **£75**

Number One 1 Windsor Villas, Lockyer St, PL1 2QD ☎ 01752 212981, ⓦ numberoneplymouth.co.uk; map

p.339. Light, airy and spacious en-suite rooms are offered in this refurbished Regency-style villa on a quiet street close to the Hoe and Barbican, with parking available. **£74**

Riverside Caravan Park Leigham Manor Drive, Marsh Mills, PL6 8LL ☎ 01752 344122, ⓦ riversidecaravanpark .com; map p.339. The nearest campsite to the centre, three miles northeast of the Barbican and close to the Drake's Trail cycle and walking route. There are riverside walks, and an outdoor pool open in summer. **£16**

EATING

Barbican Kitchen 60 Southside St, PL1 2LQ ☎ 01752 604448, ⓦ barbicankitchen.com; map p.339. Modern decor, tasty food and a casual ambience draw the crowds at this bistro, housed in the ancient Black Friars Distillery. Choose from a varied menu that runs from wild garlic risotto to slow-cooked lamb shoulder (£11–18). There are some decent set menus too. Mon–Thurs noon–2.30pm & 6–9.30pm, Fri & Sat noon–2.30pm & 5–10pm.

Quay 33 33 Southside St, PL1 2LE ☎ 01752 229345, ⓦ quay33.co.uk; map p.339. This elegant but informal harbourside spot is ideal at lunchtime for a plate of pasta

or a doorstop sandwich with salad and chips (£10–11). The evening menu usually includes Exmouth mussels (£8), pork belly (£15) and fish stew (£17). Sit upstairs for the view. Mon–Sat noon–2.30pm & 5pm–late, Sun noon–3pm & 6–8.30pm.

West Hoe Fryers 7 Radford Rd, PL1 3BY ☎ 01752 221409; map p.339. It doesn't get much simpler than this: an old-style fish shop with a queue for takeaway orders on one side and tables on the other. The fish and chips (from £5.80 to take away) might come with extras like pickled eggs and cockles. Mon–Sat noon–2pm & 5–9pm.

DRINKING

The Dolphin 14 The Barbican, PL1 2LS ☎ 01752 660876; map p.339. A local institution, this harbourside pub has an authentic atmosphere, and West Country ales

straight from the barrel. Look out for the pictures by Beryl Cook, who used to drink here. Mon–Sat 10am–midnight, Sun 11am–midnight.

Buckland Abbey

9 miles north of Plymouth, PL20 6EY • Jan to mid-Feb Sat & Sun 10am–4pm; mid-Feb to Oct daily 10am–5pm; Nov & Dec daily 10am–4pm • £11; NT • ☎ 01822 853607, ⓦ nationaltrust.org.uk/buckland-abbey • From Plymouth, take #1 or #X1 to Yelverton (4 hourly), then #55 (Mon–Sat 5 daily)

Close to the River Tavy and on the edge of Dartmoor, **Buckland Abbey** was once the most westerly of England's Cistercian abbeys. After its dissolution, Buckland was converted to a family home by the privateer Richard Grenville (cousin of Walter Raleigh), from whom the estate was acquired by Francis Drake in 1582, the year after he became mayor of Plymouth. It remained Drake's home until his death, though the house reveals few traces of his residence. There are, however, numerous maps, portraits and mementos of his buccaneering exploits on show, most famous of which is Drake's Drum, which was said to beat a supernatural warning of impending danger to the country. More eye-catching are the oak-panelled **Great Hall**, previously the nave of the abbey, a newly identified Rembrandt self-portrait, and, in the majestic grounds, a fine fourteenth-century **monastic barn**.

North Devon

Apart from a few pockets of more intense activity, **North Devon** is a tranquil, unhurried region, encompassing picture-postcard villages, wind-lashed cliffs and some of the county's finest beaches. The chief town, **Barnstaple**, is a good place to get started, from where it's an easy run to some of Devon's best surf breaks at **Woolacombe** and nearby Croyde and Saunton Sands. **Ilfracombe**, on the other hand, is a traditional resort with a modern edge, while on the coast west of the historic river-port of **Bideford**, the tourist honeypot of **Clovelly** clings to the steep slopes amid thick woods. You can escape the crowds by following the bay round to stormy **Hartland Point** at Devon's northwestern corner, though for remoteness you can't beat **Lundy Island**, a tract of wilderness in the middle of the Bristol Channel.

Barnstaple

BARNSTAPLE, at the head of the Taw estuary, makes an excellent North Devon base, well connected to the resorts of Bideford Bay, Ilfracombe and Woolacombe, as well as to the western fringes of Exmoor. The town's centuries-old role as a marketplace is perpetuated in the daily bustle around the huge timber-framed **Pannier Market** off the High Street, alongside which runs **Butchers Row**, its 33 archways now converted to a variety of uses. At the end of Boutport Street is the **Museum of Barnstaple and North Devon** (Mon–Sat: April–Oct 10am–5pm; Nov–March 10am–4pm; free; ☎01271 346747), which holds a lively miscellany that includes a collection of the eighteenth-century pottery for which the region was famous. The museum lies alongside the Taw, where footpaths make for a pleasant riverside stroll, with the colonnaded eighteenth-century **Queen Anne's Walk** – built as a merchants' exchange – providing some architectural interest.

ARRIVAL AND INFORMATION

BARNSTAPLE

By train Barnstaple's train station is on the south side of the Taw, a 5min walk from the centre. There are good connections with Exeter on the Tarka Line (Mon–Sat hourly, Sun 7 daily; 1hr 10min).

By bus The bus station is centrally located between Silver St and Belle Meadow Rd.

Destinations Bideford (every 10–20min; 30min); Croyde (Mon–Sat hourly, Sun 5 daily; 35min); Ilfracombe (every 30min; 40min).

Tourist office The local tourist office is inside the Museum of North Devon on The Square (Mon–Sat 10am–5pm; ☎01271 346747, ⒲ staynorthdevon.co.uk)

THE TARKA LINE AND THE TARKA TRAIL

North Devon is closely associated with Henry Williamson's **Tarka the Otter** (1927), which relates the travels and travails of a young otter, and is one of the finest pieces of nature writing in the English language. With parts of the book set in the Taw valley, it was perhaps inevitable that the Exeter to Barnstaple rail route – which follows the Taw for half of its length – should be dubbed the **Tarka Line**. Barnstaple itself forms the centre of the figure-of-eight traced by the **Tarka Trail**, which tracks the otter's wanderings for a distance of more than 180 miles. To the north, the trail penetrates Exmoor (see p.311) then follows the coast back, passing through Williamson's home village of **Georgeham** on its return to Barnstaple. South, the path takes in Bideford (see p.345), and continues as far as Okehampton (see p.336).

For 23 miles the trail follows a former rail line that's ideally suited to **bicycles**, and there are bike rental shops in Barnstaple and Bideford. You can pick up a *Tarka Trail* booklet and free leaflets on individual sections of the trail from tourist offices.

ACCOMMODATION

★**Broomhill Art Hotel** Muddiford, EX31 4EX, 2 miles north of Barnstaple ☎01271 850262, ⓦbroomhillart .co.uk. Striking combination of gallery, restaurant and hotel where the rooms look onto a sculpture garden. The *Terra Madre* restaurant alone is worth a visit (see below). **£75**

The Old Vicarage Barbican Terrace, EX32 9HQ ☎01271 328504, ⓦoldvicaragebarnstaple.co.uk. This well-kept Victorian house has modern double and twin rooms,

some with freestanding bathtubs and all with good-sized beds. Handily, there's on-site parking too. **£90**

Yeo Dale Hotel Pilton Bridge, EX31 1PG ☎01271 342954, ⓦyeodalehotel.co.uk. Clean B&B rooms in a converted Georgian merchant's house, just a short walk from the centre. The best ones (£120) are on the first floor, and there are cheaper doubles higher up – though these have steeply sloping ceilings. Room-only rates also available. **£85**

EATING

Monty's Caribbean Kitchen 19 Tuly St, EX31 1DH ☎01271 372985, ⓦmontyscaribbeankitchen.co.uk. Patties, jerk chicken, and ackee and saltfish feature on the menu of this modern Jamaican restaurant with small wooden tables, off Boutport St. Most dishes are £10–15. Tues & Wed 11.30am–3pm, Thurs–Sat 11.30am–3pm & 6–11pm.

Old School Coffee House 6 Church Lane, EX31 1BH ☎01271 372793. This well-preserved building from 1659 now houses a no-frills café/restaurant – nothing fancy, but brimming with atmosphere. The meals are a bit hit

and miss but the coffee and cakes are good value (try a slice of the chocolate and raisin cake for 95p). Mon–Sat 9.15am–3pm.

Terra Madre Muddiford, EX31 4EX, 2 miles north of Barnstaple ☎01271 850262, ⓦbroomhillart.co.uk. Part of the *Broomhill Art Hotel* (see above), this relaxed place specializes in Mediterranean-style cuisine in the form of lunchtime tapas or set-price three-course lunches (Wed–Sun; £17) and evening meals (Wed–Sat; £25). Mon, Tues & Sun 12.30–2.30pm, Wed–Sat noon–2.30pm & 7–8.30pm.

Ilfracombe and around

The most popular resort on Devon's northern coast, **ILFRACOMBE** is essentially little changed since its evolution into a Victorian and Edwardian tourist centre. The town has started to assume a hipper image in recent years, however, symbolized by the dramatic **Damien Hirst sculpture** *Verity*, installed at the end of the compact harbour, depicting a giant, half-flayed, pregnant woman, trampling on law tomes and with a sword upthrust – said to be an allegory of truth and justice.

In summer, if the crowds become oppressive, you can escape on a coastal tour, a fishing trip or the fifteen-mile cruise to Lundy Island (see box, p.345), all available at the small harbour. On foot, you can explore the attractive stretch of coast running east out of Ilfracombe and beyond the grassy cliffs of Hillsborough, where a succession of undeveloped coves and inlets is backed by jagged slanting rocks and heather-covered hills. There are sandy **beaches** here, though many prefer those beyond **Morte Point**, five miles west of Ilfracombe, from where the view takes in Lundy. Below the promontory, the pocket-sized **Barricane Beach**, famous for the tropical shells washed up by Atlantic currents from the Caribbean, is a popular swimming spot.

ARRIVAL AND INFORMATION   ILFRACOMBE AND AROUND

By bus Stagecoach bus #21 runs every 30min from/to Braunton (30min), Barnstaple (45min) and Bideford (1hr 30min), stopping at St James's Place Gardens in Ilfracombe, a short walk west of The Quay.

Tourist office The tourist office is at the Landmark

Theatre, on the seafront (Easter–Oct Mon–Fri 9.30am–4.30pm, Sat & Sun 10.30am–4.30pm; Oct–Easter Mon–Fri 9.30am–4.30pm, Sat 10am–4pm; ☎01271 863001, ⓦvisitilfracombe.co.uk).

ACCOMMODATION

The Collingdale Larkstone Terrace, EX34 9NU ☎01271 863770, ⓦcollingdalehotel.co.uk. Attractive Victorian house with friendly owners, where six of the nine rooms look out over the harbour. There's also a small bar and a lounge to relax in. **£80**

Ocean Backpackers 29 St James Place, EX34 9BJ ☎01271 867835, ⓦoceanbackpackers.co.uk. Excellent, central hostel that's popular with surfers. Dorms are mostly five- or six-bed, and there are doubles available and a well-equipped kitchen. Dorms **£18**, doubles **£48**

6

EATING AND DRINKING

Blacksands Bistro 3 St James Place, EX34 9BH ☎01271 523296. Cosy and welcoming restaurant with a small selection of thoughtfully prepared items. Try the baked blue cheesecake made with Stilton and leeks, or the rainbow trout, both around £14. There's a warm atmosphere and some tables outside on the heated terrace. June–Sept Tues–Sat 5–11pm, Sun noon–4pm; reduced hours in winter.

The Quay 11 The Quay, EX34 9EQ ☎01271 868090, ⓦ11thequay.co.uk. By the harbour and with great sea views, this restaurant (co-owned by artist Damien Hirst, whose works are displayed) offers European-inspired dishes using local ingredients – seared scallops, for example, or Exmoor beef. Most mains are £15–20, and drinks and snacks are available in the relaxed ground-floor bar. Daily 10.30am–late, kitchen noon–2.30pm & 6–9pm; closed Sun eve, Mon & Tues in winter.

Woolacombe and around

Woolacombe Sands is a broad, west-facing beach much favoured by surfers and families alike. At the more crowded northern end of the beach, a cluster of hotels, villas and retirement homes makes up the summer resort of **WOOLACOMBE**. At the quieter southern end lies the choice swimming and surfing spot of **Putsborough Sands** and the promontory of **Baggy Point**, where gannets, shags, cormorants and shearwaters gather in September and November.

South of here is **Croyde Bay**, another surfers' delight, more compact than Woolacombe, with stalls on the sand renting surfboards and wetsuits. South again around the headland is **Saunton Sands**, a magnificent long stretch of wind-blown coast pummelled by seemingly endless ranks of classic breakers.

ARRIVAL AND INFORMATION

WOOLACOMBE AND AROUND

By bus Service #303 links Barnstaple and Woolacombe (Mon–Sat 4–6 daily; 45min), while bus #31 runs between Woolacombe and Ilfracombe (Mon–Sat roughly hourly; 30min).

Tourist office The Esplanade (Easter–Oct daily 10am–5pm; Nov–Easter Mon, Tues, Fri & Sat 10am–1pm, sometimes also Wed & Thurs; ☎01271 870553, ⓦwoolacombetourism .co.uk).

ACCOMMODATION

North Morte Farm Mortehoe, 1 mile north of Woolacombe, EX34 7EG ☎01271 870381, ⓦnorth mortefarm.co.uk. More peaceful than many of the campsites around here, this has panoramic sea views and access to Rockham Beach, though not much shelter. Mortehoe's pubs are a short walk away. Closed Nov–Easter. Per person **£10**

Rocks Hotel Beach Rd, EX34 7BT ☎01271 870361, ⓦtherockshotel.co.uk. This surfer-friendly place close to the beach has smallish but smart, high-spec bedrooms

and bathrooms, and a breakfast room styled like a 1950s American diner. Sea-view rooms cost an extra £10. **£79**

Woolacombe Bay Hotel South St, EX34 7BN ☎01271 870388, ⓦwoolacombe-bay-hotel.co.uk. This grand building just up from the beach once housed American troops training for the Normandy landings, and is now a tidy hotel with comfortable rooms, good leisure facilities (including indoor and outdoor pools and a spa) and a restaurant overlooking the water. **£184**

SURFING IN NORTH DEVON

Devon's premier **surfing** sites are on the west-facing coast between Morte Point and the Taw estuary. While **Woolacombe Sands** and **Saunton Sands** can (and often do) comfortably accommodate armies of surfers, smaller **Croyde Bay** does get congested in summer. **Equipment** is available to rent from numerous places in the villages of Woolacombe and Croyde or from stalls on the beach (around £8–12 for 4hr or £10–15/day for a board, £8 for 4hr or £10/day for a wetsuit). You can see local surf reports and live webcams at ⓦmagicseaweed .com. If you find yourself without any waves, you can while away half an hour at the tiny **Museum of British Surfing** in Braunton, four miles east of Croyde (April–Sept Mon–Sat 11am–3pm; £2; ☎01271 815155, ⓦmuseumofbritishsurfing.org.uk), which uses interactive exhibits and old boards to tell the story of British board riding – from the early "surf bathers" of the 1920s to today's fearless big-wave surfers.

EATING AND DRINKING

Bar Electric Beach Rd, EX34 7BP ☎01271 870429, ⓦbarelectric.co.uk. Friendly hangout that stays buzzing until late, with themed food nights and a long list of drinks and meals, including pizzas and pastas (all £10–12). Easter–Dec Mon–Thurs 11am–10pm, Fri 11am–midnight, Sat & Sun 10am–midnight; kitchen Easter–Dec Mon–Fri 12.30–3pm & 5–9pm, Sat & Sun (or daily in summer) 10am–3pm & 5–9pm.

Blue Groove Hobbs Hill, Croyde, EX33 1LZ ☎01271 890111, ⓦblue-groove.co.uk. As well as burgers, steaks and seafood, this modern restaurant/bar offers a good range of international food, from enchiladas to prawn dhansak (most mains £13–15). Easter–Oct daily 9am–late; Nov & Dec Mon & Sun 10am–4pm, Fri & Sat 10am–late.

★**The Thatch** Hobbs Hill, Croyde, EX33 1LZ ☎01271 890349, ⓦthethatchcroyde.com. Perennially popular pub in the centre of Croyde, worth visiting for its ice-cold local cider and enormous stacks of nachos (£7–12). There's often live music on Fri nights, when the pub and its two beer gardens get especially busy. Mon–Thurs & Sun 8am–11pm, Fri & Sat 8am–midnight; kitchen daily 8am–10pm.

Bideford and around

Like Barnstaple, nine miles to the east, the handsome estuary town of **BIDEFORD** formed an important link in north Devon's trade network in the Middle Ages, mainly due to its **bridge**, which still straddles the River Torridge. Just northwest is the seafront village of **Westward Ho!**, which faces a broad, sandy beach blessed with fairly consistent swell. A couple of miles downstream from Bideford, the old shipbuilding port of **APPLEDORE**, lined with pastel-coloured Georgian houses, is worth visiting for a wander and a drink in one of its cosy **pubs**.

LUNDY ISLAND

There are fewer than thirty full-time residents on **Lundy**, a tiny windswept island twelve miles north of Hartland Point. Now a refuge for thousands of marine birds, Lundy has no cars, just one pub and one shop – indeed, little has changed since the Marisco family established itself here in the twelfth century, making use of the shingle beaches and coves to terrorize shipping along the Bristol Channel. The family's fortunes only fell in 1242 when one of their number, William de Marisco, was found to be plotting against the king, whereupon he was hung, drawn and quartered at Tower Hill in London. The castle erected by Henry III on Lundy's southern end dates from this time.

Today the island is managed by the **Landmark Trust**. Unless you're on a specially arranged diving or climbing expedition, **walking** along the interweaving tracks and footpaths is really the only thing to do here. The shores – mainly cliffy on the west side of the island, softer and undulating on the east – shelter a rich variety of **birdlife**, including kittiwakes, fulmars, shags and Manx shearwaters, which often nest in rabbit burrows. The most famous birds, though, are the **puffins** after which Lundy is named – from the Norse *Lunde* (puffin) and *ey* (island). They can only be sighted in April and May, when they come ashore to mate. Offshore, **grey seals** can be seen all year round.

ARRIVAL AND INFORMATION

By boat Between April and Oct, the *MS Oldenburg* sails to Lundy up to four times a week from Ilfracombe, less frequently from Bideford (around 2hr from both places; day returns £37, child £19, open returns £65). To reserve a place, call the shore office on ☎01271 863636 or visit ⓦlandmarktrust.org.uk/lundyisland/ms-oldenburg (day returns can also be booked from local tourist offices).

ACCOMMODATION

Self-catering A number of idiosyncratic Landmark Trust properties are available for self-catering for a minimum of two nights (at around £170). These range from eighteenth-century hideaways for two in a castle keep to weathered fishermen's cottages. They're hugely popular, so book well in advance (☎01628 825925, ⓦlandmarktrust.org.uk/Search-and-Book/landmark-groups/lundy).

B&B The shore office (☎01271 863636) can occasionally arrange accommodation on a bed and breakfast basis, with meals at the island's pub. **£75**

Camping Lundy has a small campsite, also run by the Landmark Trust (closed late Oct to late March; book two weeks ahead). Per person **£6**

6

ARRIVAL AND INFORMATION
BIDEFORD AND AROUND

By bus Route #21 (every 30min) handily links Bideford with Barnstaple (40min) and Westward Ho! (20min). Services #15A, #15C (Mon–Sat every 30min) and #21A (Sun hourly) connect Bideford with Appledore (15min).

Tourist office In the Burton Art Gallery and Museum, Kingsley Road (Mon–Sat 10am–4pm, Sun 11am–4pm; ☎ 01237 477676, ⊛ burtonartgallery.co.uk).

ACCOMMODATION AND EATING

Beaver Inn Irsha St, Appledore, EX39 1RY ☎ 01237 474822, ⊛ beaverinn.co.uk. At the northern tip of Appledore, this traditional pub has wonderful estuary views from its outdoor tables, regular live music and a friendly mix of visitors and locals. Snacks cost under £10, a seafood main is around £15. Daily 11am–11pm; kitchen daily noon–2.30pm & 6–9pm.

The Mount Northdown Rd, Bideford, EX39 3LP ☎ 01237 473748, ⊛ www.themountbideford.co.uk. Handsome Georgian guesthouse set in its own walled gardens, with elegantly furnished rooms and a separate guests' lounge. It's in a quiet area a few minutes outside the centre, linked by a footpath. **£90**

Clovelly

West along Bideford Bay, picturesque **CLOVELLY** was put on the map in the second half of the nineteenth century by two books: Charles Dickens' *A Message From the Sea* and *Westward Ho!* by Charles Kingsley, whose father was rector here for six years. The picture-postcard tone of the village has been preserved by strict regulations, but its excessive quaintness and the streams of visitors on summer days can make it hard to see beyond the artifice.

Beyond the **visitor centre**, where an entrance fee to the village is charged (£7.25), the cobbled, traffic-free main street plunges down past neat, flower-smothered cottages. The tethered sledges here are used for transporting goods, the only way to carry supplies up and down the hill since they stopped using donkeys. At the bottom, Clovelly's stony beach and tiny harbour snuggle under a cleft in the cliff wall.

ARRIVAL AND INFORMATION
CLOVELLY

By bus Bus #319 from Bideford Quay (Mon–Sat 4 daily; 45min) stops outside the visitor centre. The same buses then continue on to Hartland (15min).
Tourist office The visitor centre is at the top of the village

(daily: Easter–June, Sept & Oct 10am–5pm; July & Aug 9am–6pm; Nov–Easter 10am–4pm; ☎ 01237 431781, ⊛ clovelly.co.uk).

GETTING AROUND

Land Rover service If you can't face the return climb to the top of the village, make use of the Land Rover service

that leaves from behind the *Red Lion* on the quayside (Easter–Oct 11am–5pm, roughly every 15min; £2.50).

ACCOMMODATION AND EATING

★ **East Dyke Farmhouse** Higher Clovelly, EX39 5RU ☎ 01237 431216, ⊛ bedbreakfastclovelly.co.uk. Away from the old village, this 200-year-old building with a beamed and flagstoned dining room has guest rooms with fridges and private bathrooms. No credit cards. **£65**
Red Lion The Quay, EX39 5TF ☎ 01237 431237,

⊛ stayatclovelly.co.uk. Of the village's two luxurious and pricey hotels, this one enjoys the best position, right on the harbourside. It's got a congenial bar and the formal *Harbour Restaurant*, specializing in super-fresh seafood (£28 for two courses). Daily noon–3pm & 6.30–8.30pm. **£160**

Hartland and around

Three miles west of Clovelly, the inland village of **HARTLAND** holds little appeal, but the surrounding coastline is spectacular. You could arrive at **Hartland Point** along minor roads, but the best approach is on foot along the coast path. The jagged black rocks of the dramatic headland are battered by the sea and overlooked by a

solitary lighthouse 350ft up. South of Hartland Point, the saw-toothed rocks and near-vertical escarpments defiantly confront the waves, with spectacular waterfalls tumbling over the cliffs.

Hartland Abbey

1.5 miles west of Hartland, EX39 6DT • **House** Easter to early Oct Mon–Thurs & Sun 2–5pm • £12 (includes grounds) • **Grounds** Easter to early Oct Mon–Thurs & Sun 11am–5pm • £8.50 • ☎ 01237 441496, ⊛ hartlandabbey.com

Surrounded by gardens and lush woodland, **Hartland Abbey** is an eighteenth-century mansion incorporating the ruins of an abbey dissolved in 1539. The Regency library has portraits by Gainsborough and Reynolds, George Gilbert Scott designed the vaulted Alhambra Corridor and outer hall, and fine furniture, old photographs and frescoes are everywhere. A path leads a mile from the house to cliffs and a small, sandy bay.

ARRIVAL AND DEPARTURE	HARTLAND AND AROUND
By bus Stagecoach service #319 (Mon–Sat 4–5 daily) links Hartland with Clovelly (15min), Bideford (1hr) and	Barnstaple (1hr 30min).

ACCOMMODATION

2 Harton Manor The Square, off Fore St, EX39 6BL ☎ 01237 441670, ⊛ twohartonmanor.co.uk. Small, friendly B&B offering three rooms above an artist's studio – one en suite with a four-poster. Organic, locally sourced and Aga-cooked breakfasts are served in the flagstone kitchen. No credit cards. **£100**

Stoke Barton Farm Stoke, EX39 6DU, half a mile west of Hartland Abbey ☎ 01237 441238, ⊛ westcountry -camping.co.uk. Right by the fourteenth-century church of St Nectan's, this working farm offers camping as well as accommodation in basic "Pixie huts" (£45) and one room in the farmhouse is available for B&B (£60). Closed Nov– Easter. Per person **£7.50**

Southeast Cornwall

The numerous estuaries strung along the seaboard of **Southeast Cornwall** shelter a succession of quaint old fishing ports, among them **Looe**, **Polperro**, **Fowey** and **Mevagissey**. The area is also noted for its china clay industry, and the conical spoil heaps left by the mines are a feature of the landscape around **St Austell Bay**; a short distance inland, a former clay pit is home to the **Eden Project**, a visionary celebration of environmental diversity and one of the region's biggest draws. West of here, bustling **Falmouth** and the pretty village of **St Mawes** on either side of the Carrick Roads estuary are both worth a wander, as is the laidback county capital, **Truro**.

Looe

In the southeast corner of Cornwall, **LOOE** was drawing crowds as early as 1800, when the first "bathing-machines" were wheeled out; it was the arrival of the railway in 1879, though, that really packed the beaches of this river-divided resort. The handiest stretch of sand lies in front of East Looe, but you'll find cleaner water and less congestion away from the river mouth, a mile eastwards at **Millendreath**.

ARRIVAL AND INFORMATION	LOOE
By train Looe's train station is on the east bank of the river, on Station Rd. There's a rail link from Liskeard to Looe (roughly hourly, not Sun in winter; 30min).	25min); Plymouth (Mon–Sat every 2hr; 1hr 10min); Polperro (Mon–Sat 2–3 hourly, Sun hourly; 10–20min).
By bus Most buses to and from Looe stop on the eastern side of the bridge joining East Looe with West Looe.	**Tourist office** The Guildhall, Fore St (Easter to mid-Sept Mon–Sat 10am–3pm; mid-Sept to Easter Mon–Fri 10am–
Destinations Liskeard (Mon–Sat hourly, Sun every 2hr;	1pm; ☎ 01503 262072, ⊛ www.looeguide.co.uk).

ACCOMMODATION AND EATING

Meneglaze House Shutta, East Looe, PL13 1LU ☎01503 269227, ⓦlooebedandbreakfast.com. Guests at this B&B near the station are greeted with fresh flowers and home-made biscuits. Rooms have fridges and Egyptian cotton bedding, and breakfasts include hog's pudding. No children. **£84**

Old Sail Loft The Quay, East Looe, PL13 1AP ☎01503 262131, ⓦoldsailloftlooe.co. This oak-beamed former warehouse offers the freshest seafood, such as seafood tagliatelle (£15) and lemon sole (£24), plus meat-based dishes like lamb shank (£18). Mon–Thurs 5.30–9pm (last orders), Fri & Sat 11.45am–2pm & 5.30–9pm.

Schooner Point 1 Trelawney Terrace, Polperro Rd, West Looe, PL13 2AG ☎01503 262670, ⓦschooner point.co.uk. Just 100yd from Looe Bridge, this family-run guesthouse has great river views from most of its good-value rooms, which include a single (£50) with a private shower. **£90**

Polperro

Linked to Looe by frequent buses, **POLPERRO** is smaller and quainter than its neighbour, but has a similar feel. From the bus stop and car park at the top of the village, it's a five- or ten-minute walk alongside the River Pol to the pretty harbour. The surrounding cliffs and the tightly packed houses rising on each side of the stream have an undeniable charm, and the tangle of lanes is little changed since the village's heyday of pilchard fishing and smuggling. However, the influx of tourists has inevitably taken its toll, and the straggling main street – the Coombes – is now an unbroken row of tacky shops and food outlets.

ARRIVAL AND DEPARTURE   POLPERRO

By bus Polperro is served by frequent buses from Looe (Mon–Sat 2–3 hourly, Sun hourly; 15–30min) and Plymouth (Mon–Sat every 2hr; 1hr 40min).

ACCOMMODATION AND EATING

★**Blue Peter** The Quay, PL13 2QZ ☎01503 272743, ⓦthebluepeterinn.yolasite.com. Welcoming harbourside pub serving real ales and local scrumpy. The bar food is good (£11 for fish and chips) and there's live music at weekends. Mon–Sat 11am–11pm, Sun noon–10.30pm; kitchen daily noon–2.30pm & 6–8.30pm, school hols daily noon–8.30pm.

The House on the Props Talland St, PL13 2RE ☎01503 272310, ⓦhouseontheprops.co.uk. Staying at this quirky B&B right on the harbour is a bit like being on a boat, with snug rooms, wonky floors and awesome views; there's also a tearoom and restaurant on board. Closed mid-Nov to Easter. Mon & Tues 9am–4pm, Thurs–Sat 9am–8.30pm. **£85**

Penryn House The Coombes, PL13 2RQ ☎01503 272157, ⓦpenrynhouse.co.uk. Relaxed and friendly B&B with a country-house feel. The immaculately clean rooms are small but cosy – those at the back are quietest, but have no view. Parking available. **£75**

Fowey

The ten miles west from Polperro to Polruan are among south Cornwall's finest stretches of the coastal path, giving access to some beautiful, secluded **sand beaches**. There are frequent ferries across the River Fowey from Polruan, affording a fine prospect of **FOWEY** (pronounced "Foy"), a cascade of neat, pale terraces at the mouth of one of the peninsula's greatest rivers. The major port on the county's south coast in the fourteenth century, Fowey finally became so ambitious that it provoked Edward IV to strip the town of its military capability, though it continued to thrive commercially, becoming the leading port for china clay shipments in the nineteenth century.

Fowey's steep layout centres on the distinctive fifteenth-century church of **St Fimbarrus** (ⓦfoweyparishchurch.org). Below the church, the **Ship Inn**, which sports some fine Elizabethan panelling and plaster ceilings, held the local Roundhead HQ during the Civil War. From here, Fore Street, Lostwithiel Street and the Esplanade fan out, the last of which leads to a footpath that gives access to some splendid **coastal walks**. One of these passes Menabilly House, where **Daphne Du Maurier** lived for 24 years – it was the model for the "Manderley" of her novel *Rebecca*. The house is not open to the public,

6

but the path takes you down to the twin coves of **Polridmouth**, where Rebecca met her watery end. The tourist office can provide information on the eight-day **Fowey Festival** (☎01726 879500, ⓦfoweyfestival.com), which takes place each May, with talks, walks, workshops and concerts.

ARRIVAL AND INFORMATION   FOWEY

By bus Fowey is easily accessible from the west, with buses #24 and #25 running from Par (Mon–Sat every 30min, Sun every 1hr 30min; 15min) and St Austell (Mon–Sat every 30min, Sun every 1hr 30min; 45min).
By ferry Fowey can be reached by ferry every 10–15min daily from Bodinnick (foot passengers and vehicles) and

Polruan (foot passengers only); tickets cost around £2 for a foot passenger, £5 for a car and passengers (☎01726 870232, ⓦctomsandson.co.uk).
Tourist office 5 South St (Mon–Sat 10am–5pm, Sun 11am–4pm; ☎0905 151 0262, ⓦfowey.co.uk).

ACCOMMODATION AND EATING

Coombe Farm Lankelly Lane, PL23 1HW, 1 mile southwest of Fowey ☎01726 833123, ⓦcoombe farmbb.co.uk. A 20min walk from town, this B&B provides perfect rural isolation – and there's a bathing area just 300yd away. **£75**
Old Quay House 28 Fore St, PL23 1AQ ☎01726 833302, ⓦtheoldquayhouse.com. Pricey harbourside hotel with eleven compact yet fresh-feeling rooms, some of which have balconies. The restaurant, *Q*, serves plenty of fresh seafood

on set-price menus (£29 at lunch, £40 in the evening for three courses). Mon & Tues 6.30–9pm, Wed–Sun 12.30–3pm & 6.30–9pm; reduced hours in winter. **£190**
Sam's 20 Fore St, PL23 1AQ ☎01726 832273, ⓦsams cornwall.co.uk. With a menu ranging from burgers (£10–16) to seafood (£7–16.50), this place has 1960s rock'n'roll decor and friendly service. It doesn't take bookings, so arrive early or be prepared to wait. There's a late-closing lounge/bar upstairs. Daily noon–9pm (last orders).

St Austell Bay

It was the discovery of china clay, or kaolin, in the downs to the north of **St Austell Bay** that spurred the area's growth in the eighteenth century. An essential ingredient in the production of porcelain, kaolin had until then only been produced in northern China. Still a vital part of Cornwall's economy, the clay is now mostly exported for use in the manufacture of paper, paint and medicines, the green and white spoil heaps making an eerie sight in the local landscape.

The town of **ST AUSTELL** itself is fairly unexciting, but makes a useful stop for trips in the surrounding area. Its nearest link to the sea is at **CHARLESTOWN**, an easy downhill walk from the centre of town. This unspoilt port is still used for china clay shipments, and is a frequent filming location (including for *Poldark*). Behind the harbour, the **Shipwreck & Heritage Centre** (March–Oct daily 10am–5pm; £5.95; ☎01726 69897, ⓦshipwreck charlestown.com) is entered through tunnels once used to convey clay to the docks, and shows a good collection of photos and relics as well as tableaux of historical scenes.

On either side of the dock, the coarse sand and stone **beaches** have small rock pools, above which cliff walks lead around the bay.

ARRIVAL AND DEPARTURE   ST AUSTELL BAY

By train St Austell is the main rail stop in southeast Cornwall, with regular services from/to Bodmin (every 30min–1hr; 20min) and Truro (every 30min–1hr; 20min); the station is off High Cross St.
By bus Buses pull in next to St Austell's train station, off High Cross St.

Destinations Bodmin (Mon–Sat hourly; 1hr); Charlestown (Mon–Sat every 10–20min, Sun 7 daily; 10–15min); Falmouth (2 daily; 1hr); Newquay (Mon–Sat 1–2 hourly, Sun every 1–2hr; 1hr–1hr 20min); Plymouth (3 daily; 1hr 20min); Truro (Mon–Sat hourly, Sun 4 daily; 30–40min).

ACCOMMODATION AND EATING

Rashleigh Arms Charlestown Rd, PL25 3NJ ☎01726 73635, ⓦrashleigharms.co.uk. Friendly inn with St Austell and guest ales, reasonably priced food (mains £10–16)

including sandwiches and a Sunday carvery, and outdoor seating. Rooms are available upstairs or in a Georgian annexe. Daily 11am–11pm; kitchen daily noon–9pm. **£125**

The Eden Project

4 miles northeast of St Austell, PL24 2SG • Jan to mid-Feb & early to late Nov Mon–Fri 10am–4pm, Sat & Sun 9.30am–6pm; mid-Feb to March daily 10am–4pm; April–July, Sept & Oct daily 9.30am–6pm; Aug Mon–Thurs 9.30am–8pm, Fri–Sun 9.30am–6pm; late Nov to mid-Dec Mon–Thurs 10am–4pm, Fri–Sun 9.30am–8pm; mid- to late Dec daily 9.30am–8pm; last entry 1hr 30min before closing • £27.50, or £25 in advance (under-17s £14/£12.60); £23.50 (£10) if arriving by bus, by bike or on foot; £38 (£18.45) combined ticket with Lost Gardens of Heligan (see below); tickets are valid for a year when registered as a donation • ☎01726 811911, ⓦedenproject.com • The most useful bus is #101 from St Austell train station (roughly hourly; 20min)

Occupying a 160ft-deep crater whose awesome scale only reveals itself once you have passed the entrance at its lip, the **Eden Project** showcases the diversity of the planet's plant life in an imaginative way. Centre-stage are the geodesic "**biomes**" – vast conservatories made up of eco-friendly Teflon-coated, hexagonal panels. One holds groves of olive and citrus trees, cacti and other plants usually found in the warm, temperate zones of the Mediterranean, southern Africa and southwestern USA, while the larger one contains plants from the tropics, including teak and mahogany trees, with a waterfall and river gushing through. Equally impressive are the **grounds**, where plantations of bamboo, tea, hops, hemp and tobacco are interspersed with brilliant displays of flowers. In summer, the grassy arena sees **performances** of a range of music – from Van Morrison to Foals (ⓦedensessions.com) – and in winter they set up a skating rink.

6

Mevagissey and around

MEVAGISSEY was once known for the construction of fast vessels, used for carrying pilchards (officially) and contraband (less officially). Today the tiny port might display a few stacks of lobster pots, but the real business is tourism, and in summer the maze of backstreets is saturated with day-trippers, converging on the inner harbour and overflowing onto the large sand beach at **Pentewan** a mile to the north.

Four miles south of Mevagissey juts the striking headland of **Dodman Point**, cause of many a wreck and topped by a stark granite cross built by a local parson as a seamark in 1896. The promontory holds the substantial remains of an Iron Age fort, with an earthwork bulwark cutting right across the point. Curving away to the west, elegant **Veryan Bay** holds a string of exquisite inlets and coves, such as **Hemmick Beach**, a fine place for a dip with rocky outcrops affording a measure of privacy, and **Porthluney Cove**, a crescent of sand whose centrepiece is the battlemented **Caerhays Castle** (house tours mid-March to mid-June Mon–Fri 11.30am, 1pm and 2.30pm; 45min; gardens mid-Feb to mid-June daily 10am–5pm, last entry 4pm; house tours £8.50, gardens £8.50, combined ticket £13.50; ☎01872 501310, ⓦwww.caerhays.co.uk), built in 1808 by John Nash and surrounded by beautiful gardens. A little further on is the minuscule and whitewashed village of **Portloe**, fronted by jagged black rocks that throw up fountains of seaspray, giving it a poignant, end-of-the-road feel.

Lost Gardens of Heligan

Near Pentewan, PL26 6EN • Daily: April–Sept 10am–6pm; Oct–March 10am–5pm; last entry 1hr 30min before closing • £14.50, £38 combined ticket with Eden Project (see above) • ☎01726 845100, ⓦheligan.com • Bus #471 (Mon–Sat 4–8 daily) from Mevagissey (10min) and St Austell (30–40min)

A couple of miles north of Mevagissey lie the **Lost Gardens of Heligan**; these fascinating Victorian gardens had fallen into neglect and were resurrected by Tim Smit, the visionary instigator of the Eden Project, in the 1990s. A boardwalk takes you through a jungle and under a canopy of bamboo and ferns down to the Lost Valley, where there are lakes, woods and wildflower meadows.

ARRIVAL AND DEPARTURE   MEVAGISSEY AND AROUND

By bus From St Austell's station, the #24 and #471 services leave for Mevagissey (Mon–Sat 1–2 hourly, Sun 7 daily; 20min); #471 continues to the Lost Gardens of Heligan (10min).

6

ACCOMMODATION AND EATING

Alvorada 5 East Quay, PL26 6QQ ☎01726 842055. The chances are that if you choose a fish dish at this small, family-run Portuguese restaurant, it'll have been caught by the chef. Dishes include sardines, mussels with chorizo and *caldeirada* (fish casserole), with most mains around £17.50. Noon–2pm & 6.30pm–late; call for winter opening.

Wild Air Polkirt Hill, PL26 6UX ☎01726 843302, ⓦwildair.co.uk. Away from the harbour crowds, this B&B has three tastefully furnished rooms, all with en-suite or private bathrooms, and all enjoying lofty views over the harbour and coast. There's also a panoramic patio, and parking. **£85**

YHA Boswinger Boswinger, PL26 6LL, half a mile from Hemmick Beach and 3.5 miles southwest of Mevagissey ☎01726 844527, ⓦyha.org.uk/hostel/boswinger. Set in a former farmhouse, this is a remote spot a mile from the bus stop at Gorran Churchtown (Mon–Sat #471 or #G1 from St Austell and Mevagissey). Kitchen and meals available. Only groups can book Nov–Feb. Dorms **£19**, doubles **£59**

Truro

Cornwall's capital, **TRURO**, presents a mixture of different styles, from the graceful Georgian architecture that came with the tin-mining boom of the 1800s to its neo-Gothic cathedral and modern shopping centre (Lemon Quay). It's an attractive place, not overwhelmed by tourism and with a range of good-value facilities.

Truro Cathedral

St Mary's St, TR1 2AF • Mon–Sat 7.30am–6pm, Sun 9am–7pm; tours April–Oct Mon–Thurs 11am, 1hr • Free (£5 suggested donation) • ☎01872 276782, ⓦtrurocathedral.org.uk

Truro's dominant feature is its faux-medieval **cathedral**, completed in 1910 and incorporating part of the fabric of the old parish church that previously occupied the site. In the airy interior, the neo-Gothic baptistry commands attention, complete with its emphatically pointed arches and elaborate roof vaulting.

Royal Cornwall Museum

River St, TR1 2SJ • Mon–Sat 10am–4.45pm, Sun 10am–4pm • £4.50 • ☎01872 272205, ⓦroyalcornwallmuseum.org.uk

Truro's **Royal Cornwall Museum** offers a rich and wide-ranging hoard that takes in everything from the region's natural history to Celtic inscriptions. If time is tight you could confine yourself to the renowned collection of minerals on the ground floor and the upstairs galleries holding works by Cornish artists including members of the Newlyn School.

ARRIVAL AND INFORMATION

By train The train station is just off Richmond Hill, a 10min walk west of the centre.

Destinations Bodmin (hourly; 35min); Exeter (every 1–2hr; 2hr 20min); Falmouth (Mon–Sat every 30min, Sun hourly; 25min); Liskeard (hourly; 50min); Penzance (hourly; 45min); Plymouth (hourly; 1hr 15min).

By bus Buses stop centrally at Lemon Quay, or near the train station.

Destinations Falmouth (Mon–Sat every 30min, Sun hourly; 45min); Newquay (Mon–Sat 3 hourly, Sun 1–2 hourly; 55min–1hr 30min); Penzance (Mon–Sat every 30min, Sun hourly; 1hr 40min); Plymouth (5 daily; 1hr 40min–2hr 20min); St Austell (Mon–Sat hourly, Sun 3 daily; 30–40min); St Ives (Mon–Sat every 30min, Sun hourly; 1hr 35min); St Mawes (Mon–Sat 7 daily, Sun 4 daily; 1hr 5min).

Tourist office Municipal Buildings, Boscawen St (Mon–Sat 9.30am–5pm ☎01872 274555, ⓦvisittruro.org.uk).

ACCOMMODATION

Bay Tree 28 Ferris Town, TR1 3JH ☎01872 240274, ⓦbaytree-guesthouse.co.uk. Homely, restored Georgian house halfway between the train station and the town centre, with a friendly owner and shared bathrooms (one room has its own shower). Singles available. Rough Guide readers receive a discount if prebooked. No debit/ credit cards. **£65**

★Truro Lodge 10 The Parade, TR1 1QE ☎07813 755210, ⓦtrurolodge.co.uk. Relaxed B&B in a large, Georgian terraced house near the centre. Buffet breakfasts are available in the kitchen, which is accessible all day for guests' use, and there's a lounge and veranda. **£45**

EATING AND DRINKING

Charlotte's Teahouse 1 Boscawen St, TR1 2QU
☎ 01872 263706. Upstairs in the old Coinage Hall, this is
a gloriously old-fashioned spot for sandwiches (£6.50–
8.50), muffins and cream teas. The setting is Victorian,
with staff in period dress. Mon–Sat 10am–5pm.

Hooked! Tabernacle St, TR1 2EJ ☎ 01872 274700,
ⓦ hookedrestaurantandbar.co.uk. This relaxed restaurant
sports banquettes, bare brick walls and a vaulted ceiling,
and has a menu that's strong on seafood, including tapas
(£3) and more substantial dishes such as paella and
seafood curry (both £15). Mon–Sat noon–2pm & 5.30–
9pm (last orders).

Wig & Pen 1 Frances St, TR1 3DP ☎ 01872 273028,
ⓦ staustellbrewery.co.uk. The pick of Truro's pubs
serves St Austell ales and bar food, as well as brunches
and cream teas, with some tables outside. Simple bar
meals such as pastas and burgers cost £7.50–10. Mon–
Thurs 11am–11pm, Fri & Sat 11am–midnight, Sun
11am–6pm; kitchen Mon–Sat noon–3pm & 6–9pm,
Sun noon–3pm.

Falmouth

Amid the lush tranquillity of the **Carrick Roads** estuary basin, the major resort of
FALMOUTH is the site of one of Cornwall's mightiest castles, **Pendennis Castle**, and of
one of the country's foremost collections of boats in the **National Maritime Museum
Cornwall**. The town sits at the mouth of the Fal estuary, at the end of a rail branch line
from Truro and connected by ferry to Truro and St Mawes. Round Pendennis Point,
south of the centre, a long sandy bay holds a succession of sheltered **beaches**: from the
popular **Gyllyngvase Beach**, you can reach the more attractive **Swanpool Beach** by cliff
path, or walk a couple of miles further on to **Maenporth**, from where there are some
fine clifftop walks.

National Maritime Museum Cornwall

Discovery Quay, TR11 3QY • Daily 10am–5pm • £12.95 • ☎ 01326 313388, ⓦ nmmc.co.uk

Vessels from all around the world are exhibited in Falmouth's **National Maritime
Museum Cornwall**. Of every size and shape, the craft are arranged on three levels,
many of them suspended in mid-air in the cavernous Flotilla Gallery. Smaller galleries
examine specific aspects of boat-building, seafaring history and Falmouth's packet
ships, and a lighthouse-like lookout tower offers excellent views over the harbour and
estuary, with a lift descending to an underwater viewing room.

Pendennis Castle

Pendennis Head, TR11 4LP • Mid-Feb to late Feb daily 10am–4pm; late Feb to March Wed–Sun 10am–4pm; April–Sept daily 10am–6pm;
Oct daily 10am–5pm; Nov to mid-Feb Sat & Sun 10am–4pm • £8.40; EH • ☎ 01326 316594, ⓦ www.english-heritage.org.uk/visit/places
/pendennis-castle • Bus #367 from town centre

Under a mile southeast of Falmouth's harbour, **Pendennis Castle** stands sentinel
at the tip of the promontory that separates the Carrick Roads estuary from
Falmouth Bay. The extensive fortification shows little evidence of its five-month
siege by the Parliamentarians during the Civil War, which ended only when half its
defenders had died and the rest had been starved into submission. Though this is a
less-refined contemporary of the castle at St Mawes (see p.354), its site wins hands
down, the stout ramparts offering the best all-round views of Carrick Roads and
Falmouth Bay.

ARRIVAL AND INFORMATION   FALMOUTH

By train The branch rail line from Truro (Mon–Sat every
30min, Sun hourly; 30min) stops at Falmouth Town, best
for the centre, and Falmouth Docks, 2min away, near
Pendennis Castle.

By bus Most buses stop on The Moor, close to the Prince
of Wales Pier and just east of the High St.

Destinations Helston (Mon–Sat hourly, Sun 2 daily;
25–50min); Penzance (Mon–Sat 6 daily, Sun 1 daily;
55min–1hr 40min); St Austell (2 daily; 1hr); Truro (Mon–
Sat every 30min, Sun hourly; 45min).

Tourist office Prince of Wales Pier (April–Oct Mon–Sat
9.45am–3.15pm, Sun 9.45am–1pm; Nov–March Mon–
Thurs & Sat 10am–3pm; ☎ 01326 741194, ⓦ falmouth
.co.uk).

6

ACCOMMODATION

★**Falmouth Lodge** 9 Gyllyngvase Terrace, TR11 4DL ☎01326 319996, ⒲falmouthbackpackers.co.uk. Clean and friendly backpackers' hostel located a couple of minutes' walk from the beach, with a sociable lounge and kitchen. Dorms **£19**, doubles **£52**

Falmouth Townhouse 3 Grove Place, TR11 4AL ☎01326 312009, ⒲falmouthtownhouse.co.uk. Chic boutique hotel in a Georgian building just across from the Maritime Museum. It's all highly designed, with spacious guestrooms, quirky bathrooms and a buzzing bar, though some front-facing rooms suffer from street noise at night. **£75**

St Michael's Hotel and Spa Gyllyngvase Beach, TR11 4NB ☎01326 312707, ⒲stmichaelshotel.co.uk. Sleekly luxurious seaside hotel, very close to the beach and with a range of spa facilities, including an indoor pool. Rooms are bright and contemporary, the cheapest being compact "cabin rooms" (£176). The *Flying Fish* bistro provides quality modern cuisine with sea views. **£200**

EATING AND DRINKING

★**Beerwolf Books** Bells Court, off Market St, TR11 3AZ ☎01326 618474, ⒲beerwolfbooks.com. Here's a novel concept – a free house and bookshop combined. Set in a beautifully restored old building, with tables in a secluded courtyard, it makes a relaxing spot for a drink, with a great selection of local beers. Mon–Sat 10am–midnight, Sun noon–11pm.

Fuel 35–37 Arwenack St, TR11 3JG ☎01326 314499, ⒲fuelfalmouth.co.uk. This buzzy, colourful spot near the Maritime Museum on the main drag provides all-day breakfasts, coffees, cream teas, snack lunches and full meals, with friendly service and an upbeat atmosphere. Main courses such as moussaka, fishcakes and beef burgers cost around £10. Daily 8am–10pm.

Gylly Beach Café Gyllyngvase Beach, TR11 4PA ☎01326 312884, ⒲gyllybeach.com. Cool beachside hangout serving everything from baguettes to monkfish curry. Breakfast is served until 11.30am, lunch dishes are £8–12, and evening mains start at £14. There are outdoor barbecues in summer from 4pm and live music on Sun eves. Daily 9am–late.

St Mawes and around

Situated on the east side of the Carrick Roads estuary, the two-pronged **Roseland Peninsula** is a luxurious backwater of woods and sheltered creeks. The main settlement is **ST MAWES**, a tranquil old fishing port easily reached on ferries from Falmouth. Moving east from St Mawes, you could spend a pleasant afternoon poking around the southern arm of the peninsula, which holds the twelfth- to thirteenth-century church of **ST ANTHONY-IN-ROSELAND** and the **lighthouse** on St Anthony's Head, marking the entry into Carrick Roads. Two and a half miles north of St Mawes is the scattered hamlet of **ST JUST-IN-ROSELAND**, home to the strikingly picturesque **Church of St Just** (⒲stjustandstmawes.org .uk/st-just-in-roseland), which is right next to the creek and surrounded by palms and subtropical shrubbery, its gravestones tumbling down to the water's edge.

St Mawes Castle

Half a mile west of the quay, TR2 5DE • Mid-Feb to late Feb daily 10am–4pm; late Feb to March Wed–Sun 10am–4pm; April–Sept daily 10am–6pm; Oct daily 10am–5pm; Nov to mid-Feb Sat & Sun 10am–4pm • £5.40; EH • ☎01326 270526, ⒲www.english-heritage.org.uk /visit/places/st-mawes-castle

At the end of the walled seafront of St Mawes stands the sister fort of Pendennis Castle, the small and pristine **St Mawes Castle**, built during the reign of Henry VIII to a clover-leaf design. The castle owes its excellent condition to its early surrender to Parliamentary forces during the Civil War in 1646. The various rooms and gun decks contain artillery exhibits and historical background, and you can climb to the top of the tower and explore the grounds.

Trelissick

Feock, TR3 6QL, 6 miles north of St Mawes • **House** Mid-Feb to Oct daily 11am–5pm; Dec Fri–Sun 11am–7pm • **Garden** Daily: mid-Feb to Oct daily 10.30am–5.30pm; Nov to mid-Feb 10.30am–4.30pm; closes at dusk if earlier • £10.90; NT • ☎01872 862090, ⒲nationaltrust .org.uk/trelissick • The King Harry Ferry (see opposite) stops near here, as do ferries from Falmouth, St Mawes and Truro (see opposite), and the #493 bus from Truro (Mon–Sat)

On a spectacular site that was first settled in the Iron Age, eighteenth-century **Trelissick House** displays Spode china, family portraits, and exhibitions relating to the place and the family, but the real attraction is **Trelissick Garden**, celebrated for its hydrangeas and other Mediterranean species. There are impressive vistas over the River Fal, and splendid woodland walks.

ARRIVAL AND GETTING AROUND

By bus There are regular buses (#50 & #551) between Truro and St Mawes (Mon–Sat 7 daily, Sun 4 daily; 1hr), stopping off at St Just-in-Roseland (7min from St Mawes) en route.

By ferry St Mawes can be reached on frequent ferries from Falmouth's Prince of Wales Pier and Custom House Quay (£10 return). Passenger ferries from St Mawes also cross to Place on the southern arm of the peninsula (daily every 30min: April, May & Oct 9am–4.30pm;

ST MAWES AND AROUND

June–Sept 9.30am–5.30pm; £7 return).

By car The fastest road route from Truro, Falmouth and west Cornwall involves crossing the River Fal on the chain-driven King Harry Ferry (every 20min: April–Sept Mon–Sat 7.20am–9.20pm, Sun 9am–9.20pm; Oct–March Mon–Sat 7.20am–7.20pm, Sun 9am–7.20pm; cars £6 & bicycles £1 one-way, foot passengers free in exchange for a charity donation; ☎ 01872 862312, ⦿ falriver.co.uk).

ACCOMMODATION AND EATING

Little Newton Newton Rd, TR2 5BS ☎ 01326 270664, ⦿ little-newton.co.uk. Two small but smart and modern en-suite rooms are available at this B&B just off Castle Rd, a steep 10min walk up from the seafront. No debit/credit cards. Closed Nov–Feb. **£65**

St Mawes Hotel Harbourside, TR2 5DW ☎ 01326 270170, ⦿ stmaweshotel.com. Superbly sited over-looking the harbour, this place offers sober but stylish, airy rooms, a quirkily decorated restaurant offering delicious, modern European dishes (mains around £16), and a cosy

street-level bar serving snacks and local beers. Daily noon–3pm & 6–9pm. **£195**

★**Tresanton Hotel** 27 Lower Castle Rd, TR2 5DR ☎ 01326 270055, ⦿ tresanton.com. Cornwall doesn't get much ritzier than this, a slice of Mediterranean-style luxury with bright, sunny colours and a yacht and speedboat available to guests in summer. There's a fabulous Italian-inspired restaurant, too; you can have lunch (£25 for two courses) or an evening meal (mains around £20). Daily noon–3pm & 6.30–10pm. **£280**

The Lizard Peninsula

The **Lizard Peninsula** – from the Celtic *lys ardh*, or "high point" – is mercifully undeveloped. If this flat and treeless expanse can be said to have a centre, it's **Helston**, a junction for buses running from Falmouth and Truro, and to the spartan villages of the peninsula's interior and coast. Other than that it's all deserted beaches

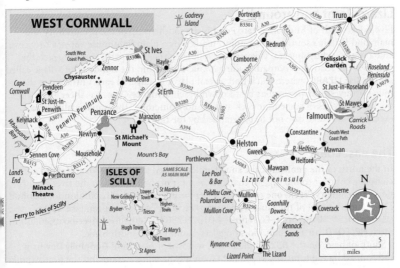

6

and windswept downland – plus **Lizard Point**, the farthest south you can go on the British mainland.

Helston

The otherwise quiet and workaday inland town of **HELSTON** is best known for its **Furry Dance** (or Flora Dance), dating from the seventeenth century. Held on May 8 (unless this falls on Sun or Mon, when the procession takes place on the preceding Sat), it's a stately procession of top-hatted men and summer-frocked women performing a solemn dance through the town's streets and gardens. You can learn something about it and absorb plenty of other local history in the eclectic **Helston Folk Museum** (Mon–Sat 10am–4pm; free; ☎01326 564027, ⊛helstonmuseum.co.uk), housed in former market buildings behind the Guildhall on Church Street.

Porthleven and around

Two and a half miles southwest of Helston, tin ore from inland mines was once shipped from **PORTHLEVEN**. Good **beaches** lie to either side: the best for swimming are around **Rinsey Head**, three miles north along the coast, including the sheltered **Praa Sands**. One and a quarter miles south of Porthleven, strong currents make it unsafe to swim at **Loe Bar**, a strip of shingle which separates the freshwater **Loe Pool** from the sea. The elongated Pool is one of two sites which claim to be the place where the sword Excalibur was restored to its watery source (the other is on Bodmin Moor). The path running along its western edge makes a fine walking route between here and Helston.

Mullion and around

The inland village of **MULLION**, five miles south of Porthleven, has a fifteenth- to sixteenth-century church dedicated to the Breton **St Mellanus** (or Malo), complete with a dog-door for canine churchgoers. A lane leads a mile and a quarter west to **Mullion Cove**, where a tiny beach is sheltered behind harbour walls and rock stacks, though the neighbouring sands at **Polurrian** and **Poldhu**, to the north, are better and attract surfers.

Lizard Point and around

Five miles south of Mullion, **Lizard Point** is the southern tip of the promontory and mainland Britain's southernmost point, marked by a plain lighthouse above a tiny cove and a restless, churning sea. If you're not following the coast path, you can reach the point via the road and footpath leading a mile south from the nondescript village called simply **THE LIZARD**, where you'll find several places to stay and eat. A little more than a mile northwest, the peninsula's best-known beach, **Kynance Cove**, has sheer 100ft cliffs, stacks and arches of serpentine rock and offshore outcrops. The water quality here is excellent – but take care not to be stranded by the tide.

The east coast

In the north of the peninsula, the snug hamlets dotted around the **River Helford** are a complete contrast to the rugged character of most of the Lizard. On the river's south side, **Frenchman's Creek**, one of a splay of serene inlets, was the inspiration for Daphne Du Maurier's novel of the same name. From Helford Passage you can take a ferry (Easter–Oct 9.30am–5pm; £6 return; ☎01326 250770, ⊛helford-river-boats.co.uk) to reach **HELFORD**, an agreeable old smugglers' haunt on the south bank.

South of here, on the B3293, the broad, windswept plateau of **Goonhilly Downs** is interrupted by the futuristic saucers of Goonhilly Satellite Station and the nearby ranks of wind turbines. As you head east, the road splits: left to **ST KEVERNE**, an inland village whose tidy square is flanked by two inns and a church; right to **COVERACK**, a fishing port in a sheltered bay. Following the coast path or negotiating minor roads south will bring you to the safe and clean swimming spot of **Kennack Sands**.

GETTING AROUND   **THE LIZARD PENINSULA**

By bus From Helston, bus #2 goes to Porthleven (Mon–Sat hourly, Sun every 2hr; 10min), #36 (Mon–Sat 5–6 daily) goes to Coverack (30–40min) and St Keverne (30–50min), and #37 (Mon–Sat 8–11 daily, Sun 3–5 daily) goes to Mullion (35min) and The Lizard (45–55min).

6

ACCOMMODATION AND EATING

★ **Blue Anchor** 50 Coinagehall St, Helston, TR13 8EL ☎ 01326 562821, ⓦ spingoales.com. Deeply traditional West Country pub, once a fifteenth-century monastery rest house, now brewing its own Spingo beer on the premises. Four B&B rooms are available in an adjacent building. Mon–Thurs & Sun 10am–midnight, Fri & Sat 10am–1am. **£75**

Mounts Bay Inn On the B3296, Mullion, TR12 7HN ☎ 01326 240221, ⓦ mountsbaymullion.co.uk. Mullion's best place for Cornish ales, snacks and meals (£6–8) with a beer garden and views over Mounts Bay. Live bands every fortnight and Cornish songs on the last Sun of the month. B&B also available. Mon–Thurs 11am–11pm, Fri & Sat 11am–midnight, Sun noon–11pm; kitchen Mon–Sat noon–2pm & 6–9pm, Sun noon–2.30pm & 6–8.30pm. **£80**

Poldhu Beach Café Poldhu Cove, near Mullion, TR12 7JB ☎ 01326 240530, ⓦ poldhu.com. The perfect beach café, with energizing breakfasts, burgers (from £4), good coffee and hot chocolate, and locally produced ice cream. Stays open late on Fri in summer for pizza nights. Daily 9.30am–4.30/5.30pm.

YHA Lizard Lizard Point, TR12 7NT ☎ 0345 371 9550, ⓦ yha.org.uk/hostel/lizard. This hostel occupies a former Victorian hotel right on the coast, with majestic views. Camping is also possible, either in your own tent or the hostel's bell tent (July–Sept only; £59) that sleeps up to five, and there's a kitchen for self-catering. Only groups can book Dec–Feb. Camping/person **£13**, dorms **£19**, doubles **£39**

The Penwith Peninsula

Though more densely populated than the Lizard, the **Penwith Peninsula** is a more rugged landscape, with a raw appeal that is still encapsulated by **Land's End**, despite the commercialization of that headland. It also boasts some excellent beaches, chief among them **Porthcurno**, as well as the quaint-but-crowded fishing village of **Mousehole** and the fascinating **St Michael's Mount**, rising out of the sea near **Penzance**. The seascapes, the quality of the light and the slow tempo of the local fishing communities made this area a hotbed of artistic activity from the late nineteenth century onwards, when **Newlyn** became associated with a distinctive school of painting, quickly followed by **St Ives**, while **Zennor** is associated with one-time resident D.H. Lawrence.

Penzance and around

Occupying a sheltered position at the northwest corner of Mount's Bay, **PENZANCE** has always been a major port, but most traces of the medieval town were obliterated at the end of the sixteenth century by a Spanish raiding party. From the top of **Market Jew Street** (from *Marghas Jew*, meaning "Thursday Market"), which climbs from the harbour and the train and bus stations, turn left into **Chapel Street** to see some of the town's finest buildings, including the flamboyant **Egyptian House**, built in 1835 to contain a geological museum but subsequently abandoned until its restoration by the Landmark Trust (ⓦ landmarktrust.org.uk) in 1973; you can now stay there. Across the street, the seventeenth-century **Union Hotel** originally held the town's assembly rooms, where news of Admiral Nelson's victory at Trafalgar and the death of Nelson himself was first announced in 1805.

6

Penlee House Gallery and Museum

Morrab Rd, TR18 4HE • Mon–Sat: April–Oct 10am–5pm; Nov–March 10.30am–4.30pm; last entry 30min before closing • £5 • ☎ 01736 363625,
Ⓦ penleehouse.org.uk

Long a centre of the local art movements, **Penlee House Gallery and Museum** holds the country's largest collection of Newlyn School artworks – impressionistic harbour scenes, frequently sentimentalized but often bathed in an evocatively luminous light. There are also displays on local archeology and history, and frequent exhibitions.

Jubilee Pool

The Promenade, TR18 4UU • Late May to Sept daily 10.30am–6pm • Swimmers £5, £3.15 after 3.30pm; spectators £2 • ☎ 01736 369214,
Ⓦ jubileepool.co.uk

Bulging into Mount's Bay from the seafront, the **Jubilee Pool** is a tidal, saltwater (though chlorinated) open-air swimming pool, built to mark the Silver Jubilee of George V in 1935. Smartly renovated following storm damage in 2014, it's a classic Art Deco design, worth a visit even if you're not taking a dip (and there's a café).

Newlyn Art Gallery

24 New Rd, Newlyn, TR18 5PZ • 10am–5pm: April–Oct Mon–Sat; Nov–March Tues–Sat • Free • ☎ 01736 363715, Ⓦ newlynartgallery.co.uk

From the Promenade, it's an easy 15–20min walk to **NEWLYN**, Cornwall's biggest fishing port, lying immediately south of Penzance. The **Newlyn Art Gallery**, near the harbour, merits a visit for its exhibitions of contemporary work, often curated by Cornish artists. Originally opened in 1895 and remodelled several times since, the gallery has a pleasant top-floor café with sea views.

St Michael's Mount

Off Marazion, TR17 0HS, 5 miles east of Penzance • **House** Mon–Fri & Sun: mid-March to June, Sept & Oct 10.30am–5pm; July & Aug 10.30am–5.30pm; last entry 45min before closing • £9.50, £14 with garden; NT • **Garden** Mid-April to June Mon–Fri 10.30am–5pm; July & Aug Thurs & Fri 10.30am–5.30pm; Sept Thurs & Fri 10.30am–5pm • £7, £14 with house • ☎ 01736 710265, Ⓦ stmichaelsmount.co.uk • At low tide the promontory can be approached on foot via a cobbled causeway (daily tide times on the website); at high tide there are boats from Marazion (£2–3)

Frequent buses from Penzance leave for **MARAZION**, the access point to **St Michael's Mount**, some four hundred yards offshore. A vision of the archangel Michael led to the building of a church on this granite pile around the fifth century, and within three centuries a Celtic monastery had been founded here. The present building derives from a **chapel** raised in the eleventh century by Edward the Confessor, who handed it over to the Benedictine monks of Brittany's Mont St Michel, whose island abbey was the model for this one. Following the Civil War, it became the residence of the St Aubyn family, who still inhabit the castle. Some of the buildings date from the twelfth century, but the later additions are more interesting, such as the battlemented **chapel** and the seventeenth-century decorations of the **Chevy Chase Room**, the former refectory. The lush **gardens** are also well worth exploring.

ARRIVAL AND DEPARTURE   PENZANCE AND AROUND

By train Penzance's train station lies on the seafront, on Station Rd.

Destinations Bodmin (roughly hourly; 1hr 15min); Exeter (roughly hourly; 3hr 15min); Plymouth (roughly hourly; 2hr); St Ives (most via St Erth; hourly; 30min–1hr 20min); Truro (roughly hourly; 40min).

By bus The bus station is next to the train station, on the seafront.

Destinations Falmouth (Mon–Sat 7 daily, Sun 1 daily;

55min–1hr 50min); Helston (Mon–Sat hourly, Sun 7 daily; 50min); Plymouth (4 daily; 2hr 50min–4hr); St Austell (2 daily; 1hr 35min–2hr); St Ives (Mon–Sat every 10–30min, Sun 2 hourly; 30min); Truro (Mon–Sat every 30min, Sun hourly; 1hr 40min).

By boat From Easter to early Nov boats depart from Penzance Quay for St Mary's on the Isles of Scilly (Mon–Sat 4–6 weekly; 2hr 45min; ☎ 01736 334220, Ⓦ islesofscilly -travel.co.uk).

ACCOMMODATION

★ **Artist Residence** 20 Chapel St, TR18 4AW ☎ 01736 365664, Ⓦ artistresidencecornwall.co.uk. Artistic licence

has been given free rein at this central hipster hotel, where each room is designed by a different artist (some rooms are quite cramped). The staff are friendly and helpful, the breakfasts are superb and there's a popular bar and restaurant. **£130**

Penzance Backpackers Alexandra Rd, TR18 4LZ ☎01736 363836, ⓦpzbackpack.com. In a quiet neighbourhood 15min from the centre, this is a tidy, good-value hostel, with en-suite dorms, a well-equipped kitchen

and a large lounge. Dorms **£17**, doubles **£38**

Warwick House 17 Regent Terrace, TA18 4DW ☎01736 363881, ⓦwarwickhousepenzance.co.uk. Located near the centre of town and the harbour, this B&B has elegant rooms decorated in blue and white – the best ones have views of the water. Two- or three-night minimum stay in summer. **£95**

EATING AND DRINKING

Admiral Benbow 46 Chapel St, TA18 4AF ☎01736 363448. Characterful pub crammed with gaudy ships' figureheads and other nautical items. The bar meals are pretty standard, but this is really a drinking pub, and the atmosphere more than compensates. Mon–Sat 11am–11pm, Sun noon–11pm; kitchen daily noon–2.30pm & 6–9.30pm.

Archie Browns Bread St, TR18 2EQ ☎01736 362828, ⓦarchiebrowns.co.uk. Vegans, vegetarians and whole-foodies will be happy in this café above a health shop, with its relaxed, friendly vibe and local art on the walls. Dishes include quiches, curries, stews and homity pie (£6–9). Mon–Sat 9am–5pm.

Old Lifeboat House Wharf Rd, TR18 4AA ☎01736 369409, ⓦoldlifeboathouse.co.uk. On the seafront,

this café-bistro delivers seafood dishes at reasonable prices (around £15 on the evening menu). Apart from the daily specials, you'll find bouillabaisse and fish pie, as well as a couple of meat and vegetarian options. You can also drop by for breakfast, a well-filled sandwich or coffee and cake. Tues–Sat 9.30am–9pm, Sun 9.30am–4pm.

★**The Shore** 13–14 Alverton St, TR18 2QP ☎01736 362444, ⓦtheshorerestaurant.uk. Simple seafood dishes are expertly prepared at this friendly, semiformal restaurant, where starters might include red mullet with chana dal, and mains like hake and steamed sole cost around £19. The desserts are memorably good too. Tues–Thurs 6.30–9pm, Fri & Sat 12.30–1.30pm & 6.30–9pm.

Mousehole

Accounts vary as to the derivation of the name of **MOUSEHOLE** (pronounced "Mowzle"), though it may be from a smugglers' cave just to the south. In any case, the name evokes perfectly this minuscule fishing port cradled in the arms of a granite breakwater, three miles south of Penzance. The village attracts more visitors than it can handle, so hang around until the crowds have departed before exploring its tight tangle of lanes, where you'll come across Mousehole's oldest house, the fourteenth-century **Keigwin House**, a survivor of the sacking of the village by Spaniards in 1595.

ARRIVAL AND DEPARTURE   MOUSEHOLE

By bus The #M6 bus (every 20–30min) connects Mousehole's harbour with Newlyn (10min) and Penzance (15min).

ACCOMMODATION AND EATING

Ship Inn Harbourside, TR19 6QX ☎01736 731234, ⓦshipinnmousehole.co.uk. Overlooking the boats, this is a perfect spot for a pint, or a crab sandwich (£12) or grilled mackerel (£13). Accommodation is available in surprisingly

modern en-suite rooms, some in an annexe (those with a view cost extra). Daily 11am–11pm; kitchen daily noon–2.30pm & 6–8.30pm. **£115**

Porthcurno

Eight miles west of Mousehole, one of Penwith's best **beaches** lies at **PORTHCURNO**, sandwiched between cliffs. On the shore to the east, a white pyramid marks the spot where the first transatlantic cables were laid in 1880. On the headland beyond lies an Iron Age fort, **Treryn Dinas**, close to the famous rocking stone called **Logan Rock**, a seventy-ton monster that was knocked off its perch in 1824 by a gang of sailors, among them a nephew of writer and poet Oliver Goldsmith. Somehow they replaced the stone, but it never rocked again.

Minack Theatre

South end of village, TR19 6JU • Exhibition Centre daily: March–Oct generally 9.30am–5.30pm, but may close at 12.30pm on Tues & Thurs when performances take place; Nov–Feb 10am–4pm; last entry 30min before closing • £5; performances cost £10–14 • ☎ 01736 810181, ⓦ www.minack.com

Steep steps lead up from the beach of tiny white shells to the **Minack Theatre**, hewn out of the cliff in the 1930s and since enlarged to hold 750 seats, though retaining the basic Greek-inspired design. The spectacular backdrop of Porthcurno Bay makes this one of the country's most inspiring theatres (providing the weather holds), where a range of plays, operas and musicals are presented from April to September – bring a cushion and a blanket. The attached **Exhibition Centre** gives access to the theatre during the day and explains the story of its creation.

ARRIVAL AND DEPARTURE
PORTHCURNO

By bus Only one bus service – #A1 – runs to and from Porthcurno, making hourly trips to Land's End (15min), Newlyn (30min) and Penzance (40min).

Land's End and around

The extreme western tip of England, **Land's End**, lies four miles west of Porthcurno. Best approached on foot along the coastal path, the 60ft turf-covered cliffs provide a platform to view the Irish Lady, the Armed Knight, Dr Syntax Head and the rest of the Land's End outcrops. Beyond, look out for the Longships lighthouse, a mile and a half out to sea; you can sometimes spot the Wolf Rock lighthouse, nine miles southwest, or even the Isles of Scilly, 28 miles away (see p.363).

Whitesand Bay

To the north of Land's End the rounded granite cliffs fall away at **Whitesand Bay** to reveal a glistening mile-long shelf of beach that offers the best swimming on the Penwith peninsula. The rollers make for good surfing and boards can be rented at **Sennen Cove**, the more popular southern end of the beach.

St Just-in-Penwith

Three miles north of Sennen Cove, the highly scenic headland of **Cape Cornwall** is dominated by the chimney of the Cape Cornwall Mine, which closed in 1870. Half a mile inland is the grimly grey village of **ST JUST-IN-PENWITH**, formerly a centre of the tin and copper industry, with rows of cottages radiating out from Bank Square. The tone is somewhat lightened by **Plen-an-Gwary**, a grassy open-air theatre where miracle plays were once staged; it was later used by Methodist preachers and Cornish wrestlers.

ARRIVAL AND DEPARTURE
LAND'S END AND AROUND

By bus #A1 and #A3 buses, both hourly, run to and from the car park at Land's End, providing easy connections to Penzance (55min) and St Ives (1hr 20min) respectively. Bus #A3 also runs between Sennen Cove and Land's End (10min), while bus #A17 runs to St Just from Penzance (Mon–Sat hourly, Sun every 2hr; 20–30min).

By plane Land's End Airport, around 1.5 miles south of St Just, handles flights to and from St Mary's in the Isles of Scilly (Mon–Sat: April–Oct 9–17 daily; Nov–March around 10 daily; 20min). For schedules call ☎ 01736 334220 or see ⓦ islesofscilly-travel.co.uk.

ACCOMMODATION

Kelynack Caravan and Camping Park Kelynack, TR19 7RE ☎ 01736 787633, ⓦ kelynackholidays.co.uk. Secluded campsite, one of the few sheltered ones on Penwith, about a mile south of St Just. There are also caravans (from £330/week) and self-catering rooms. Camping/person £8, doubles £70

Trevedra Farm 1 mile north of Sennen, TR19 7BE ☎ 01736 871818, ⓦ trevedrafarm.co.uk. Popular but spacious campsite above Gwynver Beach (at the northern end of Sennen Cove), with level pitches and sea views. There's a modern block providing good facilities, a shop, and a restaurant serving breakfast and dinner.

Closed Nov–Easter. Per person £8
YHA Land's End TR19 7NT ☎ 0345 371 9643, ⓦ yha
.org.uk/hostel/lands-end. Less than a mile south of St Just
and a half-mile from the coast path, this hostel offers a
kitchen, meals and camping facilities with a bell tent to rent
(June to mid-Sept; £59). Take the left fork past the post
office in St Just to find it. Only groups can book late Oct to
Easter. Camping/person £13, dorms £16, doubles £39

EATING

Kegen Teg 12 Market Square, St Just, TR19 7HD
☎ 01736 788562. Locally sourced ingredients go into the
tasty breakfasts, home-made cakes and ice cream served
here. You'll also find fresh juices, organic coffee and a range
of snacks – try the falafel or Welsh rarebit (around £8).
Mon–Sat 10am–5pm.

Old Success Inn Sennen Cove, TR19 7DG ☎ 01736
871232, ⓦ oldsuccess.co.uk. Excellent seaside pub
offering craft ales, baguettes (£6–7) and bar meals such as
Korean spiced chicken (£13) and local mussels (£16).
Rooms with sea views are also available (£110). Daily
11am–11pm; kitchen daily noon–9pm.

Zennor and around

Eight miles northeast of St Just, set in a landscape of rolling granite moorland, **ZENNOR** is
where D.H. Lawrence came to live with his wife Frieda in 1916. "It is a most beautiful
place," he wrote, "lovelier even than the Mediterranean". The Lawrences stayed a year and a
half in the village – long enough for him to write *Women in Love* – before being given notice
to quit by the local constabulary, who suspected them of unpatriotic sympathies (their
Cornish experiences were later described in *Kangaroo*). At the top of the lane, the church of
St Sennen displays a sixteenth-century bench carving of a mermaid who, according to local
legend, was so entranced by the singing of a chorister that she lured him down to the sea,
from where he never returned – though his song can still occasionally be heard.

Chysauster

2 miles inland from Zennor, TR20 8XA • Daily: April–June & Sept 10am–5pm; July & Aug 10am–6pm; Oct 10am–4pm • £4.60; EH •
☎ 07831 757934, ⓦ www.english-heritage.org.uk/visit/places/chysauster-ancient-village

On a windy hillside a couple of miles inland from Zennor, the Iron Age village of
Chysauster is the best-preserved ancient settlement in the southwest. Dating from
about the first century BC, it contains two rows of four buildings, each consisting of a
courtyard with small chambers leading off it, and a garden that was presumably used
for growing vegetables.

ARRIVAL AND DEPARTURE   ZENNOR AND AROUND

By bus The #A3 service from St Ives (hourly; 20min) and
#16A from Penzance (Mon–Sat 4 daily; 20–40min) stop
near the turn-off for Zennor. From here it's a short stroll into
the village.

ACCOMMODATION AND EATING

Gurnard's Head Treen, TR26 3DE, a mile west of
Zennor ☎ 01736 796928, ⓦ gurnardshead.co.uk. This
relaxed gastropub serves delicious meals (set-price menus,
otherwise mains around £17 at lunchtime, £20 eves;
booking advised) and a good selection of wines and beers.
Smallish B&B rooms are also available. Daily 8am–11pm;
kitchen daily noon–2.30pm & 6–9/9.30pm. £120

Zennor Chapel TR26 3DA ☎ 01736 798307, ⓦ zennor
chapelguesthouse.com. This guesthouse in a former
Wesleyan chapel has five en-suite rooms, each with space
for two to four people. The café downstairs turns out
breakfasts 8–9.30am (£5, not included in rate), and sells
snacks (£6.50–8), coffees and cakes throughout the
day. £80

St Ives

East of Zennor, the road runs four hilly miles on to the steeply built town of **ST IVES**.
By the time the pilchard reserves dried up around the early 1900s, the town was
beginning to attract a vibrant **artists' colony**, precursors of the wave later headed by
Ben Nicholson, Barbara Hepworth, Naum Gabo and the potter Bernard Leach, who in
the 1960s were followed by a third wave including Peter Lanyon and Patrick Heron.

6

Tate St Ives

Porthmeor Beach, TR26 1TG • March–Oct daily 10am–5.20pm; Nov–Feb Tues–Sun 10am–4.20pm; closes for one week three times a year • £9.50, £13 with Hepworth Museum • ☎ 01736 796226, ⓦ tate.org.uk/visit/tate-st-ives

The place to view the best work created in St Ives is the **Tate St Ives**, overlooking Porthmeor Beach on the north side of town. Most of the paintings, sculptures and ceramics displayed within the airy, gleaming-white building date from 1925 to 1975, with specially commissioned contemporary works also on view as well as exhibitions. The gallery's rooftop **café** is a splendid spot for a coffee.

Barbara Hepworth Museum

Barnoon Hill, TR26 1AD • March–Oct daily 10am–5.20pm; Nov–Feb Tues–Sun 10am–4.20pm; closes for one week three times a year • £7.50, £13 with Tate • ☎ 01924 247360, ⓦ tate.org.uk/visit/tate-st-ives

Not far from the Tate, the **Barbara Hepworth Museum** provides further insight into the local arts scene. One of the foremost nonfigurative sculptors of her time, Hepworth lived in the building from 1949 until her death in a studio fire in 1975. Apart from the sculptures, which are arranged in positions chosen by Hepworth in the house and garden, the museum has background on her art, from photos and letters to catalogues and reviews.

The beaches

Porthmeor Beach dominates the northern side of St Ives, its excellent water quality and surfer-friendly rollers drawing a regular crowd, while the broader **Porthminster Beach**, south of the station, is usually less busy. A third town beach, the small and sheltered **Porthgwidden**, lies in the lee of the prong of land separating Porthmeor and Porthminster, while east of town a string of magnificent golden beaches lines **St Ives Bay** on either side of the Hayle estuary.

ARRIVAL AND INFORMATION ST IVES

By train Trains from Penzance (most via St Erth; roughly hourly; 30min–1hr) arrive at the train station on Trelyon Ave, off Porthminster Beach.

By bus The bus station is on Station Hill, just off The Terrace.

Destinations Penzance (Mon–Sat 3 hourly, Sun 2 hourly;

35–55min); Plymouth (3 daily; 3hr–3hr 30min); Truro (Mon–Sat every 30min, Sun hourly; 1hr 35min).

Tourist office In St Ives library, Gabriel St (May & June daily 10am–4pm; July–Sept Mon–Sat 10am–5pm, Sun 10am–4pm; Oct–April Mon–Sat 10am–3pm; ☎ 01736 796297, ⓦ stives-cornwall.co.uk).

ACCOMMODATION

Cohort Hostel The Stennack, TR26 1FF ☎ 01736 791664, ⓦ stayatcohort.co.uk. Centrally located in a restored Wesleyan chapel school from 1845, this hostel has a clean, modern feel, with mixed or single-sex dorms, double and twin rooms, a bar and a kitchen. Only groups can book Nov–Feb. Dorms **£24**, doubles **£50**

Cornerways 1 Bethesda Place, TR26 1PA ☎ 01736 796706, ⓦ cornerwaysstives.com. Daphne du Maurier once stayed here; it's now a modern cottage conversion with friendly owners and small, bright rooms. Ask about complimentary tickets for the Tate and Hepworth galleries. No credit cards. **£100**

★ **Little Leaf** 16 Park Ave, TR26 2DN ☎ 01736 795427,

ⓦ littleleafguesthouse.co.uk. With friendly young hosts and local art on the walls, this guesthouse has six en-suite rooms, two with fantastic views. Breakfasts are fresh and use locally sourced ingredients. Two- to three-night minimum stay March–Oct. **£85**

Primrose Valley Porthminster Beach, TR26 2ED ☎ 01736 794939, ⓦ primroseonline.co.uk. Relaxed boutique hotel, a level walk from the centre and the train station and Porthminster Beach (from which it's separated by the railway). The chic, contemporary rooms, some with balconies, are fresh and light, though some are small and viewless. Closed mid-Dec to mid-Feb. **£175**

EATING

Alba Wharf Rd, TR26 1LF ☎ 01736 797222, ⓦ alba -stives.co.uk. Sleekly modern harbourfront restaurant with top-class seafood, including a superb fish soup (£8). Set-price menus (£24 & £28) are available 6–7.30pm, otherwise

mains are around £18. Daily 11am–2pm & 6–10pm.

Blas Burgerworks The Warren, TR26 2EA ☎ 01736 797272, ⓦ blasburgerworks.co.uk. This diminutive spot doles out extremely good burgers (£11–13), using local ingredients. There's just one small room with communal tables made from found or reclaimed wood. No reservations. Mid-Feb to Nov daily 5–9.30pm.

The Cornish Deli 3 Chapel St, TR26 2LR ☎01736 795100 ✪cornishdeli.com. The tables fill up quickly at this cosy café and deli, which sells excellent sandwiches (using meat from the local butcher's shop), as well as wine, Cornish chocolate, West Country cheeses and the like. In summer, bistro-style meals are served in the evenings, including tapas (£6–7) and chorizo and squid (£13). No credit cards. Mon–Sat 9.30am–4/5pm, school hols daily 9.30am–9.30pm.

★**Porthminster Café** Porthminster Beach, TR26 2EB ☎01736 795352, ✪porthminstercafe.co.uk. With its sun deck and beach location, this is an appealing venue for coffees, snack lunches and sophisticated seafood dinners (mains around £22; book ahead). Late Feb to Dec daily 9am–9.30pm; reduced hours in winter.

6

The Isles of Scilly

The **ISLES OF SCILLY** are a compact archipelago of about a hundred islands, 28 miles southwest of Land's End. None is bigger than three miles across, and only five of them are inhabited – **St Mary's**, **Tresco**, **Bryher**, **St Martin's** and **St Agnes**. In the annals of folklore, the Scillies are the peaks of the submerged land of Lyonnesse, a fertile plain that extended west from Penwith before the ocean broke in, drowning the land and leaving only one survivor to tell the tale. In fact they form part of the same granite mass as Land's End, Bodmin Moor and Dartmoor, and despite rarely rising above 100ft, they possess a remarkable variety of landscape. Points of interest include irresistible **beaches**, such as Par Beach on St Martin's; the southwest's greatest concentration of **prehistoric remains**; some fabulous **rock formations**; and the impressive **Tresco Abbey Gardens**.

Along with tourism, the main source of income is flower-growing, for which the equable climate and long hours of sunshine – their name means "Sun Isles" – make the islands ideal. The profusion of **wildflowers** is even more noticeable than the fields of narcissi and daffodils, and the heaths and pathways are often dense with marigolds, gorse, sea thrift, trefoil and poppies, not to mention a host of more exotic varieties introduced by visiting foreign vessels. The waters hereabouts are held to be among the country's best for **diving**, while between May and September, on a Wednesday or Friday evening, islanders gather for **gig races**, performed by six-oared vessels – some of them more than a hundred years old and 30ft long.

Free of traffic, theme parks and amusement arcades, the islands are a welcome respite from the tourist trail, the main drawbacks being the high cost of reaching them and the shortage of **accommodation**, most of which is on the main isle of St Mary's.

St Mary's

The majority of the resident population of just over two thousand is concentrated on the biggest island, **ST MARY'S**, which has the lion's share of facilities in its capital, **Hugh Town**, and the richest trove of prehistoric sites. The cove-fringed island is also home to **Star Castle**, a huge eight-pointed fortress that was originally built to deter Spanish invasions, and is now a four-star hotel.

Tresco

The second-largest island, **TRESCO**, presents an appealing contrast between the orderly landscape around the remains of its ancient abbey and the bleak, untended northern half. The exuberant **Abbey Garden** (daily 10am–4pm; £15; ☎01720 424108, ✪tresco.co.uk) hosts an impressive collection of subtropical plants.

Bryher

West of Tresco, **BRYHER** has the smallest population, the slow routines of island life quickening only in the tourist season. The bracing, back-to-nature feel here is nowhere

6

more evident than on the exposed western shore, where **Hell Bay** sees some formidable Atlantic storms.

St Martin's

East of Tresco, **ST MARTIN'S** has some of the archipelago's most majestic white-sand beaches – **Par Beach** deserves a special mention. There are stunning views from its cliffy northeastern end, and the surrounding waters are much favoured by scuba enthusiasts.

St Agnes

On the southwest rim of the main island group, the tidy lanes and picturesque cottages of **ST AGNES** are nicely complemented by the weathered boulders and craggy headlands of its indented shoreline. Many of the islanders still make their living by farming **flowers**, and you'll find plenty of tranquil spots even in summer.

The uninhabited isles

A visit to the Scillies would be incomplete without a sortie to the **uninhabited isles**, sanctuaries for seals, puffins and other marine birdlife. On the largest, **SAMSON**, you can poke around prehistoric and more recent remains that testify to former settlement. Some of the smaller islets are worth visiting for their delightfully deserted beaches, though the majority amount to no more than bare rocks. This chaotic profusion of rocks of all shapes and sizes, each bearing a name, is densest at the archipelago's extremities – the **Western Rocks**, lashed by ferocious seas and home to Bishop's Rock Lighthouse (Britain's tallest and most westerly lighthouse), and the milder **Eastern Isles**.

ARRIVAL AND DEPARTURE   THE ISLES OF SCILLY

Transport to the Isles of Scilly – by plane and by boat – is currently operated solely by **Isles of Scilly Travel** (☎01736 334220, ⓦislesofscilly-travel.co.uk). At time of writing, a helicopter service run by a separate company is under discussion and may begin operating in 2018; check ⓦpenzanceheliport.co.uk for updates.

By plane The departure points for flights are Land's End Airport (near St Just; Mon–Sat 9–17 daily; 20min), Newquay (Mon–Sat 3–6 daily; 30min) and Exeter (Mon–Sat 3–5 daily; 1hr); in winter (usually Nov–Feb) there are departures only from Land's End and Newquay. The fare for a one-way flight from Land's End starts at £70.

By boat Boats to St Mary's depart from Penzance's South Pier between Easter and early Nov (2hr 45min). A one-way fare from Penzance costs from £45.

GETTING AROUND AND INFORMATION

By boat Boats link each of the inhabited islands, though services are sporadic in winter. The St Mary's Boatmen's Association (☎01720 423999, ⓦscillyboating.co.uk) publishes up-to-date timetables and fares online. Ask the Association about trips to the uninhabited isles, or look out for boards advertising excursions.

By bike Cycling is the ideal way to get around (bikes can be taken on ferries from the mainland for £13 each way).

Alternatively, you can rent bikes from St Mary's Bike Hire in Porthmellon Business Park, off Telegraph Rd just outside Hugh Town (£12.50/day; ☎07552 994709, ⓦstmarys bikehire.co.uk).

Tourist office Schiller Shelter, Porthcressa beachfront, St Mary's (March–Oct Mon–Sat 9am–5pm, Sun 9am–2pm; Nov–Feb Mon–Fri 10am–2pm; ☎01720 424031, ⓦvisitislesofscilly.com).

ACCOMMODATION

St Mary's has the great majority of the **accommodation** on the islands; the smaller isles (excepting Tresco) each have two or three B&Bs only, and these are booked up early. Tresco and St Martin's have luxury hotels, and all the islands except Tresco have **campsites**, which usually close in winter. See ⓦvisitislesofscilly.com for complete accommodation lists.

Fuchsia Cottage Middle Town, St Martin's, TR25 0QN ☎ 01720 422023, ⓦ scillyman.co.uk. This simple, white-washed cottage has two rooms with en-suite or shared facilities, and home-made bread for breakfast. No debit/credit cards. Closed Nov–Feb. **£70**

★ **Mincarlo** Carn Thomas, Hugh Town, St Mary's, TR21 0PT ☎ 01720 422513, ⓦ mincarloscilly.com. With modern decor in a traditional building, this B&B has fantastic views. Most rooms have big windows, though the cheapest (on the ground floor) don't overlook the sea. The terrace is a great suntrap, and top-quality meals are available some evenings. **£92**

Old Chapel Old Town Lane, Old Town, St Mary's, TR21 0NN

☎ 01720 422100, ⓦ theoldchapelislesofscilly.co.uk. A 15min walk east of Hugh Town, this former Wesleyan meeting hall has two spacious rooms, one with a separate sun lounge. You can sit outside in the lush garden or in the conservatory. Minimum two-night stay. No debit/credit cards. **£100**

Polreath Higher Town, St Martin's, TR25 0QL ☎ 01720 422046, ⓦ polreath.com. Three smartly furnished rooms with sea views are available at this B&B, with a conservatory and garden. Daytime meals are served in the popular tearoom, as well as evening meals three times a week. The minimum stay is five days in April, one week (from Fri) at other times. No credit cards. Closed Oct–March. **£120**

6

EATING AND DRINKING

St Mary's has most of the **restaurants** and **pubs**. Each of the other inhabited islands has a pub serving food and one or two cafés, while all hotels and some B&Bs also provide meals.

Juliet's Garden Restaurant Porthloo, St Mary's, TR21 0NF ☎ 01720 422228, ⓦ julietsgardenrestaurant .co.uk. With garden terraces and panoramic sea views, this restaurant just outside Hugh Town serves snacks, cakes and teas by day, and in the evenings (for which booking is essential) dishes might include braised organic beef and pan-roasted bream fillets (mostly £13–19). Easter–Oct daily 10am–5pm, plus most eves until 9.30pm.

Seven Stones Inn Lower Town, St Martin's, TR25 0QW ☎ 01720 423777. This place boasts the best views of any Scillies pub, and offers a good selection of ales and meals – soups, salads, ciabattas, burgers (£11) and dishes like couscous with halloumi (£9.50). There's occasional live music and film screenings. April–Oct Mon–Sat

11am–11pm, Sun noon–10.30pm; Nov–March Wed & (sometimes) Fri 6–11pm, Sun noon–6pm.

★ **Turk's Head** Porth Conger, St Agnes, TR22 0PL ☎ 01720 422434. Sited just above the jetty, with plenty of outdoor seating, this pub serves superb St Agnes pasties (£4.75) as well as a range of meat, seafood and veggie dishes (around £11) to accompany local beers. Easter–Oct Mon–Sat 10.30am–11.30pm, Sun 10.30am–10.30pm; kitchen Easter–Oct daily noon–2/2.30pm & 6–8/9pm.

Vine Café Below Watch Hill, Bryher, TR23 0PR ☎ 01720 423168. Hot snacks, sandwiches and cakes are sold during the day, and there are twice-weekly set evening meals (£21; bookings only, BYOB). No debit/credit cards. Easter–Oct Mon & Thurs–Sat 10.30am–4pm, Wed & Sun 10.30am–4pm & 7–9.30pm.

Cornwall's Atlantic coast

The north Cornish coast is punctuated by some of the finest beaches in England, the most popular of which are to be found around **Newquay**, the surfers' capital, and **Padstow**, also renowned for its gourmet seafood restaurants. North of the Camel estuary, the coast features an almost unbroken line of cliffs as far as the Devon border; this gaunt, exposed terrain makes a melodramatic setting for **Tintagel Castle** and nearby **Boscastle**. There are more good beaches at **Bude**, **St Agnes** and **Polzeath**.

St Agnes and around

Though surrounded by ruined engine houses, the village of **ST AGNES** gives little hint of the conditions in which its population once lived, with the uniform grey ex-miners' cottages now fronted by immaculate flower-filled gardens, and its steep, straggling streets busy in summer with troops of holiday-makers.

At the end of a steep valley below St Agnes, **Trevaunance Cove** is the site of several failed attempts to create a harbour for the town, and now has a fine sandy beach. West of the village lies one of Cornwall's most famous vantage points, **St Agnes Beacon**, 630ft high, from which views extend inland to Bodmin Moor and even across the peninsula to St Michael's Mount. To the northwest, the headland of **St Agnes Head** has the area's largest colony of breeding kittiwakes, and the nearby cliffs also shelter fulmars and guillemots, while grey seals are a common sight offshore.

Four miles north of St Agnes, **PERRANPORTH** lies at the southern end of **Perran Beach**, a two-mile expanse of sand enhanced by caves and natural rock arches. It's very popular with surfers – boards and equipment are available to rent in summer.

<table>
<tr><td>**ARRIVAL AND DEPARTURE**</td><td style="text-align:right">**ST AGNES AND AROUND**</td></tr>
</table>

By bus The hourly #87 service goes to St Agnes from Truro (30min) and Newquay (55min), with a stop at Perranporth.

Newquay

In a superb position on a knuckle of cliffs overlooking fine golden sands and Atlantic rollers, its glorious natural advantages have made **NEWQUAY** the premier resort of north Cornwall. The "new quay" in question was built in the fifteenth century in what was already a long-established fishing port, up to then more colourfully known as Towan Blistra. The town was given a boost in the nineteenth century when a railway was constructed across the peninsula for china clay shipments; with the trains came a swelling stream of seasonal visitors.

Today, the town centre is a tacky parade of shops, bars and restaurants from which lanes lead to ornamental gardens and clifftop lawns. The main attraction is the **beaches**. A number of **surfing competitions** and festivals run through the summer, when Newquay can get very crowded – it's also popular with stag and hen parties.

The beaches

All Newquay's beaches can be reached fairly easily on foot from the centre, otherwise take bus #A5 for Porth Beach and Watergate Bay, #85 for Crantock and Holywell Bay

Close to the centre of town, **Towan Beach**, **Great Western Beach** and **Tolcarne Beach** are the most sheltered of the seven miles of firm sand that line the coast around Newquay, and all get very busy with families in high season. Together with **Porth Beach**, with its grassy headland further east, these are popular with bodyboarders and novice and intermediate surfers all year. Experienced surfers are generally more partial to **Watergate Bay** to the north, and the more exposed **Fistral Bay**, west of Towan Head. Fistral is also the venue for national and international surfing competitions.

On the other side of East Pentire Head from Fistral, **Crantock Beach** – reachable over the Gannel River by ferry or upstream footbridge – is usually less crowded, and has a

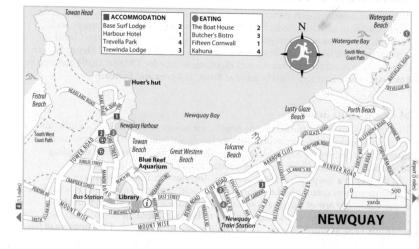

■ ACCOMMODATION		● EATING	
Base Surf Lodge	2	The Boat House	2
Harbour Hotel	1	Butcher's Bistro	3
Trevella Park	4	Fifteen Cornwall	1
Trewinda Lodge	3	Kahuna	4

NEWQUAY

TOP 5 DEVON AND CORNWALL SURF SPOTS

Croyde Bay See p.344
Fistral Bay See opposite
Watergate Bay See opposite

Polzeath See p.369
Whitesand Bay See p.360

lovely backdrop of dunes and undulating grassland. South of Crantock, **Holywell Bay** and Perran Beach (see opposite) are also very popular with surfers.

6

ARRIVAL AND DEPARTURE

NEWQUAY

By plane Newquay's airport is at St Mawgan, 5 miles northeast of town, with connections to major British and Irish cities, and linked to town by bus #A5.
Destinations London Gatwick (1–3 daily; 1hr 10min); Manchester (1–2 daily; 1hr 20min); St Mary's, Isles of Scilly (Mon–Sat 3–6 daily; 30min).
By train Newquay is served by trains from Par (Mon–Sat 6–7 daily, Sun 3–5 daily; 50min); the train station is off

Cliff Rd, a short walk east of the centre.
By bus The bus station is on Manor Rd, near the tourist office.
Destinations Bodmin (4 daily; 30–55min); Padstow (hourly; 1hr 20min–1hr 30min); Plymouth (4–5 daily; 1hr 35min–2hr); St Austell (Mon–Sat hourly, Sun every 2hr; 1hr–1hr 15min); Truro (Mon–Sat 3 hourly, Sun 1–2 hourly; 55min–1hr 30min).

INFORMATION AND ACTIVITIES

Tourist office Marcus Hill (April–Sept Mon–Fri 9.15am–5.30pm, Sat & Sun 10am–4pm; Oct–March Mon–Fri 10am–4pm, Sat & Sun 10am–3pm; ☎01637 838516, ⓦ visitnewquay.org).
Surfing Newquay's surfing buzz is infectious enough to tempt scores of non-surfheads to try their hand

every summer. Equipment is available to rent or buy from beach stalls and shops along Fore St, Tower Rd and Cliff Rd (£5–15/day for board or wetsuit rental). Dozens of local outfits arrange surfing coaching and courses year-round. For surf reports and webcam images, see ⓦ magicseaweed.com.

ACCOMMODATION

Base Surf Lodge 20 Tower Rd, TR7 1LR ☎07766 132124, ⓦ basesurflodge.co.uk; map p.366. A good central option for small groups, with fresh, private bunk rooms sleeping 2–6 people. It's surfer-friendly, with board storage facilities and free hot drinks to warm you up post-surf. Beginners should ask about their surf and stay packages, which include lessons. No credit cards. Closed Oct–March. Dorms **£25**
Harbour Hotel North Quay Hill, TR7 1HF ☎01637 873040, ⓦ harbourhotel.co.uk; map p.366. Small, luxurious hotel with stunning views from its stylish rooms, all of which have balconies. Some rooms are tiny, so check first. **£180**

Trevella Park Near Crantock, 1.5 miles southwest of town, TR8 5EW ☎01637 830308, ⓦ trevella.co.uk; map p.366. It can feel crowded at peak times, but this remains one of the better holiday parks near Newquay, with good, clean facilities for campers and a heated outdoor pool. Apart from camping pitches, they offer "Ready Tents" sleeping four (three nights £221) and static caravans sleeping six (three nights £284), both self-catering, among other options. Camping **£21**
Trewinda Lodge 17 Eliot Gardens, TR7 2QE ☎01637 877533, ⓦ trewinda-lodge.co.uk; map p.366. The owners of this B&B, close to Tolcarne Beach, can give informed advice to surfers (they also run Dolphin Surf School). Rooms are on the small side, but clean and comfortable. **£60**

EATING

The Boat House Newquay Harbour, TR7 1HT ☎01637 874062, ⓦ the-boathouse-newquay.co.uk; map p.366. Seafood is the main event at this atmospheric bar and restaurant situated right by the old harbour. The menu includes hake, haddock, crab (£11–17) and whatever else appears on the daily specials board. Easter–Nov daily 10am–11pm; kitchen Easter–June & Oct daily noon–3pm & 6–10pm, July–Sept daily noon–10pm.
Butcher's Bistro 26 Cliff Rd, TR7 2ND ☎01637 874470, ⓦ butchers-bistro.co.uk; map p.366. This small eatery is renowned for its steaks and seafood. For a real treat try the

seafood *marinière* – a big, steaming bowl of prawns, crab claws, mussels and boneless fish (£20). Daily 6–9pm; Sept–June closed Wed.
★**Fifteen Cornwall** Watergate Bay, TR8 4AA ☎01637 861000, ⓦ fifteencornwall.co.uk; map p.366. Overlooking the beach, this contemporary restaurant set up by TV chef Jamie Oliver showcases the culinary talents of trainee chefs. The Italian-inspired but locally sourced dishes are inventive and delicious; set menus are £26–40 at lunchtime, £65 in the evening, and breakfasts are also worth tucking into. Daily 8.30–10am, noon–2.30pm & 6.15–9.15pm.

6

★**Kahuna** Station Approach, TR7 2NG ☎01637 850440, ⊛kahunarestaurant.co.uk; map p.366. Mouth-watering Asian dishes from *tom yum* seafood soup to beef rendang are presented beautifully at this friendly, relaxed and modern restaurant. Mains are £12–15. Daily 6pm–late.

Padstow and around

PADSTOW attracts nearly as many holiday-makers as Newquay, but has a very different feel. Enclosed within the estuary of the Camel – the only river outlet of any size on Cornwall's north coast – the town has long retained its position as North Cornwall's principal fishing port, and can boast some of the county's best seafood **restaurants**. The **harbour** is jammed with launches and boats offering cruises in the bay, while a **ferry** (see below) carries people across the river to **ROCK** – close to the isolated church of **St Enodoc** (John Betjeman's burial place) and to the good beaches around Polzeath. Padstow is also known for its annual **Obby Oss** festival, a May Day romp when a local in horse costume prances through the town preceded by a masked and club-wielding "teaser", in a spirited reenactment of an old fertility rite.

Church of St Petroc

Church Lane, PL28 8BG · Daily 9.30am–5pm, closes 4pm in winter · ☎ 01841 533776, ⊛ padstowparishchurch.org.uk

Set on the hill overlooking Padstow, the **Church of St Petroc** is dedicated to Cornwall's most important saint, a Welsh or Irish monk who landed here in the sixth century, died in the area and gave his name to the town – "Petrock's Stow". The building has a fine fifteenth-century font, an Elizabethan pulpit and some amusing carved bench ends – seek out the one to the right of the altar depicting a fox preaching to a congregation of geese.

Prideaux Place

Half a mile west of the quay, PL28 8RP · Easter to early Oct Mon–Thurs & Sun 1.30–4pm; grounds 12.30–5pm · £9 · ☎ 01841 532411, ⊛ prideauxplace.co.uk

Padstow's ancient Prideaux family – whose Cornish origins date back to the Normans – still occupy **Prideaux Place**, an Elizabethan manor house with grand staircases, richly furnished rooms full of portraits, fantastically ornate ceilings and formal gardens. You might recognize some parts of the house, which is used extensively for location filming and has appeared in a plethora of films, including *Oscar and Lucinda* (1997).

The beaches

The area immediately west of Padstow has some fine **beaches** – all within a short walk or drive of the town. On the west side of the estuary, round **Stepper Point**, you can reach the sandy and secluded **Harlyn Bay** and, turning the corner southwards, **Constantine Bay**, the best surfing beach hereabouts. The dunes backing the beach and the rock pools skirting it make this one of the most appealing bays on this coast, though the tides can be treacherous and bathing hazardous near the rocks. Three or four miles further south, the slate outcrops of **Bedruthan Steps** were traditionally held to be the stepping-stones of a giant; they can be readily viewed from the clifftop path and the B3276, with steps descending to the broad beach below (not safe for swimming).

ARRIVAL AND DEPARTURE
PADSTOW AND AROUND

By bus Buses #A5 from Newquay (hourly; 1hr 20min) and #11A from Bodmin (Mon–Sat hourly, Sun 6 daily; 50min) pull in on Station Rd, above the harbour.

GETTING AROUND AND INFORMATION

By ferry The ferry across the river to Rock operates daily year-round, roughly every 20min during the day (£4 return; ⊛ padstow-harbour.co.uk).

By bus Bus #A5 (hourly) connects Padstow with Harlyn Bay (10min) and Constantine Bay (15min). Every 1–2hr, the same bus calls at Bedruthan (40min).

THE CAMEL TRAIL AND THE SAINTS' WAY

The old railway line between Padstow and Wadebridge has been converted into an excellent **cycle track** that forms part of the **Camel Trail**, a fifteen-mile traffic-free path that follows the river up as far as Wenfordbridge, on the edge of Bodmin Moor, with a turn-off for Bodmin. The five-mile Padstow–Wadebridge stretch offers glimpses of a variety of birdlife, especially around the small **Pinkson Creek**, habitat of terns, herons, curlews and egrets.

You can **rent bikes** from Trail Bike Hire (☎01841 532594, ⓦtrailbikehire.co.uk; £14/day) and Padstow Cycle Hire (☎01841 533533, ⓦpadstowcyclehire.com; £16/day), both on South Quay, by the start of the Camel Trail. Further up the Trail at Wadebridge, Bridge Bike Hire (☎01208 813050, ⓦbridgebikehire.co.uk; £12/day) has a greater stock, though it's still advisable to reserve.

Padstow also marks one end of the thirty-mile cross-peninsula **Saints' Way**, linking up with Fowey on Cornwall's south coast (see p.349). Leaflets and books detailing the walk are available from the tourist offices at Padstow, Bodmin and Fowey.

6

Tourist office North Quay, by the harbour (April to late July, Sept & Oct Mon–Fri 10am–5pm, Sat & Sun 10am–4pm; late July & Aug Mon–Fri 9.30am–5.30pm, Sat & Sun 10am–4.30pm; Nov–March Mon–Sat 10am–4pm; ☎01841 533449, ⓦpadstowlive.com).

ACCOMMODATION

St Petroc's Hotel New St, PL28 8EA ☎01841 532700, ⓦrickstein.com. Restaurateur Rick Stein has extended his Padstow empire to include classy accommodation, including this chic little lodging away from the harbour, with modern decor and outstanding breakfasts. But even the very small rooms are pricey. **£175**

Treverbyn House Treverbyn Rd, PL28 8DA ☎01841 532855, ⓦtreverbynhouse.com. A short walk up from the harbour, this elegant Edwardian B&B has large,

beautifully furnished rooms. Breakfast is served in the dining room or on a terrace in the garden with views over the river. No debit/credit cards. **£130**

YHA Treyarnon Bay Treyarnon, PL28 8JR, 4.5 miles west of Padstow ☎345 371 9664, ⓦyha.org.uk/hostel /treyarnon. Perfectly sited hostel in a 1930s summer villa right by the beach. Take bus #A5 from Padstow or Newquay to Constantine, then walk half a mile. Surf packages available. Camping/person **£15**, dorms **£15**, doubles **£39**, bell tents **£59**

EATING

Foodies know Padstow for its high-class **restaurants**, particularly those associated with star chef **Rick Stein**; the waiting list for a table at one of his establishments can be months long, though a weekday reservation out of season might mean booking only a day or two ahead. For something a little cheaper, try Stein's fish and chip shop or his deli, both on South Quay.

Prawn on the Lawn 11 Duke St, PL28 8AB ☎01841 532223, ⓦprawnonthelawn.com. Part fishmonger, part rough-and-ready bistro, this place is usually abuzz with cheerful diners. Menus are based on what's on display: small plates such as spiced mackerel, marinated scallops and Szechuan prawns cost £7–10, larger platters are £16–30. Book ahead. Tues–Sat noon–10pm.

★**The Seafood Restaurant** Riverside, PL28 8BY ☎01841 532700, ⓦrickstein.com. The core of Rick Stein's culinary empire, this is one of Britain's top places for fish, with most mains – Singapore chilli crab, hake *en papillote*, seafood curry – costing £25–35. Daily noon–2.30pm & 6.30–9.30pm.

Polzeath and around

Facing west into Padstow Bay, the beaches around **POLZEATH** are the finest in the vicinity, pelted by rollers that make **Hayle Bay**, in particular, one of the most popular **surfing** venues in the West Country. A mile south of Polzeath, **Daymer Bay** is more favoured by the windsurfing crowd. All the gear can be rented from shops on the beach, where you can get information on tuition, and there are campsites and bars in the vicinity.

Head east and the coastal path brings you through clifftop growths of feathery tamarisk, which flower spectacularly in July and August. From the headland of **Pentire Point**, views unfold for miles over the offshore islets of **The Mouls** and **Newland**, which foster populations of grey seals and puffins. Half a mile east, the scanty remains of an

6

Iron Age fort stand on **Rump's Point**, from where the path descends a mile or so to **Lundy Bay**, a pleasant sandy cove surrounded by green fields. Climbing again, you pass the shafts of an old antimony mine on the way to **Doyden Point**, which is picturesquely ornamented with a nineteenth-century castle folly once used for gambling parties.

Port Isaac

Beyond the inlet of **Port Quin**, the next settlement of any size is **PORT ISAAC**, wedged in a gap in the precipitous cliff wall and dedicated to the crab and lobster trade. The cramped village, whose narrow lanes lead down to a pebble beach where rock pools are exposed at low tide, has become increasingly popular with tourists in recent years thanks to its role in the British TV series *Doc Martin*.

ARRIVAL AND GETTING AROUND

By bus The area's most useful bus service is #96, which connects Polzeath with Rock (5 daily; 10min), Port Isaac (5 daily; 20min), Wadebridge (5 daily; 30min) and Camelford (2–5 daily; 45min). Coming from further afield (eg Newquay or Bodmin) involves a change at Wadebridge.

POLZEATH AND AROUND

ACCOMMODATION AND EATING

The Golden Lion Fore St, Port Isaac, PL29 3RB ☎01208 880336, ⓦthegoldenlionportisaac.co.uk. Traditional harbourside pub with bare floorboards and nautical decor. There's a separate upstairs restaurant and a small outdoor terrace. Bar meals (£8–16) are available in generous portions. Mon–Thurs & Sat noon–11pm, Fri noon–midnight, Sun noon–10.30pm; kitchen daily noon–3pm & 5–9pm.

★**The Old School Hotel** Fore St, Port Isaac, PL29 3RD ☎01208 880721, ⓦtheoldschoolhotel.co.uk. Overlooking the harbour, this place comes with quirky, contemporary rooms (some cramped), a good restaurant (mains around £15), parking and great views. Mon–Thurs & Sun noon–2.30pm & 6–9pm, Fri & Sat noon–2.30pm & 6–9.30pm. **£119**

Valley Caravan Park 200m south of Polzeath's beach, signposted up the lane behind the shop, PL27 6SS ☎01208 862391. Accommodation around Polzeath is scarce, but this is a useful campsite, with a stream running through that attracts ducks and geese. Closed late Sept to Easter. **£19**

The Waterfront Beach Rd, Polzeath, PL27 6SP ☎01208 869655, ⓦwaterfrontpolzeath.co.uk. A relaxed café/restaurant just back from the beach, with a first-floor terrace and an eclectic menu that includes burgers (£11), pizzas (£12) and seafood dishes (£12–17). Daily 9am–11pm; last food orders 9pm.

Tintagel

Despite its romantic name and its famous **castle** standing aloof on a promontory to the north, the village of **TINTAGEL** is for the most part a dreary collection of cafés and B&Bs. Apart from the castle, Tintagel has one other item of genuine interest: the **Old Post Office** on Fore Street (daily: mid-Feb, early March to early April & late Sept to Oct 11am–4pm; early April to late Sept 10.30am–5.30pm; £4, NT; ☎01840 770024, ⓦnationaltrust.org.uk/tintagel-old-post-office), a slate-built, rickety-roofed construction dating from the fourteenth century, now restored to its appearance in the Victorian era.

Tintagel Castle

Half a mile northwest of the village, PL34 0HE • Mid- to late Feb daily 10am–4pm; late Feb to March Wed–Sun 10am–4pm; April–Sept daily 10am–6pm; Oct daily 10am–5pm; Nov to mid-Feb Sat & Sun 10am–4pm • £8.40; EH • ☎01840 770328, ⓦwww.english-heritage.org.uk /visit/places/tintagel-castle

The wild and unspoilt coast around Tintagel provides an appropriate backdrop for the forsaken ruins of **Tintagel Castle**. It was the twelfth-century chronicler Geoffrey of Monmouth who first popularized the notion that this was the **birthplace of King Arthur**, son of Uther Pendragon and Ygrayne, though the visible ruins in fact belong to a Norman stronghold occupied by the earls of Cornwall. After sporadic spurts of rebuilding, the castle was allowed to decay, and most of it had been washed into the sea by the sixteenth century. The remains of a sixth-century **Celtic monastery** on the headland have provided important insights into how the country's earliest monastic houses were organized.

KING ARTHUR IN CORNWALL

Did **King Arthur** really exist? It's more likely that he was an amalgam of two people: a sixth-century Celtic warlord who united the local tribes in a series of successful battles against the invading Anglo-Saxons, and a local Cornish saint. Whatever his origins, his role was recounted and inflated by poets and troubadours in later centuries. The Arthurian legends were elaborated by the medieval chroniclers Geoffrey of Monmouth and William of Malmesbury and in Thomas Malory's epic, *Morte d'Arthur* (1485), further romanticized in Tennyson's *Idylls of the King* (1859) and resurrected in T.H. White's saga, *The Once and Future King* (1958).

Although there are places throughout Britain and Europe that claim some association with Arthur, it's England's West Country, and **Cornwall** in particular, that has the greatest concentration of places boasting a link. Here, the myths, enriched by fellow Celts from Brittany and Wales, have established deep roots, so that, for example, the spirit of Arthur is said to be embodied in the Cornish chough – a bird now almost extinct. Cornwall's most famous Arthurian site is his supposed birthplace, **Tintagel**, where Merlin apparently lived in a cave under the castle (he also resided on a rock near Mousehole, south of Penzance, according to some sources). Nearby **Bodmin Moor** is littered with places with names such as "King Arthur's Bed" and "King Arthur's Downs", while Camlan, the battlefield where Arthur was mortally wounded fighting against his nephew Mordred, is associated with Slaughterbridge, on the northern reaches of the moor near **Camelford** (which is also sometimes identified as Camelot itself). At **Dozmary Pool**, the knight Bedivere was dispatched by the dying Arthur to return the sword Excalibur to the mysterious hand emerging from the water – though Loe Pool in Mount's Bay also claims this honour. Arthur's body was supposedly carried after the battle to **Boscastle**, on Cornwall's northern coast, from where a funeral barge transported it to Avalon, identified with Glastonbury in Somerset (see p.303).

6

ARRIVAL AND INFORMATION

By bus Buses pull in on Bossiney Rd, opposite the tourist office.
Destinations Boscastle (Mon–Sat 7 daily, Sun 5 daily; 15min); Bude (5–6 daily; 50min); Camelford (Mon–Sat 7 daily, Sun 5 daily; 20min).

TINTAGEL

Tourist office Bossiney Rd (daily: April–Oct 10am–4pm; Nov–March 10am–1pm; ☎ 01840 779084, ⓦ visitboscastle andtintagel.com); it also has a small exhibition about the region's cultural heritage.

ACCOMMODATION AND EATING

Avalon Hotel Atlantic Rd, PL34 0DD ☎ 01840 770116, ⓦ theavalonhotel.co.uk. Classy guesthouse at the eastern end of the village, mixing Victorian-Gothic details with a fresh, contemporary style. Some rooms are small, but all are spotless and most have amazing views. Breakfast choices include porridge brûlée. **£89**

★ **Bosayne** Atlantic Rd, PL34 0DE ☎ 01840 770514, ⓦ bosayne.co.uk. This solid Edwardian B&B has amiable, eco-aware owners and smallish rooms with sea views and mini-fridges. Breakfasts are mainly organic with home-made bread and cakes. **£75**

★ **Charlie's** Fore St, PL34 0DA ☎ 01840 779500, ⓦ charlies.cafe. Deli and café with outdoor seating and a bright, family-friendly feel. Choose from among the pies and Scotch eggs for a superlative picnic, or settle down for brunch, sandwiches (£4–7) or burgers (£7–9). Cakes and cream teas include gluten-free options. Mon–Sat 10am–5pm.

YHA Tintagel Dunderhole Point, PL34 0DW ☎ 0345 371 9145, ⓦ yha.org.uk/hostel/tintagel. Three-quarters of a mile south of Tintagel, the offices of a former slate quarry now house this hostel with great coastal views. There's a kitchen and BBQ area but no restaurant. Closed Nov–Easter. Dorms **£17**

Boscastle

Three miles east of Tintagel, the port of **BOSCASTLE** lies compressed within a narrow ravine drilled by the rivers Jordan and Valency, and ending in a twisty harbour. One of the lime-washed cottages bordering the tidy riverfront holds the **Museum of Witchcraft and Magic** (April–Oct Mon–Sat 10.30am–6pm, Sun 11.30am–6pm; £5; ☎ 01840 250111, ⓦ museumofwitchcraftandmagic.co.uk), an absorbing, non-gimmicky account of witchcraft and sorcery through the ages, displayed in themed galleries. Above and behind, you can see more seventeenth- and eighteenth-century cottages on a circular walk that traces the valley of the Valency for about a mile to reach Boscastle's graceful parish church of **St Juliot**, tucked away in a peaceful glen, where Thomas Hardy once worked as a young architect.

ARRIVAL AND INFORMATION   BOSCASTLE

By bus There are bus stops at the car park and Boscastle Bridge, at the top of the harbour.
Destinations Bude (5–6 daily; 40min); Camelford (5 daily, 30min); Tintagel (5 daily; 10min).

Tourist office The Harbour (daily: March–Oct 10am–5pm; Nov–Feb 10.30am–4pm; ☏ 01840 250010, ☒ visitboscastle andtintagel.com).

ACCOMMODATION AND EATING

Napoleon Inn High St, PL35 0BD ☏ 01840 250204, ☒ napoleoninn.co.uk. Boscastle's excellent pubs include this traditional tavern in the upper town with tankards hanging off the ceiling, real ale, great food (mains £9–13) and Cornish singing every Tues. Daily noon–11pm; kitchen daily noon–2pm & 6–9pm.
Old Rectory St Juliot, PL35 0BT, 1.5 miles east of Boscastle ☏ 01840 250225, ☒ stjuliot.com. For a real

Thomas Hardy experience, head for this luxurious Victorian B&B, where you can stay in the author's bedroom and roam the extensive grounds. Minimum two-night stay. £95
★YHA Boscastle Harbourside, PL35 0HD ☏ 0345 371 9006, ☒ yha.org.uk/hostel/boscastle. Fine old hostel in a former stables right by the river. Rooms have two to six beds and there's a self-catering kitchen and a comfy lounge. Only groups can book Nov–Feb. Dorms £18, doubles £69

Bude and around

Just four miles from the Devon border, Cornwall's northernmost town of **BUDE** is built around an estuary surrounded by a fine expanse of sands. The town has sprouted a crop of hotels and holiday homes, though these have not unduly spoilt the place nor the magnificent cliffy coast surrounding it.

Of the excellent **beaches** hereabouts, the central **Summerleaze** is clean and spacious, but the mile-long **Widemouth Bay**, south of town, is the main focus of the holiday crowds (though bathing can be dangerous near the rocks at low tide). Surfers also congregate five miles down the coast at **Crackington Haven**, wonderfully situated between 430ft crags at the mouth of a lush valley. To the **north** of Bude, acres-wide **Crooklets** is the scene of **surfing** and life-saving demonstrations and competitions. A couple of miles further on, **Sandy Mouth** holds a pristine expanse of sand with rock pools beneath the encircling cliffs. It's a short walk from here to another surfers' delight, **Duckpool**, a tiny sandy cove flanked by jagged reefs at low tide, and dominated by the three-hundred-foot **Steeple Point**.

ARRIVAL AND INFORMATION   BUDE AND AROUND

By bus Buses stop on The Strand, running to Boscastle (5–6 daily; 40min) and Hartland (Mon–Sat 6 daily; 30–55mins).

Tourist office The Crescent car park (Mon–Sat 10am–5pm, Sun 10am–4pm; summer school hols daily 10am–7pm; ☏ 01288 354240, ☒ visitbude.info).

ACCOMMODATION AND EATING

The Bank at Bude Pethericks Mill, EX23 8TF ☏ 01288 352070, ☒ thebankatbude.co.uk. A bit out of the way – unless you're a cyclist, as it's right on the cycle path – this place offers tapas (£5–9) as well as paellas and other meat and seafood dishes (£14–25). It's a 5min walk along the riverbank from the tourist office. Easter–June, Sept & Oct Tues & Wed 6–10pm, Thurs–Sat noon–10pm; July & Aug Tues, Wed & Sun 3–10pm, Thurs–Sat noon–10pm; Nov–Easter Tues–Sat 6pm–late.
The Beach Summerleaze Crescent, EX23 8HJ ☏ 01288 389800, ☒ thebeachatbude.co.uk. Chic hotel overlooking the beach, with modern, airy rooms, swish bathrooms and an excellent restaurant (mains £17–20). The bar has an

outdoor terrace, perfect for soaking up the sunset. Daily noon–2.30/3pm & 6–9/9.30pm. £175
★Cerenety Lynstone Lane, EX23 0LR ☏ 01288 356778 or ☏ 07429 016962, ☒ cerenetycampsite.co.uk. Back-to-basics, eco-friendly camping a mile south of Bude, with grassy pitches, solar-powered showers and composting toilets. In summer, hot drinks and crêpes can be bought from a caravan on the site. £14
Life's a Beach Summerleaze Beach, EX23 8HN ☏ 01288 355222, ☒ lifesabeach.info. Right on the beach, this is a café by day, offering baguettes, burgers and drinks, and a classy bistro in the evening, with the accent on seafood (mains £18–26). Easter–Oct Mon–Sat

10.30am–3.30pm & 7–9pm, Sun 10.30am–3.30pm; reduced opening in winter, call to check.
North Shore 57 Killerton Rd, EX23 8EW ☎ 01288 354256, ⓦ northshorebude.com. Friendly hostel 5min from the centre of town, with clean and spacious rooms – including en-suite doubles – a large garden and a kitchen. Dorms £22, doubles £60

Bodmin Moor

6

Bodmin Moor, the smallest of the West Country's great moors, has some beautiful tors, torrents and rock formations, but much of its fascination lies in the strong human imprint, particularly the wealth of relics left behind by its **Bronze Age** population. Separated from these by some three millennia, the churches in the villages of **St Neot**, **Blisland** and **Altarnun** are among the region's finest examples of fifteenth-century art and architecture.

Bodmin

BODMIN's position on the western edge of Bodmin Moor, equidistant from the north and south Cornish coasts and the Fowey and Camel rivers, encouraged its growth as a trading town. It was also an important ecclesiastical centre after the establishment of a priory by St Petroc, who moved here from Padstow in the sixth century.

St Petroc's Church

Priory Rd, PL31 2DT · Daily 9am–4pm · Free · ☎ 01208 73867

After Bodmin's priory had disappeared, the town retained its prestige through its **church of St Petroc**, built in the fifteenth century and still Cornwall's largest parish church. Inside, there's an extravagantly carved twelfth-century font and an ivory casket that once held the bones of the saint. The southwest corner of the churchyard holds a sacred well.

Bodmin Jail

Berrycoombe Rd, PL31 2NR · Daily: April–Sept 9.30am–8pm; Oct–March 9.30am–6pm · £10 · ☎ 01208 76292, ⓦ bodminjail.org

The notorious **Bodmin Jail** is redolent of the public executions that were guaranteed crowd-pullers until 1862, though it didn't finally close until 1927. You can visit part of the original eighteenth-century structure, including the condemned cell and "execution pit", and some grisly exhibits chronicling the lives of the inmates. *The Governors Hall* café/restaurant stays open until 9pm.

Lanhydrock

3 miles southeast of Bodmin, PL30 5AD · **House and garden** Daily: March & Oct 11am–5pm; April–Sept 11am–5.30pm · £13.55, Nov & Dec 7.50; garden only £8.25, Nov & Dec £4.35; NT · **Grounds** Daily dawn–dusk · Free, but parking £3; NT · ☎ 01208 265950, ⓦ nationaltrust.org.uk/lanhydrock · Less than 2 miles' walk from Bodmin Parkway train station

One of Cornwall's most celebrated country houses, **Lanhydrock** originally dates from the seventeenth century but was totally rebuilt after a fire in 1881. The most prominent survivor from its Jacobean past is the long picture gallery, whose plaster ceiling depicts scenes from the Old Testament, while the servants' quarters fascinatingly reveal the daily workings of a Victorian manor house. The grounds have magnificent **gardens** with lush beds of magnolias, azaleas and rhododendrons, and a huge area of wooded parkland bordering onto the River Fowey

Blisland

BLISLAND stands in the Camel valley on the western slopes of Bodmin Moor, three miles northeast of Bodmin. Georgian and Victorian houses cluster around a village green and a church whose well-restored interior has an Italianate altar and a startlingly painted screen.

The western moor

On **Pendrift Common** above Blisland, the gigantic **Jubilee Rock** is inscribed with various patriotic insignia commemorating the jubilee of George III's coronation in 1809. From this 700ft vantage point you look eastward over the De Lank gorge and the boulder-crowned knoll of **Hawk's Tor**, three miles away. On the shoulder of the tor stand the Neolithic **Stripple Stones**, a circular platform once holding 28 standing stones, of which just four are still upright.

6

The northern tors

The northern half of Bodmin Moor is dominated by its two highest tors, both of them easily accessible from **CAMELFORD**, an unassuming local centre known for its slate industry. Four miles southeast, **Rough Tor** is the second-highest peak on Bodmin Moor at 1311ft. A short distance to the east stand **Little Rough Tor**, where there are the remains of an Iron Age camp, and **Showery Tor**, capped by a prominent formation of piled rocks. Easily visible to the southeast, **Brown Willy** is, at 1378ft, the highest peak in Cornwall, as its original name signified – Bronewhella, or "highest hill". Like Rough Tor, Brown Willy shows various faces, its sugarloaf appearance from the north sharpening into a long multi-peaked crest as you approach. The tor is accessible by continuing from the summit of Rough Tor across the valley of the De Lank, or, from the south, by footpath from Bolventor.

Bolventor and around

The village of **BOLVENTOR**, lying at the centre of the moor midway between Bodmin and Launceston, is an uninspiring place close to **Jamaica Inn**, one of the moor's chief focuses for walkers and literary sightseers alike.

Jamaica Inn

10 miles northeast of Bodmin, PL15 7TS • Museum daily 8am–9pm • £3.95 • ☏ 01566 86250, ⓦ jamaicainn.co.uk

A staging post even before the precursor of the A30 road was laid here in 1769, the inn was described as being "alone in glory, four square to the winds" by **Daphne Du Maurier**, who stayed here in 1930, soaking up inspiration for her smugglers' yarn, *Jamaica Inn*. There's a room inside devoted to the author, and the hotel also has an attached **Smugglers Museum**, illustrating the diverse ruses used for concealing contraband.

Dozmary Pool

A mile south of Bolventor

The car park at *Jamaica Inn* makes a useful place to leave your vehicle and venture forth on foot. Just a mile south is **Dozmary Pool**, another link in the West Country's Arthurian mythologies – after Arthur's death, according to some versions of the story, Sir Bedivere hurled Excalibur into this pool, where it was seized by an arm raised from the depths. Despite its proximity to the A30, the diamond-shaped lake usually preserves an ethereal air, though it's been known to run dry in summer, dealing a bit of a blow to the legend that it is bottomless.

Altarnun

Four miles northeast of Bolventor, **ALTARNUN** is a pleasant, granite-grey village snugly sheltered beneath the eastern heights of the moor. Its prominent **church**, **St Nonna's**, contains a fine Norman font and 79 bench ends carved at the beginning of the sixteenth century, depicting saints, musicians and clowns.

St Neot and the southeastern moor

Approached through a lush wooded valley, **ST NEOT** is one of the moor's prettiest villages. Its fifteenth-century **church** contains some of the most impressive stained-glass windows of any parish church in the country, the oldest glass being the fifteenth-century **Creation Window**, at the east end of the south aisle.

Golitha Falls

One of the moor's most attractive spots lies a couple of miles east of St Neot, below Draynes Bridge, where the Fowey tumbles through the **Golitha Falls**, less a waterfall than a series of rapids. Dippers and wagtails flit through the trees, and there's a pleasant woodland walk to Siblyback Lake reservoir just over a mile away.

Kilmar and Stowe's Hill

North and east of Siblyback Lake are some of Bodmin Moor's grandest landscapes. The quite modest elevations of Hawk's Tor (1079ft) and the lower Trewartha Tor appear enormous from the north, though they are overtopped by **Kilmar**, highest of the hills on the moor's eastern flank at 1280ft. **Stowe's Hill** is the site of the moor's most famous stone pile, **The Cheesewring**, a precarious pillar of balancing granite slabs, marvellously eroded by the wind. A mile or so south down Stowe's Hill stands an artificial rock phenomenon, **The Hurlers**, a wide complex of three circles dating from about 1500 BC. The purpose of these stark upright stones is not known, though they owe their name to the legend that they were men turned to stone for playing the Celtic game of hurling on the Sabbath.

Minions and Trethevy

The Hurlers are easily accessible just outside **MINIONS**, Cornwall's highest village, three miles south of which stands another Stone Age survival, **Trethevy Quoit**, a chamber tomb nearly nine feet high, surmounted by a massive capstone. Originally enclosed in earth, the stones have been stripped by centuries of weathering to create Cornwall's most impressive megalithic monument.

ARRIVAL AND INFORMATION   BODMIN MOOR

By train 3 miles outside Bodmin itself, Bodmin Parkway train station has a regular bus connection (hourly; 15min) to the centre of Bodmin.
Destinations Exeter (every 1–2hr; 1hr 40min); Penzance (every 30min–1hr; 1hr 25min); Plymouth (every 1–2hr; 40min).
By bus Most buses to and from Bodmin stop on Mount Folly, near the tourist office.

Destinations Newquay (4 daily; 35–50min); Padstow (Mon–Sat hourly, Sun 6 daily; 45min); Plymouth (4 daily; 1hr); St Austell (Mon–Sat hourly; 1hr).
Tourist office Mount Folly, Bodmin (March–May & Oct Mon–Fri 8.45am–4pm, Sat 10am–5pm; June–Sept Mon–Fri 8.45am–5pm, Sat 10am–5pm; Nov–Feb Mon–Fri 8.45am–2pm; ☎01208 76616, ⓦbodminlive.com).

ACCOMMODATION AND EATING

★ **Bedknobs** Polgwyn, Castle St, Bodmin, PL31 2DX ☎01208 77553, ⓦbedknobs.co.uk. Victorian villa in an acre of wooded garden, with three spacious and luxurious B&B rooms (the priciest with its own en-suite Airbath) and a self-catering apartment (£115). Friendly, eco-aware hosts and lots of extras. **£95**

Blisland Inn The Green, Blisland, PL30 4JK ☎01208 850739. Traditional village pub on the green, serving seven cask ales, including Blisland Bulldog, as well as Cornish fruit wine, bar snacks and full meals (£8–15). There are outdoor tables, and often live music on Sat. Mon–Sat 11.30am–11pm, Sun noon–10.30pm; kitchen Mon–Sat noon–2pm & 6.30–9pm, Sun noon–2pm.

Jamaica Inn Bolventor, PL15 7TS ☎01566 86250, ⓦjamaicainn.co.uk. Despite its fame, this inn immortalized by Daphne du Maurier has lost any trace of romance since its development into a bland hotel and restaurant complex. It occupies a grand site, though, ideal for excursions onto the moor. Mon–Sat 7.30am–midnight, Sun 7.30am–10.30pm; kitchen daily 7.30–10.30am, 11am–4pm & 5–9pm. **£89**

Roscrea 18 St Nicholas Rd, Bodmin, PL31 1AD ☎01208 74400, ⓦroscrea.co.uk. Central, friendly B&B with tasteful Victorian rooms. Breakfasts include home-made bread, jams and muesli. **£90**

East Anglia

KING'S COLLEGE CHAPEL, CAMBRIDGE

East Anglia

Strictly speaking, East Anglia is made up of just three counties – Suffolk, Norfolk and Cambridgeshire, which were settled in the fifth century by Angles from today's Schleswig-Holstein – but the term has come to be loosely applied to parts of Essex too. As a region it's renowned for its wide skies and flat landscapes, but there are a few surprises too: parts of Suffolk and Norfolk are decidedly hilly, with steep coastal cliffs; broad rivers cut through the fenlands; and Norfolk also boasts some wonderful sandy beaches. Fine medieval churches abound, built in the days when this was England's most progressive and prosperous region.

7

Heading into East Anglia from the south takes you through **Essex**, whose proximity to London has turned much of the county into an unappetizing commuter strip. Amid the suburban gloom, there are, however, several worthwhile destinations, most notably **Colchester**, once a major Roman town and now a busy place with an imposing castle, and the handsome hamlets of the bucolic **Stour River Valley** on the Essex–Suffolk border. Essex's Dedham is one of the prettiest of these villages, but the main attraction hereabouts is Suffolk's Flatford Mill, famous for its associations with the painter John Constable.

Further north, **Suffolk** boasts a string of pretty little towns that enjoyed immense prosperity from the thirteenth to the sixteenth centuries, the heyday of the wool trade. Lavenham is the prime example, but neither should you miss the old abbey town of **Bury St Edmunds**. Suffolk's county town is **Ipswich**, which has more to offer than it's given credit for, but really it's the **Suffolk coast** that is the main magnet, especially the delightful seaside resort of Southwold and neighbouring Aldeburgh, with its prestigious music festival.

Norfolk, as everyone knows thanks to Noël Coward, is very flat. It's also one of the most sparsely populated and tranquil counties in England, a remarkable turnaround from the days when it was an economic and political powerhouse – until, that is, the Industrial Revolution simply passed it by. Its capital, **Norwich**, is East Anglia's largest city, renowned for its Norman cathedral and castle; nearby are the Broads, a unique landscape of reed-ridden waterways that have been intensively mined by boat-rental companies. Similarly popular, the **North Norfolk coast** holds a string of busy, very English seaside resorts – Cromer and Sheringham to name but two – but for the most part it's charmingly unspoilt, its marshes, creeks and tidal flats studded with tiny flint villages, most enjoyably Blakeney and Cley.

Cambridge is much visited, principally because of its world-renowned university, whose ancient colleges boast some of the finest medieval and early-modern architecture in the country. The rest of **Cambridgeshire** is pancake-flat fenland, for centuries an inhospitable marshland, but now rich alluvial farming land. The cathedral town of **Ely**, settled on one of the few areas of raised ground in the fens, is an easy and popular day-trip from Cambridge, while farther up the River Ouse is the ancient port of **King's Lynn**.

SOUTHWOLD

Highlights

❶ Orford Solitary hamlet with a splendid coastal setting that makes for a wonderful weekend away. **See p.390**

❷ The Aldeburgh Festival The region's prime classical music festival takes place every summer. **See p.391**

❸ Southwold Handsome and genteel seaside town, which is perfect for walking and bathing – with the added incentive of the most inventive Under the Pier Show in the country. **See p.393**

❹ Norwich Market This open-air market is the region's biggest and best for everything from whelks to wellies. **See p.396**

❺ Holkham Bay and beach Wide bay holding Norfolk's finest beach – acres of golden sand set against pine-dusted dunes. **See p.406**

❻ Ely Isolated Cambridgeshire town, with a true fenland flavour and a magnificent cathedral. **See p.411**

❼ Cambridge With some of the finest late medieval architecture in Europe, Cambridge is a must-see, its compact centre graced by dignified old colleges and their neatly manicured courts. **See p.413**

HIGHLIGHTS ARE MARKED ON THE MAP ON P.380

LONG-DISTANCE FOOTPATHS

Given the prevailing flatness of the terrain, hiking in East Anglia is less strenuous than in most other English regions, and there are several first-rate **long-distance footpaths**. The main one is the **Peddars Way**, which runs north from Knettishall Heath, near Thetford, to the coast at Holme, near Hunstanton, where it continues east as the **Norfolk Coast Path** to Cromer – 93 miles in total (w nationaltrail.co.uk for both). At Cromer, you can pick up the 61-mile **Weavers' Way** (w ldwa.org.uk), which wends its way through the Broads to the coast at Great Yarmouth.

GETTING AROUND

EAST ANGLIA

By train Trains from London are fast and frequent: one main line links Colchester, Ipswich and Norwich, another Cambridge and Ely. Among several cross-country services, there are trains between Peterborough, Ely, Norwich and Ipswich.

By bus Beyond the major towns you'll have to rely on local buses. Services are patchy, except on the north Norfolk coast, which is well served by the Norfolk Coasthopper bus (w stagecoachbus.com/promos-and-offers/east/coasthopper).

HIGHLIGHTS

1. Orford
2. The Aldeburgh Festival
3. Southwold
4. Norwich Market
5. Holkham Bay and beach
6. Ely
7. Cambridge

EAST ANGLIA

Colchester

If you visit only one place in Essex, it should be **COLCHESTER**, a lively, medium-sized town with a **castle**, a university and an army base, just fifty miles or so northeast of London. Colchester prides itself on being England's oldest town, and there is indeed documentary evidence of a settlement here as early as the fifth century BC. Today, Colchester makes a good base for explorations of the surrounding countryside – particularly the **Stour Valley** towns of Constable Country, within easy reach a few miles to the north.

Brief history

By the first century AD, the original settlement was the region's capital under **King Cunobelin** – better known as Shakespeare's Cymbeline – and when the **Romans** invaded Britain in 43 AD they chose Colchester (Camulodunum) as their new capital, though it was soon eclipsed by London. Later, the conquering Normans built one of their mightiest strongholds here, but the conflict that most marked the town was the **Civil War**. In 1648, Colchester was subjected to a gruelling siege by the Parliamentarian army; after three months, during which the population ate every living creature within the walls and then some, the town finally surrendered and the Royalist leaders were promptly executed for their pains.

7

Colchester Castle

Castle Park, CO1 1TJ · Mon–Sat 10am–5pm, Sun 11–5pm · £7.75 · **Tours** 3–4 daily; 45min–1hr · £3 · **Park** Daily dawn–dusk · Free · ☎ 01206 282939, Ⓦ www.cimuseums.org.uk

At the heart of the towns are the remains of **Colchester Castle**, a ruggedly imposing, honey-coloured keep, set in attractive parkland stretching down to the River Colne. Begun less than ten years after the Battle of Hastings, the keep was the largest in Europe at the time, built on the site of the Temple of Claudius. Inside the keep, a **museum** holds an excellent collection of Romano-British archeological finds, notably a miscellany of coins and tombstones. The museum also runs regular **guided tours**, giving access to the Roman vaults and the castle roof, which are otherwise out of bounds. Outside, down towards the river in **Castle Park**, is a section of the old **Roman walls**, whose battered remains are still visible around much of the town centre. They were erected after Boudica had sacked the city and, as such, are a case of too little too late.

Firstsite Art Gallery

Lewis Gardens, High St, CO1 1JH · Daily 10am–5pm · Free · ☎ 01206 713700, Ⓦ firstsite.uk

In a new and stunningly handsome modern building near the castle, the **Firstsite Art Gallery** offers a varied and often challenging programme of contemporary art exhibitions. Recent exhibitors have included Ed Gold and Patrick Hough. The building itself has a lustrous metallic gold sheen and was designed by the Uruguayan architect **Rafael Viñoly**.

The High Street

Colchester's long and largely pedestrianized **High Street** follows pretty much the same route as it did in Roman times. The most arresting building here is the flamboyant **Town Hall**, built in 1902 and topped by a statue of St Helena, mother of Constantine the Great and daughter of "Old King Cole" of nursery-rhyme fame – after whom, some say, the town was named. Looming above the western end of the High Street is the town landmark, "**Jumbo**", a disused nineteenth-century water tower, considerably more imposing than the nearby **Balkerne Gate**, which marked the western entrance to Roman Colchester. Built in 50 AD, this is the largest surviving Roman gateway in the country, though with the remains at only a touch over 6ft high, it's far from spectacular.

ARRIVAL AND INFORMATION

COLCHESTER

By train Colchester has two train stations. Colchester station (a 20min walk north of the centre – follow the signs) covers mainline services, including for the Tendring peninsula. Colchester Town (on the southeast corner of the centre, about 500yd from the High St) is only for local services out along the Tendring.

Destinations (Colchester) Clacton (hourly; 30min); Ipswich (every 30min; 20min); London Liverpool Street (every 20min; 1hr); Norwich (every 30min; 1hr); Sudbury (change at Marks Tey; hourly; 40min).

Destinations (Colchester Town) Walton-on-the-Naze

(hourly; 40min).

By bus The bus station is on Osborne St, on the southeast side of the centre, near Colchester Town train station.

Destinations Chambers bus #753 (⊛ chambersbus.co.uk) links Colchester with Bury St Edmunds (Mon–Sat hourly; 2hr), Lavenham (Mon–Sat hourly; 1hr 30min) and Sudbury (Mon–Sat hourly; 50min). Other companies link Colchester with Dedham (every 1–2hr; 40min) – consult ⊛ traveline.info.

Tourist office On the ground floor of the Hollytrees Museum, just off the High St in Castle Park (Mon–Sat 10am–5pm; ☎ 01206 282920, ⊛ visitcolchester.com).

ACCOMMODATION AND EATING

The Company Shed 129 Coast Rd, West Mersea, CO5 8PA ☎ 01206 382700, ⊛ the-company-shed.co.uk. Colchester's oysters have been highly prized since Roman times and nowadays they are at their best among the oyster beds of Mersea Island, about 6 miles south of Colchester. It's here you'll find *The Company Shed*, where they serve the freshest of oysters at simple rickety tables in, to quote their own PR, a "romantically weatherbeaten shed". Romantic or not, the oysters are indeed delicious. Last orders for eating in 4pm. Tues–Sat 9am–5pm, Sun 10am–5pm.

Four Sevens Guesthouse 28 Inglis Road, CO3 3HU ☎ 01206 546093, ⊛ foursevens.co.uk. This is one of the best of the town's B&Bs, in an attractively remodelled Victorian house with six bright and breezy guest rooms decorated in an uncluttered modern style. Two of the rooms are en suite (£10 extra). It's on a leafy residential street, a brief walk southwest from the centre. **£65**

Il Padrino 11 Church St, CO1 1NF ☎ 01206 366699, ⊛ ilpadrinocolchester.co.uk. This excellent Italian café-restaurant, a few yards from the west end of the High St, serves all the classics for both lunch and dinner. There are daily specials, chalked up on a blackboard, and prices are very reasonable, with mains averaging £15 (£9 for pasta dishes), less at lunchtime. Cosy premises and attentive service. Mon noon–2.30pm, Tues–Sat noon–2.30pm & 6–10pm.

North Hill Hotel 51 North Hill, CO1 1PY ☎ 01206 574001, ⊛ northhillhotel.com. Set within an intelligently revamped older building, this appealing, mid-range hotel has seventeen guest rooms with lots of original features – especially the exposed half-timbered walls and beams. Handy central location too, just north of the High St, but North Hill can be noisy so you may prefer a room at the back. **£75**

BETRAYED AND ABUSED: BOUDICA OF THE ICENI

Boudica – aka **Boadicea** – was the wife of Prasutagus, chief of the **Iceni** tribe of Norfolk, who allied himself to the Romans during their conquest of Britain. Five years later, when the Iceni were no longer useful, the Romans attempted to disarm them; the Iceni rebelled, but were quickly brought to heel. On Prasutagus's death, the Romans confiscated his property and when Boudica protested, they flogged her and raped her daughters. Enraged, Boudica determined to take revenge, rallying the Iceni and their allies before setting off on a rampage across southeastern Britain in 60 AD.

As the ultimate symbol of Roman oppression, the **Temple of Claudius** in **Colchester** was the initial focus of hatred, but, once Colchester had been razed, Boudica turned her sights elsewhere. She laid waste to London and St Albans, massacring thousands and inflicting crushing defeats on the Roman units stationed there. Finally, the Roman governor **Suetonius Paulinus** defeated her in a pitched battle and, knowing what to expect from the Romans, Boudica chose **suicide**, thereby ensuring her later reputation as a patriotic Englishwoman who died fighting for liberty – a claim that Boudica would have found incomprehensible.

7

The Stour Valley

Six miles or so north of Colchester, the **Stour Valley** forms the border between Essex and Suffolk, and signals the beginning of East Anglia proper. The river valley is dotted with lovely little villages, where rickety, half-timbered Tudor houses and handsome Georgian dwellings cluster around medieval churches, proud buildings with square, self-confident towers. The Stour's prettiest villages are concentrated along its lower reaches – to the east of the A134 – in Dedham Vale, with **Dedham** the most appealing of them all. The vale is also known as "**Constable Country**", as it was the home of John Constable, one of England's greatest artists, and the subject of his most famous paintings. Inevitably, there's a Constable shrine – the much-visited complex of old buildings down by the river at **Flatford Mill**. Elsewhere, the best-preserved of the old south Suffolk wool towns is **Lavenham**, while neighbouring **Sudbury** has a fine museum, devoted to the work of another outstanding English artist, Thomas Gainsborough.

Brief history

7

The villages along the River Stour and its tributaries were once busy little places at the heart of East Anglia's medieval **weaving trade**. By the 1480s, the region produced more cloth than any other part of the country, but in Tudor times production shifted to Colchester, Ipswich and Norwich and, although most of the smaller settlements continued spinning cloth for the next three hundred years or so, their importance slowly dwindled. Bypassed by the Industrial Revolution, **south Suffolk** had, by the late nineteenth century, become a remote rural backwater, an impoverished area whose decline had one unforeseen consequence: with few exceptions, the towns and villages were never prosperous enough to modernize, so the architectural legacy of medieval and Tudor times survived and now pulls in second-home owners and tourists alike.

GETTING AROUND   **THE STOUR VALLEY**

By public transport Seeing the Stour Valley by public transport can be problematic – distances are small (Dedham Vale is only about ten miles long), but buses between the villages are patchy, especially on Sunday. The only local rail service is the short branch line between Marks Tey, on the London Liverpool Street to Colchester line, and Sudbury.

Flatford Mill

"I associate my careless boyhood with all that lies on the banks of the Stour," wrote **John Constable**, who was born in **EAST BERGHOLT**, ten miles northeast of Colchester, in 1776. The house in which he was born has long since disappeared, so it has been left to **FLATFORD MILL**, a mile or so to the south, to take up the painter's cause. The mill was owned by his father and was where Constable painted his most celebrated canvas, *The Hay Wain* (now in London's National Gallery), which created a sensation when it was exhibited in Paris in 1824. To the chagrin of many of his contemporaries, Constable turned away from the landscape painting conventions of the day, rendering his scenery with a realistic directness that harked back to the Dutch landscape painters of the seventeenth century.

The mill itself – not the one he painted, but a Victorian replacement – is not open to the public and neither is neighbouring **Willy Lott's Cottage**, which does actually feature in *The Hay Wain*, but the National Trust has colonized several local buildings, principally **Bridge Cottage**.

Bridge Cottage

Flatford Mill, CO7 6UL • Jan & early Feb Sat & Sun 10.30am–3.30pm; late Feb to March Wed–Sun 10am–4.30pm; April–Sept daily 10am–5pm; Oct daily 10am–4.30pm; Nov & early Dec Wed–Sun 10.30am–3.30pm • Free, but parking £4; NT • ☎ 01206 298260, ⓦ nationaltrust.org.uk/flatford • The nearest train station is at Manningtree, 2 miles away

Neat and trim and tidily thatched, **Bridge Cottage** was familiar to Constable and, although none of the artist's paintings are displayed here, it is packed with Constabilia

7

GUIDED WALKS AROUND FLATFORD MILL

Many visitors to Flatford Mill are keen to see the sites associated with Constable's paintings and, although there is something a tad futile about this – so much has changed – the National Trust does organize volunteer-led **guided walks** to several key locations; the nearest are the remains of the Dry Dock next to Bridge Cottage and the *Hay Wain* view itself. For more details, call ☎01206 298260.

---

alongside a small exhibition on the artist's life and times. The cottage also has a very pleasant riverside tearoom where you can take in the view.

Dedham

Constable went to school just upriver from Flatford Mill in **DEDHAM**, a pretty little village whose wide and lazy main street is graced by a handsome medley of old timber-framed houses and Georgian villas. The main sight is the **Church of St Mary** (daily 9am–dusk; free; ⓦ dedham-and-ardleigh-parishes.org.uk), a large, well-proportioned structure with a sweeping, sixteenth-century nave adorned by some attractive Victorian stained glass. Constable painted the church on several occasions, and today it holds one of the artist's rare religious paintings, *The Ascension* – though frankly, it's a good job Constable concentrated on landscapes. Be aware that day-trippers arrive in Dedham by the coachload throughout the summer.

ARRIVAL AND DEPARTURE   DEDHAM

By bus There is a reasonably good bus service to Dedham from Colchester (every 1–2hr; 40min).

ACCOMMODATION AND EATING

The Sun Inn High St, CO7 6DF ☎01206 323351, ⓦ thesuninndedham.com. Among Dedham's several pubs, the pick is *The Sun*, an ancient place that has been sympathetically modernized. The menu is strong on local ingredients and offers tasty Italian and British dishes, all washed down by real ales; mains average £15. They also have five en-suite rooms decorated in a creative blend of country-inn and boutique-hotel styles, from four-poster beds through to billowy, caramel-cream curtains. Kitchen Mon–Sat noon–2.30pm & 6.30–9.30pm, Sun noon–4pm & 6.30–9pm. **£145**

Stoke-by-Nayland

West of Dedham, **STOKE-BY-NAYLAND** is the most picturesque of villages, where a knot of half-timbered and pastel-painted cottages cuddle up to one of Constable's favourite subjects, **St Mary's Church** (daily 9am–5pm; free), with its pretty brick-and-stone-trimmed tower. The doors of the south porch are covered by the beautifully carved if badly weathered figures of a medieval **Jesse Tree** (purporting to show the ancestors of Christ).

ARRIVAL AND DEPARTURE   STOKE-BY-NAYLAND

By bus There is a reasonably good bus service to Stoke-by-Nayland from both Colchester (Mon–Sat every 1–2hr; 40min) and Sudbury (Mon–Sat every 1–2hr; 40min).

ACCOMMODATION AND EATING

The Angel Inn Polstead St, CO6 4SA ☎01206 263245, ⓦ angelinnsuffolk.co.uk. This agreeable country pub, with its bare-brick walls and rustic beams, offers a good-quality British menu – steak and ale pie, fish and chips – with mains around £14. *The Angel* also has half a dozen en-suite guest rooms, each of which is kitted out in pleasant style with lots of creams. Daily 10am–11pm; kitchen Mon–Sat noon–2.30pm & 6–9.30pm, Sun noon–4pm & 6–9pm. **£110**

The Crown Polstead St, CO6 4SE ☎01206 262001, ⓦ crowninn.net. *The Crown* may fancy itself just a little too much, but there's no disputing the quality of the food or the inventiveness of the menu (mains from £15). The decor is appealing too, with the open-plan restaurant spreading over several separate areas and decorated in a sort of low-key, country-house style. The same decorative approach has been followed in the eleven bedrooms, which are all kept in tip-top condition. Kitchen Mon–Sat noon–2.30pm & 6–9.30pm, Sun noon–9pm. **£150**

Sudbury

By far the most important town in this part of the Stour Valley, **SUDBURY** holds a handful of timber-framed houses that recall its days of wool-trade prosperity, though in fact its salad days were underwritten by another local industry, **silk weaving**. The town's most famous export, however, is **Thomas Gainsborough** (1727–88), the leading English portraitist of the eighteenth century. Although he left Sudbury when he was just 13, moving to London where he was apprenticed to an engraver, the artist is still very much identified with the town: his statue, with brush and palette, stands on Market Hill, the predominantly Victorian marketplace, while a superb collection of his work is on display inside the house in which he was born.

7

Gainsborough's House

46 Gainsborough St, CO10 2EU • Mon–Sat 10am–5pm, Sun 11am–5pm • £7 • ☎ 01787 372958, ⓦ gainsborough.org

Gainsborough's House possesses an outstanding collection of the artist's work distributed over a couple of main floors. Displayed here is the earliest of Gainsborough's surviving portrait paintings – his *Boy and Girl*, a remarkably self-assured work dated to 1744, though it's exhibited in two pieces as someone, somewhere, chopped up the original. Later, Gainsborough developed a fluid, flatteringly easy style that was ideal for his well-heeled subjects, who posed in becoming postures painted in soft, evanescent colours as in the particularly striking *Portrait of Abel Moysey, MP* (1771). Look out also for one of Gainsborough's specialities, his wonderful "**conversation pieces**", so called because the sitters engage in polite chitchat – or genteel activity – with a landscape as the backdrop. In his last years, the artist also dabbled with romantic paintings of country scenes – as in *A Wooded Landscape with Cattle by a Pool* – a playful variation on the serious landscape painting he loved to do best; the rest, he often said, just earned him a living.

ARRIVAL AND INFORMATION

SUDBURY

By train Sudbury station is a 5–10min walk from the centre via Station Rd, with services to Marks Tey, on the London to Colchester line (hourly; 20min).

By bus The bus station is on Hamilton Rd, just south of Market Hill. The main local bus company is H.C. Chambers (ⓦ chambersbus.co.uk).

Destinations Bury St Edmunds (Mon–Sat every 1–2hr; 1hr 10min); Colchester (Mon–Sat every 1–2hr; 50min); Lavenham (Mon–Sat hourly; 35min); Stoke-by-Nayland (Mon–Sat every 1–2hr; 40min).

Tourist office In the library, which is in the grand old Corn Exchange, near Market Hill (Mon–Thurs 9.30am–4.30pm, Fri 9.30am–4pm, Sat 10am–3.30pm; ☎ 01787 881320, ⓦ sudburytowncouncil.co.uk).

EATING AND DRINKING

Black Adder Brewery Tap 21 East St, CO10 2TP ☎ 01787 370876, ⓦ blackaddertap.co.uk. Enjoyable neighbourhood pub where the big deal is the beer – a rotating selection of real ales on draught, but always including something from Mauldons, a local brewer. There's a courtyard patio and pub grub. Mon–Thurs 11am–11pm, Fri & Sat 11am–midnight, Sun noon–10.30pm.

David's 51 Gainsborough St, CO10 2ET ☎ 01787 373919, ⓦ davidsdelicatessen.co.uk. Neat and trim café-deli, where they turn out a tasty range of salads and light meals, mostly featuring local ingredients. Try, perhaps, the scrambled eggs and pancetta on toast. Sandwiches around £3.50. Mon–Sat 9am–4pm.

Lavenham

LAVENHAM, seven miles northeast of Sudbury, was once a centre of the region's wool trade and is now one of the most visited villages in Suffolk, thanks to its unrivalled ensemble of perfectly preserved half-timbered houses. In outward appearance at least, the whole place has changed little since the demise of the wool industry, owing in part to a zealous local preservation society, which has carefully maintained the village's antique appearance. Lavenham is at its most beguiling in the triangular **Market Place**, an airy spot flanked by pastel-painted, medieval dwellings whose beams have been warped into all sorts of wonky angles by the passing of the years.

Guildhall of Corpus Christi

Market Place, CO10 9QZ • Jan to late Feb Sat & Sun 11am–4pm; March–Oct daily 11am–5pm; Nov & Dec Thurs–Sun 11am–4pm • £6.50; NT • ☏ 01787 247646, ⓦ nationaltrust.org.uk/lavenham-guildhall

On the Market Place you'll find the village's most celebrated building, the lime-washed, timber-framed **Guildhall of Corpus Christi**, erected in the sixteenth century as the headquarters of one of Lavenham's four guilds. In the much-altered interior (used successively as a prison and workhouse), there are modest exhibitions on timber-framed buildings, medieval guilds, village life and the wool industry, though most visitors soon end up in the **walled garden**, or the teashop next door.

Church of St Peter and St Paul

Church St, CO10 9SA • Daily: April–Sept 8.30am–6pm; Oct–March 8.30am–4pm • Free • ☏ 01787 247244, ⓦ lavenhamchurch.onesuffolk.net

The Perpendicular **Church of St Peter and St Paul**, located a short walk southwest of the centre, features gargoyle waterspouts and carved boars above the entrance. Local merchants endowed the church with a nave of majestic proportions and a mighty flint tower – at 141ft the highest for miles around – partly to celebrate the Tudor victory at the Battle of Bosworth in 1485 (see p.490), but mainly to show just how wealthy they had become.

ARRIVAL AND INFORMATION   LAVENHAM

By bus Buses pull in at the corner of Water and Church streets, a 5min walk from Market Place. Among several services, perhaps the most useful is Chambers bus #753 (ⓦ chambersbus.co.uk), which links Lavenham with Sudbury, Bury St Edmunds and Colchester.
Destinations Bury St Edmunds (Mon–Sat every 1–2hr;

40min); Colchester (Mon–Sat every 1–2hr; 1hr 30min); Sudbury (Mon–Sat every 1–2hr; 35min).
Tourist office Lady St, just south of Market Place (Jan to mid-March Sat & Sun 11am–3pm; mid-March to Oct daily 10am–4.45pm; Nov to mid-Dec daily 11am–3pm; ☏ 01787 248207, ⓦ heartofsuffolk.co.uk).

ACCOMMODATION AND EATING

★**The Great House** Market Place, CO10 9QZ ☏ 01787 247431, ⓦ greathouse.co.uk. Delightful, family-run hotel bang in the centre of the village. Each of the five guest rooms is decorated in a thoughtful and tasteful manner, amalgamating the original features of the old – very old – house with the new. Deeply comfortable beds and a great breakfast round it all off. The hotel restaurant specializes in classic French cuisine, with both set meals and a la carte. Main courses start at £24. Tues 7–10.30pm, Wed–Sat noon–2.30pm & 7–10.30pm, Sun noon–2.30pm. **£180**
Swan Hotel High St, CO10 9QA ☏ 01787 247477,

ⓦ theswanatlavenham.co.uk. This excellent hotel is a veritable rabbit warren of a place, its nooks and crannies dating back several hundred years. There's a lovely, very traditional, lounge to snooze in, a courtyard garden, an authentic Elizabethan Wool Hall and a wood-panelled bar. Just as appealing, most of the comfy guest rooms abound in original features, and the restaurant is first-rate too, serving imaginative British-based cuisine – roasted wood pigeon and puy lentils for example – with mains starting at around £18. Main restaurant daily noon–2pm & 7–9pm; brasserie daily noon–2.30pm & 6–9.30pm. **£180**

Bury St Edmunds

One of Suffolk's most appealing towns, **BURY ST EDMUNDS**, ten miles north of Lavenham, started out as a Benedictine monastery, founded to accommodate the remains of Edmund, the last Saxon king of East Anglia, who was beheaded by the marauding Danes in 869. Almost two centuries later, England was briefly ruled by the kings of Denmark and the shrewdest of them, **King Cnut**, granted the monastery a generous endowment and built the monks a brand-new church. It was a popular move, and the abbey prospered: by the time of its dissolution in 1539, it had become the richest religious house in the country. Most of the abbey disappeared long ago, and nowadays Bury is better known for its graceful Georgian streets, its flower gardens and its gargantuan sugar-beet plant.

Angel Hill

At the heart of the town is **Angel Hill**, a broad, spacious square partly framed by Georgian buildings, the most distinguished being the ivy-covered **Angel Hotel**, which features in Dickens' *The Pickwick Papers*. Dickens also gave readings of his work in the **Athenaeum**, the Georgian assembly rooms at the far end of the square. A twelfth-century wall runs along the east side of Angel Hill, with the bulky fourteenth-century **Abbey Gate** forming the entrance to the abbey gardens and ruins beyond.

Abbey Gardens and ruins

Abbey Gardens, off Angel Hill, IP33 1XL · Mon–Sat 7.30am–dusk, Sun 9am–dusk · Free; EH · ⓦ www.english-heritage.org.uk/visit/places/bury-st-edmunds-abbey · There's a public car park opposite the abbey, not EH-managed

Ensconced within the immaculate greenery of the **Abbey Gardens**, the **abbey ruins** are themselves like nothing so much as petrified porridge, with little to remind you of the grandiose Norman complex that once dominated the town. Thousands of medieval pilgrims once sought solace at St Edmund's altar and the cult was of such significance that the barons of England gathered here to swear that they would make King John sign their petition – the Magna Carta of 1215. A plaque marks the spot where they met beside what was once the high altar of the old abbey church, whose crumbly remains are on the far (right) side of the abbey gardens behind the Cathedral.

St Edmundsbury cathedral

Angel Hill, IP33 1LS · Daily 8.30am–6pm · Free, but £3 donation requested · ☏ 01284 748720, ⓦ stedscathedral.co.uk

Abutting the gardens, the Anglican **St Edmundsbury Cathedral** is a hangar-like structure, whose most attractive features are its Gothic lantern tower and its beautiful painted roof. The tower was completed in 2005 as part of the Millennium Project, a long-term plan to improve the church, which has also involved the installation of a vaulted ceiling under the tower and the reconstruction of the cloisters. Next door to the cathedral stands the twelfth-century **Norman Tower** (no access), a solitary structure whose rounded arches, blind arcading and dragon gargoyles once served as the main gatehouse into the abbey.

Corn Exchange and around

Bury's main commercial area lies just to the west of Angel Hill up along Abbeygate. There's been some intrusive modern planning here, but sterling Victorian buildings flank both the L-shaped **Cornhill** and the **Buttermarket**, the two short main streets, as well as the narrower streets in between. The dominant edifice is the **Corn Exchange**, whose portico is all Neoclassical extravagance with a whopping set of stone columns and a carved tympanum up above. Perhaps the Victorian merchants who footed the bill decided it was too showy after all, for they had a biblical quote inscribed above the columns in an apparent flash of modesty – "The Earth is the Lord's and the Fulness Thereof".

The Apex

Apex Gallery, 1 Charter Square, IP33 3FD · Mon–Sat 10am–5pm, Sun 10am–4pm · Free · ☏ 01284 758000, ⓦ theapex.co.uk

Attached to the Arc Shopping Centre, a brief stroll from the Cornhill, the **Apex** is Bury's glitzy new performance venue, its construction part of a sustained effort to enliven the town. The first floor here holds the **Apex Gallery**, a contemporary art gallery whose temporary exhibitions have been very well received; most of the works on display are for sale.

ARRIVAL AND DEPARTURE — BURY ST EDMUNDS

By train The station is on the northern edge of the centre, a 10min walk from Angel Hill via Northgate St.

Destinations Cambridge (hourly; 45min); Ely (every 2hr; 30min); Ipswich (hourly; 40min).

By bus The bus station, with regular Lavenham services (Mon–Sat every 1–2hr; 40min), is on St Andrew St North, just south of the Cornhill.

Tourist office In the town centre at the Apex, 1 Charter Square (Mon–Sat 10am–5pm; 01284 764667, visit-burystedmunds.co.uk).

ACCOMMODATION

Chantry Hotel 8 Sparhawk St, IP33 1RY 01284 767427, chantryhotel.com. There are seventeen guest rooms in this privately owned hotel, occupying the Georgian house at the front and the annexe behind. The decor is retro with big wooden beds and even the odd four-poster. A handy, central location on a busy street. **£100**

The Old Cannon B&B 86 Cannon St, IP33 1JR 01284 768769, oldcannonbrewery.co.uk. Bury's most distinctive B&B, a 5min walk north of the town centre. There's a handful of neat and trim modern guest rooms here, all en suite, in an intelligently recycled brewhouse, which is itself attached to a microbrewery, restaurant and bar (see below). **£130**

7

EATING AND DRINKING

Baileys 2 5 Whiting St, IP33 1NX 01284 706198, baileys2.co.uk. This cosy, modern place just off Abbeygate is the best teashop in town. The food is fresh and the menu extensive, but you need look no further than the toasties (£5.25). Mon–Sat 9am–4pm.

★**Maison Bleue** 30 Churchgate St, IP33 1RG 01284 760623, maisonbleue.co.uk. Slick and sleek seafood restaurant noted for its outstanding (French-influenced) menu, covering everything from crab and cod through to sardines and skate. Main courses average £24. Tues–Sat noon–2pm & 7–9.30pm.

★**The Nutshell** 17 The Traverse, IP33 1BJ 01284 764867, thenutshellpub.co.uk. Located at the top of Abbeygate, *The Nutshell* claims to be Britain's smallest pub and it certainly is tiny – it's only sixteen feet by seven, big enough for twelve customers or maybe fifteen, provided they can raise a pint without raising their elbows. The pub provides some sterling beers, including Greene King's full-bodied Abbot Ale and Old Speckled Hen. Daily 11am–11pm.

The Old Cannon Brasserie 86 Cannon St, IP33 1JR 01284 768769, oldcannonbrewery.co.uk. With a B&B (see above) in the adjoining brewhouse, the *Old Cannon's* restaurant-bar offers an excellent range of daily specials with due prominence given to local ingredients. Main courses are competitively priced at around £14. Mon–Sat noon–11pm, Sun noon–10.30pm; kitchen Mon–Sat noon–9pm, Sun noon–3pm.

Ipswich

IPSWICH, situated at the head of the Orwell estuary, was a rich trading port in the Middle Ages, but its appearance today is mainly the result of a revival of fortunes in the Victorian era – give or take some clumsy postwar development. The two surviving reminders of old Ipswich – **Christchurch Mansion** and the splendid **Ancient House** – plus the recently renovated **waterfront** are all reason enough to spend at least an afternoon here, and there's also the **Cornhill**, the ancient Saxon marketplace and still the town's focal point, an agreeable urban space flanked by a bevy of imposing Victorian edifices – the Italianate town hall, the old Neoclassical Post Office and the grandiose pseudo-Jacobean Lloyds building.

Ancient House

30 Buttermarket,, at corner of St Stephen's Lane, IP1 1BT • Lakeland store Mon–Sat 9am–5.30pm

From Cornhill, at the centre of town, it's just a couple of minutes' walk southeast to Ipswich's most famous building, the **Ancient House**, whose exterior was decorated around 1670 in extravagant style, a riot of pargeting and stuccowork that together make it one of the finest examples of Restoration artistry in the country. The house is now a branch of the Lakeland homewares chain, and as such you're free to take a peek inside to view yet more of the decor, including its hammer-beam roof.

Christchurch Mansion and Wolsey Gallery

Soane St, IP4 2BE • March–Oct Tues–Sat 10am–5pm, Sun 11am–5pm; Nov–Feb Tues–Sat 10am–4pm, Sun 11am–4pm • Free • ☎ 01473 433554, ⓦ cimuseums.org.uk

Christchurch Mansion is a handsome if much-restored Tudor building, sporting seventeenth-century Dutch-style gables and set in 65 acres of parkland – an area larger than the town centre itself. The labyrinthine interior is worth exploring. There are period furnishings and a good assortment of paintings by Constable and Gainsborough – the largest collection outside London – both in the main building and in the attached **Wolsey Art Gallery** (same hours).

The Waterfront

Neptune Quay, IP4 1AX, half a mile south of Cornhill

The **Waterfront** – or Wet Dock – was the largest dock in Europe when it opened in 1845. Today, after an imaginative refurbishment, it's flanked by apartments and offices, pubs, hotels and restaurants, many converted from the old marine warehouses. Walking around the Waterfront is a pleasant way to pass an hour or so – look out, in particular, for the proud Neoclassical **Customs House**.

7

ARRIVAL AND INFORMATION   IPSWICH

By train The train station is on the south bank of the River Orwell, a 10min walk from Cornhill along Princes St.
Destinations Bury St Edmunds (hourly; 35min); Cambridge (hourly; 1hr 20min); Colchester (every 30min; 20min); Ely (every 2hr; 1hr); London Liverpool Street (every 30min; 1hr); Norwich (every 30min; 40min).
By bus Buses arrive at and depart from various places around the city centre, including the Cattle Market bus

station, a 5min walk south of Cornhill on Turret Ln, and the Tower Ramparts bus station, just north of Cornhill. Timetables on ⓦ suffolkonboard.com.
Destinations Aldeburgh (Mon–Sat hourly; 2hr); Orford (Mon–Sat every 1–2hr; 1hr 50min; change at Rendlesham).
Tourist office St Stephen's Church, St Stephens Ln (Mon–Sat 9am–5pm; ☎ 01473 258070, ⓦ allaboutipswich.com).

ACCOMMODATION AND EATING

Aqua Eight 8 Lion St, IP1 1DQ ☎ 01473 218989, ⓦ aquaeight.com. Cool Asian fusion restaurant right in the heart of town. Most mains go for £10–15, but you can't go wrong with the superb steamed silver cod with ginger and spring onions in soy sauce for £21. It also has a great bar serving good East Asian-style meze and finger food. Tues–Sun noon–3pm & 6–10pm.

Salthouse Harbour Hotel Neptune Quay, IP4 1AX ☎ 01473 226789, ⓦ salthouseharbour.co.uk. Housed in

an imaginatively converted old warehouse down on the quayside, this is the city's best choice, with seventy large, modern and minimalist-style rooms whose floor-to-ceiling windows look out over Ipswich's old harbour. The hotel restaurant lives up to the same high standards, with curvy banquettes and a low-lit, warehouse-like feel. The food is hearty rather than healthy, but served with flourish and a good eye for detail. Mains £15–22. Daily noon–5pm & 6–10pm. **£150**

The Suffolk coast

The **Suffolk coast** feels detached from the rest of the county: the main road and rail lines from Ipswich to the seaport of Lowestoft funnel traffic a few miles inland for most of the way, and patches of marsh and woodland make the separation still more complete. The coast has long been plagued by erosion and this has contributed to the virtual extinction of the local fishing industry – and in the case of **Dunwich**, almost destroyed the whole town. What is left, however, is undoubtedly one of the most unspoilt shorelines in the country – if, that is, you set aside the Sizewell nuclear power station. Highlights include the sleepy isolation of minuscule **Orford** and several genteel resorts, most notably **Southwold** and **Aldeburgh**, which have both evaded the lurid fate of so many English seaside towns. There are scores of delightful **walks** around here too, easy routes along the coast that are best followed with either the appropriate OS *Explorer* map or the simplified footpath maps available at most tourist offices. The Suffolk coast is also host to East Anglia's most compelling cultural gathering, the three-week-long **Aldeburgh Festival**, which takes place every June.

GETTING AROUND   **THE SUFFOLK COAST**

By public transport Getting around the Suffolk coast requires planning; work out your route in advance on   Ⓦ traveline.info or Ⓦ suffolkonboard.com.

Sutton Hoo

Tranmer House, Sutton Hoo, IP12 3DJ · **Exhibition hall** Jan, Nov & early Dec Sat & Sun 10.30am–4pm; mid-Feb to Oct daily 10.30am–5pm · £8.50; NT · ☎ 01394 389700, Ⓦ nationaltrust.org.uk/sutton-hoo · No public transport

In 1939, a local farmer/archeologist by the name of Basil Brown investigated one of a group of burial mounds on a sandy ridge at **Sutton Hoo**, on a remote part of the Suffolk coast between Ipswich and Orford. Much to everyone's amazement, including his own, he unearthed the forty-oar burial ship of an Anglo-Saxon warrior king, packed with his most valuable possessions, from a splendid iron and tinted-bronze helmet through to his intricately worked gold and jewelled ornaments. Much of the Sutton Hoo treasure is now in London's British Museum (see p.72), but a scattering of artefacts can be seen in the **Sutton Hoo exhibition hall**, which explains the history and significance of the finds. Afterwards, you can wander out onto the burial site itself, about 500 yards away.

Orford

Some twenty miles from Ipswich, on the far side of the Tunstall Forest, two medieval buildings dominate the tiny, eminently appealing village of **ORFORD**. The more impressive is the twelfth-century **castle** (April–Oct daily 10am–5pm; Nov–March Sat & Sun 10am–4pm; £7.30, EH; Ⓦwww.english-heritage.org.uk/visit/places/orford-castle), built on high ground by Henry II, and under siege by Henry's rebellious sons within months of its completion. Most of the castle disappeared centuries ago, but the lofty keep remains, its striking stature hinting at the scale of the original fortifications. Orford's other medieval edifice is **St Bartholomew's Church**, where Benjamin Britten premiered his most successful children's work, *Noye's Fludde*, as part of the 1958 Aldeburgh Festival.

Orford Ness National Nature Reserve

Orford Quay, IP12 2NU · **Boat trips** Outward boats 10am–2pm, last boat back 5pm: mid-April to late June & Oct Sat only; July to Sept Tues–Sat · £9; NT · ☎ 01728 648024, Ⓦ nationaltrust.org.uk/orford-ness-national-nature-reserve

From the top of the castle keep, there's a great view across **Orford Ness National Nature Reserve**, a six-mile-long shingle spit that has all but blocked Orford from the sea since Tudor times. The National Trust offers **boat trips** across to the Ness from Orford Quay, 400 yards down the road from the church – and a five-mile **hiking trail** threads its way along the spit. En route, the trail passes a string of abandoned military buildings, where some of the pioneer research on radar and atomic weapons testing was carried out.

ARRIVAL AND DEPARTURE   **ORFORD**

By bus Buses to and from Orford are poor and often need advance booking. Consult Ⓦ traveline.info.

ACCOMMODATION AND EATING

Butley Orford Oysterage Market Hill, IP12 2LH ☎01394 450277, ⓦpinneysoforford.co.uk. A local institution, dishing up great fish and seafood, much of it caught and smoked locally and served in this simple café/restaurant. Hours vary, but core hours daily noon–2.15pm & 6.30–9pm.

Crown & Castle Market Hill, IP12 2LJ ☎01394 450205, ⓦcrownandcastle.co.uk. Orford's gentle, unhurried air is best experienced by staying overnight at this outstanding (albeit very expensive) hotel, which has eighteen stylish guest rooms and an excellent restaurant. Local, seasonal ingredients are the focus – rump of Suffolk lamb with broad-bean cream sauce for example – with mains around £20. Daily 12.15–2pm & 6.30–9pm. **£200**

Aldeburgh

Well-heeled **ALDEBURGH**, a small seaside town just along the coast from Orford, is best known for its annual **arts festival**, the brainchild of composer **Benjamin Britten** (1913–76), who is buried in the village churchyard alongside the tenor Peter Pears, his lover and musical collaborator. They lived by the seafront in Crag House on Crabbe Street – named after the poet, George Crabbe, who provided Britten with his greatest inspiration (see box below) – before moving to a much larger house a few miles away.

Outside of June, Aldeburgh is a relaxed and low-key coastal resort, with a small fishing fleet selling its daily catch from wooden shacks along the pebbled shore. Aldeburgh's slightly old-fashioned-shop appearance is fiercely defended by its citizens, who caused an almighty rumpus – Barbours at dawn – when Maggi Hambling's 13ft-high *Scallop* sculpture appeared on the beach in 2003. Hambling described the sculpture as a conversation with the sea and a suitable memorial to Britten; many disgruntled locals compare it to a mantelpiece ornament gone wrong.

Aldeburgh's wide **High Street** and narrow side streets run close to the **beach**, but this was not always the case – hence their quixotic appearance. The sea swallowed much of what was once an extensive medieval town long ago and today Aldeburgh's oldest building, the sixteenth-century **Moot Hall** (daily: April, May, Sept & Oct 2.30–5pm; June–Aug noon–5pm), which began its days in the centre of town, finds itself on the seashore. Several **footpaths** radiate out from Aldeburgh, with the most pleasant leading southwest to the winding estuary of the **River Alde**.

7

BENJAMIN BRITTEN AND THE ALDEBURGH FESTIVAL

Born in Lowestoft in 1913, **Benjamin Britten** was closely associated with Suffolk for most of his life. The main break was during World War II when, as a conscientious objector, Britten exiled himself to the US. Ironically enough, it was here that Britten first read the work of the nineteenth-century Suffolk poet, George Crabbe, whose *The Borough*, a grisly portrait of the life of the fishermen of Aldeburgh, was the basis of the libretto of Britten's best-known opera, *Peter Grimes*, which was premiered in London in 1945. Three years later, Britten launched the **Aldeburgh Festival** as a showpiece for his own works and those of his contemporaries. For the rest of his life he composed many works specifically for the festival, including his masterpiece for children, *Noye's Fludde*, and the last of his fifteen operas, *Death in Venice*.

By the mid-1960s, the festival had outgrown the parish churches in which it began, and moved into a collection of disused malt houses, five miles west of Aldeburgh on the River Alde, just south of the small village of **Snape**. The complex, the **Snape Maltings** (ⓦsnapemaltings .co.uk), was subsequently converted into one of the finest concert venues in the country and, in addition to the concert hall, there are now recording studios, galleries, a tearoom, and a pub, the *Plough & Sail*. The Aldeburgh Festival takes place every June for two and a half weeks. Core performances are still held at the Maltings, but a string of other local venues are pressed into service as well. Throughout the rest of the year, the Maltings hosts a wide-ranging programme of musical and theatrical events. For all programme information and bookings, go to ⓦsnapemaltings.co.uk or call the box office on ☎01728 687110. **Tickets** for the Aldeburgh Festival usually go on sale to the public towards the end of March, and sell out fast for the big-name recitals.

By bus Buses to Aldeburgh pull in along the High St and on the south side of the resort at Fort Green, heading to

Ipswich (Mon–Sat hourly; 2hr) and Saxmundham (Mon–Sat every 30min; 30min).

ACCOMMODATION

Brudenell The Parade, IP15 5BU ☎ 01728 452071, ⓦ brudenellhotel.co.uk. This bright and smart seafront hotel has something of a New England feel that sits very comfortably here in Aldeburgh. There's a pleasant sitting room downstairs with sea views and the bedrooms are thoughtfully furnished in a contemporary style. **£170**

★ **Ocean House B&B** 25 Crag Path, IP15 5BS ☎ 01728 452094, ⓦ oceanhousealdeburgh.co.uk. Housed in an immaculately maintained Victorian dwelling right on the seafront, *Ocean House* has just three traditional, en-suite guest rooms including a top-floor suite. The English breakfasts, with home-made bread, are delicious. **£100**

EATING AND DRINKING

★ **Aldeburgh Fish & Chip Shop** 226 High St, IP15 5DB ☎ 01728 452250, ⓦ aldeburghfishandchips.co.uk. One of Aldeburgh's two outstanding fish-and-chip shops – this is the original, serving takeaway only. Such is its reputation that there are often long queues at the weekend. Core hours: daily noon–2pm & 5/6–8/9pm.

The Golden Galleon 137 High St, IP15 5AR ☎ 01728 454685, ⓦ aldeburghfishandchips.co.uk. Canteen-style, sit-down fish-and-chip restaurant, sister to the *Fish & Chip Shop* along the road. Mon–Fri noon–2.30pm & 5–8pm,

Sat & Sun noon–8pm.

★ **The Lighthouse** 77 High St, IP15 5AU ☎ 01728 453377, ⓦ lighthouserestaurant.co.uk. Aldeburgh's best restaurant, a relaxed, informal and always busy place located in cosy, split-level premises. The menu favours locally sourced ingredients, featuring everything from burgers and fish and chips to venison tagine with couscous. Mains average £13 at lunchtimes, more in the evening. Daily noon–2pm & 6.30–10pm.

Dunwich and around

Tiny **DUNWICH**, about twelve miles up the coast from Aldeburgh, is probably the strangest and certainly the eeriest place on the Suffolk coast. The one-time seat of the kings of East Anglia, a bishopric and formerly a large port, Dunwich peaked in the twelfth century since when it's all been downhill: over the last millennium something like a mile of land has been lost to the sea, a process that continues at the rate of about a yard a year. As a result, the whole of the medieval city now lies underwater, including all twelve churches, the last of which toppled over the cliffs in 1919. All that survives today are fragments of the Greyfriars monastery, which originally lay to the west of the city and now dangles near the sea's edge. For a potted history of the lost city, head for the **museum** (April–Oct daily 11.30am–4.30pm; free, but donation requested; ☎ 01728 648796, ⓦ www.dunwichmuseum.org.uk) in what's left of Dunwich – little more than one small street of terraced houses built by the local landowner in the nineteenth century.

Minsmere RSPB Nature Reserve

IP17 3BY • Reserve daily 9am–9pm or dusk; visitor centre daily 9am–5pm, 4pm in winter • £9 • ☎ 01728 648281, ⓦ rspb.org .uk/minsmere

From Dunwich, it's about an hour's walk south along the coast to the **Minsmere RSPB Nature Reserve**, though there's a road here too – just watch for the sign on the more southerly of the two byroads into Dunwich. The reserve covers a varied terrain of marsh, scrub and beach, and in the autumn it's a gathering place for wading birds and waterfowl, which arrive here by the hundred. The reserve is also home to a small population of bitterns, one of England's rarest birds. You can rent binoculars from the **visitor centre** and strike out on the trails to the birdwatching hides.

By car There's no regular public transport to Dunwich, so driving is your best bet. A sprawling seashore car park gives

ready access to both the village and this slice of coast.

EATING AND DRINKING

Flora Tearooms Dunwich beach, IP17 3EN ☎01728 648433. Set right on the beach, this popular café is a large hut-like affair, where they serve steaming cups of tea and piping hot fish and chips to an assortment of birdwatchers, hikers and anglers. Daily 11am–4pm.

Southwold

Perched on robust cliffs just to the north of the River Blyth, **SOUTHWOLD** is one of the region's most charming towns, its genteel delights attracting the well-heeled and well-spoken. It was not always so: by the sixteenth century Southwold had become Suffolk's busiest fishing port, but thereafter it lost most of its fishery to neighbouring Lowestoft and today, although a small fleet still brings in herrings, sprats and cod, the town is primarily a **seaside resort** – and one with none of the crassness of many of its competitors. There are fine Georgian buildings, a long sandy beach, open heathland, a dinky harbour and even a little industry – in the shape of the Adnams brewery – but no burger bars and certainly no amusement arcades. This gentility was not to the liking of **George Orwell**, who lived for a time at his parents' house at 36 High Street (a plaque marks the spot), but he might well have taken a liking to Southwold's major music festival, **Latitude** (Ⓦlatitudefestival.co.uk), which spreads over four days in the middle of July with happy campers grubbing down in Henham Park beside the A12, about five miles west of town.

7

Market Place and around

The centre of Southwold is its triangular, pocket-sized **Market Place**, sitting at one end of the town's busy High Street and framed by attractive, mostly Georgian buildings. From here, it's a couple of hundred yards north along Church Street to **East Green**, one of the several greens that were left as firebreaks after the town was gutted by fire in 1659. On one side of East Green is **Adnams Brewery** (tours available; Ⓦtours.adnams.co.uk), on the other a stumpy old lighthouse. Close by is Southwold's architectural pride and joy, the **Church of St Edmund** (daily 9am–4pm; free), a handsome fifteenth-century structure whose solid symmetries are balanced by its long and elegantly carved windows.

The Sailors' Reading Room

East Cliff, IP18 6EL • Daily 9am–dusk • Free • Ⓦ www.southwoldsailorsreadingroom.co.uk

From Market Place, it's a short stroll along East Street to a clifftop vantage point, which offers a grand view over the beach. Also up there is the curious **Sailors' Reading Room**, where pensioners gather in the mornings to shoot the breeze in a room full of model ships, seafaring texts and vintage photos of local tars, all beards and sea boots: founded in 1864, it was designed to keep these very same men reading rather than drinking.

Under the Pier Show

Southwold pier, IP18 6BN • Daily: April–Sept 9am–7pm; Oct–March 10am–5pm • Free • ☎ 01502 7221055, Ⓦ underthepier.com

Jutting out from the beach, **Southwold pier** is the latest incarnation of a structure that dates back to 1899. Revamped and renovated a decade ago, the pier houses the usual – if rather more polite than usual – cafés and souvenir shops, but its star turn is the **Under the Pier Show**, where a series of knowingly playful machines, handmade by Tim Hunkin, provide all sorts of arcade-style sensory surprises. Try the "Pirate Practice", the "Rent-a-Dog" and the mischievous (and emotionally rewarding) "Whack-a-banker".

The harbour

At the mouth of the River Blyth is **the harbour**, an idyllic spot where fishing boats rest against old wooden jetties and nets are spread out along the banks to dry. A footpath leads west from the river mouth to a tiny foot **ferry** (April–Oct Sat & Sun 10am–5pm, plus sometimes Mon–Fri 10am–12.30pm & 2–5pm; £1; ⓦexplorewalberswick.co.uk /ferry), which shuffles across the river to Walberswick. If you're heading back towards Southwold, however, keep going along the river until you pass the *Harbour Inn* and then take the path that leads back into town across **Southwold Common**. The whole circular walk takes about thirty minutes.

ARRIVAL AND DEPARTURE   SOUTHWOLD

By bus Buses pull in along Station Rd, on the west side of the town centre.
Destinations Halesworth (on the Ipswich to Lowestoft train line; Mon–Sat hourly; 30min); Norwich (Mon–Sat every 1–2hr; 1hr 30min to 2hr).

ACCOMMODATION

The Crown 90 High St, IP18 6DP ☎01502 722275, ⓦthecrownsouthwold.co.uk. The less upmarket (and less expensive) of Adnams' two hotels in Southwold, with a dozen or so rooms above a bar/restaurant (see below). Most of the rooms are large and have been decorated in a pleasant, contemporary style. **£170**

★**Home@21** 21 North Parade, IP18 6LT ☎01502 722573, ⓦhomeat21.co.uk. Located near the pier, this seafront guesthouse occupies a well-maintained Victorian terraced house. There are three sympathetically updated guest rooms, two of which are en suite and two sea-facing. **£100**

The Swan Market Place, IP18 6EG ☎01502 722186, ⓦtheswansouthwold.co.uk. Delightful if pricey hotel occupying a splendid, recently refurbished Georgian building right at the heart of Southwold. The main building is a real period piece, its nooks and crannies holding all manner of Georgian details. Some of the guest rooms are here, others (the "Lighthouse Rooms") are in the more modern garden annexe at the back. **£200**

EATING AND DRINKING

The Crown 90 High St, IP18 6DP ☎01502 722275, ⓦthecrownsouthwold.co.uk. Deluxe bar food featuring local, seasonal ingredients, all washed down with Adnams ales. Try, for example, the roast butternut squash with puy lentils. Mains £8–19. Tables are allocated on a first-come, first-served basis. Drinks daily noon–11pm; kitchen Mon–Sat noon–2pm & 6–9pm, Sun noon–3pm & 6–9pm.

Lord Nelson 42 East St, IP18 6EJ ☎01502 722079, ⓦthelordnelsonsouthwold.co.uk. This lively neighbourhood pub, with its low-beamed ceilings, has a first-rate, locally inspired menu. Try, for example, the herring, Nelson smokes (smoked haddock and cod in sauce) or the dressed crab. Mains average £13. Drinks Mon–Sat 10.30am–11pm, Sun noon–10.30pm; kitchen daily noon–2pm & 7–9pm.

Sutherland House 56 High St, IP18 6DN ☎01502 724544, ⓦsutherlandhouse.co.uk. There's a strong local emphasis to the menu at this classy Modern British restaurant, which is housed in one of Southwold's oldest buildings. Main courses are £12–20, and they have a helpful food-miles chart attached. Daily noon–2.30pm & 6.30–8.30pm; closed Mon in winter.

Norwich

One of the five largest cities in Norman England, **NORWICH** once served a vast hinterland of East Anglian **cloth producers**, whose work was brought here by river and then exported to the continent. Its isolated position beyond the Fens meant that it enjoyed closer links with the Low Countries than with the rest of England and, by 1700, Norwich was the second-richest city in the country after London. With the onset of the Industrial Revolution, however, Norwich lost ground to the northern manufacturing towns – the city's famous mustard company, Colman's, is one of its few industrial success stories – and this has helped preserve much of the ancient street plan and many of the city's older buildings. Pride of place goes to the beautiful **cathedral** and the sterling **castle**, but the city's hallmark is its **medieval churches**, thirty or so squat flint structures with sturdy towers and sinuous stone tracery decorating the windows. Many are no longer in regular use and are now in the care of the **Norwich Historic Churches Trust** (ⓦnorwich-churches.org), whose website describes each in precise detail.

Norwich's relative isolation has also meant that the population has never swelled to any great extent and today, with just 220,000 inhabitants, it remains an easy and enjoyable city to negotiate. Yet Norwich is no provincial backwater. In the 1960s, the foundation of the **University of East Anglia** (UEA) made it much more cosmopolitan and bolstered its arts scene, while in the 1980s it attracted new high-tech companies, who created something of a mini-boom, making the city one of England's wealthiest. As East Anglia's unofficial capital, Norwich also lies at the hub of the region's **transport** network, serving as a useful base for visiting the Broads and as a springboard for the north Norfolk coast.

The Cathedral

The Close, NR1 4EH • Daily 7.30am–6pm • Free, but donation requested • ☎ 01603 218300, ⓦ cathedral.org.uk

Of all the medieval buildings in Norwich, it's the **Cathedral** that fires the imagination, a mighty, sandy-coloured structure finessed by its prickly octagonal spire, which rises to a height of 315ft, second only to Salisbury Cathedral in Wiltshire. Entered via the Hostry, a glassy, well-proportioned visitor centre, the **interior** is pleasantly light thanks to a creamy tint in the stone and the clear glass windows of much of the **nave**, where the thick pillars are a powerful legacy of the Norman builders who began the cathedral in 1096. The nave's architectural highlight is the ceiling, a finely crafted affair whose delicate and geometrically precise fan vaulting is embellished by several dozen **roof bosses**. Accessible from the south aisle of the nave are the cathedral's unique **cloisters**.

Built between 1297 and 1450, and the only two-storey cloisters left standing in England, they contain a remarkable set of sculpted **bosses**, similar to the ones in the main nave, but here they are close enough to be scrutinized without binoculars. The dominant theme is the **Apocalypse**, but look out also for the bosses depicting green men, originally pagan fertility symbols.

Cathedral precincts

Outside, in front of the main entrance, stands the medieval **Carnary Chapel**. This is the original building of Norwich School, whose blue-blazered pupils are often visible during term time – the rambling school buildings are adjacent. A statue of the school's most famous boy, **Horatio Nelson**, faces the chapel, standing on the green of the **Upper Close**, which is guarded by two ornate and imposing medieval gates (**Erpingham** and, a few yards to the south, **Ethelbert**). Beside the Erpingham gate is a memorial to **Edith Cavell**, a local woman who was a nurse in occupied Brussels during World War I. She was shot by the Germans in 1915 for helping Allied prisoners to escape, a fate that made her an instant folk hero; her grave is outside the cathedral ambulatory. Both gates lead onto the old Saxon marketplace, **Tombland**, a wide and busy thoroughfare whose name derives from the Saxon word for an open space.

Strangers' Hall

4 Charing Cross, NR2 4AL • Mid-Feb to May & Oct–Dec Wed 10am–4pm, Sun 1–4.30pm; June–Sept Wed–Fri 10am–4pm Sun 1–4.30pm • £5 • ☎ 01603 667229, ☻ museums.norfolk.gov.uk

Strangers' Hall is the city's most unusual attraction. Dating back to the fourteenth century, it's a veritable rabbit warren of a place stuffed with all manner of bygones, including ancient fireplaces, oodles of wood panelling, a Regency music room and a Georgian dining room. Allow an hour or so to explore its nooks and crannies, though the most impressive room, the Great Hall, with its church-like Gothic windows, comes right at the beginning. The hall is named after the Protestant refugees who fled here from the Spanish Netherlands to avoid the tender mercies of the Inquisition in the 1560s; at the peak of the migration, these "Strangers" accounted for around a third of the local population.

Market Place

The city's **Market Place** is the site of one of the country's largest **open-air markets** (Mon–Sat), with stalls selling everything from bargain-basement clothes to local mussels and whelks. Four very different but equally distinctive buildings oversee the market's stripy awnings, the oldest of them being the fifteenth-century **Guildhall**, a capacious flint and stone structure begun in 1407. Opposite, commanding the heights of the marketplace, are the austere **City Hall**, a lumbering brick pile with a landmark clocktower that was built in the 1930s in a Scandinavian style, and **The Forum**, a large, flashy glass structure completed in 2001. The latter is home to the city's main library and tourist office (see p.398). On the south side of Market Place is the finest of the four buildings, **St Peter Mancroft** (Mon–Sat 10am–3pm; free; ☻ stpetermancroft.org .uk), whose long and graceful nave leads to a mighty stone tower, an intricately carved affair surmounted by a spiky little spire, while inside slender columns reach up to the delicate groining of the roof.

Back outside and just below the church is **Gentlemen's Walk**, the town's main promenade, which runs along the bottom of the marketplace and abuts the **Royal Arcade**, an Art Nouveau extravagance from 1899. The arcade has been beautifully restored to reveal its swirling tiling, ironwork and stained glass.

Castle Museum and Art Gallery

Castle Meadow, NR1 3JU • Late June to late Sept Mon–Sat 10am–5pm, Sun 1–5pm; late Sept to late June Mon–Sat 10am–4.30pm, Sun 1–4.30pm • £9.15 • ☎ 01603 493625, ⓦ museums.norfolk.gov.uk

Glued to the top of a grassy mound in the centre of town – and with a modern shopping mall drilled into its side – the stern walls of **Norwich Castle** date from the twelfth century. To begin with they were a reminder of Norman power and then, when the castle was turned into a prison, they served as a grim warning to potential lawbreakers. Today, much of the castle is occupied by the **Castle Museum and Art Gallery**, whose wide-ranging displays spread over two floors around a central rotunda. Pride of place goes to the **Colman Art galleries**, which boast an outstanding selection of work by the **Norwich School**. Founded in 1803, and in existence for just thirty years, this school of landscape painters produced – for the most part – richly coloured, formally composed land- and seascapes in oil and watercolour, paintings whose realism harked back to the Dutch landscape painters of the seventeenth century. The leading figures were **John Crome** (1768–1821) – aka "Old Crome" – and **John Sell Cotman** (1782–1842).

University of East Anglia

Earlham Rd, NR4 7TJ • **UEA Campus** Open access • Free • ☎ 01603 456161, ⓦ uea.ac.uk • **Sainsbury Centre for Visual Arts** Tues–Fri 10am–6pm, Sat & Sun 10am–5pm • Free, but admission charged for some exhibitions • ☎ 01603 593199, ⓦ scva.ac.uk • Among several services, bus #25 runs to the UEA campus from the train station and Castle Meadow

The **University of East Anglia** (UEA) occupies a sprawling campus on the western outskirts of the city beside the B1108. Its buildings are resolutely modern, an assortment of concrete-and-glass blocks of varying designs, some quite ordinary, others, like the prize-winning "ziggurat" halls of residence, designed by Denys Lasdun, eminently memorable. The main reason to visit is the **Sainsbury Centre for Visual Arts**, which occupies a large, shed-like building designed by Norman Foster. Well-lit and beautifully presented, the bulk of the permanent collection spreads out over the main floor, beginning with a substantial selection of non-European – particularly Asian and African – artefacts positioned close to some of the European paintings and sculptures they influenced and/or inspired.

ARRIVAL AND INFORMATION

NORWICH

By plane Norwich Airport (ⓦ norwichairport.co.uk) serves national and international destinations and is about 4 miles north of the city centre along the A140. Park and Ride buses (ⓦ norwichparkandride.co.uk) run from the airport to the centre (Mon–Sat every 20min; 20min).

By train The station is on the east bank of the River Wensum, a 10min walk from the city centre along Prince of Wales Rd.

Destinations Cambridge (hourly; 1hr 20min); Cromer (hourly; 45min); Colchester (every 30min; 1hr); Ely (every 30min; 1hr); Ipswich (every 30min; 40min); London Liverpool Street (every 30min; 1hr 50min);

Sheringham (hourly; 1hr).

By bus Long-distance buses mostly terminate at the main bus station between Surrey St and Queen's Rd, a 10min walk from the centre. Some services also stop in the centre on Castle Meadow.

Destinations King's Lynn (hourly; 1hr 50min with one change); London Victoria (every 2–3hr; 2hr 30min–3hr 45min).

Tourist office In the Forum building, overlooking Market Place (Mon–Sat 9.30am–5.30pm, plus early July to mid-Sept Sun 10.30am–3.30pm; ☎ 01603 213999, ⓦ visitnorwich.co.uk).

ACCOMMODATION

38 St Giles 38 St Giles St, NR2 1LL ☎ 01603 662944, ⓦ 38stgiles.co.uk; map p.395. Billing itself as a cross between a B&B and a hotel, this deluxe establishment has five en-suite guest rooms of varying size and description, but all top quality. Great home-made breakfasts too. It's in a handy location, just a few yards from

the Market Place. __£120__

★**Gothic House** King's Head Yard, 42 Magdalen St, NR3 1JE ☎ 01603 631879, ⓦ gothic-house-norwich .com; map p.395. This particularly charming B&B occupies a slender, three-storey Georgian house down a little courtyard off Magdalen Street. The interior has been meticulously renovated in a period style and the two salon-style bedrooms are reached via the most charming of spiral staircases. The guest rooms are not attached to their bathrooms, but this really is no inconvenience. **£105**

Maid's Head Hotel 20 Tombland, NR3 ILB ☎01603 209955, ⓦmaidsheadhotel.co.uk; map p.395. Not everyone's cup of tea perhaps, but this chain hotel is delightfully idiosyncratic – a rabbit warren of a place with all sorts of architectural bits and pieces, from the mock-Tudor facade to the ancient, wood-panelled bar, though there is also a clumpy modern extension. The rooms are mostly large and very comfortable in a standard-issue sort of way, and the location, bang in the centre opposite the cathedral, can't be beat. If you are a light sleeper, you should avoid those rooms that overlook the street, especially at the weekend. **£120**

Number 17 17 Colegate, NR3 1BN ☎01603 764486, ⓦnumber17norwich.co.uk; map p.395. Family-run guesthouse with eight en-suite guest rooms decorated in a brisk, modern style with solid oak flooring; there are two larger family rooms as well. Good location, in one of the nicest parts of the centre. **£90**

EATING

Benedicts 9 St Benedict's St, NR2 4PE ☎01603 926080, ⓦrestaurantbenedicts.com; map p.395. All simple lines and bright whites, this appealing, family-owned restaurant offers a well-considered Modern British menu: try, for example, the locally caught sea bass or mullet with turnips, Jersey Royals and passion fruit. A two-course meal costs £30, less at lunch. Tues 6–10pm, Wed–Sat noon–2pm & 6–10pm.

★**Grosvenor Fish Bar** 28 Lower Goat Lane, NR2 1EL ☎01603 625855, ⓦfshshop.com; map p.395. A fish-and-chip shop with bells on: the funky decor is inventive, but this plays second fiddle to the delicious fish and chips (from £6), not to mention the veggie burgers, meat pies and more distinctive dishes – tuna with wasabi beans, for one. Eat in or take away. Mon–Sat 11am–7.30pm.

The Last Wine Bar 76 St George's St, NR3 1AB ☎01603 626626, ⓦlastwinebar.co.uk; map p.395. Imaginatively converted old shoe factory, a couple of minutes' walk north of the river that has an unpretentious wine bar in one section and an excellent restaurant in the other. The food is firmly Modern British, with the likes of braised lamb shank with carrots and parsnips in a rosemary jus (around £17). Mon–Sat noon–2.30pm & 6–10.30pm.

Nazma 15 Magdalen St, NR3 1LE ☎01603 618701, ⓦnazmaonline.co.uk; map p.395. The menu at this modern Indian restaurant covers all the classics, each prepared from scratch with the freshest of ingredients. Particularly strong on Bangladeshi cuisine. Eat in or take away. Mains around £11. Daily 5–11pm.

DRINKING AND NIGHTLIFE

Birdcage 23 Pottergate, NR1 1BA ☎01603 633534 ⓦthebirdcagenorwich.co.uk; map p.395. Idiosyncratic pub with a classic Art Deco exterior and a self-proclaimed "Bohemian" interior – take it all in, from the razzly furniture to the modern art and vintage postcards on the walls. It all works very well and the place casts a wide net, with light bites, board games, cocktails, cabaret and cupcakes. Mon–Wed & Sun noon–11pm, Thurs–Sat noon–midnight.

★**Kings Head** 42 Magdalen St, NR3 1JE ☎01603 620468 ⓦkingsheadnorwich.com; map p.395. The perfect drinkers' pub, with precious little in the way of distraction – there are certainly no one-armed bandits here. The outstanding selection of real ales is supplemented by an equally impressive range of bottled beers, most notably Belgian. The pub has just two smallish rooms, so you may need to be assertive to get served. Daily noon–11pm, sometimes later.

Micawbers Tavern 92 Pottergate, NR2 1DZ ☎01603 626627; map p.395. Lodged in an old beamed building on one of the city's prettiest streets, this friendly pub is a local par excellence, featuring an outstanding range of guest ales on draft. There's home-cooked food and sports TV too. Mon & Tues 5–11pm, Wed & Thurs 3–11pm, Fri 3pm–midnight, Sat noon–midnight, Sun noon–9pm.

Waterfront 139–141 King St, NR1 1QH ☎01603 632717, ⓦwaterfrontnorwich.webflow.io; map p.395. This happening club and alternative music venue, which occupies a one-time beer bottling plant, showcases some great bands, both big names and local talent, and offers club and DJ nights too. Schedule varies; see website.

ENTERTAINMENT

Cinema City Suckling House, St Andrew's St, NR2 4AD ☎0871 902 5724, ⓦpicturehouses.co.uk; map p.395. Easily the best cinema in town, featuring prime new releases plus themed evenings and cult and classic films. Also live feeds, a Kids' Club and late-night horror films.

Norwich Arts Centre 51 St Benedict's St, NR2 4PG ☎01603 660352, ⓦnorwichartscentre.co.uk; map p.395. Housed in a redundant church, this inventive and creative Arts Centre offers a wide range of media and performing arts plus an enterprising programme of participatory workshops and activities for both kids and adults.

7

7

THE NORFOLK BROADS

Three **rivers** – the Yare, Waveney and Bure – meander across the flatlands to the east of Norwich, converging on Breydon Water before flowing into the sea at Great Yarmouth. In places these rivers swell into wide expanses of water known as **broads**, which for years were thought to be natural lakes. In fact they're the result of extensive peat cutting – several centuries of accumulated diggings made in a region where wood was scarce and peat a valuable source of energy. The pits flooded when sea levels rose in the thirteenth and fourteenth centuries to create these **Norfolk Broads** (ⓦvisitthebroads.co.uk), now one of the most important wetlands in Europe – a haven for birds including kingfishers, grebes and warblers – and one of the region's major tourist attractions. Looking after the Broads, the **Broads Authority** (ⓦwww.broads-authority.gov.uk) maintains a series of information centres throughout the region.

The Norfolk Broads are crisscrossed by roads and rail lines, but the best – really the only – way to see them is **by boat**, and you could happily spend a week or so exploring the 125 miles of lock-free navigable waterways, visiting the various churches, pubs and windmills en route. Of the many **boat rental** companies, Norfolk Broads Direct (☎01603 782207, ⓦbroads.co.uk), is one of the most reputable and they have a rental outlet at The Bridge in **Wroxham**, which is just seven miles northeast of Norwich – and easy to reach by train, bus and car. Prices for cruisers start at around £700 a week for four people in peak season, but less expensive, short-term rentals are widely available too. For something rather more adventurous, you could also contact the Wroxham-based **Canoe Man** (☎01603 783777, ⓦthecanoeman.com), who organizes a whole range of activities from guided canoe trips to bushcraft expeditions.

Trying to explore the Broads by car is pretty much a waste of time, but **cyclists** and **walkers** can take advantage of the region's network of footpaths and cycle trails. There are **bike rental** points dotted around the region and walkers might consider the 62-mile **Weavers' Way**, a long-distance footpath that winds through the best parts of the Broads on its way from Cromer to Great Yarmouth.

Norwich Puppet Theatre Church of St James, Whitefriars, NR3 1TN ☎01603 629921, ⓦpuppet theatre.co.uk; map p.395. Housed in a deconsecrated medieval church beside the busy Whitefriars roundabout, this long-established puppet theatre company has an outstanding reputation for the quality of its puppets and the excellence of its shows. Some performances are aimed at young children – who are simply enraptured – while others are for adults.

Theatre Royal Theatre St, NR2 1RL ☎01603 630000, ⓦtheatreroyalnorwich.co.uk; map p.395. This is the city's major performance venue, located in a clunky modern building with a capacious auditorium. It casts its artistic net wide, from world music to opera.

North Norfolk coast

About forty miles from one end to the other, the **north Norfolk coast** is a top tourist destination, attracting a wide cross section of the British population to its long sandy beaches and seaside resorts. This stretch of coast begins (or ends) at **Cromer**, perhaps the most appealing of the larger resorts on account of its handsome setting, perched on the edge of blustery cliffs. A few miles to the west is another well-established resort, **Sheringham**, but thereafter the shoreline becomes a ragged patchwork of salt marshes, dunes and shingle spits trimmed by a string of charming villages, principally **Cley**, **Blakeney**, **Burnham Market** and **Wells-next-the-Sea**, all of which are prime targets for an overnight stay.

GETTING AROUND

NORTH NORFOLK COAST

By train There are hourly trains on the Bittern Line (ⓦbitternline.com) from Norwich to Cromer (45min) and Sheringham (1hr).

By bus Easily the most useful bus is Stagecoach's Norfolk Coasthopper (ⓦstagecoachbus.com/promos-and-offers /east/coasthopper), which runs along the coast between

Cromer and King's Lynn via a whole gaggle of coastal towns and villages, including Blakeney, Sheringham, Wells and Burnham Market; it generally sticks to the main coast road, the A149. Frequencies vary on different stretches of the route and there are more services in the summer than in the winter, but on the more popular stretches buses appear every 30min or hourly (less frequently on Sun). There are lots of different tickets and discounts; perhaps most useful is the Coasthopper Rover, which provides unlimited travel on the whole route for either one day (£10), three days (£21) or seven days (£36); tickets can be bought from the driver.

Cromer

Dramatically poised on a high bluff, **CROMER** should be the most memorable of the Norfolk coastal resorts, but its fine aspect has long been undermined by a certain shabbiness in its narrow streets and alleys. To be fair, however, things are at last on the mend, with new businesses arriving to add a touch of flair, and the town council keeps a string of clifftop mini-parks and gardens in immaculate condition. It's no more than the place deserves: Cromer has a long history, first as a prosperous medieval port – witness the tower of **St Peter and St Paul**, at 160ft the tallest in Norfolk – and then as a fashionable watering hole after the advent of the railway in the 1880s. There are three things you must do here: take a walk on the **beach**, stroll out onto the **pier**, and, of course, grab a **crab**: Cromer crabs are famous right across England and several places sell them, reliably fresh, and cooked and stuffed every which way.

7

ARRIVAL AND INFORMATION

By train From Cromer station, with trains for Norwich (hourly; 45min) and Sheringham (hourly; 10min), it's a 5min walk to the centre.

By bus Buses to Cromer, including the Norfolk Coasthopper (see opposite), stop at the east end of Cadogan Rd, on the western side of the town centre.

Tourist office The North Norfolk Information Centre is on the south side of the town centre on Louden Rd (late May to Aug Mon–Sat 10am–5pm, Sun 10am–4pm; Sept to late May daily 10am–4pm; ☎01263 512497, ⓦvisitnorfolk.co.uk).

ACCOMMODATION

Cliftonville Hotel 29 Runton Rd, NR27 9AS ☎01263 512543, ⓦcliftonvillehotel.co.uk. Among the big old mansions that line Runton Rd just west of the town centre facing out to sea, this is the smartest, its grand Edwardian foyer equipped with an impressive double staircase and oodles of wood panelling. After the foyer, the rooms beyond can't help but seem a tad mundane, but they are large and most have sea views. **£160**

Virginia Court Hotel 9 Cliff Ave, NR27 0AN ☎01263 512398, ⓦvirginiacourt.co.uk. This recently revamped, medium-sized hotel, arguably Cromer's best, has super-comfy beds, super-thick towels, and super-warm duvets. The hotel dates back to Edwardian times, hence the capacious foyer with its wide, sweeping staircase, and the atmosphere is very much that of a traditional seaside hotel, friendly and relaxed. **£140**

EATING AND DRINKING

Mary Jane's Fish & Chip Shop 27 Garden St, NR27 9HN ☎01263 511208, ⓦmaryjanes.co.uk. Many Norfolk tourists are fastidious about their fish and chips, with allegiances strongly argued and felt. This simple, family-owned place is especially popular, for the lightness of the batter and the freshness of the fish. Eat in or take away. Takeaway May–Aug Mon–Sat 11.30am–10pm, Sun noon–9.30pm; Sept–April Mon–Thurs 11.30am–9pm, Fri & Sat 11.30am–10.30pm, Sun noon–8pm.

Rocket House Café RNLI building, The Gangway, NR27 9ET ☎01263 519126, ⓦrockethousecafe.co.uk. Offering sparkling views over the beach, pier and ocean from its giant windows – and from its blustery terrace – this café has the best location in town. The food lacks subtlety, though – stick to the crabs and the salads (which start at just £5). Mon–Fri 9am–5pm, Sat & Sun 10am–5pm.

Virginia Court Hotel 9 Cliff Ave, NR27 0AN ⓦvirginiacourt.co.uk. Excellent hotel restaurant, where the emphasis is on local, seasonal ingredients – try, for example, the roast duckling with an orange and redcurrant jus. Mains average £16. Accommodation and dinner deals available. Daily: afternoon teas 2–5pm; dinner 6–8.30pm.

Felbrigg Hall

Felbrigg, NR11 8PR, 2 miles southwest of Cromer · **House** Mon–Wed, Sat & Sun: mid-Feb to late March 11am–3pm; late March to late Oct 11am–5pm · £10.40 (includes gardens & estate); NT · **Gardens & estate** Late Feb to late Oct daily 11am–5pm; Nov to late Dec Thurs–Sun 11am–3pm · £6.25; NT · ☎ 01263 837444, ⓦ nationaltrust.org.uk/felbrigg-hall-gardens-and-estate · No public transport

A charming Jacobean mansion, **Felbrigg Hall** boasts an appealing main facade where the soft hues of the ageing limestone and brick are intercepted by three bay windows, which together sport a large inscription – "Gloria Deo in Excelsis" – in celebration of the reviving fortunes of the family who then owned the place, the Windhams. The interior is splendid too, with the studied informality of both the dining and drawing rooms enlivened by their magnificent seventeenth-century plasterwork ceilings. The surrounding **parkland** divides into two, with woods to the north and open pasture to the south. A popular spot to head for is the medieval **Church of St Margaret's**, which contains a fancy memorial to William Windham I and his wife by Grinling Gibbons. Nearer the house, the **walled garden** features flowering borders, while the stables have been converted into pleasant tearooms.

Sheringham

SHERINGHAM, just five miles west of Cromer, is a popular seaside resort with an amiable, easy-going air – though frankly you're still only marking time until you hit the more appealing places further west. Apart from the shingle **beach**, the main sight is the local museum, **The Mo** (March–Oct Tues–Sat 10am–4.30pm, Sun noon–4pm; £4; ⓦ sheringhammuseum.co.uk), which focuses on the town's nautical history. An enjoyable out-of-town jaunt is on the **North Norfolk Railway**, whose steam and diesel trains shuttle along the five miles of track southwest from Sheringham to the small market town of **HOLT** (April & Oct most days; May–Sept daily; Nov–March limited service; all-day ticket £12.50; ☎ 01263 820800, ⓦ nnrailway.co.uk).

Sheringham Park

Upper Sheringham, NR26 8TL · Daily dawn to dusk · Free, but parking £5; NT · ☎ 01263 820550, ⓦ nationaltrust.org.uk/sheringham-park · Reached from Sheringham along the B1157, from Cromer along the A148 or from Cromer and Sheringham train stations by bus

Stretching over a large and distinctly hilly chunk of land just a couple of miles to the southwest of town, Sheringham Park was laid out to a design by **Humphry Repton** (1752–1818), one of England's most celebrated landscape gardeners. Repton's original design has been modified on several occasions, but the broad principles have survived, most memorably in the several **lookout points** that dot the wooded ridge running across the southern half of the park. There is also an area of heathland and a magnificent, fifty-acre **rhododendron garden**, seen at its best from late May to early June.

ARRIVAL AND INFORMATION

By train Sheringham has two stations, standing opposite each other on either side of Station Rd. One is the terminus of the privately run North Norfolk Railway (see above), the other the terminus of the Bittern Line from Norwich.
Destinations Cromer (hourly; 10min); Norwich (hourly; 1hr).

By bus Buses to Sheringham pull in on Station Approach, by the train stations.
Tourist office Station Approach, by the stations (April, May, Sept & Oct daily 10am–2pm; June–Aug Mon–Sat 10am–5pm, Sun 10am–4pm; ☎ 01263 824329, ⓦ visit northnorfolk.co.uk).

ACCOMMODATION AND EATING

★**Dales Country House Hotel** Lodge Hill, Upper Sheringham, NR26 8TJ ☎ 01263 824555, ⓦ dales countryhouse.co.uk. In a superb location on the edge of Sheringham Park, this splendid hotel occupies a rambling Edwardian mansion. The pick of the guest rooms come complete with mini-terrace, four-poster bed, oak furniture and open fireplace. The hotel also has a smashing restaurant with a menu that exhibits flair and imagination; mains start at £15. Daily noon–2pm & 6.30–9.30pm. **£150**

No. 10 Restaurant 10 Augusta St, NR26 8LA ☎01263 824400, ⓦno10sheringham.co.uk. This is the best restaurant in Sheringham – and in the prettiest of premises. The menu is well-considered, the cod fillet with spring onion risotto and red pepper sauce (£16) being a good example. Wed–Sat 6.30–10pm.

Salthouse

The tiny hamlet of **SALTHOUSE** may look inconsequential today, but the wool from the flocks of sheep that once grazed here provided a rich living for the lord of the manor and funded the construction of the **Church of St Nicholas** (daily 10am–4pm; free), an imposing and strikingly beautiful edifice stuck on top of a grassy knoll; the church's prominent position was both a reminder to the faithful and a landmark for those at sea.

ARRIVAL AND DEPARTURE   SALTHOUSE

By bus The Norfolk Coasthopper (see p.400) pulls in by The Green, a small triangular piece of grass by the A149.

7

EATING

Cookie's Crab Shack The Green, NR25 7AJ ☎01263 740352, ⓦsalthouse.org.uk. *Cookie's* has something of a cult following, not for the decor, which is simple in the extreme, but for the freshness and variety of the seafood. Crabs, prawns and smoked fish lead the maritime way, but there's lots more to choose from, including samphire, a local delicacy harvested from the surrounding mud flats and salt marshes from late June to mid-Sept. Daily: April–Sept 9am–6pm; Oct–March 10am–4pm.

Cley Marshes Nature Reserve

A149, NR25 7SA • Reserve daily dawn to dusk; visitor centre April–Oct daily 10am–5pm, Nov–March daily 10am–4pm • £5 • ☎01263 740008, ⓦnorfolkwildlifetrust.org.uk

Beside the A149, between Salthouse and Cley (see below), **Cley Marshes Nature Reserve**, with its conspicuous, roadside **visitor centre**, attracts birdwatchers like bees to a honey pot. Owned and operated by the Norfolk Wildlife Trust (NWT), the visitor centre issues permits for entering the reserve, whose saltwater and freshwater marshes, reed beds and coastal shingle ridge are accessed on several footpaths and overseen by half a dozen hides.

Cley beach to Blakeney Point

National Trust information centre Blakeney Point • April–Sept daily dawn to dusk • Free; NT • ⓦnationaltrust.org.uk/blakeney-national-nature-reserve

On the west side of the Cley Marshes Nature Reserve – and about 400 yards east of Cley village – is the mile-long byroad (Beach Rd) that leads to the shingle mounds of **Cley beach**. This is the starting point for the four-mile hike west out along the spit to **Blakeney Point**, a nature reserve famed for its colonies of terns and seals. The seal colony is made up of several hundred common and grey seals, and the old lifeboat house, at the end of the spit, is now a **National Trust information centre**. The shifting shingle can make walking difficult, so keep to the low-water mark. The easier alternative is to take one of the **boat trips** to the point from Blakeney or Morston (see box, p.404).

Cley

Once a thriving wool port, **CLEY** (more formally **Cley-next-the-Sea** and pronounced "cly") is one of the coast's most agreeable spots, beginning beside the main road with a row of flint cottages and Georgian mansions that stand beside a narrow, marshy inlet that (just) gives access to the sea. The sea once dipped further inland, which explains why the main part of the village, including the fine medieval **Church of St Margaret** (daily 9.30am–4.30pm or dusk; free), is located half a mile further inland beside an expansive green.

ARRIVAL AND DEPARTURE

CLEY

By bus The Norfolk Coasthopper (see p.400) stops outside the Picnic Fayre deli on Cley's main street (the A149).

ACCOMMODATION AND EATING

★**Cley Windmill** NR25 7RP ☎01263 740209, ⓦcleywindmill.co.uk. This outstanding B&B occupies a converted windmill that offers wonderful views over the surrounding marshes. The guest rooms, both in the windmill and the adjoining outhouses, are decorated in attractive period style and the best have splendid beamed ceilings; self-catering arrangements are possible as well. At peak times, there's a minimum two-night stay. The *Windmill's* smart and very agreeable restaurant specializes in traditional, home-made English cooking (three-course set meal £32.50/person). Advance reservations – by 10am of the same day – are required. Daily from 7.30pm, plus Sun lunch Nov–Easter. **£160**

★**Cley Smokehouse** High St, NR25 7RF ☎01263 740282, ⓦcleysmokehouse.com. Superb smokehouse selling a wide range of freshly smoked shellfish, fish and cured meats. Their kippers are near impossible to beat. Mon–Fri 9am–5pm, Sat 8.30am–5pm, Sun 9.30am–4.30pm.

Wiveton Hall fruit farm, café and farm shop

Wiveton Hall, 1 Marsh Lane, NR25 7TE • Café & shop April to early Nov Mon–Fri 10am–4.30pm, Sat & Sun 9.30am–4.30pm • Free • ☎01263 740515, ⓦwivetonhall.co.uk

Just off the A149 midway between Cley and Blakeney, **Wiveton Hall fruit farm, café and farm shop** casts its gastronomic net as widely as possible. Visitors can pick their own fruit and veg in the fields, buy local produce at the farm shop, and pop into the café, a charming rural-rustic kind of place with a homely feel and offering excellent home-made snacks and meals; the café uses the farm's produce whenever possible. From the café, it's a few yards to **Wiveton Hall** (no public access), a sprawling country house, parts of which, including some of the Dutch-style gables, date back to the seventeenth century.

Blakeney and around

Delightful **BLAKENEY**, a mile or so west of Cley, was once a bustling port, but that was before its harbour silted up; nowadays it's a lovely little place of pebble-covered cottages with a laidback nautical air. Crab sandwiches are sold from stalls at the quayside, the meandering high street is flanked by family-run shops, and footpaths stretch out along the sea wall to east and west, allowing long, lingering views over the salt marshes. At low tide, the harbour is no more than a muddy creek (ideal for a bit of quayside crabbing and mud sliding) and at high tide the waters rise just enough to allow for boat trips out into the North Sea (see box below). Blakeney is also close to the charming ruins of sixteenth-century **Binham Priory** (daily dawn–dusk; free; ☎01328 830362, ⓦwww.english-heritage.org.uk/visit/places/binham-priory).

> ### BOAT TRIPS TO BLAKENEY POINT
>
> Depending on the tides, there are **boat trips** to **Blakeney Point** (see p.403) from either Blakeney or **Morston quay**, a mile or so to the west. Passengers have a couple of hours at the point before being ferried back and also get the chance to have a close-up look at the seal colony just off the point; some boat trips just offer the seal colony. The main **operators** advertise departure times on blackboards by Blakeney quayside, or you can reserve in advance with Beans Boats (☎01263 740505, ⓦbeansboattrips.co.uk) or Bishop's Boats (☎01263 740753, ⓦbishopsboats.co.uk). All boat trips cost £12.

ARRIVAL AND DEPARTURE

By bus Buses to Blakeney pull in at the Westgate bus shelter, a couple of minutes' walk from the harbour.

ACCOMMODATION AND EATING

King's Arms Westgate St, NR25 7NQ ☎01263 740341, ⓦ blakeneykingsarms.co.uk. The best pub in Blakeney by far, this traditional boozer, with its low, beamed ceilings and rabbit-warren rooms, offers top-ranking bar food (mains average £13), largely English but with an international slant. They also have seven modest, en-suite bedrooms. Kitchen daily noon–2pm & 6–9pm. **£80**

★**The Moorings** High St, NR25 7NA ☎01263 740054, ⓦ blakeney-moorings.co.uk. Informal, cheerful little bistro where the creative menu is particularly strong on Norfolk meat, fish and shellfish. A typical main course might be sautéed lamb kidneys with pancetta, rosemary, and a white-bean ragout (£17). Tues–Sun 10.30am–9.30pm.

The White Horse Blakeney 4 High St, NR25 7AL ☎01263 740574, ⓦ whitehorseblakeney.co.uk. This well-regarded inn has nine guest rooms kitted out in a bright and cheerful version of country-house style. The *White Horse* is also noted for its food: great play is made of local ingredients, the bread is baked here daily, and they offer lunchtime snacks and a la carte suppers. Mains average £15. Kitchen Mon–Sat noon–2.30pm & 6–9pm, Sun noon–2.30pm & 6–8.30pm. **£130**

7

Wells-next-the-Sea

Despite its name, **WELLS-NEXT-THE-SEA**, some eight miles west of Blakeney, is actually a good mile or so from open water. In Tudor times, before the harbour silted up, this was one of the great ports of eastern England, a major player in the trade with the Netherlands. Those heady days are long gone – the port is now a shadow of its former self – but Wells has reinvented itself as a popular coastal resort.

The town divides into three areas, starting with the **Buttlands**, a broad rectangular green on the south side of town, lined with oak and beech trees and framed by a string of fine Georgian houses. North from here, across Station Road, lie the narrow lanes of the town centre, with **Staithe Street** being the main drag. Staithe Street leads down to the **quay**, a somewhat forlorn affair inhabited by a couple of amusement arcades and fish-and-chip shops as well as the mile-long byroad that scuttles north to the **beach**, a handsome sandy tract backed by pine-clad dunes. Shadowing this beach road is a high flood defence and the dinky, narrow-gauge **Wells Harbour Railway** (Easter to mid-Oct every 20min or so from 10.30am; £3 return). There is also a steam train from the edge of Wells to Walsingham (see p.406).

ARRIVAL AND DEPARTURE

By bus Buses stop on Station Rd, between Staithe St and the Buttlands; some also travel towards the quay.

ACCOMMODATION AND EATING

★**The Crown** The Buttlands, NR23 1EX ☎01328 710209, ⓦ crownhotelnorfolk.co.uk. This enjoyable hotel occupies an especially attractive, three-storey former coaching inn with a handsome Georgian facade. Inside, the first batch of public rooms is cosy and quaint, all low ceilings and stone-flagged floors, and upstairs the dozen guest rooms are decorated in an imaginative and especially soothing style. *The Crown* also prides itself on its food, with splendid takes on traditional British dishes. Mains average around £19, less at lunch times. Mon–Sat noon–2.30pm & 6.30–9.30pm, Sun noon–9pm. **£150**

The Merchant's House 47 Freeman St, NR23 1BQ ☎01328 711877, ⓦ the-merchants-house .co.uk. Occupying one of the oldest houses in Wells, parts of which date back to the fifteenth century, this deluxe B&B has just two cosy, en-suite guest rooms. It's handily located, just a couple of minutes' walk from the quayside. **£95**

Pinewoods Holiday Park Beach Rd, NR23 1DR ☎01328 710439, ⓦ pinewoods.co.uk. Sitting pretty behind a long line of pine-clad dunes and a splendid sandy beach, *Pinewoods* has been welcoming holiday-makers for over sixty years. It's a sprawling complex that holds touring and static caravans, beach huts and cosy wooden lodges. It is located about 15min walk from the town quay and accessible on the narrow-gauge railway (see above). The caravan pitches are open from mid-March to late Oct, the lodges from mid-March to Dec. Tariffs vary widely, and minimum stays often apply. **£170**

Holkham Hall

A149, NR23 1AB, 3 miles west of Wells • **Hall** April–Oct Mon, Thurs & Sun noon–4pm • £15 • **Park** April–Oct daily 9am–5pm • Free, but parking £3/day • ☎ 01328 713111, ⊕ holkham.co.uk

One of the most popular outings from Wells is to neighbouring **Holkham Hall**, a grand and self-assured (or vainglorious) stately home designed by the eighteenth-century architect William Kent for the first earl of Leicester – and still owned by the family. The severe, sandy-coloured Palladian exterior belies the warmth and richness of the interior, which retains much of its original decoration, notably the much-admired marble hall, with its fluted columns and intricate reliefs. The rich colours of the state rooms are an appropriate backdrop for a fabulous selection of **paintings**, including canvases by Van Dyck, Rubens, Gainsborough and Gaspar Poussin.

The **grounds** are laid out on sandy, saline land, much of it originally salt marsh. The focal point is an 80ft-high **obelisk**, atop a grassy knoll, from where you can view both the hall to the north and the triumphal arch to the south. In common with the rest of the north Norfolk coast, there's plenty of **birdlife** – Holkham's lake attracts Canada geese, herons and grebes, and several hundred deer graze the open pastures.

Holkham Bay

The **footpaths** latticing the Holkham estate stretch as far as the A149, from where a half-mile byroad – **Lady Anne's Drive** – leads north across the marshes from opposite the *Victoria Hotel* to **Holkham Bay**, which boasts one of the finest beaches on this stretch of coast, with golden sand and pine-studded sand dunes flanking a tidal lagoon. Warblers, flycatchers and redstarts inhabit the drier coastal reaches, while waders paddle about the mud and salt flats.

ARRIVAL AND DEPARTURE   HOLKHAM HALL

By bus The Norfolk Coasthopper (see p.400) stops beside the *Victoria Hotel* on the A149. This is at the north entrance of the Holkham estate (about a mile from the house) and at the south end of Lady Anne's Drive.

Little Walsingham

For centuries, **LITTLE WALSINGHAM**, six miles south of Wells, rivalled Bury St Edmunds and Canterbury as the foremost **pilgrimage site** in England. It all began in 1061 when the Lady of the Manor, a certain Richeldis de Faverches, built a replica of the **Santa Casa** (Mary's home in Nazareth) here in this remote part of Norfolk – inspired, it is said, by visions of the Virgin Mary. It brought instant fame and fortune to Little Walsingham and every medieval king from Henry III onwards made at least one trip, walking the last mile barefoot – though this didn't stop Henry VIII from destroying the shrine in the Dissolution of the 1530s. Pilgrimages resumed in earnest after 1922, an Anglo-Catholic prelude to the building of an **Anglican shrine** in the 1930s – much to the initial chagrin of the diocesan authorities. Nowadays, the village does good business out of its holy connections as well as from the **Wells & Walsingham Light Railway (WWLR)**, a steam railway which links it with Wells (mid-March to Oct 3–5 daily; 30min; £9 return; ☎ 01328 711630, ⊕ wellswalsinghamrailway.co.uk).

Shirehall Museum and Walsingham Abbey grounds

Common Place, NR22 6BP • Late March to early Nov daily 11am–4pm • £5 • ☎ 01328 820510, ⊕ walsinghamabbey.com

Little Walsingham has an attractive and singularly old-fashioned centre, beginning with **Common Place**, the main square, whose half-timbered buildings surround a quaint octagonal structure built to protect the village pump in the sixteenth century. Also on Common Place is a mildly diverting local history museum, the **Shirehall Museum**, through which you gain access to the **Walsingham abbey grounds**, whose lovely landscaped gardens stretch down to the River Stiffkey, enclosing the scant ruins of the abbey.

Anglican shrine

Common Place, NR22 6EE · Daily, all reasonable hours · Free · ☎ 01328 820255, ⓦ walsinghamanglican.org.uk

Dotted around Little Walsingham are a number of shrines catering to a variety of denominations, but the main event is the **Anglican shrine**. Flanked by attractive gardens as well as a visitor centre, where there's a small exhibition on the history of the cult, the shrine is a strange-looking building, rather like a cross between an English village hall and an Orthodox church. The interior holds a series of small chapels and a Holy Well (whose waters are reputed to have healing properties), as well as the idiosyncratic Holy House – **Santa Casa** – which contains the much revered **statue** of Our Lady of Walsingham.

ARRIVAL AND DEPARTURE
LITTLE WALSINGHAM

By bus Stagecoach (ⓦ stagecoachbus.com) service #29 runs south from Wells to Fakenham via Little Walsingham, pausing outside the Anglican Shrine (Mon–Sat hourly, Sun every 2hr; 12min).

By train From the terminus of the steam train from Wells (see opposite), it's a 5min walk south to Common Place:

from the station, turn left along Egmere Rd and take the second major right down Bridewell St.

Tourist office In the Shirehall Museum, Common Place (late March to early Nov daily 11am–4pm; ☎ 01328 820510, ⓦ visitnorthnorfolk.com).

ACCOMMODATION AND EATING

Anglican Shrine of Our Lady of Walsingham Common Place, NR22 6EE ☎ 01328 820255, ⓦ walsinghamanglican.org.uk. The Anglican Shrine offers affordable lodgings in several locations in and around the village for pilgrims and non-pilgrims alike. The rooms are simply furnished, even frugal; some are en suite, some with shared facilities. Note that during major pilgrimages, vacancies are rare. **£80**

Norfolk Riddle 2 Wells Rd, NR22 6DJ ☎ 01328 821903, ⓦ norfolkriddle.co.uk. A combined fish-and-chip shop and restaurant supplied – and owned – by local farmers. The restaurant lacks a certain cosiness, but there's no denying the tastiness of the food and by and large it's locally sourced – try, for example, the Farm Shop beef and ale pie (£11). Aug Mon–Sat 11.30am–2pm & 5–9pm, Sun 11.30am–2.30pm; rest of year Wed–Sat 11.30am–2pm & 5–9pm, Sun 11.30am–2pm.

The Burnhams

Head west from Wells and it's about five miles to tiny **BURNHAM OVERY STAITHE**, the first of a handful of villages occupying this corner of Norfolk that are collectively known as **the Burnhams**. A mile further is the pretty little village of **BURNHAM MARKET**, the leading player of the Burnhams, where a medley of Georgian and Victorian houses surrounds a dinky little green. The village attracts a well-heeled, north London crowd, most of them here to enjoy the assorted comforts of the *The Hoste* (see p.408) and/or hunker down in their second homes.

Burnham Thorpe

Straggling **BURNHAM THORPE**, a mile or so to the southeast of Burnham Market, was the birthplace of **Horatio Nelson** (see box, p.408), who was born in the village parsonage on September 29, 1758. The parsonage was demolished years ago, but the great man is still celebrated in the village's **All Saints Church**, where the lectern is made out of timbers taken from Nelson's last ship, the *Victory*, the chancel sports a Nelson bust, and the south aisle has a small exhibition on his life and times. Traditionally, the other place to head for is the village pub, where Nelson held a farewell party for the locals in 1793, but currently – and sadly – this is closed.

ARRIVAL AND DEPARTURE
THE BURNHAMS

By bus The Norfolk Coasthopper bus (see p.400) travels through Burnham Overy Staithe on the main road and stops beside the green on the Market Place in Burnham Market, but it does not pass through Burnham Thorpe.

7

SHOT TO BITS: THE UPS AND DOWNS OF BEING NELSON

Horatio Nelson (1758–1805) joined the navy at the tender age of 12, and was soon sent to the West Indies, where he met and married Frances Nisbet, retiring to Burnham Thorpe in 1787. Back in action by 1793, his bravery cost him first the sight in his right eye, and shortly afterwards his right arm. His personal life was equally eventful – famously, his infatuation with Emma Hamilton, wife of the ambassador to Naples, caused the eventual break-up of his marriage. His finest hour was during the **Battle of Trafalgar** in 1805, when he led the British navy to victory against the combined French and Spanish fleets, a crucial engagement that set the scene for Britain's century-long domination of the high seas. The victory didn't do Nelson much good – he was shot in the chest during the battle and died shortly afterwards. Subsequently, Nelson was placed in a barrel of brandy and the pickled body shipped back to England, where he was buried at St Paul's. In all the naval hullabaloo, Nelson's far-from-positive attitude to the landowners of his home village was soon glossed over: in 1797, he sent a batch of blankets back to Norfolk to keep the poor warm, railing that an average farm labourer received "not quite two pence a day for each person; and to drink nothing but water, for beer our poor labourers never taste…".

ACCOMMODATION AND EATING

The Hoste The Green, Burnham Market PE31 8HD ☎ 01328 738777, ⓦ thehoste.com. One of the most fashionable spots on the Norfolk coast, this former coaching inn has been sympathetically modernized. The hotel's guest rooms are round the back and range from the small (verging on cramped) to the much more expansive (and expensive). At the front, the *Hoste*'s antique bar, complete with its wooden beams and stone-flagged floor, is merely a foretaste of the several, chi-chi dining areas beyond. Throughout, the menu is a well-balanced mixture of "land and sea", anything from wood pigeon with strawberries to cod in beer batter. Main courses average around £18 in the evening, slightly less at lunch. Daily: brasserie noon–9.30pm; afternoon teas 3–5.30pm; dinner 6–9.30pm. **£165**

Brancaster and around

The last of the Burnhams – Burnham Deepdale – leads seamlessly into **BRANCASTER STAITHE** and then **BRANCASTER**, both of which spread along the main coastal road, the A149. Behind them, to the north, lies pristine coastline, a tract of lagoon, sandspit and creek that pokes its head out into the ocean, attracting an extravagant range of wildfowl. This is prime **walking** territory and it's best explored along the Norfolk Coast Path (see box, p.380) as it nudges its way through the marshes that back up towards the ocean. Push on west from Brancaster and it's a mile or so more to minuscule **TITCHWELL**, with its handful of flint-walled houses, old stone cross and bird reserve.

Titchwell Marsh RSPB Nature Reserve

Titchwell, PE31 8BB • Daily: reserve dawn to dusk; information centre March–Oct 10am–5pm Nov–Feb 10am–4pm • Free, but parking £5 • ☎ 01485 210779, ⓦ rspb.org.uk/titchwellmarsh

The old sea approaches to Titchwell harbour have now become **Titchwell Marsh RSPB Nature Reserve**, whose mix of marsh, reed bed, mud flat, lagoon and sandy beach attracts a wide variety of birds, including marsh harriers, bearded tits, avocets, gulls and terns. A series of footpaths explore this varied terrain, there are several well-positioned bird hides, including a super Parrinder hide, and a very helpful shop and **information centre**.

ARRIVAL AND DEPARTURE

BRANCASTER AND AROUND

By bus The Norfolk Coasthopper bus (see p.400) sticks to the A149 as it travels on from the Burnhams through Brancaster Staithe, Brancaster and Titchwell.

ACCOMMODATION AND EATING

★**Titchwell Manor Hotel** Titchwell, PE31 8BB ☎ 01485 472027, ⓦ titchwellmanor.com. Facing out towards the salt marshes that roll down to the sea, this large Victorian hotel is one of the most enjoyable on the Norfolk coast.

There are nine guest rooms in the main building, with more in the contemporary-style courtyard complex round the back. Everything is high spec, from the top-quality duvets to the bespoke furniture. The restaurant menu is very British with traditional dishes superbly prepared – anything from fish and chips with mushy peas (£13) through to lobster thermidor with new potatoes. Daily noon–9.30pm. **£170**

White Horse Brancaster Staithe, PE31 8BY ☏ 01485 210262, ⊕ whitehorsebrancaster.co.uk. This combined hotel, pub and restaurant backs straight onto the marshes, lagoons and creeks of the coast – and, even better, the Norfolk Coast Path runs along the bottom of its car park. The hotel divides into two sections: there are seven en-suite rooms in the main building, and eight more at the back with grass roofs. Brancaster is famous for its mussels and oysters, which you can try in the restaurant; the local duck and beef are also good (main courses average £16). Restaurant daily noon–2pm & 6.15–9pm. **£110**

Holme-next-the-Sea and around

HOLME-NEXT-THE-SEA, some four miles west of Titchwell, is the quietest of villages, its gentle ramble of old flint cottages and farm buildings nudging up towards the sand dunes of the coast. It's here at Holme that the Norfolk Coast Path (see box, p.380) intersects with the Peddars Way (see box, p.380), which follows the route of an old Roman road for most of its course, though it's likely that the Romans simply enhanced what was there before. Any doubts on the matter were surely quashed when, in 1998, gales uncovered a fascinating prehistoric site in the sands just off Holme, comprising a circle of timber posts surrounding a sort of inverted tree stump. Dated to around 2050 BC, **Seahenge**, as it soon became known, attracted hundreds of visitors, but fears for its safety prompted its removal to the Lynn Museum in King's Lynn (see p.410) – and there's nothing to see here today. From Holme, it's just three miles or so to **HUNSTANTON**, a kiss-me-quick resort at the west end of the north Norfolk coast.

Holme Dunes National Nature Reserve

Holme-next-the-Sea, PE36 6LQ • Daily: reserve 10am–5pm, or dusk if earlier; visitor centre April–Oct 10am–5pm • Free to walk through on the Norfolk Coast Path; £3.75 for the reserve's footpaths and bird hides; parking £5 • ☏ 01485 525240, ⊕ norfolkwildlifetrust.org.uk

The **Holme Dunes National Nature Reserve** stretches along the coast at the point where The Wash meets the North Sea. The extensive sand and mud flats here have long protected the coast and allowed for the formation of a band of sand dunes, which have, in their turn, created areas of salt- and freshwater marsh, reed beds, and Corsican pine woodland. This varied terrain attracts all sorts of **birds**, both migrants and residents.

The reserve's **visitor centre** can be reached on foot from Thornham via the Norfolk Coast Path (3 miles) and by car from Holme-next-the-Sea: from the A149, turn down Beach Road just to the west of Holme-next-the-Sea and, near the end of the road, turn right down the signed gravel track.

ARRIVAL AND DEPARTURE

HOLME-NEXT-THE-SEA AND AROUND

By bus The Norfolk Coasthopper bus (see p.400) sticks to the A149 as it travels along the southern edge of Holme-next-the-Sea; the Holme Dunes National Nature Reserve visitor centre is a 40min walk from the nearest Coasthopper bus stop.

King's Lynn

Straddling the canalized Great Ouse river just before it slides into The Wash, **King's Lynn** is an ancient port whose merchants grew rich importing fish from Scandinavia, timber from the Baltic and wine from France, while exporting wool, salt and corn. The good times came to an end when the focus of maritime trade moved to the Atlantic seaboard, but its port struggled on until it was reinvigorated in the 1970s by the burgeoning trade between the UK and the EU. Much of the old centre was demolished during the 1960s and as a result most of Lynn – as it's known locally – is not especially enticing, but it does have a cluster of especially handsome old **riverside buildings**, and its lively, open-air **markets** attract large fenland crowds.

Saturday Market Place

Behind the riverfront, the **Saturday Market Place**, the older and smaller of the town's two marketplaces, is a focal point of the old town. In addition to the Saturday market, it's home to Lynn's main parish church, **St Margaret's**, and the striking **Trinity Guildhall**, which has a wonderful, chequered flint-and-stone facade dating to 1421. Just across from the church is the former **Hanseatic Warehouse**, the most evocative of the medieval warehouses that survive along the quayside. Built around 1475, its half-timbered upper floor juts unevenly over the cobbles of St Margaret's Lane.

Custom House

A couple of minutes' walk north of the Saturday Market Place along Georgian Queen Street stands Lynn's finest building, the **Custom House**, which was erected beside Purfleet Quay in 1683. It's in a style that was clearly influenced by the Dutch, with classical pilasters, petite dormer windows and a rooftop balustrade, but it's the dinky little cupola that catches the eye. The tourist office (see opposite) is inside.

King Street and around

Beyond the Custom House, **King Street** continues where Queen Street leaves off, and is perhaps the town's most elegant thoroughfare, lined with beautifully proportioned Georgian buildings. On the left, just after Ferry Lane is **St George's Guildhall**, one of the oldest surviving guildhalls in England. It was a theatre in Elizabethan times and is now part of the popular King's Lynn Arts Centre (see opposite). At the end of King Street, the **Tuesday Market Place** is a handsome square surrounded by yet more Georgian buildings and the plodding Neoclassical **Corn Exchange** (now a theatre); it hosts King's Lynn's main market on Fridays and, yes, Tuesdays.

Lynn Museum

Market St, PE30 1NL · April–Sept Tues–Sat 10am–5pm, Sun noon–4pm; Oct–March Tues–Sat 10am–5pm · £4.35 · ☎ 01553 775001, ⓦ museums.norfolk.gov.uk

Located in the old Union Chapel by the bus station, right in the centre of town, much of the **Lynn Museum** is given over to **Seahenge**, a circle of 556 oak timbers, preserved in peat, that were found on the Norfolk coast (see p.409). The timber circle is now

---

A MYSTERIOUS LANDSCAPE: THE FENS

One of the strangest of all English landscapes, **the Fens** cover a vast area of eastern England from just north of Cambridge right up to Boston in Lincolnshire. For centuries, they were an inhospitable wilderness of quaking bogs and marshland, punctuated by clay islands on which small communities eked out a livelihood cutting peat for fuel, using reeds for thatching and living on a diet of fish and wildfowl. Piecemeal land reclamation took place throughout the Middle Ages, but it wasn't until the seventeenth century that the systematic draining of the Fens was undertaken – amid fierce local opposition – by the Dutch engineer **Cornelius Vermuyden**. This wholesale draining had unforeseen consequences: as it dried out, the peaty soil shrank to below the level of the rivers, causing frequent flooding, and the region's **windmills**, which had previously been vital in keeping the waters at bay, now compounded the problem by causing further shrinkage. The engineers had to do some rapid backtracking and the task of draining the Fens was only completed in the 1820s following the introduction of **steam-driven pumps**, leviathans which could control water levels with much greater precision than their windmill predecessors. Drained, the Fens now comprise some of the most fertile agricultural land in Europe – though at least **Wicken Fen** (see p.412) gives the flavour of what went before.

housed in an atmospheric gallery that showcases the timbers themselves, their original position and their possible purpose. The rest of the museum has displays on various aspects of life in Lynn from medieval times onwards.

ARRIVAL AND INFORMATION

KING'S LYNN

By train From King's Lynn station, it's a 5min walk to the centre via Waterloo St.

Destinations Cambridge (hourly; 50min); Ely (hourly; 30min); London King's Cross (hourly; 1hr 40min).

By bus The bus station is in the centre of town just off Market St. The Norfolk Coasthopper (see p.400) begins (and ends) its journey at King's Lynn, putting a string of Norfolk destinations within easy reach.

Tourist office In the Custom House, Purfleet Quay (Mon–Sat 10am–5pm, Sun noon–5pm; Oct–March closes 4pm; ☎ 01553 763044, ⓦ visitnorfolk.co.uk).

ACCOMMODATION AND EATING

★ **Bank House Hotel** King's Staithe Square, PE30 1RD ☎ 01553 660492, ⓦ thebankhouse.co.uk. A riverside boutique hotel in a lovely Georgian house in the heart of the town's oldest quarter. The twelve, period-style rooms are simply delightful, and there's also a wonderfully inviting bar and restaurant, whose Modern British menu features dishes like Lowestoft plaice and guinea fowl with bacon and cabbage. Mains average £12. Mon–Sat noon–9.30pm, Sun noon–8.30pm. £115

The Old Rectory 33 Goodwins Rd, off London Rd, PE30 5QX ☎ 01553 768544, ⓦ www.theoldrectory-kingslynn .com. Small, agreeable B&B in a substantial Victorian house on the southern side of town; bedrooms are decorated in a modern and reassuringly cosy style. £80

ENTERTAINMENT

King's Lynn Arts Centre 29 King St, PE30 1HA ☎ 01553 764864, ⓦ kingslynnarts.co.uk. King's Lynn at its best, the arts centre stages a wide range of performances and exhibitions.

Ely and around

Perched on a mound of clay above the Great Ouse river about thirty miles south of King's Lynn, the attractive little town of **ELY** – literally "eel island" – was to all intents and purposes a true island until the draining of the fens in the seventeenth century. Before that, the town was encircled by treacherous marshland, which could only be crossed with the help of the local "fen-slodgers" who knew the firm tussock paths. In 1070, **Hereward the Wake** turned this inaccessibility to military advantage, holding out against the Normans and forcing William the Conqueror to undertake a prolonged siege – and finally to build an improvised road floated on bundles of sticks. Since then, Ely has been associated with that rebellious Englishman, which is more than a little ridiculous as Ely is, above all else, a Norman town: it was the Normans who built the **cathedral**, a towering structure visible for miles across the flat fenland landscape and Ely's principal sight. The rest of Ely is at its busiest to the immediate north of the cathedral on the **High Street**, a slender thoroughfare lined with old-fashioned shops, and at its prettiest down by the **river**, a relaxing spot with a riverside footpath and a tearoom or two. Ely is also within easy driving distance of an undrained and unmolested chunk of fenland, the National Trust's **Wicken Fen**.

Ely Cathedral

The College, CB7 4DL • **Cathedral** June–Sept daily 7am–6.30pm; Oct–May Mon–Sat 7am–6.30pm, Sun 7am–5.30pm • Mon–Sat £8 (includes free ground-floor tour; 1hr), Sun free • **Tower tours** Mon–Sat 8/9 daily, Sun 5 daily (West Tower Sat & Sun only in winter); 1hr • Mon–Sat £7 (on top of cathedral admission), Sun £9; reserve in advance • ☎ 01353 667735, ⓦ elycathedral.org • **Stained Glass Museum** Mon–Sat 10.30am–5pm, Sun noon–4.30pm • £4.50 • ☎ 01353 660347, ⓦ stainedglassmuseum.com

Ely Cathedral is one of the most impressive churches in England, but the west facade, where visitors enter, has been an oddly lopsided affair ever since one of the transepts collapsed in a storm in 1701. Nonetheless, the remaining transept, which

PETERBOROUGH CATHEDRAL

Burgeoning **Peterborough**, some thirty miles northwest of Ely, has just one distinct – but unmissable – attraction: its superb Norman **cathedral** (Mon–Sat 9am–5pm, Sun noon–3pm; free, but donation requested; ☎01733 355315, ⓦpeterborough-cathedral.org.uk). Work on the present church began a year after the great fire of 1116 and was largely completed within the century. The one significant later addition is the thirteenth-century west **facade**, one of the most magnificent in England, made up of three deeply recessed arches, though the purity of the design is marred slightly by an incongruous central porch added in 1370. The **interior** is an exquisite example of Norman architecture. Round-arched rib vaults and shallow blind arcades line the nave, while up above the painted wooden ceiling, dating from 1220, is a wonderful illustration of medieval art, one of the most important in Europe. There are several notable tombs in the cathedral, too, beginning with that of Henry VIII's first wife, **Catherine of Aragon**, who is buried in the north aisle of the presbytery under a slab of black Irish marble.

Peterborough **train station**, with direct links to Ely and Cambridge, is a short, signposted walk across the pedestrianized town centre from the cathedral, in the Minster Precincts.

was completed in the 1180s, is an imposing structure, its dog-tooth windows, castellated towers and blind arcading possessing all the rough, almost brutal charm of the Normans.

The first things to strike you as you enter the **nave** are the sheer length of the building and the lively nineteenth-century painted ceiling, largely the work of amateur volunteers. The nave's procession of plain late Norman arches leads to the architectural feature that makes Ely so special, the **Octagon** – the only one of its kind in England – built in 1322 to replace the collapsed central tower. Its construction, employing the largest oaks available in England to support some four hundred tons of glass and lead, was one of the wonders of the medieval world, and the effect, as you look up into this Gothic dome, is simply breathtaking. You can take a **tour** of the Octagon, and of the taller **West Tower**, from which you can see the Octagon and take in the sweeping views.

When the central tower collapsed, it fell eastwards onto the **choir**, the first three bays of which were rebuilt at the same time as the octagon in the Decorated style – in contrast to the plainer Early English of the choir bays beyond. The other marvel is the **Lady Chapel**, a separate building accessible via the north transept. It lost its sculpture and its stained glass during the Reformation, but its fan vaulting remains, an exquisite example of English Gothic. The south triforium near the main entrance holds the **Stained Glass Museum**, an Anglican money-spinner exhibiting examples of this applied art from 1200 to the 1970s.

Oliver Cromwell's House

29 St Mary's St, CB7 4HF • Daily: April–Oct 10am–5pm; Nov–March 11am–4pm • £4.90 • ☎01353 662062, ⓦolivercromwells house.co.uk

Near the cathedral is **Oliver Cromwell's House**, a timber-framed former vicarage that holds a small exhibition on the Protector's ten-year sojourn in Ely, where he was employed as a tithe collector. The tourist office (see opposite) is here as well.

Wicken Fen Nature Reserve

Lode Lane, Wicken, CB7 5XP, 9 miles south of Ely • Reserve daily dawn to dusk; dragonfly centre late May to late Sept Sat & Sun 11am–4pm • £6.95; NT • ☎01353 720274 • ⓦnationaltrust.org.uk/wicken-fen-nature-reserve

Wicken Fen National Nature Reserve is one of the few remaining areas of undrained fenland and as such is an important wetland habitat. It owes its survival to a group of

Victorian entomologists who donated the land to the National Trust in 1899. The seven hundred acres are undrained but not uncultivated – sedge and reed cutting are still carried out to preserve the landscape as it is – and the reserve is easily explored by means of several clearly marked **footpaths**. The reserve holds about ten birdwatching hides and is also one of the best places in the UK to see **dragonflies**.

ARRIVAL AND INFORMATION

By train Ely is a major railway junction, with direct trains from as far afield as Liverpool, Norwich and London, as well as Cambridge. From the station, it's a 10min walk to the cathedral, straight up Station Rd and its continuation Back Hill before veering right along The Gallery.

Destinations Cambridge (every 15min; 15min); Ipswich (every 2hr; 1hr); King's Lynn (hourly; 30min); London King's

ELY AND AROUND

Cross (every 30min; 1hr); Norwich (every 30min; 1hr).

By bus Most buses, including Stagecoach express services to Cambridge (hourly; 1hr), stop on Market St immediately north of the cathedral.

Tourist office In Oliver Cromwell's House, 29 St Mary's Street (daily: April–Oct 10am–5pm; Nov–March 11am–4pm; ☎ 01353 662062, ⓦ visitely.org.uk).

ACCOMMODATION AND EATING

Peacocks Tearoom 65 Waterside, CB7 4AU ☎ 01353 661100, ⓦ peacockstearoom.co.uk. Down by the river, this popular tearoom – easily the best in town – serves a delicious range of cream teas, salads, sandwiches, soups and lunches with the odd surprise: try, for example, the chocolate courgette cake. There's also an enormous choice of teas from around the world. After the success of their tearoom, the owners ventured into B&B, offering two comfortably furnished suites in the same premises. Both are kitted out in antique style – and very pleasant they

are too. Wed–Sun 10.30am–5pm. **£135**

29 Waterside B&B 29 Waterside, CB7 4AU ☎ 01353 614329, ✉ info@29waterside.org.uk. Ely is a tad short of places to stay, but this cosy B&B, in a pair of pretty little brick cottages dating back to the 1760s, helps remedy things. Several original features have been preserved, including the beamed ceilings, and the remainder has been sympathetically modernized. If the sun is out, breakfast can be taken in the garden. **£86**

7

Cambridge and around

On the whole, **CAMBRIDGE** is a much quieter and more secluded place than Oxford, though for the visitor what really sets it apart from its scholarly rival is "**The Backs**" – the green sward of land that straddles the languid River Cam, providing exquisite views over the backs of the old colleges. At the front, the handsome facades of the colleges dominate the layout of the town centre, lining up along the main streets. Most of the older colleges date back to the late thirteenth and early fourteenth centuries and are designed to a **similar plan**, with the main gate leading through to a series of "courts", typically a carefully manicured slab of lawn surrounded on all four sides by college residences or offices. Many of the buildings are extraordinarily beautiful, but the most famous is **King's College**, whose magnificent **King's College Chapel** is one of the great statements of late Gothic architecture. There are 31 university colleges in total, each an independent, self-governing body, proud of its achievements and attracting – for the most part at least – a close loyalty from its students.

Note that most colleges have restricted opening times and some impose admission charges; during the **exam period** (late April to early June) most of them close their doors to the public at least some of the time.

King's College

King's Parade, CB2 1ST • Term time Mon–Fri 9.30am–3.30pm, Sat 9.30am–3.15pm, Sun 1.15–2.30pm; rest of year daily 9.30am–4.30pm • £9 (includes chapel) • ☎ 01223 331100, ⓦ www.kings.cam.ac.uk

Henry VI founded **King's College** in 1441, but he was disappointed with his initial efforts. So, four years later, he cleared away half of the town to make room for a

7

much grander foundation. His plans were ambitious, but the Wars of the Roses – and bouts of royal insanity – intervened and by the time of his death in 1471 very little had been finished and work on what was intended to be Henry's **Great Court** hadn't even started. This part of the site remained empty for no less than three hundred years and the Great Court complex of today – facing King's Parade from behind a long stone screen – is largely neo-Gothic, built in the 1820s to a design

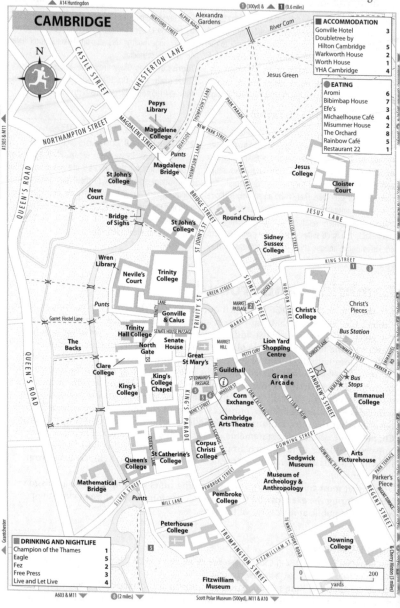

CAMBRIDGE

■ **ACCOMMODATION**
Gonville Hotel	3
Doubletree by Hilton Cambridge	5
Warkworth House	2
Worth House	1
YHA Cambridge	4

● **EATING**
Aromi	6
Bibimbap House	7
Efe's	3
Michaelhouse Café	4
Misummer House	2
The Orchard	8
Rainbow Café	5
Restaurant 22	1

■ **DRINKING AND NIGHTLIFE**
Champion of the Thames	1
Eagle	5
Fez	2
Free Press	3
Live and Let Live	4

by William Wilkins. Henry's workmen did, however, start on the college's finest building, the much-celebrated **King's College Chapel**, on the north side of today's Great Court.

King's College once enjoyed an exclusive supply of students from Eton and until 1851 claimed the right to award its students degrees without their taking any examinations. The first non-Etonians were only accepted in 1873. Times have changed, however, and King's is now one of the university's more progressive colleges – it was among the first three to admit women, in 1972, and consistently has one of the highest intakes of state-school students.

King's College Chapel
Entrance either via the main gatehouse on King's Parade or the North Gate, at the end of Senate House Passage

Committed to canvas by Turner and Canaletto, and eulogized in no fewer than three sonnets by Wordsworth, **King's College Chapel** is now internationally famous for its **boys' choir**, whose members process across the college grounds during term time in their antiquated garb to sing **evensong** (Tues–Sat at 5.30pm, plus choral services Sun 10.30am & 3.30pm) and carols on Christmas Eve. The setting for the choristers is supreme, the chapel impossibly slender, its streamlined buttresses channelling up to a dainty balustrade and four spiky turrets, though the exterior was, in a sense at least, a happy accident – its design predicated by the carefully composed interior. Here, the high and handsome **nave** has an exquisite ceiling, whose fantail tracery has a dense geometry of extraordinary complexity and delicacy. The nave is flooded with kaleidoscopic patterns of light that filter in through copious stained-glass windows. Paid for by Henry VIII, the **stained glass** was largely the work of Flemish glaziers, with the lower windows portraying scenes from the New Testament and the Apocrypha, and the upper windows the Old Testament. Above the **altar** hangs Rubens' tender *Adoration of the Magi* and an exhibition in the side **chantries** puts more historical flesh on Henry's grand plans.

7

King's Parade and around

King's College dominates **King's Parade**, the town's medieval High Street, but the higgledy-piggledy shops and cafés opposite are an attractive foil to Wilkins' architectural screen. At the northern end of King's Parade is **Great St Mary's** (May–Aug Mon–Sat 9.30am–5pm, Sun 12.30–5pm; Sept–April closes 4pm; free; ☎01223 747272, ⊕www .gsm.cam.ac.uk), the university's pet church, a sturdy Gothic structure whose **tower** (£4) offers a good view of the surrounding colleges. Opposite the church stands **Senate House**, an exercise in Palladian classicism by James Gibbs, and the scene of graduation ceremonies in late June, when champagne corks fly around the (faux) fur collars and black gowns. Behind the church is **Market Hill**, usually full of stalls selling books, records, flowers, food and souvenirs – make time for the Belgian waffle stand on the eastern edge, a student favourite.

Gonville and Caius College
Trinity St, CB2 1TA • Daily 9am–2pm • Free • ☎ 01223 332400, ⊕ cai.cam.ac.uk

The northern continuation of King's Parade is Trinity Street, a short way along which, on the left, is the cramped main entrance to **Gonville and Caius College**, known simply as Caius (pronounced "keys"), after the sixteenth-century co-founder John Keys, who latinized his name as was then the custom with men of learning. The design of the college owes much to Keys, who placed three gates on two adjoining courts, each representing a different stage on the path to academic enlightenment: at the main entrance is the **Gate of Humility**, through which the student enters the college; the **Gate of Virtue**, sporting the female figures of Fame and Wealth, marks the entrance to Caius Court; and the exquisite **Gate of Honour**, capped with sundials and decorated with classical motifs, leads onto Senate House Passage.

Clare College

Trinity Lane, CB2 1TL • No set opening hours • Summer £5; winter free • ☎ 01223 333200, ⓦ clare.cam.ac.uk

Senate House Passage continues west beyond Caius College's Gate of Honour en route to **Clare College**. Clare's plain period-piece courtyards, completed in the early eighteenth century, lead to one of the most picturesque of all the bridges over the Cam, **Clare Bridge**. Beyond lies the **Fellows' Garden**, one of the loveliest college gardens open to the public (same times as college). Back at the entrance to Clare, it's a few steps more to the North Gate of King's College, beside King's College Chapel (see p.415).

Trinity College

Trinity St, CB2 1TQ • **College** Daily 10am–4.30pm • £3 • **Wren Library** Mon–Fri noon–2pm, plus Sat during term 10.30am–12.30pm • Free • ☎ 01223 338400, ⓦ trin.cam.ac.uk

A statue of Henry VIII, who founded **Trinity College** in 1546, sits in majesty over Trinity's **Great Gate**, his sceptre replaced long ago with a chair leg – legend has it a student stole it for a prank, either switching it themselves or leaving it, only for a helpful college employee to come up with the ad hoc replacement. Beyond lies the vast asymmetrical expanse of **Great Court**, which displays a superb range of Tudor buildings, the oldest of which is the fifteenth-century clocktower. The centrepiece of the court is a delicate fountain, in which, so it's said, Lord Byron used to bathe naked with his pet bear – the college forbade students from keeping dogs.

On the far side of the Great Court, walk through "**the screens**" – the narrow passage separating the Hall from the kitchens – to reach **Nevile's Court**, where Newton first calculated the speed of sound. The west end of Nevile's Court is enclosed by one of the university's most famous buildings, the **Wren Library** (access only from The Backs). Viewed from the outside, it's impossible to appreciate the scale of the interior thanks to Wren's clever device of concealing the internal floor level by means of two rows of stone columns. Natural light pours into the white, stuccoed interior, which contrasts wonderfully with the dark lime-wood bookcases, also Wren-designed.

St John's College

St John's St, CB2 1TP • Daily: March–Oct 10am–5pm; Nov–Feb 10am–3.30pm • £10 • ☎ 01223 338600, ⓦ www.joh.cam.ac.uk

Next door to Trinity, **St John's College** sports a grandiloquent Tudor gatehouse, which is distinguished by the coat of arms of the founder, Lady Margaret Beaufort, the mother of Henry VII. Beyond, three successive courts lead to the river, but there's an excess of dull reddish brickwork here – enough for Wordsworth, who lived above the kitchens on F staircase, to describe the place as "gloomy". The arcade on the far side of Third Court leads through to the **Bridge of Sighs**, a chunky, covered bridge across the river built in 1831 but in most respects very unlike its Venetian namesake. The bridge is best viewed from the much older – and much more stylish – Wren-designed bridge a few yards to the south. The Bridge of Sighs links the old college with the fanciful nineteenth-century **New Court**, a crenellated neo-Gothic extravaganza topped by a feast of dinky stone chimneys and pinnacles.

Magdalene College

Magdalene St, CB3 0AG • **College** Daily 10am–6pm • Free • **Pepys Library** Late April to early Sept Mon–Fri 2–4pm, Sat 11.30am–12.30pm & 1.30–2.30pm; Oct to late March Mon–Sat 2–4pm • Free • ☎ 01223 332100, ⓦ www.magd.cam.ac.uk

Founded as a hostel by the Benedictines, **Magdalene College** (pronounced "maudlin") became a university college in 1542; it was also the last of the Oxbridge colleges to admit women, finally surrendering in 1988. Male students responded by wearing black armbands to symbolize the "death of education" – but, armbands or not, the college's academic results swiftly improved. The main focus of attention here is the **Pepys Library**, in the second of the college's ancient courtyards. Samuel Pepys, a Magdalene student, bequeathed his entire library to the college, where it has been displayed ever since in its original red-oak bookshelves. His famous diary is also parked here.

Jesus College

Jesus Lane, CB5 8BL • Daily 10am–5pm • Free • ☎ 01223 339339, ⓦ jesus.cam.ac.uk

The intimate cloisters of **Jesus College** are reminiscent of a monastery – appropriately, as the Bishop of Ely founded the college on the grounds of a suppressed Benedictine nunnery in 1496. Beyond the main red-brick gateway, much of the ground plan of the nunnery has been preserved, especially around **Cloister Court**, the first court on the right after the entrance and the prettiest part of the college, dripping with ivy and, in summer, overflowing with hanging baskets. Entered from the Cloister Court, the college **chapel** occupies the former priory chancel and looks like a medieval parish church, though in fact it was imaginatively restored in the nineteenth century, using ceiling designs by William Morris and Pre-Raphaelite stained glass. The poet **Samuel Taylor Coleridge** was the college's most famously bad student, absconding in his first year to join the Light Dragoons, and returning only to be kicked out for a combination of bad debts and unconventional opinions.

Sidney Sussex College

Sidney St, CB2 3HU • No set opening times • Free • ☎ 01223 338800, ⓦ sid.cam.ac.uk

The sombre, mostly mock-Gothic facade of **Sidney Sussex College** glowers over Sidney Street. The interior is fairly unexciting too, though the long, slender **chapel** is noteworthy for its fancy marble floor, hooped roof and Baroque wood panelling, as well as for being the last resting place of the skull of its most famous alumnus, **Oliver Cromwell** – though the exact location remains a closely guarded secret. Incidentally, neighbouring **Hobson Street** is named after the owner of a Cambridge livery stable, who would only allow customers to take the horse nearest the door, hence "Hobson's choice".

Christ's College

St Andrew's St, CB2 3BU • Daily 9am–4pm • Free • ☎ 01223 334900, ⓦ christs.cam.ac.uk

Close to Cambridge's central shopping area, the turreted gateway of **Christ's College** features the coat of arms of the founder, Lady Margaret Beaufort, who also founded St John's. Passing through First Court you come to the Fellows' Building, attributed to Inigo Jones, whose central arch gives access to the **Fellows' Garden**. The poet **John Milton** is said to have either painted or composed here, though there's no definite proof that he did either; another of Christ's famous undergraduates was **Charles Darwin**, who showed little academic promise and spent most of his time hunting.

CAMBRIDGE: TAKING A PUNT

Punting is the quintessential Cambridge activity, though it is, in fact, a good deal harder than it looks. First-timers find themselves zigzagging across the water and in summer "punt jams" are very common on the stretch of the River Cam beside The Backs. **Punt rental** is available at several points, including the boatyard at Mill Lane (beside the Silver Street bridge), at Magdalene Bridge, and at the Garret Hostel Lane bridge at the back of Trinity College. It's almost always possible to rent on spec, but you can usually save money if you book ahead of time – Scudamore's (☎01223 359750, ⚑scudamores.com) are as good as anyone. Hiring a punt costs around £27 per hour (and most places charge a deposit), for up to six people in each punt. Alternatively, you can hire a **chauffeured punt** from any of the rental places – either a shared punt (with strangers) for about £12 per person per hour, or your own (with friends) for around £18 per person per hour.

Queens' College

7

Silver St, CB3 9ET, but visitors' gate on Queens' Lane • March–Oct daily 10am–4.30pm; Dec–Feb Mon–Fri 10am–3pm • £3.50 • ☎01223 335511, ⚑www.queens.cam.ac.uk

Queens' College is particularly beautiful, boasting, in the **Old Court** and the **Cloister Court**, two dream-like, fairy-tale Tudor courtyards: the first of the two is a perfect illustration of the original collegiate ideal, with kitchens, library, chapel, hall and rooms all set around a tiny green. Flanking Cloister Court is the Long Gallery of the President's Lodge, the last remaining half-timbered building in the university, and the tower where Erasmus is thought to have beavered away during his four years here, probably from 1510 to 1514. Equally eye-catching is the wooden **Mathematical Bridge** over the River Cam (visible for free from the Silver Street Bridge), a copy of the mid-eighteenth-century original, which – so it was claimed – would stay in place even if the nuts and bolts were removed.

The Fitzwilliam Museum

Trumpington St, CB2 1RB • Tues–Sat 10am–5pm, Sun noon–5pm • Free • ☎01223 332900, ⚑fitzmuseum.cam.ac.uk

The **Fitzwilliam Museum** holds the city's premier fine and applied art collection in an imposing Neoclassical edifice, which was built to house the vast hoard bequeathed by Viscount Fitzwilliam in 1816. Since then, the museum has been gifted a string of private collections, most of which follow a particular specialism. The **Lower Galleries** contain a wealth of antiquities including Egyptian sarcophagi and mummies, fifth-century BC Greek vases, plus a bewildering display of early European and Asian ceramics and sections dedicated to armour, glass and pewterware. Temporary exhibitions are held here too. The **Upper Galleries** contain an eclectic assortment of mostly eighteenth, nineteenth- and early twentieth-century European paintings and sculptures, with more modern pieces by Lucian Freud, David Hockney, Henry Moore, Ben Nicholson, Jacob Epstein and Barbara Hepworth.

The Polar Museum

Lensfield Rd, CB2 1ER • Tues–Sat 10am–4pm • Free • ☎01223 336540, ⚑spri.cam.ac.uk

The pocket-sized **Polar Museum** at the Scott Polar Research Institute begins with a section devoted to the native peoples of the Arctic, with an especially enjoyable collection of Inuit soapstone sculptures. It continues with pen sketches of the European explorers who ventured to both poles with varying degrees of success and it's here you'll find a substantial set of documents – original letters, incidental artefacts and so on – relating to the fateful expedition to the South Pole led by **Captain Robert Falcon Scott** (1868–1912), after whom the institute is named.

Duxford Imperial War Museum

Duxford, CB22 4QR, 11 miles south of Cambridge • Daily: mid-March to late Oct 10am–6pm; late Oct to mid-March 10am–4pm • £16.35 • ☎ 01223 835000, ⓦ iwm.org.uk

The giant hangars of the **Duxford Imperial War Museum** dominate the eponymous airfield. Throughout World War II, East Anglia was a centre of operations for the RAF and the USAF, with the region's flat, unobstructed landscape dotted with dozens of airfields, among which Duxford was one of the more important. In total, the museum holds nearly 200 historic aircraft, a wide-ranging collection of civil and military planes from the Sunderland flying boat to Concorde and the Vulcan B2 bombers, which were used for the first and last time in the 1982 Falklands conflict; the Spitfires, however, are the enduring favourites. Most of the planes are kept in full working order and are taken out for a spin at **Duxford Air Shows**, which attract thousands of visitors. There are usually half a dozen air shows a year (as well as temporary exhibitions) and advance bookings are strongly recommended – call ahead or consult the museum website.

ARRIVAL AND INFORMATION

By train Cambridge train station is a mile or so southeast of the city centre, off Hills Rd. From here, it's an easy if tedious 20min walk into the centre, or a short bus ride; take any one of several local (Citi) buses to Emmanuel St.

Destinations Bury St Edmunds (hourly; 40min); Ely (every 30min; 15min); Ipswich (hourly; 1hr 20min); King's Lynn (hourly; 45min); London King's Cross (every 30min; 50min); London Stansted Airport (every 30min; 30min); Norwich (hourly; 1hr 20min).

By bus The long-distance bus station, with services to

CAMBRIDGE AND AROUND

7

London Victoria (every 2hr; 2hr), is just east of the city centre on Drummer St.

By car Arriving by car, you'll find much of the city centre closed to traffic and on-street parking well-nigh impossible to find, so most visitors plump for a park-and-ride car park; these are signposted on all major approaches.

Tourist office In the Guildhall, Peas Hill, just off King's Parade (April–Oct Mon–Sat 10am–5pm, Sun 11am–3pm; Nov–March Mon–Sat 10am–5pm; ☎ 01223 791500, ⓦ visitcambridge.org).

GETTING AROUND

By bike Popular with locals and students alike, cycling is an enjoyable way to get around the city. Among the small army of bike rental outlets, one of the more dependable is Rutland Cycling (☎ 01223 352728, ⓦ rutlandcycling.com),

which has an outlet close to the train station at 155 Great Northern Rd. Wherever you leave your bike, lock it securely as bike theft is not uncommon.

ACCOMMODATION

Cambridge is light on central **accommodation** so vacant rooms are often thin on the ground, but the situation improves outside term time when many of the colleges let out rooms on a B&B basis, often at bargain rates. The rooms are pretty frugal, but there again visitors can enjoy the college atmosphere; for bookings, go to ⓦ visitcambridge.org /accommodation/college-rooms.

★**Doubletree by Hilton Cambridge** Granta Place, Mill Lane, CB2 1RT ☎ 01223 259988, ⓦ doubletree3 .hilton.com; map p.414. This is the city's most appealing hotel by a long chalk, occupying a stylishly designed 1960s building a short walk from the centre. The best rooms have balconies overlooking the river (though the views are hardly riveting) and breakfasts are first-rate – as you'd expect at this price. **£210**

Gonville Hotel Gonville Place, CB1 1LY ☎ 01223 366611, ⓦ gonvillehotel.co.uk; map p.414. One of the better mid-range choices in Cambridge, this pleasantly refurbished hotel occupies a long albeit somewhat undistinguished building just set back off a busy main road. Proficient, efficient lodgings with smart, modern guest rooms. **£140**

Warkworth House Warkworth Terrace, CB1 1EE ☎ 01223 363682, ⓦ warkworthhouse.co.uk; map p.414. Welcoming, family-run B&B with a handful of straight-forward, bright and unfussy en-suite rooms. In a substantial Victorian property a shortish walk southeast of the bus station, off Parkside. **£95**

Worth House 152 Chesterton Rd, CB4 1DA ☎ 01223 316074, ⓦ worth-house.co.uk; map p.414. Friendly B&B in a pleasantly upgraded Victorian house a 20min walk from the centre. All the bedrooms are decorated in a bright modern style and have generous en-suite bathrooms. Great breakfasts too. **£120**

YHA Cambridge 97 Tenison Rd, CB1 2DN ☎ 0345 3719728, ⓦ yha.org.uk/hostel/cambridge; map p.414.

This long-established hostel occupies a substantial Victorian house and a modern annexe near the train station. Facilities include a laundry and self-catering kitchen, cycle storage, a games room and a small courtyard garden. There are just over one hundred beds in two- to six-bedded rooms, some en suite; advance reservations advised. Dorms __£20__, doubles __£60__

EATING

With most Cambridge students and staff eating in college, good-quality restaurants are comparatively thin on the ground – whereas the **takeaway** and **café** scene is on a roll.

★**Aromi** 1 Bene't St, CB2 3QN ☎01223 300117, ⓦaromi.co.uk; map p.414. The furnishings and fittings may be standard-issue modern, but, oh my word, the food here at this little café is absolutely superb: they offer authentic Sicilian food – pizza slices, focaccia and cannoli, plus a hatful of other delights. Eat in or takeaway. Expect queues at peak times. Mon–Thurs & Sun 9am–7pm, Fri & Sat 9am–8pm.

★**Bibimbap House** 60 Mill Rd, CB1 2AS ☎01223 506800; map p.414. Tiny, family-run Korean restaurant, specializing in – you guessed it – bibimbap. Portions are huge, always served with an array of delicious side dishes. Slightly out of the centre, a 5–10min walk from Parker's Piece, but worth it. Mains £12–15. Mon 5–10pm, Wed–Sun noon–3pm & 5–9/10pm.

Efe's 78 King St, CB1 1LN ☎01223 500005; map p.414. Something of a city institution, this Turkish restaurant may have uninspiring decor, but the chargrilled meats – the house speciality – are extremely tasty. Mains around £12. Mon–Fri noon–2.30pm & 6–11pm; Sat & Sun noon–11pm.

Michaelhouse Café Trinity St, CB2 1SU ☎01223 309147 ⓦmichaelhousecafe.co.uk; map p.414. Good-quality café food – snacks, salads and so forth – in an attractively renovated medieval church. Great, central location too. Mains for around £6. Mon–Sat 8am–5pm.

Midsummer House Midsummer Common, CB4 1HA ☎01223 369299, ⓦmidsummerhouse.co.uk; map p.414. This two-Michelin-starred restaurant delights with its inventive French cuisine and surprisingly unpretentious atmosphere. Everything is delicious, of course, but the friendly, good-humoured and immensely knowledgeable staff really set it apart. One for a major treat: a five-course lunch is £56.50, eight-course dinner £120. Book well ahead. Sittings Tues 7–8.30pm, Wed & Thurs noon–1.30pm & 7–8.30pm, Fri & Sat noon–1.30pm & 6.30–9.30pm.

The Orchard 47 Mill Way, Grantchester, CB3 9ND ☎01223 840230, ⓦtheorchardteagarden.co.uk; map p.414. Follow the river south out of Cambridge for a lovely 2-mile stroll or cycle through Grantchester Meadows, and reward yourself with one of the enormous scones (cream tea £5.75) at *The Orchard*. This simple tearoom with deckchairs dotted around an orchard was a favourite haunt of Rupert Brooke, among many other famous alumni. It's still a popular escape for students today – many punt all the way here. Hours vary by season, but usually daily 9.30am–5/6pm.

Rainbow Café 9a King's Parade, CB2 1SJ ☎01223 321551, ⓦrainbowcafe.co.uk; map p.414. Cramped but agreeable vegetarian restaurant with main courses – ranging from Jamaican roti cups to North African tagine – for around £10. Specializes in vegan and gluten-free food plus organic wines. Handy location, down an alley opposite King's College. Don't be surprised if there's a queue. Tues–Sat 10am–10pm, Sun 10am–3pm.

Restaurant 22 22 Chesterton Rd, CB4 3AX ☎01223 351880, ⓦrestaurant22.co.uk; map p.414. Well-regarded and long-established restaurant in cosy premises where they serve a Modern British menu with seafood at the fore. A three-course set meal will set you back about £40. Northeast of the centre, on the far side of Jesus Green and the river. Tues–Sat 7–11pm.

DRINKING AND NIGHTLIFE

Champion of the Thames 68 King St, CB1 1LN ☎01223 351464, ⓦthechampionofthethames.com; map p.414. Gratifyingly old-fashioned central pub with oodles of wood panelling, decent beer and a student/academic crowd. Daily noon–11pm.

Eagle 8 Bene't St, CB2 3QN ☎01223 505020, ⓦeagle-cambridge.co.uk; map p.414. Owned and operated by Greene King, this ancient city-centre inn, with its antique appearance and cobbled courtyard, is associated with Crick and Watson, two of the scientists who discovered DNA in 1953. It gets horribly crowded, but is still worth a pint of anyone's time – the ales are reliably good. Mon–Sat 10am–11pm, Sun 11am–10.30pm.

Fez 15 Market Passage, CB2 3PF ☎01223 519224, ⓦcambridgefez.com; map p.414. Popular city-centre club with vaguely Middle Eastern decor, good drinks deals and the requisite sticky floor. It tends to have better DJs than the competition, and some excellent one-off nights; check the website to see what's coming up. Tues & Thurs–Sat 10pm–3am, other days vary.

★**Free Press** 7 Prospect Row, CB1 1DU ☎01223 368337, ⓦfreepresskitchen.co.uk; map p.414. Classic, traditional and superbly maintained backstreet local with a great selection of real ales and single malts. Walled garden, too. Just off Parkside. Daily noon–11pm.

Live and Let Live 40 Mawson Rd, CB1 2EA ☎01223 460261; map p.414. This smashing pub, in an old corner building among a battery of terrace houses, is the epitome of the traditional local – from the pot-pourri furnishings and fittings through to the wood-panelled alcoves. Mawson Rd leads off Mill Rd in between Parker's Piece and the train station. Mon, Tues & Fri 11.30am–2.30pm & 5.30–11pm, Wed & Thurs 5.30–11pm, Sat 11.30am–2.30pm & 6–11pm, Sun noon–3pm & 7–11pm.

ENTERTAINMENT

The **performing arts** scene is at its busiest and best in term time, with numerous student drama productions, classical concerts and gigs culminating in the traditional "May Week" excesses following exam season. The most celebrated concerts are given by **King's College choir** (see p.415), while the long-established, four-day **Cambridge Folk Festival** (late July to eary Aug; ⓦ cambridgelivetrust.co.uk/folk-festival) takes place in neighbouring Cherry Hinton. The tourist office (see p.419) issues various free **listings** leaflets and brochures.

Cambridge Arts Picturehouse 38–39 St Andrew's St, CB2 3AR ☎0871 902 5720, ⓦ picturehouses.com; map p.414. Arthouse cinema with an excellent, wide-ranging programme – and a decent bar.

Cambridge Arts Theatre 6 St Edward's Passage, off King's Parade, CB2 3PJ ☎01223 503333, ⓦ cambridge artstheatre.com; map p.414. The city's main rep theatre, founded by John Maynard Keynes, and launch pad of a thousand and one famous careers; offers a top-notch range of cutting-edge and classic productions.

Cambridge Corn Exchange Wheeler St, CB2 3QE ☎01223 357851, ⓦ cambridgelivetrust.co.uk/cornex; map p.414. Revamped nineteenth-century trading hall, now the main city-centre venue for opera, ballet, musicals and comedy as well as regular rock and folk gigs.

Cambridge Junction Clifton Way, CB1 7GX ☎01223 511511, ⓦ junction.co.uk; map p.414. Rock, indie, jazz, reggae or soul gigs, plus theatre, comedy and dance at this popular arts venue. Out near the train station.

7

The West Midlands and the Peak District

IRONBRIDGE GORGE

The West Midlands and the Peak District

Birmingham, the urban epicentre of the West Midlands, is Britain's second city and was once the world's greatest industrial metropolis, its slew of factories powering the Industrial Revolution. Long saddled with a reputation as an ugly, unappealing city, Birmingham has broken free, redeveloping its central core with vim and architectural verve, its prestige buildings – especially Selfridges and the Symphony hall – helping to redefine and reshape its image. Within easy striking distance is Stratford-upon-Avon, famous as the birthplace of William Shakespeare and for the exemplary Royal Shakespeare Company (RSC). Beyond are the rural shires that stretch out towards Wales, with the bumpy Malvern Hills, one of the region's scenic highlights, in between; you could also drift north to the rugged scenery of the Peak District, whose surly, stirring landscapes enclose the attractive little spa town of Buxton.

8

Change was forced on **Birmingham** by the drastic decline in its manufacturing base during the 1980s; things were even worse in the Black Country, that knot of industrial towns clinging to the west of the city, where deindustrialization has proven particularly painful. The counties to the south and west of Birmingham – Warwickshire, Worcestershire, Herefordshire and Shropshire – comprise a rural stronghold that maintains an emotional and political distance from the conurbation. Of the four, Warwickshire is the least obviously scenic, but draws by far the largest number of visitors, for – as the road signs declare at every entry point – this is "Shakespeare Country". The prime target is **Stratford-upon-Avon**, Shakespeare's birthplace, but spare time also for the town of **Warwick**, which has a superb church and a whopping castle.

Neighbouring Worcestershire, which stretches southwest from the urban fringes of the West Midlands, holds two principal places of interest: **Worcester**, with its mighty cathedral, and Great Malvern, a mannered inland resort in the rolling contours of the **Malvern Hills**. From here, it's west again for **Herefordshire**, a large and sparsely populated county that's home to several amenable market towns, notably Hereford, where the remarkable medieval **Mappa Mundi** is displayed in the cathedral; literary **Hay-on-Wye**; and pocket-sized Ross-on-Wye, which is near a scenic stretch of the Wye River Valley. To the north is rural **Shropshire**, which has one of the region's prettiest towns, **Ludlow**, awash with antique half-timbered buildings, and the county town of Shrewsbury, close to the hiking trails of the Long Mynd. Shropshire has a fascinating industrial history, too, which you can explore in **Ironbridge Gorge**.

To the north of Birmingham and its sprawling suburbs is Derbyshire, its northern reaches dominated by the rough landscapes of the **Peak District National Park**. The park's many trails attract hikers by the thousand and one of the best bases is the appealing former spa town of **Buxton**. The Peak District is also home to the limestone

Who exactly was Shakespeare? p.437
Stratford's theatres p.440
Hiking the Malvern Hills p.445
Canoeing around Hay-on-Wye p.450
Buxton Festival p.465

The Pennine Way p.467
Ring a ring o' roses: Eyam and the plague p.469
Hiking around Bakewell p.470

ROYAL SHAKESPEARE THEATRE, STRATFORD-UPON-AVON

Highlights

❶ Staying Cool, Birmingham Stay Cool and be cool by renting an apartment at the top of the Rotunda, a Birmingham landmark, and enjoy the panoramic views. **See p.433**

❷ RSC theatres, Stratford-upon-Avon Shakespeare's birthplace is quite simply the best place in the world to see the great man's plays, performed by the pre-eminent Royal Shakespeare Company. **See p.440**

❸ Mappa Mundi, Hereford Cathedral This glorious antique map, dating to around 1000 AD, provides a riveting insight into the medieval mind with all its quirks and superstitions. **See p.447**

❹ Hay-on-Wye On the Welsh border, Hay is internationally famous as a book-lovers'

heaven – with dozens of bookshops and a world-famous annual literary festival. **See p.449**

❺ Ironbridge Gorge The first iron bridge ever constructed arches high above the River Severn – industrial poetry in motion. **See p.451**

❻ Ludlow A postcard-pretty country town with a castle, a platoon of half-timbered houses and some quality restaurants. **See p.458**

❼ Buxton Good-looking and relaxed former spa town with good hotels and restaurants; it's an ideal base for exploring the Peak District. **See p.463**

❽ Hiking in the Peak District The wonderful wilds of the Peak District are crisscrossed by hiking trails – start with an amiable stroll or two near Bakewell. **See p.470**

HIGHLIGHTS ARE MARKED ON THE MAP ON P.426

caverns of Castleton, the "Plague Village" of Eyam and the grandiose stately pile of Chatsworth House.

GETTING AROUND   THE WEST MIDLANDS AND THE PEAK DISTRICT

Birmingham has a major international **airport** and is readily accessible by **train** from all of England's big cities. It is also well served by the National Express **bus** network, with dozens of buses leaving every hour for destinations all over Britain. Furthermore, Birmingham acts as a public transport hub for the whole of the West Midlands, with trains fanning out into

HIGHLIGHTS

1. Staying Cool, Birmingham
2. RSC theatres, Stratford-upon-Avon
3. Mappa Mundi, Hereford Cathedral
4. Hay-on-Wye
5. Ironbridge Gorge
6. Ludlow
7. Buxton
8. Hiking in the Peak District

0 ——————— 10
miles

THE WEST MIDLANDS AND THE PEAK DISTRICT

the surrounding counties. However, once you leave the rail network behind you'll find local buses thin on the ground, especially in the quieter parts of Worcestershire, Herefordshire and Shropshire. The main exception is the Peak District, where a dense network of bus services will take you most places on most days.

Birmingham

If anywhere can be described as the first purely industrial conurbation, it has to be **BIRMINGHAM**. Unlike the more specialist industrial towns that grew up across the north and the Midlands, "Brum" – and its "Brummies" – turned its hand to every kind of manufacturing, gaining the epithet "the city of 1001 trades". It was here that the pioneers of the Industrial Revolution – James Watt, Matthew Boulton, Josiah Wedgwood, Joseph Priestley and Erasmus Darwin (grandfather of Charles) – formed the **Lunar Society**, an extraordinary melting pot of scientific and industrial ideas. They conceived the world's first purpose-built factory, invented gas lighting and pioneered both the distillation of oxygen and the mass production of the steam engine. Thus, a modest Midlands market town mushroomed into the nation's economic dynamo, with a population to match: in 1841 there were 180,000 inhabitants; just fifty years later that number had trebled.

Now Britain's second-largest city, with a population of over one million, Birmingham has long outgrown the squalor and misery of its boom years and today its industrial supremacy is recalled – but only recalled – by a crop of **recycled buildings**, from warehouses to old factories, and an extensive network of **canals**. This recent (and enforced) shift to a post-manufacturing economy has also been trumped by an intelligent and far-reaching revamp of the city centre that has included the construction of a glitzy **Convention Centre**, a talented reconstruction of the **Bull Ring**, the reinvigoration of the excellent **Birmingham Museum & Art Gallery**, and, at a time when other councils are nervously biting their nails, the building of a lavish, state-of-the-art **Library**. Birmingham has also launched a whole range of cultural initiatives – including the provision of a fabulous new concert hall for the **City of Birmingham Symphony Orchestra** – and boasts both a first-rate restaurant scene and a boisterous nightlife. While Birmingham doesn't have the density of attractions of a capital city, it's well worth at least a couple of days of anyone's time.

8

The Bull Ring and around

Most visitors to Birmingham arrive at **New Street Station**, formerly an unsightly modern building, but now transformed into an airy, billowing structure clad in bands of undulating stainless steel. From here, it's just a few steps to Rotunda Square, at the intersection of New and High streets, which takes its name from the soaring **Rotunda**, a handsome and distinctive cylindrical tower that is the sole survivor of the notorious **Bull Ring** shopping centre, which fulfilled every miserable cliché of 1960s town planning until its demolition in 2001. The new Bull Ring shopping centre, which replaced it, has two strokes of real invention: firstly, the architects' decision to split the shops into two separate sections, providing an uninterrupted view of the medieval spire of **St Martin's** in between; and secondly, the dramatic design of the **Selfridges'** store.

Selfridges

Bull Ring, B5 4BP • Mon–Wed 10am–8pm, Thurs & Fri 10am–9pm, Sat 9am–9pm, Sun 11am–5.30pm • ☎ 0800 123400, ⓦ selfridges.com

Birmingham's **Selfridges** is an extraordinary sight – a billowing organic swell protruding from the Bull Ring's east side, and seen to best advantage from the wide stone stairway that descends from Rotunda Square to St Martin's. Reminiscent of an inside-out octopus, Selfridges shimmers with an architectural chain mail of thousands of spun aluminium discs, an altogether bold and hugely successful attempt to create a popular city landmark.

BIRMINGHAM

DRINKING AND NIGHTLIFE

Aluna	5
The Jam House	1
The Nightingale	7
O2 Academy Birmingham	6
Old Joint Stock	2
Sunflower Lounge	4
The Wellington	3

EATING

Asha's	2
Edmunds Bistro Deluxe	5
Edwardian Tea Room	3
Fumo	4
MPW Steakhouse Bar & Grill	7
Purnells Bistro	1
Shababs Balti	6
Topokki	8

ACCOMMODATION

Back to Backs Houses	4
Radisson Blu	3
Staybridge Suites	1
Staying Cool	2

St Martin's Church

St Martin's Square, B5 5BB • Mon–Sat 10am–4pm, Sun 9am–7pm • Free • ☏ 0121 600 6020, ⓦ bullring.org

Nestling at the foot of the Bull Ring, **St Martin's Church** is a fetching amalgamation of the Gothic and the neo-Gothic, its mighty spire poking high into the sky. The church has had some hard times, attacked by the Victorians and bombed by the Luftwaffe, but the interior, with its capacious three-aisled nave, is saved from mediocrity by a delightful **Burne-Jones stained-glass window**, a richly coloured, finely detailed affair whose panes sport angels, saints, biblical figures and scenes; the window is in the south transept.

Victoria Square

Busy **New St** stretches west from the Bull Ring to the handsomely refurbished **Victoria Square**, whose wide stone stairways and assorted statues – both old and new – serve as an attractive prelude to the **Council House**, whose gables and cupola, columns and tympana – completed in 1879 – witness the thrusting self-confidence of the Victorian bourgeoisie. Across the square, and very different, is the **Town Hall** of 1834, whose classical design – by Joseph Hansom, who went on to design Hansom cabs – was based on the Roman temple in Nîmes. The building's simple, flowing lines and imposing size contrast with much of its surroundings, but it's a wonderful structure all the same, and now houses a performing arts venue.

The Birmingham Museum and Art Gallery

Chamberlain Square, B3 3DH • Mon–Thurs, Sat & Sun 10am–5pm, Fri 10.30am–5pm • Free • ☏ 0121 348 8000, ⓦ birminghammuseums .org.uk/bmag

The **Birmingham Museum and Art Gallery** (BM&AG), which occupies a grand, rambling, Edwardian building and one of its neighbours, possesses a multifaceted collection running from fine and applied art through to archeological finds. The key paintings, including the museum's prime collection of **Pre-Raphaelites**, are spread over one long floor – Floor 2 – as is the **Staffordshire Hoard** of Anglo-Saxon treasures. Note, though, that the museum's collection of paintings is too large to all be exhibited at any one time, and artworks are regularly rotated, so be sure to pick up a **plan** at reception. There's also a pleasant **café** on Floor 2 (see p.433).

The Pre-Raphaelites

The BM&AG holds a significant sample of **European** paintings and an excellent collection of eighteenth- and nineteenth-century British art, most notably a supreme muster of **Pre-Raphaelite** work. Founded in 1848, the Pre-Raphaelite Brotherhood consisted of seven young artists, of whom Rossetti, Holman Hunt, Millais and Madox Brown are the best known. The name of the group was selected to express their commitment to honest observation, which they thought had been lost with the Renaissance. Two seminal Pre-Raphaelite paintings on display are **Dante Gabriel Rossetti**'s stirring *Beata Beatrix* (1870) and **Ford Madox Brown**'s powerful image of emigration, *The Last of England* (1855). The Brotherhood disbanded in the 1850s, but a second wave of artists carried on in its footsteps, most notably **Edward Burne-Jones**, whose *Star of Bethlehem* is one of the largest watercolours ever painted, a mysterious, almost magical piece with earnest Magi and a film-star-like Virgin Mary.

The Staffordshire Hoard

Discovered by amateur detectorists in 2009, the **Staffordshire Hoard** is the largest collection of Anglo-Saxon treasure ever unearthed, consisting of nearly 4000 pieces, mostly related to warfare. Gold, silver and garnet are the three main materials, but it's the delicacy and intricacy of the work that inspires – and a selection of pieces, along with detailed explanations, is exhibited here to fine effect.

The Industrial Gallery, Gas Hall and the Waterhall Gallery

Sharing Floor 2 is the **Industrial Gallery**, which is set around an expansive atrium whose wrought-iron columns and balconies clamber up towards delicate skylights. The gallery holds a choice selection of ceramics, jewellery and stained glass retrieved from defunct churches all over Birmingham. Here also is the *Edwardian Tea Room*, one of the city's more agreeable places for a cuppa (see p.433). Elsewhere in the museum, the cavernous **Gas Hall** is an impressive venue for touring art exhibitions, while the **Waterhall Gallery**, inside the Council House, just across Edmund St from the main museum building, showcases temporary exhibitions of modern and contemporary art.

St Philip's Cathedral

Colmore Row, B3 2QB • Mon–Fri 7.30am–6.30pm, Sat & Sun 8.30am–5pm • Free • ☎ 0121 262 1840, ⓦ birminghamcathedral.com

The string of fancily carved, High Victorian stone buildings on Colmore Row provides a suitable backdrop for **St Philip's Anglican Cathedral**, a bijou example of English Baroque. Consecrated in 1715, the church is a handsome affair, its graceful, galleried interior all balance and poise, its harmonies unruffled by the Victorians, who enlarged the original church in the 1880s, when four stained-glass windows were commissioned from local boy **Edward Burne-Jones**, a leading light of the Pre-Raphaelite movement. The windows are typical of his style – intensely coloured, fastidiously detailed and distinctly sentimental. Three – the *Nativity*, *Crucifixion* and *Ascension* – are at the east end of the church beyond the high altar, the fourth – the *Last Judgement* – is directly opposite.

Centenary Square

One of the city's centrepieces, the wide, pedestrianized expanse of **Centenary Square** is framed by several of Birmingham's key buildings. These begin on the left with the showpiece **International Convention Centre** (ICC) and **Symphony Hall**. Next up is the **Birmingham Repertory Theatre**, which is attached to the super-duper **Library** and in front of this – in architectural contrast – is the older **Hall of Memory**.

Birmingham Library

Centenary Square, B1 2ND • Mon–Fri 9am–9pm, Sat 11am–5pm • Free • ☎ 0121 242 4242, ⓦ libraryofbirmingham.com

At a time when many British libraries were under threat, it was a brave move for the City Council to fund the construction of the new **Birmingham Library**, a prestige structure that was completed in 2013 to a striking design, its cubic superstructure clad with a shimmering filigree of overlapping metal rings. Local opinion seems to be divided as to whether it was a sound investment, but it's certainly a city landmark and the interior has all mod cons, while the outside terraces have views over the city centre.

Hall of Memory

Centenary Square, B1 2HF • Mon–Sat 10am–4pm • Free • ⓦ hallofmemory.co.uk

Erected in the 1920s, the distinctive **Hall of Memory** was built to commemorate the 12,320 citizens of Birmingham who died in World War I. An architectural hybrid, the Hall has a delightful mix of Art Deco and Neoclassical features rendered in Portland stone, its centrepiece a domed Remembrance chamber complete with a mournful inscription.

Gas Street Basin

Away2canal times & frequency vary; 1hr • £8 • ☎ 0121 647 7151, ⓦ away2canal.co.uk

Gas Street Basin is the hub of Birmingham's intricate canal system. There are eight canals within the city's boundaries – 32 miles' worth in total – with most dug in the late eighteenth century before the railways made them uneconomic. Much of the surviving network slices through the city's grimy, industrial bowels, but certain sections have been immaculately restored (see below), with Gas Street Basin leading the way. The Basin, which is edged by a fascinating medley of old brick buildings, lies at the junction of the Worcester and Birmingham and Birmingham Main Line canals, and its dark waters almost invariably bob with a fleet of brightly painted narrowboats; from the periphery of the Basin, Away2canal organizes **narrowboat excursions** along Birmingham's canals.

The Mailbox

Following the towpath along the canal southeast from Gas Street Basin soon brings you to **The Mailbox**, a striking reinvention of Birmingham's old postal sorting office complete with restaurants, hotels, and some of the snazziest shops in the city – including Harvey Nichols, Paul Smith and Armani.

Brindleyplace

Beside Gas Street Basin is the waterside **Brindleyplace**, which is named after James Brindley, the eighteenth-century engineer responsible for many of Britain's early canals. It's an aesthetically pleasing development, with an attractive central plaza that's popular with office staff at lunch times. The city's much-praised **Ikon Gallery** is just off the central square.

Ikon Gallery

1 Oozells Square, B1 2HS • Tues–Sun & bank hols 11am–5pm • Free • ☎ 0121 248 0708, ⓦ ikon-gallery.org

Housed in a substantial Victorian building, the first-rate **Ikon Gallery** is one of the country's most imaginative venues for touring exhibitions of contemporary art, with recent shows by the likes of Oliver Beer and Jean Painlevé. Perhaps even better, the gallery organizes all sorts of workshops, family days and special events plus guided **tours** of the gallery itself.

8

The Birmingham & Fazeley Canal

Just beyond Brindleyplace, in front of the massive dome of the Barclaycard Arena, the canal forks: the Birmingham Main Line Canal cuts west (to the left) and the more interesting **Birmingham & Fazeley Canal** leads northeast (to the right), running past a sequence of antique brick buildings en route to the quaint **Scotland St Locks**. Further on, the canal slides past a string of new apartment blocks as well as the (signed) flight of steps that clambers up to Newhall Street, about half a mile beyond the main canal junction, and a few minutes' walk from St Paul's church.

St Paul's church

St Paul's Square, B3 1QZ • Ring for opening times • ☎ 0121 236 7858, ⓦ stpaulsjq.church

On **St Paul's Square**, an attractive ensemble of old houses flank **St Paul's church**, whose rational symmetries, dating to the 1770s, are an excellent illustration of Neoclassical design. To the people who paid for it (by public subscription), though, there was much more to the building than aesthetics: gone were the mysteries of the medieval church, replaced by a church of the Enlightenment and one that proved popular with the new industrialists – both Matthew Boulton and James Watt had family pews here, though Watt never actually turned up.

Jewellery Quarter

Birmingham's long-established **Jewellery Quarter** is located to the northwest of Snow Hill station. Buckle- and toy-makers first colonized this area in the 1750s, opening the way for hundreds of silversmiths, jewellers and goldsmiths, and today there are still several hundred jewellery-related companies in the district. Most of the **jewellery shops** are concentrated along Vittoria Street and its northerly continuation, Vyse Street.

Museum of the Jewellery Quarter

75 Vyse St, B18 6HA • Tues–Sat 10.30am–5pm • £7 • ☎ 0121 348 8140, ⓦ birminghammuseums.org.uk/jewellery • A brief walk from the Jewellery Quarter train station & metro stop

The engrossing **Museum of the Jewellery Quarter** occupies a former jewellery-maker's that closed down in the early 1980s. What makes it so distinctive is that the owners just shut up shop, leaving everything intact and untouched, down to the dirty teacups. The museum details the rise, fall and rise again of the jewellery trade in Birmingham, but it's the old building that steals the show.

Back to Backs

55–63 Hurst St, B5 4TE • Feb–Dec Tues–Sun 10am–5pm • £8; NT • **Tours** Tues–Sun approx every 15min (only if prebooked); 1hr 15min–1hr 30min; advance reservations required • Included in entry fee • Booking line ☎ 0121 666 7671, ⓦ nationaltrust.org.uk/birmingham-back-to-backs

The sheer scale of the industrial boom that gripped nineteenth-century Birmingham is hard to grasp, but the raw statistics speak for themselves: in 1811, there were just 85,000 Brummies; just over a century later there were ten times more. The demand for cheap **housing** spawned the **back-to-back**, quickly erected dwellings that were one room deep and two, sometimes three storeys high, built in groups ("courts") around a courtyard where the communal privies were located. Even by the standards of the time, this was pretty grim stuff and as early as the 1870s Birmingham council banned the construction of any more. Almost all of the Birmingham courts were bulldozed in the 1970s, but one substantial set survived and this, the **Birmingham Back to Backs**, has been restored by the National Trust. The guided tour wends its way through four separate homes, each of which represents a different period from the early nineteenth century onwards, with titbits about the families who lived here and lots of period items to touch and feel; you can stay here too (see opposite).

ARRIVAL AND DEPARTURE

BIRMINGHAM

By plane Birmingham's airport is 8 miles east of the city centre off the A45 – and near the M42 (Junction 6). The terminal is beside Birmingham International train station, from where there are regular services into New St train station (every 10–15min; 10min).

By train Most intercity and many local services use New St station, in the heart of the city. There are two smaller stations – Snow Hill and Moor St, respectively a (signed) 10min walk north and 5min walk east of New St. Moor St, the quaintest of the three – with much of its Edwardian fabric intact – is used primarily by Chiltern Railways.

Destinations (New St) Birmingham International (every 10–15min; 10min); Derby (every 20min; 45min); Great Malvern (every 30min; 1hr); Hereford (every 30min;

1hr 30min); London Euston (every 30min; 1hr 25min); Shrewsbury (every 30min; 1hr); Telford (Mon–Sat every 30min, Sun hourly; 40min); Worcester Foregate (hourly; 45min).

Destinations (Snow Hill) Stratford-upon-Avon (hourly; 50min); Warwick (every 30min; 30min).

Destinations (Moor St) London Marylebone (every 30min; 1hr 50min); Stratford-upon-Avon (hourly; 45min); Worcester Foregate (hourly; 1hr).

By bus National Express long-distance buses arrive at the Birmingham Coach Station, in Digbeth, from where it's a 10min walk northwest to the Bull Ring.

Destinations London (hourly; 3hr 30min); Manchester (hourly; 3–4hr).

GETTING AROUND

Birmingham has an excellent public transport system, whose trains, buses and metro (a light railway/tram) delve into almost every urban nook and cranny. Various companies provide these services, but they are all coordinated by Transport for West Midlands, with journey planning available online (ⓦ networkwestmidlands.com).

INFORMATION

Tourist office There are currently no tourist offices in the city, but Visit Birmingham does operate an excellent and comprehensive website, ⓦ visitbirmingham.com.

ACCOMMODATION

To see Birmingham at its best, you really need to stay in the centre, preferably in the vicinity of **Centenary Square**, though chain hotels do monopolize the downtown core. A comprehensive list of options is available on Visit Birmingham's website (ⓦ visitbirmingham.com/where-to-stay).

Back to Backs Houses 52 Inge St, B5 4TE ☏ 0344 800 2070, ⓦ nationaltrustholidays.org.uk; map p.428. The most distinctive place to stay in town: the National Trust has refurbished a small block of nineteenth-century back-to-back workers' houses conveniently located just to the south of the city centre along Hurst St. Part of the complex now holds two small "cottages" – really terraced houses – kitted out in Victorian period style, but with the addition of en-suite and self-catering facilities. Each accommodates two guests. **£110**

Radisson Blu 12 Holloway Circus, Queensway, B1 1BT ☏ 0121 654 6000, ⓦ radissonblu.com/en/hotel-birmingham; map p.428. Smart hotel in a tall, sleek skyrise within a few minutes' walk of the centre. The interior is designed in routine modern-minimalist style, but the floor-to-ceiling windows of many of the bedrooms add more than a dash of élan. **£100**

Staybridge Suites Martineau Place, Corporation St, B2 4UW ☏ 0121 289 3636, ⓦ ihg.com; map p.428. Classic 1960s, city-centre office block that has been cleverly converted into a hotel, holding 179 smart, modern suites with fitted kitchenettes. Capacious breakfast area, too. **£85**

★ **Staying Cool** The Rotunda, 150 New St, B2 4PA ☏ 0121 285 1290, ⓦ stayingcool.com; map p.428. The top three floors of the Rotunda, right at the heart of the city, have been converted into fully furnished and serviced apartments. All the apartments are modern and spotless, and those on the top floor – Floor 20 – come with a balcony from where there are panoramic views over the city. The apartments can be rented for one night – no problem. **£140**

EATING

Central Birmingham has a bevy of first-rate **restaurants** with a string of smart new venues springing up in the slipstream of the burgeoning conference and trade-fair business. Birmingham's gastronomic speciality is the **balti**, a delicious Kashmiri stew cooked and served in a small wok-like dish called a *karahi*, eaten with naan bread instead of cutlery. The original balti houses are concentrated out in the suburbs of Balsall Heath, Moseley and Sparkhill to the south of the centre, which is where you should head if a balti whets your appetite.

Asha's 12 Newhall St, B3 3LX ☏ 0121 200 2767, ⓦ ashasrestaurant.co.uk; map p.428. Chic and polished Indian restaurant named after a Bollywood star – Asha Parekh – with a wide-ranging menu that covers all the classics and then some. Reservations strongly advised. Mains average £16 or £11 for a vegetarian dish. Mon–Fri noon–2.30pm & 5.30–10.30pm, Sat 5–11pm, Sun 5–10pm.

Edmunds Bistro Deluxe 6 Brindleyplace, B1 2JB ☏ 0121 633 4944, ⓦ edmundsrestaurant.co.uk; map p.428. High-life dining in smart, contemporary premises. An inventive, French-style menu features seasonal ingredients – venison with dauphinoise potato, duck liver, parsnip mousseline and hazelnut crumble is typical. Mains £16–28. Reservations well-nigh essential. Mon–Fri noon–2pm & 6–10pm, Sat 6–10pm.

Edwardian Tea Room BM&AG, Chamberlain Square, B3 3DH ☏ 0121 348 8082, ⓦ bmag.org.uk; map p.428. This canteen-style café has a great setting in one of the large and beautifully decorated halls of the museum's industrial section – check out the fancy ironwork and skylights. The food doesn't quite match up to the surroundings, but stick to the simpler dishes and you won't go far wrong: the soup and bread should hit the mark (£4.50). Mon–Thurs, Sat & Sun 10am–4.30pm, Fri 10.30am–4.30pm.

Fumo 1 Waterloo St, B2 5PG ☏ 0121 643 8979, ⓦ sancarlofumo.co.uk; map p.428. In smart modern premises, this fast-paced Italian restaurant serves up excellent and authentic Italian cuisine, from the basics (pizzas and pastas) through to more elaborate concoctions like monkfish and prawns marinated in garlic, parsley and lemon. Tapas-style mains cost around £9. Daily 11.30am–11.30pm.

★ **MPW Steakhouse Bar & Grill** The Cube, 200 Wharfside St, B1 1PR ☏ 0121 634 3433, ⓦ mpw steakhousebirmingham.co.uk; map p.428. Amazingly popular Marco Pierre White-run cocktail bar and restaurant. A no-nonsense menu features steaks (as you would expect), but there are other offerings too – for example pork belly and bramley apple with bubble and squeak and mustard sauce. One of the reasons for its popularity is the location – on the top-floor of The Cube, a high-rise office block that has been creatively reconfigured, including the addition of a sculpture-like external casing/screen. Steaks from £20, other mains from £16. Daily noon–10pm.

Purnells Bistro 11 Newhall St, B3 3NY ☏ 0121 200 1588, ⓦ purnellsbistro-gingers.com; map p.428. A side venture by Michelin-starred chef Glynn Purnell, who already operates one of the city's best restaurants – *Purnell's* – this combined cocktail bar and upmarket bistro offers a menu inspired by "rustic British fare". Quite. A la carte mains average £17 and

8

include such delights as pan-fried sea bass with olive tapenade and anchovy. Reservations recommended. Mon–Fri noon–2.30pm & 6–9.30pm, Sat noon–3.30pm & 5–9.30pm, Sun noon–4pm.

Shababs Balti 163 Ladypool Rd, Sparkbrook, B12 8LQ ☎0121 440 2893, ⓦshababs.co.uk; map p.428. Long-established and much praised balti restaurant with strikingly garish decor in the so-called "Balti Triangle" to the south of the city centre. Reckon on £7 per balti. Daily noon–10pm.

Topokki Unit 1C, Hurst St, B5 4TD ☎0121 666 7200; map p.428. Informal, canteen-style restaurant serving up delicious and authentic Korean dishes at very affordable prices – *odeng guk* (fishcake soup), for example, at £6.80. Daily noon–9pm.

DRINKING AND NIGHTLIFE

Birmingham's **pub and club scene** is one of Britain's best, with the latter spanning everything from word-of-mouth underground parties to meat-market mainstream clubs. **Live music** is strong, too, with big-name concerts at several major venues and other (often local) bands appearing at some clubs and pubs. Birmingham's showpiece **Symphony Orchestra** and **Royal Ballet** are the spearheads of the city's **classical scene**, while the city also lines up a string of top-ranking **festivals**. For details of all upcoming events, performances and exhibitions, consult either ⓦvisitbirmingham .com/explore-birmingham or ⓦlivebrum.co.uk.

Aluna 128 The Mailbox, Wharfside St, B1 1RQ ☎0121 633 9987, ⓦaluna.uk.com; map p.428. There are no real-ale fans here in this popular cocktail bar, whose over-the-top decor (orange crushed-velvet banquettes, etc) wows its twenty-something customers. There's a small canalside terrace here too. Mon–Thurs & Sun noon–midnight, Fri & Sat noon–1.30am.

★ **The Jam House** 3 St Paul's Square, B3 1QU ☎0121 200 3030, ⓦthejamhouse.com; map p.428. This jazz, funk, blues and swing club/pub pulls in artists from every corner of the globe. Great vibe; great gigs. Has a close relationship with Jools Holland. Tues & Wed 6pm–midnight, Thurs–Sat 6pm–1am.

The Nightingale 18 Kent St, B5 6RD ☎0121 622 1718, ⓦnightingaleclub.co.uk; map p.428. The king/queen of Brum's gay clubs, popular with straight folks as well. Five bars, three levels, two discos, a café-bar and even a garden. Thurs–Sat from 10pm.

Old Joint Stock 4 Temple Row West, B2 5NY ☎0121 200 1892, ⓦoldjointstocktheatre.co.uk; map p.428.

This charming pub has the fanciest decor in town – with busts and a balustrade, a balcony and chandeliers, all dating from its days as a bank. There's a medium-sized theatre studio upstairs, mostly featuring improv comedy and musical theatre. Mon–Fri 8am–11pm, Sat 9am–11pm, Sun 10am–5pm.

★ **Sunflower Lounge** 76 Smallbrook Queensway, B5 4EG ☎0121 632 6756, ⓦthesunflowerlounge.com; map p.428. Quirky pub-cum-bar in modern premises on the inner ring road near New St station. Attracts an indie/student crowd and covers many bases, with quizzes and big-screen TV plus resident DJs and live gigs. It really is cool without being pretentious – just as they say on their website. Mon, Tues & Sun noon–11.30pm, Wed–Sat noon–2am.

The Wellington 37 Bennetts Hill, B2 5SN ☎0121 200 3115, ⓦthewellingtonrealale.co.uk; map p.428. Specialist real-ale pub with a top-notch range of local brews, including those of the much-vaunted Black Country Brewery. A good selection of ciders, too. Daily 10am–midnight.

ENTERTAINMENT

Birmingham Hippodrome Hurst St, B5 4TB ☎0844 338 5000, ⓦbirminghamhippodrome.com; map p.428. Lavishly refurbished, the Hippodrome is home to the Birmingham Royal Ballet. Also features touring plays and big pre- and post-West End productions, plus a splendiferous Christmas pantomime.

Birmingham Repertory Theatre Centenary Square, B1 2EP ☎0121 236 4455, ⓦbirmingham-rep.co.uk; map p.428. Mixed diet of classics and new work featuring local and experimental writing.

The Electric Cinema 47 Station St, B5 4DY ☎0121 643 7879, ⓦtheelectric.co.uk; map p.428. Britain's oldest working cinema, housed in a handsome Art Deco building, with an inventive programme of mainstream and art-house films. Sofas and waiter service too.

O2 Academy Birmingham 16–18 Horsefair, Bristol St,

B1 1DB ☎0844 477 2000 (Ticketmaster ticket line), ⓦo2academybirmingham.co.uk; map p.428. State-of-the-art venue with three performance areas, hosting either gigs or club nights, though the big deal is the top-ranking artists who regularly appear here.

Symphony Hall ICC, Centenary Square, B1 2EA ☎0121 780 3333, ⓦthsh.co.uk; map p.428. Acoustically one of the most advanced concert halls in Europe, home of the acclaimed City of Birmingham Symphony Orchestra (CBSO; ⓦcbso.co.uk), as well as a venue for touring music and opera.

Town Hall Victoria Square, B3 3DQ ☎0121 780 3333, ⓦthsh.co.uk; map p.428. The old Town Hall, with its magnificent interior fully renovated, offers a varied programme of popular, classical and jazz music through to modern dance and ballet.

Lichfield

Spreading north from the Birmingham conurbation, the county of **Staffordshire** has one especially interesting town, **LICHFIELD**, an amenable kind of place that pulls in the day-trippers for two reasons – its magnificent sandstone **cathedral** and the birthplace of **Samuel Johnson**, whose considerable achievements are remembered at the delightful **Samuel Johnson Birthplace Museum**.

Lichfield Cathedral

19A The Close, WS13 7LD • Mon–Fri & Sun 7.30am–6pm, Sat 8am–6pm, Sun 7.30am–5pm except during services • chapter house Mon–Sat 10am–4pm, Sun 12.30–2.30pm • Free; donation requested • ☎ 01543 306100, ⓦ lichfield-cathedral.org

Begun in 1085, but substantially rebuilt on several subsequent occasions, **Lichfield Cathedral** is unique in possessing three spires – an appropriate distinction for a bishopric that once extended over virtually all of the Midlands. The magnificent **west front** of the cathedral is simply stunning, a veritable cliff face of stone graced by scores of statues of biblical figures, English kings and the supposed ancestors of Christ. Inside, the nave's soaring **vaulted roof** extends without interruption into the choir, looking rather like the ribcage of a giant beast – a distinctly eerie experience. Most impressive of all, however, is the **Lady Chapel**, at the far end of the choir, which boasts a set of magnificent sixteenth-century windows, purchased from a Cistercian abbey in Belgium in 1802. Off the north side of the nave is the **chapter house**, which is used to display the cathedral's greatest treasure, the **Chad Gospels**, a rare and exquisite example of Anglo-Saxon artistry dating to the eighth century, though at time of writing the gospels were in London for a thoroughgoing restoration.

Samuel Johnson Birthplace Museum & Bookshop

Breadmarket St, Market Square, WS13 6LG • Daily: March–Oct 10.30am–4.30pm; Nov–Feb 11am–3.30pm • Free • ☎ 01543 264972, ⓦ www.samueljohnsonbirthplace.org.uk • A 5min walk from the cathedral via Dam St, which runs along the edge of an ancient fishpond/pool, the Minster Pool

Samuel Johnson's father was a bookseller and the charming **Samuel Johnson Birthplace Museum** was once both the family home and his place of work. The museum's ground floor still serves as a **bookshop**, while up above, a series of displays explores the life and times of eighteenth-century England's most celebrated wit and critic, best known for compiling the first dictionary of the English language – a truly extraordinary achievement. The museum has busts of Johnson and his contemporaries, a few apposite paintings, plaques displaying some of the man's more famous statements, and, on the top floor, a modest collection of personal memorabilia, including Johnson's favourite armchair, his chocolate pot (chocolate was a delicacy in Georgian times) and ivory writing tablets.

ARRIVAL AND INFORMATION LICHFIELD

By train Lichfield has two train stations: Lichfield Trent Valley, on the eastern fringe of the city, and the much more convenient Lichfield City, about 10min walk south of the cathedral, from where there are frequent services to Birmingham New Street (every 20min; 40min).

By bus The station is on Birmingham Rd, near Lichfield City Station; buses run regularly to Derby (every 30min, change at Burton; 1hr 20min).

EATING AND DRINKING

Chapters 19 The Close, WS13 7LD ☎ 01543 306125, ⓦ lichfield-cathedral.org. Next door to the cathedral, this traditional café has a pleasant atmosphere and offers inexpensive home-made food, from soups and sandwiches to cakes and quiches. Mon–Sat 9am–4pm, Sun 10am–4pm.

Siam Corner Ma Ma Thai 17 Bird St, WS13 6PW ☎ 01543 411911, ⓦ siamcornermamathai.co.uk. Two short blocks southwest of the Market Square, this is a smart and modern Thai place serving all the classics; main courses average £16, or £7 for vegetarian dishes. Mon 5–10.30pm, Tues–Sun noon–2.30pm & 5–10.30pm.

Stratford-upon-Avon

Despite its worldwide fame, **STRATFORD-UPON-AVON**, some thirty miles south of Birmingham, is at heart an unassuming market town with an unexceptional pedigree. A charter for Stratford's weekly market was granted in the twelfth century and the town later became an important stopping-off point for stagecoaches between London, Oxford and the north. Like all such places, Stratford had its clearly defined class system and within this typical milieu John and Mary **Shakespeare** occupied the middle rank, and would have been forgotten long ago had their first son, **William**, not turned out to be the greatest writer ever to use the English language. A consequence of their good fortune is that, in summer at least, this pleasant little town can seem overwhelmed by the number of visitors, but don't be deterred: the **Royal Shakespeare Company** offers superb theatre and if you are willing to forgo the busiest attraction – **Shakespeare's Birthplace** – you can largely avoid the crush. Stratford's key attractions are dotted around the centre, a flat and compact slice of land spreading back from the River Avon, and three of them – as well as two more on the edge of town – are owned and operated by the excellent **Shakespeare Birthplace Trust** (see p.441).

Shakespeare's Birthplace

Henley St, CV37 6QW • Daily: late March–Oct 9am–5pm; Nov to mid-March 10am–4pm • Shakespeare Birthplace Trust combination ticket £17.50/£26.25 (see p.441) • ☎ 01789 204016, ⓦ shakespeare.org.uk/visit/shakespeares-birthplace

Top of everyone's bardic itinerary is **Shakespeare's Birthplace**, comprising a modern visitor centre and the heavily restored, half-timbered building where the great man was born, or rather, where it is generally believed he was born. The visitor centre pokes into every corner of Shakespeare's life and times, making the most of what little hard evidence there is. Next door, the half-timbered birthplace dwelling is actually two buildings knocked into one. The northern, much smaller and later part was the house of Joan, Shakespeare's sister; adjoining it is the main family home, bought by John Shakespeare in 1556 and now returned to something like its original appearance.

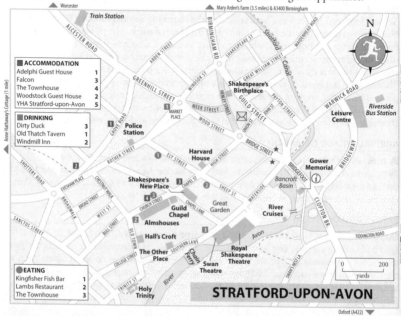

WHO EXACTLY WAS SHAKESPEARE?

Over the past hundred years or so, the deification of **William Shakespeare** (1564–1616) has been dogged by an eccentric backlash among a fringe of revisionist scholars and literary figures sometimes known as "**Anti-Stratfordians**", according to whom the famous plays and sonnets were not written by a glover's son from Stratford, but by someone else, and William Shakespeare was merely a nom de plume. A variety of candidates has been proposed for the authorship of Shakespeare's works, and they range from the vaguely plausible (Christopher Marlowe, Francis Bacon, Ben Jonson, and the Earls of Rutland, Southampton and Oxford) to the manifestly whacko (Queen Elizabeth I, King James I and Daniel Defoe, author of *Robinson Crusoe*, who was born six years after publication of the first Folio).

Lying at the root of the authorship debate are several **unresolved questions** that have puzzled scholars for years. How could a man of modest background have such an intimate knowledge of royal protocol? How could he know so much about Italy without ever having travelled there? Why did he not leave a library in his will, when the author of the plays clearly possessed a detailed knowledge of classical literature? And why, given that Shakespeare was supposedly a well-known dramatist, did no death notice or obituary appear in publications of the day?

The lack of **definite information** about Shakespeare's life has only fuelled the speculation, and the few details that have been preserved come mostly from official archives – birth, marriage and death certificates and court records. From these we know that on April 22 or 23, 1564, a certain John Shakespeare – variously described as a glovemaker, butcher, wool merchant and corn trader – and his wife, Mary, had their first son, William. We also know that William attended a local grammar school and that, at the age of 18, he married a local woman, Anne Hathaway, seven years his senior, with whom he had three children. Several years later, probably in 1587, William was forced to flee Stratford after being caught poaching. Five companies of players passed through Stratford on tour that year and it is believed that he **absconded** with one of them to London, where a theatre boom was in full swing. *Henry VI*, Shakespeare's first play, appeared soon after, followed by the hugely successful *Richard III*. Over the next decade, Shakespeare's output was prodigious. Thirty-eight plays appeared and most were performed by his own theatre troupes based in London's **Globe** theatre (see p.88), in which he had a one-tenth share.

Success secured Shakespeare the **patronage** of London's fashionable set and Queen Elizabeth I regularly attended the Globe, as did her successor, James I, whose Scottish ancestry and fascination with the occult partly explain the subject matter of *Macbeth* – Shakespeare knew the commercial value of appealing to the rich and powerful. This, as much as his extraordinary talent, ensured that his plays were the most acclaimed of the day, earning him enough money to purchase the largest house in Stratford, where he lived with his family until his death. Ultimately, however, the sketchy details of Shakespeare's life are of far less importance than the plays, sonnets and songs he left behind. Whoever wrote them – and William almost certainly did – the body of work generally attributed to him comprises some of the most inspired and exquisite English ever written.

It includes a glover's workshop, where Shakespeare's father beavered away, though he was something of a Jack the Lad, seemingly also trading grain, doing a little butchery and illegally acting as a small-time wool merchant. Despite the many historical uncertainties, the house has been attracting visitors for centuries and upstairs one of the old mullioned windows, now displayed in a glass cabinet, bears the scratch-mark signatures of some of them, including Thomas Carlyle and Walter Scott.

Shakespeare's New Place and Nash's House

22 Chapel St, CV37 6EP • Daily: late March to Oct 9am–5pm, Nov to mid-March 10am–4pm • Shakespeare Birthplace Trust combination ticket £17.50/£26.25 (see p.441) • ☎ 01789 204016, 🖥 shakespeare.org.uk/visit/shakespeares-new-place

Kept in immaculate order by the Shakespeare Birthplace Trust, the gardens of **Shakespeare's New Place** are divided into three sections. The first displays a small selection of modern sculptures with Shakespearean references along with the ground plaques that mark the layout of what were the foundations of New Place, Shakespeare's family home for the last nineteen years of his life, long ago demolished. Beyond is a neat and trim Knot Garden and this leads to the **Great Garden**, decorated with an enjoyable set of modern sculptures by Gregg Wyatt and also home to the ancient mulberry tree that, legend asserts, was grown from a cutting off the tree that the great man himself had planted. Adjoining the gardens is **Nash's House**, an attractive Tudor building once owned by Thomas Nash, the first husband of Shakespeare's granddaughter, Elizabeth Hall. The house delves into the details of Shakespeare's family life by means of a "timeline" and among the supporting exhibits are the archeological bits and pieces retrieved during a recent excavation of the New Place site.

Hall's Croft

Old Town, CV37 6BG • Daily: late March to Oct 10am–5pm, Nov to mid-March 11am–4pm • Shakespeare Birthplace Trust combination ticket £17.50/£26.25 (see p.441) • ☎ 01789 204016, ☻ shakespeare.org.uk/visit/halls-croft

Stratford's most impressive medieval building is **Hall's Croft**, the former home of Shakespeare's elder daughter, Susanna, and her physician husband, John Hall. This immaculately maintained house, with its beamed ceilings and rickety rooms, holds a good-looking medley of period furniture and paintings – and upstairs it exhibits a fascinating display on **Elizabethan medicine**. Hall established something of a reputation for his medical know-how and after his death some of his case notes were published in a volume entitled *Select Observations on English Bodies*. The best view of the building itself is at the back, in the neat walled garden.

Holy Trinity Church

Old Town, CV37 6BG • March & Oct Mon–Sat 9am–5pm, Sun 12.30–5pm; April–Sept Mon–Sat 8.30am–6pm & Sun 12.30–5pm; Nov–Feb Mon–Sat 9am–4pm & Sun 12.30–5pm • Free, but chancel £3 • ☎ 01789 266316, ☻ stratford-upon-avon.org

Dating from the thirteenth century, the mellow stonework of **Holy Trinity Church** is enhanced by its riverside setting, though the dignified proportions of this quintessentially English church are the result of several centuries of chopping and changing, culminating in the replacement of the original wooden spire with today's stone version in 1763. Inside, the nave is flanked by a fine set of stained-glass windows, some of them medieval, and bathed in light from the clerestory windows up above. Quite unusually, you'll see that the nave is built on a slight skew from the line of the chancel – to represent Christ's inclined head on the cross. William Shakespeare lies buried in the **chancel**, his remains overseen by a sedate and studious memorial plaque and effigy added just seven years after his death.

Bancroft Basin

In front of the **Royal Shakespeare Theatre**, the manicured lawns of a small riverside park stretch north as far as **Bancroft Basin**, where the Stratford Canal meets the river. This is one of the prettiest parts of Stratford, with brightly painted narrowboats bobbing in the water and a fancy pedestrian bridge leading over to the finely sculpted **Gower Memorial** of 1888, where Shakespeare sits surrounded by characters from his plays.

Anne Hathaway's Cottage

22 Cottage Lane, Shottery, CV37 9HH • Daily: late March to Oct 9am–5pm; Nov to mid-March 10am–4pm • £10.25, Shakespeare Birthplace Trust combination ticket £26.25 (see p.441) • ☎ 01789 204016, ☻ shakespeare.org.uk/visit/anne-hathaways-cottage • There's a mile-long signposted footpath from Evesham Place in the town centre (20min)

Anne Hathaway's Cottage is just over a mile west of the centre in the well-heeled suburb of Shottery. The cottage – actually an old farmhouse – is an immaculately maintained,

STRATFORD'S THEATRES

Sitting pretty beside the River Avon are the **Royal Shakespeare Company**'s two main **theatres**, the Swan and the Royal Shakespeare. There was no theatre in Stratford in Shakespeare's day and indeed the first hometown festival in his honour was only held in 1769 at the behest of London-based David Garrick. Thereafter, the idea of building a permanent home in which to perform Shakespeare's works slowly gained momentum, and finally, in 1879, the first Memorial Theatre was opened on land donated by local beer baron Charles Flower. A fire in 1926 necessitated the construction of a new theatre, and the ensuing architectural competition, won by Elisabeth Scott, produced the **Royal Shakespeare Theatre**, a red-brick edifice that has recently been remodelled and extended, its proscenium stage replaced by a thrust stage – to the horror of many and the delight of some. Attached to the main theatre is the **Swan Theatre**, a replica "in-the-round" Elizabethan stage that has also been refurbished; close by is the RSC's third theatre, formerly called The Courtyard Theatre and now The Other Place.

PERFORMANCES AND TICKETS

The RSC (☎ 01789 403493, ⓦ rsc.org.uk) works on a repertory system, which means you could stay in Stratford for a few days and see three or four different plays, and not necessarily all by Shakespeare. The RSC does indeed focus on the Bard's plays, but it offers other productions too, from new modern writing through to works by Shakespeare's contemporaries – performed at three locations, the Royal Shakespeare, the Swan and The Other Place. **Tickets** start from as little as £14 and can be bought online, by phone and in person at the Royal Shakespeare Theatre's box office. Note that some performances are sold out months in advance; though there's always the off-chance of a last-minute return or stand-by ticket (for unsold seats), don't bet on it.

8

half-timbered affair with a thatched roof and dinky little chimneys. This was the home of Anne Hathaway before she married Shakespeare in 1582, and the interior holds a comely combination of period furniture, including a superb, finely carved four-poster bed. The garden is splendid too, bursting with blooms in the summertime. The adjacent orchard features more than forty types of tree, shrub and rose mentioned in the plays, each bearing a plaque with the appropriate quotation.

Mary Arden's Farm

Station Rd, Wilmcote, CV37 9UN, 3 miles northwest of Stratford • Late March to Oct daily 9am–5pm • £13.25, Shakespeare Birthplace Trust combination ticket £26.25 (see opposite) • ☎ 01789 204016, ⓦ shakespeare.org.uk/visit/mary-ardens-farm

Mary Arden's Farm takes its name from Shakespeare's mother, who at the time of her father Robert's death in 1556 was his only unmarried daughter. Unusually for the period, Mary inherited the house and land, thus becoming one of the neighbourhood's most eligible women – John Shakespeare, eager for self-improvement, married her within a year. The house is a well-furnished example of an Elizabethan farmhouse and a platoon of costumed guides fills in the details of family life. Outside, several acres of farmland are presented as a working Tudor farm complete with rare-breed animals and a woodland area with nature trails and a wildflower meadow.

ARRIVAL AND DEPARTURE
STRATFORD-UPON-AVON

By train Stratford's main train station is on the northwest edge of town, a 10min walk from the centre.
Destinations Birmingham Snow Hill (every 30min; 1hr); London Marylebone (hourly, with one change; 2hr);

Warwick (every 2hr; 30min).
By bus Local buses arrive and depart from Bridge St; most long-distance buses pull into the Riverside bus station on the east side of the town centre, off Bridgeway.

INFORMATION

Tourist office Handily located by the bridge at the junction of Bridgeway and Bridgefoot (Mon–Sat 9am–

5.30pm, Sun 10am–4pm; ☎ 01789 264293, ⓦ discover -stratford.com). Among much else, they offer a last-minute accommodation booking service that can be especially handy at the height of summer.

Shakespeare Birthplace Trust (☎01789 204016, ⚅shakespeare.org.uk) cares for five properties – three in the town centre (Shakespeare's Birthplace, Shakespeare's New Place and Hall's Croft) and two on the outskirts (Anne Hathaway's Cottage and Mary Arden's Farm). Tickets are not available for the three individual properties in the town centre – instead you have to buy a combined ticket for £17.50, or a ticket covering all five for £26.25. You can purchase individual tickets for the two outlying attractions. Tickets are on sale at all five and are discounted online.

ACCOMMODATION

At peak periods it's pretty much essential to book well ahead. The town has a dozen or so **hotels**, the pick of which occupy old half-timbered buildings right in the centre, but most visitors choose to stay in a **B&B**; there's a particular concentration to the west of the centre, around Grove Rd and Evesham Place.

Adelphi Guest House 39 Grove Rd, CV37 6PB ☎01789 204469, ⚅adelphi-guesthouse.com; map p.436. Extremely cosy B&B in a good-looking Victorian townhouse a short walk from the centre. The owners have accumulated all sorts of interesting curios – from vintage theatrical posters to ornate chandeliers – and the five double guest rooms are all en suite. The best room, which has a four-poster, is in the attic and offers pleasing views. Top-notch home-cooked breakfasts, too. **£90**

Falcon Chapel St, CV37 6HA ☎01789 279953, ⚅falcon stratfordhotel.com; map p.436. Right in the centre of town, this chain hotel is a rambling affair whose front section, with its half-timbered facade and stone-flagged bar, dates from the sixteenth century. A corridor connects this to the modern block behind, where the rooms are neat, trim and rather well designed; the rooms in older parts of the hotel, however, are not nearly as appealing. **£110**

The Townhouse 16 Church St, CV37 6HB ☎01789 262222, ⚅stratfordtownhouse.co.uk; map p.436. Twelve deluxe, en-suite guest rooms decorated in a smart and neat modern manner and equipped with king-size beds. Two-night minimum stay at peak periods. Convenient, central location and first-rate breakfasts, plus good food in the bar/restaurant (see below). **£100**

Woodstock Guest House 30 Grove Rd ☎01789 299881, ⚅woodstock-house.co.uk; map p.436. A smart, neatly kept B&B just a 5min walk from the centre, by the start of the path to Anne Hathaway's Cottage (see p.438). The five extremely comfortable bedrooms are all en suite, decorated in a fetching modern style. Minimum two nights at peak times. **£90**

YHA Stratford-upon-Avon Hemmingford House, Wellesbourne Rd, Alveston, CV37 7RG ☎0345 371 9661, ⚅yha.org.uk/hostel/stratford-upon-avon; map p.436. Occupying a rambling Georgian mansion about two miles east of Stratford on the B4086, this medium-sized hostel has dorms, doubles and family rooms, some en suite, plus car parking and self-catering facilities. Breakfasts and evening meals are on offer, too. Local bus from Stratford's Wood St. Dorms **£18**, doubles **£39**

EATING

Kingfisher Fish Bar 13 Ely St, CV37 6LW ☎01789 292513; map p.436. The best fish-and-chip shop in town, a 5min walk from the theatres. Takeaway and sit-down. Mon–Sat 11.30am–1.45pm & 5–9.30pm.

★**Lambs Restaurant** 12 Sheep St, CV37 6EF ☎01789 292554, ⚅lambsrestaurant.co.uk; map p.436. A mouth-watering range of stylish English and continental dishes – slow-roasted lamb shank, for example – are dished up in this smart restaurant that has period features like beamed ceilings, and modern art on the walls. Daily specials around £12, other mains £14–20. Mon 5–9pm, Tues–Sat noon–2pm & 5–9.30pm, Sun noon–2pm & 6–9pm.

The Townhouse 16 Church St, CV37 6HB ☎01789 262222, ⚅stratfordtownhouse.co.uk; map p.436. Smart, appealing bar/restaurant in one of the town's oldest premises. The menu is creative with due emphasis on local ingredients – vegetable risotto, for instance, or pan-roasted turbot with braised oxtail. Mains £13–18. Rooms available, too (see above). Mon–Fri noon–3pm & 5–10pm, Sat noon–10pm, Sun noon–8pm.

DRINKING

Dirty Duck 53 Waterside, CV37 6BA ☎01789 297312, ⚅oldenglishinns.co.uk; map p.436. The archetypal actors' pub, albeit now one of a chain, which is stuffed to the gunwales every night with a vocal entourage of RSC thesps and admirers. Traditional beers in somewhat spartan premises plus a terrace for hot-weather drinking. Daily 11am–11pm.

Old Thatch Tavern Market Place, CV37 6LE ☎01789 295216, ⚅oldthatchtavernstratford.co.uk; map p.436. Ancient pub with a convivial atmosphere and a good range of beers attracting a mixed bag of tourists and locals. Fuller's ales on tap. Mon–Sat 11.30am–11pm, Sun noon–11pm.

Windmill Inn Church St, CV37 6HB ☎01789 297687, ⚅windmill-stratford-upon-avon.co.uk; map p.436. Popular pub with a rabbit-warren of rooms and low-beamed ceilings. Greene King beers, too. Daily 10am–11pm.

8

Warwick and around

Small-town **WARWICK**, just nine miles northeast of Stratford, is famous for its massive **castle**, but it also possesses several charming streetscapes, which arose in the aftermath of a great fire in 1694. An hour or two is quite enough time to nose around the town centre, though you'll need the whole day if, braving the crowds and the medieval musicians, you're also set on exploring the castle and its extensive grounds; either way, Warwick is the perfect day-trip from Stratford.

Warwick Castle

CV34 4QU • Daily: core hours June–Sept 10am–5pm; Oct–May 10am–4pm • Various ticketing options from £18 in advance (£26 on the day) • ☏ 01926 495421; recorded info ☏ 0871 265 2000, ⓦ warwick-castle.com

Towering above the River Avon at the foot of the town centre, **Warwick Castle** is often proclaimed the "greatest medieval castle in Britain". This claim is valid enough if bulk equals greatness, but actually much of the existing structure is the result of extensive nineteenth-century tinkering. It's likely that the Saxons raised the first fortress on this site, though things really took off with the Normans, who built a large motte and bailey here towards the end of the eleventh century. Almost three hundred years later, the eleventh Earl of Warwick turned the stronghold into a formidable stone castle, complete with elaborate gatehouses, multiple turrets and a keep.

Today, the **entrance** to the castle is through the old stable block at the foot of Castle St. Beyond, a footpath leads round to the imposing moated and mounded **East Gate**. Over the footbridge – and beyond the protective towers – is the main **courtyard**. You can stroll along the ramparts and climb the towers, but most visitors head straight for one or other of the special, very touristy displays installed inside the castle's many chambers and towers. The **grounds** are perhaps much more enjoyable, acres of woodland and lawn inhabited by peacocks and including a large glass **conservatory**. A footbridge leads over the River Avon to **River Island**, the site of jousting tournaments and other such medieval hoopla.

Lord Leycester Hospital

60 High St, CV34 4BH • Tues–Sun & bank hols: April–Oct 10am–5pm; Nov–March 10am–4pm • £8.50 • ☏ 01926 491422, ⓦ lordleycester.com

The fascinating **Lord Leycester Hospital**, a tangle of half-timbered buildings leaning at fairy-tale angles against the stone remains of the West Gate, represents one of Britain's best-preserved examples of domestic Elizabethan architecture. It was established as a hostel for old soldiers by Robert Dudley, Earl of Leicester – a favourite of Queen Elizabeth I – and incorporates several beamed buildings, principally the Great Hall and the Guildhall, as well as a wonderful galleried courtyard and an intimate chantry chapel. Retired servicemen (and their wives) still live here, so some of the complex is out of bounds, but you can visit a **tearoom**, the *Brethrens' Kitchen* (Feb–Nov; same hours).

St Mary's Church

Old Square, CV34 4RA • April–Sept Mon–Sat 10am–6pm, Sun 12.30–4.30pm; Oct–March Mon–Sat 10am–4.30pm, Sun 12.30–4.30pm • Free, but £2 donation suggested • ☏ 01926 403940, ⓦ stmaryswarwick.org.uk

Rebuilt in a weird Gothic-Renaissance amalgam after the fire of 1694, **St Mary's Church** may not look too exciting from the outside, but wander inside and you'll see that the flames spared the **chancel**, a simply glorious illustration of the Perpendicular style with a splendid vaulted ceiling of flying and fronded ribs. To the right of the chancel is the even more spectacular **Beauchamp Chantry Chapel**, which holds the beautiful tomb of Richard Beauchamp, Earl of Warwick, who is depicted in an elaborate, gilded-bronze suit of armour of Italian design from the tip of his swan helmet down to his mailed feet. A griffin and a bear guard Richard, who lies with his hands half-joined in prayer so that, on the Resurrection, his first sight would be of Christ Triumphant at the Second Coming. The adjacent tomb of Ambrose Dudley is of finely carved and painted alabaster, as is that of Robert Dudley – who founded the Lord Leycester Hospital (see opposite) – and his wife.

Kenilworth Castle

Castle Rd, Kenilworth, CV8 1NG • April–Sept daily 10am–6pm; Oct daily 10am–5pm; Nov to mid-Feb Sat & Sun 10am–4pm; mid- to late Feb daily 10am–4pm; March Wed–Sun 10am–4pm • £10.70; EH • ☏ 01926 852078, ⓦ www.english-heritage.org.uk/visit/places/kenilworth-castle

Begun in the twelfth century, **Kenilworth Castle**, about seven miles north of Warwick, was long one of the key strategic strongholds in the Midlands, alternately held by the monarch or a leading noble. The Dudleys acquired the castle in the sixteenth century and one of the clan, Robert, pleased Elizabeth I no end by turning the draughty fortress into an elegant palace in preparation for her visit. Thereafter, the castle fell into disrepair, but the substantial ruins of today still maintain a tremendous presence and are approached across a long causeway that formerly dammed an artificial lake. There is also an **Elizabethan Garden**, a careful replica of the garden Dudley prepared for the queen's visit.

ARRIVAL AND INFORMATION

WARWICK AND AROUND

By train Warwick station is on the northern edge of town, a 15min walk from the centre via Station and Coventry roads.
Destinations Birmingham Snow Hill or Birmingham Moor St (every 30min; 30min); Stratford-upon-Avon (every 2hr; 30min).

By bus The bus station is on Market St, yards from Market Place in the town centre.
Tourist office The old Courthouse, on the corner of Castle St and Jury St (Mon–Fri 9.30am–4.30pm, Sat 10am–4.30pm; ☏ 01926 492212, ⓦ visitwarwick.co.uk).

ACCOMMODATION AND EATING

Catalan 6 Jury St, CV34 4EW ☏ 01926 498930, ⓦ catalantapas.co.uk. This inviting café/restaurant has a wide-ranging, Mediterranean-inspired menu, but the tasty tapas are its speciality – try, for example, the sardines or the white beans, shallots and leeks in a tomato sauce. Tapas average around £7, a la carte mains £14, less at lunch times. Mon–Sat noon–2.30pm & 6–9.30pm.

Rose and Crown 30 Market Place, CV34 4SH ☏ 01926 411117, ⓦ roseandcrownwarwick.co.uk. This centrally located, independently owned place offers thirteen attractive, competitively priced guest rooms, all en suite, five above the pub and eight just across the street. Each is decorated in a bright and breezy contemporary style. The first-rate pub/restaurant offers a lively, creative menu from breakfast through to dinner. Try, for example, the Cornish lamb with green bean and caper beurre noisette. A prime selection of guest beers and house wines, too. Mains average £16. Mon–Sat 7am–11pm, Sun 8am–10.30pm. £90

Worcester and around

In geographical terms, **Worcestershire** can be compared to a huge saucer, with the low-lying plains of the Severn Valley and the Vale of Evesham, Britain's foremost fruit-growing area, rising to a lip of hills, principally the Malverns in the west and the Cotswolds (see p.256) to the south. In character, the county divides into two broad belts. To the north lie the industrial and overspill towns – Droitwich and Redditch for instance – that have much in common with the Birmingham conurbation, while the south is predominantly rural. Bang at the heart of the county is **WORCESTER**, an amenable county town, where a liberal helping of half-timbered Tudor and handsome Georgian buildings stand cheek by jowl with some fairly charmless modern developments. The biggest single influence on the city has always been the **River Severn**, which flows along Worcester's west flank. It was the river that made the city an important settlement as early as Saxon times, though its propensity to breach its banks has prompted the construction of a battery of defences which tumble down the slope from the mighty bulk of the **cathedral**, easily the town's star turn. Worcester's centre is small and compact, and, handily enough, all the key sights plus the best restaurants are clustered within the immediate vicinity of the cathedral.

Worcester Cathedral

College Yard, WR1 2LA • Daily 7.30am–6pm • Free • ☎ 01905 732900, ⓦ worcestercathedral.co.uk

Towering above the River Severn, the soaring sandstone of **Worcester Cathedral** comprises a rich stew of architectural styles dating from 1084. The bulk of the church is medieval, from the Norman transepts through to the late Gothic cloister, though the Victorians did have a good old hack at the exterior. Inside, the highlight is the thirteenth-century **choir**, a beautiful illustration of the Early English style, with a forest of slender pillars rising above the intricately worked choir stalls. Here also, in front of the high altar, is the **table-tomb** of England's most reviled monarch, **King John** (1167–1216), who certainly would not have appreciated the lion that lies at his feet biting the end of his sword – a reference to the curbing of his power by the barons when they obliged him to sign the Magna Carta. Just beyond the tomb – on the right – is **Prince Arthur's Chantry**, a delicate lacy confection of carved stonework erected in 1504 to commemorate Arthur, King Henry VII's son, who died at the age of 15. He was on his honeymoon with Catherine of Aragon, who was soon passed on – with such momentous consequences – to his younger brother, the future Henry VIII. A doorway on the south side of the nave leads to the **cloisters**, with their delightful roof bosses, and the circular, largely Norman **chapter house**, which has the distinction of being the first such building constructed with the use of a central supporting pillar.

Museum of Royal Worcester

Severn St, WR1 2ND • Mon–Sat: March–Oct 10am–5pm; Nov–Feb 10am–4pm • £6 • ☎ 01905 21247, ⓦ museumofroyalworcester.org

There was a time when Severn Street, tucked away just to the south of the cathedral, hummed with the activity of one of England's largest porcelain factories, **Royal Worcester**. Those days ended, however, when the company hit the skids and was finally rolled up in 2008 after more than one hundred and fifty years in production. Much of the old factory complex has been turned into apartments, but the **Museum of Royal Worcester** has survived, and exhibits a comprehensive collection of the ornate porcelain for which Royal Worcester was famous.

The Commandery

Sidbury, WR1 2HU • Feb–Dec Tues–Sat 10am–5pm, Sun 1.30–5pm • £5.50 • ☎ 01905 361 821, ⓦ www.worcestershire.gov.uk/museums

Occupying Worcester's oldest building, a rambling, half-timbered structure dating from the early sixteenth century, the **Commandery**, beside the busy Sidbury dual carriageway, holds several different displays tracking through the history of the Commandery and its assorted occupants. The building itself is historically important: **King Charles II** used it as his headquarters during the Battle of Worcester in 1651, the endgame of his unsuccessful attempt to regain the throne from Cromwell and the Parliamentarians, who had executed his father in 1649. The high point of the interior is the medieval **painted chamber**, whose walls are covered with intriguing cameos recalling the building's original use as a monastery hospital. Each relates to a saint with healing powers – for example St Thomas Becket is shown being stabbed in the head by a group of knights, which was enough to make him the patron saint for headaches.

Greyfriars' House and Garden

Friar St, WR1 2LZ • Mid-Feb to mid-Dec Tues–Sat 11am–4pm • £5.25; NT • ☎ 01905 23571, ⓦ nationaltrust.org.uk/greyfriars-house-and-garden

From the Commandery, it's a short step northwest along Sidbury to narrow Friar Street, whose hotchpotch of half-timbered houses and small, independent shops make it

Worcester's prettiest thoroughfare. Among the buildings is **Greyfriars**, a largely fifteenth-century townhouse whose wonky timbers and dark-stained panelling shelter a charming collection of antiques. There's an attractive walled garden here too. From Greyfriars, it's a couple of minutes' walk west to the High Street, a couple more back to the cathedral.

ARRIVAL AND INFORMATION
WORCESTER AND AROUND

By train Worcester has two train stations. The handiest for the city centre is Foregate St, from where it's about 800yd south to the cathedral along Foregate and its continuation The Cross and then High St. The other train station, Shrub Hill, is further out, about a mile to the northeast of the cathedral.
Destinations (Foregate St) Birmingham Moor St (every 30min; 1hr); Great Malvern (every 30min; 15min); Hereford (hourly; 50min).

By bus The bus station is at the back of the sprawling Crowngate shopping centre, about 600yd north of the cathedral.
Destinations Great Malvern (2 hourly; 40min); Hereford (Mon–Sat every 2hr; 1hr 20min).
Tourist office Guildhall, towards the cathedral end of the High St (Mon–Fri 9.30am–5pm, Sat 10am–4pm; ☎ 01905 726311, ⓦ visitworcestershire.org).

ACCOMMODATION

The Cardinal's Hat 31 Friar St, WR1 2NA ☎ 01905 724006, ⓦ the-cardinals-hat.co.uk. In a great central location, this old inn with its mullioned windows and wooden panelling offers a handful of attractive rooms kitted out in lavish retro-meets-period rooms. Tasty breakfasts too. **£100**
Diglis House Hotel Severn St, WR1 2NF ☎ 01905

353518, ⓦ diglishousehotel.co.uk. Medium-sized hotel in an attractive Georgian villa beside the river, about 5min walk south of the cathedral. Some of the guest rooms are in the main building, others in the modern annexe, and all are decorated in a pleasant if somewhat staid version of country-house style. The hotel's prime feature is the large conservatory overlooking the river. **£110**

EATING AND DRINKING

Mac & Jac's Café 44 Friar St, WR1 2NA ☎ 01905 731331, ⓦ macandjacs.co.uk. With a sister café in Great Malvern (see p.446), this family-run place occupies an old, half-timbered building near the cathedral. Offers a tasty range of home-made snacks and meals – try, for example, the pollack and salmon fishcake with green beans (£12). Tues–Sat 9am–5pm.
Saffrons Bistro 15 New St, WR1 2DP ☎ 01905 610505,

ⓦ saffronsbistro.co.uk. One of Worcester's best restaurants, this cheerfully decorated little place near Greyfriars is strong on local ingredients – and the proof is in the eating. Try the delicious slow-braised blade of beef with green beans, mushrooms and shallots in a red-wine sauce. Reservations advised in the evening. Mains hover around £15. Mon–Fri noon–2.15pm & 5.30–9.30pm, Sat noon–2.30pm & 5.30–10.30pm.

The Malvern Hills

One of the more prosperous parts of the West Midlands, **The Malverns** is the generic name for a string of towns and villages stretched along the eastern lower slopes of **THE MALVERN HILLS**, which rise spectacularly out of the flatlands a few miles to the southwest of Worcester. About nine miles from north to south and never more than five miles wide, the hills straddle the Worcestershire–Herefordshire boundary. Of ancient granite rock, they are punctuated by over twenty summits, mostly around

---

HIKING THE MALVERN HILLS

Great Malvern tourist office (see p.446) sells hiking maps and issues half a dozen free **Trail Guide leaflets**, which describe circular routes up to and along the hills that rise behind the town. The shortest trail is just a mile and a half, the longest four. One of the most appealing is the 2.5-mile hoof up to the top of – and back from – **North Hill** (1307ft), from where there are panoramic views over the surrounding countryside. This hike also takes in *St Ann's Well Café* (times vary; ☎ 01684 560285, ⓦ stannswell.co.uk), a sweet little café in an attractive Georgian building where you can taste the local spring water; the signposted path begins beside the *Mount Pleasant Hotel*, on Belle Vue Terrace, just to the left (south) of the top of Church Street.

1000ft high, and in between lie innumerable dips and hollows. It's easy, if energetic, walking country, with great views, and there's an excellent network of **hiking trails**, most of which can be completed in a day or half-day, with **Great Malvern** being the obvious base.

Great Malvern

Of all the towns in the Malverns, it's **GREAT MALVERN** that grabs the attention, its pocket-sized centre clambering up the hillside with the crags of North Hill beckoning beyond. The grand old houses, which congregate on and around the top of the main drag, **Church Street**, mostly date from Great Malvern's nineteenth-century heyday as a spa town when the local **spring waters** drew the Victorians here by the trainload. You can still sample the waters at the gushing **Malvhina spring** in the mini-park at the top of Church Street – or venture further afield to the spring at **St Ann's Well Café** (see box, p.445) – but the town's principal sight is its splendid **Priory Church**, yards from the Malvhina spring (Mon–Sat 9am–5pm; free; ⓦ greatmalvernpriory.org.uk). The Benedictines built one of their abbeys here at Great Malvern and, although Henry VIII closed the place down in 1538, the church's elaborate decoration and fabulous late medieval **stained-glass windows** proclaim the priory's former wealth. ·

Malvern Museum

Priory Gatehouse, Abbey Rd, WR14 3ES • Late March to Oct daily 10.30am–5pm • £2 • ☎ 01684 567811, ⓦ malvernmuseum.co.uk

Behind the Priory Church is the delicately proportioned **Priory Gatehouse**, which now holds the tiny **Malvern Museum** of local history. One of the most interesting rooms explores what life was like here in medieval times, another looks at Great Malvern's days as a spa town, with old promotional cartoons showing patients packed into soaked sheets before, their ailments cured, they hop gaily away from their crutches.

ARRIVAL AND INFORMATION

By train From Great Malvern's rustic train station, with its dainty ironwork and quaint chimneys, it's about 800yd to the town centre – take Avenue Rd, which leads to Church St, the steeply sloping main drag.
Destinations Birmingham New St (hourly; 1hr); Hereford (hourly; 35min); Worcester Foregate (every 30min; 15min).

Tourist office At the top of Church St, metres from the Priory Church (daily 10am–5pm; ☎01684 892289, ⓦ visitthemalverns.org).

ACCOMMODATION

Abbey Hotel Abbey Rd, WR14 3ET ☎01684 892332, ⓦ sarova-abbeyhotel.com. This is easily the most conspicuous hotel in Great Malvern, a few yards from the Priory Church, much of it occupying a rambling, creeper-clad Victorian building executed in a sort of neo-Baronial style. It's part of a small chain, and the guest rooms, especially in the hotel's lumpy modern wing, can be a little characterless – but they are comfortable enough and many have attractive views back over town. **£110**

The Cottage in the Wood Holywell Rd, Malvern Wells, WR14 4LG ☎01684 588860, ⓦ cottageinthewood .co.uk. Family-run hotel with a dozen or so cheery, comfortable guest rooms in the main house and a brace of small annexes. The main house is not so much a cottage as a spacious villa built as a dower house to a neighbouring estate in the late 1700s. Wooded grounds surround the hotel and there are fine views. The rooms vary considerably in size and comfort. **£110**

EATING AND DRINKING

Mac & Jac's Café 23 Abbey Rd, WR14 3ES ☎01684 573300, ⓦ macandjacs.co.uk. This bright and cheery café does its level best to source things locally (with the exception of its teas, the house speciality). It offers a particularly good range of salads – for example, beef salad with salsa verde and rocket (£8). Next door to the Malvern Museum. Tues–Sat 9am–6.30pm, Sun 10am–3.30pm.

The Morgan 52 Clarence Rd, WR14 3EQ ☎01684 578575, ⓦ wyevalleybrewery.co.uk. Just beyond the train station, this is the best pub in town, where you can sample the assorted brews of Herefordshire's much-praised Wye Valley Brewery. Drink outside on the terrace if the sun is out, or inside in the wood-panelled bar. Mon–Wed noon–3pm & 5–11pm, Thurs–Sun noon–11pm.

Herefordshire

Over the Malvern Hills from Worcestershire, the rolling agricultural landscapes of **HEREFORDSHIRE** have an easy-going charm, but the finest scenery hereabouts is along the banks of the **River Wye**, which wriggles and worms its way across the county. Plonked in the middle of Herefordshire on the Wye is the county town, Hereford, a sleepy, old-fashioned place whose proudest possession is the cathedral's remarkable medieval map, the **Mappa Mundi**. Beyond Hereford, the southeast corner of the county has one especially attractive town, **Ross-on-Wye**, a genial little place with a picturesque setting that serves as a gateway to one of the wilder portions of the **Wye River Valley**, around **Symonds Yat**, where canoeists gather in their droves.

GETTING AROUND   **HEREFORDSHIRE**

By train Herefordshire has just one rail line, linking Hereford with points north to Shrewsbury and east to Great Malvern and Worcester.

By bus Local buses provide a reasonable service between

the county's villages and towns, except on Sun when there's very little at all. For timetable details, consult ⓦ travelinemidlands.co.uk or pop into the nearest tourist office.

Hereford

A low-key county town with a spacious feel, **HEREFORD** was long a border garrison held against the Welsh, its military importance guaranteed by its strategic position beside the River Wye. It also became a religious centre after the Welsh murdered the Saxon king **Ethelbert** near here in 794. Today, with the fortifications that once girdled the city all but vanished, it's the **cathedral** – and its extraordinary medieval **Mappa Mundi** – which forms the focus of interest. The cathedral lies just to the north of the river at the heart of the city centre, whose compact tangle of narrow streets and squares is clumsily boxed in by the ring road. Taken as a whole, Hereford makes for a pleasant overnight stay, especially as it has a particularly fine hotel.

8

Hereford Cathedral

Cathedral Close, HR1 2NG • Daily 9.15am–5.30pm • Free • ☎ 01432 374200, ⓦ www.herefordcathedral.org • **Mappa Mundi** Mon–Sat: April–Oct 10am–5pm; Nov, Dec, Feb & March 10am–4pm • £6 • ⓦ themappamundi.co.uk

Hereford Cathedral is a curious building, an uncomfortable amalgamation of styles, with bits and pieces added to the eleventh-century church by a string of bishops and culminating in an extensive – and not especially sympathetic – Victorian refit. From the outside, the sandstone **tower** is the dominant feature, constructed in the early fourteenth century to eclipse the Norman western tower, which collapsed under its own weight in 1786. The crashing masonry mauled the **nave** and its replacement lacks some of the grandeur of most other English cathedrals, though the forceful symmetries of the long rank of surviving Norman arches and piers more than hint at what went before. The **north transept** is, however, a flawless exercise in thirteenth-century taste, its soaring windows a classic example of Early English architecture.

The Mappa Mundi

In the 1980s, the cathedral's finances were so parlous that a plan was drawn up to sell its most treasured possession, the **Mappa Mundi**. Luckily, the government and John Paul Getty Jr rode to the rescue, with the oil tycoon stumping up a million pounds to keep the map here and install it in a new building, the New Library, which blends in seamlessly with the older buildings it adjoins at the west end of the cloisters.

The Mappa Mundi exhibit begins with a series of interpretative panels explaining the historical background and composition of the map. Included is a copy in English, which is particularly helpful as the original, displayed in a dimly lit room just beyond, is in Latin. Measuring 64 by 52 inches and dating to about 1300, the Mappa provides an extraordinary insight into the medieval mind. It is indeed a map (as we know it) insofar as it suggests the general geography of the world – with Asia at the top and Europe and Africa below, to left and right respectively – but it also squeezes in history, mythology and theology. In the same building as the Mappa Mundi is the **Chained Library**, a remarkably extensive collection of books and manuscripts dating from the eighth to the eighteenth centuries. A selection is always open on display.

ARRIVAL AND INFORMATION   HEREFORD

By train Hereford train station is about 800yd northeast of the main square, High Town, via Station Approach, Commercial Rd and its continuation Commercial St.
Destinations Birmingham New St (hourly; 1hr 30min); Great Malvern (hourly; 30min); Ludlow (every 30min; 30min); Shrewsbury (every 30min; 1hr); Worcester

Foregate (hourly; 50min).
By bus The long-distance bus station is on the north side of the town centre, just off Commercial Rd; most local and regional buses stop in the centre on High Town.
Destinations Hay-on-Wye (Mon–Sat every 2hr; 1hr); Ross-on-Wye (Mon–Sat hourly; 1hr).

ACCOMMODATION

★**Castle House** Castle St, HR1 2NW ☎01432 356321, ⓦ castlehse.co.uk. Occupying an immaculately refurbished Georgian mansion and a neighbouring townhouse near the cathedral, it's hard to praise this medium-sized hotel too highly: the staff are obliging; the better, bigger rooms are simply delightful, with all sorts of period details; and the breakfast room has a lovely outside terrace. They have two smashing restaurants here too (see below). **£160**

No. 21 21 Aylestone Hill, HR1 1HR ☎01432 279897, ⓦ 21aylestonehill.co.uk. In a substantial, half-timbered Edwardian house just northeast of the centre, this comfortable B&B has five, en-suite guest rooms decorated in soothing shades and complete with period flourishes. It's located within easy walking distance of the centre, near the train station and beside the A465 (Aylestone Hill). **£70**

EATING AND DRINKING

The Barrels 69 St Owen St, HR1 2JQ ☎01432 274968, ⓦ wyevalleybrewery.co.uk. A popular local just 5min southeast of High Town, *The Barrels* is the home pub of the local Wye Valley Brewery, whose trademark bitters are much acclaimed. Mon–Thurs 11am–11.30pm, Fri & Sat 11am–midnight, Sun noon–11.30pm.

Cafe@allsaints All Saints Church, High St, HR4 9AA ☎01432 370415, ⓦ cafeatallsaints.co.uk. Near the cathedral, in the old church at the top of Broad St, this excellent café has become something of a local institution since it was founded by a local foodie in the late 1990s.

Serves a range of well-conceived and tasty dishes – ricotta pie with salad leaves for instance – at around £7. Mon–Sat 8am–4pm.

★**Castle House** Castle St, HR1 2NW ☎01432 356321, ⓦ castlehse.co.uk. This superb hotel (see above) has two first-rate restaurants – one formal, the other casual – and both emphasize local ingredients, with Hereford beef and Gloucestershire pork being prime examples. Prices are reasonable too, both at lunch and dinner, with mains from £10. Mon–Sat noon–2pm & 6.30–9.30pm, Sun noon–2pm & 6.30–9pm.

Ross-on-Wye

Nestling above a loop in the river fifteen miles southeast of Hereford, **ROSS-ON-WYE** is a relaxed and easy-going market town with an artsy/New Age undertow. Ross's jumble of narrow streets converges on **Market Place**, which is shadowed by the seventeenth-century **Market House**, a sturdy two-storey sandstone structure that sports a medallion bust of a bewigged Charles II. Veer right at the top of Market Place, then turn left up Church Street to reach Ross's other noteworthy building, the mostly thirteenth-century **St Mary's Church**, whose sturdy stonework culminates in a slender, tapering spire. In front of the church, at the foot of the graveyard, is a plain but rare **Plague Cross**, commemorating the three hundred or so townsfolk who were buried here by night without coffins during a savage outbreak of the plague in 1637.

ARRIVAL AND DEPARTURE   ROSS-ON-WYE

By bus Ross bus station is on Cantilupe Rd, a 4min-walk from Market Place.

Destinations Goodrich (Mon–Sat every 2hr; 20min); Hereford (Mon–Sat hourly; 1hr).

ACCOMMODATION AND EATING

★**Linden Guest House** 14 Church St, HR9 5HN ☎01989 565373, ⓦlindenguesthouse.com. Housed within a fetching Georgian building opposite St Mary's Church, this B&B has three en-suite guest rooms, each of which is cosily decorated. The cooked breakfasts are delicious too – both traditional and vegetarian. **£75**

Old Court House B&B 53 High St, HR9 5HH ☎01989 762275, ⓦtheoldcourthousebandb.co.uk. An unusual B&B in a rabbit warren of an old stone building, complete with open fires and exposed wooden beams. Has four en-suite guest rooms of varying sizes. Handily located in the centre of the town. **£80**

Pots and Pieces Teashop 40 High St, HR9 5HD ☎01989 566123, ⓦpotsandpieces.com. This appealing little café and gift shop behind the Market House sells a tasty range of snacks and light meals. The toasted teacakes are the best for miles around – make space for the home-made cakes, too. Mon–Fri 9am–4.30pm, Sat 10am–4.30pm, plus June–Aug Sun 11am–3.30pm.

Yaks N Yetis 1 Brookend St, HR9 7EG ☎01989 564963. Not the prettiest of restaurants perhaps, but this is genuine Nepalese (Gurkha) cuisine – and the staff are more than willing to help explain its intricacies. It's delicious and, with mains from around £9, economically priced too. Brookend is a continuation of Broad St, which runs north from Market Place. Tues–Sun noon–2.30pm & 6–11pm.

The Wye River Valley

Travelling south from Ross along the B4234, it's just five miles to the gaunt sandstone mass of **Goodrich Castle** (April–Oct daily 10am–5pm; Nov–March restricted hours; £7.60, EH; ⓦwww.english-heritage.org.uk/visit/places/goodrich-castle), which commands wide views over the hills and woods of the **Wye River Valley**. The castle's strategic location guaranteed its importance as a border stronghold from the twelfth century onwards and today the substantial ruins incorporate a Norman keep, a maze of later rooms and passageways and walkable ramparts. The castle stands next to the tiny village of **GOODRICH**, from where it's around a mile and a half southeast along narrow country lanes to the solitary *YHA Wye Valley Hostel* (see below), which, with the **Wye Valley Walk** running past the front door, makes a great base (in a no-frills sort of way) for **hikers**.

Symonds Yat

From Goodrich, it's a couple of miles southwest along narrow country lanes to a signed fork in the road – go straight on for the wriggly road up to the top of **Symonds Yat Rock**, one of the region's most celebrated viewpoints, rising high above a wooded loop in the River Wye. Down below is **SYMONDS YAT EAST** (which you reach if you veer right at the fork in the road), a pretty little hamlet that straggles along the east bank of the river. It's a popular spot and one that offers canoe rental and regular **river trips** (40min) – and there's a good hotel here too (see below). The road to the village is a dead end, so you have to double back to regain Goodrich (or Symonds Yat Rock), though you can cross the river to **Symonds Yat West** by means of a hand-pulled rope **ferry**, which leaves from outside the *Saracens Head Inn*.

ACCOMMODATION AND EATING   THE WYE RIVER VALLEY

Saracens Head Inn Symonds Yat East, HR9 6JL ☎01600 890345, ⓦsaracensheadinn.co.uk. There are twelve en-suite guest rooms in this village hotel beside the River Wye, each decorated in pleasant modern style with wooden floors and pastel walls. You can eat well both in the restaurant and in the bar, with the menu featuring mostly English favourites – though there are international dishes as well. Mains average £14. Kitchen daily noon–2.30pm & 6.30–9pm. **£95**

YHA Wye Valley Hostel Near Goodrich, HR9 6JJ ☎0345 371 9666, ⓦyha.org.uk/hostel/wye-valley. If you're after a remote location, this is the hostel to head for – in a Victorian rectory in its own grounds above the River Wye. There are eighty-odd beds here, in anything from two-bedded private rooms to ten-bed dorms, as well as camping and self-catering facilities, but note that advance booking is essential as the hostel is sometimes rented by groups; evening meals can also be provided on request. Formerly the *Welsh Bicknor YHA Hostel*. Open March to Oct. Camping/person **£13**, dorms **£15**, doubles **£40**

Hay-on-Wye

Straddling the Anglo-Welsh border some twenty miles west of Hereford, the hilly little town of **HAY-ON-WYE** has an attractive riverside setting and narrow, winding streets lined with an engaging assortment of old stone houses, but is known to most people for one thing – **books**. Hay saw its first bookshop open in 1961 at the instigation of **Richard Booth** (b.1938), a leftist who was determined to refloat the town's economy without recourse to the government-led regeneration schemes he hated. It worked – today just about every inch of town is given over to the trade, including the old cinema. The prestigious **Hay Festival of Literature and the Arts** (ⓦhayfestival.com) is held over ten days in late May, when England's literary world decamps here en masse.

ARRIVAL AND INFORMATION
HAY-ON-WYE

By bus Buses stop on Oxford Rd, just along from the tourist office, and run to Hereford (Mon–Sat every 2hr; 1hr).
Tourist office Oxford Rd (Easter–Oct daily 10am–4.30pm;

Nov–Easter daily 11am–1pm & 2–4pm; ☎01497 820144, ⓦhay-on-wye.co.uk).

ACCOMMODATION

Hay has plenty of **accommodation**, but everywhere gets booked up months in advance during the festival.

★**Old Black Lion** Lion St, HR3 5AD ☎01497 820841, ⓦoldblacklion.co.uk. Well-regarded old inn, which has ten en-suite guest rooms both above the pub and in two nearby buildings. The rooms vary in size and demeanour – from the plush with period details to the rather plainer, but they are all very comfortable. **£80**
Seven Stars B&B 11 Broad St, HR3 5DB ☎01497 820886, ⓦtheseven-stars.co.uk. Former town pub near the clocktower, with eight modestly sized but cosy rooms, some with original oak beams. There's also an indoor

swimming pool and sauna. **£80**
The Start B&B Hay Bridge, HR3 5RS ☎01497 821391, ⓦthe-start.net. Neatly renovated stone house on the riverbank, with three rooms boasting antique furnishings and handmade quilts. The vegetable garden provides many of the ingredients for the delicious breakfast. **£80**
★**Tinto House** 13 Broad St, HR3 5DB ☎01497 821556, ⓦtinto-house.co.uk. Charming old house with three large and sumptuous rooms, each different, and a self-contained unit in the old stable block which has splendid garden views. **£90**

EATING AND DRINKING

Blue Boar Castle St, HR3 5DF ☎01497 820884. Tasteful, wood-panelled real ale pub centred around a gently curving bar and two stone fireplaces, with a separate dining area to one side. Daily 9am–11pm; food served daily 11.30am–2pm & 6–9.30pm.
The Granary 20 Broad St, HR3 5DB ☎01497 820790. This unpretentious café-bistro offers a wide range of meals, with good veggie options. Save space for the home-made desserts. Mains £12. Daily 9am–5.30pm.
The Old Stables Tearooms Bear St, HR3 5AN ☎01497 821557, ⓦoldstablestearooms.co.uk. Barely half a dozen

tables are shoehorned into this delightful place, with chalked-up boards offering superb Welsh produce and a fantastic array of teas and home-made tarts. On a warm day, eat in the flower-filled yard. Tues–Sat 11am– 4.30pm.
Shepherd's Ice Cream Parlour 9 High Town, HR3 5AE ☎01497 821898, ⓦwww.shepherdsicecream.co.uk. Popular café/ice-cream parlour doling out local ice cream made from sheep's milk; flavours include raspberry cheesecake and banana toffee crunch. Mon–Fri 9.30am–5.30pm, Sat 9.30am–6pm, Sun 10.30am–5.30pm.

SHOPPING

Hay has over thirty **bookshops**, many of which are highly specialized, focusing on areas like travel, poetry or murder mystery.

CANOEING AROUND HAY-ON-WYE

Hay-on-Wye's environs are readily and pleasantly explored by **kayak or canoe** along the **River Wye**. In four to six days, it's possible to paddle your way downriver from Hay to Ross-on-Wye (see p.448), overnighting in tents on isolated stretches of riverbank, or holing up in comfortable B&Bs and pubs along the way. Hay's **Paddles & Pedals**, down by the river on the far side of the Clyro bridge (☎01497 820604, ⓦpaddlesandpedals.co.uk), is a reputable outfit for kayak and canoe **rental**, full of good ideas and advice. Rental of life jackets and other essential equipment (such as waterproof canisters to carry your gear) is included in the price, which works out at around £35 per canoe for 24 hours, with discounts for longer trips. They also transport their customers to and from the departure and finishing points by minibus; advance reservations essential.

Richard Booth's Bookshop 44 Lion St, HR3 5AA ☎ 01497 820322, ⓦ boothbooks.co.uk. Just beyond the main square, High Town, this slicked-up, three-floor emporium offers unlimited browsing potential. Superb stock of first edition, rare and antiquarian books. Incorporated into the rear of the bookshop is the charming little Bookshop Cinema, screening art-house films at weekends. Bookshop Mon–Sat 9am–5.30pm, Sun 10.30am–4.30pm.

Stella & Rose's Books 14 Broad St, HR3 5DB ☎ 01497 820013, ⓦ stellabooks.com. Located opposite the clock-tower, Rose's Books has a wonderful stock of rare and collectable children's and illustrated books. Daily 10am–5pm.

Shropshire

One of England's largest and least populated counties, **SHROPSHIRE** stretches from its long and winding border with Wales to the edge of the urban Black Country. The Industrial Revolution made a huge stride forward here, with the spanning of the River Severn by the very first iron bridge and, although the assorted industries that then squeezed into the **Ironbridge Gorge** are long gone, a series of museums celebrates their craftsmanship – from tiles through to iron. The gorge is also within easy striking distance of one of the prettiest towns hereabouts, **Much Wenlock**. Further west, the River Severn also flows through the county town of **Shrewsbury**, whose centre holds dozens of old half-timbered buildings, though **Ludlow**, further south, has the edge when it comes to handsome Tudor and Jacobean architecture. In between the two lie some of the most beautiful parts of Shropshire, primarily the **Long Mynd**, a prime hiking area that's readily explored from the attractive little town of **Church Stretton**.

GETTING AROUND AND INFORMATION SHROPSHIRE 8

By train There are frequent trains from Birmingham to Telford (for Ironbridge Gorge) and Shrewsbury, which is also linked to Church Stretton and Ludlow on the Hereford line.

By bus Bus services are patchy, but one small step forward has been the creation of the Shropshire Hills Shuttle bus service (mid-April to Sept Sat & Sun; every 1–2hr; ⓦ shropshirehillsaonb.co.uk) aimed at the tourist market. The shuttle noses round the Long Mynd as well as the Stiperstones and drops by Church Stretton. An adult Day Rover ticket, valid on the whole route and available from the driver, costs just £8. Timetables are available at most Shropshire tourist offices and on the website.

Website ⓦ shropshiretourism.co.uk.

Ironbridge Gorge

IRONBRIDGE GORGE, the collective title for a cluster of small villages huddled in the Severn Valley to the south of new-town Telford, was the crucible of the Industrial Revolution, a process encapsulated by its famous span across the Severn – the world's first **iron bridge**, engineered by **Abraham Darby** and opened on New Year's Day, 1781. Darby was the third innovative industrialist of that name – the first Abraham Darby started iron-smelting here back in 1709 and the second invented the forging process that made it possible to produce massive iron beams. Under the guidance of such creative figures as the Darbys and Thomas Telford, the area's factories once churned out engines, rails, wheels and other heavy-duty iron pieces in quantities unmatched anywhere else in the world. Manufacturing has now all but vanished, but the surviving monuments make the Gorge the most extensive **industrial heritage site** in England – and one that has been granted UNESCO World Heritage Site status.

The Gorge contains several museums and an assortment of other industrial attractions spread along a five-mile stretch of the Severn Valley. A thorough exploration takes a couple of days, but the highlights – the bridge itself, the **Museum of Iron** and the **Jackfield Tile Museum** – are easily manageable on a day-trip.

Ironbridge village

There must have been an awful lot of nail-biting during the construction of the **Iron Bridge** over the River Severn in the late 1770s. No one was quite sure how the new

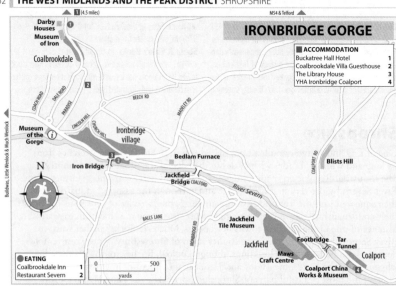

material would wear and although the single-span design looked sound, many feared

that the bridge would simply tumble into the river. To compensate, Abraham Darby used more iron than was strictly necessary, but the end result still manages to appear stunningly graceful, arching between the steep banks with the river far below. The settlement at the north end of the span was promptly renamed **IRONBRIDGE**, and today its brown-brick houses climb prettily up the hill from the bridge.

Museum of the Gorge

Wharfage, TF8 7DQ • Daily 10am–4pm • £4.50, but covered by Passport Ticket (see p.454) • ☎ 01952 433424, ⓦ www.ironbridge.org.uk /museum-of-the-gorge

Ironbridge village is also home to the **Museum of the Gorge**, in a church-like, neo-Gothic riverside warehouse about seven hundred yards west of the bridge along the main road. This provides an introduction to the Gorge's industrial history and gives a few environmental pointers too; it also houses the main visitor centre (see p.454).

Coalbrookdale Museum of Iron

Coach Rd, Coalbrookdale, TF8 7DQ • Daily 10am–4pm • £8.85, but covered by Passport Ticket (see p.454) • ☎ 01952 433424, ⓦ www .ironbridge.org.uk/coalbrookdale-museum-of-iron

At the roundabout just to the west of the Museum of the Gorge, turn right for the half-mile trip up to what was once the Gorge's big industrial deal, the **Coalbrookdale iron foundry**, which boomed throughout the eighteenth and early nineteenth centuries, employing up to four thousand men and boys. The foundry has been imaginatively converted into the **Museum of Iron**, with a wide range of displays on iron-making in general and the history of the company in particular. There are superb examples of Victorian and Edwardian ironwork here, including the intricate castings – stags, dogs and even camels – that became the house speciality. Also in the complex, across from the foundry beneath a protective canopy, are the ruins of the **furnace** where Abraham Darby pioneered the use of coke as a smelting fuel in place of charcoal.

Bedlam Furnace

TF8 7QY, about 600yd east of Ironbridge village on the B4373 • Open access • Free • ⓦ www.ironbridge.org.uk/bedlam-furnace

Heading east from the bridge along the north bank of the river, you soon pass the battered brick-and-stone remains of the **Bedlam furnace**, one of the first furnaces to use coke rather than charcoal. It was kept alight around the clock, and at night its fiery silhouette was said to have scared passers-by out of their wits – hence the name.

Blists Hill Victorian Town

Coalport Rd, TF7 5DU, about half a mile north of the River Severn – take the signed turning between the Bedlam Furnace and Coalport • Daily 10am–4.30pm • £16.25, but covered by Passport Ticket (see p.454) • ☎ 01952 433424, ⓦ www.ironbridge.org.uk/blists-hill-victorian-town

The rambling **Blists Hill Victorian Town** is the Gorge's most popular attraction, enclosing a substantial number of reconstructed Victorian buildings, most notably a school, a candle-maker's, a doctor's surgery, a pub and wrought-iron works. Jam-packed on most summer days, it's especially popular with school parties, who keep the period-dressed employees busy.

Tar Tunnel

Coalport High St, Coalport, TF8 7HT • On the north bank of the river, 500yd east of the turning to Blists Hill & on the west edge of Coalport • Daily 11am–3pm • £3.40, but covered by Passport Ticket (see p.454) • ☎ 01952 433424, ⓦ www.ironbridge.org.uk/tar-tunnel

Built to transport coal from one part of the Gorge to another, but named for the bitumen that oozes naturally from its walls, the **Tar Tunnel** may not be long, but it's certainly more than a tad spooky and you'll be issued with a hard hat for reassurance.

Coalport China Museum

Coalport High St, Coalport, TF8 7HT • Daily 10am–4pm • £8.85, but covered by Passport Ticket (see p.454) • ☎ 01952 433424, ⓦ ironbridge.org.uk/coalport-china-museum

The most easterly of the industrial sites on the north bank of the River Severn (and yards from the Tar Tunnel), the former **Coalport China works** occupies a sprawling brick complex, which incorporates the **Coalport China Museum**, which is packed with gaudy Coalport wares. There's also a workshop, where potters demonstrate their skills, and two **bottle kilns**, those distinctive conical structures that were long the hallmark of the pottery industry.

8

Jackfield

From the north bank of the Severn, take the Jackfield Bridge just east of Bedlam Furnace or the footbridge beside the Tar Tunnel

Now a sleepy little village of pretty brown-brick cottages that string along the south bank of the River Severn, **JACKFIELD** was once a sooty, grimy place that hummed to the tune of two large tile factories, Maws and Craven Dunnill. Both were built in the middle of the nineteenth century to the latest industrial design, a fully integrated manufacturing system that produced literally thousands of tiles at breakneck speed. The more easterly of the two has been turned into the **Maws Craft Centre** (ⓦmawscraftcentre.co.uk), which holds more than twenty arts, craft and specialist shops, while the other, about half a mile away to the west, boasts the Jackfield Tile Museum.

Jackfield Tile Museum

Salthouse Rd, TF8 7LJ • Daily 10am–4pm • £8.85, but covered by Passport Ticket (see p.454) • ☎ 01952 433424, ⓦ www.ironbridge.org.uk /jackfield-tile-museum

A small part of the expansive Craven Dunnill factory still produces Craven Dunnill tiles (ⓦcravendunnill-jackfield.co.uk), but mostly it's home to the outstanding **Jackfield Tile Museum**. The exhibits here include the superb "Style Gallery" and "Tiles Everywhere Galleries", where room after room illustrates many different types of tile, by style – Art Deco and Art Nouveau through to Arts and Crafts and the Aesthetic Movement – and location, from a London underground station to a butcher's shop.

ARRIVAL AND DEPARTURE   IRONBRIDGE GORGE

By bus Arriva bus #96 (ⓦarrivabus.co.uk) connects both Shrewsbury and Telford bus stations with Ironbridge village

(Mon–Sat every 2hr; 40min/15min). There's also an Arriva bus service to Much Wenlock (Mon–Sat every 2hr; 30min).

GETTING AROUND

By bus Bus services along the Gorge are limited to Gorge Connect (late July to mid-Sept Sat & Sun 10am–5pm; every 30min; ⓦ telford.gov.uk), which links Coalbrookdale in the west with Coalport in the east, taking in Ironbridge village and Blists Hill on the way.

INFORMATION

Tourist information Ironbridge Gorge tourist information (daily 10am–4pm; ☎ 01952 433424, ⓦ ironbridge .org.uk) is in the Museum of the Gorge (see p.452). In addition to local maps and information, they sell the Passport Ticket.

Admissions and passes Each museum and attraction charges its own admission fee, but if you're intending to visit several, then buy a Passport Ticket (£25), which allows access to all ten as many times as you want for year. Available at all the main sights, and through tourist information. Does not cover parking, but charges are reasonable.

ACCOMMODATION

Buckatree Hall Hotel The Wrekin, Telford, TF6 5AL ☎ 01952 641821, ⓦ buckatreehallhotel.com; map p.452. In a pleasant rural setting near the wooded slopes of The Wrekin, the distinctive 1334ft peak that rises high above its surroundings, the *Buckatree* comprises the original Edwardian house and a modern wing. Most of the rooms have balconies. Just south of the M54 and Wellington. **£65**

Coalbrookdale Villa Guesthouse 17 Paradise, Coalbrookdale, TF8 7NR ☎ 01952 433450, ⓦ www .coalbrookdalevilla.co.uk; map p.452. This B&B occupies an attractive Victorian ironmaster's house set in its own grounds about half a mile up the hill from Ironbridge village in the tiny hamlet of Paradise. Rooms are sedately decorated, country-house-style, and en suite. **£75**

The Library House 11 Severn Bank, Ironbridge village, TF8 7AN ☎ 01952 432299, ⓦ libraryhouse.com; map p.452. Enjoyable B&B, the village's best, in a charming Georgian villa yards from the Iron Bridge. Three doubles, decorated in a modern rendition of period style. **£100**

YHA Ironbridge Coalport High St, Coalport, TF8 7HT ☎ 0345 371 9325, ⓦ yha.org.uk/hostel/ironbridge -coalport; map p.452. At the east end of the Gorge in the former Coalport China factory, this YHA hostel has around eighty beds in two- to six-bedded rooms (doubles all en suite), plus a shop and a café. Popular with school groups and for activity breaks. Dorms **£16**, doubles **£40**

EATING

Coalbrookdale Inn 12 Wellington Rd, Coalbrookdale, TF8 7DX ☎ 01952 432166, ⓦ facebook.com /CoalbrookdaleInn; map p.452. On the main road across from the Coalbrookdale iron foundry, this traditional pub offers a top-notch selection of real ales plus filling pub grub. Mon–Thurs noon–2pm & 5–11.30pm, Fri–Sun noon–11.30pm.

Restaurant Severn 33 High St, Ironbridge village, TF8 7AG ☎ 01952 432233, ⓦ restaurantsevern.co.uk; map p.452. This smart little place, just a few yards from the bridge, offers an inventive menu with main courses such as venison in a cognac and cranberry sauce. In the evening, a two-course set meal costs around £28. Wed–Sat noon–4.30pm & 6–10.30pm, Sun noon–6pm.

Much Wenlock and around

The tiny town of **MUCH WENLOCK**, about six miles southwest of Ironbridge village, is an attractive little place, where a medley of Tudor, Jacobean and Georgian buildings dot the High Street – and pull in day-trippers by the score. At the foot of the High Street is the **Guildhall**, sitting pretty on sturdy oak columns, but the town's architectural high point is **Wenlock Priory**.

Wenlock Priory

5 Sheinton St, TF13 6HS • April–Sept daily 10am–6pm; Oct daily 10am–5pm; Nov–Feb Sat & Sun 10am–4pm • £5.20; EH • ☎ 01952 727466, ⓦ www.english-heritage.org.uk/visit/places/wenlock-priory

The Saxons built a monastery at Much Wenlock, but the remains of today's **Wenlock Priory** mostly stem from the thirteenth and fourteenth centuries when its successor, a Cluniac monastery founded here in the 1080s, reached the height of its wealth and power. Set amid immaculate gardens and fringed by woodland, the ruins are particularly picturesque, from the peeling stonework of the old priory church's transepts to the shattered bulk of **St Michael's chapel**.

Wenlock Edge

A magnet for hikers, the beautiful and deeply rural **Wenlock Edge** is a limestone escarpment that runs twenty-odd miles southwest from Much Wenlock. The south side of the escarpment is a gently shelving slope of open farmland, while the thickly wooded north side scarps steeply down to the Shropshire plains. Much of the Edge is owned by the National Trust (@nationaltrust.org.uk/wenlock-edge), which maintains a network of waymarked **trails** that wind through the woodland from a string of car parks along the B4371 – all graded by colour according to length and difficulty.

ARRIVAL AND DEPARTURE   MUCH WENLOCK AND AROUND

By bus Buses to Much Wenlock (@arrivabus.co.uk) stop on Queen St, in the centre of town; there are currently no buses along the length of the B4371 (Wenlock Edge).

Destinations Ironbridge village (Mon–Sat every 2hr; 30min); Shrewsbury (Mon–Sat hourly; 30min).

ACCOMMODATION AND EATING

The Raven 30 Barrow St, TF13 6EN ☎01952 727251, @ravenhotel.com. The best restaurant hereabouts, in a tastefully modernized old coaching inn just off the centre, *The Raven* offers a modern British menu served with flair amd imagination. Mains begin at £18. Daily noon–2.30pm & 6–8.30pm, Sun till 7.45pm.

YHA Wilderhope Manor Longville-in-the-Dale, TF13

6EG, 8 miles southwest of Much Wenlock ☎0345 371 9149, @yha.org.uk/hostel/wilderhope-manor. One of the YHA's most distinctive hostels, *Wilderhope Manor* occupies a remote Elizabethan mansion next to a farm. Facilities include a café, laundry and cycle storage; there are over seventy beds in two- to six-bed rooms. Dorms £22, doubles £54

Shrewsbury

SHREWSBURY, the county town of Shropshire, sits in a tight and narrow loop of the River Severn. It would be difficult to design a better defensive site and predictably the Normans built a stone castle here, one which Edward I decided to strengthen and expand in the thirteenth century, though by then the local economy owed as much to the Welsh wool trade as it did to the town's military importance. In Georgian times, Shrewsbury became a fashionable staging post on the busy London to Holyhead/Ireland route and has since evolved into a laidback, middling market town. It's the overall feel of the place that is its main appeal, rather than any specific sight, though to celebrate its associations with **Charles Darwin**, who was born here, the town is now in possession of a 40ft-high, concertina-like sculpture entitled **Quantum Leap**: it cost nigh-on half a million pounds, so many locals may well be rueing the cost rather than celebrating the artistic vision.

The city centre

The obvious place to start an exploration of Shrewsbury is the 1840s **train station**, built in a fetching neo-Baronial-meets-country-house style. Looming overhead are the ramparts of the **castle**, a pale reminder of the mighty medieval fortress that once dominated the town – the illustrious Thomas Telford turned it into the private home of a local bigwig in the 1780s. **Castle Gates** and its continuation **Castle Street/Pride Hill** cuts up from the station into the heart of the river loop where the medieval town took root. Here, on St Mary's Place, you'll find Shrewsbury's most interesting church, **St Mary's** (no set opening hours), whose architecturally jumbled interior is redeemed by a magnificent east window. From St Mary's, it's only a few steps to **St Alkmund's Church**, with its charming view of the fine old buildings of **Fish Street**, which cuts its way down to the High Street. Near here is **The Square**, which stands at the very heart of town, its narrow confines inhabited by the **Old Market Hall**, a heavy-duty stone structure dating from 1596.

From The Square, High Street snakes down the hill to become **Wyle Cop**, lined with higgledy-piggledy ancient buildings and leading to the **English Bridge**, which sweeps across the Severn in grand Georgian style to the stumpy red-stone mass of the **Abbey Church**, on Abbey Foregate (daily: April–Oct 10am–4pm, Nov–March 10.30am–3pm;

8

free; ⓦshrewsburyabbey.com). This is all that remains of the Benedictine abbey that was a major political and religious force hereabouts until the Dissolution.

ARRIVAL AND INFORMATION SHREWSBURY

By train The station is on the northeast edge of the town centre.
Destinations Birmingham (every 30min; 1hr); Church Stretton (hourly; 15min); Hereford (every 30min; 1hr); Ludlow (hourly; 30min); Telford (every 30min; 20min).
By bus Most buses pull into the Raven Meadows bus station, off Smithfield Rd, on the north side of the centre.

Destinations Ironbridge village (Mon–Sat every 2hr; 40min); Much Wenlock (Mon–Sat hourly; 30min); Telford (Mon–Sat every 2hr; 55min).
Tourist office In The Square (Mon–Sat 10am–4pm; ☏01743 258888, ⓦshropshiretourism.co.uk); shares premises with the Shrewsbury Museum & Art Gallery.

ACCOMMODATION

★**Lion and Pheasant** 50 Wyle Cop, SY1 1XJ ☏01743 770345, ⓦlionandpheasant.co.uk. Excellent, medium-sized, town-centre hotel in the shell of a former coaching inn; rooms are in pastel shades with lots of period details. Delicious breakfasts too. **£120**
Prince Rupert Hotel Butcher Row, off Pride Hill, SY1

1UQ ☏01743 499955, ⓦprinceruperthotel.co.uk. A smart and popular hotel, the *Rupert* occupies a cannily converted old building in the middle of the town centre. There are seventy comfortable guest rooms – including twelve suites – and the pick have a platoon of period details like wood panelling and exposed wooden beams. **£130**

EATING AND DRINKING

Admiral Benbow 24 Swan Hill, SY1 1NF ☏01743 244423. Popular and enterprising town-centre pub with a beer garden and a fine selection of real ales, Hereford farmhouse ciders and perry. Mon–Fri 5–11pm, Sat noon–11pm & Sun 7–10.30pm.
Golden Cross 14 Princess St, SY1 1LP ☏01743 362507, ⓦgoldencrosshotel.co.uk. This must be the best restaurant in Shrewsbury, a cosy, intimate spot (don't be deterred by the mullioned windows) with a select international menu – try,

for example, the pan-roasted, crusted fillet of sea bass. In the city centre, a 2min walk from The Square. Mains average a very reasonable £14. Tues–Sat noon–2.30pm & 5.30–9.30pm, Sun noon–2.30pm.
Good Life Coffee Shop & Restaurant Barracks Passage, SY1 1XA ☏01743 350455. Something of a local institution, this excellent café specializes in salads and vegetarian dishes from a daily menu. Locals swear by the quiches. Mains around £8. Mon–Sat 9am–4pm.

Long Mynd

Beginning about nine miles south of Shrewsbury, the upland heaths of the **Long Mynd**, some eight miles long and between two and four miles wide, run parallel to and just to the west of the A49. This is prime **walking** territory and the heathlands are latticed with footpaths, the pick of which offer sweeping views over the border to the Black Mountains of Wales. Also popular with hikers, and even more remote, are the **Stiperstones**, a clot of boggy heather dotted with ancient cairns and earthworks lying to the west of the Long Mynd.

Church Stretton

Nestled at the foot of the Mynd is **CHURCH STRETTON**, a tidy little village that makes an ideal base for hiking the area. The village also possesses the dinky parish **church of St Laurence**, parts of which – especially the nave and transepts – are Norman. Look out also for the (badly weathered) fertility symbol over the side door, just to the left of the entrance – it's a genital-splaying **sheela-na-gig**, whose sheer explicitness is eye-watering.

ARRIVAL AND INFORMATION CHURCH STRETTON

By train The train station is beside the A49 about 600yd east of High St, which forms the heart of the village.
Destinations Hereford (every 1hr–1hr 30min; 40min); Ludlow (every 1hr–1hr 30min; 15min); Shrewsbury (hourly; 15min).

By bus Most buses pull in beside the train station, but some also continue on to High St. There's also a useful Shropshire Hills Shuttle bus service (see p.451).
Tourist office The library, Church St (Mon–Sat 9.30am–1pm & 2–5pm; ☏01694 723133, ⓦchurchstretton.co.uk).

8

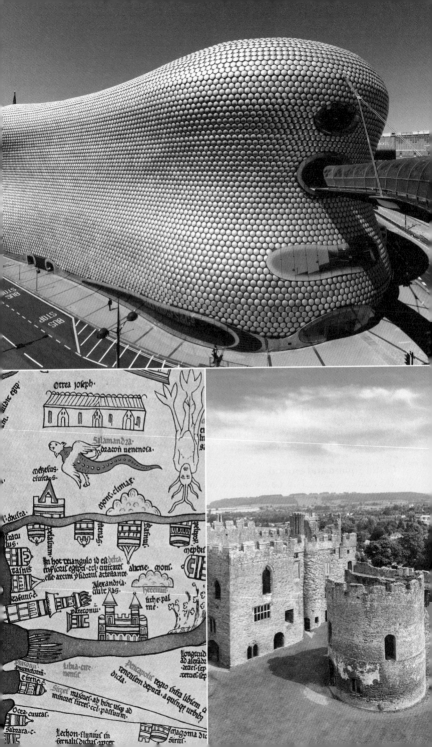

ACCOMMODATION AND EATING

★ **Berry's Coffee House** 17 High St, SY6 6BU ☎ 01694 724452, ⊛ berryscoffeehouse.co.uk. This is the dinkiest of (licensed) cafés, squeezed into antique premises in the centre of the village. They serve delicious snacks and light meals, but their salads (around £9) are especially tasty – locally smoked salmon with *Berry's* dill sauce salad gives the flavour of the menu. Daily 9am–5pm.

★ **Victoria House** 48 High St, SY6 6BX ☎ 01694 723823, ⊛ victoriahouse-shropshire.co.uk. An extraordinarily cosy little place, the most central of several excellent B&Bs. The six guest rooms – all kitted out with heavy curtains, thick carpets and iron beds – are above the owner's teashop, *Jemima's Kitchen*, which serves delicious home-made food including specialist teas and mouth-watering scones. Breakfast, as you would expect, is delicious. Wed–Sun 9.30am–4pm. **£85**

YHA Bridges Ratlinghope, SY5 0SP, 5 miles west of Church Stretton ☎ 01588 650656, ⊛ yha.org.uk /hostel/bridges. On the edge of a tiny village, this hostel occupies a converted village school, has 38 beds in four- to eight-bedded rooms, a café, camping and a self-catering kitchen. It's an ideal base for hiking to the Long Mynd or the Stiperstones. Camping/person **£8**, dorms **£19**

Ludlow

Perched on a hill in a loop of the River Teme, **LUDLOW**, thirty miles from Shrewsbury, is one of the most picturesque towns in the West Midlands – a gaggle of beautifully preserved Georgian and black-and-white half-timbered buildings packed around a craggy stone castle, with rural Shropshire forming a drowsy backdrop. These are strong recommendations in themselves, but Ludlow earns bonus points by being something of a gastronomic hidey-hole with a clutch of outstanding **restaurants**, whose chefs gather at the much-vaunted **Ludlow Food Festival** (⊛ foodfestival.co.uk), held over three days every September. The other notable knees-up is the **Ludlow Fringe Festival** (⊛ ludlowfringe.co.uk), two weeks of music, art and theatre held in late June.

Ludlow Castle

Castle Square, SY8 1AY • Jan to mid-Feb Sat & Sun 10am–4pm; mid-Feb to March & Oct–Dec daily 10am–4pm; April–July & Sept daily 10am–5pm; Aug daily 10am–6pm • £5 • ☎ 01584 873355, ⊛ ludlowcastle.com

Ludlow's large and imposing **castle** dates mostly from Norman times, its rambling ruins incorporating towers and turrets, gatehouses and concentric walls as well as the remains of the 110ft Norman **keep** and an unusual **Round Chapel** built in 1120. With its spectacular setting high above the river, the castle also offers grand views over the surrounding countryside.

Castle Square and around

The castle entrance abuts **Castle Square**, an airy rectangle whose eastern side breaks into several short and narrow lanes, with the one on the left leading through to the gracefully proportioned **Church of St Laurence** (⊛ stlaurences.org.uk), whose interior is distinguished by its stained-glass windows and exquisite misericords in the choir. From the church, it's a few paces to the **Butter Cross**, a Neoclassical extravagance from 1744, and a few more to the **Bull Ring**, home of the **Feathers Hotel**, a fine Jacobean building with the fanciest wooden facade imaginable.

Broad Street

To the south of Castle Square, the gridiron of streets laid out by the Normans has survived intact, though most of the buildings date from the eighteenth century. Steeply sloping **Broad Street** is particularly attractive, flanked by many of Ludlow's five hundred half-timbered Tudor and red-brick Georgian listed buildings. At the foot of Broad Street is Ludlow's only surviving **medieval gate**, which was turned into a house in the eighteenth century.

ARRIVAL AND INFORMATION

LUDLOW

By train Ludlow station is a 15min walk from the castle via Station Drive and Corve St – just follow the signs.

Destinations Church Stretton (hourly; 20min); Hereford (every 30min; 30min); Shrewsbury (hourly; 30min).

By bus Most long-distance buses pull in on Corve St, just north of its junction with Station Drive.

Destinations Church Stretton (Mon–Sat hourly; 30min);

Shrewsbury (Mon–Sat hourly; 1hr 15min).

Tourist office Castle Square (Mon–Sat 10am–4pm; ☎ 01584 875053, ⓦ ludlow.org.uk).

ACCOMMODATION

Dinham Hall Hotel Dinham, SY8 1EJ ☎ 01584 876464, ⓦ dinhamhall.co.uk. Handily located near the castle, this deluxe, medium-sized hotel, with its thirteen appealing rooms, occupies a rambling, bow-windowed eighteenth-century mansion, which has previously seen service as a boarding house for Ludlow School. **£140**

Ludlow Bed & Breakfast 35 Lower Broad St, ☎ 01584 876912, ⓦ sawdays.co.uk. Near the bridge over the River Teme, a 5–10min walk from the castle, this extremely cosy B&B has just two doubles in a pair of Georgian terrace cottages, which have been carefully knocked into one. Great breakfasts. **£75**

EATING

Bistro 7 7 Corve St, SY8 1DB ☎ 01584 877412, ⓦ bistro7 ofludlow.co.uk. One of Ludlow's best restaurants, featuring a lively, varied menu – from tortillas to fish pie – mostly based on local ingredients. Superb, creative vegetarian options, too. Mains average £19. Reservations advised. Tues–Sat noon–3pm & 6–10pm.

The Fish House 51 Bullring, SY1 1AB ☎ 01584 879790, ⓦ thefishhouseludlow.co.uk. First-class fishmonger's with a few tables where they serve sparkling wine and

fresh seafood – anything from a plate of smoked mackerel (£5) through to dressed crabs, oysters and prawns. Wed–Sat 9.30am–4pm.

Mortimers 17 Corve St, SY8 1DA ☎ 01584 872325, ⓦ mortimersludlow.co.uk. Top-ranking restaurant with a strong French influence, where a two-course lunch costs a very reasonable £22. Try, for example, the halibut with white beans and crayfish ragout. Reservations essential. Tues–Sat noon–2pm & 6.30–9pm.

8

Derby

Resurgent **DERBY** may be close to the wilds of the Peak District (see p.460), but it has more in common with its big-city neighbours, Nottingham and Leicester – except that here the industrial base is thriving, with **Rolls-Royce** leading the charge. Furthermore, recent attempts to spruce up the place have proved particularly successful and there's one especially diverting attraction in the centre too, the **Derby Museum and Art Gallery**. From the gallery, it's the briefest of strolls along Derby's most boho street, **Sadlergate**, to both the central **Market Place** and the **cathedral** (daily 8.30am–5.30pm; ⓦ derbycathedral.org), the city's most impressive building, whose sturdy medieval tower rises high above its Victorian surroundings. A couple of hours will do to see the sights before you hightail it to the Peak District.

Derby Museum and Art Gallery

The Strand, DE1 1BS • Tues–Sat 10am–5pm, Sun noon–4pm • Free • ☎ 01332 641901, ⓦ derbymuseums.org/locations/museum-art-gallery

Among much else, **Derby Museum and Art Gallery** exhibits a splendid collection of Derby **porcelain**, several hundred pieces tracking through its different phases and styles from the mid-eighteenth century until today. There's also a room devoted to **Bonnie Prince Charlie**, aka Charles Edward Stuart, whose march from Scotland to London to seize the crown during the Jacobite Rebellion of 1745 ended here – he turned round and headed back north, a dismal retreat that culminated in the battle of Culloden. The museum's star turn, however, is its prime collection of the work of **Joseph Wright** (1734–97), a local artist generally regarded as one of the most talented English painters of his generation. Wright was one of the few artists of his period to find inspiration in technology and his depictions of the scientific world were hugely influential – as in his *The Alchemist Discovering Phosphorus* and *A Philosopher Lecturing on the Orrery*.

ARRIVAL AND INFORMATION

DERBY

By train Derby train station is a mile to the southeast of the city centre – just follow the signs – but it's a dreary

walk, so you might as well take a bus; they leave from outside the station every few minutes.

Destinations Birmingham New Street (every 30min; 40min); Leicester (every 30min; 30min); London St Pancras (every 30min; 1hr 30min); Nottingham (every 30min; 25min).

By bus The bus station is on Morledge on the east side of the city centre. One useful service beginning here is High Peak Buses' (⊛highpeakbuses.com) TransPeak service across the Peak District via Bakewell

and Buxton to Manchester.

Destinations Ashbourne (hourly; 40min); Bakewell (hourly; 1hr 20min); Buxton (hourly; 1hr 50min); Manchester (3 daily; 3hr 30min).

Tourist office Derby tourist information centre is in a part of the Assembly Rooms, on Market Place (Mon–Sat 9.30am–8pm; ☎01332 643411, ⊛visitderby.co.uk).

EATING AND DRINKING

Brunswick Inn 1 Railway Terrace, DE1 2RU ☎01332 290677, ⊛brunswickderby.co.uk. In a handsome Georgian terrace just a couple of minutes' walk from the train station, this traditional pub, with its garden and leather banquettes, offers an impressive range of ciders and real ales, some of which are brewed on the premises. Mon–Sat 11am–11pm, Sun noon–10.30pm.

Exeter Arms 47 Sadler Gate, DE1 3NQ ☎01332 608619,

⊛exeterarms.co.uk. Occupying lovely old premises and complete with a garden terrace, this first-rate gastropub has an excellent range of draft ales and a wide-ranging, top-ranking bar menu – try, for example, the lamb with sumac yoghurt (£7.75). It's on the east side of the city centre, a 5min walk from the Assembly Rooms across the River Derwent. Mon–Fri noon–11.30pm, Sat 11am–midnight & Sun noon–10.30pm; kitchen Mon–Sat noon–9pm, Sun noon–6pm.

The Peak District

In 1951, the hills and dales of the **PEAK DISTRICT**, at the southern tip of the Pennine range, became Britain's **first National Park**. Wedged between Derby, Manchester and Sheffield, it is effectively the back garden for the fifteen million people who live within an hour's drive of its boundaries, though somehow it accommodates the huge influx with minimum fuss.

Landscapes in the Peak District come in two forms. The brooding high moorland tops of **Dark Peak**, to the east of Manchester, take their name from the underlying gritstone, known as millstone grit for its former use – a function commemorated in the millstones demarcating the park boundary. Windswept, mist-shrouded and inhospitable, the flat tops of these peaks are nevertheless a firm favourite with walkers on the **Pennine Way**, which meanders north from the tiny village of **Edale** to the Scottish border. Altogether more forgiving, the southern limestone hills of **White Peak** have been eroded into deep forested dales populated by small stone villages and often threaded by walking **trails**, some of which follow former rail routes. The limestone is riddled with complex cave systems around **Castleton** and on the periphery of **Buxton**, a pleasant former spa town lying just outside the park's boundaries and at the end of an industrialized corridor that reaches out from Manchester. Elsewhere, one of the country's most distinctive manorial piles, **Chatsworth House**, stands near **Bakewell**, a town famed locally not just for its cakes but also for its **well-dressing**, a possibly pagan ritual of thanksgiving for fresh water that takes place in about thirty local villages each summer. The well-dressing season starts in May and continues through to mid-September (get exact dates and details on ⊛welldressing.com).

As for a **base**, Buxton is perhaps your best bet, though if you're after hiking and cycling you'll probably prefer one of the area's villages – Edale or Castleton will do very nicely.

ARRIVAL AND DEPARTURE
THE PEAK DISTRICT

By train Frequent trains run south from Manchester to end-of-the-line Buxton, and Manchester/Sheffield trains stop at Hathersage and Edale.

By bus One especially useful service is High Peak Buses' (⊛highpeakbuses.com) TransPeak service, which runs

from Derby to Manchester (3 daily), with more frequent buses on parts of the route – Derby to Bakewell (hourly) and Buxton (hourly). There's also a reasonably good daily bus service from Sheffield to Castleton and Hathersage. See ⊛traveline.info.

GETTING AROUND

By bus Within the Peak District, you'll find that local bus services are reasonably frequent (less so on Sun & in

winter). Local tourist offices almost always have bus and train timetables, or see ⊛traveline.info.

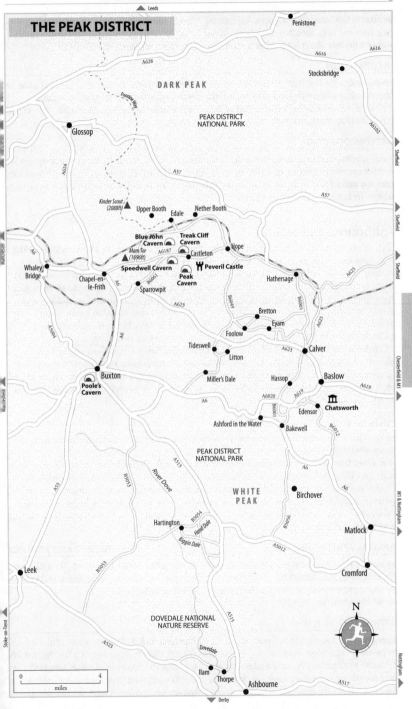

THE PEAK DISTRICT

Leeds

Penistone

A628

A616   A616

DARK PEAK

Stocksbridge

A6102

PEAK DISTRICT
NATIONAL PARK

Pennine Way

Glossop

A57

A57

A624

Kinder Scout
(2088ft)   Upper Booth   Nether Booth

Edale

Blue John   Treak Cliff
Cavern   Cavern

Mam Tor   A6187   Castleton   Hope
(1696ft)

Speedwell Cavern   Peveril Castle

Whaley   Peak
Bridge   Cavern

A6   Chapel-en-   Hathersage
le-Frith   Sparrowpit

A5004   A6   B6061   A623   B6049   Bretton   B6001

Eyam

Foolow

A625

Tideswell   Calver
Litton

A623

Miller's Dale   Hassop   Baslow

A619   A619

Buxton   A6020   Edensor   Chatsworth
Poole's   B6001
Cavern   Ashford in the Water   B6012

Bakewell

PEAK DISTRICT
NATIONAL PARK

A6   A6

A515   WHITE   Birchover
PEAK

River Dove   B5054

Hartington   Hand Dale   B5056   Matlock

Biggin Dale   A5012

A53   B5053   Cromford

Leek

N

DOVEDALE NATIONAL
NATURE RESERVE

A515

Dovedale

0   4   Ilam   Thorpe   A517
miles   Ashbourne

Derby

8

Sheffield

Sheffield

Sheffield

Chesterfield & M1

M1 & Nottingham

Nottingham

Manchester

Manchester

Midlands

Macclesfield

Stoke-on-Trent

By bike The Peak District has a good network of dedicated cycle lanes and trails, sometimes along former railway lines, and the Peak District National Park Authority (see below) operates three cycle rental outlets: at Ashbourne (☎01335 343156); Derwent, Bamford (☎01433 651261); and Parsley Hay, Buxton (☎01298 84493).

INFORMATION

Visitor centres The Peak District National Park Authority (ⓦpeakdistrict.gov.uk) operates four visitor centres, including those at Bakewell and Castleton; these supplement a platoon of town and village tourist information offices.

Maps and guides A variety of maps and trail guides are widely available at most tourist information centres.
Useful websites ⓦvisitpeakdistrict.com; ⓦpeakdistrict.gov.uk.

ACCOMMODATION

There's a plethora of accommodation in and around the Peak District National Park, mostly **B&Bs** and holiday cottages. The Peak District also holds numerous **campsites** and half a dozen or so **YHA hostels** as well as a network of YHA-operated **camping barns**. The latter are located in converted farm buildings and provide simple and inexpensive self-catering facilities. For further details, consult ⓦyha.org.uk.

Ashbourne and around

Sitting pretty on the edge of the Peaks thirteen miles northwest of Derby, **ASHBOURNE** is an amiable little town, whose stubby, cobbled **Market Place** is flanked by a happy ensemble of old red-brick buildings. Hikers tramp in and out of town en route to and from the neighbouring dales, with many wandering the popular **Tissington Trail**, which runs north from near Ashbourne for thirteen miles along the route of an old railway line. Just down the hill from the Market Place, a suspended **wooden beam** spans St John's Street. Once a common feature of English towns, but now a rarity, these **gallows** were not warnings to malcontents, but advertising hoardings.

On the western edge of Ashbourne is **St Oswald's Church** (daily 9am–4pm; free; ⓦderbyshirechurches.org/church/st-oswalds-ashbourne), a striking thirteenth-century lime- and ironstone structure. The interior is an intriguing architectural muddle, graced by handsome stained-glass windows; look out for the five superbly carved table-tombs in the Cockayne Chapel.

Dovedale

Head north from Ashbourne along the A515 and then follow the signs to Dovedale, where the main car park is on a narrow country road just beyond the hamlet of Thorpe

The **River Dove**, which wriggles its way across the Peak District, is at its scenic best four miles north of Ashbourne in the stirring two-mile gorge that comprises **Dovedale** – confusingly, other parts of the river are situated in different dales. The **hike** along the gorge is a real pleasure, and easy to boot, the only problem being the bogginess of the valley after rain, but be warned that the place heaves with visitors on summer weekends and bank holidays.

ARRIVAL AND INFORMATION   ASHBOURNE AND AROUND

By bus The bus station is conveniently located on King Edward St, off Dig St, a 3min walk from Market Place.
Destinations Buxton (every 2hr; 1hr 20min); Derby (hourly; 40min); Hartington (every 2hr; 40min).

Tourist office Market Place (March–Oct daily 10am–5pm; Nov–Feb Mon–Sat 10.30am–4pm; ☎01335 343666, ⓦvisitpeakdistrict.com).

EATING AND DRINKING

Bennetts 19 St John St, DE6 1GP ☎01335 342982. Independent department store in the centre of Ashbourne with a particularly cosy café, where they do a good line in home-made cakes, scones and sandwiches. Mon–Sat 9.30am–3.30pm.

Bramhalls Deli & Café 22 Market Place, DE6 1ES ☎01335 342631, ⓦbramhallsdeli.co.uk. Pop into this first-rate deli to stock up on local cheeses, hams, terrines, etc. There's a small café too – try the local sausages and Derbyshire oatcakes. Mon–Sat 8am–4.30pm, Sun 9am–4.30pm.

Hartington

Best approached from the east, through the boisterous scenery of Hand Dale, **HARTINGTON**, twelve miles north of Ashbourne, is one of the prettiest villages in the Peaks, with an easy ramble of stone houses zeroing in on a tiny duck pond. The village is also within walking distance of the River Dove and a sequence of handsome limestone dales, **Biggin Dale** perhaps the pick. The other excitement is cheese – the village has its own specialist **cheese shop** (⊚hartingtoncheeseshop.co.uk), which offers a raft of local and international cheeses and a selection of chutneys to lighten the gastronomic load.

ARRIVAL AND DEPARTURE   HARTINGTON

By bus Buses stop on Mill Lane in the centre of the village, yards from the duck pond.

Destinations Ashbourne (every 2hr; 40min); Buxton (every 2hr; 40min).

ACCOMMODATION

The Hayloft Church St, SK17 0AW ☎01298 84358, ⊚hartingtonhayloft.co.uk. Perhaps the best of Hartington's B&Bs, in a sympathetically converted barn near the duck pond and part of a working farm. There are just four rooms – each decorated in a straightforward modern style. **£80**

YHA Hartington Hall Hall Bank, SK17 0AT ☎0345 371 9740, ⊚yha.org.uk/hostel/hartington-hall. Well-equipped hostel whose 130-odd beds – in one- to six-bunk dorms – are squeezed into a seventeenth-century manor house, Hartington Hall, about 300yd from the centre of the village. Facilities include a self-catering kitchen, a café and cycle storage. Dorms **£15**, doubles **£40**

Cromford Mills

Mill Lane, Cromford, DE4 3RQ • **Complex** Daily 9am–5pm • Free • **Arkwright Mill & visitor centre** Daily 10.30am–4pm • £5 • ☎ 01629 823256, ⊚ cromfordmills.org.uk • 15min walk from Cromford train station

Dating from the early 1770s, **Cromford Mills**, in a slender ravine just off the A6, 18 miles north of Derby, lays claim to hold the first successful water-powered cotton-spinning mill in the world – hence its UNESCO designation. The original mill, built at the instigation of formidable industrialist Sir Richard Arkwright (1732–92), has recently been returned to something like its original appearance and is flanked by several other stone buildings, mostly mills too. Arkwright ran his mill day and night in two twelve-hour shifts, employing mostly women and children – an early example of the industrialistion that was about to sweep the country. The mills closed in the nineteenth century and the complex was long neglected, but the process of restoration is now well under way. Today the original **Arkwright Mill** and attached **visitor centre** include an excellent museum and a peek into the dark and dank mill interior.

Buxton

BUXTON, twelve miles north of Hartington, has had more than its fair share of ups and downs, but with its centre revamped and reconfigured, it is without doubt the most agreeable town in the Peak District and its several excellent B&Bs make it a perfect base for further explorations. Buxton has a long history as a **spa**, beginning with the Romans, who happened upon a spring from which 1500 gallons of pure water gushed every hour at a constant 28°C. Impressed by the recuperative qualities of the water, the Romans came here by the chariot-load, setting a trend that was to last hundreds of years. The spa's heyday came at the end of the eighteenth century with the **fifth Duke of Devonshire**'s grand design to create a northern answer to Bath or Cheltenham, a plan ultimately thwarted by the climate, but not before some distinguished buildings had been erected. Victorian Buxton may not have had quite the élan of its more southerly rivals but it still flourished, creating the rows of handsome stone houses that inhabit the town centre today. The town's **thermal baths** were closed for lack of custom in 1972, but Buxton has hung on, not least because of its splendid **festival** (see box, p.465).

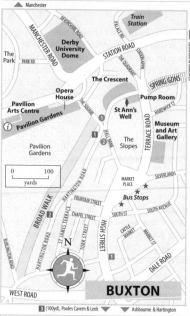

The Crescent and around

The centrepiece of Buxton's hilly, compact centre is **The Crescent**, a broad sweep of Georgian stonework commissioned by the fifth Duke of Devonshire in 1780 and modelled on the Royal Crescent in Bath. It was cleaned and scrubbed a few years ago, but has lain idle ever since and plans to turn it into a five-star hotel with thermal baths have been beset by difficulties; at the time of writing these are yet to be resolved. Facing The Crescent, and also currently empty, is the old **Pump Room**, an attractive Victorian building where visitors once sampled the local waters; next to it is a **water fountain**, supplied by St Ann's Well and still used to fill many a local water bottle. For a better view of The Crescent and the town centre, clamber up **The Slopes**, a narrow slice of park that rises behind the Pump Room, that is dotted with decorative urns. From here, it's impossible to miss the enormous **dome** of what was originally the Duke of Devonshire's stables and riding school, erected in 1789 and now part of Derby University.

Pavilion Gardens and around

Next to The Crescent, the appealing old stone buildings of **The Square** – though square it isn't – nudge up to the grandly refurbished **Buxton Opera House**, an Edwardian extravagance whose twin towers date from 1903. Stretching back from the Opera House are the **Pavilion Gardens** (Feb–Dec daily 10/10.30am–4/5pm; free), a slender string of connected buildings distinguished by their wrought-iron work and culminating in a large and glassy dome, the **Octagon**, and the **Pavilion Arts Centre**. The adjoining **park** (daily dawn–dusk; free), also known as the Pavilion Gardens and cut across by the River Wye, is especially pleasant, its immaculate lawns and neat borders graced by a bandstand, ponds, dinky little footbridges and fountains.

Buxton Museum and Art Gallery

Terrace Rd, SK17 6DA • Tues–Fri 9.30am–5.30pm, Sat 9.30am–5pm, plus April–Aug Sun 10.30am–5pm • Free • ☎ 01629 533540, ⓦ derbyshire.gov.uk/leisure/buxton_museum

Recently refurbished, the enjoyable **Buxton Museum and Art Gallery** delves into all things local, including a period room dedicated to two Victorian archeologist-cum-geologists – William Boyd Dawkins and Wilfred Jackson – who spent decades exploring the Peaks. The museum's most diverting section deals with the **petrifactioners**, who turned local semi-precious stones into ornaments and jewellery.

Poole's Cavern

Green Lane, SK17 9DH • Daily: March–Oct 9.30am–5pm; Nov–Feb 10am–4pm • Tours March–Oct daily every 20min; Nov–Feb Mon–Fri 3 daily, Sat & Sun every 20min; 50min • £9.75 • ☎ 01298 26978, ⓦ poolescavern.co.uk • Half a mile southwest of central Buxton: take the A53 towards Macclesfield/Leek and watch for the sign

The Peaks are riddled with cave systems and half a dozen have become popular tourist attractions rigged up with underground lighting. One of the better examples is

BUXTON FESTIVAL

Buxton boasts the outstanding **Buxton Festival** (box office ☎01298 72190, ⓦbuxtonfestival
.co.uk), which runs for two and a half weeks in July and features a full programme of classical
music, opera and literary readings. This has spawned the first-rate **Buxton Festival Fringe**
(☎01298 73461, ⓦbuxtonfringe.org.uk), also in July, which focuses on contemporary music,
theatre and film.

Poole's Cavern, whose network of caves culminates in a vast chamber dripping with
stalactites and stalagmites. Visitors have been popping in for centuries – apparently,
Mary, Queen of Scots, dropped by and was suitably impressed.

ARRIVAL AND INFORMATION   BUXTON

By train Buxton train station is on Station Rd, a 4min walk
from the town centre, with regular services to Manchester
Piccadilly (hourly; 1hr).

By bus Buses stop on Market Place, a 4min walk from the
Opera House.

Destinations Ashbourne (every 2hr; 1hr 20min); Bakewell

(hourly; 30min); Castleton (1 daily; 50min); Derby (hourly;
1hr 40min); Hartington (every 2hr; 40min).

Tourist office Pavilion Gardens, behind the Opera House
(daily: Feb & March 11am–4pm; April–June & Sept 10.30am–
5pm; July & Aug 10am–5pm; Oct & Nov 10.30am–4pm;
☎01298 25106, ⓦvisitbuxton.co.uk).

ACCOMMODATION

Buxton's centre is liberally sprinkled with **B&Bs** and finding somewhere to stay is rarely a problem, except during the
Buxton Festival (see box above), when advance reservations are essential.

8

Griff House 2 Compton Rd, SK17 9DN ☎01298 23628,
ⓦgriffhousebuxton.co.uk; map p.464. Cosy B&B in a
sympathetically updated Victorian house with a handful of
well-appointed, en-suite rooms. Local produce is served up
at breakfast. A 5min walk south of the centre. **£85**

★**Grosvenor House** 1 Broad Walk, SK17 6JE ☎01298
72439, ⓦgrosvenorbuxton.co.uk; map p.464. There are
eight unfussy, en-suite guest rooms in this attractive B&B,
which is located in a handsome Victorian townhouse.

The best rooms offer gentle views over the gardens.
Delicious home-made breakfasts, too. **£75**

Roseleigh 19 Broad Walk, SK17 6JR ☎01298 24904,
ⓦroseleighhotel.co.uk; map p.464. This classic, three-
storey gritstone Victorian townhouse, overlooking Pavilion
Gardens, is an excellent place to stay. The trim public rooms
are decorated in attractive Victorian style, and the en-suite
bedrooms are well appointed. Family-run and competitively
priced. **£75**

EATING

Columbine 7 Hall Bank, SK17 6EW ☎01298 78752,
ⓦcolumbinerestaurant.co.uk; map p.464. The menu at
this small and intimate restaurant, right in the centre of
Buxton, is short but imaginative; main courses, such as
saddle of monkfish with crab risotto, average £17. Pre-
theatre dinners, from about 5pm, can be reserved in
advance. May–Oct Mon–Sat 7–10pm; Nov–April Mon
& Wed–Sat 7–10pm.

Old Hall Hotel The Square, SK17 6BD ☎01298 22841,
ⓦoldhallhotelbuxton.co.uk; map p.464. A few steps
from the Opera House, in a building that dates way back,
the *Old Hall* offers good-quality, if sometimes inconsistent,
food in both its (fairly formal) restaurant and in the bar.
The menu is Modern British. Mains average £16. Pre-
theatre dinners, from about 5pm, can be reserved in
advance. Kitchen daily noon–2pm & 7–10pm.

DRINKING

Old Sun Inn 33 High St, SK17 6HA ☎01298 72375; map
p.464. This fine old pub, with its maze of antique beamed
rooms, is just south of Market Place. It's a good spot for a

fine range of real ales and above-average bar food. Daily
noon–11pm.

Castleton and around

A hikers' heaven, pocket-sized **CASTLETON**, a scenic ten miles northeast of Buxton via
Sparrowpit and the dramatic **Winnats Pass**, lies on the northern edge of White Peak,
its huddle of old stone cottages ringed by hills and set beside a babbling brook, all

beneath a ruined **castle**. It's a distinctly unpretentious place – and none the worse for that – and the hikers are joined by platoons of cyclists and cavers, all of whom gather together to prepare for the off on **Market Place**, yards from the main drag. The limestone hills pressing in on Castleton are riddled with water-worn **cave systems**, four of which have been developed as tourist attractions complete with subterranean lighting. Peak Cavern (⊚peakcavern.co.uk) and Speedwell Cavern (⊚speedwellcavern .co.uk) are within easy walking distance of Castleton Market Place, but the more interesting are slightly further afield, these being the **Blue John Cavern** and, the pick of the bunch, **Treak Cliff Cavern**.

Peveril Castle

Off Market Place, S33 8WQ • April–Oct daily 10am–5pm; Nov–March Sat & Sun 10am–4pm • £5.60; EH • ☎ 01433 620613, ⊚www .english-heritage.org.uk/visit/places/peveril-castle

Overseeing Castleton is **Peveril Castle**, from which the village takes its name. William the Conqueror's illegitimate son William Peveril raised the first fortifications here to protect the king's rights to the forest that then covered the district, but most of the remains – principally the ruinous square keep – date to the 1170s. After a stiff climb up to the keep, you can enjoy commanding views over the Hope Valley.

Treak Cliff Cavern

Buxton Rd, S22 8WP • Guided tours daily 10am–5pm; 40min • £9.75 • ☎ 01433 620571, ⊚ bluejohnstone.com • Take the signed minor road off the A6187 just west of Castleton; it's about 1 mile in total

Treak Cliff Cavern is a major source of a rare sparkling fluorspar known as **Blue John**. Highly prized for ornaments and jewellery since Georgian times, this semi-precious stone comes in a multitude of hues from blue through deep red to yellow, depending on its hydrocarbon impurities. The Treak Cliff contains the best examples of the stone *in situ* and is also the best cave to visit in its own right, dripping – literally – with ancient stalactites, flowstone and bizarre rock formations, all visible on an entertaining walking **tour** through the main cave system.

Blue John Cavern

Mam Tor, S33 8WA • Guided tours daily: April–Sept 9.30am–5pm; Oct–March 9.30am–dusk; 45min–1hr • £12 • ☎ 01433 620638, ⊚ bluejohn-cavern.co.uk • Take the signed minor road off the A6187 west of Castleton; it's about 2 miles in total

Tours of the **Blue John Cavern** dive deep into the rock, with narrow steps and sloping paths following an ancient watercourse. The **tour** leads through whirlpool-hollowed chambers to Lord Mulgrave's Dining Room, a cavern where the eponymous lord and owner once put on a banquet for his miners (heaven knows what they made of his "generosity"). A goodly sample of Blue John is on sale at the cavern gift shop.

ARRIVAL AND INFORMATION

CASTLETON AND AROUND

By train There are no trains to Castleton – the nearest you'll get is Hope, a couple of miles or so east along the valley on the Manchester–Sheffield line. Regular buses run from very close to Hope train station to Castleton (every 1–2hr; 10min); walk down Station Rd to the bus stop on the main road.
Destinations (from Hope) Edale (hourly; 7min); Hathersage (hourly; 7min); Manchester Piccadilly (hourly; 1hr); Sheffield (hourly; 30min).

By bus Castleton's main bus stop is on the main street, How Lane (the A6187).

Destinations Bakewell (3 daily; 2hr); Buxton (1 daily; 50min); Hope (every 1–2hr; 10min).

Tourist office A combined tourist office and Peak District exhibition centre is on the west side of the village, just off the main street (daily: April–Oct 10am–5pm; Nov–March 10.30am–4.30pm; ☎ 01629 816572, ⊚ peakdistrict.gov.uk).

Maps The tourist office sells hiking leaflets and maps, which are invaluable for a string of walking routes that take you up to the bulging hilltops and along the dales that surround Castleton.

ACCOMMODATION AND EATING

Castleton heaves with visitors throughout the summer, but especially on bank holidays and at the weekend, when accommodation should be booked in advance.

THE PENNINE WAY

When it was opened in 1965, the 268-mile-long **Pennine Way** (ⓦnationaltrail.co.uk) was the country's first official long-distance footpath. A dramatic route by any standard, the trail stretches north from the boggy plateau of the Peak District's Kinder Scout (see below) to the Yorkshire Dales and then crosses Hadrian's Wall and the Northumberland National Park, before entering Scotland to fizzle out at the village of **Kirk Yetholm**. One of the most popular walks in the country, either taken in sections or completed in two to three weeks, the wild countryside of the Pennine Way is a challenge in the best of weather and you must certainly arrive properly equipped. Information centres along the route – like the one at Edale village (see below) – stock a selection of guides, maps and associated trail leaflets and can offer advice. Some hikers, however, stick to Wainwright's *Pennine Way Companion*, first published in 1968 and re-edited in 2012.

1530 The Restaurant Cruck Barn, Cross St, S33 8WH ☎01433 621870, ⓦ1530therestaurant.co.uk. Located in an old stone building near the centre of the village, this bright and breezy restaurant specializes in Italian cuisine – from pizzas and pastas through to more ambitious dishes, like the sea bass with artichokes and sun-dried tomatoes. Mains average £12. Mon & Wed–Fri 5.30–11pm, Sat & Sun 1–11pm.

Causeway House Back St, S33 8WE ☎01433 623291, ⓦcausewayhouse.co.uk. The cream of the crop, this B&B occupies an old and well-tended stone cottage just north of Market Place. There are five guest rooms, three en suite, all tastefully kitted out to make the most of the cottage's original features. **£75**

Ramblers' Rest Back St, S33 8WR ☎01433 620125, ⓦramblersrest-castleton.co.uk. Four spick and span, modern, en-suite guest rooms shoehorned into an old stone building just to the north of Market Place. Parking and a small garden for guests, too. **£80**

YHA Castleton Losehill Hall Castleton Rd, S33 8WB, signed off the A6187 just to the east of Castleton ☎0345 371 9628, ⓦyha.org.uk/hostel/castleton-losehill-hall. The YHA has spent a bucket refurbishing this Victorian Neo-Gothic mansion set in its own grounds to the north of the village. It's a well-equipped hostel with a self-catering kitchen, café, laundry, cycle storage and drying room, and its many beds are parcelled up into two- to six-bedded rooms, most of which are en suite. Dorms **£18**, doubles **£30**

Edale village

There's almost nothing to **EDALE VILLAGE**, about five miles from Castleton, except for a slender, half-mile trail of stone houses, which march up the main street from the train station, with a couple of pubs, an old stone church and a scattering of B&Bs on the way – and it's this somnambulant air that is its immediate appeal. The village is also extremely popular with walkers, who arrive in droves throughout the year to set off on the **Pennine Way** (see box above) – the route's traditional starting point is the *Old Nag's Head* at the top of the village. If that sounds too daunting, note that there are lots of more manageable alternatives, including an excellent **circular walk** (9 miles; 5hr) that takes in the first part of the Pennine Way, leading up onto the bleak, gritstone tabletop of **Kinder Scout** (2088ft), below which Edale cowers.

ARRIVAL AND INFORMATION   EDALE VILLAGE

By train Located at the southern end of the village, Edale train station is on the Sheffield–Manchester line.
Destinations Hope, for Castleton (hourly; 7min); Hathersage (hourly; 15min); Manchester Piccadilly (hourly; 45min); Sheffield (hourly; 35min).

Tourist information From Edale train station, it's 400yd

or so up the road to the Moorland Centre (Jan & Feb daily 9.30am–3.30pm; March & Oct Mon–Fri 10am–3.30pm, Sat & Sun 9.30am–4.30pm; April–Sept daily 9.30am–5pm; Nov Sat & Sun 9.30am–4.30pm; closed Dec; ☎01433 670207, ⓦpeakdistrict.gov.uk), who sell all manner of trail leaflets and hiking guides and can advise on local accommodation.

ACCOMMODATION AND EATING

Cheshire Cheese Inn Edale Rd, Hope, S33 6ZF ☎01433 620381, ⓦthecheshirecheeseinn.co.uk. Two attractively renovated old stone cottages with a cosy/folksy bar downstairs and four pleasant en-suite guest rooms up above.

They serve the best food hereabouts – good-quality, very English dishes featuring local, seasonal ingredients with mains at about £12. Just north of Hope on the road to Edale. Tues–Fri noon–3pm & 6–11pm, Sat noon–11.30pm,

8

Sun noon–10pm; kitchen Tues–Fri noon–2pm & 6–9pm, Sat noon–9pm, Sun noon–7.30pm. £85

Stonecroft S33 7ZA ☎01433 670262, ⓦstonecroft guesthouse.co.uk. Arguably the pick of the several B&Bs in Edale village, this detached Edwardian house offers two, en-suite doubles and one single guest room, each of which is decorated in an unfussy traditional style. On the main street, just short of the *Old Nag's Head*. Caters well for dietary restrictions. £100

Upper Booth Camping West of Edale village on the way to Kinder Scout, S33 7ZJ ☎01433 670250, ⓦupper boothcamping.co.uk. This campsite and camping barn is a popular spot for walkers on the Pennine Way. Car parking £5 extra. Camping/person £8, camping barn/person £10

YHA Edale Rowland Cote, Nether Booth, S33 7ZH, 2 miles east of Edale ☎0345 371 9514, ⓦyha.org.uk /hostel/edale. This large hostel has a good range of facilities, including a laundry, café and a self-catering kitchen, and also offers an extensive range of outdoor activities. These must be booked in advance – as must accommodation, which is parcelled up into two- to six-bedded rooms. The hostel is signed from the road into Edale, or you can hike across the fields from the nearby Moorland Centre (see p.467). Dorms £18, doubles £60

Hathersage

Hilly **HATHERSAGE**, six miles east of Castleton, has a hard time persuading people not to shoot straight past on their way to the heart of the Peaks. This pretty little town is, however, worth at least an hour of anyone's time, the prime target being the much-restored **Church of St Michael and All Angels**, a good-looking stone structure perched up on the hill on its eastern edge. The views out over the surrounding countryside are delightful and, enclosed within a miniature iron fence in the churchyard, is the **grave** – or at least what legend asserts to be the grave – of Robin Hood's old sparring partner, **Little John**.

In the 1800s, Hathersage became a **needle-making centre** with a string of factories billowing out dust and dirt. The metalworking tradition was revived by Sheffield designer **David Mellor** (1930–2009), whose cutlery factory – now run by his son – occupies the distinctive **Round Building**, a gritstone edifice with a sweeping lead roof half a mile south of town. There's a **Design Museum** (Mon–Sat 10am–5pm, Sun 11am–5pm; ☎01433 650220, ⓦdavidmellordesign.com) here too, as well as a café and shop.

ARRIVAL AND DEPARTURE
HATHERSAGE

By train The station, on the Manchester–Sheffield line, is about 500yd south of the Main Rd (A6187). Destinations Edale (hourly; 15min); Manchester Piccadilly (hourly; 1hr); Sheffield (hourly; 20min).

By bus Buses pull into the centre of the village at the A6187/B6001 junction – yards from the *George Hotel*. Destinations Bakewell (3 daily; 45min); Castleton (hourly; 30min); Eyam (Mon–Sat every 2hr; 30min).

ACCOMMODATION AND EATING

George Hotel Main Rd, S32 1BB ☎01433 650436, ⓦgeorge-hotel.net. In an immaculately maintained former coaching inn, this very good hotel has twenty or so comfortable rooms decorated in a modern rendition of country-house style. The excellent restaurant features British cuisine with a twist – try, for example, the spring-onion-stuffed rabbit saddle. Two-course set meal £33. Mon–Thurs & Sun noon–2.30pm &

6.30–9pm, Fri & Sat noon–2.30pm & 7–10pm. £120

YHA Hathersage Castleton Rd, S32 1EH ☎0345 371 9021, ⓦyha.org.uk/hostel/hathersage. In a substantial Victorian house and annexe on the main road just to the west of the *George*, this frugal hostel has its beds divided up into two- to six-bunk rooms. There is a café, a lounge and a self-catering kitchen. Dorms £15, doubles £50

Eyam

Within a year of September 7, 1665, the lonely lead-mining settlement of **EYAM** (pronounced "Eem"), six miles south of Hathersage, had lost almost half of its population of 750 to the bubonic plague, a calamity that earned it the enduring epithet "**The Plague Village**". The first victim was one George Viccars, a journeyman tailor who is said to have released some infected fleas into his lodgings from a package of cloth he had brought here from London. Acutely conscious of the danger to neighbouring villages, **William Mompesson**, the village rector, speedily organized a self-imposed quarantine, arranging for food to be left at places on the parish boundary. Payment was made with coins left in pools

RING A RING O' ROSES: EYAM AND THE PLAGUE

As the people of Eyam began to drop like flies from the **plague** in the autumn of 1665, they resorted to **folkloric remedies** to stave off the threat. Some, thinking it to be a miasma, kept coal braziers alight day and night in the hope that the smoke would push the infection back into the sky from where it was thought to have come. Others tried herb infusions and draughts of brine or lemon juice; yet more applied poultices and used leeches. When all else failed, **charms and spells** were wheeled out – the plucked tail of a pigeon laid against the sore supposedly drew out the poison. All, of course, had no effect and the death toll mounted. The horrors of a plague-ridden England were recorded in the *Ring o' roses* nursery rhyme that remains in use today, culminating in the gloomy "We all fall down".

of disinfecting vinegar in holes chiselled into the old boundary stones – and these can still be seen at **Mompesson's Well**, half a mile up the hill to the north of the village along Edge Road.

Church of St Lawrence and around

Church St, S32 5QH • Easter–Sept Mon–Sat 9am–6pm, Sun 1–5.30pm; Oct–Easter Mon–Sat 9am–4pm, Sun 1–5.30pm • Free • 📞 01433 630930, 🌐 eyam-church.org

In the **graveyard** of the **Church of St Lawrence** – of medieval foundation but revamped in the nineteenth century – stands a conspicuous, eighth-century carved Celtic cross, and close by is the distinctive table-tomb of Mompesson's wife, Catherine, whose sterling work nursing sick villagers caused her early death. Rather more cheerful is the grave of one **Harry Bagshaw** (d. 1927), a local cricketer whose tombstone shows a ball breaking his wicket with the umpire's finger raised above, presumably – on this occasion – to heaven.

The old **Plague Cottages**, where Viccars and his neighbours met their untimely end, are just along the street from the church – and each carries a memorial plaque.

8

Eyam Hall

Main St, S32 5QW • Mid-Feb to Oct Wed–Sun 10.30am–4.30pm; early Nov Sat & Sun 10.30am–3.30pm; mid-Nov to mid-Dec Wed–Sun 10.30am–3.30pm • £8.09 • 📞 01433 639565, 🌐 nationaltrust.org.uk/eyam-hall-and-craft-centre

Dating from the late seventeenth century, **Eyam Hall** is a fine example of a Jacobean manor house, its sombre gritstone exterior a perfect match for its Peakland surroundings. Eleven generations of the same family – the Wrights – lived here and the house reflects their changing tastes.

Eyam Museum

Hawkhill Rd • April–Oct Tues–Sun 10am–4pm • £2.50 • 📞 01433 631371, 🌐 eyam-museum.org.uk

Just up the hill on the north side of the village, the old Methodist chapel has been turned into the **Eyam Museum**, whose several displays examine the course of the plague as it ripped through the village. There's also an enjoyable section on the bubonic plague as a whole – its transmission, symptoms and social aftermath. Interestingly, the shortage of labour after the plague panicked many members of the landed gentry, who turned to the law to create new rules and regulations – anything but improve the conditions of their agricultural labourers.

ARRIVAL AND DEPARTURE   EYAM

By bus Buses stop on The Square, beside the green at the east end of the village, with most then proceeding west along the lengthy main street, Church St/Main Rd.

Destinations Baslow (every 2hr; 10min); Hathersage (Mon–Sat every 2hr; 30min); Sheffield (Mon–Sat every 2hr; 1hr).

ACCOMMODATION AND EATING

Village Green Café The Square, S32 5RB • 📞 01433 631293, 🌐 cafevillagegreen.com. The pick of the two cafés on The Square, a cosy, family-run place with pavement terrace. Home-made soups and sandwiches lead the

gastronomic way. Mon & Thurs–Sun 9.15am–4pm.
YHA Eyam Hawkhill Rd, S32 5QP • 📞 0345 371 9738, 🌐 yha.org.uk/hostel/eyam. This well-equipped hostel occupies an idiosyncratic Victorian house, whose ersatz

medieval towers and turrets overlook Eyam from amid wooded grounds on Hawkhill Rd, a good, half-mile ramble up from Eyam Museum (see p.469). The hostel has a café, self-catering facilities, cycle storage and a lounge, with sixty-odd beds in two- to six-bed rooms; advance reservations are recommended. Dorms £18, doubles £40

Baslow

Well-heeled **BASLOW**, spreading out from the busy A623/A619 junction just four miles southeast of Eyam, is an unassuming little village, whose oldest stone cottages string prettily along the River Derwent. The only building of any real note is **St Anne's Church**, (@stannesbaslow.org.uk) a medieval structure whose chunky stone spire pokes up above the Victorian castellations of its nave, but Baslow is very handy for Chatsworth (see opposite) and it also has one of the Peaks' best hotels, *Fischer's Baslow Hall* (see below).

ARRIVAL AND DEPARTURE
BASLOW

By bus The main bus stop is beside St Anne's Church, near the A623/A619 junction.

Destinations Bakewell (hourly; 20min); Buxton (every 2hr; 1hr); Eyam (every 2hr; 15min); Sheffield (hourly; 45min).

ACCOMMODATION AND EATING

★ **Fischer's Baslow Hall** Calver Rd (A623), DE45 1RR ☎01246 583259, @fischers-baslowhall.co.uk. In its own immaculate grounds, *Fischer's* is picture-postcard perfect, a handsome Edwardian building made of local stone with matching gables and a dinky canopy over the front door. The interior is suitably lavish and the service attentive, while rooms occupy both the main building and the Garden House annexe next door. The restaurant is superb too, and has won several awards for its imaginative cuisine – Modern British at its best – with a three-course set meal, for example, costing £78. Daily noon–2pm & 7–10pm. £230

Bakewell and around

Amenable **BAKEWELL**, flanking the banks of the River Wye about thirty miles north of Derby, is famous for both its **Bakewell Pudding** and its **Bakewell Tart**. The former is much more distinctive (and less commonplace), being a sweet and slippery almond-flavoured confection – now with a dab of jam – invented here around 1860 when a cook botched a recipe for strawberry tart. Almost a century before this fortuitous mishap, the Duke of Rutland set out to turn what was then a remote village into a prestigious spa, thereby trumping the work of his rival, the Duke of Devonshire, in Buxton. The frigidity of the water made failure inevitable, leaving only the prettiness of **Bath Gardens** at the heart of the town centre as a reminder of the venture. Bakewell is within easy striking distance of the big tourist attraction hereabouts, **Chatsworth House** (see opposite).

Ashford in the Water

Minuscule **ASHFORD IN THE WATER**, just over a mile to the west of Bakewell along the River Wye, is one of the prettiest and wealthiest villages in the Peaks, its old stone cottages nuzzling up to a quaint medieval church. It was not always so. Ashford was once a poor lead-mining settlement with sidelines in milling and agriculture, hence the

HIKING AROUND BAKEWELL

Bakewell is a popular starting point for short hikes out into the easy landscapes that make up the town's surroundings, with one of the most relaxing excursions being a four-mile loop along the banks of the **River Wye** to the south of the centre. Chatsworth (see opposite) is also within easy hiking distance – about seven miles there and back – or you could venture out onto one of the best-known hikes in the National Park – the **Monsal Trail**, which cuts eight miles north through some of Derbyshire's finest limestone dales using part of the old Midland Railway line. The trail begins at Coombs viaduct, one mile southeast of Bakewell, and ends at Topley Pike Junction, three miles east of Buxton.

name of the (impossibly picturesque) **Sheepwash Bridge**. There was, however, a bit of a boom when locals took to polishing the dark limestone found on the edge of the village (and nowhere else), turning it into so-called **Ashford black marble** – much to the delight of Buxton's petrifactioners (see p.464).

ARRIVAL AND INFORMATION BAKEWELL AND AROUND

By bus Buses to Bakewell stop on – or very close to – central Rutland Square; there are no trains.

Destinations Baslow (hourly; 20min); Buxton (hourly; 30min); Castleton (3 daily; 2hr); Derby (hourly; 1hr 20min);

Hathersage (3 daily; 45min); Sheffield (hourly; 1hr).

Tourist office Handy location in the Old Market Hall, Bridge St (April–Oct daily 9.30am–5pm; Nov–March daily 10.30am–4.30pm; ☎ 01629 816558, ⊛ peakdistrict.gov.uk).

ACCOMMODATION AND EATING

★**Hassop Hall** Hassop, DE45 1NS, 3 miles north of Bakewell on the B6001 ☎ 01629 640488, ⊛ hassophall .co.uk. Hidden away in the heart of the Peaks, the solitary hamlet of Hassop is home to the wonderful *Hassop Hall*, a handsome stone manor house with just 13 guest rooms. The interior has kept faith with the Georgian architecture – modernization has been kept to a subtle minimum – and the views out over the surrounding parkland are delightful. The hotel restaurant is also first-class, with a two-course set meal costing £32. Daily noon–1.30pm & 7–8.30pm. **£110**

Old Original Bakewell Pudding Shop The Square, DE45 1BT ☎ 01629 812193, ⊛ www.bakewellpudding

shop.co.uk. Bakeries all over town claim to make Bakewell Pudding to the original recipe, but the most authentic are served up here. They sell the pudding in several sizes. Mon–Sat 8.30am–6pm, Sun 9am–5pm.

Riverside House Hotel Fennel St, Ashford in the Water, DE45 1QF ☎ 01629 814275, ⊛ riversidehouse hotel.co.uk. The plush and lush *Riverside House* occupies a handsome Georgian building by the banks of the Wye. There are a dozen or so extremely well-appointed rooms here, each decorated in a full-blown country-house style, and the hotel takes justifiable pride in both its gardens and its restaurant. Daily noon–1.30pm & 7–9pm. **£150**

8

Chatsworth House

Bakewell, DE45 1PN • Daily: late March to late May & Sept–Dec 11am–5pm; late May to Aug 10.30am–5pm; gardens open until slightly later • £19.90; gardens only £12.90 • ☎ 01246 565300, ⊛ chatsworth.org

Fantastically popular, and one of the finest stately homes in Britain, **Chatsworth House** was built in the seventeenth century by the first Duke of Devonshire. It has been owned by the family ever since and though several of them have done a fair bit of tinkering – the sixth duke, for instance, added the north wing in the 1820s – it's still remarkably harmonious. The property is best seen from the B6012, which meanders across the estate to the west of the house, giving a full view of its vast Palladian frontage, whose clean lines are perfectly balanced by the undulating partly wooded parkland rolling in from the south and west.

Many visitors forgo the **house** altogether, concentrating on the grounds – an understandable decision given the predictability of the assorted baubles accumulated by the family over the centuries. Nonetheless, among the maze of grandiose rooms and staircases there are several noteworthy highlights, including the ornate ceilings of the **State Apartments** and, in the State Bedroom, the four-poster bed in which George II breathed his last. And then there are the **paintings**. Among many, Frans Hals, Tintoretto, Veronese, Reynolds, Van Dyck and Lucian Freud all have a showing, and there's even a Rembrandt.

Back outside, the **gardens** are a real treat and owe much to the combined efforts of Capability Brown, who designed them in the 1750s, and Joseph Paxton (designer of London's Crystal Palace), who had a bash seventy years later. Among all sorts of fripperies, there are water fountains, modern sculptures, a rock garden, an artificial waterfall, a grotto and a folly as well as a nursery and greenhouses. Afterwards, you can wend your way to the **café** in the handsomely converted former stables.

ARRIVAL AND DEPARTURE CHATSWORTH HOUSE

On foot The best way to approach is on one of the paths which network the estate; Bakewell (4 miles; see opposite) and Baslow (2 miles; see opposite) make good starting points.

By bus Buses from several neighbouring towns, including Sheffield, Derby and Buxton, pull into the bus stop a 2min walk from Chatsworth House.

The East Midlands

VIEW DOWN BARN HILL, STAMFORD

9

The East Midlands

Many tourists bypass the East Midlands' four major counties – Nottinghamshire, Leicestershire, Northamptonshire and Lincolnshire – on their way to more obvious destinations, an understandable mistake given that the region seems, at first sight, to be short of star attractions. Nevertheless, though the county towns of Nottingham, Leicester and Northampton are at heart industrial – sometimes post-industrial – cities, they each have enough sights and character to give them appeal, while Lincoln, with its superb cathedral, is in parts a fine old city. What's more, the countryside hereabouts is sprinkled with historic market towns, pretty villages and prestigious country homes.

Of the county towns, **Nottingham** has perhaps the most to offer, not least an enjoyable castle and a cutting-edge art gallery, while the rest of **Nottinghamshire** holds Byron's Newstead Abbey, the pleasing Harley Gallery and, even better, Elizabethan **Hardwick Hall** (just over the border in Derbyshire, but covered in this chapter). Nottinghamshire is also home to **Southwell**, with its splendid minster, and the market town of **Newark**, which played a prominent role in the Civil War. To the south, **Leicester** boasts an excellent art gallery and its county – **Leicestershire** – offers Market Bosworth, an amiable country town famous as the site of the Battle of Bosworth Field, and a particularly intriguing church at Breedon-on-the-Hill. Leicestershire also lies adjacent to the easy countryside of **Rutland**, where you'll find another pleasant county town, Oakham. Rutland and **Northamptonshire** benefit from the use of limestone as the traditional building material and rural Northamptonshire is studded with handsome stone villages and towns – most notably Fotheringhay – as well as a battery of country estates.

Lincolnshire is very different in character from the rest of the region, an agricultural hidey-hole that remains surprisingly remote, its wide-skied landscapes at their prettiest in the band of rolling hills that comprise the **Lincolnshire Wolds**. Locals sometimes call it the "forgotten county", but this was not always the case: throughout medieval times the county flourished as a centre of the wool trade with Flanders, its merchants and landowners becoming some of the wealthiest in England. Reminders of the high times are legion, beginning with the majestic **cathedral** that rises above **Lincoln**; equally enticing is the splendidly intact stone town of **Stamford**. Out in the sticks, the county's most distinctive feature is the **Lincolnshire Fens**, whose pancake-flat fields, filling out much of the south of the county and extending deep into Cambridgeshire, have been reclaimed from the marshes and the sea. Fenland villages are generally short of charm, but their parish churches, whose spires regularly interrupt the wide-skied landscape, are simply stunning; Gedney and Long Sutton have two of the finest.

Very different again is the **Lincolnshire coast**, whose long sandy beach extends, with a few marshy interruptions, from Mablethorpe to Skegness, the region's main resort. The coast has long attracted holiday-makers from the big cities of the East Midlands and Yorkshire, hence its trail of bungalows, campsites and caravan parks, though significant chunks of the seashore are now protected as nature reserves, with the **Gibraltar Point National Nature Reserve** being the pick.

LINCOLN CATHEDRAL

Highlights

❶ Newstead Abbey One-time hidey-hole of Lord Byron, this intriguing old mansion has superb period rooms, with lots of Byron memorabilia, plus delightful gardens. **See p.482**

❷ Hardwick Hall A beautifully preserved Elizabethan mansion that was home to the formidable Bess of Hardwick, one of the leading figures of her age. The gardens and surrounding parkland are charming, too. **See p.483**

❸ Lincoln Cathedral One of the finest medieval cathedrals in the land, dominating this fine old city and seen to best advantage on a guided tour. **See p.498**

❹ Gibraltar Point National Nature Reserve Escape the crowds and enjoy the wonderful birdlife at this first-class coastal nature reserve. **See p.503**

❺ Stamford Lincolnshire's prettiest town, with its cobbled lanes, lovely old churches, and ancient limestone buildings, well deserves an overnight stay. **See p.505**

HIGHLIGHTS ARE MARKED ON THE MAP ON P.476

0
miles

N

HUMBER BRIDGE
Barton-upon-Humber

NORTH LINCOLNSHIRE

Scunthorpe

Grimsby
Cleethorpes

Brigg

Caistor

Saltfleet

Barnsley

SOUTH YORKSHIRE

Doncaster

Rotherham

Robin Hood Airport
Bawtry

Market Rasen

Louth

Mablethorpe

Sheffield

Gainsborough

THE WOLDS

Skegne

Ingoldm

Worksop

Retford

Chesterfield

Clowne
Bolsover

Carburton

Clumber Park

Lincoln

Horncastle

Cuckney

Ollerton

Sherwood Forest National Nature Reserve

Edwinstowe

Woodhall Spa

Hardwick Hall

Mansfield

NOTTINGHAMSHIRE

Newark-on-Trent

Tattershall Castle
Coningsby

LINCOLNSHIRE

Alfreton

Newstead Abbey

Southwell

Southwell Workhouse

Eastwood

Hucknall

Ilkeston

Beeston

Nottingham

Sleaford

Boston

Heckington

Derby

West Bridgford

Colston Bassett

Grantham

Fosdyke

The Wash

Long Eaton

THE FENS

Welland

East Midlands Airport

Loughborough

Melton Mowbray

Holbeach

East Light Lighthouse

Gedney

Sutto Bridge

Calke Abbey
Breedon-on-the-Hill

Spalding

Long Sutton

Ashby-de-la-Zouch

Coalville

Clipsham

LEICESTERSHIRE

RUTLAND

Oakham
Whitwell

Hambleton

Rutland Water

Stamford

Burghley House

Wisbech

Market Bosworth

Bosworth Field

Hinckley

Leicester

Tugby

Hallaton

Upphingham
Lyddington

Fotheringhay

Peterborough

March

Nuneaton

Lutterworth

Medbourne

Market Harborough

Corby

Oundle

Bedford Levels

CAMBRIDGESHIRE

Chatteris

Ely

Coventry

Rugby

NORTHAMPTONSHIRE

Kettering

Wellingborough

Ashby St Ledgers

Brixworth

Daventry

Northampton

St Neots

Bedford

Stoke Bruerne

Towcester

Newport Pagnell

Sandy

Biggleswade

Royston

Banbury

Brackley

Milton Keynes

BEDFORDSHIRE

THE EAST MIDLANDS

HIGHLIGHTS

1 Newstead Abbey
2 Hardwick Hall
3 Lincoln Cathedral
4 Gibraltar Point National Nature Reserve
5 Stamford

Gibraltar Po Nature Reser

By train and bus Travelling between the cities of the East Midlands by train or bus is simple and most of the larger towns have good regional links, too. Things are very different in the country, however, where bus services are distinctly patchy, nowhere more so than in Lincolnshire.

By plane The region's international airport, East Midlands (ⓦ eastmidlandsairport.com), is located just off the M1 between Derby, Nottingham and Leicester. There are buses from the airport to these three major cities – the operator is currently Trentbarton (ⓦ trentbarton.co.uk/skylink247).

Nottingham

With a population of around 320,000, **NOTTINGHAM** is one of England's big cities. A one-time lace manufacturing and pharmaceutical centre (the Boots chain began here), today it's famous for its association with **Robin Hood**, the legendary thirteenth-century outlaw. Hood's bitter enemy was, of course, the **Sheriff of Nottingham**, but unfortunately his home and lair – the city's imposing medieval castle – is long gone, replaced by a handsome Palladian mansion that is still called, somewhat confusingly, **Nottingham Castle**. Nowadays, Nottingham is at its most diverting in and around both the castle and the handsome **Market Square**, which is also the centre of a heaving, teeming weekend nightlife scene. Within easy striking distance of the city is the former coal-mining village of **Eastwood**, home to the **D.H. Lawrence Birthplace Museum**.

Brief history
Controlling an important crossing point over the River Trent, the Saxon town of **Nottingham** was built on one of a pair of sandstone hills whose 130ft cliffs looked out over the river valley. In 1068, William the Conqueror built a castle on the other hill, and the Saxons and Normans traded on the low ground in between, the Market Square. The castle was a military stronghold and royal palace, the equal of the great castles of Windsor and Dover, and every medieval king of England paid regular visits. In August 1642, Charles I stayed here too, riding out of the castle to raise his standard and start the Civil War – not that the locals were overly sympathetic. Hardly anyone joined up, even though the king had the ceremony repeated on the next three days.

After the Civil War, the Parliamentarians slighted the castle and, in the 1670s, the ruins were cleared by the Duke of Newcastle to make way for a palace, whose continental – and, in English terms, novel – design he chose from a pattern book, probably by Rubens. Beneath the castle lay a handsome, well-kept market town until the second half of the eighteenth century, when the city was transformed by the expansion of the lace and hosiery industries. Within the space of fifty years, Nottingham's population increased from ten thousand to fifty thousand, the resulting slums becoming a hotbed of radicalism.

The worst of the slums were cleared in the early twentieth century, when the city centre assumed its present structure, with the main commercial area ringed by alternating industrial and residential districts. Thereafter, crass postwar development, adding tower blocks, shopping centres and a ring road, ensconced and embalmed the remnants of the city's past.

The Market Square
One of the best-looking central squares in England, Nottingham's **Market Square** remains the heart of the city, an airy open plaza whose shops, offices and fountains are overseen and overlooked by the grand neo-Baroque **Council House**, completed as part of a make-work scheme in 1928. Just off the square there's also a statue honouring one of the city's heroes, the former manager of Nottingham Forest FC, **Brian Clough** (1935–2004), shown in his characteristic trainers and tracksuit. Clough won two European cups with Forest, a remarkable achievement by any standards, but his popularity came just as much from his forthright personality and idiosyncratic

NOTTINGHAM

Tram Line & Stop — T

utterances. One quote will suffice to show the mettle of the man – "I wouldn't say I was the best manager in the business, but I was in the top one."

Nottingham Castle

Castle Place, NG1 6EJ • Mid-Feb to mid-Nov daily 10am–5pm; mid-Nov to mid-Feb Wed–Sun 10am–3pm; last entry 1hr before closing • £8 • **Cave tours** Noon, 1pm, 2pm & 3pm: mid-Feb to mid-Nov daily; mid-Nov to mid-Feb Wed–Sun; 45min • £5 • ☎ 0115 876 1400, ⓦ nottinghamcastle.org.uk

From the Market Square, it's a five-minute walk to **Nottingham Castle**, whose heavily restored medieval gateway edges the immaculately maintained gardens, whose lawns, flower borders and trees slope up to the squat, seventeenth-century ducal **palace**. Parts of the castle will be closed during **major renovation works** (2018–20), but the end result should feature a gallery exploring the city's radical, rebellious past – from its support for Parliament against the king through to its espousal of Chartism. There is also likely to be a display of the small but exquisite medieval **alabaster carvings** for which Nottingham once had an international reputation and, on the top floor, the capacious and handsome **picture gallery** will undoubtedly survive – and continue to display its enjoyable collection of mostly English nineteenth- and early twentieth-century paintings.

Just outside the main entrance, two sets of steps lead down into the maze of ancient **caves** that honeycomb the sandstone cliff below – one set being **King David's Dungeon**, the other **Mortimer's Hole**. Both are open for tours, but Mortimer's Hole is the more atmospheric, a 300ft shaft along which, so the story goes, the young Edward III and his accomplices crept in 1330 to capture his mother, Isabella, and her lover, Roger Mortimer. The two had staged a coup four years earlier in which Edward's hapless father, Edward II, was murdered, but they were unable to keep a firm hold on power, with Edward III proving too shrewd for them. Edward had his revenge on Mortimer, who came to a grisly end, but the remarkable Isabella was allowed to simply step back from politics, living out her days in comfort (and probably acute boredom).

The Lace Market

Once key to the city's fortunes, Nottingham's lace industry boomed in the nineteenth century, its assorted warehouses and factories flanking the narrow streets of a compact area known as the **Lace Market**, beginning just to the east of the Market Square. The lace industry has pretty much disappeared but the buildings haven't, with **Stoney Street** the most architecturally striking, its star turn being the **Adams Building**, whose handsome stone-and-brick facade combines both neo-Georgian and neo-Renaissance features. Take a peek also at neighbouring **Broadway**, where a line of impressive red-brick buildings perform a neat swerve halfway along the street. The district grew up round a much older structure, the **church of St Mary's** (daily 9am–5pm; free; Ⓦ stmarysnottingham.org), an imposing, medieval Gothic building with Saxon origins. The church interior is fairly routine, but there is a particularly interesting memorial on the wall of the nave to a Lieutenant James Still, who died of yellow fever while serving in a British anti-slaving squadron off Sierra Leone in 1821 – and the memorial's rant against slavery cheers the soul.

National Justice Museum

High Pavement, NG1 1HN · Daily 10am–5.30pm · £11 · Ⓣ 0115 952 0555, Ⓦ nationaljusticemuseum.org.uk

The Lace Market abuts **High Pavement**, the administrative centre of Nottingham in Georgian times, and it's here that you'll find **Shire Hall**, whose Neoclassical columns, pilasters and dome date from the 1770s. Shire Hall now houses the **National Justice Museum**, which explores and explains the workings of the law by means of semi-interactive displays. The building is perhaps more interesting than the hoopla, incorporating two superbly preserved Victorian courtrooms, an Edwardian police station, some spectacularly unpleasant old cells and a prisoners' exercise yard.

Nottingham Contemporary

Weekday Cross, NG1 2GB · Tues–Sat 10am–6pm, Sun 11am–5pm; bank hols 10am–5pm · Free · Ⓣ 0115 948 9750, Ⓦ nottinghamcontemporary.org

In a handy, central location, **Nottingham Contemporary** is the city's premier art gallery, though from the outside it looks like something assembled from an IKEA flat pack. The gallery's temporary exhibitions are consistently strong; hit shows have included the early paintings of David Hockney, a wonderful, all-encompassing display on Haitian voodoo, and a solo exhibition by Wu Tsang.

D.H. Lawrence Birthplace Museum

8a Victoria St, Eastwood, NG16 3AW, off Nottingham Rd · Tours Tues–Sat 10am–4pm (4 daily) · £6.90 · Ⓣ 0115 917 3824 · Buses link Nottingham's Victoria bus station with Eastwood (every 20min; 30min; Ⓣ 01773 712265, Ⓦ trentbarton.co.uk)

D.H. Lawrence (1885–1930) was born in the pit village of **Eastwood**, about seven miles northwest of Nottingham. The mines hereabouts closed years ago, and Eastwood is, to be frank, something of a post-industrial eyesore, but Lawrence's earliest home has survived, a tiny, red-brick terraced house refurbished as the **D.H. Lawrence Birthplace Museum**. None of the furnishings and fittings are Lawrence originals, which isn't too surprising given that the family moved out when he was two, but it's an appealing evocation of the period, interlaced with biographical insights into the author's life. Afterwards, enthusiasts can follow the three-mile **Blue Line Trail** round those parts of Eastwood with Lawrence associations: the walk takes an hour or so, and a brochure is available at the museum. Interestingly, few locals thought well of Lawrence – and the sexual scandals hardly helped. Famously, he ran off with Frieda, the wife of a Nottingham professor, and then there was the *Lady Chatterley's Lover* obscenity trial, but much of his local unpopularity was caused by the author's move to the political right until, eventually, he espoused a cranky and unpleasant form of (Nietzschean) elitism.

ARRIVAL AND INFORMATION

By train Nottingham train station is on the south side of the city centre, a 10min walk (just follow the signs), or a tram ride, from Market Square.
Destinations Birmingham (every 30min; 1hr 20min); Leicester (every 30min; 20min); Lincoln (hourly; 1hr); London (every 30min; 1hr 45min); Newark (every 30min; 30min); Oakham (hourly; 1hr 15min, change at Leicester).
By bus Most long-distance buses arrive at the Broad

Marsh bus station, down the street from the train station, but some – including services to north Nottinghamshire (see opposite) – pull in at the Victoria bus station, a 5min walk north of Market Square.
Tourist office Market Square, on the ground floor of the Council House, 1 Smithy Row (Mon–Sat 9.30am–5.30pm, plus selected Sun 11am–5pm; ☎0844 477 5678, ⓦ experiencenottinghamshire.com).

ACCOMMODATION

★**Harts Hotel** Standard Hill, Park Row, NG1 6GN ☎0115 988 1900, ⓦhartsnottingham.co.uk; map p.478. Nottingham may be short of good places to stay, but this chic hotel does much to fill the gap. The thirty-odd stylish guest rooms have ultramodern fixtures and fittings, Egyptian-cotton bed linen and contemporary paintings on the wall. Completed in 2002, the hotel's inventive use of space – from the inviting reception area onwards – is its special hallmark. Handy location, plus

a smashing restaurant next door (see below). **£140**
The Walton Hotel 2 North Road, The Park, NG7 1AG ☎0115 947 5215, ⓦthewaltonhotel.com; map p.478. Garners mixed reviews, but this 28-room hotel does occupy a good-looking, nineteenth-century building and its annexe on the edge of the city centre – a 15min walk from Market Square, beside Derby Road. The rooms vary considerably, though the best are cheered by a smattering of period furnishings and fittings. **£125**

EATING

Annie's Burger Shack 5 Broadway, NG1 1PR ☎0115 684 9920, ⓦanniesburgershack.com; map p.478. This large and extremely busy burger joint has been a real local hit, attracting a young and lively crowd, who chomp away at a wide range of top-ranking burgers, including the "Deathray" (with jalapeños, peppers and chilli paste). Craft ales, stouts and ciders too – but come early or expect to queue. Burgers average £10. Mon–Thurs noon–10pm, Fri & Sat noon–11pm, Sun 11am–10pm.
Edin's 15 Broad St, NG1 3AJ ☎0115 924 1112, ⓦedins nottingham.co.uk; map p.478. This city-centre café-bar has a laidback vibe, with its pocket-sized open kitchen, boho furniture and jazzy, bluesy soundtrack. The menu is short, unpretentious and inexpensive; mains cost as little as £7, but there are also snacks such as the bread and cheese board. Mon–Sat 9.30am–11.30pm, Sun 9.30am–9pm.
Harts Restaurant Standard Hill, Park Row, NG1 6GN ☎0115 988 1900, ⓦhartsnottingham.co.uk; map p.478. One of the city's most acclaimed restaurants, occupying a tastefully remodelled wing of the old general hospital and offering a creative international menu – try,

for example, the sea bream bouillabaisse. Reservations recommended. Mains average £21. Daily noon–2.15pm & 6–10pm, Sun till 9pm.
★**Masala Junction** 301 Mansfield Road, NG5 2DA ☎0115 962 2366, ⓦmasalajunction.co.uk; map p.478. The best Indian restaurant in Nottingham, its menu featuring canny amalgamations of different regional cooking styles. It's in an attractively refurbished former bank, about a mile from the city centre up along Mansfield Road (buses from Lower Parliament St). Mains around £14. Mon–Thurs 5.30–10.30pm, Fri & Sat 5.30–11pm.
★**World Service** Newdigate House, Castle Gate, NG1 6AF ☎0115 847 5587, ⓦworldservicerestaurant.com; map p.478. Chic restaurant with bags of decorative flair in charming premises up near the castle, complete with a delightful terrace. A Modern British menu, including delights like rack of lamb with butternut squash, is prepared with imagination and flair. In the evenings, mains start around £20, but there are great deals at lunchtimes (two-course set menu £17). Mon–Fri noon–2pm & 7–10pm, Sat noon–2pm & 6.30–10pm, Sun noon–3.30pm.

DRINKING AND NIGHTLIFE

Central Nottingham's **pubs** literally heave on the weekend and are not for the faint-hearted – and anyone over thirty years old may well feel somewhat marooned. That said, there are several particularly engaging places amid all the argy-bargy.

★**Boilermaker** 36 Carlton St, NG1 1NN ☎0115 986 6333, ⓦboilermakerbar.co.uk; map p.478. Don't be deterred by the glum, anonymous exterior, this is Nottingham's coolest cocktail bar, set in a large, almost shed-like space with boho decor – and it has superb cocktails. First come, first served, so come early. Mon–Fri 5pm–1am, Sat 2pm–1am, Sun 7pm–1am.

Broadway Cinema Bar Broadway Cinema, 14 Broad St, NG1 3AL ☎0115 952 6611, ⓦbroadway.org.uk; map p.478. Informal, fashionable (in an arty sort of way) bar serving an eclectic assortment of bottled beers to a cinema-keen clientele. Filling, inexpensive bar food too. Much to its credit, Broadway has played a key role in boosting Nottingham's creative credentials – hence the city's clutch of artist-led collectives. Mon–Wed 9am–11pm, Thurs 9am–midnight, Fri & Sat 9am–1am, Sun 10am–11pm.

Lincolnshire Poacher 161 Mansfield Rd, NG1 3FR ☎0115 941 1584, ⓦcastlerockbrewery.co.uk/pubs/lincolnshire-poacher; map p.478. Popular and relaxed pub, where the decor is pleasantly traditional and the customers take their real ales (fairly) seriously. About half a mile from the Market Square. Mon–Wed 11am–11pm, Thurs & Fri 11am–midnight, Sat 10.30am–midnight, Sun noon–11pm.

★**Ye Olde Trip to Jerusalem** Brewhouse Yard, NG1 6AD ☎0115 947 3171, ⓦtriptojerusalem.com; map p.478. Carved into the sandstone cliff below the castle, this ancient inn – said to be the oldest in England – may well have been a meeting point for soldiers gathering for the Third Crusade. Its cave-like bars, with their rough sandstone ceilings and antique furniture, are delightfully secretive and there's a good range of ales too. Mon–Thurs & Sun 11am–11pm, Fri & Sat 11am–midnight.

ENTERTAINMENT

Broadway Cinema 14 Broad St, NG1 3AL ☎0115 952 6611, ⓦbroadway.org.uk; map p.478. The best cinema in the city, featuring a mixed bag of mainstream and avant-garde films.

Motorpoint Arena & National Ice Centre Bolero Square, Lace Market, NG1 1LA ☎0843 373 3000, ⓦmotorpointarenanottingham.com; ⓦnational-ice-centre.com; map p.478. Major performance venue that seems to change its name (and sponsor) with surprising regularity. Big-name acts perform here – from music through to shows and comedy. The Arena is inside the National Ice Centre, with its prime ice-skating facilities.

Nottingham Playhouse Wellington Circus, NG1 5AF ☎0115 941 9419, ⓦnottinghamplayhouse.co.uk; map p.478. Long-established theatre offering a wide-ranging programme of plays – Shakespeare through to Ayckbourn – plus dance, music and comedy, often with a local twist or theme. There's also a delightful piece of modern art beside the entrance – Anish Kapoor's whopping, reflective *Sky Mirror*.

Theatre Royal & Royal Concert Hall Theatre Square, NG1 5ND ☎0115 989 5555, ⓦtrch.co.uk; map p.478. Two venues with one set of contact details: the Theatre Royal is an attractive, well-maintained Victorian theatre and the nearby Concert Hall dates from the 1980s. Many of the big names in live music, both popular and classical, play at one or the other.

SHOPPING

Five Leaves Bookshop 14a Long Row, NG1 2DH ☎0115 837 3097, ⓦfiveleavesbookshop.co.uk; map p.478. UK bookshops may be having a bumpy ride, but this new and independent place bucks the trend, with a well-chosen selection of titles with a radical twist. Down an alley opposite the tourist office. Mon–Sat 10am–5.30pm, Sun noon–4pm.

Paul Smith 20 Low Pavement, NG1 7DN ☎0115 968 5990, ⓦpaulsmith.co.uk; map p.478. Nottingham's Paul Smith (b.1946) worked in a clothing factory as a young man, but only developed a passion for art and design after a bike accident left him incapacitated for six months. He opened his first small shop on Byard Lane in 1970, since when he has gone on to become one of the major success stories of contemporary British fashion, his trademark multicoloured stripes proving popular on every continent. The Byard Lane shop closed in 2017 but the flagship store on Low Pavement is worth a visit. Both shops: Mon–Sat 10am–6pm, Sun 11am–5pm.

Rough Trade 5 Broad St, NG1 3AJ ☎0115 896 4012, ⓦroughtrade.com; map p.478. To have a Rough Trade outlet here in Nottingham is a real coup – take your pick from the stacks of vinyl and selected books on the ground floor or visit the dimly lit café up above. Mon–Sat 10am–8pm, Sun 11am–7pm.

9

Northern Nottinghamshire

Rural **northern Nottinghamshire**, with its gentle rolling landscapes and large ducal estates, was transformed in the nineteenth century by **coal** – deep, wide seams of the stuff that spawned dozens of collieries, and colliery towns, stretching up across the county and on into Yorkshire. Today, the mines have all gone, their passing marked only by the occasional pithead winding wheel, left, bleak and solitary, to commemorate the thousands of men who laboured here.

The suddenness of the pit closure programme imposed by Thatcher and her Conservative administration in the 1980s and 1990s knocked the stuffing out of the area, but one prop of its slow revival has been the tourist industry. The countryside in between these former mining communities holds several enjoyable attractions, the best known of which is **Sherwood Forest** – or at least the patchy remains of it – with one chunk of woodland preserved in the **Sherwood Forest National Nature Reserve**, supposedly where Robin Hood did his canoodling with Maid Marian. Byron is a pipsqueak in the celebrity stakes by comparison with Robin, but his family home – **Newstead Abbey** – is here too, as is **Hardwick Hall**, a handsome Elizabethan mansion built at the behest of one of the most powerful women of her day, Bess of Hardwick (1521–1608). Newstead Abbey and Hardwick Hall are publicly owned, but a third estate, **Welbeck Abbey**, remains in ducal hands and it's here that you'll find the excellent and enjoyable **Harley Gallery**.

Newstead Abbey

Ravenshead, NG15 8NA, 10 miles north of Nottingham on the A60 • **House** Sat, Sun & some hols noon–4pm; last entry 1hr before closing • £8 • **Gardens & grounds** Daily 9am–5pm or dusk • Vehicles £6; pedestrians & cyclists £1 • ☎ 01623 455900, ⓦ newsteadabbey.org.uk • A regular Pronto bus (every 20min; 40min; ☎ 01773 712265, ⓦ trentbarton.co.uk) leaves Nottingham's Victoria bus station for Mansfield, and stops at the gates of Newstead Abbey

In 1539, **Newstead Abbey** was granted by Henry VIII to Sir John Byron, who demolished most of the church and converted the monastic buildings into a family home. Much later, in 1798, **Lord Byron** (1788–1824) inherited the estate, but by then it was little more than a ruin; he restored part of the complex during his six-year residence (1808–14), but most of the present structure actually dates from later renovations, which maintained much of the shape and feel of the medieval original while creating the warren-like mansion that exists today.

Inside, a string of intriguing period rooms begins with the neo-Gothic Great Hall and Byron's bedroom (one of the few rooms to look pretty much like it did when he lived here) and then continues on into the Library, which holds a collection of the poet's possessions, from letters and an inkstand through to his pistols and boxing gloves. A further room contains a set of satirical, cartoon-like watercolours entitled *The Wonderful History of Lord Byron & His Dog* by his friend Elizabeth Pigot – there's a portrait of the self-same dog, **Boatswain**, in the south gallery, and a conspicuous memorial bearing an absurdly extravagant inscription to the mutt in the delightful walled garden at the back of the house. Beyond the house lie the main **gardens**, a secretive and subtle combination of lake, Gothic waterfalls, yew tunnels and Japanese-style rockeries, complete with idiosyncratic pagodas.

Sherwood Forest

The main entrance to the Sherwood Forest National Nature Reserve is half a mile north of Edwinstowe village, about 20 miles north of Nottingham via the A614 • Daily dawn–dusk • Free, but parking £3 (April–Dec only) • ☎ 01623 823202, ⓦ nottinghamshire.gov.uk • The Sherwood Arrow bus (ⓦ stagecoachbus.com) links Nottingham's Victoria bus station with Worksop via the visitor centre (hourly; 1hr)

Most of **Sherwood Forest**, once a vast royal woodland of oak, birch and bracken covering all of northern Nottinghamshire, was cleared in the eighteenth century. It's difficult today to imagine the protection all the greenery provided for generations of outlaws, the most famous of whom was of course **Robin Hood**. There's no "true story" of Robin's life – the earliest reference to him, in Langland's *Piers Plowman* of 1377, treats him as a fiction – but to the balladeers of fifteenth-century England, who invented most of Hood's folklore, this was hardly the point. For them, he was a symbol of yeoman decency, a semi-mythological opponent of corrupt clergymen and evil officers of the law; in the early tales, Robin may show sympathy for the peasant, but he has rather more respect for the decent nobleman, and he's never credited with robbing the rich to give to the poor. This and other parts of the legend, such as Maid Marian and Friar Tuck, were added later.

Robin Hood may lack historical authenticity, but it hasn't discouraged the county council from spending thousands of pounds sustaining the **Major Oak**, the creaky tree where Maid Marian and Robin are supposed to have plighted their troth. The Major Oak is on a pleasant one-mile woodland walk that begins beside the visitor centre at the main entrance to **Sherwood Forest National Nature Reserve**, which comprises 450 acres of ancient gnarled oak and silver birch crisscrossed with footpaths.

Welbeck Abbey

Welbeck, Worksop, S80 3LW, about 25 miles north of Nottingham or 2 miles north of Cuckney • **Harley Gallery** Mon–Sat 10am–5pm, Sun 10am–4pm • Free • **Portland Collection** Daily 11am–4pm • Free • **Welbeck Abbey tours** Aug to early Sept 3 daily; 1hr 30min; book ahead • £18 • **Welbeck Abbey extended tours** Early Sept 2 daily; 2hr 30min; book ahead • £26.50 • ☎ 01909 501700, ⓦ harleygallery.co.uk

Firmly in ducal hands, the picturesque stone buildings of the **Welbeck Abbey estate** are dotted over a large chunk of land to the northwest of Edwinstowe. Here, on the western edge of the estate, the old gasworks has been tastefully turned into the pocket-sized **Harley Gallery**, which hosts changing exhibitions by contemporary artists, while the adjacent **Portland Collection** showcases an appealing assortment of ducal knick-knacks, from portraits, cameos and rare books to silverware and paintings, all regularly rotated. Locally at least, the most famous member of the family, whose various branches are named Cavendish, Portland and Newcastle, was the **Fifth Duke of Portland** (1800–79), known as the "burrowing duke" for the maze of gas-lit tunnels that he built underneath his estate – they are still there, but not open to the public. Naturally enough, many thought he was bonkers, but the truth may be far more complex; Mick Jackson's novel *The Underground Man* portrays the duke as shy and haunted by his obsessions. Across from the gallery, there is also a café and a first-rate **farm shop**, which attracts happy eaters from far and wide, and it's also possible to visit the **main house** on a guided tour (extended tours also available in early Sept), which takes in several Edwardian rooms plus the rather splendid eighteenth-century Great Hall.

Hardwick Hall

Doe Lea, Chesterfield, Derbyshire, S44 5QJ • **Hardwick Hall & gardens** Wed–Sun: Mid-Feb to Oct 11am–5pm; mid-Nov to mid-Dec 11am–3pm • Hall & gardens £14; gardens only £7; NT • **Parkland** Daily 9am–6pm (or dusk if sooner) • Free, but parking £4; NT • ☎ 01246 850430, ⓦ nationaltrust.org.uk/hardwick-hall • **Hardwick Old Hall** April–Sept Wed–Sun 10am–6pm; Oct Wed–Sun 10am–5pm; Nov–March Sat & Sun (daily in school hols) 10am–4pm • £6.50; EH • ☎ 01246 850431, ⓦ www.english-heritage.org.uk/visit/places/hardwick-old-hall • No public transport; by car via M1 (Junction 29), then signposted from roundabout at the top of the slip road)

Born the daughter of a minor Derbyshire squire, Elizabeth, Countess of Shrewsbury (1527–1608) – aka **Bess of Hardwick** – became one of the leading figures of Elizabethan England, renowned for her political and business acumen. She had a penchant for building and her major achievement, **Hardwick Hall**, begun when she was 62, has survived in amazingly good condition. The house was the epitome of fashion, a balance of symmetry and ingenious detail in which the building's rectangular lines are offset by line upon line of windows – there's actually more glass than stone – while up above, her giant-sized initials (E.S.) hog every roof line.

The highlights of the labyrinthine mansion are on its top floor (closed late Dec), home to the breathtaking **High Great Chamber**, where Bess received her most distinguished guests. The Chamber boasts an extraordinary, brightly painted plaster

9

frieze celebrating the goddess Diana, the virgin huntress – designed, of course, to please the Virgin Queen herself. Next door, the **Long Gallery** features eye-catching furnishings and fittings, from splendid chimneypieces and tapestries through to a set of portraits, including one each of the queen and Bess. Bess could exercise here while keeping out of the sun – at a time when any hint of a tan was considered decidedly plebeian.

Outside, the **garden** makes for a pleasant wander and, beyond the ha-ha, rare breeds of cattle and sheep graze the **parkland**. Finally – and rather confusingly – Hardwick Hall is next to **Hardwick Old Hall**, Bess's previous home, but now little more than a broken-down if substantial ruin (combined tickets are available; £20).

Southwell

SOUTHWELL, some fourteen miles northeast of Nottingham, is a well-heeled little town distinguished by **Southwell Minster**, whose perky twin towers are visible for miles around, and by the fine Georgian mansions facing it along Church Street.

Southwell Minster

Church St, NG25 0HD • Mon–Sat 8am–6pm or dusk; Sun hours depend on services • Free, but £5 donation requested • ☎ 01636 812649 • ⓦ southwellminster.org

The Normans built **Southwell Minster** at the beginning of the twelfth century and, although some elements were added later, their design predominates, from the imposing west towers to the dog-tooth decoration and the clerestory's bull's-eye windows. Inside, the splendid Norman nave leads to the north transept, where there's a fine alabaster tomb of Archbishop Sandys, who died in 1588; the red-flecked alabaster effigy is so precise that you can see the furrows on his brow and the crow's feet round his eyes. His children are depicted kneeling below; it's assumed that Sandys was one of the first bishops to marry – and beget – after the break with Rome changed the rules. Beyond the nave, the choir is Early English and a side door leads through to the remarkable **chapter house**, which is embellished with naturalistic foliage from the late thirteenth century – some of the earliest carving of its type in England.

Southwell Workhouse

Upton Road, NG25 0PT • Mid-Feb to Oct daily noon–5pm • £8.65; NT • ☎ 01636 817260, ⓦ nationaltrust.org.uk/the-workhouse-southwell

About a mile from the minster, on the edge of town out on the road to Newark, stands **Southwell Workhouse**, a substantial three-storey brick building that looks like a prison, but is in fact a rare survivor of the Victorian workhouses (see p.691) that once dotted every corner of the country. Most were knocked down or redeveloped years ago, but this one remained almost untouched, though its bare rooms and barred windows make the whole experience rather depressing.

ARRIVAL AND DEPARTURE   SOUTHWELL

By bus There are regular NCT (Nottingham City Transport; ⓦ nctx.co.uk) buses to Southwell from King Street in central Nottingham; buses stop near the minster.

EATING

Saracen's Head Market Place, NG25 0HE ☎ 01636 812701, ⓦ saracensheadhotel.com. Metres from the Minster is the rambling *Saracen's Head*, which dates back to the fourteenth century and has one major claim to fame: it was here that Charles I spent a sleepless night before being handed over to his enemies in Newark (see opposite). Several of the downstairs rooms have been restored to their original half-timbered appearance, with furniture and fittings to match – a pleasant spot for lunch (mains average £10) or afternoon tea (Fri–Sun 2–5pm; £13). Mon–Sat noon–2.30pm & 5–8pm, Sun 6–8pm.

Newark

From Nottingham, it's about twenty miles northeast to **NEWARK**, an old and really rather good-looking river port and market town that was once a major staging point on the Great North Road. Fronting the town as you approach from the west are the gaunt riverside ruins of **Newark Castle** (daily dawn–dusk; free), all that's left of the mighty medieval fortress that was pounded to pieces during the Civil War by the Parliamentarians. Opposite, just across the street to the north, is former **Ossington Coffee Palace**, a flashy structure whose Tudor appearance is entirely fraudulent – it was built in the 1880s as a temperance hotel by a local bigwig, in an effort to save drinkers from themselves. From here, it's just a couple of minutes' walk east through a network of narrow lanes and alleys to the **Market Place**, an expansive square framed by attractive Georgian and Victorian facades.

Church of St Mary Magdalene

Church Walk, NG24 1JS • Mon–Sat 8.30am–4pm, but often closed for lunch; May–Sept also Sun noon–4pm • Free • ☎ 01636 706473

Standing just off the Market Place, the mostly thirteenth-century **church of St Mary Magdalene** is a handsome if badly weathered structure whose massive spire (236ft) soars high above the town centre. Inside, look out for the pair of medieval Dance of Death panel paintings, behind the reredos in the choir's Markham Chantry Chapel. One panel has a well-to-do man slipping his hand into his purse, the other shows a ghoulish, carnation-carrying skeleton pointing to the grave – an obvious reminder to observers of their mortality.

National Civil War Centre

14 Appletongate, NG24 1JY • Daily: April–Sept 10am–5pm; Oct–March 10am–4pm • £8 • ☎ 01636 655765, ⓦ nationalcivilwarcentre.com

Newark played a leading role in the Civil War as a Royalist stronghold, and endured three Parliamentary sieges. The **National Civil War Centre**, housed in a thoroughly refurbished former school behind St Mary Magdalene, describes these military comings and goings in some detail, all illuminated by short films and a few archeological bits and pieces. The Centre also has details of Newark's **Civil War Trail**, which takes in those local sites associated with the conflict, most notably the **Queen's Sconce**, the well-preserved, star-shaped, earthen fortification on the southwest side of town near the River Trent.

ARRIVAL AND INFORMATION

NEWARK

By train Newark has two train stations: Newark Castle on the Nottingham–Lincoln line is on the west side of the River Trent, a 5min walk from the castle, while the larger Newark North Gate station, on the main London–Edinburgh line, is to the northeast of the centre at the far end of Appletongate.

Destinations Lincoln (1–2 hourly; 30min); London (every 30min; 1hr 30min); Nottingham (2 hourly; 30min).

By bus Newark bus station is on Lombard St, on the south side of the town centre.

Destinations Nottingham (2 hourly; 1hr); Southwell (hourly; 30min).

Tourist office In the National Civil War Centre (daily: April–Sept 10am–5pm, Oct–March 10am–4pm; ☎ 01636 655765).

EATING AND DRINKING

★**Gannets** 35 Castlegate, NG24 1AZ ☎ 01636 702066, ⓦ gannetsinnewark.co.uk. This bright and breezy modern café/restaurant has been popular with locals for the last few decades. It's an informal sort of place with shared tables and a wide-ranging, well-priced menu, in which the salads and bakes are special highlights, though there is much more – lasagnes, risottos, jacket potatoes and a real local favourite, the carrot cake. Also caters to most dietary requirements. Mon–Fri & Sun 8.30am–4pm, Sat 8.30am–5pm.

9

Leicester

At first glance, **LEICESTER**, some 25 miles south of Nottingham, seems a resolutely modern city, but further inspection reveals traces of its medieval and Roman past as a settlement on the Fosse Way (now the A46) linking Exeter and Lincoln. In 2012, Leicester's national profile was boosted by the discovery of the remains of **Richard III** beneath a council car park in the centre – the body was originally brought here after the Battle of Bosworth Field (see p.490). There followed a prolonged legal battle with York as to who should keep the king's skeleton, but Leicester won and the body has now been reinterred in Leicester Cathedral. This was, however, small beer compared with Leicester's general delirium when their **football** team won the English Premier League title in 2016, at odds which started out at 5000/1.

Skeleton and football apart, it's probably fair to say that Leicester has a reputation for looking rather glum, but the centre is on the move, with the addition of **Highcross**, a large and glitzy shopping centre, and the creation of a Cultural Quarter equipped with both a flashy performance venue, **Curve Theatre**, and a first-rate independent cinema,

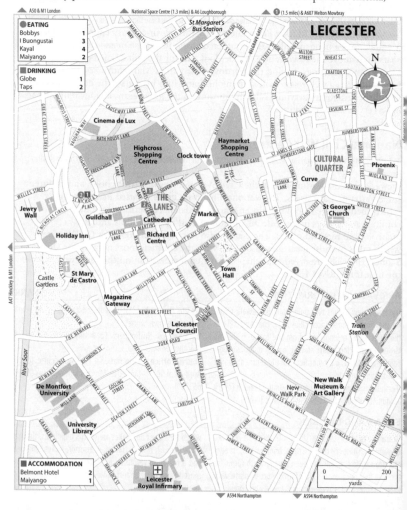

LEICESTER

EATING
Bobbys	1
I Buongustai	3
Kayal	4
Maiyango	2

DRINKING
Globe	1
Taps	2

ACCOMMODATION
Belmont Hotel	2
Maiyango	1

LEICESTER'S FINEST FESTIVALS

The crowded terraced streets on and around Belgrave Road are the hub for the city's principal Hindu festival, **Diwali** (Ⓦ visitleicester.info), the Festival of Light, held in October or November, when thousands of lamps illuminate proceedings. In addition, the city's sizeable African-Caribbean community holds England's second-biggest street festival (after Notting Hill Carnival; see box, p.124). It's called the **Leicester Caribbean Carnival** (Ⓦ facebook.com /LeicesterCaribbeanCarnival), and it's held on the first weekend in August.

the **Phoenix**. The star attractions are, however, the **New Walk Museum and Art Gallery**, which features an exemplary collection of German Expressionist paintings, and the intriguing **King Richard III Visitor Centre**. Leicester is also distinctive in its make-up: more than a third of the population is Asian and indeed the city elected England's first Asian MP, Keith Vaz, in 1987. The traditional focus of the Asian community is **Belgrave Road** and its environs, an area of terraced houses about a mile to the northeast of the centre.

Brief history

The **Romans** chose this site beside the River Soar to keep an eye on the rebellious Corieltauvi, constructing a fortified town here beside the Fosse Way in about 47 AD. Later, the Emperor Hadrian kitted the place out with huge public buildings, though the Danes, who overran the area in the eighth century, were not overly impressed and didn't even bother to pilfer much of the stone. Later still, the town's medieval castle became the base of the earls of Leicester, the most distinguished of whom was **Simon de Montfort**, who forced Henry III to convene the first English Parliament in 1265. Since the late seventeenth century, Leicester has been a centre of the **hosiery trade** and it was this industry that attracted a stream of Asian immigrants to settle here from the 1950s onwards.

The Clock Tower and around

The most conspicuous buildings in Leicester's bustling centre are the two large shopping centres, the ultramodern **Highcross** and the clumpy **Haymarket**, but the proper landmark is the Victorian **Clock Tower** of 1868, standing in front of the Haymarket and marking the spot where seven streets meet. One of the seven is Cheapside, which leads to Leicester's open-air **market** (Mon–Sat), one of the best in the country and the place where the young **Gary Lineker**, now the UK's best-known football pundit, worked on the family stall. Good-hearted Gary remains a popular figure hereabouts and has been made a freeman of the city, which, among other things, gives him the right to graze his sheep in front of the town hall. Another of the seven streets is Silver Street (subsequently Guildhall Lane), which passes through **The Lanes**, where a medley of small, independent shops gives this part of the centre real character.

Leicester Cathedral

St Martin's, LE1 5PZ • Mon–Sat 10am–5pm, Sun 12.30–2.30pm (dependent on services) • Free, suggested donation £3 • Ⓣ 0116 261 5200, Ⓦ leicestercathedral.org

Abutting Guildhall Lane is **Leicester Cathedral**, a much-modified eleventh-century structure incorporating two finely carved porches – a stone one at the front and an earlier timber version at the rear. The interior, with its clutch of Gothic arches, holds several interesting side chapels, in one of which is a splendid wooden tabernacle, as well as the conspicuous stone **tomb of Richard III**.

King Richard III Visitor Centre

4a St Martin's, LE1 5DB • Mon–Fri & Sun 10am–4pm, Sat & bank hols 10am–5pm • £8.95 • Ⓣ 0300 300 0900, Ⓦ kriii.com

Across the street from the cathedral, Leicester's old Grammar School is a substantial Victorian redbrick that has been turned into the ambitious **King Richard III Visitor Centre**

9

after the royal body was discovered in 2012 beneath the adjoining car park, where Greyfriars church had once stood. The Centre has four distinct sections. The first examines Richard's reign and the battle of Bosworth Field that ended it; the second explores the nature of Richard's disability – he suffered from curvature of the spine – and relates the story of how the body was discovered, a remarkable tale in itself. The third section comprises a replica of Richard's skeleton with the various wounds the king suffered at the Battle of Bosworth Field clearly observable. This is really intriguing stuff – and it's all immaculately presented. The fourth and final section gives visitors the chance to peer down into the makeshift grave where the body was found.

The Jewry Wall

A five-minute stroll from the cathedral, beside the large St Nicholas Circle roundabout, you'll spot the conspicuous **church of St Nicholas**; beside that, in a small dell, lie the foundations of Emperor Hadrian's public baths, which culminate in the **Jewry Wall**, a substantial chunk of Roman masonry some 18ft high and 73ft long. The baths were a real irritation to the emperor: the grand scheme was spoilt by the engineers, who miscalculated the line of the aqueduct that was to pipe in the water, and so bathers had to rely on a hand-filled cistern replenished from the river – not what Hadrian had in mind at all.

Castle Gardens and around

Near the Roman ruins, **Castle Gardens** is a narrow strip of a park that runs alongside a canalized portion of the River Soar. It's a pleasant spot and one that incorporates the overgrown mound where Leicester's Norman castle motte once stood. Beyond the motte, at the far end of Castle Gardens, you emerge on The Newarke; turn left and follow the road round, and in a jiffy you'll reach **Castle View**, a narrow lane spanned by the Turret Gateway, a rare survivor of the city's medieval castle. Just beyond the gateway is **St Mary de Castro**, a rambling old church with a chunky crocketed tower; curiously, Chaucer may well have got married here.

New Walk Museum and Art Gallery

53–55 New Walk, LE1 7EA • Mon–Sat 10am–5pm, Sun 11am–5pm • Free • ☎ 0116 225 4900, ⓦ visitleicester.info

The **New Walk** is a long and agreeable pedestrianized promenade that's home to the city's best museum, the **New Walk Museum and Art Gallery**. The museum covers a lot of ground, from dinosaurs to geology and beyond, but one highlight is its collection of Ancient Egyptian artefacts, featuring mummies and hieroglyphic tablets brought back to Leicester in the 1880s. The museum also holds an enjoyable collection of paintings and, although these are rotated regularly, you're likely to see a good range of works by British artists as well as an outstanding collection of German Expressionist works, mostly sketches, woodcuts and lithographs by artists such as Otto Dix and George Grosz.

The National Space Centre

Exploration Drive, LE4 5NS, 2 miles north of the city centre, off the A6 • Mon–Fri 10am–4pm, Sat & Sun 10am–5pm • £14, under-17s £11 • ☎ 0116 261 0261, ⓦ spacecentre.co.uk • Bus #54 links the train station with Abbey Lane, a 5min walk from the Space Centre

On the outskirts of Leicester, the **National Space Centre** is devoted to all things astronomical, with a string of themed galleries plus a planetarium and a 135m-high Rocket Tower. The emphasis is on the interactive, which makes the place very popular with kids.

ARRIVAL AND INFORMATION   **LEICESTER**

By train Leicester train station is on London Rd, on the southeast edge of the city centre.

Destinations Birmingham (every 30min; 1hr); Lincoln (hourly; 2hr); London (every 30min; 1hr 15min); Nottingham (every 30min; 30min); Oakham (hourly; 30min); Stamford (hourly; 40min).

By bus St Margaret's bus station is on the north side of the centre, just off Gravel St.

Destinations Ashby-de-la-Zouch (hourly; 1hr 20min); Market Bosworth (hourly; 1hr 10min).

Tourist office In the centre at 51 Gallowtree Gate (Mon–Sat 9.30am–5.30pm, Sun 10am–4pm; ☎0116 299 4444, ⓦvisitleicester.info).

ACCOMMODATION

★**Belmont Hotel** 20 De Montfort Square, LE1 7GR ☎0116 254 4773, ⓦbelmonthotel.co.uk; map p.486. A particularly pleasant and proficient hotel in an attractively modernized Victorian property, about 300yd south of the train station via London Rd. Independently owned, it's popular with business folk and tourists alike, and the 74 rooms vary in size and character, though all are extremely well-appointed. **£100**

Maiyango 13–21 St Nicholas Place, LE1 4LD ☎0116 251 8898, ⓦmaiyango.com; map p.486. This small, independent hotel has fourteen slick modern rooms, each with bespoke artwork and handmade furniture. Their "superior" rooms have rain showers, whereas the larger "deluxe" rooms opt for walk-in wet rooms and bathtubs – and both have king-size beds. The hotel is also in a handy location, a brief walk from Leicester's main sights and shopping centres. There's a first-rate restaurant on site, too (see below). **£170**

EATING

Bobbys 154 Belgrave Rd, LE4 5AT ☎0116 266 0106, ⓦeatatbobbys.com; map p.486. In operation for more than forty years, *Bobbys* is something of a local institution. It's an unpretentious, family-run place with simple decor, where they serve all things vegetarian; £15 will cover a meal for two. At the junction with MacDonald Road. Mon–Fri 11am–10pm, Sat & Sun 10am–10pm.

I Buongustai 82 Granby St, LE1 1DJ ☎0116 367 0511, ⓦfacebook.com/BuongustaiLeicester; map p.486. Unusual little café – with just three tables and takeaway – that specializes in Italian street food at bargain prices. The calzone, for instance cost just £3, and very tasty they are too. Mon–Fri 9am–5.30pm & Sat 9am–4pm.

★**Kayal** 153 Granby St, LE1 6FE ☎0116 255 4667, ⓦkayal restaurant.com; map p.486. Outstanding South Indian restaurant offering a well-conceived menu covering all the classic dishes and then some – try the Kayal fish curry (£12), or the Njandu crab curry (£14), influenced by Portuguese seafarers. In a handy location near the train station. Mon–Fri noon–3pm & 6–11pm, Sat & Sun noon–10pm.

★**Maiyango** 13–21 St Nicholas Place, LE1 4LD ☎0116 251 8898, ⓦmaiyango.com; map p.486. Chi-chi lounge-bar and restaurant beneath the hotel of the same name (see above). The restaurant zeroes in on local, seasonal ingredients and the menu is wide-ranging – try the parmesan and truffle spelt risotto, for example, or the soy-marinated trout. Afterwards, you can relax in the rooftop terrace bar. Mains average £18. Restaurant: Mon–Wed 6–11pm, Thurs & Fri noon–2pm & 6–11pm, Sat noon–midnight, Sun noon–4pm & 6–11pm.

DRINKING

Globe 43 Silver St, LE1 5EU ☎0116 253 9492, ⓦwww.eversosensible.com/globe; map p.486. Popular and traditional pub in an attractive old building at the heart of the city. Smashing range of real ales, and filling bar food too. Mon–Thurs & Sun 11am–11pm, Fri & Sat 11am–1am.

Taps 10 Guildhall Lane, LE1 5FQ ☎0116 253 0904, ⓦtaps-leicester.com; map p.486. Inventive bar and restaurant, whose main claim to fame is the beer taps at many of the tables – help yourself and pay later (yes, the taps are monitored as they dispense). Excellent range of bottled beers too, plus vaulted cellars that date back yonks, and an above-average menu – lamb shank with mash and apricot gravy, for example, for just £15. Mon–Sat noon–11.30pm.

ENTERTAINMENT

Curve Rutland St, LE1 1SB ☎0116 242 3595, ⓦcurve online.co.uk; map p.486. The heart of the Cultural Quarter, Curve is Leicester's leading performing arts venue, offering a varied programme from within its startlingly dramatic glass facade.

Phoenix 4 Midland St, LE1 1TG ☎0116 242 2800, ⓦwww.phoenix.org.uk; map p.486. Just a couple of minutes' walk from Curve, the Phoenix is an outstanding art-house cinema, one of the best in the Midlands.

Leicestershire

Shaped rather like a fox's head, **Leicestershire** is perhaps one of the more anonymous of the English shires, its undulating landscapes comprising an apparently haphazard mix of the industrial, post-industrial and rural with Leicester itself (see p.486) plumb in the middle. The star turn is the pretty little village of **Market Bosworth**, or rather the neighbouring **Bosworth Battlefield Heritage Centre**, near where – at the Battle of Bosworth Field – Richard III met a sticky and untimely end in 1485. Less well known are the county's most intriguing church, **St Mary and St Hardulph**, perched high above tiny **Breedon-on-the-Hill**, and **Calke Abbey**, technically over the boundary in Derbyshire and not an abbey at all, but an intriguing country house whose faded charms bear witness to the declining fortunes of the landed gentry.

Market Bosworth

The thatched cottages and Georgian houses of pocket-sized **MARKET BOSWORTH**, some thirteen miles west of Leicester, fan out from a dinky **Market Place**, which was an important trading centre throughout the Middle Ages. From the sixteenth to the nineteenth centuries, the dominant family hereabouts were the Dixies, merchant-landlords who were not universally admired: the young Samuel Johnson, who taught at the **Dixie Grammar School** – its elongated facade still abuts the Market Place – disliked the founder, Sir Wolstan Dixie, so much that he recalled his time there "with the strongest aversion and even a sense of horror". The Dixies mostly ended up at the **Church of St Peter** (daily 8.30am–dusk), a sturdy structure just north of Market Place, whose chancel holds the early eighteenth-century **tomb** of John Dixie, one-time rector, who is honoured by a long hagiographic plaque and the striking effigy of his weeping sister.

Bosworth Field

Sutton Cheney, Nuneaton, CV13 0AD, just south of Market Bosworth • **Heritage Centre** Daily: April–Oct 10am–5pm; Nov–March 10am–4pm • £8.95 • ☎ 01455 290429, ⓦ bosworthbattlefield.org.uk • The Centre is clearly signed, but there is also an unsigned, 2km-long lane from the south side of Market Bosworth's Market Place

Market Bosworth is best known for the **Battle of Bosworth Field**, which was fought on hilly countryside near the village in 1485. This was the last and most decisive battle of the Wars of the Roses, an interminably long-winded and bitterly violent conflict among the nobility for control of the English Crown. The victor was Henry Tudor, subsequently Henry VII, and he defeated Richard III (1452–85), who famously died on the battlefield. In desperation, Shakespeare's villainous Richard cried out "A horse, a horse, my kingdom for a horse," but in fact the defeated king seems to have been a much more phlegmatic character. Taking a glass of water before the fighting started, he actually said, "I live a king: if I die, I die a king". What happened to Richard's body after the battle was long a matter of conjecture, but in 2012 his skeleton was unearthed in the centre of Leicester beneath a council car park (see p.487).

THE PORK PIE: A GASTRONOMIC DELIGHT?

Melton Mowbray, some eighteen miles northeast of Leicester, is famous for its **pork pies**, an extraordinarily popular English delicacy made of compressed balls of meat and gristle encased in wobbly jelly and thick pastry. To many, the pie's appeal is unaccountable, but in 2009 the EU accorded the pie Protected Geographical Status, a coveted designation if ever there was one. Pork pies were the traditional repast of the foxhunting fraternity, for whom Melton Mowbray was long a favourite haunt. The antics of some of the aristocratic huntsmen are legend – in 1837 the Marquis of Waterford literally painted the town's buildings red, hence the saying. Today, connoisseurs swear by the pork pies of Dickinson & Morris and, although their products are widely distributed, you may want to go to their shop at 10 Nottingham St, just off the Market Place (Mon–Sat 8am–5pm; ⓦ porkpie.co.uk), to sample (or gawp at) the full range, from the tiny to the enormous.

The **Bosworth Battlefield Heritage Centre** features a lucid and well-illustrated description of the battle and explains its historical context in intriguing detail. There is also a section on recent archeological efforts to verify the actual site of the battle: when it was set up in the 1970s, the Heritage Centre followed eighteenth-century tradition in claiming that the battle took place on adjacent Ambion Hill and a circular 1.5-mile **Battle Trail** was laid out accordingly. In the event, it turns out that the battlefield was actually a couple of miles further west in marshy ground on what is now private land, so there has been some tinkering; the Battle Trail now offers views over to the actual battlefield, and it does still make for an enjoyable ramble. On the way you'll pass **King Richard's Well**, a rough cairn where the king was supposed to have had his final drink. Pick up a trail map at the Heritage Centre before you set out.

ARRIVAL AND DEPARTURE

MARKET BOSWORTH

By bus There are regular services from Leicester to Market Bosworth's Market Place (hourly; 1hr 10min).

ACCOMMODATION AND EATING

Softleys 2 Market Place, CV13 0LE ☎ 01455 290464, ⓦ softleys.com. In the centre of the village, this first-rate, family-run hotel has three well-appointed bedrooms decorated in a homely version of country-house style. The rooms serve as an adjunct to the restaurant, where the menu is lively, creative and locally sourced wherever possible – the lamb is especially good. Mains average around £19. Tues–Thurs noon–1.45pm & 6.30–9pm, Fri & Sat noon–1.45pm & 6.30–9.30pm, Sun noon–2.30pm. **£100**

Calke Abbey

Near the hamlet of Ticknall, DE73 7LE • **House** Early March to Oct daily 11am–5pm • £13.50 (includes gardens and park); NT; timed tickets only • **Gardens** Feb–Oct daily 10am–5pm • £9.10 (includes park); NT • **Park** Daily 7.30am–7.30pm (dusk if sooner) • £3.60; NT • ☎ 01332 863822, ⓦ nationaltrust.org.uk/calke-abbey • No public transport

The eighteenth-century facade of **Calke Abbey**, set deep in the countryside about 25 miles northwest of Leicester, is all self-confidence, its acres of dressed stone and three long lines of windows polished off with an imposing Greek Revival portico. This all cost oodles of money and the Harpurs, and then the Harpur-Crewes, who owned the estate, were doing very well until the finances of the English country estate changed after World War I. Then they simply hung on, becoming the epitome of faded gentility and refusing to make all but the smallest of changes – though they did finally plump for electricity in 1962. In 1985, the estate was passed to the National Trust, who decided not to bring in the restorers and have kept the house in its dishevelled state – and this is its real charm.

In the **house**, the entrance hall sets the scene, its walls decorated with ancient, moth-eaten stuffed heads from the family's herd of prize cattle. Beyond is the Caricature Room, whose walls are lined with satirical drawings, some by the leading cartoonists of their day. Further on are more animal heads and glass cabinets of stuffed birds in the capacious Saloon; an intensely cluttered Miss Havisham-like Drawing Room; a chaotic at-home School Room; and an endearingly dilapidated top floor. After you've finished in the house, you can stroll out into the **gardens**, pop into the Victorian estate **church**, and wander through wooded **parkland**.

Breedon-on-the-Hill

Sitting pretty just off the A42, some 9km from Calke Abbey, the hamlet of **BREEDON-ON-THE-HILL** lies at the foot of the large, partly quarried hill from which it takes its name. A steep footpath and a winding, half-mile byroad lead up from the village to the summit, from where there are commanding views over the surrounding countryside. The site of an Iron Age hillfort and an eighth-century Anglo-Saxon monastery, today the hill provides a grand setting for the village's fascinating **church**.

9

Church of St Mary and St Hardulph

DE73 8AJ • Daily 9.30am–4pm, sometimes later in summer • Free • ☎ 01530 564372, ⓦ breedonchurches.co.uk • There are no buses to the church; the village is poorly served, too

A sturdy edifice that mostly dates from the thirteenth century, the **Church of St Mary and St Hardulph** has an evocative interior holding a finely preserved set of Georgian pews, a large and intricately carved box-pew dating to the seventeenth century, and a trio of exquisite alabaster tombs. Even more rare, however, are a number of **Anglo-Saxon carvings** that include individual saints and prophets as well as panels in which a dense foliage of vines is inhabited by a tangle of animals and humans. The carvings are quite extraordinary, and the fact that the figures look Byzantine rather than Anglo-Saxon has fuelled much academic debate.

Rutland

To the east of Leicestershire lies **Rutland**, England's smallest county – at least when it's not low tide on the Isle of Wight – a well-heeled pocket of steeply rolling hills just eighteen miles from north to south. Rutland has three places of note: **Oakham**, the amiable county town, and **Uppingham** – both rural centres with some elegant Georgian architecture – and the prettier, much smaller ironstone hamlet of **Lyddington**.

Oakham

The prosperity of **OAKHAM**, twenty miles east of Leicester, is bolstered by Oakham School, one of the region's more exclusive private schools, and by its proximity to **Rutland Water**, a large reservoir whose assorted facilities attract cyclists, ramblers, sailors and birdwatchers by the hundred. Oakham's stone terraces and Georgian villas are too often interrupted to assume much grace, but the town does have its architectural moments, particularly in the L-shaped **Market Place**, where a brace of sturdy awnings shelter the old water pump and town stocks, and where **Oakham School** is housed in a series of impressive ironstone buildings.

Oakham Castle

Market Place, LE15 6DR • Mon & Wed–Sat 10am–4pm, Sun noon–4pm • Free • ☎ 01572 757578, ⓦ oakhamcastle.org

Footsteps from the Market Place stands **Oakham Castle**, a large banqueting hall that was once part of a twelfth-century fortified house. The hall is a good example of Norman domestic architecture and surrounding the building are the grassy banks of the castle that once protected it. Inside, the whitewashed walls are covered with **horseshoes**, the result of an ancient custom by which every lord or lady, king or queen, is obliged to present an ornamental horseshoe when they first set foot in the town.

All Saints' Church

Church St, LE15 6AA • Daily dawn to dusk • Free • ☎ 01572 724007, ⓦ oakhamteam.uk/oakham

A narrow lane leads from the Market Place to **All Saints' Church**, whose heavy tower and spire rise high above the town. Dating from the thirteenth century, the

---

OUTDOORS AT RUTLAND WATER

The gentle waters and easy, green hills of **Rutland Water** (ⓦ rutlandwater.org.uk) have made it a major centre for outdoor pursuits. There's **sailing** at Rutland Sailing Club (ⓦ rutlandsc.co.uk); **cycle hire** with Rutland Cycling (ⓦ rutlandcycling.com); and a **Watersports Centre** at Whitwell on the north shore (ⓦ anglianwater.co.uk). Rutland Water also attracts a wide range of waterfowl, which prompted the establishment of a **nature reserve** with numerous hides and a **Birdwatching Centre** (ⓦ rutlandwater.org.uk/awbc). The reserve is home to a successful Osprey breeding project.

church is an architectural hybrid, its solemn interior distinguished by a handsome timber ceiling and intense medieval carvings along the columns of the nave and choir, with Christian scenes and symbols set alongside dragons, grotesques, devils and demons.

ARRIVAL AND DEPARTURE — OAKHAM

By train Rutland's only train station is here in Oakham on Station Rd, on the northwest side of town, a 10min walk from Market Place.
Destinations Birmingham (hourly; 1hr 20min); Leicester (hourly; 30min); Melton Mowbray (hourly; 10min);

Stamford (hourly; 15min).
By bus The bus station is on John St, just off the High St, a 5min walk west of the Market Place.
Destinations Lyddington (Mon–Sat hourly; 25min); Uppingham (Mon–Sat hourly; 15min).

ACCOMMODATION AND EATING

Castle Cottage Café Church Passage, off Church St, LE15 6DR ☎ 01572 757952, ⓦ castlecottagecafe.co.uk. Cosy little café at the back of All Saints' Church featuring a tempting range of moderately priced home-made dishes. They do a particularly good line in cakes and salads. Mon–Fri 10am–4pm, Sat 8.30am–4.30pm, plus dinner specials.

Hambleton Hall Hambleton, LE15 7PL ☎ 01572 756991, ⓦ hambletonhall.com. Just a couple of miles from Oakham, overlooking Rutland Water in tiny Hambleton, this opulent hotel occupies an imposing Baronial-Gothic mansion set in its own immaculate grounds. It's seriously expensive – and seriously luxurious. **£300**

Uppingham

The **High Street**, the narrow main street of **UPPINGHAM**, six miles from Oakham, has the uniformity of style Oakham lacks, its course flanked by motly eighteenth-century bow-fronted shops and ironstone houses. It's the general appearance that pleases, rather than any individual sight, but the town is famous as the home of **Uppingham School**, founded in 1587, a bastion of privilege tucked away within imposing, fortress-like buildings.

ARRIVAL AND DEPARTURE — UPPINGHAM

By bus Buses pull in along North St East, just to the north of the High St.

Destinations Lyddington (Mon–Sat hourly; 5min); Oakham (Mon–Sat hourly; 15min).

ACCOMMODATION AND EATING

Lake Isle 16 High St East, LE15 9PZ ☎ 01572 822951, ⓦ lakeisle.co.uk. A tastefully modernized eighteenth-century townhouse, with rooms decorated in a pleasant rendition of traditional style. The restaurant is first-rate too,

offering a superb and varied menu from guinea fowl to local venison; main courses average £17. Mon 7–9pm, Tues–Thurs noon–2pm & 7–9pm, Fri & Sat noon–2pm & 6.30–9.30pm, Sun noon–2pm. **£90**

Lyddington

LYDDINGTON, about two miles south of Uppingham, is a sleepy little village of honey-coloured cottages that straggle along a meandering main street, backed by plump hills and broadleaf woodland. The most conspicuous building here is the **Church of St Andrew**, whose weathered stonework stands adjacent to **Lyddington Bede House** (April–Oct Wed–Sun 10am–5pm; £5.40; EH), a beautifully restored set of seventeenth-century almshouses, whose origins were as a country retreat for the bishops of Lincoln. The highlight is the light and airy Great Chamber, with its exquisitely carved oak cornices, but look out also for the tiny ground-floor rooms, which were occupied by impoverished locals until the 1930s.

ARRIVAL AND DEPARTURE — LYDDINGTON

By bus Buses travel along the main street – and there's a stop outside the *Old White Hart* (see p.494).

Destinations Oakham (Mon–Sat hourly; 25min); Uppingham (Mon–Sat hourly; 5min).

Old White Hart 51 Main St, LE15 9LR ☎ 01572 821703, ⓦ oldwhitehart.co.uk. This most convivial of pubs, with its wooden floors and beamed ceilings, occupies a handsome stone building and modern extension in the centre of Lyddington. It has fourteen bright and breezily decorated rooms and serves delicious food, both in the bar and in the restaurant; mains around £14. Mon–Sat noon–2pm & 6.30–9pm, Sun noon–2.30pm. **£100**

Northampton

Spreading north from the River Nene, **NORTHAMPTON** is a workaday town whose modern appearance largely belies its ancient past. Throughout the Middle Ages, this was one of central England's most important towns, a flourishing commercial hub whose now demolished castle was a popular stopping-off point for travelling royalty. A fire in 1675 burnt most of the medieval city to a cinder, and the Georgian town that grew up in its stead was itself swamped by the Industrial Revolution, when Northampton swarmed with **boot- and shoemakers**, whose products shod almost everyone in the British Empire. Errol Flynn kitted himself out with several pairs of Northampton shoes and boots when he was in repertory here in 1933, but he annoyed his suppliers no end by hightailing it out of town after a year, leaving a whopping debt behind him – justifying David Niven's cryptic comment, "You can count on Errol Flynn, he will always let you down".

Church of All Saints

George Row, NN1 1DF • Mon–Sat 10am–5pm • Free • ☎ 01604 632845, ⓦ allsaintsnorthampton.co.uk

Right in the centre of town, the **Church of All Saints** is Northampton's finest building, its unusually secular appearance stemming from its finely proportioned, pillared portico and towered cupola. A statue of a bewigged Charles II in Roman attire surmounts the portico, a (flattering) thank-you for his donation of a thousand tonnes of timber after the Great Fire of 1675 had incinerated the earlier church. Inside, the handsome interior holds a sweeping timber gallery and a quartet of Neoclassical pillars, which lead the eye up to the fancy plasterwork decorating the ceiling.

Northampton Museum and Art Gallery

4 Guildhall Rd, NN1 1DP • Closed till 2018/19 • ☎ 01604 838111, ⓦ northampton.gov.uk/museums

Closed for a thoroughgoing refit and expansion, the **Northampton Museum and Art Gallery** celebrates the town's industrial heritage with a wonderful collection of **shoes and boots**, from silk slippers, clogs and antique court shoes through to riding boots, Ottoman sandals and celebrity footwear.

Charles Rennie Mackintosh House

78 Derngate, NN1 1UH • Feb to mid-Dec Tues–Sun & bank hols 10am–5pm; last entry 4pm • £7.50 • ☎ 01604 603407, ⓦ 78derngate.org.uk

In 1916–17, the Scottish architect **Charles Rennie Mackintosh** (1868–1928), the most celebrated proponent of Art Nouveau in the UK, played a key role in the remodelling of this Northampton house on behalf of two, well-heeled newly-weds, Florence and Wenman Bassett-Lowke. Since the redesign, 78 Derngate – the **Charles Rennie Mackintosh House** – has had a chequered history, but in recent years it has been painstakingly restored and now shows to fine effect many of the man's stylistic hallmarks, most notably the strong, almost stern, right angles that are set against the flowing lines of floral-influenced decorative motifs. The adjacent buildings are now part of the site too, holding a café and exhibition space.

CLOCKWISE FROM TOP ROBIN HOOD STATUE OUTSIDE NOTTINGHAM CASTLE (P.478); CALKE ABBEY (P.491); GIBRALTAR POINT (P.503) >

By train Northampton train station is on the western edge of the city centre, a 10min walk from All Saints' church.

Destinations Birmingham (every 30min; 1hr); London Euston (every 30min; 1hr).

By bus North Gate bus station is on Bradshaw St, a short walk from All Saints, with regular Leicester services (every 30min; 1hr 20min).

Tourist office In the former county courthouse across from All Saints on George Row (Mon–Fri 8am–5.30pm, plus April–Sept Sat 10am–2pm; ☎01604 367997, ⓦnorthamptonshire.gov.uk).

EATING

Charles Rennie Mackintosh House Café 76 Derngate, NN1 1UH ☎01604 230166, ⓦ78derngate.org.uk. This pleasantly turned-out café offers a straightforward menu of home-cooked dinners – for example, fish and chips (£9) – and afternoon teas. Feb to mid-Dec Tues–Sun 10am–4.30pm.

Northamptonshire

Running northeast to southwest and sliced by the M1, **Northamptonshire** holds four medium-sized, semi-industrial towns – Kettering, Corby, Wellingborough and **Northampton** (see p.494) and a scattering of stone villages set amid rolling countryside. Of the villages, two standouts are the postcard-pretty hamlet of **Ashby St Ledgers**, and tiny **Fotheringhay**, where Mary, Queen of Scots came to her untimely end.

Ashby St Ledgers

The **Gunpowder Plot** (see box below) was hatched in **ASHBY ST LEDGERS**, immediately to the west of the M1, about fifteen miles northwest of Northampton. Since those heated conversations, nothing much seems to have happened here and the village's one and only street, flanked by handsome limestone cottages and a patch of ancient grazing land, still leads to the conspiratorial **manor house** (no access), a beautiful Elizabethan complex set around a wide courtyard. Also of interest is the village church, **St Mary and St Leodegarius** (no fixed opening times), which contains some wonderful, if faded, medieval murals: the clearest is the large painting in the nave of St Christopher carrying the infant Jesus.

Fotheringhay

Hard to believe today, but **FOTHERINGHAY**, a delightful hamlet nestling by the River Nene about thirty miles northeast of Northampton, was once an important centre of feudal power with both a weekly market and a castle. The castle was demolished long ago, but the magnificent **Church of St Mary and All Saints**, rising mirage-like above the green riverine meadows, recalls Fotheringhay's medieval heyday.

THE GUNPOWDER PLOT

Many of England's Catholics were delighted when the Protestant **Queen Elizabeth I** died in 1603, but when her successor, **James I** (1603–25), proved even less sympathetic to their cause, a small group, under the leadership of a certain **Robert Catesby**, began to plot against the king. The conspirators met here at Ashby St Ledgers, where they hatched the simplest of plans: first they rented a cellar under Parliament and then they filled it with barrels of gunpowder – enough to blow Parliament sky high. The preparations were in the hands of **Guy Fawkes**, an ardent Catholic and experienced soldier, but the authorities discovered this so-called **Gunpowder Plot** on the eve of the attack, November 4, 1605, and the conspirators were soon rounded up and dispatched. It's quite possible that James's men knew of the plot long before November and allowed it to develop for political (anti-Catholic) reasons. Fawkes himself was tortured, tried and executed and he is still burnt in effigy across the UK on **Bonfire Night** (Nov 5).

Fotheringhay Castle ruins

Signposted down a short and bumpy lane on the bend of the road as you come into the village from Oundle • Daily 24hr • Free

Precious little remains of **Fotheringhay Castle**, but the fortress witnessed two key events – the birth of Richard III in 1452 and the beheading of Mary, Queen of Scots, in 1587. On the orders of Elizabeth I, Mary – who had been imprisoned for nearly twenty years – was beheaded in the castle's Great Hall with no one to stand in her support, apart, that is, from her dog, which is said to have rushed from beneath her skirts as her head hit the deck. Thereafter, the castle fell into disrepair and nowadays only a grassy mound, the outline of earthen ramparts and a marshy ditch remain to mark where it once stood.

Church of St Mary and All Saints

Fotheringhay, PE8 5HZ • Daily 9am–5pm (4pm in winter) • Free • ⓦ friends-of-fotheringhay-church.co.uk

Begun in 1411 and 150 years in the making, Fotheringay's **Church of St Mary and All Saints** is a paradigm of the Perpendicular, its exterior sporting wonderful arching buttresses, its nave lit by soaring windows and the whole caboodle topped by a splendid octagonal lantern tower. The interior is a tad bare, but there are two fancily carved medieval pieces to inspect – a painted pulpit and a sturdy stone font – and two cumbersome memorials to the Dukes of York.

EATING AND DRINKING

FOTHERINGHAY

The Falcon PE8 5HZ ☎ 01832 226254, ⓦ thefalcon-inn .co.uk. This excellent pub/restaurant, which occupies a neat stone building with a modern patio, offers an imaginative menu – lamb shank and artichoke for example – with delicious main courses costing around £15. Daily noon–11pm; kitchen Mon–Sat noon–2pm & 6–9pm, Sun noon–3pm.

Lincoln

Reaching high into the sky from the top of a steep hill, the triple towers of **LINCOLN**'s magnificent **cathedral** are visible for miles across the surrounding flatlands. The cathedral, along with the neighbouring **castle**, are the city's main tourist draws – although, for a smallish place, Lincoln also packs in several good places to eat and one outstanding hotel. The key sights are best seen over a leisurely weekend, not least in December during Lincoln's lively open-air **Christmas market**, and there's also a brand-new attraction on the southeast edge of town, **The International Bomber Command Centre** (ⓦ internationalbcc .co.uk), which celebrates the Allied airmen of World War II.

Brief history

High ground is in short supply in Lincolnshire, so it's no surprise that the steep hill which is today surmounted by Lincoln Cathedral was fortified early, firstly by the **Celts**, who called their settlement Lindon, "hillfort by the lake", a reference to the pools formed by the River Witham in the marshy ground below. In 47 AD the **Romans** occupied Lindon and built a fortified town, which subsequently became **Lindum Colonia**, one of the four regional capitals of Roman Britain. During the reign of William the Conqueror the construction of the **castle** and **cathedral** initiated Lincoln's medieval heyday – the town boomed, first as a Norman power base and then as a centre of the wool trade with Flanders, until 1369 when the wool market was transferred to neighbouring Boston. It was almost five hundred years before Lincoln revived, its recovery based upon the manufacture of agricultural machinery and drainage equipment for the neighbouring fenlands. As the nineteenth-century town spread south down the hill and out along the old Roman road – the Fosse Way – so Lincoln became a place of precise class distinctions: the **Uphill** area, spreading north from the cathedral, became synonymous with middle-class respectability, **Downhill** with the proletariat, a distinction which finally disappeared with the development of **Lincoln University**, whose campus abuts the old city harbour, **Brayford Pool**.

9

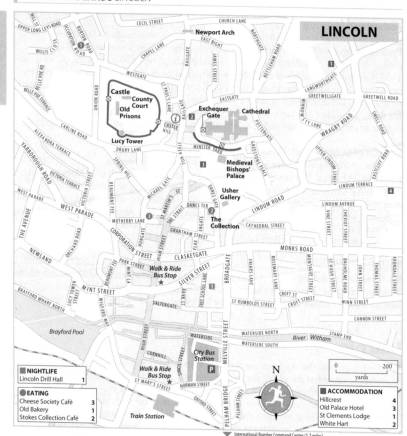

Lincoln Cathedral

Minster Yard • July & Aug Mon–Fri 7.15am–8pm, Sat & Sun 7.15am–6pm; Sept–June Mon–Sat 7.15am–6pm, Sun 7.15am–5pm •
Access restricted during services • £8 (includes tour; see box below), free Sun • ☎ 01522 561600, ⓦ lincolncathedral.com

Lincoln Cathedral is best approached from the west, through the fancy stone arches of
the medieval **Exchequergate**, beyond which soars the glorious main facade, a veritable
cliff face of blind arcading mobbed by decorative carving. The west front's apparent
homogeneity is, however, deceptive, and further inspection reveals two phases of
construction – the small stones and thick mortar of much of the facade belong to the
original church, completed in 1092, whereas the longer stones and finer courses date
from the early thirteenth century. These were enforced works: in 1185, an earthquake
shattered much of the Norman church, which was then rebuilt under the auspices of

---

GUIDED TOURS OF LINCOLN CATHEDRAL

The cathedral offers three types of **guided tour**. The first, the **Floor Tour** (Mon–Sat 2–3 daily;
30min; free with the price of admission), is a quick trot around the cathedral's defining features;
the second, the **Roof Tour** (Mon–Sat 1–2 daily; 1hr 30min; £4), takes in parts of the church
otherwise out of bounds, as does the third, the **Tower Tour** (March–Nov Sat 3 daily; 1hr
30min; £4). Advance reservations are advised for the Tower and Roof tours.

THE LINCOLN IMP

The **Lincoln imp**, carved high on a column in Lincoln Cathedral, had long been a source of legend, but it was the entrepreneurial James Ward Usher who turned the wee beastie into a tidy profit in the 1880s, selling Lincoln imp tie-pins, cuff-links, spoons, brooches and beads. Usher also popularized the traditional legend of the imp, a tall tale in which a couple of imps are blown to Lincoln by a playful wind. They then proceed to hop around the cathedral, until one of them is turned to stone for trying to talk to the angels carved into the roof of the Angel Choir. His chum makes a hasty exit on the back of a witch, but the wind is still supposed to haunt the cathedral, awaiting its opportunity to be mischievous again.

Bishop Hugh of Avalon, the man responsible for most of the present cathedral, with the notable exception of the (largely) fourteenth-century central tower.

The mighty **interior** is a fine example of Early English architecture, with the nave's pillars conforming to the same general design yet differing slightly, their varied columns and bands of dark Purbeck marble contrasting with the oolitic limestone that is the building's main material. Looking back up the nave from beneath the **central tower**, you can also observe a major medieval cock-up: Bishop Hugh's roof is out of alignment with the earlier west front, and the point where they meet has all the wrong angles. It's possible to pick out other irregularities, too – the pillars have bases of different heights, and there are ten windows in the nave's north wall and nine in the south – but these are deliberate features, reflecting a medieval aversion to the vanity of symmetry.

Beyond the nave lies **St Hugh's Choir**, more jumbled architecturally but with some exquisite medieval misericords, and beyond that is the open and airy **Angel Choir**, completed in 1280 and famous for the tiny, finely carved **Lincoln imp** (see box above), which embellishes one of its columns; helpfully, there's a light trained on it, but it costs 20p to switch it on. Finally, a corridor off the choir's north aisle leads to the wooden-roofed **cloisters** and the splendid, polygonal **chapter house**, where Edward I and Edward II convened gatherings that prefigured the creation of the English Parliament.

Medieval Bishops' Palace

Minster Yard, LN2 1PU • April–Oct & bank hols Wed–Sun 10am–5/6pm; Nov–March Sat & Sun 10am–4pm; last entry 30min before closing • £5.50; EH • ☎ 01522 527468, ⓦ www.english-heritage.org.uk/visit/places/Lincoln-medieval-bishops-palace

Hidden behind a gated wall immediately to the south of the cathedral are the ruins of what would, in its day, have been the city's most impressive building. This, the **Medieval Bishop's Palace**, once consisted of two grand halls, a lavish chapel, kitchens and ritzy private chambers, but today the most coherent survivor is the battered and bruised **Alnwick Tower** – where the entrance is. The damage was done during the Civil War when a troop of Roundheads occupied the palace until they themselves had to evacuate after a fierce fire. Nonetheless, the ruins are suitably fetching, with wide views over the surrounding flatlands.

Lincoln Castle

Castle Hill, LN1 3AA • Daily: April–Sept 10am–5pm; Oct–March 10am–4pm • £13.80; prison & Magna Carta only £11.50; wall walkway only £6 • ☎ 01522 554559, ⓦ lincolncastle.com

Intact and forbidding, the gateway, walls and towers of **Lincoln Castle** incorporate bits and pieces from the twelfth to the nineteenth centuries with the **wall walkway** offering great views over town. The wall encloses a large central courtyard dotted around which are law courts, a heritage skills centre and two former **Victorian prisons**. The debtors' prison serves as the entrance to a newly constructed **vault**, which was built to display several rare documents, most memorably one of the four surviving copies of the **Magna Carta**.

Behind the vault is the old felons' prison, where you can wander several floors of cells and visit a truly remarkable **prison chapel**. Here, the prisoners were locked in high-sided

9

cubicles designed so that they could see the pulpit but not each other. This approach was not only applied to the chapel: prisoners were kept in perpetual **solitary confinement**, even compelled to wear masks in the exercise yard. This so-called Pentonville System of "Separation and Silence", introduced here in 1846, was based on the pseudo-scientific theory that crime is a contagious disease, but unfortunately for the theorists it drove so many prisoners crazy that it had to be abandoned thirty years later; nobody ever bothered to dismantle the chapel.

Castle Hill and around

Not a hill at all, **Castle Hill** is in fact a wide, short and level cobbled street that links Lincoln's castle and cathedral. It's a charming spot and from here it's a brief stroll to the **Newport Arch**, a much-weathered chunk of Roman wall dating to the second century AD and once the main north gate into Lincoln. In the opposite direction, **Steep Hill** and then **The Strait** cut an antique route down to the centre and are flanked by sweet little shops and a handful of well-preserved medieval stone houses.

The Collection

Danes Terrace, LN2 1LP • Daily 10am–4pm • Free • ☎ 01522 782040, ⊛ thecollectionmuseum.com

Occupying two contrasting buildings – a striking modern structure and a really rather grand 1920s edifice close by – **The Collection** is Lincoln's main museum. Pride of place in the more modern building is the city's extensive collection of archeological artefacts, from prehistoric times onwards, while the older building, aka the **Usher Gallery**, features a regularly rotated selection of fine and applied art, including English landscape paintings, sculptures, porcelain, watches and clocks.

ARRIVAL AND INFORMATION

LINCOLN

By train Lincoln train station is on St Mary's Street, on the south side of the centre.

Destinations Leicester (hourly; 2hr); Newark (1–2 hourly; 30min); Nottingham (hourly; 1hr); Stamford (hourly; 2hr–2hr 30min, min of one change).

By bus The brand-new bus station is next door to the train station.

Tourist office 9 Castle Hill, between the cathedral and the castle (April–Sept Mon–Sat 10am–5pm, Sun 10.30am–4pm; Oct–March daily 11am–3pm; ☎01522 545458, ⊛ visitlincoln.com).

GETTING AROUND

By Walk & Ride From both the train and bus stations, it's a steep, 20min walk up to the cathedral, or you can take the Walk & Ride minibus (Mon–Sat 9am–2pm & 4–5pm, every 20min; single £1.50), which loops through the city centre. Another handy Walk & Ride stop is on Silver St, just off High St.

ACCOMMODATION

Hillcrest 15 Lindum Terrace, LN2 5RT ☎01522 510182, ⊛ hillcresthotel-lincoln.co.uk; map p.498. Traditional, very English hotel in a large red-brick house that was originally a Victorian rectory. Sixteen comfortable rooms with all mod cons plus a large, sloping garden. About 10min walk from the cathedral. **£100**

★Old Palace Hotel Minster Yard, LN2 1PU ☎01522 580000, ⊛ theoldpalace.org; map p.498. Easily the best place to stay in Lincoln, this excellent hotel occupies a rambling, largely nineteenth-century mansion – once a bishops' palace – within earshot of the cathedral. The hotel has 32 rooms, half in the main building, including a tower suite, and the remainder in an immaculately reconfigured 1920s chapel. The hotel's grand drawing room is in the former library and most of the furniture has been made by local carpenters. Smashing views, too. **£90**

St Clements Lodge 21 Langworthgate, LN2 4AD ☎01522 521532, ⊛ stclementslodge.co.uk; map p.498. In a smart, modern house a short walk from the cathedral, this comfortable B&B has three cosy, en-suite rooms. Home-made breakfasts – try the haddock or the kippers. **£85**

White Hart Bailgate, LN1 3AR ☎01522 526222, ⊛ whitehart-lincoln.co.uk; map p.498. Antique former coaching inn, whose public rooms have received a fairly humdrum revamp. The bedrooms are in a more traditional, country-house style and the pick overlook the cathedral. Curiously, it was here in an upstairs room during World War I that a local engineering firm set about designing a motorized gun at the behest of the government. To camouflage their intentions, the new behemoths were called water carriers – hence "tanks" – and the name stuck. **£100**

EATING

★**Cheese Society Café** 1 St Martin's Lane, LN2 1HY ☎01522 511003, ⓦthecheesesociety.co.uk; map p.498. This bright and breezy little café is something of a gastronomic landmark hereabouts, its menu featuring all things cheesy, from rarebits and raclettes – all with salads – through to an especially delicious stilton, red wine and walnut pâté. There are non-cheesy options, too, plus a good range of beers and ciders. Mains at £9. Mon–Fri 10am–4.30pm, Sat 10am–5pm.

★**Old Bakery** 26 Burton Rd, LN1 3LB ☎01522 576057, ⓦtheold-bakery.co.uk; map p.498. Cosy, rural-chic restaurant, where the menu is both well considered and inventive – try, for example, the grilled polenta and cherry tomatoes with Gorgonzola and green olive purée. Has an excellent wine cellar, too. Reservations recommended. Mains average £18. Tues & Wed 7–8.30pm, Thurs–Sat noon–1.30pm & 7–8.30pm, Sun noon–1.30pm.

Stokes Collection Café Danes Terrace, LN2 1LP ☎01522 523548, ⓦstokes-coffee.co.uk; map p.498. Attached to Lincoln's principal museum (see opposite), this cheerful modern café is a self-service affair where they do a tasty line in crêpes, sandwiches and salads. They also have a line-up of special musical events, mainly jazz and classical. The owners, the Stokes family, have been roasting coffee and blending tea in Lincoln for several generations. Daily 10am–4pm.

ENTERTAINMENT

Lincoln Drill Hall Free School Lane, LN2 1EY ☎01522 873891, ⓦlincolndrillhall.com; map p.498. Lincoln's prime arts and entertainment venue, featuring everything from stand-up and theatre to classical concerts, rock and pop.

The Lincolnshire Wolds and the coast

Northeast of Lincoln, the **Lincolnshire Wolds** are a narrow band of chalky land whose rolling hills and gentle valleys are particularly appealing in the vicinity of **Louth**, a trim little place where conscientious objectors were sent to dig potatoes during World War II. South of Louth, the Wolds dip down to both **Woodhall Spa**, a one-time Victorian spa that served as the HQ of the Dambusters as they prepared for their celebrated Ruhr raid in 1943, and the imposing remains of **Tattershall Castle** nearby. East of the Wolds lies the **coast**, with its bungalows, campsites and caravans parked behind a sandy **beach** that extends, with a few marshy interruptions, north from **Skegness**, the main resort, to Mablethorpe and ultimately Cleethorpes. At its worst, the coast's amusement-arcade commercialism can be hard to warm to, but small portions have been preserved and protected, most notably at the **Gibraltar Point Natural Nature Reserve**, just south of Skegness.

Louth

Henry VIII didn't much care for Lincolnshire, describing it as "one of the most brutal and beestlie counties of the whole realm", his contempt based on the events of 1536, when thousands of northern peasants rebelled against his religious reforms. The insurrection – the Lincolnshire Rising, which led on to the **Pilgrimage of Grace** in Yorkshire – began at **LOUTH**, about 25 miles from Lincoln, now a pleasant country town with narrow streets and old brick terraces surrounded by woods and farmland.

Church of St James

Westgate, LN11 9YD • Easter–Christmas Mon–Sat 10.30am–4pm; Christmas–Easter no fixed hours • Free • ☎01507 610247, ⓦstjameschurchlouth.com

Louth's one outstanding building is the **Church of St James**, a handsome medieval structure topped with a mighty Perpendicular spire, set on a grassy knoll on the west side of the centre. The interior is delightful too, illuminated by slender windows and capped by a handsome Georgian timber roof decorated with dinky little angels.

9

By bus Louth bus station is on the east side of – and a 5min walk from – the centre.

Destinations Lincoln (Mon–Sat 6 daily; 1hr); Skegness (hourly; 2hr).

EATING

The Coffee Shop St James's Church, Westgate, LN11 9YD ☎ 01507 603118. This volunteer-run café has just a few tables and chairs inside the church, but the home-made cakes are simply delicious – locals set out early to get a slice of the lemon drizzle. Easter–Christmas Mon–Sat 10.30am–4pm.

Woodhall Spa and around

Set in a generous chunk of woodland, **WOODHALL SPA**, some nineteen miles from Lincoln, is one of the county's most engaging villages, its long main street – **The Broadway** – flanked by Victorian and Edwardian houses and shops, reminders of the time when visitors gathered here to sample the local spring water, rich in iodine and bromine. Nowadays, the village maintains a genteel and relaxed air, and is kept afloat by its **golf course**, generally reckoned to be one of the best in England.

The Cottage Museum

Iddesleigh Road, off The Broadway, LN10 6SH • April–Oct daily 12.30am–4.30pm; sometimes opens earlier, see website for details • £3.50 • ☎ 01526 352456, ⓦ cottagemuseum.co.uk

Tiny and extraordinarily cute, the **Cottage Museum** outlines the evolution of Woodhall Spa from genteel Victorian spa to golfing retreat via World War II, when several thousand servicemen were billeted around here. During the war, the RAF requisitioned a local mansion, Petwood, and turned it into the Officers' Mess of 617 Squadron, the **Dambusters**, famous for their bombing raid of May 16, 1943. The raid was planned to deprive German industry of water and electricity by breaching several dams in the Ruhr valley, a mission made possible by Barnes Wallis's famous bouncing bomb; Petwood – and the old Officers' Bar – has survived and is now a hotel (see opposite).

Kinema in the Woods

Coronation Rd, LN10 6QD • Tickets £6.50 • ☎ 01526 352166, ⓦ thekinemainthewoods.co.uk

An unexpected delight, the **Kinema in the Woods** is flanked by forest, but is only five minutes' walk from The Broadway – just follow the signs. Opened in 1922, the Kinema is one of England's few remaining picture houses where the film is projected from behind the screen, and at weekends a 1930s organ rises in front of the screen to play you through the ice-cream break. It's all very delightful – and very nostalgic too.

Tattershall Castle

Sleaford Road, Tattershall, LN4 4LR • Mid-Feb to Oct daily 11am–5pm; early Nov Sat & Sun 11am–3pm • £6.40; NT • ☎ 01526 342543, ⓦ nationaltrust.org.uk/tattershall-castle

From Woodhall Spa, it's about four miles southeast to **Tattershall Castle**, a massive, moated, red-brick keep that towers above the surrounding flatlands. There's been a castle here since Norman times, but it was Ralph Cromwell, the Lord High Treasurer, who built the present quadrangled tower in the 1440s. A veteran of Agincourt, Cromwell was familiar with contemporary French architecture and it was to France that he looked for his basic design – in England, keeps had been out of fashion since the thirteenth century. Cromwell's quest for style explains Tattershall's contradictions: though the castle walls are sixteen feet thick, there are lots of lower-level windows and three doorways. In effect, it's a medieval keep as fashion accessory, a theatricality that continues with the grand chimneypieces inside the castle, though otherwise the interior is almost entirely bare.

ARRIVAL AND INFORMATION

By bus Most buses stop on The Broadway, with regular Lincoln services (Mon–Sat every 1–2hr; 50min).

Tourist office At the Cottage Museum (same times; ☏ 01526 352456).

ACCOMMODATION AND EATING

★**Petwood Hotel** Stixwould Rd, LN10 6QG ☏ 01526 352411, ⓦ petwood.co.uk. Set in immaculate gardens, Petwood's handsome half-timbered gables shelter a fine panelled interior and fifty large, well-appointed bedrooms decorated in unfussy, modern style. The all-English breakfasts are excellent and so are the dinners (mains from £16) featuring local, seasonal ingredients. Here also, in prime condition, is the old Officers' Bar of the Dambusters, complete with incidental memorabilia. Daily 6.30–9pm. **£120**

Skegness

SKEGNESS has been a busy resort ever since the railways reached the Lincolnshire coast in 1875. Its heyday was before the 1960s, when the Brits began to take themselves off to sunnier climes, but it still attracts tens of thousands of city-dwellers who come for the wide, sandy **beaches** and attractions ranging from nightclubs to bowling greens. Every inch the traditional English seaside town, Skegness outdoes its rivals by keeping its beaches sparklingly clean and its parks spick-and-span. That said, the seafront, with its rows of souvenir shops and amusement arcades, can be dismal, especially on a rainy day, and you may well decide to sidestep the whole thing by heading south along the coast to the **Gibraltar Point National Nature Reserve**.

Gibraltar Point National Nature Reserve

Gibraltar Rd, PE24 4SU, 3 miles south of Skegness • Reserve daily dawn–dusk; visitor centre daily 10am–3pm • Free • ☏ 01754 898057, ⓦ lincstrust.org.uk/gibraltar-point

At the **Gibraltar Point National Nature Reserve**, a network of clearly signed footpaths patterns a narrow strip of salt- and freshwater marsh, sand dune and beach that attracts an inordinate number of birds, both resident and migratory. There are numerous hides dotted around and a brand-new **visitor centre** has been built to replace an earlier version, which was badly damaged by floods.

ARRIVAL AND INFORMATION

By bus & train Skegness's bus and train stations are adjacent, about 10min walk from the seashore – cut across Lumley Square and head straight up the main street to the landmark clocktower.
Destinations (bus) Lincoln (2–4 daily; 2hr).

Destinations (train) Boston (hourly; 30min); Nottingham (hourly; 2hr).
Tourist office Inside the Embassy Theatre, close to the clocktower on Grand Parade (core hours: daily 9.30am–4pm; ☏ 01507 613100, ⓦ visitlincolnshire.com).

ACCOMMODATION

Best Western Vine Hotel Vine Rd, Seacroft, PE25 3DB ☏ 01754 610611, ⓦ vinehotelskegness.com. Skegness has scores of bargain-basement hotels, B&Bs and guesthouses, but this pleasant hotel is a cut above its rivals. It occupies a rambling old house, partly clad in ivy, but the decor is firmly modern. Located on a quiet residential street about three-quarters of a mile from the clocktower, on the road to Gibraltar Point. **£80**

The Lincolnshire Fens

The Fens, that great chunk of eastern England extending from Boston in Lincolnshire right down to Cambridge, encompass some of the most productive farmland in Europe. Give or take the occasional hillock, this pancake-flat, treeless terrain has been painstakingly reclaimed, from the marshes and swamps which once drained into the intrusive stump of **The Wash**, an indentation of the North Sea, a process that has taken almost two thousand years. In earlier times, outsiders were often amazed by the dreadful conditions hereabouts,

9

but they did spawn the distinctive culture of the so-called **fen-slodgers**, who embanked small portions of marsh to create pastureland and fields, supplementing their diets by catching fish and fowl and gathering reed and sedge for thatching and fuel. This local economy was threatened by the large-scale land reclamation schemes of the late fifteenth and sixteenth centuries, and time and again the locals sabotaged progress by breaking down new banks and dams. But the odds were stacked against the saboteurs, and a succession of great landowners eventually drained huge tracts of the fenland – and by the 1790s the fen-slodgers' way of life had all but disappeared.

Nonetheless, the **Lincolnshire Fens** remain a distinctive area, with a scattering of introverted little villages spread across the flatlands within easy striking distance of the A17. Several of these villages are distinguished by their imposing **medieval churches** – St Mary Magdalene's in **Gedney** and St Mary's in **Long Sutton** for example – and their soaring spires are seen to best advantage in the pale, watery sunlight and wide skies of the fenland evening. But it's above the rough-edged old port of **Boston**, Lincolnshire's second-largest settlement, that you'll find the most impressive church of all, mighty St Botolph's.

Boston

As it approaches The Wash, the muddy River Witham weaves its way through **BOSTON**, which is named after St Botwulf, the Anglo-Saxon monk-saint who first established a monastery here in 645 AD. In the fourteenth century, Boston became England's second-largest seaport, its flourishing economy dependent on the wool trade with Flanders. Revelling in their success, local merchants built a church here that witnessed their wealth – the magnificent **St Botolph's** – but by then Boston was in decline. The town's fortunes only revived in the late eighteenth century when, after the nearby fens had been drained, it became a minor agricultural centre. A singular mix of fenland town and seaport, Boston is an unusual little place that is at its liveliest on **market days** – Wednesday and Saturday – when you'll hear lots of Polish voices: in recent years, Eastern Europeans have come here in their hundreds to work in food processing and agriculture.

St Botolph's Church

Church St, PE21 6NW • **Church** Mon–Sat 8.30am–4pm, Sun 7.30am–4pm • Free • **Tower** Mon–Sat 10am–3.30pm & Sun 1–3.30pm • £5 • ☎ 01205 354670, ⓦ parish-of-boston.org.uk

The massive bulk of **St Botolph's** looms over the River Witham, its exterior embellished by the high-pointed windows and elaborate tracery of the Decorated style. Most of the church dates from the fourteenth century, but the huge and distinctive tower – whose lack of a spire earned the church the nickname the "**Boston Stump**" – is of later construction, and the octagonal lantern is later still. Down below, St Botolph's light and airy **nave** is an exercise in the Perpendicular, all soaring columns and high windows, a purity of design that is simply stunning. Look out also for the **misericords** in the chancel (a 50p leaflet gives the lowdown on all sixty), which sport a charming mixture of vernacular scenes, from organ-playing bears and a pair of medieval jesters squeezing cats in imitation of bagpipes through to a schoolmaster birching a boy, watched by three more awaiting the same fate – or perhaps they are just watching and laughing. A separate chapel commemorates the church's most famous vicar, **John Cotton** (1584–1652), who helped stir the Puritan stew during his tenure, encouraging a stream of Lincolnshire dissidents to head off to the colonies of New England to found their "New Jerusalem"; Cotton emigrated himself in 1633. From beside the nave, a narrow and tortuous 365-step spiral staircase leads up the **tower** to a balcony, from where there are panoramic views over Boston and the fens.

The Guildhall

South St, PE21 6HT • Wed–Sat 10.30am–3.30pm • Free • ☎ 01205 365954, ⓦ www.bostonguildhall.co.uk

A creaky affair, the **Guildhall** incorporates a series of period rooms, including an antique Council Chamber, several old prison cells and the court room where, in 1607, several of the Pilgrim Fathers were (probably) tried and sentenced: they got thirty days for their failed attempt to escape religious persecution by slipping across to Holland. They may have been imprisoned here too, but no one is really sure. The Guildhall also exhibits a fascinating hotchpotch of historical artefacts, notably a copy of the Book of Martyrs, an inflammatory anti-Catholic text written by Boston's own John Foxe (1517–87).

ARRIVAL AND INFORMATION   BOSTON

By train It's a 15min walk east from Boston train station to the town centre: head along Station Approach, and at the end turn left onto Queen St, then take another left for West St. Keep going until Bridge St; turn left onto it and cross the river for the central Market Place.
Destinations Grantham (hourly; 1hr); Lincoln (hourly; 1hr 10min with 1 change); Skegness (hourly; 40min).

By bus The bus station is also to the west of the River Witham, just north of West St on St George's Rd – and a 5min walk away from Market Place.
Destinations Lincoln (every 1–2hr; 1hr 45min).
Tourist office In the Guildhall, on South Street (Wed–Sat 10.30am–3.30pm; ☎ 01205 365954, ⓦ boston.gov.uk).

Church of St Mary Magdalene, Gedney

Church End, PE12 0BU, 17 miles from Boston via the A17 • Daily dawn–dusk • Free

The scattered hamlet of **GEDNEY** is home to the remarkable **Church of St Mary Magdalene**. Seen from a distance the church seems almost magical, or at least mystical, its imposing lines in striking contrast with its fen-flat surroundings. Up close, the triple-aisled nave is beautiful, its Norman arcade splendid, and a battery of windows lights the exquisite Renaissance alabaster effigies of husband and wife Adlard and Cassandra Welby, facing each other on the south wall near the chancel. Curiously, their tomb is decorated with a corn-on-the-cob motif – one of the earliest representations of this American import to be found in England.

Long Sutton

A modest farming centre, **LONG SUTTON**, a couple of miles from Gedney, limps along its main street until it reaches its trim Market Place. Here, the **church of St Mary** (daily dawn–dusk; free) has preserved many of its Norman features, with its arcaded tower supporting the oldest lead spire in the country, dating from around 1200. Long Sutton once lay on the edge of the five-mile-wide mouth of the **River Nene**, where it emptied into The Wash. This was the most treacherous part of the road from Lincoln to Norfolk, and for centuries locals had to guide travellers across the mud flats and marshes on horseback. In 1831, the River Nene was embanked and then spanned with a wooden bridge at **Sutton Bridge**, a hamlet just two miles east of Long Sutton. The present swing bridge, with its nifty central tower, was completed in 1894.

Stamford and around

Tucked away in the southwest corner of Lincolnshire, **STAMFORD**, 35 miles from Boston, is delightful, a handsome little limestone town of yellow-grey seventeenth- and eighteenth-century buildings, which slope up from the River Welland. The town's salad days were as a centre of the medieval wool and cloth trade, when wealthy merchants built its medley of stone churches and houses. Stamford was also the home of William Cecil, Elizabeth I's sagacious chief minister, who built his splendid mansion, **Burghley House**, close by.

The town survived the collapse of the wool trade, prospering as an inland port after the Welland was made navigable to the sea in 1570, and, in the eighteenth century, as a staging point on the Great North Road from London. More recently, Stamford escaped the three main threats to old English towns – the Industrial Revolution, wartime

9

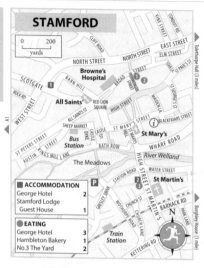

bombing and postwar development – and was designated the country's first Conservation Area in 1967. Thanks to this, its unspoilt streets readily lend themselves to period drama and filmmaking, and although it's the harmony of Stamford's architecture that pleases rather than any specific sight, there are still a handful of buildings of some special interest as well as an especially charming **High Street**.

Church of All Saints

All Saints' Place, PE9 2AG • Mon–Sat 9am–5pm, Sun 9am–7pm • Free • W stamfordallsaints.org.uk

A convenient place to start an exploration of Stamford, the **Church of All Saints** stands at the western end of the town centre, its beautiful facade a happy amalgamation of Early English and Perpendicular. Entry is via the south porch, an ornate structure with a fine – if badly weathered – crocketted gable. Beyond, though much of the interior is routinely Victorian, the nave's carved capitals are of great delicacy. Look out also for an engaging folkloric carving of the Last Supper behind the high altar that dates to the 1870s.

Browne's Hospital

Broad St, PE9 1PF • **Guided tours** Late May to Sept by arrangement; advance booking required • £3.50/person, but minimum £30/tour • **Open days** Two per year, spring & autumn, 11am–4pm • Free • ☎ 01780 763153, W stamfordcivicsociety.org.uk

A stone's throw from All Saints, wide and good-looking Broad Street is home to **Browne's Hospital**, the most extensive of the town's surviving almshouses, a substantial complex dating from the late fifteenth century. The cottages and the green towards the rear are rarely open to the public, but the old **dormitory** at the front, with its splendid wood-panelled ceiling, is usually included on the guided tour as is the adjacent **chapel**, which holds some fine stained-glass windows and appealingly folksy misericords.

Church of St Mary

St Mary's St, PE9 2DS • No regular opening hours • Free • W stamfordbenefice.com

A brief stroll from Broad Street, sitting pretty just above the main bridge over the River Welland, the **Church of St Mary** boasts a splendid spire, which rises high above its cramped surroundings. The interior is small but airy and incorporates an imposing reredos, a batch of Victorian stained glass and the **Corpus Christi** (or north) chapel, whose intricately embossed, painted and panelled ceiling dates back to the 1480s.

Church of St Martin

23 High St St Martin's, PE9 2NT • Daily 9.30am–4pm • Free • ☎ 01780 753356, W achurchnearyou.com/stamford-baron-st-martin

The sombre, late fifteenth-century **Church of St Martin** shelters the magnificent tombs of the lords Burghley, beginning with a recumbent William Cecil (1520–98) carved beneath twin canopies, holding his rod of office and with a lion at his feet. Immediately behind are the early eighteenth-century effigies of John Cecil, the fifth Lord Burghley (1648–1700), and his wife, with the couple depicted as Roman aristocrats, propped up on their elbows, John to stare across the nave commandingly, Anne to gaze at him.

Burghley House

9

Barnack Rd, PE9 3JY · **House & gardens** Mid-March to Oct Mon–Thurs, Sat & Sun 11am–5pm · £18, £16 in advance · **Park** Daily 8am–6pm (dusk if sooner) · Free · ☎ 01780 752451, ⊛ burghley.co.uk · The main entrance is signposted 1.5miles southeast of Stamford

Now famous for the prestigious Burghley Horse Trials (⊛ burghley-horse.co.uk), held over four days in late August and/or early September, Stamford's **Burghley House** is an extravagant Elizabethan mansion standing in parkland landscaped by Capability Brown. Completed in 1587 after 22 years in the making, the house sports a mellow-yellow ragstone exterior, embellished by dainty cupolas, a pyramidal clocktower and skeletal balustrading, all to a plan by **William Cecil**, the long-time adviser to Elizabeth I. However, with the notable exception of the Tudor kitchen, little remains of Burghley's Elizabethan interior and, instead, the house bears the heavy hand of John Cecil, who toured France and Italy in the late seventeenth century, buying paintings and commissioning furniture, statuary and tapestries. To provide a suitable setting for his old masters, John brought in Antonio Verrio and his assistant Louis Laguerre, who between them covered many of Burghley's walls and ceilings with frolicking gods and goddesses. These gaudy and gargantuan murals are at their most engulfing in the **Heaven Room**, an artfully painted classical temple that adjoins the **Hell Staircase**, where the entrance to the inferno is through the gaping mouth of a cat.

ARRIVAL AND INFORMATION

STAMFORD AND AROUND

By train Stamford's pretty station is on the south side of the River Welland, a 5–10min walk from the centre.
Destinations Cambridge (hourly; 1hr 10min); Leicester (hourly; 40min); Oakham (hourly; 15min).

By bus The bus station is on Sheepmarket, off All Saints' St.
Tourist office In the Stamford Arts Centre, 27 St Mary's Street (Mon–Sat 9.30am–5pm; ☎ 01780 755611, ⊛ southwestlincs.com).

ACCOMMODATION

★**George Hotel** 71 High St St Martin's, PE9 2LB ☎ 01780 750750, ⊛ georgehotelofstamford.com; map p.506. Stamford's most celebrated hotel by a country mile, *The George* is a sympathetically renovated old coaching inn, which comes complete with flagstone floors and antique furnishings; the most appealing of the plush rooms overlook a cobbled courtyard. Its Georgian facade supports one end of the gallows that span the street – not a warning

to criminals, but a traditional advertising hoarding. There's a good restaurant, too (see below). <u>£200</u>
Stamford Lodge Guest House 66 Scotgate, PE9 2YB ☎ 01780 482932, ⊛ stamfordlodge.co.uk; map p.506. In an attractive, Georgian stone house on the north side of the town centre, this smartly turned-out establishment has five, en-suite guest rooms decorated in a warm and cosy version of period style. <u>£95</u>

EATING

George Hotel 71 High St St Martin's, PE9 2LB ☎ 01780 750750, ⊛ georgehotelofstamford.com; map p.506. *The George* has two excellent restaurants – one formal, the other, the *Garden Room*, much more informal. At the latter, a wide-ranging menu covers everything from hamburgers to lobster spaghetti, all prepared to a high standard; mains average £18. Finish off with a drink at the hotel's delightfully antiquated *York Bar*. Garden Room daily noon–10pm.
Hambleton Bakery 1 Ironmonger St, PE9 1PL ☎ 01780 754327, ⊛ hambletonbakery.co.uk; map p.506. A small

regional chain offering a first-rate range of breads – rye, sourdough and so forth – plus muffins and cakes. Takeaway only. Mon–Sat 8am–5pm.
No.3 The Yard 3 Ironmonger St, PE9 1PL ☎ 01780 756080, ⊛ no3theyard.co.uk; map p.506. Inside a creatively refurbished old building, at the back of a scrappy courtyard, this enjoyable spilt-level restaurant has an excellent Modern British menu – try, for example, the smoked haddock with pancetta. Mains hover around £16. Tues–Sat 11.30am–2pm & 6.30–9.30pm, Sun noon–3pm.

STAMFORD SHAKESPEARE COMPANY

One of the most enjoyable of Stamford's several festivals is the **Stamford Shakespeare Company**'s (☎ 01780 756133, ⊛ stamfordshakespeare.co.uk) open-air performances of the great man's works set in the grounds of **Tolethorpe Hall**, an Elizabethan mansion just outside Stamford. The season lasts from June to August, with the audience protected from the elements by a vast canopy.

The Northwest

SUNSET ACROSS MORECAMBE BAY

The Northwest

Ask most Brits about northwest England and they'll probably mention football and rain – stereotypes that don't come close to summarizing this exciting region of dynamic urban centres, pretty countryside, iconic seaside resorts and historic towns. One of the world's great industrial cities, Manchester has transformed its cityscape in recent decades to place itself firmly in the vanguard of modern British urban design, and complements its top-class visitor attractions with lively cafés and an exciting music scene. Just thirty miles west, revitalized Liverpool has kept apace of the "northern renaissance", too, and is a city of great energy and charm.

The southern suburbs of Manchester bump into the steep hills of the **Pennine range**, and to the southwest the city slides into pastoral **Cheshire**, a county of rolling green countryside whose dairy farms churn out the famed crumbly white cheese. The county town, **Chester**, with its complete circuit of Roman walls and partly Tudor centre, is as alluring as any of the country's northern towns, capturing the essence of one of England's wealthiest counties.

The historical county of **Lancashire** reached industrial prominence in the nineteenth century primarily due to the cotton-mill towns around Manchester and the thriving port of Liverpool – although neither city is part of the county today. Resorts along the coast between Southport and Morecambe once formed the mainstay of the northern British holiday, though only **Blackpool** is really worth visiting for its own sake, a rip-roaring resort which has stayed at the top of its game by supplying undemanding entertainment with more panache than its neighbours. However, **Morecambe**, with its Art Deco *Midland Hotel*, is easily combined with a visit to the historically important city of **Lancaster** and its hilltop Tudor castle. Finally, the Crown dependency of the **Isle of Man**, just 25 miles off the coast, provides a rugged terrain almost as rewarding as that of the Lake District, but without the seasonal overcrowding.

GETTING AROUND

THE NORTHWEST

By train Both Manchester and Liverpool are well served by trains, with regular high-speed connections to the Midlands and London, and up the west coast to Scotland. The major east–west rail lines in the region are the direct routes between Manchester, Leeds and York, and between Blackpool, Bradford, Leeds and York. The Lancaster–Leeds line slips through the Yorkshire Dales and further south, the Manchester–Sheffield line provides a rail approach to the Peak District.

By bus The major cities, as well as Chester, are connected by frequent bus services.

Manchester

MANCHESTER has had a global profile for more than 150 years, since the dawn of the industrial revolution. But today's elegant core of converted warehouses and glass skyscrapers is a far cry from the smoke-covered sprawl George Orwell once described as

WHITWORTH ART GALLERY, MANCHESTER

Highlights

❶ Manchester's Northern Quarter Lose yourself in chic shops, café-bars and happening music venues in this vibrant warehouse district. **See p.518**

❷ Whitworth Art Gallery, Manchester An ambitious £15m transformation has created a light-filled gallery space that blends seamlessly with the surrounding park. **See p.519**

❸ City walls, Chester The handsome old town of Chester is best surveyed from the heights of its Roman walls. **See p.527**

❹ Culture in Liverpool From the artistic hub of the Baltic Triangle to Antony Gormley's Crosby Beach statues, this dynamic city pulses with creative energy. **See p.530**

❺ Blackpool Pleasure Beach Bright, bawdy and brash, Britain's cheekiest resort is constantly reinventing itself. **See p.541**

❻ Lancaster Castle From the dungeons to the ornate courtrooms, the castle is a historical tour de force. **See p.543**

❼ Sunset across Morecambe Bay Drink in one of the country's finest sunsets at the bar in the Art Deco *Midland Hotel*. **See p.545**

❽ Sea-kayaking, the Calf of Man Taking to the water in a kayak allows you to view local seal colonies, seabirds, and the Isle of Man's stunning rugged coast from a unique perspective. **See p.550**

HIGHLIGHTS ARE MARKED ON THE MAP ON P.512

"the belly and guts of the nation". Its renewed pre-eminence expresses itself in various ways, most swaggeringly in its **football**, as home to the world's most famous and wealthiest clubs – Manchester United and Manchester City, respectively – but also in a thriving **music scene** that has given birth to world-beaters as diverse as the Hallé Orchestra and Oasis. Moreover, the city's celebrated concert halls, theatres, clubs and cafés feed off the cosmopolitan drive provided by the country's largest **student** population outside London and a high-profile **LGBT+** community.

HIGHLIGHTS

1. Manchester's Northern Quarter
2. Whitworth Art Gallery, Manchester
3. City walls, Chester
4. Culture in Liverpool
5. Blackpool Pleasure Beach
6. Lancaster Castle
7. Sunset across Morecambe Bay
8. Sea-kayaking, the Calf of Man

THE NORTHWEST

MANCHESTER ORIENTATION

If Manchester can be said to have a centre, it's **Albert Square** and the cluster of buildings surrounding it – the Town Hall, the Central Library and the *Midland Hotel*, originally built in the railway age to host visitors to Britain's greatest industrial city. South of here, the former Central Station now functions as the **Manchester Central** convention centre, with the Hallé Orchestra's home, **Bridgewater Hall**, just opposite. **Chinatown** and the **Gay Village** are just a short walk to the east, while to the northeast, the revamped **Piccadilly Gardens** provides access to the hip **Northern Quarter**. To the southwest is the **Castlefield** district, site of the **Museum of Science and Industry**, and flashy **Spinningfields**, incongruous home of the People's History Museum. The central spine of the city is **Deansgate**, which runs from Castlefield to the cathedral and, in its northern environs, displays the most dramatic core of urban regeneration in the country, centred on the unalloyed modernity of **Exchange Square**.

10

There are plenty of sights, too: the centre possesses the **Manchester Art Gallery**, the **National Football Museum** and the fantastic **People's History Museum** as well as the **Museum of Science and Industry**, while further south is **The Whitworth Art Gallery**, and, to the west, the revamped **Salford Quays**, which are home to the prestigious **Lowry arts centre**, complete with a handsome selection of L.S. Lowry paintings, the stirring and stunning **Imperial War Museum North**, and **MediaCityUK**, the new northern base of the BBC.

Brief history

Despite a **history** stretching back to Roman times, and pockets of surviving medieval and Georgian architecture, Manchester is first and foremost a **Victorian manufacturing city**. Its rapid growth set the pace for the flowering of the Industrial Revolution elsewhere – transforming itself in just a hundred years from little more than a village to the world's major cotton centre. The spectacular rise of **Cottonopolis**, as it became known, arose from the manufacture of vast quantities of competitively priced imitations of expensive Indian calicoes, using water and then steam-driven machines developed in the late eighteenth and nineteenth centuries.

Rapid industrialization brought immense wealth for a few but a life of misery for the majority. The discontent came to a head in 1819 when eleven people were killed at the **Peterloo Massacre**, in what began as a peaceful demonstration against the oppressive **Corn Laws**. Things were, however, even worse when the 23-year-old Friedrich Engels came here in 1842 to work in his father's cotton plant: the grinding poverty he recorded in his *Condition of the Working Class in England* was a seminal influence on his later collaboration with **Karl Marx** in the *Communist Manifesto*.

The **Manchester Ship Canal**, constructed in 1894 to entice ocean-going vessels into Manchester and away from burgeoning Liverpool, played a crucial part in sustaining Manchester's competitiveness. From the late 1950s, however, the docks, mills, warehouses and canals were in dangerous decline. The main engine of change turned out to be the devastating **IRA bomb**, which exploded outside the Arndale shopping centre in June 1996, wiping out a fair slice of the city's commercial infrastructure. Rather than simply patching things up, the city council embarked on an ambitious rebuilding scheme, which transformed the face of Manchester forever. In 2017, the resilience of the city was demonstrated once again as performers took to the stage for One Love, a benefit concert for those affected by the tragic suicide bombing at Manchester Arena on May 22, which killed 22 people.

Albert Square

Most of Manchester's panoply of **neo-Gothic** buildings and monuments date from the city's heyday in the second half of the nineteenth century. One of the more fanciful is

10

CENTRAL MANCHESTER

Metrolink Trams (T)

TRINITY WAY

A56 & M62

A664 Rochdale

Victoria Station

Stoller Hall

National Football Museum

Chetham's School of Music

Triangle (Corn Exchange)

NORTHERN QUARTER

ANCOATS

Cathedral

Arndale Centre

Royal Exchange Theatre

St Ann's

People's History Museum

John Rylands Library

Piccadilly Gardens

SPINNINGFIELDS

CHINATOWN

Manchester Art Gallery

Piccadilly Gardens Bus Station

Opera House

Town Hall

Chorlton Street Coach Station

GAY VILLAGE

Piccadilly Station

Museum of Science & Industry

Central Library

Free Trade Hall

International Convention Centre

Great Northern

ST JOHN'S

Midland Hotel

PETERSFIELD

Manchester Central

Bridgewater Hall

CASTLEFIELD

Roman Fort

Beetham Tower

DEANSGATE LOCKS

The Hacienda

Rochdale Canal

Oxford Road Station

HOME

Salford Central Station

River Irwell

Deansgate Station

MANCUNIAN WAY

ACCOMMODATION

ABode	2
Arora	4
Great John Street	3
Hilton Chambers	1
Midland	7
Motel One	6
Radisson Blu Edwardian	5
YHA Manchester	8

Old Trafford (2.5 miles), A56 & Chester   Manchester Airport (9.5 miles), M63 & M56   The Dancehouse (100yd), Dimitri's (500yd), Eighth Day (700yd), Lime Tree (700yd), RNCM (700yd), Manchester Museum (0.6 miles), Rudy's Pizza (0.9 miles), Whitworth Art Gallery (1 mile), Yuzu (2 miles), Yang Sing (4 miles), Rusholme & Didsbury

0   200   yards

● EATING

Australasia	8	Richmond Tea Rooms	11
Dimitri's	12	Rudy's Pizza	4
Eighth Day	13	Sam's Chop House	6
Federal Café Bar	2	Takk	7
Home Sweet Home	3	Trof NQ	1
The Koffee Pot	5	Yang Sing	10
Lime Tree	15	Yuzu	9
Mughli Charcoal Pit	14		

■ DRINKING

Big Hands	15
Britons Protection	11
Circus Tavern	8
Cloud 23	9
Corbières	5
Mr Thomas' Chop House	6
Sand Bar	13
The Temple	10

■ NIGHTLIFE

Albert Hall	7
Band on the Wall	1
The Castle Hotel	3
The Deaf Institute	14
Matt & Phreds	2
O2 Apollo Manchester	16
O2 Ritz Manchester	12
Soup Kitchen	4

● SHOPPING

Afflecks	5
Craft & Design Centre	1
Oklahoma	3
Piccadilly Records	4
Retro Rehab	2

the shrine-like, canopied **monument** to Prince Albert, Queen Victoria's husband, perched prettily in the middle of the trim little square that bears his name – **Albert Square**. The monument was erected in 1867, six years after Albert's death, supposedly because the prince had always shown an interest in industry, but perhaps more to curry favour with the grieving queen. Overlooking the prince is Alfred Waterhouse's magnificent, neo-Gothic **Town Hall** (Mon–Fri 9am–5pm; free), whose mighty clocktower, completed in 1877, pokes a sturdy finger into the sky, soaring high above its gables, columns and arcaded windows.

St Peter's Square and around

Just south of the Town Hall is **St Peter's Square**, home to the revamped **Central Library**. Footsteps away, over on Peter Street, the **Free Trade Hall** was the home of the city's Hallé Orchestra for more than a century – until Bridgewater Hall was completed in 1996. The Italianate facade survived intense wartime bombing and is now a protected part of the *Radisson Blu Edwardian Hotel*, whose modern tower block rises up behind at a (fairly) discreet distance.

Central Library

St Peter's Square, M2 5PD • Mon–Thurs 9am–8pm, Fri & Sat 9am–5pm • Free • ☎ 0161 234 1983, ⓦ manchester.gov.uk/centrallibrary • St Peter's Square Metrolink

The circular **Central Library** was built in 1934 as the world's largest municipal library, a self-consciously elegant, classical construction. After a four-year closure, it reopened, beautifully refurbished and extended, in 2014, with its showpiece domed **reading room** restored; check out the display case of sweet wrappers, found stuffed down the desks here over the last eighty years. The **children's library** is modelled on *The Secret Garden* by local author Frances Hodgson Burnett.

10

Manchester Art Gallery

Mosley St, M2 3JL • Daily 10am–5pm, till 9pm Thurs • Free • ☎ 0161 235 8888, ⓦ manchesterartgallery.org • St Peter's Square Metrolink

Manchester Art Gallery, as well as attracting big-name exhibitions by contemporary artists, holds an invigorating collection of eighteenth- and nineteenth-century art. Spread across **Floor 1**, these works are divided by theme – Face and Place, Expressing Passions and so on – rather than by artist (or indeed school of artists), which makes it difficult to appreciate the strength of the collection, especially when it comes to its forte, the Pre-Raphaelites. There's much else – views of Victorian Manchester, a Turner or two, a pair of Gainsboroughs, and Stubbs's famous *Cheetah and Stag with Two Indians* to name but a few. **Floor 2** features temporary exhibitions and crafts, while the **Ground Floor**'s Manchester Gallery is devoted to a visual history of the city. The **Clore Art Studio** is fun for kids.

Petersfield

South of St Peter's Square, on **Lower Mosley Street**, stands Britain's finest concert hall, **Bridgewater Hall**, balanced on shock-absorbing springs to guarantee the clarity of the sound. The apartment block at the corner of Lower Mosley Street and Whitworth Street West bears the name of the site's previous occupant, the infamous **Hacienda Club**, the spiritual home of Factory Records, an independent label that defined a generation of music through such bands as Joy Division, New Order and the Happy Mondays before closing down in 1997. Across the road on Tony Wilson Place is Manchester's glitzy new cultural hub, **HOME** (see p.525), a merger between Manchester heavyweights Cornerhouse and the former Library Theatre Company. It comprises two theatres, five cinema screens, gallery space, and production and broadcast facilities; each of the three floors has a low-key bar or restaurant with additional outdoor seating for when the sun shines.

Turn left along Whitworth Street West and you'll spot the string of café-bars and restaurants that have been shoehorned along the Rochdale canal's **Deansgate Locks**, a pattern repeated along and across the street in the old railway arches abutting Deansgate Station. Look up and you'll see the striking **Beetham Tower**, easily the tallest skyscraper in Manchester and home to a glitzy hotel.

Castlefield and St John's

Just west of Deansgate Station, the tangle of railway viaducts and canals that lie sandwiched between Water Street, Liverpool Road and Deansgate make up pocket-sized **Castlefield**. It was here that the country's first man-made canal, the Bridgewater Canal, brought coal and other raw materials to the city's warehouses throughout the eighteenth century. By the early 1960s, the district was an eyesore, but an influx of money cleaned it up, and it now boasts cobbled canalside walks, attractive café-bars and the **Castlefield Urban Heritage Park** (always open; free), centred on the excavated and partially reconstructed *Mamucium* Roman fort, from which the name "Manchester" is derived.

Exciting changes are afoot west of Lower Byrom St around the old ITV Granada studios; newly labelled **St John's** (@stjohnsmanchester.com) is a neighbourhood to watch, particularly as **Factory**, an impressive arts space which will be a permanent home for the Manchester International Festival (see box, p.525), is slated to open in 2020.

Museum of Science and Industry

Liverpool Rd, M3 4FP · Daily 10am–5pm · Free, but admission charge for special exhibitions · ☎ 0161 832 2244, @ msimanchester.org.uk · Deansgate-Castlefield Metrolink

One of the most impressive museums of its type in the country, the **Museum of Science and Industry** mixes technological displays and blockbuster exhibitions with trenchant analysis of the social impact of industrialization. Key points of interest include the **Power Hall**, which trumpets the region's remarkable technological contribution to the Industrial Revolution by means of a hall full of steam engines, some of which are fired up daily. There's more steam in the shape of a working replica of Robert Stephenson's *Planet*, whose original design was based on the *Rocket*, the work of Robert's father George. Built in 1830, the *Planet* reliably attained a scorching 30mph but had no brakes; the museum's version does, however, and it's used at weekends (noon–4pm; £2, children £1), dropping passengers a couple of hundred yards away at the **Station Building**, the world's oldest passenger railway station.

The **1830 Warehouse** features a sound-and-light show that delves into the history of the city's immense warehouses, and the **Air and Space Hall**, which barely touches on Manchester at all, features vintage planes, cutaway engines and space exploration displays.

Spinningfields

From the old to the uber-new, Castlefield blends into **Spinningfields**, a glitzy, corporate district that's home to law courts, financial HQs, designer shops and a crop of see-and-be-seen bars and restaurants, including a swanky rooftop terrace bar as the cherry on the top of shiny corporate high-rise, No. 1 Spinningfields. There are also a couple of standout cultural attractions that bookend the district.

People's History Museum

Left Bank, M3 3ER · Daily 10am–5pm, until 8pm second Thursday of the month · Free · ☎ 0161 838 9190, @ phm.org.uk · Deansgate-Castlefield Metrolink

The superb **People's History Museum** explores Britain's rich history of radicalism and the struggles of marginalized people to acquire rights and extend suffrage – ideas that developed out of the workers' associations and religious movements of the industrial city and which helped to shape the modern world. Housed in a former pump house and an ultramodern, four-storey extension, the galleries use interactive displays – including coffins and top hats – to trace a compelling narrative from the Peterloo Massacre of 1819 onwards. As the gallery shows, this moment became the catalyst for agitation that led to the 1832 Reform Act, and subsequent rise of the egalitarian Chartist movement; the museum will play a big part in the 2019 two-hundred-year anniversary. The galleries go on to explore the struggle for female suffrage, the Communist party in Britain, Oswald Mosley's fascists, and the working-class origins of football and pop music, and include the finest collection of trade union banners in the country.

John Rylands Library

Deansgate, M3 3EH · **Library** Mon & Sun noon–5pm, Tues–Sat 10am–5pm · **Tour and treasures** Rare books can be seen close up every third Thurs of month 3–4pm (booking required) · Free · ☎ 0161 306 0555, @ www.library.manchester.ac.uk/rylands · Metroshuttle #1, #2

Nestling between Spinningfields and the north end of Deansgate, **John Rylands Library** is the city's supreme example of Victorian Gothic – notwithstanding the presence of an unbecoming modern entrance wing. The architect who won the original commission, Basil Champneys, opted for a cloistered neo-Gothicism of narrow stone corridors, delicately crafted stonework, stained-glass windows and burnished wooden panelling. The library, which has survived in superb condition, now houses specialist collections of rare books and manuscripts.

Deansgate and around

Deansgate cuts through the city centre from the Rochdale canal to the cathedral, its architectural reference points ranging from Victorian industrialism to post-millennium posturing. One landmark is the **Great Northern** mall, flanking Deansgate between Great Bridgewater and Peter streets. This was once the **Great Northern Railway Company's Goods Warehouse**, a great sweep of brickwork dating back to the 1890s, originally an integral part of a large and ambitious trading depot with road and rail links on street level and subterranean canals down below.

10

St Ann's Square

Slender **St Ann's Square** is tucked away off the eastern side of Deansgate, not all that far from the cathedral. Flanking the square's southern side is **St Ann's Church** (Tues–Sat 10am–5pm; free), a trim sandstone structure whose Neoclassical symmetries date from 1709, though the stained-glass windows are firmly Victorian. At the other end of the square is the **Royal Exchange**, which houses the much-lauded **Royal Exchange Theatre**. Formerly the Cotton Exchange, this building employed seven thousand people until trading finished on December 31, 1968 – the old trading board still shows the last day's prices for American and Egyptian cotton.

Manchester Cathedral and around

Exchange Station Approach, Victoria St, M3 1SX • Mon–Sat 8.30am–6.30pm, Sun 8.30am–7pm • Free • **Tours** Mon–Fri 11am & 2.30pm, Sat 1pm, Sun 2.30pm; 30min • Free, but £3 donation suggested • Ⓦ manchestercathedral.org • Victoria Metrolink

Manchester's **cathedral** dates back to the fifteenth century, though its Gothic lines have been hacked about too much to have any real architectural coherence. Actually, it's surprising it's still here at all: in 1940, a 1000lb bomb all but destroyed the interior, knocking out most of the stained glass, which is why it's so light inside today.

Exchange Square

A pedestrian high street – **New Cathedral Street** – runs north from St Ann's Square to **Exchange Square**, with its water features, public sculptures and massive department stores (primarily Selfridges and Harvey Nichols). On the southeast side of the square stands the whopping **Arndale Centre**, once a real Sixties eyesore, but now a modern shopping precinct, clad in glass.

Chetham's School of Music

Long Millgate, M3 1SB • Library Mon–Fri timed entry, 10am, 11am, noon, 1.30pm, 2.30pm & 3.30pm • Free • ☎ 0161 834 7961, Ⓦ chethamsschoolofmusic.com • Victoria Metrolink

The choristers in Manchester Cathedral are trained at **Chetham's School of Music**. This fifteenth-century manor house became a school and a free public library in 1653 and was turned into a music school in 1969. There are free recitals during term time, and you can visit the oak-panelled **Library** with its handsome carved eighteenth-century bookcases. Along the side corridor is the main **Reading Room**, where Marx and Engels beavered away on the square table that still stands in the windowed alcove. There's no public access to the rest of the complex, except to **Stoller Hall**, a 500-seat concert hall (see p.525) that had its grand opening in 2017.

10

National Football Museum

Urbis Building, Cathedral Gardens, M4 3BG • Mon–Sun 10am–5pm • Free except for special exhibitions • ☎ 0161 605 8200, ⓦ nationalfootballmuseum.com • Victoria Metrolink

Manchester's **National Football Museum**, housed in a suitably spectacular structure – the sloping, six-storey glass Urbis building near Victoria train station – houses some true treasures of the world's most popular game. Here you can see the 1966 World Cup Final ball, Maradona's "Hand of God" shirt, and the only surviving version of the Jules Rimet world cup trophy. They also display the personal collection of Sir Stanley Matthews (1915–2000), considered one of the greatest English footballers of all time.

Piccadilly

Piccadilly is another area earmarked by developers for regeneration. Exciting projects in the pipeline include a four-storey food-and-drink venue at **Mayfield Depot** (ⓦ mayfield manchester.co.uk) and renovation of the Grade I listed Fire Station on London Road. **Piccadilly Gardens** (Piccadilly Gardens Metrolink), historically the largest green space in the city, has also recently been spruced up; this family-friendly space has a fountain and water jets, and a pavilion at one end to screen off the traffic. Regular events, including a food **market** (Thurs–Sat 10am–5pm), keep the gardens lively.

The Northern Quarter and Ancoats

Oldham Street, which shoots off northeast from Piccadilly Gardens, is the shabby gateway to the hip **Northern Quarter**. Traditionally, this is Manchester's garment district and you'll still find old-fashioned shops and wholesalers selling clothes, shop fittings, mannequins and hosiery alongside the more recent designer shops, music stores and trendy café-bars. The side wall of iconic indie emporium Afflecks (see p.525) sports a colourful series of **mosaics** depicting Manchester legends – from stars of Coronation Street to the Stone Roses. As rents in the Northern Quarter rise, the arty types are spilling over into **Ancoats**, an area of conservation across busy Great Ancoats Street. It's here in the old red-brick factory buildings that you'll find the newest and most innovative new restaurants and bars popping up (see p.522).

Chinatown

From Piccadilly Gardens, it's a short walk south to **Chinatown**, whose grid of narrow streets stretch north–south from Charlotte to Princess Street between Portland and Mosley streets and are dotted with Chinese restaurants, supermarkets and bakeries. The inevitable **Dragon Arch**, at Faulkner and Nicolas, provides the focus for the annual Chinese New Year celebrations.

Along Oxford Road

A couple of blocks out of the Gay Village (see box opposite), you'll come to the junction of Whitworth Street and **Oxford Road**, the latter cutting a direct route south through a string of impressive Manchester University buildings towards The Whitworth Art Gallery.

Manchester Museum

Oxford Rd, M13 9PL • Daily 10am–5pm • Free • ☎ 0161 275 2648, ⓦ www.museum.manchester.ac.uk

The university's Gothic Revival **Manchester Museum** boasts a diverse collection spread over five floors, with displays on rocks, minerals and prehistoric life, meteorites, animal life, the human body and biomedical research. It also boasts one of the country's finest collections outside of the British Museum on **Ancient Egypt**. The **Vivarium** is dedicated to the conservation of reptiles and amphibians, with plenty of frogs, snakes and lizards

MANCHESTER'S GAY VILLAGE AND PRIDE

The side roads off Portland Street lead down to the Rochdale canal, where **Canal Street** forms the heart of Manchester's thriving **Gay Village**: the pink pound has filled this area of the city with canalside cafés, clubs, bars and businesses, though these days it's as busy with hooting hen-nighters as with LGBT+ punters. Always lively, the village is packed to bursting point during Manchester's huge **Pride** festival (weekend tickets £22.50, day tickets £16.50; ⓦfestival .manchesterpride.com), which usually occurs on the last weekend of August. The village is closed off as thousands of people descend for music – big-name performers have included Beth Ditto and Boy George – comedy, theatre and exhibitions, all celebrating the lesbian, gay, bi and transgender community.

10

to handle, while new high-tech space **The Study** (ⓦthestudymcr.com) is an interactive learning and exhibition facility on the top floor of the museum's Grade II listed Alfred Waterhouse building.

Whitworth Art Gallery

Corner of Oxford Rd & Denmark Rd, M15 6ER • Mon–Wed & Fri–Sun 10am–5pm, Thurs 10am–9pm • Free • ☏ 0161 275 7450, ⓦ www.whitworth.manchester.ac.uk

The university's **Whitworth Art Gallery** reopened in 2015 after a £15 million renovation project to double and extend its public space into the surrounding Whitworth Park. A lively rota of exhibitions showcases contemporary artists, designers and performers, as well as the gallery's fine collection of pre-1880s and modern art, and the country's widest range of textiles outside London's Victoria and Albert Museum. The glass walls and walkways of the award-winning gallery space blends seamlessly with the park, and sculpture by the likes of Emily Young, Nathan Coley and Dorothy Cross have augmented the already spectacular collection that included work by Epstein, Hepworth and Moore.

Salford Quays

After the Manchester Ship Canal opened in 1894, **Salford docks** played a pivotal role in turning the city into one of Britain's busiest seaports. Following their closure in 1982, which left a post-industrial mess just a couple of miles to the west of the city centre, an extraordinarily ambitious redevelopment transformed **Salford Quays**, as it was rebranded, into a hugely popular waterfront complex with its own gleaming apartment blocks, shopping mall and arts centre, **The Lowry**. Also here is the splendid **Imperial War Museum North** and the **MediaCityUK** site.

The Lowry

Pier 8, Salford Quays, M50 3AZ • Galleries Mon–Fri & Sun 11am–5pm, Sat 10am–5pm • Free • ☏ 0843 208 6000, ⓦ thelowry.com • Harbour City/MediacityUK Metrolink

Perched on the water's edge, **The Lowry** is the quays' shiny steel arts centre. The **Galleries**, which host sixteen different exhibitions each year, are largely devoted to the paintings of **Lawrence Stephen Lowry** (1887–1976), the artist most closely associated with Salford. The earlier paintings – those somewhat desolate, melancholic portrayals of Manchester mill workers – are the most familiar, while later works, repeating earlier paintings but changing the greys and sullen browns for lively reds and pinks, can come as a surprise.

Imperial War Museum North

The Quays, Trafford Wharf North, M17 1TZ • Daily 10am–5pm • Free • ☏ 0161 836 4000, ⓦ iwm.org.uk • MediacityUK Metrolink

A footbridge across the Manchester Ship Canal links The Lowry with the startling **Imperial War Museum North**, which raises a giant steel fin into the air, in a building designed by the architect Daniel Libeskind. The interior is just as striking, its angular lines serving as a dramatic backdrop to the displays, which kick off with the Big Picture, when the walls of the main hall are transformed into giant screens to show regularly rotated, fifteen-minute, surround-sound films. Superb themed displays fill six separate exhibition areas – the "Silos" – focusing on everything from women's work in the World Wars to the 9/11 attacks (with a 23ft section of crumpled steel recovered from the World Trade Center wreckage).

MediaCityUK

Salford, M50 2EQ • BBC tours Mon–Thurs 10.30am, 12.30pm & 3pm (Thurs in school term time, radio studio tour only), Sat & Sun times vary; 1hr 30min • £11.75 • Book on ⓦ bbc.co.uk/showsandtours • MediaCityUK Metrolink

In 2011, the BBC moved 26 of its London-based departments up north to **MediaCityUK**, a vast, purpose-built workspace for creative and digital businesses. ITV followed suit in 2013, the *Coronation Street* set arrived in 2014, and the whole place has a certain pizzazz, with telly types buzzing about on Segway scooters, and trendy bars and restaurants open until the early hours. The BBC offer insanely popular though mildly underwhelming **tours** (the highpoint of which is the sound studio and its semi-anechoic chamber), but you don't have to join a tour to wander around the piazza and visit the **Blue Peter garden**, transplanted here from London complete with Shep's paw print.

The National Cycling Centre

Stuart St, M11 4DQ, 2 miles east of the city centre ☎ 0161 223 2244 option 3, ⓦ nationalcyclingcentre.com • Daily 7.30am–10pm • Tours 10am–4pm, £45 for up to 14 people, booking essential • From Piccadilly Gardens (Stop D) take bus #216 to Sport City; or Velopark Metrolink

Opposite Man City's football ground (see box opposite), in an area being touted as "sports city", the **National Cycling Centre** is the home of British Cycling and one of the fastest and busiest velodromes in the world. Its stunning, Olympic-standard loop of Siberian pine track, angled at 42.5°, is in constant use, with hour-long taster sessions (bikes and coach provided) available to anyone aged nine and over; arrive early and you might well catch the end of a Team GB training session. Also on site is a world-class indoor **BMX track** and the start of 7.5 miles of **mountain-bike** trails. Elsewhere in the city, the centre's facilities include an outdoor BMX track and a mountain-bike skills zone.

ARRIVAL AND DEPARTURE   MANCHESTER

By plane Manchester International Airport (☎ 0161 489 3000, ⓦ manchesterairport.co.uk) is 10 miles south of the city centre. There's an excellent train service to Manchester Piccadilly (£5 single; 20min); the new Metrolink (£4.20 single; 45min; see below) runs daily to Deansgate-Castlefield; the taxi fare is around £25.

By train Of Manchester's three stations, Piccadilly, on the east side of the centre, sees the largest number of long-distance services, some of which continue on to Oxford Road, just south of the centre. On the city's north side, Victoria Station mainly sees services to Lancashire and Yorkshire. All three stations are connected to the centre via the free Metroshuttle bus service (see opposite); Piccadilly and Victoria are also on the Metrolink tramline (see opposite).

Destinations from Manchester Piccadilly Barrow-in-Furness (Mon–Sat 7 daily, Sun 3 daily; 2hr 15min); Birmingham (hourly; 1hr 30min); Blackpool (hourly; 1hr 10min); Buxton (hourly; 1hr); Carlisle (8 daily; 1hr 50min); Chester (every 30min; 1hr–1hr 20min); Lancaster (hourly; 1hr); Leeds (hourly; 1hr); Liverpool (every 30min; 50min); London (hourly; 2hr 20min); Newcastle (10 daily; 3hr); Oxenholme (4–6 daily; 40min–1hr 10min); Sheffield

(hourly; 1hr); York (every 30min; 1hr 30min).

Destinations from Manchester Oxford Road Blackpool (hourly; 1hr 15min); Carlisle (8 daily; 1hr 50min); Chester (hourly; 1hr); Lancaster (8 daily; 1hr); Leeds (10 daily; 1hr); Liverpool (every 30min; 50min); Oxenholme (8 daily; 1hr 10min); Penrith (8 daily; 1hr 40min); Sheffield (hourly; 1hr); York (hourly; 1hr 30min).

Destinations from Manchester Victoria Blackpool (6 daily; 1hr 30min); Leeds (every 30min; 1hr 20min); Liverpool (hourly; 35min).

By bus Most long-distance buses use Chorlton Street Coach Station, about halfway between Piccadilly train station and Albert Square, though some regional buses also leave from Shudehill Interchange, between the Arndale Centre and the Northern Quarter.

Destinations Birmingham (6 daily; 3hr); Blackpool (5 daily; 1hr 40min); Chester (3 daily; 1hr); Leeds (6 daily; 2hr); Liverpool (hourly; 40min); London (every 1–2hr; 4hr 30min–6hr 45min); Newcastle (6 daily; 5hr); Sheffield (4 daily; 2hr 40min).

Travel information For information on train and bus services, contact TFGM (☎ 0871 200 2233, ⓦ tfgm.com).

MANCHESTER FOOTBALL TOURS

Manchester is, of course, home to two mega Premier League football teams. It's tough to get tickets for matches if you're not a season-ticket-holder, but **guided tours** placate out-of-town fans who want to gawp at the silverware and sit in the dug-out. You'll need to book in advance.

Old Trafford Sir Matt Busby Way, off Warwick Rd, M16 0RA ☎0161 868 8000, ⓦmanutd.com; Old Trafford Metrolink; map p.514. The self-styled "Theatre of Dreams" is the home of Manchester United, arguably the most famous football team in the world. Stadium tours include a visit to the club museum. Tours daily (except match days) 9.40am–4.30pm; £18.

Etihad Stadium Sport City, off Alan Turing Way, M11 3FF ☎0161 444 1894, ⓦmcfc.co.uk; Etihad Campus Metrolink; map p.514. United's formerly long-suffering local rivals, Manchester City, became the world's richest club in 2008 after being bought by the royal family of Abu Dhabi. They play at the revamped Etihad Stadium, east of the city centre. Tours daily 9am–5pm; £17.

10

GETTING AROUND

On foot About a 30min walk from top to bottom, central Manchester is compact enough to cover on foot.
By bus Three free Metroshuttle bus services (ⓦtfgm.com) weave across the centre of town, linking the city's train stations and NCP car parks with all the major points of interest; Metroshuttle #1 runs Mon–Fri every 10min 7am–7pm, Sat every 10min 8.30am–6.30pm, Sun & public hols every 12min 9.30am–6pm; Metroshuttle #2 runs every 10min Mon–Fri 6.30am–6.30pm, Sat 8.30am–6.30pm, Sun & public hols every 12min 9.35am–6pm; Metroshuttle #3 runs every 10min Mon–Fri 7.25am–7.20pm, Sat 8.35am–6.25pm, Sun & public hols every 12min 9.40am–6.05pm.
By taxi Mantax (☎0161 230 3333) and Streetcars (☎0161 228 7878) are two reliable taxi firms.
By tram Metrolink trams (ⓦmetrolink.co.uk) whisk through the city centre bound for the suburbs, along an ever-expanding network of routes. Services run from approximately 6am–12.30am (Mon–Thurs), with last trams running later on Fridays and Saturdays, and Sunday services between around 7am–10.30pm. Ticket machines are on the platform; single journeys cost from £1.20, while day and weekend Travelcards (from £5 off-peak) are good value.

INFORMATION AND TOURS

Tourist information Manchester Visitor Centre is at 1 Piccadilly Gardens, on the corner of Portland Street (Mon–Sat 9.30am–5.30pm, Sun 10.30am–4.30pm; ☎0871 222 8223, ⓦvisitmanchester.com); it has a useful blog.
Listings information In print, Thursday's *City Life* supplement in the *Manchester Evening News* (ⓦmanchester eveningnews.co.uk) covers popular events, while *The Skinny*, widely available in the Northern Quarter, is a hip and independent monthly freebie. Online, there's intelligent and incisive guidance on ⓦcreativetourist.com, while ⓦconfidentials.com/manchester has informative restaurant and bar reviews.
Walking tours The Visitor Centre has details of the city's many walking tours, including a street art tour of the northern quarter (from £7). There's also a 3hr pay-what-you-can walking tour that leaves from the Alan Turing Memorial in Sackville Gardens (11am Tues, Fri, Sat & Sun; ⓦfreetour.com/manchester).

ACCOMMODATION

There are many city-centre **hotels**, especially budget chains, which means that you have a good chance of finding a smart, albeit generic, en-suite room in central Manchester for around £60–70 at almost any time of the year – except when City or United are playing at home. Less expensive **guesthouses** and **B&Bs** are concentrated some way out of the centre, mainly on the southern routes into the city. Prices often halve midweek.

HOTELS

ABode 107 Piccadilly, M1 2DB ☎0161 247 7744, ⓦabodemanchester.co.uk; Piccadilly Gardens Metrolink; map p.514. Part of a small chain of boutique hotels, this gem occupies a former cotton warehouse a stone's throw from Piccadilly Station. Rooms are light and elegant, with high ceilings and polished wooden floors. **£85**
Arora 18–24 Princess St, M1 4LG ☎0161 236 8999, ⓦmanchester.arorahotels.com; Piccadilly Gardens/ St Peter's Square Metrolink; map p.514. Four-star with more than 100 neat, modern rooms in a listed building in a great central location opposite the Manchester Art Gallery. The convivial, obliging staff pride themselves on offering a "real Manchester welcome". Good online discounts. **£99**
★ **Great John Street** Great John St, M3 4FD ☎0161 831 3211, ⓦeclectichotels.co.uk/great-john-street; Deansgate-Castlefield Metrolink; map p.514. Deluxe hotel in an imaginatively refurbished old school building

10

not far from Deansgate, with thirty individual, spacious and comfortable suites, some split-level. The on-site bar-cum-restaurant has an open fire and deep sofas, with a gallery breakfast room up above. Nice rooftop garden, too. They've also recently opened sister hotel *King Street Townhouse*. **£250**

Midland Peter St, M60 2DS ☎ 0161 236 3333, ⓦ qhotels .co.uk; St Peter's Square Metrolink; map p.514. Once the terminus hotel for the old Central Station – and where Mr Rolls first met Mr Royce – this building was the apotheosis of Edwardian style and is still arguably Manchester's most iconic hotel. The public areas today are returned to their former glory, with bedrooms in immaculate chain style. *Mr Cooper's House and Garden*, attached to the hotel, is wonderful for pre-theatre cocktails. **£130**

Motel One London Rd, M1 2PF ☎ 0161 200 5650, ⓦ motelone.com; Piccadilly Metrolink; map p.514. Not much to look at from the outside, but the location couldn't be more central and the stylish lobby leads to clean, modern rooms. The fixed room prices are higher at the weekend. **£69**

Radisson Blu Edwardian Peter St, M2 5GP ☎ 0161 835 9929, ⓦ radissonblu-edwardian.com; St Peter's

Square Metrolink; map p.514. The Neoclassical facade is all that's left of the Free Trade Hall; inside, this five-star hotel has a sleek modern interior full of natural light, tasteful rooms, and all the extras you'd expect – spa, gym and the trendy *Opus One* bar. **£120**

HOSTELS

Hilton Chambers 15 Hilton St, M1 1JJ ☎ 0161 236 4414 ⓦ hattersgroup.com/manchester-hilton -chambers; Piccadilly Gardens Metrolink; map p.514. Part of a small regional chain, this newish hostel is right in the heart of the Northern Quarter, and a great location for exploring the city's nightlife. A range of different rooms and some great communal spaces, including an outdoor deck. Rates reduce considerably midweek. Dorms **£21**, doubles **£82**

YHA Manchester Potato Wharf, Castlefield, M3 4NB ☎ 0845 371 9647, ⓦ yha.org.uk/hostel/manchester; Deansgate-Castlefield Metrolink; map p.514. Excellent hostel overlooking the canal that runs close to the Museum of Science and Industry, with 35 rooms (thirty four-bunk, two five-bunk and three doubles). Facilities include laundry, self-catering and a café. Dorms **£20**, doubles **£40**

EATING

Rivalling London in the breadth and scope of its **cafés** and **restaurants**, Mancunians are justly baffled at Michelin not awarding any restaurant in the city a star (yet). Most options are in the city centre, with the vast majority of new openings in the Northern Quarter and Ancoats. If you have the time, head a couple of miles along Wilmslow Road to **Didsbury**, a leafy suburb with several excellent places to eat, or to **Altrincham**, 8 miles outside the city, which has an outstanding food market (ⓦ altrinchammarket.co.uk).

CAFÉS AND CAFÉ-BARS

Eighth Day 107–111 Oxford Rd, M1 7DU ☎ 0161 273 1850, ⓦ 8thday.coop; Metroshuttle #2; map p.514. Manchester's oldest organic vegetarian café has a shop, takeaway and juice bar upstairs, with a great-value café/restaurant downstairs. Mon–Fri 9am–7pm, Sat 10am–5pm.

Federal Café Bar 9 Nicholas Croft, Northern Quarter, M4 1EY ☎ 0161 425 0974, ⓦ federalcafe.co.uk; Shudehill Metrolink; map p.514. Manchester's latest independent coffee shop-cum-bar has queues out of the door for its all-day brunch (try the smashed avo on sourdough toast with bacon for £8.50), strong coffee (flat white £2.60) and superb cocktails (around £8). Mon–Fri 7.30am–6pm, Sat 8am–6pm, Sun 8am–5pm.

Home Sweet Home 49–41 Edge St, Northern Quarter, M4 1HW ☎ 0161 224 9424, ⓦ homesweethomenq .com; Shudehill Metrolink; map p.514. Queues snake round the block for this gem, which serves huge portions of American/Tex Mex-influenced mains (from £8), luscious milkshakes and generous slices of the most extravagantly decorated cakes you will ever have seen. Mon–Thurs & Sun 9am–10pm, Fri 9am–11pm, Sat 9am–midnight.

The Koffee Pot 84–86 Oldham St, Northern Quarter, M4 1LE ☎ 0161 236 8918, ⓦ thekoffeepot.co.uk; Market St Metrolink; map p.514. Beloved by hungover hipsters, this is *the* place for a Full English (£5.80) or Veggie (£5.60) brekkie (served until 2pm) amid much Formica and red leatherette. Often packed. Mon 7.30am–4pm, Tues–Fri 7.30am–11pm, Sat 9am–11pm, Sun 9am–4pm; note the kitchen closes at 9pm Tues–Sat.

★ **Richmond Tea Rooms** Richmond St, Gay Village, M1 3HZ ☎ 0161 237 9667, ⓦ www.richmondtearooms .com; Metroshuttle #1; map p.514. Without question the most brilliantly conceived tearoom in Manchester, with an amazing Tim Burton-esque *Alice in Wonderland* theme. The sumptuous afternoon teas (£6.50–23.50) are the stuff of local legend, while the adjoining cocktail lounge is a super-stylish place to kick off an evening. Mon–Thurs 11am–9pm, Fri 11am–10pm, Sat 10am–10pm, Sun 10am–9.30pm.

Takk 6 Tariff St, Northern Quarter, M1 2FF ⓦ takkmcr .com; Shudehill Metrolink; map p.514. Cool yet cosy Icelandic coffee bar with a living-room feel, home-made cakes, hipster brunch (blueberry pie porridge £4), a changing roster of sandwiches (£6), Nordic art and, of course, superior coffee. Mon–Fri 8am–5pm, Sat 9am–5pm, Sun 10am–5pm.

Trof NQ 8 Thomas St, Northern Quarter, M4 1EU ☎ 0161 833 3197, ⓦ trofnq.co.uk; Shudehill Metrolink; map p.514. Three storeys of cool, relaxed café-bar populated by trendy young things. It's ideal for a late breakfast or early afternoon drink, and hosts open-mic nights, poetry readings and DJ sets. Mon & Tues 10am–midnight, Wed & Thurs 10am–1am, Fri 10am–3am, Sat 9am–3am, Sun 9am–midnight.

RESTAURANTS

Australasia 1 The Ave, Spinningfields, M3 3AP ☎ 0161 831 0288, ⓦ australasia.uk.com; Metroshuttle #1 or #2; map p.514. A remarkable glass pyramid on street level leads down under (get it?) to Australasia, a buzzing, white-tiled restaurant that's arguably the star of the Spinningfield dining scene. Food is Modern Oz meets Pacific Rim and pricey but well-regarded (mains from £15, with the Australian Wagyu steak fillet a whopping £60). Daily noon–midnight.

★**Dimitri's** 1 Campfield Arcade, Deansgate, M3 4FN ☎ 0161 839 3319, ⓦ dimitris.co.uk; Metroshuttle #1 or #2; map p.514. Long-established Manchester favourite: pick and mix from the Greek/Spanish/Italian menu (particularly good for vegetarians) and enjoy it at a semi-alfresco arcade table with a Greek coffee or Lebanese wine; you'll think you're in the Med. Mon–Thurs & Sun 11am–midnight, Fri & Sat 11am–2am.

★**Lime Tree** 8 Lapwing Lane, West Didsbury, M20 2WS ☎ 0161 445 1217, ⓦ thelimetreerestaurant.co.uk; West Didsbury Metrolink; map p.514. The finest local food, with a menu that chargrills and oven-roasts as if its life depended on it, using produce from its own smallholding. Main courses cost £14 and up, less at lunchtime. Reservations recommended. Mon & Sat 5.30–10pm, Tues–Fri noon–2.30pm & 5.30–10pm, Sun noon–8pm.

Mughli Charcoal Pit 30 Wilmslow Rd, M14 5TQ ☎ 0161 248 0900, ⓦ mughli.com; map p.514. Out by the Whitworth Art Gallery, this stylish Indian restaurant is a standout in the area traditionally known as "curry mile". Mouth-watering meat, veggie and vegan dishes include butter paneer (£11) and charred lamb chops (£10.50) – there's even a mild "little mughal" for children (£6.50). Mon–Thurs 5pm–midnight, Fri 5pm–12.30am, Sat 4pm–12.30am, Sun 2–10.30pm.

Rudy's Pizza 9 Cotton St, Ancoats, M4 5BF ☎ 07931 162059, ⓦ rudyspizza.co.uk; map p.514. Super-light handstretched pizza the Neapolitan way, this place gets rave reviews (and has long queues). On afternoons from Wed to Sat they stay open for drinks only as the chefs are busy making dough. Prices from £4.90 for a Marinara and you'll pay £15 for a bottle of the house wine. Tues 5–10pm, Wed–Sat noon–3pm & 5–10pm, Sun noon–6pm.

Sam's Chop House Chapel Walks, off Cross St, M2 1HN ☎ 0161 834 3210, ⓦ samschophouse.com; Market St Metrolink; map p.514. One of three good chop houses in the city, the restaurant attached to this wonderful old-world pub is a hidden gem. It has a Victorian gas-lit feel and a delightful menu of English food (mains £14–16) – and they really know their wine, too. Mon–Sat noon–3pm & 5.30–11pm, Sun noon–8pm.

Yang Sing 34 Princess St, M1 4JY ☎ 0161 236 2200, ⓦ yang-sing.com; St Peter's Square Metrolink; map p.514. One of the best Cantonese restaurants in the country, with authentic dishes ranging from a quick-fried noodle plate to the full works. For the most interesting food, stray from the printed menu; ask the friendly staff for advice. Sister restaurant, the *Little Yang Sing* on George St, slightly cheaper, is also worth stopping by. Mains from £12. Mon–Sat noon–11.30pm, Sun noon–10.30pm.

★**Yuzu** 39 Faulkner St, M1 4EE ☎ 0161 236 4159, ⓦ yuzumanchester.co.uk; St Peter's Square Metrolink; map p.514. Outstanding Japanese in Chinatown with a shortish menu of exceptionally executed sashimi (from £10.50), tempura (from £5.90) dishes and more, plus a tempting range of sake. Tues–Sat noon–2pm & 5.30–10pm.

DRINKING

From Victorian boozers to designer cocktail bars, Manchester does **drinking** in style, while its musical heritage and large student population keep things lively and interesting.

★**Big Hands** 296 Oxford Rd, M13 9NS ☎ 0161 272 7779, ⓦ facebook.com/BigHandsBar; map p.514. Right by the Academy venues, this intimate, uber-cool bar is popular with students, usually post-gig as it has a late licence. Mon–Fri 10am–2am, Sat noon–3am, Sun 6pm–1am.

Britons Protection 50 Great Bridgewater St, M1 5LE ☎ 0161 236 5895, ⓦ facebook.com/britonsprotection; map p.514. Cosy old pub with a couple of small rooms, a backyard beer garden and all sorts of Victorian detail – most splendidly the tiles and the open fires in winter. Boasts over 300 whiskies and a large mural depicting the Peterloo Massacre. Mon–Thurs 11am–11.30pm, Fri noon–12.30am, Sat 11am–midnight, Sun noon–11pm.

Circus Tavern 86 Portland St, M1 4GX ☎ 0161 236 5818; map p.514. Manchester's smallest pub, this Victorian drinking hole is a favourite city-centre pit stop. You may have to knock to get in; when you do, you're confronted by the landlord in the corridor pulling pints. Daily 11am–11pm.

10

10

Cloud 23 Beetham Tower, 301 Deansgate, M3 4LQ ☎ 0161 870 1670, ⓦ cloud23bar.com; map p.514. Manchester's highest and most popular cocktail bar, with a 23rd-floor glass overhang. Expensive, but worth it for the view of the city and Pennines beyond. Mon–Thurs & Sun 11am–1am, Fri & Sat 11am–2am.

Corbières 2 Half Moon St, just off St Ann's Square, M2 7BS ☎ 0161 834 3381; map p.514. Look for the Gaudí-esque wall art flanking the door of this long-standing subterranean, slightly dank drinking cellar with arguably the best jukebox in Manchester. Mon–Thurs 11am–11pm, Fri & Sat 11am–midnight, Sun 2–10.30pm.

★ **Mr Thomas' Chop House** 52 Cross St, M2 7AR ☎ 0161 832 2245, ⓦ tomschophouse.com; map p.514. Victorian classic with Dickensian nooks and crannies. Office workers, daytime drinkers, old goats and students all call it home, and

there's good-value, traditional food too. Mon–Thurs 11am–11pm, Fri & Sat 11am–midnight, Sun noon–10.30pm.

Sand Bar 120 Grosvenor St, M1 7HL ☎ 0161 273 1552, ⓦ www.sandbarmanchester.co.uk; map p.514. Between the university and the city centre, this is a brilliant modern take on the traditional pub, where students, lecturers and workers shoot the breeze. There's a great selection of beers and wines. Mon–Wed & Sun noon–midnight, Thurs noon–1am, Fri & Sat noon–2am.

The Temple 100 Great Bridgewater St, M1 5JW ☎ 0161 228 9834; map p.514. Teeny-tiny subterranean boozer in an old public toilet, with an amazing jukebox and bags of atmosphere, if not much elbow room. It's run by the same people as *Big Hands* (see p.523) and shares its nonchalant, fun-time vibe. Mon–Thurs & Sun noon–midnight, Fri & Sat noon–1am.

NIGHTLIFE

Manchester has an excellent **live-music** scene, of course, and a mercurial roster of **clubs**; note too that many of the city's hip **café-bars** (see p.522) host regular club nights. See print and online listings (see p.521) for information.

Albert Hall 27 Peter St, M2 5QR ☎ 0844 858 8521, ⓦ alberthallmanchester.com; map p.514. Former Wesleyan chapel that's now an atmospheric live-music venue hosting a select programme of high-quality, slightly left-field artists. Hours vary.

★ **Band on the Wall** 25 Swan St, Northern Quarter, M4 5JZ ☎ 0161 834 1786, ⓦ bandonthewall.org; map p.514. This legendary Northern Quarter joint remains true to its commitment to "real music": it's one of the city's best venues to see live bands – from world and folk to jazz and reggae – and it hosts club nights to boot. Box office Mon–Sat 5–9pm. Mon–Thurs 9am–1am, Fri & Sat 9am–3am, Sun noon–5pm.

The Castle Hotel 66 Oldham St, Northern Quarter, M4 1LE ☎ 0161 237 9485, ⓦ thecastlehotel.info; map p.514. Genuinely good 200-year-old pub with cask and craft ales and an extremely intimate backroom gig space. Jake Bugg played to just seventy-odd people here months before hitting the big time. Hosts regular spoken word nights too. Mon–Thurs noon–1am, Fri noon–2am, Sun noon–midnight.

★ **The Deaf Institute** 135 Grosvenor St, M1 7HE ☎ 0161 276 9350 ⓦ thedeafinstitute.co.uk; map p.514. A mile down Oxford Rd, this bar and music hall sits in a funky makeover of the elegant Victorian former deaf institute. Mostly folk, indie and r'n'b, with lots of up-and-coming

talent, and a raft of great club nights. Sister venue *Gorilla* (ⓦ thisisgorilla.com) on Whitworth Street is also excellent. Mon–Thurs & Sun 10am–midnight, Fri & Sat 10am–3am.

Matt & Phreds 64 Tib St, Northern Quarter, M4 1LW ☎ 0161 831 7002, ⓦ mattandphreds.com; map p.514. The city's finest jazz bar, offering everything from swing to gritty New Orleans blues. Mon–Thurs & Sat 6pm–late, Fri 5pm–late.

O2 Apollo Manchester Stockport Rd, M12 6AP ☎ 0844 477 7667, ⓦ academymusicgroup.com/o2apollo manchester; map p.514. Medium-sized theatre auditorium for all kinds of concerts; a brilliant place to see big names up close, with bags of atmosphere. Hours vary.

O2 Ritz Manchester Whitworth St West, M1 5NQ ☎ 0161 236 3234, ⓦ academymusicgroup.com /o2ritzmanchester; map p.514. This legendary dance hall has been around for decades (it's where The Smiths first played) and has a sprung dancefloor that really boings when things get going. Jumping live music and plenty of fun club nights, including a roller disco. Hours vary.

Soup Kitchen 31–33 Spear St, Northern Quarter, M1 1DF ☎ 0161 236 5100, ⓦ soupkitchenmcr.co.uk; map p.514. Soup-specializing canteen with a basement club/live-music venue that's among Manchester's finest. Mon–Wed & Sun noon–11pm, Thurs noon–1am, Fri & Sat noon–4pm.

ENTERTAINMENT

The artist-led **Manchester International Festival** (see box opposite) is a biennial eighteen-day culture fest, but a range of mainstream and fringe **theatres** also produce a lively, year-round programme. As for **classical music**, Manchester is blessed with the North's most highly prized **orchestra**, the Hallé, which is resident at Bridgewater Hall. Other acclaimed names include the **BBC Philharmonic** and the **Manchester Camerata** chamber orchestra (ⓦ manchestercamerata.com), who perform at a variety of venues.

MANCHESTER INTERNATIONAL FESTIVAL

Manchester is well-established as a leading light on the UK arts and music scene and the biennial **Manchester International Festival** (2018, 2020, etc) pulls together an impressive array of performers, directors and theatre companies to celebrate Manchester doing things a bit differently. Radical plays are premiered, new arty concepts are trialled (opera for babies, anyone?) and big names – including Damon Albarn, Björk, New Order, Punchdrunk, Sir Kenneth Branagh and Jane Horrocks – collaborate with the best directors and producers in the industry. Traditionally at various public venues across Manchester, the festival will have a permanent £110m state-of-the-art home once new arts venue **The Factory** opens in St John's in 2020 (ⓦ stjohnsmanchester.com).

10

CLASSICAL MUSIC

Bridgewater Hall Lower Mosley St, M2 3WS ⓣ 0844 907 9000, ⓦ bridgewater-hall.co.uk; map p.514. Home of the Hallé Orchestra, the BBC Philharmonic and the Manchester Camerata; also a full programme of chamber, pop, classical and jazz concerts.

Royal Northern College of Music (RNCM) 124 Oxford Rd, M13 9RD ⓣ 0161 907 5200, ⓦ rncm.ac.uk; Metroshuttle #2; map p.514. Top-quality classical and modern jazz concerts.

THEATRE, CINEMA AND DANCE

The Dancehouse 10 Oxford Rd, M1 5QA ⓣ 0161 237 9753, ⓦ thedancehouse.co.uk; Metroshuttle #2; map p.514. Home to the Northern Ballet School and the eponymous theatre troupe; venue for dance, drama and comedy.

★ **HOME** 2 Tony Wilson Place, M15 4FN ⓣ 0161 200 1500, ⓦ homemcr.org; Deansgate-Castlefield Metrolink; map p.514. A new sleek centre for contemporary arts, with two theatres, five cinema screens, changing art exhibitions in a flexible gallery space, recitals and talks, plus a bookshop,

café and ground-floor bar.

The Lowry Pier 8, Salford Quays, M50 3UB ⓣ 0843 208 6000, ⓦ thelowry.com; Harbour City Metrolink; map p.514. This quayside venue hosts many of the biggest shows, including major National Theatre touring productions, most recently *La Strada* and *War Horse*.

Opera House 3 Quay St, M3 3HP ⓣ 0844 871 3018, ⓦ manchesteroperahouse.com; Deansgate-Castlefield Metrolink; map p.514. Major venue for touring West End musicals, drama, comedy and concerts.

Royal Exchange Theatre St Ann's Square, M2 7DH ⓣ 0161 833 9833, ⓦ royalexchange.co.uk; Market St Metrolink; map p.514. The theatre-in-the-round in the Royal Exchange is the most famous stage in the city, with a Studio Theatre (for works by new writers) alongside.

Stoller Hall Hunts Bank, M3 1DA ⓣ 0333 130 0967, ⓦ stollerhall.com; map p.514. Manchester's major new £8.7 million concert hall is attached to the world-renowned Chetham School of Music. With a focus on chamber music, the hall also hosts family concerts, workshops and masterclasses.

SHOPPING

As well as the out-of-town Trafford Centre, the high-end boutiques on **King Street**, and the **department stores** around Market Street and Exchange Square, the Northern Quarter has a plethora of smaller independent stores catering for all tastes. If you're around between mid-November and mid-December, make for the **Christmas Market**, when Albert Square is packed with nearly 350 stalls and a lot of Christmas cheer.

Afflecks 52 Church St, Northern Quarter, M4 1PW ⓣ 0161 839 0718, ⓦ afflecks.com; Piccadilly Gardens Metrolink; map p.514. A Manchester institution, where more than fifty independent stalls are spread over four floors mixing everything from goth outfits to retro cocktail dresses and quirky footwear. Mon–Fri 10.30am–6pm, Sat 10am–6pm, Sun ground and first floors only 11am–5pm.

Craft & Design Centre 17 Oak St, Northern Quarter, M4 5JD ⓣ 0161 832 4274, ⓦ craftanddesign.com; Shudehill Metrolink; map p.514. The city's best place to pick up ceramics, fabrics, earthenware, jewellery and decorative art – there's also a good little café. Mon–Sat 10am–5.30pm.

Oklahoma 74–76 High St, Northern Quarter, M4 1ES ⓣ 0161 834 1136, ⓦ okla.co.uk; Shudehill Metrolink; map p.514. Hidden behind large wooden doors, this charming gift-shop-cum-veggie-café is packed with fun knick-knacks and fripperies, with some pretty jewellery too. Mon–Thurs & Sun 10am–6pm, Fri & Sat 10am–7pm.

Piccadilly Records 53 Oldham St, Northern Quarter, M1 1JR ⓣ 0161 839 8008, ⓦ piccadillyrecords.com; Piccadilly Gardens Metrolink; map p.514. The enthusiastic staff, many of them DJs themselves, are more than willing to navigate you through the shelves of collectibles and vinyl towards some special gem, whatever your taste. Mon–Sat 10am–6pm, Sun 11am–5pm.

Retro Rehab 91 Oldham St, Northern Quarter, M1 1JR ☎ 0161 839 2050, ⓦ retro-rehab.co.uk; Piccadilly Gardens Metrolink; map p.514. Gorgeously feminine dresses abound, be they reworked vintage styles or genuine 1950s pieces, in this wonderful little boutique that prides itself on the range of its fashions and accessories from across several decades. Mon–Sat 10am–6pm, Sun noon–4pm.

DIRECTORY

Hospital Manchester Royal Infirmary, Oxford Rd ☎ 0161 276 1234.
Left luggage Facilities at Piccadilly train station on platform 10 (Mon–Sat 7am–11pm, Sun 8am–11pm; ☎ 0161 236 8667, ⓦ left-baggage.co.uk).
Police There's a 24hr police counter in an extension of the town hall on the corner of Lloyd and Mount St.
Post office 26 Spring Gardens.

Chester

CHESTER, forty miles southwest of Manchester across the Cheshire Plain, is home to a glorious two-mile ring of medieval and Roman **walls** that encircles a kernel of Tudor and Victorian buildings, all overhanging eaves, mini-courtyards, and narrow cobbled lanes, which culminate in the raised arcades called the "**Rows**". The compact centre of this little city is full of easy charms that can be explored on foot, and taken altogether Chester has enough in the way of sights, restaurants and atmosphere to make it an enjoyable base for a day or two. Though traditionally viewed as rather staid compared to near neighbours Manchester and Liverpool, it's gradually acquiring a bit of an edge, and with new cultural centre Storyhouse due to open on Hunter Street in 2017 (ⓦ storyhouse.com), it's one to watch.

The Rows

Intersecting at **The Cross**, the four main thoroughfares of central Chester are lined by **The Rows**, galleried shopping arcades that run along the first floor of a wonderful set of half-timbered buildings with another set of shops down below at street level. This engaging tableau, which extends for the first 200 or 300 yards of each of the four main streets, is a blend of genuine Tudor houses and Victorian imitations. There's no clear explanation of the origin of The Rows – they were first recorded shortly after a fire wrecked Chester in 1278 – but it seems likely that the hard bedrock that lies underneath the town centre prevented its shopkeepers and merchants from constructing the cellars they required, so they built upwards instead. The finest Tudor buildings are on **Watergate Street**, though **Bridge Street** is perhaps more picturesque. From The Cross, it's also a brief walk along **Eastgate Street** to one of the old town gates, above which is perched the filigree **Eastgate Clock**, raised in honour of Queen Victoria's Diamond Jubilee.

Chester Cathedral

St Werburgh St, off Northgate St, CH1 2DY • Mon–Sat 9am–6pm, Sun 11am–4pm • Free, but £3 donation suggested • **Cathedral at Height tours** Regular, but check website for specific times; 1hr • £8, children (over-8s only) £6 • ☎ 01244 324756, ⓦ chestercathedral.com

North of The Cross, along **Northgate Street**, rises the neo-Gothic **Town Hall**, whose acres of red and grey sandstone look over to the **cathedral**, a much modified red sandstone structure dating back to the Normans. The **nave**, with its massive medieval pillars, is suitably imposing, and on one side it sports a splendid sequence of Victorian Pre-Raphaelite mosaic panels that illustrate Old Testament stories in melodramatic style. Close by, the **north transept** is the oldest and most Norman part of the church – hence the round-headed arch and arcade – and the adjoining **choir** holds an intricately carved set of fourteenth-century choir stalls with some especially beastly misericords. The atmospheric East Cloister leads to a gorgeously tranquil **garden**.

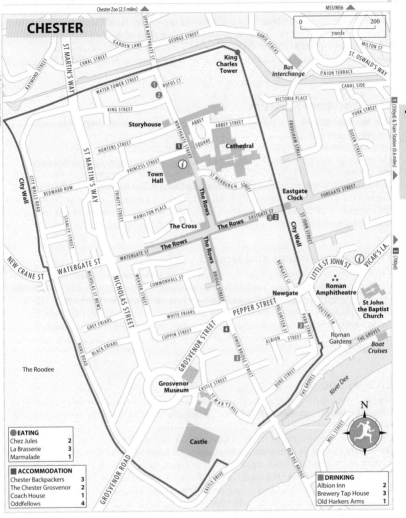

The **Cathedral at Height** tour, an enjoyable rootle around the building's previously hidden spaces, takes you up onto the roof for panoramic views over five counties – you'll even spot Liverpool's cathedrals.

Around the city walls

East of the cathedral, steps provide access to the top of the **city walls** – a two-mile girdle of medieval and Roman handiwork that's the most complete in Britain, though in places the wall is barely above street level. You can walk past all its towers, turrets and gateways in an hour or so, and most have a tale or two to tell. The fifteenth-century **King Charles Tower** in the northeast corner is so named because Charles I stood here in 1645 watching his troops being beaten on Rowton Moor, two miles to the southeast, while the earlier **Water Tower** at the northwest corner once stood in the river – evidence of the changes brought about by the gradual silting of the River Dee. South from the Water Tower you'll see the **Roodee**, England's oldest racecourse, laid out on a silted tidal pool where Roman ships once unloaded wine, figs and olive oil from the Mediterranean, and slate, lead and silver from their mines in North Wales. Races are still held here throughout the year.

The Grosvenor Museum

27 Grosvenor St, CH1 2DD • Mon–Sat 10.30am–5pm, Sun 1–4pm • Free; £3 donation requested • ☎ 01244 972197, ⓦ grosvenormuseum .westcheshiremuseums.co.uk

Scores of sculpted tomb panels and engraved headstones once propped up the wall to either side of the Water Tower, evidence of some nervous repair work undertaken when the Roman Empire was in retreat. Much of this stonework was retrieved by the Victorians and is now on display at the **Grosvenor Museum**, which also has interesting background displays on the Roman Empire in general and Roman Chester in particular. At the rear of the museum is **20 Castle Street**, a period house with nine rooms tricked out to represent domestic scenes from 1680 to 1925.

The Roman Gardens and around

Immediately to the east of one of the old city gates, **Newgate**, a footpath leads into the **Roman Gardens** (open access), where a miscellany of Roman stonework – odd bits of pillar, coping stones and incidental statuary – is on display. Footsteps away, along Little St John Street, is the shallow, partly excavated bowl that marks the site of the **Roman Amphitheatre** (open access); it is estimated to have held seven thousand spectators, making it the largest amphitheatre in Britain, but frankly it's not much to look at today.

Chester Zoo

Off the A41, 2 miles north of Chester, CH2 1EU • Daily: April–Sept 10am–5/6pm; Oct–March 10am–4/4.30pm; last admission 1hr before closing • £26, £24 in winter; under-16s £24/£20 • ⓦ chesterzoo.org • Buses #1 or #X8 from the new Chester Bus Interchange or opposite the train station

Chester's most popular attraction is **Chester Zoo**, one of the best in Europe. It is also the second largest in Britain (after London's), with over eleven thousand animals spread over a hundred landscaped acres. The zoo is well known for its **conservation projects** and has had notable success with its Asiatic lions and giant Komodo dragons. Animals are grouped by region in large paddocks viewed from a maze of pathways, from the monorail or the waterbus, with main attractions including the baby animals, the Tropical Realm and the Chimpanzee Forest, which has the biggest climbing frame in the country.

ARRIVAL AND INFORMATION

By train The train station is a 10min walk northeast of the centre, down City Road and Foregate Street from the central Eastgate Clock. Bus #40 (Mon–Sat 7.30am–7pm, Sun 9.30am–5pm; every 12min) links the station with the city centre.

Destinations Birmingham (5 daily; 2hr); Liverpool (every 30min; 45min); London (every 20min; 3hr 30min); Manchester (every 30min; 1hr–1hr 20min).

By bus The new Bus Interchange opened at Gorse Stacks in the northeast of the city centre in June 2017. All long-distance and most local buses stop here, including the free #200 Shopper Hopper running between here and the Town Hall (for Chester Market and Storyhouse; daily 8am–6pm, every 15min).

Destinations Liverpool (every 20min; 1hr 20min); Manchester (3 daily; 1hr).

Tourist information Chester's information centre (March–Oct Mon–Sat 9am–5.30pm, Sun 10am–5pm; Nov–Feb Mon–Fri 9.30am–4.30pm, Sat 10am–5pm, Sun 10am–4pm; ☎ 01244 405340, ⓦ visitchester.com) is in the Town Hall on Northgate St.

ACCOMMODATION

Chester is a popular tourist destination and although most of its visitors are day-trippers, enough of them stay overnight to sustain dozens of **B&Bs** and a slew of **hotels**. At the height of the summer and on high days and holidays – like Chester Races – advance booking is strongly recommended, either direct or via the tourist office.

Chester Backpackers 67 Boughton, CH3 5AF ☎ 01244 400185, ⓦ chesterbackpackers.co.uk; map p.527. Close to the city walls and a 5min walk from the train station, in a typically Chester mock-Tudor building. En-suite doubles and two dorms (8- and 15-bed). Dorms **£20**, doubles **£38**

The Chester Grosvenor Eastgate St, CH1 1LT ☎ 01244 324024, ⓦ chestergrosvenor.co.uk; map p.527. Superb luxury hotel in an immaculately maintained Victorian building in the centre of town. Extremely comfortable bedrooms and a whole host of facilities, not least a full-blown spa (charges apply) and posh chocolatier Rococo on site. Continental breakfast is included, but it's an extra £7.50 for a cooked breakfast. Rack rates are vertiginous, but look for special offers online. **£280**

Coach House Chester 39 Northgate St, CH1 2HQ ☎ 01244 351900, ⓦ coachhousechester.co.uk; map p.527. All eight rooms at this city centre gastropub were fully renovated in 2017 – in time for the opening of nearby Storyhouse. Cosy and contemporary, but with gorgeous period features, and all have en-suite bathrooms. **£100**

★**Oddfellows** 20 Lower Bridge St, CH1 1RS ☎ 01244 895700, ⓦ oddfellowschester.com; map p.527. Quirky boutique hotel packed with look-at-me touches – from the typewriters climbing the reception walls, to the set table-for-two affixed to the ceiling, to the neon "Good Night" sign en route to the eighteen comfortable, individually styled bedrooms. There's a buzzy bar scene – including the *Secret Garden* – and popular restaurant on site too. **£179**

EATING

★**Chez Jules** 71 Northgate St, CH1 2HQ ☎ 01244 400014, ⓦ chezjules.com; map p.527. There's a classic brasserie menu – salade nicoise to rib-eye steak – at this popular spot in an attractive half-timbered building. In the evenings, main courses begin at around £10, with a terrific-value, two-course prix fixe menu (Mon–Sat noon–6pm, Sun noon–5.30pm) for £12.95 and a two-course lunch for £9.95. Mon–Sat noon–10.30pm, Sun noon–9.30pm.

★**La Brasserie** Chester Grosvenor, Eastgate St, CH1 1LT ☎ 01244 324024, ⓦ chestergrosvenor.com; map p.527. In the same hotel as the Michelin-starred *Simon Radley's*, where the a la carte menu sits at a cool £75, this is a much more affordable yet smart brasserie that serves inventive French and fusion cooking. Main courses average £20, and it's also a great place for a coffee and pastry. Light bites daily 11.30am–9pm; a la carte Mon–Thurs noon–2.30pm, 5.30–9pm, Fri & Sat noon–2.30pm, 5.30–9.30pm, Sun noon–8.30pm.

Marmalade 67 Northgate St, CH1 2HQ ☎ 01244 314565, ⓦ marmalade-chester.co.uk; map p.527. An amenable little licensed café with tasty food – filling breakfasts, sandwiches and salads (all around £5) are made using all local produce (and a lot of it is – or can be – gluten-free). Mon–Fri 8am–7.30pm, Sat 9am–7.30pm, Sun 10am–4pm.

DRINKING

Albion Inn Corner of Albion and Park streets, CH1 1RN ☎ 01244 340345, ⓦ albioninnchester.co.uk; map p.527. A Victorian terraced pub in the shadow of the city wall – no fruit machines, no muzak, just good old-fashioned decor (and a World War I theme), tasty bar food and a great range of ales. Hilariously unwelcoming signs outside – basically, if you're on a hen or stag do, or have a child in tow, forget it. Mon–Thurs & Sat noon–3pm & 5–11pm, Fri noon–11pm, Sun noon–2.30pm & 7–10.30pm.

Brewery Tap House 52–54 Lower Bridge St, CH1 1RU ☎ 01244 340999, ⓦ the-tap.co.uk; map p.527. Up the cobbled ramp, this converted medieval hall, once owned by the royalist Gamul family and confiscated by Parliament after the English Civil War, serves a good selection of ales from local brewery Spitting Feathers in a tall, barn-like room with whitewashed walls. Mon–Sat noon–11pm, Sun noon–10.30pm.

★**Old Harkers Arms** 1 Russell St, CH3 5AL ☎ 01244 344525, ⓦ brunningandprice.co.uk/harkers; map p.527. Canalside real-ale pub imaginatively sited in a former warehouse about 500 yards northeast of Foregate Street. Quality bar food too (until 9.30pm). Mon–Sat 10.30am–11pm, Sun noon–10.30pm.

Liverpool

Standing proud in the 1700s as the empire's second city, **LIVERPOOL** faced a dramatic change of fortune in the twentieth century, suffering a series of harsh economic blows and ongoing urban deprivation. The postwar years were particularly tough, but the outlook changed again at the turn of the millennium, as economic and social regeneration brightened the centre and old docks, and the city's stint as European Capital of Culture in 2008 transformed the view from outside. Today Liverpool is a dynamic, exciting place with a Tate Gallery of its own, a series of innovative museums and a fascinating social history. And of course it also makes great play of its musical heritage – as well it should, considering that this is the place that gave the world The Beatles.

The main sights are scattered throughout the centre of town, but you can easily walk between most of them. The **River Mersey** provides one focus, whether crossing on the famous ferry to the **Wirral** peninsula or taking a tour of the Albert Dock. **Beatles** sights could easily occupy another day. If you want a cathedral, they've "got one to spare" as the song goes; plus there's a fine showing of British art in the celebrated **Walker Art Gallery** and **Tate Liverpool**, a multitude of exhibits in the terrific **World Museum Liverpool**, a revitalized arts and nightlife urban quarter centred on **FACT**, Liverpool's showcase for film and the media arts, and a whole new cutting-edge creative district known as the **Baltic Triangle**.

Brief history

Liverpool gained its charter from King John in 1207, but remained a humble fishing village for half a millennium until the booming slave trade prompted the building of the first dock in 1715. From then until the abolition of slavery in Britain in 1807, Liverpool was the apex of the **slaving triangle** in which firearms, alcohol and textiles were traded for African slaves, who were then shipped to the Caribbean and America where they were in turn exchanged for tobacco, raw cotton and sugar. After the abolition of the trade, the port continued to grow into a seven-mile chain of docks, not only for freight but also to cope with wholesale European emigration, which saw nine million people leave for the Americas and Australasia between 1830 and 1930. During the 1970s and 1980s Liverpool became a byword for British economic malaise, but the waterfront area of the city was granted **UNESCO World Heritage** status in 2004, spurring major refurbishment of the city's magnificent municipal and industrial buildings.

St George's Hall

St George's Place, off Lime St, L1 1JJ • Daily 10am–5pm • Free; walking tour £4.95 (booking essential) • ☎ 0151 233 3020, Ⓦ liverpoolcityhalls.co.uk

Emerging from Lime Street Station, you can't miss **St George's Hall**, one of Britain's finest Greek Revival buildings and a testament to the wealth generated from transatlantic trade. Now primarily an exhibition venue, but once Liverpool's premier concert hall and crown court, its vaulted Great Hall features a floor tiled with thirty thousand precious Minton tiles (usually covered over, but open for a week or two in Aug), while the Willis organ is the third largest in Europe. You can take a self-guided tour, or call for details of the guided tours.

Walker Art Gallery

William Brown St, L3 8EL • Daily 10am–5pm • Free; audio tour £2.50 • ☎ 0151 478 4199, Ⓦ liverpoolmuseums.org.uk/walker

Liverpool's **Walker Art Gallery** houses one of the country's best provincial art collections. The city's explosive economic growth in the eighteenth and nineteenth centuries, a time when British painting began to blossom, is illustrated by such luminaries as native Liverpudlian George Stubbs, England's greatest animal painter. Impressionists and Post-Impressionists, including Degas, Sickert, Cézanne and Monet, take the collection into more modern times and tastes, before the final round of galleries of contemporary British art. Paul Nash, Lucian Freud, Ben Nicholson, David Hockney and John Hoyland all have work here, much of it first displayed in the Walker's biennial John Moores Exhibition.

10

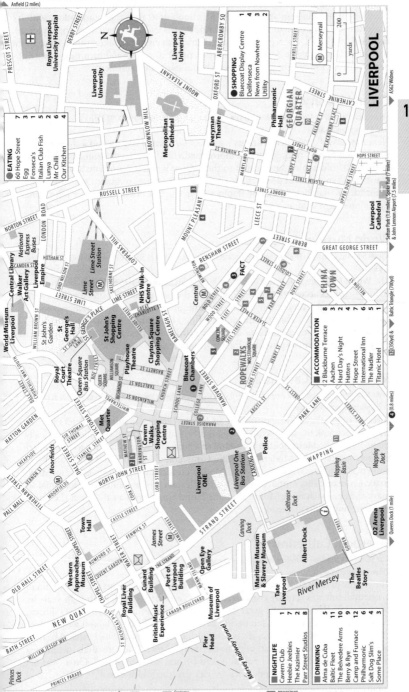

LIVERPOOL

● SHOPPING
Bluecoat Display Centre 1
Delifonseca 4
News from Nowhere 3
Utility 2

● EATING
60 Hope Street 7
Egg 3
Fonseca's 1
Italian Club Fish 5
Lunya 2
Mr Chilli 6
Our Kitchen 4

■ ACCOMMODATION
2 Blackburne Terrace 8
Aachen 3
Hard Day's Night 2
Hatters 4
Hope Street 7
International Inn 6
The Nadler 5
Titanic Hotel 1

■ NIGHTLIFE
Cavern Club 1
Heebie Jeebies 7
The Kazimier 2
Parr Street Studios 8

■ DRINKING
Alma de Cuba 5
Baltic Fleet 11
The Belvedere Arms 10
Berry & Rye 9
Camp and Furnace 12
Philharmonic 6
Salt Dog Slim's 4
Some Place 3

Although the paintings are up on the first floor, don't miss the ground-floor with its Sculpture gallery, excellent Big Art for Little Artists gallery (aimed at young children), and the Craft and Design gallery, which displays changing exhibits from a large applied arts collection – glassware, ceramics, fabrics, precious metals and furniture – largely retrieved from the homes of the city's early industrial businessmen.

Central Library

10

William Brown St, L3 8EW · Mon–Fri 9am–8pm, Sat 9am–5pm, Sun 10am–5pm · Free · ☎ 0151 233 3069 , ⓦ liverpool.gov.uk/libraries /find-a-library/central-library

Next to the Walker Gallery, the city's spectacular **Central Library** had a three-year, £50 million facelift back in 2013. Approached via a "Literary Pavement" celebrating the city's considerable contribution to the written word, it centres on a stunning atrium crowned by an elliptical dome made of around 150 pieces of glass. Don't miss the beautiful circular **Picton Reading Room** and, in the **Oak Room**, a copy of John James Audubon's huge *Birds of America*.

World Museum Liverpool

William Brown St, L3 8EN · Daily 10am–5pm · Free; planetarium £2.50, children £1.50 · ☎ 0151 478 4393, ⓦ liverpoolmuseums .org.uk/WML

The **World Museum Liverpool** is a great family attraction. The dramatic six-storey atrium provides access to an eclectic series of themed exhibits of broad appeal – from natural history to ethnography, insects to antiquities, dinosaurs to space rockets. Excellent sections for children include the Bug House and the newly reopened Mummy Room, plus a hands-on discovery centre. The planetarium and theatre have daily shows, with times posted at the information desk.

Metropolitan Cathedral

On the hill behind Lime St, off Mount Pleasant, L3 5TQ · Daily 7.30am–6pm · Free; £3 admission to crypt · ☎ 0151 709 9222, ⓦ liverpoolmetrocathedral.org.uk

After an original grandiose project of Sir Edwin Lutyens to outdo St Peter's in Rome was left incomplete (and eventually demolished in the 1980s), the idiosyncratically shaped Catholic **Metropolitan Cathedral** of Christ the King was built to Sir Frederick Gibberd's spectacular Modernist design. Consecrated in 1967, and denigratingly known as "Paddy's Wigwam" or the "Mersey Funnel", the building is anchored by sixteen concrete ribs supporting the landmark stained-glass lantern. Ceremonial steps mark the approach from Mount Pleasant/Hope Street, with a café-bar at the bottom and four huge bells at the top.

Liverpool Cathedral

Hope St, L1 7AZ · Daily 8am–6pm · Free, but donation requested · **Tower & audio tour** Daily 10am–5pm · £5.50 · ⓦ liverpoolcathedral.org.uk

The Anglican **Liverpool Cathedral** looks much more ancient than the Metropolitan Cathedral, but was actually completed eleven years later, in 1978, after 74 years in construction. The last of the great British neo-Gothic structures, Sir Giles Gilbert Scott's masterwork claims a smattering of superlatives: Britain's largest and the world's fifth-largest cathedral, the world's tallest Gothic arches and the highest and heaviest bells. Contemporary visual art adds to the unique feel of the cathedral, including a neon sign by Tracey Emin: "I Felt You And I Knew You Loved me". On a clear day, a trip up the 330ft tower is rewarded by views to the Welsh hills.

10

Ropewalks and around

At the heart of Liverpool's regenerating city centre, **Ropewalks**, the former warehouse and factory district roughly between Bold Street and Duke Street, is anchored by **FACT** (Foundation for Art and Creative Technology; 88 Wood Street; galleries Tues–Sun 11am–6pm; free; ⊚fact.co.uk), with its galleries, community projects, cinema screens, café and bar. Just north of Duke Street, in Wolstenholme Square, is *Penelope*, a huge modern sculpture of coloured plexiglass spheres on giant interwoven stalks, created by sculptor Jorge Pardo for the 2006 Biennial; it's especially striking when illuminated at night.

A short walk northwest over Hanover Street – and almost in the shadow of the enormous **Liverpool ONE** shopping complex – is the beautifully proportioned Bluecoat Chambers on School Lane, which was built in 1717 as an Anglican boarding school for orphans. Today it houses **The Bluecoat** (⊚www.thebluecoat.org.uk), long a mainstay of Liverpool's cultural life, complete with artists' studios and venues for exhibitions, courses and performances. There's also a fantastic **Bluecoat Display Centre** (see p.539), where contemporary crafts are for sale.

Western Approaches Museum

1–3 Rumford St, off Chapel St, L2 8SZ • March–Oct Mon–Thurs & Sat 10.30am–4.30pm (closed Nov–Feb) • £8 • ⊚liverpoolwarmuseum.co.uk

Not far from the waterfront, the **Western Approaches Museum** reveals an underground labyrinth of rooms, formerly headquarters for the Battle of the Atlantic during World War II. The massive Operations Room vividly displays all the technology of a 1940s nerve centre – wooden pushers and model boats, chalkboards and ladders.

The waterfront

Dominating the waterfront are the so-called **Three Graces** – namely the Port of Liverpool Building (1907), Cunard Building (1913) and, most prominently, the 322ft-high Royal Liver Building (1910), topped by the "Liver Birds", a couple of cormorants that have become the symbol of the city. As the waterfront has developed in the last decade or so, it has sprouted a number of attractions, including **Tate Liverpool**, the excellent **Maritime Museum**, the **Beatles Story**, the impressive **Museum of Liverpool** and the marvellous **Open Eye** gallery.

Museum of Liverpool

Pier Head, L3 1DG • Daily 10am–5pm • Free • ☎ 0151 478 4545, ⊚liverpoolmuseums.org.uk/mol

Huge and flashy, in a show-stopping Danish-designed building, the brilliant **Museum of Liverpool** opened in 2011. Spread over three floors, the galleries play on Liverpool's historic status as the "second city of Empire", exploring the complex political and life histories that have unfolded in a community whose wealth and social fabric were built on international trade. Children will enjoy "Little Liverpool", a gallery where they can design and build their own city, while anyone with any interest in popular culture will have an absolute ball at "Wondrous Place", a memorabilia-rich celebration of sports and music.

FERRY ACROSS THE MERSEY

Though the tumult of shipping which once fought the current in Liverpool has gone, the **Pier Head** landing stage remains the embarkation point for the **Mersey Ferry** (☎0151 330 1444, ⊚merseyferries.co.uk) to Woodside (for Birkenhead) and Seacombe (Wallasey). Straightforward ferry shuttles (£2.80 return) operate during the morning and evening rush hours. At other times the boats run circular fifty-minute "river explorer" **cruises** (hourly: Mon–Fri 10am–4pm, Sat & Sun 10am–6pm; £9), which you can combine with a visit to the **Spaceport** space exploration visitor attraction at Seacombe (Tues–Fri 10am–3pm, Sat & Sun & bank hols 10am–5pm; £9.50, with ferry £14.50; ☎0151 330 1444, ⊚spaceport.org.uk).

THE BEATLES TRAIL

Mathew Street, ten minutes' walk west of Lime Street Station, is now a little enclave of Beatles nostalgia, most of it bogus and typified by the **Cavern Walks Shopping Centre**, with a bronze statue of the boys in the atrium. **The Cavern** club where the band was first spotted by Brian Epstein, saw 275 Beatles' gigs between 1961 and 1963; it closed in 1966 and was partly demolished in 1973, though a latter-day successor, the *Cavern Club* at 10 Mathew St, complete with souvenir shop, was rebuilt on the original site. The *Cavern Pub*, across the way, boasts a coiffed Lennon mannequin lounging against the wall and an exterior "Wall of Fame" highlighting the names of all the bands who appeared at the club between 1957 and 1973 as well as brass discs commemorating every Liverpool chart-topper since 1952 – the city has produced more UK No. 1 singles than any other. There's more Beatlemania at **The Beatles Shop**, 31 Mathew Street (Ⓦthebeatleshop.co.uk), which claims to have the largest range of Beatles gear in the world.

For a personal and social history, head to the Albert Dock for **The Beatles Story** (daily: April–Oct 9am–7pm, Nov–March 10am–6pm; £15.95; Ⓦ beatlesstory.com), which traces the band's rise from the early days to their disparate solo careers. Then it's on to the two houses where John Lennon and Paul McCartney grew up. Both **20 Forthlin Rd**, home to the McCartney family from 1955 to 1964, and the rather more genteel **Mendips**, where Lennon lived with his Aunt Mimi and Uncle George between 1945 and 1963, are only accessible on pre-booked **National Trust** minibus tours (£23, NT members £9.50; ☎0844 800 4791), which run from both the city centre and Speke Hall, seven miles south (times for tours vary). The experience is disarmingly intimate, whether you're sitting in John Lennon's bedroom – which has its original wallpaper – on a replica bed looking out, as he would have done, onto his front lawn, or simply entering Paul's tiny room and gazing at pictures of his childhood.

BEATLES TOURS

Phil Hughes ☎0151 228 4565 or ☎07961 511223, Ⓦtourliverpool.co.uk. Small (eight-seater) minibus tours run daily on demand with a Blue Badge guide well versed in The Beatles and Liverpool life (4hr; £120 min tour price, 5+ £25/person). Includes city-centre pick ups/drop-offs and refreshments.

Magical Mystery Tour ☎0151 236 9091, Ⓦcavern club.org; or book at tourist offices. Tours on the multicoloured Mystery Bus (daily from 10am; 2hr; £17.95) leave from Albert Dock.

Open Eye Gallery

19 Mann Island, L3 1BP • Tues–Sun 10.30am–5.30pm; closed during exhibition takeovers, which take place four times a year and last approximately 12 days • Free • ☎0151 236 6768, Ⓦ openeye.org.uk

On the new Mann Island development just by the Museum of Liverpool sits the **Open Eye Gallery**, dedicated to photography and related media. As well as presenting an impressive programme of international exhibitions, it contains a permanent archive of around 1600 prints from the 1930s onwards.

British Music Experience

Cunard Building, L3 1DS • Daily 9am–7pm, Thurs until 9pm • Last entry 1hr 30min before closing • £16, children £11 • ☎0344 3350655, Ⓦ britishmusicexperience.com

The British Music Experience is an essential stop if you have an interest in British culture and pop music – or if you have children in tow. It's a fun and interactive experience with loads of memorabilia from 1945 onwards on display, plus a hands-on instrument studio.

Albert Dock

Five minutes' walk south of Pier Head is **Albert Dock**, built in 1846 when Liverpool's port was a world leader. Its decline began at the beginning of the twentieth century, as the new deep-draught ships were unable to berth here, and the dock last saw service in 1972. A decade later the site was given a refit, and it is now one of the city's most popular areas, full of **attractions** – including the **Beatles Story** (see box above) – and bars and restaurants.

Merseyside Maritime Museum

Albert Dock, L3 4AQ • Daily 10am–5pm • Free • ☎ 0151 478 4499, ⓦ liverpoolmuseums.org.uk/maritime

The **Merseyside Maritime Museum** fills one wing of the Dock; there's lots to see, even if some of the exhibits are looking a little tired. The basement houses **Seized!**, giving the lowdown on smuggling and revenue collection, along with **Emigrants to a New World**, an illuminating display detailing Liverpool's pivotal role as a springboard for more than nine million emigrants. Other galleries tell the story of the Battle of the Atlantic and of the three ill-fated liners – the *Titanic*, *Lusitania* and *Empress of Ireland*.

10

International Slavery Museum

The unmissable **International Slavery Museum**, on the third floor of the Maritime Museum, manages to be both challenging and chilling, as it tells dehumanizing stories of slavery while examining contemporary issues of equality, freedom and racial injustice.

Tate Liverpool

Albert Dock, L3 4BB • Daily 10am–5.50pm • Free, except for special exhibitions • ⓦ tate.org.uk/liverpool

The country's national collection of modern art from the north, **Tate Liverpool** holds popular retrospectives of artists such as Mondrian, Dalí, Magritte and Calder, along with an ever-changing display from its vast collection, and temporary exhibitions of artists of international standing. There's also a full programme of events, talks and tours.

Crosby Beach

Mariners Rd, L23 6SX/Hall Rd West, L23 8TA, Crosby • Trains from Lime St to Hall Road Station; every 30min; 20min

Seven miles north of Liverpool city centre, **Crosby Beach** was an innocuous, if picturesque, spot until the arrival in 2005 of Antony Gormley's haunting **Another Place** installation, spread along more than two miles of the shore. An eerie set of a hundred life-size cast-iron statues, each cast from Gormley's own body, are buried at different levels in the sand, all gazing out to sea and slowly becoming submerged as high tide rolls in.

ARRIVAL AND DEPARTURE   LIVERPOOL

By plane Liverpool John Lennon Airport (☎ 0870 129 8484, ⓦ liverpoolairport.com) is 8 miles southeast of the city centre; it has an information desk (daily 8am–6pm). The Airlink #500 bus (5.45am–11.45pm; every 30min; £2.20) runs from the entrance into the city. A taxi to Lime Street costs around £15.

By train Mainline trains pull in to Lime Street Station, northeast of the city centre.

Destinations Birmingham (hourly; 1hr 40min); Chester (every 30min; 45min); Leeds (hourly; 1hr 40min); London Euston (hourly; 2hr 20min); Manchester (hourly; 50min); Sheffield (hourly; 1hr 45min); York (11 daily; 2hr 15min).

By bus National Express buses use the station at Liverpool ONE, on Canning Place.

Destinations Chester (12 daily; 1hr); London (9 daily; 5hr 10min–6hr 40min); Manchester (hourly; 1hr).

By ferry Ferries to and from the Isle of Man, run by the Isle of Man Steam Packet Company (☎ 0872 299 2992, ⓦ steam -packet.com), dock at the terminals just north of Pier Head, not far from James Street Merseyrail station. From Belfast Stena Line (☎ 0844 770 7070, ⓦ stenaline.co.uk) dock over the water on the Wirral at Twelve Quays, near Woodside ferry terminal (ferry or Merseyrail to Liverpool).

GETTING AROUND

By bus Local buses depart from Queen Square and Liverpool ONE bus station. The anti-clockwise circular CityLink service is a perfect way to see the sights (every 12min; day tickets from £3)

By train The suburban Merseyrail system (trains from

Chester) calls at four underground stations, including Lime Street and James Street (for Pier Head and the Albert Dock).

By bike The largest public bicycle scheme outside of London, Citybike (☎ 0151 374 2034, ⓦ citybikeliverpool .co.uk) has bikes from £3 a day, with stations citywide.

INFORMATION AND TOURS

Tourist information The best online source of information is ⓦ visitliverpool.com. There are visitor centres at Albert Dock, Anchor Courtyard (daily 10am–4.30pm; ☎ 0151 707

0729, ⓦ albertdock.com) and Liverpool John Lennon Airport (daily 8am–6pm; ☎ 0151 907 1057). Merseytravel (☎ 0151 236 7676, ⓦ merseytravel.gov.uk) has travel centres at

Queen Square and the Liverpool ONE Interchange.

Listings The *Liverpool Echo*'s website (ⓦ liverpoolecho .co.uk/whats-on) is always current; while the hip ⓦ the doublenegative.co.uk and ⓦ creativetourist.com will see you right. *The Skinny* (ⓦ theskinny.co.uk) also publishes a useful, widely available monthly freebie.

Beatles tours Among the most popular jaunts in the city are those around the Fab Four's former haunts (see box, p.535).

Football tours You're unlikely to get a ticket for a Liverpool game, but there are daily tours around the museum, trophy room and dressing rooms (£17; museum only £10; ⓦ liverpoolfc.com). Everton, the city's other Premiership side, also offers tours (Mon, Wed, Fri 11am & 1pm, Sun 10am, noon & 2pm; ☎ 0151 530 5212; £12; ⓦ evertonfc.com).

Walking tours ⓦ visitliverpool.com has details of local guides (most Easter–Sept; from £5).

10

ACCOMMODATION

Budget chains are well represented in Liverpool, with *Premier*, *Travel Inn*, *Ibis*, *Express* (*Holiday Inn*) and others all with convenient city-centre locations, including down by Albert Dock and near Mount Pleasant.

2 Blackburne Terrace 2 Blackburne Terrace, L8 7PJ ☎ 0151 708 5474, ⓦ www.2blackburneterrace.com; map p.531. Beautiful B&B in a grand Georgian house set back from Blackburne Place, with just four elegant and individually designed rooms boasting high thread-count linens, original artworks and cutting-edge technology. With welcoming hosts and a sumptuous breakfast, this is a hidden, high-end gem. You'll save around £80 by staying midweek. **£270**

Aachen 89–91 Mount Pleasant, L3 5TB ☎ 0151 709 3477, ⓦ aachenhotel.co.uk; map p.531. The best of the Mount Pleasant budget choices, with a range of good-value rooms (with and without en-suite showers), big "eat-as-much-as-you-like" breakfasts, and a bar. **£95**

Hard Day's Night North John St, L2 6RR ☎ 0151 668 0476, ⓦ harddaysnighthotel.com; map p.531. Up-to-the-minute four-star close to Mathew Street. Splashes of vibrant colour and artful lighting enhance the elegant decor. The Lennon and McCartney suites (£950/750 respectively) are the tops. Breakfast not included. **£120**

Hatters 56–60 Mount Pleasant. L3 5SD ☎ 0151 709 5570, ⓦ hattershostels.com/liverpool-hostel; map p.531. Though it's housed in the former YMCA building – with an institutional feel and gymnasium-size dining hall – *Hatters* has clean rooms, friendly staff and a great location. Standard facilities, including internet. Prices fluctuate wildly according to what's on. Dorms **£28**, doubles **£100**

★ Hope Street 40 Hope St, L1 9DA (entrance on Hope Place) ☎ 0151 709 3000, ⓦ hopestreethotel.co.uk;

map p.531. In an unbeatable location between the cathedrals, this former Victorian warehouse retains its original elegant brickwork and cast-iron columns but now comes with hardwood floors, huge beds and luxurious bathrooms. Fabulous breakfasts, too, served in the highly rated *London Carriage Works* restaurant. Flash sales, held three times a year, offer bargain rooms; register for the email newsletter to snap one up. **£152**

★ International Inn 4 South Hunter St, off Hardman St, L1 9JG ☎ 0151 709 8135, ⓦ internationalinn.co.uk; map p.531. Converted Victorian warehouse in a great location, with modern en-suite rooms sleeping two to ten people, and 32 new double and twin "Cocoon Pods". Dorms **£20**, doubles **£45**, pods **£55**

The Nadler 29 Seel St, L1 4AU ☎ 0151 705 2626, ⓦ nadlerhotels.com/the-nadler-liverpool.html; map p.531. Smack in the heart of the Ropewalks this converted warehouse, with more than 100 minimalist rooms that complement the building's original brickwork and well-appointed modern art pieces. Rooms include a "mini-kitchen". Prices are almost halved midweek. **£119**

★ Titanic Hotel Stanley Dock, Regent Rd, L3 0AN ☎ 0151 559 1444, ⓦ titanichotelliverpool.com; map p.531. This vast warehouse was converted into a designer hotel and spa for a cool £53million. Light-filled rooms have views of the next-door tobacco warehouse or the Mersey, all have exposed brick ceilings, classy decor and en-suite bathrooms with a drench shower. It's a long walk or short taxi ride into the city; free parking. **£165**

EATING

Many Liverpool venues morph from breakfast hangout to dinner spot to late-night live-music space, making categorization tricky. Most **eating** choices are in three distinct areas – at Albert Dock, around Hardman and Hope streets in the Georgian Quarter, and along Berry and Nelson streets, the heart of Liverpool's Chinatown. Alternatively, take a short taxi ride out to Lark Lane in Aigburth, close to Sefton Park, where a dozen eating and drinking spots pack into one short street.

★ 60 Hope Street 60 Hope St, L1 9BZ ☎ 0151 707 6060, ⓦ 60hopestreet.com; map p.531. The star of the Liverpool gastronomic scene, set in a Georgian terrace, serves British cuisine (mains around £22) with creative

flourishes – roast rump of Cumbrian lamb with broccoli purée, for example – and an extensive wine list. It takes some nerve to offer, as a dessert, deep-fried jam sandwich with Carnation milk ice cream (£8.50), but the confidence

10

is justified. Just around the corner on Falkner St, they also operate *The Quarter*. Mon–Sat noon–2.30pm & 5–10.30pm, Sun noon–8pm.

Egg 16–18 Newington, L1 4AD ☎ 0151 707 2755, ⓦ eggcafe.co.uk; map p.531. Up on the third floor, this plant-strewn bohemian café serves excellent vegan and vegetarian food with good set-meal deals. Also a nice place for a chai. Mon–Fri 9am–10.30pm, Sat & Sun 10am–10.30pm.

★**Fonseca's** 12 Stanley St, L1 6AF ☎ 0151 255 0808, ⓦ delifonseca.co.uk; map p.531. Bistro with a changing blackboard menu of Italian and British delights, including Welsh black beef braised in local Wapping ale, and crayfish and chicken pie (mains around £13). The small deli counter downstairs offers a sample of the wares at the newer *Delifonseca*, 30min away on the dockside (see opposite). Mon–Thurs noon–2.30 & 5–9pm, Fri & Sat noon–10pm.

Italian Club Fish 128 Bold St, L1 4JA ☎ 0151 707 2110, ⓦ theitalianclubfish.co.uk; map p.531. Proper Italian seafood place with a menu that adapts to what's fresh – try the *Sauté Di Maurizio* (£17.95). There are also a few token meat and vegetarian dishes, all around £13. Over the road

is *Italian Club*, its slightly cooler, younger sister. Mon–Sat 10am–10pm, Sun noon–9pm.

Lunya 18–20 College Lane, L1 3DS ☎ 0151 706 9770, ⓦ lunya.co.uk; map p.531. Gorgeous Catalan and Spanish deli-restaurant in the heart of Liverpool ONE, with a vast tapas selection (from around £5) and menus running the gamut from suckling pig banquet to vegan. Mon & Tues 10am–9pm, Wed & Thurs 10am–9.30pm, Fri 10am–10pm, Sat 9am–10.30pm, Sun 10am–8.30pm.

Mr Chilli 92 Seel St, L1 4BL ☎ 0151 709 5772, ⓦ mrchilli .co.uk; map p.531. *Mr Chilli* is widely held to be the best Sichuan restaurant in Liverpool, with dishes – many of them fiery – at around £8, and famous hot pots for £10/person (min two). Mon & Tues noon–midnight, Wed–Sun noon–2am.

Our Kitchen 84b Bold St, L1 4HR ☎ 0151 709 0606, ⓦ ourkitchen.co.uk; map p.531. Brand-new Scandi-feel veggie & vegan restaurant on cool Bold St. Brunch is superb, with dishes like huevos rancheros with poached eggs or spicy tofu for £7.95; later in the day plump for an awesome Buddha Bowl filled with fresh organic produce. Juices, smoothies and tonics from £2.25. Mon–Fri 8am–10pm, Sat 9am–10pm, Sun 10am–8pm.

DRINKING

You'll enjoy a perfect evening's **bar-hopping** along Seel Street, while cutting-edge **Baltic Triangle**, the old industrial warehouse district south of Chinatown, has become the go-to quarter for the artsy crowd.

Alma de Cuba St Peter's Church, Seel St, L1 4BH ☎ 0151 702 7394, ⓦ alma-de-cuba.com; map p.531. It may have far more candles now than when it was a church – and even more in the mezzanine restaurant – but the mirrored altar is still the focus of this bar's rich, dark Cuban-themed interior. Daily 11am–2am.

Baltic Fleet 33a Wapping, L1 8DQ ☎ 0151 709 3116, ⓦ balticfleetpubliverpool.com; map p.531. Restored, no-nonsense, quiet pub with age-old shipping connections and an open fire, just south of the Albert Dock. Beer brewed on site and good pub grub on offer. Mon–Thurs & Sun noon–11pm, Fri noon–midnight, Sat 11am–midnight.

The Belvedere Arms 5 Sugnall St, L7 7EB ☎ 0151 709 0303; map p.531. Teeny-tiny two-roomed backstreet pub; punters spill outside when the sun shines. Changing ales and a splendid selection of gin. Daily noon–11pm.

★**Berry & Rye** 48 Berry St, L1 4JQ ⓔ berryandrye @gmail.com; map p.531. You'll have to hunt hard – or ask a likely local – to find this unmarked bar, but once you're in it's a delight. An intimate, bare-brick gin and whiskey joint with knowledgeable bartenders, turn-of-the-twentieth-century music – often live – and well-crafted cocktails (from £6.50). Mon–Sat 5pm–2am, Sun 7pm–1am.

★**Camp and Furnace** 67 Greenland St, L1 0BY ☎ 0151 708 2890, ⓦ campandfurnace.com; map p.531. The city's most creative and exhilarating venue is in the Baltic Triangle. Its huge warehouse spaces – one boasting the city's biggest public screen, one with a mighty furnace at one end, a cosier bar area – host festival-style food slams (Fri), massive, communal Sunday roasts, all sorts of parties and pop-ups, art installations, live performances, the lot. Do not miss it. Mon–Thurs 9am–10pm, Fri & Sat 10am–2am, Sun 10am–midnight/1am.

★**Philharmonic** 36 Hope St, L1 9BX ☎ 0151 707 2837, ⓦ nicholsonspubs.co.uk; map p.531. Liverpool's finest traditional watering hole where the main attractions – beer aside – are the mosaic floors, tiling, gilded wrought-iron gates and the marble decor in the gents. Daily 11am–midnight.

Salt Dog Slims 79–83 Seel St, L1 4BB ☎ 0151 709 7172, ⓦ saltdogslims.com; map p.531. American-style bar that's a lot of fun, with a young, friendly crowd wolfing delicious hot dogs (from £3.50) washed down with plenty of beers, backed by a solidly indie soundtrack. Upstairs is the supposedly secret *81 Ltd*, which rocks a Prohibition-era speakeasy vibe, though perhaps a tad self-consciously. Mon–Fri 3pm–2am, Sat & Sun 1pm–2am.

★**Some Place** 43 Seel St, L1 4AZ; map p.531. A green light above an unmarked doorway hints at what lies up the incense-heavy staircase – an utterly gorgeous absinthe bar that is every inch a bohemian fantasy. Savour an absinthe cocktail (from £4.50), drink in the meticulous decor and channel your inner Oscar Wilde. Wed, Thurs & Sun 9pm–late, Fri & Sat 8pm–late.

NIGHTLIFE

Liverpool's **club scene** is famously unpretentious, with posing playing second fiddle to drinking and dancing, while particularly rich in home-grown live music. Popular annual **festivals** include Beatles Week (last week of Aug; ⓦ cavernclub.org/beatleweek) and the Liverpool International Music Festival (Aug bank hol; ⓦ limfestival.co.uk), with big-name acts playing across the city.

Cavern Club 10 Mathew St, L2 6RE ☎ 0151 236 1965, ⓦ cavernclub.org; map p.531. The self-styled "most famous club in the world" has live bands, from Beatles tribute acts to indie pop and rock, at the weekends, along with occasional backstage tours and special events. The atmosphere is always high-spirited, and even though this is not the very same *Cavern* club of the Beatles' days (see box, p.535), there's a certain thrill to it all. Entry fee Thurs–Sun nights. Daily from 10am.

Heebie Jeebies 80–82 Seel St, L1 4BH ☎ 0151 708 7001, ⓦ facebook.com/Officialheebiejeebies; map p.531. Student favourite in a huge brick-vaulted room. Mainly indie and soul, with some live bands. Outdoor

courtyard too. Daily 1pm–3am.

★**The Kazimier** 4–5 Wolstenholme Square, L1 4BE ☎ 0151 324 1723, ⓦ thekazimier.co.uk; map p.531. A super-creative, split-level place with a magical garden space (entrance at 32 Seel St); *the* place to come for cabaret-style club nights, gigs and eclectic events. Hours vary but generally noon–midnight.

Parr Street Studios Parr St, L1 4JN ☎ 0151 707 1050, ⓦ parrstreet.co.uk; map p.531. Dynamic working recording studios – the UK's biggest outside London – hosting a long list of big names and home to bars/performance spaces Studio 2 and The Attic. Check website for details of what's on when.

ARTS AND ENTERTAINMENT

On the classical music scene, the **Royal Liverpool Philharmonic Orchestra** dominates; it's ranked with Manchester's Hallé as the best in the region. The **Liverpool Biennial** (July–Oct; free; ⓦ biennial.com) is a world-renowned contemporary arts festival that takes place in various public spaces and galleries across the city; the next Biennial is 2018.

CLASSICAL MUSIC AND THEATRE

Everyman Theatre Hope St, L1 9BH ☎ 0151 709 4776, ⓦ everymanplayhouse.com; map p.531. Iconic, remodelled theatre staging a mix of classics with a twist, blockbusters and new writing. The theatre's stunning portrait wall – 105 aluminium shutters featuring life-size photographs of everyday people – is a celebration of its inclusive ethos.

Liverpool Empire Lime St, L1 1JE ☎ 0870 606 3536, ⓦ liverpooltheatres.com/empire.htm; map p.531. The city's largest theatre, a venue for touring West End shows and large-scale opera and ballet productions.

Philharmonic Hall Hope St, L1 9BP ☎ 0151 709 3789, ⓦ liverpoolphil.com; map p.531. Home to the Royal Liverpool Philharmonic Orchestra, and with a full programme of other concerts.

Playhouse Theatre Williamson Square, L1 1EL ☎ 0151 709 4776, ⓦ everymanplayhouse.com; map p.531. Sister theatre to the Everyman, staging bold productions of great plays in the three-tier main house and new plays in the seventy-seat Studio.

Royal Court Theatre Roe St, L1 1HL ☎ 0870 787 1866, ⓦ royalcourtliverpool.co.uk; map p.531. Art Deco theatre and concert hall, which sees regular plays, music and comedy acts.

CINEMA

Picturehouse at FACT Wood St, L1 4DQ ☎ 0871 704 2063, ⓦ picturehouses.co.uk; map p.531. The city's only independent cinema screens new films, re-runs, cult classics and festivals.

SHOPPING

Liverpool is fabulous for shopping, with the brilliantly designed **Liverpool ONE** shopping complex holding pretty much all the names, a stretch of independent stores on **Bold Street** and arty originals in the **Baltic Triangle**.

Bluecoat Display Centre College Lane, L1 3BZ ☎ 0151 709 4014, ⓦ www.bluecoatdisplaycentre.com; map p.531. Established in 1959, this contemporary crafts and design gallery curates, exhibits and promotes jewellery, textiles, ceramics and more. Mon–Sat 10am–5.30pm, Sun noon–5pm.

Delifonseca Brunswick Dock, L3 4BN ☎ 0151 255 0808, ⓦ delifonseca.co.uk; map p.531. The new food

hall of this acclaimed, two-site bistro offers a vast array of fine deli foods and wines. Daily 8am–9pm.

News From Nowhere 96 Bold St, L1 4HY ☎ 0151 708 7270, ⓦ newsfromnowhere.co.uk; map p.531. Proper radical bookshop in the heart of Bold Street, packed to the rafters with left-leaning literature, music and more, and with an informative noticeboard. Mon–Sat 10am–5.45pm, Sun (Dec only) 11am–5pm.

Utility 8 Paradise Place, L1 8BQ ☎ 0151 702 9116, ⓦ utilitydesign.co.uk; map p.531. Stylish, design-led Liverpool store with three outlets across the city, two of them on Bold Street. This one, in Liverpool ONE, has the longest hours. Make a beeline for the quality Scouse souvenirs, particularly the brilliant · wheelie-bin desk tidy. Mon–Fri 9.30am–8pm, Sat 9am–7pm, Sun 11am–5pm.

Blackpool

10

BLACKPOOL remains Britain's archetypal seaside resort. Alongside its Golden Mile, piers, amusement arcades, tram and donkey rides, fish-and-chip restaurants, candyfloss stalls, and glitzy show venues, it boasts six miles of beach – the tide ebb is half a mile, leaving plenty of sand at low tide – a revamped **prom** and an increasingly attractive, gentrified centre.

It was the coming of the railway in 1846 that made Blackpool what it is today: Blackpool's own "Eiffel Tower" on the seafront and other refined diversions were built to cater to the tastes of the first influx of visitors, but it was the Central Pier's "open-air dancing for the working classes" that heralded the crucial change of accent. Suddenly Blackpool was favoured destination for the "Wakes Weeks", when whole Lancashire mill towns descended for their annual holiday.

Where other British holiday resorts have suffered from the rivalry of cheap foreign packages, Blackpool has gone from strength to strength. Underneath the populist veneer there's a sophisticated marketing approach, which balances ever more elaborate rides and public art installations with well-grounded traditional entertainment. And when other resorts begin to close up for the winter, Blackpool's main season is just beginning, as more than half a million light bulbs create the **Illuminations** that decorate the prom from early September to early November.

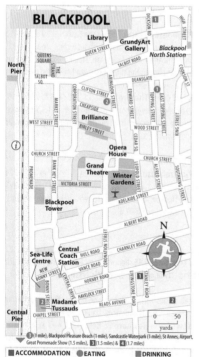

The Blackpool Tower

Promenade, FY1 4BJ · **Tower** Mon–Fri 10am–4.45pm, Sat & Sun 10am–6.15pm · Free entry to tower, but charges for attractions; for multi-attraction all-day tickets from £30, book online 24hr in advance · **Circus** 1–3 shows daily; 2hr · £16.95, or included in package · ☎ 01253 622242, ⓦ theblackpooltower.com

Between Central and North piers stands the 518ft-high **Blackpool Tower**, erected in 1894 when it was thought that the northwest really ought not to be outdone by Paris. Ride up to the top for the stunning view and an unnerving walk on the see-through glass floor. The all-day ticket covers all the other tower attractions, including the gilt Edwardian ballroom (otherwise £7.95), with its Wurlitzer organ tea dances and big band evenings, plus dungeon, children's entertainers, adventure playground, cafés and amusements. From the earliest days, there's also been a Moorish-inspired **circus** held between the tower's legs.

■ ACCOMMODATION		● EATING		■ DRINKING	
The Big Blue	3	Michael Wan's	1	Funny Girls	1
FouRooms	2	Notarianni	3	The Pump and	
Number One	4	Yorkshire		Truncheon	2
Raffles	1	Fisheries	2		

BLACKPOOL – BEHIND THE SCENES

There is, after all, an alternative Blackpool – one of history, heritage and even a spot of culture. Scene of party political conferences over the decades, the **Winter Gardens** (Coronation Street) opened to fanfares in 1878. Among the motley array of cafés, bars and amusements, seek out the extraordinary **Spanish Hall Suite** (in the form of a carved galleon), and the **Opera House** honours board – Lillie Langtry, George Formby and Vera Lynn are all present. From in front of the Opera House, follow Abingdon Street to Queen Street and the porticoed Central Library, next to which the **Grundy Art Gallery** (Mon–Sat 10am–5pm; free) might tempt you in to see its Victorian oils and watercolours, contemporary art and special exhibitions. **North Pier**, the first pier to be opened (1863) on the Blackpool seafront, is now a listed building. Head northbound from here on the tram to the **Imperial Hotel**, whose wood-panelled No. 10 Bar is covered with photographs and mementos of every British prime minister since Lloyd George.

10

The Comedy Carpet

Right outside Blackpool Tower, **The Comedy Carpet** is one of the country's most engaging pieces of public art – a 2200m-square, cross-shaped pavement comprising jokes and catchphrases from around a thousand comedians and writers, both old-school and new, in a dazzling typographic display that recalls a music hall playbill. Opened in 2011 by end-of-the-pier stalwart Ken Dodd, it's a unique celebration of British comedy and a marvellous way to spend an hour.

Blackpool Pleasure Beach

525 Ocean Blvd, FY4 1EZ • April–Nov daily from 10am • £6, though rides are extra; wristband £32.50, cheaper if booked online • ⓦ blackpoolpleasurebeach.com

The major draw in town is **Blackpool Pleasure Beach** on the South Promenade, just south of South Pier. Entrance to the amusement park is relatively cheap, but you'll have to fork out for the superb array of white-knuckle rides including the 235ft-high "Big One". The wonderful antique wooden roller coasters ("woodies" to aficionados) may seem like kids' stuff, but each is unique – the original "Big Dipper" was invented at Blackpool in 1923 and still thrills, as does the "Grand National" (1935). Caution: do not disregard the warning at the thrilling "Valhalla" ride – you will indeed get (very) wet, so maybe save this one until the end of the day. Recuperate in the park's champagne and oyster bar, which adds a bit of class to the otherwise relentless barrage of fairground noise, shrieking, jangling and fast food.

Great Promenade Show

South of the Pleasure Beach, from the Sandcastle Waterpark down to Squire's Gate, FY4 1BB • Free

Perhaps nowhere sums up the "new" Blackpool better than the **Great Promenade Show**, a set of ambitious outdoor sculptures, installations and soundscapes set along a mile or so of the new promenade. All relating to some aspect of Blackpool's history or its natural environment, these include the mighty **High Tide Organ**, which gives off haunting music when "played" by the swell of the waves, a set of sculptures of circus characters by **Sir Peter Blake**, and the world's largest **disco ball**, named "They Shoot Horses, Don't They?"

ARRIVAL AND INFORMATION   BLACKPOOL

By train The town's main train station, Blackpool North, is just off Talbot Road, a few minutes' walk northeast of the town centre, with two smaller stations, Blackpool South, just north of the Pleasure Beach on Waterloo Road,

and Blackpool Pleasure Beach. There are regular trains to Manchester (hourly; 1hr 10min).
By bus Buses pull in at the new Blackpool Central Coach Station, behind the Coral Island arcade at the junction of

Central Drive and New Bonny Street.

Tourist office Festival House, on the Promenade (Mon & Tues 9am–6pm, Wed–Sat 9am–5pm, Sun 10am–4pm; ⓣ01253 478222, ⓦvisitblackpool.com). Excellent purpose-built information centre selling discounted admission tickets for all major Blackpool attractions (except the Pleasure Beach), and travel passes.

GETTING AROUND

By tram Electric trams (ⓦblackpooltransport.com) cover the length of the promenade, from Fleetwood, north of Blackpool, to Starr Gate, south of the Pleasure Beach. Prices vary, but the cheapest option is to buy a travel pass online or from the tourist office (see above) that is valid for local buses and trams (1/3/7-day, £5/11/14); you'll pay more if you buy on board.

ACCOMMODATION

Bed-and-breakfast **prices** are generally low (from £25/person, even less on a room-only basis or out of season), but rise at weekends and during the Illuminations. To avoid the noisy crowds in peak season, make for the North Shore, beyond North Pier (the grid west of Warbreck Hill Road has hundreds of options).

The Big Blue Ocean Blvd, Pleasure Beach, FY4 1ND ⓣ01253 400045, ⓦbigbluehotel.com; map p.540. Spacious family rooms with games consoles and separate children's area, plus boutique-style, dark-wood executive rooms. There's a bar and brasserie, parking and a gym. It's next to the Pleasure Beach (and Blackpool South train station), and most rooms look out on the rides. **£135**

★ **FouRooms** 60 Reads Ave, FY1 4DE ⓣ01253 752171, ⓦfouroomsblackpool.co.uk; map p.540. One of Blackpool's best boutique hotels, a tastefully converted Victorian townhouse with airy rooms and original dark-wood fittings. The four suites are individually furnished, and staff are keen to help. **£129**

★ **Number One** 1 St Luke's Rd, FY4 2EL ⓣ01253 343901, ⓦnumberoneblackpool.com; map p.540. There's no other B&B quite like this – an extraordinarily lavish boutique experience hosted by the ultra-amiable Mark and Claire. There are just three extravagantly appointed rooms here, with more at *Number One South Beach* nearby. Parking available. **£100**

Raffles 73–77 Hornby Rd, FY1 4QJ ⓣ01253 294713, ⓦraffleshotelblackpool.co.uk; map p.540. Nice place back from Central Pier and away from the bustle, with well-kept rooms, a bar, and traditional tearooms attached. Winter rates are a good deal. **£84**

EATING

Michael Wan's Mandarin 27 Clifton St, FY1 1JD ⓣ01253 622687, ⓦmichaelwansmandarin.co.uk; map p.540. Delicious and authentic Asian food served up in contemporary surroundings by charming staff. Signature dishes include zesty lemon chicken (£11.90) and Szechuan twice-cooked pork (£11.50). Tues–Fri noon–3pm & 4.30pm–midnight, Sat noon–1.45pm & 5.30–11.45pm, Sun 5.30–10.15pm.

Notarianni 9 Waterloo Rd, FY4 1AF ⓣ01253 342510, ⓦnotarianni.co.uk; map p.540. Now with the third- and fourth-generation of Italians at the helm, this ice-cream parlour is a Blackpool institution. No fancy flavours here; they only serve vanilla. The banana split (£4.50) is unmissable. Daily 10am–8pm.

Yorkshire Fisheries 14–16 Topping St, FY1 3AQ ⓣ01253 627739, ⓦyorkshirefisheries.co.uk; map p.540. Behind the Winter Gardens, this sit-down and takeaway fish-and-chip shop is commonly agreed to be the best in the centre of town. Mon–Sat 11.30am–7pm, Sun noon–6pm.

DRINKING AND NIGHTLIFE

Blackpool has a plethora of **theme bars** and any number of places for **karaoke** or **dancing**. Family-oriented fun revolves around musicals, veteran TV comedians, magicians, ice dance, tribute bands, crooners and stage spectaculars put on at a variety of end-of-pier and historic venues.

Funny Girls 5 Dickson Rd, off Talbot Rd, FY1 2AX ⓣ01253 649194, ⓦfunnygirlsonline.co.uk; map p.540. A Blackpool institution – a transvestite-run bar with nightly cabaret shows that attract long (gay and straight) queues. It's a hen-party favourite and not to everyone's tastes, but the best place in town if you fancy some unabashedly bawdy Blackpool fun.

The Pump and Truncheon 13 Bonny St, FY1 4AR (behind Madame Tussauds) ⓣ01253 624099, ⓦbit.ly/Truncheon; map p.540. If you're after something a little more low-key, this traditional backstreet pub is a gem. Craft beers, cask ales and CAMRA discount – and they serve pizza for less than a tenner.

ENTERTAINMENT

The Grand Theatre Church St, FY1 1HT ☎ 01253 290190, ⓦ blackpoolgrand.co.uk; map p.540. Built in 1894 for the town's more refined audiences, the Grand has a tradition of distinguishing itself from other amusements, putting on performances of Shakespeare as well as more popular variety shows.

Opera House Winter Gardens, Church St, FY1 1HL

☎ 01253 625252, ⓦ wintergardensblackpool.co.uk; map p.540. Set in the Winter Gardens, the Opera House has a star-studded history that includes such populist greats as Charlie Chaplin, George Formby and Vera Lynn. These days you'll find a variety of shows on offer, including West End hits. Also in the Winter Gardens is the Empress Ballroom, which is a majestic gig venue (same contact details).

10

Lancaster

LANCASTER, Lancashire's county town, dates back at least as long ago as the Roman occupation, though only scant remains survive from that period. A Saxon church was later built within the ruined Roman walls as Lancaster became a strategic trading centre, and by medieval times a **castle** had been built on the heights above the river. Lancaster later developed into an important port on the slave trade triangle, and it's the **Georgian buildings** from that time – especially those around the castle – that give the town much of its character. Many people choose to stay here on the way to the Lakes or Dales to the north; and it's an easy side-trip the few miles west to the resort of **Morecambe** and to neighbouring **Heysham village**, with its ancient churches, or east through the **Forest of Bowland**.

Lancaster Castle

Castle Park, LA1 1YJ • Daily 9.30am–5pm • £8 • **Tours** Every 30min Mon–Fri 10am–4pm, Sat & Sun 10.30am–4pm; 1hr 30min • Included in entry price • ☎ 01524 64998, ⓦ lancastercastle.com

The site of **Lancaster Castle** has been the city's focal point since Roman times. The Normans built the first defences here, at the end of the eleventh century – two hundred years later it became a **crown court**, a role it maintains today, and until 2011 it was a working prison. Currently, about a third of the battlemented building can be visited on an entertaining hour-and-a quarter-long tour, though court sittings sometimes affect the schedules.

Lancaster City Museum

Market Square, LA1 1HT • Tues–Sun 10am–5pm • Free • ☎ 01524 64637, ⓦ lancashire.gov.uk/leisure-and-culture/museums /lancaster-maritime-museum

Drop into the former Town Hall to peruse the **Lancaster City Museum**. While hardly groundbreaking, exhibits do a good job of illustrating the history of Lancaster. One of the rooms holds the **Kings Own Royal Regiment Museum**, and the landscapes and portraits on the stairway are a nice local touch.

Lancaster Maritime Museum

Custom House, St George's Quay, LA1 1RB • Daily: April–Oct 10am–5pm; Nov–March 12.30–4pm • £3 • ☎ 01524 382264, ⓦ lancashire.gov.uk /leisure-and-culture/museums/lancaster-maritime-museum

Down on the banks of the River Lune – which lent Lancaster its name – one of the eighteenth-century quayside warehouses is taken up by part of **Lancaster Maritime Museum**. The museum amply covers life on the sea and inland waterways of Lancashire, including the role of Lancaster's residents in the highly profitable slave trade.

Williamson Park

Quernmore Rd, LA1 1UX • Daily: April–Sept 10am–5pm; Oct–March 10am–4pm • Free; butterfly house £3.90, under-16s £2.90 • ☏ 01524 33318, ⓦ lancaster.gov.uk/parks-and-open-spaces/williamson-park

For a panorama of the town, Morecambe Bay and the Cumbrian fells, take a steep 25-minute walk up Moor Lane (or a taxi from the bus station) to the beautifully maintained **Williamson Park**, Lancaster's highest point. Funded by local statesman and lino magnate Lord Ashton, the park's centrepiece is the 220ft-high **Ashton Memorial**, a Baroque folly raised by his son in memory of his second wife. The revamped tropical **Butterfly House** is a must if you have children with you.

10

ARRIVAL AND DEPARTURE
LANCASTER

By train Trains pull in at Meeting House Lane, a 5min walk from the town centre.

Destinations Carlisle (every 30min–1hr; 50min); Manchester (every 30min–1hr; 1hr); Morecambe (every 30min–1hr; 10min).

By bus The bus station is on Cable St, a 5min walk from the tourist office.

Destinations Carlisle (4–5 daily; 1hr 20min); Kendal (hourly; 1hr); Manchester (2 daily; 2hr); Windermere (hourly; 1hr 45min).

INFORMATION AND TOURS

Tourist office The Storey, Meeting House Lane, off Castle Hill, LA1 1TH (Mon–Sat 10am–5pm; ☏ 01524 582394, ⓦ visitlancaster.org.uk).

Canal cruises Contact Lancaster Canal Boats (☏ 01524 389410, ⓦ budgietransport.co.uk).

ACCOMMODATION

Toll House Penny St, LA1 1XT ☏ 01524 599900, ⓦ www.thwaites.co.uk/hotels-and-inns/inns/toll-house -at-lancaster. Recently refurbished, this elegant townhouse has 28 oddly shaped rooms, all with airy high ceilings and flatscreen TVs. It's worth popping in the bar for a pint of good local ale too. **£95**

★**The Sun Hotel and Bar** 63 Church St, LA1 1ET ☏ 01524 66006, ⓦ thesunhotelandbar.co.uk. The city centre's only four-star hotel is in a handsome Georgian building, with sixteen contemporary rooms (some with king-sized beds, all with fine bathrooms) above a relaxed bar-restaurant. **£90**

EATING AND DRINKING

The Borough 3 Dalton Square, LA1 1PP ☏ 01524 64170, ⓦ theboroughlancaster.co.uk. Great for informal dining, this roomy gastropub – in a refurbished 1824 building – has a rigorously sourced local and organic menu. Moderately priced tapas-style platters offer smoked fish, Lancashire cheese and the like, while mains range from ostrich to salmon. Nine smart new rooms upstairs too (£95). Kitchen Mon–Thurs & Sun 8–11am & noon–9pm, Fri & Sat 8–11am & noon–9.30pm.

The Music Room Sun St, LA1 1EW ☏ 01524 65470, ⓦ facebook.com/themusicroomcafe. A quirky, stylish little place with a marvellous glass frontage, serving top-quality coffees (it has its own roaster), teas and melt-in-the-mouth cake. The best place in town to take a break.

Mon–Sat 10am–5pm.

Water Witch Canal towpath, Aldcliffe Lane, LA1 1SU ☏ 01524 63828, ⓦ waterwitchlancaster.co.uk. Relaxing canalside pub named after an old canal packet boat. There is an impressive range of real ales and continental lagers, and the food is a cut above pub grub (sharing platters from £10). Kitchen Mon–Fri noon–9pm, Sat noon–9.30pm, Sun noon–8pm.

★**Whale Tail** 78a Penny St, LA1 1XN ☏ 01524 845133, ⓦ whaletailcafe.co.uk. Tucked away in a yard and up on the first floor, this cheery veggie and wholefood café serves good breakfasts, quiche, moussaka and baked potatoes. Mon–Sat 9am–4.30pm, Sun 10am–3pm.

ON YOUR BIKE

Lancaster promotes itself as a **cycling centre**, and miles of canal towpaths, old railway tracks and riverside paths provide excellent traffic-free routes around the Lune estuary, Lancaster Canal and Ribble Valley, southeast of Lancaster. Typical is the easy riverside path to the **Crook O'Lune** beauty spot, where you can reward yourself with a bacon buttie and an Eccles cake at *Woodie's* famous snack bar. For bike hire, contact **Leisure Lakes Bikes** (from £10/4hr; 103–105 Penny St, LA1 1XN; ☏ 01524 844389, ⓦ leisurelakesbikes.com).

THE FOREST OF BOWLAND

The remote **Forest of Bowland** (⊛forestofbowland.com), designated an Area of Outstanding Natural Beauty, is a picturesque drive east from Lancaster. The name forest is used here in its traditional sense of "a royal hunting ground" – it's a captivating landscape of remote fells and farmland with plenty of walks and is populated by rare birds like the golden plover, short-eared owl, snipe and merlin. Head east on the A683, turning off towards High Bentham; once at the village turn right at the sign for the station and you begin the fifteen-mile slog down an old drovers' track (now a very minor road) known as the **Trough of Bowland**. This winds through heather- and bracken-clad hills before ending up at the compact village of Slaidburn. If you've got time, it's worth pushing ahead to **Clitheroe**, a tidy little market town overlooked by a Norman keep.

10

NIGHTLIFE

The Dukes Moor Lane, LA1 1QE ☎01524 598500, ⊛dukes-lancaster.org. Lancaster's arts centre is the main cultural destination in town, with cinemas and stages for all manner of theatre and dance performances, exhibition space and a café-bar.

Yorkshire House 2 Parliament St, LA1 1DB ☎01524 64679, ⊛bit.ly/YorkshireHouse. Down-to-earth real ale boozer with a cracking alternative live-music venue upstairs, pulling in a young crowd. Mon–Wed 7pm–midnight, Thurs 7pm–1am, Sat 2pm–1am, Sun 7–11.30pm.

Morecambe and Heysham

The seaside resort of **MORECAMBE** lies five miles west of Lancaster – there's a pleasant cycle path between the two, and there are bus and train services that can whizz you there in ten minutes. The sweep of the bay is the major attraction, with the Lake District fells visible beyond, while the **Stone Jetty** features bird motifs and sculptures – recognizing Morecambe Bay as Britain's most important wintering site for wildfowl and wading birds. A little way along the prom stands the statue of one of Britain's most treasured comedians – Eric Bartholomew, who took the stage name **Eric Morecambe** when he met his comedy partner, Ernie Wise.

Heysham Village

Three miles southwest of Morecambe – you can walk here along the promenade – the shoreside **HEYSHAM VILLAGE** is centred on a group of charming seventeenth-century cottages and barns. Proudest relic is the well-preserved Viking hog's-back tombstone in Saxon **St Peter's Church**, set in a romantic churchyard below the headland. Don't miss the local **nettle beer**, brewed since Victorian times and served in the village tearooms.

ARRIVAL AND DEPARTURE   MORECAMBE AND HEYSHAM

By bus and train Morecambe's bus and train stations are close together near Central Drive; both receive regular services from Lancaster (10min); the train is far cheaper.

ACCOMMODATION

Midland Hotel The Promenade, Marine Road West, LA4 4BU ☎0845 850 3502, ⊛englishlakes.co.uk/the-midland. Lovely four-star Art Deco hotel whose comfortable rooms extend the Modernist theme. Even if you're not staying it's worth popping into the electric-blue bar, and taking a drink onto the terrace to watch the sunset. **£125**

The Isle of Man

The **Isle of Man** (locally called **Ellan Vannin**), almost equidistant from Ireland, England, Wales and Scotland, is one of the most beautiful spots in Britain, a mountainous, cliff-fringed island just 33 miles by 13. There's peace and quiet in abundance, walks around the unspoilt hundred-mile coastline, rural villages and steam trains straight out of a 1950s picture book – a yesteryear ensemble if ever there was one.

10

Many true Manx inhabitants, who comprise a shade under half of its 87,500 population, insist that the Isle of Man is not part of England, nor even of the UK. Indeed, although a Crown dependency, the island has its own government, **Tynwald**, arguably the world's oldest democratic parliament, which has run continuously since 979 AD. To further complicate matters, the island maintains a unique associate status in the EU (islanders were not allowed a vote in the recent Brexit referendum), and also has its own sterling currency (worth the same as the mainland currency), its own laws, an independent postal service, and a Gaelic-based language which is taught in schools and seen on dual-language road signs.

All roads lead to the capital, **Douglas**, the only town of any size. From the summit of **Snaefell**, the island's highest peak, you get an idea of the island's varied scenery, the finest parts of which are to be found in the seventeen officially designated National Glens. Most of these are linked by the 95-mile **Raad Ny Foillan** (Road of the Gull) coastal footpath, which passes several of the island's numerous hillforts, Viking ship burials and Celtic crosses. Scenery aside, the main tourist draw is the **TT (Tourist Trophy) motorcycle races** held in the two weeks around the late May bank holiday, a frenzy of speed and burning rubber that has shattered the island's peace annually since 1907.

ARRIVAL AND DEPARTURE
THE ISLE OF MAN

By plane The cheapest way to get to the Isle is by air, with several budget airlines – among them Flybe (W flybe .com); and easyJet (W easyjet.com) – offering flights from many British and Irish regional airports.

By ferry Ferries or the quicker fastcraft (Manannan), both run by the Isle of Man Steam Packet Company (T 0872 299 2992, W steam-packet.com), leave from Heysham (ferries; 1 or 2 daily; 3hr 30min) and Liverpool (fastcraft; 1 or 2 daily March–Nov; 2hr 30min).

GETTING AROUND

Travel passes "Island Explorer" tickets – sold at Douglas's Welcome Centre (see below) – give one (£16), three (£32), or seven (£47) days' unlimited travel on all buses and trains.

Car rental Most rental outfits have offices at the airport or can deliver cars to the Sea Terminal in Douglas. Contact Athol (T 01624 820092, W athol.co.im); Mylchreests (T 0800 019 0335, W mylchreests.com); or 4Hire (T 01624 820820, W 4hire.co.im).

Transport website W gov.im/publictransport.

INFORMATION

Manx National Heritage (W manxnationalheritage.im) run thirteen heritage sites and museums around the Isle of Man including the Old House of Keys, the House of Manannan, Castle Rushen and the Laxey Wheel. They also offer money-saving passes including a 14-Day Holiday pass (£20, available from any attraction).

Tourist information The Welcome Centre in the Sea Terminal building at Douglas (Mon–Sat 8am–6pm, plus Sun 10am–2pm May–Sept only); T 01624 686766, is the best place for island-wide information.

Useful websites W gov.im, W visitisleofman.com and W www.iomguide.com.

Douglas

Dubbed "the Naples of the North" by John Betjeman, **DOUGLAS** has developed since its 1950s heyday of seaside holiday-making into a major offshore financial centre. The seafront vista has changed little since Victorian times, and is still trodden by heavy-footed carthorses pulling trams (April–Sept, 9am–5.30pm; £3). On Harris Promenade the opulent Edwardian **Gaiety Theatre** sports a lush interior that can be seen on fascinating two-hour tours (Easter–Oct, Sat 10am; £8.50, call ahead; T 01624 600555, W www.villagaiety.com).

Further up Harris Promenade, approaching Broadway, the **Villa Marina gardens** display classic Victorian elegance with their colonnade walk, lawns and bandstand. The main sight, however, is the **Manx Museum**, on the corner of Kingswood Grove and Crellin's Hill (Mon–Sat 10am–5pm; free), which helps the visitor get to grips with Manx culture and heritage from the Vikings to the Victorians. Finally, out on **Douglas Head** – the point looming above the southern bay – the town's Victorian camera obscura has been restored for visits (May–Sept Sat 1–4pm, Sun & bank hols 11am–4pm; weather dependent, open when flag is flying; £2).

ARRIVAL AND DEPARTURE   DOUGLAS

By plane Ronaldsway Airport (☎01624 821600, ⌨gov .im) is 10 miles south of Douglas, close to Castletown. A regular bus runs into town, while a taxi costs around £20. Car hire is available at the airport.

By ferry The Isle of Man Steam Packet Company (⌨steam-packet.com) ferries from Liverpool, Heysham, Dublin, and Belfast arrive at the Sea Terminal (April–Oct 7am–8pm; Nov–March 8am–6/8pm), close to the centre of town, at the south end of the promenade.

By train The Steam Railway (March–Nov 9.50am– 4.50pm; £5.20–12.40 return) extends for 15 miles and

connects Douglas to Port Soderick, Santon, Castletown, Port St Mary and Port Erin. The Douglas station is alongside the river and fishing port, at the top end of the North Quay. Meanwhile, the Manx Electric Railway (March–Nov daily 9.40am–4.40pm; some later departures in summer; £4.40–14 return), which runs for 17.5 miles from Douglas to Snaefell, departs from the northern end of the seafront at Derby Castle Station.

By bus The Lord Street terminal, the hub of the island's dozen or so bus routes, is 50yd west of the Sea Terminal's forecourt taxi rank.

10

GETTING AROUND AND TOURS

By bus Buses #1, #1H, #2, #2A, #11, #12 and #12A run along Douglas's promenade from North Quay; you can also take a horse-drawn tram.

Bike rental Eurocycles, 8a Victoria Rd, off Broadway (Mon–Sat 9am–5.30pm; ☎01624 624909, ⌨eurocycles

.co.im).

Cruises Seasonal pleasure cruises on the *MV Karina* head out from Douglas Sea Terminal (daily April–Oct, weather permitting; ☎01624 861724 or ☎07624 493592, ⌨iompleasurecruises.com).

ACCOMMODATION

The Claremont Hotel Loch Promenade, IM1 2LX ☎01624 617068, ⌨claremonthoteldouglas.com. Recently renovated throughout, the centrally located 56-room *Claremont* boasts sea views and gym access for all guests. **£150**

The Mereside 1 Empire Terrace, IM2 4LE ☎01624 676355, ⌨hqbar.im. Small, family-owned B&B just off the Central Promenade, with well-appointed if slightly old-fashioned rooms. There's a good bar/restaurant downstairs. **£80**

The Sefton Harris Promenade, IM1 2RW ☎01624 645500, ⌨seftonhotel.co.im. Next to the Gaiety Theatre, this four-star has spacious rooms – some of which

have been modernized – offering either a sea view or a balcony overlooking the impressive internal water garden. Facilities include gym, an underground car park, a bar and restaurant. **£125**

The Town House Loch Promenade, IM1 2LX ☎01624 626125, ⌨thetownhouse.im. This aparthotel is set over three floors and offers 15 individually designed suites with complimentary telephone calls. Service is excellent. **£120**

Welbeck Hotel Mona Drive, IM2 4LF ☎01624 675663, ⌨welbeckhotel.com. A traditional mid-sized family-run seaside hotel, with well-maintained, comfortable rooms and friendly service. It lies 100yd from the seafront, up the hill. **£90**

EATING

The food scene in Douglas is increasingly sophisticated and many of the independent cafés and restaurants are focusing on seasonal Manx produce. In the summer months, the places below get busy in the evenings, so always book ahead.

★**Café Tanroagan** 9 Ridgeway St, IM1 1EW ☎01624 612355, ⌨tanroagan.co.uk. The best fish and seafood on the island, straight off the boat, served simply or with an assured Mediterranean twist in a relaxed, contemporary setting. Dinner reservations essential. Mains around £20. Mon–Fri 12.30–2.30pm & 6–9.30pm, Sat 6–9.30pm.

L'Experience 1 Summer Hill, IM2 4PH ☎01624 623103, ⌨lex.co.im. This seemingly unexceptional whitewashed shack is in fact a long-standing French bistro that serves up meat dishes as well as daily caught fish specials, and good lunchtime dishes; £18 average for a

main. Mon & Wed–Sat noon–2pm & 7–11pm.

Little Fish Café 31 North Quay, IM1 4LB ☎01624 622518, ⌨littlefishcafe.com. This stylish quayside eatery offers freshly brewed coffee and a breakfast, brunch and evening menu featuring locally sourced ingredients. Tues–Sat 11am–9pm, Sun 10am–3pm.

Noa Bakehouse Fort St, IM1 2LJ ☎01624 618063, ⌨bit.ly/NoaBakehouse. An open-plan industrial space made cosy with eclectic decor and the smell of coffee and fresh baking. Locals descend for the delicious breakfasts (until 11am) and brunch and lunch (until 3pm). Daily

specials such as Manx lamb burger with Moroccan spices are around £7.50. Mon–Sat 8am–4pm, Sun 10am–2pm.
The Ticket Hall Douglas Station, North Quay, IM1 1JE, ☏ 01624 627888, ⊛ ticket-hall.com. A very handy and pleasantly traditional café in the former ticket office at Douglas Station. Serving brunch 8–11am and hot lunches and daily specials noon–2.30pm, otherwise only drinks and snacks. Daily 8am–4pm, Fri & Sat 7–9.30pm.

DRINKING

The Bridge North Quay, IM1 4LQ ☏ 01624 675 268 ⊛ facebook.com/TheBridgeIOM. Cosy and comfortable quayside pub, with a lovely outdoor patio. The pub food here is of a high standard, the staff are friendly and there's plenty of choice at the bar. Mon–Thurs noon–11pm, Fri & Sat noon–midnight, Sun noon–6pm.
Queen's Hotel Queen's Promenade, IM2 4NL ☏ 01624 674438, ⊛ facebook.com/thequeensisleofman. This old seafront pub at the top end of the promenade is the best place for alfresco drinks, with picnic tables looking out over the sweeping bay. Daily noon–1am.
Rovers Return 11 Church St, IM1 2AG ☏ 01624 611101, ⊛ facebook.com/TheRoversReturnPubIoM. Cosy old local where you can try the local Manx beers, including "Old Bushy Tail". Daily 11am–11pm.

Laxey

Filling a narrow valley, the straggling village of **LAXEY**, seven miles north of Douglas, spills down from its train station to a small harbour and long, pebbly beach, squeezed between two bulky headlands. The Manx Electric Railway from Douglas drops you at the station used by the Snaefell Mountain Railway (see below). Passengers disembark and then head inland and uphill to Laxey's pride, the **"Lady Isabella" Great Laxey Wheel** (April–Nov daily 9.30am–5pm; £8), which is smartly painted in red and white. With a diameter of more than 72ft it's said to be the largest working water wheel in the world. In **Old Laxey**, around the harbour, half a mile below the station, large car parks attest to the popularity of the beach and river.

Snaefell

Every hour (30min in high season), the tramcars of the **Snaefell Mountain Railway** (April–Nov daily 10.15am–3.45pm; £12 return) begin their thirty-minute climb from Laxey through increasingly denuded moorland to the island's highest point, the top of **Snaefell** (2036ft) – the Vikings' "Snow Mountain" – from where, on a clear day, you can see England, Wales, Scotland and Ireland. At the summit, most people are content to pop into the café and bar and then soak up the views for the few minutes until the return journey. But with a decent map and good weather, you could follow the trails back down to Laxey instead (approx. 5.5 miles).

Maughold

Bus #16 direct from Ramsey (Mon–Fri 6 daily)

The Manx Electric Railway trains stop within a mile and a half of **MAUGHOLD**, seven miles northeast of Laxey, a tiny hamlet just inland from the cliff-side lighthouse at Maughold Head. The isolation adds to the attraction of its **parish church**, with its outstanding collection of early Christian and Norse carved crosses – 44 pieces, dating from the sixth to the thirteenth century, and ranging from fragments of runic carving to a 6ft-high rectangular slab.

Peel

The main settlement on the west coast, **PEEL** (bus #4, #5 or #6 hourly from Douglas) is one of the most Manx of all the island's towns, with an imposing medieval **castle** rising across the harbour and a popular sandy **beach** running the length of its eastern promenade.

TYNWALD DAY

The trans-island A1 (hourly buses #5 or #6 from Douglas) follows a deep twelve-mile-long furrow between the northern and southern ranges from Douglas to Peel. A hill at the crossroads settlement of **ST JOHN'S**, nine miles along, is the original site of **Tynwald**, the ancient Manx government, which derives its name from the Norse *Thing Völlr*, meaning "Assembly Field". Nowadays the word refers to the Douglas-based **House of Keys and Legislative Council** (tours Mon 2pm & Fri 10am; free; ☎01624 685520), but acts passed in the capital only become law once they have been proclaimed here on **July 5** (ancient Midsummer's Day), in an annual open-air parliament that also hears the grievances of the islanders.

Until the nineteenth century the local people arrived with their livestock and stayed a week or more – in true Viking fashion – to thrash out local issues, play sports, make marriages and hold a fair. Now **Tynwald Day** begins with a service in the chapel, followed by a procession, a fair and concerts.

10

Peel Castle

M5 1TB • April–Nov daily 10am–4/5pm • £6, audioguide £5

What probably started out as a flint-working village on a naturally protected spot gained significance with the foundation of a **monastery** in the seventh or eighth century, parts of which remain inside the ramparts of the red sandstone **Peel Castle**. The site became the residence of the Kings of Mann until the mid-thirteenth century, when they moved to Castle Rushen in Castletown. It's a fifteen-minute walk from the town around the river harbour and over the bridge to the castle.

House of Manannan

M5 1TA • Daily 10am–5pm • £10

The excellent harbourside **House of Manannan** heritage centre is named after the island's ancient sea god. You should allow at least two hours to get around this splendid three-floor participatory museum, where you can listen to Celtic legends in a replica roundhouse, wander through a replica kipper factory and even examine the contents and occupants of a life-sized Viking ship.

EATING AND DRINKING   PEEL

Cod and Castle 16 Shore Road, IM5 1QH ☎01624 840624, ⓦfacebook.com/thecodandcastle. Traditional seafront chippie with a few tables, or get takeaway and cross the road to the beach. Manx Queenies (lightly battered Queen scallops) are a local speciality (£4.50). Mon–Sat 11.30am–9pm, Sun 11.30am–8pm.

Creek Inn The Quayside, IM5 1AT ☎01624 842216, ⓦthecreekinn.co.uk. Popular quayside pub opposite the House of Manannan, serving real ale, with monthly guest beers, and a delicious array of specials. Live music at the weekends. Daily from 10am–midnight; food served noon–10pm.

Port Erin

The small, time-warped resort of **PORT ERIN**, at the southwestern tip of the island, a one-hour train ride from Douglas, has a wide, fine sand beach backing a deeply indented bay sitting beneath green hills. To stretch your legs, head up the promenade past the golf club to the entrance of Bradda Glen, where you can follow the path out along the headland to Bradda Head.

ARRIVAL AND DEPARTURE   PORT ERIN

By bus Buses #1 and #2 from Douglas/Castletown, and #8 from Peel/St John's, stop on Bridson St, across Station Road and opposite the *Cherry Orchard* aparthotel.

By train Trains pull in on Station Rd, a couple of hundred yards above and back from the beach.

10

Rowany Cottier Spaldrick, IM9 6PE ☎01624 832287, ⓦrowanycottier.com. Port Erin's best B&B, in a detached house overlooking the bay, opposite the entrance to Bradda Glen. No credit cards. **£48**

Port St Mary and around

Two miles east of Port Erin, the fishing harbour still dominates little **PORT ST MARY**, with its houses strung out in a chain above the busy dockside. The best beach is away to the northeast, reached from the harbour along a well-worked Victorian path that clings to the bay's rocky edge.

From Port St Mary, a minor road runs out along the Meayll peninsula towards **CREGNEASH**, the oldest village on the island. The **Cregneash Village Folk Museum** (April–Nov daily 10am–4/5pm; £6) is a picturesque cluster of nineteenth-century thatched crofts populated by craftspeople in period costume; there's a tearoom and information centre. Local views are stunning, and it's just a short walk south to **The Chasms**, a headland of gaping rock cliffs swarming with gulls and razorbills.

The footpath continues around Spanish Head to the turf-roofed **Sound Visitor Centre** (daily 10am–4/5pm; free), which also marks the end of the road from Port St Mary. There's an excellent café (see below), with windows looking out across The Sound to the **Calf of Man**.

By train Regular steam trains run to Port Erin or back to Douglas from Port St Mary. The station is a 10min walk from the harbour along High St, Bay View Road and Station Road.

By bus Hourly buses from the harbour serve Port Erin and Douglas.

★**Aaron House** The Promenade, Port St Mary, IM9 5DE ☎01624 835702, ⓦaaronhouse.co.uk. High up on the Promenade, this guesthouse lovingly re-creates a Victorian experience and features brass beds and claw-foot baths in some of the rooms, with home-made scones and jam in the parlour and splendid breakfasts. The bay views from the front are superb. **£40**

The Café at the Sound Sound Road, IM9 5PZ, 2.5 miles south of Port St Mary ☎01624 838123, ⓦbit.ly /TheCafeAtTheSound. This incredible Modernist building has a hard to beat location overlooking the Calf of Man – weather permitting, nab a table outside. Freshly made sandwiches from £4.95 and fish and chips (£11.95) all day with a fancier evening menu and daily specials. All local produce. April–Oct Sun–Thurs 9am–5pm, Fri & Sat 9am–9pm; Nov–March daily 10am–4/5pm.

Castletown and around

From the twelfth century until 1869, **CASTLETOWN** was the island's capital, but then the influx of tourists and the increase in trade required a bigger harbour and Douglas

---

THE CALF OF MAN

It is worth making the effort to visit the **Calf of Man**, a craggy, heath-lined nature reserve lying off the southwest tip of the Isle of Man, where resident wardens monitor the seasonal populations of kittiwakes, puffins, choughs, razorbills, shags, guillemots and others, and grey seals can be seen all year round basking on the rocks.

There are no scheduled tours but **boats** can be chartered (May–Sept, weather permitting) from Port St Mary (Gemini Charter; wildlife and fishing trips; ☎01624 832761, ⓦgeminicharter. co.uk) and Port Erin pier (Shona Boat Trips; Calf of Man round trips or drop off/pick up; ☎07624 322765 or ☎07624 480682, ⓦbit.ly/Shonaboat). You can also **sea-kayak** around this spectacular coast. **Adventurous Experiences** (☎01624 843034, ⓦadventurousexperiences. com) runs trips from evening paddles (£55) to full-day excursions (from £85) – no experience is required, but the location might change depending on sea conditions.

took over. Its sleepy harbour and low-roofed cottages are dominated by **Castle Rushen** (April–Nov, daily 10am–4/5pm; £8), formerly home to the island's legislature and still the site of the investiture of new lieutenant-governors.

Old House of Keys

Parliament Square, IM9 1LA • April–Nov daily 10am–4pm • Free • **Debates** Daily 11am & 2.45pm • £6 • ☎ 01624 648017

Across the central Market Square and down Castle Street in tiny Parliament Square you'll find the **Old House of Keys**. Built in 1821, this was the site of the Manx parliament, the Keys, until 1874 when it was moved to Douglas. The frock-coated Secretary of the House meets you at the door and shows you into the restored debating chamber, where visitors are included in a highly entertaining participatory session of the House, guided by a hologram Speaker.

Rushen Abbey

Ballasalla, IM9 3DB, 2 miles north of Castletown • Daily April–Nov 10am–4/5pm • £8 • Buses #1, #2, #8, #11, #12 from Castletown or steam railway

The island's most important medieval religious site, **Rushen Abbey** lies two miles north of Castletown at Ballasalla ("place of the willows"). A Cistercian foundation of 1134, it was abandoned by its "White Monks" in the 1540s and was subsequently used as a school. The excavated remains themselves – low walls, grass-covered banks and a sole church tower from the fifteenth century – would hold only specialist appeal were it not for the excellent interpretation centre, which explains much about daily life in a Cistercian abbey.

ARRIVAL AND DEPARTURE

By bus Buses #8 (from Peel/Port Erin) and #1 (from Douglas) stop in the main square.

By train Castletown Station is a 5min walk from the centre, out along Victoria Road from the harbour.

CASTLETOWN AND AROUND

Destinations include Ballabeg, Colby, Port St Mary and Port Erin to the south and Ballasalla, Santon, Port Soderick and Douglas to the north.

EATING AND DRINKING

The Abbey Restaurant Ballasalla, IM9 3DB, 2 miles north of Castletown ☎ 01624 822393 🌐 theabbey.im. Located next to Rushen Abbey, this restaurant and café serves up modern European cuisine complemented by a predominately Southern European wine list. The venue is child-friendly and also boasts a spacious outdoor garden and a private dining room. Wed–Sat 10am–10pm, Sun noon–3.30pm.

Cumbria and the Lakes

SUNRISE OVER WINDERMERE

Cumbria and the Lakes

The Lake District is England's most hyped scenic area, and for good reason. Within an area a mere thirty miles across, sixteen major lakes are squeezed between the country's highest mountains – an almost alpine landscape of glistening water, dramatic valleys and picturesque stone-built villages. Most of the region lies within the Lake District National Park (slightly expanded in 2016 to touch borders with the Yorkshire Dales National Park and named a UNESCO World Heritage Site in 2017), which, in turn, falls entirely within the county of Cumbria. The county capital is Carlisle, a place that bears traces of a pedigree stretching back to Roman times, while both the isolated western coast and market towns like Kendal and Penrith counter the notion that Cumbria is all about its lakes.

11

Given a week you could easily see most of the famous settlements and lakes – a circuit taking in **Windermere**, with the towns of **Ambleside**, Windermere and **Bowness** dotted around it, **Coniston**, with its own lake and famous peak, the Wordsworth houses in **Grasmere**, the picture-postcard village of **Hawkshead**, and the more dramatic northern scenery near **Keswick** and **Ullswater** would give you a fair sample of the whole. But it's away from the more obvious sights that the Lakes really begin to pay dividends, in the dramatic valleys of **Langdale**, **Wasdale** and **Eskdale**, villages such as the foodie haven of **Cartmel**, or over on the coast's less-visited destinations: **Ravenglass** – access point for the **Ravenglass and Eskdale Railway** – and the attractive Georgian port of **Whitehaven**.

ARRIVAL AND INFORMATION

By bus National Express coaches connect London and Manchester with Windermere, Ambleside, Grasmere and Keswick.

By train Trains (ⓦ virgintrains.co.uk/train-to/lake-district) leave the West Coast main line at Oxenholme, north of Lancaster, for the branch-line service to Kendal and Windermere (ⓦ lakesline.co.uk).

Websites ⓦ golakes.co.uk and, for the National Park, ⓦ lakedistrict.gov.uk.

GETTING AROUND

By train The Cumbrian Coast Line (ⓦ cumbriancoastline.co.uk) and Furness Line (ⓦ furnessline.co.uk) between them offer a useful passenger service along the coast between Carlisle, Barrow-in-Furness, and Carnforth (on the main Lancaster–Carlisle line). Rail enthusiasts also shouldn't miss the short Ravenglass–Eskdale ride (see p.575).

By bus The North West 7-day megarider Gold (£27.30, family £55; ⓦ stagecoachbus.com/northwest) allows unlimited travel for a week on the entire regional bus network. Note that some local services run only through the busy summer months.

By car Before deciding to explore the Lake District in your own vehicle, be aware that narrow roads, heavy holiday traffic and an almost total lack of free parking can make for a frustrating experience. You're better off – at least during the summer, when local buses are most abundant – leaving your car at your accommodation and using public transport where possible.

WRAY CASTLE

Highlights

① Windermere Enjoy the changing seasons and serene views with a cruise on England's largest lake. **See p.559**

② Wray Castle Picnic in the grounds of this extraordinary Victorian holiday home on the shores of Windermere. **See p.563**

③ Old Dungeon Ghyll Hotel, Langdale The hikers' favourite inn – cosy rooms, stone-flagged floors and open fires – has England's most famous mountains on the doorstep. **See p.565**

④ Brantwood, Coniston Water John Ruskin's elegant home and inspiring garden are beautifully sited on Coniston Water. **See p.568**

⑤ Via Ferrata, Honister Pass The Lake District's biggest thrill sees you scrambling, climbing and hanging on for dear life along the old miners' route up Fleetwith Pike. **See p.574**

⑥ Ravenglass and Eskdale Railway It's a great day out on the narrow-gauge railway from coast to mountains. **See p.575**

⑦ Wordsworth House, Cockermouth Costumed staff and authentic surroundings bring the eighteenth century back to life at the birthplace of William Wordsworth. **See p.578**

⑧ Carlisle Castle Cumbria's mightiest castle dominates the county town. **See p.582**

HIGHLIGHTS ARE MARKED ON THE MAP ON P.556

Kendal and around

The self-billed "Gateway to the Lakes" (though just outside the National Park and nearly ten miles from Windermere), **KENDAL** is the largest of the southern Cumbrian towns. It offers rewarding rambles around the "yards" and "ginnels" (courtyards and alleys) on both sides of Highgate and Stricklandgate, the main streets, and while the old Market Place long since succumbed to development, traditional stalls still do business outside the Westmorland Shopping Centre every Wednesday and Saturday. Outside Kendal, the main trips are to the stately homes

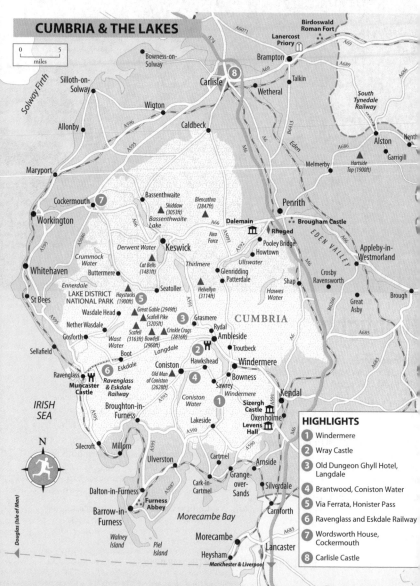

CUMBRIA & THE LAKES

0   5
miles

HIGHLIGHTS

1 Windermere
2 Wray Castle
3 Old Dungeon Ghyll Hotel, Langdale
4 Brantwood, Coniston Water
5 Via Ferrata, Honister Pass
6 Ravenglass and Eskdale Railway
7 Wordsworth House, Cockermouth
8 Carlisle Castle

of **Sizergh Castle** and **Levens Hall**, just a few miles to the south, both of which have beautifully kept gardens.

Kendal Museum

Station Rd, LA9 6BT • Tues–Sat 10am–4pm; closed Christmas week • £2 • ☎ 01539 815597, ⊛ kendalmuseum.org.uk

The **Kendal Museum** holds the district's natural history and archeological finds, and town history displays. You'll also find collections related to **Alfred Wainwright** (1907–91), Kendal's former borough treasurer and honorary clerk at the museum. Wainwright moved to Kendal in 1941, and in 1952, dissatisfied with the accuracy of existing maps, he embarked on his series of painstakingly handwritten walking guides, with mapped routes and delicately drawn views. They have been hugely popular guidebooks ever since, which many treat as gospel in their attempts to "bag" ascents of the 214 fells he recorded.

Abbot Hall

LA9 5AL • Mon–Sat 10.30am–5pm (Nov–Feb closes at 4pm), plus July & Aug Sun noon–4pm • Joint ticket £9.90 • **Art Gallery** £7.70 • ☎ 01539 722464, ⊛ abbothall.org.uk • **Museum** £5.50 • ☎ 01539 722464, ⊛ lakelandmuseum.org.uk

The town's two main cultural attractions are at the Georgian **Abbot Hall**, by the river near the parish church. The principal hall houses the **Art Gallery**, concentrating in particular on the works of the eighteenth-century "Kendal School" of portrait painters, most famously George Romney. Across the way, the former stables contain the **Museum of Lakeland Life and Industry**, where reconstructed house interiors and workshops exhibit rural trades and crafts, from spinning and weaving to shoemaking and tanning.

Sizergh Castle

Off A591, LA8 8DZ, 3 miles south of Kendal • **House** Easter–Oct Tues–Sun & bank hols noon–4pm • £10.50 (includes gardens); NT • **House tours** Easter–Oct Tues–Fri & Sun 11am & 11.20am; 45min • £1 (on top of entry fee); NT • **Gardens** Daily: Easter–Oct 10am–5pm; Nov–Easter 10am–4pm • £6.50; NT • ☎ 01539 560951, ⊛ nationaltrust.org.uk/sizergh • Bus #555 from Kendal

Sizergh Castle owes its "castle" epithet to the fourteenth-century peel tower at its core, one of the best examples of the towers built as safe havens during the region's medieval border raids. The rooms themselves are largely Elizabethan, and aside from the informative **tours** you can wander around at will. On a sunny day, it's worth exploring the **gardens** too, with their rockeries and kitchen garden.

Levens Hall

Off A6, LA8 0PD, 6 miles south of Kendal • **House** Easter to mid-Oct Mon–Thurs & Sun noon–4pm • £13.50 (includes gardens) • **Gardens** Easter to mid-Oct Mon–Thurs & Sun 10am–5pm • £9.90 • ☎ 01539 560321, ⊛ levenshall.co.uk • Bus #555 from Kendal

The sturdy, fortress-like stone towers at **Levens Hall** date right back to the fourteenth century, but the interior was refurbished in the classic Elizabethan manner – all heavy oak panels and ornate plaster – between 1570 and 1640. House stewards are on hand to point out the oddities and curios – for example, the dining room is panelled not with oak but with goat's leather, printed with a deep-green floral design. Outside are beautifully trimmed topiary **gardens**, featuring yews in the shape of pyramids, peacocks and top hats.

> ### CLIMB EVERY MOUNTAIN
> **Kendal mint cake**, a tooth-challenging, energy-giving, solid block of sugar and peppermint oil, was apparently invented by accident in the mid-nineteenth century. The familiar retro-packaged Romney's brand (from Kendal) is on sale throughout the Lakes, and their proudest boast is still that Kendal mint cake was carried to the top of Everest during Hillary's ascent of 1953.

ARRIVAL AND DEPARTURE

By train Kendal's station is a 10min walk from the centre. Destinations Oxenholme (for Carlisle, Lancaster or Manchester; hourly; 5min); Windermere (hourly; 20min).
By bus The bus station is on Blackhall Road (off Stramongate), with main routes including the #599 (to Windermere, Ambleside and Grasmere) or #555 (to Keswick or Lancaster).

KENDAL AND AROUND

Destinations Ambleside (hourly; 40min); Grasmere (hourly; 1hr); Keswick (hourly; 1hr 30min); Lancaster (hourly; 1hr); Windermere/Bowness (hourly; 30min).

ACCOMMODATION

Bolt Hole 40 Greenside, LA9 4LD ☎ 01539 720385, ⓦ beechhouse-kendal.co.uk. Self-contained self-catering apartments, complete with wood-burning stoves, richly coloured fabrics, and black-and-white bathrooms with gleaming roll-top baths. Per apartment **£100**

★ **Punch Bowl Inn** Crosthwaite, LA8 8HR, 5 miles west of Kendal ☎ 015395 68237, ⓦ the-punchbowl.co.uk. A super-stylish country inn – the earth-toned rooms with exposed beams and superb bathrooms, while the restaurant serves locally sourced food (from pot-roast woodpigeon to local lamb; mains £14–20). Rooms are individually priced, up to £310, with highest rates at weekends and holidays. **£170**

EATING AND DRINKING

★ **Grain Store** Brewery Arts Centre, 122 Highgate, LA9 4HE ☎ 01539 725133, ⓦ breweryarts.co.uk. The arts centre bistro has a mix-and-match menu of Mediterranean dishes – anything from local pork-and-chilli bangers to salmon skewers (£5–9) – plus a range of gourmet pizzas (£8–9.50). You can also get pizza, tapas and real ales in the adjacent *Vats Bar*, and there's often a weekday lunch service in holiday periods. Mon–Fri noon–2.30pm & 5.30–11pm, Sat noon–11pm, Sun 2–10.30pm.
Waterside Café Gulfs Rd, bottom of Lowther St, LA9 4DZ ☎ 01539 729743, ⓦ watersidekendal.co.uk. A handy place by the river for veggie and vegan wholefood snacks or meals (mains from £7.95), such as poached pear salad or falafel burgers. Mon–Sat 8.30am–4pm.

ENTERTAINMENT

Brewery Arts Centre 122 Highgate, LA9 4HE ☎ 01539 725133, ⓦ breweryarts.co.uk. Hub of everything that's happening in town, with cinema, theatre, galleries and concert hall, not to mention all-day café (closed Sun), bistro (see above) and the lively *Vats Bar*.

Cartmel and Holker Hall

Around eighteen miles southwest of Kendal, the pretty village of **CARTMEL** is something of an upmarket getaway, with its Michelin-starred restaurant-with-rooms, winding country lanes and cobbled market square brimming with inns and antique shops. You're in luck if you're looking to buy a handmade doll's house or embroidered footstool, while in the **Cartmel Village Shop** on the square they sell the finest sticky-toffee pudding known to humanity. Quite what the original monks of Cartmel would have made of all this is anyone's guess – the village first grew up around its twelfth-century Augustinian priory and is still dominated by the proud **Church of St Mary and St Michael** (daily 9am–5.30pm; guided tours Wed April–Oct 11am & 2pm, £3; ⓦ cartmelpriory.org.uk).

Holker Hall

Cark-in-Cartmel, LA11 6PU, 2 miles west of Cartmel • Easter–Oct Wed–Sun: house 11am–4pm, gardens 10.30am–5pm • £12.50, gardens only £8.50, house only £8; under-15s free • ☎ 01539 558328, ⓦ holker.co.uk

A couple of miles west of Cartmel lies **Holker Hall**, one of Cumbria's most glorious country estates. The impressive 25-acre **gardens**, both formal and woodland, are the highlight for many, and a celebrated annual garden festival (June) is held here, as well as spring and winter markets. You don't have to pay the entrance fee to visit the excellent Food Hall and Courtyard Café, both of which are also open on Saturdays and in winter (when the hall is otherwise closed).

L'Enclume Cavendish St, LA11 6PZ ☎01539 536362, ⓦlenclume.co.uk. One of England's most critically acclaimed dining experiences, overseen by the masterful Simon Rogan. Expect a succession of artfully constructed dishes, accompanied by intensely flavoured jellied cubes, mousses or foams, wild herbs, hedgerow flowers and exotic roots; lunch is £49, dinner £130. The dozen highly individual rooms and suites (up to £350, depending on location and size) mix antique French furniture and designer fabrics. Restaurant closed for two weeks in winter. Food served Tues–Sun noon–1.30pm & 6.30–8.30pm. **£170**

Ulverston

ULVERSTON is an attractive if faintly down-at-heel place of dappled grey limestone cottages, a jumble of cobbled alleys and traditional shops zigzagging off the central **Market Place**. Stalls are still set up here and in the surrounding streets every Thursday and Saturday.

11

Laurel and Hardy Museum

Brogden St, LA12 7AH • Easter–Oct daily 10am–5pm, at other times call first • £5 • ☎ 01229 582292, ⓦ laurel-and-hardy-museum.co.uk

Ulverston's most famous son is Stan Laurel (born Arthur Stanley Jefferson), the whimpering, head-scratching half of the comic duo. They're celebrated in a mind-boggling collection of memorabilia at the **Laurel and Hardy Museum**, inside a rear entrance of the Roxy Cinema behind Coronation Hall.

ARRIVAL AND DEPARTURE   **ULVERSTON**

By train Ulverston train station is a few minutes' walk from the town centre – head down Prince's Street and turn right at the main road for County Square.
Destinations Manchester (hourly; 2hr) via Lancaster (40min);

Carlisle (hourly; 2hr 20min) via Barrow-in-Furness (20min).
By bus Buses arrive on Victoria Road, near the library.
Destinations Kendal (Mon–Sat hourly, Sun 3 daily; 1hr); Windermere (Mon–Sat 5 daily; 45min).

ACCOMMODATION AND EATING

Bay Horse Canal Foot, LA12 9EL, 1.5 miles east of Ulverston ☎01229 583972, ⓦthebayhorsehotel.co.uk. A cosy old inn on the Leven estuary, with gorgeous views and fine Cumbrian cuisine. Six of the nine rooms open onto a river-view terrace, while dining in the olde-worlde bar or candlelit conservatory focuses on steaks, lamb, fresh fish, and game in season (mains around £20; fixed-price 2 courses £25, 3 courses £31). Lunch served Tues–Sun noon–2pm, dinner daily at 8pm. **£120**

Gillam's 64 Market St, LA12 7LT ☎01229 587564, ⓦgillams-tearoom.co.uk. An excellent tearoom – with summer terrace garden – that's wholly organic, Fair Trade and veggie. Tues–Sat 9am–5pm, Sun 10am–4pm.
Sefton House 34 Queen St, LA12 7AF ☎01229 582190, ⓦseftonhouse.co.uk. Amiable B&B in an attractive Georgian house that also holds Ulverston's best café, the rather wonderful *Natterjacks*, which is an afternoon/evening hangout for the local arts and music crowd. Mon–Fri 3–10pm. **£65**

Windermere town

WINDERMERE TOWN was all but nonexistent until 1847 when a railway terminal was built here, making England's longest lake (after which the town is named) an easily accessible resort. Windermere remains a major gateway and transport hub for the lakes, but there's precious little else to keep you in the slate-grey streets. All the traffic pours a mile downhill to Windermere's older twin town – Bowness, actually on the lake – but you should stay long enough to make the twenty-minute stroll up through the woods to **Orrest Head** (784ft), from where you get a 360-degree panorama from the Yorkshire fells to Morecambe Bay. The path begins by the *Windermere Hotel* on the A591, across from Windermere train station.

Brockhole Lake District Visitor Centre

Brockhole, LA23 1LJ, 3 miles northwest of Windermere town • Daily: Easter–Oct 10am–5pm; Nov–Easter 10am–4pm • Free • ☎ 01539 446601, ⓦ brockhole.co.uk • Buses between Windermere and Ambleside run past the visitor centre, or you can take the cruise launch from Waterhead, near Ambleside (see box, p.562)

The Lake District National Park Authority has its main visitor centre at **Brockhole**, a late Victorian mansion set in lush grounds on the shores of Windermere, northwest of Windermere town. It's the single best place to get to grips with what there is to see and do in the Lakes, with some excellent natural history and geological displays, lovely gardens and a big range of activities (separate fees apply), including bike hire, adventure playground, watersports and high-ropes treetop adventures.

ARRIVAL AND INFORMATION

By train Windermere is as far into the Lakes as you can get by train, on the branch line from Oxenholme, via Kendal. Destinations Kendal (hourly; 15min) and Oxenholme (for London, Carlisle, Lancaster, Manchester or Penrith; hourly; 20min).

By bus All buses (including National Express coaches from London and Manchester) stop outside Windermere train station.

Destinations Ambleside (hourly; 15min); Bowness (every 20–30min; 15min); Brockhole Visitor Centre (every 20–30min; 7min); Carlisle (3 daily; 2hr 20min); Grasmere (every 20–30min; 30min); Kendal (hourly; 25min); Keswick (hourly; 1hr).

Tourist office Brockhole aside, Windermere's local tourist office is on Victoria Street (daily: April–Oct 8.30am–5pm, Nov–March 9am–4.30pm; ☎ 01539 446499, ⓦ windermere info.co.uk), 100yd from the train station.

GETTING AROUND

Bike rental Country Lanes, at the train station (☎ 01539 444544, ⓦ countrylaneslakedistrict.co.uk), provides bikes (£20–30/day) plus route maps for local rides.

ACCOMMODATION

★**Archway** 13 College Rd, LA23 1BU ☎ 01539 445613, ⓦ archwayguesthouse.co.uk. Four trim rooms in a Victorian house known for its breakfasts – traditional Full English or American, pancakes, kippers, home-made yoghurt and granola, smoked haddock and the like. **£80**

Brendan Chase 1–3 College Rd, LA23 1BU ☎ 01539 445638, ⓦ brendanchase.co.uk. Popular place with overseas travellers, providing a friendly welcome, a good breakfast and eight comfortable rooms (some en suite). **£60**

Holbeck Ghyll Holbeck Lane, LA23 1LU, 3 miles north of Windermere town ☎ 01539 432375, ⓦ holbeckghyll .com. Luxurious rooms either in the main house or in the lodge or suites in the grounds (with room-and-dinner prices up to £550/night). There's a sherry decanter in every room, seven acres of gardens, and excellent food (dinner included in the price). **£320**

Lake District Backpackers High St, LA23 1AF, across from the tourist office ☎ 01539 446374, ⓦ lake districtbackpackers.co.uk. Nineteen backpackers' beds in small dorms, with a women-only room plus a couple of private rooms available on request. There's a kitchen too, though the price includes a tea-and-toast breakfast. No credit cards. Dorms **£16.50**, doubles **£39**

YHA Windermere High Cross, Bridge Lane, LA23 1LA, 2 miles north of Windermere ☎ 0845 371 9352, ⓦ yha.org .uk/hostel/windermere. The local YHA hostel is a revamped old mansion with magnificent lake views; you can camp here too. Camping/person **£12**, dorms **£19**, doubles **£29**

EATING

First Floor Lakeland Ltd, Alexandra Buildings, LA23 1BQ, behind the train station ☎ 01539 488100. Occupying a first-floor gallery, this superior café's snacks, lunches and high teas attract peak-period queues. Daily filled baguettes, tortilla wraps, soups, meat and cheese platters, salads, cakes and puddings, plus a seasonally changing menu covering dishes such as salmon, rocket and radicchio salad. Most dishes £5–7.50. Mon–Fri 9.30am–5.30pm, Sat 9am–5pm, Sun 10.30am–4pm.

Francine's 27 Main Rd, LA23 1DX ☎ 01539 444088, ⓦ francinesrestaurantwindermere.co.uk. Drop in during the day for anything from a pain au chocolat or a sandwich to a big bowl of mussels (lunch dishes mostly £6–10). Dinner sees the lights dimmed for a wide-ranging continental menu, from pork belly confit to seafood casserole. Mains £12–16. Café Tues–Sun 10am–2.30pm, restaurant Tues–Sun 6–11pm.

Hooked Ellerthwaite Square, LA23 1BU ☎ 01539 448443, ⓦ hookedwindermere.co.uk. Fabulous contemporary seafood place serving fish straight from the Fleetwood boats. Typical dishes include hake with chorizo, fava beans and garlic, or Thai-style sea bass. Starters are

£6–8, mains around £22. Tues–Sun 5.30–10pm; check website for occasional closures.

Lamplighter Dining Rooms High St, LA23 1AF ☎ 01539 443547, ⓦ www.lamplighterdiningrooms.com. Very popular local choice for bistro meals, served in the hotel's bar/dining room. Expect classics (fish and chips, burgers, rack of lamb, steaks), and big portions; most dishes £15–20. There's also a cracking carve-your-own Sun lunch. April–Oct Mon–Thurs 4–9pm, Fri 4–9.30pm, Sat noon–9.30pm, Sun noon–9pm; check website for off-season hours.

Bowness and Windermere

BOWNESS-ON-WINDERMERE spills back from its lakeside piers in a series of terraces lined with guesthouses and hotels. There's been a village here since the fifteenth century and a ferry service across the lake for almost as long – these days, however, you could be forgiven for thinking that Bowness begins and ends with its best-known attraction, the **World of Beatrix Potter**. At ten and a half miles long, a mile wide in parts and a shade over 200ft deep, the **lake** itself – **Windermere**, incidentally, never "Lake" Windermere – is the heavyweight of Lake District waters. On a busy summer's day, crowds swirl around the trinket shops, cafés, ice-cream stalls and lakeside seats, but you can easily escape onto the water or into the hills, and there are lots of attractions around town to fill a rainy day.

11

The World of Beatrix Potter

Old Laundry, Crag Brow, LA23 3BX • Daily 10am–5.30pm • £7.50, children £3.95 • ☎ 01539 488444, ⓦ hop-skip-jump.com

You either like Beatrix Potter or you don't, but it's safe to say that the elaborate 3D story scenes, audiovisual "virtual walks", themed tearoom and gift shop here at the interactive **World of Beatrix Potter** find more favour with children than the more formal Potter attractions at Hill Top and Hawkshead.

Blackwell

LA23 3JT, 1.5 miles south of Bowness, off A5074 • Daily 10.30am–5pm • £8.80, under-16s free • ☎ 01539 446139, ⓦ blackwell.org.uk

Mackay Hugh Baillie Scott's **Blackwell** was built in 1900 as a lakeside holiday home, and boasts a superbly restored Arts and Crafts interior. Lakeland motifs – trees, flowers, birds and berries – abound, while temporary exhibits focus on furniture and decorative art. There's an informative introductory talk (usually weekdays at 2.30pm), plus a tearoom, craft shop and gardens. Parking is available; alternatively, you can walk from Bowness in about 25 minutes (although along a busy road).

Lakeside and Haverthwaite Railway

Haverthwaite station, LA12 8AL, on A590 • Easter–Oct 6–7 departures daily • £6.80 return; £16.20 including cruise boat from Bowness • ☎ 01539 531594, ⓦ lakesiderailway.co.uk

From Bowness piers, boats head to the southern reaches of Windermere at Lakeside. This is the terminus of the **Lakeside and Haverthwaite Railway**, whose steam-powered engines puff gently over four miles of track along the River Leven and through the woods of Backbarrow Gorge. Boat arrivals from Bowness connect with train departures throughout the day and, as well as the boat-and-train combination, there are also joint tickets for the Lakes Aquarium and the nearby Lakeland Motor Museum.

Lakeland Motor Museum

Backbarrow, near Newby Bridge, LA12 8TA • Daily 9.30am–4.30pm • £8.50; combo tickets available with lake cruise (£16.20) and steam railway (£14.60) • ⓦ lakelandmotormuseum.co.uk

The **Lakeland Motor Museum** has a smashing landmark riverside home to show off its 30,000-plus motoring history exhibits. It's a dream for petrolheads and nostalgia buffs alike, as it's simply stuffed with vintage vehicles and memorabilia, from boneshaker bikes and Bentleys to DeLoreans and Dinky toys.

Lakes Aquarium

On the quay at Lakeside, Newby Bridge, LA12 8AS • Daily 10am–4.30pm • £6.95; joint ticket with the boat ride from Bowness, £15.95 • ☎ 01539 530153, ⊚ lakesaquarium.co.uk

The **Lakes Aquarium** is centred on the fish and animals found along a lakeland river. There's a pair of frisky otters (fed daily, 10.30am & 3pm), plus rays from Morecambe Bay, not to mention a walk-through tunnel aquarium containing huge carp and diving ducks (fed daily, 11am & 4pm). Enthusiastic staff are on hand to explain what's going on.

ARRIVAL AND DEPARTURE
BOWNESS AND WINDERMERE

By bus The open-top #599 bus from Windermere town train station stops at the lakeside piers (every 20–30min; 15min). For onward routes to Ambleside and Grasmere you have to return first to Windermere town station.

By ferry The traditional ferry service is the chain-guided contraption from Ferry Nab on the Bowness side (10min walk from the cruise piers) to Ferry House, Sawrey (every 20min; Mon–Sat 7am–10pm, Sun 9am–10pm; 50p, bike and cyclist £1, cars £4.40), providing access to Hill Top and to Hawkshead beyond. There's also a useful pedestrian launch service between Bowness piers and Ferry House, Sawrey (see box below), saving you the walk down to the car ferry.

GETTING AROUND

Cross Lakes Experience A connecting boat-and-minibus shuttle service (Easter–Oct, up to ten departures daily; ☎ 01539 448600, ⊚ lakedistrict.gov.uk/crosslakes) runs from Bowness pier 3 to Beatrix Potter's house at Hill Top (£10.40 return), and then to Hawkshead (£11.95) and Coniston Water (£21).

ACCOMMODATION

Angel Inn Helm Rd, LA23 3BU ☎ 01539 444080, ⊚ theangelinnbowness.com. A dozen chic rooms – all bright, with thick-pile carpets and patterned curtains – bring a bit of country style to Bowness. Snacks, wraps and sandwiches and posh pub food are served in the contemporary bar downstairs, back restaurant or terraced garden. **£95**

Linthwaite House Crook Rd, LA23 3JA, 1 mile south of Bowness ☎ 01539 488600, ⊚ linthwaitehouse.com. Contemporary boutique style grafted onto an ivy-covered country house set high above Windermere. A conservatory and terrace offer fabulous lake and fell views, and you can work up an appetite for dinner with a walk in the gardens to the hotel's private tarn. Rates run up to £300, suites up to £460, dinner included. **£225**

★**Number 80** 80 Craig Walk, LA23 2JS ☎ 01539 443584, ⊚ number80bed.co.uk. Colin and Mandy's quiet townhouse offers quirky, stylish B&B in four rather dramatic, earth-toned double rooms – a grown-up space for couples (no pets, no children). **£90**

EATING AND DRINKING

Bowness has plenty of places offering pizza, fish and chips, a Chinese stir-fry or a budget café meal – a stroll along pedestrianized **Ash Street** and up **Lake Road** shows you most of the possibilities.

★**Hole in t'Wall** Fallbarrow Rd, LA23 3DH ☎ 01539 443488, ⊚ www.robinsonsbrewery.com. For a drink and a bar meal (£9–12) you can't beat the town's oldest hostelry, with stone-flagged floors, open fires and real ales, plus a terrace-style beer garden that's a popular spot on summer evenings. Mon–Sat 11am–11pm, Sun noon–10.30pm.

WINDERMERE CRUISES

Windermere Lake Cruises (⊚ windermere-lakecruises.co.uk) operates services from Bowness to Lakeside ("Yellow Cruise"; return £11; 1hr 30min), Bowness to Ambleside via the Visitor Centre at Brockhole ("Red Cruise"; return £10.50; 1hr 10min), and a 45min Islands Cruise (return £8). There's also a service from Ambleside that calls at Wray Castle and Brockhole ("Green Cruise"; return £8; 45min). The **Freedom-of-the-Lake ticket** (one-day £19.50) is valid on all routes, while the **Walkers Ticket** (£10.50) allows you to catch a ferry from Ambleside to Wray Castle, walk four miles to Ferry House and then travel back by water via Bowness, Brockhole and Ambleside.

> **TOP 5 LAKE DISTRICT VIEWS**
> **Castlerigg Stone Circle** Keswick. See p.571 **Loughrigg Terrace** Grasmere. See p.565
> **Cat Bells** Derwent Water. See p.571   **Orrest Head** Windermere. See p.559
> **Hardknott Roman Fort** Eskdale. See p.575

Ambleside and around

Five miles northwest of Windermere, **AMBLESIDE** town centre consists of a cluster of grey-green stone houses, shops, pubs and B&Bs (and the tiny landmark of **Bridge House**, a seventeenth-century cottage built over a stream) hugging a circular one-way system, which loops round just south of the narrow gully of stony Stock Ghyll. Huge car parks soak up the day-trip trade, but actually Ambleside improves the longer you spend here, with some enjoyable local walks and also the best selection of accommodation and restaurants in the area. The rest of town lies a mile south at **Waterhead**, where the cruise boats dock, overlooked by the grass banks and spreading trees of Borrans Park. Four miles away, Victorian neo-Gothic **Wray Castle** is a great place to visit for the day.

11

The Armitt

Rydal Rd, LA22 9BL • Mon–Sat 10am–5pm, check website for winter hours • £5 • ☎ 01539 431212, ⓦ armitt.com

For some background on Ambleside's history, stroll a couple of minutes from the centre along Rydal Road to **The Armitt**, a library and gallery which catalogues the very distinct contribution to Lakeland society made by writers and artists from John Ruskin to Beatrix Potter.

Wray Castle

Low Wray, LA22 0JA, 4 miles south of Ambleside • Easter–Oct daily 10am–5pm, last admission 4pm • £10 • ⓦ nationaltrust.org.uk/wray-castle • Windermere Lake Cruises service from Waterhead or Brockhole (see box opposite), or bus #505 to Low Wray turn-off and 1 mile walk

Take the boat across to Wray and walk up through the grounds to magnificent **Wray Castle**, a castellated, mock-Gothic mansion built in the 1840s by a wealthy couple as their retirement home. Appealingly, it's not presented as a period piece but rather a family-friendly attraction where you are positively begged to walk on the grass and sit on the chairs. House **tours** (every hour or so) are available to explain the finer points of the architecture and history, but in the end it's the freedom to play and picnic in lovely surroundings that's the real draw.

ARRIVAL AND INFORMATION   AMBLESIDE AND AROUND

By bus All buses in town stop on Kelsick Rd, opposite the library.
Destinations Windermere (every 30min–1hr; 14min); Grasmere (every 30min–1hr; 13min); Keswick (hourly; 45min); Hawkshead/Coniston (every 1–2hr; 20min/30min); and Langdale (5–6 daily; 30min) via Elterwater (17min).

By ferry There are ferry services from Bowness and Lakeside; it's a 15min walk into Ambleside from the piers at Waterhead.
Tourist office Central Buildings, Market Cross (Mon–Sat 9am–5.30pm, Sun 10am–5pm; ☎ 01539 432582, ⓦ lakelandgateway.net.

GETTING AROUND

Bike rental Ghyllside Cycles, The Slack (Mon–Sat 9.30am–5.30pm; ☎ 01539 433592, ⓦ ghyllside.co.uk), rents out   bikes at around £25/day.

ACCOMMODATION

Lake Rd, running between Waterhead and Ambleside, is lined with **B&Bs**, as are Church St and Compston Road. Fancier places lie out of town, especially a mile to the south at Waterhead by the lake, which is also where you'll find Ambleside YHA. The nearest **campsite**, *Low Wray*, is three miles south and also right by the lake.

11

WALKS FROM AMBLESIDE

A couple of good walks are accessible straight from the town centre. First, from the footbridge across the river in Rothay Park you can strike up across **Loughrigg Fell** (1099ft). Dropping down to Loughrigg Terrace overlooking Grasmere, you then cut south at Rydal on the A591 and follow the minor road back along the River Rothay to Ambleside – a total of 6 miles (4hr).

The walk over **Wansfell to Troutbeck** and back (6 miles; around 4hr) is a little tougher. Stock Ghyll Lane runs up the left bank of the tumbling stream to **Stock Ghyll Force** waterfall. The path then rises steeply to **Wansfell Pike** (1581ft) and down into Troutbeck village, where you can have lunch either at the *Mortal Man* or the nearby *Queen's Head* (recently rebuilt after a fire), both just a short walk from the village centre. The return cuts west onto the flanks of Wansfell and back to Ambleside.

Compston House Compston Rd, LA22 9DJ ☎ 01539 432305, ⓦ compstonhouse.co.uk. There's a breezy New York vibe in this traditional Lakeland house, where the American style extends from the rooms to the breakfasts – home-made pancakes and maple syrup, fluffy omelettes and the like. **£95**

Low Wray Campsite Low Wray, LA22 0JA, 3 miles south of Ambleside ☎ 01539 463862, ⓦ ntlakescampsites .org.uk, ⓦ 4windslakelandtipis.co.uk or ⓦ luxury-yurt -holidays.co.uk. The beautiful National Trust site on the western shore of the lake is a glampers' haven. As well as tent pitches (prices vary according to location – some sites are bang on the water's edge), there are wooden camping pods for couples and families (from £35), tipis (part-week from £200, full week from £360) and bell tents (part-week from £199, full week from £385). Bike and kayak hire make it great for families too. Closed Nov–Easter. Per person **£8.50**

★ **Randy Pike** On B5286, LA22 0JP, 3 miles south of Ambleside ☎ 01539 436088, ⓦ randypike.co.uk. Two amazing, boutique B&B suites open out on to the gardens

of what was once a Victorian gentleman's hunting lodge. It's a grown-up, romantic retreat, and you can either stay put with the snack larder, terrace and gardens, or be whizzed down to the owners' *Jumble Room* restaurant in Grasmere (see p.566) for dinner. Prices are £25 higher at weekends. **£200**

Riverside Under Loughrigg, LA22 9LJ ☎ 01539 432395, ⓦ riverside-at-ambleside.co.uk. Charming guesthouse, half a mile (10min walk) from Ambleside across Rothay Park. Six large, light country-pine-style rooms available, including a river-facing four-poster (£140) with an en-suite spa bath. **£110**

YHA Ambleside Waterhead, LA22 0EU, 1 mile south of Ambleside ☎ 0845 371 9620, ⓦ yha.org.uk/hostel /ambleside. The YHA's flagship regional hostel has an impressive lakeside location (most rooms have a water view), and 250 beds divided among neatly furnished small dorms, twins, doubles and family rooms (including 11 en-suites). Tour and activity bookings, and licensed bar and restaurant. Dorms **£25**, doubles **£56**

EATING AND DRINKING

★ **Apple Pie** Rydal Rd, LA22 9AN ☎ 01539 433679, ⓦ applepieambleside.co.uk. The best café and bakery in town has a secluded patio-garden and plenty of room inside for lounging around. Breakfast is served until 11am (with free tea/coffee refills); they also have BLTs, soup and quiche, along with trademark home-made pies that come savoury (say, broccoli and stilton or sausage and cider) or sweet (a luscious Bramley apple variety laced with cinnamon and raisins). Dishes around £8. Mon–Fri 9am–5.30pm, Sat & Sun 8.30am–5.30pm; winter hours may be reduced.

Doi Intanon Market Place, LA22 9BU ☎ 01539 432119, ⓦ ambleside-thai-restaurant.com. Ambleside's popular Thai restaurant makes a welcome change, with a standard stir-fry and curry menu bolstered by specials such as a fiery vegetable jungle curry or a grilled chicken appetizer wrapped in pandan leaves. Most mains £9–12. Daily 6–10pm.

Golden Rule Smithy Brow LA22 9AS ☎ 01539 432257, ⓦ www.robinsonsbrewery.com. The beer-lovers' and climbers' favourite pub – this is a cosy place for a post-hike pint (six real ales usually available) and a read of the

Wainwright, with no jukebox, pool table or other distractions besides the dart board. No meals. Daily 11am–midnight.

★ **Lucy's On A Plate** Church St, LA22 0BU ☎ 01539 432288, ⓦ lucysofambleside.co.uk. Quirky, hugely enjoyable, informal bistro – if they know you're coming, you'll probably find yourself name-checked on the menu. Daytime café dishes (brunch, dips, pastas, salads, soup and sandwiches; £5–10) give way to a dinner menu (mains £14–19) that is "sourced locally, cooked globally". Mon–Fri 5–10.30pm, Sat & Sun 11am–10.30pm; last orders 9.30pm.

Zeffirelli's Compston Rd, LA22 9AD ☎ 01539 433845, ⓦ zeffirellis.com. *Zeffirelli's* independent cinema has five screens at three locations in town. The restaurant attached to the Compston Road screens is famous for its wholemeal-base pizzas, plus Italian-with-a-twist pastas and salads, all vegetarian (pizzas and mains around £12). The menu is available at lunch and dinner, but *Zeff's* is also open from 10am as a café for tea, coffee and snacks. There's a great music-bar upstairs, plus an associated fine-dining veggie restaurant (*Fellini's*) elsewhere in town. Daily 10am–10pm.

Great Langdale

Three miles west of Ambleside along the A593, Skelwith Bridge marks the start of **Great Langdale**, a U-shaped glacial valley overlooked by the rocky summits of the **Langdale Pikes**, the most popular of the central Lakeland fells. You can get to the pretty village of **Elterwater** – where there's a tiny village green overlooked by the excellent *Britannia Inn* (see below) – by bus, which then continues on to the **Old Dungeon Ghyll Hotel** (see below) at the head of the valley. Three miles from Elterwater, at **Stickle Ghyll** car park, Harrison Stickle (2414ft), Pike of Stickle (2326ft) and Pavey Ark (2297ft) form a dramatic backdrop, though many walkers go no further than the hour-long climb to **Stickle Tarn** from Stickle Ghyll. Another car park, a mile further west up the valley road by the *Old Dungeon Ghyll Hotel*, is the starting point for a series of more hardcore hikes to resonant Lakeland peaks like Crinkle Crags (2816ft) or Bowfell (2960ft).

ARRIVAL AND DEPARTURE   GREAT LANGDALE

By bus From Ambleside, the #516 Langdale Rambler bus runs to Elterwater (5–6 daily; 17min) and the *Old Dungeon* *Ghyll* (5–6 daily; 30min).

11

ACCOMMODATION AND EATING

Britannia Inn Elterwater, LA22 9HP ☎ 01539 437210, ⊕ thebritanniainn.com. Halfway up the valley, this popular pub on Elterwater's green has nine recently refurbished, cosy rooms – cosy being the key word, since there's not a lot of space in a 500-year-old inn. Rates are at least £10 higher at weekends. A wide range of beers and good-value food – home-made pies and Cumberland sausage to beer-battered haddock (mains £12.50–16) – is served either in the dining room (booking advised) or front bar. Kitchen daily noon–2pm & 6–9pm. **£125**

Great Langdale Campsite LA22 9JU ☎ 01539 463862, ⊕ ntlakescampsites.org.uk, ⊕ luxury-yurt-holidays.co.uk, or ⊕ basecamptipi.co.uk. The National Trust's stupendously sited Langdale campsite has gone stellar since camping pods (from £35) and yurts (from £365 for 4 days) and nordic tipis (£50) were added into the mix. The bar at the *Old Dungeon Ghyll* is a 5min walk away. Per person **£8.50**

★ **Old Dungeon Ghyll** LA22 9JY ☎ 01539 437272, ⊕ odg .co.uk. The Lakes' most famous inn is decidedly old-school – well-worn oak, floral decor, four-poster beds – but walkers can't resist its unrivalled location. Dinner (£25, reservations essential) is served at 7.30pm in the dining room, though all the action is in the stone-flagged *Hikers' Bar*, which has real ales and hearty pub food (from £12). Daily noon–9pm. **£116**

Grasmere and around

Four miles northwest of Ambleside, **GRASMERE** consists of an intimate cluster of grey-stone houses on the old packhorse road that runs beside the babbling River Rothay. Pretty it certainly is, but in high summer its charms are submerged by the hordes who descend on the trail of the village's most famous former resident, **William Wordsworth** (1770–1850). The poet, his wife Mary, sister Dorothy and other members of his family are buried beneath the yews in **St Oswald's churchyard**, around which the river makes a sinuous curl. There's little else to the village, save its gift shops, galleries, tearooms and hotels, though the **lake** is just a ten-minute walk away; tremendous views unfold from **Loughrigg Terrace**, on its southern reaches. A four-mile circuit of Grasmere and adjacent **Rydal Water** takes around two hours, with the route passing Wordsworth haunts **Rydal Mount** and **Dove Cottage**.

Dove Cottage

Town End, LA22 9SH, half a mile southeast of Grasmere • Daily: March–Oct 9.30am–5.30pm; Nov–Feb 10am–4.30pm; check Jan opening hours for closures • £8.95 • ☎ 01539 435544, ⊕ wordsworth.org.uk • Buses #555 and #599

Dove Cottage, home to William and Dorothy Wordsworth from 1799 to 1808, was the place where Wordsworth wrote some of his best poetry. Guides, bursting with anecdotes, lead you around the cottage rooms, little changed now but for the addition of electricity

THE LAKE POETS

William Wordsworth dominates the literary landscape of the Lakes like no other. Born in Cockermouth in 1770, he was sent to school in Hawkshead before a stint at Cambridge, a year in France and two in Somerset. In 1799 he returned to the Lake District, settling in Grasmere, where he spent the last two-thirds of his life with his wife Mary and sister Dorothy, who not only transcribed his poems but was an accomplished diarist as well.

Wordsworth and fellow poets **Samuel Taylor Coleridge** and **Robert Southey** formed a clique that became known as the "Lake Poets", a label based more on their fluctuating friendships and their shared passion for the region than on any common subject matter in their writings. A fourth member of the Cumbrian literary elite was the critic and essayist **Thomas De Quincey**, chiefly known today for his *Confessions of an English Opium-Eater*. One of the first to fully appreciate the revolutionary nature of Wordsworth's and Coleridge's collaborative *Lyrical Ballads*, De Quincey became a long-term guest of the Wordsworths in 1807, taking over Dove Cottage from them in 1809.

11

and internal plumbing. In the adjacent **museum** are paintings, manuscripts (including that of "Daffodils") and mementos of the so-called "Lake Poets" (see box above) Robert Southey and Samuel Taylor Coleridge, as well as "opium-eater" Thomas De Quincey, who also lived in the cottage for several years.

Rydal Mount

Rydal, LA22 9LU, 2 miles southeast of Grasmere • March–Oct daily 9.30am–5pm; Nov–Feb Wed–Sun 11am–4pm; closed for 3 weeks in Jan • £7.50, gardens only £4.50 • ☎ 01539 433002, ⓦ rydalmount.co.uk • Buses #555 and #599

At Dove Cottage Wordsworth had been a largely unknown poet of straitened means, but by 1813 he'd written several of his greatest works (though not all had yet been published) and had been appointed Westmorland's Distributor of Stamps, a salaried position which allowed him to take up the rent of a comfortable family house. **Rydal Mount** remained Wordsworth's home from 1813 until his death in 1850, and the house is still owned by descendants of the poet. You're free to wander around what is essentially still a family home, as well as explore Wordsworth's cherished garden.

ARRIVAL AND DEPARTURE
GRASMERE AND AROUND

By bus The #555 (between Kendal and Keswick) and the #599 (from Kendal, Bowness, Windermere and Ambleside) stop on the village green.

ACCOMMODATION AND EATING

Daffodil Keswick Rd, LA22 9PR ☎ 01539 463550, ⓦ daffodilhotel.co.uk. This huge slate Victorian-era lakefront hotel, the landmark at the southern village entrance, has been given a complete contemporary makeover. Its lakeview rooms and suites, restaurant-with-a-view and up-to-the-minute spa add another string to Grasmere's increasingly boutique bow. **£175**

★**Grasmere Independent Hostel** Broadrayne Farm, LA22 9RU, 1.3 miles north of Grasmere ☎ 01539 435055, ⓦ grasmerehostel.co.uk. A stylish gem of a backpackers' hostel, with 24 beds in carpeted en-suite rooms – the price goes up a quid at weekends and two on bank holidays. There's an impressively equipped kitchen, and even a sauna, with the local pub just a few hundred yards away. Dorms **£22**

How Foot Lodge Town End, LA22 9SQ, half a mile southeast of Grasmere ☎ 01539 435366, ⓦ howfoot lodge.co.uk. You won't get a better deal on good-quality B&B accommodation than in this light-filled Victorian villa just a few yards from Dove Cottage. **£78**

★**Jumble Room** Langdale Rd, LA22 9SU ☎ 01539 435188, ⓦ thejumbleroom.co.uk. Funky, relaxed dining spot, where the menu roams the world – blue swimmer crab risotto, Thai salmon salad, or fish in organic beer batter – and, once ensconced, no one's in any hurry to leave. Mains £15–25. Wed–Sun 5.30–9.30pm, plus Mon in summer; closed 2 weeks in Dec.

Moss Grove Organic Grasmere, LA22 9SW ☎ 01539 435251, ⓦ mossgrove.com. Stunning, revamped Victorian-era hotel that's been designed along organic, low-impact lines – thus, handmade beds of reclaimed timber, wallpaper coloured with natural inks, and windows

screened by natural wood blinds. £159
Thorney How Independent Hostel Off Easedale Rd, LA22 9QW, 0.75 miles north of Grasmere ☏ 01539 435597, ⓦ thorneyhow.co.uk. This, the first-ever hostel bought by the YHA (back in 1931), now trades as an indie backpacker hostel, overseen by friendly owners. It's been spruced up recently, though a café-bar, film nights and bike hire already make it a great night's stay. Dorms £23.50, doubles £47

Coniston and around

Coniston Water is not one of the most immediately imposing of the lakes, yet it has a quiet beauty that sets it apart from the more popular destinations. The nineteenth-century art critic and social reformer John Ruskin made the lake his home, and today his isolated house, **Brantwood**, on the northeastern shore, provides the most obvious target for a day-trip. **Arthur Ransome** was also a frequent visitor, his local memories and experiences providing much of the detail in his *Swallows and Amazons* children's books.

Coniston village

The small, slate-grey village of **CONISTON** hunkers below the craggy and copper-mine-riddled bulk of **The Old Man of Coniston** (2628ft), which most fit walkers can climb in under two hours. In the village itself, **John Ruskin's grave** lies in St Andrew's original churchyard beneath a beautifully worked Celtic cross.

Ruskin Museum

Yewdale Rd, LA21 8DU · Easter to mid-Nov daily 10am–5.30pm; mid-Nov to Easter Wed–Sun 10.30am–3.30pm · £6 · ☏ 01539 441164, ⓦ ruskinmuseum.com

The highly entertaining local museum is named after Coniston's most famous resident but is devoted to all aspects of local life and work, from pre-history to the exploits of Donald Campbell (see box below). Ruskin's fascinating ideas and theories are also given an airing – not to mention his socks, matriculation certificate from Oxford, and letters, manuscripts, sketchbooks and watercolours.

Coniston Water

Lake Rd, LA21 8AN · **Steam Yacht Gondola** Easter–Oct, 4–5 times daily from 11am, weather permitting · £11 · ☏ 01539 432733, ⓦ nationaltrust.org.uk/steam-yacht-gondola · **Coniston Launch** Easter–Oct hourly 10.45am–5pm; Nov–Easter up to 5 daily · £11.25 (north route) or £16.95 (south) · ☏ 01768 775753, ⓦ conistonlaunch.co.uk

Coniston Water is hidden out of sight, half a mile southeast of the village. As well as boat and kayak rental from the pier, there are two lake cruise services, which both call at Ruskin's Brantwood as well as various other points around the lake. The National Trust's restored **Steam Yacht Gondola** is the historic choice, while the **Coniston Launch** runs the solar-powered wooden vessels "Ruskin" and "Ransome" on two routes around the lake, north and south. You can stop off at any pier en route, and local walking leaflets are available, as well as special cruises throughout the year.

CONISTON'S SPEED KING

On January 4, 1967, **Donald Campbell** set out to better his own world water-speed record (276mph, set three years earlier in Australia) on the glass-like surface of Coniston Water. Just as his jet-powered *Bluebird* hit an estimated 320mph, however, a patch of turbulence sent it into a somersault. Campbell was killed immediately and his body and boat lay undisturbed at the bottom of the lake until both were retrieved in 2001. Campbell's grave is in the small village cemetery behind the *Crown Hotel*, while the *Bluebird* tailfin is displayed in a purpose-built gallery at the local museum, where you can find out more about Campbell and that fateful day.

Brantwood

Off B5285, LA21 8AD, 2.5 miles southeast of Coniston • Mid-March to Nov daily 10.30am–5pm; Dec to mid-March Wed–Sun 10.30am–4pm • £7.50, gardens only £5.20, under-16s free • ☏ 01539 441396, ⊕ brantwood.org.uk

Sited on a hillside above the eastern shore of Coniston Water, **Brantwood** was home to John Ruskin from 1872 until his death in 1900. Ruskin was the champion of J.M.W. Turner and the Pre-Raphaelites and the foremost Victorian proponent of the supremacy of Gothic architecture. His **study** and **dining room** boast superlative lake views, bettered only by those from the **Turret Room** where he used to sit in later life in his bathchair. Exhibition rooms and galleries display Ruskin-related arts and crafts, while the excellent *Jumping Jenny Tearooms* has an outdoor terrace with lake views.

ARRIVAL AND GETTING AROUND

By bus The #505 "Coniston Rambler" bus (from Kendal, Windermere, Ambleside or Hawkshead) stops on the main road through Coniston village. The "Ruskin Explorer" ticket (available on the bus; from £18) includes return travel on the #505 from Windermere, a return trip on the Coniston Launch to Brantwood and entry to Brantwood itself.

CONISTON AND AROUND

Cross Lakes Experience The boat-and-minibus service from Bowness (Easter–Oct daily; ☏ 01539 448600, ⊕ lake district.gov.uk) runs as far as the *Waterhead Hotel* pier (for Brantwood and lake services), at the head of Coniston Water, half a mile out of the village.

ACCOMMODATION

Bank Ground Farm Coniston Water, LA21 8AA, 2 miles southeast of Coniston ☏ 01539 441264, ⊕ bankground .com. The lakeside farmhouse was the original model for Holly Howe Farm in *Swallows and Amazons* and later used in the 1970s film. Seven traditionally furnished rooms have oak beams and carved beds, and there's also a farmhouse tearoom. **£90**

Black Bull Inn Coppermines Rd, LA21 8DU, by the bridge ☏ 01539 441335, ⊕ blackbullconiston.co.uk. The village's best pub has a variety of reasonable B&B rooms (£10 more expensive at the weekends). It also brews its own beer, while local lamb, sausage and trout are menu mainstays (bar meals £11–18). **£100**

Church House Inn Torver, LA21 8AZ, 2 miles south of Coniston ☏ 015394 49159, ⊕ thechurchhouseinn.com. Anyone after good food should drop by for a meal (mains £12–20; generous Sun roast £12.95), but there are also five comfortable, small and charming B&B rooms with a modern "country cottage" look, offering very good value (plus hook-ups for a few motorhomes out the back). **£79**

YHA Coniston Holly How Far End, LA21 8DD ☏ 0845 371 9511, ⊕ yha.org.uk/hostel/coniston-holly-how. Well-equipped hostel in a big old slate house (with some four-bed family rooms; £69) set in its own gardens just a few minutes' walk north of the centre on the Ambleside road. It's popular with schools and families for its café, bar (with real ale), outdoor activities, and unusually spacious dorms. Good meals available too. Dorms **£21.50**

EATING

Bluebird Café Lake Rd, LA21 8AN ☏ 01539 441649, ⊕ thebluebirdcafe.co.uk. The big, covered outdoor terrace with lake views makes this the perfect place to watch the comings and goings of the boats. On the menu are Cumberland sausage butties, soups and sandwiches, jacket potatoes and salads (£3.50–8); also good for a decent coffee and a cake. Daily: Feb half term to Nov 9.30am–5.30pm; Dec to Feb half term 10am–4.30pm.

★**Swallows & Amazons Tearoom** Bank Ground Farm, Coniston Water, LA21 8AA, 2 miles southeast of Coniston ☏ 01539 441264, ⊕ swallowsandamazons.net. For a drive, cycle or walk with a café at the end of it, this place is worth a special trip. Lunches, cakes and ice cream are served at the farmhouse associated with Arthur Ransome and his adventure stories; try the farmhouse taster, with locally sourced game terrine and lamb cutlet (£15) or a spinach pancake with smoked salmon (£11). 11am–5pm: Easter–Oct Thurs–Sun; daily during school hols.

Hawkshead and around

HAWKSHEAD, midway between Coniston and Ambleside, wears its beauty well, its handful of whitewashed eighteenth-century cottages and cobbles backed by woods and fells, all barely affected by modern intrusions. Seemingly oversized car parks at the edge of this little village take the strain, and when the crowds of day-trippers leave, Hawkshead regains its natural tranquillity. It's a major stop on both the **Beatrix Potter**

and **Wordsworth** trails (Potter's house, Hill Top, is nearby, while William and his brother went to school here), and makes a handy base for days out in **Grizedale Forest**.

Beatrix Potter Gallery

Main St, LA22 0NS • Feb half term to Easter Mon–Thurs, Sat & Sun 10am–4pm; Easter–May Mon–Thurs, Sat & Sun 10am–5pm, June–Aug daily 10am–5pm, Oct Mon–Thurs, Sat & Sun 10am–5pm • £6.30, discount available for Hill Top visitors; NT • ☏ 01539 436355, Ⓦ nationaltrust.org.uk/beatrix-potter-gallery-and-hawkshead

Hawkshead's **Beatrix Potter Gallery** occupies rooms once used by Potter's solicitor husband, William Heelis, and contains an annually changing selection of her original sketchbooks, drawings, watercolours, letters and manuscripts. Those less devoted to the "Tales" will find displays on Potter's life as a keen naturalist, conservationist and early supporter of the National Trust more diverting.

Tarn Hows

LA21 8DP • Daily 24hr • Free, but parking £5/2hr or £7.50/day • ☏ 015394 41456, Ⓦ nationaltrust.org.uk/tarn-hows-and-coniston • Seasonal buses sometimes run to the tarn

Beatrix Potter bequeathed her farms and land in the Lake District to the Trust on her death, including the local beauty spot **Tarn Hows**, whose glistening waters are circled by woodland, paths and picnic spots. Tarn Hows is a two-mile walk from Hawkshead (or Coniston) on country lanes and paths; it takes about an hour to walk around the tarn.

Hill Top

Near Sawrey, LA22 0NF, 2 miles southeast of Hawkshead • Mon–Thurs, Sat & Sun: Feb half term to May & Sept–Oct 10.30am–4.30pm, June–Aug 10am–5.30pm • £10.40, garden free; NT • ☏ 01539 436269, Ⓦ nationaltrust.org.uk/hill-top

Beatrix Potter's beloved house, **Hill Top**, lies close to Hawkshead in the gorgeous hamlet of Near Sawrey. A Londoner by birth, Potter bought the farmhouse here with the proceeds from her first book, *The Tale of Peter Rabbit*, and retained it as her study long after she moved out following her marriage in 1913. Bear in mind that entry is by timed ticket: you'll probably have to wait in line to enter the small house, and sell-outs are possible, especially in school holidays (you can't book in advance).

Grizedale Forest

LA22 0QJ, 2.5 miles southwest of Hawkshead • Daily 24hr; Grizedale Forest Centre Easter–Oct daily 10am–5pm, Nov–Easter daily 10am–4pm • Free • ☏ 0300 067 4495, Ⓦ forestry.gov.uk/grizedale • Cross Lakes Experience bus from Hawkshead

Grizedale Forest extends over the fells separating Coniston Water and Hawkshead from Windermere, and the picnic spots, open-air sculptures, children's activities, cycle trails and treetop adventure course make for a great day out away from the main lakes. The best starting point is the **Grizedale Forest Centre**, where there's a café and information point.

Go Ape

LA22 0QJ • Sessions daily Feb half term & Easter–Oct, otherwise weekends only and closed certain other days in season • £33–45, advance booking essential • ☏ 0845 519 3342, Ⓦ goape.co.uk

Go Ape, a high-ropes adventure course in the thick of Grizedale Forest, has you frolicking in the tree canopy for a couple of hours. You get a quick safety briefing and then make your own way around the fixed-ropes course – fantastic fun involving zipwires, Tarzan swings and aerial walkways.

ARRIVAL AND DEPARTURE   **HAWKSHEAD AND AROUND**

By bus The main bus service to Hawkshead is the #505 Coniston Rambler between Windermere, Ambleside and Coniston.

GETTING AROUND

Cross Lakes Experience The shuttle bus service (Easter–Oct daily; ☎01539 448600, ⦿lakedistrict.gov.uk) runs from Hawkshead to Grizedale and to Hill Top, and on to Sawrey for boat connections back to Bowness.

By bike Grizedale Forest Centre (⦿velobikes.co.uk/pages/hire, ☎01229 581116) rents bikes at £20/4hr, or £25/day.

ACCOMMODATION AND EATING

Ann Tyson's Guest House Wordsworth St, LA22 0PA ☎01539 436405, ⦿anntysons.co.uk. Wordsworth briefly boarded at this quaint B&B on an old cobbled street, and now you can too. Two double bedrooms, plus space for an extra single bed. You can also rent the whole place on a self-catering basis. **£76**

★ Drunken Duck Inn Barngates crossroads, LA22 0NG, 2 miles north of Hawkshead off B5285 ☎01539 436347, ⦿drunkenduckinn.co.uk. Stylish restaurant-with-rooms in a beautifully located 400-year-old inn. Smallish standard rooms are cheapest, weekend stays cost at least £140,

and there's more deluxe accommodation too (up to £325 a night). Bar meals at lunch (sandwiches, or dishes from belly pork to roast cod, £6–13) give way to more modish dining in the evening, with local sourcing a priority (mains £22; reservations essential). Daily noon–4pm & 6–9pm. **£105**

Yewfield Hawkshead Hill, LA22 0PR, 2 miles northwest of Hawkshead off B5285 ☎01539 436765, ⦿yewfield.co.uk. Splendid vegetarian guesthouse set among organic vegetable gardens and wildflower meadows. The house is a Victorian Gothic beauty, filled with Oriental artefacts and art from the owners' travels. Closed Dec & Jan. **£105**

11

Keswick and around

Standing on the shores of **Derwent Water**, the market town of **KESWICK** makes a good base for exploring the northern Lake District, particularly delightful **Borrowdale** to the south of town or the heights of Skiddaw (3053ft) and Blencathra (2847ft), which loom over Keswick to the north. Granted its **market** charter by Edward I in 1276 – held in the main Market Place on Saturdays – Keswick was an important wool and leather centre until around 1500, when these trades were supplanted by the discovery of local graphite. Keswick went on to become an important pencil-making town; the entertaining **Derwent Pencil Museum**, (daily 9.30am–5pm; £4.95; ⦿pencilmuseum.co.uk) tells the whole story.

Castlerigg Stone Circle

Castle Lane, CA12 4RN • Daily 24hr • Free

Don't miss Keswick's most mysterious landmark, **Castlerigg Stone Circle**, where 38 hunks of volcanic stone, the largest almost 8ft tall, form a circle 100ft in diameter set against a magnificent mountain backdrop. Take the Threlkeld rail-line path (signposted by the *Keswick Country House Hotel*) and follow the signs for around a mile and a half.

Derwent Water

Keswick Launch departures: Easter–Oct daily, Nov–Easter Sat & Sun only • £9.75 return, £2.10 per stage • ☎01768 772263, ⦿keswick-launch.co.uk

The shores of **Derwent Water** lie five minutes' walk south of the town centre. It's ringed by crags and studded with islets, and is most easily seen by hopping on the **Keswick Launch**, which runs around the lake calling at several points en route. You can jump off the launch at any of the half a dozen piers on Derwent Water for a stroll, but if you've only got time for one hike, make it up **Cat Bells** (take the launch to Hawes End), a superb vantage point (1481ft) above the lake's western shore – allow two and a half hours for the scramble to the top and a return to the pier along the wooded shore.

Bassenthwaite Lake

Regular buses along the eastern shore, including the #554 and the #73

Keswick's other lake is **Bassenthwaite**, a couple of miles northwest of town – any pub-quiz fan will know that Bassenthwaite is actually the only "lake" in the Lake District (all the

11

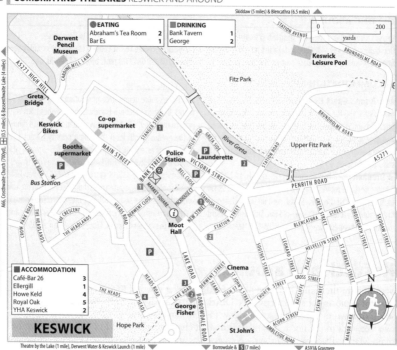

EATING
Abraham's Tea Room	2
Bar Es	1

DRINKING
Bank Tavern	1
George	2

ACCOMMODATION
Café-Bar 26	3
Ellergill	1
Howe Keld	4
Royal Oak	5
YHA Keswick	2

KESWICK

others are known as waters or meres). Families will enjoy both **Mirehouse** stately home (ⓦ mirehouse.com) and the **Lake District Wildlife Park** (ⓦ lakedistrictwildlifepark.co.uk), the latter a pioneering conservation project.

Bassenthwaite is also known for its **ospreys**, which nest and breed each year on the shore below Dodd Wood (usually from April to late Aug/Sept, ⓦ ospreywatch.co.uk). From a viewing platform at the wood you'll get to see the birds fishing and feeding, or you can get even closer with the nest-cam at nearby **Whinlatter Forest Park**, west of Keswick along the B5292. This is a great place for mountain bikers, and there's a forest high-ropes Go Ape adventure course here too.

Borrowdale

It is difficult to overstate the beauty of **Borrowdale**, a valley of river flats and yew trees, lying at the head of Derwent Water and overshadowed by Scafell Pike, the highest mountain in England, and Great Gable, reckoned as one of the finest-looking. At the straggling hamlet of **Rosthwaite**, seven miles south of Keswick, there are a couple of hotels with public bars, while another mile up the valley there's a café and a car park at Seatoller. From here, it's twenty minutes' walk down a minor road to the hamlet of **Seathwaite**, the base for walks up **Scafell Pike** (3205ft). The classic ascent is a tough eight-mile (6hr) loop walk from Seathwaite, heading up the thrilling Corridor Route then descending via Esk Hause.

ARRIVAL AND DEPARTURE   KESWICK AND AROUND

By bus Buses (including National Express services from Manchester and London) use the terminal in front of the large Booths supermarket, off Main Street. Some local services are seasonal.
Destinations Ambleside (hourly; 50min); Buttermere

(2 daily; 50min); Carlisle (3 daily; 1hr 10min); Cockermouth (every 30min–1hr; 30min); Grasmere (hourly; 40min); Honister (Easter–Oct 4 daily; 40min); Kendal (hourly; 1hr 30min); Rosthwaite (every 30min–1hr; 25min); Seatoller (every 30min–1hr; 30min); Windermere (hourly; 1hr).

GETTING AROUND

By bus Local services include the #77A (Easter–Oct only; down the west side of Derwent Water, via the access point for Cat Bells) and the scenic #78 "Borrowdale Rambler", which runs south down the B5289 to Seatoller. You can use either service all day with the "Honister Rambler" ticket (from £8).

By bike Keswick Bikes, 133 Main Street (daily 9am–5pm; ☎ 01768 775202, ⓦ keswickbikes.co.uk), rents out bikes from £25/day.

INFORMATION AND TOURS

Tourist office National Park Information Centre, Moot Hall, Market Square (daily: April–Oct 9.30am–5.30pm; Nov–March 9.30am–4.30pm; ☎ 0845 901 0845, ⓦ lake district.gov.uk).

Guided walks For a good walk in good company – lakeside rambles to mountain climbs – contact Pace the Peaks (regular walks Easter–Sept; £15; booking essential; ⓦ pacethepeaks.co.uk).

ACCOMMODATION

B&Bs and **guesthouses** cluster around Southey, Blencathra, Church and Eskin streets, in the grid off the A591 (Penrith road). Smarter guesthouses and **hotels** line The Heads, overlooking Hope Park, a couple of minutes south of the centre on the way to Derwent Water, while nearby Borrowdale has several fine old inns and country-house hotels.

11

Café-Bar 26 26 Lake Rd, CA12 5DQ ☎ 01768 780863; map p.572. Four stylishly decorated rooms on the first floor offer a chintz-free B&B base right in the town centre, while downstairs is a funky café-bar. It's £95 at the weekend. **£75**

★ **Ellergill** 22 Stanger St, CA12 5JU ☎ 01768 773347, ⓦ ellergill.co.uk; map p.572. Owners Robin and Clare have grafted a chic European feel onto their restored Victorian house, and offer classy B&B with five rooms. **£75**

★ **Howe Keld** 5–7 The Heads, CA12 5ES ☎ 01768 772417, ⓦ howekeld.co.uk; map p.572. The Fishers' boutique guesthouse puts local crafts and materials centre stage, with furniture and floors handcrafted from Lake District trees, plus green-slate bathrooms and carpets of Herdwick wool. Breakfast is terrific, from the daily home-baked organic bread to veggie rissoles and other specialities. **£115**

Royal Oak Rosthwaite, CA12 5XB, 7 miles south of Keswick ☎ 01768 777214, ⓦ royaloakhotel.co.uk; map p.572. The Borrowdale hikers' favourite – rooms in a traditional inn with stone-flagged bar, where a hearty lakeland dinner (no choice, but vegetarian alternative available) is served promptly at 7pm, and a bacon-and-eggs breakfast at 8.30am. Rates include dinner, and bed and breakfast. **£134**

YHA Keswick Station Rd, CA12 5LH ☎ 0845 371 9746, ⓦ yha.org.uk/hostel/keswick; map p.572. Once a riverside woollen mill, Keswick's YHA is more budget hotel than hostel these days, but still good value. It's big (84 beds in 21 rooms) but you're still advised to book, especially for a twin-bedded or family room. Dorms **£23.50**, doubles **£56**

EATING

Abraham's Tea Room George Fisher, 2 Borrowdale Rd, CA12 5DA ☎ 01768 772178, ⓦ georgefisher.co.uk; map p.572. Keswick's celebrated outdoors store has a top-floor tearoom for home-made soups, big breakfasts, open sandwiches and other daily specials (£5–9). Mon–Fri 10am–5pm, Sat 9.30am–5pm, Sun 10.30am–4.30pm.

Bar Es 1 New St, CA12 5BH ☎ 01768 775222, ⓦ esbarkeswick.co.uk; map p.572. On the right night Bar Es can be a real buzz (it's best to book at weekends in summer) – have a drink in the downstairs bar, munch "Mexican-inspired tapas" and then move upstairs for hearty portions of chorizo stew and beans, quesadillas, or their slow-cooked beef enchiladas (around £12 a head). Daily 5–11pm, kitchen closes 9pm.

DRINKING

Bank Tavern 47 Main St, CA12 5DS ☎ 01768 772663, ⓦ banktavern.co.uk; map p.572. Resolutely traditional pub with a great range of beers (usually half a dozen real ales available), and a terrace at the back looking towards Market Square. Also enjoys a local reputation for its classic bar meals – bangers and mash to rib-eye steak (£9–14) – which can mean a crush at meal times. Daily 11am–11pm; kitchen daily noon–9pm.

George St John St, CA12 5AZ ☎ 01768 772076, ⓦ georgehotelkeswick.co.uk; map p.572. If you're looking to down a pint or two of local Jennings ale at a traditional pub with bags of character, you won't do better than this 350-year-old inn. There's also a good bistro menu available: slow-roast lamb to venison casserole, local trout to fish and chips (mains £11–16). Mon–Thurs & Sun 11am–11pm, Fri & Sat 11am–midnight; kitchen Mon–Thurs noon–2.30pm & 5.30–9pm, Fri–Sun noon–4.30pm & 5.30–9.30pm.

There's a fair amount going on in Keswick throughout the year, including the **jazz festival** (ⓦ keswick.org) and **mountain festival** (ⓦ keswickmountainfestival.co.uk), both in May, a **beer festival** in June (ⓦ keswickbeerfestival.co.uk), and the **Keswick Agricultural Show** (Aug bank hol, ⓦ keswickshow.co.uk).

Theatre by the Lake Lake Rd, CA12 5DJ ☎ 01768 774411, ⓦ theatrebythelake.com; map p.572. England's loveliest theatre hosts a full programme of drama, concerts, exhibitions, readings and talks. "Words By The Water", a literature festival, takes place here in the spring.

Honister Pass

Near the head of Borrowdale at Seatoller, the B5289 road cuts west, snaking up and over the dramatic **Honister Pass**, en route to Buttermere. At the top lie the unassuming buildings of **Honister Slate Mine** – an unexpectedly great place for daredevil adventurers, with its deep mine tours and mountain activities. Come suitably clothed – it's wet or windy up here at the best of times.

Honister Slate Mine

Honister Pass, CA12 5XN · **Visitor centre, shop and café** Daily 9am–5pm · Free · **Tours** Daily 10.30am, 12.30pm & 3.30pm; 1hr 30min · From £13.50; reservations essential · ☎ 01768 777230, ⓦ honister.com

Slate has been quarried on Honister since the eighteenth century. **Honister Slate Mine**, the last remaining working slate mine in England, was rescued by local entrepreneurs in 1996 and is now operating again as a sustainable, commercial enterprise. To get an idea of what traditional mining entailed, you can don a hard hat and lamp to join one of the hugely informative guided **tours**, which lead you through narrow tunnels into illuminated, dripping caverns.

Via Ferrata

Daily departures from Honister Slate Mine · Classic £38, Xtreme £45; reservations essential · ☎ 01768 777714, ⓦ honister.com

Honister features England's first **Via Ferrata** – a dramatic Alpine-style three-hour mountain climb using a fixed cableway and harness, which allows visitors to follow the old miners' route up the exposed face of Fleetwith Pike (2126ft), the peak right above the mines. There are two options, labelled "Classic" and "Extreme"; both are terrifying and exhilarating in equal measure. Although you don't need climbing experience, check out the photos and videos on the website first to see what you're in for.

By bus The #77/77A runs up to Honister from Keswick on a circular route, coming either via Borrowdale (40min) or via Whinlatter and Buttermere (1hr). Buses run April–Sept only.

Buttermere

Ringed by peaks and crags, the tranquil waters and lakeside paths of **Buttermere** make a popular day-trip from Keswick, with the best approach being the sweeping descent into the valley from Honister Pass. There's no real village here – just a few houses and farms, a couple of hotels and a youth hostel, a café and large car park. The four-mile, round-lake stroll circling Buttermere shouldn't take more than a couple of hours. You can always detour up Scarth Gap to the peak known as **Haystacks** (1900ft) if you want more of a climb and views.

ARRIVAL AND DEPARTURE

By bus The #77 from Keswick travels via Whinlatter Pass (1hr 15min), and the #77A travels via Honister Pass (1hr).

Buses run April–Sept only.

Eskdale

Eskdale is perhaps the prettiest of the unsung Lake District valleys, reached from Ambleside on a long, twisting and alarmingly steep drive via the dramatic Hardknott Pass and **Hardknott Roman Fort** (daily 24hr; free), which commands a strategic and panoramic position. Eskdale can also be accessed less dramatically from the Cumbrian coast by road or the Ravenglass and Eskdale Railway (see below). However you arrive, you end up in the heart of superb walking country around the hamlet of **Boot**, where there's an old mill to explore and several local trails.

ARRIVAL AND DEPARTURE

11

By car There's parking at Dalegarth station and at a couple of other designated areas in Eskdale, but the valley road is very narrow and side-of-the-road parking is impossible. Come by train if you can for a hassle-free day out.

By train There are year-round services on the Ravenglass and Eskdale Railway (see below), with stops at Eskdale Green (for *Stanley House*) and Dalegarth Station, the latter a short walk from Boot and around 1.5 miles from the *Woolpack Inn*.

ACCOMMODATION AND EATING

Eskdale Campsite Eskdale, Hardknott Pass road, CA19 1TF, just east of Boot ☎01946 723253, ⓦeskdale camping.com. Small, beautifully sited campsite, just a short walk from the railway and the valley's pubs. For camping without canvas they also have ten heated "pods" (£45.50). Closed two weeks in Jan, and all of Feb. **£12.80**

★ Stanley House Eskdale Green, CA19 1TF ☎01946 723327, ⓦstanleyghyll-eskdale.co.uk. Self-catering/ B&B with a home-from-home feel and contemporary air. Accommodation is in a dozen spacious rooms, while downstairs is a huge open-plan kitchen-diner, plus lounge

with woodburner. The genial owners – who also run the *Woolpack Inn* – can arrange a lift to the pub. **£110**

★ Woolpack Inn Eskdale, Hardknott Pass road, CA19 1TH, 1 mile east of Boot ☎01946 723230, ⓦwoolpack .co.uk. Friendly country inn whose weather-beaten facade conceals a cosy B&B and popular bar. Their seven rooms enjoy a smart urban chic feel, while downstairs the bar sports leather sofas and wood-fired pizza oven. It's strong on Cumbrian real ales, and the beer garden has spectacular fell views. Bar hours flexible but around 10am–10pm; bar meals noon–9pm, pizza noon–10pm. **£80**

Ravenglass and around

A sleepy coastal village at the estuary of three rivers, the Esk, Mite and Irt, **RAVENGLASS** is the starting point for the wonderful narrow-gauge **Ravenglass and Eskdale Railway**. It's worth taking some time to look around, though, before hopping on the train or heading out to **Muncaster Castle**, the other main local attraction. The single main street preserves a row of characterful nineteenth-century cottages facing out across the estuarine mud flats and dunes – the northern section, across the Esk, is a **nature reserve** where black-headed gulls and terns are often seen (get there by crossing over the mainline railway footbridge).

Ravenglass and Eskdale Railway

Ravenglass station, CA18 1SW • March–Oct, at least 5 trains daily (up to 15 daily in school summer hols); also most winter weekends, plus Christmas, New Year and Feb half-term hols • £13.90 return • ☎01229 717171, ⓦravenglass-railway.co.uk

Opened in 1875 to carry ore from the Eskdale mines to the coastal railway, the 15-inch-gauge track of the **Ravenglass and Eskdale Railway** winds seven miles up through the Eskdale Valley to Dalegarth Station near Boot. The ticket lets you break your journey and get off and take a walk from one of the half-dozen stations en route;

the full return journey, without a break, takes an hour and forty minutes. Alternatively, take your bike up on the train (prebooking essential; £3.50/bike) and cycle back from Dalegarth down the traffic-free **Eskdale Trail** (8.5 miles, 2hr; route guide available from Ravenglass and Dalegarth stations).

Muncaster Castle

A595, CA18 1RQ, 1 mile east of Ravenglass • Late March to late Oct; castle Mon–Fri & Sun noon–4pm; gardens and bird centre daily 10.30am–5pm; bird displays daily 2.30pm; check website for out-of-season openings • £14, £11 without castle entrance • ☎ 01229 717614, ⓦ muncaster.co.uk • There's a footpath (30min) from Ravenglass

The **Muncaster Castle** estate, a mile east of Ravenglass, provides one of the region's best days out. Apart from the ghost-ridden rooms of the castle itself, there are also seventy acres of well-kept **grounds and gardens**, at their best in spring and autumn, as well as an entertaining **hawk and owl centre** where they breed endangered species (including England's own barn owl).

11

ARRIVAL AND DEPARTURE

RAVENGLASS AND AROUND

By train As well as the narrow-gauge line to Eskdale, Ravenglass is on the Cumbrian Coast line. There are hourly services to Barrow-in-Furness (50min), Carlisle (1hr 50min), Carnforth (1hr 50min) and Lancaster (2hr).

Wasdale

Wasdale is all about the mountains, which encircle three-mile long **Wast Water**, England's deepest lake. Awesome 1700ft screes plunge to its eastern shore, separating Wast Water from Eskdale to the south, while the highest peaks in England – Great Gable and the Scafells – frame **Wasdale Head**, the tiny settlement at the top of the lake. Apart from a few farms and cottages, and a single inn, the valley head is a remote yet starkly beautiful environment – mountain hikers know all about it, and can access some of the toughest, most rewarding lakeland peaks and circuits from here.

Wasdale has its softer side too, starting in the approach village of **Gosforth**, with its Viking-era cross, just off the A595. Beyond here, through forestry plantations and farmland, lie several scattered hamlets; the foot of the lake is just a mile and a half east of the village of **Nether Wasdale**, where there's overflow accommodation and places to eat. The drive in is a treat – bracken-covered walls hide the fields from view, while the roads cross little stone bridges and pass farm shops selling jars of bramble jelly or bags of new potatoes. Beyond Nether Wasdale the road hugs Wast Water's western shore, with occasional parking spots by bosky groves, stony coves and little promontories.

Wasdale Head

The road ends a mile beyond Wast Water at **Wasdale Head**, a clearing between the mountain ranges where you'll find the *Wasdale Head Inn*, one of the most celebrated in all the lakeland. British mountain climbing was born here in the days when the inn's landlord and champion liar was the famous Will Ritson (there's an annual **"World's Biggest Liar"** festival in his honour just down the road at Santon; ⓦ santonbridgeinn. com). Black-and-white photographs pinned to the panelled rooms inside show Victorian gents in hobnailed boots and flat caps scaling dreadful precipices with nonchalant ease. The inn's gone a bit upmarket since those days, but still attracts a genuine walking and climbing crowd, unfazed by the general lack of TV or mobile phone reception in the valley.

For a true measure of your own insignificance, take a walk down to Wast Water and along the eastern lakeshore path, approaching the unnerving, implacable screes – beware of tackling the tricky "footpath" across them, marked on some maps.

St Olaf's church

St Olaf's, reputedly **England's smallest church**, lies a couple of hundred yards from the *Wasdale Head Inn*, encircled by evergreens and dwarfed by the surrounding fells. The small cemetery contains graves and memorials to several of those killed while climbing them. Wasdale's had a church since medieval times and though no one knows quite how old this plain chapel is, its current appearance – moss-grown slate roof and all – dates from a complete overhaul in 1892. A path over Eskdale Moor, via Burnmoor Tarn, was the former "corpse road" along which the dead were carried for burying in Eskdale church, as St Olaf's had no consecrated churchyard until 1901.

ARRIVAL AND DEPARTURE   WASDALE HEAD

By car There's a public car park near the head of the lake and another close to the *Wasdale Head Inn*, but the spaces fill quickly with hikers, even on the grottiest of days. There are other parking places down the side of the lake.

INFORMATION

Information and supplies For everything you might need, from advance information to last-minute outdoor gear and supplies, contact the *Wasdale Head Inn* (☏ 01946 726229, ⓦ wasdale.com). Their Barn Door Shop, next to the inn (daily: Easter–Oct 9am–5pm; Nov–Easter 9am–4pm) is the only proper store for miles, and has a full range of outdoor clothes, equipment, camping gear, maps and guides – and the staff give great local walking advice. They also sell basic foodstuffs, including those crucial slabs of Kendal mint cake to get you up any mountain.

ACCOMMODATION

★**Burnthwaite Farm** Wasdale Head, CA20 1EX ☏ 01946 726242, ⓦ burnthwaite.co.uk. The last building in the valley – up a driveable track from the parking area near the inn – is a handsome old working sheep farm with six traditional B&B rooms (only two en suite, £76) inside a whitewashed farmhouse. All rooms have up-close-and-personal views of Lingmell, the adjacent mountain. There is also a self-catering apartment (sleeps four; from £395/week, or £60/night when available). A big farmhouse breakfast sets you up for the day. No credit cards. **£66**

Wasdale Campsite Wasdale Head, CA20 1EX ☏ 01946 726220, reservations on ☏ 01539 463862, ⓦ national trust.org.uk. The National Trust's Wasdale site is a mile from the pub, under glowering mountains at the head of the lake. There's a basic store, showers and a laundry room beneath the trees, and a couple of camping pods for softies (sleep two adults and a child; from £35). Open all year. Per person **£13.50**

★**Wasdale Head Inn** Wasdale Head, CA20 1EX ☏ 01946 726229, ⓦ wasdale.com. In addition to the excellent bar there are nine en-suite guest rooms in the main building of this famous inn; three "superior rooms" (£130) in the adjacent cottage conversion offer more space. The inn also runs six self-catering apartments in a converted barn (sleeping two to five; £470–540/week, short breaks and winter discounts available), a nearby B&B (£70), and another campsite (£5/person) with campers' toilets, hot showers (£1) and a wash-up area. **£118**

Whitehaven and around

Around twenty miles up the coast from Ravenglass, some fine Georgian houses mark out the centre of **WHITEHAVEN** – one of the few grid-planned towns in England and easily the most interesting destination on Cumbria's west coast. Whitehaven had a long history of trade in coal, but its rapid economic expansion was largely due to the booming slave trade – the town spent a brief period during the eighteenth century as one of Britain's busiest ports, importing sugar, rum, spices, tea, timber and tobacco.

The Beacon Museum

West Strand, on the harbour, CA28 7LY • Tues–Sun 10am–4.30pm, plus school and bank hols; last admission 3.45pm • £5 • ☏ 01946 592302, ⓦ thebeacon-whitehaven.co.uk

The best place to swot up on Whitehaven's local history is the enterprising **Beacon Museum** on the harbour with interactive exhibitions covering a variety of themes from slaving and smuggling to the history of the nuclear industry at nearby Sellafield.

You could easily spend a couple of hours here, teaching yourself how to build a ship, tie a sailor's knot or dress like a Roman centurion.

Rum Story

Lowther St, CA28 7DN • 10am–4.30pm: Easter–Sept daily; Oct–Easter Mon–Sat; closed 2nd week in Jan • £5.95 • ☎ 01946 592933, ⓦ rumstory.co.uk

Housed in the eighteenth-century shop, courtyard and warehouses of the Jefferson family, the **Rum Story** museum is where you can learn about rum, the navy, temperance and the hideousness of the slaves' Middle Passage, among other matters.

ARRIVAL AND DEPARTURE

WHITEHAVEN AND AROUND

By train From Whitehaven's train station (services to St Bees and Ravenglass, or north to Carlisle) you can walk around the harbour to The Beacon in less than 10min.

By bike Whitehaven is the start of the 140-mile C2C cycle route to Sunderland/Newcastle – a metal cut-out at the harbour marks the spot.

ACCOMMODATION

★**Lowther House** 13 Inkerman Terrace, CA28 7TY ☎ 01946 63169, ⓦ lowtherhouse-whitehaven.com. A highly personal, period restoration of an old Whitehaven house, with three charming rooms (one with harbour and sea views). You're welcomed with tea and cake, and breakfast is a chatty affair around your host's kitchen table. __£90__

St Bees

Five miles south of Whitehaven (and easily reached by train or bus), lie long sands, a few hundred yards west of the coastal village of **St Bees**. The steep, sandstone cliffs of **St Bees Head** to the north are good for windy walks and birdwatching, while the headland's lighthouse marks the start of Alfred Wainwright's 190-mile **Coast-to-Coast Walk** to Robin Hood's Bay.

Cockermouth

There's a lot to admire about the attractive small town and market centre of **COCKERMOUTH** – impressive Georgian facades, tree-lined streets and riverside setting – and there's no shortage of local attractions, not least the logical first stop on the **Wordsworth** trail, namely the house where the future poet was born. In the smartened-up Market Place (with monthly farmers' **markets**) there are more reminders of bygone days, including a pavement plaque teaching you the basics of talking Cumbrian.

Wordsworth House

Main St, CA13 9RX • Easter–Oct Mon–Thurs, Sat & Sun 11am–5pm, last admission 4pm • £7.50, admission by timed ticket on busy days; NT • ☎ 01900 824805, ⓦ nationaltrust.org.uk/wordsworth-house

The **Wordsworth House**, where William and sister Dorothy spent their first few years, is presented as a functioning eighteenth-century home – with a costumed cook sharing recipes in the kitchen and a clerk completing the ledger with quill and ink.

Jennings Brewery

Brewery Lane, CA13 9NE • Tours Feb, Nov & Dec Thurs–Sat 1.30pm; March–Oct Wed–Sat 1.30pm; 1hr 30min • £9 • ☎ 0845 129 7190, ⓦ www.jenningsbrewery.co.uk

Follow your nose in town, after the heady smell of hops, and you're likely to stumble upon **Jennings Brewery**, near the river. Jennings have been brewers in Cockermouth since 1874 and you don't have to step far to sample their product, available in any local pub. Or you can take the brewery **tour**, which ends with a free tasting in the bar.

ARRIVAL AND DEPARTURE COCKERMOUTH

By bus All buses stop on Main Street, with the most useful service being the #X4/X5 (hourly, Sun every 2hr) from Penrith (1hr 30min) and Keswick (35min).

ACCOMMODATION AND EATING

★**Bitter End** 15 Kirkgate, CA13 9PJ ☎ 01900 828993, ⊕ bitterend.co.uk. The cosiest pub in town also contains Cumbria's smallest brewery, producing ales like "Farmers", "Cockersnoot" and "Cuddy Lugs". Food ranges from steak and ale pie to cajun chicken (dishes £10–13). Mon–Fri 4–11pm, Sat & Sun 11am–11pm; kitchen Mon & Tues 4–9pm, Wed–Fri & Sun noon–2pm & 4–9pm, Sat noon–9pm.

Merienda 7a Station St, CA13 9QW ☎ 01900 822790, ⊕ merienda.co.uk. Bright and breezy café-bar offering breakfasts (from £3), light lunches (around £7) and evening meals (mains from £13). Also open Fri nights for tapas and music. Mon–Thurs & Sat 8am–9pm, Fri 8am–10pm, Sun 9am–9pm.

★**Six Castlegate** 6 Castlegate, CA13 9EU ☎ 01900 826786, ⊕ sixcastlegate.co.uk. Period-piece house that retains its lofty Georgian proportions, impressive carved staircase and oak panelling, though the half-dozen B&B rooms are contemporary country in style. **£85**

Ullswater

Wordsworth declared **Ullswater** "the happiest combination of beauty and grandeur, which any of the Lakes affords", a judgement that still holds good. At almost eight miles, it's the second-longest lake in the National Park, with a dramatic serpentine shape that's overlooked by soaring fells, none higher than **Helvellyn** (3114ft), the most popular of the four 3000ft mountains in Cumbria. Cruises depart from the tiny village of **Glenridding**, at the south of the lake, and also call at lovely **Pooley Bridge**, the hamlet at the head of the lake. Meanwhile, at **Gowbarrow Park**, three miles north of Glenridding, the hillside still blazes green and gold in spring, as it did when the Wordsworths visited in April 1802; it's thought that Dorothy's recollections of the visit in her diary inspired William to write his famous "Daffodils" poem. The car park, tearooms and ferry dock here mark the start of a walk up to the 70ft falls of **Aira Force** (40min return).

ARRIVAL AND INFORMATION ULLSWATER

By bus Buses from Penrith, Keswick and Bowness/ Windermere) stop on the main road in Glenridding.
By boat The Glenridding steamer pier is a 5min walk from the centre. There's pay-and-display parking by the pier.
By car Parking along the lake is difficult, especially in summer, but it's easy to park in Glenridding and use the bus or boat to visit local attractions. Use the large pay-and-display car park by the visitor centre.
Tourist office National Park Information Centre, in the main car park at Glenridding (Easter–Oct daily 9.30am–5.30pm; Nov–Easter Sat & Sun 9.30am–3.30pm, weather dependent; ☎ 07769 956144, ⊕ lakedistrict.gov.uk).

ULLSWATER LAKE SERVICES

Ullswater steamer services started in 1859, and the lake still has a year-round ferry and cruise service provided by The Ullswater Navigation & Transit Company (☎ 01768 482229, ⊕ ullswater -steamers.co.uk). Services run from Glenridding to Howtown (45min; £6.60 single, £10.40 return), and from Howtown on to Pooley Bridge (1hr 5min; £9.30 each way) and back again. The one-day hop-on, hop-off "Round the Lake" pass (£13.50) also nets you a fifty percent discount on the Ravenglass and Eskdale Railway (see p.575). You can buy tickets at the piers or on board.

In school and summer holidays there are up to nine **daily departures** from Glenridding (basically an hourly service), down to between three and six a day at other times of the year – only Christmas Eve and Christmas Day have no sailings. The same company also runs a separate **Glenridding–Aira Force ferry** (June–Sept 6 daily; £5.20 each way; 20min).

> ### CLIMBING HELVELLYN
>
> The climb to the summit of **Helvellyn** (3114ft) forms part of a day-long circuit from Glenridding. The most frequently chosen approach is via the infamous **Striding Edge**, an undulating rocky crest offering the most direct access via a steep and dangerous scramble. The classic return is via the less demanding and less exposed **Swirral Edge**, where a route leads down to **Red Tarn** – the highest Lake District tarn – then follows the beck down to Glenridding past Helvellyn youth hostel. The Swirral Edge route is also the best way *up* Helvellyn if you don't fancy chancing Striding Edge (or you can try the even easier west face, from Thirlmere on the A591). Either approach from Glenridding makes for a seven-mile (5–6hr) round walk.

ACCOMMODATION AND EATING

★**The Quiet Site** Watermillock, CA11 0LS ☎ 07768 727016, ⓦ thequietsite.co.uk. The eco-friendly choice for cool campers is this hilltop site with sweeping views, around 2.5 miles north of Ullswater. Grassy camping pitches, a dozen camping pods (from £35) and a bar-in-a-barn (open most summer evenings) offer a bit of glamping comfort. Check website for seasonal rate hikes. __£20__

Sharrow Bay 2 miles south of Pooley Bridge, CA10 2LZ, on the Howtown road ☎ 01768 486301, ⓦ sharrowbay .co.uk. Halfway down Ullswater's eastern shore, *Sharrow Bay* offers a breathtaking setting and excellent food. Needless to say, it's London prices in the country (rooms up to £400 a night, suites up to £700) but there are few places

anywhere in England that compare. The dining room is open to nonresidents (reservations essential); afternoon tea here (£25) is famous, while lunch and dinner (£65) are classy, formal affairs – and the desserts are renowned. Lunch noon–2pm, afternoon tea at 4pm, dinner 7–9pm. __£165__

YHA Helvellyn Greenside, CA11 0QR ☎ 0845 371 9742, ⓦ yha.org.uk/hostel/helvellyn. Walkers wanting an early start on Helvellyn stay at this basic hostel, dramatically sited 900ft up in the foothills around 1.5 miles from Glenridding. There are lots of beds (and private rooms available for families; £50) while the nearest pub, the *Travellers Rest*, is a mile away. Dorms __£21.40__

Penrith and around

The nearest town to Ullswater – just four miles from the head of the lake – is **PENRITH**, whose deep-red buildings are constructed from the same rust-red sandstone used to build **Penrith Castle** in the fourteenth century; this is now a romantic, crumbling ruin, opposite the train station. The town itself is at its best in the narrow streets, arcades and alleys off **Market Square**, and around **St Andrew's churchyard**, where the so-called "Giant's Grave" is actually a collection of pre-Norman crosses and "hogback" tombstones.

Dalemain

A592, CA11 0HB, 2 miles north of Pooley Bridge or 3 miles southwest of Penrith • **House** Easter–Oct Mon–Thurs & Sun 10.30am–3.30pm • £11.50 (includes gardens & tearoom) • **Gardens & tearoom** Mon–Thurs & Sun: Feb–Easter & Nov to mid-Dec 11am–3pm; Easter–Oct 10am–4.30pm • £8.50 • ☎ 01768 486450, ⓦ dalemain.com • No public transport

Residence to the same family since 1679, the country house of **Dalemain** started life in the twelfth century as a fortified tower, but has been added to by successive generations, culminating with a Georgian facade grafted on to a largely Elizabethan house. Its grounds are gorgeous and, rather remarkably, inside you're given the run of the public rooms, which the Hasell family still use.

Rheged

Redhills, CA11 0DQ, 1.5 miles southwest of Penrith • Daily 10am–5.30pm • Free; admission to one film £6.50, each extra film £5 • ☎ 01768 868000, ⓦ rheged.com • Bus #X4/X5 from Penrith or Keswick/Cockermouth

Rheged – a Cumbrian "visitor experience", just outside Penrith – is billed as Europe's largest earth-covered building, and blends in admirably with the surrounding fells – from the main road you wouldn't know it was there. An impressive atrium-lit underground visitor centre fills you in on the region's history, and you'll also find souvenir shops, food outlets, galleries, workshops, demonstrations and play areas. The staple visit, though, is for the big-screen 3D **cinema**, which shows family-friendly movies.

ARRIVAL AND DEPARTURE
PENRITH AND AROUND

By train Penrith train station is 5min walk south of Market Square and the main street, Middlegate.
Destinations Carlisle (every 30min; 20min), with onward services to Glasgow/Edinburgh; Lancaster (every 30min; 40min), with onward services to London; Manchester (hourly; 1hr 40min).

By bus The bus station is on Albert St, behind Middlegate. Regular Ullswater, Keswick, Cockermouth and Carlisle services.

ACCOMMODATION AND EATING

Askham Hall Askham, CA10 2PF, 6 miles south of Penrith ☎01931 712350, ☻askhamhall.co.uk. Country-house living at its most gracious – the Lowther family's *Askham Hall* boasts stunning rooms, a heated outdoor pool and gorgeous gardens. There's both elegant restaurant dining (bookings essential) and the *Kitchen Garden Café*, which has an outdoor wood-fired oven for pizzas. Restaurant daily 7–9.30pm; café March & Nov Fri & Sun 11am–4pm, Easter to mid-Oct Mon–Fri & Sun 10am–5pm. **£190**

Brooklands 2 Portland Place, CA11 7QN ☎01768 863395, ☻brooklandsguesthouse.com. Handsome 1870s townhouse whose colour-coordinated B&B rooms have country pine furniture and small but snazzy bathrooms. **£95**

Crake Trees Manor Crosby Ravensworth, CA10 3JG, 15 miles southeast of Penrith ☎01931 715205, ☻craketreesmanor.co.uk. A gorgeous barn-conversion B&B in the nearby Eden Valley. Rooms have slate floors, antique beds, serious showers and fluffy, wrap-me-up towels; or consider the self-catering Brewhouse (sleeps two; from £260 for three nights), or the cosy Shepherds' Hut (sleeps two; £75–85). **£100**

★ George and Dragon Clifton, CA10 2ER, 3 miles northeast of Askham/south of Penrith ☎01768 865381, ☻georgeanddragonclifton.co.uk. This revamped eighteenth-century inn is a class act – country-chic rooms (up to £160) feature big beds with brocade headboards and slate-floor bathrooms, while the informal downstairs bar and restaurant (around £35 for three courses) sources pretty much everything from the adjacent Lowther estate. Kitchen daily noon–2.30pm & 6–9pm. **£95**

Carlisle and around

The county capital of Cumbria, **CARLISLE** has been fought over for more than 2000 years, ever since the construction of Hadrian's Wall – part of which survives at nearby **Birdoswald Roman Fort**. The later struggle with the Scots defined the very nature of Carlisle as a border city: William Wallace was repelled in 1297 and Robert the Bruce eighteen years later, but Bonnie Prince Charlie's troops took Carlisle in 1745 after a six-day siege, holding it for six weeks before surrendering to the Duke of Cumberland. It's not surprising, then, that the city trumpets itself as "historic Carlisle", and it's well worth a night's stop.

POTTY PENRITH

Potfest (☻potfest.co.uk), Europe's biggest ceramics show, takes place in Penrith over two consecutive weekends (late July/early Aug). The first is **Potfest in the Park**, with ceramics on display in marquees in front of Hutton-in-the-Forest country house, as well as larger sculptural works laid out in the grounds. This is followed by the highly unusual **Potfest in the Pens**, which sees potters displaying their creations in the unlikely setting of the covered pens at Penrith's cattle market, just outside town on the A66. Here, the public can talk to the artists, learn about what inspires them and sign up for free classes.

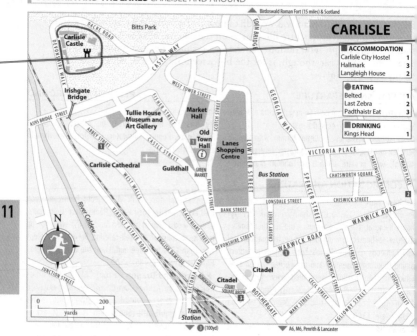

Carlisle Cathedral

Castle St, CA3 8TZ • Mon–Sat 7.30am–6.15pm, Sun 7.30am–5pm • Free, £5 donation requested • ☎ 01228 548151,
ⓦ carlislecathedral.org.uk

Carlisle Cathedral was founded in 1122 but embraces a considerably older heritage.
Christianity was established in sixth-century Carlisle by St Kentigern (often known as
St Mungo), who became the first bishop and patron saint of Glasgow. Parliamentarian
troops during the Civil War caused much destruction, but there's still plenty to admire
in the ornate fifteenth-century choir stalls and the glorious **East Window**, which features
some of the finest pieces of fourteenth-century stained glass in the country.

Tullie House Museum and Art Gallery

Castle St, CA3 8TP • April–Oct Mon–Sat 10am–5pm, Sun 11am–5pm; Nov–March Mon–Sat 10am–4pm, Sun noon–4pm • £7.70,
under-18s free • ☎ 01228 618718, ⓦ tulliehouse.co.uk

Among other wide-ranging attractions, the wonderful **Tullie House Museum and Art
Gallery** takes an imaginative approach to Carlisle's turbulent past, with special emphasis
put on life on the edge of the Roman Empire. Climbing a reconstruction of part of
Hadrian's Wall, you learn about catapults and stone-throwers, while other sections
elaborate on domestic life, work and burial practices.

Carlisle Castle

Bridge St, CA3 8UR • April–Sept daily 10am–6pm; Oct daily 10am–5pm; Nov–March Sat & Sun 10am–4pm • £6.80; EH • Guided tours
Easter–Oct daily; ask at the entrance • ☎ 01228 591922, ⓦ www.english-heritage.org.uk/visit/places/carlisle-castle

With a thousand years of military occupation of the site, **Carlisle Castle** is loaded with
significance – not least as the place where, in 1568, Elizabeth I kept Mary Queen of
Scots as her "guest". Guided **tours** help bring the history to life; don't leave without
climbing to the battlements for a view of the Carlisle rooftops.

Birdoswald Roman Fort

Gilsland, Brampton, CA8 7DD, 15 miles northeast of Carlisle • April–Sept daily 10am–6pm; Oct daily 10am–5pm; Nov–March Sat & Sun 10am–4pm • £6.10; EH • ☎ 01697 747602, ⓦ www.english-heritage.org.uk/visit/places/birdoswald-roman-fort-hadrians-wall

One of sixteen major fortifications along Hadrian's Wall, **Birdoswald Fort** has all tiers of the Roman structure intact, while a drill hall and other buildings have been excavated. There's a tearoom and picnic area at the fort.

ARRIVAL AND INFORMATION

By train The train station is right in the town centre. Carlisle is on the West Coast mainline (for London–Manchester–Scotland services), with additional coastal services to Whitehaven, and cross-country trains to Newcastle. The Settle to Carlisle Railway, the magnificent scenic railway through the Yorkshire Dales (ⓦ settle-carlisle.co.uk), also ends its run at Carlisle (see box, p.604).

CARLISLE AND AROUND

Destinations Lancaster (every 30min–1hr; 1hr); Newcastle (hourly; 1hr 20min–1hr 40min); Whitehaven (hourly; 1hr 10min).

Tourist office Old Town Hall, Green Market (March, April, Sept & Oct Mon–Sat 9.30am–5pm; May–Aug Mon–Sat 9.30am–5pm, Sun 10.30am–4pm; Nov–Feb Mon–Sat 10am–4pm; ☎ 01228 598596, ⓦ discovercarlisle.co.uk).

ACCOMMODATION

Carlisle City Hostel 36 Abbey St, CA3 8TX ☎ 01228 545637, ⓦ carlislecityhostel.com; map p.582. Carlisle's indie hostel makes a great budget base, with four bright bunk rooms offering flexible accommodation for groups or families. One room is available as a private double/triple (£50), another as a family room (£74). There's a kitchen, free tea and coffee, bike storage and secure lockers, and the location is excellent. Dorms **£19**

Hallmark Court Square, CA1 1QY ☎ 01228 531951, ⓦ hallmarkhotels.co.uk; map p.582. Right outside the train station, the boutique-style *Hallmark* has a chic look, sleek rooms with big beds, and a contemporary bar and brasserie. **£95**

Langleigh House 6 Howard Place, CA1 1HR ☎ 01228 530440, ⓦ langleighhouse.co.uk; map p.582. Nicely presented Victorian townhouse B&B – furnishings reflect the period, and original features abound. **£76**

EATING

Belted 20–34 Warwick Rd, CA1 1DN ☎ 01228 528941, ⓦ beltedburgers.co.uk; map p.582. The place to go if you're after a full-on burger experience (around £12 a head), with meat sourced from prime Scots beef, in a big, bustling, barn-like setting. Vegetarians can opt for the mushroom or beetburger instead. Good range of bottled craft beers, too. Tues–Sun 11am–11pm.

Last Zebra 6 Lowther St, CA3 8DA ☎ 01228 593600, ⓦ thelastzebra.co.uk; map p.582. Quirky lounge bar and grill serving cosmopolitan food at lunch and dinner – mussels to local lamb, burgers to piri-piri chicken (mains £10–28) – and good cocktails. Mon–Fri 11am–midnight, Sat 11am–1am, Sun noon–11pm.

Padthaistr Eat In the car park by Nelson Bridge, between the train station and the river, CA3 0BB ☎ 07970 030658; map p.582. Amazingly tasty Thai takeaway food at around £5 a portion, sold out of a red van; something of a local institution. Mon–Sat 11.30am–3pm.

DRINKING

Kings Head 31 Fisher St, CA3 8RF ⓦ kingsheadcarlisle .co.uk; map p.582. Recently given a much-needed facelift, this reliable, old-style pub right in the centre of town specializes in real ale; there are always a few guest beers on tap, plus local brews by Yates. Service can occasionally be surly. Mon–Thurs 10am–11pm, Fri 10am–midnight, Sat 11am–midnight, Sun noon–11pm.

11

Yorkshire

WHITBY

Yorkshire

It's easy to be glib about Yorkshire – to outsiders it's the archetypal "up North" with all the clichés that implies, from flat caps to grim factories. For their part, many Yorkshire locals are happy to play up to these prejudices, while nursing a secret conviction that there really is no better place in the world to live. In some respects, it's a world apart, its most distinctive characteristics – from the broad dialect to the breathtaking landscapes – deriving from a long history of settlement, invention and independence. It's hard to argue with Yorkshire's boasts that the beer's better, the air's cleaner and the people are friendlier.

The number-one destination is undoubtedly **York**, established by the Vikings and for centuries England's second city; the region's **Norse heritage** is still evident in Yorkshire dialect words, such as -gate ("street", from the Norse *gata*), dale ("valley"), tarn ("pond") and force ("waterfall"). York's mixture of medieval, Georgian and Victorian architecture is repeated in towns such as **Beverley**, Richmond and **Ripon**, while the Yorkshire **coast**, too, retains something of its erstwhile grandeur – Bridlington and Scarborough boomed in the nineteenth century and again in the postwar period, though it's in smaller resorts like **Whitby** and Robin Hood's Bay that the best of the coast is to be found today. A renewed vigour has infused the maritime city of **Hull**, which hopes to emulate the remarkable city-centre transformations of once-industrial **Leeds** and **Sheffield** to the south and west of the county, where **Bradford** also makes a fine diversion on the way to **Haworth**, home of the Brontë sisters.

The **Yorkshire Dales**, to the northwest, form a patchwork of stone-built villages, limestone hills, serene valleys and majestic heights. The county's other National Park, the **North York Moors**, is divided into bleak upland moors and a tremendous rugged coastline between Robin Hood's Bay and Staithes.

GETTING AROUND
YORKSHIRE

By train Fast trains on the East Coast main line link York to London, Newcastle and Edinburgh. Leeds is served by trains from London, and is at the centre of the integrated Metro bus and train system that covers most of West and South Yorkshire. There are services to Scarborough (from York) and Whitby (from Middlesbrough), while the Settle to Carlisle line, to the southern and western Dales, can be accessed from Leeds, as can Hull.

Transport passes The North Country Rover ticket (northernrailway.co.uk/tickets/rail-rover-tickets), £93 for four days in eight) covers train travel north of Leeds, Bradford and Hull and south of Newcastle and Carlisle.

York and around

YORK is the North's most compelling city, a place whose history, said George VI, "is the history of England". This is perhaps overstating things a little, but it reflects the significance of a metropolis that stood at the heart of the country's religious and political life for centuries, and until the Industrial Revolution was second only to London in population and importance. These days a more provincial air hangs over the

AKBAR'S RESTAURANT, BRADFORD

Highlights

❶ Jorvik & Jorvik Dig, York Travel through time to Viking York, then seek out new discoveries at Jorvik Dig. **See p.593**

❷ Fountains Abbey Enjoy views of the atmospheric ruins of Fountains Abbey set in spectacular Studley Water Garden. **See p.598**

❸ Malham It's a breathtaking hike from Malham village to the glorious natural amphitheatre of Malham Cove. **See p.603**

❹ Haworth Visiting the moorland home of the talented and ultimately tragic Brontë sisters is an affecting experience, despite the crowds. See p.609

❺ Bradford curry houses Bradford's Indian restaurants provide wonderful opportunities for gastronomic exploration. **See p.611**

❻ National Coal Mining Museum A working coal mine until the mid-1980s, now a museum; you can even head underground, if you're brave enough. **See p.618**

❼ Ferens Art Gallery Hull's 2017 stint as European Capital of Culture marked the city's transformation into a hub for the arts. **See p.622**

❽ Whitby Follow in the footsteps of Count Dracula and Captain James Cook in this spectacularly pretty former whaling port. See p.632

HIGHLIGHTS ARE MARKED ON THE MAP ON P.588

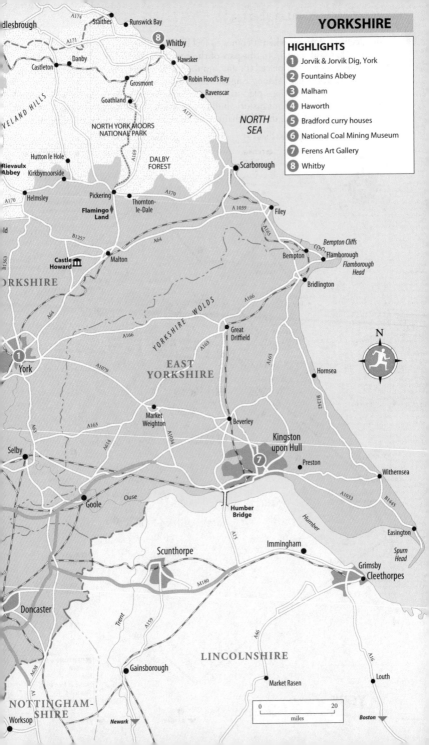

HIGHLIGHTS

1. Jorvik & Jorvik Dig, York
2. Fountains Abbey
3. Malham
4. Haworth
5. Bradford curry houses
6. National Coal Mining Museum
7. Ferens Art Gallery
8. Whitby

ddlesbrough

A174

Staithes

Runswick Bay

A171

8 Whitby

Danby

Hawsker

Castleton

Grosmont

Robin Hood's Bay

Goathland

Ravenscar

VELAND HILLS

NORTH YORK MOORS
NATIONAL PARK

A169

NORTH
SEA

DALBY
FOREST

Hutton le Hole

Scarborough

RIEVAULX
ABBEY

Kirkbymoorside

A170

Helmsley

Pickering

A170

ld

Thornton-
le-Dale

A1039

Filey

A64

B1257

Flamingo
Land

A165

Castle
Howard

Malton

Bempton Cliffs

CO₂

Bempton

Flamborough

ORKSHIRE

A64

Flamborough
Head

Bridlington

A166

YORKSHIRE WOLDS

A166

A163

Great
Driffield

A166

N

A1079

EAST
YORKSHIRE

A165

1 York

Hornsea

A59

B1242

A163

Market
Weighton

A1034

Beverley

Selby

A614

Kingston
upon Hull

7

Preston

Withernsea

Goole

Ouse

Humber
Bridge

A1033

B1445

A15

Easington

Humber

Spurn
Head

Scunthorpe

Immingham

Grimsby

M180

Cleethorpes

Doncaster

Trent

A159

A46

A638

Gainsborough

LINCOLNSHIRE

A16

Worksop

Market Rasen

Louth

NOTTINGHAM-
SHIRE

Newark

0   20
miles

Boston

city, except in summer when it comes to feel like a heritage site for the benefit of tourists. That said, no trip to this part of the country is complete without a visit to York, which is also well placed for any number of **day-trips**, the most essential being to **Castle Howard**, the gem among English stately homes.

The **minster** is the obvious place to start, and you won't want to miss a walk around the old city **walls**. Standout historic buildings include the Minster's Treasurer's House, Georgian Fairfax House, the Merchant Adventurers' Hall, and the stark remnants of

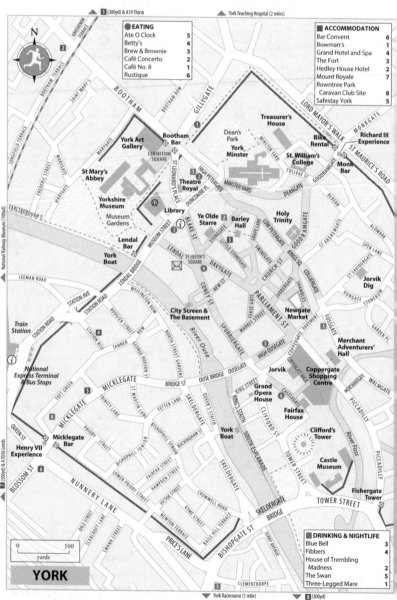

EATING

Ate O Clock	5
Betty's	4
Brew & Brownie	3
Café Concerto	2
Café No. 8	1
Rustique	6

ACCOMMODATION

Bar Convent	6
Bowman's	1
Grand Hotel and Spa	4
The Fort	3
Hedley House Hotel	2
Mount Royale	7
Rowntree Park Caravan Club Site	8
Safestay York	5

DRINKING & NIGHTLIFE

Blue Bell	3
Fibbers	4
House of Trembling Madness	2
The Swan	5
Three-Legged Mare	1

YORK

12

York's **Castle**; the medieval city is at its most evocative around the streets known as Stonegate and the **Shambles**. The city's favourite family attraction, **Jorvik Viking Centre**, isn't far from here. The two major museum collections are the incomparable **Castle Museum** and the **National Railway Museum** (where the appeal goes way beyond railway memorabilia), while the **Museum Gardens** (ⓦyorkmuseumgardens.org.uk) between Exhibition Square and the river are home to the evocative ruins and gardens of **St Mary's Abbey** and the child-friendly **Yorkshire Museum**. Recent redevelopment work has extended the gardens to the back of **York Art Gallery**.

Brief history

An early **Roman** fortress of 71 AD in time became a city – Eboracum, capital of the empire's northern European territories and the base for Hadrian's northern campaigns. Later, the city became the fulcrum of **Christianity** in northern England: on Easter Day in 627, Bishop Paulinus, on a mission to establish the Roman Church, baptized King Edwin of Northumbria in a small timber chapel here. Six years later the church became the first minster and Paulinus the first archbishop of York.

In 867 the city fell to the **Danes**, who renamed it **Jorvik**, and later made it the capital of eastern England (Danelaw). Later Viking raids culminated in the decisive **Battle of Stamford Bridge** (1066) six miles east of the city, where English King Harold defeated Norse King Harald – a pyrrhic victory in the event, for Harold's weakened army was defeated by the Normans just a few days later at the Battle of Hastings, with well-known consequences for all concerned.

The **Normans** devastated much of York's hinterland in their infamous "Harrying of the North". Stone walls were thrown up during the thirteenth century, when the city became a favoured Plantagenet retreat and commercial capital of the north, its importance reflected in the new title of Duke of York, bestowed ever since on the monarch's second son. Although Henry VIII's Dissolution of the Monasteries took its toll on a city crammed with religious houses, York remained wedded to the Catholic cause, and the most famous of the Gunpowder Plot conspirators, **Guy Fawkes**, was born here. During the **Civil War** Charles I established his court in the city, which was strongly pro-Royalist, inviting a Parliamentarian siege. Royalist troops, however, were routed by Cromwell and Sir Thomas Fairfax at the **Battle of Marston Moor** in 1644, another seminal battle in England's history, which took place six miles west of York.

The city's eighteenth-century history was marked by its emergence as a social centre for Yorkshire's landed elite. While the Industrial Revolution largely passed it by, the arrival of the **railways** brought renewed prosperity, thanks to the enterprise of pioneering "Railway King" George Hudson, lord mayor during the 1830s and 1840s. The railway is gradually losing its role as a major employer, as is the traditional confectionery industry, and incomes are now generated by new service and bioscience industries – not forgetting, of course, the 6.9 million annual tourist visits.

York Minster

Minster Yard, YO1 7HH • Mon–Sat 9am–5pm, Sun 12.45–5pm • £10 (including undercroft), combined ticket with tower £15; admission ticket valid for 12 months • **Tours** Mon–Sat 10am–3pm, on the hour; access to "Revealing York Minster" and the Orb included; 1hr • Included in entry price • ☎01904 557200, ⓦyorkminster.org

York Minster ranks as one of the country's most important sights. Seat of the Archbishop of York, it is Britain's largest Gothic building and home to countless treasures, not least of which is an estimated half of all the medieval stained glass in England. The first significant foundations were laid around 1080 by the first Norman archbishop, Thomas of Bayeux, and it was from the germ of this Norman church that the present structure emerged.

The stained-glass windows

Nothing else in the minster can match the magnificence of the **stained glass** in the nave and transepts. The **West Window** (1338) contains distinctive heart-shaped upper tracery (the "Heart of Yorkshire"), while in the nave's north aisle, the second bay window (1155) contains slivers of the oldest stained glass in the country. The greatest of the church's 128 windows, however, is the majestic **East Window** (1405), at 78ft by 31ft the world's largest area of medieval stained glass in a single window.

The undercroft, treasury and crypt

The Minster's foundations, or **undercroft**, have been turned into a museum, featuring a new interactive gallery "Revealing York Minster". Among precious relics in the adjoining **treasury** is the eleventh-century *Horn of Ulf*, presented to the minster by a relative of the tide-turning King Canute. There's also access from the undercroft to the **crypt**, the spot that transmits the most powerful sense of antiquity, as it contains sections of the original eleventh-century church, including pillars with fine Romanesque capitals. Access to the undercroft, treasury and crypt is from the south transept, which is also the entrance to the **central tower**, which you can climb for exhilarating rooftop views over the city.

Around the walls

The city's superb **walls** date mainly from the fourteenth century, though fragments of Norman work survive, particularly in the gates (known as "bars"), and the northern sections still follow the line of the Roman ramparts. **Monk Bar** is as good a point of access as any, tallest of the city's four main gates and host to the small **Richard III Experience** (daily: April–Oct 10am–5pm; Nov–March 10am–4pm; £5; ☎01904 615505, ⓦrichardiiiexperience.com). For just a taste of the walls' best section – with great views of the minster and acres of idyllic-looking gardens – take the ten-minute stroll west from Monk Bar to Exhibition Square and **Bootham Bar**, the only gate on the site of a Roman gateway and marking the traditional northern entrance to the city. A stroll round the walls' entire two-and-a-half-mile length will also take you past the southwestern **Micklegate Bar**, long considered the most important of the gates since it marked the start of the road to London; it's now home to the Henry VII Experience (April–Oct 10am–4pm; Nov–March 10am–3pm; £5; ☎01904 615505).

York Art Gallery

Exhibition Square, YO1 7EW · Daily 10am–5pm · £7.50; free access to garden · ☎ 01904 687687, ⓦ yorkartgallery.org.uk

York Art Gallery houses an impressive collection of early Italian, British and northern European paintings, some of which are on display in the Burton Gallery. The gallery's extensive recent renovations made space for its notable British studio ceramics collection, which now has a permanent home in two of the first-floor state-of-the-art exhibition spaces. The ground floor hosts a year-round series of special exhibitions and events and a café (daily 10am–4.45pm); a second entrance leads directly from the Museum Gardens.

Yorkshire Museum

Museum Gardens, YO1 7FR · Daily 10am–5pm · £7.50 · ☎ 01904 687687, ⓦ yorkshiremuseum.org.uk

In the beautiful Museum Gardens, next to the romantic ruins of St Mary's Abbey, sits the majestic Grade I listed building of the **Yorkshire Museum**. Five exciting, hands-on galleries comprise the "History of York", a multiscreen, audiovisual display; "Extinct", which covers dinosaurs and more recently extinct creatures; "Meet the People of the Empire" (Roman York); the "Power and the Glory" (Medieval York); and "Enquiry", about how archeology and science can uncover the past.

Stonegate

One of York's most picturesque streets, **Stonegate** is as ancient as the city itself. Originally the Via Praetoria of Roman York, it's now paved with thick flags of York stone, which were once carried along here to build the minster (hence the name). The Tudor buildings that line it retain their considerable charm – **Ye Olde Starre Inne** at no. 40, one of York's original inns, is on every tourist itinerary (you can't miss the sign straddling the street).

Barley Hall

Off Stonegate, YO1 8AR • Daily: April–Oct 10am–5pm, Nov–March 10–4pm • £6, under-17s £3; joint ticket with Jorvik £14/£9.25 • ☎ 01904 615505, ⓦ barleyhall.co.uk

Step through an alley known as Coffee Yard (opposite *Ye Olde Starre Inne*) to find **Barley Hall**, a fine restoration of a late medieval townhouse with a lively museum where you can learn about fifteenth-century life by, among other things, playing period games and trying on costumes. Barley Hall is one of the Jorvik group of attractions.

The Shambles

York's most famous street, and one which appears regularly on its promotional brochures, **The Shambles** could be taken as the epitome of the medieval city. Almost impossibly narrow and lined with perilously leaning timber-framed houses, it was the home of York's butchers (the word "shambles" derives from the Old English for slaughterhouse) – old meat hooks still adorn the odd house.

Jorvik

Coppergate Shopping Centre, YO1 9WT • Daily: April–Oct 10am–5pm; Nov–March 10am–4pm • £10.25, under-17s £7.25; joint ticket with Jorvik Dig £14.45/£11; joint ticket with Barley Hall £14/£9.25 • ☎ 01904 615505, ⓦ jorvikvikingcentre.co.uk

Excavations of Coppergate in 1976 uncovered York's original Viking settlement, now largely buried beneath a shopping centre. But at adjacent **Jorvik**, visitors are propelled in "time capsules" on a ride through a reconstructed version of the tenth-century Viking city, immersing you in the sights, sounds and even the smells of the times. You also get to see how artefacts unearthed from the original site were used, and watch live-action domestic scenes on actual Viking-age streets, with constipated villagers, axe-fighting and other singular attractions.

Jorvik Dig

St Saviourgate, YO1 8NN • Daily 10am–5pm • £6.50, under-17s £6; joint ticket with Jorvik £14.45/£11; pre-booking advised • ☎ 01904 615505, ⓦ digyork.com

Where Jorvik shows what was unearthed at Coppergate, the associated attraction that is **Jorvik Dig** illustrates the science involved. Housed five minutes' walk away from the museum, in the medieval church of St Saviour, on St Saviourgate, a simulated dig allows children to take part in a range of excavations in the company of archeologists, using authentic tools and methods. There's an on-site exhibition **Looking Back at Hungate** (included in admission, or £2.50), which has some interesting artefacts from a five-year archeological excavation of local Roman, Viking and medieval remains.

Clifford's Tower

Tower St, YO1 9SA • Daily 10am–6pm • £5; EH • ☎ 01904 646940, ⓦ www.english-heritage.org.uk/visit/places/cliffords-tower-york

There's precious little left of **York Castle**, one of two established by William the Conqueror. Only the perilously leaning **Clifford's Tower** remains, a stark stone keep built between 1245 and 1262 to replace the original wooden keep burned down in 1190 AD when it was being used as a refuge by hundreds of Jews trying to escape anti-Semitic riots in the city.

12

Of a rare quatrefoil (clove-leaf) design, perhaps an experiment to improve sight lines between the top of the keep and the base of the walls, it once had two floors with a supporting central column. Controversial plans are afoot to build a large visitor centre into the mound that the tower sits on.

Castle Museum

Eye of York, YO1 9WD • Daily 9.30am–5pm • £10 • ☎ 01904 687687, ⓦ yorkcastlemuseum.org.uk

Housed in what was once a couple of prisons, displays in the wonderfully inventive **Castle Museum** begin with a series of period rooms from the seventeenth century to the 1980s. There's a large room devoted to Victorian attitudes to birth, marriage and death, followed by a wonderful reconstruction of the sights and sounds of York's Kirkgate during the final years of the nineteenth century, often staffed by people dressed-in authentic costume. There are displays, too, of period kitchens, plus a superb re-creation of the fashion, music and news stories of the 1960s. Finally, the cells in the basement of the prison building contain an affecting series of real-life stories, told by video recordings of actors projected onto cell walls, gleaned from the prison's records.

The National Railway Museum

Leeman Rd, a 10min walk from the train station, YO26 4XJ • Daily 10am–6pm • Free • ☎ 0844 815 3139, ⓦ nrm.org.uk • A "road train" shuttles visitors here from Duncombe Place next to York Minster (April–Oct daily every 30min; £2)

The **National Railway Museum** is a must if you have even the slightest interest in railways, history, engineering or Victoriana. The Great Hall alone features some fifty restored locomotives dating from 1829 onwards, among them *Mallard*, at 126mph the fastest steam engine ever built. After a lengthy on-site £4.2 million restoration, the **Flying Scotsman** is back on the tracks as a working exhibit (ⓦ flyingscotsman.org.uk); it returns to the museum in winter. Engines aside, you can't help but love the sheer Britishness of the Station Hall with its Royal carriages, railway memorabilia and real-life stories.

Castle Howard

15 miles northeast of York off the A64, YO60 7DA • Late March to late Oct & late Nov to mid-Dec house daily 11am–4pm; grounds 10am–5pm; grounds also open Jan to late March & Nov to mid-Dec • £18.95; grounds only £11.95 • ☎ 01653 648333, ⓦ castlehoward.co.uk • Tours run from York (see opposite), or catch a Yorkshire Coastliner bus from York, Malton or Pickering, or summer-only Moorsbus (see p.626) from Helmsley

Immersed in the deep countryside of the Howardian Hills, **Castle Howard** is the seat of one of England's leading aristocratic families and among the country's grandest stately homes. The grounds especially are worth visiting, and you could easily spend the best part of a day here. The colossal main house was designed by **Sir John Vanbrugh** in 1699 and was almost forty years in the making – remarkable enough, even were it not for the fact that Vanbrugh was, at the start of the commission at least, best known as a playwright and had no formal architectural training. Shrewdly, Vanbrugh recognized his limitations and called upon **Nicholas Hawksmoor**, who had a major part in the house's structural design – the pair later worked successfully together on Blenheim Palace.

Vanbrugh also turned his attention to the estate's thousand-acre **grounds**, where he could indulge his playful inclinations – the formal gardens, clipped parkland, towers, obelisks and blunt sandstone follies stretch in all directions, sloping gently to two artificial lakes. The whole is a charming artifice of grand, manicured views – an example of what three centuries, skilled gardeners and pots of money can produce.

ARRIVAL AND DEPARTURE YORK AND AROUND

By train Trains arrive at York Station, just outside the city walls, a 10min walk from the historic core.

Destinations Durham (every 10min; 50min); Harrogate (hourly; 30min); Hull (hourly; 1hr); Leeds (every 10–15min; 25min); London (every 30min; 2hr); Manchester (every 15min; 1hr 25min); Newcastle (every 15min; 1hr); Scarborough (hourly; 50min); Sheffield (every 15–30min; 45min).

By bus National Express buses and most other regional bus services drop off and pick up on Rougier St, 200yd north of the train station, or on Station Road itself. Companies include East Yorkshire (for Hull, Beverley and Bridlington; ⓦ eyms.co.uk) and Yorkshire Coastliner/City Zap (for Leeds, Castle Howard, Pickering, Scarborough and Whitby; ⓦ yorkbus.co.uk).

Destinations Beverley (Mon–Sat hourly, Sun 7 daily; 1hr 10min); Hull (Mon–Sat hourly, Sun 7 daily; 1hr 35min); Leeds (Mon–Sat every 15min, Sun every 30min; 50min–1hr 20min); Pickering (hourly; 1hr 8min); Scarborough (hourly; 1hr 40min); Whitby (4–6 daily; 2hr 13min).

GETTING AROUND

On foot The historic core is easily explored on foot; from the minster in the north, for example, to Castle Museum in the south is about a 10min walk. Indeed, one of the best ways to explore the city is to circumnavigate it atop the splendid city walls.

By taxi There are taxi ranks at Duncombe Place and the train station, or call Streamline Taxis on ☎ 01904 656565.

INFORMATION AND TOURS

Tourist office 1 Museum St, on the corner with Blake Street (Mon–Sat 9am–5pm, July & Aug to 5.30pm, Sun 10am–4pm; ☎ 01904 550099, ⓦ visityork.org). There is also a smaller tourist office at the train station.

Listings information The monthly *What's On York* (ⓦ whatsonyork.com) provides detailed entertainment, events, festival and exhibition listings for the city. Online guide YORK:PM (ⓦ york-pm.co.uk) is another useful local resource.

Bus tours City tours by bus – pick up details at the tourist office – cost around £10. Stephensons of Easingwold (☎ 01347 838990, ⓦ stephensonsofeasingwold.co.uk) operates services to Castle Howard for £10 return, along with several routes to the Dales.

Walking tours The York Association of Voluntary Guides

(☎ 01904 550098, ⓦ avgyork.co.uk) offers a free historic guided tour of the city (daily: April–Oct 10.15am & 1.15pm, Nov–March 10.15am & 2.15pm, plus June–August 6.15pm; 2hr), from outside the York Art Gallery – just turn up. The tourist office has details of other tours, which start at around £6.

River cruises The best river operator is YorkBoat (☎ 01904 628324, ⓦ yorkboat.co.uk; Feb–Nov; cruises from £10, families £27; 45min–1hr), who run cruises with commentary from King's Staith and Lendal Bridge.

York Pass The York Pass (☎ 01904 550099, ⓦ yorkpass .com) gives free entry to over thirty attractions, not only in the city (eg Barley Hall, Clifford's Tower, Jorvik Dig and Fairfax House) but also elsewhere (Castle Howard and the North York Moors Railway); it costs £38/£50/£65 for one/two/three days respectively, with reductions if you buy it online.

12

ACCOMMODATION

The main **B&B** concentration is in the side streets off Bootham (immediately west of Exhibition Square), with nothing much more than a 10min walk from the centre.

★**Bar Convent** 17 Blossom St, YO24 1AQ ☎ 01904 464902, ⓦ bar-convent.org.uk; map p.590. Unique opportunity to stay in a working convent. The grand Georgian building houses a museum and café as well as nine single rooms, twins, doubles and a family room (en-suite a little more expensive), self-catering kitchen and guest lounge. Single £44, double £74

Bowman's 33 Grosvenor Terrace, YO30 7AG ☎ 01904 622204, ⓦ bowmansguesthouse.co.uk; map p.590. Six spotless rooms in a friendly renovated Victorian terrace B&B off Bootham, within easy reach of the city centre. They provide a permit for free on-street parking. £80

★**Grand Hotel and Spa** Station Rise, YO1 6GD ☎ 01904 891949, ⓦ thegrandyork.co.uk; map p.590. Splendid five-star hotel and spa a 2min walk from the train station, housed in what was the 1906 headquarters of the North Eastern Railway. Bags of character, with wonderful views of the walls and the minster, luxurious rooms, a fine-dining restaurant and relaxing bar. £180

The Fort Little Stonegate, YO1 8AX ☎ 01904 639573,

ⓦ thefortyork.co.uk; map p.590. An interesting idea – a "boutique hostel" in the city centre, offering rooms and dorms decorated on themes (log cabin, deep-sea creatures) at a knock-down price. Dorms £22, doubles £85

Hedley House Hotel 3 Bootham Terrace, YO30 7DH ☎ 01904 637404, ⓦ hedleyhouse.com; map p.590. Friendly, comfortable small hotel that is at its best in summer, when the outdoor area with jacuzzi comes into its own. There is a spa and hot-room yoga available on site. Free car parking on first-come, first served basis. £115

Mount Royale The Mount, YO24 1GU ☎ 01904 628856, ⓦ www.mountroyale.co.uk; map p.590. Lots of antiques, super garden suites (and cheaper rooms), and a heated outdoor pool in summer. Plus a hot tub, sauna and steam room, and a well-regarded restaurant. £125

Rowntree Park Caravan Club Site Terry Ave, YO23 1JQ ☎ 01904 658997, ⓦ caravanclub.co.uk; map p.590. A wonderful site, the best-located in the city, a 10min walk from the centre, with a back gate that opens onto a street of delis, gastropubs and shops. Open to non-members.

Mainly for caravans and motorhomes, but with a small tent enclosure – those with tents must arrive on foot. Advance booking essential, especially at weekends. Motorhome plus two adults £26

Safestay York Micklegate House, 88–90 Micklegate, YO1 6JX ☎ 01904 627720, ⓦ safestayyork.co.uk; map p.590. In a handsome 1752 building in the centre of the city, with many impressive features. Beds are in dorms (sleeping 4 to 14) and private rooms, all en suite; prices drop during the week and for multi-night stays. Dorms £21, doubles £80

EATING

Ate O Clock 13a High Ousegate, YO1 8RZ ☎ 01904 644080, ⓦ ateoclockyork.co.uk; map p.590. The name is dreadful, but the – largely Mediterranean – food is excellent, and there's attentive service and a relaxed atmosphere. Lunch dishes such as risotto come in around £8.50, while main dishes are around £14–20. Music most Fri evenings. Tues–Thurs noon–3.30pm & 5.50–9.30pm, Fri noon–3.30pm & 5.50–10pm, Sat & Sun noon–10pm.

Betty's 6–8 St Helen's Square, YO1 8QP ☎ 01904 659142, ⓦ bettys.co.uk; map p.590. Famous across Yorkshire, *Betty's* specializes in cakes and pastries like granny used to make (or not) – try a hot buttered pikelet (£2.95) or a Yorkshire fat rascal (£4.10) – plus hot dishes and puddings from around £6. No reservations. In the basement there's a mirror with the signatures of the hundreds of Allied airmen who used *Betty's* as an unofficial mess during World War II. Daily 9am–9pm.

Brew & Brownie 5 Museum St, YO1 7DT ☎ 01904 647420, ⓦ brewandbrownie.co.uk; map p.590. This buzzing café is usually busy with students and thirty-somethings enjoying strong coffee and stupendous home-made cakes. Brunch and light lunches not to be missed either – a stack of American pancakes for £6.25, or the Eeh

Bah Gum sharing plate for £15. Yorkshire-sourced produce where possible. Mon–Sat 9am–5pm, Sun 9.30–4pm.

Café Concerto 21 High Petergate, YO1 7EN ☎ 01904 610478, ⓦ cafeconcerto.biz; map p.590. Relaxed, belle epoque-style bistro facing the minster, with sheet-music-papered walls and waiting staff in robust aprons. Food is modern European; there are papers to browse. Daily 9am–9pm.

★**Café No. 8** 8 Gillygate, YO31 7EQ ☎ 01904 653074, ⓦ cafeno8.co.uk; map p.590. Limited menu using excellent locally sourced produce (Masham sausages, Yorkshire beef and lamb, Ryedale ice cream, beer from Masham) in unpretentious surroundings. Mains cost around £10 during the day, and £14–17 in the evening, or have two courses midweek for £12.50. Its heated garden is a popular spot, and they now have a café in the Art Gallery (see p.596). Mon–Fri noon–10pm, Sat & Sun 9am–10pm.

Rustique 28 Castlegate, YO1 9RP ☎ 01904 612744, ⓦ rustiqueyork.co.uk; map p.590. French-style bistro serving excellent-value Gallic food and wine. There are a couple of set menus (two courses £14.95, three £17.95); a la carte features all the classics, including steak frites, moules marinière and confit de canard. Mon–Sat noon–10pm, Sun noon–9pm.

DRINKING AND NIGHTLIFE

Blue Bell Fossgate, YO1 9TF ☎ 01904 654904; map p.590. Built in 1798, the *Blue Bell* is a tiny, friendly local with two rooms, oak-panelling and good real ales. When landlord John took over in 2015, he upheld the traditional pub values: no mobile phones or swearing. Mon–Thurs 11am–11pm, Fri & Sat 11am–12.30am, Sun noon–10.30pm.

Fibbers 3 Toft Green, YO1 6JT ☎ 01904 651250, ⓦ fibbers .co.uk; map p.590. York's primary live-music venue, *Fibbers* regularly puts on local and nationally known bands in a lively atmosphere. Hours changeable; check online.

★**House of Trembling Madness** 48 Stonegate, YO1 8AS ☎ 01904 640009, ⓦ tremblingmadness.co.uk; map p.590. A wonderfully atmospheric attic pub (it's above their shop) with exposed beams and a medieval hall feel. Bar snacks are exceptional and so is the range of craft ales,

lagers and ciders. Arrive early to avoid the queue. Mon–Sat 10am–midnight, Sun 11am–midnight.

★**The Swan** 16 Bishopgate, YO23 1JH ☎ 01904 634968; map p.590. Proper local, a Tetley Heritage Inn that offers convivial surroundings, well-kept real ale and a really friendly atmosphere a few minutes from the city centre. Mon–Wed 4–11pm, Thurs 4–11.30pm, Fri 3pm–midnight, Sat noon–midnight, Sun noon–10.30pm.

Three-Legged Mare 15 High Petergate, YO1 7EN ☎ 01904 638246, ⓦ threeleggedmareyork.co.uk; map p.590. A converted shop provides an airy outlet for York Brewery's own quality beer. No kids, no jukebox, no video games. It's named after a three-legged gallows – it's there on the pub sign, with a replica in the beer garden. Mon–Sat 11am–midnight, Sun 11am–11pm.

ENTERTAINMENT

York has its fair share of theatres and cinemas, and **classical music concerts** and recitals are often held in the city's churches and York Minster. Major annual events include the **Viking Festival** (ⓦ jorvik-viking-festival.co.uk) every Feb and the **Early Music Festival** (ⓦ ncem.co.uk), perhaps the best of its kind in the country, held in July. The city is also famous for its **Mystery Plays** (ⓦ ympst.co.uk), traditionally held every four years – the next are planned for 2018.

The Basement 13–17 Coney St, below City Screen cinema, YO1 9QL ☎01904 612940, ⓦthebasementyork .co.uk; map p.590. An intimate venue with a variety of nights – from music to comedy to arts events. The first Wed of every month is "Café Scientifique" – a free evening of discussion surrounding current issues in science. Live music events are scattered through the week, along with cabaret, burlesque and club nights. Most nights 8–11pm.
City Screen 13–17 Coney St, YO1 9QL ☎0871 902 5726, ⓦpicturehouses.co.uk; map p.590. The city's independent cinema is the art-house choice, with three screens, a riverside café-bar, and licensed restaurant.
Grand Opera House Cumberland St at Clifford St, YO1 9SW ☎0844 871 3024, ⓦatgtickets.com; map p.590. Musicals, ballet, pop gigs and family entertainment in all its guises.
The National Centre for Early Music St Margaret's Church, Walmgate, YO1 9TL ☎01904 632220, ⓦncem .co.uk; map p.590. Not just early music, but also folk, world and jazz.

Harrogate

HARROGATE – the very picture of genteel Yorkshire respectability – owes its landscaped appearance and early prosperity to the discovery of Tewit Well in 1571. This was the first of more than eighty ferrous and sulphurous **hot springs** that, by the nineteenth century, were to turn the town into one of the country's leading spas. With this in mind, tours of the town should begin with the **Royal Baths**, facing Crescent Road, first opened in 1897 and now restored to their late Victorian finery. You can experience the beautiful Moorish-style interior during a session at the **Turkish Baths and Health Spa** (from £15.50, booking recommended especially at weekends; ☎01423 556746, ⓦturkishbathsharrogate.co.uk).

12

The Royal Pump Room and around

Pump Room Crown Place, HG1 2RY • Mon–Sat 10.30am–4pm, Sun 2–4pm • £4 • ☎01423 556188 • **Mercer Art Gallery** • Tues–Sat 10am–5pm, Sun 2–5pm • Free • ☎01423 556188

Just along from the Royal Baths stands the **Royal Pump Room**, built in 1842 over the sulphur well that feeds the baths. Today it houses a small local museum with eclectic exhibits from Victorian bikes to an Egyptian collection. The town's earliest surviving spa building, the old Promenade Room of 1806, is just 100yd from the Pump Room on Swan Road – now housing the **Mercer Art Gallery** and its changing fine art exhibitions. The nearby 17-acre **Valley Gardens** are a delightful place to stretch your legs (entrance just over the zebra crossing).

RHS Harlow Carr

Crag Lane, 1.5 miles west of the centre, HG3 1QB • Daily March–Oct 9.30am–6pm, Nov–Feb 9.30am–4pm • £11 • ☎01423 565418, ⓦrhs.org.uk • Bus #X6A (every 20min) or follow the path from Valley Gardens through Pinewoods

The botanical gardens at **Harlow Carr** are the northern showpiece of the Royal Horticultural Society. The woodland and wildflower meadow are a wonderful place to wander, but there are also formal rose gardens, an alpine house and kitchen gardens to explore. Year-round events are hosted, including **Live Music Sundays** in July and August (1–4pm), and **Betty's** (daily 9am–5.30pm) have a branch of their popular tearooms overlooking the grounds.

ARRIVAL AND INFORMATION   HARROGATE

By train The station is on Station Parade, on the eastern edge of the town centre. There are regular services from/to Leeds (every 30min; 37min).
By bus The bus station is next to the train station on Station Parade and is served by #36 buses from/to Leeds (every 15min–1hr; 40min) and Ripon (every 15min–1hr; 32min).
Tourist office In the Royal Baths on Crescent Road, HG1 2WJ (April–Oct Mon–Sat 9am–5.30pm, Sun 10am–1pm; Nov–March Mon–Sat 9.30am–5pm; ☎01423 537300, ⓦvisitharrogate.co.uk).

ACCOMMODATION

Acorn Lodge Studley Rd, HG1 5JU ☎01423 525630, ⓦacornlodgeharrogate.co.uk. A guesthouse with big-hotel aspirations (luxury fittings, individual decor, jacuzzi, in-room massages) but B&B friendliness (and tariffs). Well placed for the town centre (a 5min walk). **£94**

The Grafton 1–3 Franklin Mount, HG1 5EJ ☎01423 508491, ⓦgraftonhotel.co.uk. Just a 10min walk from town, and close to the International Conference Centre, the hotel's thirteen stylish rooms all have drape curtains and tasteful decor. The helpful owners will lend you a permit for parking. Price drops £20 Sun–Thurs. **£135**

Studley Swan Rd, HG1 2SE ☎01423 560425, ⓦstudley hotel.co.uk. Mid-sized independent hotel with attached Thai restaurant. The attractive rooms vary in size and cost, and service is good, though the restaurant can get very busy. You can find surprisingly good rates online. **£119**

EATING AND DRINKING

Betty's 1 Parliament St, HG1 2QU ☎01423 814070, ⓦbettys.co.uk. *Betty's* has a uniquely old-fashioned air, with a wrought-iron canopy, large bowed windows, a light airy room and waiting staff in starched linen. While they are known for cakes (from £2.95), speciality teas and coffees, they also offer delicious breakfasts and mains – try the Swiss breakfast rösti (£11.85). No reservations (except for afternoon tea Fri–Sun), so you may have to wait. They have another outlet at RHS Gardens Harlow Carr (see p.597). Daily 9am–9pm.

10 Devonshire Place HG1 4AA ☎01423 202356. A bit of a walk east of town, but worth it. An old coaching inn with bags of character, it can get crowded (especially for the brill pub quiz on Sunday night), but always has a fantastic atmosphere.

There's a bottle shop tucked away as you walk in. Mon–Thurs 3pm–midnight, Fri–Sun noon–midnight.

Le D2 Bower Rd, HG1 1BB ☎01423 502700, ⓦled2 .co.uk. Quality French food and excellent service in unpretentious surroundings, and at affordable prices – one course for £9.95 at lunch and three courses for £19.95 in the evening (includes a drink). Tues–Thurs noon–2pm & 6pm–late, Fri & Sat noon–2pm & 5.30pm–late.

The Tannin Level 5 Raglan St, HG1 1LE ☎01423 560595, ⓦtanninlevel.co.uk. Popular brasserie, smartly understated, with a Michelin-trained cook and super locally sourced food. Express two courses £13.95, a la carte mains around £15–25. Tues–Fri noon–2pm & 5.30–9pm, Sat noon–2pm & 5.30–9.30pm.

Ripon and around

The attractive market town of **RIPON**, eleven miles north of Harrogate, is centred upon its small **cathedral** (Mon–Sat 8.30am–6pm, Sun noon–5pm; donation requested; ☎01765 602072, ⓦriponcathedral.info), which can trace its ancestry back to its foundation by St Wilfrid in 672; the original crypt below the central tower can still be reached down a stone passage. The town's other focus is its **Market Place**, linked by narrow Kirkgate to the cathedral (market day is Thurs, with a farmers' market on the third Sun of the month). Meanwhile, three restored buildings – prison, courthouse and workhouse (which was expanded in 2017) – show a different side of the local heritage, under the banner of the **Yorkshire Law and Order Museums** (all daily: Workhouse 11am–4pm; Prison & Police and Courthouse 1–4pm; combined ticket £12; ☎01765 690799, ⓦriponmuseums.co.uk). Just four miles away lies **Fountains Abbey**, the one Yorkshire monastic ruin you must see.

Fountains Abbey and Studley Royal Water Garden

4 miles southwest of Ripon off the B6265, HG4 3DY • Feb & March daily 10am–5pm; April–Oct daily 10am–6pm; Oct–Jan Sat–Thurs 10am–5pm; free guided tours of abbey April–Oct daily • £15; NT & EH • ☎01765 608888, ⓦfountainsabbey.org.uk • #139 bus from Ripon (Mon, Thurs & Sat 4 daily; 15min)

It's tantalizing to imagine how the English landscape might have appeared had Henry VIII not dissolved the monasteries, and the substantial ruins at **Fountains Abbey** gives a good idea of what might have been. The abbey was founded in 1133 by thirteen dissident Benedictine monks and formally adopted by the Cistercian order two years later. Within a hundred years, Fountains had become the wealthiest Cistercian foundation in England, supporting a magnificent **abbey church**. The almost-intact **Perpendicular Tower**, 180ft high, looms over the whole ensemble, while equally grandiose in scale is the undercroft of the **Lay Brothers' Dormitory** off the cloister, a stunningly vaulted space over 300ft long that was used to store the monastery's annual harvest of fleeces. Its sheer size gives some idea of the abbey's entrepreneurial scope; the estate produced some thirteen tons of wool annually, most of it sold to Venetian and Florentine merchants who toured the monasteries.

Studley Royal Water Garden

A riverside walk, marked from the visitor centre car park, takes you through Fountains Abbey to a series of ponds and ornamental gardens, harbingers of **Studley Royal Water Garden** (same times as the abbey), which can also be entered via the village of Studley Roger, where there's a separate car park. This lush medley of lawns, lake, woodland and **Deer Park** was laid out in 1720 to form a setting for the abbey, and there are some scintillating views from the gardens, though it's the cascades and water gardens that command most attention.

ARRIVAL AND INFORMATION
RIPON AND AROUND

By bus Ripon is served by #36 buses from/to Harrogate (every 10–25min; 35min) and Leeds (every 20–35min; 1hr 30min); the bus station is just off Market Place.
Tourist information Ripon Town Hall, Market Place

(April–Oct Mon–Sat 10am–5pm, Sun 10am–1pm; Nov–March Thurs & Sat 10am–4pm; closes daily 1–1.30pm year-round; ☏01765 604625, ☻visitharrogate.co.uk).

ACCOMMODATION AND EATING

The Old Deanery Minster Rd, HG4 1QS ☏01765 600003, ☻theolddeanery.co.uk. Luxurious contemporary hotel opposite the cathedral with eleven charming rooms. The

innovative menu (main courses from £15.95) features dishes such as belly of pork or fried stone bass. Mon–Sat noon–2pm & 7–9pm, Sun 12.30–2.30pm. **£125**

12

The Yorkshire Dales

The **Yorkshire Dales** – "dales" from the Norse word *dalr* (valley) – form a varied upland area of limestone hills and pastoral valleys at the heart of the Pennines. Protected as a National Park (or, in the case of Nidderdale, as an Area of Outstanding Natural Beauty), there are more than twenty main dales covering 680 square miles, crammed with opportunities for outdoor activities. Most approaches are from the south, via the superbly engineered **Settle to Carlisle Railway**, or along the main A65 road from towns such as **Skipton**, **Settle** and **Ingleton**. Southern dales like **Wharfedale** are the most visited, while neighbouring **Malhamdale** is also immensely popular due to the fascinating scenery squeezed into its narrow confines around **Malham** village. **Ribblesdale** is more sombre, its villages popular with hikers intent on tackling the famous **Three Peaks** – the mountains of Pen-y-ghent, Ingleborough and Whernside. To the northwest lies the more remote **Dentdale**, one of the least known but most beautiful of the valleys, and further north still **Wensleydale** and **Swaledale**, the latter of which rivals Dentdale as the most rewarding overall target. Both flow east, with Swaledale's lower stretches encompassing the appealing historic town of **Richmond**.

GETTING AROUND AND INFORMATION
THE YORKSHIRE DALES

On foot The Pennine Way cuts right through the heart of the Dales, and the region is crossed by the Coast-to-Coast Walk, but the principal local route is the 84-mile Dales Way (☻dalesway.org.uk). Shorter guided walks (5–13 miles; April–Oct Sun & bank hols; free) are organized by the National Park Authority and Dalesbus Ramblers (☻dalesbusramblers.org.uk).
By bike The Dales has a network of over 500 miles of bridleways, byways and other routes for mountain bikers

(download routes on ☻yorkshiredales.org.uk). The main touring cycle route is the circular 130-mile Yorkshire Dales Cycle Way (☻www.cyclethedales.org.uk), which starts and finishes in Skipton.
By public transport Bus timetables (☻dalesbus.org) are available at tourist offices across the region, as are *Dales Explorer* timetable booklets, or consult ☻wymetro.com.
National Park Centres There are useful National Park Centres (☻yorkshiredales.org.uk) at Grassington,

Aysgarth Falls, Malham, Reeth and Hawes (April–Oct daily 10am–5pm; Nov–March Sat & Sun 10am–4pm; Hawes is also open weekdays Feb & March, but all sites close in Jan).

Skipton

Skipton (Anglo-Saxon for "sheep town") sits on the Dales' southern edge, at the intersection of the two routes that cradle the National Park and Area of Outstanding Natural Beauty – the A65 to the western and the A59/61 to the eastern dales. A pleasant market town with a long history, it is defined by its **castle** and **church**, by its long, wide and sloping **High Street**, and by a **water system** that includes the Leeds and Liverpool Canal, its spur the Springs Canal and the Eller Beck.

ARRIVAL AND INFORMATION   SKIPTON

By train Trains run from/to Leeds (every 30min–2hr; 54min) and Bradford (every 30min; 49min), and there's a daily service to London (every 30min; 3hr 10min with one change). The train is by far the best way of getting to Dentdale/Ribblesdale: Dent (every 2hr; 46min); Settle (every 30min–1hr 25min; 30min–1hr).
By bus Buses run from Skipton up Wharfedale towards

Buckden (every 2hr; 1hr), to Malham (every 2–3hr; 35min) and Settle (every 2hr; around 40–50min). Links to the rest of the Dales are more difficult, and usually involve using trains and/or changing buses.
Tourist office Town Hall, High Street (Mon–Sat 9.30am–4pm; ☎ 01756 792809).
Useful website ⓦ welcometoskipton.com.

ACCOMMODATION AND EATING

Herriot's Hotel Broughton Rd, BD23 1RT ☎ 01756 792781, ⓦ herriotsforleisure.co.uk. A short walk along the canal towpath from the centre of Skipton, in a Victorian listed building, the boutique-style hotel and its restaurant, *Rhubarb*, both offer cheerful decor and lots of original features. Rooms vary in size and price, and there are frequent packages available. __£125__
The Woolly Sheep Inn 38 Sheep St, BD23 1HY ☎ 01756

700966, ⓦ woollysheepinn.co.uk. Pleasant town-centre Timothy Taylor tavern which offers a good range of pub food (from £11) along with sandwiches, steaks and pasta dishes. The nine rooms are comfortable and well furnished, though some are small. Convivial, but pub noise can reach some of the rooms at weekends. Mon–Wed 10am–11pm, Thurs 10am–midnight, Fri & Sat 10am–1am, Sun noon–11pm; kitchen Mon–Sat 11.30am–9pm, Sun noon–8pm. __£80__

Ilkley

The small town of **ILKLEY** holds a special place in the iconography of Yorkshire out of all proportion to its size, largely because it's the setting of the county's unofficial anthem, *On Ilkley Moor baht 'at*. Vibrant and stylish, Ilkley has plenty to see, including an interesting church, a **toy museum** (ⓦ ilkleytoymuseum.co.uk) and enough top-end shops, bars and restaurants to keep visiting urbanites happy.

All Saints Church

Church St, LS29 9DS • Office hours Mon & Thurs 9.30am–2.30pm, Tues 9am–noon • ☎ 01943 816035

Ilkley's parish church, **All Saints**, was established in AD 627 by King Edwin of Northumbria and Bishop Paulinus of York, whose carved heads you can see in the entrance porch. Inside, highlights include three impressive eighth-century Saxon crosses, a family pew dating from 1633 and a Norman font made of Ilkley Moor stone with a seventeenth-century font cover complete with pulley and counterweight for raising and lowering it. Tucked in just behind the church, **Ilkley Manor House** (ⓦ manorhouse.ilkley .org) stands on the site of a Roman fort (you can see a section of the original Roman wall at the rear of the building).

Ilkley Moor

A 20min walk from the town centre

Dominating Ilkley's southern skyline is its famous **moor**, somehow smaller yet more forbidding than you might expect. Far from being a remote wilderness, it is very much part of the town's fabric: a place where people can walk, climb or ponder the immensities of time reflected in its ancient rock formations and prehistoric markings. Look out for the Swastika Stone, the Twelve Apostles, the famous Cow and Calf, and a host of cup-and-ring marked rocks. For a bite to eat or a dip in its eighteenth-century open-air plunge pool, you can also visit the **White Wells Spa Cottage Café** on Wells Road (pool open when the flag is flying, usually Sat & Sun 10am–5pm, plus school hols Mon–Fri 2–5pm; ☎01943 608035).

ARRIVAL AND INFORMATION   ILKLEY

By train Ilkley station, in Station Plaza in the town centre, is the terminus of a line which links the town to Leeds and Bradford (every 30min; 31min).

By bus The bus station is next to the train station.

Destinations Bolton Abbey (Mon, Wed & Sat 3 daily; 17min); Harrogate (every 2hr; 55min), Leeds (every 30min; 1hr); Malham (6 daily; 1hr 10min); Skipton (hourly; 30min).

Tourist office Station Road, LS29 8HB (April–Sept Mon–Sat 9.30am–4.30pm; Oct–March Mon–Sat 10am–4pm, Tues from 10.30am; ☎01943 602319, ⓦvisitilkley.com).

EATING AND DRINKING

Bar t'at Ale and Wine Bar 7 Cunliffe Rd, LS29 9DZ ☎01943 608888, ⓦmarkettowntaverns.co.uk. With an irresistible name, a huge selection of wines and beers and a good atmosphere, this place also offers a decent range of light lunches, sandwiches, and main meals (£9.50–12.50), though service can be slow. Daily noon–11pm; kitchen Mon–Thurs noon–8pm, Fri & Sat noon–9pm, Sun noon–6pm.

The Box Tree 35–37 Church St, LS29 9DR ☎01943 608484, ⓦtheboxtree.co.uk. One of Yorkshire's handful of Michelin-starred restaurants, offering inventive modern French cuisine in mellow surroundings. There are fixed-price menus at £37.50 (lunch), £47.50 (dinner), £65 (called a la carte, though it's not) and £80 (gourmand). Wed & Thurs 7–9.30pm, Fri & Sat noon–2pm & 7–9.30pm,

Sun noon–3pm.

The Flying Duck 16 Church St, LS29 9DS ☎01943 609587, ⓦwharfedalebrewery.com. Occupying the town's oldest pub building, this real ale pub sports old stone walls, beamed ceilings and stone-flagged and wooden-floored rooms. Also has its own brewery in a barn at the rear. Mon–Thurs & Sun noon–11pm, Fri & Sat noon–12.30am.

Piccolino 31–33 Brook St, LS29 8AE ☎01943 605827, ⓦindividualrestaurants.com. Large Italian restaurant in the centre of Ilkley, one of a chain across the country. The star attraction is a roof terrace (with a retractable roof and heaters – this is England after all), which has terrific views across the town. Good food (mains around £16–23) and helpful staff. Mon–Sat 10am–11pm, Sun 10am–10.30pm.

12

Wharfedale

The River Wharfe runs south from just below Wensleydale, eventually joining the Ouse south of York. The best of **Wharfedale** starts just east of Skipton at **Bolton Abbey**, and then continues north in a broad, pastoral sweep scattered with villages as picture-perfect as any in northern England. The popular walking centre of **Grassington** is the main village.

Bolton Abbey

BOLTON ABBEY, five miles east of Skipton, is the name of a whole village rather than an abbey, a confusion compounded by the fact that the place's main monastic ruin is known as **Bolton Priory** (daily 8am–dusk; free; ☎01756 710238, ⓦboltonpriory.org.uk). The priory is the starting point for several popular riverside **walks**, including a section of the **Dales Way** footpath that follows the river's west bank to take in Bolton Woods and the **Strid** (from "stride"), an extraordinary piece of white water two miles north of the abbey, where softer rock has allowed the river to funnel into a cleft just a few feet wide. Beyond the Strid, the path emerges at **Barden Bridge**, four miles from the priory, where **Barden Tower** shelters The Priests House, a wedding venue which is sometimes open for Sunday lunch (ⓦthepriestshouse.com).

ARRIVAL AND INFORMATION   BOLTON ABBEY

By train For a fun excursion, ride the Embsay & Bolton Abbey Steam Railway (late July and Aug five daily; rest of year schedule varies, check website; day rover £11;

☎01756 710614, ⓦembsayboltonabbeyrailway.org.uk). Trains run between Embsay, 1.5 miles east of Skipton, to Bolton Abbey station, around a mile from the abbey ruins – a journey of 15min.

Tourist information The main source of information is the estate office (Bolton Abbey, ☎ 01756 718009, ⓦ boltonabbey.com).

ACCOMMODATION AND EATING

Cavendish Pavilion One mile north of Bolton Abbey along the river, D23 6AN ☎ 01756 710245, ⓦ cavendish pavilion.co.uk. Restaurant and café on the Bolton Abbey estate serving roasts, casseroles and the like at good prices. Daily: March–Oct 10am–5pm; Nov–Feb 10am–4pm.

Grassington

GRASSINGTON is Wharfedale's main village, nine miles northwest of Bolton Abbey. The cobbled Market Square is home to several inns, a few gift shops and, in a converted lead-miner's cottage, a small **Folk Museum** (April–Oct daily 2–4.30pm; free; ☎ 01756 753287, ⓦ grassingtonfolkmuseum.org.uk), which is filled with domestic equipment and artefacts relating to local crafts and farming.

ARRIVAL AND INFORMATION   GRASSINGTON

By bus #72/72R buses to Grassington run roughly hourly (X43 on Sun and bank hols) from Skipton (33min) and then, six times a day, on up the B6160 to Kettlewell, Starbotton and Buckden in upper Wharfedale.

National Park Centre Hebden Road, across from the bus stop (April–Oct daily 10am–5pm; for winter hours, check with the centre; ☎ 01756 751690, ⓦ yorkshiredales .org.uk).

ACCOMMODATION AND EATING

★ **Angel Inn** Hetton, 4 miles southwest of Grassington, BD23 6LT ☎ 01756 730263, ⓦ angelhetton.co.uk. The Dales' gastropub par excellence has nine immaculate rooms and suites that are either in the charming cottage next door to the inn, or just over the road in a converted barn. Main courses from £17.95. Kitchen Mon–Thurs noon–2.15pm & 6–8.30pm, Fri & Sat noon–2.15pm & 6–9.30pm, Sun noon–2.30pm & 6–8.30pm. **£150**

Grassington Lodge 8 Wood Lane, BD23 5LU ☎ 01756 752518, ⓦ grassingtonlodge.co.uk. A splash of contemporary style – coordinated fabrics, hardwood floors, Dales photographs – together with a pleasant front terrace enhances this comfortable village guesthouse. **£90**

Upper Wharfedale

KETTLEWELL (a Norse/Old English compound name for "bubbling spring") is the main centre for **Upper Wharfedale**, and it has plenty of local B&B accommodation plus a youth hostel. It was also one of the major locations for *Calendar Girls*, the 2003 based-on-a-true-story film of doughty Yorkshire ladies who bared all for a charity calendar.

ARRIVAL AND DEPARTURE   UPPER WHARFEDALE

By bus There's a Sun and bank hol bus service (#800) from Leeds to Hawes, connecting the top end of Wharfedale with Wensleydale, via Ilkley, Grassington and Kettlewell, among other stops. It takes 3hr 10min for the whole trip, and 1hr 5min from Kettlewell to Hawes.

ACCOMMODATION AND EATING

Blue Bell Inn Kettlewell, BD23 5DX ☎ 01756 760230, ⓦ bluebellkettlewell.co.uk. Pretty seventeenth-century coaching inn that's very much a traditional pub and serves good, no-nonsense pub grub (lasagne, steak and ale pie and the like; main courses £10–15). Daily specials are a cut above the usual fare. Daily noon–11pm; kitchen Mon–Fri noon–2.30pm & 5–8pm, Sat noon–9pm, Sun noon–8pm. **£85**

Racehorses Hotel Kettlewell, BD23 5QZ ☎ 01756 760233, ⓦ racehorseshotel.co.uk. Comfortable, refurbished hotel in what was once the *Blue Bell Inn*'s stables. The food is a cut above your standard bar food (home-made paté, for example, or rare-breed belly pork); main courses start at £11. Daily noon–2pm & 6–9pm. **£90**

Malhamdale

A few miles west of Wharfedale lies **Malhamdale**, one of the National Park's most heavily visited regions, thanks to its three outstanding natural features of **Malham Cove**,

Malham Tarn and **Gordale Scar**. All three attractions are within easy hiking distance of **Malham village**.

Malham

MALHAM village is home to barely a couple of hundred people who inhabit the huddled stone houses on either side of a bubbling river. Appearing in spectacular fashion a mile to the north, the white-walled limestone amphitheatre of **Malham Cove** rises 300ft above its surroundings. After a breath-sapping haul to the top, you are rewarded with fine views and the famous limestone pavement, an expanse of clints (slabs) and grykes (clefts) created by water seeping through weaker lines in the limestone rock. A simple walk (or summer shuttle-bus ride) over the moors abruptly brings **Malham Tarn** into sight, its waterfowl protected by a nature reserve on the west bank. Meanwhile, at **Gordale Scar** (also easily approached direct from Malham village), the cliffs are if anything more spectacular than at Malham Cove. The classic circuit takes in cove, tarn and scar in a clockwise **walk from Malham** (8 miles; 3hr 30min).

ARRIVAL AND INFORMATION   MALHAMDALE

By bus Malham village is served year-round by bus from Skipton (3 daily; 35min) and the seasonal Malham Tarn shuttle (Easter–Oct Sun & bank hols 3 daily; 25min) which runs between Settle and the National Park Centre.

National Park Centre At the southern edge of the village (April–Oct daily 10am–5pm; for winter hours, check with centre; ☎01729 833200, ⓦyorkshiredales.org.uk).

Website A good online source of tourist information is ⓦmalhamdale.com.

ACCOMMODATION AND EATING

★**Buck Inn** Cove Road, BD23 4DA ☎01729 830317, ⓦthebuckmalham.co.uk. Pleasant pub that's popular with walkers. Given the good, locally sourced food – especially sausages, pies and steaks (main courses £10–22) – eleven comfortable rooms, and a relaxed attitude to muddy boots, this is the ideal base for a walking holiday. Daily noon–9pm. **£95**

Miresfield Farm Across the river from the Buck Inn and Lister Arms, BD23 4DA ☎01729 830414, ⓦmiresfield-farm.com. The first house in the village, by the river, with lovely rural views. The country-pine-bedecked rooms vary in size, and there's a small campsite with toilet and shower. Breakfast available. **£64**

YHA Malham Centre of village, next to the Lister Arms pub, BD23 4DB ☎0845 371 9529, ⓦyha.org.uk/hostel/malham. A purpose-built and newly renovated hostel that's a good bet for families and serious walkers. Open all year with midweek prices often slashed by half. Check-in 5–10.30pm. Dorms **£30**, doubles **£69**

Ribblesdale

The river Ribble runs south along the western edges of the Yorkshire Dales, starting in the bleak uplands near the Ribblehead Viaduct, flowing between two of Yorkshire's highest mountains, **Ingleborough** and **Pen-y-ghent**, and through the village of **Horton in Ribblesdale** and on to **Settle**, the upper dale's principal town.

Settle

West of Malhamdale, Ribblesdale is entered from **SETTLE**, starting point of the **Settle to Carlisle Railway** (see box, p.604). The small town has a typical seventeenth-century market square (market day Tues), still sporting its split-level arcaded shambles, and the **Museum of North Craven Life** (April–Oct Tues 10.30am–4.30pm & Thurs–Sun 12.30–4.30pm; £2.50; ☎01524 251388), which contains odds and ends from the history of the town and of the construction of the railway. The museum is housed in the eccentric Folly, dating from the 1670s and earning its name from the strange combination of styles, and the curiously upside-down look created by the fact that there are far more windows on the ground floor than on the first and second – it seems surprising that it hasn't fallen down.

12

THE SETTLE TO CARLISLE RAILWAY

The 72-mile **Settle to Carlisle** line – hailed by some as "England's most scenic railway" – is a feat of Victorian railway engineering that has few equals in Britain. In particular, between Horton and Ribblehead, the line climbs 200ft in five miles, before crossing the famous 24-arched **Ribblehead viaduct** and disappearing into the 2629yd Blea Moor Tunnel. Meanwhile, the station at **Dent Head** is the highest, bleakest mainline station in England. The journey through the Yorkshire Dales and Eden Valley from Settle to Carlisle takes 1hr 40min, so it's easy to do the full **return trip** in one day (£20.90). If you're short of time, ride the most dramatic section between Settle and Garsdale (30min). There are connections to Settle from Skipton (20min) and Leeds (1hr); full **timetable** details are available from ⓦ settle-carlisle.co.uk.

ARRIVAL AND INFORMATION SETTLE

By train The train station, less than a 5min walk from Market Place, down Station Road, is served by the famous Settle to Carlisle railway (see box above).

By bus #580 buses connect Settle with Skipton (Mon–Sat; every 2hr; 40min); #11 buses go north to Horton-in-Ribblesdale (Mon–Sat every 2hr; 21min); while #581 (every 2hr; 31min) runs to the western Dales. The Malham

Tarn shuttle (Dalesbus #881; Easter–Oct Sun & bank hol; 3 daily) makes a stop at Settle en route to Malham (25min) and Ingleton (25min).

Tourist information In the town hall, just off Market Place, BD24 9EJ (Mon, Tues, Thurs–Sat 9.30am–4pm, Wed & Sun 9.30am–1pm; closed Sun in winter; ☎ 01729 825192). They can provide hiking maps and pamphlets.

ACCOMMODATION AND EATING

The Lion Duke St, BD24 9DU ☎ 01729 822203, ⓦ thelion settle.co.uk. The ground-floor inn offers a fantastic range of locally sourced fish, meats, cheese, pies and sausages (mains £10.50–21), and guest rooms are comfortable and contemporary. Mon–Thurs & Sun 8am–9pm, Fri & Sat 8am–10.30pm. __£95__

Ye Olde Naked Man Café Market Place, BD24 9EJ ☎ 01729 823230. For non-alcoholic drinks and traditional hot food, cakes and scones, this unfussy tearoom is your best bet. They also have a takeaway sandwich bar and shop selling local produce. Daily 9am–5pm.

Horton in Ribblesdale

The valley's only village of any size is **HORTON IN RIBBLESDALE**, a noted walking centre which is the usual starting point for the famous **Three Peaks Walk**: namely a 25-mile, 12-hour circuit of Pen-y-ghent (2273ft), Whernside (2416ft) – Yorkshire's highest point – and Ingleborough (2373ft).

ARRIVAL AND INFORMATION HORTON IN RIBBLESDALE

By bus The #11 service from Settle runs every 2hr (20min).

Tourist and hiking information The *Pen-y-ghent Café* (see below; ☎ 01729 860333) doubles as a tourist office and unofficial headquarters for the Three Peaks walk. They operate a clocking-in/clocking-out system; walkers who complete

the route within a 12hr period become eligible to join the Three Peaks of Yorkshire Club. Note that they do not provide automatic back-up should walkers fail to return, though can make arrangements for this if notified at least a day in advance. Opening hours are complicated, so phone to check.

EATING

Pen-y-ghent Café BD24 0HE ☎ 01729 860333. A local institution for more than forty years, not only supplying much-needed hot drinks, snacks and meals, but also information and advice to walkers. Phone in advance to

confirm hours. Roughly Feb half term to mid-Oct Mon & Wed–Sun 9am–5.30pm (Sat & Sun 8am in summer); Jan & Feb hours vary.

The western Dales

The **western Dales** is a term of convenience for a couple of tiny dales running north from **Ingleton**, and for **Dentdale**, one of the loveliest valleys in the National Park. Ingleton has the most accommodation, but **Dent** is by far the best target for a quiet night's retreat, with a cobbled centre barely altered in centuries.

Ingleton and around

The straggling slate-grey village of **INGLETON** sits upon a ridge at the confluence of two streams, the Twiss and the Doe, whose beautifully wooded valleys are easily the area's best features. The 4.5-mile **Waterfalls Trail** (daily Nov–March 9am–2.30pm, April–Aug 9am–7pm, Sept & Oct 9am–4pm; £6; ☎01524 241930, ⓦingletonwaterfallstrail.co.uk) is a lovely circular walk (2hr 30min) taking in both valleys, and providing viewing points over its waterfalls.

Just 1.5 miles out of Ingleton on the Ribblehead/Hawes road (B6255) is the entrance to the **White Scar Cave** (tours 10am–5pm: Feb–Oct daily, Nov–Jan weather permitting Sat & Sun; 1hr 20min; £9.95; ☎01524 241244, ⓦwhitescarcave.co.uk). It's worth every penny for the tour of dank underground chambers, contorted cave formations and glistening stalactites.

ARRIVAL AND INFORMATION   INGLETON AND AROUND

By bus Buses stop at the tourist office: the #80 runs from/to Lancaster (every 30min; 1hr 10min) and the #581 and #881 from/to Settle (every 30min; 25min).

Tourist office Community Centre car park, Main St (daily:

Easter–Sept 10am–4.30pm; Nov–March 11am–3pm; ☎01524 241049).

Website ⓦvisitingleton.co.uk.

ACCOMMODATION AND EATING

The Inglesport Café Main St, LA6 3EB ☎01524 241146. On the first floor of a hiking supplies store, this café dishes up hearty breakfasts, soups, and potatoes with everything. Mon–Fri 9am–5pm, Sat & Sun 9am–5.30pm.

Riverside Lodge 24 Main St, LA6 3HJ ☎01524 241359, ⓦriversideingleton.co.uk. Clean and tidy, with eight bedrooms decorated individually (if a little fussily) and

named after flowers. There's a small sauna and play room, and an optional evening meal at £15. **£70**

YHA Ingleton Sammy Lane, LA6 3EG ☎015242 41444, ⓦyha.org.uk/hostel/ingleton. This YHA hostel is in an attractively restored Victorian stone house, set in its own gardens, close to the village centre. Reception 7–10am & 5–11pm. Dorms **£24**, doubles **£52**

Dentdale

In the seventeenth and eighteenth centuries, **Dentdale** supported a flourishing hand-knitting industry, later ruined by mechanization. These days, the hill-farming community supplements its income through tourism and craft ventures, and in **DENT** village itself the main road soon gives way to grassy cobbles.

ARRIVAL AND INFORMATION   DENTDALE

By train While the famous Settle to Carlisle railway (see box opposite) might seem a good alternative to the bus, be warned that Dent station is over 4 miles from the village itself.

By bus Most of Dent's bus connections are with towns outside Yorkshire – Sedbergh (April–Oct 5 daily; 15min),

Kirkby Stephen and Kendal (Sat 1 daily; 50min) – though there is a service to Settle.

Tourist information Dentdale Heritage Centre, Dent, LA10 5QJ (daily 11am–4pm; ☎01539 625800, ⓦmuseums intheyorkshiredales.co.uk).

Website ⓦdentdale.com.

ACCOMMODATION AND EATING

★George & Dragon Dent, LA10 5QL ☎01539 625256, ⓦthegeorgeanddragondent.co.uk. Opposite the fountain in the centre of the village, the *George & Dragon* is bigger and more expensive than the nearby *Sun*, with ten comfortable rooms (though some are small and all are a little tired), good service and a

convivial bar. There's an extensive menu of traditional pub food with a twist (try, for example, the terrine of Cumberland sausage and black pudding) – mains cost between £8.50 and £16.50. Daily 11am–11pm; kitchen daily noon–2pm & 6–8.30pm. **£80**

Wensleydale

The best known of the Dales, if only for its cheese, **Wensleydale** is also the largest. With numerous towns and villages, the biggest and busiest being **Hawes**, it has plenty

12

of appeal to non-walkers, too; many of its rural attractions will be familiar to devotees of the **James Herriott** books and TV series.

Hawes

HAWES is Wensleydale's chief town, main hiking centre, and home to its tourism, cheese and rope-making industries. It also claims to be Yorkshire's highest market town; it received its market charter in 1699, and the weekly Tuesday market is still going strong. In the same building as the National Park Centre (see opposite), the recently revamped **Dales Countryside Museum** (April–Oct daily 10am–5pm; closed Jan; for winter hours phone ahead; £4.80; ☎01969 666210, ⓦwww.dalescountrysidemuseum.org.uk) focuses on local trades and handicrafts.

You'll find another attraction a 15min-walk south of the town centre; the **Wensleydale Creamery** on Gayle Lane has a café and restaurant, and of course a cheese shop – you only pay to enter the adjacent museum and cheese-making viewing gallery (daily 10am–4pm; £2.95; ☎01969 667664, ⓦwensleydale.co.uk). The first cheese in Wensleydale was made by medieval Cistercian monks from ewes' milk; after the Dissolution local farmers made a version from cows' milk which, by the 1840s, was being marketed as "Wensleydale" cheese.

Askrigg

The mantle of "Herriot country" lies heavy on **ASKRIGG**, six miles east of Hawes, as the TV series *All Creatures Great and Small* was filmed in and around the village. Nip into the *King's Arms* on Main Street, where you can see stills from the programme.

Aysgarth

The ribbon-village of **AYSGARTH**, straggling along and off the A684, sucks in Wensleydale's largest number of visitors due to its proximity to the **Aysgarth Falls**, half a mile below. A marked nature trail runs through the surrounding woodlands and there's a big car park and excellent **National Park Centre** on the north bank of the River Ure (see opposite).

Bolton Castle

Castle Bolton village, DL8 4ET • Feb–March daily 10am–4pm; April–Oct daily 10am–5pm (restricted winter opening, call for details) • £8.50, gardens only £4 • ☎ 01969 623981, ⓦ boltoncastle.co.uk

The foursquare battlements of **Bolton Castle** are visible from miles away. Completed in 1399, its Great Chamber, a few adjacent rooms and the castle gardens have been restored, and there's also a café that's a welcome spot if you've hiked here – a superb circular **walk** (6 miles; 4hr) heads northeast from Aysgarth via Castle Bolton village, starting at Aysgarth Falls and climbing up through Thoresby.

ARRIVAL AND GETTING AROUND   WENSLEYDALE

By bus The #156 route runs along Wensleydale from Leyburn to Hawes (every 2hr; 50 min), calling at Aysgarth and Bolton Castle. Less frequently, the #59 runs once a day along a similar route (1 daily; 47min). The Little White Bus runs from Hawes to Garsdale (2–4 daily; 23min). A post-bus service runs between Hawes and Northallerton (Mon–Fri 3 daily; 1hr 45min). There's also a summer Sun and bank holiday service (#800) connecting Hawes to Leeds (3hr).

HERE FOR THE BEER

If you're a beer fan, the handsome Wensleydale market town of **Masham** (pronounced Mass'm) is an essential point of pilgrimage. At **Theakston brewery** (tours daily 11am–3pm; £7.75, reservations advised; ☎01765 680000, ⓦtheakstons.co.uk), sited here since 1827, you can learn the arcane intricacies of the brewer's art and become familiar with the legendary Old Peculier ale. The **Black Sheep Brewery**, set up in the early 1990s by one of the Theakston family brewing team, also offers tours (four daily, evening tours Thurs & Fri, but call for availability; £9.50; ☎01765 680101, ⓦblacksheepbrewery.com). Both are just a few minutes' signposted walk out of the centre.

INFORMATION

Tourist information There are National Park Centres at Hawes Dales Countryside Museum, Station Yard, DL8 3NT (daily 10am–5pm; closed Jan, for winter hours, check with centre; ☎01969 666210; ⑩yorkshiredales .org.uk) and at Aysgarth, by the river (April–Oct daily 10am–5pm; for winter hours check with centre; ☎01969 662910).

Useful website ⑩wensleydale.org.

ACCOMMODATION AND EATING

Herriot's Main St, Hawes, DL8 3QW ☎01969 667536, ⑩herriotsinhawes.co.uk. Small, friendly guesthouse in an eighteenth-century building off the market square. There are just six rooms – some of which have fell views. Good hearty breakfasts are cooked to order. **£80**

Herriot's Kitchen Main St, Hawes, DL8 3QW ☎01969 667536, ⑩herriotsinhawes.co.uk. Light lunches, Yorkshire cream teas and cakes, plus preserves made on the premises.

Mon, Tues & Fri–Sun 11am–3pm.

The Old Dairy Farm Widdale, 3 miles west of Hawes, DL8 3LX ☎01969 667070, ⑩olddairyfarm.co.uk. Once the home of the original Wensleydale dairy herd, this farm offers luxurious and contemporary accommodation, with fine dining available (main courses around £15). While nonresidents are welcome to dine, there are no fixed opening hours – it is essential to phone first. **£140**

Swaledale

Narrow and steep-sided in its upper reaches beyond the tiny village of Keld, **Swaledale** merges rocky and rugged in its central tract around Thwaite and Muker before more typically pastoral scenery cuts in at **REETH**, the dale's main village and market centre (market day is Fri). Its desirable cottages sit around a triangular green, where you'll find a couple of pubs, a hotel, a **National Park Centre** (see above) and the **Swaledale Museum** (May–Oct daily 10am–5pm; £3; ☎01748 884118, ⑩swaledalemuseum.org), containing an interesting hotchpotch of material on the geology, industry, domestic life and people of the valley. Downriver, the dale opens out into broad countryside and the splendid historic town of **Richmond**.

Richmond

RICHMOND is home to the Dales' single most tempting destination, a magnificent **castle**, whose extensive walls and colossal keep cling to a precipice above the River Swale. Indeed, the entire town is an absolute gem, centred on a huge cobbled market square backed by Georgian buildings, hidden alleys and gardens. Market day is Saturday, augmented by a farmers' market on the third Saturday of the month.

Richmond Castle

Riverside Rd, DL10 4QW • April–Sept daily 10am–6pm; Oct daily 10am–5pm; Nov–March Sat & Sun 10am–4pm • £5.70; EH • ☎01748 822493, ⑩www.english-heritage.org.uk/visit/places/richmond-castle

Most of medieval Richmond sprouted around its **castle**, which, dating from around 1071, is one of the oldest Norman stone fortresses in Britain. The star turn is, without doubt, the massive **keep** – which was built between 1150 and 1180 – with its stone staircases, spacious main rooms and fine battlements. From the top, the **views** down into the town, across the turbulent Swale and out across the gentle countryside, are out of this world. For more splendid views, with the river roaring below, take a stroll along Castle Walk, around the outside of the curtain walls.

Green Howards Museum

Trinity Church Square, DL10 4QN • Mon–Sat 10am–4.30pm (plus Sun July & Aug) • £4.50 • ☎01748 825561, ⑩greenhowards.org.uk

Fully revamped in 2014, this regimental collection of 35,000 objects (not all on display) has some fascinating items including a key to Hitler's office and the first poppy to be laid on The Cenotaph in London. By focusing on the real-life stories, the **Green Howards Museum** avoids being just for those with a specialist interest; ask staff about the painting of Henry Tandey that Hitler used for propaganda, or the first footballer to be awarded the Victoria Cross.

12

Richmondshire Museum

Ryder's Wynd, off the Victoria Rd roundabout at the top of King St, DL10 4JA • April–Oct Mon–Sat 10.30am–4.30pm • £3.50 • ☎ 01748 825611, ⓦ richmondshiremuseum.org.uk

For a fascinating chunk of Richmond history, visit the charming **Richmondshire Museum**, off the northern side of the market square. It's full of local treasures, covering subjects as varied as lead mining and toys through the ages, with reconstructed houses and shops re-creating village life, and even the set from the TV series *All Creatures Great and Small*.

Theatre Royal

Victoria Rd, DL10 4DW • Tours on the hour mid-Feb to mid-Nov Mon–Sat 10am–4pm; £5 • ☎ 01748 825252, ⓦ georgiantheatre royal.co.uk

Richmond's tiny Georgian **Theatre Royal** (1788) has the diminutive feel of a toy theatre made from a shoe box. One of England's oldest theatres, it features a sunken pit with boxes on three sides and a gallery above; it is open for both performances and tours.

Easby Abbey

1 mile southeast of town, DL10 7EU • April–Sept daily 10am–6pm; Oct daily 10am–5pm; Nov–March daily 10am–4pm • Free; EH • ⓦ www.english-heritage.org.uk/visit/places/easby-abbey

A signposted walk runs along the north bank of the River Swale out to the golden stone walls of **Easby Abbey**. The evocative ruins are extensive, and in places – notably the thirteenth-century refectory – still remarkably intact.

12

ARRIVAL AND INFORMATION   SWALEDALE

By train There are regular services into Wensleydale and lower Swaledale on the heritage Wensleydale Railway from Leeming to Redmire, and to Darlington, 10 miles to the northeast, on the main east-coast train line.

By bus The main transport hub is Richmond, where buses stop in the market square. Bus #159 runs between Masham, Leyburn and Richmond, while bus #30 runs up the valley along the B6270 as far as Keld, 8 miles north of Hawes and at the crossroads of the Pennine Way and the Coast-to-Coast path.

Destinations from Richmond Keld (Mon–Sat 4 daily; 1hr); Leyburn (hourly; 25 min); Masham (Mon–Sat hourly; 55min); Ripon (Mon–Sat hourly; 1hr 15min).

Tourist office Richmond Library, Queens Rd (Mon & Thu 10am–6pm, Tues & Fri 10am–5pm, Wed 10am–noon, S 10am–1pm; ☎ 01609 532980, ⓦ richmond.org).

National Park Centre Hudson House, Reeth (April–O daily 10am–5pm; Nov, Dec, Feb & March Sat & Sun 10am 4pm; ☎ 01748 884059, ⓦ hudsonhouse.org).

ACCOMMODATION AND EATING

Frenchgate Hotel 59–61 Frenchgate, Richmond, DL10 7AE ☎ 01748 822087, ⓦ thefrenchgate.co.uk. Georgian townhouse hotel with eight rooms and walled gardens. Its food (set menu £39) has an excellent reputation – spiced loin of Yorkshire rabbit, for example, or Reg's duck breast. Mon–Fri 7.30–9.30am, noon–2pm & 6–9.30pm, Sat & Sun 8–10am, noon–2pm & 6–9.30pm. **£118**

Frenchgate House 66 Frenchgate, Richmond, DL10 7AG ☎ 01748 823421, ⓦ 66frenchgate.co.uk. Eight immaculately presented rooms, plus breakfast with the best – panoramic – view in town. **£95**

King's Arms High Row, Reeth, DL11 6SY ☎ 01748 884259, ⓦ thekingsarms.com. Attractive eighteenth-century inn on the green, offering a range of meals and snacks using locally sourced food, and rooms – all of which are en suite. Daily 11am–11pm; kitchen daily noon–2.30pm & 6–9pm. **£70**

★**Millgate House** Millgate, Richmond, DL10 4JN

☎ 01748 823571, ⓦ millgatehouse.com. Shut the b green door of this Georgian house and enter a world books, antiques, embroidered sheets, handmade toiletrie scrumptious breakfasts and the finest (and least preciou hosts you could wish for. No credit cards. **£125**

Rustique Finkle St, Richmond, DL10 4QB ☎ 0174 821565, ⓦ rustiqueyork.co.uk. The clue to *Rustique* ambience lies in its name – it concentrates on rural Fren food and wine in a bistro setting. The atmosphere is bu and cheerful, and the food's lovely, and very reasonab priced (two courses £14.95, three for £17.95). Dai noon–9pm.

Whashton Springs Near Whashton, DL11 7JS, 3 mil north of Richmond on Ravensworth Rd ☎ 0174 822884, ⓦ whashtonsprings.co.uk. This working Dal farm offers a peaceful night in the country in rooms the main house or round the courtyard) filled wi family furniture. **£80**

Haworth

Of English literary shrines, probably only Stratford sees more visitors than the quarter of a million who swarm annually into the village of **HAWORTH**, eight miles north of Bradford, to tramp the cobbles once trodden by the Brontë sisters. In summer the village's steep Main Street is lost under huge crowds, herded by multilingual signs around the various stations on the **Brontë trail**. The most popular local walk runs to **Brontë Falls** and **Bridge**, reached via West Lane (a continuation of Main St) and a track from the village, signposted "Bronte Falls"; and to **Top Withens**, a mile beyond, a ruin fancifully (and erroneously) thought to be the model for the manor, Wuthering Heights (allow 3hr for the round trip). The moorland setting beautifully evokes the flavour of the book, and to enjoy it further you could walk on another two and a half miles to **Ponden Hall**, claimed by some to be Thrushcross Grange in *Wuthering Heights*.

Brontë Parsonage Museum

Church St, BD22 8DR • Daily: April–Oct 10am–5.30pm; Nov–March 10am–5pm • £8.50 • ☎ 01535 642323, ⓦ bronte.org.uk

Behind the parish church is the **Brontë Parsonage Museum**, a modest Georgian house bought by Patrick Brontë in 1820 and in which he planned to bring up his family. After the tragic early loss of his wife and two eldest daughters, the surviving four children – Anne, Emily, Charlotte and their dissipated brother, Branwell – spent most of their short lives in the place, which is furnished as it was in their day, filled with the sisters' pictures, books, manuscripts and personal treasures. Between 2016 and 2020, Brontë200 celebrates the bicentenary of the births of these four, and special events are taking place here and across the globe (see website for details). The **parish church** in front of the parsonage contains the family vault; Charlotte was married here in 1854.

12

ARRIVAL AND INFORMATION

HAWORTH

By train The nicest way of getting to Haworth is on the steam trains of the Keighley and Worth Valley Railway (Easter week, school hols, June, July & Aug daily; rest of the year Sat & Sun; day rover ticket £16; ☎ 01535 645214, ⓦ kwvr.co.uk); regular trains from Leeds or from Bradford's Forster Square station run to Keighley, from where the steam train takes 18min to Haworth.

By bus Bus #662 from Bradford Interchange runs to Keighley (every 10–30min; 50min); change there for the #663, #664 (not Sun) or #665 (every 20–30min; 16–24min).

Tourist office 2–4 West Lane (daily: April–Sept 10am–5pm; Oct–March Mon, Tues, Thurs–Sun 10am–4pm, Wed 10.30am–4pm; ☎ 01535 642329, ⓦ haworth-village .org.uk).

ACCOMMODATION

Apothecary 86 Main St, BD22 8DP ☎ 01535 643642, ⓦ theapothecaryguesthouse.co.uk. Traditional guesthouse opposite the church, in a seventeenth-century building with oak beams, millstone grit walls and quaint passages. The rear rooms, breakfast room and attached café have moorland views. **£60**

Wilsons of Haworth 15 West Lane, BD22 8DU ☎ 01535 643209, ⓦ wilsonsofhaworth.co.uk. Top-end B&B with all the bells and whistles you might expect in a quality boutique hotel; its five luxurious rooms (four doubles and a single), are in a converted row of weavers' cottages within sight of the Brontë Parsonage Museum. **£79**

YHA Haworth Longlands Hall, Lees Lane, BD22 8RT, a mile from Haworth ☎ 0845 371 9520, ⓦ yha.org.uk /hostel/haworth. YHA hostel – a little in need of a refurb – overlooking the village; Bradford buses stop on the main road nearby. Only open to groups Mon–Fri Nov to mid-Feb. Dorms **£13**, doubles **£39**

Bradford and around

BRADFORD has always been a working town, booming in tandem with the Industrial Revolution, when just a few decades saw it transform from a rural seat of woollen manufacture to a polluted metropolis. In its Victorian heyday it was the world's biggest producer of worsted cloth, its skyline etched black with mill chimneys, and its hills clogged with some of the foulest back-to-back houses of any northern city. A look at the Venetian-Gothic **Wool Exchange** building on Market Street, or a walk through **Little Germany**, northeast of the city centre (named for the German wool merchants who populated the area in the second half of the 1800s) provides ample evidence of the wealth of nineteenth-century Bradford.

Contemporary Bradford, perhaps the most multicultural centre in the UK outside London, is valiantly rinsing away its associations with urban decrepitude, and while it can hardly yet be compared with neighbouring Leeds as a visitor attraction, it has two must-see attractions in the **National Science and Media Museum** and the industrial heritage site of **Saltaire**. The major annual event is the **Bradford Festival** (ⓦbradfordfestival.org.uk), a three-day multicultural celebration of art, music, theatre and dance, held in late July.

National Science and Media Museum

Little Horton Ln, BD1 1NQ • Daily 10am–6pm • Free, screenings £9 • ⓣ 0844 856 3797, ⓦ scienceandmediamuseum.org.uk

The main interest in the centre of Bradford is provided by the superb **National Science and Media Museum**, which wraps itself around one of Britain's largest cinema screens showing daily **IMAX** and 3D film screenings. Exhibitions are devoted to every nuance of film and television, including topics like digital imaging, light and optics, and computer animation with fascinating detours into the mechanics of advertising and news-gathering.

Saltaire

4 miles northwest of Bradford towards Keighley, BD17 7EF • 1853 Gallery Mon–Fri 10am–5.30pm, Sat & Sun 10am–6pm • Free • ⓣ 01274 531163, ⓦ saltsmill.org.uk • Trains run from Bradford Forster Square, or take bus #678 from the Interchange

The city's extraordinary outlying attraction of **Saltaire** was a model industrial village built by the industrialist Sir Titus Salt. Still inhabited today, the village was constructed between 1851 and 1876, and centred on **Salt's Mill**, which, larger than London's St Paul's Cathedral, was the biggest factory in the world when it opened in 1853. The mill was surrounded by schools, hospitals, parks, almshouses and some 850 homes, yet for all Salt's philanthropic vigour the scheme was highly paternalistic: of the village's 22 streets, for example, all – bar Victoria and Albert streets – were named after members of his family, and although Salt's workers and their families benefited from far better living conditions than their contemporaries elsewhere, they certainly were expected to toe the management line. Salt's Mill remains the fulcrum of the village, the focus of which is the **1853 Gallery**, three floors given over to the world's largest retrospective collection of the works of Bradford-born **David Hockney**.

ARRIVAL AND DEPARTURE

BRADFORD AND AROUND

By train Bradford has two train stations: Bradford Forster Square, just north of the city centre, offers routes to suburbs, towns and cities to the north and west of the city, while Bradford Interchange, off Bridge St, south of the city centre, serves destinations broadly south and west of the city.

Destinations from Bradford Forster Square Ilkley (every 30min; 31min); Keighley (every 30min; 20min); Leeds (every 30min; 22min); Skipton (every 30min; 39min).

Destinations from Bradford Interchange Halifax (every 15min; 12min); Leeds (every 15min; 23min); Manchester (every 30min; 1hr); Todmorden (every 30min; 35min).

By bus Bradford Interchange is the departure point for regional buses to the rest of West Yorkshire; as well as National Express coaches for long-distance services (travel centre Mon, Wed, Thurs & Fri 8.30am–5.30pm, Tue 9am–5.30pm, Sat 9am–4.30pm; ⓣ 0113 245 7676).

Destinations Leeds (every 30min; 30–45min); Liverpool (every 30min–2hr; 3–4hr); London (every 25–90min; 5–6hr); Manchester (every 10min–2hr; 1–2hr).

GETTING AROUND AND INFORMATION

By bus Bradford's handy free citybus service (Mon–Fri 7am–7pm, every 10min) links the Interchange with Forster Square, Kirkgate, Centenary Square, the National Media Museum, the University and the West En.

HIP HEBDEN BRIDGE

Hebden Bridge's independent galleries, bookshops and boutiques give it more of an artsy vibe than might be expected from a small mill town set in a deep valley. Community spirit has ensured that the cooperative-run town hall got a £3.7 million development that repurposed the Grade II listed building into a hub for creative business (Ⓦ hebdenbridgetownhall.org.uk); the 1921 picture house is civic-owned (Ⓦ hebdenbridgepicturehouse.co.uk); and the 120-seat Little Theatre produces a range of independent plays (Ⓦ hblt.co.uk). The annual **Hebden Bridge Arts Festival** (Ⓦ hebdenbridgeartsfestival.co.uk) at the end of June sees open studios and gardens, live gigs at various venues and free street theatre.

Hebden Bridge is easily accessed by train from Manchester, Leeds or Bradford, or it's a beautiful drive over the moors from Haworth. Nearby **Heptonstall** is also worth a visit for its connections to poets Ted Hughes and Sylvia Plath – the latter is buried in the churchyard here.

(Ⓣ 0113 245 7676, Ⓦ wymetro.com).
Tourist office Britannia House, Broadway (April–Sept Mon–Sat 10am–5pm, Oct–March Mon 10.30am–4pm, Tues–Sat 10am–4pm; Ⓣ 01274 433678, Ⓦ visitbradford .com).

EATING AND DRINKING

With nearly a quarter of its population having roots in south Asia, Bradford is renowned for its hundreds of **Indian restaurants**, and in 2016 was crowned "Curry Capital of Britain" for the sixth year in a row. Meanwhile, a burgeoning craft beer scene has seen an explosion of independent brew pubs opening along Westgate and North Parade.

Akbar's 1276 Leeds Rd, BD3 8LF Ⓣ 01274 773311, Ⓦ akbars.co.uk. The original in a chain that now has branches across the north of England (and one in Birmingham). It's famed for the quality of its south Asian cuisine, offering a wide range of chicken, lamb and prawn curries, and is hugely popular, so at weekends you may end up waiting, even when you've booked. Most dishes well under £10. Mon–Fri 5pm–midnight, Sat 4pm–midnight, Sun 2–11.30pm.

Bradford Brewery 22 Rawson Rd, BD1 3SQ Ⓣ 01274 397054, Ⓦ bradfordbrewery.com. In a period building with quirky decor, this is one of the craft beer places blazing a trail in Bradford. Great selection of ales and craft lagers, cheap and tasty pub grub (chilli and nachos £5), nice people, and a beer garden. Mon–Thurs & Sun noon–11pm, Fri & Sat noon–1am.

Mumtaz 386–410 Great Horton Rd, BD7 3HS Ⓣ 01274 522533, Ⓦ mumtaz.co.uk. With its smart decor and delicious Kashmiri food – a range of *karahi* and biryani dishes, with meat, fish and vegetarian options – *Mumtaz* has won plaudits from everyone from Dawn French to Amir Khan. No alcohol. Around £30/person. Mon–Thurs & Sun 11am–midnight, Fri & Sat 11am–1am.

Prashad Vegetarian Cuisine 137 Whitehall Rd, Drighlington, BD11 1AT Ⓣ 0113 285 2037, Ⓦ prashad .co.uk. Located five miles southeast of Bradford, this family-run vegetarian restaurant specialises in masterfully crafted Gujarat and Punjab dishes. The seven-course tasting menu (£46/person) shows off the very best of local produce and tantalizing spices. Tues–Fri 5–11pm, Sat noon–11pm, Sun noon–10pm.

12

Leeds

Yorkshire's commercial capital, and one of the fastest-growing cities in the country, **LEEDS** has undergone a radical transformation in recent years. There's still a true northern grit to its character, but any trace of grime has been removed from the impressive Victorian buildings and the city – along with its well-connected suburbs – is revelling in its new persona as a booming financial, commercial and cultural centre. The renowned **shops**, **restaurants**, **bars** and **clubs** provide one focus of a visit to contemporary Leeds – it's certainly Yorkshire's top destination for a day or two of conspicuous consumption and indulgence. Museums include the impressive **Royal Armouries**, which hold the national arms and armour collection, while the **City Art Gallery** has one of the best collections of British twentieth-century art outside London.

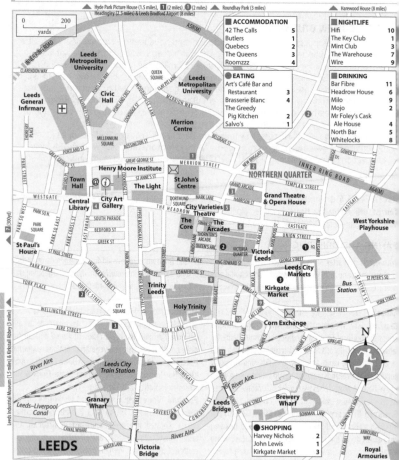

LEEDS

ACCOMMODATION	
42 The Calls	5
Butlers	1
Quebecs	2
The Queens	3
Roomzzz	4

EATING	
Art's Café Bar and Restaurant	3
Brasserie Blanc	4
The Greedy Pig Kitchen	2
Salvo's	1

NIGHTLIFE	
Hifi	10
The Key Club	1
Mint Club	3
The Warehouse	7
Wire	9

DRINKING	
Bar Fibre	11
Headrow House	6
Milo	9
Mojo	2
Mr Foley's Cask Ale House	4
North Bar	1
Whitelocks	5

SHOPPING	
Harvey Nichols	2
John Lewis	1
Kirkgate Market	3

City Art Gallery

The Headrow, LS1 3AA • Mon & Tues 10am–5pm, Wed noon–5pm, Thurs–Sat 10am–5pm, Sun 1–5pm • Free • ☎ 0113 247 8256, ⓦ leeds.gov.uk

Sharing a recently restored Victorian building with the Central Library, the **City Art Gallery** has an important collection of largely nineteenth- and twentieth-century paintings, prints, drawings and sculptures, some on permanent display, others rotated. There's an understandable bias towards pieces by **Henry Moore** and **Barbara Hepworth**, both former students at the Leeds School of Art; Moore's *Reclining Woman* lounges at the top of the steps at the gallery entrance – near where you'll also find the ornate Art Nouveau café with its grand marble columns.

Henry Moore Institute

The Headrow, LS1 3AH • Tues–Sun 11am–5.30pm (8pm Wed) • Free • ☎ 0113 246 7467, ⓦ henry-moore.org

The City Art Gallery connects with the adjacent **Henry Moore Institute**, which, despite its misleading name, is devoted not to Moore himself but to temporary exhibitions of sculpture from all periods and nationalities.

Royal Armouries

Armouries Drive, LS10 1LT • Daily 10am–5pm • Free • ☎ 0113 220 1999, ⓦ armouries.org.uk • Bus #28, #70 from city centre or free water taxi in summer

On the south side of the riverbank beckons the spectacular glass turret and gunmetal grey bulk of the **Royal Armouries**, purpose-built to house the **arms** and **armour** collection from the Tower of London. One of the best museums of its type in the world, its five enormous galleries hold beautifully displayed weapons for war, tournaments and hunting, and armour and other artefacts dating from Roman times onwards. Particularly spectacular are the reconstruction of a tiger hunt; the Indian elephant armour (the heaviest armour in the world) consisting of 8500 iron plates; fabulously decorated ceremonial suits of full plate armour; a Sikh "quoit turban" which carried a blood-curdling array of throwing quoits; garrotting wires and knives; Samurai, Mongol and Indian armour and weapons; and many ornate guns, from a reconstruction of an enormously long Essex punt gun to an exquisite Tiffany-decorated Smith and Wesson .44 Magnum.

ARRIVAL AND INFORMATION
LEEDS

By train National and local Metro trains use Leeds Station in the city centre.

Destinations Bradford (every 20min; 20min); Carlisle (every 2hr; 2hr 40min); Harrogate (every 30min; 34min); Hull (hourly; 1hr); Knaresborough (every 30min; 45min); Lancaster (4 daily; 2hr); Liverpool (hourly; 1hr 50min); London (every 30min; 2hr 20min); Manchester (every 15min; 1hr); Scarborough (every 30min–1hr; 1hr 20min); Settle (every 2hr; 1hr); Sheffield (every 10–15min; 40min–1hr 25min); Skipton (every 15–30min; 45min); Wakefield (Westgate & Kirkgate; every 10–15min; 12min); York (every 10–15min; 25min).

By bus The bus station is to the east of the centre behind Kirkgate Market, on St Peter's Street, though many buses stop outside the train station as well. Buses run from the bus station to all parts of the city, the suburbs, the rest of West Yorkshire and, via National Express, the rest of the country.

Destinations Bradford (10–30min; 25min); Halifax (every 30min; 1hr 16min); London (hourly; 4hr 25min); Manchester (every 30min–1hr; 1hr 5min–1hr 45min); Wakefield (every 10min; 31min); York (hourly; 1hr).

Public transport information The Metro Travel Centres at the bus and train stations have up-to-date service details for local transport; information is also available from Metroline (☎ 0113 245 7676, ⓦ wymetro.com).

Tourist office Visit Leeds, City Art Gallery shop ☎ 0113 378 6977, ⓦ visitleeds.co.uk (Mon–Sat 10am–5pm, Sun 11am–3pm).

12

ACCOMMODATION

There's a good mix of **accommodation** in Leeds. Cheaper lodgings lie out to the northwest in the student area of Headingley, though these are a train, bus or taxi ride away.

★ **42 The Calls** 42 The Calls, LS2 7EW ☎ 0113 244 0099, ⓦ 42thecalls.co.uk; map p.612. Converted riverside grain mill, where rooms come with great beds and sharp bathrooms. Being next to the Centenary footbridge, it can sometimes suffer from noisy passers-by. **£89**

Butlers Cardigan Rd, Headingley, LS6 3AG, 1.5 miles northwest of the centre ☎ 0113 274 4755, ⓦ butlers hotel.co.uk; map p.612. This hotel offers cosy and traditionally furnished rooms on a suburban street, breakfast is an extra £4. **£69**

Quebecs 9 Quebec St, LS1 2HA ☎ 0113 244 8989, ⓦ quebecshotel.co.uk; map p.612. The ultimate city-boutique lodgings, boasting glorious Victorian oak panelling and stained glass, offset by chic rooms. Online deals can cut costs considerably. Limited parking. **£170**

The Queens City Square, LS1 4DY ☎ 0113 242 1323, ⓦ qhotels.co.uk; map p.612. This luxurious 4-star option sports an imposing Art Deco facade and is located bang in the centre of town, right next to the train station. Standard rooms are a little small, but smart. Valet parking £15.95/24hr. **£100**

Roomzzz 12 Swine Gate, LS1 4AG ☎ 0113 233 0400, ⓦ roomzzz.co.uk; map p.612. Self-catering, one- and two-bedroom apartments in contemporary style, at several locations – Swine Gate is the most central. All come with great kitchens and widescreen TVs. Reduced rates if you book more than a week in advance. **£88**

EATING

★ **Art's Café Bar and Restaurant** 42 Call Lane, LS1 6DT ☎ 0113 243 8243, ⓦ artscafebar.co.uk; map p.612. A relaxed hangout for drinks, dinner or a lazy Sunday brunch. Mediterranean flavours dominate the well-priced menu, and the wine list is excellent. Mains £10.95–16.50. Mon–Fri noon–11pm, Sat noon–late, Sun noon–9pm.

★ **Brasserie Blanc** Victoria Mill, Sovereign St, LS1 4BJ ☎ 0113 220 6060, ⓦ brasserieblanc.com; map p.612.

One of the twenty restaurants established by French celebrity chef Raymond Blanc all over the country, the Leeds branch is a 5min walk from the train station. Housed in an old mill, with plain brick walls, vaulted ceilings and iron pillars, it offers good food in smart but unstuffy surroundings at unthreatening prices. Set two-course menus from £11.50 (lunch) and £14 (dinner). Mon–Fri 10am–10pm, Sat 9am–10.30pm, Sun 9am–9pm (bar open all day).

The Greedy Pig Kitchen 58 North St, LS2 7PN ☎07477 834227, ⓦthegreedypigkitchen.co.uk; map p.612. This little spot just outside the city-centre ring road is where those in the know go for brunch. Full English is £7 (they do

a veggie version too) and all the ingredients are local sourced. Small plate dining on Thurs, Fri & Sat evening only. Tues & Wed 7am–3pm, Thurs & Fri 7am–3pm 5.30–9pm, Sat 8.30am–1.30pm & 5.30–9pm.

Salvo's 115 Otley Rd, Headingley, LS6 3PX ☎0113 27 5017, ⓦsalvos.co.uk; map p.612. Mention pizza to Leed locals and they'll think of *Salvo's*, though there's a class Italian menu as well – mains £15.95–19.50 – and a choic list of daily specials. It really is worth the trek out fro the centre. Mon–Thurs noon–2pm & 6–10pm, F noon–2pm & 5.30–10.30pm, Sat noon–10.30pm, Su noon–9pm.

DRINKING

The newly coined Northern Quarter, north of the Grand Theatre and Opera House, is booming. A short walk in any directio and you'll stumble on one of Leeds's many independent brew pubs packed out with young creatives sipping local ales.

Bar Fibre 168 Lower Briggate LS1 6LY ☎0870 120 0888, ⓦbarfibre.com; map p.612. One of Leeds's finest gay-friendly bars comes with plenty of attitude. There's food during the day at *Café Mafiosa*, and regular alfresco parties in the courtyard outside (summer) and roaring fires inside (winter). Mon–Wed & Sun noon–1am, Thurs & Fri noon–3am, Sat noon–4am.

Headrow House Bramleys Yd, 10 The Headrow, LS1 6PU ☎0113 245 9370; map p.612. Low-key and with a friendly vibe, this venue has something for everyone (beer hall, decent restaurant, live music and a stunning roof terrace). Mon–Thurs noon–11pm/midnight, Fri noon– 2am, Sat 11am–3am, Sun 11am–11pm.

Milo 10–12 Call Lane, LS1 6DN ☎0113 245 7101; map p.612. Unpretentious, intimate and offbeat bar, with DJs most evenings, ringing the changes from old soul and reggae to indie and electronica. Mon–Thurs 5pm–2am, Fri 4pm–3am, Sat noon–3am, Sun noon–2am.

★**Mojo** 18 Merrion St, LS1 6PQ ☎0113 244 6387, ⓦmojobar.co.uk; map p.612. A great bar with classic tunes ("music for the people" – an eclectic mix with a swerve towards soul), American food, and a classy drinks

menu with lots of cocktails. Mon–Wed 4pm–3am, Thurs Fri & Sun 4pm–4am, Sat noon–3am.

Mr Foley's Cask Ale House 159 The Headrow, LS1 5R ☎0113 242 9674, ⓦmrfoleysleeds.co.uk; map p.612 Super Victorian pub near the Town Hall, with several bar on different levels, draught beers listed on a blackboar with strengths and tasting notes, and bottled beers fro around the world. Food is served, too, from around a five Mon–Thurs noon–11pm, Fri & Sat 11am–1am, Su noon–10pm.

North Bar 24 New Briggate, LS1 6NU ☎0113 242 454 ⓦnorthbar.com; map p.612. The city's beer specialist ha a massive selection of guest beers (more Belgian tha bitter) plus cold meats and cheeses to nibble on. This plac is part of the hugely successful North Bar group, with grea pubs popping up across the city. Mon & Tues 11am–1am Wed–Sat 11am–2am, Sun noon–midnight.

Whitelocks Turk's Head Yard, off Briggate, LS1 6H ☎0113 245 3950, ⓦwhitelocksleeds.com; map p.61 Leeds's oldest and most atmospheric pub retains its tradition Victorian decor and a good choice of beers. Mon–Thu 11am–midnight, Fri & Sat 11am–1am, Sun 11am–11pm

NIGHTLIFE

For information about **what's on**, your best bets are the fortnightly listings magazine *The Leeds Guide* (ⓦleedsguid .co.uk) or the daily *Yorkshire Evening Post* (ⓦyorkshireeveningpost.co.uk).

Hifi 2 Central Rd, LS1 6DE ☎0113 242 7353, ⓦthehifi club.co.uk; map p.612. Small club playing everything

from Stax and Motown to hip-hop or drum 'n' bass. Liv comedy from top comics.

LEEDS CONCERTS AND FESTIVALS

Temple Newsam, four miles east of Leeds city centre (see p.616), hosts numerous events, from concerts and plays to rock gigs and opera. Roundhay Park is the other large outdoor venue for concerts, while Bramham Park, ten miles east of the city, hosts the annual **Leeds Festival** (ⓦleeds festival.com) at the end of August with rock/indie music on five stages. August bank holiday weekend heralds the **West Indian Carnival** (ⓦleedscarnival.co.uk) in the Chapeltown area of Leeds.

The Key Club 66 Merrion St, LS2 8LW ☎ 0113 244 1573, ⓦ slamdunkmusic.com/the-key-club; map p.612. Took on the mantle of best live music spot after closure of the renowned Cockpit, although the focus is strictly on rock. Cheap bar, young crowd, and club nights Tues, Fri & Sat.

Mint Club 8 Harrison St, LS1 6HD ☎ 0113 244 3168, ⓦ themintclub.com; map p.612. Up-to-the-minute house tunes (there's a "no-cheese" policy), and the best chill-out space in the city.

The Warehouse 19–21 Somers St, LS1 2RG ☎ 0113 234 3535, ⓦ www.theleedswarehouse.com; map p.612. A mix of house, electro and techno – plus an epic sound system – brings in clubbers from all over the country, especially for Saturday's Technique night.

Wire 2–8 Call Lane, LS1 6DN ☎ 0113 234 0980, ⓦ wire club.co.uk; map p.612. A good indie/alternative dance/rock/electronic club associated with *Hifi* (see opposite) with weekly club nights and individual events.

ENTERTAINMENT

City Varieties Swan St, LS1 6LW ☎ 0113 243 0808, ⓦ www.cityvarieties.co.uk; map p.612. One of the country's last surviving music halls, this place hosts a wide range of acts and was from 1953 to 1983 the venue for the TV series *The Good Old Days*.

Grand Theatre and Opera House 46 New Briggate, LS1 5NZ ☎ 0870 121 4901, ⓦ leedsgrandtheatre.com; map p.612. The regular base of Opera North (ⓦ operanorth.co.uk) – who organize programming in the first-floor Howard Assembly Room – and Northern Ballet (ⓦ northernballet

.com), but also puts on a full range of theatrical productions.

Hyde Park Picture House Brudenell Rd, Headingley, LS6 1JD ☎ 0113 275 2045, ⓦ hydeparkpicturehouse .co.uk; map p.612. The place to come for classic cinema with independent and art-house shows alongside more mainstream films; get there on bus #56.

West Yorkshire Playhouse Quarry Hill, LS2 7UP ☎ 0113 213 7700, ⓦ wyp.org.uk; map p.612. The city's most innovative theatre has two stages, plus a bar, restaurant and café.

SHOPPING

Leeds is one of the best cities outside the capital for **shopping**, with numerous independent shops, a throng of classy emporia in the beautifully restored **Victoria Leeds** (ⓦ victorialeeds.co.uk) – the "Knightsbridge of the North" which includes brand-new landmark Victoria Gate – and other arcades that open off **Briggate**. Other options include the shopping complex **The Light** (ⓦ thelightleeds.co.uk), the city-centre malls, such as the **Merrion Centre** (ⓦ merrion centre.co.uk) off Merrion St and the **Trinity Leeds complex** (ⓦ trinityleeds.com) in Albion Street, not forgetting the eight hundred traders in Kirkgate.

Harvey Nichols 107–11 Briggate, LS1 6AZ ☎ 0113 204 8888, ⓦ harveynichols.com/leeds; map p.612. Harvey Nicks, who opened their first branch outside London here in the Victoria Quarter in 1996, are the lodestone for this chi-chi shopping district. Mon–Sat 10am–7pm, Sun 10.30am–5pm.

John Lewis Victoria Gate, Harewood St, LS2 7AR ⓦ johnlewis.com; map p.612. This extravagant five-storey flagship store opened at the end of 2016; most

talked about for its impressive architecture and plush decor, it also stocks Yorkshire suppliers such as the Harrogate Candle Company. Mon–Fri 9.30am–7pm, Sat 9am–7pm, Sun 10.30am–5pm.

Kirkgate Market Vicar Lane, LS2 7HY ⓦ leeds.gov.uk; map p.612. The largest covered market in the north of England, housed in a superb Edwardian building. If you're after tripe, haberdashery or big knickers, this is the place to come. Mon–Sat 8am–5.30pm.

Around Leeds

Beyond the city, a number of major attractions are accessible by bus or train: north of town lies the stately home **Harewood House**, while south of Leeds, the neighbouring town of **Wakefield** is home to the stunning **Hepworth Gallery** and not far from the **National Coal Mining Museum** and the **Yorkshire Sculpture Park**.

Thackray Museum

Beckett St, LS9 7LN, 2 miles northeast of the centre • Daily 10am–5pm, last admission 3pm • £8 • ☎ 0113 244 4343, ⓦ thackraymedical museum.co.uk • Bus #16 #42 #49 #50 #50A or #61 from the city centre (all around 15min, all stop outside the museum)

Essentially a medical history museum, and a hugely entertaining one, the **Thackray Museum**, next to St James's Hospital, has displays on subjects as diverse as the history

12

of the hearing aid and the workings of the human intestine. It's gruesome, too, with a film of a Victorian limb amputation in a gallery called "Pain, pus and blood".

Leeds Industrial Museum

Off Canal Rd, between Armley and Kirkstall Rd, LS12 2QF, 2 miles west of the centre • Tues–Sat 10am–5pm, Sun 1–5pm • £3.80 •
Ⓦ leeds.gov.uk, ☎ 0113 263 7861 • Bus #15 from Leeds railway station

For Leeds's industrial past, visit the vast **Leeds Industrial Museum**. There's been a mill on the site since at least the seventeenth century, and the present building was one of the world's largest woollen mills until its closure in 1969. Although most of its displays naturally centre on the **woollen industry**, and famous offshoots like Hepworths and Burtons, the cinema and printing in the local area are also covered.

Kirkstall Abbey

Abbey Rd, LS5 3EH, about 3 miles northwest of the city centre • **Abbey** Tues–Sun: April–Sept 10am–4.30pm; Oct–March 10m–4pm •
Free • **Museum** Tues–Fri & Sun 10am–5pm, Sat noon–5pm • £4.50 • ☎ 0113 230 5492, Ⓦ leeds.gov.uk • Buses #33, #33A or #757 from
city centre

The bucolic ruins and cloisters of **Kirkstall Abbey**, which was built between 1152 and 1182 by Cistercian monks from Fountains Abbey (see p.598), are well worth a visit. The former gatehouse now provides the setting for the family-friendly **Abbey House Museum**, which takes a look at Victorian Leeds.

Temple Newsam

Off Selby Rd, LS15 0AE, 4 miles east of Leeds • **House** Tues–Sun: April–Sept 10.30am–5pm; Oct–March 10.30am–4pm • £6 • **Rare breeds farm** Tues–Sun: April–Sept 10am–5pm; Oct–March 10am–4pm • £3.80 • ☎ 0113 264 7321, Ⓦ leeds.gov.uk • On Sun bus #63a runs to the house from central Leeds and during the rest of the week #19 and #19a run to Whitkirk, from where it is a 1-mile walk; during hols (Easter to Oct half term), #10 bus runs directly to the house

The Tudor-Jacobean house of **Temple Newsam** shows many of the paintings and much of the decorative art owned by Leeds City Art Gallery. There are paintings from the sixteenth to the nineteenth centuries, furniture (including a number of Chippendale pieces), textiles and tapestries, silver, porcelain and pottery. The estate is over fifteen thousand acres and also contains Europe's largest **rare breeds farm**, where you can see four breeds of pigs, six of sheep, eight of poultry and no fewer than nine of cattle.

Harewood House

Harewood, LS17 9LG, 7 miles north of Leeds • Opening hours vary widely according to day and season; check website for full details •
Freedom ticket, covering all parts of house and gardens £16.50 • ☎ 0113 218 1010, Ⓦ harewood.org • Frequent buses run to Harewood
from Leeds, including the #36 (Mon–Sat every 15min, Sun every 30min)

Harewood House – still the home of the Earl and Countess of Harewood – is one of the UK's greatest country mansions. It was created in the mid-eighteenth century by an all-star team: designed by John Carr of York, with interiors by Robert Adam, furniture by Thomas Chippendale, and paintings by Turner, Reynolds, Titian and El Greco, all sitting in beautiful **grounds** landscaped by Capability Brown. Tours take in the below-stairs kitchen and servants' quarters as well as innumerable galleries, halls, reception rooms and staircases, dripping with antiques and priceless art treasures, while added attractions include an adventure playground and gardens – including the famous bird garden. Numerous special events, special-interest tours and talks on things like beekeeping, photography and food keep things lively. Incidentally, the village is pronounced "Harewood" as it is spelt, while the house is pronounced "Harwood".

CLOCKWISE FROM TOP ROYAL ARMOURIES, LEEDS (P.613); HUMBER STREET, HULL (P.623); CASTLE HOWARD (P.594) ›

The Hepworth Wakefield

Gallery Walk, Wakefield, WF1 5AW • Tues–Sun 10am–5pm • Free; parking £5 • ☎ 01924 247360, ⊛ hepworthwakefield.org • From Leeds, take a train to Wakefield Westgate and walk, or a bus to Wakefield city centre, then a local bus to Bridge St (next to the gallery); alternatively, Wakefield's FreeCityBus (9.30am–3pm; ⊛ wymetro.com) links all major parts of town, including the Hepworth Gallery

Established in May 2011, **The Hepworth** was the largest new gallery to open outside London for decades. Inside a cuboid concrete riverside building designed by Sir David Chipperfield, it has ten display areas housing a wonderful collection of Dame Barbara Hepworth's work – not only finished sculptures, but also working models in plaster and aluminium, lithographs and screen prints. You can even see her original workbench and tools. Other contemporary artists are represented, too, and a flow of new exhibits is assured by close cooperation with the Tate. There's a café and shop, and a children's playground within its pleasant surroundings, which are set to be developed into a vast landscaped garden.

National Coal Mining Museum

Caphouse Colliery, Overton, WF4 4RH, about 10 miles south of Leeds, halfway between Wakefield and Huddersfield (on the A642, signposted from M1) • Tours daily 10am–5pm; last tour 3.15pm; 1hr 30min • Free • ☎ 01924 848806, ⊛ ncm.org.uk • Train from Leeds to Wakefield Westgate, then from the station the #128 bus goes right past the museum, while #232 passes nearby

While the gentry enjoyed the comforts of life in grand houses like Harewood (see p.616), just a few miles away generations of Yorkshiremen sweated out a living underground. Mining is now little more than a memory in most parts of Yorkshire, but visitors can get all too vivid an idea of pit life through the ages at the excellent **National Coal Mining Museum**. Based in a former pit, Caphouse Colliery, the highlight is an underground **mine tour** (warm clothes required; arrive early in school hols; no under-5s) with a former miner as your guide.

Yorkshire Sculpture Park

West Bretton, outside Wakefield, WF4 4LG, a mile from the M1 (junction 38) • Daily 10am–6pm (galleries, restaurant and café 10am–5pm) • Free, but parking £5 for 1–2hr, £8/day • ☎ 01924 832631, ⊛ ysp.co.uk • Train from Leeds to Wakefield Westgate, then bus #96 (Mon–Sat) – a fair bit of walking is necessary

The Yorkshire country estate at West Bretton now serves as the **Yorkshire Sculpture Park**. Trails and paths run across five hundred acres of eighteenth-century parkland, past open-air "gallery spaces" for some of Britain's most famous sculptors; there are also three indoor galleries for exhibitions. The two big local names represented here are Henry Moore (1898–1986), born in nearby Castleford, and his contemporary Barbara Hepworth (1903–75), from Wakefield. The **visitor centre** is the place to check on current exhibitions and pick up a map – the restaurant has great views over Moore's monumental pieces.

Sheffield and around

Yorkshire's second city, **SHEFFIELD** remains linked with its steel industry, in particular the production of high-quality cutlery. As early as the fourteenth century the carefully fashioned, hard-wearing knives of hard-working Sheffield enjoyed national repute, while technological advances later turned the city into one of the country's foremost centres of heavy and specialist engineering. Unsurprisingly, it was bombed heavily during World War II, and by the 1980s the steel industry's subsequent downturn had tipped parts of Sheffield into dispiriting decline. The subsequent revival has been rapid, however, with the centre utterly transformed by flagship architectural projects. Steel, of course, still underpins much of what Sheffield is about; museum collections tend to focus on the region's industrial heritage, complemented by the startling science-and-adventure exhibits at **Magna**, which was built in a disused steelworks at **Rotherham**, the former coal and iron town a few miles northeast of the city.

Sheffield's **city centre** is very compact and easily explored on foot. The hub of the city is the **Winter Garden**, as well as the attractive **Peace Gardens** (named in hope immediately after World War II) nearby, with their huge bronze water features and converging ceramic-lined rills that represent the rivers that gave Sheffield steel mills their power. Southeast of here, clubs and galleries exist alongside the arts and media businesses of the **Cultural Industries Quarter**. To the northeast, spruced-up warehouses and cobbled towpaths line the canal basin, **Victoria Quays**. The **Devonshire Quarter**, east of the Peace Gardens and centred on Division Street, is the trendiest shopping area.

Winter Garden

Surrey St, S1 2HH • Mon–Sat 8am–8pm, Sun 8am–6pm • Free • ☎ 0114 273 6895, ⓦ sheffield.gov.uk

A minute's walk east of the Peace Gardens, the stunning **Winter Garden** is a potent symbol of the city's regeneration. A twenty-first-century version of a Victorian conservatory on a huge scale (230ft long, and around 70ft high and wide), it's created from unvarnished, slowly weathering wood and polished glass, and filled with more than two thousand seasonally changing plants and towering trees.

Millennium Gallery

Arundel Gate, S1 2PP • Mon–Sat 10am–5pm, Sun 11am–4pm • Free • ☎ 0114 278 2600, ⓦ museums-sheffield.org.uk

Backing onto the Winter Garden are the **Millennium Galleries**, consisting of the **Metalwork Gallery**, which is devoted to the city's world-famous cutlery industry, including an introduction to the processes involved and a collection of fine silver and stainless steel cutlery, and the diverting **Ruskin Gallery**. Based on the cultural collection founded by John Ruskin in 1875 to "improve" the working people of Sheffield, this includes manuscripts, minerals, watercolours and drawings, all relating in some way to the natural world.

12

Sheffield Cathedral

Church St, S1 1HA • Visitor centre open Mon 8am–5pm, Tues–Fri 8.30am–6.30pm (5pm in school hols), Sat 9.30am–4pm, Sun 7.30am–5pm • Details of recitals and tours available on ☎ 0114 279 7412, ⓦ sheffieldcathedral.org

The **Cathedral Church of St Peter and St Paul**, to give **Sheffield Cathedral** its full title, was a simple parish church before 1914, and subsequent attempts to give it a more dignified bearing have frankly failed. It's a mishmash of styles and changes of direction, and you'd need a PhD in ecclesiastical architecture to make any sense of it. That said, the magnificent **Shrewsbury Chapel**, at the east end of the south aisle, is worth a look. Built around 1520, it contains the tombs of the fourth and sixth Earls of Shrewsbury, whose alabaster effigies adorn their tombs.

Kelham Island Museum

Alma St, S3 8RY • Mon–Thurs 10am–4pm, Sun 11am–4.45pm • £6 • ☎ 0114 272 2106, ⓦ simt.co.uk

Fifteen minutes' walk north of the cathedral, the **Kelham Island Museum** reveals the breadth of the city's **industrial output** – cutlery, of course, but also Barnes Wallis's 22ft-long Grand Slam bomb, the Sheffield Simplex roadster, and the gigantic River Don steam engine. Many of the old machines are still working, arranged in period workshops where craftspeople show how they were used.

Weston Park Museum

Weston Bank, S10 2TP • Mon–Sat 10am–5pm, Sun 11pm–4pm • Free • ☎ 0114 278 2600, ⓦ museums-sheffield.org.uk • Bus #51 or #52 from city centre, or Sheffield University tram

You can put the city's life and times into perspective a mile or so west of the centre at the **Weston Park Museum**. Here the imaginatively themed and family-friendly galleries draw together the city's extensive archeology, natural history, art and social history collections.

Magna

Magna Way, Rotherham, S60 1FD • Mon–Fri 10am–2pm, Sat & Sun 10am–5pm • £10.95, family ticket from £28.95 • ☎ 01709 720002, ⓦ visitmagna.co.uk • Bus #X1 (every 10min) from either Sheffield or Rotherham Interchanges, or a 15min taxi ride from Sheffield

Housed in a former steelworks building in **ROTHERHAM**, about six miles northeast of Sheffield and just off the M1, **Magna** is the UK's best science adventure centre. The vast internal space comfortably holds four gadget-packed **pavilions**, themed on the elements of earth, air, fire and water. You're encouraged to get your hands on a huge variety of interactive exhibits, games and machines – operating a real JCB, filling diggers and barrows, blasting a rock face or investigating a twister, for example. On the hour, everyone decamps to the main hall for the **Big Melt**, when the original arc furnace is used in a bone-shaking light and sound show that has visitors gripping the railings.

ARRIVAL AND DEPARTURE

By train Sheffield's train station is on the eastern edge of the city centre.

Destinations Leeds (every 12min; 40min–1hr 19min); London (hourly; 2hr 30min); York (every 30min; 53min).

By bus Sheffield Interchange bus and coach station lies about 200yd north of the train station. Buses run to and from most regional and national centres – including all the main South Yorkshire towns; London (hourly; 3hr 45min); Birmingham (every 30min; 2hr 5min); Liverpool (hourly; 2hr 50min) and Manchester (every 30min; 1hr).

GETTING AROUND AND INFORMATION

By bus Local buses depart from High Street or Arundel Gate.

By tram The Supertram system (ⓦ supertram.com) connects the city centre with the Meadowhall shopping centre (see opposite), Halfway, Herdings Park, Malin Bridge and Middlewood, with the stations in between giving comprehensive access to most of the city and connections to the Park and Ride scheme.

Transport information For fare and timetable information, visit the Mini Interchange travel centre on Arundel Gate, behind the Crucible Theatre (Mon–Fri 7am–6pm, Sat 9am–5pm; ☎ 01709 515151, ⓦ sypte.co.uk).

Tourist office Unit 1, The Winter Garden (Mon–Fri 9.30am–1pm & 1.30–5pm, Sat 9.30am–1pm & 1.30–4pm; ☎ 0114 275 7754, ⓦ welcometosheffield.co.uk).

ACCOMMODATION

Houseboat Hotels Victoria Quays, S2 5SY ☎ 07776 144693, ⓦ houseboathotels.com. Something different – two moored houseboats, available by the night, with en-suite bathrooms and kitchens. You get exclusive use of your own boat, sleeping up to four people (£190) and priced accordingly. **£130**

Leopold Hotel 2 Leopold St, S1 2GZ ☎ 0114 252 4000, ⓦ leopoldhotel.co.uk. Once a boys' grammar school, this place is immaculately modernized but retains some original features. Centrally located, the hotel backs onto remodelled Leopold Square, which has an appealing array of places to eat. **£99**

Mercure St Paul's Hotel 119 Norfolk St, S1 2JE ☎ 0114 278 2000, ⓦ mercure.com. Sandwiched between the Peace Gardens and Tudor Square, this modern hotel couldn't be more central. Comfortable rather than innovative, with understated (if a little anodyne) decor and fine views over the city the higher you go. **£94**

EATING

★ Forum Kitchen + Bar 127–129 Devonshire St, S3 7SB ☎ 0114 272 0569, ⓦ forumsheffield.co.uk. A vibrant and recently refurbed mixture of bar, café, music venue and boutique mall, with a lively clientele who use it as a breakfast stop, lunch spot, after-work bar, dinner venue, comedy club and night club. Mon–Wed 8am–1am, Thurs 8am–2am, Fri 8am–3am, Sat 9am–3am, Sun 10am–1pm.

Nonna's 535–541 Ecclesall Rd, S11 8PR ☎ 0114 268 6166, ⓦ nonnas.co.uk. Italian bar/restaurant with a great reputation and a family feel. Authentic Italian cuisine (menus have English descriptions). Evening mains £9.95 and up. Mon–Sat 8.30am–11pm, Sun 9am–10.30pm.

Silversmiths 111 Arundel St, S1 2NT ☎ 0114 270 6160 ⓦ silversmiths-restaurant.com. A "kitchen nightmare" turned around in 2008 by Gordon Ramsay in his TV show, city-centre *Silversmiths* supplies top-notch Yorkshire food from local ingredients – venison sausages and pies, spinach tart with Yorkshire Blue cheese – in a 200-year-old silversmith's workshop. Pre-theatre three-course menu for £18.95 or three-course seasonal Sunday roast for £25. Reservations recommended. Tues–Thurs 10am–9.30pm, Fri & Sat 10am–9.45pm, Sun noon–2.30pm.

DRINKING AND NIGHTLIFE

For the best insight into what makes Sheffield tick as a party destination take a night-time walk along **Division St** and **West St** where competing theme and retro bars go in and out of fashion. Locals and students also frequent the bars and pubs of **Ecclesall Rd** (the so-called "golden mile"), out of the centre to the southwest.

★ **Devonshire Cat** 49 Wellington St, Devonshire Green, S1 4HG ☎ 0114 279 6700, ⓦ devonshirecat.co.uk. Renowned ale house with wide variety of domestic and imported beers, plus good pub food (£7.75–14.25) with drinks matched to every selection. Daily noon–2am; kitchen Mon–Sat noon–9pm, Sun noon–8pm.

★ **Fat Cat** 23 Alma St, S3 8SA ☎ 0114 249 4801, ⓦ thefatcat.co.uk. Bought by real ale enthusiasts in 1981 after a brewery sell-off, the *Fat Cat* is now a Sheffield institution offering a wide range of bottled and draft beers, ciders and country wines, and a hearty pub-grub menu (meals around £4.50). With its open fires, polished mahogany bar and etched mirrors, and its total absence of flashing gaming machines and piped music, this is pub-going as it used to be. Mon–Thurs & Sun noon–11.30pm, Fri & Sat noon–midnight; kitchen Mon–Fri noon–3pm & 6–8pm, Sat noon–7pm, Sun noon–3pm.

Leadmill 6–7 Leadmill Rd, S1 4SE ☎ 0114 221 2828, ⓦ leadmill.co.uk. In the Cultural Industries Quarter, this venue hosts live bands and DJs most nights of the week, as well as screenings and comedy nights.

Plug 14 Matilda St, S1 4QD ☎ 0114 279 5039, ⓦ the-plug.com. Mid-sized music venue featuring everything from live acoustic folk to diverse club nights, including the award-winning "Jump Around". Check online for hours.

ENTERTAINMENT

Crucible, Lyceum and Studio 55 Norfolk St, S1 1DA ☎ 0114 249 6000, ⓦ sheffieldtheatres.co.uk. Sheffield's theatres put on a full programme of theatre, dance, comedy and concerts. The *Crucible*, of course, has hosted the World Snooker Championships for thirty years. It also presents the annual Music in the Round festival of chamber music (May), and the Sheffield Children's Festival (late June or July).

Sheffield City Hall Barker's Pool, S1 2JA ☎ 0114 278 9789, ⓦ sheffieldcityhall.com. Year-round programme of classical music, opera, mainstream concerts, comedy and club nights, in a magnificent, renovated concert hall.

Showroom 7 Paternoster Row, S1 2BX ☎ 0114 275 7727, ⓦ showroom.org.uk. The biggest independent cinema outside London, and also a popular workstation and meeting place, with a relaxed café-bar.

12

SHOPPING

Sheffield has all the national chain stores and other shops you'd expect in the city centre, with top-end shops concentrated particularly along **Fargate** and **High St** on one side of the Peace Gardens and budget alternatives along **The Moor** on the other. The trendiest shopping is to be found in the **Devonshire Quarter**, based on Division St, while due south there's an **indoor market** at 77 The Moor (Mon–Sat 8.30am–5.30pm).

Meadowhall Centre S9 1EP ☎ 0845 600 6800, ⓦ meadowhall.co.uk. Since it opened in 1990 on the site of a derelict steelworks, out-of-town Meadowhall has pulled in thirty million shoppers a year. Free parking is a boon, or it's an easy tram ride three miles east of the centre. Mon–Fri 10am–9pm, Sat 9am–8pm, Sun 11am–5pm.

Antiques Quarter A621 and surrounding roads ⓦ sheffieldantiquesquarter.co.uk. To the south of the city centre, along Abbeydale and Broadfield roads and easily reached by bus, you'll find a horde of delightful independent antique dealers and an auction house. For exact shop locations and opening hours, check online.

Hull

HULL – officially **Kingston upon Hull** – dates back to 1299, when it was laid out as a seaport by Edward I. It quickly became England's leading harbour, and was still a vital garrison when the gates were closed against Charles I in 1642, the first serious act of rebellion of what was to become the English Civil War. Fishing and **seafaring** have always been important here, and today's city maintains a firm grip on its heritage with a number of superb visitor attractions, including the excellent **Museum Quarter** in the **Old Town**. The city's stint as **UK City of Culture** in 2017 saw a massive investment in arts and culture across the city; the revitalization is particularly noticeable in the burgeoning **Fruit Market** district between the Marina and river (ⓦ fruitmarkethull.co.uk), where new galleries and cool cafés have opened.

Ferens Art Gallery

Queen Victoria Square, HU1 3RA • Mon–Sat 10am–5pm (Thurs 7.30pm), Sun 11am–4.30pm • Free • ☎ 01482 300300, ⓦ hcandl.co.uk/ferens

When it reopened in April 2017 after a multi-million pound refurbishment, **Ferens Art Gallery** attracted more than 10,000 visitors in its first weekend. The world-class gallery has a permanent collection of paintings and sculpture with works by Frans Hals, David Hockney and Antonio Canaletto. Visiting exhibitions have included SKIN – major works by Lucian Freud, Ron Mueck and Spencer Tunick – and the prestigious Turner Prize.

The Maritime Museum

Queen Victoria Square, HU1 3DX • Mon–Sat 10am–5pm (Thurs 7.30pm), Sun 11am–4.30pm • Free • ☎ 01482 300300, ⓦ hullcc.gov.uk

The city's maritime legacy is covered in the **Maritime Museum**, housed in the Neoclassical headquarters of the former Town Docks Offices. With displays on fishing, whaling and sailing, this provides a valuable record of centuries of skill and expertise, not to mention courage and fortitude, now fading into the past. Highlights include the whaling gallery, with whale skeletons, fearsome exploding harpoons, the sort of flimsy boats in which whalers of old used to chase the leviathans of the deep, and oddities such as a whalebone seat and a blubber cauldron.

The Museums Quarter

Between High St & the River Hull, HU1 1NQ • All attractions Mon–Sat 10am–5pm, Sun 11am–4.30pm • Free • ☎ 01482 300300, ⓦ hullcc.gov.uk

12

Over towards the River Hull, you reach the **Museums Quarter** and **High Street**, which has been designated an "Old Town" conservation area thanks to its crop of former merchants' houses and narrow cobbled alleys. At its northern end stands **Wilberforce House**, the former home of William Wilberforce, which contains fascinating exhibits on slavery and its abolition, the cause to which he dedicated much of his life. Next door is **Streetlife**, devoted to the history of transport in the region and centred on a 1930s street scene. The adjoining **Hull and East Riding Museum** is even better, with showpiece attractions including vivid displays of Celtic burials and an impressive full-size model of a woolly mammoth.

The Deep

Tower St, HU1 4DP • Daily 10am–6pm, last entry 5pm • £12.50, children £10.50 (discount online) • ☎ 01482 381000 , ⓦ thedeep.co.uk

Protruding from a promontory overlooking the River Humber, Hull's splendid aquarium, **The Deep**, is just ten minutes' walk from the old town. Its educational displays and videos wrap around an immense 30ft-deep, 2.3-million-gallon viewing tank filled with sharks, rays and octopuses. There's an underwater tunnel along the bottom of the tank, together with a magical glass lift in which you can ascend or descend through the water.

ARRIVAL AND DEPARTURE   HULL

By train Hull's train station is situated in the Paragon Interchange off Fensway. There are direct trains between London and Hull, while the city is also linked to the main London–York line via Doncaster as well as to the East Yorkshire coast.
Destinations Bempton (hourly; 55min); Beverley (Mon–Sat every 25min, Sun 6 daily; 13min); Bridlington (every 30min; 42min); Filey (around 10 daily; 1hr10min); (Leeds (hourly; 1hr); London (6 daily; 2hr 45min); Scarborough

(every 2hr; 1hr 30min); York (hourly; 1hr 10m).
By bus The bus station is near the train station in the Paragon Interchange off Fensway. Buses run to all parts of the region including York (2hr) and the East Coast (1hr 40min to Bridlington; 2hr 30min to Scarborough).
By ferry Daily crossing to/from Rotterdam and Zeebrugge (Bruges) from the ferry terminal, 3 miles from the city centre (ⓦ poferries.com).

INFORMATION AND TOURS

Visitor information There's a volunteer-run hub in Hull railway station, where you can pick up the entertaining

"Fish Trail" leaflet, a self-guided trail that kids will love. See also ⓦ visithullandeastyorkshire.com.

Walking tour Paul Schofield (☎ 01482 878535, ⓦ tourhull .com) is an English Heritage-accredited guide who leads historic Old Town tours (from the tourist office; Mon, Fri & Sat 10am & 2pm, Sun 11am & 2pm; £4), as well as tours of some of Hull's best pubs.

ACCOMMODATION

Holiday Inn Hull Marina Castle St, HU1 2BX ☎ 0871 9422 9043, ⓦ hihullmarinahotel.co.uk. Rooms at the city's best central hotel overlook the marina, and there's a restaurant and bar, plus an indoor pool, gym, sauna and plenty of parking. <u>£114</u>

Kingston Theatre Hotel 1–2 Kingston Square, HU2 8DA ☎ 01482 225828, ⓦ kingstontheatrehotel.com. This straightforward, good-value hotel on the city's prettiest square, across from Hull New Theatre, is a 5min walk from the city centre, yet in a quiet neighbourhood. Street parking only (but there's a public car park nearby). <u>£110</u>

EATING AND DRINKING

Cerutti's 10 Nelson St, HU1 1XE ☎ 01482 328501, ⓦ ceruttis.co.uk. Facing the old site of the Victoria Pier (now replaced by a wooden deck overlooking the river), this first-floor Italian restaurant is especially good for fish dishes. The atmosphere is busy and friendly, and there are frequent special events including live jazz. Main courses are around £13–23, but look out for two- and three-course deals. Mon–Fri noon–2pm & 6.45–9.30pm, Sat 6.45–9.30pm.

The George The Land of Green Ginger, HU1 2EA ☎ 01482 226373. Venerable pub on Hull's most curiously named street – see if you can find England's smallest window. Mon noon–6pm, Tues–Thurs noon–11.00pm, Fri & Sat noon–midnight, Sun noon–10pm.

Pave Café-Bar 16–20 Princes Ave, HU5 3QA ☎ 01482 333181, ⓦ pavebar.co.uk. Nice laidback atmosphere with lots going on – live jazz/blues and comedy nights, and readings by the likes of Alexei Sayle, Will Self and Simon Armitage – and a comprehensive menu of home-cooked food served till 7pm (most mains well under £10). Mon–Thurs & Sun 11am–11.00pm, Fri & Sat 11am–11.30pm.

Thieving Harry's 73 Humber St, HU1 1UD ☎ 01482 214141, ⓦ thievingharrys.co.uk. A cornerstone of the Fruit Market regeneration, quirky *Thieving Harry's* "food + stuff" has mismatched chairs, a cool vibe, gorgeous views and tasty food (poached egg on toast with charred avocado and bacon £6). Mon–Thurs 10am–4pm, Fri & Sat 9am–midnight, Sun 9am–4pm.

ENTERTAINMENT

Hull Venue ⓦ cityplanhull.co.uk. A major state-of-the-art music and events complex set to open in 2018. Check the website for updates.

Hull Truck Theatre Company 50 Ferensway, HU2 8LB

☎ 01482 323638, ⓦ hulltruck.co.uk. Renowned theatre, where, among other high-profile works, many of the plays of award-winning John Godber see the light of day.

Beverley

With its tangle of old streets, cobbled lanes and elegant Georgian and Victorian terraces **BEVERLEY**, nine miles north of Hull, is the very picture of a traditional market town. More than 350 of its buildings are listed, and though you could see its first-rank offerings in a morning, it makes an appealing place to stay.

Beverley Minster

Minster Yard North, HU17 0DP • April–Oct Mon–Sat 9am–5.30pm, Sun noon–4.30pm; Nov–March Mon–Sat 9am–4pm, Sun noon–4.30pm; services Thurs & Sun (see website) • Free, but donation requested • **Roof tours** Thurs (by prior appointment only) & Sat 11am; 1hr • £10; advance booking only • ☎ 01482 868540, ⓦ beverleyminster.org.uk

The town is dominated by the fine, Gothic twin towers of **Beverley Minster**. The **west front**, which crowned the work in 1420, is widely considered without equal, its survival due in large part to architect Nicholas Hawksmoor, who restored much of the church in the eighteenth century. The carving throughout is magnificent, particularly the 68 misericords of the oak **choir** (1520–24), one of the largest and most accomplished in England. Much of the decorative work here and elsewhere is on a musical theme. Beverley had a renowned guild of itinerant minstrels, which provided funds in the sixteenth century for the carvings on the transept aisle capitals, where you'll be able to pick out players of lutes, bagpipes, horns and tambourines.

St Mary's

Corner of North Bar Within and Hengate, HU17 8DL • Mon–Sat 11.30am–3pm, Sun before and after services only • Free • ☎ 01482 869177, ⓦ stmarysbeverley.org

Cobbled Highgate runs from the minster through town, along the pedestrianized shopping streets and past the main Market Square, to Beverley's other great church, **St Mary's**, which nestles alongside the **North Bar**, sole survivor of the town's five medieval gates. Inside, the chancel's painted panelled ceiling (1445) contains portraits of English kings from Sigebert (623–37) to Henry VI (1421–71), and among the carvings the favourite novelty is the so-called "Pilgrim's Rabbit", said to have been the inspiration for the White Rabbit in Lewis Carroll's *Alice in Wonderland*.

ARRIVAL AND INFORMATION — BEVERLEY

By train Beverley's train station on Station Square is just a couple of mins' walk from the town centre and the minster. Destinations Bridlington (every 30min; 30min); Hull (every 30min; 15min); Sheffield (hourly; 1hr 41min).
By bus The bus station is at the junction of Walkergate and Sow Hill Road, with the main street just a minute's walk away. Destinations Bridlington (hourly; 1hr) Driffield (hourly;

25min); Hull (every 30min–1hr; hourly; 40min); Scarborough (hourly; 1hr 16min).
Tourist office 34 Butcher Row in the main shopping area (April–Sept Mon–Fri 9.30am–5.30pm, Sat 9.30am–4.30pm, Sun 10am–3.30pm; Oct–March Mon–Fri 10am–5pm, Sat 10am–4.30pm; ☎ 01482 391672, ⓦ visithull andeastyorkshire.com).

ACCOMMODATION AND EATING

★ **Cerutti 2** Station Square, HU17 0AS ☎ 01482 866700, ⓦ ceruttis.co.uk. Occupying what was once the station waiting rooms, *Cerutti 2*, run by the same family as *Cerutti's* in Hull, specializes in fish, though there are meat and vegetarian options too (mains around £12–23). Popular with locals, so it's as well to book, especially at weekends. Tues–Sat noon–2pm & 6.45–9.30pm.
King's Head Hotel 37–38 Saturday Market, HU17 9AH ☎ 01482 868103, ⓦ kingsheadpubbeverley.co.uk. Tucked into a corner of busy Saturday Market, this period building has contemporary decor inside. It's a Marston's

pub, with food from £7, and it can be noisy, especially at weekends, but the rear rooms are quieter, and earplugs are provided. Mon–Thurs 9am–11pm, Fri & Sat 9am–1am, Sun 11am–11pm; kitchen Mon–Sat 10am–9pm, Sun 10am–8pm. **£100**
YHA Beverley Friary Friar's Lane, HU17 0DF ☎ 0845 371 9004, ⓦ yha.org.uk/hostel/beverley-friary. Beautiful medieval monastic house in the shadow of the minster. What it lacks in luxury it makes up for in atmosphere, location and, of course, economy. Limited parking. Dorms **£18**, triples **£69**

The East Yorkshire coast

The **East Yorkshire coast** curves south in a gentle arc from the mighty cliffs of Flamborough Head to Spurn Head, a hook-shaped promontory formed by relentless erosion and shifting currents. There are few parts of the British coast as dangerous – indeed, the Humber lifeboat station at **Spurn Point** is the only one in Britain permanently staffed by a professional crew. Between the two points lie a handful of tranquil villages and miles of windswept dunes and mud flats. The two main resorts, **Bridlington** and **Filey**, couldn't be more different, but each has its own appeal.

Bridlington and around

The southernmost resort on the Yorkshire coast, **BRIDLINGTON** has maintained its harbour for almost a thousand years. The seafront promenade looks down upon the town's best asset – its sweeping sandy **beach**. It's an out-and-out family resort, which means plenty of candyfloss, fish and chips, rides, boat trips and amusement arcades. The historic core of town is a mile inland, where in the largely Georgian Bridlington Old Town the **Bayle Museum** (Easter–Oct Mon–Fri 11am–4pm; £2; ☎01262 674308) presents local history in a building that once served as the gateway to a fourteenth-century priory.

Around fourteen miles of precipitous 400ft-high cliffs gird **Flamborough Head**, just to the northeast of Bridlington. The best of the seascapes are visitable on the peninsula's north side, accessible by road from Flamborough village.

Bempton

From **BEMPTON**, two miles north of Bridlington, you can follow the clifftop path all the way round to Flamborough Head or curtail the journey by cutting up paths to Flamborough village. The **RSPB sanctuary** at **Bempton Cliffs**, reached along a quiet lane from Bempton, is the best single place to see the area's thousands of cliff-nesting birds.

RSPB Bempton Cliffs

1 mile from Bempton, YO15 1JF • Visitor centre daily 9.30am–5pm (4pm in winter) • £4 • ☎ 01262 4222212, ⓦ rspb.org.uk

A quarter of a million seabirds nest in these cliffs, including fifteen thousand pairs of gannets, and the second-largest **puffin colony** in the country, with several thousand returning to the cliffs each year. Late March and April is the best time to see the puffins, but the reserve's **visitor centre** can advise on other breeds' activities. There are six clifftop viewpoints (three of them wheelchair accessible), plus a beautiful picnic spot.

Filey

12

FILEY, half a dozen miles north up the coast from Bempton, is at the very edge of the Yorkshire Wolds (and technically in North Yorkshire). It has a good deal more class as a resort than Bridlington, retaining many of its Edwardian features, including some splendid panoramic gardens. It, too, claims miles of wide sandy beach, stretching most of the way south to Flamborough Head and north the mile or so to the jutting rocks of **Filey Brigg**, where a nature trail wends for a couple of miles through the surroundings.

ARRIVAL AND GETTING AROUND
THE EAST YORKSHIRE COAST

By train Bridlington and Filey are linked by the regular service between Hull and Scarborough, and there are regular trains between York and Scarborough, further up the coast.

By bus There are buses from York to Bridlington (every 2hr; 2hr), plus a service from Hull to Scarborough (every 2hr; 2hr 50min) via Bridlington and Filey. There's also an hourly service between Bridlington, Filey and Scarborough.

The North York Moors

Virtually the whole of the **North York Moors**, from the Hambleton and Cleveland hills in the west to the cliff-edged coastline to the east, is protected by one of the country's finest National Parks. The heather-covered, flat-topped hills are cut by deep, steep-sided valleys, and views here stretch for miles, interrupted only by giant cultivated forests. This is great walking country; footpaths include the superb **Cleveland Way**, one of England's premier long-distance National Trails, which embraces both wild moorland and the cliff scenery of the North Yorkshire coast. Barrows and ancient forts provide memorials of early settlers, mingling on the high moorland with the battered stone crosses of the first Christian inhabitants and the ruins of great monastic houses such as **Rievaulx Abbey**.

GETTING AROUND
THE NORTH YORK MOORS

By train The steam trains of the North Yorkshire Moors Railway (see box, p.629) run between Pickering and Grosmont and on to Whitby. At Grosmont you can connect with the regular trains on the Esk Valley line, running either 6 miles east to Whitby and the coast, or west through more remote country settlements (and ultimately to Middlesbrough).

By bus The main bus approaches to the moors are from Scarborough and York to the main towns of Helmsley and Pickering. There are two seasonal services that connect Pickering and Helmsley to everywhere of

interest in the National Park. Moorsbus (☎ 01751 477216, ⓦ moorsbus.org) and the Moors Explorer from Hull (☎ 01482 592929 or ⓦ eyms.co.uk) both have several departures on summer weekends, fewer at other times (at least every Sun & bank hols).

INFORMATION

National Park Visitor Centres There are two National Park Visitor Centres for the North York Moors, one in Danby (daily: April–July & Sept–Oct 10am–5pm; Aug 9.30am–5.30pm; for winter hours check with centre; ☎ 01439 772737), and the other in Sutton Bank (same hours; ☎ 01845 597426). Both offer exhibitions, pamphlets and

maps, a café and a shop. The National Park's website is ⓦ northyorkmoors.org.uk.

Cleveland Way Project Provides maps and information about the route, including an annual, downloadable accommodation guide (☎ 01439 770657, ⓦ nationaltrail .co.uk/cleveland-way).

Thirsk

The market town of **THIRSK**, 23 miles north of York, made the most of its strategic crossroads position on the ancient drove road between Scotland and York and on the historic east–west route from dales to coast. Its medieval prosperity is clear from the large, cobbled **Market Place** (markets Mon & Sat), while well-to-do citizens later endowed the town with fine Georgian houses and halls. However, Thirsk's main draw is its attachment to the legacy of local vet Alf Wight, better known as James Herriott. Thirsk was the "Darrowby" of the Herriott books, and the vet's former surgery, at 23 Kirkgate, is now the hugely popular **World of James Herriott** (daily: March–Oct 10am–5pm; Nov–Feb 10am–4pm; £8.50; ☎ 01845 524234, ⓦ worldofjamesherriot.org), and is crammed with period pieces and Herriott memorabilia.

ARRIVAL AND INFORMATION

By train The train station is a mile west of town on the A61 (Ripon road); minibuses connect the station with the town centre.
Destinations Middlesbrough (hourly; 44min); Manchester (hourly; 1hr 50min); London (every 2hr; 2hr 30min).

By bus Buses stop in the Market Place.
Destinations Northallerton (every 2hr; 25–30min); Ripon (every 2hr; 41min); York (every 1–2hr; 1hr).
Tourist office 93a Market Place (Mon–Sat 10am–4pm; ☎ 01845 522755, ⓦ visit-thirsk.org.uk).

ACCOMMODATION AND EATING

Gallery 18 Kirkgate, YO7 1PQ ☎ 01845 523767, ⓦ gallery bedandbreakfast.co.uk. An award-winning B&B with three comfortable rooms and excellent breakfasts in an eighteenth-century Grade II listed building. It's on a main street, and can get noisy when the pubs close. **£70**

Golden Fleece Market Place, YO7 1LL ☎ 01845 523108, ⓦ goldenfleecehotel.com. There are good rooms and a pleasant busy atmosphere in this charming old coaching inn, nicely located on Thirsk's large cobbled square. They serve locally sourced food, too. Daily noon–9pm. **£95**

Osmotherley and around

Eleven miles north of Thirsk, the little village of **OSMOTHERLEY** huddles around its green. The pretty settlement gets by as a hiking centre, since it's a key stop on the **Cleveland Way** as well as starting point for the brutal 42-mile **Lyke Wake Walk** to Ravenscar, south of Robin Hood's Bay.

Mount Grace Priory

Half a mile off the A19, DL6 3JG • April–Sept daily 10am–6pm; Oct daily 10am–5pm; Nov–March Sat & Sun 10am–4pm • £6.60; NT & EH ☎ 01609 883494, ⓦ nationaltrust.org.uk, ⓦ english-heritage.org.uk • #80/#89 from Northallerton, then a 30min walk

An easy two-mile walk from Osmotherley via Chapel Wood Farm, the fourteenth-century **Mount Grace Priory** is the most important of England's nine Carthusian ruins. The Carthusians took a vow of silence and lived, ate and prayed alone in their two-storey cells, each separated from its neighbour by a privy, small garden and high walls. The foundations of the cells are still clearly visible, and one has been reconstructed to suggest its original layout.

Sutton Bank

The main A170 road enters the National Park from Thirsk as it climbs 500ft in half a mile to **Sutton Bank** (960ft), a phenomenal **viewpoint** from where the panorama extends across the Vale of York to the Pennines on the far horizon. While you're here, call in at the **National Park Visitor Centre** (see opposite) half a mile further up the road, to pick up information on the **walks** and off-road **bike rides** you can make from here.

Kilburn

To the south of the A170, the **White Horse Nature Trail** (2–3 miles; 1hr 30min) skirts the crags of Roulston Scar en route to the **Kilburn White Horse**, northern England's only turf-cut figure, 314ft long and 228ft high. You could make a real walk of it by dropping a couple of miles down to pretty **KILBURN** village (a minor road also runs from the A170, passing the White Horse car park), which has been synonymous with woodcarving since the days of "Mouseman" Robert Thompson (1876–1955), whose woodcarvings are marked by his distinctive mouse motif. The **Mouseman Visitor Centre** (Easter–Oct daily 10am–5pm; Nov & Dec Wed–Sun 11am–4pm; £4.50; ☎01347 869102, ⊛robert thompsons.co.uk) displays examples of Thompson's personal furniture.

12

Coxwold

Most visitors to the attractive village of **COXWOLD** come to pay homage to the novelist **Laurence Sterne**, who is buried by the south wall (close to the porch) in the churchyard of **St Michael's**, where he was vicar from 1760 until his death in 1768. **Shandy Hall**, further up the road past the church (house May–Sept Wed & Sun 11am–4.30pm; gardens May–Sept Mon–Fri & Sun 11am–4.30pm; tours Wed & Sun 2.45pm & 3.45pm, or by appointment; house & gardens £5, gardens only £3; ☎01347 868465, ⊛laurencesternetrust.org.uk), was Sterne's home, now a museum crammed with literary memorabilia. It was here that he wrote *A Sentimental Journey through France and Italy* and the wonderfully eccentric anti-novel *The Life and Opinions of Tristram Shandy, Gentleman*.

Helmsley and around

One of the moors' most appealing towns, **HELMSLEY** makes a perfect base for visiting the western moors and **Rievaulx Abbey**. Local life revolves around a large cobbled market square (market Fri), which is dominated by a boastful monument to the second earl of Feversham, whose family was responsible for rebuilding most of the village in the nineteenth century. The old **market cross** now marks the start of the 110-mile **Cleveland Way**. Signposted from the square, it's easy to find **Helmsley Castle** (April–Sept daily 10am–6pm; Oct–Nov daily 10am–5pm; Nov–March Sat & Sun 10am–4pm; £6.20, EH; ☎01439 770442, ⊛www.english-heritage.org.uk/visit/places/helmsley-castle), its unique twelfth-century D-shaped keep ringed by massive earthworks.

Rievaulx Abbey

Just over 2 miles northwest of Helmsley, YO62 5LB • April–Sept daily 10am–6pm; Oct to early Nov daily 10am–5pm; mid-Nov to March Sat & Sun 10am–4pm • £8.50; EH • ☎ 01439 798228, ⊛ www.english-heritage.org.uk/visit/places/rievaulx-abbey

From Helmsley you can easily walk across country to **Rievaulx Abbey** on a signposted path (1hr 30min). Founded in 1132, the abbey became the mother church of the

Cistercians in England, quickly developing into a flourishing community with interests in fishing, mining, agriculture and the woollen industry. At its height, 140 monks and up to five hundred lay brothers lived and worked here, though numbers fell dramatically once the Black Death (1348–49) had done its worst. The end came with the Dissolution, when many of the walls were razed and the roof lead stripped – the beautiful ruins, however, still suggest the abbey's former splendour.

Rievaulx Terrace

YO62 5LJ, 2 miles northwest of Helmsley • Feb–Oct daily 10am–5pm • £5.40; NT • ☎ 01439 798340 (summer) or ☎ 01439 748283 (winter), ⓦ nationaltrust.org.uk/rievaulx-terrace

Although they form some sort of ensemble with the abbey, there's no access between the ruins and **Rievaulx Terrace**. This half-mile stretch of grass-covered terraces and woodland was laid out as part of Duncombe Park in the 1750s, and was engineered partly to enhance the views of the abbey. The resulting panorama over the ruins and the valley below is superb, and this makes a great spot for a picnic.

ARRIVAL AND INFORMATION   HELMSLEY AND AROUND

By bus Buses from Scarborough (every 1hr 15min; 1hr 36min) and Pickering (every 1hr 15min; 35min) stop on or near the Market Place. In addition, seasonal Moorsbus services (April–Oct; ☎ 01751 477217, ⓦ moorsbus.org), connect Helmsley to most places in the National Park.

ACCOMMODATION, EATING AND DRINKING

Black Swan Market Place, YO62 5BJ ☎ 01439 770466, ⓦ blackswan-helmsley.co.uk. An interesting Tudor/Georgian ex-coaching inn right on the main square, with a comfortable bar, airy restaurant, award-winning tearoom, refurbished rooms and charming, attentive staff. Daily: 11am–11pm, later at weekends; tearoom 10am–5.30pm; restaurant 7.30–9.30pm. **£144**

Feathers Hotel Market Place, YO62 5BH ☎ 01439 770275, ⓦ feathershotelhelmsley.co.uk. Pub serving restaurant food – all the staples, from £11.95 – and with a surprisingly large choice of rooms. Mon–Sat 11.30am–midnight, Sun 11.30am–1pm; kitchen Mon–Fri noon–2.30pm & 5.30–9pm, Sat noon–9pm, Sun noon–8.30pm. **£79**

★Feversham Arms 1 High St, YO62 5AG ☎ 01439 770766, ⓦ fevershamarmshotel.com. One of Yorkshire's top hotels, multi-award-winning, luxurious yet unpretentious. It has a pool, underground car park, spa and a terrific fine-dining restaurant. Look out for special deals. Mon–Sun noon–2.30pm & 6.45–9.30pm, Sun 12.30–2.30pm & 6.45–9.30pm. **£190**

Star Inn Harome, YO62 5JE, 2 miles southeast of Helmsley ☎ 01439 770397, ⓦ thestaratharome.co.uk. The *Star* is not only a spectacularly beautiful thatched inn, but a restaurant which regained its Michelin star in 2015. Food is classic British and surprisingly affordable (main courses around £19–30), and the atmosphere is blessedly unpretentious. Accommodation is available in a separate building, and there's an associated shop/deli across the road. Mon 6–11pm, Tues–Sat 11.30am–3pm & 6–11pm, Sun noon–11pm; kitchen Mon 6.15–9.30pm, Tues–Sat 11.30am–2pm & 6.15–9.30pm, Sun noon–6pm. **£180**

Hutton le Hole

Eight miles northeast of Helmsley, one of Yorkshire's quaintest villages, **HUTTON LE HOLE**, has become so great a tourist attraction that you'll have to come off-season to get much pleasure from its stream-crossed village green and the sight of sheep wandering freely through the lanes. Apart from the sheer photogenic quality of the place, the big draw is the family-oriented **Ryedale Folk Museum** (mid-Jan to March & Nov to early Dec daily 10am–4pm; April to Oct 10am–5pm; £7.50; ☎ 01751 417367, ⓦ ryedalefolkmuseum.co.uk), where local life is explored in a series of reconstructed buildings, notably a sixteenth-century house, a glass furnace, a crofter's cottage and a nineteenth-century blacksmith's shop.

ARRIVAL AND INFORMATION   HUTTON LE HOLE

By bus The #174 travels from/to Pickering once on Mon (30min).

National Park Information Centre At Ryedale Folk Museum (see above).

ACCOMMODATION AND EATING

The Barn Guest House Hutton-le-Hole, YO62 6UA ☏ 01751 417311, ⊛ thebarnguesthouse.com. Comfortable en-suite rooms, plus tearooms serving home-made cakes, scones, sandwiches and hot specials. Food served March–Oct daily 10.30am–4.30pm. **£79**

The Crown Hutton-le-Hole, YO62 6UA ☏ 01751 417343, ⊛ crownhuttonlehole.com. Spacious real ale pub where you can sit outside and enjoy the peace of the village. They serve traditional, freshly cooked food, too; you can eat well for under a tenner. Typically daily 11am–10pm (later when busy); kitchen Mon–Thurs 11.45am–2.15pm & 5.30–8.15pm, Fri & Sat 11.45am–2.30pm & 5.30–8.30pm, Sun 11.45am–6pm; winter closed Mon & Tues.

Pickering

The biggest centre for miles around, **PICKERING** takes for itself the title "Gateway to the Moors", which is pushing it a bit, though it's certainly a handy halt if you're touring the villages and dales of the **eastern moors**. Its most attractive feature is its motte and bailey **castle** on the hill north of the Market Place (daily: April–Sept 10am–6pm; Oct–Nov 10am–5pm; £4.90, EH; ☏ 01751 474989, ⊛ www.english-heritage.org.uk/visit/places/pickering-castle), reputedly used by every English monarch up to 1400 as a base for hunting in nearby Blandsby Park. The other spot worth investigating is the **Beck Isle Museum of Rural Life** on Bridge Street (Feb–Nov daily 10am–5pm; £6; ☏ 01751 473653, ⊛ www.beckislemuseum.org.uk), which has reconstructions of a gents' outfitters and barber's shop, a case full of knickers, and a painting of two giant Welsh guardsmen produced by Rex Whistler for a children's party. **Market** day in town is Monday, and there's a farmers' market on the first Thursday of the month.

12

ARRIVAL AND DEPARTURE   PICKERING

By train The steam trains of the North Yorkshire Moors Railway (see box below) run between Pickering and Grosmont and on to Whitby. The station is a 5min signposted walk from the main street.

By bus Buses stop outside the library and tourist office, opposite the Co-op in the centre of town.

Destinations Helmsley (hourly; 35min); Scarborough (hourly; 53min); Whitby (4–6 daily; 1hr 4min); York (hourly; 1hr 10min).

ACCOMMODATION AND EATING

The White Swan Market Place, YO18 7AA ☏ 01751 472288, ⊛ white-swan.co.uk. Delightful traditional coaching inn, fully refurbished and updated, with contemporary and traditional bedrooms, and fine Modern British food (mains from £13.95). Daily 7.30am–11pm; kitchen daily noon–2pm & 6.45–9pm. **£149**

THE NORTH YORKSHIRE MOORS RAILWAY

The **North Yorkshire Moors Railway** (☏ 01751 472508, ⊛ nymr.co.uk) provides a double whammy of nostalgia: first there's the rolling stock, station furniture and smell of steam conjuring up images of bygone travel (especially to those who remember rail in the mid-twentieth century); and then the countryside through which the trains pass is reminiscent of an England which in many places has disappeared. Lately, the railway has been attracting a younger generation, too, as a result of its connection with the **Harry Potter films**: Goathland Station was used in the first of the Harry Potter films as **Hogsmeade**, where Harry and co disembarked from the *Hogwarts Express*.

The line, completed by George Stephenson in 1835 just ten years after the opening of the Stockton and Darlington Railway, connects **Pickering** with the Esk Valley (Middlesbrough–Whitby) line at **Grosmont**, eighteen miles to the north. Scheduled **services** operate year-round (limited to weekends and school hols Nov–March), and a **day-return ticket** costs £24. Daily services also run on the Esk Valley line from Grosmont to the nearby seaside resort of Whitby from April to early November, with a return fare from Pickering of £29.

The North Yorkshire coast

The **North Yorkshire coast** is the southernmost stretch of a cliff-edged shore that stretches almost unbroken to the Scottish border. **Scarborough** is the biggest resort, with a full set of attractions and a terrific beach. Cute **Robin Hood's Bay** is the most popular of the coastal villages, with fishing and smuggling traditions, while bluff **Staithes** – a fishing harbour on the far edge of North Yorkshire – has yet to tip over into a full-blown tourist trap. **Whitby**, between the two, is the best stopover, with its fine sands, good facilities, abbey ruins, Georgian buildings and maritime heritage – more than any other local place Whitby celebrates Captain Cook as one of its own. Two of the best sections of the **Cleveland Way** start from Whitby: southeast to Robin Hood's Bay (six miles) and northwest to Staithes (eleven miles), both along thrilling high-cliff paths.

Scarborough

The oldest resort in the country, **SCARBOROUGH** first attracted early seventeenth-century visitors to its newly discovered mineral springs. To the Victorians it was "the Queen of the Watering Places", but Scarborough saw its biggest transformation after World War II, when it became a holiday haven for workers from the industrial heartlands. All the traditional ingredients of a beach resort are still here, from superb, clean sands and kitsch amusement arcades to the more refined pleasures of its tight-knit old-town streets and a genteel round of quiet parks and gardens. Be sure to drop into the **Church of St Mary** (1180), below the castle on Castle Road, whose graveyard contains the tomb of Anne Brontë (see p.609), who died here in 1849.

12

Rotunda Museum
Vernon Rd, YO11 2PS • Tues–Sun 10am–5pm • £3 • ☎ 01723 353665, ⓦ scarboroughmuseumstrust.com
The second-oldest purpose-built museum in the country (the oldest is in Oxford), the **Rotunda Museum** was constructed to the plans of William Smith, the founder of English geology, and opened in 1829. A fascinating building in its own right, it includes in its venerable shell some high-tech displays on geology and local history. The Dinosaur Coast Gallery is particularly child-friendly.

Art Gallery
The Crescent, YO11 2PW • Tues–Sun 10am–5pm • £3 • ☎ 01723 384503 ⓦ scarboroughartgallery.co.uk
Scarborough's **Art Gallery**, housed in an Italianate villa, contains the town's permanent collection – largely the work of local artists, and including paintings, posters and photography – which gives an insight into the way the town has been depicted over the centuries.

Scarborough Castle
Castle Rd, YO11 1HY • April–Sept daily 10am–6pm; Oct daily 10am–5pm; Nov to mid-Feb Sat & Sun 10am–4pm • £5.90; EH • ☎ 01765 608888, ⓦ www.english-heritage.org.uk/visit/places/scarborough-castle
There's no better place to acquaint yourself with the local layout than **Scarborough Castle**, mounted on a jutting headland between two golden-sanded bays. Bronze and Iron Age relics have been found on the wooded castle crag, together with fragments of a fourth-century Roman signalling station, Saxon and Norman chapels and a Viking camp, reputedly built by a Viking with the nickname of Scardi (or "harelip"), from which the town's name derives.

The bays
One fun way to explore **North Bay** is aboard the miniature **North Bay Railway** (Feb–Oct daily 10/11am–4pm; day return £3.90; ☎01723 368791, ⓦnbr.org.uk), which runs for just under a mile between Scarborough's **Sea Life Centre and Marine Sanctuary** at Scalby Mills (daily 10am–5pm; £18, £9.50 online; ☎01723 373414, ⓦvisitsealife.com

/scarborough) and Peasholme Park. For unique entertainment, head to the park for **naval warfare**, when miniature man-powered naval vessels battle it out on the lake (July & Aug Mon, Thurs & Sat; £4; details from the tourist office).

To explore the bays from the water, board one of the pleasure steamers that ply the coastline on one-hour **cruises** or zip across to Casty Rocks on a **speedboat** to view seals and seabirds. All boat tours depart from the harbourside throughout the day between Easter and October (ⓦscarboroughboats.webs.com).

The **South Bay** is more refined, backed by the Valley Gardens and the Italianate meanderings of the South Cliff Gardens, and topped by an esplanade from which a **hydraulic lift** (Feb–Nov daily 9.30am–5pm; 90p) chugs down to the beach.

ARRIVAL AND DEPARTURE SCARBOROUGH

By train The train station is at the top of town facing Westborough.

Destinations Hull (every 2hr; 1hr 30min); Leeds (hourly; 1hr 16min); York (hourly; 50min).

By bus Buses pull up outside the train station or in the surrounding streets. National Express services (direct from London) stop in the car park behind the station.

Destinations Bridlington (hourly; 1hr 18min); Filey (hourly; 30min); Helmsley (hourly; 1hr 30min); Hull (hourly; 1hr 30min); Leeds (hourly; 2hr 40min); Pickering (hourly; 1hr); Robin Hood's Bay (hourly; 38min); Whitby (hourly; 1hr); York (hourly; 1hr 35min).

GETTING AROUND AND INFORMATION

By bus Open-top seafront buses (Feb–Nov daily from 9.30am, every 12–20min; £2 single) run between North Bay to the Spa Complex in South Bay.

Tourist offices Scarborough has two tourist information points; one inside the Stephen Joseph Theatre (Mon–Sat 10am–6pm), and the other by the harbour in RNLI Scarborough (daily 9am–5pm).

ACCOMMODATION

Crescent Hotel The Crescent, YO11 2PP ☎01723 360929, ⓦthecrescenthotel.com. A spacious, slightly old-fashioned hotel catering for both holiday-makers and business folk, with friendly, helpful staff, comprehensive facilities and a fine restaurant, all housed in mid-nineteenth-century splendour. **£107**

Crown Spa Hotel The Esplanade, YO11 2AG ☎01723 357400, ⓦcrownspahotel.com. On the south cliff, overlooking the town, this elegant and traditional hotel and spa brings a bit of luxury to Scarborough. Sea views are extra, but worth it. **£150**

YHA Scarborough Burniston Rd, YO13 0DA, 2 miles north of town ☎01723 361176, ⓦyha.org.uk/hostel /scarborough. In an early seventeenth-century watermill a 15min walk from the sea, this is a good hostel for families with kids. Dorms **£13**, private rooms sleeping four **£60**

EATING AND DRINKING

Café Fish 19 York Place, at the intersection with Somerset Terrace, YO11 2NP ☎01723 500301, ⓦcafe fish.co.uk. More of a top-end fish restaurant than a fish-and-chip shop, where a two-course dinner with wine could feature fish curry, steamed mussels or Thai fishcakes, and will cost from about £30. Gets very busy at weekends. Daily 5.30–10pm.

Café Italia 36 St Nicholas Cliff, YO11 2ES ☎01723 501973. Enchanting, tiny, authentic Italian coffee bar. They stick to what they're good at: excellent coffee, ice cream and cakes. Daily 9am–9pm.

Golden Grid 4 Sandside, YO11 1PE ☎01723 360922, ⓦgoldengrid.co.uk. The harbourside's choicest fish-and-chip establishment, "catering for the promenader since 1883". Offers grilled fish, crab and lobster, a fruits-de-mer platter and a wine list alongside the standard crispy-battered fry-up. Decent portions of fish from £7.80. Easter–Oct Mon–Thurs 10am–8.30pm, Fri 10am–9pm, Sat 10am–9.30pm, Sun 11am–6.30pm; Nov–Easter opens daily 11am, closing varies.

ENTERTAINMENT

Scarborough Open Air Theatre Burniston Rd, YO12 6PF ☎01723 818111, ⓦscarboroughopenairtheatre .com. Europe's largest open-air theatre, built in 1932, hosts a range of top-end concerts and gigs by the likes of Jessie J, Elton John and Status Quo.

Stephen Joseph Theatre Westborough, YO11 1JW ☎01723 370541, ⓦsjt.uk.com. Housed in a former Art Deco cinema, this premieres every new play of local playwright Alan Ayckbourn and promotes strong seasons of theatre and film. There's a good, moderately priced café/ restaurant and a bar open Mon–Sat.

12

Robin Hood's Bay

The most heavily visited spot on this stretch of coast, **ROBIN HOOD'S BAY** is made up of gorgeous narrow streets and pink-tiled cottages toppling down the cliff-edge site, evoking the romance of a time when this was both a hard-bitten fishing community and smugglers' den par excellence. From the upper village, lined with Victorian villas, now mostly B&Bs, it's a very steep walk down the hill to the harbour. The **Old Coastguard Station** (Jan, March, Nov & Dec Sat & Sun 10am–4pm, Feb daily 10am–4pm, April–Oct daily 10am–5pm, late Dec Mon–Wed, Sat & Sun 10am–4pm; free; NT; ☎01947 885900; ⓦnationaltrust.org.uk/yorkshire-coast) has been turned into a visitor centre with displays relating to the area's geology and sealife. When the tide is out, the massive rock beds below are exposed, split by a geological fault line and studded with fossil remains. Robin's Hood's Bay is the traditional finishing point for Alfred Wainwright's 190-mile **Coast-to-Coast Walk** from St Bees, but you might prefer to take the much shorter circular walk (2.5 miles) to **Boggle Hole** and its youth hostel, a mile south, returning inland via the path along the old Scarborough–Whitby railway line.

ARRIVAL AND GETTING AROUND   ROBIN HOOD'S BAY

By bus Robin Hood's Bay is connected to Whitby by Arriva #93 buses (hourly; 20min) and to Scarborough by Arriva #93 buses (hourly; 40min).

By bike A couple of miles northwest of Robin Hood's Bay

at Hawsker, on the A171, Trailways (☎01947 820207, ⓦtrailways.info) is a bike rental outfit based in the old Hawsker train station, perfectly placed for day-trips in either direction along the disused railway line.

INFORMATION

Tourist information Though you can pick up a lot of information at the Old Coastguard Station (see above), the nearest official tourist office is in Whitby (see p.634).

ACCOMMODATION AND EATING

Bay Hotel On the harbour, YO22 4SJ ☎01947 880278, ⓦbayhotel.info. At the traditional start or end of the Coast-to-Coast Walk, this inn offers rooms and bar meals, with main courses at around £9–11. Mon–Sat 11am–11pm, Sun noon–11pm; kitchen daily noon–2pm & 6.30–9pm. __£70__

Swell Café Old Chapel, Chapel St ☎01947 880180, ⓦswellcafe.co.uk. A gift shop and café in an old Wesleyan Chapel, built in 1779, where John Wesley himself once preached. They serve a good range of snacks, sandwiches,

cakes, teas and coffees, and alcoholic drinks, and there are great coastal views from its terrace tables. Daily 9.30am–3.30pm, or later if busy.

YHA Boggle Hole Boggle Hole, Fylingthorpe, YO22 4UQ ☎0845 371 9504, ⓦyha.org.uk/hostel/boggle-hole. In a former mill in a wooded ravine about a mile south of Robin Hood's Bay at Mill Beck, this outstanding hostel has a great location practically on the beach. Dorms __£18__, doubles __£59__

Whitby

If there's one essential stop on the North Yorkshire coast it's **WHITBY**, with its historical associations, atmospheric ruins, fishing harbour, lively music scene and intrinsic charm. The seventh-century clifftop **abbey** here made Whitby one of the key foundations of the early Christian period, and a centre of great learning. Below, on the harbour banks of the River Esk, for a thousand years the local herring boats landed their catch until the great **whaling** boom of the eighteenth century transformed the fortunes of the town. Melville's *Moby Dick* makes much of Whitby whalers such as William Scoresby, and James Cook took his first seafaring steps from the town in 1746, on his way to becoming a national hero. All four of Captain Cook's ships of discovery – the *Endeavour*, *Resolution*, *Adventure* and *Discovery* – were built in this town.

Walking around Whitby is one of its great pleasures. Divided by the River Esk, the town splits into two halves joined by a swing bridge: the cobbled **old town** to the east, and the newer (mostly eighteenth- and nineteenth-century) town across the bridge, generally known as **West Cliff**. **Church Street** is the old town's main thoroughfare, barely changed in aspect since the eighteenth century, though now lined with tearooms and

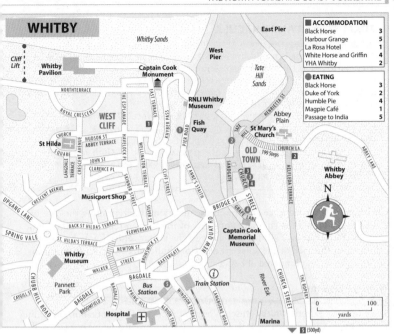

gift shops. Parallel **Sandgate** has more of the same, the two streets meeting at the small **marketplace** where souvenirs and trinkets are sold, and which hosts a farmers' market every Thursday.

Captain Cook Memorial Museum

Grape Lane, YO22 4BA • Daily: Feb–March 11am–3pm; April–Oct 9.45am–5pm • £5.70 • ☎ 01947 601900, ⊛ cookmuseumwhitby.co.uk

Whitby, understandably, likes to make a fuss of Captain Cook, who served an apprenticeship here from 1746–49 under John Walker, a Quaker shipowner. The **Captain Cook Memorial Museum**, housed in Walker's rickety old house, contains an impressive amount of memorabilia, including ships' models, letters and paintings by artists seconded to Cook's voyages.

Church of St Mary

Abbey Plain, YO22 4JT • Daily 10am–4pm

At the north end of Church Street, you climb the famous **199 steps** of the Church Stairs – now paved, but originally a wide wooden staircase built for pall-bearers carrying coffins to the **Church of St Mary** above. This is an architectural amalgam dating back to 1110, boasting a Norman chancel arch, a profusion of eighteenth-century panelling, box pews unequalled in England and a triple-decker pulpit – note the built-in ear trumpets, added for the benefit of a nineteenth-century rector's deaf wife.

Whitby Abbey

Abbey Lane, YO22 4JT • April–Sept daily 10am–6pm; Oct daily 10am–5pm; Nov–March Sat & Sun 10am–4pm • £7.60; EH • ☎ 01947 603568, ⊛ www.english-heritage.org.uk/visit/places/whitby-abbey

The clifftop ruins of **Whitby Abbey** are some of the most evocative in England. Its monastery was founded in 657 by St Hilda of Hartlepool, daughter of King Oswy of Northumberland, and by 664 had become important enough to host the **Synod of Whitby**, an event of seminal importance in the development of English

BRAM STOKER AND DRACULA

The story of **Dracula** is well known, but it's the exact attention to the geographical detail of Whitby – little changed since Bram Stoker first wrote the words – which has proved a huge attraction to visitors. Using first-hand observation of a town he knew well – he stayed at a house on the West Cliff, now marked by a plaque – Stoker built a story which mixed real locations, legend and historical fact: the grounding of Count Dracula's ship on Tate Hill Sands was based on an actual event reported in the local papers.

It's hardly surprising that the town has cashed in on its **Dracula Trail**. The various sites – Tate Hill Sands, the abbey, church and steps, the graveyard, Stoker's house – can all be visited, while down on the harbourside the Dracula Experience attempts to pull in punters to its rather lame horror-show antics. Keen interest has also been sparked among the **Goth** fraternity, who now come to town en masse a couple of times a year (in late spring and around Halloween) for a vampire's ball, concerts and readings.

Christianity. It settled once and for all the question of determining the date of Easter, and adopted the rites and authority of the Roman rather than the Celtic Church. You'll discover all this and more in the **visitor centre** (same hours), which is housed in the shell of the adjacent mansion, built after the Dissolution using material from the plundered abbey.

Whitby Museum

Pannett Park, YO21 1RE • Tues–Sun 9.30am–4.30pm • £5 • ☏ 01947 602908, ⓦ whitbymuseum.org.uk

The gloriously eclectic **Whitby Museum** features more Cook memorabilia, including various objects and stuffed animals brought back as souvenirs by his crew, as well as casefuls of exhibits devoted to Whitby's seafaring tradition, its whaling industry in particular. Some of the best and largest fossils of Jurassic period reptiles unearthed on the east coast are also preserved here.

ARRIVAL AND INFORMATION

By train Whitby's station is in the centre of town on Station Square, just south of the swing bridge, next to the bus station. Whitby is the terminus of the Esk Valley line, which runs from Middlesbrough and connects with the steam trains of the North Yorkshire Moors Railway at Grosmont, which run south to Pickering (see box, p.629).
Destinations Danby (4–5 daily; 40min); Great Ayton (4–5 daily; 1hr 5min); Grosmont (4–5 daily; 16min); Middlesbrough (4–5 daily; 1hr 30min).

By bus The bus station is next to the train station in the centre of town.
Destinations Robin Hood's Bay (hourly; 19min); Staithes (every 30min; 30min); York (4–6 daily; 2hr).
Tourist office On the corner of Langborne Rd and New Quay Rd, opposite the train station (May–Oct daily 9.30am–5pm; Nov–April Thurs–Sun 9.30am–4.30pm; ☏ 01723 383636, ⓦ discoveryorkshirecoast.com or ⓦ visitwhitby.com).

ACCOMMODATION

Black Horse 91 Church St, YO22 4BH ☏ 01947 602906, ⓦ the-black-horse.com; map p.633. Four simple en-suite guest rooms above this fine old pub (see opposite), each named after one of Captain Cook's ships. **£60**
Harbour Grange Spital Bridge, Church St, YO22 4BF ☏ 01947 600817, ⓦ whitbybackpackers.co.uk; map p.633. Backpackers' hostel right on the river (eastern side) with 24 beds from a double up to an eight-bed dorm. Self-catering kitchen and lounge; 11.30pm curfew. **£18**
★**La Rosa Hotel** 5 East Terrace, YO21 3HB ☏ 01947 606981, ⓦ larosa.co.uk; map p.633. Eccentric B&B with themed rooms done out in extravagantly individual style courtesy of auctions, eBay and car boot sales. Great fun, with

terrific views of the harbour and the abbey. Breakfast picnic delivered in a basket to your door. Street parking. **£110**
White Horse and Griffin 87 Church St, YO22 4BH ☏ 01947 604857, ⓦ whitehorseandgriffin.com; map p.633. In the centre of Whitby's old town, with wonderful views of the harbour. Nicely renovated rooms with many original features. It's full of character, but can be noisy. **£120**
YHA Whitby Abbey House, East Cliff, YO22 4JT ☏ 0845 371 9049, ⓦ yha.org.uk/hostel/whitby; map p.633. Flagship hostel in a Grade I listed building next to the Abbey Visitor Centre. Stunning views, good facilities and a Victorian conservatory, tearoom and restaurant. Rates include breakfast and entry to the abbey. Dorms **£15**, doubles **£59**

WHITBY MUSIC SCENE

Whitby has a strong **local music** scene, with an emphasis on folk and world music. During the annual **Whitby Folk Week** (W whitbyfolk.co.uk), held the week preceding the August bank holiday, the town is filled day and night with singers, bands, traditional dancers, storytellers and music workshops. Not-for-profit Musicport (W musicportfestival.com) put on gigs from big names in the world/folk scene and hold a renowned annual World Music Festival at Whitby Pavilion in October. The shop of the same name, Musicport (16 Skinner Street; ☎01947 603475, W musicportshop.com), is a great spot to find out more about live music in the town.

EATING

Black Horse 91 Church St, YO22 4BH ☎01947 602906, W the-black-horse.com; map p.633. Lovely pub (parts date from the seventeenth century) in the old town, with real ales and food served all day, including tapas, Yorkshire cheeses and local seafood. Easter–Nov Mon–Sat 11am–11pm, Sun noon–11pm; Dec–Easter daily noon–4pm & 7–11pm.

★**Duke of York** 124 Church St, YO22 4DE ☎01947 600324, W dukeofyork.co.uk; map p.633. In a great position at the bottom of the 199 steps, this is a warm and inviting pub, with beams, nautical memorabilia, church pews and views across the harbour and West Cliff. Come for good real ales, modern pub food and music. Mon–Thurs & Sun 11am–11pm, Fri 11am–11.30pm, Sat 11am–midnight; kitchen daily noon–9pm.

★**Humble Pie** 163 Church St, YO22 4AS ☎07919 074954, W humblepie.tccdev.com; map p.633. Tiny sixteenth-century building serving a range of pies, cooked fresh to order – steak, stout and leek, Romany, Homity, haggis and neep, and many more – with mash and peas. The decor is 1940s, with World War II background music. All pies £5.99; soft drinks only. Mon–Sat noon–8pm, Sun noon–4pm.

Magpie Café 14 Pier Rd, YO21 3PU ☎01947 602058, W www.magpiecafe.co.uk; map p.633. Said by Rick Stein to be one of the best fish-and-chip shops in the country, the *Magpie* has served food from its 1750-built premises since the start of World War II. To call it a fish-and-chip shop is a bit disingenuous – although it provides the normal takeaway service, it also serves lesser-known fish like Woof and John Dory in its restaurant (from £10.95) and has an extensive wine list. Closed at time of writing because of a fire, but hoping to reopen for the 2018 season.

Passage to India 30–31 Windsor Terrace, YO1 1ET ☎01947 606500, W passagetoindia.eu; map p.633. Stylish tandoori restaurant near the station, with bright red-and-black decor, great food, and friendly, efficient service. Mains £8–12; look out for the tandoori king prawn *karahi* or the Lam Kam. Mon–Thurs 5pm–midnight, Fri 5.30pm–1am, Sat noon–1am, Sun noon–midnight.

12

Staithes

At the northernmost border of the Yorkshire coast is the fishing village of **STAITHES**, an improbably beautiful grouping of huddled stone houses around a small harbour, backed by the severe outcrop of Cowbar Nab, a sheer cliff face that protects the northern flank of the village. James Cook worked here in a draper's shop before moving to Whitby, and he's remembered in the **Captain Cook and Staithes Heritage Centre**, on the High Street (Feb–Nov daily 10am–5pm; Dec & Jan Sat & Sun 10am–5pm; £3; ☎01947 841454, W captaincookatstaithes.co.uk), which recreates an eighteenth-century street, among other interesting exhibits. Other than this, you'll have to content yourself with pottering about the rocks near the harbour – there's no beach to speak of – or clambering the nearby cliffs for spectacular views. At **Boulby**, a mile and a half's trudge up the coastal path (45min), you're walking on the highest cliff (670ft) on England's east coast.

ARRIVAL AND DEPARTURE   STAITHES

On foot There's a fine coastal walk from Whitby, passing pretty Runswick Bay and the village of Sandsend (around 4hr).

By bus The X4 runs daily between Staithes and Whitby (every 30min; 30min).

ACCOMMODATION AND EATING

Endeavour House 1 High St, TS13 5BH ☎01947 841029 (rooms), ☎07969 054556 (restaurant), W endeavour -restaurant.co.uk. Three lovely doubles in this restaurant-B&B located in a two-centuries-old house by the harbour. Parking available in municipal (£6/day) and private (Glen Vale, £5/day) car parks. There's also a restaurant, run separately from the B&B, currently operating as a pop-up. Opening times vary – phone for details. **£100**

The Northeast

TYNE BRIDGE AT NIGHT, NEWCASTLE

13

The Northeast

Post-industrial Tyne and Wear is home to the Northeast's major metropolis, the dynamic and distinctive city of Newcastle upon Tyne. Crammed with cultural attractions, great shops and an exceptionally energetic nightlife, Newcastle is up there with the most exciting cities in England. The bulk of the Northeast is, however, formed by the remote and beautiful county of Northumberland, an enticing medley of delightful market towns, glorious golden beaches, wooded dells, wild uplands and an unsurpassed collection of historical monuments. South of Northumberland lies the county of Durham, famous for its lovely university town and magnificent twelfth-century cathedral.

While its most recent past is defined by industry and in particular post-industrial hardship, the Northeast has an eventful early history: Romans, Vikings and Normans have all left dramatic evidence of their colonization, none more cherished than the 84-mile-long **Hadrian's Wall**, built by the Romans in 122 AD to contain the troublesome tribes of the far north. Thousands come each year to walk along parts, or all, of the Wall, or to cycle the nearby National Route 72. Neighbouring Northumberland National Park also has plenty for outdoors enthusiasts, with the huge **Kielder Water** reservoir, and surrounding footpaths and cycleways.

As well as Roman ruins, medieval **castles** scatter the region, the best-preserved being Alnwick, with its wonderful gardens, and stocky Bamburgh, on the coast. The shoreline round here, from Amble past Bamburgh to the Scottish border town of Berwick-upon-Tweed – and officially the end of Northumberland – is simply stunning, boasting miles of pancake-flat, dune-backed beach and a handful of off-shore islands. Reached by a tidal causeway, the lonely little islet of **Lindisfarne** – Holy Island – where early Christian monks created the Lindisfarne Gospels, is the most famous, while not far away to the south, near Seahouses, the **Farne Islands** are the perfect habitat for large colonies of seabirds including puffins, guillemots and kittiwakes.

South of Northumberland, the counties of **Durham** and **Tyne and Wear** better illustrate the Northeast's industrial heritage. It was here in 1825 that the world's first railway opened – the Darlington and Stockton line – with local coal and ore fuelling the shipbuilding and heavy-engineering companies of Tyneside. Abandoned coalfields, train lines, quaysides and factories throughout the area have been transformed into superb, child-friendly tourist attractions.

GETTING AROUND   **THE NORTHEAST**

By public transport The main East Coast train line runs along the coast from London King's Cross to Edinburgh, calling at Darlington, Durham, Newcastle and Berwick-upon-Tweed, while cross-country trains and buses serve smaller towns and villages inland. In the more remote areas public transport is spotty, so it's best to have your own car or bike.

LINDISFARNE CASTLE, HOLY ISLAND

Highlights

❶ Newcastle nightlife From raucous clubs and chic wine bars to cosy boozers and chilled-out indie gigs, there's something for everybody. **See p.649**

❷ Hadrian's Wall Walk the length of the greatest Roman monument in England. **See p.652**

❸ Northumberland castles Northumberland is littered with beautiful castles, telling of a violent past ridden with ferocious battles and embittered family feuds. **See p.658**

❹ Holy Island A brooding lump of rock reached by a tidal causeway, this is a cradle of

Christianity, where the splendid, illuminated Lindisfarne Gospels were created. **See p.664**

❺ Durham Cathedral Said to be the finest Norman building in Europe, this awe-inspiring cathedral soars above the River Wear. **See p.667**

❻ Beamish Museum Exceptional open-air museum that recreates the Northeast's industrial past. **See p.671**

❼ Killhope Lead Mining Museum Put on a hard hat and get down the pit to see what life was really like for the Weardale coal miners. **See p.674**

HIGHLIGHTS ARE MARKED ON THE MAP ON P.640

THE NORTHEAST

HIGHLIGHTS

1. Newcastle nightlife
2. Hadrian's Wall
3. Northumberland castles
4. Holy Island
5. Durham Cathedral
6. Beamish Museum
7. Killhope Lead Mining Museum

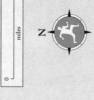

N

NORTH SEA

SCOTLAND

Edinburgh

Edinburgh

Norham Castle

Coldstream

Cornhill-on-Tweed

Branxton

Kirk Yetholm

THE CHEVIOT HILLS

Byrness

REDESDALE

Greenhaugh

Tarset

Stannersburn

KIELDER
FOREST PARK

Kielder

Kielder
Water

Belvedere

Falstone

Kielder
Waterside

Tower

NORTHUMBERLAND NATIONAL PARK

Otterburn

Cambo

Cragside

Rothbury

Newton-on-the-Moor

Morpeth

Ashington

Amble

Warkworth

Alnmouth

Alnwick

Craster

Dunstanburgh Castle

Embleton

Newton-by-the-Sea

Beadnell

Seahouses

Farne Islands

Bamburgh

Waren Mill

Holy Island

Belford

Beal

Scremerston

Berwick-upon-Tweed

Chillingham Castle

Eglingham

Wooler

Ford

Etal

Etal Castle

Heatherslaw Light Railway

Crookham

The Cheviot
(2674ft)

B6525

A697

A1

B1340

A1

A697

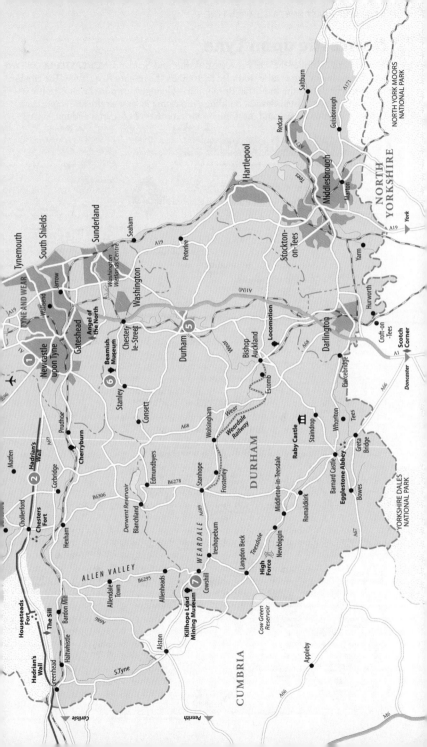

13

Newcastle upon Tyne

The de facto capital of the area between Yorkshire and Scotland, **NEWCASTLE UPON TYNE** was named for its "new castle" founded in 1080 on the mighty River Tyne. The city hit the limelight during the Industrial Revolution – Grainger Town in the city's centre is lined with elegant, listed classical buildings, indicating its past wealth and importance as one of Britain's biggest and most important exporters of coal, iron and machinery.

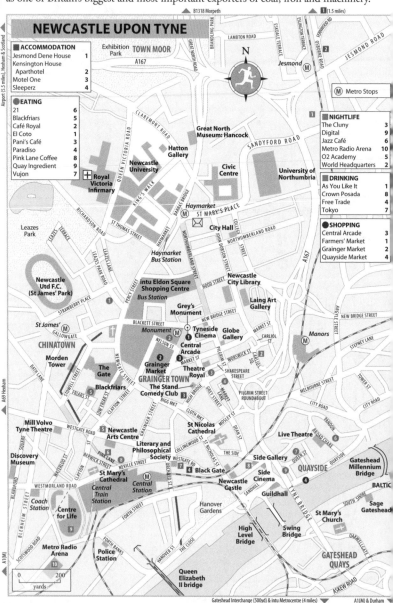

NEWCASTLE UPON TYNE

ACCOMMODATION
Jesmond Dene House	1
Kensington House Aparthotel	2
Motel One	3
Sleeperz	4

EATING
21	6
Blackfriars	5
Café Royal	2
El Coto	1
Pani's Café	3
Paradiso	4
Pink Lane Coffee	8
Quay Ingredient	9
Vujon	7

NIGHTLIFE
The Cluny	3
Digital	9
Jazz Café	6
Metro Radio Arena	10
O2 Academy	5
World Headquarters	2

DRINKING
As You Like It	1
Crown Posada	8
Free Trade	4
Tokyo	7

SHOPPING
Central Arcade	3
Farmers' Market	1
Grainger Market	2
Quayside Market	4

Metro Stops

0 200 yards

13

Although the decline of industry damaged Newcastle badly, today the city has emerged from its post-industrial difficulties with barely a smut on its face. Its reputation for lively nightlife is just the tip of the iceberg; visitors flock here for its collection of top-class art galleries, museums and flourishing theatre scene – not to mention the shopping.

Newcastle Castle

Castle Garth, NE1 1RQ • Daily 10am–5pm • £6.50, purchased at the Black Gate • ☎ 0191 230 6300, ⓦ newcastlecastle.org.uk

Anyone arriving by train from the north will get a sneak preview of the **Castle**, as the rail line splits the keep from its gatehouse, the **Black Gate**, on St Nicholas Street. A wooden fort was built here over an Anglo-Saxon cemetery by Robert Curthose, illegitimate eldest son of William the Conqueror, but the present keep dates from the twelfth century. There's a great view from the rooftop over the river and city.

St Nicholas Cathedral

At the junction of St Nicholas St and Mosley St, NE1 1DF • Mon–Fri & Sun 7.30am–6pm, Sat 8am–4pm • Free, donation requested • ☎ 0191 232 1939, ⓦ stnicholascathedral.co.uk

St Nicholas Cathedral, dating mainly from the fourteenth and fifteenth centuries, is remarkable chiefly for its tower; erected in 1470, it is topped with a crown-like structure of turrets and arches supporting a lantern. Inside, behind the high altar, is one of England's largest funerary brasses, commissioned by Roger Thornton, the Dick Whittington of Newcastle, who arrived in the city penniless and died its richest merchant in 1429.

Quayside

From between the castle and the cathedral a road known simply as The Side – formerly the main road out of the city, and home to the excellent **Side Gallery** – descends to Newcastle's **Quayside**. The river is spanned by seven bridges in close proximity, the most prominent being the looming **Tyne Bridge** of 1928, symbol of the city. Immediately west is the hydraulic **Swing Bridge**, erected in 1876 by Lord Armstrong so that larger vessels could reach his shipyards upriver, while modern road and rail lines cross the river on the adjacent **High Level Bridge**, built by Robert Stephenson in 1849 – Queen Victoria was one of the first passengers to cross, promoting the railway revolution. Beyond the Tyne Bridge is an area of riverside apartments, landscaped promenades, public sculpture and pedestrianized squares, along with a series of fashionable bars and restaurants centred on the graceful **Gateshead Millennium Bridge**, the world's first tilting span, designed to pivot to allow ships to pass.

NEWCASTLE ORIENTATION

Visitors are encouraged to think of the city as **Newcastle Gateshead**, an amalgamation of the two conurbations straddling the Tyne. On Gateshead Quays are the **BALTIC** contemporary arts centre and Norman Foster's **Sage** music centre, and on the opposite side, Newcastle's **Quayside** is where you'll find much of the city's nightlife. The city splits into several distinct areas, with just a few minutes' walk between them. The **castle** and **cathedral** occupy the heights immediately above the River Tyne, while north of here lies the city centre, **Grainger Town**. Chinatown and the two big draws of the **Discovery Museum** and **Centre for Life** are west of the centre, while east is the renowned **Laing Gallery** and, a short walk along the river, the old industrial **Ouseburn** area, home to an alternative cultural scene, interesting galleries, the excellent **Seven Stories** children's museum and some popular bars. In the north of the city, on the university campus, is the **Great North Museum: Hancock**; further north, through the landscaped Exhibition Park, is the **Town Moor**, 1200 acres of common land where freemen of the city – including Jimmy Carter and Bob Geldof – are entitled to graze cattle.

13

A WEEKEND IN NEWCASTLE

FRIDAY NIGHT

There's no point in wasting time: put on your glad rags and head into town for a raucous night out, Geordie-style. Warm up with a pint at the **Crown Posada**, and then move on to sleek *Tokyo* for a cocktail or three and some dancing. Hardcore party people can finish up their night at a **club** – *World Headquarters* and *Digital* are the pick of the bunch.

SATURDAY

Blow the cobwebs away with a breezy walk along the **Quayside**, admiring the melee of beautifully constructed bridges and striking modern buildings that fringe the riverbank. Spend an hour or two in the contemporary art museum, **The Baltic**, and then pop back over the river to the old town, stopping off at the diminutive **Side Gallery**. After all that art, it's time for lunch at lively Sardinian café, *Pani*. In the afternoon, indulge your inner child at the colourful **Seven Stories** literature museum in Ouseburn. While you're in the area, don't miss a visit to the **Biscuit Factory**, if only for a cup of coffee and a cake in their cute café. The best place to spend Saturday night is at the artsy **Cluny** bar, particularly if there's live music or a theatre recital going on.

SUNDAY

Explore Newcastle's architectural heritage – take a trip up to the gloomy **castle** and the adjacent **cathedral**, and then follow the ruins of the old city wall and medieval towers along **Stowell Street**. For lunch you could choose one of the many **Chinese restaurants** near the wall, or tuck into a large Sunday roast at the snug and traditional *Blackfriars*. Walk off your meal and expand your scientific knowledge at the **Centre of Life** museum, and the nearby **Discovery Museum**. If you're all partied and museumed out, put your feet up and munch on popcorn at Newcastle's art-house cinema, **The Tyneside**.

BALTIC

By the Millennium Bridge, Gateshead Quays, NE8 3BA • Mon & Wed–Sun 10am–6pm, Tues 10.30am–6pm • Free • ☎ 0191 478 1810, ⓦ balticmill.com

Fashioned from an old brick flourmill, **BALTIC** sits on the Gateshead riverbank, by the Millennium Bridge. Designed to be a huge visual "art factory", it's second only in scale to London's Tate Modern. There's no permanent collection here – instead there's an ever-changing calendar of exhibitions and local community projects, as well as artists' studios, education workshops, an art performance space and cinema, plus a rooftop restaurant with uninterrupted views of the Newcastle skyline.

Sage Gateshead

St Mary's Square, Gateshead Quays, NE8 2JR • Daily 9am–late • ☎ 0191 443 4666, ⓦ sagegateshead.com

Sitting on the riverbank, the **Sage Gateshead** is an extraordinary billowing steel, aluminium and glass concert hall complex, best seen at night when it glows with many colours. It's home to the Royal Northern Sinfonia orchestra and Folkworks, an organization promoting British and international traditional music, and there's something on most nights – from music concerts to workshops and lectures, as well as the Gateshead International Jazz Festival every April. The public concourse provides marvellous river and city views, and there are bars, a café and a brasserie.

Ouseburn

The **Ouseburn area**, fifteen minutes' walk up the River Tyne from Millennium Bridge, was once at the heart of Newcastle's industrial activities but became a derelict backwater in the mid-twentieth century. A jumble of old Victorian mills and warehouses, Ouseburn has seen a remarkable rejuvenation, as artists, musicians, businesses and even residents move in. Lime Street, home to quirky live-music venue, **The Cluny** (see p.649), artists' workshops and the nationally renowned **Seven Stories**, is the hub, but there are plenty of attractions nearby including Europe's biggest commercial art space, the **Biscuit Factory** (see box opposite), plus an art-house cinema, riding stables and a small working farm.

Seven Stories

30 Lime St, NE1 2PQ • Tues–Sat 10am–5pm, Sun & bank hols 10am–4pm • £7.70, under-17s £6.60 • ☎ 0300 330 1095 ext 300, Ⓦ sevenstories.org.uk

Housed in a beautifully converted Victorian riverside mill and spread over seven floors, **Seven Stories** celebrates the art of children's books through displays of original artwork, manuscripts and related documents. The bright, interactive exhibitions change regularly but highlights include original sketches taken from Noel Streatfield's *Ballet Shoes*, material from *Charlie and the Chocolate Factory* by Roald Dahl, Philip Pullman's early drafts, and the unpublished novel by Enid Blyton, *Mr Tumpy's Caravan*. Kids get the opportunity to dress up and create their own artworks; there is also a simple café.

Grainger Town

The heart of the city is known as **Grainger Town**, one of the best-looking city centres in Britain. Thrown up in a few short mid-nineteenth-century years by businessmen-builders and architects such as Richard Grainger, Thomas Oliver and John Dobson, the area is known for its classical stone facades lining splendid, wide streets and, in particular, **Grey Street**, named for the second Earl Grey (he of the tea), prime minister from 1830 to 1834. In 1832, Grey carried the Reform Act – which granted seats in the House of Commons to large cities that had developed during the Industrial Revolution, like Newcastle – through parliament, an act commemorated by **Grey's Monument** at the top of the street. The restored **Grainger Market** (Mon–Sat 9am–5.30pm, Ⓦ graingermarket.org.uk), nearby, was Europe's largest covered market when built in the 1830s, and is today home to the smallest branch of Marks & Spencer, known as the Original Penny Bazaar.

Centre for Life

Times Square, NE1 4EP • Mon–Sat 10am–6pm, Sun 11am–6pm; last admission 4pm • £13, under-18s £7.50 • ☎ 0191 243 8210, Ⓦ life.org.uk

A five-minute walk west of Central Station, the sleek buildings of the **Centre for Life** reach around the sweeping expanse of Times Square. This ambitious "science village" project combines bioscience and genetics research with a science visitor centre that aims to convey the secrets of life using the latest entertainment technology. Children find the whole thing enormously rewarding – from the sparkling Planetarium to the motion simulator – so expect to spend a good three hours here, if not more.

Discovery Museum

Blandford Square, NE1 4JA • Mon–Fri 10am–4pm, Sat & Sun 11am–4pm • Free • ☎ 0191 232 6789, Ⓦ twmuseums.org.uk

The **Discovery Museum** concentrates on the maritime history of Newcastle and Tyneside, and their role in Britain's scientific and technological developments. Highlights include the *Turbinia* – the first ship to be powered by a steam turbine – which dominates the museum entrance, and the Newcastle Story, a walk through the city's past with tales from animatronic characters along the way.

Literary and Philosophical Society

23 Westgate Rd, NE1 1SE • Mon, Wed & Thurs 9.30am–7pm, Tues 9.30am–8pm, Fri 9.30am–5pm, Sat 9.30am–1pm • Free • ☎ 0191 232 0192, Ⓦ litandphil.org.uk

Known as the **Lit and Phil**, this temple-like public library and learned society occupies one of the city's finest Georgian buildings: the domed roof, stucco ceilings and

13

wrought-iron galleries are well worth a look. Established in 1825, it now runs a programme of recitals, jazz concerts, talks and exhibitions.

Laing Art Gallery

New Bridge St, NE1 8AG • Tues–Sat 10am–5pm, Sun 2–5pm • Free • ⓦ laingartgallery.org.uk

The **Laing Art Gallery**, in the east of the city, is home to the northeast's premier art collection: the permanent display is a sweep through British art from the seventeenth century to today, featuring sculpture from Henry Moore and a large collection of John Martin's fiery landscapes, along with a smattering of Pre-Raphaelites, a group much admired by the English industrial barons. Another permanent display highlights a superb collection of Newcastle silver dating from the seventeenth century and some colourful 1930s glassware by George Davidson.

Newcastle University

A short walk north of Haymarket Metro are two sites of interest on the **Newcastle University** campus.

Great North Museum: Hancock

Barras Bridge, NE2 4PT • Mon–Fri 10am–5pm, Sat 10am–4pm, Sun 11am–4pm • Free, planetarium £2.50 • ☎ 0191 208 6765, ⓦ greatnorthmuseum.org.uk

The **Great North Museum: Hancock** has an engaging mishmash of natural history exhibits – there's a knobbly T-Rex skeleton, some stuffed animals and an aquarium – historical artefacts such as the large-scale replica Hadrian's Wall, and a planetarium.

Hatton Gallery

Kings Rd, NE1 7RU • Mon–Sat 10am–5pm • Free • ☎ 0191 208 6059, ⓦ hattongallery.org.uk

Just across the street from the Great North Museum is the newly reopened bijou **Hatton Gallery** (ⓦ hattongallery.org.uk), famous for housing the only surviving example of German Dadaist Kurt Schwitters' *Merzbau* (a sort of architectural collage).

ARRIVAL AND DEPARTURE	NEWCASTLE UPON TYNE

By plane Newcastle International Airport is 6 miles north of the city (☎ 0871 882 1121, ⓦ newcastleairport.com). It is linked by the Metro to Central Station (every 7–15min 5.45am–midnight; 22min; £4.70) and beyond. You can also take a taxi into the centre (around £18).

By train Central Station is a 5min walk from the city centre or Quayside, and has a Metro station.

Destinations Alnmouth (hourly; 25min); Berwick-upon-Tweed (hourly; 45min); Carlisle (hourly; 1hr 30min); Darlington (frequent; 35min); Durham (frequent; 15min); Hexham (every 30min; 40min); London (every 30min; 2hr 45min–3hr 15min); York (frequent; 1hr).

By bus National Express coaches stop on St James's Boulevard/Churchill St, not far from Central Station, while regional buses stop at Haymarket bus station (Haymarket Metro). Gateshead Interchange is a big bus station served by local and national buses, linked by Metro to the city centre.

Destinations Alnmouth (every 30min; 1hr 30min); Alnwick (every 30min; 1hr 20min); Bamburgh (Mon–Sat 3 daily, Sun 2 daily; 2hr 30min); Beamish (April–Oct daily, Nov–March Sat & Sun; every 30min; 1hr); Berwick-upon-Tweed (Mon–Sat 8 daily; 2hr 30min); Carlisle (Mon–Sat hourly; 2hr 10min); Craster (Mon–Sat 7 daily, Sun 4 daily; 1hr 50min); Durham (Mon–Sat every 30min, Sun 4–6 daily; 50min)

THE GEORDIE NATION

Tyneside and Newcastle's native inhabitants are known as **Geordies**, the word probably derived from a diminutive of the name "George". There are various explanations of who George was (King George II, railwayman George Stephenson), all plausible, none now verifiable. Geordies speak a highly distinctive dialect and accent, heavily derived from Old English. Phrases you're likely to come across include: haway man! (come on!), scran (food), a'reet (hello) and propa belta (really good) – and you can also expect to be widely addressed as "pet" or "flower".

NEWCASTLE ART GALLERIES

Biscuit Factory 16 Stoddart St, Ouseburn, NE1 2NP ☎0191 261 1103, ⓦthebiscuitfactory.com. Britain's largest commercial art gallery, displaying and selling anything from pendulum clocks and carved wooden tables to ceramic teapots and quirky necklaces. Free. Mon–Fri 10am–5pm, Sat 10am–6pm, Sun 11am–5pm.

Globe Gallery 47 Pilgrim St, NE1 6QE ☎0191 597 9377, ⓦglobegallery.org. Contemporary arts space that supports local, up-and-coming artists; it hosts a variety of exhibitions and one-off events.

Free. Wed–Sat noon–5pm.

Northern Print Stepney Bank, Ouseburn, NE1 2NP ☎0191 261 7000, ⓦnorthernprint.org.uk. Little gallery that sells affordable prints by local artists. You can also learn how to make prints at the studio's workshop. Free. Wed–Sat noon–4pm.

Side Gallery 5–9 Side, NE1 3JE ☎0191 232 2208, ⓦamber-online.com. A long-established, collectively run space with a strong specialism in social documentary photography. Free. Tues–Sun 11am–5pm.

Hexham (hourly; 50min); Middlesbrough (Mon–Sat every 30min; 1hr); Rothbury (Mon–Sat hourly, Sun 2 daily; 1hr 30min); Seahouses (Mon–Sat 3 daily, Sun 2 daily; 2hr 10min); Warkworth (daily every 30min; 1hr 20min).

GETTING AROUND

By Metro The convenient, easy-to-use Tyne and Wear Metro (daily 5.30am–midnight, every 5–10min or 10–20min in the evening) connects the city centre with the airport and runs out to the suburbs. You can buy a Metro Day Saver ticket for unlimited rides in all zones (£5).

By bus All city and local buses stop at Eldon Square shopping centre. Quaylink buses connect major attractions in Newcastle and Gateshead Quays with Newcastle Central Station, Haymarket Bus Station and Gateshead Interchange. Buses run frequently daily (day ticket from £5.10).

By bike Rent bikes at The Cycle Hub, Quayside (☎0191 276 7250, ⓦthecyclehub.org). Town bikes £10/2hr.

By taxi There are taxi ranks at Haymarket, Grey St (near the Theatre Royal) and outside Central Station. To book, contact Noda Taxis (☎0191 222 1888, ⓦnoda-taxis.co.uk).

INFORMATION AND TOURS

Tourist information Up-to-date visitor information is available online (ⓦnewcastlegateshead.com) and maps and brochures are available at hotels and attractions across Newcastle and Gateshead.

Public transport information Nexus Traveline has shops at the Central Station, Haymarket, Monument and Gateshead Metro stations (☎0191 202 0747, ⓦnexus.org.uk).

Tours City tours and various tours to Hadrian's Wall, Northumberland and Durham are run by Newcastle City Tours (from £40 per group of seven people max; ☎07780 958679, ⓦnewcastlecitytours.co.uk) while River Escapes Cruises' sightseeing boats (£6/10/12; ☎01670 785666, ⓦriverescapes.co.uk) depart most weekends throughout the year, and other days in summer, from the Quayside. A hop-on hop-off, open-top sightseeing bus departs from Central Station (April–June, Sept & Oct Sat & Sun only, July & Aug daily; every 30min–1hr; £8; ☎01789 299123, ⓦcity-sightseeing.com). Saddle Skedaddle (ⓦskedaddle .co.uk) organizes C2C (sea-to-sea) cycle tours and trips to Hadrian's Wall from £250/3 days.

ACCOMMODATION

Budget **hotel chains** offer plenty of good-value rooms in the city centre and down by the Quayside, while the biggest concentration of small hotels and guesthouses lies a mile north of the centre in popular, student-filled Jesmond, along and off Osborne Road: take bus #33 from Central Station or Haymarket.

★**Jesmond Dene House** Jesmond Dene Rd, Jesmond, NE2 2EY ☎0191 212 3000, ⓦjesmonddenehouse .co.uk; map p.642. An imposing Arts and Crafts house in a very peaceful wooded valley. The sleek, boldly decorated rooms are decked out in decadent velvet and silk furnishings and have enormous bathrooms with underfloor heating. There's fine dining in the garden-room restaurant and breakfasts are particularly luxurious, with smoked salmon, a range of cooked meats and champagne on offer. Rates vary; book well in advance. **£110**

Kensington House Aparthotel 5 Osborne Rd, Jesmond, NE2 2AU ☎0191 281 8175, ⓦkensingtonaparthotel.com; map p.642. Twenty-three upmarket apartments of varying sizes, conveniently situated near Jesmond Metro. The decor is modern and sleek, with wood floors, cream carpets and marble kitchen surfaces. Beds are kitted out with luxurious Egyptian cotton sheets and feather down duvets. Six apartments have wheelchair access. **£115**

Motel One 15–25 High Bridge, NE1 1EW ☎0191 211 1090, ⓦmotel-one.com/en; map p.642. This new 222-bed

13

budget chain hotel has retained period features while embracing modern style. Rooms are small but perfectly formed and staff go the extra mile. Breakfast extra. **£59**

Sleeperz 15 Westgate Rd, NE1 1SE ☎0191 261 6171, ⓦ sleeperz.com/newcastle; map p.642. A great-value option in the heart of town, part of a little chain that marries functionality with good design. Despite the city-centre location, the 98 compact but comfortable rooms provide a quiet respite from Saturday-night mayhem, and there's a funky breakfast bar/café downstairs. **£52**

EATING

Newcastle has a great variety of places to eat, from expensive, top-quality restaurants showcasing the talents of young and creative chefs, to fun, relaxed cafés and budget-friendly Chinese restaurants (mostly around Stowell Street in Chinatown). The popular chain restaurants are down by the Quayside.

21 Trinity Gardens, NE1 2HH ☎0191 222 0755, ⓦ 21newcastle.co.uk; map p.642. Parisian-style bistro with crisp white tablecloths, leather banquettes, a classic French menu and slick service. Expect dishes like confit of duck with Lyonnaise potatoes (£20.50) or smoked haddock with softly poached hen's egg (£18.20), and delicious desserts – the Florentine doughnut with strawberry jam and crème Chantilly (£7.20) is particularly good. Mon–Sat noon–2.30pm & 5.30–10.30pm, Sun noon–8pm.

★ Blackfriars Friars St, NE1 4XN ☎0191 261 5945, ⓦ blackfriarsrestaurant.co.uk; map p.642. Housed in a beautiful stone building dating to 1239, *Blackfriars* offers superb traditional British dishes made with local ingredients. Mains (from £15) could include pork loin with a bacon and cheese floddie (potato cakes, originating from Gateshead, and traditionally eaten for breakfast) or a Doddington cheese and onion Wellington with chive cream sauce. For afters, dig into sticky toffee pudding with green grape ice cream and Brown Ale caramel (puddings from £6). Book ahead. Mon–Sat noon–2.30pm & 5.30pm–late, Sun noon–4pm.

Café Royal 8 Nelson St, NE1 5AW ☎0191 231 3000, ⓦ sjf.co.uk; map p.642. Bright and buzzy café with great smoothies, coffees and delectable home-made breads and cakes – try the raspberry scones with clotted cream (£3.50) or hazelnut twists (£2). Mon–Sat 8am–6pm, Sun 10am–3.30pm.

El Coto 21 Leazes Park Rd, NE1 4PF ☎0191 261 0555, ⓦ elcoto.co.uk; map p.642. Cute and cosy, this great tapas place has an extensive, good-value menu featuring all the usuals, such as *patatas bravas* and marinated sardines – dishes cost around £5, though paella goes for £10 per person. Daily noon–11pm.

Pani's Café 61–65 High Bridge St NE1 6BX ☎0191 232 4366, ⓦ paniscafe.co.uk; map p.642. On a side street below the Theatre Royal, this lively Sardinian café has won a loyal clientele for its good-value sandwiches, pasta and salads (mains around £8). Mon–Sat 10am–10pm.

Paradiso 1 Market Lane, NE1 6QQ ☎0191 221 1240, ⓦ paradiso.co.uk; map p.642. Mellow café-bar hidden down an alley off Pilgrim Street – the snack food in the daytime becomes more substantial at night, with truffle risotto, salmon steaks and the like. There are set menus throughout the day (two courses: lunchtime £9.95, evening £16.95) as well as a la carte. You can dine outdoors on the terrace in good weather. Mon–Thurs 11am–2.30pm & 5–10.30pm, Fri & Sat 11am–10.45pm.

Pink Lane Coffee 1 Pink Lane, NE1 5DW ☎07841 383085, ⓦ pinklanecoffee.co.uk; map p.642. The best coffee in town: their beans are slow roasted and the milk is Northumbrian Pedigree. Exposed light bulbs, reclaimed furniture and brickwork tiling makes for an uber-hip interior. Mon–Fri 7.30am–6pm, Sat 9am–5pm, Sun 10am–4pm.

Quay Ingredient 4 Queen St, Quayside, NE1 3UG ☎0191 447 2327, ⓦ quayingredient.co.uk; map p.642. Teeny tiny and popular, so it's best to get here early for brunch at weekends. Full English (£6.95) or eggs benedict (£5.95), plus sandwiches and salads (from £4.95) and delicious cakes (sweet muffin £1). Great coffee, too. Daily 8am–5pm.

Vujon 29 Queen St, NE1 3UG ☎0191 221 0601, ⓦ vujon.com; map p.642. The city's classiest Indian restaurant, housed in an elegant building by the Quayside, serving dishes a cut above the ordinary, from venison Jaipur-style with chilli jam (£15.90) to the spicy duck *salan* (£14.90). Daily 5.30–11.30pm.

DRINKING

Newcastle's boisterous pubs, bars and clubs are concentrated in several areas: in the **Bigg Market** (between Grey St and Grainger St), around the **Quayside** and in the developing **Ouseburn** area, where bars tend to be quirkier and more sophisticated; in **Jesmond**, with its thriving student-filled strip of café-bars; and in the mainstream leisure-and-cinema complex known as **The Gate** (Newgate St). The main **LGBT+** area, known as the "Pink Triangle", focuses on the Centre for Life, spreading out to Waterloo Street and Westmorland and Scotswood roads.

As You Like It Archbold Terrace, NE2 1DB ☎0191 281 2277, ⓦ asyoulikeitjesmond.com; map p.642. The top bar in the Jesmond area sits incongruously beneath an ugly tower block. This funky bar/restaurant has a relaxed vibe, exposed brick walls and a mishmash of furniture. The Supper Club, a club night on Fri & Sat (10pm–2am) features jazz, blues and soul. Mon–Thurs & Sun noon–midnight, Fri & Sat noon–2am.

Crown Posada 31 Side, NE1 3JE ☎ 0191 232 1269, ⓦ sjf .co.uk; map p.642. A proper old man's boozer: local beers and guest ales in this small wood-and-glass-panelled Victorian pub. You might fancy the dark, malty Hadrian's Gladiator (£3.80) or opt for the golden, hoppy Tyneside Blonde (£3.80). Mon–Wed noon–11pm, Thurs 11am–11pm, Fri 11am–midnight, Sat noon–midnight, Sun noon–10.30pm.

★ **Free Trade** St Lawrence Rd, NE6 1AP ☎ 0191 265 5764; map p.642. Walk along the Newcastle Quayside past the Millennium Bridge and look for the shabby pub on the hill, where you are invited to "drink beer, smoke tabs" with the city's pub cognoscenti. Cask beer from local microbreweries, a great free juke box and superb river views from the beer garden. Mon–Thurs 11am–11pm, Fri & Sat 11am–midnight, Sun noon–11pm.

Tokyo 17 Westgate Rd, NE1 1SE ☎ 0191 232 1122, ⓦ tokyonewcastle.co.uk; map p.642. The dark, sleek main bar is handsome enough, but follow the tealights up the stairs to the outdoor "garden" bar lined by plants and trees, giving the area a secret, exclusive feel. A pre-club favourite for Shindig (see below). Mon, Tues & Sun 5pm–midnight, Wed & Thurs 5pm–1am, Fri & Sat 5pm–2am.

NIGHTLIFE

Newcastle's biggest club night is **Shindig**, taking place on Saturdays and switching locations around the city. See ⓦ shindiguk.com for the latest. Gigs, club nights and the gay scene are reviewed exhaustively in *The Crack* (monthly; free; ⓦ thecrackmagazine.com), available in shops, pubs and bars.

CLUBS

Digital Times Square, NE1 4EP ☎ 0191 261 9755, ⓦ yourfutureisdigital.com/newcastle; map p.642. The city's top club, with an amazing sound system pumping out a variety of musical genres. If you like cheesy classics, look out for Born in the Sixties nights; while house, funk and disco fans will get their fix on Saturday's Love nights. Mon & Thurs 10.30pm–2.30am, Fri & Sat 11pm–3.30am.

World Headquarters Carliol Square, East Pilgrim St, NE1 6UF ☎ 0191 281 3445, ⓦ welovewhq.com; map p.642. Smallish and down-to-earth club that's always packed. Music is a medley of house, hip-hop, soul and r'n'b and reggae. Downstairs there's a comfy lounge area with squashy sofas and a pool table. Entry fee around £10. Fri & Sat 10.30pm–3am.

LIVE MUSIC VENUES

★ **The Cluny** 36 Lime St, Ouseburn, NE1 2PQ ☎ 0191 230 4474, ⓦ thecluny.com; map p.642. Based in an old whisky bottling plant, this is the best small music venue in the city, with something going on most nights, from quirky indie bands to contemporary punk-pop. *Cluny 2*, around the corner at 34 Lime Street (same hours), is its spacious sister venue, with less frequent gigs. Mon–Fri noon–11pm, Fri & Sat noon–1am, Sun noon–10.30pm.

Jazz Café 23–25 Pink Lane, NE1 5DW ☎ 0191 232 6505, ⓦ jazzcafe-newcastle.co.uk; map p.642. Slick and intimate jazz club in inauspicious surroundings, hosting top-quality jazz from 9.30pm on Friday and Saturday nights. Tues–Thurs 11am–11pm, Fri & Sat 11am–1am.

Metro Radio Arena Arena Way, NE4 7NA ☎ 0844 493 4567, ⓦ metroradioarena.co.uk; map p.642. The biggest concert and exhibition venue in the Northeast; star appearances have included Lady Gaga, Dolly Parton and The Killers. Book popular gigs well in advance.

02 Academy Westgate Rd, NE1 1SW ☎ 0844 477 2000, ⓦ o2academynewcastle.co.uk; map p.642. Housed in the former bingo hall, this mainstream venue hosts a variety of big names and local talent.

ENTERTAINMENT

Live Theatre 27 Broad Chare, NE1 3DQ ☎ 0191 232 1232, ⓦ live.org.uk; map p.642. Enterprising theatre company that aims to find and develop local, and particularly young, talent – the attached *Caffe Vivo* is good for coffee by day and pre-theatre meal deals by night.

Mill Volvo Tyne Theatre 111 Westgate Rd, NE1 4AG ☎ 0844 493999, ⓦ millvolvotynetheatre.co.uk; map p.642. Beautifully restored Victorian theatre with a wide range of plays, comedy shows and gigs.

Side Cinema 3 Side, NE1 3JE ☎ 0191 232 2000, ⓦ amber-online.com; map p.642. A quaintly dishevelled fifty-seat cinema: they run an imaginative programme combining art-house movies with live music.

The Stand Comedy Club 31 High Bridge, NE1 1EW ☎ 0191 300 9700, ⓦ thestand.co.uk; map p.642. Great venue for comedy downstairs, with great pub food and a lovely courtyard upstairs. Laidback and friendly, with something showing every night of the week.

Theatre Royal 100 Grey St, NE1 6BR ☎ 0844 811 2121, ⓦ theatreroyal.co.uk; map p.642. Grand venue for drama, opera, dance, musicals and comedy; also hosts the annual RSC season in Nov.

Tyneside Cinema 10 Pilgrim St, NE1 6QG ☎ 0845 217 9909, ⓦ tynesidecinema.co.uk; map p.642. The city's premier art-house cinema, with coffee, light meals and movie talk in the Art Deco cinema café. The gorgeous restored decor includes Persian-inspired gilded stucco, stained glass and mosaic floors.

13

SHOPPING

Newcastle has two shopping centres, the central intu Eldon Square (ⓦintu.co.uk/eldonsquare) and the vast intu Metrocentre (ⓦintu.co.uk/metrocentre), 4 miles west of the city centre.

Central Arcade Grainger Town, NE1 6EG; map p.642. A classy Edwardian arcade with a barrel-vaulted roof. Several high-end chain stores here include Office, Jones, Space NK and JG Windows (with its lovely window display of musical instruments). Daily 9am–5pm.

Farmers' Market Grey's Monument, NE1 7AL; map p.642. Central market selling wonderful locally sourced fruit and veg, jams, meats and fish. First Fri of each month 9.30am–2.30pm.

Grainger Market Grainger Town, NE1 5JQ;

ⓦgraingermarket.org.uk; map p.642. One of the city's oldest and best shopping experiences: a centrally located Georgian market painted in pastel colours and featuring old-fashioned fishmongers, butchers and a hardware store alongside delis, gift shops and a French café. Mon–Sat 9am–5.30pm.

Quayside Market NE1 3DE; map p.642. Busy, popular market down on the quayside selling locally produced food, clothes and arts and crafts including jewellery. Sun 9.30am–4pm.

DIRECTORY

Hospital Royal Victoria Infirmary, Queen Victoria Rd (ⓣ0191 233 6161, ⓦwww.newcastle-hospitals.org.uk) has 24hr A&E services and a Minor Injuries Unit (daily 8am–9pm). The Westgate Walk-in Centre at Newcastle General Hospital, Westgate Road, is open daily (8am–8pm).

Police Newcastle City Centre Police Station, Forth Banks ⓣ0191 214 6555.

Around Newcastle

There are a number of attractions near Newcastle, all accessible by Metro. The train runs east towards **Wallsend**, where **Segedunum** fort marks the beginning of Hadrian's Wall, while out at Jarrow, **Bede's Museum** pays homage to Christianity's most important historian. Further out again is the splendid **Washington Wildfowl Centre** near Sunderland, while the Angel and the Goddess of the North are two striking pieces of public art south and north of Newcastle respectively.

Wallsend and Segedunum

Budle St, Wallsend, NE28 6HR, 4 miles east of Newcastle • June to mid-Oct 10am–6pm • £5.95 • ⓣ0191 236 9347, ⓦsegedunumromanfort.org.uk • Metro to Wallsend

Wallsend was the last outpost of Hadrian's great border defence and **Segedunum**, the "strong fort" a couple of minutes' signposted walk from the Metro station, has been admirably developed as one of the prime attractions along the Wall. The grounds contain a fully reconstructed bathhouse, complete with heated pools and colourful frescoes, while the "wall's end" itself is visible at the edge of the site, close to the river and Swan Hunter shipyard. From here, the **Hadrian's Wall Path** (see box, p.653) runs 84 miles westwards to Bowness-on-Solway in Cumbria; you can get your walk "passport" stamped inside the museum.

Jarrow Hall

On the edge of Jarrow, NE32 3DY, 5 miles east of Newcastle • Daily: Feb & March 10am–4.30pm; April–Sept 10am–5.30pm • £5 • ⓣ0191 424 1585, ⓦjarrowhall.org.uk • Newcastle Metro to Jarrow, from where it's a 20min walk through the industrial estate

Jarrow Hall sits at the edge of the town of **JARROW** – ingrained on the national consciousness since the 1936 **Jarrow Crusade**, when 201 people marched three hundred miles down to London to protest against the government's refusal to ease unemployment and poverty in the Northeast. The complex is made up of the eighteenth-century Jarrow Hall House; a reconstructed Anglo Saxon Farm and Village; and the **Bede Museum**, which explores the life of Venerable Bede (673–735 AD), who lived here as a boy. Bede grew up to become one of Europe's greatest scholars and England's first historian – his *History of the English Church and People*, describing the struggles of the island's early Christians, was completed at Jarrow in 731.

Angel of the North

6 miles south of Newcastle upon Tyne, off A167 (signposted Gateshead South), NE9 7TY • Bus #21 from Eldon Shopping Centre; there's car parking at the site

Since 1998, Antony Gormley's 66ft-high **Angel of the North** has stood sentinel over the A1 at Gateshead. A startling steel colossus that greets anyone travelling up from the south by rail or road, it's sited on top of a former coal-mining site, and has become both a poignant eulogy for the days of industry and a symbol of resurgence and regeneration.

Goddess of the North

Cramlington, NE23 8AU, 9 miles north of Newcastle upon Tyne • Daily dawn–dusk, café & visitor centre July & Aug 10am–4pm • Ⓦ northumberlandia.com • Cramlington's train station is 2.5 miles from the site, or take bus #X13 from Newcastle

The Angel of the North (see above) has a rival in Charles Jencks' **Goddess of the North** (or *Northumberlandia*), a gigantic landscaped sculpture laid out as a park. Made out of 1.5 million tonnes of earth from Shotton mine and an epic 34m-high and 400m-long, the recumbent naked Goddess was unveiled in 2013.

Washington Wildfowl and Wetlands Centre

Pattinson, NE38 8LE, 10 miles east of Newcastle • Daily: April–Oct 9.30am–5.30pm; Nov–March 9.30am–4.30pm • £9.45 • ☎ 0191 416 5454, Ⓦ wwt.org.uk • Bus #8 from Sunderland (Mon–Sat only) stops at the Waterview Park, a short walk from the wildfowl centre; from Newcastle, take the Metro to Washington

Taking up one hundred acres of the north bank of the River Wear in Pattinson, the popular **Washington Wildfowl and Wetlands Centre** is a lush conservation area of meadows, woods and wetlands that acts as a winter habitat for migratory birds, including geese, waders and ducks. In summer, you can watch fluffy ducklings hatch in the Waterfowl Nursery.

Sunderland

SUNDERLAND is fifteen miles southeast of Newcastle and shares that city's long history, river setting and industrial heritage – but cannot match its architectural splendour. However, it's worth a trip to visit the Sunderland Museum, easily accessible by Metro from Newcastle.

Sunderland Museum

Burdon Road, SR1 1PP • Mon–Sat 10am–4pm, Sun noon–4pm • Free • ☎ 0191 561 2323

The **Sunderland Museum** does a very good job of telling the city's history, relating how Sunderland ships were once sent around the world, and also has much to say about the city's other major trades, notably its production of lustreware and glass. The **Winter Gardens**, housed in a steel-and-glass hothouse, invite a treetop walk to view the impressive polished-steel column of a water sculpture.

Riverside

Across the River Wear, the landscaped **Riverside** is actually the oldest settled part of the city: walk up Fawcett Street and then Bridge Street from the centre and cross Wearmouth Bridge (around 20min). Along the north bank of the river, in front of the university buildings, the early Christian church of **St Peter** (674 AD) is the elder sibling of St Paul's Church at Jarrow and displays fragments of the oldest stained glass in the country.

By Metro The main stop for Metros from Newcastle (30–35min) is in the central train station opposite The Bridges shopping centre.

Website ⓦ seeitdoitsunderland.co.uk is a great site for visitors; it also lists visitor information points around the city where you can pick up maps and brochures.

Hadrian's Wall

Hadrian's Wall (ⓦhadrianswallcountry.co.uk) was constructed in 122 AD at the behest of the Roman emperor Hadrian. Keen for peace and safety within his empire, fearing attacks from Pictish Scotland, Hadrian commissioned a long wall to act as a border, snaking its way from the Tyne to the Solway Firth. It was built up to a height of 15ft in places and was interspersed by milecastles, which functioned as gates, depots and mini-barracks. The best-preserved portions of the Wall are concentrated between **Chesters Roman Fort**, four miles north of Hexham, and Haltwhistle, sixteen miles to the west, which passes **Housesteads Roman Fort**, **Vindolanda** and the **Roman Army Museum**. Most people come to walk or cycle the length of the Wall, but if you're only planning to walk a short stretch, start off at Housesteads and head west for sweeping views. There are plenty of interesting places to stay and eat around and along the Wall, including the handsome market town of **Hexham** (see p.654).

Chesters Roman Fort

4 miles north of Hexham, NE46 4EU • April–Sept daily 10am–6pm; Oct & Nov daily 10am–5pm; Nov–April Sat & Sun 10am–4pm • £6.60; EH ◀ ⓣ 01434 681379, ⓦ www.english-heritage.org.uk/visit/places/chesters-roman-fort-and-museum-hadrians-wall

Beautifully sited next to the gurgling River Tyne, **Chesters Roman Fort**, otherwise known as Cilurnum, was built to guard the Roman bridge over the river. Enough remains of the original structure to pick out the design of the fort, but the highlight is down by the river where the vestibule, changing room and steam range of the garrison's **bathhouse** are still visible, along with the furnace and the latrines.

Housesteads Roman Fort

Around 8 miles west of Chesters, NE47 6NN • Daily: April–Sept 10am–6pm; Oct–March 10am–4pm • £7.50; EH & NT • ⓣ 01434 344525, ⓦ www.english-heritage.org.uk/visit/places/housesteads-roman-fort-hadrians-wall

Housesteads Roman Fort is one of the most popular sites on the Wall. The fort is of standard design but for one enforced modification – forts were supposed to straddle the line of the Wall, but here the original stonework follows the edge of the cliff, so Housesteads was built on the steeply sloping ridge to the south. Enter via the tiny

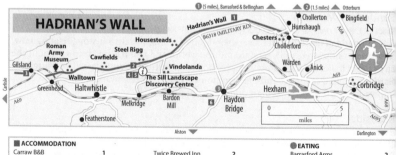

■ ACCOMMODATION				● EATING	
Carraw B&B	1	Twice Brewed Inn	2	Barrasford Arms	2
Hadrian's Wall Camping		Willowford Farm	3	Battlesteads Country	
and Caravan Site	4	YHA The Sill	5	Inn and Restaurant	1
Langley Castle	6			General Havelock Inn	3

ALONG HADRIAN'S WALL

The best way to visit the Wall is to walk or cycle the length of it. The **Hadrian's Wall Path** (⟳ nationaltrail.co.uk/hadrians-wall-path) runs for 84 miles alongside the Wall itself from Wallsend (see p.650) to Bowness-on-Solway. It takes on average seven days to complete and there's an optional Passport system (May–Oct) involving collecting a series of stamps to prove you've done it. If you want to walk only short routes, you can link up with the AD122 bus (see below) that runs along Hadrian's Wall between mid-April and October. Alternatively, the **National Route 72** (signposted NCN 72; ⟳ www.sustrans.org.uk), shares some of the same route as the Hadrian Wall Path, and runs from South Shields to Ravenglass in Cumbria. There's bike hire in Newcastle (see p.647).

museum, and walk across to the south gate; next to this lies the ruins of a garrison of up to one thousand infantrymen. It's not necessary to pay for entrance to the fort if you're simply walking along the Wall west from here; the three-mile hike takes in wonderful views as it meanders past **Crag Lough** and over to **Steel Rigg** (which has a car park).

Vindolanda

13 miles west of Hexham, NE47 7JN, turn-off at Bardon Mill is signposted • Daily: mid-Feb to late March & Oct 10am–5pm; April–Sept 10am–6pm; Nov & Dec 10am–4pm • £7, combined ticket with Roman Army Museum £11 • ☎ 01434 344277, ⟳ vindolanda.com

The garrison fort of **Vindolanda** is believed to have been built and occupied before the construction of the Wall itself. Guarding the important central section of the east–west supply route across Britain, a series of early forts in this location were built of timber, eventually replaced with a stone construction during Hadrian's reign. Preserved beneath the remains of the stone fortress, these early forts are now being excavated – around three to four hundred volunteers take part every day. The museum contains the largest collection of Roman leather items ever discovered on a single site – sandals, purses, an archer's thumb guard – and a fascinating series of **writing tablets** dating to 90 AD. The earliest written records found in Britain, they feature shopping lists, duty rotas and even a birthday party invitation from one Claudia Severa to Sulpicia Lepidina.

Roman Army Museum

20 miles west of Hexham, CA8 7JB • Daily: mid-Feb to end March & Oct 10am–5pm; April–Sept 10am–6pm; Nov & Dec 10am–4pm • £5.75, combined ticket with Vindolanda £11 • ☎ 01434 344277, ⟳ vindolanda.com

The **Roman Army Museum** aims to illustrate how the Roman soldiers stationed here lived. There's everything from armour and weapons – including javelins, shields and swords – to a full-size chariot and a wagon. It's all very entertaining, and successfully brings to life the ruins you may just have seen at Vindolanda.

ARRIVAL AND GETTING AROUND

HADRIAN'S WALL

By train The nearest train stations are on the Newcastle–Carlisle line at Corbridge, Hexham, Bardon Mill and Haltwhistle.

By bus The little #AD122 (known as the "Hadrian's Wall bus"; Easter–Oct up to five times daily in each direction) runs from Newcastle to Corbridge, Hexham, and all the Wall sites and villages, before heading on to Carlisle and Bowness-on-Solway (the end of the Hadrian's Wall Path). There's also a year-round hourly service on the #685 bus between Newcastle and Carlisle, and other local services from Carlisle and Hexham, which provide access to various points along the Wall.

INFORMATION AND TOURS

Information The Sill Landscape Discovery Centre, Military Rd (☎ 01434 605555, ⟳ northumberlandnationalpark.org .uk) is a National Park hub that introduces visitors to the natural and human history of Hadrian's Wall. It has an exhibition centre and shop, a café and an 86-bed youth hostel.

Tours Wild Dog Outdoors (☎ 01434 688386, ⟳ wilddog outdoors.co.uk) runs tours of the wall and forts suitable for all ages. Guides dress up as Celts or Romans and most of the walks set out from Cawfields, a lesser-known, but well-preserved section on the wall. From £20/2hr.

13

ACCOMMODATION

In addition to the B&Bs in the countryside around the Wall, Hexham (see below), Haltwhistle and Corbridge have a good selection of accommodation.

★**Carraw B&B** Military Rd, Humshaugh, NE46 4DB ☎01434 689857, ⓦcarraw.co.uk; map p.652. It's not often you can say "I've slept on Hadrian's Wall", but here you can – this beautiful B&B, run by a friendly couple, is built right next to Hadrian's masterpiece and boasts stunning views. Lovely homely touches, like home-made shortbread and cake on arrival, hot-water bottles and luxurious toiletries make this place really special. Delicious breakfasts – the nutty granola is a winner. Supper £12.50. **£105**

Hadrian's Wall Camping and Caravan Site Melkridge Tilery, NE49 9PG, 2 miles north of Melkridge ☎01434 320495, ⓦhadrianswallcampsite.co.uk; map p.652. Friendly, family-run site half a mile from the Wall, with showers, café, washing machine and dryer, and bike storage; breakfast and evening meals available. There's also a heated bunk room sleeping 10 people (£15/person). Open all year. Camping **£12**, camper van **£15**

Langley Castle A686, Langley-on-Tyne, 2 miles south of Haydon Bridge, NE47 5LU ☎01434 688888, ⓦwww .langleycastle.com; map p.652. There are suitably regal rooms – four-poster beds, sumptuous furnishings and beautiful bathrooms with saunas and spa baths – in this turreted medieval castle. The cheaper rooms are in the grounds, looking onto the castle. There's also an atmospheric restaurant, cocktail bar, lounge and gardens. **£195**, castle rooms **£245**

Twice Brewed Inn Military Rd, NE47 7AN ☎01434 344534, ⓦtwicebrewedinn.co.uk; map p.652. This friendly community pub close to new hub The Sill (see p.653) has simple en-suite rooms that have been recently redecorated. On site there's a microbrewery and beer garden; breakfast is included, but must be ordered the night before. **£85**

★**Willowford Farm** Gilsland, CA8 7AA ☎01697 747962, ⓦwillowford.co.uk; map p.652. Strictly speaking just over the Northumbrian border in Cumbria, but this farmhouse B&B still makes a lovely, tranquil base to explore the Wall. Rooms are in converted farm buildings and decked out with pretty wooden beams and large beds. Packed lunch £6. **£88**

★**YHA The Sill** Military Road, Bardon Mill, NE47 7AN ☎0800 019 1700, ⓦyha.org.uk/sill-hadrians-wall; map p.652. Opened in summer 2017, this 86-bed hostel, attached to The Sill information centre, has doubles, triples and four-bed rooms, some of them en suite. Dorms **£15**, doubles **£39**

EATING

★**Barrasford Arms** Barrasford, NE48 4AA, 9 miles north of Hexham ☎01434 681237, ⓦbarrasfordarms .co.uk; map p.652. Endearingly local, welcoming and homely, this country pub serves great traditional British food with a French twist; dishes could include pan-roasted lamb rump with creamy mash, wilted spinach, onion gravy and onion rings (£16) and for pudding, sticky toffee pudding with butterscotch sauce (£6.50). Booking advisable. Tues–Sat noon–midnight, Sun noon–11pm; snacks served all day; kitchen Tues–Sat noon–2pm & 6–9pm, Sun noon–3pm.

Battlesteads Country Inn and Restaurant Wark-on-Tyne, NE48 3LS, 12 miles north of Hexham ☎01434 230209, ⓦbattlesteads.com; map p.652. In a charming little village by a trickling stream, this locally renowned restaurant with a lovely beer garden uses fresh produce sourced from within a 30-mile radius. Leave room for their famed whisky and marmalade bread-and-butter pudding (£5.75). Best to book. Food served daily noon–3pm & 6.30–9.30pm.

General Havelock Inn 9 Ratcliffe Rd, Haydon Bridge, NE47 6ER ☎01434 684376; map p.652. Eighteenth-century inn that specializes in tasty Modern British food, from crab cakes and Cumberland sausages to chocolate brûlée and ice-cream sundaes. Great locally brewed ales on offer, too. Main meals average around £17 (bar menu cheaper). Daily noon–3pm & 5pm–midnight; kitchen daily noon–3pm & 6–11pm.

Hexham

HEXHAM is the only significant stop between Newcastle and Carlisle, and however keen you are on seeing the Wall, you'd do well to spend a night at this handsome market town – or even make it your base.

The focal point is the **abbey**, whose foundations were originally part of a fine Benedictine monastery founded by St Wilfrid in 671. Claimed, according to contemporaneous accounts, to be the finest this side of the Alps, the church – or rather its gold and silver – proved irresistible to the Vikings, who savaged the place in 876. It was rebuilt in the eleventh century as part of an Augustinian priory, and the town grew up in its shadow.

13

Hexham Abbey

NE46 3NB • Daily 9.30am–5pm • ⓦ hexhamabbey.org.uk

The stately exterior of **Hexham Abbey** dominates the west side of the central marketplace. Entry is through the south transept, where there's a bruised but impressive first-century tombstone honouring Flavinus, a standard-bearer in the Roman cavalry, who's shown riding down his bearded enemy. The memorial lies at the foot of the broad, well-worn steps of the canons' **night stair**, one of the few such staircases – providing access from the monastery to the church – to have survived the Dissolution. The chancel, meanwhile, displays the inconsequential-looking **frith-stool**, an eighth-century stone chair that was once believed to have been used by St Wilfrid.

The Old Gaol

Hallgate, NE46 1XD • Feb, March, Oct & Nov Tues & Sat 11am–4.30pm; April–Sept Tues–Sat 11am–4.30pm • £3.95 • ⓣ 01434 652349, ⓦ hexhamoldgaol.org.uk

Britain's first purpose-built prison, **Hexham Old Gaol** occupies a solid sandstone building to the east of the abbey. It was commissioned by the powerful Archbishop of York in 1330, and constructed using stone plundered from the Roman ruins at Corbridge. Inside there's an entertaining museum extolling the virtues and pitfalls of medieval crime and punishment.

ARRIVAL AND INFORMATION   HEXHAM

By train The train station sits on the northeastern edge of the town centre, a 10min walk from the abbey.
Destinations Carlisle (hourly; 50min); Haltwhistle (hourly; 20min); Newcastle (hourly; 50min).
By bus The bus station is Loosing Hill, a 10min stroll east of the abbey.

Destinations Bellingham (Mon–Sat hourly; 45min); Newcastle (hourly; 50min).
Tourist office In the library at Queens Hall, Beaumont St (Mon 9am–6pm, Tues–Thurs 9am–5pm, Friday 9am–6pm, Sat 9.30am–5pm; ⓣ 01670 620250).
Websites ⓦ hadrianswallcountry.co.uk, ⓦ visithexham.net.

ACCOMMODATION

The County Hotel Priestpopple, NE46 1PS ⓣ 01434 608444, ⓦ countyhotelhexham.co.uk. A refurbished pub with seven spacious and elegant en-suite rooms. The staff are incredibly welcoming and there's great food served here, too. Street parking. **£110**

Hallbank Hallgate, behind the Old Gaol, NE46 1XA ⓣ 01434 605567, ⓦ hallbankguesthouse.co.uk. A restored house in a quiet town-centre location, with eight very comfortable rooms and an associated coffee shop/restaurant. Evening meals available on request. **£120**

EATING AND DRINKING

★**Bouchon Bistrot** 4–6 Gilesgate, NE46 3NJ ⓣ 01434 609943, ⓦ bouchonbistrot.co.uk. Very stylish restaurant in a handsome terraced townhouse, serving sophisticated French dishes such as crispy duck confit with gratin potatoes (£15.95), and crème brûlée (£5.50). Mon–Sat noon–2pm & 6–9.30pm.

Dipton Mill Inn Dipton Mill Rd, NE46 1YA, 2 miles south of Hexham ⓣ 01434 606577, ⓦ diptonmill.co.uk. A lovely, traditional country pub covered in ivy. While the food is excellent – good pub grub like steak and kidney pie and vegetable casserole – it's most famous for the home-brewed ales, made at Hexhamshire Brewery. Try

Old Humbug, named after the landlord. Mon–Sat noon–2.30pm & 6–11pm, Sun noon–3pm; kitchen Mon–Sat noon–2.30pm & 6.30–8.30pm, Sun noon–2pm.

★**Rat Inn** Anick, NE46 4LN, 2 miles northeast of Hexham ⓣ 01434 602814, ⓦ theratinn.com. In a glorious hillside location overlooking Hexham, this quaint pub has a roaring fire in winter and a pretty summer garden. The food is all locally sourced – try the braised local beef in Allendale beer (£10.50). Booking essential for Sun lunch. Mon–Sat noon–11pm, Sun noon–10.30pm; kitchen Mon–Sat noon–2pm & 6–9pm, Sun noon–3pm.

Northumberland National Park

Northwest Northumberland, the great triangular chunk of land between Hadrian's Wall and the coastal plain, is dominated by the wide-skied landscapes of **Northumberland National Park** (ⓦ northumberlandnationalpark.org.uk), whose four

13

hundred windswept square miles rise to the **Cheviot Hills** on the Scottish border. The bulk of the park is taken up by **Kielder Water and Forest nature reserve**, a superb destination for watersports and outdoor activities; the small town of **Bellingham** on the eastern edge of the park makes a good base for the reserve, as do **Rothbury** and **Wooler**, both of which also provide easy access to some superb walking in the craggy Cheviots.

Kielder Water and Forest

Surrounded by 250 acres of dense pine forest, **Kielder Water and Forest** is the largest reservoir in England; the mass of woodlands and wetlands means that **wildlife** is abundant – you might spot badgers, deer, otters, ospreys and red squirrels. The road from Bellingham follows the North Tyne River west and skirts the forested edge of the lake, passing an assortment of visitor centres, waterside parks, picnic areas and anchorages that fringe its southern shore. Mountain biking, hiking, horseriding and fishing are some of the land-based activities on offer, and of course watersports (waterskiing, sailing, kayaking and windsurfing) are hugely popular, too.

The skies here are some of the darkest in Europe and star-gazing can be magical; award-winning **Kielder Observatory** (wkielderobservatory.org) hosts over forty night-time events a month (booking essential). **Kielder Waterside**, on the western flank of the reservoir, is the best place to head if you're visiting for the first time and need to get your bearings.

Kielder Waterside

NE48 1BT • Birds of Prey Centre daily 10.30am–4pm • Flying demonstrations summer 1.30pm & 3pm, Oct–March 2pm • £7, children £4.50 • ☎ 01434 251000, w kielderwaterside.com

Kielder Waterside Park is a purpose-built hub of lodges (see below) with cafés and a restaurant, a visitor centre (see below), bike hire (see below) and a Birds of Prey Centre where you can see a variety of handsome, sharp-taloned beasts, from owls and falcons to vultures and ospreys.

ARRIVAL AND INFORMATION   KIELDER WATER AND FOREST

By bus The #880 from Hexham serves the visitor centres of Tower Knowe, Kielder Waterside (by request) and Kielder Castle via Bellingham (2 daily Tues & Sat). The #714 from Newcastle upon Tyne runs on Sun (1 daily) to Tower Knowe, Kielder Waterside (by request) and Kielder Castle.

Visitor centres Tower Knowe: from Bellingham, the first visitor centre you come to as you head anti-clockwise round the reservoir (daily: April–June & Sept 10am–5pm; July & Aug 10am–6pm; Oct 10am–4pm; ☎ 0845 155 0236). Kielder Waterside: western flank of the reservoir (Feb–Oct daily 9am–5pm; ☎ 01434 251000). Kielder Castle: at the northernmost point of the reservoir (daily 10am–5pm; ☎ 01434 250209).

GETTING AROUND

By bike The Bike Place (w thebikeplace.co.uk) has two hire centres at Kielder Castle Visitor Centre (daily 9.30am–5.30pm; ☎ 01434 250457) and at Kielder Waterside (daily 9.30am–6pm; ☎ 01434 250144); both offer day rental from £15/2hr.

By car For parking, you can buy a ticket at your first stop (£5) that's valid for all other car parks throughout the day.

By ferry The 60-seater Osprey Ferry (☎ 01434 251000) sails round the reservoir, with stops at Kielder Waterside, Tower Knowe and occasionally Belvedere. Tickets (day pass £6.75, short journeys from £4.40) are available at Tower Knowe; prior booking is necessary.

ACCOMMODATION AND EATING

Hollybush Inn Greenhaugh, NE48 1PW, 12 miles east of Kielder Water ☎ 01434 240391, w hollybushinn.net. Super little pub in a remote village serving great ales and food, and with seven simple and attractive bedrooms upstairs or in the quiet cottage next door. **£85**

Kielder Lodges Kielder Waterside Park, NE48 1BT ☎ 0845 155 0236, or Hoseasons ☎ 0345 498 6060, w hoseasons.co.uk. Scandinavian-style self-catering lodges, all with access to the park's pool, sauna, bar and restaurant. Bring plenty of midge repellent. Two-night

13

minimum stay; rates vary widely. From **£60**
★ **Pheasant Inn** Stannersburn, NE48 1DD ☎ 01434 240382, ⓦ thepheasantinn.com. A traditional country pub on the road from Bellingham, the *Pheasant Inn* has eight very comfortable bedrooms (including one family room). The highlight is the food, though, served downstairs in the cosy restaurant; expect game pies, Northumbrian cheeses and plenty of fish (mains around £12 in the evening). Booking recommended. Food served noon–2pm & 6.30–8.30pm. **£110**

Rothbury and around

ROTHBURY, straddling the River Coquet thirty miles northeast of Hexham, prospered as a late Victorian resort because it gave ready access to the forests, burns and ridges of the **Simonside Hills**. The small town remains a popular spot for walkers, with several of the best local trails beginning from the **Simonside Hills** car park, a couple of miles southwest of Rothbury. Nearby, the estates of **Cragside** and **Wallington** are good options if you want to take a break from hiking.

Cragside

1 mile east of Rothbury, NE65 7PX · **House** March–Oct daily 11am–5pm · £17 (includes gardens); NT · **Gardens** March–Oct daily 10am–6pm; Nov–Feb Fri–Sun 11am–4pm · £11; NT · ☎ 01669 620333, ⓦ nationaltrust.org.uk/cragside

Victorian Rothbury was dominated by Sir William, later the first Lord Armstrong, the wealthy nineteenth-century arms manufacturer, shipbuilder and engineer who built his country home at **Cragside**, a mile to the east of the village. He hired Richard Norman Shaw, one of the period's top architects, who produced a grandiose Tudor-style mansion entirely out of place in the Northumbrian countryside. Armstrong was an avid innovator, and in 1880 Cragside became the first house in the world to be lit by hydroelectric power. The surrounding **gardens**, complete with the remains of the original pumping system, are beautiful and there's a pleasant tearoom for a light snack.

Wallington

13 miles south of Rothbury, NE61 4AR · House March–Oct daily noon–5pm; gardens year-round daily 10am–dusk · £12.40; NT · ☎ 01670 773967, ⓦ nationaltrust.org.uk/wallington

South of Rothbury, down the B6342, stands **Wallington**, an ostentatious mansion rebuilt in the 1740s by Sir Walter Blackett, the coal- and lead-mine owner. The house is known for its Rococo plasterwork and William Bell Scott's Pre-Raphaelite murals of scenes from Northumbrian history. Children will love the collection of doll's houses, one of which has thirty-six rooms and was originally fitted with running water and a working lift. However, it's the magnificent **gardens and grounds** that are the real delight, with lawns, woods and lakes laced with footpaths. There are events, concerts and activities throughout the year, as well as a café and farm shop on site.

ARRIVAL AND INFORMATION   ROTHBURY AND AROUND

By bus Buses from Newcastle via Morpeth stop outside the *Queen's Head* pub in the centre (hourly; 1hr 20min).
Information Help and advice for visitors to Northumberland National Park is available at the Coquetdale Centre near the cross on Church St (daily 9.30am–5pm; ☎ 01669 621462, ⓦ northumberlandnationalpark.org.uk).

ACCOMMODATION

★ **Hillcrest** Rothbury, NE65 7TL ☎ 01669 621944, ⓦ hillcrestbandb.co.uk. Superb B&B in a pretty Georgian house, with two beautifully decorated bedrooms – wooden floorboards, antique furniture, exposed walls and the like – with an intriguing past (the owner will explain). Wonderful breakfasts, too. **£85**

Thistleyhaugh Longframlington, NE65 8RG, 5 miles east of Rothbury ☎ 01665 570629. Gorgeous, ivy-smothered Georgian farmhouse with five luxurious chintzy bedrooms. They serve delicious three-course dinners (7pm; £20) and hearty breakfasts. **£80**

★ **Tosson Tower** Great Tosson, NE65 7NW, 2 miles southwest of Rothbury ☎ 01669 620228, ⓦ tossontowerfarm.com. Seven lovely rooms on this little working farm in a quiet hamlet with spectacular views out over the Cheviot Hills. Four charming self-catering cottages also available for longer stays. **£90**

13

TOP 5 NORTHUMBRIAN CASTLES
Alnwick Castle See p.660
Bamburgh Castle See p.662
Chillingham Castle See p.658
Dunstanburgh Castle See p.661
Warkworth Castle See p.659

Wooler and around

Stone-terraced **WOOLER** – rebuilt after a terrible fire in the 1860s – is a one-street market town twenty miles north of Rothbury. It's the best base for climbs up **The Cheviot** (2674ft), seven miles to the southwest and the highest point in the Cheviot Hills. From *YHA Wooler* at 30 Cheviot St, it's four hours there and back; from Hawsen Burn, the nearest navigable point, it's two hours walking there and back. Wooler is also a staging post on the Pennine Way and the lovely **St Cuthbert's Way** (from Melrose in Scotland to Lindisfarne).

Chillingham Castle

6 miles southeast of Wooler, NE66 5NJ • April–Oct daily noon–5pm • £9.50 • ☎ 01668 215359, ⓦ chillingham-castle.com

Chillingham Castle started life as an eleventh-century tower. The castle was augmented at regular intervals until the nineteenth century, but from 1933 was largely left to the elements for fifty years, until the present owner set about restoring it in his own individualistic way: bedrooms, living rooms and even a grisly torture chamber (designed to "cause maximum shock") are decorated with historical paraphernalia.

Chillingham Wild Cattle

Between Alnwick and Belford, signposted The Wild White Cattle, NE66 5NP • Tours April–Oct Mon–Fri hourly 10am–noon & 2–4pm, Sun 10am–noon; winter by appointment • £16 • ⓦ chillinghamwildcattle.com

In 1220, Chillingham Castle's adjoining 365 acres of parkland were enclosed to protect the local wild cattle for hunting and food. And so the **Chillingham Wild Cattle** – a fierce, primeval herd with white coats, black muzzles and black tips to their horns – have remained to this day, cut off from mixing with domesticated breeds. It's possible to visit these unique relicts, who number around ninety, but only in the company of a warden, as the animals are potentially dangerous, and also need to be protected from outside infection. The visit takes about two hours and involves a short country walk before viewing the cattle at a safe distance – the closest you're likely to get to big-game viewing in England. Bring strong shoes or walking boots if it's wet.

ARRIVAL AND INFORMATION
WOOLER AND AROUND

By bus The bus station is set back off High St. Destinations Alnwick (Mon–Sat 9 daily; 45min); Berwick-upon-Tweed (Mon–Sat 9 daily; 50min); Newcastle (Mon–Sat 2 daily; 1hr 15min).

Tourist office Cheviot Centre, Padgepool Place (Mon–Sat 10am–4.30pm, plus Sun 10am–2pm Easter to Oct; ☎ 01668 282123).

ACCOMMODATION AND EATING

Milan 2 High St, through the arch of the Black Bull hotel, NE71 6BY ☎ 01668 283692, ⓦ milan-restaurant.co.uk. Good-value Italian restaurant with exposed brick walls and a jolly ambience, serving large pizzas (from £7.50), pasta dishes (from £7.95) and plenty of meat and fish options. It's a very popular place, so book ahead. Daily 5–10pm.

Tilldale House 34 High St, NE71 6BG ☎ 01668 281450, ⓦ tilldalehouse.co.uk. Snug seventeenth-century stone cottage in the middle of town with three en-suite bedrooms. With enormous, soft beds, deep-pile carpets, an open fire and great breakfasts, it makes a very cosy and enticing base after a long day hiking in the hills. **£75**

The Northumberland coast

Stretching 64 miles north of Newcastle up to the Scottish border, the low-lying **Northumberland coast** is the region's shining star, stunningly beautiful and packed with

13

impressive sights. Here you'll find mighty fortresses at **Warkworth**, **Alnwick** and **Bamburgh** and magnificent Elizabethan ramparts surrounding **Berwick-upon-Tweed**; in between there are glorious sandy beaches, the site of the Lindisfarne monastery on **Holy Island**, and the seabird and nature reserve of the **Farne Islands**, reached by boat from Seahouses.

Warkworth

WARKWORTH, a peaceful coastal hamlet set in a loop of the River Coquet a couple of miles from Amble, is best seen from the north, from where the grey stone terraces of the long main street slope up towards the commanding remains of **Warkworth Castle**. From the castle, the main street sweeps down into the village, flattening out at Dial Place and the Church of St Lawrence before curving right to cross the River Coquet; just over the bridge, a signposted quarter-mile lane leads to the **beach**, which stretches for five miles from Amble to Alnmouth.

Warkworth Castle

Castle Terrace, NE65 0UJ • April–Oct daily 10am–5pm; rest of the year usually Sat & Sun only, see website for details; Duke's Rooms April–Sept Mon, Sun & bank hols only • £6.20, combined ticket with hermitage £8.90; EH • ☎ 01665 711423, Ⓦ www.english-heritage.org.uk/visit /places/warkworth-castle-and-hermitage

Ruined but well-preserved, **Warkworth Castle** has Norman origins, but was constructed using sandstone during the fourteenth and fifteenth centuries. Home to generations of the Percy family, the powerful earls of Northumberland, it appears as a backdrop in several scenes of Shakespeare's *Henry IV, Part II*. The cross-shaped keep contains a great hall, a chapel, kitchens, storerooms and the Duke's Rooms, which are kitted out in period furniture and furnishings.

Warkworth Hermitage

Castle Terrace, NE65 0UJ • Weather permitting April–Oct Mon, Sun & bank hols (plus Fri & Sat in July & Aug) 11am–5pm; rest of the year limited opening hours, see website for details • £4.30, combined ticket with castle £8.90; EH • ☎ 01665 711423, Ⓦ www.english-heritage.org.uk /visit/places/warkworth-castle-and-hermitage

A path from the churchyard heads along the right bank of the Coquet to the boat that shuttles visitors across to **Warkworth Hermitage**, a series of simple rooms and a claustrophobic chapel that were hewn out of the cliff above the river some time in the fourteenth century, but abandoned by 1567. The last resident hermit, one George Lancaster, was charged by the sixth earl of Northumberland to pray for his noble family, for which lonesome duty he received around £15 a year and a barrel of fish every Sunday.

ARRIVAL
WARKWORTH

By bus The #X18 (Newcastle to Berwick) stops here, but it's quicker to take the train to Alnmouth, then the bus.

Destinations Alnmouth (every 30min; 10min), Berwick (every 2hr; 2hr 10min), Newcastle (hourly; 1hr 30min).

Alnmouth

It's three miles north from Warkworth to the seaside resort of **ALNMOUTH**, whose narrow centre is strikingly situated on a steep spur of land between the sea and the estuary of the Aln. This lovely setting has been a low-key holiday spot since Victorian times, and is particularly popular with golfers: the village's nine-hole course, right on the coast, was built in 1869 (it's claimed to be the second oldest in the country) and dune-strollers really do have to heed the "Danger – Flying Golf Balls" signs which adorn Marine Road.

ARRIVAL AND DEPARTURE
ALNMOUTH

By train Trains pass through from Berwick (every 2hr; 20min) and Newcastle (hourly; 30min).

By bus There are local bus services from Alnwick and

Warkworth, and the regular #X18 Newcastle–Berwick bus also passes through Alnmouth and calls at its train station, 1.5 miles west of the centre.

Red Lion 22 Northumberland St, NE66 2RJ ☎01668 30584, ⓦredlionalnmouth.com. Six spacious and modern rooms, with pine furniture, cream walls and fresh bathrooms, above a popular, traditional pub. The beer garden is perfect for sunny days, and the menu has everything from big open sandwiches (from £4.95) to sirloin steak (£17.50). Restaurant Mon–Sat noon–3pm & 4–9pm, Sun noon–8pm. __£85__

Alnwick

The appealing market town of **ALNWICK** (pronounced "Annick"), thirty miles north of Newcastle and four miles inland from Alnmouth, is renowned for its **castle** and **gardens** – seat of the dukes of Northumberland – which overlook the River Aln. It's worth spending a couple of days here, exploring the medieval maze of streets, the elegant gatehouses on Pottergate and Bondgate and the best **bookshop** in the north.

Alnwick Castle

NE66 1NQ • April–Oct daily 10am–5.30pm • £15.50; castle and garden £26.10 • ☎01665 511100, ⓦalnwickcastle.com

The Percys – who were raised to the dukedom of Northumberland in 1750 – have owned **Alnwick Castle** since 1309. In the eighteenth century, the first duke had the interior refurbished by Robert Adam in an extravagant Gothic style – which in turn was supplanted by the gaudy Italianate decoration preferred by the fourth duke in the 1850s. There's plenty to see inside, including remains from Pompeii, though the **interior** can be crowded at times – not least with families on the *Harry Potter* trail, since the castle doubled as Hogwarts School in the first two films.

Alnwick Garden

NE66 1YU • April–Oct & late Nov to early Jan daily 10am–6pm; Grand Cascade and Poison Garden closed in winter • Summer £12.10, winter £7; garden and castle £26.10 • ☎01665 511350, ⓦalnwickgarden.com

The grounds of the castle are taken up by the huge and beautiful **Alnwick Garden**, designed by an innovative Belgian team and full of quirky features such as a bamboo labyrinth maze, a serpent garden involving topiary snakes, and the popular **Poison Garden**, filled with the world's deadliest plants. The heart of the garden is the computerized Grand Cascade, which shoots water jets in a regular synchronized display, while to the west is Europe's largest treehouse, which has a restaurant within (see below). The walled Roots and Shoots community veg garden (no ticket required) is a delight.

Barter Books

Alnwick station, NE66 2NP • Daily 9am–7pm • ☎01665 604888, ⓦbarterbooks.co.uk

Housed in the Victorian train station on Wagonway Road, and containing visible remnants of the ticket office, passenger waiting rooms and the outbound platform, the enchanting **Barter Books** is one of the largest secondhand bookshops in England. With its sofas, murals, open fire, coffee and biscuits – and, best of all, a model train that runs on top of the stacks – it is definitely worth a visit.

By bus The station is on Clayport St, a couple of minutes' walk west of the marketplace.
Destinations Bamburgh (Mon–Sat 7 daily, Sun 4 daily; 1hr 15min); Berwick-upon-Tweed (Mon–Sat 6 daily, Sun 3 daily; 1hr); Craster (Mon–Fri 7 daily, Sat 4 daily; 35min); Wooler (Mon–Sat 9 daily; 45min).

Tourist office 2 The Shambles, off the marketplace (April–June, Sept & Oct Mon–Sat 9.30am–5pm, Sun 10am–4pm; July & Aug daily 9am–5pm; Nov–March Mon–Fri 9.30am–4.30pm, Sat 10am–4pm; ☎01665 622152, ⓦvisitalnwick.org.uk).

Alnwick Garden Treehouse Alnwick Gardens, NE66 1YU ☎01665 511852, ⓦalnwickgarden.com. Glorious restaurant in the enormous treehouse in Alnwick Gardens (you don't have to pay the garden entry fee to visit). There's

13

an open fire in the middle of the room and even tree trunks growing through the floor. A set menu is available at lunch and dinner (two courses £19.95/£28.50) with lots of local produce cooked to perfection (mains include English rack of lamb or stuffed field mushrooms). Booking essential. Mon & Tues noon–3pm, Wed–Sat noon–3pm & 6.30–9.15pm, Sun noon–8pm.

Station Buffet Barter Books Wagonway Road, NE66 2NP 📞01665 604888, 🌐barterbooks.co.uk. Set in the old station waiting room at Barter Books, this unique café serves home-made food including cooked breakfasts (9–11.30am), hamburgers, sandwiches, salads and cakes (meals around £7). Daily 9am–7pm.

Tate House 11 Bondgate Without, NE66 1PR 📞01665 660800, 🌐stayinalnwick.co.uk. In a pretty Victorian house opposite Alnwick Gardens, the ten comfortable bedrooms are available on a "room only" basis, with spotless bathrooms and nice little touches such as hot-water bottles, iPod docks and DVD players. Ten percent off breakfast at *The Plough* across the road. **£65**

YHA Alnwick 4–38 Green Batt, NE66 1TU 📞01665 604661, 🌐yha.org.uk/hostel/alnwick. A handsome Victorian courthouse nicely converted into a hostel with some private rooms. You're a stroll away from the gardens and castle, and there's a bus stop right outside the front door. Dorms **£18.50**, doubles **£39**

Craster and around

The tiny fishing village of **CRASTER** – known for its kippers – lies six miles northeast of Alnwick, right on the coast. It's a delightful little place, with its circular, barnacle-encrusted harbour walls fronting a cluster of tough, weather-battered little houses and the cheery *Jolly Fisherman* pub. Other villages worth visiting round here include **Newton-on-Sea** and **Beadnell**, both exuding wind swept, salty charm. The **coastline** between Dunstanburgh and Beadnell is made up of the long sandy beaches that Northumberland is famous for.

Dunstanburgh Castle

Dunstanburgh Rd, NE66 3TT • April–Sept daily 10am–6pm; Oct daily 10am–4pm; Nov–March Sat & Sun 10am–4pm • £5; NT & EH • 📞01665 576231, 🌐www.english-heritage.org.uk/visit/places/dunstanburgh-castle

Looming in the distance, about a thirty-minute walk northwards up the coast from Craster, is stunning **Dunstanburgh Castle**. Built in the fourteenth century, in the wake of civil war, its shattered remains occupy a magnificent promontory, bordered by sheer cliffs and crashing waves.

ARRIVAL   CRASTER AND AROUND

By bus Buses #X18 and #418 run to Alnwick (Mon–Sat 11 daily, Sun 3 daily; 35min).

ACCOMMODATION

Old Rectory Howick, NE66 3LE, 2 miles south of Craster 📞01665 577590, 🌐oldrectoryhowick.co.uk. Just 400yds from the wind-whipped North Sea, this fantastic B&B sits in its own peaceful grounds and has extremely pretty bedrooms and comfortable sitting areas. Superb breakfasts feature plenty of cooked options, including Craster kippers. **£90**

EATING AND DRINKING

There's not much in the way of fine dining round these parts; most villages simply have a traditional pub serving decent meals. Craster's beloved **kippers** are smoked at L. Robson & Sons (📞01665 576223, 🌐kipper.co.uk) in the centre of the village; they also sell salty oak-smoked salmon.

Jolly Fisherman 9 Haven Hill, NE66 3TR 📞01665 576461, 🌐thejollyfishermancraster.co.uk. Located just above the harbour, this pub has sea views from its back window and a lovely summer beer garden. Not surprisingly for a pub opposite L. Robson & Sons, it serves plenty of fish – crab sandwiches, kipper pâté and a famously good crabmeat, whisky and cream soup. Mon–Sat 11am–11pm, Sun noon–11pm; ktchen Mon–Fri 11am–3pm & 5–8.30pm, Sun noon–7pm.

Ship Inn Low Newton-by-the-Sea, NE66 3EL, 5 miles north of Craster 📞01665 576262, 🌐shipinnnewton

.co.uk. Great, rustic pub in a coastal hamlet serving dishes using ingredients from local suppliers – there's plenty of L. Robson smoked fish on the menu. Mains from £7. Ales are supplied by their own brewery next door. Dinner reservations essential in evening. April–Oct Mon & Tues 11am–10.30pm, Wed–Sat 11am–11pm, Sun & bank hols noon–10pm, Nov–March Mon–Wed 11am–5pm, Thurs–Sat 11am–11pm, Sun noon–6pm; kitchen April–Oct daily noon–2.30pm plus Wed–Sat 7–8pm, Nov–March daily noon–2.30pm plus Thurs–Sat 7–8pm.

13

Seahouses and the Farne Islands

Around ten miles north from Craster, beyond the small village of Beadnell, lies the fishing port of **SEAHOUSES**, the only place on the local coast that could remotely be described as a resort. It's the embarkation point for boat trips out to the wind swept **Farne Islands**, a rocky archipelago lying a few miles offshore.

The Farne Islands

Owned by the National Trust and maintained as a nature reserve, the **Farne Islands** (ⓦnationaltrust.co.uk/farne-islands) are the summer home of hundreds of thousands of migrating seabirds, notably puffins, guillemots, terns, eider ducks and kittiwakes, and home to the only grey seal colony on the English coastline. A number of boat trips potter around the islands – the largest of which is Inner Farne – offering birdwatching tours, grey seal-watching tours and the Grace Darling tour, which takes visitors to the lighthouse on Longstone Island, where the famed local heroine (see p.664) lived.

ARRIVAL AND INFORMATION   SEAHOUSES AND THE FARNE ISLANDS

By bus The bus stop is on King St, near the post office. The #X18 runs between Berwick (every 2hr; 1hr) and Alnwick (every 2hr; 1hr).

By boat Weather permitting, several operators in Seahouses run daily boat trips (2–3hr; from £15; National Trust landing fee £7–9) starting at around 10am. Wander down to the quayside, contact either the National Trust Shop or the tourist office (closed at time of writing; see above), or book online

in advance at ⓦfarne-islands.com. During the breeding season (May–July) landings are restricted to morning trips to Staple Island and afternoons to Inner Farne.

Tourist information National Trust Shop, 16 Main St (ⓣ01665 721099), by the Seahouses traffic roundabout. The tourist office is located in the main car park but was closed at the time of writing; see ⓦseahouses.org for the latest information.

ACCOMMODATION

★**St Cuthberts** 198 Main st, Seahouses, NE68 7UB ⓣ01665 720456, ⓦstcuthbertshouse.com. Award-winning B&B in a beautifully converted 200-year-old chapel a mile inland from the harbour. Rooms cleverly incorporate period features like the original arched windows with

lovely modern touches such as wet rooms, flatscreen TVs, comfy dressing gowns and slippers. Breakfast is all locally sourced, from the sausages and the eggs to the kippers and the honey. **£105**

Bamburgh

One-time capital of Northumbria, the little village of **BAMBURGH**, just three miles from Seahouses, lies in the lee of its magnificent **castle**. Attractive stone cottages – holding the village shop, a café, pubs and B&Bs – flank each side of the triangular green, and at the top of the village on Radcliffe Road is the diminutive **Grace Darling Museum**. From behind the castle it's a brisk, five-minute walk to two splendid sandy **beaches**, backed by rolling, tufted dunes.

Bamburgh Castle

Half a mile from Bamburgh, NE69 7DF • Mid-Feb to Oct daily 10am–5pm; Nov to mid-Feb Sat & Sun 11am–4.30pm • £10.85 • ⓣ01668 214515, ⓦbamburghcastle.com

Solid and chunky, **Bamburgh Castle** is a spectacular sight, its elongated battlements crowning a formidable basalt crag high above the beach. Its origins lie in Anglo-Saxon times, but it suffered a centuries-long decline – rotted by sea spray and buffeted by winter storms, the castle was bought by Lord Armstrong (of Rothbury's Cragside; see p.657) in 1894, who demolished most of the structure to replace it with a hybrid castle-mansion. Inside there's plenty to explore, including the sturdy keep that houses an unnerving armoury packed with vicious-looking pikes, halberds, helmets and muskets; the King's Hall, with its marvellous teak ceiling that was imported from Siam (Thailand) and carved in Victorian times; and a medieval kitchen complete with original jugs, pots and pans.

13

Grace Darling Museum

Radcliffe Rd, NE69 7AE • Easter–Sept daily 10am–5pm; Oct–Easter Tues–Sun 10am–4pm • Free • ☎ 01668 214910, ⓦ rnli.org.uk

The **Grace Darling Museum** celebrates the life of famed local heroine Grace Darling. In September 1838, a gale dashed the steamship *Forfarshire* against the rocks of the Farne Islands. Nine passengers struggled onto a reef where they were subsequently saved by Grace and her lighthouseman father, William, who left the safety of the Longstone lighthouse to row out to them. *The Times* trumpeted Grace's bravery, offers of marriage and requests for locks of her hair streamed into the Darlings' lighthouse home, and for the rest of her brief life Grace was plagued by unwanted visitors – she died of tuberculosis aged 26 in 1842, and was buried in Bamburgh, in the churchyard of the thirteenth-century St Aidan's.

ARRIVAL AND INFORMATION
                                                                    BAMBURGH

By bus A regular bus service links Alnwick and Berwick-upon-Tweed with Bamburgh, stopping on Front St, by the green. **Destinations** Alnwick (Mon–Sat hourly; 1hr 10min); Berwick-upon-Tweed (Mon–Sat every 2hr; 40min); Seahouses (Mon–Sat hourly; 10min). **Website** ⓦ bamburgh.org.uk

ACCOMMODATION AND EATING

Copper Kettle 21 Front St, NE69 7BW ☎ 01668 214315. Sweet little tearoom, with a sunny sitting area out the back, serving tasty cakes, teas and coffees – try the fruit loaf or the tempting carrot cake with icing. Also light meals such as sandwiches (£5), jacket potatoes (£6.50) and pies (£6). Daily 11am–6pm.

Victoria Hotel 1 Front St, NE69 7BP ☎ 01668 214431, ⓦ strhotels.co.uk/victoria-hotel. This smart boutique hotel has elegant rooms in a variety of sizes – one with lovely castle views – a couple of relaxing bars and a more expensive brasserie (dinner only). Pets are welcome for an additional charge of £7.50/night. **£90**

Holy Island

It's a dramatic approach to **HOLY ISLAND** – only accessible at low tide – past the barnacle-encrusted marker poles that line the three-mile-long causeway. Topped with a stumpy **castle**, the island is small (just 1.5 miles by one), sandy and bare, and in winter it can be bleak, but come summer day-trippers clog the car parks as soon as the causeway is open. Even then, though, **Lindisfarne** (as the island was once known) has a distinctive and isolated atmosphere. Give the place time and, if you can, stay overnight, when you'll be able to see the historic remains without hundreds of others cluttering the views. The island's surrounding tidal mud flats, salt marshes and dunes have been designated a **nature reserve**.

Brief history

It was on Lindisfarne that St Aidan of Iona founded a monastery at the invitation of King Oswald of Northumbria in 634. The monks quickly established a reputation for scholarship and artistry, the latter exemplified by the **Lindisfarne Gospels**, the apotheosis of Celtic religious art, now kept in the British Library. The monastery had sixteen bishops in all, the most celebrated being the reluctant **St Cuthbert**, who never settled here – within two years, he was back in his hermit's cell on the Farne Islands, where he died in 687. His colleagues rowed the body back to Lindisfarne, which became a place of pilgrimage until 875, when the monks abandoned the island in fear of marauding Vikings, taking Cuthbert's remains with them.

Lindisfarne Priory

TD15 2RX • Feb daily 10am–4pm; March & Nov–Jan Sat & Sun 10am–4pm; April–Sept daily 10am–6pm; Oct daily 10am–5pm • £6.50; EH • ☎ 01289 389200, ⓦ www.english-heritage.org.uk/visit/places/lindisfarne-priory

Located just off the village green are the tranquil, pinkish sandstone ruins of **Lindisfarne Priory**, which dates from the Benedictine foundation. The **museum** next door displays a collection of incised stones that constitute all that remains of the first monastery.

Lindisfarne Castle

13

TD15 2SH • **Castle** Closed until April 2018 • **Gardens** Daily dawn–dusk • Free • ☎ 01289 389244, ⓦ nationaltrust.org.uk/lindisfarne-castle

Stuck on a small pyramid of rock half a mile away from the village, **Lindisfarne Castle** was built in the middle of the sixteenth century to protect the island's harbour from the Scots. It was, however, merely a decaying shell when Edward Hudson, the founder of *Country Life* magazine, stumbled across it in 1901. He promptly commissioned Edwin Lutyens (1869–1944) to turn it into an Edwardian country house, and installed a charming walled garden in the castle's former vegetable gardens, to designs by Gertrude Jekyll. Only the garden remains open while the castle undergoes major restoration work, due to be completed in April 2018.

ARRIVAL AND INFORMATION

HOLY ISLAND

By bus The #477 bus from Berwick-upon-Tweed to Holy Island (35min) is something of a law unto itself given the interfering tides, but basically service is daily in Aug and twice-weekly the rest of the year.

Crossing the causeway The island is cut off by tides for about 5hr a day. Consult tide timetables at a tourist office, in the local paper or at ⓦ holyisland.northumberland .gov.uk.

Castle shuttle A minibus trundles the half a mile to the castle from the main car park, The Chare (every 20min 10.20am–4.20pm; £1).

Website ⓦ lindisfarne.org.uk

ACCOMMODATION AND EATING

Due to the size of the island and the small number of B&Bs, it's imperative to **book in advance** if you're staying overnight.

★**Bamburgh View** Fenkle St, TD15 2SR ☎ 01289 389212, ⓦ lindisfarne.org.uk/bamburghview. Sweet, friendly B&B very near the priory, with three airy, wood-floored rooms, good showers and generous breakfasts. **£90**

St Aidan's Winery TD15 2RX, in the modern building behind the green ☎ 01289 389230, ⓦ lindisfarne -mead.co.uk. If you're keen to sample some of the world-famous Lindisfarne mead, this is the place to come. They also sell home-made chutneys, biscuits and jams. Hours depend on tides.

The Ship Marygate, TD15 2SJ ☎ 01289 389311, ⓦ the shipinn-holyisland.co.uk. The best pub on the island; friendly and traditional, with open fires and wood-panelled walls. The ales are good, as is the inexpensive pub grub. They have four cosy, en-suite rooms upstairs. **£110**

Berwick-upon-Tweed

Before the union of the English and Scottish crowns in 1603, **BERWICK-UPON-TWEED**, twelve miles north of Holy Island, was the quintessential frontier town, changing hands no fewer than fourteen times between 1174 and 1482, when the Scots finally ceded the stronghold to the English. Interminable cross-border warfare ruined Berwick's economy, turning the prosperous Scottish port of the thirteenth century into an impoverished English garrison town. By the late sixteenth century, Berwick's fortifications were in a dreadful state and Elizabeth I, fearing the resurgent alliance between France and Scotland, had the place rebuilt in line with the latest principles of military architecture. Berwick was reborn as an important seaport between 1750 and 1820, and is still peppered with elegant **Georgian mansions** dating from that period.

Berwick's **walls** – one and a half miles long and still in pristine condition – are now the town's major attraction, but look out for panels that mark the **Lowry Trail**; L.S. Lowry (1887–1976) was a regular visitor to Berwick and his sketches and paintings of local landmarks are dotted about town.

Town walls

No more than 20ft high but incredibly thick, the Elizabethan **town walls** are protected by ditches on three sides and the Tweed on the fourth, and strengthened by immense bastions. It's possible to walk a mile-long circuit (45min) around Berwick, and to take in wonderful views out to sea, across the Tweed and over the orange-tiled rooftops of the town.

13

Barracks

TD15 1DF • April–Sept Mon–Fri 10am–6pm; Oct 10am–4pm • £4.90; EH • ☎ 01289 304493, ⓦ www.english-heritage.org.uk/visit/places /berwick-upon-tweed-barracks-and-main-guard

The town's finely proportioned **Barracks**, designed by Nicholas Hawksmoor (1717) functioned as a garrison until 1964, when the King's Own Scottish Borderers regiment decamped. Inside there's the rather specialist **By the Beat of the Drum** exhibition, tracing the lives of British infantrymen from the Civil War to World War I, as well as the **King's Own Scottish Borderers Museum** and the **Berwick Museum and Art Gallery**, which has a collection of works donated by Sir William Burrell.

ARRIVAL AND DEPARTURE
BERWICK-UPON-TWEED

By train From the train station it's a 10min walk down Castlegate and Marygate to the town centre.
Destinations Durham (every 30min; 1hr 10min); Edinburgh (hourly; 45min); Newcastle (hourly; 45min).
By bus Most regional buses stop on Golden Square (where Castlegate meets Marygate), though some may also stop

in front of the train station.
Destinations Bamburgh (Mon–Sat every 2hr; Sun 3 daily 45min); Holy Island (Aug 2 daily, rest of the year 2 weekly 35min); Newcastle (Mon–Sat hourly; 2hr 15min); Wooler (Mon–Sat 6 daily; 1hr).

INFORMATION AND TOURS

Tourist office Berwick TIC and Library, Walkergate (Mon–Fri 9am–5pm, Sat 10am–5pm; ☎ 01670 622155).
Tours The tourist office can book you onto a walking tour

(Easter–Oct Mon–Fri 11am; £7; ⓦ explore-northumberland .co.uk) which includes the walls and an eighteenth-century gun bastion not usually open to the public.

ACCOMMODATION

Marshall Meadow Hotel 3 miles north of Berwick-Upon-Tweed, TD15 1UT ☎ 01289 331133, ⓦ marshall meadowshotel.co.uk. An eighteenth-century country house set in delightful grounds. The 19 en-suite guest rooms are traditional – but without chintz – and very clean. The oak-panelled restaurant has a menu of comforting seasonal dishes, featuring local produce. **£109**
Queen's Head 6 Sandgate, TD15 1EP ☎ 01289 307852, ⓦ queensheadberwick.co.uk. One of the best pubs in

town has six snug rooms, including a family room. Great evening meals and breakfasts, too (mains around £15). **£99**
YHA Berwick Dewars Lane, TD15 1HJ ☎ 0845 371 9676, ⓦ yha.org.uk/hostel/berwick. Set in a remarkable eighteenth-century granary building which, thanks to a fire in 1815, has a lean greater than that of the Leaning Tower of Pisa. Thirteen en-suite rooms, some private and family, plus a bistro and gallery. Dorms **£18**, doubles **£78**

EATING AND DRINKING

Barrel's Alehouse 59–61 Bridge St, TD15 1ES ☎ 01289 308013, ⓦ facebook.com/TheBarrelsAleHouse. Atmospheric pub specializing in (frequently changing) cask ales, lagers and stouts. It's also a great music venue, hosting an eclectic mix of jazz, blues, rock and indie bands. Daily noon–midnight.

The Maltings Eastern Lane, TD15 1AJ ☎ 01289 330999, ⓦ maltingsberwick.co.uk. Berwick's arts centre has a year-round programme of music, theatre, comedy, film and dance and a licensed café, the *Maltings Kitchen*. Café Mon–Wed 9.30am–4pm, Thurs–Sat 9.30am–4pm & 5.45–7.30pm.

Durham

The handsome city of **DURHAM** is best known for its beautiful Norman **cathedral** – there's a tremendous view of it as you approach the city by train from the south – and for its flourishing university, founded in 1832. Together, these form a little island of privilege in what's otherwise a moderately sized, working-class city. It's worth visiting for a couple of days – there are plenty of attractions, but it's more the overall atmosphere that captivates, enhanced by the omnipresent golden stone, slender bridges and the glint of the river. The heart of the city is the **marketplace**, flanked by the Guildhall and St Nicholas Church. The cathedral and church sit on a wooded peninsula to the west, while southwards stretch narrow streets lined with shops and cafés.

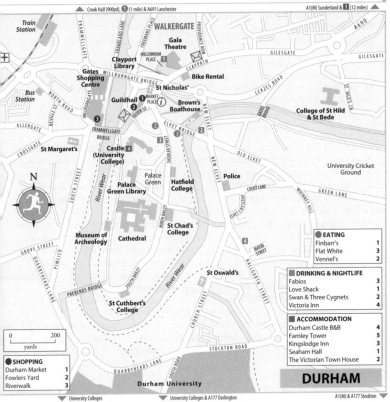

SHOPPING

Durham Market	1
Fowlers Yard	2
Riverwalk	3

EATING

Finbarr's	1
Flat White	3
Vennel's	2

DRINKING & NIGHTLIFE

Fabios	3
Love Shack	1
Swan & Three Cygnets	2
Victoria Inn	4

ACCOMMODATION

Durham Castle B&B	4
Farnley Tower	5
Kingslodge Inn	3
Seaham Hall	1
The Victorian Town House	2

DURHAM

Brief history

Durham's history revolves around its cathedral. Completed in just forty years, the cathedral was founded in 1093 to house the shrine of **St Cuthbert**, arguably the Northeast's most important and venerated saint (see box, p.668). Soon after Cuthbert was laid to rest here, the bishops of Durham were granted extensive powers to control the troublesome northern marches of the Kingdom (a rabble of invading Picts from Scotland and revolting Norman earls, ruling as semi-independent **Prince Bishops**, with their own army, mint and courts of law. At the peak of their power in the fourteenth century, the office went into decline, especially in the wake of the Reformation), yet the bishop's clung to the vestiges of their authority until 1836, when they ceded them to the Crown. The bishops abandoned Durham Castle for their palace in Bishop Auckland (see p.671) and transferred their old home to the fledgling Durham University, England's third-oldest seat of learning after Oxford and Cambridge.

Durham Cathedral

DH1 3EH • Mon–Sat 9.30am–6pm, Sun 12.30–5.30pm • Donation requested; Open Treasure ticket (£7.50) covers entry to the Monks' Dormitory, the Great Kitchen and the Treasures of St Cuthbert • **Tours** April–Oct Mon–Sat 2–3 daily; 1hr • £5 • ☎ 0191 386 4266, ⓦ durhamcathedral.co.uk

From the marketplace, it's a five-minute walk up Saddler Street to **Durham Cathedral**, considered a supreme example of the Norman-Romanesque style. The awe-inspiring **nave** used pointed arches for the first time in England, raising the vaulted ceiling to new and dizzying heights. The weight of the stone is borne by massive pillars, their heaviness

13

ST CUTHBERT

Born in North Northumbria in 653, **Cuthbert** spent most of his youth in Melrose Abbey in Scotland, from where he moved briefly to Lindisfarne Island, which was at that time a well-known centre of religious endeavour. Preferring the peace and rugged solitude of the Farne Islands, he lived on Inner Farne for thirty years. News of his piety spread, however, and he was head-hunted to become Bishop of Lindisfarne, a position he accepted reluctantly. Uncomfortable in the limelight, he soon returned to Inner Farne, and when he died his remains were moved to Lindisfarne before being carted off to Durham Cathedral.

relieved by striking Moorish-influenced geometric patterns. A door on the western side gives access to the **tower**, from where there are beautiful views. Separated from the nave by a Victorian marble screen is the **choir**, where the dark Restoration stalls are overshadowed by the 13ft-high **bishop's throne**. Beyond is the **Chapel of the Nine Altars**, which dates from the thirteenth century. Here, and around the **Shrine of St Cuthbert**, much of the stonework is of local Weardale marble, each dark shaft bearing its own pattern of fossils. Cuthbert himself lies beneath a plain marble slab, his shrine having gained a reputation over the centuries for its curative powers. The legend was given credence in 1104, when the saint's body was exhumed in Chester-le-Street for reburial here, and was found to be completely uncorrupted, more than four hundred years after his death on Lindisfarne. Almost certainly, this was the result of his fellow monks having (unintentionally) preserved the body by laying it in sand containing salt crystals.

Back near the entrance, at the west end of the church, is the **Galilee Chapel**; begun in the 1170s, its light and exotic decoration is in imitation of the Great Mosque of Córdoba. The chapel contains the simple tombstone of the **Venerable Bede** (see p.650), the Northumbrian monk credited with being England's first historian. Bede died at the monastery of Jarrow in 735, and his remains were transferred to the cathedral in 1020.

Open Treasure

A large wooden doorway opposite the cathedral's main entrance leads into the spacious cloisters, which are flanked by the most intact set of medieval monastic buildings in the UK. These now house **Open Treasure**, a display exploring the history of Christianity in northeast England, which kicks off in the fourteenth-century **Monks' Dormitory** with its magnificent oak-beamed ceiling, where interactive displays evoke the sights, sounds and smells of life in a medieval monastery. The **Collections Gallery** showcases some of the most precious manuscripts from the cathedral's collections; while the spectacular **Great Kitchen** – one of only two surviving medieval monastic kitchens in the UK – is a setting for The Treasures of St Cuthbert, featuring beautifully preserved Anglo-Saxon artefacts.

Palace Green Library

Palace Green, DH1 3RN • Mon noon–5pm, Tues–Sun 10am–5pm • Free, although entry fee for changing exhibitions • ☎ 0191 334 2972, ⓦ dur.ac.uk/palace.green/whatson

Palace Green Library, between the cathedral and the castle, shows off a wonderful collection of the university's treasures, including medieval manuscripts and incunabula – early printed books. The library is divided into four separate galleries, two of which host permanent exhibitions that are free to view: **Living on the Hills: 10,000 years of Durham**; and the **DLI Collection: Courage, Comrades, Community**. The Durham Light Infantry (DLI) were one of the most famous county regiments in the British Army and the exhibit tells the story from their beginnings in 1181, via World War I (when it lost twelve thousand soldiers) to its last parade in 1968. Other exhibitions change but could feature anything from Japanese enamel pots to Chinese imperial textiles and ancient Egyptian relics. The *Courtyard Café* (daily 9.30am–4pm) is on the ground floor.

Durham Castle

13

DH1 3RW • Tours daily: Easter & July–Sept 10am, 11am, noon, 2pm, 3pm, 4pm & 5pm; rest of the year 2pm, 3pm & 4pm; 50min • £5 • ☎ 0191 334 3800, ⓦ durhamworldheritagesite.com

Durham Castle lost its medieval appearance long ago, as each successive Prince Bishop modernized the building according to the tastes of the time. The university was bequeathed the castle in the nineteenth century and subsequently renovated the old keep as a hall of residence. It's only possible to visit the castle on a **guided tour**, departing from outside Palace Green Library, highlights of which include the enormous hanging staircase and the underground Norman chapel, one of the few surviving interiors from the period. It's notable for its lively Romanesque carved capitals, including a green man, and what may be the earliest surviving depiction anywhere of a mermaid. Note that out of term time you can stay here (see below).

Crook Hall

Frankland Lane, Sidegate, DH1 5SZ • Mon–Wed & Sun 10am–5pm • April–Oct £7.50, Nov–March £5.50 • ☎ 0191 384 8028, ⓦ crookhallgardens.co.uk

Around half a mile north of the centre, **Crook Hall** is a hidden gem. A rare mix of medieval, Jacobean and Georgian architecture, with origins dating from the twelfth century, it's said to be one of the oldest inhabited houses in the area. You can explore its rambling rooms, complete with period furniture and rickety staircases, as well as a series of beautifully tended, themed gardens, including the ethereal Silver and White garden, the Shakespeare Garden, planted with herbs used in Elizabethan times, and the delightful Secret Walled Garden. Book **afternoon tea** in the manor house tearooms in advance (£24.50) or drop in at the **Garden Gate Café and shop** at the gatehouse (sandwiches from £5).

ARRIVAL AND INFORMATION

DURHAM

By train Durham's train station is on North Rd, a 10min walk from the centre of the city.

Destinations Berwick-upon-Tweed (every 30min; 1hr 10min), Darlington (frequent; 20min); London (every 30min–1hr; 3hr); Newcastle (frequent; 15min); York (frequent; 50min).

By bus It's a 5min walk to the city centre from the bus station on North Rd.

Destinations Bishop Auckland (frequent; 30min);

Darlington (every 20min; 1hr 10min); Middlesbrough (every 30min; 55min); Newcastle (Mon–Sat every 30min, Sun 4–6 daily; 50min); Stanhope (Mon–Fri 4 daily; 45min).

Tourist information There are visitor information points dotted around the city. From mid-April to mid-Sept volunteer "pointers" on Market Square give out information (ⓦ durhampointers.co.uk).

Website ⓦ thisisdurham.com

GETTING AROUND

By bus The Cathedral Bus is a minibus service running two routes around Durham via the train station, the bus station, the marketplace and the cathedral. Tickets cost £1 and are valid all day (Mon–Sat).

ACCOMMODATION

Durham Castle B&B DH1 3RW ☎ 0191 334 4106, ⓦ dur.ac.uk; map p.667. Out of term time you can have the unique experience of staying in Durham Castle. Accommodation ranges from standard rooms with shared bathrooms to two grand "state rooms" (£250), one with a four-poster and seventeenth-century tapestries. Breakfast is served in the thirteenth-century Great Hall. **£100**

Farnley Tower The Avenue, DH1 4DX ☎ 0191 375 0011, ⓦ farnley-tower.co.uk; map p.667. A 10min walk up a steep hill west from the centre, this fine stone Victorian house has thirteen comfortable rooms with bright, coordinated fabrics. The best rooms have sweeping city views. **£95**

Kingslodge Inn Waddington St, DH1 4BG ☎ 0191 370 9977, ⓦ kingslodgeinn.co.uk; map p.667. The 23 en-suite rooms at this newly reopened inn aren't spacious, but they are comfortable and clean. The pub-restaurant is usually fairly quiet. Free on-site car park, a rarity in central Durham. **£95**

Seaham Hall Lord Byron's Walk, Seaham, SR7 7AG, 12 miles northeast of Durham ☎ 0191 516 1400, ⓦ seaham-hall.co.uk; map p.667. Perched on a clifftop overlooking the sea, this hip, exclusive hotel makes a great coastal base for city sightseeing – Durham is only a 20min drive away. It's known for its luxurious spa and pampering

13

treatments and has a wonderful restaurant; spa, dinner, bed and breakfast packages are available. **£195**

The Victorian Town House 2 Victoria Terrace, DH1 4RW ☎0191 370 9963, ⓦdurhambedandbreakfast .com; map p.667. This friendly and tranquil B&B features three en-suite rooms: one twin, one double and one family room. It's located on a quiet and attractive backstreet backed by gardens and is a 5min walk from the station. **£95**

EATING

Finbarrs Aykley Heads House, HH1 5TS ☎0191 307 7033, ⓦfinbarrsrestaurant.co.uk; map p.667. This chic restaurant with crisp white tablecloths serves up anything from full English breakfasts and banana pancakes to dinners of Moroccan lamb with golden raisins; the sweet cherry and pistachio sundaes are delicious. Mains from £15. Mon–Sat noon–2.30pm & 6–9.30pm, Sun noon–2.30pm & 6–9pm.

Flat White 21a Elvet Bridge, DH1 3AA ☎07936 449291, ⓦflatwhitekitchen.com; map p.667. Durham's hippest café, serving barista-standard coffee and hearty sandwiches served on wooden boards (£5). Sit outside in the sun, or inside at tables made from old sewing machines. It has a fancier sister restaurant on Saddler St too. Mon–Sat 8am–4pm, Sun 10am–6pm.

Vennel's 71 Saddler's Yard, Saddler St, DH1 3NP ☎0191 375 0571; map p.667. Named after the skinny alley or "vennel" where it stands – near the junction with Elvet Bridge – this café serves up generous sandwiches, salads, quiche (£5–6) and tasty cakes in its sixteenth-century courtyard. Mon–Sat 9.30am–5.30pm, Sun 10.30am–5.30pm.

DRINKING AND NIGHTLIFE

Walkergate is the area to head for if you're after loud, lively bars and mainstream nightclubs pumping out cheesy music, but there are also plenty of quieter establishments and more traditional, laidback pubs. Durham's **clubs**, frequented by students during the week and locals at the weekends, don't generally have a dress code, but the locals tend to make an effort.

Fabios 66 Sadler St, DH1 3NP ☎0191 383 9290, ⓦfabiosdurham.com; map p.667. Just above *La Spaghettata* pizzeria, *Fabios* occupies a series of rooms filled with comfy, rug-draped sofas and chalked-up black-boards offering drinks from around £3. The atmosphere is cool and relaxed, with music a melange of rap, r'n'b and dance. Daily 6pm–2am.

Love Shack Walkergate, DH1 1WA ☎0191 384 5757, ⓦloveshackdurham.com; map p.667. Large, popular club with two bars, snug booths and a sleek dancefloor. Music is an energetic mix of contemporary club tunes and cheesy classics. Wed–Fri 10pm–2am, Sat 8pm–2am.

Swan & Three Cygnets Elvet Bridge, DH1 3AF ☎0191 384 0242; map p.667. Sitting proudly at the end of Elvet Bridge overlooking the River Wear, this loud and cheery pub serves cheap drinks and is filled with a mixed crowd of locals and students. Mon–Sat 11am–11pm, Sun noon–10.30pm.

Victoria Inn 86 Hallgarth St, DH1 3AS ☎0191 386 5269, ⓦvictoriainn-durhamcity.co.uk; map p.667. With its three open fires and rickety wooden stools, this cosy traditional pub specializes in local ales – try the creamy Tyneside Blonde or the hoppy Centurion Bitter – and stocks more than thirty Irish whiskeys. Mon–Sat noon–3pm & 6–11pm, Sun noon–3pm & 7–11pm.

ENTERTAINMENT

In addition to shows at the Gala Theatre, you can catch regular **classical concerts** at venues around the city, including the cathedral. Ask the tourist office for more details.

Gala Theatre Millennium Place, DH1 1WA ☎0191 332 4041, ⓦgaladurham.co.uk; map p.667. A modern venue staging music of all kinds, plus theatre, cinema, dance and comedy.

SHOPPING

As well as the indoor market (see below), Durham has a monthly **farmer's market** in the Market Place (third Thurs of the month 9am–4pm; ⓦthisisdurham.com).

Durham Market Market Place, DH1 3NJ ⓦdurham markets.co.uk; map p.667. Durham's Indoor Market holds a variety of stalls including a haberdashers, sweet shop and fishmongers. Mon–Sat 9am–5pm.

Fowlers Yard Silver St, DH1 3RA ⓦfowlersyarddurham .co.uk; map p.667. A series of workshops behind the marketplace showcasing local trades and crafts. Drop by to watch the craftspeople at work, commission a piece or buy off the cuff. Opening hours vary.

Riverwalk DH1 4SL ⓦtheriverwalk.co.uk; map p.667. Shopping development undergoing a much-needed revamp but stores including vintage Ding Dong and gentleman's outfitters Woven remain open.

Around Durham

The county of Durham has shaken off its grimy reputation in recent years and recast itself as a thriving tourist area. The well-to-do market towns of **Bishop Auckland** and **Barnard Castle** make great day-trips from Durham, and there's plenty of excellent walking and cycling in the wilds of the two Pennine valleys, **Teesdale** and **Weardale**. You'll find some top-class museums in the area, too, including **Beamish**, **Locomotion** and the **Bowes Museum**.

Beamish Museum

10 miles north of Durham, DH9 0RG • Daily: April–Oct 10am–5pm; Nov–March 10am–4pm • £19, under-17s £11 • ☏ 0191 370 4000, ⓦ beamish.org.uk • Waggonway #28/28A runs from Newcastle (every 30min Mon–Sat, hourly Sun); from Durham catch a bus to Chester-le-Street to connect with the #28/28A

The open-air **Beamish Museum** spreads out over three hundred acres, with buildings taken from all over the region painstakingly reassembled in six main sections linked by restored trams and buses. Complete with costumed shopkeepers, workers and householders, four of the sections show life in 1913, before the upheavals of World War I, including a **colliery village** complete with drift mine (regular tours throughout the day) and a large-scale recreation of the high street in a **market town**. Two areas date to 1825, at the beginning of the northeast's industrial development, including a **manor house**, with horse yard, formal gardens, vegetable plots and orchards. You can ride on the beautifully restored steam-powered carousel, the **Steam Galloper**, which dates from the 1890s, and the **Pockerley Waggonway**, which is pulled along by a replica of George Stephenson's *Locomotion* (see p.672), the first passenger-carrying steam train in the world.

Bishop Auckland

BISHOP AUCKLAND, a busy little market town eleven miles southwest of Durham, grew up slowly around its showpiece building, **Auckland Castle**, and became famous throughout England as the homeland of the mighty Prince Bishops. Today the town has paled into lesser significance but still offers enough for a pleasant hour or two's wander.

Auckland Castle

DL14 7NR • **Castle** Closed into 2018 for extensive restoration work; see online for times and charges • **Deer park** Daily 7am–dusk • Free • ☏ 01388 602576, ⓦ aucklandcastle.org

Looking more like an opulent Gothic mansion than a traditional fortress, **Auckland Castle** served for 900 years as a private palace for the Prince Bishops of Durham, who stood second in power only to the King of England. The castle is one of the most important and best-preserved medieval bishops' palaces in Europe and today it's being transformed into an arts, faith and heritage destination; an extension will house the UK's first **Faith Museum**, the original seventeenth-century walled garden is being revamped, and a mining art gallery (which includes works by prominent local mining artists Tom McGuinness and Norman Cornish), Spanish gallery and welcome building are opening in the adjoining Market Place. These will open in stages between 2017 and 2020, with Auckland Castle itself reopening in May 2018. Meanwhile, you can stroll around the 200-acre **Deer Park**, or book tickets for the summer spectacular open-air show, **Kynren** (ⓦ elevenarches.org), which features the castle as a backdrop to a reenactment of 2000 years of history.

Binchester Roman Fort

1.5 miles north of Bishop Auckland, DL14 8DJ • Daily: Easter–June & Sept 11am–5pm; July & Aug 10am–5pm • £2.55 • ☏ 0191 370 8712, ⓦ durham.gov.uk

From the town's marketplace, it's a pleasant twenty-minute walk along the banks of the River Wear to the remains of **Binchester Roman Fort**. While most of the stone fort and a civilian settlement that occupied the area remain hidden beneath surrounding fields,

13 the bathhouse with its sophisticated underground heating system (hypocaust) is visible. Excavations are ongoing.

By train Bishop Auckland is the end of the line for trains from Darlington (26min); the station is on Newgate St.

By bus Buses terminate at Saddler St. There are frequent services to Durham (40min) and Newcastle (1hr 25min).

Locomotion (National Railway Museum Shildon)

Shildon, DL4 2RE, 12 miles south of Durham • Daily 10am–5pm • Free • ☎ 01388 777999, Ⓦ nrm.org.uk • Trains from Durham and Darlington to Bishop Auckland stop at Shildon station, a 2min walk from the museum. Buses #1 and 1B (to Crook and Tow Law) run from Darlington (Mon–Sat every 30min), stopping at Dale Rd, a 15min walk from the museum

The first passenger train in the world left from the station at Shildon in 1825 – making this the world's oldest railway town. It's a heritage explored in the magnificently realized **Locomotion** (also known as NRM Shildon), the regional outpost of York's National Railway Museum. It's less a museum and more an experience, spread out around a 1.5-mile-long site, with the attractions linked by free bus from the reception building. Depots, sidings, junctions and coal drops lead ultimately to the heart of the museum, **Collection** – a gargantuan steel hangar containing an extraordinary array of seventy locomotives, dating from the very earliest days of steam. With interactive children's exhibits, summer steam rides, rallies and shows, it makes an excellent family day out.

Barnard Castle

Affectionately known as "Barney", the honey-coloured market town of **BARNARD CASTLE** lies fifteen miles southwest of Bishop Auckland. The middle of the town is dominated by the splendid octagonal **Market Cross**; built in 1747 and formerly functioning as a market for dairy and butter, it now serves a more mundane purpose as a roundabout.

The castle

Galgate, DL12 8PR • Daily: April–Sept 10am–6pm; Oct 10am–5pm; Nov–March Sat & Sun 10am–4pm • £5.40; EH • ☎ 01833 638212, Ⓦ www.english-heritage.org.uk/visit/places/barnard-castle

The skeletal remains of the town's **castle** sit high on a rock overlooking the River Tees. It was founded in 1125 by the powerful Norman baron Bernard de Balliol – thus the town's name – and later ended up in the hands of Richard III. Richard's crest, in the shape of a boar, is still visible carved above a window in the inner ward.

Bowes Museum

Half a mile east of the town centre, DL12 8NP • Daily 10am–5pm • £10.50, under-16s free • ☎ 01833 690606, Ⓦ bowesmuseum.org.uk

Castle aside, the prime attraction in town is the grand French-style chateau that constitutes the **Bowes Museum**. Begun in 1869, the chateau was commissioned by John and Josephine Bowes, a local businessman and MP and his French actress wife, who spent much of their time in Paris collecting ostentatious treasures and antiques. Don't miss the

---

TRAILS AND CYCLEWAYS

Coast-to-Coast (C2C) Ⓦ c2c-guide.co.uk. This demanding cycle route runs 140 miles from Whitehaven to Sunderland.

Hadrian's Wall Path Ⓦ hadrianswallcountry.co.uk. An 84-mile waymarked trail allowing you to walk the length of this atmospheric Roman monument.

National Route 72 Ⓦ hadrian-guide.co.uk. Cycle path that starts in the Lake District and heads to the Northumberland coast, running the length of Hadrian's Wall.

Pennine Way Ⓦ thepennineway.co.uk. This 270-mile-long footpath starts in the Peak District National Park, runs along the Pennine ridge through the Yorkshire Dales, up into Northumberland, across the Cheviots, and finishes in the Scottish Borders.

beautiful **Silver Swan**, a life-size musical automaton dating from 1773 – every afternoon at 2pm it puts on an enchanting show, preening its shiny feathers while swimming along a river filled with jumping fish.

Egglestone Abbey

mile southeast of Barnard Castle, DL12 9TN • Daily 10am–6.30pm • Free; EH • ⓦ www.english-heritage.org.uk/visit/places/egglestone-abbey

It's a fine mile-long walk from the castle, southeast (downriver) through the fields above the banks of the Tees, to the lovely shattered ruins of **Egglestone Abbey**, a minor foundation dating from 1195. A succession of wars and the Dissolution destroyed most of it, but you can still see the remnants of a thirteenth-century church and the remains of the monks' living quarters, including an ingenious latrine system.

ARRIVAL AND INFORMATION   BARNARD CASTLE

By bus Buses stop either side of Galgate.
Destinations Bishop Auckland (Mon–Sat 6 daily; 50min); Darlington (Mon–Sat every 30min; Sun hourly; 45min); Middleton-in-Teesdale (Mon–Sat hourly; 35min); Raby

Castle (Mon–Sat hourly; 15min).
Tourist information There's a visitor information point at The Witham arts centre, 3 Horsemarket (Tues–Sat 10am–4pm).

ACCOMMODATION

Homelands 85 Galgate, DL12 8ES ☎ 01833 638757, ⓦ homelandsguesthouse.co.uk. An assortment of pretty rooms with floral soft furnishings and comfortable beds.

The owners are very knowledgeable about the area and can recommend plenty of good walks. Breakfast is great, with delicious fruit salads and generous cooked options. **£85**

EATING AND DRINKING

Blagraves House 30–32 The Bank, DL12 8PN ☎ 01833 637668, ⓦ blagraves.com. Supposed to be the oldest house in Barnard Castle, dating back 500 years, this refined restaurant – oozing atmosphere, with its low oak wooden beams, open log fires and plush furnishings – specializes in traditional British cuisine. Dishes such as pan-fried fillet of beef cost from £23. Tues–Sun 7–10pm.

Fernaville's Rest Whorlton, DL12 8XD ☎ 01833 627341, ⓦ fernavilles.com. Cosy country pub, with open fires and flagstone floors, in a picturesque village four miles east of Barnard Castle. The food is traditional pub grub which changes seasonally – try the shepherd's pie with red cabbage, apple and kale (£12.90). Daily 5–10pm; kitchen daily 5.30–8.30pm.

Teesdale

TEESDALE extends twenty-odd miles northwest from Barnard Castle, its pastoral landscapes on the lower reaches beginning calmly enough but soon replaced by wilder Pennine scenery. Picturesque little villages like **Middleton-in-Teesdale** and Romaldkirk pepper the valley, while natural attractions include the stunning **Cow Green Reservoir** in Upper Teesdale, home to the indigenous Teesdale violet and the blue spring gentian.

Raby Castle

Staindrop, DL2 3AH, 8 miles northeast of Barnard Castle • **Castle** Easter to Sept Mon–Wed & Sun 12.30–4.30pm (weekdays by guided tour only) • £12 (includes park & gardens) • **Park & gardens** Easter to Sept Mon–Wed & Sun 11am–5pm • £7 • ☎ 01833 660202, ⓦ rabycastle.com

Eight miles from Barnard Castle, up the A688, beckon the splendid, sprawling battlements of **Raby Castle**, reflecting the power of the Neville family, who ruled the local roost until 1569. The Neville estates were confiscated after the "Rising of the North", the abortive attempt to replace Elizabeth I with Mary Queen of Scots, with Raby subsequently passing to the Vane family in 1626, who still own it today. You can explore the interior, with its lavish bedrooms, dining room, kitchen and drawing rooms, which are filled with furniture and artwork dating from the sixteenth and seventeenth centuries.

Middleton-in-Teesdale

Surrounded by magnificent, wild countryside laced with a myriad of public footpaths and cycling trails, the attractive town of **MIDDLETON-IN-TEESDALE** is a popular base for

13

walkers and cyclists. A relaxed little place, it was once the archetypal "company town", owned lock, stock and barrel by the London Lead Company, which began mining here in 1753. Just a few miles out of town is a famous set of waterfalls, **Low Force** and **High Force**.

High Force

DL12 0XH · Daily: Easter–Oct 10am–5pm; Nov–Easter 10am–4pm · £1.50 · ⓦ highforcewaterfall.com

Heading on the B6277 northwest out of Middleton-in-Teesdale, you'll first pass the turning off to the rapids of **Low Force**. Another mile up the road is the altogether more spectacular **High Force** (from the Norse "foss", meaning waterfall), a 70ft cascade that tumbles over an outcrop of the Whin Sill ridge and into a deep pool. The waterfall is on private Raby land (see p.673) and is reached by a short woodland walk.

ARRIVAL AND INFORMATION   MIDDLETON-IN-TEESDALE

By bus There are hourly bus services to Middleton-in-Teesdale from Barnard Castle (35min).

Tourist office Market Place (restricted hours, though usually daily 10am–1pm; ☎ 01833 641001).

ACCOMMODATION AND EATING

★**The Old Barn** 12 Market Place, DL12 0QG ☎ 01833 640258, ⓦ theoldbarn-teesdale.co.uk. In a very central location next to the tourist office, this sympathetically converted barn has three attractive B&B rooms with rustic furniture, elegant iron beds and Egyptian cotton sheets. There's a little patio garden to chill out in after a hard day's walking. **£75**

Rose & Crown Romaldkirk, DL12 9EB, 4 miles southwest of Middleton-in-Teesdale ☎ 01833 650213, ⓦ rose-and-crown.co.uk. Beautiful ivy-clad eighteenth-century coaching inn set on the village green and next to a pretty Saxon church. Beneath the tastefully decorated rooms is a refined restaurant (mains from £16), serving accomplished dishes such as pan-fried wood pigeon with juniper-berry sauce and grilled pancetta, plus a cosy bar with a wood fire. Restaurant Mon–Sat 6.30–9pm, Sun noon–2.30pm; bar meals daily noon–2.30pm and 6.30–9pm. **£140**

Weardale

Sitting to the north of Teesdale, the valley of **WEARDALE** was once hunting ground reserved for the Prince Bishops, but was later transformed into a major centre for lead mining and limestone quarrying; this industrial heritage is celebrated at the excellent **Killhope Lead Mining musueum** and the **Weardale Museum** near Irehopesburn. The main settlement is **Stanhope**, a small market town with a pleasant open-air heated swimming pool (£4; times at ⓦ stanhopehosting.co.uk/pool), perfect for cooling off after a long walk in the hills. Just to the east is the village of **Wolsingham**, a renowned pilgrimage centre in the Middle Ages, and neighbouring **Frosterley** which features the remnants of an eleventh-century chapel.

Weardale Museum

Ireshopeburn, DL13 1HD, 9 miles west of Stanhope · Easter, May, June, Sept & Oct Wed–Sun 1.30–4.30pm; July & Aug daily 1.30–4.30pm · £3 · ☎ 01388 517433, ⓦ www.weardalemuseum.co.uk

At Ireshopeburn, west of Stanhope, the **Weardale Museum** tells the story of the dale, in particular its lead mining and the importance of Methodism (the faith of most of the county of Durham's lead miners). There's a reconstructed miner's house as well as the "Wesley Room", dedicated to the founder of Methodism, John Wesley, and filled with his writings, books and belongings.

Killhope Lead Mining Museum

5 miles west of Ireshopeburn and 12 miles east of Stanhope, DL13 1AR · April–Oct daily 10.30am–5pm · £8.60 (includes mine visit) · ☎ 01388 537505, ⓦ www.killhope.org.uk · Request stop on bus #101 (see opposite), contact Weardale Travel (☎ 01388 528235, ⓦ weardale-travel.co.uk)

If you're keen to learn about Weardale's mining past, a visit to **Killhope Lead Mining Museum**, five miles west of Ireshopeburn, is an absolute must. After many successful years as one of the richest mines in Britain, Killhope shut for good in 1910, and now houses a terrific, child-friendly museum that brings to life the difficulties and dangers f a mining life. The site is littered with preserved machinery and nineteenth-century buildings, including the Mine Shop where workers would spend the night after finishing a late shift. The highlight of the visit comes when you descend Park Level Mine – you'll be given wellies, a hard hat and a torch – in the company of a guide who expounds entertainingly about the realities of life underground, notably the perils of the "Black Spit", a lung disease which killed many men by their mid-forties.

ARRIVAL AND INFORMATION
WEARDALE

By bus Bus #101 runs roughly hourly (Mon–Sat) between Bishop Auckland and Stanhope, calling at Wolsingham and Frosterley.

Information Durham Dales Centre, Stanhope, houses

the tourist office (daily: April–Oct 9am–5pm; Nov–March 9am–4pm; ☎01388 527650, ⓦdurhamdalescentre.co.uk) and a café.

GETTING AROUND

By bus Apart from #101, buses are relatively irregular and sporadic round these parts. Contact the Weardale Bus Company (☎01388 528235, ⓦweardale-travel.co.uk).

By train Weardale Railway is a volunteer-run steam line

which chugs along from Bishop Auckland (see p.671) to Stanhope, stopping at Wolsingham and Frosterley on request. For timetables and fares see ⓦweardale-railway .org.uk.

ACCOMMODATION

★**Dowfold House** Crook, DL15 9AB, 6 miles east of Wolsingham ☎01388 762473, ⓦdowfoldhouse.co.uk. Wonderful, relaxed B&B in a Victorian house surrounded by lush gardens and with splendid views out over Weardale.

Breakfast, served in the elegant dining room, is the highlight, with lashings of free-range eggs, locally sourced sausages and bacon, home-made bread and jams. __£90__

EATING AND DRINKING

★**Black Bull** Frosterley, DL13 2SL ☎01388 527784, ⓦblackbullfrosterley.com. Hop off the Weardale Railway (see above) and into this traditional pub with beams, ranges, oak tables and flagstone floors. The ales are excellent, as is the

food, which is hearty and delicious; mains, like herb-crusted lamb shoulder with apricot and walnut stuffing, start at £10. Thurs–Sat 11am–11pm, Sun 11am–5pm; food served Thurs–Sat noon–3pm & 7–9pm, Sun noon–2.30pm.

Allen Valley

The B6295 climbs north out of Weardale into Northumberland, soon dropping into the **Allen Valley**, where heather-covered moorland shelters small settlements that once made their living from lead mining. The dramatic surroundings are easily viewed from a series of river walks accessible from either of the main settlements: **Allenheads**, at the top of the valley, twelve miles from Stanhope, where handsome stone buildings stand close to the river, or **Allendale Town**, another four miles north. Allendale is a quiet, rural spot – New Year's Eve excepted, when the villagers celebrate pagan-style by throwing barrels of burning tar onto a huge, spluttering bonfire – and is a good place to base yourself for local walking; it has a small supermarket and several friendly pubs, all centred on the market square.

ARRIVAL AND GETTING AROUND
ALLEN VALLEY

By bus Service #668 runs from Hexham to Allendale (Mon–Sat 4 daily; 40min) and Allenheads (Mon–Sat 3 daily; 55min).

EATING AND DRINKING

Allenheads Inn Allenheads, NE47 9HJ ☎01434 685200, ⓦallenheadsinn.co.uk. A popular stop for cyclists on the C2C route, this pub provides beer and inexpensive bar meals, and has seven rooms which get booked up quickly in summer. Mon–Thurs 4–11pm, Fri & Sat 12.30pm–midnight, Sun 12.30–10.30pm. __£80__

King's Head Market Place, Allendale, NE47 9BD

☎01434 683 681, ⓦthekingsheadallendale.com. A handsome eighteenth-century stone-built pub run by two ex-police officers and serving Marston's cask ales and Jennings' Cumberland Ale as well as classic pub grub: fish and chips, scampi and burgers. In summer you can eat outside on the village square. Daily noon–11pm.

13

Blanchland

A trans-moorland route into Northumberland, the B6278 cuts north from Weardale at Stanhope for ten wild miles to **BLANCHLAND**, a handful of lichen-stained stone cottages huddled round an L-shaped square that was once the outer court of a twelfth-century abbey. The village has been preserved since 1721, when Lord Crewe bequeathed his estate to trustees on condition that they restored the old buildings, as Blanchland had slowly fallen into disrepair after the abbey's dissolution.

ARRIVAL AND DEPARTURE
BLANCHLAND

By bus Service #733 connects Blanchland with Consett (Mon–Fri 3 daily; 30min).

EATING AND DRINKING

★ **Lord Crewe Arms Hotel** DH8 9SP ☎ 01434 675251, ⓦ lordcrewearmsblanchland.co.uk. Once the abbot's lodge, this hotel's nooks and crannies are an enticing mixture of medieval and eighteenth-century Gothic, including the vaulted basements, two big fireplaces and a priest's hideaway stuck inside the chimney. You can eat in the restaurant (mains from £15), or more cheaply in the public bar in the undercroft. Restaurant Mon–Fri noon 2.30pm & 6–9pm, Sat noon–3.30pm & 6–9pm, Sun noon–3pm & 6.30–8.30pm; bar food Mon–Sat noon 8.30pm, Sun 6.30–8.30pm. **£172**

Tees Valley

Admittedly not much of a tourist hotspot in comparison to Northumberland or Durham, the **Tees Valley** – once an industrial powerhouse and birthplace of one of the greatest developments in Britain, the public steam railway – nevertheless has some enjoyable attractions. **Darlington**, with its strong railway heritage, is a pleasant place to spend a day, while Middlesbrough's **MIMA** and Hartlepool's **Maritime Experience** (daily: April–Oct 10am–5pm; Nov–March 11am–4pm; £9.25, under-16s £7; ☎01429 860077, ⓦhartlepoolsmaritimeexperience.com) are all worthwhile, the latter particularly if you have children to entertain.

Darlington

Abbreviated to "Darlo" by the locals, the busy market town of **DARLINGTON** hit the big time in 1825, when George Stephenson's "Number 1 Engine", later called *Locomotion*, hurtled from here to nearby Stockton-on-Tees at the terrifying speed of fifteen miles per hour. The town subsequently grew into a rail-engineering centre, and it didn't look back till the closure of the works in 1966. The origins of the rest of Darlington lie deep in Saxon times. The monks carrying St Cuthbert's body from Ripon to Durham (see p.666) stopped here, the saint lending his name to the graceful riverside church of **St Cuthbert**. The market square, one of England's largest, spreads beyond the church up to the restored and lively **Victorian covered market** (Mon–Sat 8am–5pm).

Head of Steam
North Rd Station, a 20min walk up Northgate from the marketplace, DL3 6ST • April–Sept Tues–Sun 10am–4pm, Oct–March Wed–Sun 11am–3.30pm • £4.95 • ☎ 01325 460532, ⓦ www.darlington.gov.uk

Darlington's railway history is celebrated at the wonderful little **Head of Steam** museum which is actually the restored 1842 passenger station on the original Stockton and Darlington railway route. The highlight is Stephenson's *Locomotion No. 1*, a tiny wood-panelled steam engine, the first-ever steam train to carry fare-paying passengers. Other locomotives jostle for space alongside, including the shiny, racing-green *Derwent*, the oldest surviving Darlington-built steam train. These, along with a collection of station and line-side signs, uniforms, luggage, a reconstructed ticket office and carriages successfully bring to life the most important era in Darlington's existence.

ARRIVAL AND INFORMATION   **DARLINGTON**

By train The train station is on Bank Top, a 10min walk from the central marketplace: from the train station walk up Victoria Rd to the roundabout and turn right down Feethams. Destinations Bishop Auckland (frequent; 25min); Durham (frequent; 20min); Newcastle (frequent; 35min).
By bus Most buses stop outside the Town Hall on Feethams.

Destinations Barnard Castle (Mon–Sat every 30min, Sun hourly; 45min); Bishop Auckland (Mon–Sat every 30min, Sun hourly; 1hr); Durham (every 20min; 1hr 10 min).
Information Leaflets on the region are available at the library on Crown St (Mon & Tues 9am–6pm, Thurs 10am–6pm, Wed & Fri 9am–5pm, Sat 9am–4pm; ☎ 01325 462034).

ACCOMMODATION

Clow Beck House Croft-on-Tees, 2 miles south, DL2 2SP ☎ 01325 721075, ⓦ clowbeckhouse.co.uk. Very welcoming B&B with thirteen individually decorated rooms named after flowers and set round a pretty landscaped garden. The owner is also an accomplished chef, creating delicious breakfasts – the Skipton sausage is very tasty – and evening meals (mains from £17). **£140**

Rockliffe Hall Hurworth-on-Tees, 5 miles south, DL2 2DU ☎ 01325 729999, ⓦ rockliffehall.com. Swanky hotel in a red-brick Victorian Gothic pile between the villages of Croft-on-Tees and Hurworth, which lays claim to having the UK's longest golf course. The rooms are cool and luxurious, and there's a spa, as well as three restaurants. **£175**

EATING AND DRINKING

★ Bay Horse 45 The Green, Hurworth, 5 miles south, DL2 2AA ☎ 01325 720663, ⓦ thebayhorsehurworth com. This exquisite pub has a roaring fire, exposed wooden beams, comfy bar stools and chalked-up menus. Tuck into delicious meals such as braised daube of beef

(£22) and make sure that you leave room for their puds; the sticky toffee pudding with salted caramel sauce (£7) is fabulous. Mon–Sat 11am–11pm, Sun noon–10.30pm; kitchen Mon–Sat noon–2.30pm & 6–9.30pm, Sun noon–4pm & 6.30–8.30pm.

Middlesbrough Institute of Modern Art

Centre Square Middlesbrough, TS1 2AZ, 15 miles east of Darlington • Tues, Wed, Fri & Sat 10am–4.30pm, Thurs 10am–7pm, Sun noon–4pm • Free • ☎ 01642 726720, ⓦ visitmima.com • 10min walk from the train station

The stunning **Middlesbrough Institute of Modern Art (MIMA)** is one of the few tourist draws in the industrial town of Middlesbrough. Bringing together its municipal art collections, changing exhibitions concentrate on fine arts and crafts from the early twentieth century to the present day, with a heavy emphasis on ceramics and jewellery. The collection features work by David Hockney, L.S. Lowry and Tracey Emin, among others.

Saltburn

South of the Tees estuary along the coast, it's not a difficult decision to bypass the kiss-me-quick tackiness of Redcar in favour of **SALTBURN**, twelve miles east of Middlesbrough, a graceful Victorian resort in a dramatic setting overlooking extensive sands and mottled red sea-cliffs. Soon after the railway arrived in 1861 to ferry Teessiders out to the seaside on high days and holidays, Saltburn became a rather fashionable spa town boasting a hydraulic **inclined tramway**, which still connects upper town to the pier and promenade, and ornate **Italian Gardens** that are laid out beneath the eastern side of town.

ARRIVAL AND INFORMATION   **SALTBURN**

By train There are regular train services from Newcastle (1hr 40min) and Durham (1hr 30min) via Darlington (50min) and Middlesbrough (25min).
By bus Frequent buses from Middlesbrough stop outside the train station (40min).

Information Some tourist information is available at the library on Windsor Rd (Mon & Wed–Fri 9am–12.30pm, 1.30–6.30pm, Tues 1.30–6.30pm, Sat 10am–12.30 & 1.30–4pm, Sun noon–4pm; ☎ 01287 622422)
Website ⓦ redcar-cleveland.gov.uk.

TOURISTS AT STONEHENGE, C.1900

Contexts

History

England's history is long and densely woven. From obscure beginnings, England came to play a leading role in European affairs and more latterly, with the expansion of the British Empire, the world. What follows is therefore a necessarily brief introduction: we have offered some more detailed reference materials in our "Books" section (see p.707).

The Stone Age

England has been inhabited for the best part of half a million years, though the earliest archeological evidence, dating from around 250,000 BC, is scant, comprising the meagre remains of bones and flint tools from the **Stone Age** (**Palaeolithic**). The comings and goings of these migrant peoples were dictated by the fluctuations of successive Ice Ages. The next traces – mainly roughly worked flint implements – were left much later, around 40,000 BC, by cave-dwellers at Creswell Crags in Derbyshire, Kent's Cavern near Torquay and Cheddar Cave in Somerset. The last spell of intense cold began some 17,000 years ago, and it was the final thawing of this **last Ice Age** around 5000 BC that caused the British Isles to become separated from the European mainland.

The sea barrier did little to stop further migrations of nomadic hunters, drawn by the rich forests that covered ancient Britain. In about 3500 BC a new wave of colonists arrived from continental Europe, probably via Ireland, bringing with them a **Neolithic culture** based on farming and the rearing of livestock. These tribes were the first to make some impact on the environment, clearing forests, enclosing fields, constructing defensive ditches around their villages and digging mines to obtain flint used for tools and weapons. Fragments of Neolithic pottery have been found near Peterborough and in Wiltshire, but the most profuse relics are their graves, usually stone-chambered, turf-covered mounds (called **long barrows**). These are scattered throughout the country, but the most impressive are at Belas Knap in Gloucestershire and at Wayland's Smithy in Oxfordshire.

The Bronze Age

The transition from the Neolithic to the **Bronze Age** began around 2500 BC with the importation from northern Europe of artefacts attributed to the **Beaker Culture** – named for the distinctive cups found at many burial sites. In England as elsewhere, the spread of the Beaker Culture along European trade routes helped stimulate the development of a comparatively well-organized social structure with an established aristocracy. Many of England's stone circles were completed at this time, including **Avebury** and **Stonehenge** in Wiltshire, while many others belong entirely to the Bronze Age – for example, the Hurlers and the Nine Maidens on Cornwall's Bodmin Moor. Large numbers of earthwork forts were also built in this period, suggesting endemic tribal warfare, a situation further complicated by the appearance of bands of **Celts**,

5000 BC	3952 BC	2500 BC	55 BC
As the ice sheets retreat, the sea floods in, separating Britain from continental Europe.	The date of the Creation – as determined by the careful calculations of the Venerable Bede (673–735).	The start of the Bronze Age – and the construction of dozens of stone and timber circles.	First Roman invasions of Britain, under Julius Caesar.

who arrived in numbers from central Europe around 600 BC, though some historians have disputed the whole notion of a Celtic migration, preferring instead the idea of cultural diffusion along well-established trade routes.

The Iron Age

By 500 BC, the **Britons** – with or without a significant Celtic infusion – had established a sophisticated farming economy and a social hierarchy that was dominated by a druidic priesthood. Familiar with Mediterranean artefacts through their far-flung trade routes, they developed better methods of metalworking, ones that favoured **iron** rather than bronze, from which they forged not just weapons but also coins and ornamental works, thus creating the first recognizable English art. Their principal contribution to the landscape was a network of hillforts and other defensive works stretching over the entire country, the greatest of them at **Maiden Castle** in Dorset, a site first fortified during the Neolithic period. Maiden Castle was also one of the first English fortifications to fall to the Romans, in 43 AD.

Roman invasion

Coming at the end of a long period of commercial probing, the Roman invasion began hesitantly, with small cross-Channel incursions led by **Julius Caesar** in 55 and 54 BC. Britain's rumoured mineral wealth was a primary motive, but the spur to the eventual conquest that came nearly a century later was anti-Roman collaboration between the British Celts and their cousins in France. The subtext was that the **Emperor Claudius**, who led the invasion, owed his power to the army and needed a military triumph. The death of the king of southeast England, Cunobelin – Shakespeare's Cymbeline – presented Claudius with a golden opportunity and in August **43 AD** a substantial Roman force landed in Kent, from where it fanned out, soon establishing a base along the estuary of the Thames. Joined by a menagerie of elephants and camels for the major battles of the campaign, the Romans soon reached **Camulodunum** (Colchester) – the region's most important city – and within four years were dug in on the frontier of south Wales.

Resistance and defeat

Resistance to the Romans was patchy. **Caractacus** of the Catuvellauni orchestrated a guerrilla campaign from Wales until he was captured in about 50 AD, but this was nothing when compared with the revolt of the East Anglian Iceni, under their queen **Boudica** (or Boadicea) in 60 AD. The Iceni sacked Camulodunum and Verulamium (St Albans), and even reached the undefended new port of Londinium (London), but the Romans rallied and exacted a terrible revenge. The rebellion turned out to be the last major act of resistance and it would seem that most of the southern tribes acquiesced to their absorption into the empire. In the next decades, the Romans extended their control, subduing Wales and the north of England by 80 AD. They did not, however, manage to conquer Scotland and eventually gave up – as signified by the construction of **Hadrian's Wall** in 130 AD. Running from the Tyne to the Solway, the wall marked the northern limit of the Roman Empire, and stands today as England's most impressive remnant of the Roman occupation.

43 AD	60 AD	130	313
The Roman emperor Claudius invades Britain – and he means business.	An affronted and enraged Boudica and her Iceni sack Roman Colchester.	Hadrian's Wall completed; Scots kept at bay (at least for a while).	Emperor Constantine makes Christianity the official religion of the Roman Empire.

Roman England

The written history of England begins with the **Romans**, whose rule lasted nigh on four centuries. For the first time, the country began to emerge as a clearly identifiable entity with a defined political structure. Peace also brought prosperity. Commerce flourished and cities prospered, including the northerly Roman town of Eboracum (York) and **Londinium**, which soon assumed a pivotal role in the commercial and administrative life of the colony. Although Latin became the language of the Romano-British ruling elite, local traditions were allowed to coexist alongside imported customs, so that Celtic gods were often worshipped at the same time as Roman ones, and sometimes merged with them. Perhaps the most important legacy of the Roman occupation, however, was the introduction of **Christianity** from the third century on, becoming firmly entrenched after its official recognition by the Emperor Constantine in 313.

The Anglo-Saxons

By the middle of the fourth century, Roman England was subject to regular **raids** by a confusing medley of Germanic Saxons, Picts from Scotland and itinerant Scots from northern Ireland. Economic life declined, rural areas became depopulated, and as central authority collapsed, so a string of military commanders usurped local authority. By the start of the fifth century England had become irrevocably detached from what remained of the Roman Empire and within fifty years the **Saxons** had begun settling England themselves. This marked the start of a gradual conquest that culminated in the defeat of the native Britons in 577 at the Battle of Dyrham (near Bath) and, despite the despairing efforts of such semi-mythical figures as **King Arthur**, the last independent Britons were driven deep into Cumbria, Wales and the southwest. So complete was the Anglo-Saxon domination, through conquest and intermarriage, that some ninety percent of English place names today have an Anglo-Saxon derivation.

The Anglo-Saxons went on to divide England into the **kingdoms** of Northumbria, Mercia, East Anglia, Kent and Wessex. In the eighth century, the central English region of **Mercia** was the dominant force, its most effective ruler being **King Offa**, who was responsible for the greatest public work of the period, **Offa's Dyke**, an earthwork marking the border with Wales from the River Dee to the River Severn. Yet, after Offa's death, **Wessex** gained the upper hand, and by 825 the Wessex kings had taken fealty from all the other English kingdoms.

Christianity wins the day

At first, the pagan Anglo-Saxons had little time for **Christianity**, which only survived among the Romano-Britons in the westerly extremities of the country. This was soon to change. In 597, at the behest of Pope Gregory I, **St Augustine** landed on the Kent coast accompanied by forty monks. **Ethelbert**, the overlord of all the English south of the River Humber, received the missionaries and gave Augustine permission to found a monastery at **Canterbury** (on the site of the present cathedral), where the king himself was soon baptized, followed by ten thousand of his subjects at a grand Christmas ceremony. Despite some short-term reversals thereafter, the Christianization of England proceeded quickly, so that by the middle of the seventh century all of the Anglo-Saxon kings had at least nominally adopted the faith. Tensions between the Augustinian missionaries and the

597	793	796	1066
St Augustine lands in Kent with instructions to convert Britain to Christianity.	In a surprise attack, Viking raiders destroy the monastery at Lindisfarne.	Death of King Offa, the most powerful king in England and long-time ruler of Mercia.	King Harold, the last Saxon king of England, catches an arrow in the eye at the Battle of Hastings.

Romano-British (Celtic) monks inevitably arose, but were resolved by the **Synod of Whitby** in 663, when it was agreed that the English Church should follow the rule of Rome, thereby ensuring a realignment with the European cultural mainstream.

The Viking onslaught

The supremacy of Wessex in the early ninth century was short-lived. Carried here by their remarkable longboats, the **Vikings** – by this time mostly **Danes** – had started to raid the east coast towards the end of the eighth century. Emboldened by their success, these raids grew in size and then turned into a migration. In 865, a substantial Danish army landed in East Anglia, and within six years they had conquered Northumbria, Mercia and East Anglia. The Danes then set their sights on Wessex, whose new king was the formidable and exceptionally talented **Alfred the Great**. Despite the odds, Alfred successfully resisted the Danes and eventually the two warring parties signed a truce, which fixed an uneasy border between Wessex and Danish territory – the **Danelaw** – to the north. Ensconced in northern England and the East Midlands, the Danes soon succumbed to Christianity and internal warfare, while Alfred modernized his kingdom and strengthened its defences.

Alfred died in 899, but his successor, **Edward the Elder**, capitalized on his efforts, establishing Saxon supremacy over the Danelaw to become the de facto overlord of all England. The relative calm continued under Edward's son, **Athelstan** and his son, **Edgar**, who became the first ruler to be crowned **king of England** in 973. However, this was but a lull in the Viking storm. Returning in force, the Vikings milked Edgar's son **Ethelred the Unready** ("lacking counsel") for all the money they could, but payment of the ransom (the Danegeld) brought only temporary relief and in 1016 Ethelred hot-footed it to Normandy, leaving the Danes in command. The first Danish king of England was **Cnut**, a shrewd and gifted ruler, but his two disreputable sons quickly dismantled his carefully constructed Anglo-Scandinavian empire and the Saxons promptly regained the initiative.

1066

In 1042, the resurgent Saxons anointed Ethelred's son, **Edward the Confessor**, as king of England. It was a poor choice. Edward was more suited to be a priest than a king and he allowed power to drift into the hands of his most powerful subject, Godwin, Earl of Wessex, and his son Harold. On Edward's death, the Witan – effectively a council of elders – confirmed **Harold** as king, ignoring several rival claims including that of William, Duke of Normandy. William's claim was a curious affair, but he always insisted – however improbable it may seem – that the childless Edward the Confessor had promised him his crown. Unluckily for Harold, his two main rivals struck at the same time. First up was his alienated brother **Tostig** along with his ally King Harald of Norway, a giant of a man reckoned to be seven feet tall. They landed with a Viking army in Yorkshire and Harold marched north to meet them. Harold won a crushing victory at the battle of **Stamford Bridge**, but then he heard that **William of Normandy** had invaded the south. Rashly, he dashed south without gathering reinforcements, a blunder that cost him his life: Harold was famously defeated at the **Battle of Hastings** in 1066 and, on Christmas Day, William the Conqueror was installed as king in Westminster Abbey.

1085	1190	1216	1220
The Normans start work on the Domesday Book, detailing who owns what, does what and lives where.	King Richard complains that in England it is "cold and always raining," and joins the Third Crusade.	King John loses the Crown Jewels in The Wash (not the wash); much royal grumpiness ensues.	Work begins on York Minster and Salisbury Cathedral – heady days for stone masons.

The Normans

William I imposed a Norman aristocracy on his new subjects, reinforcing his rule with a series of strongholds, the grandest of which was the **Tower of London**. Initially, there was some resistance, but William crushed these sporadic rebellions with great brutality – Yorkshire and the north were ravaged and the fenland resistance of Hereward the Wake was brought to a savage end. Perhaps the single most effective controlling measure was the compilation of the **Domesday Book** in 1085–86. Recording land ownership, type of cultivation, number of inhabitants and their social status, it afforded William an unprecedented body of information about his subjects, providing a framework for the administration of taxation, judicial structure and ultimately feudal obligations.

William died in 1087, and was succeeded by his son **William Rufus**, an ineffectual ruler but a notable benefactor of religious foundations. Rufus died in mysterious circumstances – killed by an unknown assailant's arrow while hunting in the New Forest – and the throne passed to **Henry I**, William I's youngest son. Henry spent much of his time struggling with his unruly barons, but at least he proved to be more conciliatory in his dealings with the Saxons, even marrying into one of their leading families. On his death in 1135, the accession was contested, initiating a long-winded civil war that was only ended when Henry II secured the throne.

The early Plantagenets (1154–1216)

Energetic and far-sighted, **Henry II**, the first of the **Plantagenets**, kept his barons in check and instigated profound administrative reforms, most notably the introduction of trial by jury. Nor was England Henry's only concern, his inheritance bequeathing him great chunks of France. This territorial entanglement was to create all sorts of problems for his successors, but Henry himself was brought low by his attempt to subordinate Church to Crown. This went terribly awry in 1170, when he (perhaps unintentionally) sanctioned the murder in Canterbury Cathedral of his erstwhile drinking companion **Thomas Becket**, whose canonization just three years later created an enduring Europe-wide cult.

The last years of Henry's reign were riven by quarrels with his sons, the eldest of whom, **Richard I** (or Lionheart), spent most of his ten-year reign crusading in the Holy Land. Neglected, England fell prey to the scheming of Richard's brother **John**, the villain of the Robin Hood tales, who became king in his own right after Richard died of a battle wound in France in 1199. Yet John's inability to hold on to his French possessions and his rumbling dispute with the Vatican over control of the English Church alienated the English barons, who eventually forced him to consent to a charter guaranteeing their rights and privileges, the **Magna Carta**, which was signed in 1215 at Runnymede, on the Thames.

The later Plantagenets (1216–1399)

The power struggle with the barons continued into the reign of **Henry III**, but Henry's successor, **Edward I**, who inherited the throne in 1272, was much more in control of his kingdom than his predecessors. Edward was a great law-maker, but he also became preoccupied with military matters, spending years subduing Wales and imposing

1237	1256	1277
The Treaty of York, signed by Henry III of England and Scotland's Alexander II, sets the Anglo-Scottish border.	The calendar is getting out of sync, so in England a decree installs a leap year – one leap day every four years.	Well armed and well organized, Edward I of England embarks upon the conquest of Wales.

English jurisdiction over Scotland. Fortunately for the Scots – it was too late for Wales – the next king of England, **Edward II**, proved to be completely hopeless, and in 1314 Robert the Bruce inflicted a huge defeat on his guileless army at the battle of **Bannockburn**. This spelled the beginning of the end for Edward, who ultimately died under suspicious circumstances – likely murdered by his wife Isabella and her lover Roger Mortimer – in 1327.

Edward III began by sorting out the Scottish imbroglio before getting stuck into his main enthusiasm – his (essentially specious) claim to the throne of France. Starting in 1337, the resultant **Hundred Years War** kicked off with several famous English victories, principally Crécy in 1346 and Poitiers in 1356, but was interrupted by the outbreak of the **Black Death** in 1349. The plague claimed about one and a half million English souls – some one third of the population – and the scarcity of labour that followed gave the peasantry more economic clout than they had ever had before. Predictably, the landowners attempted to restrict the concomitant rise in wages, thereby provoking the widespread rioting that culminated in the **Peasants' Revolt** of 1381. The rebels marched on London under the delusion that they could appeal to the king – now **Richard II** – for fair treatment, but they soon learned otherwise. The king did indeed meet a rebel deputation in person, but his aristocratic bodyguards took the opportunity to kill the peasants' leader, **Wat Tyler**, a prelude to the enforced dispersal of the crowds and mass slaughter.

Running parallel with this social unrest were the clerical reforms demanded by the scholar **John Wycliffe** (1320–84), whose acolytes made the first translation of the Bible into English in 1380. Another sign of the elevation of the common language was the success enjoyed by **Geoffrey Chaucer** (c.1343–1400), a wine merchant's son, whose *Canterbury Tales* was the first major work written in the vernacular and one of the first English books to be printed.

The houses of Lancaster and York (1399–1485)

In 1399, **Henry IV**, the first of the **Lancastrian** kings, supplanted the weak and indecisive Richard II. Henry died in 1413 and was succeeded by his son, the bellicose **Henry V**, who promptly renewed the Hundred Years War with vigour. Henry famously defeated the French at the battle of **Agincourt**, a comprehensive victory that forced the French king to acknowledge Henry as his heir in the Treaty of Troyes of 1420. However, Henry died just two years later and his son, **Henry VI** – or rather his regents – all too easily succumbed to a French counter-attack inspired by **Joan of Arc** (1412–31); by 1454, only Calais was left in English hands.

It was soon obvious that the new monarch, **Henry VI**, was mentally unstable. Consequently, as he drifted in and out of sanity, two aristocratic factions attempted to take control: the Yorkists, whose emblem was the white rose, and the Lancastrians, represented by the red rose – hence the protracted **Wars of the Roses**. The Yorkist **Edward IV** seized the crown in 1471 and held onto it until his death in 1483, when he was succeeded by his 12-year-old son **Edward V**, whose reign was cut short after only two months: he and his younger brother were murdered in the Tower of London, probably at the behest of their uncle, the Duke of Gloucester, who was crowned **Richard III**. Richard did not last long either: in 1485, he was defeated (and killed) at the battle of Bosworth Field by **Henry Tudor**, Earl of Richmond, who took the throne as Henry VII.

1290	1295	1314
Edward I of England expels the Jews from his kingdom, one of several medieval pogroms.	Edward I much vexed when France and Scotland sign a treaty of mutual assistance – the start of the "Auld Alliance".	At the Battle of Bannockburn, Robert the Bruce's Scots destroy an English army.

The Tudors (1485–1603)

The opening of the **Tudor** period brought radical transformations. A Lancastrian through his mother's line, **Henry VII** promptly reconciled the Yorkists by marrying Edward IV's daughter Elizabeth, thereby ending the Wars of the Roses at a stroke. It was a shrewd gambit and others followed. Henry married his daughter off to James IV of Scotland and his eldest son Arthur to Catherine, the daughter of Ferdinand and Isabella of Spain – and by these means England began to assume the status of a major European power.

Henry's son, **Henry VIII**, is best remembered for his multiple marriages, but much more significant was his separation of the English Church from Rome and his establishment of an independent Protestant Church – the **Church of England**. This is not without its ironies. Henry was not a Protestant himself and the schism between Henry and the pope was triggered not by doctrinal issues but by the failure of his wife **Catherine of Aragon** – widow of his elder brother – to provide Henry with male offspring. Failing to obtain a decree of nullity from Pope Clement VII, he dismissed his long-time chancellor Thomas Wolsey and turned instead to **Thomas Cromwell**, who helped make the English Church recognize Henry as its head. One of the consequences was the **Dissolution of the Monasteries**, which conveniently gave both king and nobles the chance to get their hands on valuable monastic property in the late 1530s.

In his later years, Henry became a corpulent, syphilitic wreck, six times married but at last furnished an heir, **Edward VI**, who was only nine years old when he ascended the throne in 1547. His short reign saw **Protestantism** established on a firm footing, with churches stripped of their images and Catholic services banned, yet on Edward's death most of the country readily accepted his fervently Catholic half-sister **Mary**, daughter of Catherine of Aragon, as queen – England's first female monarch to reign in her own right. She returned England to the papacy and married the future Philip II of Spain, forging an alliance whose immediate consequence was war with France. The marriage was deeply unpopular and so was Mary's decision to begin persecuting Protestants, executing the leading lights of the English Reformation – Hugh Latimer, Nicholas Ridley and Thomas Cranmer, the archbishop of Canterbury.

Elizabeth I

Queen Mary, or "Bloody Mary" as many of her subjects called her, died in 1558 and the crown passed to her half-sister, **Elizabeth I**. The new queen looked very vulnerable. The country was divided by religion – Catholic against Protestant – and threatened from abroad by Philip II of Spain, the most powerful ruler in Europe. Famously, Elizabeth eschewed marriage and, although a Protestant herself, steered a delicate course between the two religious groupings. Her prudence sat well with the English merchant class, who were becoming the greatest power in the land, its members mostly opposed to foreign military entanglements. An exception, however, was made for the piratical activities of the great English seafarers of the day, captains like Walter Raleigh, Martin Frobisher, John Hawkins and Francis Drake, who made a fortune raiding Spain's American colonies. Inevitably, Philip II's irritation with the raiding took a warlike turn, but the **Spanish Armada** he sent against England in 1588 was defeated, thereby establishing England as a major European sea power. Elizabeth's reign also saw the efflorescence of a specifically English Renaissance – **William Shakespeare** (1564–1616) is the obvious name – the only major fly in the royal ointment being the queen's reluctant execution of her cousin and rival **Mary, Queen of Scots**, in 1587.

1349	1380s	1485
The Black Death reaches England and moves on into Scotland the year after.	Geoffrey Chaucer begins work on *The Canterbury Tales* and changes the face of English literature forever.	Battle of Bosworth Field ends the Wars of the Roses. Richard III does not say "*A horse, a horse, my kingdom for a horse*".

The early Stuarts (1603–49)

James VI of Scotland – son of Mary, Queen of Scots – succeeded Elizabeth as **James I** of England in 1603, thereby uniting the English and Scottish crowns. James quickly moved to end hostilities with Spain and adopted a policy of toleration towards the country's Catholics. Inevitably, both initiatives offended many Protestants, whose worst fears were confirmed in 1605 when **Guy Fawkes** and a group of Catholic conspirators were discovered preparing to blow up king and Parliament in the so-called **Gunpowder Plot** (see p.496). During the ensuing hue and cry, many Catholics met an untimely end and Fawkes himself was hanged, drawn and quartered. At the same time, many Protestants felt that the English state was irredeemably corrupt and some of the more dedicated **Puritans** fixed their eyes on establishing a "New Jerusalem" in North America following the foundation of the first permanent **colony** in Virginia in 1608. Twelve years later, the **Pilgrim Fathers** landed in New England, establishing a colony that would absorb about a hundred thousand Puritan immigrants by the middle of the century.

Meanwhile, James was busy alienating his landed gentry. He clung to an absolutist vision of the monarchy – the **divine right of kings** – that was totally out of step with the Protestant leanings of the majority of his subjects and he also relied heavily on court favourites. It could only lead to disaster, but in the end it was to be his successor who reaped the whirlwind.

Charles I and the Civil War

Charles I inherited James's penchant for absolutism, ruling without Parliament from 1629 to 1640, but he over-stepped himself when he tried to impose a new Anglican prayer book on the Scots, who rose in revolt, forcing Charles to recall Parliament in an attempt to raise the money he needed for an army. This was Parliament's chance and they were not going to let it slip. The **Long Parliament**, as it became known, impeached several of Charles's allies – most notably Archbishop Laud, who was hung out to dry by the king and ultimately executed – and compiled its grievances in the Grand Remonstrance of 1641.

Facing the concerted hostility of Parliament, the king withdrew to Nottingham where he raised his standard, the opening act of the **Civil War**. The Royalist forces ("Cavaliers") were initially successful, leading to the complete overhaul of key regiments of the Parliamentary army ("Roundheads") by **Oliver Cromwell** and his officer allies. The **New Model Army** Cromwell created was something quite unique: singing psalms as they went into battle and urged on by preachers and "agitators", this was an army of believers whose ideological commitment to the parliamentary cause made it truly formidable. Cromwell's revamped army cut its teeth at the battle of Naseby and thereafter simply brushed the Royalists aside. Meanwhile, an increasingly desperate Charles attempted to sow discord among his enemies by surrendering himself to the Scots, but as so often with Charles's plans, they came unstuck: the Scots handed him over to the English Parliament, by whom – after prolonged negotiations, endless royal shenanigans and more fighting – he was ultimately **executed** in January 1649.

The Commonwealth

For the next eleven years, England was a **Commonwealth** – at first a true republic, then, after 1653, a **Protectorate** with Cromwell as the Lord Protector and commander in chief.

1536	1588	c. 1592	1603
Anne Boleyn, the second wife of Henry VIII is executed for treason.	Spanish Armada meets a watery end; England gleeful; Elizabeth I relieved.	First performance of Shakespeare's *Henry VI, Pt 1*, at the Rose Theatre, London.	King James unites the crowns of Scotland and England.

Cromwell reformed the government, secured advantageous commercial treaties with foreign nations and used his New Model Army to put the fear of God into his various enemies. The turmoil of the Civil War and the pre-eminence of the army unleashed a furious legal, theological and political debate throughout the country. This milieu spawned a host of leftist sects, the most notable of whom were the **Levellers**, who demanded wholesale constitutional reform, and the more radical **Diggers**, who proposed common ownership of all land. Nonconformist religious groups also flourished, prominent among them the pacifist **Quakers**, led by the much persecuted George Fox (1624–91), and the **Dissenters**, to whom the most famous writers of the day, John Milton (1608–74) and John Bunyan (1628–88), both belonged.

Cromwell died in 1658 to be succeeded by his son **Richard**, who ruled briefly and ineffectually, leaving the army unpaid while one of its more ambitious commanders, **General Monk**, conspired to restore the monarchy. Charles II, the exiled son of the previous king, entered London in triumph in May 1660.

The Restoration

A **Stuart** was back on the English throne, but **Charles II** had few absolutist illusions – the terms of the **Restoration** were closely negotiated and included a general amnesty for all those who had fought against the Stuarts, with the exception of the regicides – that is, those who had signed Charles I's death warrant. Nonetheless, there was a sea change in public life with the re-establishment of a royal court and the foundation of the **Royal Society**, whose scientific endeavours were furthered by Isaac Newton (1642–1727). The low points of Charles's reign were the **Great Plague** of 1665 and the 1666 **Great Fire of London**, though the London that rose from the ashes was an architectural showcase for Christopher Wren (1632–1723) and his fellow classicists. Politically, there were still underlying tensions between the monarchy and Parliament, but the latter was more concerned with the struggle between the **Whigs** and **Tories**, political factions representing, respectively, the low-church gentry and the high-church aristocracy. There was a degree of religious toleration too, but its brittleness was all too apparent in the anti-Catholic riots of 1678.

James II and the Glorious Revolution

James II, the brother of Charles II, came to the throne in 1685. He was a Catholic, which made the bulk of his subjects uneasy, but there was still an indifferent response when the Protestant **Duke of Monmouth**, the favourite among Charles II's illegitimate sons, raised a rebellion in the West Country. Monmouth was defeated at Sedgemoor, in Somerset, in July 1685 and nine days later he was beheaded at Tower Hill. Neither was any mercy shown to his supporters: in the **Bloody Assizes** of Judge Jeffreys, hundreds of rebels and suspected sympathizers were executed or deported. Yet if James felt secure he was mistaken; he showed all the traditional weaknesses of his family, from his enthusiasm for the divine right of kings to an over-reliance on sycophantic favourites. Even worse, as far as the Protestants were concerned, he built up a massive standing army, officered it with Roman Catholics and proposed a **Declaration of Indulgence**, removing anti-Catholic restrictions. The final straw was the birth of James's son, which threatened to secure a Catholic succession, and, thoroughly

1605	**1642**	**1660**
Gunpowder Plot: Guy Fawkes et al plan to blow up the Houses of Parliament, but fail.	The Civil War begins when Charles I raises his standard in Nottingham – three times.	The Restoration: Charles II takes the throne – and digs up the body of Oliver Cromwell to hammer home his point.

KINGS AND QUEENS SINCE 1066

HOUSE OF NORMANDY
William I (William the Conqueror) 1066–87
William II (William Rufus) 1087–1100
Henry I 1100–35
Stephen 1135–54

HOUSE OF PLANTAGENET
Henry II 1154–89
Richard I (Richard the Lionheart) 1189–99
John 1199–1216
Henry III 1216–72
Edward I 1272–1307
Edward II 1307–27
Edward III 1327–77
Richard II 1377–99

HOUSE OF LANCASTER
Henry IV 1399–1413
Henry V 1413–22
Henry VI 1422–61 & 1470

HOUSE OF YORK
Edward IV 1461–70 & 1471–83
Edward V 1483
Richard III 1483–85

HOUSE OF TUDOR
Henry VII 1485–1509
Henry VIII 1509–47
Edward VI 1547–53

Mary I 1553–58
Elizabeth I 1558–1603

HOUSE OF STUART
James I 1603–25
Charles I 1625–49
Commonwealth and Protectorate 1649–60
Charles II 1660–85
James II 1685–88
William III and Mary II 1688–94
William III 1694–1702
Anne 1702–14

HOUSE OF HANOVER
George I 1714–27
George II 1727–60
George III 1760–1820
George IV 1820–30
William IV 1830–37
Victoria 1837–1901

HOUSE OF SAXE-COBURG-GOTHA
Edward VII 1901–10

HOUSE OF WINDSOR
George V 1910–36
Edward VIII 1936
George VI 1936–52
Elizabeth II 1952–

alarmed, powerful Protestants now urged **William of Orange**, the Dutch husband of James II's Protestant daughter Mary, to save them from "popery" – and that was precisely what he did. William landed in Devon in 1688 and, as James's forces melted away, he speedily took control of London in the **Glorious Revolution** of 1688. This was the final postscript to the Civil War – although it was a couple of years before James and his remaining Jacobites were finally defeated in Ireland at the **Battle of the Boyne**.

The last Stuarts

William and Mary became joint sovereigns after they agreed a **Bill of Rights** defining the limitations of the monarchy's power and the rights of its subjects. This, together with the **Act of Settlement of 1701**, made Britain a **constitutional monarchy**, in which the roles of legislature and executive were separate and interdependent. The model was broadly consistent with that outlined by the philosopher and political thinker **John Locke** (1632–1704), whose essentially Whig doctrines of toleration and social

1669	1678	1684	1703
Samuel Pepys gives up his diary, after nine years of detailed jottings.	John Bunyan, the Protestant preacher and reformer, writes his *Pilgrim's Progress*.	Isaac Newton observes gravity – but is probably not hit on the head by an apple.	"The Great Storm", a week-long hurricane, blasts through southern England.

contract were gradually embraced as the new orthodoxy. Meanwhile, William, ruling alone after Mary's death in 1694, mainly regarded England as a prop in his defence of Holland against France, a stance that defined England's political alignment in Europe for the next sixty years.

After William's death, the crown passed to **Anne**, the second daughter of James II. Anne was a Protestant – an Anglican to be exact – but her popularity had more to do with her self-proclaimed love of England, which came as something of a relief after William's marked preference for the Dutch. During Anne's reign, English armies won a string of remarkable victories on the Continent, beginning with the Duke of Marlborough's triumph at Blenheim in 1704, followed the next year by the capture of Gibraltar, establishing a British presence in the Mediterranean. These military escapades were part of the Europe-wide **War of the Spanish Succession**, a long-winded dynastic squabble that rumbled on until the 1713 Treaty of Utrecht pretty much settled the European balance of power for the rest of the century. Otherwise, Anne's reign was distinguished mainly for the 1707 **Act of Union**, uniting the English and Scottish parliaments.

Despite her seventeen pregnancies, none of Anne's children survived into adulthood. Consequently, when she died in 1714, the succession passed from the Stuarts to the Hanoverians in the person of the Elector of Hanover, a non-English-speaking Protestant who became George I of England – all in accordance with the terms of the Act of Settlement.

The Hanoverians

During **George I**'s lacklustre reign, power leached into the hands of a Whig oligarchy led by a chief minister – or prime minister – the longest serving of whom was **Robert Walpole** (1676–1745). Elsewhere, plans were being hatched for a **Jacobite Rebellion** in support of **James Edward Stuart**, the "Old Pretender", son of the usurped James II. Its timing appeared perfect: Scottish opinion was moving against the Union, which had failed to bring Scotland tangible economic benefits, and many English Catholics supported the Jacobite cause too, toasting the "king across the water". In 1715, the Earl of Mar raised the Stuart standard in Scotland and gathered an army of more than ten thousand men. Mar's rebellion took the government by surprise. They had only four thousand soldiers in the north, but Mar dithered until he lost the military advantage. There was an indecisive battle at Sheriffmuir, but by the time the Old Pretender landed in Scotland in December 1715, six thousand veteran Dutch troops had reinforced government forces. The rebellion disintegrated rapidly and James slunk back to exile in France with his tail between his legs.

Under **George II**, England became embroiled in yet another dynastic squabble, the War of the Austrian Succession (1740–48), but this played second fiddle to another **Jacobite Rebellion**, this one in 1745, when the "Young Pretender", **Charles Stuart** (Bonnie Prince Charlie), assembled a Highland army and marched south, reaching Derby, just 100 miles from London. There was panic in the capital, but the Prince's army proved too small – he had failed to rally the Lowland Scots, never mind the English – and his supply lines too over-extended to press home his advantage, and the Jacobites turned tail. A Hanoverian army under the Duke of Cumberland caught up with them at **Culloden Moor** near Inverness in April 1746, and hacked them to pieces.

1707	1715	1745
The Act of Union merges the Scottish Parliament into the English Parliament.	First Jacobite Rebellion: James Stuart ("The Old Pretender") raises a Scottish army, but is defeated.	Second Jacobite Rebellion: Charles Stuart (Bonnie Prince Charlie) invades England with a Scots army, but is defeated at Culloden.

The prince lived out the rest of his life in drunken exile, while in Scotland wearing tartan, bearing arms and playing bagpipes were all banned. Most significantly, the government prohibited the private armies of the highland chiefs, thereby destroying the military capacity of the clans.

Empire and colonies

Towards the end of George II's reign, the **Seven Years War** (1756–63) harvested England a bounty of overseas territory in India and Canada at the expense of France; and then, in 1768, with **George III** now on the throne, **Captain James Cook** stumbled upon New Zealand and Australia, thereby extending Britain's empire still further. Amid the imperial bonanza, the problem was the deteriorating relationship with the thirteen colonies of North America, which came to a head with the **American Declaration of Independence** and Britain's subsequent defeat in the **Revolutionary War** (1775–83). The debacle helped fuel a renewed struggle between king and Parliament, enlivened by the intervention of John Wilkes, first of a long and increasingly vociferous line of parliamentary radicals. It also made the British reluctant to interfere in the momentous events taking place across the Channel, where France, long its most consistent foe, was convulsed by revolution. Out of the turmoil emerged the most daunting of enemies, **Napoleon Bonaparte** (1769–1821), whose stunning military progress was interrupted by Nelson at **Trafalgar** in 1805 and finally stopped ten years later by the Duke of Wellington (and the Prussians) at **Waterloo**.

The Industrial Revolution

England's triumph over Napoleon was underpinned by its financial strength, which was itself born of the **Industrial Revolution**, the switch from an agricultural to a manufacturing economy that transformed the face of the country within a century. The earliest mechanized production was in the northern **cotton mills**, where cotton-spinning progressed from a cottage industry to a highly productive factory-based system. Initially, river water powered the mills, but the technology changed after James Watt patented his **steam engine** in 1781. Watt's engines needed **coal**, which made it convenient to locate mills and factories near coal mines, a tendency that was accelerated as **ironworks** took up coal as a smelting fuel, vastly increasing the output from their furnaces. Accordingly, there was a shift of population towards the Midlands and the north of England, where the great coal reserves were located, and as the industrial economy boomed and diversified, so these regions' towns mushroomed at an extraordinary rate. Sheffield was a steel town, Stoke-on-Trent was famed for its pottery, Manchester possessed huge cotton warehouses, and Liverpool had the docks, where raw materials from India and the Americas flowed in and manufactured goods went out. Commerce and industry were also served by improving transport facilities, principally the digging of a network of **canals**, but the great leap forward came with the arrival of the **railway**, heralded by the Stockton–Darlington line in 1825 and followed five years later by the Liverpool–Manchester railway, where George Stephenson's *Rocket* made its first outing.

Boosted by a vast influx of immigrant workers, the country's population rose from about eight and a half million at the beginning of George III's reign to more than fifteen million by its end. As the factories and their attendant towns expanded, so the

1781	1783	1815	1819
Opening of the Iron Bridge – the first iron bridge the world had ever seen – over the River Severn.	End of the American War of Independence – the American colonies break from Britain.	Final defeat of Napoleon at the battle of Waterloo.	Peterloo Massacre: in Manchester, the cavalry wade into a crowd who are demanding parliamentary reform. Scores are killed.

rural settlements of England declined, inspiring the elegiac pastoral yearnings of Samuel Taylor Coleridge and William Wordsworth, the first great names of the **Romantic movement**. Later Romantic poets such as Percy Bysshe Shelley and Lord Byron took a more socially engaged position, but much more dangerous to the ruling class were the nation's factory workers, who grew restless when mechanization put thousands of them out of work.

The Chartists – and social reform

Industrial discontent coalesced in the **Chartists**, a broad-based popular movement that demanded parliamentary reform – the most important of the industrial boom towns were still unrepresented in Parliament – and the repeal of the hated **Corn Laws**, which kept the price of bread artificially high to the advantage of the large landowners. Class antagonisms came to boiling point in 1819, when the local militia bloodily dispersed a demonstration in support of parliamentary reform in Manchester in the so-called **Peterloo Massacre**.

Tensions continued to run high throughout the 1820s, and in retrospect it seems that the country may have been saved from a French-style revolution by a series of judicious parliamentary acts: the **Reform Act** of 1832 established the principle (if not actually the practice) of popular representation; the **New Poor Law** of 1834 did something to alleviate the condition of the most destitute; and the repeal of the Corn Laws in 1846 cut the cost of bread. Furthermore, there was such a furore after six Dorset labourers – the **Tolpuddle Martyrs** – were transported to Australia in 1834 for joining an agricultural trade union that the judiciary decided it was prudent to overturn the judgement six years later.

Significant sections of the middle classes supported progressive reform too, as evidenced by the immense popularity of **Charles Dickens** (1812–70), whose novels railed against poverty and injustice. Indeed, they had already played a key reforming role in the previous century when John Wesley (1703–91) and his **Methodists** led the anti-slavery campaign. As a result of their efforts, **slavery** was banned in Britain in 1772 and throughout the British Empire in 1833 – albeit long after the seaports of Bristol and Liverpool had grown rich from the trade. The middle classes weren't always a progressive force, though; the New Poor Law attempted to provide shelter for the destitute but, due to middle-class fears that workers would take advantage of free shelter, conditions were made hard – as a matter of policy – and the "**workhouses**" were much feared.

The Victorians

Blind and insane, **George III** died in 1820. His two sons, **George IV** and **William IV**, were succeeded in their turn by his niece, **Victoria**, whose long reign witnessed the zenith of British power. The economy boomed – typically the nation's cloth manufacturers boasted that they supplied the domestic market before breakfast, the rest of the world thereafter – and the British trading fleet was easily the mightiest in the world. The fleet policed an empire upon which, in that famous phrase of the time, "the sun never set" and Victoria became the symbol of both the nation's success and the imperial ideal. There were extraordinary intellectual achievements too – as typified by the publication

1824	1834	1841
Charles Dickens's father is imprisoned as a debtor; his son never forgets.	Tolpuddle Martyrs: agricultural workers from Dorset are transported to Australia for daring to organize.	Thomas Cook organizes his first package tour, taking hundreds of Leicester temperance campaigners to Loughborough. More trips are planned.

of Charles Darwin's *On the Origin of Species* in 1859 – and the country came to see itself as both a civilizing agent and the hand of (a very Protestant) God on earth. Britain's industrial and commercial prowess was best embodied by the engineering feats of **Isambard Kingdom Brunel** (1806–59) and by the **Great Exhibition** of 1851, a display of manufacturing achievements without compare.

With trade at the forefront of the agenda, much of the political debate crystallized into a conflict between the Free Traders – led by the Whigs, who formed the **Liberal Party** – and the Protectionists under Bentinck and **Disraeli**, guiding light of the **Conservatives**, descended from the Tories. Parliament itself was long dominated by the duel between Disraeli and the Liberal leader **Gladstone**, the pre-eminent statesmen of the day. It was Disraeli who eventually passed the Second Reform Bill in 1867, further extending the electoral franchise, but it was Gladstone's first ministry of 1868–74 that ratified some of the century's most far-reaching legislation, including compulsory education and the full legalization of trade unions.

Foreign entanglements

In 1854 troops were sent to protect the Ottoman empire against the Russians in the **Crimea**, an inglorious fiasco whose horrors were relayed to the public by the first-ever press coverage of a military campaign and by the revelations of Florence Nightingale, who was appalled by the lack of medical care for the soldiers. The **Indian Mutiny** – or more accurately Indian Rebellion – of 1857 was a further shock to the imperial system, exposing the fragility of Britain's hold over the Indian subcontinent, though the status quo was brutally restored and Victoria took the title Empress of India after 1876. Thereafter, the British army was flattered by a series of minor wars against poorly armed Asian and African opponents, but promptly came unstuck when it faced the Dutch settlers of South Africa in the **Boer War** (1899–1902). The British ultimately fought their way to a sort of victory, but the discreditable conduct of the war prompted a military shake-up at home that was to be of significance in the coming European conflict.

World War I and its aftermath (1914–39)

Victoria died in 1901, to be succeeded by her son, **Edward VII**, whose leisurely lifestyle has often been seen as the epitome of the complacent era to which he gave his name. It wasn't to last. By 1910, all the major European powers were enmeshed in a network of rival military alliances and these were switched on – almost accidentally – by the assassination of the Habsburg Archduke Franz Ferdinand in late June, 1914; a few weeks later, with **George V** now on the throne, the British declared war on Germany in alliance with France and Russia. Hundreds of thousands volunteered for the British army, but their enthusiastic nationalism was not enough to ensure a quick victory and **World War I** dragged on for four miserable years, its key engagements fought in the trenches that zigzagged across northern France and Belgium. Britain and its allies eventually prevailed, but the number of dead – tragically increased by 1918's devastating **Spanish flu** pandemic – beggared belief, undermining the authority of the British ruling class, whose generals had shown a lethal combination of incompetence and indifference to the plight of their men. Many people looked admiringly at the Soviet Union, where Lenin and his Bolsheviks had rid themselves of the tsar and seized control in 1917.

1858	1892	1865	1909
Isambard Kingdom Brunel builds the iron-hulled SS *Great Eastern*, the largest ship in the world.	Liverpool Football Club founded – years before Chelsea.	William Booth from Nottingham founds the Salvation Army, in the East End of London.	Lord Baden-Powell forms the "British Boy Scouts".

After the war ended in 1918, the sheer weight of public opinion pushed Parliament into extending the **vote** to all men 21 and over and to women over 30. This tardy liberalization of women's rights owed much to the efforts of the Suffragists and the more radical **Suffragettes**, led by Emmeline Pankhurst and her daughters Sylvia and Christabel, but the process was only completed in 1929 when women were at last granted the vote at 21. The royal family itself was shaken in 1936 by the **abdication of Edward VIII**, following his decision to marry a twice-divorced American, Wallis Simpson. In the event, the succession passed smoothly to his brother **George VI**, but the royals had to play catch-up to regain their popularity among the population as a whole.

Trouble and turmoil

During this period, the **Labour Party** supplanted the Liberals as the second-largest party, its strength built on an alliance between the working-class trade unions and middle-class radicals. Labour formed its first government in 1923 under **Ramsay MacDonald** (1866–1937), but the publication of the **Zinoviev Letter**, a forged document that purported to be a letter from the Soviets urging British leftists to promote revolution, undermined MacDonald's position and the Conservatives were returned with a large parliamentary majority in 1924. Two years later, a bitter dispute between the nation's pit men and the mine-owners spread to the railways, the newspapers and the iron and steel industries, thereby escalating into a **General Strike**. The strike lasted nine days and involved half a million workers, provoking the government into draconian action – the army was called in, and the strike was broken. The economic situation deteriorated even further after the crash of the New York Stock Exchange in 1929, which precipitated a worldwide depression. Unemployment topped 2.8 million in 1931, generating mass demonstrations that peaked with the **Jarrow March** from the northeast of England to London in 1936.

The empire reorganizes

Abroad, the structure of the **British Empire** was undergoing profound changes. After the cack-handed way in which the British had dealt with Dublin's 1916 Easter Rising, the status of **Ireland** was bound to change. There was a partial resolution in 1922 with the establishment of the Irish Free State, but the six counties of the mainly Protestant North (two-thirds of the ancient province of **Ulster**) chose to "contract out" and stay part of the United Kingdom – and this was to cause endless problems later. In 1926, the **Imperial Conference** recognized the autonomy of the British dominions, comprising all the major countries that had previously been part of the empire. This agreement was formalized in the 1931 Statute of Westminster, whereby each dominion was given an equal footing in a Commonwealth of Nations, though each still recognized the British monarch.

World War II

When Hitler set about militarizing Germany in the mid-1930s, the British government adopted a policy of appeasement. Consequently, when Britain declared war on Germany after Hitler's invasion of Poland in September 1939, the country was poorly prepared. After embarrassing military failures during the first months of **World War II**, the discredited government was replaced in May 1940 by a national coalition headed

1912	1926	1946	1951
The *Titanic* sinks, and Captain Scott and his men die on the ice in the Antarctic.	Britain's first-ever General Strike: the army break a nine-day walkout in support of the coal miners.	Death of John Maynard Keynes, one of the most influential economists of all time.	Britain's first supermarket opens in south London.

by the charismatic **Winston Churchill** (1874–1965)– days before the British army made a forced evacuation from Dunkirk. These were bleak and uncertain days for Britain, but the tide turned when the Germans invaded the **USSR** in 1941, and Churchill found he had a new and powerful ally. Further reinforcements arrived in December 1941, when the **US** declared war on both Germany and Japan after the Japanese had made a surprise attack on Pearl Harbor. The involvement of both the United States and the Soviet Union swung the military balance, and by early 1943 the Germans were doomed to defeat – though it took two more years to finish Hitler off.

In terms of casualties, World War II was not as calamitous as World War I, but its impact upon British civilians was much greater. In its first wave of **bombing** of the UK, the Luftwaffe caused massive damage to industrial centres such as London, Hull, Coventry, Manchester, Liverpool, Southampton and Plymouth. Later raids, intended to shatter morale rather than factories and docks, battered the cathedral cities of Canterbury, Exeter, Bath, Norwich and York. By 1945, nearly a third of the nation's houses had been destroyed or damaged, over 58,000 civilians had lost their lives, and nearly a quarter of a million soldiers, sailors and airmen had been killed.

Postwar England (1945–79)

Hungry for change (and demobilization), voters in 1945's postwar election replaced Churchill with the Labour Party under **Clement Attlee** (1883–1967), who set about a radical programme to **nationalize** the coal, gas, electricity, iron and steel industries. In addition, the early passage of the National Insurance Act and the National Health Service Act gave birth to what became known as the **welfare state**. However, despite substantial American aid, rebuilding the economy was a huge task that made **austerity** the keynote, with the rationing of food and fuel remaining in force long after 1945. This cost the Labour Party dearly in the general election of 1951, which returned the Conservatives to power under the leadership of an ageing Churchill. The following year, King George VI died and was succeeded by his elder daughter, who, as **Queen Elizabeth II**, remains on the throne today.

Meanwhile, Britain, the United States, Canada, France and the Benelux countries defined their postwar international commitments in 1949's **North Atlantic Treaty**, a counterbalance to Soviet power in Eastern Europe. Nevertheless, there was continuing confusion over Britain's imperial – or rather post-imperial – role and this bubbled to the surface in both the incompetent **partition of India** in 1947 and the **Suez Crisis** of 1956, when Anglo-French and Israeli forces invaded Egypt to secure control of the Suez Canal, only to be hastily recalled following international (American) condemnation; the resignation of the Conservative prime minister, **Anthony Eden** (1897–1977), followed. His replacement, pragmatic, silky-tongued **Harold Macmillan** (1894–1986), accepted the end of empire, but was still eager for Britain to play a leading international role – and the country kept its nuclear arms, despite the best efforts of the **CND** (Campaign for Nuclear Disarmament).

Boom and bust

The dominant political figure in the 1960s was Labour's **Harold Wilson** (1916–95), a witty speaker and skilled tactician who was prime minister twice (1964–70 and 1974–76). The

1955	1962	1967	1970
Fashion designer Mary Quant opens her first shop in London. Skirt hems are about to rise.	The Beatles hit the big time with their first single, *Love Me Do*.	First withdrawal from an ATM in Britain – at a branch of Barclays.	First Glastonbury Festival held – music lovers get used to mud.

Sixties saw a boom in consumer spending, pioneering social legislation (primarily on homosexuality and abortion), and a corresponding cultural upswing, with London becoming the hippest city on the planet. But the good times lasted barely a decade: the Conservatives returned to office in 1970 and although the new prime minister, the ungainly **Edward Heath** (1916–2005), led Britain into the brave new world of the **European Economic Community** (**EEC**), the 1970s was an era of recession and industrial strife. Labour returned to power in 1974, but ultimately a succession of public-sector strikes and mistimed decisions handed the 1979 general election to the Conservatives under new leader **Margaret Thatcher** (1925–2013). The pundits were amazed by her success, but as events proved, she was primed and ready to break the unions and anyone else who crossed her path.

Thatcher and Major (1979–97)

Thatcher went on to win three general elections, but pushed the UK into a period of sharp social polarization. While taxation policies and easy credit fuelled a consumer boom for the professional classes, the erosion of manufacturing and weakening of the welfare state impoverished a swathe of the population. Thatcher won an increased majority in the 1983 election, thanks largely to the successful recapture of the **Falkland Islands**, a remote British dependency in the south Atlantic, retrieved from the occupying Argentine army in 1982. Her electoral domination was also assisted by the fragmentation of the Labour opposition, particularly following the establishment of the Social Democratic Party, which had formed in response to what it perceived as the radicalization of the Labour Party, but ended up amalgamating with what remained of the Liberal Party to form the **Liberal Democrats** in 1988.

Trouble and strife

Social and political tensions surfaced in sporadic urban rioting and the year-long **miners' strike** (1984–85) against colliery closures, a bitter industrial dispute in which the police were given unprecedented powers to restrict the movement of citizens. The violence in Northern Ireland also intensified, and in 1984 IRA bombers came close to killing the entire Cabinet, who were staying in a Brighton hotel during the Conservatives' annual conference. The divisive politics of Thatcherism reached their apogee when the desperately unpopular **Poll Tax** led to her overthrow by Conservative

THE ROYALS – AND DIANA

The 1990s were a troubled time for the **Royal Family**, whose credibility fissured with the break-up of the marriage of Prince Charles and Diana. Revelations about the cruel treatment of Diana by both the (unfaithful) prince and his entourage damaged the royals' reputation and suddenly the institution itself seemed an anachronism, its members stiff, old-fashioned and dim-witted. By contrast, **Diana**, who was formally divorced from Charles in 1994, appeared warm-hearted and glamorous, so much so that her death in a car accident in Paris in 1997 may actually have saved the Royal Family as an institution. In the short term, Diana's death had a profound impact on the British, who joined in a media-orchestrated exercise in public grieving unprecedented in modern times.

1975	1985	1994	1999
First North Sea oil comes ashore.	The bitter, year-long miners' strike is crushed by Margaret Thatcher.	The Channel Tunnel opens to traffic.	The Scottish Parliament and the National Assemblies for Wales and Northern Ireland take on devolved powers.

colleagues who feared annihilation if she led them into another general election. The beneficiary was **John Major** (b.1943), a notably uninspiring figure who nonetheless managed to win the Conservatives a fourth term of office in 1992, albeit with a much reduced Parliamentary majority. While his government presided over a steady growth in economic performance, they gained little credit amid allegations of mismanagement, incompetence and feckless leadership, all overlaid by endless tales of Tory "sleaze", with revelations of extramarital affairs and financial crookery gleefully recounted by the British press. There was also the small matter of ties with Europe: a good chunk of the Conservative Party wanted a European free-trade zone, but nothing more, whereas the **Maastricht Treaty** of 1992, which the UK government signed, seemed to imply an element of political union with the EEC (now rebranded as the **European Union** or **EU**); right-wing Tories were apoplectic and their frequent and very public demonstrations of disloyalty further hobbled the Major government.

The Blair years

Wracked by factionalism in the 1980s, the **Labour Party** regrouped under Neil Kinnock and then John Smith, though neither of them reaped the political rewards. These dropped into the lap of a new and dynamic young leader, **Tony Blair** (b.1953), who soon pushed the party further away from traditional left-wing socialism. Blair's cloak of idealistic, media-friendly populism worked to devastating effect, sweeping the Labour Party to power in the **general election of May 1997** on a wave of genuine popular optimism. There were immediate rewards in enhanced relations with the EU and progress in the Irish peace talks, and Blair's electoral touch was soon repeated in Labour-sponsored **devolution referenda**, whose results semi-detached Scotland and Wales from their more populous neighbour in the form of a Scottish Parliament and Welsh Assembly.

Labour won the **general election of June 2001** with another thumping parliamentary landslide. This second victory was, however, accompanied by little of the optimism of the one before. Few voters fully trusted Blair, and his administration had by then established an unenviable reputation for the laundering of events to present the government in the best possible light. Nonetheless, the ailing Conservative Party failed to capitalize on these shortcomings, leaving Blair streets ahead of his political rivals in the opinion polls when the hijacked planes hit New York's World Trade Center on **September 11, 2001**. Blair rushed to support President Bush, joining in the attack on Afghanistan and then, to widespread horror, sending British forces into **Iraq** alongside the Americans in 2003. Saddam Hussein was deposed with relative ease, but neither Bush nor Blair had a coherent exit strategy, and back home Blair was widely seen as having spun Britain into the war by exaggerating the danger Saddam presented with his supposed – indeed nonexistent – **WMDs** (Weapons of Mass Destruction).

Domestic investment

On the domestic front, Blair proceeded with a massive and much-needed investment in **public services** during his second term, with education and health being the prime beneficiaries. There was also a concerted attempt to lift (many of) the country's poorer citizens out of poverty. These efforts secured little recognition, though, partly due to the

2005	2007	2009
The Civil Partnership Act gives same-sex couples legal recognition of their relationships.	Smoking banned in enclosed public places in England and Wales.	Economic crisis prompts the Bank of England to reduce interest rates to a record low of 0.5 percent: misery for savers; (some) pleasure for spenders.

methods Labour used, characterized by impenetrable bureaucracy and lack of trust in its public-sector workforce. The result was a top-down, command-and-control system in which central government imposed all sorts of targets – performance indicators and the like – in a welter of initiatives and regulation that confused almost everyone.

The financial crash and its immediate aftermath

Blair won a **third general election in May 2005**, but only after promising to step down before the following one – by any standard, a rather odd way to secure victory. Perhaps regretting his promise, Blair proceeded to huff and puff but eventually, in 2007, he stepped down and was succeeded by his colleague and arch-rival, **Gordon Brown** (b.1951). It was not a happy succession: Brown, previously Chancellor of the Exchequer, proved to be an extraordinarily tin-eared prime minister, who even managed to secure little credit for his one major achievement, the staving-off of a banking collapse during the worldwide **financial crisis** that hit the UK hard in the autumn of 2007–08. Brown's bold decision to keep public investment high by borrowing vast sums of money almost certainly prevented a comprehensive economic collapse in 2008–09, though equally his failure to properly regulate the banks beforehand helped create the crisis in the first place.

In the build-up to the **general election of 2010**, both main political parties, as well as the Liberal Democrats, spoke of the need to **cut public spending** more or less drastically, manoeuvring the electorate away from blaming the bankers for the crash. In the event, none of the three was able to secure a Parliamentary majority in the general election, but an impasse was avoided when the Liberal Democrats swapped principles for power to join a **Conservative–Liberal Democrat coalition**, which took office in May 2010 with Conservative David Cameron as prime minister.

The Cameron years

An old Etonian with a PR background, **David Cameron** (b.1966) made a confident and sure-footed start as prime minister, keeping his ideological cards well hidden (if indeed he had any), while his government set about a concerted attack on the public sector on the pretext of the need for **austerity** following the financial crash. All seemed set fair, with the Liberals suitably supine, but key policy initiatives soon began to run aground and the coalition zigzagged between decision and revision, for example in its plans to transform (that is, part privatize) the NHS.

There was also the matter of Scotland, where the **Scottish National Party** (SNP) had galvanized support for Scottish independence. In the event, the **Scottish independence referendum** of September 2014 gave a slight victory to the unionists, and the United Kingdom survived. The most remarkable feature of the referendum, though, was the high turnout – an astounding 84 percent.

Despite the less than impressive record of his government, Cameron managed to win an overall majority in the **general election of 2015** by promising strong fiscal management – and yet more austerity. The Conservative election manifesto also committed to a referendum on the UK's membership of the EU – partly as a sop to Eurosceptics within the party and partly to head off an emergent **UKIP**, an EU-hating, right-wing party led by

2011	**2012**	**2013**
Murdoch media empire in crisis over illegal phone-hacking: *News of the World* newspaper closed.	London hosts the Olympic Games.	Same-sex marriage legalized in England.

the shrewd **Nigel Farage** (b.1964). Cameron, who wanted to stay in the EU, seems to have been quietly confident that the "remainers" would win by a country mile, but in the **EU membership referendum** of June 23, 2016, almost 52 percent of the population voted to leave the EU; Cameron was toast – and promptly resigned.

Into the future

After Cameron's departure, **Theresa May** (b.1956) was elected Prime Minister from within the ranks of the Conservative Party. Initially, it seemed a sound choice: an experienced politician and long-serving Home Secretary, May was reckoned to be reliable and efficient. However, it soon became obvious that Brexit negotiations with the EU would both strain the resources of the British government and sharpen divisions within the Tory Party about the speed of leaving the EU – and what, exactly, leaving actually meant. Still, the Tories thought, they were in no electoral danger as the unexpected new leader of the Labour Party, **Jeremy Corbyn** (b.1949), was far too left-wing to gain any traction – and many more right-wing Labour MPs agreed, whispering away in order to plot Corbyn's downfall.

And so it was that May called the **general election of June 2017**, which she presumed would be a romp. It wasn't. May's campaign was extraordinarily inept, but rather more surprisingly a fair chunk of the population warmed to the much-maligned Labour leader – social media buzzed with photos of a young Corbyn being arrested for protesting South Africa's apartheid policies. Then there was the Labour manifesto: no ifs, no more austerity, plus a renationalization of key industries and the abolition of student fees. Somehow, suddenly, there seemed to be a sea change in the popular mood and, although the Conservatives actually won the election by a nose – albeit with the help of a controversial confidence-and-supply deal with Northern Ireland's populist, right-wing **DUP** – austerity, their key policy plank, was left looking dead in the water. It is impossible to know whether Corbyn's rise is a temporary blip, but for many left-leaning Brits seeing Corbyn feted by thousands of festivalgoers at Glastonbury was a treat indeed.

2015	2016	2017
Conservatives win the general election under David Cameron.	British narrowly votes to leave the EU (51.9 percent). Many leave voters express "Regrexit"; remainers unimpressed.	Conservative PM, Theresa May, calls a snap election – disaster for her, but an unexpected boost for Labour; a hung parliament.

Architecture

If England sometimes seems a bit like a historical theme park, it's because physical evidence of its long history is so very ubiquitous. Despite the best efforts of Victorian modernizers, the Luftwaffe and twentieth-century town planners, every corner of the country has some landmark worthy of attention, be it a Neolithic burial site or a postmodern addition to a world-famous gallery.

Pre-1066 origins

Dating from the **fourth millennium BC**, the oldest traces of building in England are the **Neolithic long barrows** (burial sites), and habitations, consisting of concentric rings of ditches and banks. The most famous prehistoric monument is the stone circle of **Stonehenge** on Salisbury Plain, which was begun in around 3000 BC and extensively modified over the next thousand years. This, as well as nearby **Avebury**, probably had an astronomical and sacred significance. Less grandiose **stone circles and rows** survive from the Lake District to Bodmin Moor, while **hut circles** on the moors of the West Country are associated with the Bronze Age – **Grimspound**, on Dartmoor, is one of the best examples, dating from about 1200 BC. The **Celts**, who arrived in numbers around 600 BC, left behind a series of hilltop defensive works, ranging from simple circular earthworks to the vast complex of **Maiden Castle** in Dorset. The best-preserved Iron Age village is **Chysauster**, Cornwall, consisting of stone houses arranged in pairs. The **Romans** brought order, peace and a slew of **public buildings**, including the surviving amphitheatre in **Chester** and baths in **Bath**. Two of Roman Britain's principal towns, **Colchester** and **St Albans**, retain impressive remains, while the palace at **Fishbourne** in West Sussex, built around 75 AD, is a prime example of a wealthy provincial villa.

The most enduring relics of **Anglo-Saxon** construction were **stone-built churches**, though those that survived were subject to constant modifications, as was the case with two of the earliest English churches, both in **Canterbury** – St Peter and St Paul, and the town's first cathedral, both dating from around 600 AD. The later Anglo-Saxon era was punctuated by Viking incursions, though an emergent native style can be discerned in the churches and monasteries erected in the tenth century, many of which show a penchant for quirky decoration, as in the spiral columns in the crypt at St Wystan's Church in Repton, Derbyshire.

Norman architecture

In the early eleventh century, Anglo-Saxon England's architectural insularity faded away as continental influences arrived from across the Channel. When Edward the Confessor rebuilt **Westminster Abbey** (1050–65), he followed the Norman – or Romanesque – style, while French architectural styles became the dominant influence in both castles and churches following the Norman conquest of 1066. The earliest Norman castles followed a "motte and bailey" design, consisting of a central tower (or keep) placed on a mound (the motte) encircled by one or more courts (the baileys). Most such castles were built of wood until the time of the Plantagenet Henry II, though some were stone-constructed from the beginning, including those at **Rochester** and **Colchester** and the **White Tower** at the **Tower of London**, the most formidable of all the Norman strongholds.

Once the Normans had secured the country, they set about transforming English churches. Many – for example at **Canterbury**, **York**, **St Albans**, **Winchester**, **Worcester** and **Ely** – were rebuilt along Romanesque lines, with cruciform ground plans and massive cylindrical columns topped by semicircular arches. The finest Norman church was **Durham Cathedral**, begun in 1093 and boasting Europe's first example of large-scale ribbed vaulting. An increasing love of decoration was evident in the spectacular zigzag and diamond patterns on Durham's colossal piers as well as in the elaborately carved capitals and blind arcading of Canterbury Cathedral.

The Transitional style

The twelfth century witnessed a dramatic increase in the wealth and power of England's monastic houses. The **Cistercians** were responsible for some of the most splendid foundations, establishing an especially grand group of self-sufficient monasteries in Yorkshire – **Fountains**, **Rievaulx** and **Jervaulx** – which all featured examples of the pointed arch, an idea imported from northern France. The reforming Cistercians favoured a plain style, but the native penchant for decoration gradually infiltrated their buildings, as at **Kirkstall Abbey** (c.1152), near Leeds. Other orders, such as the **Cluniacs**, showed a preference for greater elaboration from much earlier, as in the extravagantly ornate west front of Norfolk's **Castle Acre** priory (1140–50).

Profuse carved decoration and pointed arches were distinctive elements in the evolution of a **Transitional style**, which, from the middle of the twelfth century, represented a shift away from the purely Romanesque. The use of the pointed arch, alongside improvements in masonry techniques and the introduction of new systems of buttressing and vaulting, meant taller buildings, proportionally larger windows and more slender piers.

Early English style

Gothic architecture began in earnest in the last quarter of the twelfth century, when Gothic motifs were used at **Roche Abbey** and **Byland**, both in Yorkshire, but it was the French-designed **choir** at **Canterbury Cathedral** (1175–84) that really established the new style. This first phase of English Gothic, lasting through most of the thirteenth century, is known as **Early English** (or Pointed or Lancet), and was given its full expression in what is regarded as the first truly Gothic cathedral in England, **Wells**, largely completed by 1190. **Lincoln Cathedral** takes the process of vertical emphasis further, with wall-shafts soaring all the way to the ceiling, while adding an even greater profusion of decoration. The strong influence of Lincoln, however, was resisted by the builders of **Salisbury Cathedral** (1220–65), one of the most homogeneous of the Early English churches.

The Decorated and Perpendicular styles

The development of complicated **tracery** is one of the chief characteristics of the **Decorated** style, which reached its apotheosis around the end of the thirteenth and the beginning of the fourteenth century, when the cathedral at **Exeter** was almost completely rebuilt with a dense exuberance of rib vaulting and multiple moulding on its arches and piers. **York Minster**, rebuilt from 1225 and the largest of all English Gothic churches, introduced **lierne vaulting**, whereby a subsidiary, essentially ornamental, rib is added to the roof complex. Intricately carved roof bosses and capitals are other common features of Decorated Gothic, as is the use of the **ogee curve**.

The prevalent style in the late fourteenth century was the **Perpendicular**, the first post-Norman architecture unique to England and one that emphasized a more rectilinear, less flamboyant design. In **Gloucester Cathedral** (rebuilt 1337–57), for example, this can be seen in the massive east window, in which the tracery is organized in vertical compartments, to maximize light, while the cloister features the first fully developed **fan vault**.

The Wars of the Roses impeded the construction of new "prestige" buildings in the second half of the fifteenth century, though many parish churches eagerly embraced the new Perpendicular style and work did begin on the remarkable **King's College Chapel**,

Cambridge. This was only completed after the Tudors took power, its fan vaulting extended over the whole nave and harmonized with the windows and wall panelling. The Tudors commissioned a number of new buildings too, including Henry VII's splendid **St George's Chapel** at Windsor and **Henry VII's Chapel** in Westminster Abbey, where the dense sculptural detail took vaulting to the limit.

The Renaissance

The impact of **Renaissance** architecture during the Tudor period was largely confined to small decorative features, such as the Italianate embellishments at **Hampton Court Palace**. The championing of new and innovative designs often devolved to powerful landowners, as typified by the grand mansions of **Burghley House**, Lincolnshire (1552–87), **Longleat**, Wiltshire (1568–80), and **Hardwick Hall**, Derbyshire (1591–96) – celebrated in local rhyme as "Hardwick Hall, more glass than wall".

The full spirit of the Renaissance did not find total expression in England until **Inigo Jones** (1573–1652) began to apply the lessons learned from his visits to Italy, and in particular from his familiarity with Palladio's rules of proportion and symmetry. Appointed Royal Surveyor in 1615, Jones changed the direction of English architecture, with prominent London works including the **Banqueting House**, Whitehall (1619–22); the **Queen's House** at Greenwich (1617–35); and **St Paul's Church**, Covent Garden (1630s), the focal point of the first planned city square in England.

Wren and the Baroque

The artistic heir of Inigo Jones, **Christopher Wren** (1632–1723) had already established himself as a mathematician and astronomer before turning to architecture shortly after the Restoration of 1660. Wren's work was never so wholeheartedly Italianate as that of Jones, and his first building, Oxford's **Sheldonian Theatre**, demonstrated an eclectic style that combined orthodox classicism with **Baroque** inventiveness and French and Dutch elements. The bulk of his achievement is to be seen in London, where the **Great Fire of 1666** led to a commission for the building of no fewer than 53 churches. The most striking of these buildings display a remarkable elegance and harmony, notably **St Bride** in Fleet Street, **St Mary-le-Bow** in Cheapside, **St Stephen Walbrook** alongside Mansion House and, most monumental of all, **St Paul's Cathedral** (1675–1710), with its massive central dome.

Wren also rebuilt, extended or altered several royal palaces, including **Hampton Court** (1689–1700). Other secular works include **Trinity College Library**, Cambridge (1676–84), the **Tom Tower of Christ Church**, Oxford (1681–82) – a rare work in the Gothic mode – and, grandest of all, **Greenwich Hospital** (1694–98), a magnificent foil to Inigo Jones' nearby Queen's House, and to Wren's own Royal Observatory (1675).

Hawksmoor and Vanbrugh

Work at Greenwich Hospital was continued by Wren's pupil, **Nicholas Hawksmoor** (1661–1736), whose distinctively muscular Baroque is seen to best effect in his London churches, primarily **St George-in-the-East** (1715–23) and **Christ Church**, Spitalfields (1723–29). His exercises in Gothic pastiche include the western towers of **Westminster Abbey** (1734) and **All Souls College**, Oxford (1716–35), while the mausoleum at Castle Howard in Yorkshire (1729) shows close affinities with the Roman Baroque.

The third great English architect of the Baroque era was **John Vanbrugh** (1664–1726), principally known as a dramatist and lacking any architectural training when he was commissioned to design a new country seat at **Castle Howard** (1699–1726). More flamboyant than either Hawksmoor or Wren, Vanbrugh went on to design numerous other grandiose houses, of which the outstanding example is the gargantuan **Blenheim Palace** (1705–20), the high point of English Baroque.

Gibbs and Palladianism

The peace that followed the Treaty of Utrecht (1713) precipitated a rush to the continent by English aristocrats and artisans. The most obvious effect was the rebirth in England of the **Palladian** architecture introduced by Inigo Jones a century before – a style that was to dominate eighteenth-century secular architecture. The movement was championed by a Whig elite led by **Lord Burlington** (1694–1753), whose own masterpiece was **Chiswick House** in London (1725), a domed villa closely modelled on Palladio's Villa Rotonda. Burlington collaborated with the decorator, garden designer and architect **William Kent** (1685–1748) on such stately piles as **Holkham Hall** in Norfolk (1734), whose imposing portico and ordered composition typify the break with Baroque dramatics.

The most influential architect of religious buildings at that time was **James Gibbs** (1682–1754), whose masterpiece, London's **St Martin-in-the-Fields** (1722–26), with its steeple sprouting above a pedimented portico, was widely imitated as a model of how to combine the Classical and Gothic. Elsewhere, Gibbs designed **Senate House** (1722–30) and King's College's **Gibbs Building** (1723–49), both in Cambridge, and Oxford's **Radcliffe Camera** (1737–49), which drew heavily on his knowledge of Roman styles.

The Palladian idiom was further disseminated by such men as **John Wood** (1704–54), designer of **Liverpool Town Hall** (1749–54), but better known for the work he did in **Bath**, helping to transform the city into a paragon of town planning. His showpieces there are **Queen Square** (1729–36) and the **Circus** (1754), the latter completed by his son, **John Wood the Younger** (1728–81), who went on to design Bath's **Royal Crescent** (1767–74). **Robert Adam** (1728–92), the most versatile architect of his day, designed the city's **Pulteney Bridge** (1769–74). His forte, however, was in designing elaborate decorative interiors, best displayed in **Syon House** (1762–69) and **Osterley Park** (1761–80), both on the western outskirts of London, and **Kenwood** (1767–79) on Hampstead Heath. Adam's chief rival was the more fastidious **William Chambers** (1723–96), whose masterpiece, **Somerset House** on London's Strand (1776–98), is an academic counterpoint to Adam's dashing originality.

The nineteenth century

The greatest architect of the late eighteenth and early nineteenth centuries was **John Nash** (1752–1835), his Picturesque country houses built in collaboration with landscapist **Humphrey Repton** (1752–1818). Nash is associated above all with the style favoured during the **Regency** period, a decorous style that made plentiful use of stucco. A prolific worker, Nash was responsible for much of the present-day appearance of **resorts** such as Weymouth, Clifton (in Bristol) and Brighton, site of his orientalized Gothic palace, the **Brighton Pavilion**. In central **London**, his constructions include **Haymarket Theatre** (1820), the church of **All Souls**, Langham Place (1822–25), and **Clarence House** (1825), not to mention the layout of **Regent's Park** and **Regent Street** (from 1811), and the remodelling of **Buckingham Palace** (1826–30). The pared-down Classical experiments of Nash's contemporary, **Sir John Soane** (1753–1837), presented a serious-minded contrast to Nash's extrovert creations. Little remains of his greatest masterpiece, the **Bank of England** (1788–1833), but his idiosyncratic style is well illustrated by two other London buildings – his own home, now **Sir John Soane's Museum** on Lincoln's Inn Fields (1812–13), and **Dulwich Art Gallery** (1811–14).

Many exponents of the Picturesque also dabbled in **Gothic** architecture, and when Parliament voted a million pounds for the construction of new Anglican churches in 1818, two-thirds were built in some version of this style, inaugurating the so-called **Gothic Revival**. Its was confirmed when the **Houses of Parliament** were rebuilt in neo-Gothic style after the fire of 1834. The contract was given to **Charles Barry** (1795–1860), designer of the Classical Reform Club, but his collaborator, **Augustus Welby Pugin** (1812–52), was to become the unswerving apostle of the neo-Gothic. Another eminent architect, **George Gilbert Scott** (1811–78) expressed his neo-Gothic predilections in the extravagances of **St Pancras Station** (1868–74) and the **Albert Memorial** (1863–72), both

LANDSCAPE GARDENING

One area in which English designers excelled in the eighteenth century was **landscape gardening**, whose finest exponent was **Capability Brown** (1716–83). All over England, Brown and his acolytes modified the estates of the landed gentry into idealized "Picturesque" landscapes, often enhancing the view with a romantic "ruin" or some exotic structure such as a Chinese pagoda or Indian temple. One of Brown's earliest and most spectacular designs was at **Stowe** in Buckinghamshire, while **Chatsworth** in the Peak District combined his vision with the talents of **Joseph Paxton** (1803–65), who contributed to the estate in the following century.

ased on Flemish and north Italian models, while **Truro Cathedral** (1880–1910) was a cholarly exercise in French-influenced Gothic.

Nonetheless, the Victorian age was nothing if not eclectic: many public buildings ontinued to draw on Renaissance and Classical influences – notably the town halls of 3irmingham (1832–50) and Leeds (1853–58) – and the Catholic **Westminster Cathedral** 1895–1903) was a neo-Byzantine confection. The architectural stew was further enriched y a string of engineer-architects, who employed cast iron and other manufactured naterials in such works as Joseph Paxton's glass-and-iron **Crystal Palace** (1851, burned own in 1936). The materials' potential was similarly exploited in **Newcastle Central Station** 1846–55), one of a generation of monumental railway stations incorporating Classical notifs and rib-vaulted iron roofs.

John Ruskin (1819–1900) and his disciple **William Morris** (1834–96), leader of the Arts nd Crafts Movement, rejected these industrial technologies in favour of traditional naterials – brick, stone and timber – worked in traditional ways. Morris was not an rchitect himself, but he did plan the interior of his own home, the Red House in Bexley 1854), from designs by Philip Webb (1831–1915). The Arts and Crafts Movement also nfluenced **Charles Voysey** (1851–1941), whose clean-cut cottages and houses eschewed all stentation, depending instead on the meticulous and subtle use of local materials for their ffect. The originality of Voysey's work and that of his contemporaries **M.H. Baillie Scott** 1865–1945) and **Ernest Newton** (1856–1922) was later debased by scores of speculative uburban builders, though not before their refreshingly simple style had found recognition rst in Germany and then across the rest of Europe.

he twentieth century

Revivalist tendencies prevailed in England throughout the early decades of the twentieth century, typified by **Edwin Lutyens** (1869–1944), whose work moved from the Arts and Crafts style through to classicized structures, neo-Georgianism and the one-off, faux-medieval astle Drogo on the edge of Dartmoor (1910–30). An awareness of more radical trends did, owever, surface in isolated projects in the 1930s, for example **Senate House** in London's 3loomsbury (1932), designed by **Charles Holden** (1875–1960), who was also responsible for ome of London's Underground stations, notably **Arnos Grove** (1932). The **Tecton group**, led y the Russian immigrant Berthold Lubetkin (1901–90), also created several examples of the ustere International Modern style, most notably London Zoo's **Penguin Pool** (1934). The JK's first public building built in the Modernist style was the sleek, streamlined **De La Warr** avilion in Bexhill-on-Sea, Sussex, designed by Erich Mendelsohn and Serge Chermayeff in 935, and described by Mendelsohn as a "horizontal skyscraper".

945 to 1980

he German bombing of World War II created a national **housing crisis** of immense limensions: by 1945, nearly a third of the nation's houses had been destroyed or damaged. City planners up and down the country set about the problem with vim and gusto – but, vith one or two notable exceptions, they got the solutions very wrong. Terraced houses vere associated with slums, so they were knocked down by the thousand, but all too often they were replaced by **tower blocks** in a pale imitation of the Modernist style proclaimed by the likes of Corbusier: Modernism had gained a foothold in England after London's 1951 **Festival of Britain**. As if that wasn't enough, speed of reconstruction – rather than quality – was often the key criterion and, convinced that the car was the future, roads were ploughed through a host of English cities almost willy-nilly.

Nevertheless, there were some noteworthy architectural achievements in the 1950s and 1960s, including **Basil Spence**'s (1907–76) startling replacement of the bombed **Coventry Cathedral** (1951–59); Denys Lasdun's (1914–2001) ziggurats at the **University of East Anglia** in Norwich (1963); and the **Royal Festival Hall** (1949–51), a triumphant Modernist departure from the traditional model for classical music venues.

1980 to 2000

In the late twentieth century, English architecture was stranded between a popular dislike for the modern and a general reluctance among its practitioners to return to the past. In this climate, a string of leading architects adjusted to the new state of play by adopting a more fluent, sinuous or even whimsical style in their new commissions – and the public responded well. **Norman Foster** (b.1935) chipped in with the glass-tent terminal at **Stansted Airport** (1991) and **Michael Hopkins** (b.1935) produced both the eye-catching Mound Stand for **Lord's Cricket Ground** (1985–87) and the wood-panelled auditorium at the **Glyndebourne Opera House** (1994). Even the money-is-power **Lloyd's Building** (1978–86) by **Richard Rogers** (b.1933) was partly redeemed by its hive-like interior.

The 2000s and beyond

In London, the early years of the twenty-first century produced a brigade of prestigious public buildings including Rogers' **Millennium Dome** (1999, now the O2 Arena) erected in Greenwich; the spectacular transformation of Giles Gilbert Scott's South Bank power station into **Tate Modern** (2000) by Herzog & de Meuron; the Olympic Games **Aquatic Centre** (Zaha Hadid, 2011); and, by the Norman Foster group, both the **Great Court** (2000) at the British Museum and the **Greater London Assembly** building (2002). Exciting and fresh work also appeared in less likely places, for example, within, the hallowed Victorian frontage of **St Pancras Station**, overhauled and reopened to great acclaim in 2007, and at Richard Rogers' controversial but ultimately triumphant **Terminal 5** at Heathrow Airport (2008). Yet more contentious were the city-slicker skyscrapers that, in a vulgar assertion of the (phallic) power of money, transformed London's skyline. Behemoths like **The Gherkin** (officially 30 St Mary Axe, 2004), **Heron Tower** (Kohn Pederson Fox, 2011), Renzo Piano's **Shard** (2012), the **Cheesegrater** (Leadenhall Building, 2014) and – perhaps the worst of the lot – the **Walkie Talkie** (20 Fenchurch St, 2014) were generally well received by both architects and business leaders, but many Londoners find them daunting and aesthetically distasteful.

Beyond London

Outside the capital, most of Britain's big cities have invested in eye-catching, prestige developments, with prime examples being Gateshead's **BALTIC** arts centre (Ellis Williams Architects, 2002); Manchester's stunning **Imperial War Museum North** (Daniel Libeskind, 2002); **Nottingham Contemporary** art gallery (Caruso St John, 2009); Brighton's **i360 Tower** (Marks Barfield, 2016); Leicester's **Curve** theatre (Rafael Viñoly, 2008); and **Sage Gateshead** (Foster and Partners, 2004). Also of special note is the redevelopment of Liverpool's Paradise Street as **Liverpool One**, opened in 2008–09. Most of these structures are stand-alone – or nearly stand-alone – but in Birmingham they have shown more ambition, reconfiguring the whole of the city centre by not only refurbishing existing buildings (such as the Ikon Gallery and The Rotunda) but also erecting superb new structures, among which three stand out: the billowing **Selfridges** department store (Future Systems, 2003); the netted **Birmingham Library** (Francine Houben, 2013); and **The Cube** tower block, complete with its startling cladding (MAKE, Ken Shuttleworth, 2010).

Books and literature

A tour of literary England could take several lifetimes. Many of the world's most famous writers were born, lived and died here, leaving footprints that reach into every corner of the country. Writers' birthplaces, houses, libraries and graves are a staple of local tourist industries, while in places like Stratford-upon-Avon and Grasmere, literature and tourism have formed a symbiotic bond. The quintessential bookish destination is Hay-on-Wye, a town on the Anglo–Welsh border devoted to the buying, selling and enjoyment of books – its annual literary festival (every May) is the nation's biggest book-related jamboree.

Literary England

For readers and book-lovers of all ages, there's something deeply satisfying about immersing yourself in **English literature**'s natural fabric, whether it's tramping the Yorkshire moors with the Brontë sisters or exploring the streets of Dickens's Rochester. And for every over-trumpeted sight in "Shakespeare Country" or "Beatrix Potter's Lakeland" there are dozens of other locales that contemporary English writers have made unquestionably their own, from Martin Amis's London to P.D. James's East Anglia. To plan a route following in the footsteps of your favourite author, turn to Itineraries (see p.25).

Shakespeare Country

Warwickshire in the West Midlands is – as the road signs attest – "Shakespeare Country", though to all intents and purposes it's a county with just one world-famous destination – **Stratford-upon-Avon**, birthplace in 1564 of England's greatest writer. So few facts about **Shakespeare**'s life are known that Stratford can be a disappointment for the serious literary pilgrim, its buildings and sights hedged with "reputedlys" and "maybes" – after 500 years, still the only incontrovertible evidence is that he was born in Stratford, and lived, married, had children and died there. Real Shakespeare country could just as easily be London, where his plays were written and performed (there was no theatre in Stratford in Shakespeare's day). But, from the house where he was (probably) born to the church in which he's (definitely) buried, Stratford at least provides a coherent centre for England's Shakespeare industry – and it's certainly the most atmospheric place to see a production by the Royal Shakespeare Company.

Wordsworth's Lake District

William Wordsworth and the **Lake District** are inextricably linked, and in the streets of Cockermouth (where he was born), Hawkshead (where he went to school) and Grasmere (where he lived most of his life), you're never very far from a sight associated with the poet and his circle. Wordsworth's views on nature and the natural world stood at the very heart of all his poetry, and it's still a jolt to encounter the very views that inspired him – from his carefully tended garden at Rydal Mount to the famous daffodils of Gowbarrow Park. It wasn't just Wordsworth either. The "**Lake Poets**" of popular description – Wordsworth, Samuel Taylor Coleridge and Robert Southey – formed a clique of fluctuating friendships with a shared passion for the Lakes at its core.

Haworth and the Brontës

Quite why the sheltered life of the **Brontë** sisters, Charlotte, Emily and Anne, should exert such a powerful fascination is a puzzle, though the contrast of their pinched provincial existence in the Yorkshire village of **Haworth** with the brooding moors and tumultuous

POETIC ENGLAND

From *The Canterbury Tales* onwards, **English poets** have taken inspiration from the country's people and landscape. Traditionally, much was made of England's rural lives and trades, by poets as diverse as Northamptonshire "peasant poet" John Clare and A.E. Housman, whose nostalgic *A Shropshire Lad* is one of English poetry's most favoured works. For poets like Cumbria's Norman Nicholson it was working people, their dialect and industry that inspired, while in Yorkshire-born (and later Devon resident) Ted Hughes, savage English nature found a unique voice. Perhaps there's something about the north in particular that engages and enrages poets: Philip Larkin, famously, spent the last thirty years of his life in Hull; the self-proclaimed "bard of Salford", John Cooper Clarke, skewered Manchester in his early machine-gun-style punk poems; and Huddersfield-born Simon Armitage continues to report "from the long, lifeless mud of the River Colne". Meanwhile, dub poet Linton Kwesi Johnson uses Jamaican patois in devastating commentaries on the English social condition ("Inglan is a bitch"); and London's poet-rapper Kate Tempest weighs in on poverty, class and consumerism.

passions of their novels may well form part of the answer. Their old home in the village parsonage and the family vault in the parish church only tell half the story. As Charlotte later recalled, "resident in a remote district ... we were wholly dependent on ourselves and each other, on books and study, for the enjoyments and occupations of life". Charlotte's *Jane Eyre*, the harrowing story of a much-put-upon governess, sprang from this domestic isolation, yet it was out on the bleak moors above Haworth that inspiration often struck, and where work like Emily's *Wuthering Heights* and Anne's *The Tenant of Wildfell Hall* progressed from mere parlour entertainments to melodramatic studies of emotion and obsession.

Dickensian England

The name of **Charles Dickens** has passed into the language as shorthand for any city's filthy stew of streets and gallery of grotesques. But although any dark alley or old curiosity shop in London might still be considered "Dickensian", it's a different matter trying to trace the author through his works. He was born in **Portsmouth**, but spent his younger years in Kent's **Chatham** and **Rochester**, the setting for most of his last book, *The Mystery of Edwin Drood*. Is this Dickensian England? Perhaps, though many of the most famous books – including *Oliver Twist*, *David Copperfield*, *Bleak House* and *Little Dorrit* – are set or partly set in a **London** that Dickens unquestionably made his own. His unhappy early experiences of the city – the boot-blacking factory at the age of 12, his father's spell in a debtors' prison, working as a law clerk – form the basis of many of Dickens' most trenchant pieces. Yet only one of his London houses survives (now the Charles Dickens Museum in Bloomsbury), and he only lived in that for two years. To the north then, finally, for Dickensian England, to the fictional "Coketown" of *Hard Times*. Dickens went to Preston and other **Lancashire** mill towns to gather material for his "state-of-the-nation" satire about the social and economic conditions of factory workers, while in **Barnard Castle** (County Durham) he found the heartbreaking neglect of schoolchildren that underpinned the magnificent *Nicholas Nickleby*.

Criminal England

Contemporary **crime writers** have moved well beyond the enclosed country-house mysteries of Agatha Christie. Colin Dexter's morose Inspector Morse flits between Town and Gown in **Oxford** in a cerebral series of whodunnits, while in the elegantly crafted novels of P.D. James it's the remote coast and isolated villages of **East Anglia** that often provide the backdrop. The other English "Queen of Crime", Ruth Rendell, set her long-running Inspector Wexford series in "Kingsmarkham" – inspired by Midhurst in **West Sussex**, surely the most crime-ridden country town after over twenty Wexford novels. **London**, of course, preoccupies many writers, from Derek Raymond or Jake Arnott recreating Sixties villainy to Rendell again, writing as Barbara Vine, at home with the capital's suburban misfits, drop-outs and damaged. Val McDermid, and her spirited private eye, Kate Brannigan, nail contemporary **Manchester**, and the seedier side of the city also gets a good kicking in the noir novels of Nicholas Blincoe. **Yorkshire** of the 1970s and 1980s is dissected in David Peace's majestic Red Riding quartet about corrupt police; Reginald Hill's popular Dalziel and Pascoe series portrays a more traditional pair of Yorkshire detectives, but in his Joe Sixsmith private-eye novels it's a reimagined **Luton** that forms the backdrop. Graham Greene gave us seedy **Brighton** first, and Peter James's policeman, Roy Grace, digs further into its underbelly, while in **Portsmouth** it's Graham Hurley's Joe Faraday charged with keeping the peace. Britain's rural areas don't escape the escalating body count either. Peter Robinson's Inspector Banks series is set in the **Yorkshire Dales**, and for Stephen Booth and his Derbyshire detective Ben Cooper it's the wilds of the **Peak District**.

A bibliography

The bibliography we've given here is necessarily selective, and entirely subjective. The ★ symbol indicates titles that are especially recommended.

TRAVELS AND JOURNALS

Peter Ackroyd *London: The Biography; Albion.* The capital is integral to much of Ackroyd's work and in *London* the great city itself is presented as a living organism, with themed chapters covering its fables, follies and foibles. Meanwhile, in the massively erudite *Albion*, Ackroyd traces the very origins of English culture and imagination.

★**Bill Bryson** *Notes From A Small Island.* After twenty years living and working in England, Bryson set off on one last tour of Britain before returning to the States – though in the end he couldn't resist his new country and now lives in Hampshire. His snort-with-laughter observations set the tone for his future travel, history and popular science bestsellers.

Paul Kingsnorth *Real England.* Kingsnorth's personal journey through his own "private England" is partly a lament for what's being lost – village greens, apple varieties, independent shops, waterways, post offices – and partly a heartfelt howl against globalization.

Olivia Laing *To the River.* This acclaimed account of the author's midsummer walk along Sussex's River Ouse from source to sea is beautifully written and observed, inter-weaving nature writing, history and folklore.

Stuart Maconie *Pies and Prejudice; Adventures on the High Teas.* A Lancastrian exile explores the north of England in *Pies,* in which you can find out where the north starts (Crewe station, apparently) and unravel the arcane mysteries of

northern dialect, dress and delicacies. *Adventures* continues his engaging investigation of the country, this time the mythical "Middle England" so beloved of social commentators.

Ian Marchant *The Longest Crawl.* The pub – so central to English life and landscape – is dissected in this highly entertaining account of a month-long crawl across the country, involving pork scratchings, funny beer names and lots of falling over.

J.B. Priestley *English Journey.* The Bradford-born playwright and author's record of his travels around the country in the 1930s say nothing about contemporary England, but in many ways its quirkiness and eye for English eccentricity formed the blueprint for the later Brysons and Therouxs.

W.G. Sebald *Rings of Saturn.* Intriguing, ruminative book that is a heady mix of novel, travel and memoir, focusing ostensibly on the author's walking tour of Suffolk.

Iain Sinclair *London Orbital.* After spending a couple of years walking around the "concrete necklace" of the M25, the erudite Sinclair delves into the dark and mysterious heart of suburban London.

Paul Theroux *The Kingdom by the Sea.* Travelling around the British coast in its entirety in 1982 to find out what the British are really like leaves Theroux thoroughly bad-tempered. No change there then.

GUIDEBOOKS

★**Simon Jenkins** *England's Thousand Best Churches; England's Thousand Best Houses.* A lucid, witty pick of England's churches and houses, divided by county and with a star rating – for the book on houses Jenkins includes all sorts of curiosities, from caves in Nottingham to prefabs in Buckinghamshire. Sales were so good that Jenkins has had further stabs at the same format with *England's 100 Best Views* (2014), *England's Best Cathedrals* (2016) and

even *Britain's 100 Best Railway Stations* (2017).

Sam Jordison and Dan Kieran *Crap Towns; Crap Towns II; Crap Towns Returns: Back by Unpopular Demand.* The books that made local councils all over England as mad as hell – utterly prejudiced but tongue-in-cheek accounts of the worst places to live in the country. We daren't even repeat the names of the "winners", as we'll only get letters of complaint (or cheers of agreement).

WINDOWS ONTO ENGLAND'S PAST

In his celebrated diary, **Samuel Pepys** recorded an eyewitness account of daily life in London from 1660 until 1669, covering momentous events like the Great Plague and the Great Fire – alongside his assorted romantic liaisons. The plague of 1665 also takes centre stage in *Journal of a Plague Year* by **Daniel Defoe** (author of *Robinson Crusoe*), a fictional "observation" of London's tribulations actually written sixty years later, while the same author's *Tour Through the Whole Island of Great Britain* (1724) was an early sort of economic guide to the country in the years immediately before the Industrial Revolution. Later, the changing seasons in a Hampshire village were recorded by **Gilbert White**, whose *Natural History of Selborne* (1788) is still seen as a masterpiece of nature writing. By 1830, **William Cobbett** was bemoaning the death of rural England and its customs in *Rural Rides*, while decrying both the growth of cities and the iniquities suffered by the exploited urban poor. These last were given magnificent expression in *The Condition of the Working Class in England*, an unforgettable portrait of life in England's hellish industrial towns, published in 1844 as **Friedrich Engels** worked in his father's Manchester cotton mills. Journalist **Henry Mayhew** would later do something similar for the Victorian capital's downtrodden in his mighty *London Labour and the London Poor* (1851). **George Orwell** was therefore following a well-worn path when he published his dissections of 1920s and 1930s working-class and under-class life, *Down and Out in Paris and London* (1933) and *The Road to Wigan Pier* (1937), giving, respectively, a tramp's-eye view of the world, and the brutal effects of the Great Depression on the industrial communities of Lancashire and Yorkshire. A later period of English transformation was recorded in *Akenfield* (1969), the surprising bestseller by **Ronald Blythe** that presented life in a rural Suffolk village on the cusp of change. Craig Taylor's update, *Return to Akenfield* (2006), and **Richard Askwith**'s *The Lost Village* (2008) show that interest in ordinary English rural life endures today, while in *The Plot* (2009), **Madeleine Bunting** presents an innovative through-the-ages biography of a secluded acre of land owned by her father that gets to the very heart of the English spirit.

Iain Pattinson *Lyttleton's Britain*. Great British jazz man and bandleader Humphrey Lyttleton presented the roving radio comedy panel game *I'm Sorry I Haven't A Clue* for forty years until his death in 2008. His barbed town introductions ("... from the Malvern Hills ... it is possible to catch a sight of Birmingham, despite the many, clearly posted warning signs") form a laugh-out-loud gazetteer to many of England's towns and cities.

A. Wainwright *A Pictorial Guide to the Lakeland Fell* (7 vols). More than mere guidebooks could ever be, the beautifully produced small-format volumes of handwritten notes and sketches (produced between 1952 and 1966) have led generations up the Lake District's mountains and down through its dales. The originals have now been revised to take account of changing routes and landscapes.

HISTORY, SOCIETY AND POLITICS

Julian Baggini *Welcome to Everytown: A Journey into the English Mind*. The prolific Baggini's "Everytown" is Rotherham – or rather postcode S66, supposedly containing the most typical mix of household types in the country. As a philosopher, his six-month stay there wasn't in search of the English character, but rather their "folk philosophy" (ie, what they think). The result? A surprising, illuminating view of mainstream English life as of 2007.

Catherine Bailey *Black Diamonds – the Rise and Fall of an English Dynasty*. Thoroughly researched book telling the tale of the feuding, coal-owning Fitzwilliam family, powerful aristocrats who were holed up in Wentworth, their lavish Yorkshire mansion, for generation after generation.

Andy Beckett *When the Lights Went Out*. Enough time has elapsed to make 1970s Britain seem like a different world (the title refers to the power cuts during the industrial unrest of 1974), but Beckett's lively history brings the period to life.

John Campbell *The Iron Lady: Margaret Thatcher*. Campbell has been mining the Thatcher seam for years now and this abridged paperback version, published in 2012, hits many political nails right on the head. By the same author, and equally engaging, is his 1987 *Aneurin Bevan and the Mirage of British Socialism*, plus his biography of Roy Jenkins.

Lynsey Hanley *Estates*. The story of social housing (the council "estates" of the title) hardly sounds like a winning topic, but Hanley's "intimate history" brilliantly reveals how class structure is built into the very English landscape (albeit a land that tourists rarely see).

Christopher Hill *The World Turned Upside-Down; God's Englishman: Oliver Cromwell and the English Revolution*. A pioneering Marxist historian, Hill (1912–2003) transformed the way the story of the English Civil War and the Commonwealth was related by means of a string of superbly esearched, well-written texts – among which these are two f the best.

★ **Eric Hobsbawm** *Industry and Empire*. Ostensibly an conomic history of Britain from 1750 to the late 1960s harting Britain's decline and fall as a world power, Mobsbawm's (1917–2012) great skill was in detailed analysis f the effects on ordinary people. See also *Captain Swing*, ocusing on the eponymous labourers' uprisings of nineteenth-entury England; *Age of Extremes: The Short Twentieth Century 1914–1991*; and his magnificent trilogy, *The Age of Revolution 1789–1848*, *The Age of Capital 1848–1875*, and *The Age of Empire: 1875–1914*; there's simply nothing better.

David Horspool *Why Alfred Burned the Cakes*. Little is known of the life of Alfred the Great, king of Wessex, and arguably the first king of what would become "England", but Horspool adds a welcome new dimension to the myths and legends. And in case you were wondering about the cakes, Alfred probably didn't.

Roy Jenkins *Churchill: A Biography*. Churchill biographies abound (and the man himself, of course, wrote up – and magnified – his own life), but politician and statesman Jenkins adds an extra level of understanding. Jenkins (1920–2003) specialized in political biographies of men of power, so you can also read his take on the likes of Gladstone, Asquith and Roosevelt.

Owen Jones *Chavs: The Demonization of the Working Class*. A trumpet blast from the political left – and a yell of moral/political outrage at the way the media treat the working class. The youthful Jones is articulate, fiery and witty – and followed up *Chavs* with the equally trenchant, howl-inducing *The Establishment: And how they get away with it*.

★ **David Kynaston** *Austerity Britain, 1945–51*. Comprehensive vox pop that gives the real flavour of postwar England. Everything is here, from the skill of a Dennis Compton cricket innings through to the difficulties and dangers of hewing coal down the pit, all in a land where there were "no supermarkets, no teabags, no Formica, no trainers … and just four Indian restaurants". Also recommended are Kynaston's follow-up volumes *Family Britain, 1951–57* and *Modernity Britain, 1957–1962*.

Diane Purkiss *The English Civil War: A People's History*. The story of English revolution, given a human face – the clue is in the subtitle. Purkiss dodges the battles and armies, focusing instead on the men who fought and the women who fed and tended to them. If you like it, try Purkiss's follow-up *Literature, Gender and Politics During the English Civil War*.

★ **Andrew Rawnsley** *The End of the Party*. Arguably Britain's most acute political journalist, Rawnsley cross-examines and dissects New Labour under Blair and Brown

ZEITGEIST NOVELS

Which postwar English novels best capture the spirit of the age in which they were written? Here are our choices.

1984, George Orwell (1949). When the clocks strike thirteen in the first sentence, you know something's wrong with wartime England.

Lucky Jim, Kingsley Amis (1954). "Angry Young Man" writes funniest book of the decade.

Saturday Night and Sunday Morning, Alan Sillitoe (1958). Factory life and sexual shenanigans in working-class Nottingham.

Billy Liar, Keith Waterhouse (1959). Cloying Yorkshire provincialism meets laugh-out-loud fantasy on the eve of the Swinging Sixties.

A Clockwork Orange, Anthony Burgess (1962). Droogs, crime and violence in a dystopian England.

The History Man, Malcolm Bradbury (1975). The "campus novel" par excellence.

London Fields, Martin Amis (1989). Literary London's favourite bad boy writes ferociously witty, baleful satire or pretentious drivel – you decide.

The Buddha of Suburbia, Hanif Kureishi (1990). Youth culture, identity and the immigrant experience.

Fever Pitch, Nick Hornby (1992). Did the modern masculine obsession with football start here?

Bridget Jones's Diary, Helen Fielding (1996). Thirty-something female neurosis, rehashed from an original newspaper column (and then again in film).

White Teeth, Zadie Smith (2000). Mixed families, mixed races, mixed religions, mixed England.

Saturday, Ian McEwan (2005). One of England's finest contemporary writers addresses the state of the nation and upper-middle-class angst.

South of the River, Blake Morrison (2007). The first heavyweight literary despatch from the decade of Blair and New Labour.

One Day, David Nicholls (2009). Dexter and Emma. Short-term pleasure and long-term commitment battle it out.

Life after Life, Kate Atkinson (2013). Clever, interrogative stuff in a world with no absolutes.

Autumn, Ali Smith (2016). The first post-Brexit novel: elegiac, surreal, funny and sad.

to withering effect. Different target, same approach – *In It Together: The Inside Story of the Coalition Government*.

Sheila Rowbotham *Hidden from History*. Last published in 1992, this key feminist text provides an uncompromising account of 300 years of women's oppression in Britain alongside a cogent analysis of the ways in which key female figures have been written out of history.

Simon Schama *A History of Britain* (3 vols). British history, from 3000 BC to 2000 AD, delivered at pace by the TV-famous historian and popularizer, Simon Schama. The prolific Schama can't half bang it out – even in his seventies, he's showing no signs of slowing down.

James Sharpe *Remember, Remember the Fifth of November; Dick Turpin*. A crisp retelling of the 1605 Gunpowder Plot, *Remember, Remember* also puts the whole episode – and the resultant Bonfire Night – into historical context. In *Dick Turpin*, subtitled "The Myth of the English Highwayman", Sharpe stands and delivers a broadside to the commonly accepted notion of Turpin and his ilk – not romantic robbers but brutal villains after all. If you warm to Sharpe's themes, then move onto his *A Fiery & Furious People: A History of Violence in England*.

Lytton Strachey *Queen Victoria*. Strachey (1880–1932) is often credited with establishing a warmer, wittier, more all-encompassing form of biography with his *Queen Victoria* (1921), following on from his groundbreaking *Eminent Victorians* (1918). Many others have followed in trying to understand the long-serving monarch, but few match Strachey's economy and wit.

A.J.P. Taylor *English History 1914–45*. Thought-provoking, scintillatingly well-written survey by one of Britain's finest populist historians (1906–90). When it first appeared in 1965 it was the fifth and final volume of the Oxford History of England. See also *The Origins of the Second World War*, *The Struggle for Mastery of Europe 1848–1918* and *The First World War: An Illustrated History*, a penetrating analysis of how the war started and why it went on for so long and including a savage portrayal of Britain's high command; first published in 1963, but never surpassed.

★**E.P. Thompson** *The Making of the English Working Class*. A seminal text – essential reading for anyone who wants to understand the fabric of English society. It traces the trials and tribulations of England's emergent working class between 1780 and 1832.

ART, ARCHITECTURE AND ARCHEOLOGY

John Betjeman *Ghastly Good Taste, Or, A Depressing Story of the Rise and Fall of English Architecture*. Classic one-hundred-page account of England's architecture written by one of the country's shrewdest poet-commentators. First published in 1970.

William Gaunt *Concise History of English Painting*. Books covering the broad sweep of English painting are thin on the ground, but this succinct and excellently illustrated book provides a useful introduction to its subject, covering the Middle Ages to the twentieth century in just 288 pages; it is, however, a little dated – it was published in 1964.

Owen Hatherley *A Guide to the New Ruins of Great Britain*. There's no good news from this angry rant of a book, which rails against – and describes in detail – the 1990s architectural desecration of a string of British cities in the name of speculation masquerading as modernization.

Nikolaus Pevsner *Pevsner Architectural Guides: Buildings of England*. If you want to know who built what, when, and how (rather than why), look no further than this landmark architectural series, in 46 county-by-county volumes. This serious-minded, magisterial project was initially a one-man show, but after Pevsner died in 1983 later authors revised his text, inserting newer buildings but generally respecting the founder's tone.

Francis Pryor *Home: A Time Traveller's Tales from Britain's Prehistory*. The often arcane discoveries of working archeologists are given fascinating new exposure in Pryor's lively archeological histories of Britain. Everything from before the Romans to the sixteenth century is examined through the archeologist's eye, unearthing a more sophisticated native culture than was formerly recognized along the way. This latest book concentrates on family life, but other Pryor titles include *Britain in the Middle Ages*; *Britain BC* and *Britain AD*.

Brian Sewell *Naked Emperors: Criticisms of English Contemporary Art*. Trenchant, idiosyncratic, reviews – often attacks – on contemporary art from this leading critic and arch debunker of pretension, who died in 2015. Few would want to plough through all 368 pages of the assembled reviews – but dip in and yelp with glee, or splutter with indignation.

Sixty years of English pop

England's heritage as a source of inspirational rock'n'roll is indisputable: the country's historic role as the hub of the British Empire, absorbing immigrants from around the world, and its openness to US culture have allowed it to assimilate diverse styles and rhythms – jazz, blues, soul and reggae – and have bred a distinctive domestic brand of popular music. Local acts soaked up the delicious musical juices seeping out of the shebeens, developing, for example, a taste for ska matched only in Kingston, Jamaica, and a predominantly white audience for US black music that Tamla Motown would envy. England's best music has come from its cities, nourished by fashions from the urban mix and flavours from the cultural melting pot. Here is a brief survey of some of its major cities, region by region, and the musical legacies they have created.

London

Inevitably, **London** is home to the widest range of international influences. Traditionally, artists on the way up had to make the trek to the capital to perform, record and sign a contract. Management and publishing companies lurked on the cheaper outskirts of the West End entertainment district, and there was a domestic "Tin Pan Alley" centred on **Denmark Street**. In the 1950s, entrepreneurs such as Larry Parnes created menacing-sounding stage personae (**Tommy Steele**, **Marty Wilde** and **Billy Fury**) and stalked the cappuccino bars of Soho to find compliant star material they could reshape as the ideal "all-round entertainer". The whole sordid scene was spoofed in the 1959 film *Espresso Bongo*, starring **Cliff Richard**.

As the industry blossomed in the early 1960s, the demonic **Rolling Stones** provided contrast and foil to The Beatles' thumbs-up attitude, bringing shade and cool to the otherwise permanent sunshine of pop music. Acts such as **The Who** and **The Small Faces** were among the most successful of the "**beat groups**" who terrified the locals before heading to the US, following in the wake of the Fab Four, in a "British Invasion". The archetypal Sixties' London band, **The Kinks**, recorded some of the most thoughtful, poignant and enduring pop charmers of the era, in between bouts of scrapping onstage.

Swinging London was still the place to be when a wave of hippy lifestyles and free love washed over England from sunny California, while the now-demolished *UFO* on Tottenham Court Road kick-started British psychedelia, booking **Pink Floyd** and **Soft Machine** in as house bands, and promoting the **14 Hour Technicolor Dream** at Alexandra Palace in 1967 – London's most notorious gig of the decade. Several bands playing a new style of hard rock sprang from the meeting of classic rhythm guitar bands with these new influences: **Jethro Tull** formed in 1967, and **Led Zeppelin** in 1968; **Iron Maiden** got their act together in 1975.

Glitter to punk and beyond

When the Sixties' beautiful dreams wore off, English pop turned to primitive stomping, hard guitar riffs and androgynous sex appeal with **glam rock** and **glitter**. For a while, East-End-boy-turned-bopping-elf **Marc Bolan** and his band T. Rex ruled the roost, but iconic British rock band **Queen** and gender-bending, genre-creating **David Bowie** – whose loss in 2016 was keenly felt, especially in his birthplace of Brixton – proved more enduring, their legacies continuing to this day. In the mid- to late Seventies, **punk rock**, a movement whose roots lay both in US garage bands and early 1960s British pop, smashed its way onto the scene. The iconoclastic **Sex Pistols** were joined by such bourgeoisie-baiting bands as **The Clash**, **The Damned** and **Siouxsie & The Banshees**, and for a few ecstatic months, punk ruled. The flame burned out quickly, however, and was followed by a confusing mix of **post-punk** scenes pulling in different directions, from rockabilly to a skinhead revival with a taste for high-speed **ska**.

Those left unmoved by this lack of glamour turned to the fashion wars of nightclubs, and a squadron of **New Romantics** headed by such London-formed acts as **Duran Duran**, **Spandau Ballet**, **Culture Club** and **Adam & The Ants**. Chart success led to world-cracking tours; George Michael even took **Wham!** from London to Beijing in 1985 as the first western pop act to gig in Red China.

In the late 1980s, the rise of ecstasy and affection for the **house** and **techno** scenes of Chicago and Detroit laid the groundwork for the UK's enduring dance music culture, which for many began at Danny Rampling's euphoric *Shoom* night in Southwark. In the mainstream, the decade's frills and ruffles eventually gave way to a search for "roots" and a back-to-basics movement in which the substance of lyrics and melody were considered more important than looks. The Nineties' quest for authenticity threw up a slew of big names, including **Blur**, **Suede** and **Elastica** in London, and saw Camden reinvented as the capital of **Britpop**; London more broadly was at the centre of the decade's **Cool Britannia** vibe, spearheaded by the rather less authentic (but inarguably fun) style and music of the **Spice Girls**.

New century, new sounds

For a moment, the Camden school endured in the shape of **The Libertines** (and their offshoots **Dirty Pretty Things**), but it was soon overshadowed by the harsh, hectic East London **grime** sound and South London's more minimal **dubstep**, both bastardized fusions of hip-hop, RnB, house and the weirder end of the dance spectrum. Grime remains one of London's defining sounds, with originator **Dizzee Rascal** still going strong, and artists such as Stormzy, Novelist and JME heading up 2017's **Grime 4 Corbyn**, a show of support for the shaggy-bearded Labour leader.

The London scene is, however, broad enough to take in a gamut of other musical styles, from folk-influenced acts like **Laura Marling** to the smart, provocative pop of **Florence + the Machine**. British jazz and, particularly, soul have had a renaissance in recent years. **Sam Smith** and **Adele** have been wildly successful – both providing title tracks for Bond films – and the influence of **Amy Winehouse** can hardly be overstated. The trend for performer-producers continues unabated, from **James Blake**'s dreamy electronica to **FKA twigs**' multi-layered, sensuous tracks.

In 2016, the Brooklyn-based **Afropunk** festival came to London, with plenty of black British musical talent in the line-up – Birmingham-born soul singer **Laura Mvula**, rapper/poet **Akala** and singer-songwriter **Lianne La Havas**. The festival's resounding success shows that, as ever, London's musical strength lies in its diversity.

Liverpool, Manchester and the northwest

As one of England's major ports, postwar **Liverpool** was home to a substantial immigrant population – Irish and West Indians in particular – with strong commercial links to the New York pop scene via the maritime traffic between the two cities. When they hit big in 1963, **The Beatles** brought moptops, R&B and genuine passion to a pop scene stuffed with insipid novelty tunes and crooning balladeers. From *Please Please Me* to *Hey Jude*, their music furnished a constant reassuring backing track to the rest of the decade. Their success yanked the whole Merseyside music scene into the national spotlight, from **Cilla Black** to **Billy J. Kramer & The Dakotas**, but when The Beatles made the long drive down to London, the media attention moved away. Britain's most influential and long-serving DJ **John Peel** flew the flag for Liverpool in the 1970s, but Liverpudlian pop had to wait until the next decade for its resurgence, in the form of **The Teardrop Explodes** and **Echo & the Bunnymen**. Throughout the Eighties and Nineties, kids would hook up at Probe Records before moving on for a night raving at local superclub, *Cream*. Meanwhile, Beatle-influenced melodic pop rippled on in the love songs to heroin of **The La's** and the robust beauties of **The Boo Radleys** and continued in the 2000s in such flavours as **The Zutons**, **The Coral** and **Ladytron**.

Manchester's contribution to English pop music is, if anything, even more impressive than Liverpool's. The city boasts or boasted Morrissey's beloved Salford Lads' Club, Factory Records, Granada TV, the BBC's main northern studios and *Wigan Casino* – home of Northern Soul, a genre growing in popularity once again (Scouser Craig Charles's *Funk and Soul Show* is BBC 6 Music's most successful programme). The list of Manchester bands is endless; from Sixties pop success stories such as **Herman's Hermits** up to today, the city's role as musical capital of the north continues unchallenged. Manchester and its environs was the second city of English punk, and it nurtured a more sardonic, thoughtful crop of post-punk acts, including **Buzzcocks**, **The Fall** and Macclesfield's **Joy Division**, that showed more genuine artistry and greater resilience than the London bands. Two Eighties bands, **The Smiths** and **New Order**, despite coming from opposite ends of the pop spectrum, stand out in particular. While Morrissey's ruminations on confused sexuality, shyness and solitude gave a voice to a generation left cold by the mainstream pop world of the mid-Eighties, it was New Order that had the more far-reaching effect. Embracing the new hedonism of synth-powered dance music, they inspired an ecstasy-driven dance-all-night lifestyle that ultimately created local superclub **The Haçienda**. From this developed the **Madchester** scene that threw up **The Happy Mondays**, **The Stone Roses**, **The Charlatans** and **James**.

After Madchester, the scene lost some of its energy – the early Nineties' most successful Mancunian act was manufactured boy band, **Take That**. But the city retained its swagger in the soap-opera squabbles of **Oasis**'s Gallagher brothers, and its taste for downbeat realism with bands such as **The Verve**, **Doves**, **Elbow** and Wigan's **Starsailor**.

ENGLAND'S POP SHRINES

Alley of love, Brighton Hometown of some of England's finest pop stars, Brighton was also the location of the main beachfront action in the movie of The Who's mod opera, *Quadrophenia*.

Glastonbury Home to the country's biggest and oldest music festival, which takes place on a Somerset farm miles from town and attracts some 175,000 people.

Town & Country Club, Leeds The city's best-loved major venue for the final years of the last millennium (now corporatized as the O2 Academy).

Eric's, Liverpool Crucible of the alternative and underground scene from the Seventies onward; on the same street as *The Cavern*.

Abbey Road Studios, London The Beatles' permanent recording HQ in the capital, and birthplace to countless classic recordings from Pink Floyd to Radiohead.

Soho, London Stand in the centre of Soho Square, throw a brick in any direction and you'll hit a revered institution, recording company office, musicians' unlicensed club

or aspiring superstar. Seek out 23 Heddon St for that essential Ziggy Stardust tribute pic.

Isle of Wight Following the famous 1970 festival, it was 32 years before the island dared/was allowed to host another such event and the second-coming Isle of Wight Festival is now a musical mainstay. The more alternative, folksy Bestival also originated on the island.

Salford Lads' Club, Manchester Featured on the cover of The Smiths' album *The Queen Is Dead*, the club once boasted Allan Clarke of The Hollies among its members.

The Twisted Wheel, Manchester Northern Soul venue par excellence, which played it fast, loud, heavy and all night long. The list of visiting bands reads like a Motown/Stax greatest-hits set.

The Leadmill, Sheffield Boasting more than 25 years as the city's top venue, the *Leadmill* has been an A-listed must-play gig for acts as diverse as Cabaret Voltaire, Killing Joke and The Libertines; it's still going strong today.

The Midlands

While **Brumbeat** donated its fair share of acts to the early to mid-Sixties scenes – with **Spencer Davis Group** and **Traffic** deserving special attention for pushing basic beat music forward to the edge of psychedelia – it was not till the era of **Black Sabbath**, at the end of the decade, that Brummie pop came alive. Then – as chart pop grew to thrive on hairstyles, glitter and dinosaur stomp – local boy **Roy Wood** escaped The Move and Electric Light Orchestra to emerge as front man to **Wizzard**, while **Slade**'s Noddy Holder sported trousers even more raucous than his gravelly voice. At the tail-end of the Seventies, **The Beat** and Coventry's **The Specials** were at the forefront of a ska revival, and a decade later, all the best "Grebo" bands talked like they had day jobs as Brummie diesel mechanics.

Though Nottingham hasn't had as much impact on the UK's music scene, there have been some notable exceptions, like electro-punk duo **Sleaford Mods** (formed 2007) and innovative indie trio **London Grammar** (2012).

The West Country

England's southwest has always had a reputation for left-field mavericks, from Dorset's **PJ Harvey** to Cornwall's dance iconoclast **Aphex Twin**. The region's biggest city, and one of England's great ports, **Bristol** has been associated since the 1990s with trip-hop, a catch-all term encompassing artists as diverse as **Portishead**, **Tricky** and **Massive Attack**, who rejected the guitar-led Britpop scene in favour of a darker, spacier and more down-tempo sound. Perhaps more to be expected from such a rural area, there's a strong folk tradition, with acts such as Devonian **Seth Lakeman** combining traditional and modern influences. Also noteworthy are rock band **Muse**, known for their complex compositions and frontman Matt Bellamy's incredible vocal range.

Yorkshire and the northeast

Hull weighs in with Mick Ronson and Mick Woodmansey, the linchpins of Bowie's **Spiders From Mars** in the early Seventies; **Everything But the Girl**, who emerged transcendent in the Eighties; and pop punks and local darlings **The Housemartins**, who delighted in articulating the depressing realities normally scorned by chart acts. Rival **Leeds** responded with such politicized bands as **The Mekons**, **Gang of Four** and **Chumbawamba**, while **Soft Cell** and **Sisters of Mercy** provided a counterpart to the pop cheeriness of the post-punk era, paving the way for **The Wedding Present**'s guitar onslaught. The **Kaiser Chiefs** and the **Pigeon Detectives** spearheaded a new wave of Leeds-based indie rockers in the early 2000s, which morphed into the altogether odder indie of **alt-J** (stylised as Δ) the following decade.

Dave Berry and **Joe Cocker** led **Sheffield**'s Steel City invasion in the Sixties, with the punishing stylings of **Def Leppard**, **Cabaret Voltaire** and others maintaining the city's metal-bashing traditions long after the cutlery factories had closed down. The city has also given us a stylish brand of pop in the form of the glossy magazine tunes of **The Human League** and elegant sophistication of **ABC**. **Pulp**'s domination of the thinking-teen's playlist kept the city in the limelight in the 1990s, while **Warp Records** championed an eclectic selection of techno, ambient and rock music. By the late 2000s, though, the baton of elegant sneering, backed up by solid musicianship, had been passed to the **Arctic Monkeys**, and frontman Alex Turner's side band, **The Last Shadow Puppets**.

Newcastle's pop pedigree ranges from **The Animals** in the 1960s through to folk/rock band **Lindisfarne**, punk heroes **Penetration** and **Angelic Upstarts**, Police frontman **Sting**, plus **Dubstar** in the Nineties and **Maxïmo Park** in the 2000s. Heavy-metal, heavy-duty **Satan** also came from Newcastle – while **Durham** sent us the mixed charm and cynicism of **Prefab Sprout** in the Eighties. Softer warblers have included **Cheryl** (sometimes known with the surname Tweedy, Cole or Fernandez-Versini), ah bless, and the mercurial **Bryan Ferry**, a bit less ah bless.

Film

England has produced some of the world's greatest films, actors and directors, but for all that it's well-nigh impossible to get critics to agree on what exactly constitutes an English film. Take sci-fi-horror classic *Alien* – a 20th Century Fox movie that launched the career of New York's Sigourney Weaver, but was filmed at London's Shepperton Studios, was directed by Tyne and Wear-born Ridley Scott and featured English RADA-trained classical actor John Hurt. Or the multi-garlanded *Slumdog Millionaire*, set in Mumbai with a largely Indian cast but adapted for the screen and directed by Englishmen Simon Beaufoy and Danny Boyle and financed entirely in the UK. We've concentrated on covering films that are at least set in England (with one or two rare exceptions). The ★ symbol indicates films that are especially recommended.

THE 1930S AND 1940S

★ **Brief Encounter** (David Lean, 1945). Wonderful weepie in which Trevor Howard and Celia Johnson teeter on the edge of adultery after a chance encounter at a railway station. Noël Coward wrote the clipped dialogue, and the flushed, dreamy soundtrack features Rachmaninov's *Piano Concerto No.2*.

Brighton Rock (John Boulting, 1947). A fine adaptation of Graham Greene's novel, featuring a young and scary Richard Attenborough as the psychopathic Pinkie, who marries a witness to one of his crimes in order to ensure her silence. Beautiful cinematography and good performances, with a real sense of film noir menace.

Fires Were Started (Humphrey Jennings, 1943). This outstanding wartime documentary relates the experiences of a group of firemen through one night of the Blitz. The use of real firemen rather than professional actors, and the avoidance of formulaic heroics, gives the film great power as a tribute to the courage of ordinary people who fought, often uncelebrated, on the home front.

★ **Great Expectations** (David Lean, 1946). Another early film by one of Britain's finest directors (see above), this superb rendition of a Dickens novel features magnificent performances by John Mills as Pip and Finlay Currie as Abel Magwitch. The scene in the graveyard will (should) make your hair stand on end. Lean was later responsible for *Lawrence of Arabia* and *Bridge on the River Kwai*.

Henry V (Laurence Olivier, 1944). With dreamlike Technicolor backdrops, this rousing piece of wartime propaganda is emphatically cinematic rather than "theatrical", the action spiralling out from the Globe Theatre itself. Olivier is a brilliantly charismatic king, and the atmospheric pre-battle scene where he goes disguised among his men is heartachingly muted.

I Know Where I'm Going! (Michael Powell and Emeric Pressburger, 1945). Powell and Pressburger made some of the finest British films of all time (see also *A Matter of Life and Death*, *The Life and Death of Colonel Blimp*, *Black Narcissus*, *The Red Shoes* and *A Canterbury Tale*), all of which expose the peculiarities of the British character and reveal hidden depths and longings. In this delightful romance, Wendy Hiller's modern young woman, who knows what she wants and how to get it, is stymied in her goals by the mysterious romanticism of the Scottish islands and their inhabitants.

Jane Eyre (Robert Stevenson, 1943). Joan Fontaine does a fine job of portraying Jane, and Orson Welles is a suavely sardonic Rochester – the scene where he is thrown from his horse in the mist hits the perfect melodramatic pitch. With the unlikely tagline "A Love Story Every Woman Would Die a Thousand Deaths to Live!", it briefly features a young Elizabeth Taylor as a dying Helen Burns.

Kind Hearts and Coronets (Robert Hamer, 1949). As with the best of the Ealing movies, this is a savage comedy on the cruel absurdities of the British class system. With increasing ingenuity, Dennis Price's suave and ruthless anti-hero murders his way through the d'Ascoyne clan (all brilliantly played by Alec Guinness) to claim the family title.

★ **Rebecca** (Alfred Hitchcock, 1940). Hitchcock does Du Maurier: Laurence Olivier is wonderfully enigmatic as Maxim de Winter, and Joan Fontaine glows as his meek second wife, living in the shadow of her mysterious predecessor.

The Thirty-Nine Steps (Alfred Hitchcock, 1935). Hitchcock's best-loved British movie, full of wit and bold acts of derring-do. Robert Donat stars as innocent Richard Hannay, inadvertently caught up in a mysterious spy ring. In a typically perverse Hitchcock touch, he spends a generous amount of time handcuffed to Madeleine Carroll, fleeing across the Scottish countryside, before the action returns to London for the film's great music-hall conclusion.

★ **Wuthering Heights** (William Wyler, 1939). The version of Emily Brontë's novel that everyone remembers, with Laurence Olivier as the dysfunctional Heathcliff and Merle Oberon as Cathy. It's tense, passionate and wild, and lays proper emphasis on the Yorkshire landscape, the best of all possible places for doomed lovers.

1950 TO 1970

Billy Liar! (John Schlesinger, 1963). Tom Courtenay is Billy, stuck in a dire job as an undertaker's clerk in a northern town, spending his time creating extravagant fantasies. His life is lit up by the appearance of Julie Christie, who holds out the glamour and promise of swinging London.

Carry On Screaming (Gerald Thomas, 1966). One of the best from the Carry On crew, with many of the usual suspects (Kenneth Williams, Charles Hawtrey, Joan Sims) hamming it up with the usual nudge-nudge merriment in a Hammer Horror spoof.

Far From the Madding Crowd (John Schlesinger, 1967). An imaginative adaptation of Hardy's doom-laden tale of the desires and ambitions of wilful/wishful Bathsheba Everdene. Julie Christie is a radiant and spirited Bathsheba, Terence Stamp flashes his blade to dynamic effect, Alan Bates is quietly charismatic as dependable Gabriel Oak, and the West Country setting is sparsely beautiful.

Kes (Ken Loach, 1969). The unforgettable story of a neglected Yorkshire schoolboy who finds solace and liberation in training his kestrel. As a still-pertinent commentary on poverty and an unforgiving school system, it's bleak but idealistic. Pale and pinched David Bradley, who plays Billy Casper, is hugely affecting. Loach at the top of his game.

★ **The Ladykillers** (Alexander Mackendrick, 1955). Alec Guinness is fabulously toothy and malevolent as "Professor Marcus", a murderous con man who lodges with a sweet little old lady, Mrs Wilberforce (Katie Johnson), in this skewed Ealing comedy.

A Man for All Seasons (Fred Zinnemann, 1966). Sir Thomas More takes on Henry VIII in one of British history's great moral confrontations. Robert Bolt's wry screenplay, muted visuals and a heavenly host of theatrical talent (including Orson Welles as Cardinal Wolsey) add to the spectacle if not the tension, which is where the film dithers.

★ **Night and the City** (Jules Dassin, 1950). Great film noir, with Richard Widmark as an anxious nightclub hustler on the run. It's gripping and convincingly sleazy, and the London streetscapes have an Expressionist edge of seedy horror.

Saturday Night and Sunday Morning (Karel Reisz, 1960). Reisz's monochrome captures all the grit and dead-end grind of Albert Finney's life working in a Nottingham bicycle factory – and his anarchic rejection of pretty much everything that surrounds him. The way out: heavy drinking and heavy petting (if not more).

★ **This Sporting Life** (Lindsay Anderson, 1963). One of the key British films of the 1960s, and a classic of the gritty "kitchen sink" genre. It's the story of a Northern miner turned rugby league star with the young Richard Harris giving a great (and singularly muscular) performance as the inarticulate anti-hero, able only to express himself through physical violence.

THE 1970S AND 1980S

★ **Babylon** (Franco Rosso, 1980). A moving account of black working-class London life. We follow the experiences of young Blue through a series of encounters that reveal the nation's insidious racism. Good performances and a great reggae soundtrack: an all too rare example of Black Britain taking centre stage in a British movie.

Distant Voices, Still Lives (Terence Davies, 1988). Beautifully realized autobiographical tale of growing up in Liverpool in the 1940s and 1950s. The mesmeric pace is punctuated by astonishing moments of drama, and the whole is a very moving account of how a family survives and triumphs, in small ways, against the odds.

★ **Get Carter** (Mike Hodges, 1971). Vivid British gangster movie, featuring a hard-nosed, hard-case Michael Caine as the eponymous hero-villain, returning to his native Newcastle to avenge his brother's death. Great use of its northeastern locations and a fine turn by playwright John Osborne as the local godfather.

Hope and Glory (John Boorman, 1987). A glorious auto-biographical feature about the Blitz seen through the eyes of 9-year-old Bill, who revels in the liberating chaos of bomb-site playgrounds, tumbling barrage balloons and debris shrapnel.

The Last of England (Derek Jarman, 1987). Jarman's most abstract account of the state of Eighties Britain. Composed of apparently unrelated shots of decaying London landscapes, rent boys, and references to emblematic national events such as the Falklands War, this may not be to all tastes, but it is a fitting testament to Jarman's unique talent.

My Beautiful Laundrette (Stephen Frears, 1985). A slice of Thatcher's Britain, with a young, on-the-make Pakistani man, Omar, opening a ritzy laundrette in London. His lover, Johnny (Daniel Day-Lewis), is an ex-National Front glamour boy, angry and inarticulate when forced by the acquisitive Omar into a menial role in the laundrette. The racial, sexual and class dynamics of their relationship mirror the tensions in the city itself.

Withnail and I (Bruce Robinson, 1986). Richard E. Grant is superb as the raddled, drunken Withnail, a "resting" actor with a penchant for drinking lighter fluid. Paul McGann is the "I" of the title – a bemused spectator of Withnail's wild excesses, as they abandon their grotty London flat for a remote country cottage, and the attentions of Withnail's randy Uncle Monty (Richard Griffiths).

THE 1990S

Bhaji on the Beach (Gurinder Chadha, 1993). An Asian women's group takes a day-trip to Blackpool in this issue-laden but enjoyable picture. A lot of fun is had contrasting the seamier side of British life with the mores of the Asian aunties, though the male characters are cartoon villains all.

East Is East (Damien O'Donnell, 1999). Seventies Salford is the setting for this lively tragi-comedy, with a Pakistani chip-shop owner struggling to keep control of his seven children as they rail against the strictures of Islam and arranged marriages. Inventively made, and with some delightful performances.

Elizabeth (Shekhar Kapur, 1998). Cate Blanchett is stunning in this visually beautiful, gothic production, where the young, innocent Elizabeth slowly adapts to the role of the "Virgin Queen" to secure her survival. It's better than its sequel *Elizabeth: The Golden Age* (2007), which also stars Blanchett, and focuses on the defeat of the Spanish Armada – but don't take it as historical gospel.

The Full Monty (Peter Cattaneo, 1997). Set in Sheffield, where six unemployed former steel workers throw caution to the wind and become male strippers, their boast being that all will be revealed in the "full monty". Unpromising physical specimens all, they score an unlikely hit with the locals. The film was itself an unlikely worldwide hit, and the long-awaited striptease is a joy to behold (well, almost).

Howards End (James Ivory, 1992). A superb Anthony Hopkins leads the way in this touching recreation of E.M. Forster's celebrated novel. From the prolific Merchant Ivory team, who produced a string of exquisite period films, renowned for their elegiac settings.

Lock, Stock and Two Smoking Barrels (Guy Ritchie, 1998). Ritchie may be much derided for his marriage to Madonna and his mockney accent, but this – his breakout film – was a witty and inventive comedy-meets-heist movie that gave gangland heavies a "geezer" reboot.

The Madness of King George (Nicholas Hytner, 1994). Adapted from a witty Alan Bennett play, this royal romp is handsomely staged, with the king's loopy antics (a wonderfully nuanced performance from Nigel Hawthorne) played out against a cartoon-like court and its acolytes.

Rupert Everett is superb as the effete Prince Regent.

★**Nil by Mouth** (Gary Oldman, 1997). With strong performances by Ray Winstone as a brutish south Londoner and Kathy Burke as his abused wife, this brave and bleak picture delves deep into domestic violence and drug/drink addiction. Brace yourself.

The Remains of the Day (James Ivory, 1993). Kazuo Ishiguro's masterly novel of social and personal repression translates beautifully to the big screen. Anthony Hopkins is the overly decorous butler who gradually becomes aware of his master's fascist connections, Emma Thompson the housekeeper who struggles (unsuccessfully) to bring his deeply suppressed feelings to the surface. Call a counsellor.

Richard III (Richard Loncraine, 1995). A splendid film version of a renowned National Theatre production, which brilliantly transposed the action to a fascist state in the 1930s. The infernal political machinations of a snarling Ian McKellen as Richard are heightened by Nazi associations, and the style of the period imbues the film with the requisite glamour, as does languorously drugged Kristin Scott-Thomas as Lady Anne.

Secrets and Lies (Mike Leigh, 1996). Serious-minded, slice-of-life ensemble drama charting a dysfunctional family's hidden secrets, from infidelity to reconciliation – and all seen through the prism of class. Mike Leigh at his most penetrating.

Sense and Sensibility (Ang Lee, 1995). Ah, the English and their period dramas. They are all here – Rickman, Winslett, Thompson, Grant, Robert Hardy et al – in this tone-perfect re-creation of Jane Austen's sprightly story of love, money and, of course, manners.

★**Trainspotting** (Danny Boyle, 1996). High-octane dip into the heroin-scarred world of a group of young Scotsmen both at home and in London; includes what must be the best cinematic representation of a heroin fix ever.

Wonderland (Michael Winterbottom, 1999). One Bonfire Night in London as experienced by three unhappy sisters. Winterbottom's use of real locations, natural light and 16mm film gives it a naturalistic air that's also dreamlike, an effect heightened by Michael Nyman's haunting score.

THE 2000S

24 Hour Party People (Michael Winterbottom, 2002). Steve Coogan plays the entrepreneurial/inspirational Tony Wilson (1950–2007) – the man of many quotes – in this fast-moving recreation of the early days of Manchester's Factory Records. Stunning soundtrack, too.

Atonement (Joe Wright, 2007). This adaptation of Ian McEwan's highly literary novel of misunderstanding and regret benefits from strong performances from Keira Knightley and James McAvoy, as well as fluent plotting.

Bend It Like Beckham (Gurinder Chadha, 2003). Immensely successful film focusing on the coming of age

of a football-loving Punjabi girl in a suburb of London. Both socially acute and comic.

★**Bronson** (Nicolas Winding Refn, 2009). The subject matter may seem unappetizing – Welsh criminal Bronson (Tom Hardy) is reputed to be the most violent man ever locked up in a British prison – and it's not easy viewing, but Refn's take on this unusual anti-hero is inventive, creative and insightful. Notable also for the appearance of a Rough Guide author as an extra – but blink and you'll miss him.

Control (Anton Corbijn, 2007). Ian Curtis, the lead singer of Joy Division, committed suicide in 1980 at the age of 23.

This biopic tracks his life in and around Manchester, based on the account provided by his wife, Deborah. Some have raved over Sam Riley's portrayal of Curtis, others have been less convinced, but as an evocation of the Northwest – and pioneering Factory Records – it's hard to beat.

Dirty Pretty Things (Stephen Frears, 2003). A tumbling mix of melodrama, social criticism and black comedy, this forceful, thought-provoking film explores the world of Britain's illegal migrants.

Fish Tank (Andrea Arnold, 2009). Arnold delves deep into working-class life in this searing coming-of-age tale in which a volatile teenager struggles to make sense of things – and the attentions of her mum's boyfriend. Arnold's breakthrough movie, which used CCTV to tell a story of obsession in Glasgow, was *Red Road* (2006), and there's also her excellent *Wuthering Heights* (2011), which reveals a lyrical eye for the natural world in an arty, elemental reworking of Emily Brontë's romantic tragedy.

Gosford Park (Robert Altman, 2001). Astutely observed upstairs-downstairs murder mystery set in class-ridden 1930s England. The multi-layered plot is typical of the director, the script, from Julian Fellowes, is more nuanced than some of his later TV work, and the who's who of great British actors is led by the superb Maggie Smith.

Harry Potter and the Philosopher's Stone (Chris Columbus, 2001). The first film adaptation of J.K. Rowling's world-conquering seven-book series, eight films in all. They are all enjoyable romps (which get progressively darker) with excellent ensemble casts – Spall, Gambon, Rickman et al.

The series did wonders for the English tourist industry, and boosted the pension pots of a platoon of British actors.

In the Loop (Armando Iannucci, 2009). Look what we have to put up with from our politicians, screams Iannucci, in this satire on the opaque and corrupt meanderings of our leaders and their assorted advisors.

★**Sexy Beast** (Jonathan Glazer, 2000). Gangster thriller distinguished by the performances of Ray Winstone and more especially Ben Kingsley, who plays one of the hardest, meanest criminals ever. Delightful cameos by an evil Ian McShane and a debauched James Fox, too.

Shaun of the Dead (Edgar Wright, 2004). Shuffling and shambolic zombies roam and groan on the streets of London in this zom-com, horror-romp that made a name for Simon Pegg. Wright and Frost's "Cornetto Trilogy" was completed with buddy-cop movie homage *Hot Fuzz* (2007) and pub-crawl/apocalyptic sci-fi flick *The World's End* (2013).

This is England (Shane Meadows, 2007). British cinema rarely ventures into the East Midlands, but this is where Shane Meadows is at home. Set in the early 1980s, this thoughtful film deals with a young working-class lad who falls in with skinheads – the good-hearted ones to begin with, the racists thereafter.

★**Vera Drake** (Mike Leigh, 2004). Moving story of a 1950s working-class woman, who performs illegal abortions from the goodness of her heart – and without thought for either money or the legal consequences. Her actions eventually threaten to destroy her and her close-knit family, and serve as a powerful counterblast to the anti-abortion lobby.

2010 ONWARDS

★**Catch me Daddy** (Daniel Wolfe, 2014). Rippling and gripping tale of a young British-Pakistani woman, who breaks family convention by running away with her white boyfriend. Bleak Yorkshire moorland settings add to the gloom as she is hunted down by her male relatives – with a bitter, tragic ending. No sentimental get-out clause here.

Dreams of a Life (Carol Morley, 2011). Haunting drama-doc on the life and unnoticed death of Joyce Carol Vincent – heartbreakingly portrayed by Zawe Ashton – whose body was found in her London flat two years after her death. How did it happen? How could a life of promise end so sadly? No conclusions, but so very moving.

I, Daniel Blake (Ken Loach, 2016). Hear Loach's howl of rage as unemployed Daniel, the epitome of a decent man, is scuppered and skewered by a benefits system seemingly designed to crush him. How Loach hates the Tories – and what their austerity policies have done.

The King's Speech (Tom Hooper, 2010). Colin Firth is suitably repressed as the vocally challenged King George VI, who is given the confidence to become king by Geoffrey Rush's exuberant Australian speech therapist. Superb performances also from Helena Bonham Carter as his imperious wife (later to become the Queen Mother) and Guy Pearce as the spoiled, self-indulgent Edward VIII.

Made in Dagenham (Nigel Cole, 2010). Good-hearted, good-natured film about the struggle for equal pay in the car industry in 1960s England. Sweet packaging for a tough industrial message.

Mr Nice (Bernard Rose, 2010). Picaresque tale of one-time drug king and (supposedly) very good egg, Howard Marks (Mr Nice himself) from baffled beginnings to stoned (very stoned) fame and fortune via imprisonment and hostile drug cartels. Rhys Ifans is perfect as the drug-addled hero, Chloë Sevigny as his wife.

Mr Turner (Mike Leigh, 2014). One of Leigh's most ambitious films, elbowing into the last years of the eponymous artist's life. The curmudgeonly Turner (1775–1851) is played by Timothy Spall with consummate skill. A talented supporting cast – Dorothy Atkinson, Marion Bailey et al – add pace and vigour.

★**Sightseers** (Ben Wheatley, 2012). Murder, mayhem, sadism and psychosis on a caravan holiday in the Midlands and the North. Never, but never before, has Crich Tramway Museum seemed so dangerous. This is horror with ironic flair – so avert your eyes strategically or prepare to grimace.

Small print and index

ABOUT THE AUTHORS

Rob Andrews has written or contributed to the Rough Guides to Devon and Cornwall; Italy; Sardinia; Sicily; Bath, Bristol and Somerset; and England. He lives in Bristol.

Samantha Cook was born in London and has lived in the city all her life. In addition to the London and Southeast chapters of this guide, she has written, edited and contributed to many other Rough Guides, including London; Kent, Sussex and Surrey; and *Best Places to Stay in Britain on a Budget*.

Matthew Hancock and Amanda Tomlin are authors of *The Rough Guide to Dorset, Hampshire and the Isle of Wight* and the *Pocket Rough Guide to Porto*. Matthew Hancock is also co-author of *The Rough Guide to Portugal* and author of the *Pocket Rough Guide to Lisbon*.

Phil Lee has been writing for Rough Guides for well over twenty years. His other books in the series include Norway, Norfolk & Suffolk, Amsterdam, Mallorca & Menorca and The Netherlands. He lives in Nottingham, where he was born and raised.

David Leffman has been writing guidebooks for Rough Guides, Dorling Kindersley and others since 1992, and has lived in the UK, Australia and China.

Rachel Mills is a freelance writer and editor based on the Kent coast, or in her campervan somewhere in the UK. She is a co-author for Rough Guides to India, Vietnam and Ireland, as well as England.

Alice Park is a freelance editor and writer. She has edited numerous guidebooks and has written about Switzerland, Austria and Germany as well as her native South London.

Claire Saunders grew up in Brighton and now lives in nearby Lewes, where she works as a freelance editor and writer. She updated the Sussex sections of this book, and is the co-author of *The Rough Guide to Kent, Sussex and Surrey*.

Matthew Teller is a writer, journalist and broadcaster. He writes for media worldwide, is the author of *The Rough Guide to the Cotswolds, Stratford-upon-Avon and Oxford* among other titles, and produces and presents documentaries for BBC Radio.

A ROUGH GUIDE TO ROUGH GUIDES

Published in 1982, the first Rough Guide – to Greece – was a student scheme that became a publishing phenomenon. Mark Ellingham, a recent graduate in English from Bristol University, had been travelling in Greece the previous summer and couldn't find the right guidebook. With a small group of friends he wrote his own guide, combining a contemporary, journalistic style with a thoroughly practical approach to travellers' needs.

The immediate success of the book spawned a series that rapidly covered dozens of destinations. And, in addition to impecunious backpackers, Rough Guides soon acquired a much broader readership that relished the guides' wit and inquisitiveness as much as their enthusiastic, critical approach and value-for-money ethos. These days, Rough Guides include recommendations from budget to luxury and cover more than 120 destinations around the globe, from Amsterdam to Zanzibar, all regularly updated by our team of roaming writers.

Browse all our latest guides, read inspirational features and book your trip at **roughguides.com**.

Rough Guide credits

Editors: Rebecca Hallett, Natasha Foges, David Leffman
Layout: Nikhil Agarwal
Cartography: Rajesh Chhibber, Richard Marchi
Picture editor: Michelle Bhatia
Proofreader: Susanne Hillen
Managing editor: Edward Aves
Assistant editor: Payal Sharotri

Production: Jimmy Lao
Cover photo research: Nicole Newman
Editorial assistant: Aimee White
Senior DTP coordinator: Dan May
Programme manager: Gareth Lowe
Publishing director: Georgina Dee

Publishing information

This eleventh edition published February 2018 by
Rough Guides Ltd,
80 Strand, London WC2R 0RL
11, Community Centre, Panchsheel Park,
New Delhi 110017, India
Distributed by Penguin Random House
Penguin Books Ltd, 80 Strand, London WC2R 0RL
Penguin Group (USA), 345 Hudson Street, NY 10014, USA
Penguin Group (Australia), 250 Camberwell Road,
Camberwell, Victoria 3124, Australia
Penguin Group (NZ), 67 Apollo Drive, Mairangi Bay,
Auckland 1310, New Zealand
Penguin Group (South Africa), Block D, Rosebank Office
Park, 181 Jan Smuts Avenue, Parktown North, Gauteng,
South Africa 2193
Rough Guides is represented in Canada by DK Canada, 320
Front Street West, Suite 1400, Toronto, Ontario M5V 3B6
Printed in Singapore
© Rough Guides, 2018
Maps © Rough Guides
Contains Ordnance Survey data © Crown copyright and
database rights 2018

All rights reserved. No part of this publication may be
reproduced, stored in or introduced into a retrieval system,
or transmitted in any form, or by any means (electronic,
mechanical, photocopying, recording or otherwise) without
the prior written permission of the copyright owner.

736pp includes index
A catalogue record for this book is available from the
British Library
ISBN: 978-0-24130-628-4
The publishers and authors have done their best to
ensure the accuracy and currency of all the information in
The Rough Guide to England, however, they can accept
no responsibility for any loss, injury, or inconvenience
sustained by any traveller as a result of information or
advice contained in the guide.
1 3 5 7 9 8 6 4 2

MIX
Paper from
responsible sources
FSC
www.fsc.org   FSC™ C018179

Help us update

We've gone to a lot of effort to ensure that the eleventh
edition of **The Rough Guide to England** is accurate
and up-to-date. However, things change – places get
"discovered", opening hours are notoriously fickle,
restaurants and rooms raise prices or lower standards.
If you feel we've got it wrong or left something out,
we'd like to know, and if you can remember the
address, the price, the hours, the phone number, so
much the better.

Please send your comments with the subject line
"**Rough Guide England Update**" to mail@uk.roughguides
.com. We'll credit all contributions and send a copy of the
next edition (or any other Rough Guide if you prefer) for
the very best emails.

Acknowledgements

Rob Andrews I'd like acknowledge the huge assistance
given by Evelina at Visit England, Claire Pickup at Bath
Tourism, Lesley Gillilan at Destination Bristol and Rosa
Pedley at Visit Cornwall, and to thank Becca Hallett for
expert editing.

Samantha Cook Thanks to Natasha and Becca for diligent
editing; to Alice and Claire, great co-authors both; and to
Greg Ward for everything.

Matthew Hancock and Amanda Tomlin Thanks to
Olivia and Alex Hancock-Tomlin for their additional
research.

Phil Lee Thank you to my editor, Rebecca Hallett, for
the fine quality of your editing – hard to beat. Special
thanks also to Simon Gribbon in Leicester; Kerry McGinty
in Stratford-upon-Avon; Rabia Raza in Birmingham; and
Lydia Rusling in Lincoln.

David Leffman Thanks to Becca for her editorial work, and
to Rajesh and Richard for the excellent cartography.

Rachel Mills Thank you to Ed Aves, Becca Hallett and David
Leffman in the RG editorial team; Andy Parkinson at Visit
Manchester; Joe Keggin at Visit Liverpool; Ubiquity PR; YHA
youth hostels; Hope and Glory PR; NewcastleGateshead
Initiative; Visit Blackpool; Visit Hull and East Yorkshire; Mark
Hibbert PR; Visit Northumberland; and Visit Yorkshire.

Alice Park Many thanks to my fellow London guide
authors for their contributions: Samantha Cook, Matt
Norman and Neil McQuillian. At Rough Guides, huge
thanks to the editorial supergroup of Edward Aves,
Rebecca Hallett and Natasha Foges.

Claire Saunders Thank you to Becca, for another
smooth and stress-free edit, and to my splendid
Southeast co-author Sam.

Readers' updates

Thanks to all the readers who have taken the time to write in with comments and suggestions (and apologies if we've inadvertently omitted or misspelt anyone's name):

Amy Adams; Chris Allen; Sandra Ball; Vanessa Bennett; Claudia Berettoni; Mary Birch; Finnian Brewer; Matt Burrows; Chris Bush; Lorenza Canepa; Will Carey; Peter Carney; Georgina Church; Leanne Cromie; Matthew Crowther; Sam Dalley; Peter and Carol Delbridge; Tom Edwards; Fergus Ewbank; Rachel Faulkner; Heather Finlay; Helen Gibbons; Heather Gifford-Jenkins; Kitty Gilbert; Laura Hampton; Sam Hanson; James Harrison; James Horrocks; Dave Hough; Jo Hudson-Cook; Helen Hughes; Jerry Hyde; Ashley Jackson; Margaret Jailler; Gary Jenkins; Matthew Johnson; Feroza Kassam; Hayley Kitto; Trina King; Belinda Kirk; Rachel Knott; Lewis Lawson; Clare Leedale; Adam Legg; Shy Lewis; Alice Lowe; Gigi Mann; Alex Manners; Sophie Mason; Thomas Maxwell; John Bury Meaker; Belinda Mercer; Jamie Milton; Cheryl Morris; Shadyn Nikzad; Harley Nott; Zennor Pascoe; Allie Pinder; Sophie Pitt; Sara Priddle; Nicky Primavesi; Gabriel Quiro; Joe Rodriguez; Lucy Sambrook; Ben Selvaratnam; Alan Sharp; Samantha Sims; Robin Simpson; Gary Snapper; Owen Stephen; Diana Stoica; Koji Takeuchi; Jake Tibbits; Michael Tracey; Rachel White; Jacqui Wieksza; Anna Wilson-Barnes; Geoff Wisher; Jen Workers.

Photo credits

All photos © Rough Guides, except the following:
(Key: t-top; c-centre; b-bottom; l-left; r-right)

1 4Corners: Arcangelo Piai
2 Getty Images: R A Kearton
4 Corbis: Paul Williams - Funkystock/imageBROKER
5 Alamy Stock Photo: Loop Images Ltd
9 Alamy Stock Photo: Cath Harries (tr). **Corbis:** Atlantide Phototravel (tl); Paul Harris/JAI (b)
11 Alamy Stock Photo: Ian G Dagnall (t). **Corbis:** Neil Farrin/JAI (b)
13 Alamy Stock Photo: (b); Graham Prentice (c). **Randy Pike:** Andy Hill (t)
14 AWL Images: Alan Copson
15 4Corners: Natalie Sternberg (b). **Alamy Stock Photo:** Charles Bowman (c). **Getty Images:** Matt Cardy (t)
16 Corbis: Alan Copson/JA (b); Design Pics (t)
17 Alamy Stock Photo: Jeff Morgan 09 (b). **Corbis:** Martyn Goddard (t). **Getty Images:** Jim Dyson (cr). **Thermae Bath Spa:** Matt Cardy (cl)
18 4Corners: Sandra Raccanello (c). **Blackpool Pleasure Beach** (b). **Getty Images:** Christopher Furlong (t)
19 Alamy Stock Photo: DB Pictures (bl); Simon Reddy (tr). **Getty Images:** Christopher Furlong (b). **Robert Harding Picture Library:** Adam Burton (tl)
20 honister.com (cr). **Latitude:** Pawel Libera (b). **Robert Harding Picture Library:** James Emmerson (t)
21 4Corners: Maurizio Rellini (b). **Aldeburgh Music:** Robert Workman (c). **Getty Images:** Education Images/UIG (t)
22 Getty Images: Roger Coulam (b). **People's History Museum** (c). **Robert Harding Picture Library:** Adam Burton (tr)
23 Alamy Stock Photo: MediaWorldImages (b). **Dreamstime.com:** Elenarostunova (t)
24 Corbis: David Cheshire/Loop Images
26 Corbis: Ashley Cooper
48–49 Robert Harding Picture Library: Neil Farrin
51 Alamy Stock Photo: Elena Chaykina (t)
71 Getty Images: Erin Smallwood (t). **Robert Harding Picture Library:** Mark Mawson (b)
103 London Design Museum: Hufton + Crow (tr). **Robert Harding Picture Library:** Adina Tovy (br)
135 Getty Images: View Pictures/UIG
147 Whitstable Oyster Festival: Jon Lambert (t)
173 Alamy Stock Photo: Carolyn Clarke (tl). **Watts Gallery Artists' Village** (bl)
182–183 Corbis: Guy Edwardes/2020VISION/Nature Picture Library
185 Getty Images: Louise Heusinkveld

205 colin@vertiworks.co.uk (t). **Dreamstime.com:** Matt Jacques (b)
234–235 Getty Images: Andrea Pucci
237 Alamy Stock Photo: Francisco Martinez
255 Cheltenham Racecourse (t). **Getty Images:** Eurasia Press/Photononstop (b)
280–281 Getty Images: Adrian Dennis/AFP
283 Alamy Stock Photo: incamerastock
301 Corbis: Tim Graham (t)
316–317 Getty Images: PhotoAlto/Neville Mountford-Hoare
319 Alamy Stock Photo: incamerastock
347 Robert Harding Picture Library: Sebastian Wasek
376–377 Getty Images: Tim Stocker Photography
379 Robert Harding Picture Library: Neale Clark
422–423 Getty Images: Dave Porter Peterborough UK
425 Royal Shakespeare Company: Peter Cook
439 Corbis: Alan Copson/JAI
457 Getty Images: The Print Collector (bl). **Robert Harding Picture Library:** Ian Dagnall (br). **Selfridges Birmingham:** (t)
472–473 Getty Images: Travelpix Ltd
475 Corbis: Tom Martin/JAI
495 Alamy Stock Photo: John Kershaw (br). **Corbis:** Frank Fell/Robert Harding World Imagery (t). **Lincolnshire Wildlife Trust:** Barrie Wilkinson (bl)
508–509 Getty Images: Ian Bramham Photography
511 The Whitworth Art Gallery, The University Of Manchester: Alan Williams
533 Alamy Stock Photo: Ian Canham (t). **Blackpool Pleasure Beach** (b)
552–553 Corbis: Jeremy Lightfoot/Robert Harding World Imagery
555 Corbis: Allan Baxter
567 honister.com (br)
584–585 Getty Images: John Dowle
587 Getty Images: Andrea Pistolesi
617 Alamy Stock Photo: Ian Pilbeam (br)
636–637 Getty Images: Danny Birrell Photography
639 Alamy Stock Photo: Ian Dagnall
663 Beamish Museum Limited: (b). **Corbis:** Axiom Photographic (t). **Getty Images:** Nick Cable (c)
678 Corbis: Chris Hellier

Cover: *Lavenham High Street, Suffolk* **AWL Images:** Alan Copson

Index

Maps are marked in grey

Map symbols

The symbols below are used on maps throughout the book

International boundary	★ Transport stop	Tin mine	⚔ Battlefield
Chapter boundary	⊖ London Underground station	Mosque	Tree/arboretum
Regional boundary	⊖ DLR Station	Zoo/animal park	Nature reserve
Motorway	✈ International airport	Monument	Golf Course
Major road	⊞ Hospital	Swimming pool	Lighthouse
Minor road	P Parking	Bridge	Mountains
Pedestrian road	Fortress	Mountain peak	Swamp
Steps	Point of interest	Viewpoint	Abbey
Footpath	Ruins/archeological site	Synagogue	Stadium
Railway	Stately/historic home	Country park	Church (regional)
Ferry route	Castle	Waterfall	Building
River/coastline	Museum	Cave	Market
Wall	Gardens	Gate	Church
Cable car	@ Internet access	Statue	Christian cemetery
Gorge	(i) Information centre	Surf beach	Park
Rocks	Post office	Bird watching	Beach
Vineyard	Boat	Orchard/cider farm	Pedestrianized area

Listings key

- Accommodation
- Eating
- Drinking/nightlife
- Shopping